APA Handbook of

Psychology and Juvenile Justice

APA Handbooks in Psychology® Series

APA Handbook of Industrial and Organizational Psychology—three volumes
Sheldon Zedeck, Editor-in-Chief

APA Handbook of Ethics in Psychology—two volumes
Samuel J. Knapp, Editor-in-Chief

APA Educational Psychology Handbook—three volumes
Karen R. Harris, Steve Graham, and Tim Urdan, Editors-in-Chief

APA Handbook of Research Methods in Psychology—three volumes
Harris Cooper, Editor-in-Chief

APA Addiction Syndrome Handbook—two volumes
Howard J. Shaffer, Editor-in-Chief

APA Handbook of Counseling Psychology—two volumes
Nadya A. Fouad, Editor-in-Chief

APA Handbook of Behavior Analysis—two volumes
Gregory J. Madden, Editor-in-Chief

APA Handbook of Psychology, Religion, and Spirituality—two volumes
Kenneth I. Pargament, Editor-in-Chief

APA Handbook of Testing and Assessment in Psychology—three volumes
Kurt F. Geisinger, Editor-in-Chief

APA Handbook of Multicultural Psychology—two volumes
Frederick T. L. Leong, Editor-in-Chief

APA Handbook of Sexuality and Psychology—two volumes
Deborah L. Tolman and Lisa M. Diamond, Editors-in-Chief

APA Handbook of Personality and Social Psychology—four volumes
Mario Mikulincer and Phillip R. Shaver, Editors-in-Chief

APA Handbook of Career Intervention—two volumes
Paul J. Hartung, Mark L. Savickas, and W. Bruce Walsh, Editors-in-Chief

APA Handbook of Forensic Psychology—two volumes
Brian L. Cutler and Patricia A. Zapf, Editors-in-Chief

APA Handbook of Clinical Geropsychology—two volumes
Peter A. Lichtenberg and Benjamin T. Mast, Editors-in-Chief

APA Handbook of Human Systems Integration—one volume
Deborah A. Boehm-Davis, Francis T. Durso, and John D. Lee, Editors-in-Chief

APA Handbook of Men and Masculinities—one volume
Y. Joel Wong and Stephen R. Wester, Editors-in-Chief

APA Handbook of Psychology and Juvenile Justice—one volume
Kirk Heilbrun, Editor-in-Chief

APA Handbooks in Psychology

APA Handbook of Psychology and Juvenile Justice

Kirk Heilbrun, *Editor-in-Chief*
David DeMatteo and Naomi E. S. Goldstein, *Associate Editors*

American Psychological Association • Washington, DC

Published by
American Psychological Association
750 First Street, NE
Washington, DC 20002-4242
www.apa.org

To order
APA Order Department
P.O. Box 92984
Washington, DC 20090-2984
Tel: (800) 374-2721; Direct: (202) 336-5510
Fax: (202) 336-5502; TDD/TTY: (202) 336-6123
Online: www.apa.org/pubs/books/
E-mail: order@apa.org

In the U.K., Europe, Africa, and the Middle East, copies may be ordered from
American Psychological Association
3 Henrietta Street
Covent Garden, London
WC2E 8LU England

AMERICAN PSYCHOLOGICAL ASSOCIATION STAFF
Gary R. VandenBos, PhD, *Publisher*
Julia Frank-McNeil, *Senior Director, APA Books*
Theodore J. Baroody, *Director, Reference, APA Books*
Patricia D. Mathis, *Reference Editorial Manager, APA Books*
Kristen L. Knight, *Senior Reference Editor, APA Books*

Typeset in Berkeley by Cenveo Publisher Services, Columbia, MD

Printer: Bang Printing, Brainerd, MN
Cover Designer: Naylor Design, Washington, DC

Library of Congress Cataloging-in-Publication Data

APA handbook of psychology and juvenile justice / Kirk Heilbrun, PhD, Editor-in-Chief. — First edition.
pages cm. — (APA handbooks in psychology series)
Includes bibliographical references and index.
ISBN 978-1-4338-1967-4 — ISBN 1-4338-1967-8
1. Juvenile delinquency—United States—Psychological aspects. 2. Forensic psychology—United States.
3. Juvenile justice, Administration of—United States. 4. Juvenile delinquents—Mental health—United States.
5. Criminal psychology. I. Heilbrun, Kirk.
HV9104.A822 2015
364.360973—dc23
2014049594

British Library Cataloguing-in-Publication Data
A CIP record is available from the British Library.

Printed in the United States of America
First Edition

http://dx.doi.org/10.1037/14643-000

To Patty, Anna, and Christopher.
—*Kirk Heilbrun*

To Christina, Emma, and Jake.
—*David DeMatteo*

To Josh, Maia, and Hillary.
—*Naomi E. S. Goldstein*

Contents

Editorial Board

About the Editor-in-Chief

Kirk Heilbrun, PhD, is a professor and interim head of the department of psychology at Drexel University, and codirector of the Pennsylvania Mental Health and Justice Center of Excellence. He received his doctorate in clinical psychology in 1980 from the University of Texas at Austin and completed postdoctoral fellowship training from 1981 to 1982 in psychology and criminal justice at Florida State University. His current research focuses on juvenile and adult offenders, legal decision making, forensic evaluation associated with such decision making, and diversion. Dr. Heilbrun is the author of numerous articles on forensic assessment, violence risk assessment and risk communication, and the treatment of offenders with mental disorders, and he has published 10 books (*Principles of Forensic Mental Health Assessment,* 2001; *Forensic Mental Health Assessment: A Casebook,* with Geoffrey R. Marczyk and David DeMatteo, 2002; *Forensic Mental Health Assessment: A Casebook, Second Edition,* with David DeMatteo, Stephanie Brooks Holliday, and Casey LaDuke, 2014; *Juvenile Delinquency: Prevention, Assessment, and Intervention,* with Naomi E. Sevin Goldstein and Richard E. Redding, 2005; *Wrightsman's Psychology and the Legal System, Sixth Edition,* with Edie Greene, William H. Fortune, and Michael T. Nietzel, 2006; *Wrightsman's Psychology and the Legal System, Seventh Edition,* with Edie Greene, 2010; *Wrightsman's Psychology and the Legal System, Eighth Edition,* with Edie Greene, 2013; *Foundations of Forensic Mental Health Assessment,* with Thomas Grisso and Alan Goldstein, 2009; *Evaluating the Risk of Violence in Adults,* 2009; and *The Sequential Intercept Model and Criminal Justice: Promoting Community Alternatives for Individuals With Serious Mental Illness,* with Patricia A. Griffin, Edward P. Mulvey, David DeMatteo, and Carol A. Schubert, 2015). His practice interests also center on forensic assessment, and he directs a clinic in this area in the department of psychology at Drexel University. He is board certified in clinical psychology and in forensic psychology (American Board of Professional Psychology) and has previously served as president of both the American Psychological Association's Division 41 (American Psychology–Law Society) and the American Board of Forensic Psychology. Dr. Heilbrun received the 2004 Distinguished Contributions to Forensic Psychology Award and the 2008 Beth Clark Distinguished Service Contribution Award from the American Academy of Forensic Psychology.

Contributors

Katelyn Affleck, MA, Department of Psychology, Fordham University, Bronx, NY

Robert P. Archer, PhD, Department of Psychiatry and Behavioral Sciences, Eastern Virginia Medical School, Norfolk

Linda J. Baum, PhD, School of Psychology and Counseling, Regent University, Virginia Beach, VA

Sandra L. Bloom, MD, School of Public Health, Department of Health Management and Policy, Drexel University, Philadelphia, PA

Etta Brodersen, MA, Department of Psychology, Simon Fraser University, Burnaby, British Columbia, Canada

Leah Brogan, Doctoral Candidate, Department of Psychology, Drexel University, Philadelphia, PA

Laurie Chassin, PhD, Department of Psychology, Arizona State University, Tempe

Alisa Clark, BA, University of New Mexico School of Medicine, Albuquerque

Theodore Corbin, MD, MPP, College of Medicine, Department of Emergency Medicine, and School of Public Health, Department of Health Management and Policy, Drexel University, Philadelphia, PA

Dewey Cornell, PhD, Curry School of Education, Department of Human Services, University of Virginia, Charlottesville

Keith R. Cruise, PhD, MLS, Department of Psychology, Fordham University, Bronx, NY

Brian P. Daly, PhD, Department of Psychology, Drexel University, Philadelphia, PA

Jessica Feierman, JD, LLM, Juvenile Law Center, Philadelphia, PA

Julian D. Ford, PhD, University of Connecticut Health Center, Department of Psychiatry, University of Connecticut School of Medicine, Farmington

Erika Fountain, BA, Department of Psychology, Georgetown University, Washington, DC

Meghann Galloway, MS, Department of Psychology and Thomas R. Kline School of Law, Drexel University, Philadelphia, PA

Christy Giallella, Doctoral Candidate, Department of Psychology, Drexel University, Philadelphia, PA

Thomas Grisso, PhD, Department of Psychiatry, University of Massachusetts Medical School, Worcester

Lucy A. Guarnera, MA, Department of Psychology, University of Virginia, Charlottesville

Emily Haney-Caron, MS, Department of Psychology and Thomas R. Kline School of Law, Drexel University, Philadelphia, PA

Erica J. Harris, MD, Department of Emergency Medicine, Drexel University College of Medicine, Philadelphia, PA
Natalie A. Harrison, BA, Department of Psychology and Disruptive Behavior Clinic, University of Alabama, Tuscaloosa
Anna Heilbrun, Doctoral Candidate, Curry School of Education, Department of Human Services, University of Virginia, Charlottesville
Scott W. Henggeler, PhD, Family Services Research Center, Department of Psychiatry and Behavioral Sciences, Medical University of South Carolina, Charleston
Aimee K. Hildenbrand, MS, Department of Psychology, Drexel University, Philadelphia, PA
Robert D. Hoge, PhD, CPsych, Department of Psychology, Carleton University, Ottawa, Ontario, Canada
Shelly L. Jackson, PhD, Institute of Law, Psychiatry, and Public Policy, Department of Psychiatry and Neurobehavioral Sciences, University of Virginia School of Medicine, Charlottesville
Wesley G. Jennings, PhD, College of Behavioral and Community Sciences, Department of Criminology, University of South Florida, Tampa
Jessica Jones Coburn, MA, Institute of Law, Psychiatry and Public Policy, Department of Psychiatry and Neurobehavioral Sciences, University of Virginia School of Medicine, Charlottesville
Eva R. Kimonis, PhD, School of Psychology, University of New South Wales, Sydney, Australia
Robert T. Kinscherff, PhD, JD, William James College, Newton, MA, and National Center for Mental Health and Juvenile Justice, Delmar, NY
Gerald P. Koocher, PhD, ABPP, Dean's Office, College of Science and Health, DePaul University, Chicago, IL
Casey LaDuke, MS, Department of Psychology, Drexel University, Philadelphia, PA
Raina Lamade, PhD, School of Psychology, Fairleigh Dickinson University, Teaneck, NJ
Kimberly Larson, JD, PhD, Department of Psychiatry, University of Massachusetts Medical School, Worcester, and William James College, Newton, MA
Marsha Levick, JD, Juvenile Law Center, Philadelphia, PA
Benjamin Locklair, Doctoral Candidate, Department of Psychology, Drexel University, Philadelphia, PA
Beatriz Luna, PhD, Departments of Psychiatry, Pediatrics, and Psychology, Laboratory of Neurocognitive Development, University of Pittsburgh, Pittsburgh, PA
Emily A. M. MacDougall, MA, Department of Psychology and Disruptive Behavior Clinic, University of Alabama, Tuscaloosa
Andre D. Mansion, MA, Department of Psychology and Sandra Day O'Connor College of Law, Arizona State University, Tempe
Robert J. McMahon, PhD, Institute for the Reduction of Youth Violence, Department of Psychology, Simon Fraser University, Burnaby, British Columbia, Canada, and Child and Family Research Institute, Vancouver, British Columbia, Canada
Sharon Messenheimer Kelley, JD, MS, Department of Psychology, Drexel University, Philadelphia, PA
Samantha L. Morin, MA, Department of Psychology, Fordham University, Bronx, NY
Megan Murphy, Doctoral Candidate, Department of Psychology, Drexel University, Philadelphia, PA

Alison G. Nagel, MA, Department of Psychology, University of Virginia, Charlottesville
Brandon Nichter, MA, Department of Psychology, Arizona State University, Tempe
Candice L. Odgers, PhD, Sanford School of Public Policy, Duke University, Durham, NC
Danielle Pandika, MA, Department of Psychology, Arizona State University, Tempe
Lindsey Peterson, Doctoral Candidate, Department of Psychology, Drexel University, Philadelphia, PA
Robert A. Prentky, PhD, School of Psychology, Fairleigh Dickinson University, Teaneck, NJ
Jennifer M. Reingle Gonzalez, PhD, University of Texas Health Science Center, Houston
N. Dickon Reppucci, PhD, Department of Psychology, University of Virginia, Charlottesville
John Rich, MD, MPH, School of Public Health, Department of Health Management and Policy, Drexel University, Philadelphia, PA
Linda Rich, MA, College of Medicine, Center for Nonviolence and Social Justice, Drexel University, Philadelphia, PA
Christina Riggs Romaine, PhD, Department of Psychology, Wheaton College, Norton, MA
Sue Righthand, PhD, Clinical Psychologist, Rockland, ME, and Department of Psychology, University of Maine, Orono
Lourdes M. Rosado, JD, LLM, Juvenile Law Center, Philadelphia, PA
Michael A. Russell, PhD, Methodology Center and Bennett Pierce Prevention Research Center for the Promotion of Human Development, Pennsylvania State University, University Park
Randall T. Salekin, PhD, Department of Psychology and Disruptive Behavior Clinic, University of Alabama, Tuscaloosa
Mary Ann Scali, JD, MSW, National Juvenile Defender Center, Washington, DC
Catherine Shaffer, MA, Department of Psychology, Simon Fraser University, Burnaby, British Columbia, Canada
Elizabeth P. Shulman, PhD, Department of Psychology, Brock University, St. Catharines, Ontario, Canada
Christopher Slobogin, JD, LLM, Vanderbilt University Law School, Nashville, TN
Laurence Steinberg, PhD, Department of Psychology, Temple University, Philadelphia, PA
Jodi L. Viljoen, PhD, Department of Psychology, Simon Fraser University, Burnaby, British Columbia, Canada
Gina M. Vincent, PhD, Department of Psychiatry, Systems and Psychosocial Advances Research Center and the Law and Psychiatry Program, University of Massachusetts Medical School, Worcester
Janet I. Warren, DSW, LCSW, Institute of Law, Psychiatry, and Public Policy, Department of Psychiatry and Neurobehavioral Sciences, University of Virginia School of Medicine, Charlottesville
Melinda Wolbransky, JD, PhD, John Jay College of Criminal Justice, New York, NY, and Drexel University, Philadelphia, PA
Jennifer L. Woolard, PhD, Department of Psychology, Georgetown University, Washington, DC
Catherine Wright, LSW, Department of Psychiatry, University of Pittsburgh, Pittsburgh, PA
Amanda D. Zelechoski, JD, PhD, ABPP, Department of Psychology, Valparaiso University, Valparaiso, IN
Heather Zelle, PhD, JD, Institute of Law, Psychiatry, and Public Policy, University of Virginia, Charlottesville

Series Preface

The *APA Handbook of Psychology and Juvenile Justice* is the 18th publication to be released in the American Psychological Association's *APA Handbooks in Psychology*® series, instituted in 2010. The series comprehends both single volumes and multivolume sets focused on core subfields, or on highly focused content areas and emerging subfields. A complete listing of the series titles to date can be found on p. ii.

Each publication in the series is primarily formulated to address the reference interests and needs of researchers, clinicians, and practitioners in psychology. Each also addresses the needs of graduate students for well-organized and highly detailed supplementary texts, whether to "fill in" their own specialty areas or to acquire solid familiarity with other specialties and emerging trends across the breadth of psychology. Many of the sets additionally bear strong interest for professionals in pertinent complementary fields (i.e., depending on content area), be they corporate executives and human resources personnel; psychiatrists; doctors, nurses, and other health personnel; teachers and school administrators; counselors; legal professionals; and so forth.

Under the direction of small and select editorial boards consisting of top scholars in the field, with chapters authored by both senior and rising researchers and practitioners, each reference commits to a steady focus on best science and best practice. Coverage converges on what is currently known in the particular topical area (including basic historical reviews) and the identification of the most pertinent sources of information in both the core and evolving literature. Volumes and chapters alike pinpoint practical issues; probe unresolved and controversial topics; and highlight future theoretical, research, and practice trends. The editors provide guidance to the "dialogue" among chapters through internal cross-referencing that demonstrates a robust integration of topic. The user is thus offered a clear understanding of the complex interrelationships within each field.

With the imprimatur of the largest scientific and professional organization representing psychology in the United States and the largest association of psychologists in the world, and with content edited and authored by some of its most respected members, the *APA Handbooks in Psychology* series is an indispensable and authoritative reference resource to turn to for researchers, instructors, practitioners, and field leaders alike.

Gary R. VandenBos
APA Publisher

Introduction

The contributions of psychology to the juvenile justice system are important and growing. Historically, psychology has played a role in the development and operation of a separate system for adolescents charged with offending. It has the potential to continue, in a greatly expanded fashion, these contributions to understanding and preventing juvenile offending and to assessment, rehabilitation, and legal decision making with justice-involved youths. In assembling this handbook, however, our primary goal was not simply to provide an overview of these contributions. This book has a foundational premise: Advances in science should help inform the various tasks and decisions that affect the juvenile justice system, from the daily decisions by juvenile court judges to far-reaching decisions of the U.S. Supreme Court on juvenile matters; from appraisal of the risk and needs of a given youth to the legislative policy affecting all juveniles in a given jurisdiction; and from the appropriate training of professionals who deliver services to the enhanced public safety that results from carefully designed and effectively delivered programs for justice-involved youths.

We approached the topic with the view that psychology's most important contributions to juvenile justice are interdisciplinary and empirical. One cannot expect to make meaningful contributions to the legal system without recognizing the nature and structure of applicable law. Within that context, however, questions arise about why and how frequently adolescents become involved in offending, how long they continue, what influences serve as risk and protective factors, how adolescents might be assessed and rehabilitated in relevant and effective ways, and how important information about human development, assessment, and intervention might best be conveyed to juvenile justice professionals.

Many of these questions are clearly interdisciplinary in scope. This handbook provides relevant information from different specializations within psychology, including clinical, cognitive, developmental, educational, family, forensic, neuropsychology, and social. It also includes perspectives from other behavioral sciences (e.g., sociology, criminology), natural sciences (e.g., biology), and mental health professions (e.g., psychiatry, social work) in an attempt to identify the most important sources of information to address the major questions on which we focus.

These questions are also empirical—or at least have empirical components—and have been subjected to research yielding findings that allow us to identify patterns of outcomes that in turn provide some of the best guidance that psychology and other fields can offer to juvenile justice. In emphasizing the importance of empirical evidence, we have inevitably excluded some of the work that has been done in juvenile justice but has not been subjected to good outcome research—or that has been investigated and found wanting. We also recognize that some contributions to juvenile justice have been irrelevant, ineffective, or even actively harmful. We hope that the present approach, in which we identify important domains and discuss the relevant evidence and subsequent implications for research, policy, and practice, will be helpful to those seeking information about established and more recent contributions that are empirically supported or show strong promise of becoming so.

Each of the handbook editors—Kirk Heilbrun, editor-in-chief, and David DeMatteo and Naomi E. S. Goldstein, associate editors—is an applied researcher and scholar with great interest in building and operating effective juvenile systems. Each of us has also been responsible for the provision of services to youths. Our interest in applying science to policy and practice, therefore, is tempered by the recognition of the oft-daunting challenges in doing so.

PART I: OVERVIEW

Reviews such as those provided in this book can be helpful in this respect. To be genuinely useful, however, such reviews must be relevant, current, accurate, and translational. Juvenile justice is an enormous topic. Identifying aspects of psychological science that potentially offer the most impact requires some initial structuring. This handbook is divided into seven domains, which are discussed in depth in Chapter 1: law, human development, patterns of offending, risk factors for offending, forensic assessment, interventions and costs, and training and ethics. Our goal was to select scientific and scholarly contributions that are relevant to these areas and have a great deal of potential to influence the field in the coming decades. Such reviews must be current and accurate; outdated science or misinterpreted studies typically detract from the potential to contribute. Moreover, those reviewing the material must, through critical analysis and prioritization, translate findings and theories into implications for policy and practice. Without this final step, the potential impact of this material would also be considerably diminished. The following sections offer a brief preview of the seven domains and the chapters therein, all contributed by individuals with expertise in that particular area.

PART II: LAW

The past decade has seen a number of important developments in case law regarding the eligibility of adolescents for capital punishment and life-without-parole sentences when charged as adults. Scientific evidence on adolescent development has also influenced other U.S. Supreme Court decisions. Marsha Levick and Jessica Feierman review this evidence and these decisions in Chapter 2.

The concept of preventive justice for adolescents, in contrast to the existing retributive and rehabilitative models of juvenile justice, involves an individualized prevention approach that more clearly incorporates biological, psychological, and sociological research on offending into practice. It appears to have the potential to have a major impact on the juvenile system in the next decade, both because it explicitly calls for the inclusion of scientific knowledge and because of its primary prevention goal. Christopher Slobogin discusses this concept in Chapter 3.

PART III: HUMAN DEVELOPMENT

Adolescents are different from adults in important ways. Cognitive, emotional, and behavioral changes in developmental maturity parallel neurological changes that occur during puberty, throughout adolescence, and into early adulthood. These developmental differences are relevant to the legal system in areas such as due process rights, legal procedure, and post-adjudication treatment and sanctions. Elizabeth P. Shulman and Laurence Steinberg address these issues in detail in Chapter 4.

Recent scientific advances have allowed researchers to investigate brain development among adolescents. This research has provided a better understanding of the neurological and psychosocial changes occurring during adolescence and into young adulthood, as discussed by Beatriz Luna and Catherine Wright in Chapter 5. In addition, in Chapter 6, Alison G. Nagel, Lucy A. Guarnera, and N. Dickon Reppucci review adolescent development and mental health and how each factor affects juveniles' decision making.

PART IV: PATTERNS OF OFFENDING

From the 1980s into the early 1990s, juvenile violent crime increased substantially. More recently, however, juvenile violent crime rates have dropped considerably. Offending rates also differ on the basis of race, age, and gender. See Chapter 7, by Jennifer L. Woolard and Erika Fountain for a thorough examination of trends in juvenile offending statistics and patterns of juvenile offending.

Furthermore, the juvenile offending literature has identified a relatively small proportion of juvenile offenders who persist as serious offenders into adulthood, whereas a larger proportion stop offending and cease involvement with the criminal justice system in early adulthood. Michael A. Russell and Candice L. Odgers discuss this in Chapter 8 and incorporate additional considerations such as the age–crime curve and its relationship to gender and different populations.

PART V: RISK FACTORS FOR OFFENDING

The fourth domain examined in this book involves risk factors for offending. Describing factors empirically associated with greater risk for crime has involved taking a public health perspective (e.g., "What are the influences directly associated with the enhanced risk of a specified outcome such as offending?") rather than a clinical or disease orientation (e.g., "What is the diagnosis of offenders?" or "What symptoms of psychopathology do offenders display?"). Although there are symptoms of mental, emotional, and behavioral disorders that should be targeted in juvenile justice–involved youths, the identification of criminogenic risk factors that can then be modified through intervention appears to offer a more direct path to the prevention and risk reduction of offending. The risk–need–responsivity model for the assessment and treatment of offenders has been a useful approach to organizing the appraisal of risk and need (Andrews, Bonta, & Hoge, 1990). In Chapter 9, Robert D. Hoge discusses this model as applied to juvenile offending.

Individual-level risk factors differ by age and may interact with other individual-, family-, and societal-level risk factors. Individual static risk factors (which do not change through planned intervention) include early aggression and onset of offending, number of arrests, and number of placements. Juvenile psychopathic characteristics, a cluster of traits and behaviors identified by researchers, have some relationship with offending risk. In Chapter 10, Gina M. Vincent, Eva R. Kimonis, and Alisa Clark address juvenile psychopathy. Juvenile substance use is a robust dynamic individual risk factor related to juvenile offending, which makes it a frequent and appropriate rehabilitation target for youths in the juvenile justice system. In Chapter 13, Laurie Chassin, Andre D. Mansion, Brandon Nichter, and Danielle Pandika examine juvenile substance use as a risk factor. School and employment difficulties are risk factors as well. Discussed in detail by Dewey Cornell and Anna Heilbrun in Chapter 11, these school risk factors include bullying and being the victim of bullying, highlighting the importance of threat assessment and prevention in schools. Students dropping out of school creates a related school-based risk factor for justice involvement. Such dropout is related to the application of zero tolerance policies for school misconduct, as discussed by Brian P. Daly, Aimee K. Hildenbrand, Emily Haney-Caron, Naomi E. S. Goldstein, Meghann Galloway, and David DeMatteo in Chapter 12.

Adolescents are quite susceptible to peer influence. This susceptibility is likely to be exacerbated in youths who have disrupted family dynamics, particularly little interaction with their parents. Wesley G. Jennings and Jennifer M. Reingle Gonzalez address the particular problem of gangs as a formalized set of antisocial peers in Chapter 14.

Traumatic life experiences, adverse experience, and victimization are also associated with enhanced risk for juvenile offending, although the ways in which such experiences might result in offending are not yet clear. Amanda D. Zelechoski explores these issues in Chapter 15.

PART VI: FORENSIC ASSESSMENT

Psychological assessment of justice-involved youths helps better inform legal decision making and rehabilitative interventions. A number of legal questions are the subject of such juvenile forensic assessments. First, in Chapter 16 Kirk Heilbrun and Benjamin Locklair provide an overview of forensic assessment with juveniles, noting foundational principles and practice guidelines. Then, additional chapters address the most common questions arising in the course of juvenile forensic assessment. David DeMatteo, Melinda Wolbransky, and Casey LaDuke present a fuller discussion of risk assessment of juveniles in Chapter 17, as do Robert A. Prentky, Sue Righthand, and Raina Lamade in Chapter 29. Robert T. Kinscherff offers a detailed examination of the assessment of juveniles' treatment needs and amenability in Chapter 18. In Chapter 19, Randall T. Salekin, Emily A. M. MacDougall, and Natalie A. Harrison review the assessment of sophistication–maturity of youths in the juvenile justice system, which, as one of the three primary criteria helping to inform juvenile commitment decisions, is also considered in transfer and reverse-transfer decisions.

Some specialized instruments have been developed for juvenile contexts, but other psychological tests and measures originally developed for clinical usage also provide relevant and reliable information when used as part of juvenile forensic evaluations. They tend to be well validated and carefully normed and can help appraise various capacities such as risk, need, and sophistication. Robert P. Archer and Linda J. Baum examine the use of clinical instruments in forensic contexts in Chapter 20.

The question of whether a justice-involved youth is transferred into criminal court—or charged initially as an adult with the possibility of being transferred into the juvenile system—is an important one that may be in the jurisdiction of the juvenile court (for transfer decisions) or the criminal court (for reverse transfers). In Chapter 21, Kimberly Larson and Thomas Grisso provide an in-depth look at forensic psychological assessment in the context of transfer and commitment decisions.

Miranda v. Arizona (1966), which clarified the constitutional basis of the rights to silence and counsel during custodial interrogation, applies to juvenile as well as criminal suspects. When these rights are not sufficiently understood—which is more often true with youths than with adults—suspects may find themselves particularly vulnerable to offering incriminating statements during police questioning. In Chapter 22, Naomi E. S. Goldstein, Sharon Messenheimer Kelley, Lindsey Peterson, Leah Brogan, Heather Zelle, and Christina Riggs Romaine elaborate on the role of forensic assessment in evaluating *Miranda* waiver capacity.

Although the U.S. Supreme Court has never described a standard for juvenile competence to stand trial that differs from the adult standard articulated in *Dusky v. United States* (1960), some jurisdictions may apply the *Dusky* standard somewhat differently because of the age of those involved. Janet I. Warren, Shelly L. Jackson, and Jessica Jones Coburn provide more information about forensic assessment and restoration of juvenile competence to stand trial in Chapter 23.

PART VII: INTERVENTIONS AND COSTS

The goals of the juvenile justice system, which were almost exclusively rehabilitative when the separate juvenile system was developed, have fluctuated over time to incorporate a greater recognition of procedural rights and a stronger emphasis on public safety. Rehabilitation remains a core component, however. This section of the book reviews information about interventions and costs in the juvenile justice system.

Particularly in the past decade or two, there has been an increased focus on treatment in juvenile justice since the "get-tough" approach seen in the 1980s and 1990s. This shift has partly been a function of the enhanced understanding of adolescents' cognitive, emotional, behavioral, and neurological development; it is also a reflection of empirical evidence demonstrating that some approaches to juvenile rehabilitation are effective. Interventions designed to reduce risk by targeting an individual's risk factors are particularly promising, as discussed by Jodi L. Viljoen, Etta Brodersen, Catherine Shaffer, and Robert J. McMahon in Chapter 24.

Such promise is particularly noteworthy for treatments delivered in the community that incorporate multiple domains, including family, school, and peers. See Chapter 26 for an overview of community-based interventions for youths in the juvenile justice system by Scott W. Henggeler. For a variety of reasons, however, it is sometimes more appropriate to commit a youth to residential placement; evidence on treatment in this context is reviewed by Keith R. Cruise, Samantha L. Morin, and Katelyn Affleck in Chapter 28.

One particularly important development during the past decade involves the enhanced focus on trauma and adverse experience among justice-involved youths. As explored by Jessica Feierman and Julian D. Ford in Chapter 25, trauma-informed care reflects recognition of the high rates of traumatic exposure among juvenile justice–involved youths and is designed to address the effects of trauma on emotion, cognition, and behavior.

Among the larger cohort of justice-involved youths, some subgroups have been identified for specific interventions. These groups include young men of color who present at emergency rooms for gunshot injuries (see Chapter 27 for a discussion by John Rich, Erica J. Harris, Sandra L. Bloom, Linda Rich, and Theodore Corbin) and adolescents who offend sexually against peers and younger children (see Chapter 29 for a discussion by Robert A. Prentky, Sue Righthand, and Raina Lamade).

PART VIII: TRAINING AND ETHICS

Finally, there are some unusual challenges in training juvenile justice professionals to the appropriate level of expertise and certain distinctive ethics questions that arise in work with justice-involved youths. Expertise is complex, involving appreciation of how the legal system functions, how youths are developmentally distinct from adults, how the juvenile system may itself be distinctive within the larger system, and how some of the more common kinds of psychopathology are often seen in juveniles. The MacArthur Foundation collaborated with others to develop a juvenile court training curriculum, which seeks to foster competence and an expanded knowledge base across five modules relevant to juvenile justice. The second version of this curriculum, its applicability in training, and its dissemination across the United States are described by Lourdes M. Rosado and Mary Ann Scali in Chapter 30.

In Chapter 31, Gerald P. Koocher and Robert T. Kinscherff discuss ethical issues that arise in the course of work with justice-involved youths. These issues include not only considerations that would apply in any kind of legal context, but also matters that are distinctive or even unique to the nature of adolescence and the particular legal procedures that apply with juveniles.

Kirk Heilbrun
Editor-in-Chief
David DeMatteo and Naomi E. S. Goldstein
Associate Editors

References

Andrews, D. A., Bonta, J., & Hoge, R. D. (1990). Classification for effective rehabilitation: Rediscovering psychology. *Criminal Justice and Behavior*, *17*, 19–52. http://dx.doi.org/10.1177/0093854890017001004

Dusky v. United States, 362 U.S. 402 (1960).

Miranda v. Arizona, 348 U.S. 436 (1966).

Part I

OVERVIEW

Chapter 1

PSYCHOLOGY AND JUVENILE JUSTICE: HUMAN DEVELOPMENT, LAW, SCIENCE, AND PRACTICE

Kirk Heilbrun, David DeMatteo, Naomi E. S. Goldstein, Benjamin Locklair, Megan Murphy, and Christy Giallella

Psychology has an extensive history of contributions to the juvenile justice system. From the establishment of the first juvenile court in Chicago in 1899 to the assessment of and interventions with adolescents charged as juveniles, from research on developmental differences to that on patterns of juvenile delinquency, the field of psychology has a strong presence in advancing knowledge and promoting informed decision making in juvenile justice. Psychological research has identified important ways in which adolescents differ from adults, with significant implications for policy and practice, and has illustrated how risk factors and criminogenic needs can be applied to the prevention of offending, the diversion of less serious offenders, and the rehabilitation of more serious offenders. A psychelegal analysis of a series of U.S. Supreme Court decisions has shown that such research has substantially influenced the Court's thinking in making decisions regarding the death penalty and other sentencing options for adolescents convicted as adults (see Chapter 2, this handbook).

Such an analysis of law is important in this handbook. But there are actually seven domains that will be considered in this broad area. In the present chapter, we offer an overview of these seven domains to prime the reader for the more detailed discussions in each of the chapters that follow. As noted in the introduction to the handbook, the domains comprise law, human development, patterns of offending, risk factors for offending, forensic assessment, interventions and costs, and training and ethics.

LAW

Juvenile justice is a delicate balancing act between the philosophical ideals of paternalism and personhood. On one hand, juveniles are entitled to protection and paternalistic care because of their age, maturity level, and need for guidance. On the other hand, juveniles are autonomous beings, capable of independent thought and action. To complicate matters, today's conceptualization of juvenile justice must accommodate and balance the often-competing interests of the child, the child's caretakers, and the government.

Childhood as Distinct

Modern society conceptualizes childhood as a special period in one's life—a time of learning, growing, and developing—and childhood is seen as a critical time for nurturing and guiding youths into being productive members of society. However, the current conceptualization of childhood does not reflect or even resemble prior conceptualizations of childhood. Historically, children were not given special status or consideration and were instead treated simply as the property of their parents and expected to conduct themselves as miniature adults (Elrod & Ryder, 2011). Similarly, children caught violating societal laws were typically subject to the same standards, procedures, and consequences as adults.

Societal treatment of young offenders has changed dramatically over the years, and it continues to evolve today. Juvenile courts were designed to rehabilitate wayward youths. However, through the years, the juvenile court model has moved away

http://dx.doi.org/10.1037/14643-001
APA Handbook of Psychology and Juvenile Justice, K. Heilbrun (Editor-in-Chief)

from a primarily rehabilitative scheme into something that looks more like the adult criminal justice system, with increasing procedural protections and more frequent waivers into adult court.

The development of the first juvenile court in the United States at the end of the 19th century ushered in a new era for the handling of juvenile offenders (Platt, 1977). The first juvenile court (in Cook County, Illinois) was the first of its kind to create a separate legal process for juvenile offenders, and it focused on rehabilitation. Soon after its inception, juvenile courts emerged throughout the United States. The development of a legal framework designed specifically for juveniles marked a significant conceptual shift in how society viewed juvenile culpability and the state's role dealing with youthful offenders. Children who broke the law were no longer designated as criminals but rather as delinquents who were capable of being rehabilitated.

Initially, juvenile courts operated under the legal doctrine of *parens patriae* ("parent of, or for, the country"), meaning that the state assumed the authority to make decisions for the benefit of children in a fashion similar to that of a parent. Under a *parens patriae* philosophy, juvenile courts were granted wide discretionary power to intervene in the best interests of the child. For example, in *Commonwealth v. Fisher* (1905), 14-year-old Frank Fisher was indicted for larceny and sentenced to 7 years in the house of refuge for rehabilitation. Frank's father brought suit, alleging that Frank had been denied a trial by jury and other aspects of due process. He further argued that Frank's crime was only a minor offense and that his 7-year sentence was significantly longer than any sentence he would have received in adult court. The Supreme Court of Pennsylvania disagreed with Frank's father and upheld the constitutionality of the juvenile court, stating that due process protections were not necessary when the state acts under its *parens patriae* powers because the action "is not for the punishment of offenders, but for the reformation of children" (*Commonwealth v. Fisher*, 1905, p. 49).

Expansion of Due Process Protections to Juveniles

Theoretically, the juvenile court system provided less due process protection but a greater concern for the interests of the juvenile. However, in *Kent v. United States* (1966), the U.S. Supreme Court noted that this compensating benevolence benefit may not actually exist in practice. Instead, juveniles may receive what the Court characterized as the "worst of both worlds"—"neither the protection accorded to adults nor the solicitous care and regenerative treatment postulated for children" (*Kent*, 1966, pp. 555–56). At issue in *Kent* was the transfer—without a hearing—of a 16-year-old offender from juvenile court to adult court. After a series of appeals, the U.S. Supreme Court held that for Kent's transfer to be valid, he should have been afforded certain due process protections, including representation by counsel, a hearing, and access to probation and social records that would be considered in the transfer decision. After nearly 60 years of wide discretion and informal *parens patriae* procedures, *Kent v. United States* marked the beginning of a trilogy of Supreme Court cases expanding due process protections and advancing juvenile justice reform.

Soon after *Kent v. United States*, the Supreme Court heard the landmark case *In re Gault* (1967), which extended many (but not all) due process rights to juvenile court proceedings. In *Gault*, a 15-year-old offender was adjudicated delinquent for making lewd phone calls to his neighbor. At the delinquency hearing, there were no sworn witnesses and no formal record of the proceedings. On appeal, the Supreme Court issued a landmark ruling holding that the Fourteenth Amendment and the Bill of Rights do not provide protection exclusively for adults (*In re Gault*, 1967). The Court extended juvenile due process rights to include notice of charges, the right to counsel, the right against self-incrimination, and the right to confront and cross-examine witnesses. Interestingly, in a dissent, Justice Stewart cautioned that by requiring many of the same due process guarantees in juvenile cases, the Court was converting rehabilitative juvenile proceedings into adversarial criminal proceedings.

Three years after *In re Gault*, the Supreme Court took another step toward making procedure in juvenile courts more similar to that in adult courts. In the case of *In re Winship* (1970), the Court raised the standard of proof necessary in delinquency cases and held that the state must prove its case beyond a reasonable doubt rather than merely by a preponderance of the evidence. The Court noted that the risks relating to loss of liberty in juvenile proceedings were similar to the risks in adult proceedings, which required the use of the same standard.

In re Gault and *In re Winship* significantly expanded the due process protections afforded to juveniles, but juveniles are still not afforded all of the same procedural protections as adults. For example, in *McKeiver v. Pennsylvania* (1971), the Supreme Court held that the right to a jury trial did not extend to juvenile court proceedings. In so holding, the Court reasoned that juries have a tendency to make court proceedings more adversarial and would disrupt the informal atmosphere of the juvenile court. The Court feared that trial by jury would essentially abolish any meaningful distinctions between juvenile and criminal proceedings.

Categorical Sentencing Exceptions for Juveniles

As noted by the Court in *McKeiver v. Pennsylvania* (1971), even with the expansion of several due process rights to juvenile courts, there are still meaningful distinctions between juvenile and criminal proceedings. These distinctions are on both a philosophical level—rehabilitation versus punishment—and a more practical jurisdictional level. Juvenile courts only have jurisdiction over youths until a certain statutorily defined age, which varies by state (Elrod & Ryder, 2011). As such, some juveniles who commit serious offenses might be more appropriately handled in the criminal system, where the court retains jurisdiction over them for a longer period of time. Today, all states have methods to transfer a juvenile from juvenile court to criminal court. Depending on the jurisdiction, this process is known as *waiver, certification, remand, bindover*, or *transfer* (Elrod & Ryder, 2011). When adolescents are prosecuted in criminal court, they are subject to the same penalties that can be imposed on adults—except for a few categorical exceptions, including bans on juvenile death penalty and some life-without-parole decisions. We present a brief review of some of the more notable categorical exemptions for juvenile offenders in this section, but a more in-depth discussion of these constitutional sentencing limits can be found in Chapter 2 of this handbook.

In *Thompson v. Oklahoma* (1988), the U.S. Supreme Court held that the Eighth Amendment forbids imposition of the death penalty on offenders who were younger than age 16 when their crimes were committed. Nearly 20 years later, in *Roper v. Simmons* (2005), the Supreme Court extended the categorical ban on the death penalty to those younger than age 18 when their crimes were committed. Before *Thompson* and *Roper*, there was no categorical ban on the death penalty for juvenile offenders, although the Court had a history of prohibiting the execution of certain juvenile offenders on the basis of individual characteristics and maturity. For example, in *Eddings v. Oklahoma* (1982), the Court held that it was a violation of the Eighth Amendment to impose the death penalty on a 16-year-old convicted of murder without first considering his unhappy upbringing and emotional disturbances as potential mitigating factors. In a narrow 5–4 decision in *Roper*, the Court held that the execution of juvenile offenders constituted cruel and unusual punishment and was therefore prohibited by the Eighth Amendment.

More recently, the U.S. Supreme Court further limited the penalties that may be imposed on juvenile offenders. In *Graham v. Florida* (2010), the Court held that the Eighth Amendment prohibits a sentence of life without parole for juveniles younger than age 18 who commit a nonhomicide offense. In its holding, the Court held that the Eighth Amendment "forbid[s] States from making the judgment at the outset that [juvenile] offenders never will be fit to reenter society" (*Graham v. Florida*, 2010, p. 2030). Finally, in *Miller v. Alabama* (2012), the Court held that the Eighth Amendment prohibits the imposition of mandatory juvenile life-in-prison sentences without the possibility of parole even in cases involving juvenile homicide offenders. Although the Court did not categorically ban life without parole for juvenile homicide offenders, it banned the mandatory imposition of such punishment.

Preventive Justice for Adolescents

In light of the shortcomings of the current juvenile justice system, Slobogin and Fondacaro (2011) were the first to advocate for an individualized prevention approach to juvenile justice (see Chapter 3, this handbook). According to this position, the current juvenile justice system is failing because it does not incorporate social science research on juveniles and juvenile offending into practice. As such, the juvenile justice system is an inefficient hodgepodge of four different philosophies: rehabilitation, adult retribution, diminished retribution, and individual prevention. In Slobogin and Fondacaro's view, retributive and rehabilitative models of juvenile justice are both problematic. Retributive models, especially adult retribution, contribute to long-term incarceration and high recidivism rates among juveniles. Similarly, rehabilitation as it is currently structured is too broad, has the tendency to excuse adolescents for their antisocial behavior, and does not focus on principles of effective treatment. Using biological, psychological, and sociological research regarding juveniles, Slobogin and Fondacaro argued that an individualized prevention model of juvenile justice would lead to far better results. Furthermore, they argued that because it is so difficult to deter juveniles from committing crime, society should focus time and resources on juvenile crime prevention (Slobogin & Fondacaro, 2011).

The proposed individualized prevention model is based on principles of risk management, and it proposes several radical changes to the existing juvenile justice framework. Specifically, Slobogin and Fondacaro (2011) recommended eliminating status offenses and expanding the jurisdiction of juvenile courts to well beyond age 18. They also recommended that that the degree of intervention imposed by the court should be directly proportional to the degree of risk posed by the juvenile (Slobogin & Fondacaro, 2011). In addition, they proposed abolishing the juvenile transfer system and instead focusing on the risk level of each individual juvenile offender.

HUMAN DEVELOPMENT

The juvenile justice system was founded on the idea that adolescents are different from adults and that they should be treated differently by the legal system. It was also founded on the principle of rehabilitation, recognizing developmental differences that affect young people's responses to intervention and their ability to mature into law-abiding adults. Although the juvenile justice system has trended toward more punitive sanctions for juveniles since *Kent v. United States* (1966) and *In re Gault* (1967), research into human development has flourished, and knowledge about adolescent development continues to affect the justice system. As policies and interventions for justice-involved youths are developed, it is essential to understand and account for differences between adolescents and adults that could have an impact on legally relevant behavior. Developmentally responsive treatment for juveniles could reduce rates of reoffending, improving public safety and reducing costs. Part II of this handbook is devoted to understanding human development in the context of juvenile justice. Developments in the juvenile justice system during the 20th century reflected the understanding that juveniles have rehabilitative needs related to their development and that special protections and procedures are needed, at times, for youths to benefit from the due process rights they are guaranteed (*In re Gault*, 1967; Melton, Petrila, Poythress, & Slobogin, 2007).

Adolescents are different from adults in important ways that are relevant to the legal system. They are more likely to engage in antisocial behavior than adults; antisocial behavior tends to increase during adolescence until age 17 and then decline steadily into adulthood (Piquero, Farrington, & Blumstein, 2003). Although some young offenders engage in criminal activity during adulthood, the vast majority desist from antisocial behavior and lead productive, law-abiding lives (Steinberg, 2009). Differences in psychosocial, cognitive, and neurological development can account for this pattern and help to explain delinquent behavior.

These differences also raise questions about juveniles' functioning within the legal system. Do juveniles fully understand and appreciate their rights? Can adolescents be held to the same standard of criminal responsibility as adults, given differences in maturity levels? Because they are still developing across a number of domains, do juveniles demonstrate more promise for rehabilitation? Are they more amenable to treatment and responsive to interventions? Developmentally related differences between adolescents and adults are pertinent to the legal system in a variety of ways that are relevant to due process rights, legal procedure, and postadjudication treatment and sanctions. These differences are addressed in detail in Chapter 4 of this handbook.

Psychosocial Development

Adolescents, with their incomplete developmental maturation, demonstrate a number of psychosocial deficits relative to adults. Differences in maturity are seen in a number of areas, including risk taking, reward sensitivity, independent functioning, susceptibility to peer influence, future orientation, emotion regulation, and decision making. Cognitive, emotional, and behavioral changes in developmental maturity parallel neurological changes that occur during puberty, throughout adolescence, and into adulthood.

Adolescents display heightened risk-taking behavior, which may lead to interactions with the legal system. In a large national study of such risk taking among youths, high school students reported engaging in risky behaviors at high rates, such as texting while driving (32.8% of students), drinking alcohol (38.7%), using marijuana (23.1%), getting into physical fights (32.8%), having unprotected sex (39.8% of sexually active students), and smoking cigarettes (18.1%; Eaton et al., 2012). Adolescents perceive risk at similar levels to adults, and they can accurately identify the risks associated with particular behaviors and situations. However, adolescents are more sensitive to potential rewards than are adults, which may explain the higher rates of risky behavior (Steinberg, 2009). This reward sensitivity has been demonstrated across a number of studies using a variety of measures (e.g., behavioral, self-report), and it aligns with neurological changes that occur during puberty (e.g., Crone, Bunge, Latenstein, & van der Molen, 2005; Steinberg et al., 2009).

Adolescence is a period of development in which young people work to establish independent self-identities. Youths demonstrate difficulties in this area; compared with adults, adolescents have considerable difficulty resisting peer influence (Steinberg & Monahan, 2007). They are much more likely to engage in risk-taking behavior (e.g., aggressive driving) when their friends are present, and they make decisions similar to adults when alone. Adults do not demonstrate this effect of peer influence, performing similarly regardless of the presence of peers (Gardner & Steinberg, 2005).

In addition to heightened risk taking during adolescence and sensitivity to peer influence, youths also demonstrate deficits in their ability to consider the future consequences of their behavior (Steinberg et al., 2009). As adolescents develop into adults, this ability improves. However, teenagers are notably short sighted when making decisions. In addition to deficits in everyday decision making, youths also display problems with setting long-term goals and working toward them (Byrnes, 2002). Adolescents' abilities to make thoughtful, mature decisions are also affected by their increased levels of impulsivity, relative to adults. Impulsivity appears to decrease in a linear fashion after age 10, and the ability to delay gratification increases throughout adolescence (Steinberg et al., 2008).

There is also evidence that adolescents experience emotions more intensely and have more difficulty regulating their emotions, which may contribute to legally relevant behavior (Kemp, 2010). This is a particularly important consideration for young people who also experience mental health problems. The many developmental issues discussed, in combination with mental health problems and emotional dysregulation, can interact and have substantial legal implications (e.g., competency, criminal responsibility, treatment planning).

Brain Development

Technological advances in brain science in recent decades have allowed researchers to investigate brain development among adolescents. This research has helped psychologists understand and explain neurological and psychosocial changes that happen during this transitional period and well into young adulthood (see Chapter 5, this handbook).

The frontal lobe, which controls executive functioning, undergoes a significant decline in gray matter through the process of synaptic pruning and increased myelination (Paus, 2005). These changes occur during adolescence and contribute to the development of adultlike cognitive abilities. By age 16, teenagers reach adult-level performance on a number of cognitive tasks, such as information processing, logical reasoning, and working memory (e.g., Conklin, Luciana, Hooper, & Yarger, 2007; Hooper, Luciana, Conklin, & Yarger, 2004). However, improvements in executive functioning capacities and the development of connections to other areas of the brain that regulate social and emotional responses continue throughout the adolescent years and into early adulthood, leading to slower maturation of response inhibition, planning, and the ability to consider consequences (Paus, 2005; Steinberg, 2009).

Other localized brain areas (e.g., parietal lobe, striatum) and important connections among brain regions continue to develop into adulthood (Luna, Padmanabhan, & O'Hearn, 2010). This incomplete neural development partially explains why adolescents can perform similarly to adults in many lab-based experiments of executive functioning, yet often demonstrate significant immaturity of judgment when confronted with the social and emotional demands of real-world situations (Steinberg, 2009).

In addition to structural brain changes during the adolescent years, there is a remodeling of the dopaminergic system that leads to a dramatic increase in dopaminergic activity and redistribution of dopamine receptors in cortical and subcortical areas of the brain during puberty (Steinberg, 2009). These changes in dopaminergic activity are linked to increases in reward sensitivity and reward-seeking behaviors during adolescence (Steinberg, 2009). Although this heightened tendency to seek out rewards can lead to interaction with the legal system, research has suggested that such sensation-seeking behavior is normative during the adolescent period. Unfortunately, cognitive control mechanisms, which can modulate increases in sensation-seeking behavior, are not fully developed and interconnected in adolescence, thereby further compromising capacities for mature decision making and risk avoidance (Luna, Paulsen, Padmanabhan, & Geier, 2013). Connections between the social and emotional system of the brain and the cognitive control system are formed and strengthened later in development, improving older adolescents' and young adults' abilities to control their behavior and conform it to social and legal requirements (Steinberg, 2009).

Adolescence is a period of human development in which significant changes occur across a number of domains, and teenagers differ from adults in ways that can influence their legally relevant behaviors. As the understanding of adolescent development continues to improve, research on psychosocial and neurological differences between adolescents and adults can increasingly inform policy and practice in the juvenile justice system.

PATTERNS OF OFFENDING

Several important questions can be addressed by reviewing data on the frequency, nature, and persistence of juvenile offending. That is the focus of the two chapters in this domain.

Juvenile Offending Statistics

Although the prevalence is decreasing, juvenile violent crime remains a significant social and legal concern in the United States. In the 1980s and 1990s, the Violent Crime Index—which tracks murder, forcible rape, aggravated assault, and robbery—revealed a dramatic spike in juvenile violent crime rates, which jumped 64% between 1980 and 1994 (Butts & Travis, 2002). The rise was highest in juvenile murder rates, which showed a 99% increase over this same period (Butts & Travis, 2002). Although this heightened level of juvenile violent crime was influenced by a wide range of social and historical forces, some scholars have attributed it largely to the introduction of crack cocaine in the mid-1980s (Greenwood & Turner, 2011). Gangs relied on minority youths to distribute the drug in the disorganized—and often violent—street-level market.

More recently, though, juvenile crime rates have dropped in an equally dramatic manner, reaching their lowest point in 32 years (Butts, 2013). Puzzanchera's (2013) recently published statistics from the Office of Juvenile Justice and Delinquency Prevention (OJJDP), part of the U.S. Department of Justice, provided a snapshot of the decrease in all manner of crimes committed by juvenile offenders. The OJJDP data are drawn from the FBI's Uniform Crime Reports, a database in which state and local law enforcement voluntarily report crime and arrest rates; however, only the latter records demographic details of the perpetrators. For example, between 1980 and 2010, the juvenile arrest rate for burglary plummeted 74%, and the arrest rate for weapons violations has fallen 32% since 2006 (Puzzanchera, 2013). Even more recently, between 2009 and 2010, the OJJDP statistics showed that juvenile arrest rates for murder dropped 14%, robbery dropped 14%, aggravated assault dropped 10%, and rape dropped 8% (Puzzanchera, 2013).

Although this trend is a positive development after the spike in the 1980s and 1990s, the Uniform Crime Reports data do not offer a complete picture of the rates of juvenile crime. After all, arrest rates reflect where communities are devoting their policing resources and attention, not actual rates of offending; a drop in burglary arrests, for example, could simply indicate that such crimes are not being pursued as intently in an era of decreased law enforcement budgets (Greenwood & Turner, 2011). Still, even if the magnitude of the drop might be exaggerated, the data speak to an across-the-board decrease in juvenile crime.

Despite the trend toward lower juvenile arrest rates, the absolute number of juveniles arrested is still substantial. For example, although juveniles made up a relatively small proportion of all arrestees in 2010, law enforcement personnel across the United States arrested 1.6 million juveniles (Puzzanchera, 2013). In 2012, just more than 60,000 juveniles were arrested for violent crimes alone (Butts, 2013). Although these numbers might seem small, when taken alongside self-reported survey data, they suggest that by age 23, nearly one in three Americans has been arrested (Brame, Turner, Paternoster, & Bushway, 2012).

These arrest rates also show marked differences among various demographic groups on the basis of race, age, and gender. Racial and ethnic minorities are overrepresented in the juvenile justice system in terms of both arrests and contact with the system (Leiber, 2003; Pope & Feyerherm, 1995); for example, in 2010 African American youths were arrested 10 times more often than Caucasian youths (Puzzanchera, 2013). Additionally, there are demographic differences when it comes to the age of juvenile offenders. In 2010, youths younger than age 15 accounted for 27% of all juvenile arrests for Violent Crime Index offenses and 28% for all juvenile arrests for Property Crime Index offenses (Puzzanchera, 2013). Gender differences in juvenile arrest rates were also reported. Criminal justice statistics from 2010 indicate that females accounted for 18% of juvenile Violent Crime Index arrests, 38% of juvenile Property Crime Index arrests, and 45% of juvenile larceny–theft arrests (Puzzanchera, 2013). Perhaps most interesting, these demographic differences in arrest rates are interrelated. Data drawn from the National Longitudinal Survey of Youth in 1997 suggested that although African American males under age 23 were arrested at a rate 1.3 times higher than that of their Caucasian peers, there was no significant difference in arrest rates between African American and Caucasian females (Brame, Bushway, Paternoster, & Turner, 2014).

Persistence Versus Desistance Into Adulthood

This handbook (see Chapter 8) also explores reasons for desistence and persistence of juvenile offending into adulthood. Most delinquent youths tend to stop offending sometime in late adolescence or early adulthood, but a small percentage become chronic lifetime offenders (Mulvey, 2011). Le Blanc and Fréchette (1989) estimated that 30% to 60% of adolescents arrested by the police or convicted in court will have a criminal record as adults.

One robust finding that has been observed in nearly all Western cultures is the existence of a bell-shaped age–crime curve illustrating the relationship between offending and age (Farrington, 1986; Piquero, Farrington, & Blumstein, 2007). According to the age–crime curve, offending behavior generally increases in late childhood, peaks in the teenage years between ages 15 and 19, and then declines in the early 20s (Farrington, 1986; Piquero et al., 2007). Although a bell-shaped relationship between age and offending is fairly robust, the exact shape of the age–crime curve varies in certain populations. For example, the age–crime curve peaks earlier for girls than for boys, and young males from disadvantaged neighborhoods appear to have a higher and wider age–crime curve, which suggests that they may outgrow delinquency later or may have started engaging in criminal offending during adulthood (Elliott, Pampel, & Huizinga, 2004; Fabio, Tu, Loeber, & Cohen, 2011).

Research from the Pathways to Desistance Study, the most comprehensive data set currently available involving serious juvenile offenders, has suggested that most youths who commit felonies greatly reduce their offending over time (Mulvey, 2011). This study suggested that 91% of serious adolescent offenders in the study decreased their illegal activity in the 3 years after court involvement. Interestingly, longer stays in juvenile institutions were not associated with a lower risk of recidivism. In fact, institutional placement was associated with increased offending levels in those individuals with the lowest level of offending. Additionally, community-based supervision and aftercare were associated with decreased recidivism, higher school attendance, and higher work attendance. Finally, substance use was found to be a major contributor to continued criminal activity by serious adolescent offenders (Mulvey, 2011).

RISK FACTORS FOR OFFENDING

Categorization of Risk and Protective Factors

Risk factors and protective factors associated with serious, violent, and chronic juvenile offending have been widely studied and enjoy considerable empirical support (e.g., Cottle, Lee, & Heilbrun, 2001; Hawkins et al., 2000; Loeber, Farrington, Stouthamer-Loeber, Moffitt, & Caspi, 1998; see Heilbrun, Goldstein, & Redding, 2005). Broadly defined, risk factors are internal or external variables predictive of negative outcomes, such as antisocial behavior, delinquency, or recidivism. Some risk factors may be merely correlated with negative outcomes, and others have a causal relationship to a negative outcome. Conversely, protective factors can be conceptualized as internal or external influences that decrease the likelihood of a negative outcome or increase the likelihood of a positive outcome.

Both risk factors and protective factors are cumulative, so the ability to predict delinquent behavior increases or decreases as a function of the number of factors present and the number of data sources relied on (see, e.g., Grisso, 2013; Hawkins et al., 2000). Additionally, risk and protective factors can combine and interact with one another, and the salience of risk and protective factors may change throughout life stages. For example, risk factors related to the family appear to have the greatest influence when youths are young, whereas community-related risk factors (e.g., delinquent peers) have a larger effect during adolescence when peers play a larger role in one's life (DeMatteo & Marczyk, 2005).

Research into the risk factors for juvenile offending has primarily focused on two areas: factors associated with initial delinquent behavior and factors associated with recidivism. A distinction between static and dynamic risk factors is frequently made. Static factors are unchangeable through planned intervention (e.g., gender, criminal history), whereas dynamic factors (or "criminogenic needs") are potentially changeable. Such dynamic factors include influences such as social support networks, educational level, substance use, and employment (Andrews & Bonta, 2010). Dynamic factors can be further divided into stable and acute risk factors (Hanson & Harris, 2001). Both stable and acute risk factors are potentially changeable, but stable risk factors are more resistant to change and include characteristics such as procriminal associates and antisocial personality disorder. Acute factors, by contrast, may change quickly and include things such as mood and cooperation with authorities (Hanson & Harris, 2001).

Risk–Need–Responsivity Model

The risk–need–responsivity model for the assessment and treatment of offenders is based on three core principles: risk, needs, and responsivity (Andrews, Bonta, & Hoge, 1990). The risk principle asserts that criminal behavior can be reliably predicted and, once predicted, an offender's level of treatment should directly correspond to the offender's risk of recidivism—so higher risk offenders, for example, should receive more intensive services (Andrews et al., 1990). The need principle asserts that the criminogenic needs of offenders should be assessed and targeted in treatment. Finally, the responsivity principle outlines how treatment should be provided. It has two components: general and specific responsivity. To maximize an offender's ability to learn as part of a rehabilitative intervention, general responsivity calls for the use of cognitive social learning techniques to influence behavior. Specific responsivity principles take into account the individual characteristics of each offender, such as strengths, learning style, personality, and demographic characteristics, to maximize treatment efficacy. The risk–need–responsivity model has been used with increasing success to assess and rehabilitate juvenile offenders in the United States and elsewhere.

Specific Risk and Protective Factors Related to Juvenile Delinquency

Risk and protective factors related to juvenile offending fall into a wide variety of psychological, medical, biological, behavioral, and social domains (DeMatteo & Marczyk, 2005). In addition, many of these risk and protective factors operate at the individual, family, and community levels of functioning (see, e.g., Hawkins et al., 2000; Melton et al., 2007).

Individual factors. Individual-level risk factors for juvenile criminality and recidivism vary greatly on the basis of age and often interact with other individual, familial, and societal-level risk factors. Core static individual-level risk factors associated with juvenile offending include a history of early aggression, early onset of criminal offending, age at first adjudication, number of prior arrests, and number of out-of-home placements or institutionalizations (Cornell, Peterson, & Richards, 1999; Farrington & Hawkins, 1991; Heilbrun, 1997; Loeber & Farrington, 2001). In addition, juvenile psychopathy—a relatively stable cluster of personality traits (see Chapter 10, this handbook)—has also been found to be an important and useful predictor of antisocial behavior in early adulthood (Gretton, Hare, & Catchpole, 2004; Lynam, Miller, Vachon, Loeber, & Stouthamer-Loeber, 2009). Moreover, traumatic life experiences and violent victimization are related to an increased risk of juvenile delinquency; however, the specific pathways by which traumatic life events lead to juvenile delinquency are not yet well understood (see Chapter 14, this handbook). More important, all of the individual-level risk factors we have mentioned have demonstrated a robust relationship with juvenile offending. However, because of their static nature, the historical variables are not the target of intervention strategies. However, interventions may target dynamic attributes related to historical variables—such as treating anger problems in an individual with a long history of temper loss.

Juvenile substance use is a robust dynamic individual risk factor related to juvenile offending (see, e.g., Elliott, Huizinga, & Ageton, 1985; Stouthamer-Loeber, Wei, Loeber, & Masten, 2004). As such, it is also frequently the target of rehabilitative treatment for juvenile offenders. Although substance use is a strong predictor of juvenile criminality and recidivism, the predictive utility of substance use as a risk factor for juvenile offending decreases as youths get older (U.S. Department of Health and Human Services, 2001). Other individual-level dynamic risk factors related to juvenile offending and recidivism include drug dealing, high impulsivity, high negative emotionality (e.g., fear, anger), hyperactivity, and beliefs and attitudes favorable to antisocial behavior (Hawkins et al., 2000; Loeber et al., 1998).

Research has also focused on identifying protective factors, including high academic achievement, intolerant attitudes toward deviance, being female, high accountability, high IQ, commitment to school, high educational achievement, associations with nondelinquent peers, and residing in a neighborhood with a low crime rate (e.g., DeMatteo & Marczyk, 2005; Howell, 2003; U.S. Department of Health and Human Services, 2001). A positive social orientation, perceived sanctions for transgressions, supportive relationship with parents, parental monitoring, and recognition for involvement in conventional activities may also be protective factors against juvenile offending (Shader, 2001).

Family factors. Important family risk factors for juvenile delinquency include interfamilial violence; low levels of parental involvement; high levels of parental hostility, conflict, and aggression; parental criminality; inadequate parental supervision; early parental loss; and emotional deprivation (DeMatteo & Marczyk, 2005). Some research has suggested a relationship between being raised in a single-parent household and juvenile delinquency (McCord, Widom, & Crowell, 2001), but other research has postulated that socioeconomic conditions may instead account for this apparent relationship (Crockett, Eggebeen, & Hawkins, 1993).

Educational and employment factors. Difficulties at school or with employment are empirically supported risk factors for juvenile offending. Academic risk factors associated with delinquent behavior among juveniles include low academic achievement, poor academic performance, low commitment to school, dropping out of school, school overcrowding, truancy, and frequent school transitions (e.g., Hawkins et al., 2000; Hinshaw, 1992; Kashani, Jones, Burnby, & Thomas, 1999). In addition, suspension and expulsion have been linked to increased delinquent behavior (McCord et al., 2001). Finally, bullying at school has been linked to later antisocial behavior (see Hawkins et al., 1999).

Peer factors. The influence of peer groups plays a strong role in juvenile behavior during adolescence. Research has consistently found that adolescents who associate with delinquent youths tend to have higher levels of delinquent and antisocial behavior (e.g., Farrington, 1989; Lipsey & Derzon, 1998). Furthermore, youths who have little interaction with their parents tend to be more highly influenced by delinquent peer behavior (Steinberg, 1987). Living in a neighborhood with high levels of poverty and crime also increases the likelihood that adolescents will engage in offending behavior (McCord et al., 2001). Relatedly, gang membership has been shown to be more predictive of antisocial behavior than the presence of delinquent peers (Battin, Hill, Abbott, Catalano, & Hawkins, 1998; DeMatteo & Marczyk, 2005).

FORENSIC ASSESSMENT

Over the years, the juvenile justice system has embraced a number of different goals and priorities, from treatment and rehabilitation to tougher sanctions for more "blameworthy" juvenile offenders. For all such legal decisions, however, the individual characteristics of the juveniles have remained relevant. Psychological assessment of juveniles within the juvenile justice system plays an important role in their procedural and substantive treatment in a variety of legal contexts, discussed briefly here and in more detail in subsequent chapters in this handbook.

As the field of forensic mental health assessment has matured, practitioners and researchers have developed principles and guidelines for effective and ethical assessment practice with adults (see Heilbrun, Grisso, & Goldstein, 2009). Although many of these apply comparably to assessments conducted within the juvenile justice system, such juvenile assessments present some distinctive challenges that require modification to some of these principles (see Chapter 15, this handbook).

Risk Assessment

Particularly in the 1990's-era "get-tough" environment of juvenile justice, which prioritized protection of the community and deemphasized the rehabilitative and *parens patriae* roles of the juvenile court, assessments for juvenile offenders' risks for certain outcomes (e.g., violence or recidivism) became increasingly relevant to their dispositions. Juvenile offenders' risk for violence or reoffense may affect their prospects for assignment to a diversion program, their waiver to adult criminal court, or their postadjudication dispositions (Hoge & Andrews, 2010). As with adults, the contemporary prevailing approach to risk assessment with juveniles is strongly influenced by the risk–need–responsivity model, in which the juveniles' risk and needs are weighed against protective factors as well as their potential to benefit from risk-reducing interventions (Andrews & Bonta, 2010; see Chapters 16 and 28, this handbook).

Treatment Needs and Amenability

The type of treatment an individual juvenile offender needs—and the likelihood that the juvenile will engage with and benefit from that treatment—is a relevant consideration for a juvenile court. For purposes of rehabilitation, the assessment of treatment needs and amenability is vital to the court's ability to reach appropriate and maximally beneficial postadjudication dispositions and placements. Treatment needs and amenability have also become a key consideration in determining the appropriateness of transfer to adult criminal court (Chen & Salekin, 2012; see Chapter 17, this handbook).

Sophistication–Maturity

Under the public safety–oriented paradigm that came into vogue in the 1990s, the transfer of juvenile offenders to criminal court became increasingly common. Along with other considerations (typically risk, treatment needs, and treatment amenability), the individual juvenile's sophistication and maturity are core aspects of the decision regarding whether that juvenile is considered appropriate for such transfer (Salekin, 2002). Assessment of a juvenile's sophistication and maturity also provides useful information for treatment and intervention planning.

Forensic Uses of Clinical Instruments

Although a number of specialized instruments have been developed specifically for use with the juvenile justice population (see, e.g., Borum, Bartel, & Forth, 2003), instruments designed for non–justice-involved clinical populations remain in common use in forensic contexts. The clinical instruments that are applied appropriately in forensic settings are typically well validated and extensively normed, and the information they provide is relevant to various functional and legal capacities. Intellectual assessment, for instance, may be an important component of assessing a juvenile's sophistication, and personality assessment (particularly when relevant to constructs such as psychopathic traits) may be relevant to considerations of risk or treatment amenability (Chen & Salekin, 2012).

Transfer and Commitment

The expanded use of transfer of juveniles into criminal court has included various mechanisms, such as waiver from juvenile court or direct filing of charges in criminal court, under either statutory guidance or prosecutorial discretion (Heilbrun, Leheny, Thomas, & Huneycutt, 1997). In addition, the enactment of sexually violent predator statutes, which mandate sex offender registration and allow for postsentence civil commitment of sex offenders, have made it possible for juvenile sex offenders to be civilly committed after they have aged out of the juvenile justice system (Caldwell, 2013).

Miranda Waiver Capacity

In *Miranda v. Arizona* (1966), the Supreme Court held that individuals who are being interrogated in the custody of the police are entitled to exercise certain constitutional rights against self-incrimination. *Miranda* and other Supreme Court decisions have established that statements made to police in the course of custodial interrogation are inadmissible unless the individual being interrogated makes a knowing, intelligent, and voluntary waiver of *Miranda* rights. Relevant research has demonstrated, however, that these rights (and the implications of waiving them) are often poorly understood, particularly by juveniles; this has created the potential for investigatory overreaching and false confessions (Oberlander & Goldstein, 2001).

Competence to Stand Trial

Although the Supreme Court has not articulated a constitutional standard for youths' competence to proceed in the juvenile justice system different from the criminal standard in *Dusky v. United States* (1960), individual states have set their own standards through case law and statutes. In most jurisdictions, these requirements are very similar to the adult standards. A few states have incorporated the consideration of developmental maturity as part of this standard, however (O'Donnell & Gross, 2012). Whatever the standard, forensic assessment provides relevant information about juveniles' competence-related functional and legal capacities and the likelihood that incompetence can be remediated and restored.

INTERVENTIONS AND COSTS

The juvenile justice system was founded on a model of rehabilitation, which recognized that the needs of children and adolescents differ from those of adults and should be met through a specialized system (Melton et al., 2007). However, the goals of the system have shifted over the years, with varying levels of emphasis on treatment and punishment. During the 1980s and 1990s, a get-tough movement characterized the system and associated treatment and supervision policies (Melton et al., 2007). For instance, the juvenile justice system instituted mandatory minimum sentencing, juvenile sex offender lifetime registration, increased transfer to criminal court, and harsher dispositions that emphasized punishment (Bishop & Feld, 2012). During the late 20th century, there was also a widely held belief that nothing works (Melton et al., 2007) in the treatment of juvenile offenders (Martinson, 1974).

Recent Emphasis on Rehabilitation

In the past 15 years, the pendulum has swung back to an increased focus on treatment in the juvenile justice system. The revocation of the death penalty for juveniles (*Roper v. Simmons*, 2005) and limits on life without parole for those younger than age 18 (*Graham v. Florida*, 2010; *Miller v. Alabama*, 2012) reflect this movement. This shift also parallels and incorporates advancements in the understanding of adolescents' cognitive, emotional, behavioral, and neurological development. Moreover, advances in scientific methodology and treatment outcome research have allowed researchers to investigate the effectiveness of interventions, revealing that effective treatments do exist for youths in the juvenile justice system. Contrary to prior beliefs, these youths do have the potential for rehabilitation, and effective treatments can be replicated and disseminated. Part VI of this handbook reviews the status of interventions within the juvenile justice system, as well as the associated costs.

The recent shift toward treatment within the juvenile justice system is supported by a wide range of key stakeholders. Public opinion supports rehabilitation, federal and state agencies publicly promote the use of evidence-based treatments to reduce crime, and the government has increased funding for treatment outcome research (Bishop & Feld, 2012). The OJJDP launched an initiative to identify effective programs for juvenile offenders (i.e., Blueprints for Violence Prevention) and provided grants to disseminate effective programs (Mihalic, Irwin, Elliott, Fagan, & Hansen, 2001). Other lists of effective programs have been compiled (e.g., National Registry of Evidence-Based Programs and Practices; OJJDP's Model Programs Guide), and states have enacted legislation and advanced initiatives to promote the use of empirically supported interventions. For instance, in 1997 Washington State was the first to adopt legislation that supported the use of evidence-based treatments to reduce crime, and many states have since followed suit (Henggeler & Schoenwald, 2011).

The use of ineffective treatments increases costs to society and to individual youths. Untreated psychological symptoms can develop into greater, more costly problems in the future (e.g., social, academic, and legal difficulties; Borduin & Schaeffer, 1998; Snyder, 2002). Ineffective treatments also fail to decrease the risk of future criminal behavior and associated long-term costs (e.g., legal fees, property destruction, unemployment; Schaeffer & Borduin, 2005). Conversely, treatments with empirical support can reduce rates of reoffending and, subsequently, the related economic and emotional costs to society, victims, and individual youths. In fact, economic analyses of evidence-based programs have demonstrated that effective interventions can save millions of dollars by reducing recidivism and the frequency of out-of-home placements. Public and government support for effective programs, coupled with the cost-effectiveness of these interventions, highlight the importance of continuing to develop, evaluate, and disseminate intervention programs for youths in the juvenile justice system.

Interventions in the Juvenile Justice System

Because of the emphasis on evidence-based programming, researchers, policymakers, and clinicians have begun investigating what works and what does not work with youths involved with the juvenile justice system. Consistent with a public health model, effective treatments for juvenile offenders are generally identified as those that reduce illegal behaviors and simultaneously meet youths' individual treatment needs (Henggeler & Schoenwald, 2011). Treatment outcome research and meta-analytic reviews have demonstrated the effectiveness of a number of specific interventions and have identified characteristics of effective programs.

Effective programs target dynamic criminogenic risk factors—factors that are changeable and known to be associated with reoffending (Henggeler & Schoenwald, 2011; Lipsey, 2009). Such risk factors can be present in multiple aspects of youths' lives, including at the individual level (e.g., impulsivity, aggression), within the family (e.g., poor parental supervision), among peers (e.g., deviant peer group), and in the broader community (e.g., high-crime neighborhood; Loeber, Burke, & Pardini, 2009; Murray & Farrington, 2010). Interventions that attempt to reduce risk by targeting known risk factors have demonstrated promise for effectively treating youths in the juvenile justice system (see Chapter 23, this handbook).

Programming that addresses youths' needs using a multisystem approach also appears to generate positive outcomes. Just as risk factors can be present at multiple levels, effective treatments address youths' risks and needs in a variety of relevant contexts, including those that involve the individual youth, family, peer group, school, and community (Henggeler & Schoenwald, 2011). Treatments for individual factors that use a behavioral or cognitive–behavioral approach and are therapeutic rather than punitive appear to demonstrate positive effects (Lipsey, 2009). In addition, treatment that is delivered in natural environments tends to be more effective, and community-based treatments appear to demonstrate greater reductions in recidivism and more positive outcomes (Henggeler & Schoenwald, 2011). Reviews of interventions consistently reveal positive outcomes among a few specific programs (Mihalic, Fagan, Irwin, Ballard, & Elliott, 2002), all of which are community based. Multisystemic therapy, functional family therapy, and multidimensional treatment foster care exemplify these empirically supported approaches to treating youths in the juvenile justice system—they target known risk factors, utilize behavioral strategies, and use a multisystem approach (Chamberlain & Smith, 2003; Sheidow & Henggeler, 2005).

Although community-based treatments appear to demonstrate greater positive effects than residential placement, residential placements will continue as a public safety measure and as a sanction for those youths who violate probation. Evidence is mixed about the effectiveness of treatment in residential settings, with many researchers and scholars asserting that residential placement has negative effects (e.g., Dodge, 2008) and others suggesting that setting does not matter if treatment is good (Lipsey, 2009).

During the past decade, juvenile justice and mental health providers have begun focusing on the impact of trauma on justice-involved youths and the implementation of trauma-informed strategies in their care (Ko et al., 2008). Rates of traumatic exposure are much higher among juvenile offenders than among their nondelinquent peers, with more than 90% of youths in detention having experienced a traumatic event and more than 50% having experienced more than five events (Abram, Teplin, McClelland, & Dulcan, 2003). Traumatic experiences, such as abuse or neglect, are associated with increased risk and elevated rates of delinquent behavior (Ryan & Testa, 2005). Trauma-informed care reflects recognition of the high rates of traumatic exposure among juvenile justice–involved youths and is designed to address the effects of trauma on emotion, cognition, and behavior (see Chapter 24, this handbook).

Treatments for justice-involved youths must also be tailored to their particular needs, and focused interventions for specific target populations in the juvenile justice system are being developed. Reviews of treatments used in juvenile justice settings have demonstrated that effective programs are individualized, responsive to youths' needs, and delivered with the intended quality of and fidelity to the model (Henggeler & Schoenwald, 2011; Lipsey, 2009). There has been an increased emphasis on specification, and interventions have been developed to meet the needs of particular target populations, including trauma-related treatment for young men of color (see Chapter 26, this handbook) and treatments for juvenile sex offenders (see Chapter 28, this handbook).

Federal and state initiatives support efforts to develop and identify treatments and intervention strategies with the empirical support to reduce rates of reoffending and increase positive outcomes among youths. Ongoing research and discussion about what works and what does not work for justice-involved youths is essential to reducing recidivism, increasing public safety, decreasing costs, and meeting the needs of youths.

TRAINING AND ETHICS

A long line of jurisprudence has recognized the legal significance of the developmental differences between adults and juveniles (see Chapters 2 and 3, this handbook). Similarly, mental health professionals' recognition of important developmental differences has been sharpened by important scientific research findings in the past 2 decades regarding the impact of human development on the functioning of justice-involved adolescents (see Chapters 4–6, this handbook). However, legal and mental health professionals have often failed to collaborate as effectively as possible. Part of the problem is related to training; professionals in each field typically lack specialized training in the knowledge and methodology of the other. As a result, misunderstandings remain commonplace—and the empirically informed effectiveness of the juvenile justice system is diminished as a result.

The juvenile justice system and the professionals who provide justice-related services must remain cognizant of the particular developmental, clinical, and legal considerations relevant to juveniles. To this end, the MacArthur Foundation has funded the development of a juvenile court training curriculum that seeks to foster competence and an expanded knowledge base across five modules relevant to juvenile justice: (a) adolescent development; (b) evaluation, screening, and assessment in juvenile justice; (c) special education and disability rights; (d) legal questions about youths' capacities; and (e) communicating with youths, including interviews and colloquies.

Forensic and clinical psychological practices differ in a number of important ways as well. Whereas contact with a psychologist or other mental health professional is typically voluntary in the clinical context, the assessment and treatment of justice-involved adolescents is much more likely to be controlled by the court, by juvenile parole or probation, and by placements and other service providers after the adjudication of delinquency. Communications with a psychologist in a clinical setting are (with certain exceptions) confidential, but such confidentiality is far more limited for justice-involved youths. The consequences of a psychologist's involvement may differ substantially depending on the setting. In clinical contexts, the psychologist's recommendations affect the individual's treatment; in forensic settings, they may mean the difference between a community and a residential placement.

Similarly, psychological practice (both clinical and forensic) with adults differs in important ways from practice with juveniles. The differences in cognitive and emotional maturity between the two populations have important implications for informed consent. Adults are developmentally better equipped to understand the nature and the purpose of the psychologist's role and how the information they provide will be used. All of these differences raise ethical issues specific to the practice of forensic psychology with juveniles—considerations that are not always squarely addressed by the *Ethical Principles of Psychologists and Code of Conduct* (American Psychological Association, 2010) or the *Specialty Guidelines for Forensic Psychology* (American Psychological Association, 2013). Part VII of this handbook provides a fuller discussion of the training and ethical issues specific to the juvenile justice system.

CONCLUSION

Current perspectives drawn from the field of psychology have much to offer the juvenile justice system and the youths who are involved in it. In this chapter, we have reviewed seven domains in which particularly important and timely contributions have been made: legal, human development, offending patterns, risk factors, forensic assessment, interventions and costs, and training and ethics. This handbook provides chapters in each of these domains, offering a detailed review and analysis of scientific advances and their implications for policy and practice. This should be useful in promoting public safety, informed legal decision making, effective assessment and interventions, and the training of those who make policy and practice in juvenile justice.

References

Abram, K., Teplin, L., McClelland, G., & Dulcan, M. (2003). Cormorbid psychiatric disorders in youth in juvenile detention. *Archives of General Psychiatry*, *60*, 1097–1108. http://dx.doi.org/10.1001/archpsyc.60.11.1097

American Psychological Association. (2010). *Ethical principles of psychologists and code of conduct (2002, amended June 1, 2010*). Retrieved from http://www.apa.org/ethics/code/index.asp

American Psychological Association. (2013). *Specialty guidelines for forensic psychology*. Retrieved from http://www.apa.org/practice/guidelines/forensic-psychology.aspx

Andrews, D. A., & Bonta, J. (2010). *The psychology of criminal conduct* (5th ed.). New Providence, NJ: Matthew Bender.

Andrews, D. A., Bonta, J., & Hoge, R. D. (1990). Classification for effective rehabilitation: Rediscovering psychology. *Criminal Justice and Behavior*, *17*, 19–52. http://dx.doi.org/10.1177/0093854890017001004

Battin, S. R., Hill, K. G., Abbott, R. D., Catalano, R. F., & Hawkins, J. D. (1998). The contribution of gang membership to delinquency beyond delinquent friends. *Criminology*, *36*, 93–116. http://dx.doi.org/10.1111/j.1745-9125.1998.tb01241.x

Bishop, D., & Feld, B. (2012). Trends in juvenile justice policy and practice. In B. Feld & D. Bishop (Eds.), *The Oxford handbook of juvenile crime and juvenile justice* (pp. 898–935). New York, NY: Oxford University Press.

Borduin, C. M., & Schaeffer, C. M. (1998). Violent offending in adolescence: Epidemiology, correlates, outcomes, and treatment. In T. P. Gullotta, G. R. Adams, & R. Montemayor (Eds.), *Delinquent violent youth: Theory and interventions* (pp. 144–174). Newbury Park, CA: Sage.

Borum, R., Bartel, P., & Forth, A. (2003). *Manual for the Structured Assessment of Violence Risk in Youth, version 1.1*. Tampa: University of South Florida.

Brame, R., Bushway, S. D., Paternoster, R., & Turner, M. G. (2014). Demographic patterns of cumulative arrest prevalence by ages 18 and 23. *Crime and Delinquency*, *60*, 471–486. http://dx.doi.org/10.1177/0011128713514801

Brame, R., Turner, M. G., Paternoster, R., & Bushway, S. D. (2012). Cumulative prevalence of arrest from ages 8 to 23 in a national sample. *Pediatrics*, *129*, 21–27. http://dx.doi.org/10.1542/peds.2010-3710

Butts, J. A. (2013). *Violent youth crime in U.S. falls to new 32-year low* (Research and Evaluation Data Bits 2013–04). New York, NY: Research and Evaluation Center, John Jay College of Criminal Justice, City University of New York.

Butts, J. A., & Travis, J. (2002). *The rise and fall of American youth violence: 1980 to 2000*. Washington, DC: Urban Institute, Justice Policy Center.

Byrnes, J. P. (2002). The development of decision-making. *Journal of Adolescent Health*, *31*(Suppl.), 208–215. http://dx.doi.org/10.1016/S1054-139X(02)00503-7

Caldwell, M. F. (2013). Accuracy of sexually violent person assessments of juveniles adjudicated for sexual offenses. *Sex Abuse: A Journal of Research and Treatment*, *25*, 516–526.

Chamberlain, P., & Smith, D. K. (2003). Antisocial behavior in children and adolescents: The Oregon multidimensional treatment foster care model. In A. Kazdin & J. Weisz (Eds.), *Evidence-based psychotherapies for children and adolescents* (pp. 282–300). New York, NY: Guilford Press.

Chen, D. R., & Salekin, R. T. (2012). Transfer to adult court: Enhancing clinical forensic evaluations and informing policy. In E. L. Grigorenko (Ed.), *Handbook of juvenile forensic psychology and psychiatry* (pp. 105–125). http://dx.doi.org/10.1007/978-1-4614-0905-2_8

Commonwealth v. Fisher, 213 Pa. 48, 62 A. 198 (Pa. 1905).

Conklin, H. M., Luciana, M., Hooper, C. J., & Yarger, R. S. (2007). Working memory performance in typically developing children and adolescents: Behavioral evidence of protracted frontal lobe development. *Developmental Neuropsychology*, *31*, 103–128. http://dx.doi.org/10.1207/s15326942dn3101_6

Cornell, D. G., Peterson, C. S., & Richards, H. (1999). Anger as a predictor of aggression among incarcerated adolescents. *Journal of Consulting and Clinical Psychology*, *67*, 108–115. http://dx.doi.org/10.1037/0022-006X.67.1.108

Cottle, C. C., Lee, R. J., & Heilbrun, K. (2001). The prediction of criminal recidivism in juveniles: A meta-analysis. *Criminal Justice and Behavior*, *28*, 367–394. http://dx.doi.org/10.1177/0093854801028003005

Crockett, L. J., Eggebeen, D. J., & Hawkins, A. J. (1993). Father's presence and young children's behavioral and cognitive adjustment. *Journal of Family Issues*, *14*, 355–377. http://dx.doi.org/10.1177/019251393014003002

Crone, E. A., Bunge, S. A., Latenstein, H., & van der Molen, M. W. (2005). Characterization of children's decision making: Sensitivity to punishment frequency, not task complexity. *Child Neuropsychology*, *11*, 245–263. http://dx.doi.org/10.1080/092970490911261

DeMatteo, D., & Marczyk, G. (2005). Risk factors, protective factors, and the prevention of antisocial behavior among juveniles. In K. Heilbrun, N. E. S. Goldstein, & R. E. Redding (Eds.), *Juvenile delinquency: Prevention, assessment, and intervention* (pp. 19–44). New York, NY: Oxford University Press.

Dodge, K. A. (2008). Framing public policy and prevention of chronic violence in American youth. *American Psychologist*, *63*, 573–590. http://dx.doi.org/10.1037/0003-066X.63.7.573

Dusky v. United States, 362 U.S. 402 (1960).

Eaton, D. K., Kann, L., Kinchen, S., Shanklin, S., Flint, K. H., Hawkins, J., . . . Wechsler, H.; Centers for Disease Control and Prevention. (2012). Youth risk behavior surveillance—United States, 2011. *MMWR Surveillance Summaries*, *61*, 1–162.

Eddings v. Oklahoma, 455 U.S. 104 (1982).

Elliott, D. S., Huizinga, D., & Ageton, S. S. (1985). *Explaining delinquency and drug use*. Thousand Oaks, CA: Sage.

Elliott, D. S., Pampel, F., & Huizinga, D. (2004). *Youth violence: Continuity and desistance. A supplemental report to Youth Violence: A report of the Surgeon General*. Boulder: Center for the Study and Prevention of Violence, Institute of Behavior Science, University of Colorado.

Elrod, P., & Ryder, R. S. (2011). *Juvenile justice: A social, historical and legal perspective*. Sudbury, MA: Jones & Bartlett.

Fabio, A., Tu, L. C., Loeber, R., & Cohen, J. (2011). Neighborhood socioeconomic disadvantage and the shape of the age-crime curve. *American Journal of Public Health*, *101*(Suppl. 1), S325–S332. http://dx.doi.org/10.2105/AJPH.2010.300034

Farrington, D. P. (1986). Age and crime. In M. Tonry & N. Morris (Eds.), *Crime and justice: An annual review of research* (Vol. 7, pp. 189–250). Chicago, IL: University of Chicago Press.

Farrington, D. P. (1989). Early predictors of adolescent aggression and adult violence. *Violence and Victims*, *4*, 79–100.

Farrington, D. P., & Hawkins, D. (1991). Predicting participation, early onset and later persistence in officially recorded offending. *Criminal Behaviour and Mental Health*, *1*, 1–33.

Gardner, M., & Steinberg, L. (2005). Peer influence on risk taking, risk preference, and risky decision making in adolescence and adulthood: An experimental study. *Developmental Psychology*, *41*, 625–635. http://dx.doi.org/10.1037/0012-1649.41.4.625

Graham v. Florida, 560 U.S. 48 (2010).

Greenwood, P. W., & Turner, S. (2011). Juvenile crime and juvenile justice. In J. Q. Wilson & J. Petersilia (Eds.), *Crime and public policy* (pp. 88–129). New York, NY: Oxford University Press.

Gretton, H. M., Hare, R. D., & Catchpole, R. E. (2004). Psychopathy and offending from adolescence to adulthood: A 10-year follow-up. *Journal of Consulting and Clinical Psychology*, *72*, 636–645. http://dx.doi.org/10.1037/0022-006X.72.4.636

Grisso, T. (2013). *Forensic evaluation of juveniles* (2nd ed.). Sarasota, FL: Professional Resource Press.

Hanson, R. K., & Harris, A. J. R. (2001). A structured approach to evaluating change among sexual offenders. *Sexual Abuse: A Journal of Research and Treatment*, *13*, 105–122.

Hawkins, J. D., Herrenkohl, T., Farrington, D. P., Brewer, D., Catalano, R. F., & Harachi, T. W. (1999). A review of predictors of youth violence. In R. Loeber & D. P. Farrington (Eds.), *Serious and violent juvenile offenders: Risk factors and successful interventions* (pp. 106–146). http://dx.doi.org/10.4135/9781452243740.n7

Hawkins, J. D., Herrenkohl, T. I., Farrington, D. P., Brewer, D., Catalano, R. F., Harachi, T. W., & Cothern, L. (2000). *Predictors of youth violence* (Juvenile Justice Bulletin). Washington, DC: U.S. Department of Justice, Office of Justice Programs, Office of Juvenile Justice and Delinquency Prevention.

Heilbrun, K. (1997). Prediction versus management models relevant to risk assessment: The importance of legal decision-making context. *Law and Human Behavior*, *21*, 347–359. http://dx.doi.org/10.1023/A:1024851017947

Heilbrun, K., Goldstein, N. E. S., & Redding, R. E. (Eds.). (2005). *Juvenile delinquency: Prevention, assessment, and intervention*. New York, NY: Oxford University Press.

Heilbrun, K., Grisso, T., & Goldstein, A. (2009). *Foundations of forensic mental health assessment*. New York, NY: Oxford University Press.

Heilbrun, K., Leheny, C., Thomas, L., & Huneycutt, D. (1997). A national survey of U.S. statutes on juvenile transfer: Implications for policy and practice. *Behavioral Sciences and the Law*, *15*, 125–149. http://dx.doi.org/10.1002/(SICI)1099-0798(199721)15:2<125::AID-BSL265>3.0.CO;2-R

Henggeler, S. W., & Schoenwald, S. K. (2011). *Evidence-based interventions for juvenile offenders and juvenile justice policies that support them*. Ann Arbor, MI: Society for Research in Child Development. Retrieved from http://files.eric.ed.gov/fulltext/ED519241.pdf

Hinshaw, S. P. (1992). Externalizing behavior problems and academic underachievement in childhood and adolescence: Causal relationships and underlying mechanisms. *Psychological Bulletin*, *111*, 127–155. http://dx.doi.org/10.1037/0033-2909.111.1.127

Hoge, R. D., & Andrews, D. A. (2010). *Evaluation for risk of violence in juveniles*. http://dx.doi.org/10.1093/med/9780195370416.001.0001

Hooper, C. J., Luciana, M., Conklin, H. M., & Yarger, R. S. (2004). Adolescents' performance on the Iowa Gambling Task: Implications for the development of decision making and ventromedial prefrontal cortex. *Developmental Psychology*, *40*, 1148–1158. http://dx.doi.org/10.1037/0012-1649.40.6.1148

Howell, J. C. (2003). *Preventing and reducing juvenile delinquency: A comprehensive framework*. Thousand Oaks, CA: Sage.

In re Gault, 387 U.S. 1 (1967).

In re Winship, 397 U.S. 358 (1970).

Kashani, J. H., Jones, M. R., Burnby, K. M., & Thomas, L. A. (1999). Youth violence: Psychosocial risk factors, treatment, prevention, and recommendations. *Journal of Emotional and Behavioral Disorders*, *7*, 200–210. http://dx.doi.org/10.1177/106342669900700402

Kemp, K. (2010). *Characteristics of developmental immaturity: A cross-disciplinary survey of psychologists* (Doctoral dissertation). Retrieved from http://idea.library.drexel.edu/handle/1860/3490

Kent v. United States, 383 U.S. 541 (1966).

Ko, A., Ford, J., Kassam-Adams, N., Berkowitz, S., Wilson, C., Wong, M., . . . Layne, C. (2008). Creating trauma-informed systems: Child welfare, education, first responders, health care, juvenile justice. *Professional Psychology: Research and Practice*, *39*, 396–404. http://dx.doi.org/10.1037/0735-7028.39.4.396

Le Blanc, M., & Fréchette, M. (Eds.). (1989). *Male criminal activity from childhood through youth: Multilevel and developmental perspectives*. http://dx.doi.org/10.1007/978-1-4612-3570-5

Leiber, M. J. (2003). *The contexts of juvenile justice decision making: When race matters*. Albany, NY: SUNY Press.

Lipsey, M. (2009). The primary factors that characterize effective interventions with juvenile offenders: A meta-analytic review. *Victims and Offenders*, *4*, 124–147.

Lipsey, M. W., & Derzon, J. H. (1998). Predictors of violent or serious delinquency in adolescence and early adulthood: A synthesis of longitudinal research. In R. Loeber & D. P. Farrington (Eds.), *Serious and violent juvenile offenders: Risk factors and successful interventions* (pp. 86–105). Thousand Oaks, CA: Sage.

Loeber, R., Burke, J., & Pardini, D. (2009). Perspectives on oppositional defiant disorder, conduct disorder, and psychopathic features. *Journal of Child Psychology and Psychiatry*, *50*, 133–142. http://dx.doi.org/10.1111/j.1469-7610.2008.02011.x

Loeber, R., & Farrington, D. P. (Eds.). (2001). *Child delinquents: Development, intervention and service needs*. Thousand Oaks, CA: Sage.

Loeber, R., Farrington, D. P., Stouthamer-Loeber, M., Moffitt, T. E., & Caspi, A. (1998). The development of male offending: Key findings from the first decade of the Pittsburgh youth study. *Studies on Crime and Crime Prevention*, *7*, 141–171.

Luna, B., Padmanabhan, A., & O'Hearn, K. (2010). What has fMRI told us about the development of cognitive control through adolescence? *Brain and Cognition*, *72*, 101–113. http://dx.doi.org/10.1016/j.bandc.2009.08.005

Luna, B., Paulsen, D. J., Padmanabhan, A., & Geier, C. (2013). The teenage brain: Cognitive control and motivation. *Current Directions in Psychological Science*, *22*, 94–100. http://dx.doi.org/10.1177/0963721413478416

Lynam, D. R., Miller, D. J., Vachon, D., Loeber, R., & Stouthamer-Loeber, M. (2009). Psychopathy in adolescence predicts official reports of offending in adulthood. *Youth Violence and Juvenile Justice*, *7*, 189–207. http://dx.doi.org/10.1177/1541204009333797

Martinson, R. (1974). What works? Questions and answers about prison reform. *Public Interest*, *35*, 22–54.

McCord, J., Widom, C. S., & Crowell, N. A. (Eds.). (2001). *Juvenile crime, juvenile justice*. Washington, DC: National Academy Press.

McKeiver v. Pennsylvania, 403 U.S. 528 (1971).

Melton, G. B., Petrila, J., Poythress, N. G., & Slobogin, C. (2007). *Psychological evaluation for the courts: A handbook for mental health professionals and lawyers* (3rd ed.). New York, NY: Guilford Press.

Mihalic, S., Fagan, A., Irwin, K., Ballard, D., & Elliott, D. (2002). *Blueprints for violence prevention replications: Factors for implementation success*. Boulder, CO: Center for the Study and Prevention of Violence.

Mihalic, S., Irwin, K., Elliott, D., Fagan, A., & Hansen, D. (2001). *Blueprints for violence prevention* (Juvenile Justice Bulletin). Washington, DC: U.S. Department of Justice. Retrieved from https://www.ncjrs.gov/pdffiles1/ojjdp/187079.pdf

Miller v. Alabama, 132 S. Ct. 2455 (2012).

Miranda v. Arizona, 348 U.S. 436 (1966).

Mulvey, E. P. (2011). *Highlights from pathways to desistance: A longitudinal study of serious adolescent offenders*. Washington, DC: U.S. Department of Justice, Office of Juvenile Justice and Delinquency Prevention.

Murray, J., & Farrington, D. (2010). Risk factors for conduct disorder and delinquency: Key findings from longitudinal studies. *Canadian Journal of Psychiatry*, *55*, 633–642.

Oberlander, L. B., & Goldstein, N. E. (2001). A review and update on the practice of evaluating *Miranda* comprehension. *Behavioral Sciences and the Law*, *19*, 453–471. http://dx.doi.org/10.1002/bsl.453

O'Donnell, P. C., & Gross, B. (2012). Developmental incompetence to stand trial in juvenile courts.

Journal of Forensic Sciences, *57*, 989–996. http://dx.doi.org/10.1111/j.1556-4029.2012.02093.x

Paus, T. (2005). Mapping brain maturation and cognitive development during adolescence. *Trends in Cognitive Sciences*, *9*, 60–68. http://dx.doi.org/10.1016/j.tics.2004.12.008

Piquero, A., Farrington, D., & Blumstein, A. (2003). The criminal career paradigm: Background and recent developments. *Crime and Justice*, *30*, 359–506. Retrieved from http://www.jstor.org/stable/1147702

Piquero, A. R., Farrington, D. P., & Blumstein, A. (2007). *Key issues in criminal career research: New analyses of the Cambridge Study in Delinquent Development*. http://dx.doi.org/10.1017/CBO9780511499494

Platt, A. M. (1977). *The child savers: The invention of delinquency* (2nd ed.). Chicago, IL: University of Chicago Press.

Pope, C. E., & Feyerherm, W. (1995). *Minorities and the juvenile justice system: Research summary* (Report No. NCJ-145849). Washington, DC: U.S. Department of Justice, Office of Juvenile Justice and Delinquency Prevention.

Puzzanchera, C. (2013). *Juvenile arrests 2010*. Washington, DC: U.S. Department of Justice, Office of Juvenile Justice and Delinquency Prevention.

Roper v. Simmons, 543 U.S. 551 (2005).

Ryan, J. P., & Testa, M. F. (2005). Child maltreatment and juvenile delinquency: Investigating the role of placement and placement instability. *Children and Youth Services Review*, 27, 227–249. http://dx.doi.org/10.1016/j.childyouth.2004.05.007

Salekin, R. T. (2002). Clinical evaluation of youth considered for transfer to adult criminal court: Refining practice and directions for science. *Journal of Forensic Psychology Practice*, 2, 55–72. http://dx.doi.org/10.1300/J158v02n01_03

Schaeffer, C. M., & Borduin, C. M. (2005). Long-term follow-up to a randomized clinical trial of multisystemic therapy with serious and violent juvenile offenders. *Journal of Consulting and Clinical Psychology*, 73, 445–453. http://dx.doi.org/10.1037/0022-006X.73.3.445

Shader, M. (2001). *Risk factors for delinquency: An overview*. Washington, DC: U.S. Department of Justice, Office of Justice Programs, Office of Juvenile Justice and Delinquency Prevention.

Sheidow, A., & Henggeler, S. (2005). Community-based treatments. In K. Heilbrun, N. E. Sevin Goldstein, & R. Redding (Eds.), *Juvenile delinquency* (pp. 257–281). New York, NY: Oxford University Press.

Slobogin, C., & Fondacaro, M. R. (2011). *Juveniles at risk: A plea for preventive justice*. http://dx.doi.org/10.1093/acprof:oso/9780199778355.001.0001

Snyder, H. (2002). *Juvenile arrests 2000*. Washington, DC: U.S. Department of Justice.

Steinberg, L. (1987). Single parents, stepparents, and the susceptibility of adolescents to antisocial peer pressure. *Child Development*, *58*, 269–275. http://dx.doi.org/10.2307/1130307

Steinberg, L. (2009). Adolescent development and juvenile justice. *Annual Review of Clinical Psychology*, *5*, 459–485. http://dx.doi.org/10.1146/annurev.clinpsy.032408.153603

Steinberg, L., Albert, D., Cauffman, E., Banich, M., Graham, S., & Woolard, J. (2008). Age differences in sensation seeking and impulsivity as indexed by behavior and self-report: Evidence for a dual systems model. *Developmental Psychology*, *44*, 1764–1778. http://dx.doi.org/10.1037/a0012955

Steinberg, L., Graham, S., O'Brien, L., Woolard, J., Cauffman, E., & Banich, M. (2009). Age differences in future orientation and delay discounting. *Child Development*, *80*, 28–44. http://dx.doi.org/10.1111/j.1467-8624.2008.01244.x

Steinberg, L., & Monahan, K. C. (2007). Age differences in resistance to peer influence. *Developmental Psychology*, *43*, 1531–1543. http://dx.doi.org/10.1037/0012-1649.43.6.1531

Stouthamer-Loeber, M., Wei, E., Loeber, R., & Masten, A. S. (2004). Desistance from persistent serious delinquency in the transition to adulthood. *Development and Psychopathology*, *16*, 897–918. http://dx.doi.org/10.1017/S0954579404040064

Thompson v. Oklahoma, 487 U.S. 815 (1988).

U.S. Department of Health and Human Services. (2001). *Youth violence: A report of the Surgeon General*. Rockville, MD: Author.

Part II

LAW

CHAPTER 2

CHILDREN IN THE JUSTICE SYSTEM: THE LEGAL FRAMEWORK

Marsha Levick and Jessica Feierman

More than 100 years ago, the first juvenile court was established in Cook County, Illinois (Champion, 1992; Illinois Juvenile Court Act of 1899). The original purpose of the court was to separate juvenile offenders from adult offenders, to provide opportunities for rehabilitation and treatment, to create a more informal setting in which to adjudicate criminal conduct by children, and to limit the consequences of children's criminal conduct (Ross, 1995; Zimring, 2005). Within 25 years, almost every state in the United States had established a juvenile justice system (Snyder & Sickmund, 1999).

The early juvenile justice system favored informality over process and the best interests of children over consideration for their due process or other constitutional rights (Ross, 1995). Before 1966, the nation's juvenile courts functioned with little scrutiny from outsiders—either the public or the appellate courts (Steinberg & Schwartz, 2000). Except for two earlier instances in which the U.S. Supreme Court acknowledged the particular vulnerability of youths with respect to police interrogations and confessions, juvenile courts for the most part operated outside constitutional boundaries and behind closed doors.

In 1966, the U.S. Supreme Court's decision in *Kent v. United States* changed this landscape. *Kent* involved a challenge to transfer proceedings under the District of Columbia's Juvenile Court Act. For the first time, the Court held that certain constitutionally mandated due process protections were required in juvenile court. Holding that procedures to transfer a child to adult court must meet the essentials of due process and fair treatment, *Kent* ushered in a period of profound change for the juvenile justice system (Ross, 1995). Over the next 5 years, the Court underscored the importance of procedural protections for youths in juvenile court, firmly establishing juveniles' right to counsel, notice of charges, protection from self-incrimination, confrontation (*In re Gault*, 1967), and proof beyond a reasonable doubt (*In re Winship*, 1970). In subsequent cases, the Court grappled with the parameters of these protections; over time, the Court established a patchwork of rights in which youths in juvenile court are granted some, but not all, of the procedural rights of adults in criminal proceedings. In these cases, the Court acknowledged the continued importance of allowing states to experiment with operating separate juvenile justice systems and creating rehabilitative programming for youths. During this era, the legal impact of the separate juvenile justice system varied from case to case. In some cases, the Court pointed to the informality of the juvenile justice system to justify lesser protections for youths than for adults. In other cases, the Court was clear that because the juvenile justice system deprives young people of liberty and exposes them to harsh consequences, procedural protections are vital.

Portions of this chapter are adapted from "Kids Really Are Different: Looking Past *Graham v. Florida*," by M. Levick, 2010, *Criminal Law Reporter, 87*, 664–667. Copyright 2010 by Marsha Levick. Adapted with permission; "*J.D.B. v. North Carolina*: The U.S. Supreme Court Heralds the Emergence of the 'Reasonable Juvenile' in American Criminal Law," by M. Levick, 2011, *Criminal Law Reporter, 89*, 753–757. Copyright 2011 by Marsha Levick. Adapted with permission; "From a Trilogy to Quadrilogy: *Miller v. Alabama* Makes It Four in a Row for U.S. Supreme Court Cases That Support Differential Treatment of Youth," by M. Levick, 2012, *Criminal Law Reporter, 91*, 749–756. Copyright 2012 by Marsha Levick. Adapted with permission; and "The Eighth Amendment Evolves: Defining Cruel and Unusual Punishment Through the Lens of Childhood and Adolescence," by M. Levick, J. Feierman, S. Messenheimer, M. Goldstein, and K. Mordecai, 2012, *University of Pennsylvania Journal of Law and Social Change, 15*, 285–321. Copyright 2012 by the University of Pennsylvania Law School. Adapted with permission.

http://dx.doi.org/10.1037/14643-002
APA Handbook of Psychology and Juvenile Justice, K. Heilbrun (Editor-in-Chief)

The constitutionalization of the juvenile court was the dominant story in juvenile justice until the late 1980s and early 1990s, when increases in violent juvenile crime caused by the lethal combination of crack cocaine and guns spread throughout the country (Blumstein, 2002). The prominence accorded to images of and stories about violent juvenile offenders sparked a new wave of juvenile justice reform, aimed at limiting the jurisdiction of juvenile court and expanding the jurisdiction of the adult criminal justice system over young offenders. Convinced that the country was headed toward a generation of increasingly violent teens, or "superpredators" (Becker, 2001),[1] legislators quickly enacted laws that sought to ensure that youths charged with the most serious offenses would be prosecuted as adults (Steinberg & Schwartz, 2000; Torbet et al., 1996). As yet another period of transformation swept over the juvenile court, the focus on rehabilitation for juveniles was almost completely eclipsed by concerns for public safety, incapacitation, and retribution—the latter being core attributes of the adult criminal justice system (Holland & Mlyniec, 1995). At the same time, youthful offenders in the criminal justice system bore the full brunt of adult punishment, receiving not only lengthy sentences, but sentences of life without parole and even death.[2]

As a result of the "adultification" of juvenile offending in the public discourse and, increasingly, in state legislatures, researchers associated with the MacArthur Foundation's Research Network on Adolescent Development and Juvenile Justice began conducting studies and compiling research that demonstrated striking and highly relevant differences between children and adolescents on one hand and adults on the other (Steinberg & Schwartz, 2000).[3] In particular, the research highlighted key traits among juveniles that illustrated their reduced blameworthiness for their criminal conduct (Steinberg & Schwartz, 2000). Researchers focused on three distinct qualities of adolescence—immaturity of judgment, susceptibility to negative peer pressure, and a capacity for change and rehabilitation based on the inherently transient nature of adolescence (Grisso et al., 2003; Scott, Reppucci, & Woolard 1995; Steinberg & Cauffman, 1996; Steinberg & Scott, 2003).

Beginning in 2005, in the case of *Roper v. Simmons*, the Supreme Court responded to the research and began to articulate a jurisprudence that recognized that these distinctions between youths and adults have constitutional relevance. This legal theory was soon extended by the Supreme Court to two life-without-parole cases (*Graham v. Florida*, 2010; *Miller v. Alabama*, 2012) and to a case involving the validity of a juvenile confession (*J.D.B. v. North Carolina*, 2011). In the short span of 7 years, the Court had established a distinct juvenile jurisprudence recognizing that children are not just miniature adults and that the law must take this reality into account.

CONSTITUTIONALIZATION OF JUVENILE COURT

Between 1966 and 1970, the U.S. Supreme Court decided three seminal cases that set the stage for much of the current treatment of youths in the justice system. In *Kent v. United States* (1966), *In re Gault* (1967), and *In re Winship* (1970), the Court clearly established that constitutional protections extend to youths and apply to the juvenile justice system. As the Court explained, "Neither the Fourteenth Amendment nor the Bill of Rights is for adults alone" (*In re Gault*, 1967, p. 13). Whereas two earlier cases, *Haley v. Ohio* (1948) and *Gallegos v. Colorado* (1962), had established that youths are entitled to constitutional protections during

[1]John Dilulio is largely credited with creating the superpredator myth (Becker, 2001). Dilulio subsequently retracted this belief (Becker, 2001). For background information, see Bennet (1996) and Bazelon (2000; arguing that rejections to the infancy defense are unfounded and unsupported by empirical data).

[2]At the time of the Supreme Court's decision in *Roper v. Simmons* (2005), in which the Court struck the juvenile death penalty under the Eighth Amendment, 72 children were being held on death row in the United States. Also, 19 states allowed executions of people younger than age 18: Alabama, Arizona, Arkansas, Delaware, Florida, Georgia, Idaho, Kentucky, Louisiana, Mississippi, Nevada, New Hampshire, North Carolina, Oklahoma, Pennsylvania, South Carolina, Utah, Texas, and Virginia (*Roper v. Simmons*, 543 U.S. 564).

[3]The MacArthur Foundation formally convened the research network in 1995 (Steinberg & Schwartz, 2000). The foundation saw a need for "a scientific initiative that would address the implications of adolescent development for the construction of rational juvenile justice policy and law" (Steinberg & Schwartz, 2000, pp. 3–4). Led by distinguished Temple University psychology professor Laurence Steinberg, the research network brought a developmental lens to issues such as competence to stand trial, culpability, and the impact of different interventions (Steinberg & Schwartz, 2000).

confessions, this new set of cases was particularly instructive because they centered on the role of such protections in juvenile court.[4]

The first case of the trio, *Kent v. United States* (1966), concerned the constitutionality of the procedures by which the juvenile court could waive a young person's case to adult court. Morris A. Kent Jr., age 16, was accused of breaking and entering a woman's home, taking her wallet, and raping her (*Kent v. United States*, 1966). The juvenile court had exclusive jurisdiction over the case (*Kent v. United States*, 1966). The Juvenile Court Act permitted waiver after "full investigation" for a

> child sixteen years of age or older . . . charged with an offense which would amount to a felony in the case of an adult, or any child charged with an offense which if committed by an adult is punishable by death or life imprisonment. (*Kent v. United States*, 1966, p. 547)

The statute did not provide any further guidance or standards by which the juvenile court should make the determination about whether to waive the case to adult court.

Kent's attorney had him examined by a psychiatrist and also filed a motion with the court arguing that Kent should remain in juvenile court, stating that he would offer proof that with the proper treatment Kent could be rehabilitated (*Kent v. United States*, 1966). The attorney also argued that he should be given access to Kent's social services record, compiled while Kent was previously under probation supervision (*Kent v. United States*, 1966). Kent had initially come under the supervision of the juvenile court at age 14 for house break-ins and an attempted purse snatching (*Kent v. United States*, 1966).

The juvenile court held no hearing; did not confer with Kent, Kent's parents, or counsel; and did not rule on the motions (*Kent v. United States*, 1966). The court's order noted only that after "'full investigation, I do hereby waive jurisdiction of petitioner and direct that he be 'held for trial for (the alleged) offenses under the regular procedure' of the [district court]" (*Kent v. United States*, 1966, p. 546). The court made no findings and provided no reasons for the waiver. At trial in the adult court, Kent was found guilty of six counts of housebreaking and robbery and sentenced to 30 to 90 years in prison (*Kent v. United States*, 1966).[5]

Kent appealed on a number of grounds; the Supreme Court considered only the validity of the waiver of jurisdiction to adult court (*Kent v. United States*, 1966). The Court underscored that procedural protections were warranted because the decision was "critically important" (*Kent v. United States*, 1966, p. 553). If tried in adult court, a young person would be "taken from the Receiving Home for Children and transferred to jail along with adults" and "exposed to the possibility of a death sentence, instead of treatment for a maximum, in Kent's case, of five years, until he is 21" (*Kent v. United States*, 1966, pp. 553–554).

The opinion was seminal in a number of ways. Most important, it held that constitutional protections apply to proceedings affecting youths in the juvenile justice system. The Court explained,

> There is no place in our system of law for reaching a result of such tremendous consequences without ceremony—without hearing, without effective assistance of counsel, without a statement of reasons. It is inconceivable that a court of justice dealing with adults, with respect to a similar issue, would proceed in this manner. It would be extraordinary if society's special concern for children, as reflected in the District of Columbia's Juvenile Court Act, permitted this procedure. We hold that it does not. (*Kent v. United States*, 1966, p. 554)

Although the court recognized that the juvenile court is distinct from adult court, it also concluded that the distinctions do not justify a deprivation of appropriate procedures (*Kent v. United States*, 1966). The D.C. juvenile court's

[4]*Gallegos v. Colorado* held that the confession obtained from a 14-year-old boy, who had been held for days without seeing his parents, a lawyer, or any other adult friend, was obtained in violation of due process. *Haley v. Ohio* held that a murder confession by a 15-year-old boy after 5 hours of interrogation starting at midnight, by police officers working in relays without advising him of his rights, and without the advice of friends, family, or counsel, should have been excluded as in violation of due process.

[5]He was also found not guilty by reason of insanity, which required immediate placement in an adult psychiatric facility. The time served in this facility would count toward his total prison sentence (*Kent v. United States*, 1966).

> objectives are to provide measures of guidance and rehabilitation for the child and protection for society, not to fix criminal responsibility, guilt and punishment. The State is *parens patriae*, rather than prosecuting attorney and judge. But the admonition to function in a "parental" relationship is not an invitation to procedural arbitrariness. (*Kent v. United States*, 1966, pp. 554–555)[6]

According to the Supreme Court, a waiver hearing need not comport with all procedures available in a criminal trial. It must, however, "measure up to the essentials of due process and fair treatment" (*Kent v. United States*, 1966, p. 562). At a minimum, this would require a statement of reasons by the trial court, thus allowing for meaningful review of the decision; the right to a hearing before a waiver order, the right to counsel, and the right of counsel to review the social records at issue (*Kent v. United States*, 1966). The Court had set forth a key standard of fair treatment for evaluating procedures in juvenile court. This standard continues to govern questions of due process in juvenile court today.

In *Kent v. United States* (1966), the Court paid particular attention to the importance of counsel for children, explaining, "These rights are meaningless—an illusion, a mockery—unless counsel is given an opportunity to function" and "the right to representation by counsel is not a formality. It is not a grudging gesture to a ritualistic requirement. It is of the essence of justice" (p. 561). Just 1 year later, the Court further developed the jurisprudence granting children procedural protections, and clarifying the importance of attorneys in juvenile court, in *In re Gault* (1967).

Gerald Gault was a 15-year-old boy committed to a secure juvenile facility for 5 years after being adjudicated delinquent for making a lewd phone call (*In re Gault*, 1967). Gault received no notice of the charges and was unrepresented at his adjudicatory hearing (*In re Gault*, 1967). Testimony at the hearing was unsworn, and the complainant was not present. There was no transcript of the hearing, nor was there a memorandum or record (*In re Gault*, 1967). Gault was adjudicated guilty and sentenced to 5 years in a juvenile facility (*In re Gault*, 1967). If he had been an adult, the penalty would have been a fine of between $5 and $50 or imprisonment for no more than 2 months (*In re Gault*, 1967).

The Court noted that,

> from the inception of the juvenile court system, wide differences have been tolerated—indeed insisted upon—between the procedural rights accorded to adults and those of juveniles. In practically all jurisdictions, there are rights granted to adults which are withheld from juveniles. (*In re Gault*, 1967, p. 14)

The Court also traced the history of the juvenile court, emphasizing its core rehabilitative goals:

> The early reformers . . . believed that society's role was not to ascertain whether the child was "guilty" or "innocent," but "What is he, how has he become what he is, and what had best be done in his interest and in the interest of the state to save him from a downward career." The child—essentially good, as they saw it—was to be made "to feel that he is the object of (the state's) care and solicitude," not that he was under arrest or on trial. The rules of criminal procedure were therefore altogether inapplicable. The apparent rigidities, technicalities, and harshness which they observed in both substantive and procedural criminal law were therefore to be discarded. The idea of crime and punishment was to be abandoned. The child was to be "treated" and "rehabilitated" and the procedures, from apprehension through institutionalization, were to be "clinical" rather than punitive. (*In re Gault*, 1967, p. 15)

The Court noted that these reforms had been justified by establishing the state's role as *parens patriae* and characterizing the proceedings as

[6]Two prior cases had established constitutional protections for youths, though in the context of police interrogations rather than juvenile court procedures (*Gallegos v. Colorado*, 1962; *Haley v. Ohio*, 1948).

nonadversarial, but questioned whether the notion of *parens patriae* appropriately fit the quasi-criminal context of the juvenile court (*In re Gault*, 1967).

The Court then emphasized the problems with the juvenile court in which the "highest motives and most enlightened impulses" (*In re Gault*, 1967, p. 17) had led to a system that was problematic in practice. Children risked exposure to arbitrary treatment but did not necessarily receive careful individualized treatment (*In re Gault*, 1967). Indeed, the Court cited significant research that juvenile justice systems were not providing children the care they needed or having the intended consequence of reducing juvenile offending. Thus, concluded the Court, children were exposed to "the worst of both worlds," receiving "neither the protections accorded to adults nor the solicitous care and regenerative treatment postulated for children" (*In re Gault*, 1967, p. 18, n. 23).

Echoing the conclusions from *Kent v. United States* (1966), the Court underscored the importance of procedural protections for children that ensure basic fairness. The court exposes juveniles to harsh consequences, the Court stated, so it must also grant due process. "It would be extraordinary if our Constitution did not require the procedural regularity and the exercise of care implied in the phrase 'due process.' Under our Constitution, the condition of being a boy does not justify a kangaroo court" (*In re Gault*, 1967, pp. 27–28). The Court therefore held that children in adjudicatory hearings were entitled to the right to counsel, to confrontation, and to protection from self-incrimination (*In re Gault*, 1967).

At the same time, the Court emphasized that proper procedures need not undermine the substantive goals of the juvenile justice system: "The observance of due process standards, intelligently and not ruthlessly administered, will not compel the States to abandon or displace any of the substantive benefits of the juvenile process" (*In re Gault*, 1967, p. 21).

Only a few years later, the Supreme Court again underscored the importance of certain procedural rights in juvenile court. *In re Winship* (1970) involved a 12-year-old boy who was alleged to have entered a locker and stolen $112 from a woman's purse. The trial court adjudicated him delinquent, admitting that there might not be enough evidence to prove the case beyond a reasonable doubt, which would have been required in adult criminal court (*In re Winship*, 1970).

The Supreme Court held that "the same considerations that demand extreme caution in factfinding to protect the innocent adult apply as well to the innocent child" (*In re Winship*, 1970, p. 365) and therefore that the reasonable doubt standard must be applied in juvenile court. Relying on its previous decision in *In re Gault* (1967), the Court reiterated that a juvenile cannot be deprived of due process simply because the offense is not called a crime or because the goal was not to punish but to "save the child" (*In re Winship*, 1970, p. 365). According to the Court, *Gault* made it clear that "civil labels and good intentions do not themselves obviate the need for criminal due process safeguards in juvenile courts" (*In re Winship*, 1970, pp. 365–366) and that the consequences of juvenile proceedings were comparable to those of felony prosecutions.

Again, the Court stressed that applying procedural due process protections to youths would not blur the lines between juvenile and criminal prosecutions:

> Nor do we perceive any merit in the argument that to afford juveniles the protection of proof beyond a reasonable doubt would risk destruction of beneficial aspects of the juvenile process. Use of the reasonable-doubt standard during the adjudicatory hearing will not disturb New York's policies that a finding that a child has violated a criminal law does not constitute a criminal conviction, that such a finding does not deprive the child of his civil rights, and that juvenile proceedings are confidential. Nor will there be any effect on the informality, flexibility, or speed of the hearing at which the factfinding takes place. And the opportunity during the post-adjudicatory or dispositional hearing for a wide-ranging review of the child's social history and for his individualized treatment will remain unimpaired. Similarly, there will be no

> effect on the procedures distinctive to juvenile proceedings that are employed prior to the adjudicatory hearing. (*In re Winship*, 1970, pp. 366–367)

Kent v. United States (1966), *In re Gault* (1967), and *Winship* thus clarified that youths were entitled to constitutional protections in juvenile court and that a core test for such protections was whether they comport with fundamental fairness under the Due Process Clause of the Constitution.

PARAMETERS OF JUVENILE DUE PROCESS

In this first set of cases regarding constitutional procedures in juvenile court (*Kent v. United States*, 1966; *In re Gault*, 1967; *In re Winship*, 1970), the Supreme Court noted that not every criminal procedural protection would attach in juvenile court. In the next trio of cases we discuss—*McKeiver v. Pennsylvania* (1971), *Breed v. Jones* (1975), and *Schall v. Martin* (1984)—the Court further defined the parameters of when—and which—protections would apply.

Just a year after *In re Winship* (1970), the Supreme Court was called on to decide whether the constitutional right to a jury trial attaches in juvenile court. In *McKeiver v. Pennsylvania* (1971), a plurality of the Court (four justices) concluded that due process did not require jury trials for juveniles. The *McKeiver v. Pennsylvania* case involved two consolidated cases, one from Pennsylvania and another from North Carolina. The Pennsylvania case concerned Joseph McKeiver, a 16-year-old charged with robbery, larceny, and receiving stolen goods, and Edward Terry, a 15-year-old with delinquency charges of assault and battery on a police officer and conspiracy (*McKeiver v. Pennsylvania*, 1971). The North Carolina charges arose out of a series of civil rights demonstrations by Black adults and children protesting school assignments and a school consolidation plan (*McKeiver v. Pennsylvania*, 1971). All but one of the children in the North Carolina case were charged with willfully impeding traffic (*McKeiver v. Pennsylvania*, 1971). The other child, James Lambert Howard, was charged with willfully making riotous noise, interrupting and disturbing school, defacing school furniture, and disorderly conduct in the school (*McKeiver v. Pennsylvania*, 1971). In both the Pennsylvania and North Carolina cases, the youths were adjudicated delinquent with no right to trial by jury (*McKeiver v. Pennsylvania*, 1971). In the North Carolina case, the general public was excluded, over the objections of counsel for the youth (*McKeiver v. Pennsylvania*, 1971).

The Supreme Court observed that although "the Due Process Clause has a role to play" (*McKeiver v. Pennsylvania*, 1971, p. 541) in juvenile court, not all rights that attach in criminal procedures would also be granted in juvenile court. Instead, "our task here with respect to trial by jury, as it was in *Gault* with respect to other claimed rights 'is to ascertain the precise impact of the due process requirement'" (*McKeiver v. Pennsylvania*, 1971, p. 541, citing *In re Gault*, 1967, pp. 13–14). The Court concluded that "little, indeed, is to be gained by any attempt simplistically to call the juvenile court proceeding either 'civil' or 'criminal.' The Court carefully has avoided this wooden approach" (*McKeiver v. Pennsylvania*, 1971, p. 541). Thus, each decision about the application of procedural protections would require the Court to consider the impact on the nature of juvenile court and the extent to which a procedural right would change the goals and functioning of the juvenile court.

The Pennsylvania youth argued that their proceedings were "substantially similar to a criminal trial," both because youths are held pre- and post-adjudication in facilities that resemble jails and prisons and because the trial processes are similar in both juvenile and adult court, including motions to suppress, rules of evidence, public trials, plea bargaining, and defenses (*McKeiver v. Pennsylvania*, 1971, p. 541). The North Carolina youth urged that the requirement of a jury trial would not deprive them of the "supposed benefits of the juvenile court system" (*McKeiver v. Pennsylvania*, 1971, p. 542), including the intake procedure, flexible sentencing, and focus on rehabilitation. They emphasized that "adjudication of factual issues on the one hand and disposition of the case on the other are very different matters with very different purposes" (*McKeiver v. Pennsylvania*, 1971, p. 542) and therefore that a jury trial would not undermine the key goals of providing rehabilitative interventions for juveniles.

A plurality of the Court rejected these arguments, concluding that there was no constitutional right to a jury trial in juvenile court. Despite the "sweeping rationale" of the *Gault* decision, the Court would not extend all adult criminal procedural rights to juvenile court (*McKeiver v. Pennsylvania*, 1971). The Court expressed concern that,

> there is a possibility, at least, that the jury trial, if required as a matter of constitutional precept, will remake the juvenile proceeding into a fully adversary process and will put an effective end to what has been the idealistic prospect of an intimate, informal protective proceeding. (*McKeiver v. Pennsylvania*, 1971, p. 545)

The Court further explained that the jury trial would bring to the juvenile system "the traditional delay, the formality, and the clamor of the adversary system, and, possibly, the public trial" (*McKeiver v. Pennsylvania*, 1971, p. 550). The distinction between juvenile and adult court, therefore, was not simply a question of disposition and treatment, but also of courtroom procedures and how both the youth and the judge would participate in the courtroom. The plurality rejected the plaintiffs' argument for the right to a jury trial, justifying the opinion in large part on the importance of recognizing differences between children and adults and protecting the separate juvenile system (*McKeiver v. Pennsylvania*, 1971).

In reaching this decision, the plurality failed to fully address the plaintiffs' concerns about the need for procedural protection. The Court noted,

> of course there have been abuses. The Task Force Report has noted them. We refrain from saying at this point that those abuses are of constitutional dimension. They relate to the lack of resources and of dedication rather than to inherent unfairness. (*McKeiver v. Pennsylvania*, 1971, pp. 547–548)

Without consideration of why the right to a jury trial is essential in the adult system, the Court asserted that "the imposition of the jury trial on the juvenile court system would not strengthen greatly, if at all, the fact-finding function" of the court (*McKeiver v. Pennsylvania*, 1971, p. 547).

The Court also did not directly respond to the plaintiffs' arguments that a jury trial would not undermine the juvenile court process—either because juvenile procedures already resembled adult procedures or because the key distinction was in the treatment and sentencing of adjudicated youths, not the adjudicatory process. Instead, the Court painted the jury trial as a threat to the existence of a separate juvenile system: "Meager as has been the hoped-for advance in the juvenile field, the alternative would be regressive, would lose what has been gained, and would tend once again to place the juvenile squarely in the routine of the criminal process" (*McKeiver v. Pennsylvania*, 1971, p. 547). Thus, the Court held,

> if the formalities of the criminal adjudicative process are to be superimposed upon the juvenile court system, there is little need for its separate existence. Perhaps that ultimate disillusionment will come one day, but for the moment we are disinclined to give impetus to it. (*McKeiver v. Pennsylvania*, 1971, p. 551)

The decision underscored the importance of a distinct juvenile justice system, but also revealed a Supreme Court unwilling to fully separate procedure from substance in its analysis of how the justice system should function.

Whereas the *McKeiver v. Pennsylvania* (1971) decision opened questions about the reach of the Constitution's protections, the decision of the Court a few years later in *Breed v. Jones* (1975) clarified that the Court had not wholly abandoned its commitment to due process in juvenile proceedings. At issue in *Breed* was whether the constitutional prohibition on double jeopardy was violated when a young person faced both an adjudicatory hearing in juvenile court and a criminal trial in adult court for the same charges (*Breed v. Jones*, 1975). The Court concluded, unanimously, that requiring a youth to face the same charges in both proceedings violated the constitution (*Breed v. Jones*, 1975).

The defendant in *Breed v. Jones* (1975) was accused of a juvenile delinquency offense for actions that would have constituted armed robbery for an adult. He was 17 at the time of the offense (*Breed v. Jones*,

1975). After an adjudicatory hearing in juvenile court, with testimony from witnesses, the juvenile court concluded that the allegations were true and ordered that the defendant be detained (*Breed v. Jones*, 1975). At a later hearing, the juvenile court held that the defendant was "'unfit for treatment as a juvenile,' and ordered that he be prosecuted as an adult" (*Breed v. Jones*, 1975, p. 524). The parties agreed that he was put in jeopardy in the adult proceedings but disagreed as to whether the juvenile adjudication also placed him in jeopardy (*Breed v. Jones*, 1975).

The Court, relying on its holdings in *In re Gault* (1967) and *In re Winship* (1970) establishing procedural protections in juvenile court, determined that it was "too late in the day" (*Breed v. Jones*, 1975, p. 529) to conclude that the juvenile proceeding did not put the young person in jeopardy:

> Although the juvenile-court system had its genesis in the desire to provide a distinctive procedure and setting to deal with the problems of youth, including those manifested by antisocial conduct, our decisions in recent years have recognized that there is a gap between the originally benign conception of the system and its realities. With the exception of *McKeiver v. Pennsylvania*, 403 U.S. 528, 91 S.Ct. 1976, 29 L.Ed.2d 647 (1971), the Court's response to that perception has been to make applicable in juvenile proceedings constitutional guarantees associated with traditional criminal prosecutions. *In re Gault*, 387 U.S. 1, 87 S.Ct. 1428, 18 L.Ed.2d 527 (1967); *In re Winship*, 397 U.S. 358, 90 S.Ct. 1068, 25 L.Ed.2d 368 (1970). (*Breed v. Jones*, 1975, p. 529)

The Court once again noted the drastic consequences of juvenile adjudications, quoting both *Gault*'s and *Winship*'s conclusions that such proceedings subject a youth to loss of liberty, impose stigma, and constitute "incarceration against one's will, whether it is called 'criminal' or 'civil'" (*Breed v. Jones*, 1975, p. 530). According to the Court, "The rehabilitative goals of the system are admirable, but they do not change the drastic nature of the action taken" (*Breed v. Jones*, 1975, p. 530, n. 12).

The Court also rejected the argument that a double jeopardy right attaching in juvenile court would diminish the capacity of the juvenile court to operate in a flexible manner. The juvenile court could still transfer youth to the adult system, but would have to do so before adjudication. This would allow the juvenile court "the flexibility needed to deal with youthful offenders who cannot benefit from the specialized guidance and treatment contemplated by the system" (*Breed v. Jones*, 1975, pp. 532–533).

The Court not only underscored the importance of constitutional protections in *Breed v. Jones* (1975), it also emphasized again the importance of the juvenile system's unique rehabilitative role:

> What concerns us here is the dilemma that the possibility of transfer after an adjudicatory hearing presents for a juvenile. . . . Because of that possibility, a juvenile, thought to be the beneficiary of special consideration, may in fact suffer substantial disadvantages. If he appears uncooperative, he runs the risk of an adverse adjudication, as well as of an unfavorable dispositional recommendation. If, on the other hand, he is cooperative, he runs the risk of prejudicing his chances in adult court if transfer is ordered. We regard a procedure that results in such a dilemma as at odds with the goal that, to the extent fundamental fairness permits, adjudicatory hearings be informal and nonadversary. . . . Knowledge of the risk of transfer after an adjudicatory hearing can only undermine the potential for informality and cooperation which was intended to be the hallmark of the juvenile-court system. (*Breed v. Jones*, 1975, p. 540)

To ensure that the juvenile benefits from special consideration, then, his or her Fifth Amendment right to be free of double jeopardy must apply in juvenile as well as adult court.

The Court again considered the special circumstances of youth in juvenile court in the case of *Schall v. Martin* (1984), but reached a very different conclusion. The *Schall* Court held that it did not violate due process to hold a youth in pretrial detention without a probable cause finding (*Schall v. Martin*, 1984). The case was brought by three sets of class representatives on behalf of all similarly situated youths (*Schall v. Martin*, 1984). The class representatives were accused of serious offenses—robbery, assault, and larceny (*Schall v. Martin*, 1984). The relevant statute permitted detention for a juvenile if "'(a) there is a substantial probability that he will not appear in court on the return date;' or '(b) there is a serious risk that he may before the return date commit an act which if committed by an adult would constitute a crime'" (*Schall v. Martin*, 1984, p. 256, n. 1). The plaintiffs challenged only section (b), the provision allowing for preventive detention (*Schall v. Martin*, 1984). The Court concluded that the statute met the due process requirement of fundamental fairness and rejected the plaintiffs' arguments (*Schall v. Martin*, 1984).

The Court's holding emphasized that "juveniles . . . are always in some form of custody" (*Schall v. Martin*, 1984, p. 265). The Court stressed the state interest in public safety and noted that although children have a right to freedom from institutional restraints, that interest was qualified because children's freedom is always curtailed, whether in an institution or their own home. "Children, by definition, are not assumed to have the capacity to take care of themselves. They are assumed to be subject to the control of their parents, and if parental control falters, the State must play its part as parens patriae" (*Schall v. Martin*, 1984, p. 265). This was a drastic shift in focus from the earlier recognition in *In re Winship* (1970), *In re Gault* (1967), and *Breed v. Jones* (1975) of the serious consequences of juvenile adjudications, with a focus on the loss of liberty as well as the potential harsh reality of juvenile incarceration. To justify the position that, legally, being in the custody of the state was not that different from being in the custody of one's parents, the Court also painted a rosy picture of the conditions of detention:

> Nonsecure detention involves an open facility in the community, a sort of "halfway house," without locks, bars, or security officers where the child receives schooling and counseling and has access to recreational facilities. . . . Secure detention is more restrictive, but it is still consistent with the regulatory and parens patriae objectives relied upon by the State. Children are assigned to separate dorms based on age, size, and behavior. They wear street clothes provided by the institution and partake in educational and recreational programs and counseling sessions run by trained social workers. Misbehavior is punished by confinement to one's room. (*Schall v. Martin*, 1984, p. 271)

Strangely, the majority's characterization of the facts, citing testimony from the trial, was completely contradicted by the dissent. The dissent described the conditions as harsh and institutional, quoting the district court's finding that "the juveniles are subjected to strip-searches, wear institutional clothing and follow institutional regimen" (*Schall v. Martin*, 1984, p. 290) and highlighted the risk to youths of assault, sexual assault, and exposure to negative influences from other youths in juvenile facilities.

The majority also concluded that detention of juveniles could be justified by the state's interest in protecting youths. The opinion emphasized that unique characteristics make youths more susceptible to negative influences, including peer pressure, and less capable of mature judgment and therefore that "society has a legitimate interest in protecting the juvenile from the consequences of his criminal activity" (*Schall v. Martin*, 1984, p. 266). Thus, the Court reasoned, the differences between teenagers and adults justified detaining a juvenile more readily than an adult (*Schall v. Martin*, 1984).[7] The decision laid the groundwork for an understanding that the unique characteristics of youths, and of juvenile

[7]The majority also suggested that the rule they applied here did not differ from the rule applied in adult court. The characterization of the rule applied to adults is questionable at best. In fact, the standard for adults required a "timely judicial determination of probable cause as a prerequisite to detention" (*Gerstein v. Pugh*, 1975, p. 126).

court, permitted the court to apply lesser standards of constitutional protection for juveniles than for adults.[8]

As should be evident from the preceding discussion, the decisions during this era of constitutionalization swung between affording juveniles all of the procedural protections granted adults charged or convicted of crimes and the Court's reliance on the unique characteristics of the juvenile court, or the characteristics of juveniles, to justify a different standard with fewer constitutional protections for juveniles. These tensions are still echoed in today's opinions on juvenile justice (Feierman & Shah, 2007).

INFLUENCE OF ADOLESCENT DEVELOPMENT RESEARCH ON CHILDREN'S STATUS UNDER THE CONSTITUTION

The Supreme Court cases of the 1960s through 1980s focused on establishing the parameters of due process in juvenile court. Beginning in 2005, a new wave of challenges came before the Supreme Court in which the Court was asked to consider the impact of emerging adolescent development and neuroscientific research on the rights of children sentenced as adults or subject to police interrogation. These cases have added to the existing body of case law concerning juveniles in the justice system, linking scientifically established distinctions between youths and adults with increased protections for youths.

In the first of these cases, *Roper v. Simmons* (2005), the U.S. Supreme Court was asked to review the constitutionality of the juvenile death penalty. In banning the juvenile death penalty as violating the Eighth Amendment's proscription on cruel and unusual punishments, the *Roper v. Simmons* Court relied heavily on the emerging body of research describing the distinct emotional and psychological attributes of youths (*Roper v. Simmons*, 2005). The Court cited medical, psychological, and sociological studies, as well as common experience, which all showed that children younger than age 18 are less culpable and more amenable to rehabilitation than adults who commit similar crimes (*Roper v. Simmons*, 2005). The *Roper* Court reasoned that because juveniles have reduced culpability, they cannot be subjected to the harshest penalty reserved for the most depraved offenders; punishment for juveniles must be moderated to some degree to reflect their lesser blameworthiness (*Roper v. Simmons*, 2005). The Court's holding that juveniles are less culpable than adults was premised on three core research findings on children and adolescents: (a) Relative to adults, juveniles have a "lack of maturity and an undeveloped sense of responsibility"; (b) they "are more vulnerable or susceptible to negative influences and outside pressures, including peer pressure"; and (c) their characters are "not as well formed" (*Roper v. Simmons*, 2005, pp. 569–570).

Central to the Supreme Court's determination about juvenile culpability in *Roper v. Simmons* (2005) was its understanding that the personalities of adolescents are "more transitory" and "less fixed" (p. 570) than those of adults. The Court further explained that,

> indeed, "[t]he relevance of youth as a mitigating factor derives from the fact that the signature qualities of youth are transient; as individuals mature, the impetuousness and recklessness that may dominate in younger years can subside." Johnson v. Texas, 509 U.S. 350 . . ., 368, 113 S.Ct. 2658 (1993); see also Steinberg & Scott 1014 ("For most teens, [risky or antisocial] behaviors are fleeting; they cease with maturity as individual identity becomes settled. Only a relatively small proportion of adolescents who experiment in risky or illegal activities develop entrenched patterns of problem behavior that persist into adulthood"). (*Roper v. Simmons*, 2005, p. 570)

[8]A similar standard was subsequently applied by the Supreme Court to the question of school searches. The Court concluded that the Fourth Amendment did apply to schools, but the balance between the "privacy interests of schoolchildren" and the "substantial need of teachers and administrators for freedom to maintain order in the schools" allowed searches without probable cause as long as they were "reasonable" (*New Jersey v. T.L.O.*, 1985, p. 341; see also *Earls v. Pottawatomie School District*, 2002; *Safford Unified School District v. Redding*, 2009; *Vernonia School District 47J v. Acton*, 1995).

The Court noted that this transient nature of a youth's personality was consistent with psychological and psychiatric practice:

> It is difficult even for expert psychologists to differentiate between the juvenile offender whose crime reflects unfortunate yet transient immaturity, and the rare juvenile offender whose crime reflects irreparable corruption. See Steinberg & Scott 1014–1016. As we understand it, this difficulty underlies the rule forbidding psychiatrists from diagnosing any patient under 18 as having antisocial personality disorder, a disorder also referred to as psychopathy or sociopathy, and which is characterized by callousness, cynicism, and contempt for the feelings, rights, and suffering of others. (*Roper* v. *Simmons*, 2005, p. 573)

As a result, the Court's holding rested in part on the incongruity of imposing a final and irrevocable penalty on an adolescent, who had capacity to change and grow. "It would be misguided to equate the failings of a minor with those of an adult, for a greater possibility exists that a minor's character deficiencies will be reformed" (*Roper* v. *Simmons*, 2005, p. 570). The Court underscored that the state was not permitted to extinguish the juvenile's "potential to attain a mature understanding of his own humanity" (*Roper* v. *Simmons*, 2005, p. 573).

Although the Court's decision in *Roper* v. *Simmons* (2005) set the stage for a new constitutional jurisprudence concerning youths under the Eighth Amendment, the notion that certain offenders might be less blameworthy for their criminal conduct and thus ineligible for the harshest and most extreme penalties had already gained traction with the Court in 2002, when the Court reconsidered its prior case law upholding the death penalty for offenders with intellectual disabilities (who were then called mentally retarded). In *Atkins* v. *Virginia* (2002), the Court for the first time held that such defendants were categorically less blameworthy for their criminal conduct, including murder, than unimpaired adult offenders.[9] They were thus ineligible for the death penalty (*Atkins* v. *Virginia*, 2002). *Roper* followed *Atkins*' blueprint in holding that all juveniles younger than age 18 were likewise categorically less blameworthy than adults and could not receive the most serious sentence available—a sentence of death, reserved for the most serious offenses (*Roper* v. *Simmons*, 2005). The Court embraced the developmental research articulating the differences between juvenile and adult offenders (*Roper* v. *Simmons*, 2005)[10] and reversed its prior 1989 decision in *Stanford* v. *Kentucky* (1989), which had left the death penalty in place for 16- and 17-year-old juvenile offenders.[11]

Five years later, the Court was presented with another opportunity to consider the constitutional relevance of the adolescent development research in *Graham* v. *Florida* (2010), a case challenging the constitutionality of a sentence of life without parole for a juvenile convicted of a nonhomicide offense. Petitioner Terence Graham was 16 when he was charged with armed burglary with assault or battery, a first-degree felony carrying a maximum penalty of life imprisonment without the possibility of parole, and attempted armed robbery, a second-degree felony carrying a maximum penalty of 15 years' imprisonment. Under Florida law, it is within a prosecutor's discretion whether to charge 16- and 17-year-olds as adults or juveniles for most felony crimes. Graham's prosecutor elected to charge Graham as an adult. Under a plea agreement, the Florida trial court sentenced Graham to probation and withheld adjudication

[9]In *Penry* v. *Lynaugh* (1989), the Court had been asked to specifically rule the execution of any defendant with mental retardation to be a violation of the Eighth Amendment. The Court declined that invitation in 1989, ruling instead that mental retardation could—and should—be considered as a mitigating factor by the jury in determining the appropriateness of the death penalty, but the presence of mental retardation did not necessarily render the defendant categorically ineligible for that sentence.

[10]See, generally, Erikson (1968), which describes and defines the notion of an identity crisis within the context of youth identities; Arnett (1992), which explains the underlying factors behind reckless behavior in adolescents; and Steinberg and Scott (2003), exploring the research and theories behind concerns raised by the criminal culpability of children.

[11]One year before *Stanford*, the Court handed down *Thompson* v. *Oklahoma* (1988), in which a plurality (including Justice Stevens, joined by Justices Brennan, Marshall, and Blackmun) determined that "standards of decency" (*Thompson* v. *Oklahoma*, 1988, p. 830) did not permit the execution of an individual who commits a crime while younger than age 16.

of guilt as to both charges and sentenced Graham to concurrent 3-year terms of probation. Graham was required to spend the first 12 months of his probation in the county jail, but he received credit for the time he had served awaiting trial and spent about 6 months in jail.

Approximately 6 months later, Graham's probation officer filed with the trial court an affidavit asserting that Graham had violated the conditions of his probation; the court found that Graham had violated his probation by committing a home invasion robbery, by possessing a firearm, and by associating with people engaged in criminal activity. The trial court adjudicated Graham guilty of the earlier charges, revoked his probation, and sentenced him to life in prison for the burglary. Because Florida has abolished its parole system, the life sentence left Graham with no possibility of release except executive clemency. He challenged his sentence under the Eighth Amendment's Cruel and Unusual Punishments Clause, but the State First District Court of Appeal affirmed. The U.S. Supreme Court granted review (*Graham v. Florida*, 2010).

The Court held that such a severe and irrevocable punishment was not appropriate for a less culpable juvenile offender (*Graham v. Florida*, 2010). In banning the sentence, Justice Kennedy, writing for the majority, underscored that case law, developmental research, and neuroscience all recognize that children are different from adults—they are less culpable for their actions and at the same time have a greater capacity to change and mature. In addition to noting the three essential characteristics that distinguish youths from adults for culpability purposes—lack of maturity and responsibility, increased vulnerability to peer pressure, and malleability of their characters—Justice Kennedy further noted,

> no recent data provide reason to reconsider the Court's observations in *Roper* about the nature of juveniles. As petitioner's *amici* point out, developments in psychology and brain science continue to show fundamental differences between juvenile and adult minds. For example, parts of the brain involved in behavior control continue to mature through late adolescence. Juveniles are more capable of change than are adults, and their actions are less likely to be evidence of "irretrievably depraved character" than are the actions of adults. (*Graham v. Florida*, 2010, p. 68, citing *Roper v. Simmons*, 2005, p. 570)

As in *Roper*, the majority made it clear in *Graham v. Florida* that the constitutionality of a particular punishment for juveniles (i.e., whether it is cruel and unusual under the Eighth Amendment) is directly tied to prevailing research on adolescent development and that juvenile status is central to that analysis (*Graham v. Florida*, 2010).

Specifically, the Court ruled in *Graham v. Florida* (2010) that juveniles cannot be sentenced to life without a meaningful and realistic opportunity for parole for nonhomicide offenses. The Court explained,

> the juvenile should not be deprived of the opportunity to achieve maturity of judgment and self-recognition of human worth and potential. . . . Life in prison without the possibility of parole gives no chance for fulfillment outside prison walls, no chance for reconciliation with society, no hope. (*Graham v. Florida*, 2010, p. 79)

The defendant's age and the fact that the offenses were nonhomicide crimes were the salient factors in the *Graham* Court's decision: "The age of the offender and the nature of the crime each bear on the analysis" (*Graham v. Florida*, 2010, p. 69). As *Graham* recognized, because juveniles are more likely to be reformed than adults, it is inappropriate to impose on them a sentence with no meaningful opportunity for release. Such a sentence "improperly denies the juvenile offender a chance to demonstrate growth and maturity" (*Graham v. Florida*, 2010, p. 73).

As in *Roper v. Simmons* (2005), the Court adopted a categorical ban on life-without-parole sentences for juveniles convicted of nonhomicide offenses. Without a categorical rule, the Court noted that an "unacceptable likelihood exists that the brutality or coldblooded nature of any particular crime would overpower mitigating arguments based on youth as a matter of course" (*Graham v. Florida*, 2010, p. 78). Were the Court to allow a case-by-case assessment of culpability, courts might not "with sufficient accuracy distinguish the few incorrigible juvenile offenders from the many that have the capacity to change" (*Graham v. Florida*, 2010, p. 77). Juvenile nonhomicide offenders are "not sufficiently culpable to merit that punishment" (*Graham v. Florida*, 2010, p. 95). The categorical rule "gives all juvenile non-homicide offenders a chance to demonstrate maturity and reform" (*Graham v. Florida*, 2010, p. 51). At the same time, the *Graham* Court recognized that some juvenile offenders may never be released. As Justice Kennedy wrote, "A State need not guarantee an offender eventual release" (*Graham v. Florida*, 2010, p. 82). The ban on life-without-parole sentences is not a promise of a return to society—it is merely a requirement that juvenile offenders be provided the opportunity to be considered for release within some reasonable period of time before the completion of their sentences.

Additionally, in striking life-without-parole sentences in *Graham v. Florida* (2010), the Court held that none of the legitimate penological goals that support such sentences for adult offenders—retribution, deterrence, incapacitation, and rehabilitation—"provides an adequate justification" (*Graham v. Florida*, 2010, p. 71) for imposing the sentence on juveniles. The Court echoed its earlier holding in *Roper v. Simmons* (2005), emphasizing the reduced blameworthiness of juvenile offenders in rejecting both retribution and deterrence as proffered rationales for the sentence (*Graham v. Florida*, 2010). Its rejection of incapacitation in defense of life-without-parole sentences went further, however, underscoring the folly of making irrevocable judgments about youths:

> To justify life without parole on the assumption that the juvenile offender forever will be a danger to society requires the sentencer to make a judgment that the juvenile is incorrigible. The characteristics of juveniles make that judgment questionable. . . . Even if the State's judgment that Graham was incorrigible was later corroborated by prison misbehavior or failure to mature, the sentence was still disproportionate because that judgment was made at the outset. A life without parole sentence denies the juvenile offender a chance to demonstrate growth and maturity. Incapacitation cannot override all other considerations, lest the Eighth Amendment's rule against disproportionate sentences be a nullity. (*Graham v. Florida*, 2010, pp. 72–73)

The goal of rehabilitation was likewise dismissed, because the Court found that the punishment of life without parole is simply at odds with the rehabilitative ideal. "By denying the defendant the right to reenter the community, the State makes an irrevocable judgment about that person's value and place in society"—a judgment inconsistent with a juvenile nonhomicide offender's "capacity for change and limited moral culpability" (*Graham v. Florida*, 2010, p. 74). Indeed, the juvenile must be given an opportunity to demonstrate the capacity to change—not only at the time of sentencing, but even over the course of time as he or she matures (*Graham v. Florida*, 2010, p. 73).

Thus, at the core of the Court's opinion is the understanding that youths cannot be labeled as incorrigible because they have the capacity to mature and develop.

In 2011, in *J.D.B. v. North Carolina*, the Supreme Court was asked to consider whether the young age of a suspect should matter in applying the *Miranda v. Arizona* (1966) custody analysis to determine whether a suspect should be advised of his *Miranda* rights during a police interrogation. This issue had previously come before the Court in 2004 in *Yarborough v. Alvarado*. *Yarborough* came to the Court on a writ of certiorari by the State of California from a decision of the Ninth Circuit (*Yarborough v. Alvarado*, 2004). The question at issue was whether Alvarado's age (17 at the time of his police interrogation) was relevant to the determination of whether he would have felt free to terminate the questioning (*Yarborough v. Alvarado*, 2004). During the course of the interrogation, the defendant, 17-year-old Alvarado, confessed to his participation in a homicide (*Yarborough v. Alvarado*, 2004). He was not given a *Miranda* warning before making a statement to the police (*Yarborough v. Alvarado*, 2004). Police are required to issue *Miranda* warnings when an individual is in custody, an objective determination that considers whether the individual would have felt free to leave or terminate the questioning (*Miranda v. Arizona*, 1966). The California Supreme Court had concluded, without considering Alvarado's youth or inexperience, that he was not in custody at the time of questioning (*Yarborough*, 2004). The federal district court agreed; the Ninth Circuit U.S. Court of Appeals reversed, and the U.S. Supreme Court granted review.

Because the case reached the Supreme Court through a habeas petition under the Antiterrorism and Effective Death Penalty Act of 1996, the Supreme Court was required only to decide whether the state court decision was "objectively unreasonable" (*Yarborough v. Alvarado*, 2004, p. 665). The Supreme Court held that a state court decision that failed to take account of the juvenile's age as part of the *Miranda v. Arizona* (1966) custody analysis was not "objectively unreasonable" (*Yarborough v. Alvarado*, 2004, p. 665) under the deferential standard of the act. "Whether the [state court] was right or wrong is not the pertinent question under [the act]" (*J.D.B. v. North Carolina*, 2011, p. 2405); whereas the Court in *Yarborough* acknowledged that accounting for a juvenile's age under *Miranda* "could be viewed as creating a subjective inquiry" (*Yarborough v. Alvarado*, 2004, p. 654), the Court did not address whether such a view would be correct under law. Indeed, Justice O'Connor, in her concurrence, acknowledged that a suspect's age may indeed be relevant to the custody inquiry (*Yarborough v. Alvarado*, 2004).

The Court was given the opportunity to address this issue of youth status squarely in *J.D.B. v. North Carolina* in 2011. J.D.B. was a 13-year-old middle school student in Chapel Hill, North Carolina, when he was removed from his classroom by a uniformed police officer and escorted to a conference room. There he was interrogated by the uniformed officer, a school resource officer, the assistant principal, and an adult administrative intern for approximately 30 to 45 minutes. The door to the conference room was closed. J.D.B. was questioned about recent break-ins in his neighborhood. J.D.B. was not advised that he was free to leave the room or end the interrogation, nor was he advised of his *Miranda* rights at the outset of the interview. During the course of the interrogation, the assistant principal urged J.D.B. to "do the right thing," warning J.D.B. that "the truth always comes out in the end" (*J.D.B. v. North Carolina*, 2011, p. 2399).

Ultimately, J.D.B. confessed to the officer that he and a friend were responsible for the break-ins (*J.D.B. v. North Carolina*, 2011). Only at this point did the officer tell J.D.B. that he did not have to answer his questions and that he was free to leave. J.D.B. indicated he understood his rights, provided further details to the officer, and ultimately drafted a written statement. J.D.B. was permitted to return home at the end of the school day (*J.D.B. v. North Carolina*, 2011).

J.D.B. was charged in juvenile court with breaking and entering and larceny (*J.D.B. v. North Carolina*, 2011). His lawyer moved to suppress his statement to the officer obtained during J.D.B.'s interrogation at school, arguing that J.D.B. had been interrogated in a custodial setting without being first provided *Miranda* warnings. The juvenile court denied the motion, finding J.D.B. was not "in custody" for the purposes of *Miranda* during the interrogation at school. A divided panel of the North Carolina Court of Appeals affirmed (*In re J.D.B.*, 2009). The North Carolina Supreme Court likewise affirmed, over two dissents, adopting the lower court's finding that J.D.B. was not in custody and expressly "declin[ing] to extend the test for custody to include consideration of the age . . . of an individual subject to questioning by police" (*J.D.B. v. North Carolina*, 2011, p. 2401, citing *In re J.D.B.*, 2009, p. 140).

The U.S. Supreme Court reversed (*In re. J.D.B.*, 2011). The Court held that,

> so long as the child's age was known to the officer at the time of police questioning, or would have been objectively apparent to a reasonable officer, its inclusion in the custody analysis is consistent with the objective nature of that test. (*J.D.B. v. North Carolina*, 2011, p. 2404)

The Court was emphatic in its view that youth is a fact that "generates commonsense conclusions about behavior and perception" (*J.D.B. v. North Carolina*, 2011, p. 2414, quoting *Yarborough v. Alvarado*, 2004, p. 674) and that such "conclusions" are "self-evident to anyone who was once a child himself, including any police officer or judge" (*J.D.B. v. North Carolina*, 2011, p. 2403). The Court wrote,

> in short, officers and judges need no imaginative powers, knowledge of developmental psychology, training in cognitive science, or expertise in social and cultural anthropology to account for a child's age. They simply need the common sense to know that a 7-year old is not a 13-year old and neither is an adult. (*J.D.B.*, 2011, p. 2408)

More important, the Court wrapped its "commonsense" approach in both the research that had guided its prior rulings in *Roper v. Simmons* (2005) and *Graham v. Florida* (2010) and decades of Supreme Court case law that has consistently recognized the link between juvenile status and legal status. Referencing its own prior decisions, as well as state laws and practices, the majority noted that "'our history is replete with laws and judicial recognition' that children cannot be viewed simply as miniature adults" (*J.D.B. v. North Carolina*, 2011, p. 2404, citing *Eddings v. Oklahoma*, 1982, p. 115). The Court's observation that age yields "objective conclusions" (*J.D.B. v. North Carolina*, 2011, p. 2398) about youths' susceptibility to influence or outside pressures was drawn directly from cases such as *Roper* and *Eddings*, cases that relied on research that confirmed widely held assumptions about youths. As the Court noted,

> the law has historically reflected the same assumption that children characteristically lack the capacity to exercise mature judgment and possess only an incomplete ability to understand the world around them. . . . Like this Court's own generalizations, the legal disqualifications placed on children as a class . . . exhibit the settled understanding that the differentiating characteristics of youth are universal. (*J.D.B. v. North Carolina*, 2011, pp. 2403–2404)

Underscoring the relevance of these demonstrated differences, the Court rejected the arguments of the state and the dissent that allowing consideration of age to inform the custody analysis would undercut the intended clarity of the *Miranda v. Arizona* (1966) test. Instead, the majority noted that "ignoring a juvenile defendant's age will often make the [*Miranda*] inquiry more artificial . . . and thus only add confusion" (*J.D.B. v. North Carolina*, 2011, p. 2407). The Court faulted the state's and the dissent's argument that *Miranda* only works with a one-size-fits-all analysis, insisting that age was both a relevant and an objective circumstance that could not be excluded from the custody analysis "simply to make the fault line between custodial and non-custodial 'brighter'" (*J.D.B. v. North Carolina*, 2011, p. 2407).

The Court repeated its recognition decades earlier in *Miranda v. Arizona* (1966) itself that, because "the inherently coercive nature of custodial interrogation 'blurs the line between voluntary and involuntary statements,' . . . [the] Court in *Miranda* adopted a set of prophylactic measures designed to safeguard the constitutional guarantee against self-incrimination" (*J.D.B. v. North Carolina*, 2011, p. 2401). As the Court explained, the *Miranda* custody test was necessary "precisely because the voluntariness test is an inadequate barrier when custodial interrogation is at stake" (*J.D.B. v. North Carolina*, 2011, p. 2408, citing *Miranda*, 1966, p. 458). The Court understood that custodial interrogation can be so coercive as to "induce a frighteningly high percentage of people to confess to crimes they never committed" (*J.D.B. v. North Carolina*, 2011, p. 2401, citing *Corley v. United States*, 2009), only heightening the concern for safeguarding the rights of juvenile suspects. The Court stated, "The risk is all the more troubling—and recent studies suggest—when the subject of custodial interrogation is a juvenile" (*J.D.B. v. North Carolina*, 2011, p. 2401).

Last, the Court tethered its ruling to the accepted view in "all American jurisdictions . . . that a person's childhood is a relevant circumstance" (*J.D.B. v. North Carolina*, 2011, p. 2404, citing Restatement (3d) of Torts [2005] § 10, Comment b., p 117) in ascertaining what the so-called reasonable person would have done in the particular circumstance at issue. The Court noted that the common law has reflected the reality that children are not adults and that questions of liability routinely take proper account of age. The Court distinguished age from "other personal characteristics that, even when known to police, have no objectively discernible relationship to a reasonable person's understanding of his freedom of action" (*J.D.B. v. North Carolina*, 2011, p. 2404). The Court concluded,

> to hold, as the State requests, that a child's age is never relevant to whether a suspect has been taken into custody—and thus to ignore the very real differences between children and adults—would be to deny children the full scope of the procedural safeguards that *Miranda* guarantees to adults. (*J.D.B. v. North Carolina*, 2011, p. 2408)

The Court thus opened the door to a broader examination of age in other contexts, with potentially far-reaching implications for children involved in the justice system. There are many other situations in which a "reasonable person" or "reasonableness" test is used to determine either the legality of the conduct or the blameworthiness of the individual in the criminal law. The degree to which these determinations must now yield to consideration of the age of the individual in question is likely to be one of the next frontiers in the shifting boundaries between children and adults in U.S. law generally and criminal law specifically (Levick & Tierney, 2012).

The next and most recent Supreme Court case to address the unique characteristics of youth was *Miller v. Alabama*, decided by the Court in 2012. Evan Miller and Kuntrell Jackson were both convicted of murder for crimes they committed when they were 14 years old (*Miller v. Alabama*, 2012).[12] Miller was convicted of first-degree murder; Jackson was convicted of felony murder. Although he participated in the robbery of a video store clerk, Jackson did not directly cause the death of the victim; one of his codefendants shot the victim (*Miller v. Alabama*, 2012). Under prevailing Alabama and Arkansas law, both Miller and Jackson were mandatorily sentenced to life without parole; the sentencing courts had no discretion whatsoever to impose lesser sentences (*Miller v. Alabama*, 2012). Both sentences were affirmed on appeal and, in the case of Jackson, affirmed as well in postconviction proceedings. The U.S. Supreme Court granted review in both cases and issued its opinion on June 25, 2012 (*Miller v. Alabama*, 2012).

Although the petitioners had asked the Court to categorically prohibit all life-without-parole sentences for juveniles convicted of either murder or felony murder, the Court limited its holding to proscribing only mandatory sentences of life without parole for juveniles convicted of homicide (*Miller v. Alabama*, 2012). From the outset of her opinion, Justice Kagan, writing for the majority, made it clear that the social science and other scientific research that had informed the Court's decisions in *Roper v. Simmons* (2005), *Graham v. Florida* (2010), and *J.D.B. v. North Carolina* (2011) dictated a similar outcome in *Miller*. Consequently, although affording narrow specific relief, *Miller* strengthened the Court's "kids are different" constitutional jurisprudence (*Miller v. Alabama*, 2012). With regard to mandatory juvenile life-without-parole sentences, Justice Kagan observed that "such a [sentencing] scheme prevents those meting out punishment from considering a juvenile's 'lessened culpability' and 'greater capacity for change,' and runs afoul of our cases' requirement of individualized sentencing for defendants facing the most serious penalties" (*Miller v. Alabama*, 2012, p. 2460, quoting *Graham v. Florida*, 2010, p. 51).

Significantly, the language quoted above not only built on the distinctions between youths and adults but also linked the Court's death penalty jurisprudence with its cases reviewing juvenile sentences under the Eighth Amendment. Justice Kagan specifically noted that *Miller v. Alabama* (2012) implicated "two strands of precedent reflecting our concern with proportionate punishment" (p. 2458). In the first strand, the Court has adopted categorical bans on sentences reflecting a mismatch between the culpability of the offender and the severity of the punishment (*Miller v. Alabama*, 2012). This proportionality analysis drove the Court to strike the death penalty for nonhomicide crimes in *Kennedy v. Louisiana* (2008) and to similarly prohibit its imposition

[12]For ease of reference, the *Jackson* and *Miller* cases are referred to collectively as *Miller* or *Miller v. Alabama*.

on mentally retarded defendants in *Atkins v. Virginia* (2002). Of course, this express concern with proportionality also led to the Court's holdings in *Roper v. Simmons* (2005) and *Graham v. Florida* (2010).

The second strand of the Court's precedents involve cases prohibiting the mandatory imposition of the death penalty, requiring instead individualized sentencing hearings in which the sentencer considers the offender's individual characteristics and attributes as well as the specific circumstances of the offense before sentencing the individual to death (*Miller v. Alabama*, 2012).[13] Here, Justice Kagan specifically acknowledged the Court's recent analogy of juvenile life without parole to the death penalty itself in *Graham v. Florida* (2010),[14] providing the foundation for the Court's requirement of individualized, nonmandatory sentencing hearings in the juvenile life-without-parole cases as well.

Addressing the proportionality of a juvenile life-without-parole sentence, Justice Kagan set forth the key governing principle: "*Roper* and *Graham* establish that children are constitutionally different from adults for purposes of sentencing. Because juveniles have diminished culpability and greater prospects for reform . . . 'they are less deserving of the most severe punishments'" (*Miller v. Alabama*, 2012, p. 2464, quoting *Graham v. Florida*, 2010, p. 119). The Court reiterated its prior core findings about adolescents: They are less mature and more prone to reckless, impulsive, and heedless risk taking; they are particularly vulnerable to negative peer pressure; and, because adolescence is inherently a period of transition, they are less likely to be found "irretrievably depraved" (*Miller v. Alabama*, 2012, p. 2475, quoting *Roper v. Simmons*, 2005, p. 570). The Court cited the uncontroverted body of research and social science confirming these findings and noted that the evidence of these unique attributes of youth had become even stronger since *Roper* and *Graham* were decided (*Miller v. Alabama*, 2012).

More important, in extending the rationale of *Graham v. Florida* (2010) from nonhomicide cases to the homicide cases before it in *Miller v. Alabama* (2012), the Court held that "none of what is said about children—about their distinctive (and transitory) mental traits and environmental vulnerabilities—is crime specific" (*Miller v. Alabama*, 2012, p. 2465). In other words, the unique characteristics of youth are present and relevant whatever offense the youth commits. Justice Kagan repeated a two-part corollary to the Court's holding in *Graham:* "An offender's age is relevant to the Eighth Amendment," and "criminal procedure laws that fail to take defendants' youthfulness into account at all would be flawed" (*Miller v. Alabama*, 2012, p. 2462, quoting *Graham v. Florida*, 2010, p. 76).[15]

Building on the Court's jurisprudence in capital cases, the Court concluded that the "mitigating qualities of youth" (*Miller v. Alabama*, 2012, p. 2455) must be considered before a sentence of death may be imposed. Justice Kagan stressed the striking similarity between the Court's observations in earlier cases considering the constitutionality of the death penalty as applied to juveniles, in which the Court had underscored that "youth is more than a chronological fact" (*Miller v. Alabama*, 2012, p. 2467), and the question posed by the imposition of mandatory life-without-parole sentences on juvenile homicide offenders. Justice Kagan wrote,

> such mandatory penalties, by their nature, preclude a sentencer from taking account of an offender's age and the wealth of characteristics and circumstances attendant to it. Under these schemes, every juvenile will receive the same sentence as every other—the 17-year-old and the 14-year-old, the

[13]See *Woodson v. North Carolina* (1976; plurality opinion; see also *Lockett v. Ohio*, 1976).

[14]In *Graham*, Justice Kennedy wrote that life-without-parole sentences "share some characteristics with death sentences that are shared by no other sentences." Justice Kennedy further observed that sentencing a juvenile to die in prison alters the remainder of his or her life "by a forfeiture of his life that is irrevocable" (*Graham v. Florida*, 2010, p. 69).

[15]Although Chief Justice Roberts appears to have disavowed this core aspect of the *Graham* holding in his concurrence in *Miller*, he specifically concurred with it in *Graham* itself, acknowledging there that an "offender's juvenile status can play a central role" (*Graham v. Florida*, 2010, p. 90) in considering the proportionality of a particular sentence.

> shooter and the accomplice, the child from a stable household and the child from a chaotic and abusive one. And still worse, each juvenile . . . will receive the same sentence as the vast majority of adults committing similar homicide offenses—but really, as *Graham* noted, a *greater sentence* than those adults will serve. In meting out the death penalty, the elision of all these differences would be strictly forbidden. And once again, *Graham* indicates that a similar rule should apply when a juvenile confronts a sentence of life (and death) in prison. (*Miller v. Alabama*, 2012, pp. 2467–2468)

Justice Kagan concluded, "So *Graham* and *Roper* and our individualized sentencing cases alike teach us that in imposing a State's harshest penalties, *a sentencer misses too much if he treats every child as an adult* [emphasis added]" (*Miller v. Alabama*, 2012, p. 2467).

What the Court meant by treating children like children was also spelled out by the Court:

> Mandatory life without parole for a juvenile precludes consideration of his chronological age and its hallmark features—among them, immaturity, impetuosity, and failure to appreciate risks and consequences. It prevents taking into account the family and home environment that surrounds him—and from which he cannot usually extricate himself—no matter how brutal or dysfunctional. It neglects the circumstances of the homicide offense, including the extent of his participation in the conduct and the way familial and peer pressures may have affected him. . . . This mandatory punishment disregards the possibility of rehabilitation even when the circumstances most suggest it. (*Miller v. Alabama*, 2012, p. 2468)

Thus, courts must recognize that children are different not only because of their developmental status, but also because of their day-to-day reality. They lack the freedom to choose their family or home, so they cannot be as accountable for actions that may be connected with their environment.

Finally, Justice Kagan addressed the Court's decision to forego a categorical ban on life-without-parole sentences for juveniles convicted of homicide. Although the Court viewed its requirement for individualized sentencing determinations that would take account of "youth (and all that accompanies it)" (*Miller v. Alabama*, 2012, p. 2469) to sufficiently address the challenges by Miller and Jackson, the Court was also clear that *Miller* must be read in the context of *Roper v. Simmons* (2005) and *Graham v. Florida* (2010). Thus, although a state is not required to guarantee eventual release, a state "must provide some meaningful opportunity to obtain release based on demonstrated maturity and rehabilitation" (*Miller v. Alabama*, 2012, p. 2469, citing *Graham v. Florida*, 2010, p. 123). Justice Kagan further observed, "Given all we have said in *Roper* and *Graham*, and this decision about children's diminished culpability and heightened capacity for change, we think appropriate occasions for sentencing juveniles to this harshest possible penalty will be uncommon" (*Miller v. Alabama*, 2012, p. 2469).

In a concurring opinion joined by Justice Sotomayor, Justice Breyer wrote separately to express his view that, at least in the case of Kuntrell Jackson, who was convicted of felony murder, *Graham* forbids sentencing Jackson to life without parole unless the state proved that Jackson "kill[ed] or intend[ed] to kill" the robbery victim (*Miller v. Alabama*, 2012, p. 2475, citing *Graham v. Florida*, 2010, p. 50). In Justice Breyer's opinion, *Graham*'s reasoning precludes the imposition of this sentence "where the juvenile himself neither kills nor intends to kill the victim" (*Miller v. Alabama*, 2012, p. 2476; Keller, 2012).

IMPLICATIONS OF THE COURT'S JURISPRUDENCE FOR CHILDREN IN THE JUSTICE SYSTEM

Although the juvenile justice system is now more than a century old, there is barely 50 years of case law from the U.S. Supreme Court defining its legal and constitutional parameters. Although it is beyond the purview of this chapter, the Supreme Court has repeatedly considered how the status of being a child affects that child's legal status in scenarios well beyond the juvenile or criminal justice systems. From reproductive rights to free speech and school searches, the Court, while grappling with fitting children into the Constitution, has now unequivocally acknowledged that youth status drives legal status—that is, in virtually every legal or constitutional area, a child's age must be taken into account in defining the child's legal rights.

Since 2005, with respect to children charged with crimes and subject to prosecution in the criminal justice system, the Supreme Court has been consistent in recognizing that there are constitutionally relevant differences between youths and adults and that those differences warrant increased protections for youths. Although it is unclear precisely how these rulings will affect youths in the juvenile justice or adult criminal justice system going forward, we suggest some potential areas of impact.

First, nothing in the Court's language on how adolescent development reduces culpability, as set forth in *Roper v. Simmons* (2005), *Graham v. Florida* (2010), and *Miller v. Alabama* (2012), limits those conclusions to sentencing cases. Indeed, the fact that the Supreme Court explicitly relied on those cases in its discussion regarding the application of *Miranda v. Arizona*'s (1966) requirements to juveniles illustrates how the decisions may have a wide reach in coming years.

In addition, the link between adolescent development and reduced culpability may extend beyond sentencing and apply to assessments of blameworthiness in a variety of contexts. For example, a strong argument can be made that the criminal culpability of a juvenile convicted of felony murder should be limited to the juvenile's personal participation in the underlying felony. The premise of felony murder is that the defendant is guilty of a murder without directly killing or intending to kill. The felony murder doctrine is often justified by a *transferred intent* theory, where the intent to kill may be inferred from an individual's intent to commit the underlying felony because a reasonable person would know that death is a possible result of felonious activities (*Miller v. Alabama*, 2012, p. 2476). The research and jurisprudence on adolescent decision making has demonstrated that young people may not have the requisite capacity for such foresight. As Justice Breyer observed in *Miller*, "The ability to consider the full consequences of a course of action and to adjust one's conduct accordingly is precisely what we know juveniles lack capacity to do effectively" (*Miller v. Alabama*, 2012, p. 2476). As a result, "to apply the doctrine of transferred intent here, where the juvenile did not kill, to sentence a juvenile to life without parole would involve . . . 'fallacious reasoning'" (*Miller v. Alabama*, 2012, pp. 2476–2477).

The Court's conclusion in *J.D.B. v. North Carolina* (2011) that the research on adolescent development and decision making requires that courts recognize a "reasonable juvenile" standard may also have far-reaching implications. A reasonable-person standard is explicitly incorporated into the defenses of duress, justified use of force, and provocation. It is also an element of the crime of negligent homicide and, as described above, felony murder. In all of these contexts, the Supreme Court's jurisprudence on youth could be read to support a reduced culpability for youth (Levick & Tierney, 2012).

The Court's holding in *J.D.B. v. North Carolina* (2011) that adolescent status is relevant to the *Miranda v. Arizona* (1966) custody determination also suggests that the Court may apply the developmental research to support procedural protections for youths in a variety of contexts. This might have consequences for laws relating to confessions, self-incrimination, and competency. Moreover, this legal approach may call into question earlier decisions of the 1960s, 1970s, and 1980s that were less protective of procedural protections in the juvenile court context.

Finally, the developmental approach may also suggest that more protective standards apply to the assessment of juvenile conditions. The harm experienced by young people may be more severe or long lasting than that experienced by adults held under similar circumstances or subjected to similar abuses. At the same time, the responsibility of officials—juvenile correctional officers, counselors, and social workers—to ensure the well-being of youth will be greater. Thus, standards for the use of isolation and strip searches, as well as the protection from abuse, may look different for juveniles than for adults (Levick, Feierman, Messenheimer, Goldstein, & Mordecai, 2012).

The doctrinal developments of the past 10 years presage a possible new period of reform in which we reexamine how juvenile offenders are managed and treated. The focus on adolescent development suggests a renewed commitment to the view, present at the founding of the original juvenile court, that youths are different from adults. Although grounded in common sense and experience more than a century ago, that view is now strongly supported by scientific research. This developmental approach may also suggest that youths warrant greater, not lesser, procedural protections than adults, adding greater clarity to the constitutionalization of the juvenile court that began with *Kent v. United States* (1966), *In re Gault* (1967), and *In re Winship* (1970).

References

Antiterrorism and Effective Death Penalty Act of 1996, Pub. L. 104–132, 110 Stat. 1214 (1996).

Arnett, J. (1992). Reckless behavior in adolescence: A developmental perspective. *Developmental Review*, *12*, 339–373. http://dx.doi.org/10.1016/0273-2297(92)90013-R

Atkins v. Virginia, 536 U.S. 304 (2002).

Bazelon, L. A. (2000). Exploding the superpredator myth: Why infancy is the preadolescent's best defense in juvenile court. *New York University Law Review*, *75*, 159–198.

Becker, E. (2001, February 9). As ex-theorist on young "superpredators," Bush aide has regrets. *New York Times*. Retrieved from http://www.nytimes.com/2001/02/09/us/as-ex-theorist-on-young-superpredators-bush-aide-has-regrets.html

Bennet, W. J. (1996). *Body count: Moral poverty and how to win America's war against crime and drugs*. New York, NY: Simon & Schuster.

Blumstein, A. (2002). Youth, guns, and violent crime. *Future of Children*, *12*, 38–53. http://dx.doi.org/10.2307/1602737

Breed v. Jones, 421 U.S. 519 (1975).

Champion, D. J. (1992). *The juvenile justice system, delinquency, processing, and the law* (5th ed.). Upper Saddle River, NJ: Prentice Hall.

Earls v. Pottawatomie School District, 536 U.S. 822 (2002).

Eddings v. Oklahoma, 455 U.S. 104 (1982).

Erikson, E. H. (1968). *Identity: Youth and crisis*. New York, NY: Norton.

Feierman, J., & Shah, R. (2007). Protecting personhood: Legal strategies to combat the use of strip searches on youth in detention. *Rutgers Law Review*, *60*, 67–103.

Gallegos v. Colorado, 370 U.S. 49 (1962).

Gerstein v. Pugh, 420 U.S. 103 (1975).

Graham v. Florida, 560 U.S. 48 (2010).

Grisso, T., Steinberg, L., Woolard, J., Cauffman, E., Scott, E., Graham, S., . . . Schwartz, R. (2003). Juveniles' competence to stand trial: A comparison of adolescents' and adults' capacities as trial defendants. *Law and Human Behavior*, *27*, 333–363. http://dx.doi.org/10.1023/A:1024065015717

Haley v. Ohio, 332 U.S. 596 (1948).

Holland, P., & Mlyniec, W. J. (1995). Whatever happened to the right to treatment? The modern quest for a historical promise. *Temple Law Review*, *68*, 1791–1835.

Illinois Juvenile Court Act, Ill. Laws 131. (1899).

In re Gault, 387 U.S. 1 (1967).

In re J.D.B., 674 SE 2d 795 (2009).

In re Winship, 397 U.S. 358 (1970).

J.D.B. v, North Carolina, 131 S. Ct. 2394 (2011).

Keller, E. (2012). Constitutional sentences for juveniles convicted of felony murder in the wake of *Roper*, *Graham*, and *J.D.B. Connecticut Public Interest Law Journal*, *11*, 297–326.

Kennedy v. Louisiana, 554 U.S. 407 (2008).

Kent v. United States, 383 U.S. 541 (1966).

Levick, M. (2010). Kids really are different: Looking past *Graham* v. *Florida*. *Criminal Law Reporter*, *87*, 664–667.

Levick, M. (2011). *J.D.B. v. North Carolina*: The U.S. Supreme Court heralds the emergence of the "reasonable juvenile" in American criminal law. *Criminal Law Reporter*, *89*, 753–757.

Levick, M. (2012). From a trilogy to a quadrilogy: *Miller v. Alabama* makes it four in a row for U. S. Supreme Court cases that support differential treatment of youth. *Criminal Law Reporter*, *91*, 749–756.

Levick, M., Feierman, J., Messenheimer, S., Goldstein, M., & Mordecai, K. (2012). The Eighth Amendment evolves: Defining cruel and unusual punishment through the lens of childhood and adolescence. *University of Pennsylvania Journal of Law and Social Change*, *15*, 285–321.

Levick, M. L., & Tierney, E. A. (2012). The United States Supreme Court adopts a reasonable juvenile standard in *J.D.B. v. North Carolina* for purposes of the *Miranda* custody analysis: Can a more reasoned justice system for juveniles be far behind? *Harvard Civil Rights–Civil Liberties Law Review*, *47*(2), 1–33.

Lockett v. Ohio, 438 U.S. 586 (1976).

McKeiver v. Pennsylvania, 403 U.S. 528 (1971).

Miller v. Alabama, 132 S. Ct. 2455 (2012).

Miranda v. Arizona, 348 U.S. 436 (1966).

New Jersey v. T.L.O., 469 U.S. 325 (1985).

Penry v. Lynaugh, 492 U.S. 302 (1989).

Restatement of Torts (Third) (2005).

Roper v. Simmons, 543 U.S. 551 (2005).

Ross, C. J. (1995). Disposition in a discretionary regime: Punishment and rehabilitation in the juvenile justice system. *Boston College Law Review*, *36*, 1038–1059.

Safford Unified School District v. Redding, 557 U.S. 364 (2009).

Schall v. Martin, 467 U.S. 253 (1984).

Scott, E., Reppucci, N., & Woolard, J. (1995). Evaluating adolescent decision making in legal contexts. *Law and Human Behavior*, *19*, 221–244. http://dx.doi.org/10.1007/BF01501658

Snyder, H. N., & Sickmund, M. (1999). *Juvenile offenders and victims: 1999 national report*. Washington, DC: National Center for Juvenile Justice. Retrieved from https://www.ncjrs.gov/html/ojjdp/nationalreport99/toc.html

Stanford v. Kentucky, 482 U.S. 361 (1989).

Steinberg, L., & Cauffman, E. (1996). Maturity of judgment in adolescence: Psychosocial factors in adolescent decision making. *Law and Human Behavior*, *20*, 249–272. http://dx.doi.org/10.1007/BF01499023

Steinberg, L., & Scott, E. S. (2003). Less guilty by reason of adolescence: Developmental immaturity, diminished responsibility, and the juvenile death penalty. *American Psychologist*, *58*, 1009–1018. http://dx.doi.org/10.1037/0003-066X.58.12.1009

Steinberg, L., & Schwartz, R. G. (2000). Developmental psychology goes to court. In T. Grisso & R. G. Schwartz (Eds.), *Youth on trial: A developmental perspective on juvenile justice* (pp. 9–31). Chicago, IL: University of Chicago Press.

Thompson v. Oklahoma, 487 U.S. 815 (1988).

Torbet, P., Gable, R., Hurst, I. V. H., Montgomery, I., Syzmanski, L., & Thomas, D. (1996). *State responses to serious and violent juvenile crime*. Washington, DC: Office of Juvenile Justice and Delinquency Prevention. Retrieved from https://www.ncjrs.gov/pdffiles/statresp.pdf

Vernonia School District 47J v. Acton, 515 U.S. 646 (1995).

Woodson v. North Carolina, 428 U.S. 289 (1976).

Yarborough v. Alvarado, 541 U.S. 652 (2004).

Zimring, F. E. (2005). *American juvenile justice*. New York, NY: Oxford University Press. http://dx.doi.org/10.1093/acprof:oso/9780195181166.001.0001

CHAPTER 3

PREVENTIVE JUSTICE FOR ADOLESCENTS

Christopher Slobogin

The evolution of the juvenile justice system in the United States can be described in terms of three overlapping phases, the first focused on rehabilitation, the second on retribution, and the third on the diminished culpability of juveniles. Since its invention at the turn of the 20th century, the juvenile justice system has aimed at rehabilitating wayward youths (Faust & Brantingham, 1974). In the latter third of the 20th century, the child-saving rhetoric of the juvenile court's early years gave way to a more vehement insistence that juveniles be held accountable for their actions; as a result, although the rehabilitative ideal was never abandoned entirely, the number of juveniles transferred to adult court increased significantly, and juvenile sentences lengthened (Redding, 2006). More recently, the U.S. Supreme Court has relied on its own intuition and on developmental and neurological science in concluding that juveniles are less blameworthy and less deterrable than adults (see Chapters 4 and 5, this handbook, for a fuller discussion) and are thus entitled to some leniency under the Constitution—at least in the context of the death penalty and life without parole. In this most recent phase, a renewed emphasis has also been placed on the potential for adolescents to reform, or to grow out of, their antisocial tendencies.

In this chapter, I suggest that, in light of new scientific developments, the juvenile justice system is primed to enter a fourth phase, in which the dominant goal becomes prevention of juvenile crime. Of course, all three previous phases aimed at protecting the public, through treatment programs, imprisonment, or both. But in this chapter—building on the thesis of a book I coauthored with Mark Fondacaro titled *Juveniles at Risk: A Plea for Preventive Justice* (Slobogin & Fondacaro, 2011)—I argue that the primary goal of juvenile justice should be public safety. In other (social science) words, the goal should be risk management. In a prevention regime, rehabilitation would still be a very important goal, but it would be narrowly focused on managing criminogenic risk and would take place in the community as often as possible. Retribution—punishment based on desert—would be a juvenile justice goal only to the extent that implementing it is necessary to ensure respect for and compliance with the legal system; thus, although desert would still play a major role at the adjudication phase, it would be deemphasized at the disposition phase, where risk assessment would hold sway. This reorientation of the aims of juvenile justice toward prevention makes the most legal, economic, and scientific sense, given what is now known about juveniles, juvenile crime, and ways of reducing juvenile criminal behavior.

Ironically, a major obstacle to this agenda is the diminished culpability rationale that reformers involved in the third phase of the juvenile court's

Parts of this chapter are adapted from "Treating Juveniles Like Juveniles: Getting Rid of Transfer and Expanded Adult Court Jurisdiction," by C. Slobogin, 2013, *Texas Tech Law Review, 46*, pp. 103–132. Copyright 2013 by the Texas Tech Law Review. Adapted with permission. Further parts of this chapter are also from Slabogin (2012) and Slobogin and Fondacuro (2011).

http://dx.doi.org/10.1037/14643-003
APA Handbook of Psychology and Juvenile Justice, K. Heilbrun (Editor-in-Chief)

development have advanced as a way of mitigating overly punitive policies. The diminished culpability rationale—which could also be called the diminished retribution or diminished desert rationale—posits that juveniles are significantly less blameworthy than adults because of their immaturity, their unformed character, and their underdeveloped neurological controls (Scott & Steinberg, 2008). This rationale has been remarkably successful at helping to end the juvenile death penalty and mandatory life-without-parole sentences for juveniles. However, the conceptualization of juvenile offenders as less culpable versions of adults plays into the hands of those who want to maintain transfer and other punitive policies that treat juveniles like adults. Although the diminished culpability rationale facilitates discounted sentences for juveniles, it also justifies carrying out those sentences in adult court, where culpability is king. Moreover, because the scientific evidence indicates that, from mid-adolescence onward, juveniles are not significantly different from adults in terms of traditional culpability doctrine, the diminished culpability rationale does not require or justify sentences that are significantly shorter than adult sentences. In light of the inordinate length of today's adult dispositional practices, juvenile dispositions can justifiably still be quite long even if the diminished culpability model ultimately wins the day.

The best rationale for treating juveniles differently than adults is not their lesser culpability but their lesser deterrability—more precisely, the fact that criminal sanctions do not have the same deterrent effect on juveniles as they do on adults. The lesser deterrability rationale has long sanctioned separate justice systems for people with mental disabilities, on the theory that the prospect of criminal punishment is less likely to inhibit crimes by these types of individuals and that an alternative, prevention-oriented commitment regime is therefore necessary ("Developments in the Law," 1974, p. 1233). A version of that rationale can also justify a juvenile justice system, because juveniles as a group are demonstrably less risk averse and more impulsive than adults. In contrast to the lesser culpability idea, which is focused on punishing juveniles (albeit less harshly than adults), the lesser deterrability rationale is focused on preventing juveniles from reoffending. In terms of the purposes of punishment, a prevention-oriented juvenile justice system aims not at retribution or general deterrence, but at specific deterrence and rehabilitation. Incapacitation as incarceration also plays a significant role, but only as a last resort.

In the first part of this chapter, I summarize why, compared with the diminished culpability model (and thus compared with the adult model as well), a prevention-oriented system of juvenile justice is a much better fit with what is known about the causes of juvenile crime and how to reduce it. In the second part of the chapter, I then describe the components of a juvenile system based on prevention, including the ways in which juvenile court jurisdiction, adjudication, and dispositions would differ from the juvenile court of today. In the last part, I explain why, if prevention is the goal of juvenile justice, the transfer of juvenile offenders to adult court makes little sense.

CONCEPTUALIZING JUVENILE JUSTICE

Most policymakers accept the proposition that juvenile offenders should be treated differently than adult offenders. Most also agree that this goal is best achieved by maintaining a separate juvenile justice system. The question addressed here is which of two rationales—the diminished culpability rationale or the individual prevention rationale—provides the best justification for these propositions.

Diminished Culpability Rationale

The diminished culpability model had its genesis as far back as 1980 with the promulgation of the American Bar Association's Juvenile Justice Standards (Institute of Judicial Administration, 1980, pp. 34–35). A number of scholars, including Frank Zimring (2000, pp. 279–282), Barry Feld (1988, p. 912), and Elizabeth Scott and Laurence Steinberg (2008), have endorsed a version of this model. Bolstered by developmental and neurobiological research over the past 2 decades, these scholars have made the intuitively appealing argument that juveniles are less mature in legally relevant ways, including their relatively diminished capacity to deliberate about their actions, consider consequences, and resist peer pressure.

This body of work has had considerable, and deserved, success at reorienting the debate about juvenile justice, not just in academia but in courts and legislatures. In *Roper v. Simmons* (2005), the U.S. Supreme Court partially relied on the diminished culpability concept and Scott and Steinberg's (2008) work in holding that, under the Eighth Amendment's Cruel and Unusual Punishments Clause, juveniles are exempt from the death penalty. The Court relied on similar reasoning in *Graham v. Florida* (2010), which found unconstitutional mandatory life-without-parole sentences for juveniles who commit nonhomicide crimes, and in *Miller v. Alabama* (2012) and *Jackson v. Arkansas* (2012), which struck down mandatory life-without-parole sentences for any crime committed by a juvenile. The diminished culpability rationale may also help explain some of the recent legislative activity that has led to the reduction of transfer jurisdiction (Scott, 2013, pp. 552–553).

Despite its intuitive attractiveness, however, the diminished culpability model has at least three serious drawbacks. First, in describing the lesser culpability of juveniles, the model stretches the implications of developmental research beyond what it will bear. Juveniles are less culpable than adults, but they are not as impaired in their judgment as advocates of the diminished retributive model seem to think. Second, the diminished culpability model inhibits the ability of the juvenile justice system to make optimal use of the many treatment innovations that have developed over the past 2 decades. The best way to reduce juvenile recidivism is through community-based programs that are an awkward fit in a system based on retributive punishment. Third, the model's focus on culpability—the same metric that informs adult criminal justice—undermines the argument for a separate juvenile justice system and, as discussed in the third part of this chapter, facilitates maintenance of a wide-ranging but counterproductive transfer mechanism.

The relative culpability of juveniles can be viewed from both a legal and an empirical perspective. From the legal perspective, the Supreme Court's juvenile sentencing cases clearly hold that juveniles do not deserve the ultimate penalties available for adults—capital punishment and mandatory life without parole (*Miller v. Alabama*, 2012; *Roper v. Simmons*, 2005). The key question now, however, is whether, as a matter of legal doctrine, the diminished capacity rationale will have any significant impact on other types of penalties for juveniles. Chief Justice Roberts predicted in *Miller* that life with parole and lesser sentences are now on the chopping block in the juvenile offender context (p. 2482). Perhaps so, but the majority opinion in *Miller* focused on the inability of mandatory penalties to reflect individualized desert determinations, not on the absolute length of the sentence. After recounting how juveniles are different from adults in terms of culpability, deterrability, characterological stability, and reformability, Justice Kagan emphasized that it is "the mandatory penalty schemes at issue here" that "prevent the sentencer from taking account of these central considerations" (*Miller v. Alabama*, p. 2466). She also relied heavily on *Graham*'s equation of life-without-parole sentences and the death penalty, noting, as had *Graham*, that both types of sentences are "irrevocable" (*Miller v. Alabama*, p. 2466.).

On the basis of these pronouncements, one could easily conclude that, even if the Court were to become more activist in its Eighth Amendment jurisprudence (which many Court observers believe is extremely unlikely; see, e.g., Stinneford, 2013), it will focus on dispositional rigidity rather than on sentence duration in determining whether a disposition is cruel and unusual. Thus, for instance, the Court is more likely to strike down statutes that impose a mandatory 20-year sentence on every adolescent armed robber older than age 13 than to reject a 30-year sentence imposed on a 14-year-old armed robber after due consideration of blameworthiness, treatability, and other factors. If that is the case, then as a legal matter, the diminished culpability rationale is not likely to require deep discounts in maximum sentences for juveniles. Worthwhile noting in this regard is that Simmons, Graham, Miller, and Jackson, the litigants in the Supreme Court's four juvenile cases (*Roper v. Simmons*, 2005; *Graham v. Florida*, 2010; *Miller v. Alabama*, 2012; and *Jackson v. Arkansas*, 2012, respectively), were, or are likely to be, resentenced to multiple-decade prison terms despite their Eighth Amendment victories (see Slobogin, 2013). Not surprisingly, several states have vowed to continue to impose very hefty sentences on juveniles, despite the Court's decisions (Slobogin, 2013).

Even if the courts were to take a more explicitly empirical perspective, they are unlikely to conclude that deep mitigation is justified on the basis of youth. Research measuring youthful capacities has indicated that mid- and late adolescents, the juveniles who commit the bulk of crimes among those younger than age 20, possess a fairly high degree of cognitive maturity. Laurence Steinberg and Elizabeth Cauffman (2000), the preeminent researchers in this area, concluded that, although 14- through 16-year-olds are more impulsive, less risk averse, more prone to peer influence, and less fully formed characterologically than adults, adolescents' judgments regarding antisocial conduct are not significantly different from those of young adults. For instance, they found that, on a scale ranging from 1 to 5, the capacity of eighth graders to make good (prosocial) decisions was 2.86; of 10th graders, 2.77; and of 12th graders, 2.94, compared with 3.1 for young adults (Cauffman & Steinberg, 2000, pp. 752, 756). These differences were found to be statistically significant, but in absolute terms they vary only by .33 on a 5-point scale, and thus do not suggest a huge divergence between mid-adolescent and young adult prosocial development. Indeed, as Steinberg and Cauffman have noted, 17-year-olds generally "possess the intellectual and psychosocial capacities that permit the exercise of good judgment, even under difficult circumstances" (pp. 398–399).

These findings have significant and discouraging implications for efforts to mitigate punitive juvenile justice policies. The commentary to the American Bar Association Juvenile Justice Standards, which adopted the diminished responsibility approach, suggested that a juvenile who commits a crime that would warrant a 20-year sentence if committed by an adult should receive a sentence of only 3 years (Institute of Judicial Administration, 1980, pp. 39–40). If empirical information is any guide, that is wishful thinking from a desert perspective. Nothing in the developmental literature comes close to suggesting that a 16-year-old who commits a serious felony is only one-sixth as culpable as a 21-year-old adult who commits the same crime. Even Barry Feld (1997, p. 188), another advocate of the diminished culpability model, has suggested only a 40% to 50% discount for a 16-year-old offender, and presumably a smaller one still for a 17-year-old. Furthermore, his discounts appear to be based not on empirical assessments, but rather on simply dividing the period between 13 and 18 into thirds, with 14-year-olds receiving a 66% to 75% discount, 26-year-olds receiving a 40% to 50% discount, and 18-year-olds being treated as adults. Feld (1998) came closer to describing the import of developmental research when he stated that "while younger offenders may be less criminally responsible than more mature violators, they do not differ as inherently or fundamentally as the legal dichotomy between juvenile and criminal courts suggest" (p. 245).

A second set of empirical findings that is hard to reconcile with the diminished responsibility rationale concerns the best methods of reducing recidivism. Research has repeatedly shown that noncoercive sanctions are better than prisons at reducing juvenile recidivism (Lipsey, 2009). Multisystemic therapy (MST) and other community-based programs outperform treatment programs that take place in detention facilities because they address key risk factors—such as family and peer dynamics, substance abuse, and poor school performance—in the systems in which they occur and because they avoid the criminological effects of incarceration (see Slobogin & Fondacaro, 2011, Appendix). Unfortunately, however, because an effective MST regimen usually takes only about 4 months, it would be inappropriately lenient for virtually any person convicted of a felony in a juvenile justice system in which disposition is supposed to be proportionate to desert (see McGarvey, 2012). If, instead, a juvenile is transferred to adult court, programs such as MST are probably out of the question given the fact that transfer is reserved for those juveniles who have committed more serious crimes.

These observations lead to the third problem with the diminished responsibility rationale. If juvenile dispositions are to be measured in terms of the same metric used in adult court—culpability—why maintain a separate juvenile system? As Feld (1999, p. 389) has argued, the diminished responsibility of juveniles can be accommodated through sentencing discounts in the adult system. In other words, a diminished capacity rationale for juvenile punishment can lead to the conclusion that all juveniles should be tried in adult court, a result that very few juvenile advocates desire (and one that even Feld [2007, pp. 255–256] repudiated in later writing).

Individual Prevention Rationale

A juvenile justice system based on the goal of individual prevention is not focused on desert and thus avoids the pitfalls of the diminished culpability approach. At the same time, it encounters other problems familiar to anyone who has perused the literature on theories of punishment. The individual prevention model more easily accommodates empirical findings about the differences between youths and adults and the best methods of reducing recidivism. However, it also raises concerns about abuses of discretion that can occur in connection with determining levels of risk. Those concerns in part explain the continued attractiveness of the diminished culpability model, which sets relatively determinate minimum and maximum time limits on disposition. With a few tweaks, however, the individual prevention model can avoid its most pressing defects and provide a superior theoretical basis for a separate juvenile system.

The case for the individual prevention model is explicitly based on science—in particular, the robust empirical conclusion that juveniles are much more reckless than adults (see, e.g., Arnett, 1992, p. 344; Mathias, Marsh-Richard, & Dougherty, 2008, p. 697). That finding not only supports the conclusion that juveniles are less culpable than adults but is also consistent with the notion that they are less deterrable. The Supreme Court itself has recognized this fact in cases such as *Roper v. Simmons* (2005), *Graham v. Florida* (2010), and *Miller v. Alabama* (2012). As Justice Kennedy stated in both *Roper* and *Graham*, "The same characteristics that render juveniles less culpable than adults suggest . . . that juveniles will be less susceptible to deterrence" (*Roper v. Simmons*, 2005, p. 571; *Graham v. Florida*, 2010, p. 2028). In *Miller*, Justice Kagan repeated this conclusion, referring to youths' "transient rashness, proclivity for risk, and inability to assess consequences" and "their immaturity, recklessness and impetuosity" in explaining not only their "lessened . . . 'moral culpability,'" but also their failure to "consider potential punishment" (pp. 2464–2465).

The fact that juveniles are less deterrable than adults provides the justification for handling juvenile offenders in a system separate from the adult criminal justice system, just as people with mental disability, considered undeterrable because of their mental impairments, are subject to civil commitment rather than criminal punishment ("Developments in the Law," 1974, p. 1233). Of course, the typical juvenile offender is not as impaired as the typical person subject to civil commitment. The claim here, however, is not that juveniles are excused for their behavior; it is that they are not as responsive to the dictates of criminal law as are adults and thus can justifiably be subject to a separate system of justice. The U.S. Supreme Court endorsed an analogous proposition in *Kansas v. Hendricks* (1997), which upheld preventive commitment of adult sex offenders who are not psychotic but who are less deterrable than the "ordinary recidivist" (see also *Kansas v. Crane*, 2002, p. 420).

For reasons already suggested, once prevention is accepted as the primary goal of juvenile justice, community dispositions in lieu of incarceration are easily justifiable if they are effective at reducing recidivism. Indeed, if community dispositions are superior to incarceration in this regard, a strong argument can be made that the U.S. Constitution requires such dispositions on the grounds that they are the least drastic means of achieving the government's objective—prevention (Janus & Logan, 2003, p. 357). Moreover, any detention that does take place must be governed by the same least-drastic-means principle, meaning that periodic review is needed to ensure that the detained individual represents a high risk and to guarantee that treatment is being provided to reduce that risk (*Kansas v. Hendricks*, 1997, p. 364).

The criticisms of the individual prevention model come in three varieties. The first is that preventive dispositions are insufficient as a deterrent. The second is that a prevention-oriented regime is unfair, both because it can result in disparate sentences for the same offense and because it might sanction people more or less than they deserve, thus diluting their accountability and diminishing public support for the law (Scott & Steinberg, 2008). The third criticism is that, even if such a system can be considered fair in the abstract, it is impossible to implement without significant abuse (Scott & Steinberg, 2008, pp. 90–91).

Without some official reaction to antisocial behavior, recidivism would undoubtedly increase. Not as clear is how significant that official reaction must be to achieve the optimal amount of deterrence (see Tonry, 2006, p. 28). One way of examining that issue in the juvenile context is to look at research comparing the general deterrent effect of sanctions imposed after transfer to dispositions in juvenile court, which are normally much more lenient than adult court sanctions. To date, only one major study has found a significant deterrent effect associated with transfer. Steven Levitt's (1998) examination of national juvenile crime statistics between 1978 and 1993 concluded that crime among youths reaching the age of criminal responsibility (18) significantly decreased in those states in which an appreciable difference existed between juvenile and adult court sentences, but not in those states that tended to sentence juveniles in a similar fashion, regardless of whether they ended up in juvenile or adult court. However, Levitt's study appears to have conflated the effects of deterrence and incapacitation; those states with stiffer penalties in adult court detained youths longer, and thus reduced the potential for reoffending (Lee & McCrary, 2009). Every other deterrence study has found that transfer did not lower juvenile crimes rates, decreased them only marginally, or actually increased them (Cohn & Mialon, 2011; Lee & McCrary, 2009; McCrary & Sanga, 2011; Redding, 2010). Richard Redding (2010) has concluded that "the bulk of the evidence suggests that transfer laws, at least as currently implemented and publicized, have little or no general deterrent effect in preventing serious juvenile crime" (p. 3).

One could nonetheless justifiably wonder whether deterrent power would be lost vis-à-vis imprisonment in the adult system if, as was suggested above, the juvenile system became more oriented toward community-based treatment such as MST. Several considerations should allay such concerns. First, for reasons already noted, youth are relatively oblivious to sanctions (Redding, 2010), which may mean that general deterrence is not a significant motivator in this setting. To the extent that it is, as developed in more detail below, in a prevention-oriented system detention would still be a routine option for those convicted of serious crimes, and repeat offenders would be more likely to be detained because of their elevated risk. Thus, the deterrent effect that definite and routine incarcerative sentences might bring over indefinite and less predictable detention would not be significant. Indeed, indeterminacy in sanctions may even enhance deterrence (Kahan, 1997, pp. 137–141).

Several observations can be also made about the concern that a preventive regime would be insufficiently attentive to the goals of achieving justice and ensuring accountability. In response to the concern that a preventative regime is unjust, Slobogin and Fondacaro (2011, p. 54) argued that a system that looks at an offender's history and character, as a preventive regime does, is much more likely to achieve fair results—that is, results that reflect an appropriate disposition of an individual's case—than one that focuses solely on the accused's offense. James Whitman (2013) recently put this point well when he stated that "there are as many kinds of justice as there are offenders" (p. 39), a tenet he claims was understood and approved both by the premodern common-law judges who shaped the substantive criminal law and by adherents of the "modern penalism" that informed the Model Penal Code. It is likely that much of the public today agrees that there are as many kinds of justice as there are offenders (see Cullen, Fisher, & Applegate, 2000, p. 34). If these observations have validity, a juvenile justice system that bases disposition solely on the *actus reus* and *mens rea* of the offense will almost always result in injustice.

Even if the system were to rely on blame for a specific offense as its metric, however, the goal of fairness—in the sense of consistent results—is unlikely to be achieved. Accurate calibrations of blame, based on often indecipherable mental phenomena at the time of the act, are usually difficult and often impossible (Slobogin, 2007, pp. 42–48). Prosecutorial charging discretion, jury decision-making discretion, and judicial sentencing discretion make a mockery of the idea that the same crime triggers the same time (see Baron-Evans & Stith, 2012, pp. 1683–1684; Finkel, 1995, pp. 134, 166, 248; Slobogin, 2009, pp. 36–37). In contrast, as discussed further below, a preventive regime can at least rely on concrete probability estimates and evidence-based risk management techniques in trying to treat similar levels of risk equally.

The criticism that a preventive regime does not hold offenders responsible for their conduct (or character) is also inaccurate. First, offenders in a preventive regime would still be held accountable because they would be found guilty and receive a sentence, which for very serious crimes will usually involve, under classic risk management principles of the type applied to people with mental disability, a period of detention before resorting to community-based programs. Just as important, in a system properly focused on risk management, offenders are constantly reminded that they are responsible for their actions and that they have significant control over the nature and duration of the state's restrictions on them (see Slobogin & Fondacaro, 2011, pp. 58–59).

The third complaint against a preventive regime is that the risk assessments and treatment programs necessary to make a risk management system work are untrustworthy and that the resulting uncertainty will lead to improper detentions and ineffective rehabilitation. These types of objections are exaggerated. First, for reasons developed below, no juvenile disposition should take place in the absence of a conviction for a statutorily defined crime. Second, the aforementioned least-drastic-means principle would generally prohibit any type of detention unless the government could prove a substantial probability that the detention is necessary to prevent a serious crime (in the second part of this chapter, I suggest that this threshold should approximate a 40% probability of serious crime, as demonstrated by an actuarial assessment); if such a showing is not possible, intervention would have to take place in the community. Third, although risk assessment is clearly not an exact science, modern assessment instruments of the type described in other chapters of this book reduce the inevitable influence of bias because they set out relatively clear decision-making criteria and produce a concrete probability estimate that sets a baseline for the ultimate conclusion of risk. Modern risk evaluation may even be better at bias reduction than desert-based schemes that rely on amorphous mental states and inconsistent culpability rules. Even with the advent of determinate sentencing, racial and other disparities have proliferated (Baron-Evans & Stith, 2012, p. 1683), and transfer decisions, despite their explicit or implicit focus on "objective" offense characteristics, have exacerbated that situation (Meyers, 2005, p. 127).

A further curb on abuses of discretion in a preventive regime is that interventions in such a regime—whether they take place in detention or in the community—would be subject to continuous review (*Kansas v. Hendricks*, 1997, p. 353). In short, mistakes are correctable in a system based on prevention. In a desert-based regime, in contrast, once culpability is determined, it is immutable.

Finally, analogous to desert proportionality, a risk proportionality principle should apply in a prevention-oriented juvenile justice system. Risk proportionality would require proof of increasingly greater risk to prolong the intervention. On the basis of both risk proportionality reasoning and concerns about abuse, Slobogin and Fondacaro (2011, p. 92) proposed that even those offenders who are considered at high risk for the commission of serious crime should usually be released by the end of juvenile court jurisdiction.

In the next two parts of the chapter, I further develop these various aspects of a prevention-oriented juvenile justice system.

RISK MANAGEMENT REGIME FOR JUVENILE JUSTICE

Traditionally, the juvenile court exerted *act jurisdiction* over those who allegedly committed crimes or were charged with status offenses (e.g., incorrigibility; disobedience) before age 18, and it exercised *dispositional jurisdiction* over convicted individuals until age 21 or so. However, the court also had *transfer jurisdiction* over youths older than age 14 or 15, which allowed it to transfer juveniles out of juvenile court to adult court if they were considered unamenable to treatment. More recently, although a number of states have eliminated status offenses, most have also lowered the maximum ages for act and dispositional jurisdiction or the minimum age for transfer eligibility, or both, and the transfer decision now is focused more on culpability than treatability (Redding & Mrozoski, 2005).

In an individual prevention regime, the maximum age for act jurisdiction might increase beyond 18, the maximum age for dispositional jurisdiction would definitely increase, and transfer jurisdiction would disappear. At the adjudication stage, in addition to criminal acts typically prosecuted in adult courts, low-level crimes that are normally not prosecuted but that are associated with high risk for future crime would become an explicit basis for jurisdiction and a high priority for intervention and risk management. At the dispositional stage, assessments of risk and treatability would dominate; culpability would not be relevant unless ignoring it would undermine compliance with the law.

Age Requirement

Because undeterrability provides the rationale for intervention under the individual prevention approach, the age of eligibility for that regime should end when relative undeterrability ends. Of course, the various personal characteristics and circumstances associated with a significant degree of undeterrability do not disappear suddenly at a particular age and will vary in strength at different ages for different people. The research is unclear as to when these characteristics change for most people. At this point, all that can be said is that the traditional cutoff age of 18 would not be inconsistent with research regarding risk perception, temporal perspective, the effects of peer pressure, or one's stake in life.

However, the maximum age for act jurisdiction could ultimately be extended beyond age 18 for policy reasons grounded in research. For example, social scientists have noted that our culture has nudged the dividing line between adolescence and adulthood to the early 20s as young people take longer to acquire the education and skills necessary to compete in the modern economy (Fondacaro, Dunkle, & Pathak, 1998). Neuroscience research indicating that frontal lobe development continues well into the 3rd decade also supports expansion of act jurisdiction beyond age 18, to sometime in the early 20s (Lebel, Walker, Leemans, Phillips, & Beaulieu, 2008).

Additionally, dispositional age should extend well beyond 18. Although several states allow juvenile courts to exercise dispositional jurisdiction up to age 21 (Brummer, 2002), a preventive regime might exercise jurisdiction up to age 25. A significant differential of 7 years or so between age and dispositional jurisdiction makes sense for several reasons. First, for juveniles who commit a crime in their later adolescence, an intervention program lasting into the early 20s may be necessary. Under the juvenile system as it operates now, juvenile offenders are often transferred to adult court simply because a treatment program cannot be completed by the time a juvenile offender ages out (see *Commonwealth v. O'Brien*, 1996; *In re Appeal in Maricopa County*, 1983). The pressure to engage in this counterproductive practice would be reduced if the gap between act and dispositional age jurisdiction were larger (and, of course, it would be eliminated if, as proposed in the last part of this chapter, transfer jurisdiction were abolished).

A second reason to prefer such a differential is the converse of the situation just described. Sometimes adult criminal courts will convict a person older than age 18 who could nonetheless benefit from juvenile programs. The act–dispositional age differential would permit adult courts to engage in "reverse transfer" at the dispositional stage in those cases in which the court believes a juvenile facility would be more appropriate and less criminogenic than an adult prison.

Third, a differential between age and dispositional jurisdiction would allow longer detention of those juvenile offenders who are at very high risk for violent offending and have failed to respond to community-based, multisystemic interventions. Indeed, for extremely high-risk juveniles, extended detention (even beyond age 25) might be prudent.

The last section of this chapter also has more to say about this aspect of the regime.

Act Requirement

A pure preventive detention regime would not require a conviction for crime but rather only proof of risk, which could come from biological tests or evidence of other innocent factors that are indicative of risk, such as marital status, age, or psychiatric diagnosis. Although reliance on these types of factors to determine dangerousness is controversial (Netter, 2007), except for race their use in a regime that is explicitly based on risk is neither unconstitutional nor violative of subconstitutional norms (Monahan, 2006). Moreover, of course, excluding consideration of such factors could seriously undermine the efficacy of risk assessment (see, Slobogin, 2012, pp. 203–206).

Nonetheless, without a conviction for crime, preventive intervention should not take place. In part, this is because risk assessment is difficult without some history of antisocial conduct. The primary reason for requiring a conviction as a threshold, however, is the principle of legality. The principle of legality, applicable in both criminal and civil settings, posits that government power must be limited by permitting deprivations of liberty only for rule violations that are capable of being avoided—that is, violations of rules that (a) are known in advance and (b) require an affirmative choice to engage in harmful conduct (Jeffries, 1985).

Certainly, a juvenile's commission of an act that would be prosecuted as a crime in adult court would satisfy this conduct requirement. In addition, however, in a prevention-oriented system, some antisocial behaviors associated with relatively trivial crimes that are typically not prosecuted or not taken seriously in adult court could form the basis for juvenile court if they have been linked in the empirical literature with high risk for future crime. Some examples of such acts might include behaviors associated with "early starter," life-course persistent offending, such as bullying (Brubacher, Fondacaro, Brank, Brown, & Miller, 2009) and cruelty to animals (Ascione, 2001), as well as complicity in theft crimes that occur in association with delinquent peers. These types of offenses, often ignored or minimized in adult court, might well be common triggering acts in an individual prevention regime.

At the same time, to meet the demands of the legality principle, all acts that serve as the basis for juvenile court jurisdiction would need to be codified by statute. Furthermore, vague status offenses such as incorrigibility, or constitutionally protected activity such as gang membership, should not be grounds for intervention, even if they are associated with risk. As the U.S. Supreme Court has recognized, relatively precise codification of the acts that can trigger arrest and prosecution is necessary to curb abuses of discretion by police, prosecutors, and judges and to provide concrete notice to the public about the types of conduct to be avoided (*Kolender v. Lawson*, 1983).

Mental State Requirement

The *mens rea*, or mental state, requirement prevents conviction for conduct that is purely accidental. Furthermore, for some types of adult crimes, only harms that the perpetrator intended to occur or was aware might occur as a result of his or her actions can be the basis for an adjudication of guilt; harms that a reasonable person in the perpetrator's shoes would have anticipated—say, an injury due to speeding or resulting from a shot fired near a group of people—but that the actor did not actually anticipate or foresee cannot lead to criminal liability in these situations (LaFave, 2010, pp. 277–290). In most jurisdictions for most crimes, however, nonaccidental, negligent behavior, defined in terms of what a reasonable person would have foreseen or known, is a sufficient basis for criminal liability (LaFave, 2010, pp. 277–290).

An individual prevention regime for juveniles would continue to prohibit guilt adjudications for merely accidental harm, both because it is not likely to be a risk factor and because liability in this situation would be anathema under legality reasoning. However, it would permit adjudications of guilt for negligent crime, defined in terms of what a reasonable adult would have perceived or known. Some theorists have argued that negligence in juvenile court should be defined with reference to the reasonable juvenile, not the reasonable adult (Aronson, 2009, p. 921), but in a preventive regime, this limitation on liability would not make sense. Negligent crime can be a significant risk factor. Juvenile offenders may often engage in behavior oblivious to risks that adults could easily foresee. When an adolescent commits an act that harms or endangers someone, an unawareness that the harm would occur or that the risk was present should not prevent assertion of juvenile court jurisdiction for the purpose of reducing the likelihood of repeat occurrences unless even a reasonable adult would not have foreseen the consequences.

Thus, the juvenile code in a preventive regime might consist of relatively simple prohibitions on killing, raping, stealing, drug dealing, and trying to engage in these types of crimes, as well as a prohibition on engaging in conduct that endangers others, without the complicated *mens rea* terminology that sometimes accompanies these provisions in adult statutes. Juveniles would have a defense if such conduct was purely accidental and nonnegligent or if they could prove self-defense or some other objective justification recognized in adult court. Otherwise, however, once the criminal act is proven to have been committed by the juvenile, the only remaining questions would be whether the offender posed a risk sufficient to warrant intervention and, if so, what type of intervention could reduce that risk.

Before discussing these latter issues, it must be emphasized that, in contrast to a culpability-based regime in which proof of a crime should, at least in theory, mandate punishment of some kind, proof of an antisocial act does not and should not require intervention in a preventive system. From the prevention perspective, involvement in the juvenile justice system might well be an inadvisable disposition (Mendel, 2011, pp. 2–4). Many juveniles who have acted in an antisocial matter are unlikely to recidivate even if no intervention takes place, and others may not need any type of judicially imposed disposition but rather can be handled through intelligent use of the educational system, social welfare programs, or community efforts that have no connection with government (see Dowd, 2011). The juvenile justice system should be the last—not the first—resort when prevention is the goal.

Risk (Dangerousness) Requirement

Once a conviction occurs and it is determined that official intervention is necessary, a formal risk assessment should take place. Although risk assessment techniques are becoming increasingly sophisticated, they can still result in significant error when used to predict reoffending. A special problem in the juvenile context is the fast-changing nature of adolescence. A person's cognitive, emotional, interpersonal, and physical capacities at age 13 are quite different than they are at age 15 or age 17 (Cicchetti & Rogosch, 2002). Even at the same age, stability may be the exception; Thomas Grisso (1998) has characterized youths as "moving targets" (p. 141) because they are constantly trying out different identities, beliefs, values, and personas. Moreover, key risk factors at one age might not be significant at later ages. For instance, aggressive behavior during preadolescence is more unusual and more predictive than aggressive behavior during mid-adolescence. Bad parenting is more relevant to risk if it occurs during earlier years than in later years, and bad peer influence is a more potent risk factor during adolescence than preadolescence (Steinberg & Schwartz, 2000, pp. 26–28).

In determining how to evaluate these risks, one must recognize that each of the three dominant risk assessment techniques—commonly labeled *unstructured clinical*, *structured clinical*, and *actuarial*—presents its own methodological challenges. Unstructured clinical prediction is most problematic. First, research has firmly established that predictions based on unstructured clinical judgment, although typically better than chance, are less valid than actuarial predictions by a significant magnitude (Ægisdóttir et al., 2006, p. 360; Janus & Prentky, 2003, pp. 1455–1458). Second, clinical predictions are hard to assess in terms of error rates because the clinical method varies from evaluator to evaluator. Third, experts relying on clinical prediction can at most make general statements about an offender's propensities, such as "the offender poses a higher than average risk." These types of statements can mean different things to different evaluators and in any event are not susceptible to verification. Finally, laboratory research and evidence from actual cases has indicated that, despite its more questionable reliability, clinical prediction testimony presented by the government is extremely influential with judges and juries, much more so than actuarial prediction (see, e.g., Krauss, Lieberman, & Olson, 2004; Slobogin, 2007, pp. 122–125). Clinical testimony that a person is likely to be violent is difficult to rebut even with effective cross-examination and opposing witnesses (Diamond, Casper, Heiert, & Marshall, 1996). Fact finders appear to attribute too much weight to this type of testimony precisely because it is so vague.

Structured clinical judgment, sometimes also called *structured professional judgment* (SPJ), shares some of the same drawbacks. Although the variables that influence the risk assessment are more likely to be known, they can still vary from evaluator to evaluator. Furthermore, if not based on statistically weighted scores and linked to statistically derived probability estimates, ultimate conclusions about risk reached through SPJ are almost as imprecise as traditional clinical judgments. That is to say, SPJ at most produces conclusions about whether risk is high, low, or medium, and the definitions of high, low, and medium remain murky.

Actuarial risk assessment largely avoids all of these deficiencies. It provides error rate information and permits comparison of one offender with another in terms of risk because it is based on statistical analysis of large groups of offenders. Even when, as often occurs, group error rates are high, they are useful because they provide the fact finder with information about how much weight to give the evidence (Saks, 2003, p. 1168).

Precisely because of its nomothetic nature, however, actuarial prediction suffers from a number of other problems, all of them potentially serious. First, the population on which the actuarial device is validated may be quite different from the population to which it is applied; for instance, one of the most popular adult actuarial devices, the Violence Risk Assessment Guide, was developed in Canada, using a predominantly White group of offenders. This inadequacy can be minimized through cross-validation on other samples, as has occurred with the Violence Risk Assessment Guide (Rice, Harris, & Hilton, 2010, pp. 104–105), or by validating the instrument on a local population. Evaluators must also ensure that the instrument has in fact been validated. Although some juvenile assessment instruments, such as the Structured Assessment of Violence Risk in Youth and the Youth Level of Service/Case Management Inventory, have been subject to numerous cross-checks, the psychometric properties of many other instruments have not been adequately tested (Borum, Lodewijks, Bartel, & Forth, 2010; Hoge, 2010).

A second problem with some actuarial devices is their reliance solely on static risk factors, such as prior offenses and gender. Because these risk factors never change, the probability estimates the instruments produce are inelastic, a feature that is, at the least, counterintuitive in the juvenile setting. In any event, in the juvenile context the Supreme Court is not willing to assume that offenders cannot reform (*Graham v. Florida*, 2010).

A third methodological problem that afflicts the accuracy of any risk assessment technique but that is especially obvious in connection with actuarial prediction is the definition of the outcome measure. Many risk assessment instruments are validated on the commission of any crime, or on any violent act. For instance, the Early Assessment Risk List was designed to assess "the potential for antisocial, aggressive or violent conduct" (Augimeri, Enebrink, Walsh, & Depeng, 2010, p. 45), language that could encompass behavior ranging from shoplifting to homicide. The follow-up period used for validation purposes also varies significantly. Arguably, an offender who is at risk for committing a simple assault within 5 years, even if the risk is high, should be handled very differently than an offender who is at risk of committing assault within 5 weeks or an offender who is at risk for aggravated assault, rape, or homicide. Most risk assessment instruments have difficulty addressing these nuances, and clinical judgment, even if it is focused on the individual's history of such behavior, can do so only in a vaguely empirical way.

Although these problems with actuarial risk assessment are not fatal and have rarely led to successful admissibility challenges (Otto & Petrila, 2002), they counsel three limitations on the use of such instruments in the legal setting (Heilbrun, Douglas, & Yasuhara, 2009). First, actuarial prediction that is not based on large derivation and validation samples that are similar to the population to which they are applied should be prohibited or discounted significantly. Second, actuarial instruments must include dynamic as well as static risk factors. Third, statements about a particular probability level derived from an actuarial assessment should be specific about the type of antisocial behavior contemplated (e.g., violent, nonviolent) and the period during which it might occur (e.g., 2 months, 2 years).

Summing up the various concerns about risk assessment, Lorraine Johnstone (2011) stated that "it would be foolhardy for any practitioner or policymaker to proceed with confidence in the uncritical application of any of the available risk assessment protocols to youth" (p. 142). With this caution in mind, Slobogin and Fondacaro (2011) proposed a hybrid approach to risk assessment that relies on both actuarial and SPJ methods, depending on the context. In those situations in which a serious up-or-down decision needs to be made—that is, a decision as to whether detention is permissible after conviction in juvenile court or as to whether transfer should occur (if transfer jurisdiction is not abolished)—the government should be required to rely on actuarial risk assessments and meet a fairly high probability threshold before the deprivation of liberty may occur or be continued.
In all other situations, the SPJ model makes the most sense (see also Monahan & Skeem, 2014).

Use of pure SPJ protocols is not appropriate when the detention or transfer decision must be made. Although these protocols are more structured than traditional clinical assessment, they result in an opinion that is still subjective in nature and thus prone to the same biases as clinical assessment; as noted earlier, the reference points, or range of probabilities, associated with the conclusion that a person is a high, medium, or low risk after an SPJ assessment are not known. In contrast, despite its flaws, when actuarial assessment meets the criteria described above, it provides a specific probability estimate that has been scientifically validated. That estimate forces the legal decision maker to decide how much of a risk an individual must pose before intervention may occur.

As to the precise risk probability that the government would need to demonstrate before detention or transfer could occur, Slobogin and Fondacaro (2011) proposed a sliding scale based on the risk-proportionality reasoning introduced in the first part of this chapter. If the predicted risk is of serious violence, a 30% to 40% probability might suffice, whereas a prediction of simple assault or property theft would require a greater probability before detention could occur. If the actuarial instrument does not permit distinctions between serious and less serious crime, or no such instrument exists, then the government should have to show the person's previous conduct is consistent with a high risk of committing serious crime. Furthermore, the juvenile should be permitted, in an adversarial proceeding, to contest the actuarial assessment not only directly, through challenging whether the risk factors relied on exist, but also through rebuttal clinical testimony describing protective factors that the actuarial device does not encompass (Slobogin & Fondacaro, 2011, pp. 71–76).

Other than with front-end decisions involving detention or transfer, risk management based on SPJ methodology ought to hold sway. A relatively subjective approach is justifiable when a one-time decision about liberty deprivation is not involved because now the goal is to generate the rehabilitative regime most likely to reduce recidivism, which will need to be based on highly individualized assessments and adjusted on a periodic basis. The best-researched version of risk-relevant rehabilitation for the type of regime proposed here is known as the risk–need–responsivity model, the model that forms the theoretical basis for the Youth Level of Service/Case Management Inventory (see Andrews, Bonta, & Wormith, 2011). The risk principle matches the level of program intensity to the offender's risk level, with low-risk offenders receiving minimal intervention and the highest risk offenders receiving significant attention. The need principle targets criminogenic needs and those that are functionally related to criminal behavior, as opposed to the broader needs offenders might have if the aim is simply to improve their lives. The responsivity principle matches the style and model of intervention to the offender's learning style and abilities.

Under the risk–need–responsivity model, evaluation of an offender's risk, needs, and responsivity should be continuous and, if the offender is incarcerated, risk assessments that include dynamic factors should take place periodically to determine whether the risk threshold necessary to justify continued detention is met. Recall also that, under the risk proportionality principle, the longer detention lasts, the greater the degree of risk that must be shown. Unless the individual commits a new offense or the degree of risk is extremely high (as demonstrated by an actuarial assessment), no juvenile offender should be detained for more than a few years.

TRAVESTY OF TRANSFER

The major components of a preventive juvenile justice system are not that different from the most forward-looking juvenile justice systems today. But another aspect of the proposed preventive justice system—the abolition of transfer jurisdiction—would be a significant departure from every juvenile court jurisdiction in the United States. Nonetheless, if prevention is the goal, there is no good reason to retain transfer jurisdiction, whether the purported purpose of transfer is deterrence, rehabilitation, incapacitation, or retribution.

General and Specific Deterrence

The chapter has already discussed the minimal impact transfer has in terms of general deterrence. Transfer does even worse as a specific deterrence mechanism. Transfer to adult court is generally associated with higher rearrest rates than the rearrest rates of those offenders who stay in juvenile court. Summarizing six studies that controlled for numerous variables such as offense severity, prior offenses, and age, Richard Redding's (2010) review noted that "all of the studies found higher recidivism rates among offenders who had been transferred to criminal court, compared with those who were retained in the juvenile system" (p. 6). Redding (2010) bluntly concluded, "Transfer substantially increases recidivism" (p. 6; see also McGowan et al., 2007). A more recent study comparing transferred and nontransferred youths in Arizona, matched on more variables than previous studies, found that although transferred youths who committed property crimes were more likely to recidivate on release, those who committed violent crimes were less likely to reoffend (Mulvey & Schubert, 2012). The latter finding, however, needs to be considered in light of the fact that the follow-up period for the study was 4 years, during most of which the youths who were transferred and convicted for violent crimes were presumably in prison.

The fact that transfer is apparently not an effective means of generating specific deterrence is not surprising. Research has indicated that the stigmatizing effect of the *felon* label, the sense of injustice that an adolescent feels at being tried as an adult, the education in crime provided by adult prisoners, and the brutalizing effect of prison life can all contribute to a continued life of crime (Redding, 2010, pp.7–8). Perhaps an even more important explanation for the specific deterrence effects that researchers have found, however, is that treatment options in the juvenile systems are almost always superior to those found in the adult criminal system (Bilchik, 1999, p. 2).

Rehabilitation

If rehabilitation is the goal, transfer makes little sense. Given the traditional rehabilitative focus of the juvenile court, it stands to reason that the juvenile court system will have more to offer than the adult system in terms of treatment. In fact, both objective observers and youths themselves believe that adult facilities are less treatment oriented and more security focused than juvenile facilities (Bishop & Frazier, 2000, pp. 254–257, 259–260). Even adult systems that make an effort at providing rehabilitative services are not likely to provide the relatively short-term, community-based programs that are often the most effective means of reducing recidivism in juvenile offenders. Yet under automatic transfer laws, even first-time offenders who have never had the benefit of the juvenile system's superior resources can be sent to adult prisons (Grissom, 2011).

A more subtle disadvantage of transfer in connection with the rehabilitative goal is that it undermines efforts to pressure courts and legislatures into improving treatment options in the juvenile system. When good juvenile court programs do not exist, transfer to adult court provides an easy dispositional alternative. The transfer decision can thus be heavily influenced by economics or, as the transfer provisions at issue in the Supreme Court's decision in *Kent v. United States* (1966) put it, "The likelihood of reasonable rehabilitation of the juvenile . . . by the use of procedures, services and facilities currently available to the Juvenile Court" (p. 567). A majority of state transfer statutes explicitly provide, consistent with this provision, that one factor to consider in determining whether transfer should occur is whether treatment programs are available within the jurisdiction (Heilbrun, Leheny, Thomas, & Huneycutt, 1997, pp. 128–143).

Unfortunately, this factor is often dispositive in transfer decision making. Numerous courts have transferred a juvenile to adult court solely because of a lack of accessible programs. For instance, one court waived juvenile court jurisdiction for a 14-year-old because the state's experts testified that the state lacked adequate facilities to deal with a 14-year-old homicide offender (*State v. Simpson*, 1992). Another court transferred a youth who became violent when he consumed alcohol because the jurisdiction offered no substance abuse program (*In re R.M.*, 1993; see also *Commonwealth v. Cessna*, 1988). In perhaps the most egregious case (thankfully, now mooted by the Supreme Court's decision in *Roper*), the court rejected the argument that "the state has an obligation not to execute a juvenile who is deemed to be amenable to treatment but for whom the state offers no appropriate treatment program" (*Stanford v. Commonwealth*, 1987, p. 792). Courts also routinely refuse to consider a juvenile offender as treatable when the only pertinent programs are in another jurisdiction (*Dillard v. State*, 1981; *P.K.M. v. State*, 1989).

These types of decisions led Slobogin and Fondacaro (2011) to conclude that "if transfer were eliminated, courts would have to confront the problems caused by the current paucity of treatment programs and might become more willing to force legislatures to [provide] them" (p. 80). This judicial impetus is necessary. According to one estimate, only 15,000 juvenile offenders per year participate in MST and similar regimes; despite the success of these programs, legislatures have not been willing to scale them up (Henggeler & Shoenwald, 2011, p. 8). From a crime prevention perspective, that failure is shortsighted.

Incapacitation

Long sentences imposed by adult courts clearly have a more significant incapacitative impact than shorter juvenile sentences. However, a proper utilitarian analysis of incapacitative effects must take into account the extent to which incarceration in adult prison is necessary to protect the public. There are several reasons to believe that, on this score, the cost of transfer is greater than the benefit.

First, under the transfer laws of most states, the majority of juveniles who are transferred are not assessed for risk (see, e.g., Arizona Juvenile Court Rules of Procedure, 2013, Rule 34). Transfer is often automatically or implicitly triggered by the nature of the offense, which may or may not bear a relationship to dangerousness (Slobogin, 1999, pp. 317–327). If, instead, transfer is based on an individualized assessment of amenability to treatment—which is supposed to happen in most states with respect to at least some types of juvenile offenders—assessment of risk is more likely. Even in this situation, however, the transfer decision is often focused not on reoffense risk per se, but on other factors that are examined independently of their relationship to risk—factors such as age, the seriousness of the offense, the maturity of the juvenile, or the availability of treatment programs in juvenile court (Slobogin, 1999). As a result, many juveniles who are transferred are probably at low risk for committing a serious crime; in fact, research has indicated that a substantial percentage of juveniles who are transferred are charged with property crimes (Beresford, 2000, p. 794; Brandt, 2006, pp. 77–78; Shook, 2005, p. 266). A system that incarcerates such people in adult prisons is not an optimal incapacitative mechanism.

A second reason transfer is not a good incapacitative mechanism is that most people who offend during their adolescent years desist from offending sometime in their 20s, even when they are not incarcerated (Moffitt, 1993). Young adults find jobs, get married, and in general acquire stakes in life that militate against a life of crime (Sampson & Laub, 1994; Williams & Hawkins, 1986, pp. 561–566). Neurobiological and developmental research has confirmed that a person's impulsivity and susceptibility to peer influence significantly diminishes in the early to mid-20s (see Slobogin & Fondacaro, 2011, pp. 20–26 for summary of research). Thus, if the goal is public safety, prolonged incarceration of people who commit crimes as adolescents is excessive.

Prolonged incarceration is also counterproductive. As the research on deterrence has implied, prison is criminogenic (see also Lee & McCrary, 2009, p. 7). Transfer may keep a troublesome youth off the streets, but it increases the probability that youth will turn to crime once back in the community (McCrary & Sanga, 2011, pp. 9–12). Also important is the fact that adolescents in adult prisons are highly likely to be the victims of crime themselves, a fact that must be weighed on the cost side of the ledger (Mulvey & Schubert, 2012, pp. 4–5). In short,the safety both of the public and of juvenile offenders would be enhanced by moving from detention-heavy policies to those that focus on community-based corrections (Mendel, 2011, p. 27).

Finally, if incapacitation is necessary, the juvenile system is capable of carrying it out. The persistently violent offender probably needs to be detained in a secure setting, but such detention does not need to be provided by the adult system. Juvenile detention facilities are also criminogenic, but not nearly as much as adult prisons (Fagan, 2002; Hjalmarsson, 2009).

Retribution

The foregoing discussion suggests that retribution is the strongest, and perhaps the only, justification for transfer. The argument in this vein is that certain crimes demand prolonged punishment that only the adult system can provide. If retribution is defined solely from a deontological perspective—that is, a perspective that does not take into account the consequences of reliance on desert—and desert is based solely on the offense (rather than on the whole person), this argument is persuasive. A 17-year-old who commits murder, attempted murder, aggravated rape, armed robbery, a major drug offense, or any other offense that would warrant a sentence of 10 years or longer if committed by an adult will generally have to be transferred to adult court if a retributively appropriate sentence is to be imposed, even assuming a robust discount for youth and juvenile dispositional jurisdiction extending to age 21 or further into young adulthood.

Retribution does not have to be defined in deontological terms, however. A consequentialist approach to desert analysis might consider the effects of failing to adhere to the "morally correct" punishment warranted by desert. What will be the real-world impact of a system that does not give juvenile offenders their retributive due?

One hypothesis is that people upset with punishment that is perceived to be lenient will be more prone to take matters into their own hands or in some other way express disdain for the legal system. For instance, Paul Robinson (2008), who has developed the concept of empirical desert, has argued that if punishment routinely fails to track empirically derived lay views on deserved punishment, the result will be more noncompliance with the law in general, because people will lose respect for a government that is substantively unjust (p. 144). He and his colleagues have conducted research that purports to support that position (Robinson, Goodwin, & Reisig, 2010, pp. 1999–2007). Other research, however, has indicated that except when punishment represents a radical departure from lay norms, the hypothesized generalized noncompliance effects do not occur or occur only trivially (Slobogin & Brinkley-Rubinstein, 2012, pp. 101–108). Furthermore, to the extent such noncompliance effects do occur, they are at least as likely when punishment departs from utilitarian precepts as when it departs from retributive ones (Slobogin & Brinkley-Rubinstein, 2012).

More important, no comparable research has been conducted in the context of juvenile justice. Even if punishments that diverge from desert do have general noncompliance effects when they are imposed on adults, the same divergence in the juvenile context might not have similar impact.

One study found, for instance, that "adult punishment and long incarceration are approved, for the most part, only as a means to protect the public from violent young criminals; however, if other more lenient sanctions are effective, they are favored over incarceration" (Scott & Steinberg, 2008, p. 281). This finding suggests not only that retribution is not perceived to be as important in the juvenile context as in the adult context, but also that, to the extent the public supports transfer, it does so largely as a means of protecting its members, not as a means of exacting desert.

Nonetheless, particularly dramatic cases might severely test the proposition that desert can be ignored in fashioning dispositions for juvenile offenders. During an 8-day period in 1978, when he was 15 years old, Willie Bosket committed or tried to commit five armed robberies in or around the New York City subway system, in the course of which two individuals were killed and a third wounded (Butterfield, 1995, pp. 213–215). Sentenced in juvenile court to only 5 years, his case created such an outcry in New York that Governor Carey, who had previously been opposed to increasing transfer jurisdiction, called a special session of the legislature to consider juvenile justice reform (Butterfield, 1995, pp. 226–227). The result was a law that lowered adult jurisdiction to 15 and permitted prosecution of youths as young as 13 if charged with murder (New York Penal Law, 2009, §10.00[18]). Proving to some observers the wisdom of this legislative change, within 4 months of his release from juvenile court jurisdiction in 1983, Bosket assaulted and robbed a man. While serving the resulting sentence during the next 10 years, he assaulted several court officials and prison guards and also committed arson (Butterfield, 1989). Today, serving a prison term of 25 years to life, Bosket is housed in a special Plexiglas-lined cell with four video cameras trained on him at all times. Visitors may only talk to him through a window in the cell (Eligon, 2008).

In light of the New York legislature's immediate response to Bosket, one might conclude that a regime that did away with transfer would not survive its first Bosket-type case. Ideally, however, politicians would resist the idea that 13- to 17-year-old murderers should be sentenced to life terms simply because a vocal portion of the citizenry demands it. They could try to allay the fears of those worried about public safety by citing the research that identifies more effective, less costly crime prevention measures. And they might be able to combat retribution-driven concerns by asking the public to focus on the offender's full life story. In Bosket's case, for instance, had public authorities not only disclosed Bosket's offenses but also emphasized that he had begun offending at age 9 soon after his father was put in prison for life on a murder conviction, that his mother had nothing to do with him from an early age, and that he was in and out of reformatories that did little but warehouse him, the public's vengeful urges might have been assuaged (Butterfield, 1995, pp. 135–149, 176–178).

If that seems Pollyannaish and a more robust legislative response is thought to be needed, a juvenile justice system without transfer could include a dispositional safety valve, which would permit preventive confinement to continue past age 25 for those offenders who (like Bosket?) are "dangerous beyond their control" (*Kansas v. Hendricks*, 1997, p. 358). The latter language was the Supreme Court's way of describing a narrow subset of adult offenders who may be detained beyond their sentence on risk grounds, without violating substantive due process. Only a few offenders would qualify for such detention, however. As the Court put it in a later case, to permit this type of preventive detention

> there must be proof of serious difficulty in controlling behavior . . . sufficient to distinguish the dangerous . . . offender whose serious mental illness, abnormality, or disorder subjects him to civil commitment from the dangerous but typical recidivist convicted in an ordinary criminal case. (*Kansas v. Crane*, 2002, p. 413)

Although this safety valve might seem to be transfer in disguise, it differs from transfer in two essential ways. First, the decision to confine for a longer period of time does not occur at the front end, before it can be known whether treatment and the aging process will minimize the person's risk, but only after the offender has demonstrated dangerousness beyond control. Second, the disposition remains indeterminate, which means that release before the "deserved" length of punishment is always a possibility. As the Supreme Court stated in *Graham v. Florida* (2010), "[a] State is not required to guarantee eventual freedom" to juveniles, but it must provide "some meaningful opportunity for release based on demonstrated maturity and rehabilitation" (p. 130).

CONCLUSION

A scientifically based juvenile justice system would forthrightly focus on prevention rather than on the early 20th century notion of socialization through rehabilitation or the late 20th century notion of retribution. In a preventive system, transfer jurisdiction would be abolished, act jurisdiction would end at around age 18, and dispositional jurisdiction would end at age 25, with extensions for those few serious offenders who are dangerous beyond their control. These age thresholds are consistent with empirical research that has indicated that (a) after age 17, non–mentally disordered people tend to possess the capacities demanded by any account of criminal culpability and (b) through age 24, the brain is still maturing and character is still forming so that interventions are most likely to have significant effect up to that point (Fishbein et al., 2009, p. 429; Steinberg, Cauffman, Woolard, Graham, & Banich, 2009, p. 592).

Under this regime, a 17-year-old who commits a crime could be subject to juvenile court jurisdiction for as long as 8 years, and offenders who are younger at the time of their crimes might be under that jurisdiction for a longer period of time. However, most juveniles—even those who commit serious crimes—would not be subject to detention for anywhere near the full length of juvenile court jurisdiction, because (a) research has indicated that most treatment regimes can be completed more quickly, (b) desistance will often occur well before age 25, and (c) program personnel would know that even detention in juvenile facilities is criminogenic and thus should be as short lived as possible. This preventive justice system can optimize both the protection of society and the welfare of youthful offenders.

References

Ægisdóttir, S., White, M. J., Spengler, P. M., Maugherman, A. S., Anderson, L. A., Cook, R. S., . . . Rush, H. D. (2006). The Meta-Analysis of Clinical Judgment Project: Fifty-six years of accumulated research on clinical versus statistical prediction. *Counseling Psychologist, 34*, 341–382. http://dx.doi.org/10.1177/0011000005285875

Andrews, D., Bonta, J., & Wormith, S. (2011). The risk-need-responsivity (RNR) model. *Criminal Justice and Behavior, 38*, 735–755. http://dx.doi.org/10.1177/0093854811406356

Arizona Juvenile Court Rules of Procedure (2013). Retrieved from http://www.azcourts.gov/rules/RecentAmendments/RulesofProcedurefortheJuvenileCourt.aspx

Arnett, J. (1992). Reckless behavior in adolescence: A developmental perspective. *Developmental Review, 12*, 339–373. http://dx.doi.org/10.1016/0273-2297(92)90013-R

Aronson, J. (2009). Neuroscience and juvenile justice. *Akron Law Review, 42*, 917–930.

Ascione, F. (2001). Animal abuse and youth violence. *Juvenile Justice Bulletin, 9*. Retrieved from http://www.ncjrs.org/html/ojjdp/jjbul2001_9_2/contents.html

Augimeri, L., Enebrink, P., Walsh, M., & Depeng, J. (2010). Gender-specific childhood risk assessment tools: Early Assessment Risk Lists for Boys (EARL-20B) and Girls (EARL-21G). In R. Otto & K. Douglas (Eds.), *Handbook of violence risk assessment* (pp. 43–62). New York, NY: Routledge.

Baron-Evans, A., & Stith, K. (2012). *Booker* rules. *University of Pennsylvania Law Review, 160*, 1631–1743.

Beresford, L. (2000). Is lowering the age at which juveniles can be transferred to adult criminal court the answer to juvenile crime? A state-by-state assessment. *San Diego Law Review, 37*, 783–848.

Bilchik, S. (1999, December). *Juvenile justice: A century of change* (Juvenile Justice Bulletin). Washington, DC: U.S. Department of Justice, Office of Justice Programs, Office of Juvenile Justice and Delinquency. Retrieved from http://www.ncjrs.gov/pdffiles1/ojjdp/178995.pdf

Bishop, D., & Frazier, C. (2000). Consequences of transfer. In J. Fagan & F. Zimring (Eds.), *The changing borders of juvenile justice: Transfers of adolescents to adult court* (pp. 227–276). Chicago, IL: University of Chicago Press.

Borum, R., Lodewijks, H., Bartel, P., & Forth, A. (2010). Structured Assessment of Violence Risk in Youth (SAVRY). In R. Otto & K. Douglas (Eds.), *Handbook of violence risk assessment* (pp. 63–79). New York, NY: Routledge.

Brandt, D. E. (2006). *Delinquency, development, and social policy*. New Haven, CT: Yale University Press. http://dx.doi.org/10.12987/yale/9780300108941.001.0001

Brubacher, M. R., Fondacaro, M. R., Brank, E. M., Brown, V. E., & Miller, S. A. (2009). Procedural justice in resolving family disputes: Implications for childhood bullying. *Psychology, Public Policy, and Law, 15*, 149–167. http://dx.doi.org/10.1037/a0016839

Brummer, C. (2002). Extended juvenile jurisdiction: The best of both worlds? *Arkansas Law Review, 54*, 777–845.

Butterfield, F. (1989, April 20). Jailed “monster” gets more prison time for stabbing a guard. *New York Times*, p. A1.

Butterfield, F. (1995). *All God’s children: The Bosket family and the tradition of American violence*. New York, NY: Random House.

Cauffman, E., & Steinberg, L. (2000). (Im)maturity of judgment in adolescence: Why adolescents may be less culpable than adults. *Behavioral Sciences and the Law, 18*, 741–760. http://dx.doi.org/10.1002/bsl.416

Cicchetti, D., & Rogosch, F. A. (2002). A developmental psychopathology perspective on adolescence. *Journal of Consulting and Clinical Psychology, 70*, 6–20. http://dx.doi.org/10.1037/0022-006X.70.1.6

Cohn, J., & Mialon, H. (2011). *The impact of juvenile transfer laws on juvenile crime* (Emory Public Law Research Paper No. 10-103). Retrieved from http://ssrn.com/abstract=1606002 http://dx.doi.org/10.2139/ssrn.1606002

Commonwealth v. Cessna, 537 A.2d 834 (1988).

Commonwealth v. O’Brien, 673 N.E.2d 552 (Mass. 1996).

Cullen, F., Fisher, B., & Applegate, B. (2000). Public opinion about punishment and corrections. *Crime and Justice, 27*, 1–79.

Developments in the law: Civil commitment of the mentally ill. (1974). *Harvard Law Review, 87*, 1190–1400.

Diamond, S. S., Casper, J. D., Heiert, C. L., & Marshall, A.-M. (1996). Juror reactions to attorneys at trial. *Journal of Criminal Law and Criminology, 87*, 17–47. http://dx.doi.org/10.2307/1143971

Dillard v. State, 623 P.2d 395 (Idaho 1981).

Dowd, N. (2011). *Justice for kids: Keeping kids out of the juvenile justice system*. New York, NY: New York University Press.

Eligon, J. (2008, September 22). Two decades in solitary. *New York Times*, p. A 25.

Fagan, J. (2002). This will hurt me more than it hurts you: Social and legal consequences of criminalizing delinquency. *Notre Dame Journal of Law, Ethics and Public Policy, 16*, 1–41.

Faust, F., & Brantingham, P. (1974).The invention of the juvenile court. In F. Faust & P. Brantingham (Eds.), *Juvenile justice philosophy: Readings, cases and comments* (pp. 550–557). St. Paul, MN: West.

Feld, B. (1988). The juvenile court meets the principle of offense: Punishment, treatment, and the difference it makes. *Boston University Law Review, 68*, 821–915.

Feld, B. (1997). Abolish the juvenile court: Youthfulness, criminal responsibility, and sentencing. *Journal of Criminal Law and Criminology, 88*, 68–136. http://dx.doi.org/10.2307/1144075

Feld, B. (1998). Juvenile and criminal justice systems’ responses to youth violence. *Crime and Justice, 24*, 189–260. http://dx.doi.org/10.1086/449280

Feld, B. (1999). The transformation of the juvenile court—Part II: Race and the “crack down” on youth crime. *Minnesota Law Review, 84*, 327–395.

Feld, B. (2007). A century of juvenile justice: A work in progress or a revolution that failed? *Northern Kentucky Law Review, 34*, 189–256.

Finkel, N. (1995). *Commonsense justice: Jurors’ notions of the law*. Cambridge, MA: Harvard University Press.

Fishbein, D., Sheppard, M., Hyde, C., Hubal, R., Newlin, D., Serin, R., . . . Alesci, S. (2009). Deficits in behavioral inhibition predict treatment engagement in prison inmates. *Law and Human Behavior, 33*, 419–435. http://dx.doi.org/10.1007/s10979-008-9163-7

Fondacaro, M. R., Dunkle, M. E., & Pathak, M. K. (1998). Procedural justice in resolving family disputes: A psychosocial analysis of individual and family functioning in late adolescence. *Journal of Youth and Adolescence, 27*, 101–119. http://dx.doi.org/10.1023/A:1022832932752

Graham v. Florida, 560 U.S. 48 (2010).

Grisso, T. (1998). *Forensic evaluation of juveniles*. Sarasota, FL: Professional Resource Press.

Grissom, B. (2011, March 24). Report: Hundreds of youths in adult prisons. *Texas Tribune*. Retrieved from http://www.texastribune.org/2011/03/24/report-hundreds-of-youths-in-adult-prisons

Heilbrun, K., Douglas, K., & Yasuhara, K. (2009). Violence risk assessment: Core controversies. In J. Skeem, K. Douglas, & S. Lilienfeld (Eds.), *Psychological science in the courtroom: Controversies and consensus* (pp. 333–357). New York, NY: Guilford Press.

Heilbrun, K., Leheny, C., Thomas, L., & Huneycutt, D. (1997). A national survey of U.S. statutes on juvenile transfer: Implications for policy and practice. *Behavioral Sciences and the Law, 15*, 125–149. http://dx.doi.org/10.1002/(SICI)1099-0798(199721)15:2<125::AID-BSL265>3.0.CO;2-R

Henggeler, S., & Schoenwald, S. (2011). Evidence-based interventions for juvenile offenders and juvenile justice policies that support them. *Social Policy Report*, *25*, 1–16. Retrieved from http://files.eric.ed.gov/fulltext/ED519241.pdf

Hjalmarsson, R. (2009). Juvenile jails: A path to the straight and narrow or to hardened criminality. *Journal of Law and Economics*, *52*, 779–809. http://dx.doi.org/10.1086/596039

Hoge, R. (2010). Youth Level of Service/Case Management Inventory. In R. Otto & K. Douglas (Eds.), *Handbook of violence risk assessment* (pp. 81–95). New York, NY: Routledge.

In re Appeal in Maricopa County, 674 P.2d 841 (Ariz. 1983).

In re R.M., 648 S.W.2d 406 (Tex. Ct. App. 1983).

Institute of Judicial Administration. (1980). *American Bar Association standards relating to juvenile delinquency and sanctions*. Retrieved from http://www.americanbar.org/content/dam/aba/migrated/sections/criminaljustice/PublicDocuments/JJ_Standards_Juvenile_Delinquency_and_Sanctions.authcheckdam.pdf

Jackson v. Arkansas, 521 U.S. 346 (2012).

Janus, E., & Logan, W. (2003). Substantive due process and the involuntary confinement of sexually violent predators. *Connecticut Law Review*, *35*, 319–384.

Janus, E., & Prentky, R. (2003). Forensic use of actuarial risk assessment with sex offenders: Accuracy, admissibility and accountability. *American Criminal Law Review*, *40*, 1433–1499.

Jeffries, J. (1985). Legality, vagueness and the construction of penal statutes. *Virginia Law Review*, *71*, 189–244. http://dx.doi.org/10.2307/1073017

Johnstone, L. (2011). Assessing and managing violent youth: Implications for sentencing. In B. McSherry & P. Keyzer (Eds.), *Dangerous people: Policy, prediction, and practice* (pp. 123–145). New York, NY: Routledge Press.

Kahan, D. (1997). Ignorance of the law is an excuse—But only for the virtuous. *Michigan Law Review*, *96*, 127–154. http://dx.doi.org/10.2307/1290142

Kansas v. Crane, 534 U.S. 407 (2002).

Kansas v. Hendricks, 541 U.S. 346 (1997).

Kent v. United States, 383 U.S. 541 (1966).

Kolender v. Lawson, 461 U.S. 352 (1983).

Krauss, D. A., Lieberman, J. D., & Olson, J. (2004). The effects of rational and experiential information processing of expert testimony in death penalty cases. *Behavioral Sciences and the Law*, 22, 801–822. http://dx.doi.org/10.1002/bsl.621

LaFave, W. (2010). *Criminal law* (5th ed.). St. Paul, MN: West.

Lebel, C., Walker, L., Leemans, A., Phillips, L., & Beaulieu, C. (2008). Microstructural maturation of the human brain from childhood to adulthood. *NeuroImage*, *40*, 1044–1055. http://dx.doi.org/10.1016/j.neuroimage.2007.12.053

Lee, D., & McCrary, J. (2009). *The deterrence effect of prison: Dynamic theory and evidence* (Berkeley Program in Law and Economics Working Paper). Retrieved from http://emlab.berkley.edu/~jmccrary/lee_and_mccrary2009.pdf

Levitt, S. (1998). Juvenile crime and punishment. *Journal of Political Economy*, *106*, 1156–1185. http://dx.doi.org/10.1086/250043

Lipsey, M. (2009). The primary factors that characterize effective interventions with juvenile offenders: A meta-analytic overview. *Victims and Offenders*, *4*, 124–147. http://dx.doi.org/10.1080/15564880802612573

Mathias, C. W., Marsh-Richard, D. M., & Dougherty, D. M. (2008). Behavioral measures of impulsivity and the law. *Behavioral Sciences and the Law*, *26*, 691–707. http://dx.doi.org/10.1002/bsl.841

McCrary, J., & Sanga, S. (2011). *Youth offenders and the deterrence effect of prison*. Retrieved from http://www.researchgate.net/publication/228187834

McGarvey, S. (2012). Juvenile justice and mental health: Innovation in the laboratory of human behavior. *Jurimetrics*, *3*, 97–120.

McGowan, A., Hahn, R., Liberman, A., Crosby, A., Fullilove, M., Johnson, R., . . . Stone, G.; Task Force on Community Preventive Services. (2007). Effects on violence of laws and policies facilitating the transfer of juveniles from the juvenile justice system to the adult justice system: A systematic review. *American Journal of Preventive Medicine*, 32(Suppl.), 7–28. http://dx.doi.org/10.1016/j.amepre.2006.12.003

Mendel, R. (2011). *No place for kids: The case for reducing juvenile incarceration*. Baltimore, MD: Annie E. Casey Foundation. Retrieved from http://www.aecf.org/resources/no-place-for-kids-full-report

Meyers, D. (2005). *Boys among men: Trying and sentencing juveniles as adults*. Westport, CT: Praeger.

Miller v. Alabama, 132 S. Ct. 2455 (2012).

Moffitt, T. (1993). Adolescence-limited and life-course-persistent antisocial behavior: A developmental taxonomy. *Psychological Review*, *100*, 674–701.

Monahan, J. (2006). A jurisprudence of risk assessment: Forecasting harm among prisoners, predators, and patients. *Virginia Law Review*, *92*, 391–435.

Monahan, J., & Skeem, J. L. (2014). The evolution of violence risk assessment. *CNS Spectrums, 19*, 419–424. http://dx.doi.org/10.1017/S1092852914000145

Mulvey, E., & Schubert, C. (2012, December). *Transfer of juveniles to adult court: Effects of a broad policy in one court* (Juvenile Justice Bulletin). Washington, DC: U.S. Department of Justice, Office of Justice Programs, Office of Juvenile Justice and Delinquency Prevention. Retrieved from http://www.ojjdp.gov/pubs/232932.pdf

Netter, B. (2007). Using group statistics to sentence individual criminals: An ethical and statistical critique of the Virginia risk assessment program. *Journal of Criminal Law and Criminology, 97*, 699–729.

New York Penal Law (2009). St. Paul, MN: Thompson-Reuters.

Otto, R., & Petrila, J. (2002). Admissibility of testimony based on actuarial scales in sex offender commits: A reply to Doren. *Sex Offender Law Report, 3*, 1–4.

P.K.M. v. State, 780 P.2d 395 (Alaska Ct. App. 1989).

Redding, R. (2006). Adult punishment for juvenile offenders: Does it reduce crime? In N. Dowd, D. Singer, & R. Fretwell (Eds.), *Handbook of children, culture and violence* (pp. 375–394). Thousand Oaks, CA: Sage.

Redding, R. (2010, June). *Juvenile transfer laws: An effective deterrent to delinquency?* (Juvenile Justice Bulletin). Washington, DC: U.S. Department of Justice, Office of Justice Programs, Office of Juvenile Justice and Delinquency Prevention.

Redding, R., & Mrozoski, B. (2005). Adjudicatory and dispositional decision making in juvenile justice. In K. Heilbrun, N. E. Sevin Goldstein, & R. E. Redding (Eds.), *Juvenile delinquency: Prevention, assessment and intervention* (pp. 232–256). New York, NY: Oxford University Press.

Rice, M., Harris, G., & Hilton, N. Z. (2010). The Violence Risk Appraisal Guide and Sex Offender Risk Appraisal Guide for violence risk assessment. In R. Otto & K. Douglas (Eds.), *Handbook of violence risk assessment* (pp. 99–119). New York, NY: Routledge.

Robinson, P. (2008). *Distributive principles of criminal law: Who should be punished how much?* New York, NY: Oxford University Press. http://dx.doi.org/10.1093/acprof:oso/9780195365757.001.0001

Robinson, P., Goodwin, G., & Reisig, M. (2010). The disutility of injustice. *New York University Law Review, 85*, 1940–2033.

Roper v. Simmons, 543 U.S. 551 (2005).

Saks, M. (2003). The legal and scientific evaluation of forensic science (especially fingerprint expert testimony). *Seton Hall Law Review, 33*, 1167–1187.

Sampson, R. J., & Laub, J. H. (1994). Urban poverty and the family context of delinquency: A new look at structure and process in a classic study. *Child Development, 65*, 523–540. http://dx.doi.org/10.2307/1131400

Scott, E. (2013). *Miller* v. *Alabama* and the (past and) future of juvenile crime regulation. *Law and Inequality, 31*, 535–558.

Scott, E., & Steinberg, L. (2008). *Rethinking juvenile justice: Adolescent development and the regulation of youth crime*. Cambridge, MA: Harvard University Press.

Shook, J. (2005). Contesting childhood in the US justice system: The transfer of juveniles to adult criminal court. *Childhood, 12*, 461–478. http://dx.doi.org/10.1177/0907568205058604

Slobogin, C. (1999). Treating kids right: Deconstructing and reconstructing the amenability to treatment concept. *Journal of Contemporary Legal Issues, 10*, 299–333.

Slobogin, C. (2007). *Proving the unprovable: The role of law, science, and speculation in adjudicating culpability and dangerousness*. New York, NY: Oxford University Press.

Slobogin, C. (2009). The death penalty in Florida. *Elon Law Review, 1*, 17–63.

Slobogin, C. (2012). Risk assessment. In J. Petersilia & K. Reitz (Eds.), *Oxford handbook on sentencing and corrections* (pp. 196–214). New York, NY: Oxford University Press.

Slobogin, C. (2013). Treating juveniles like juveniles: Getting rid of transfer and expanded adult court jurisdiction. *Texas Tech Law Review, 46*, 103–132.

Slobogin, C., & Brinkley-Rubinstein, L. (2012). Putting desert in its place. *Stanford Law Review, 65*, 77–135.

Slobogin, C., & Fondacaro, M. (2011). *Juveniles at risk: A plea for preventive justice*. New York, NY: Oxford University Press. http://dx.doi.org/10.1093/acprof:oso/9780199778355.001.0001

Stanford v. Commonwealth, 734 S.W. 2 781 (Ken. 1987).

State v. Simpson, 836 S.W. 2d 75 (Miss. Ct. App. 1992).

Steinberg, L., & Cauffman, E. (2000). A developmental perspective on jurisdictional boundaries. In J. Fagan & F. Zimring (Eds.), *The changing borders of juvenile justice: Transfers of adolescents to adult courts* (pp. 379–406). Chicago, IL: University of Chicago Press.

Steinberg, L., Cauffman, E., Woolard, J., Graham, S., & Banich, M. (2009). Are adolescents less mature than adults? Minors' access to abortion, the juvenile death penalty, and the alleged APA "flip-flop." *American Psychologist, 64*, 583–594. http://dx.doi.org/10.1037/a0014763

Steinberg, L., & Schwartz, R. (2000). Developmental psychology goes to court. In T. Grisso & R. Schwartz (Eds.), *Youth on trial: A developmental perspective on juvenile justice* (pp. 9–31). Chicago, IL: University of Chicago Press.

Stinneford, J. (2013, March). *The illusory Eighth Amendment*. Paper presented at University of Florida Junior Scholars Roundtable, Gainesville, FL.

Tonry, M. (2006). Purposes and functions of sentencing. *Crime and Justice, 34*, 1–52. http://dx.doi.org/10.1086/503374

Whitman, J. (2013, March). *The failure of retributivism in the American common law*. Paper presented at Vanderbilt University Law School Roundtable, Nashville, TN.

Williams, K., & Hawkins, R. (1986). Perceptual research on general deterrence: A critical review. *Law and Society Review, 20*, 545–572. http://dx.doi.org/10.2307/3053466

Zimring, F. (2000). Penal proportionality for the young offender: Notes on immaturity, capacity, and diminished responsibility. In T. Grisso & R. Schwartz (Eds.), *Youth on trial: A developmental perspective on juvenile justice* (pp. 271–289). Chicago, IL: University of Chicago Press.

Part III

HUMAN DEVELOPMENT

CHAPTER 4

HUMAN DEVELOPMENT AND JUVENILE JUSTICE

Elizabeth P. Shulman and Laurence Steinberg

Adolescence is a key developmental period for legally relevant psychological capacities. These capacities include higher level cognitive capabilities, such as the ability to appreciate the consequences of one's actions, as well as capacities that require coordination between thoughts and feelings, such as the ability to regulate one's impulses and behave autonomously in the face of social pressure. Acquisition of such capacities proceeds gradually and unevenly. Individuals differ in the rates at which they mature psychologically and, for a given individual, one capacity may develop more rapidly than another. Some youths may attain adult levels of maturity in these capacities well before they reach the age of legal majority (usually age 18). Others may not reach the pinnacle of their abilities until early adulthood. Further complicating matters is the fact that an individual's ability to exercise legally relevant cognitive and psychosocial capacities may be compromised under certain conditions, such as when fatigued or emotionally aroused. This is true even of adults but may be exaggerated for adolescents because their cognitive and psychosocial capacities are still maturing.

The "in-betweenness" of adolescents—the fact that they possess some, but not all, of the psychological capacities expected of adults, or an intermediate degree of them—leaves ample room for disagreement among lawmakers and jurists about how they should be treated under the law. Whereas scientists recognize development as a continuous and gradual process, the law often relies on binary classifications where chronological age is concerned, defining individuals as either children or adults. Children are assumed, under the law, to be vulnerable, dependent, and incapable of informed and mature decision making (*Bellotti v. Baird*, 1979). They are therefore afforded special protections, denied certain rights, and held less than fully accountable for their actions. Adults, however, are presumed to be fully competent and responsible. Adolescents do not fit either of these profiles.

Lawmakers have traditionally responded to the uncertain developmental status of adolescents by legislating that they be treated either as children or as adults depending on the specific policy question. In the United States, different age delineations are drawn for acts such as driving, purchasing alcohol, voting, and receiving certain types of medical care without parental consent (e.g., reproductive and mental health treatment). In criminal and juvenile law, the contradictory legislative impulses to protect adolescents as minors and hold them accountable as adults has produced a nexus of complicated, and sometimes conflicting, regulations that vary from one jurisdiction to the next. For instance, many state laws would permit a 17-year-old to be prosecuted as an adult on charges of child pornography for taking an erotic photograph of herself and sending it to her boyfriend, a scenario in which the adolescent is cast simultaneously as an adult (as the sender of the photo) and a child (as its subject).

The juvenile justice system was established for the express purpose of treating accused minors (those younger than age 18) differently than adults, on the basis of minors' lesser culpability and greater

http://dx.doi.org/10.1037/14643-004
APA Handbook of Psychology and Juvenile Justice, K. Heilbrun (Editor-in-Chief)

potential for reform. Yet, state laws now vary substantially with respect to the age at which a child can be prosecuted as an adult. In 16 states, age 14 is the lower age limit for transfer to criminal court; in Kansas, Vermont, and Wisconsin, the lower limit is age 10; and 21 states and the District of Columbia impose no absolute lower age limit at all for certain crimes (Office of Juvenile Justice and Delinquency Prevention, 2012). Statutes also vary with regard to whether the decision to transfer a minor from the juvenile to the adult criminal justice system for a given offense is made on a case-by-case basis or is mandatory.

HISTORICAL SHIFTS IN THE PERCEPTION OF ADOLESCENTS UNDER THE LAW

Today, the United States differs from most of the industrialized world in its willingness to prosecute and sentence juvenile offenders as adults. In most other developed countries, age 18 is a bright-line distinction. Offenders younger than that age are processed consistently as juveniles, as was true in the United States for most of the 20th century. During the final decades of the 20th century, however, a spate of "get-tough" policies were implemented. As a result, in the United States, many more individuals younger than age 18 are now transferred out of the juvenile justice system and tried as adults than had been before 1990.

Indeed, many of the questions discussed in this chapter, such as whether adolescents should be held to the same standards of culpability as adults or whether minors are competent to stand trial in criminal court, would not have been topics of discussion in a handbook chapter on human development and juvenile justice as recently as 30 years ago. In a sense, the importance of developmental science for discussions of children and youths in the justice system is a recent development, necessitated by relatively new changes in policy and practice that have blurred the previously clear distinctions between adolescents and adults. To appreciate the nuances of these legal questions and the role that developmental science has played in shaping policy, it helps to have some familiarity with the U.S. juvenile justice system.

Two perspectives, reflected in the following quotations, capture the disparity of opinions that influenced the evolution of juvenile justice jurisprudence during the 20th century:

> Why is it not just and proper to treat these juvenile offenders, as we deal with the neglected children, as a wise and merciful father handles his own child whose errors are not discovered by the authorities?—Judge Julian Mack (1909, p. 7)
>
> Juvenile offenders are "criminals who happen to be young, not children who happen to be criminal."—Albert Regnery (1985, p. 65)

The creation in 1899 of a separate justice system in the United States for children and youths was premised on the belief that juveniles differ from adults in ways that are relevant to how the law should respond to their bad behavior. Ben Lindsey, founder and judge of the Denver Juvenile Court, for example, asserted that there were no bad kids—only bad conditions that led to bad conduct. The purpose of his court, as he explained in a 1927 magazine article, was to save young offenders, not to punish them. Like other social reformers who helped to establish the juvenile court during the Progressive Era at the turn of the 20th century, Lindsey believed that the state's primary concern with regard to juvenile offenders was to promote their welfare and, therefore, that the state had an obligation to provide these youths with assistance and rehabilitative services. In his court, Lindsey carried out this mission with the aid of probation officers, social workers, physicians, and psychiatrists. As such, Judge Lindsey's court exemplified the rehabilitative model that informed juvenile justice policy for most of the 20th century. (Lindsey was so committed to the protection of the youths who came through his court that, when he was voted off the bench in 1927, he burned the juvenile court records rather than risk a breach of confidentiality or attempts at retribution; Denver Public Library, 2011.) Because of their belief that concepts such as criminal responsibility and punishment had no place in the juvenile court, the founders implemented a unique lexicon for the juvenile court that serves as a continual reminder of its distinction from the criminal court. Juveniles commit *offenses*, as opposed to crimes; at the conclusion of a *proceeding* (rather than a trial), they may be *adjudicated delinquent* rather than found guilty; delinquent youths receive *dispositions*, not sentences.

Before the U.S. juvenile court was established, only young children were deemed incapable of criminal responsibility for their transgressions. The tradition, derived from English common law, was that individuals younger than age 7, because of their limited capacity to appreciate the wrongfulness of their acts, were incapable of committing a crime. This was known as the *infancy defense*. Common law also presumed that children between the ages of 7 and 14 were not criminally responsible for their behavior, but that this presumption was rebuttable. In practice, most accused youths in this age range were tried and punished as adults. Youths older than age 14, in contrast, were regarded as possessing the same capacities as adults. With the founding of the juvenile court, this common-law scheme was jettisoned in favor of a bright-line distinction—typically drawn at age 18[1]—which classified youth as either children or adults and resulted in their being processed accordingly in either the juvenile or the criminal justice system.

Until the late 20th century, the rehabilitative model held sway in juvenile justice policy, and the juvenile court's operations were directed toward the ultimate goal of reforming young offenders. In theory, if not always in practice, this orientation guided the adjudicative process in juvenile court and the types of dispositions that were imposed. Delinquency dispositions were open ended, which made sense given their purported rehabilitative purpose. Under the rehabilitative model, treatment delivered through the juvenile justice system was seen as ending when the "patient" was "cured," as would medical treatment for an illness. Consequently, the duration of a disposition was not contingent on the seriousness of the offense. The principle of penal proportionality—the idea that a punishment's severity should be proportional to the seriousness of the crime and the perpetrator's criminal responsibility—was not an essential consideration in delinquency proceedings. Juvenile court judges were free to formulate dispositions based on their perceptions of youths' needs, irrespective of the nature or severity of their criminal conduct. In effect, the rehabilitative model cast juvenile court judges in the role of parents; it assumed that judges would act in the best interests of delinquent youths and, accordingly, gave them a wide berth to respond in whatever manner they saw fit.

Gault and Its Repercussions

Despite the earnest intentions of the reformers who established it, the juvenile court was, by many accounts, unsuccessful in realizing the rehabilitative ideal on which it was founded (e.g., Feld, 2007a). By the 1960s, the juvenile court was under attack from both the right and the left sides of the political spectrum, with conservatives objecting to the court's emphasis on rehabilitation over punishment and public safety and liberals decrying the system's perceived abuses of judicial discretion and failure to help youth reform (Feld, 2007b). The first successful assault on the juvenile court was launched by youth advocates who argued that the court had failed to deliver on its promise of providing rehabilitative services to delinquent youths. They further reasoned that, given that rehabilitative intent served as the justification for denying juveniles the procedural rights afforded to adult criminal defendants, these rights should now be extended to juvenile defendants. At the time, juveniles had no right to legal counsel, and their court proceedings lacked the fact-finding procedures that are central to an adversarial criminal trial. Yet, dispositions could be long term and intrusive. For some, dispositions involved confinement in correctional facilities that, to the adjudicated youths, would have seemed like prison. This push for reform culminated in the landmark 1967 U.S. Supreme Court ruling in *In re Gault*. In its decision in this case, the Court

[1]Today, 18 remains the jurisdictional dividing line between juvenile and criminal courts in most states, although some use 17 or, less commonly, 16.

extended due process protections to juveniles for the adjudication component of their delinquency proceedings, thereby effecting a fundamental change in the operation the juvenile court.

Gerald Gault, the subject of *In re Gault* (1967), was 15 years old when he was arrested for making inappropriate telephone calls to his next-door neighbor—calls later described by the Supreme Court as being "of the irritatingly offensive, adolescent, sex variety" (p. 4). Gault was arrested and brought before a juvenile court judge without being given notice of the charges against him or being informed of the option to have an attorney to represent him. The neighbor who received the calls did not provide testimony at the delinquency hearing. Instead, the arresting officer described to the juvenile court what the neighbor had reported. The judge's disposition committed Gerald to the Arizona State Industrial School for a period of as long as 6 years for a crime that would have carried a sentence in criminal court of at most 2 months in jail and a $50 fine. These facts made *Gault* an ideal case on which to challenge the informality of juvenile court proceedings.

When Gault's appeal of his disposition reached the Supreme Court, the Court flatly rejected the state's proffered justification for the informality of delinquency proceedings. Justice Abe Fortas, who wrote the majority opinion, described Gault's proceeding as a "kangaroo court" and noted that "the essential difference between Gerald's case and a normal criminal case is that safeguards available to adults were discarded in Gerald's case" (*In re Gault*, 1967, p. 29). The opinion asserted that the juvenile court's mission of rehabilitating youths would not be impeded by affording minors constitutional protections in the adjudication of their cases. The Court went further, questioning the juvenile court's effectiveness in carrying out its rehabilitative mission and citing a study that found high rates of recidivism among youths who had been processed through the juvenile justice system. In the end, the decision in *Gault* held that youths undergoing adjudication in delinquency proceedings were similar to criminal defendants in that they faced a potential loss of liberty; thus, they were entitled under the U.S. Constitution to certain due process protections, including a right to notice of the charges, a right to confront witnesses against them, a privilege against self-incrimination, and, most important, a right to counsel. This decision, although apparently not intended to fundamentally alter the rehabilitative mission of the juvenile court ("the features of the juvenile system which its proponents have asserted are of unique benefit will not be impaired by constitutional domestication"; *In re Gault*, 1967, p. 22), nonetheless profoundly transformed the climate of the juvenile court. By ordering constitutional protections for juveniles, the Court turned delinquency proceedings into adversarial affairs—not unlike criminal trials—and in so doing made the juvenile court judge's role less like that of a parent, whose job is to promote the delinquent child's well-being, and more like that of a criminal court judge, whose job is to arbitrate the defendant's guilt.

By affording juveniles these procedural rights, *In re Gault* (1967) reinforced a line of reasoning that had been introduced a year earlier in the lesser known case of *Kent v. United States* (1966), which concerned the process through which juvenile courts transfer (or waive) juvenile cases to criminal court. In *Kent*, the Court held that (a) juveniles are entitled to a hearing before a waiver can occur, (b) juveniles' attorneys must be given access to the records used to inform the waiver decision, and (c) juvenile court judges are required to provide the reasons for their decision to waive a case to criminal court. In addition to being noteworthy because of the specific rights it enumerated, *Kent* is important because among the criteria the Court suggested judges might use in making waiver decisions, it listed "the sophistication and maturity of the juvenile" (p. 567). Consideration of adolescents' psychological maturity relative to that of adults and the relevance of this question to criminal culpability would become paramount in the Supreme Court's juvenile justice jurisprudence 4 decades later.

The Supreme Court's ruling in the case of *In re Winship* (1970) made the juvenile court even more like the criminal court. The justices declared that juvenile courts needed to use evidentiary standards on par with those of criminal courts, meaning that the state needed to prove a juvenile defendant's guilt "beyond a reasonable doubt." Previously, the prevailing standard for the juvenile court had been a "preponderance of evidence"—the standard used in civil proceedings. The following year, however, in *McKeiver v. Pennsylvania* (1971), the Court moved in the other direction, holding that juvenile court defendants did not have the right to a jury (as adult defendants do). Thus, whereas *Winship* made juvenile court proceedings more like criminal court proceedings, *McKeiver* upheld one of the important differences between the two courts. One of the Court's arguments for denying juveniles a right to a jury trial was that the introduction of a jury would make the juvenile court proceeding too adversarial. The Supreme Court further argued that extending all the protections of criminal court to juvenile court could lead to the elimination of the juvenile court altogether, an outcome the justices apparently wished to avoid, despite deep skepticism about the juvenile justice system:

> The juvenile concept held high promise. We are reluctant to say that, despite disappointments of grave dimensions, it still does not hold promise, and we are particularly reluctant to say . . . that the system cannot accomplish its rehabilitative goals. (*McKeiver v. Pennsylvania*, 1971, p. 547)

After *Winship* and *McKeiver*, the Court ruled on several additional cases that helped to clarify the distinctions and commonalities between juvenile and criminal court proceedings, sometimes extending juveniles the rights and protections afforded to adults and sometimes withholding them.[2]

However, as reflected in the *McKeiver v. Pennsylvania* (1971) opinion, the juvenile court system's capacity to rehabilitate young people—one of its primary reasons for existing—was in serious doubt by the 1970s. When violent juvenile crime rates rose in the late 1980s, the juvenile system's damaged reputation helped to fuel a wave of legislative reforms that increasingly redefined juveniles as adults for purposes of adjudication and punishment (Scott, 2013b). Whereas the Supreme Court decisions of the 1960s and 1970s blurred the distinction between the juvenile and criminal courts, the legislative reforms of the 1980s and 1990s blurred the distinction between juvenile and adult defendants. In pushing for the passage of a 1997 House of Representatives bill designed to reclassify offenders as young as 14 as adults, a congressman from Florida warned that "our youngest career criminals are getting away with the most heinous crimes over and over again. . . . Wake up!" (Gray, 1997). A California legislator who had introduced a similar bill opined that "juveniles have become more violent and deadly" (Mansnerus, 1993). By the end of the 20th century, the image of the young offender and the rhetoric surrounding juvenile justice policy were fundamentally reversed from what they had been at the start of the century.

Trying Juveniles as Adults

As violent youth crime increased in the 1990s, so did attacks on the juvenile court. The media propagated images of teenage street gangs spreading fear in urban neighborhoods. Even some scholars jumped on board; DiIulio described young offenders as remorseless "superpredators," who were "perfectly capable of committing the most heinous acts of physical violence for the most trivial reasons" and who "place zero value on the lives of their victims" (1995, p. 4; see also Bennett, DiIulio, & Walters, 1996). (DiIulio would later express regret for his role in propagating this characterization of young offenders; E. Becker, 2001.) In accordance with this depiction of youth crime, critics of the juvenile court rejected the notion that young criminals were dependent and vulnerable children, deserving of special protections. Under the mantra of "adult time for adult crime," legislators instituted state laws intended to subject young offenders to increasingly harsh punishments, often administered by the criminal courts, and that sometimes involved confinement in correctional facilities previously reserved for individuals age 18 and older.

These modern reformers used several legislative strategies to achieve their aim of treating juvenile offenders more like adults. During the 1980s and 1990s, these reformers effected legislation in

[2]A passage from *Kent* sums up this Supreme Court's view on juvenile proceedings: "We do not mean . . . to indicate that the [juvenile court] hearing to be held must conform with all the requirements of a criminal trial . . . but we do hold that the hearing must measure up to the essentials of due process and fair treatment" (p. 562).

27 states to lower the minimum age at which juvenile cases could be transferred to criminal court (Griffin, 2008). As a result, 14 is now the most common statutory minimum age for criminal prosecution; however, several states have lower age limits, and 22 states have no statutory minimum age at all. Under many statutes, the decision to transfer a case from juvenile to criminal court need not involve consideration of the juvenile defendant's maturity or nonamenability to treatment. Often, the transfer decision is based, instead, on the youth's criminal record and the seriousness of the offense.

One means by which the modern reformers brought about change in the legal treatment of minors was through the expansion of judicial waiver (a procedure in which a judge remands a juvenile case to criminal court). In the original formulation of the juvenile court, judicial waiver was intended to serve as a means of excluding a small number of youths from the juvenile court's jurisdiction—typically older youths suspected of serious violent crimes whom the judge perceived as unlikely to be rehabilitated by the juvenile system. The reforms of the 1980s and 1990s expanded the universe of transfer-eligible offenses to include less serious offenses (Griffin, 2008). As a result, many states now have long lists of offenses that subject a juvenile to criminal prosecution, including nonviolent transgressions such as destruction of property and drug offenses. Indeed, it is possible in most states today for youths charged with property and drug offenses to be tried and sentenced as adults. Furthermore, modern reform efforts led 13 states to enact presumptive waiver laws that make transfer to criminal court the default procedure for certain cases, absent judicial intervention to remand the case to juvenile court (Griffin, 2008).

Some states, as part of their efforts to allow for harsher punishment of juvenile offenders, implemented blended sentencing statutes, which allow juveniles convicted of designated felonies to be subjected to stiff sentences in juvenile court that can be continued through the transfer of the youth to adult prison when he or she reaches age 18. Most blended sentencing statutes include a provision that allows for the reassessment of the youth at age 18 to determine whether he or she should serve the adult portion of the sentence or have that portion suspended (e.g., if the youth has evidenced reform through adherence to institutional regulations or conditions of probation).

Other legislative reforms enacted during the final decades of the 20th century had an even greater impact on the legal treatment of children and adolescents who violate the law. Before 1970, nearly all juvenile cases that wound up in criminal court got there via judicial waiver (Griffin, Addie, Adams, & Firestine, 2011), but new laws enacted in the 1980s and 1990s gave criminal courts automatic jurisdiction over certain youths (i.e., without judicial discretion as to whether a case should be transferred to the criminal court). Under some automatic (or "legislative") waiver statutes, youths are categorized as adults and excluded from juvenile court jurisdiction solely on the basis of their age and the offense with which they are charged. Another means by which a minor may be automatically tried as an adult is by state law specifying an age other than 18 as the threshold for criminal court jurisdiction. At present, 12 states have statutory exclusion laws that draw the dividing line for juvenile court jurisdiction at age 16 or 17 instead of 18 (including Illinois, though it does so only for felony offenses). These states account for the vast majority of cases nationwide in which individuals younger than age 18 are tried as adults (Griffin et al., 2011). Other waiver statutes provide for prosecutorial discretion; they empower the prosecutor to choose whether to pursue a case in juvenile or criminal court.

Each year in the United States, whether through judicial transfer, automatic waiver, or prosecutorial discretion, more than 200,000 individuals younger than age 18 are tried as adults (Griffin et al., 2011). As judicial discretion has been increasingly restricted by automatic waiver and prosecutorial discretion statutes, judicial waiver has become rarer. Indeed, the impetus behind mandatory waiver, statutory exclusion, and prosecutorial discretion statutes was to shift discretion from judges, who were perceived as soft on crime by modern reformers, to prosecutors and legislators, who were not assumed to hold this bias. Even now, despite some jurisprudential retreat from the get-tough policies of the late 20th century, very young juveniles can still be subjected to severe sentences, including (if they are convicted of homicide) life in prison without the possibility of parole.

DEVELOPMENTAL CONCERNS: CULPABILITY AND COMPETENCE

The processing and sentencing of juveniles as adults raises two different sets of questions about developmental differences between adolescents and adults. The first concerns juveniles' adjudicative and procedural competence, which in this chapter refers to juveniles' competence to act as a defendant in criminal court and to make decisions about legal matters. The second set of questions concerns juveniles' criminal culpability, which refers to the degree to which juveniles should be held to the same standards of criminal responsibility as adults.[3]

Although both sets of questions address psychological differences between adolescents and adults, discussions of juveniles' competence and culpability are not the same. This is because the psychological capacities relevant to competence and culpability are not identical. Adjudicative and procedural competence requires the ability to make informed decisions—for example, whether to submit to an interrogation by a law enforcement agent, testify in one's own defense, or accept the terms of a plea agreement. Therefore, with respect to trying juveniles as adults, the question concerning competence is whether minors are less capable than adults of making informed decisions and, if so, whether this deficiency warrants added or special protections. In this sense, the debate surrounding juveniles' adjudicative competence is similar to debates surrounding other aspects of minors' competence, such as their competence to consent to a medical procedure or participate in a research study.

In contrast, the debate surrounding adolescents' criminal culpability centers on the extent to which juveniles are responsible for their behavior, which therefore affects the degree to which they should be punished for their wrongdoing, in light of the principle of penal proportionality discussed earlier. Whereas questions about competence hinge on the juvenile's ability to make legal decisions after an alleged offense has occurred, questions about culpability revolve around the juvenile's mental and developmental states at the time of an offense.

Some psychological capacities are relevant to questions of both competence and culpability; others are not. For instance, the ability to anticipate the downstream consequences of one's actions might affect an adolescent's decision to participate in a potentially injurious act (and is therefore relevant to the juvenile's culpability for any resulting harm). It might also influence a juvenile's response to police interrogation (and is therefore relevant to assessing, among other things, whether a juvenile suspect can understand the implications of answering police officers' questions vs. remaining silent). However, the ability of a juvenile defendant to comprehend the difference between the goals of a prosecutor and those of a judge is relevant to his or her competence to stand trial, but has nothing to do with the youth's responsibility for the offense. It is possible, therefore, for a juvenile to be fully responsible for an offense but incompetent to stand trial in a criminal proceeding. Conversely, it is possible for a juvenile to be less than fully responsible for an offense but competent to stand trial.

Adjudicative and Procedural Competence

The constitutional requirements of due process for a criminal proceeding are only satisfied if the defendant is competent to stand trial. According to the criteria set forth in *Dusky v. United States* (1960) and *Godinez v. Moran* (1993), a competent defendant must be able to understand the charges levied against him or her, comprehend the nature of court proceedings, and meaningfully participate in his or her legal defense (Grisso, 2005; Scott & Grisso, 2005). The legal standard for adjudicative competence emerged originally out of debates over whether due process was violated when adults with mental illness or intellectual disability were compelled to stand trial. However, since the 1990s, discussions about competence have expanded to

[3]In this chapter, we focus primarily on adolescents' competence and culpability as defendants in criminal court because the relative immaturity of adolescents' psychosocial capacities in comparison to those of adults is particularly germane in that setting. However, we should note that questions of youths' competence and culpability are relevant in the juvenile court as well.

include whether developmental immaturity (apart from mental illness or disability) should be viewed as a factor that can compromise adjudicative competence (Grisso, 2005).

Prior analyses have delineated the specific psychological capacities that are required to meet the standards for adjudicative competence, often referred to as the *Dusky criteria* (Grisso, 2002). These capacities include the abilities to comprehend the nature and purpose of the legal proceedings; identify and communicate relevant information to counsel; reason about pertinent information in a logical fashion; and apply information to one's own situation in an accurate, rational manner. However, criminal trials represent only one stage of the processing of a criminal case, and many cases never reach that stage because they are resolved through plea bargains. Competence with respect to other phases of processing, such as police interrogations and plea negotiations, may require capacities that are distinct from those required to stand trial. Legal scholars have therefore made a distinction between adjudicative competence, which refers to competence to stand trial, and decisional competence, which refers to the ability to make informed choices in legal contexts other than the trial (e.g., police interrogation, plea bargaining) with an appreciation of the implications of various alternative courses of action (Bonnie, 1992). Despite the distinctions noted by scholars between these two types of competence, the Supreme Court held in *Godinez v. Moran* (1993) that the standard of competence for standing trial should be regarded as applying to other phases of legal processing as well (Redding & Frost, 2002).

Whether juveniles demonstrate competence in legal contexts is clearly relevant when they are processed as adults in criminal court because the *Dusky* criteria apply to all criminal defendants regardless of age. However, as procedures and punishments in the juvenile court have come to resemble those in the criminal court, questions of competence have become important considerations for youths tried as juveniles as well (Redding & Frost, 2002). Legal scholars disagree about whether the competence standards for juvenile court should be identical to or less stringent than those for criminal court, but the majority of states, citing the potentially serious outcomes of juvenile proceedings, have implemented some minimum standard of competence for juvenile court (Redding & Frost, 2002; Scott & Grisso, 2005).

Minors differ from adults in several ways that may make them less competent in an adjudicative context. At the most basic level, younger individuals have less life experience than adults and have therefore had less opportunity to acquire knowledge about the judicial process (e.g., the roles played by different participants). Also, children and adolescents have less advanced cognitive abilities than adults. The more complex the cognitive skill in question, the longer it takes to develop (see Kuhn, 2009, for a review of cognitive development in adolescence). For example, the ability to simply recall a previously seen face does not improve with age beyond ages 12 to 13, but the ability to remember several pieces of information and manipulate that information to solve a problem improves through ages 16 to 17 (Luciana, Conklin, Hooper, & Yarger, 2005). In a legal context, more advanced cognitive abilities could aid a youth in discriminating pertinent from irrelevant details of a past event, remembering the roles and motivations of the different participants in a legal proceeding, and choosing rationally among the alternative courses of action presented to him or her.

Children and adolescents also differ from adults in what psychologists term *psychosocial capacities*—abilities that require the coordination of cognition and affect and are relevant to adaptive decision making and social functioning. These capacities include impulse control, future orientation, and risk–reward calculation, as well as the ability to exercise these capacities (to control one's impulses, remain focused on a long-term goal, and appropriately weigh risks relative to rewards) while under stress, emotional arousal, or social influence. Development of these psychosocial capacities proceeds gradually and continues throughout adolescence (see, e.g., Cauffman et al., 2010; Figner, Mackinlay, Wilkening, & Weber, 2009; Galván & Rahdar, 2013; Gardner & Steinberg, 2005; Steinberg et al., 2008; Steinberg, Cauffman, Woolard, Graham, & Banich, 2009; Steinberg & Monahan, 2007).

For example, when asked to solve a difficult puzzle in the fewest moves possible, younger adolescents (ages 10–15) spent less time planning their moves before trying to solve it than did older adolescents and young adults (ages 16–17 and 18–21), who in turn spent less time than adults (ages 22–30), suggesting declining levels of impulsivity with increasing age (Steinberg et al., 2008). Also, when playing an exciting (emotionally arousing) version of a card game in which participants had the opportunity to earn money, adolescents took more risks and considered fewer pieces of available information than adults, whereas on a less arousing version of the game, adolescents performed comparably to adults, suggesting that adults' decision making is less compromised by emotional arousal than is adolescents' (Figner et al., 2009). With respect to adjudicative and decisional competence, age differences in these psychosocial capacities could result in juvenile suspects being more likely to provide a confession to police without fully considering other options or inadvisably refusing a plea bargain in favor of a chance at a not guilty verdict at trial (Grisso et al., 2003).

Immaturity in cognitive or psychosocial capacities may render juveniles less able than adults to make competent decisions throughout the adjudicative process, including whether to submit to an interrogation (and, if so, how to respond to questions); whether to provide information to one's defense attorney (and, if so, how completely to disclose important facts); whether to testify in one's defense; and whether to accept a plea bargain (Grisso et al., 2003). Juveniles may be able to make better choices in some cases by relying on the advice of adults. However, adults are not always present, do not always provide good advice, and do not necessarily have the same interests as the adolescent (e.g., a mother who is frustrated with her adolescent may want him or her to receive a stiff sentence).

The laboratory studies reviewed above shed light on the developmental course of cognitive and psychosocial capacities in general, rather than in a legal context. However, several studies have used the MacArthur Competence Assessment Tool–Criminal Adjudication to investigate age difference in performance on tasks designed to have direct relevance to legal proceedings (for reviews, see Grisso, 2005; Fogel, Schiffman, Mumley, Tillbrook, & Grisso, 2013). This tool assesses the functional abilities required for the multiple components of adjudicative competence. It includes scales that gauge the degree to which an individual demonstrates understanding (i.e., comprehension of courtroom procedures, the role of various personnel, and defendants' rights), reasoning (i.e., recognition of information relevant to a legal defense and the ability to make legal decisions rationally using available information), and appreciation (i.e., the ability to apply information to one's own situation and fully grasp the potential consequences of different legal decisions). For the most part, these studies, which compare the performance of children, adolescents, and adults on the MacArthur Competence Assessment Tool–Criminal Adjudication (especially if they used samples that are representative of those likely to be involved in the justice system), have found that individuals age 15 and younger demonstrate lower levels of competence than do those age 16 and older, who perform comparably to adults (Dreyer & Hart, 2008; Grisso et al., 2003; Pierce & Brodsky, 2002; Warren, Aaron, Ryan, Chauhan, & DuVal, 2003). The evidence to date strongly has suggested that youths younger than age 15 are at greater risk than older individuals of being incompetent to stand trial or to make important legal decisions that arise before or during criminal trial proceedings (e.g., whether to accept a proffered plea agreement).

As noted above, competence to stand trial is only one aspect of legal competence, which also includes the competence to make legal decisions outside the courtroom. The most frequently studied aspect of noncourtroom legal decision making concerns adolescents' responses to interrogation by law enforcement officials (Kassin et al., 2010), including individuals' ability to understand and make decisions about their Miranda rights, once in police custody: to remain silent rather than respond to police questioning and to have legal representation. In this area of inquiry, researchers have found age differences in individuals' (a) comprehension of *Miranda* warnings (e.g., Grisso, 1980; Redlich, Silverman, & Steiner, 2003), (b) decisions to waive the right to counsel (Viljoen, Klaver, & Roesch, 2005),

(c) decisions about whether to confess to a crime they have committed (Grisso et al., 2003; Redlich et al., 2003; Viljoen et al., 2005), and (d) susceptibility to making false confessions (Drizin & Leo, 2004; Kassin, 2008).

Generally speaking, these studies have indicated that adolescents—especially those younger than 16—are (comparable to adults) less likely to understand their rights, more likely to waive their right to remain silent, more likely to confess, and more likely to make a false confession. The outcomes of these studies have prompted many advocates to call for greater protections for juveniles during interrogations, including mandatory videotaping and the presence of an adult during questioning (Kassin et al., 2010).

The various skills required for competence in legal contexts are founded on different underlying psychological capacities, most of which undergo developmental change during adolescence. Age differences in certain aspects of adjudicative competence, such as the abilities to understand court proceedings and to reason about alternative options, parallel age differences in other domains of competence (e.g., granting informed consent) because such competencies draw on similar cognitive capacities (e.g., basic information processing and logical reasoning) that evolve in adolescence. In contrast, although psychosocial development also demonstrates prolonged maturation (beyond mid-adolescence), immaturity in psychosocial capacities (e.g., impulse control, risk aversion, resistance to peer pressure, and future orientation) may not always result in reduced competence to stand trial because immaturity in these capacities is less likely to impair adolescents' judgment under the particular conditions in which legal decisions are made. As argued elsewhere, immaturity with respect to psychosocial capacities may, however, be relevant to assessments of criminal responsibility (see Steinberg et al., 2009).

One aspect of decisional competence that drew judicial attention recently is the ability to appraise whether one is in police custody. Being able to make this determination has legal significance because, under U.S. criminal law, police officers are only required to provide a *Miranda* warning if the individual to be questioned is in custody. Statements made to law enforcement while in custody are inadmissible unless the individual has been notified of these rights and waived them. In contrast, if an individual is not in custody, anything said to a police officer can be used as evidence in a legal proceeding, even if the individual has not been informed of his or her rights. Therefore, an individual who is not in police custody but believes he is may provide a confession, not realizing (because he was not informed of his *Miranda* rights) that he does not have an obligation to respond to police questioning. The police officer may then claim that the confession was given freely and voluntarily, even though the suspect may not have perceived it to be so.

This situation was at the center of *J.D.B. v. North Carolina* (2011), a 2011 U.S. Supreme Court case involving a 13-year-old adolescent who was taken out of class and interrogated by two police officers in a middle school conference room in the presence of two school administrators. The boy was suspected of having committed two home break-ins and thefts. Initially, the boy denied having stolen the property. However, after further questioning by one of the police investigators and the urging of a school administrator to do the right thing, J.D.B. eventually admitted that he and a friend had indeed committed the burglaries. The boy had not been read his *Miranda* warning, however, nor was he informed, until after confessing, that he was free to leave the conference room. Nor had the boy been given the opportunity by the officers or the administrators to speak with his primary caregiver (his grandmother) before he was questioned.

At issue was whether J.D.B.'s confession was admissible (*J.D.B. v. North Carolina*, 2011). The boy's defense attorney moved that the results of the interrogation be suppressed on the grounds that the confession was involuntary because it was conducted in a custodial setting in which the police officers failed to notify J.D.B. of his rights. The trial court denied the motion, arguing that J.D.B. was not in custody and that his confession was therefore voluntary. Both the appellate court and the state supreme court concurred with the trial court.

The U.S. Supreme Court, however, disagreed with the lower courts. In prior cases, the Court had determined that, in deciding whether issuing a *Miranda* warning is necessary, a police officer is required to take into account all of the "circumstances surrounding the interrogation" (*Stansbury v. California*, 1994, p. 322), including any circumstance that "would have affected how a reasonable person" in the suspect's position "would perceive his or her freedom to leave" (*Stansbury v. California*, 1994, p. 325). In its decision, the Court declared that a police officer must consider the age of the individual being questioned when deciding whether to inform the interrogee of his or her rights: "A reasonable child subjected to police questioning will sometimes feel pressured to submit when a reasonable adult would feel free to go" (p. 2403). Also important, the Court noted that the relevant variable is the age of the interrogee, not the officer's judgment of that person's appraisal of the situation. "A child's age is far more than a chronological fact," the majority opinion noted in *J.D.B.*:

> It is a fact that . . . generates commonsense conclusions about behavior and perception. . . . Such conclusions apply broadly to children as a class. And, they are self-evident to anyone who was a child once himself, including any police officer or judge. (p. 2403)

Thus, in *J.D.B.*, the Court determined that—at least in the narrow context of police issuing *Miranda* warnings—juveniles' legal decision making should be held to a different standard than adults', purely on the basis of age. As such, the Court's finding could have implications for future cases that hinge on questions of juveniles' competence to make legal decisions (e.g., competence to waive *Miranda* rights and to stand trial; Guggenheim & Hertz, 2012; Kohlman, 2012).

Criminal Culpability

The Supreme Court's acknowledgment in *J.D.B. v. North Carolina* (2011) that juveniles and adults differ in ways that necessitate differential treatment under the law is the product of an evolution in the Court's jurisprudence that can be traced back through several recent cases, most of which concerned the death penalty. In these earlier cases, the central issue was whether juveniles should be held to the same standards of criminal responsibility as adults and, accordingly, subject to the same punishments. The constitutional question before the Court was whether a punishment that is permissible for adults violates the Eighth Amendment's prohibition against cruel and unusual punishment when imposed on a minor. Consequently, the justices considered, in these cases, whether a specific sentence was unusual when applied to a juvenile (e.g., if only a minority of states allowed or imposed the death penalty in cases involving minors), as well as whether the sentence was cruel, in the sense that it was disproportionate to the defendant's degree of responsibility for the criminal act. Our discussion here focuses mostly on the latter question, because the former is an empirical question beyond the scope of our discussion.

The Supreme Court has many times been asked to delineate the legal standing of minors with respect to various rights and responsibilities. In deciding such cases, the Court's typical approach has been to look to prior legal decisions, existing state law, and foundational legal principles. However, in the landmark case of *Roper v. Simmons* (2005), in which the Court abolished the juvenile death penalty, the Court departed from tradition by giving meaningful weight to scientific findings indicating that adolescents, as a group, are different from adults in legally relevant ways. Consideration of scientific evidence of developmental differences between juveniles and adults had been largely omitted from prior cases, including two other juvenile death penalty cases decided in the 1980s: *Thompson v. Oklahoma* (1988), which banned capital punishment for individuals younger than age 16, and *Stanford v. Kentucky* (1989), which affirmed 16 as the minimum age for eligibility for capital punishment. In *Thompson* and *Stanford*, the Court's decisions were based primarily on an analysis of whether the punishment was unusual, as evidenced by a national consensus opposing the execution of minors ages 15 and younger (*Thompson*) or 16 and older (*Stanford*). For evidence of consensus (or lack thereof), the Court looked to extant state statutes.

In another death penalty case that predated *Roper v. Simmons* (2005), the Court had raised the possibility that psychological immaturity might diminish a youth's culpability. In *Eddings v. Oklahoma* (1982), the Court, while not banning the juvenile death penalty outright, opined that the age of a criminal defendant, as well as his or her "mental and emotional development" (p. 116), should be taken into account as potential mitigating factors during sentencing. The decision in the case declared that "youth is more than a chronological fact. It is a time and condition of life when a person may be most susceptible to influence and to psychological damage" (p. 115). This assertion was consistent with the Court's statements about juveniles in the earlier case of *Bellotti v. Baird* (1979), which concerned minors' access to abortion. In this decision (which struck down a Massachusetts law requiring minors to obtain parental consent before seeking an abortion, but did not bar all such parental consent laws), the Court explicitly recognized the developmental immaturity of juveniles and, in particular, "their inability to make critical decisions in an informed, mature manner" (p. 634). Therefore, even before the Court abolished the juvenile death penalty in *Roper*, it had already acknowledged the existence of legally relevant developmental differences between adolescents and adults.

In these earlier cases, the Court made its determinations about juveniles' immature psychological capacities without reference to developmental science. It was therefore remarkable when *Roper v. Simmons* (2005) the Court exhibited a willingness to consider scientific evidence of developmental differences between adolescents and adults. Writing for the majority, Justice Anthony Kennedy pointed to developmental research findings (as well as common sense) in outlining three key differences between adolescents and adults that made it difficult to classify juveniles as among the worst of offenders: (a) their immaturity and an underdeveloped sense of responsibility, which compromised their decision-making ability (noting that this was the very reason that states limited many juveniles' rights); (b) their heightened susceptibility to external influence, including peer pressure, which gave them less control over their environment; and (c) their still-developing character. All three differences make adolescents less responsible for their behavior than adults and, accordingly, less culpable for their crimes.[4] The third difference also makes adolescents better candidates for rehabilitation.

Kennedy went on to reason that the same characteristics that render juveniles less culpable also reduce the chances that they will be deterred by the possibility of capital punishment, thereby undercutting one of the chief arguments of death penalty proponents (i.e., that it deters would-be criminals). In earlier Supreme Court cases, the differences between adolescents and adults were treated as a matter of common sense. In *Roper v. Simmons* (2005), by contrast, the Court supported its claims about the nature of young offenders by citing the multiple *amicus* briefs it had received (including one from the American Psychological Association) describing the scientific evidence for legally relevant differences between adolescents and adults. For example, with respect to juvenile offenders' tendencies toward ill-considered and impetuous behaviors, Justice Kennedy quoted the finding by Arnett (1992) that "adolescents are overrepresented statistically in virtually every category of reckless behavior" (*Roper v. Simmons*, 2005, p. 569). Regarding juvenile offenders' potential for reform, he quoted Steinberg and Scott's (2003) observation that

> for most teens, [risky or antisocial] behaviors are fleeting; they cease with maturity as individual identity becomes settled. Only a relatively small proportion of adolescents who experiment in risky or illegal activities develop entrenched patterns of problem behavior that persist into adulthood. (*Roper v. Simmons*, 2005, p. 570)

Thus, it is clear that the Court drew on behavioral research findings in considering its conclusions about the lesser culpability and greater potential for reform of juvenile relative to adult offenders.

[4]For the first two differences, it is fairly obvious how they mitigate culpability. With respect to juveniles' unformed character, it has been argued that this circumstance mitigates culpability because it makes it difficult to conclude that an act was attributable to a perpetrator's irredeemably "bad" character. This is relevant to calculations of culpability because if the perpetrator of a bad act has good character, it raises the possibility that the act was committed for reasons that were partly out of his or her control (Scott, 2013a).

However, the *Roper* Court was also presented with newer research findings from neuroscience pointing to differences between adolescents' and adults' brain development. For example, during the oral arguments, the following exchange transpired between one of the attorneys and Justice Stephen Breyer:

> *Justice Breyer:* Now, I thought that the—the scientific evidence simply corroborated something that every parent already knows, and if it's more than that, I would like to know what more.
>
> *Mr. Waxman:* Well, it's—I think it's—it's more than that in a couple of respects. It—it explains, corroborates, and validates what we sort of intuitively know, not just as parents but in adults that—that—who live in a world filled with adolescents. And—and the very fact that science—and I'm not just talking about social science here, but the important neurobiological science that has now shown that these adolescents are—their character is not hard-wired. (U.S. Supreme Court, 2004, p. 40)

It is less obvious how the introduction of this relatively new neurobiological evidence influenced the Court's reasoning. The Court's opinion in *Roper v. Simmons* (2005), although expressly referring to developmental science in support of the view that adolescents are different from adults, made no explicit reference to brain science—understandably, given that at the time *Roper* was decided, the field of adolescent brain science was still in its infancy. Still, it seems very likely that research on brain development influenced the Court's thinking, given how often this evidence was raised in various *amicus* briefs.

The theory that the Court's reasoning in *Roper v. Simmons* (2005) was heavily influenced by developmental science is supported by another interesting aspect of the decision—that it appeared to give much greater weight to the question of whether the juvenile death penalty was proportional (or cruel) than to whether it was unusual (in the Eighth Amendment sense; Scott, 2013b). At the time when *Roper* was decided, many states had laws allowing minors to be executed—the juvenile death penalty was uncommon in practice, but not at all statutorily unusual. Indeed, the plethora of state laws permitting the practice had been pivotal in the Court's earlier decision in *Stanford* to uphold the death penalty for 16- and 17-year-olds; it would have been possible for the Court, in *Roper*, to reach a similar conclusion about the absence of a national consensus against the practice. The greater consideration of the proportionality of the juvenile death penalty and lesser consideration of national consensus surrounding it in *Roper* (compared with *Stanford v. Kentucky*, 1989) could have been due to the Court's consideration of both the behavioral developmental findings and the newer findings related to adolescents' neurobiological immaturity. Indeed, in subsequent decisions that applied the logic of *Roper* to the question of life sentences without the possibility of parole (LWOP) for juvenile offenders, the Court's decisions made explicit reference to both developmental psychology and neuroscience.

The first of these LWOP cases was *Graham v. Florida* (2010), in which the Court prohibited the imposition of LWOP on juveniles convicted of crimes other than homicide. Referencing its ruling in *Roper v. Simmons* (2005), the majority opinion stated, "No recent data provide reason to reconsider the Court's observations in *Roper* about the nature of juveniles. As petitioner's amici point out, developments in psychology and brain science continue to show fundamental differences between juvenile and adult minds" (p. 2026). As in *Roper*, the Court's decision suggests that the justices weighed whether juvenile LWOP was cruel more heavily than whether it was unusual, because it was hardly uncommon (Scott, 2013b); at the time of the ruling, a large majority of states (37) permitted juveniles to be sentenced to LWOP for nonhomicide offenses. The Court's analysis was consistent with its post-*Roper* view of juveniles as less culpable and more redeemable than adults. The same rationale was applied in *Miller v. Alabama* (2012), in which the Court barred states from applying mandatory life sentences to juveniles, even in cases of homicide; it ruled that no juvenile could be sentenced to LWOP without an individualized consideration of whether the sentence was appropriate—the kind of case-by-case consideration that had previously been reserved for death sentences. In its decision in *Miller*, the Court went even further down the path of establishing definitively that children are different by opining that LWOP sentences for juveniles ought to be rare: "But given all we have said in *Roper*, *Graham*, and this decision about children's diminished culpability and heightened capacity for change, we think appropriate occasions for sentencing juveniles to this harshest possible penalty will be uncommon" (*Miller v. Alabama*, 2012, p. 2469).

In addition to the evidence emerging from behavioral research on age-related changes in psychosocial maturity (reviewed previously), the Court's new reluctance to subject juveniles to LWOP was explicitly informed by neuroscience findings that corroborated behavioral evidence of protracted development. A detailed review of the literature on adolescent brain development is beyond the scope of this chapter, but the overarching conclusion from this work is that individuals' brains show continued development throughout adolescence and into the 3rd decade of life. Moreover, the region of the brain that is last to reach maturity—the prefrontal cortex—is an area that plays a critical role in many of the psychological capacities that are most relevant to judgments of culpability (and to some aspects of adjudicative competence), such as modulation of emotions and behavioral impulses, gauging of risk and reward, and the ability to anticipate long-term consequences (see Steinberg, 2008, for a review). Not only is the developmental neuroscience consistent with the position that juveniles are less criminally responsible than adults, it is also consistent with the view that adolescents' brains—and therefore their behaviors—are more alterable than adults'. At any age, the neural wiring of a person's brain can change in response to experience, but there is sound evidence that adolescence is a period of heightened neuroplasticity, for better or for worse. In general, the neuroscientific evidence (like the behavioral evidence) supports the views expressed by the majority of the Supreme Court in *Roper*, *Graham*, and *Miller*, and by the youth advocates of the late 19th century who founded the juvenile court, that juveniles are different from adults and should be considered less culpable for their wrongdoing and more capable of reform. The characterization of adolescents as less responsible for their acts and more amenable to rehabilitation is not new, but the Court's use of science to buttress anecdotal evidence and personal experience is (Steinberg, 2013).

OUTCOMES FOR ADOLESCENT OFFENDERS

The putative capacity of young offenders to reform has served as a key part of the Supreme Court's justification for shielding juveniles from the harshest punishments and is a philosophical cornerstone of the juvenile justice system. It makes sense, then, to consider the evidence regarding whether young offenders are in fact capable of reform and, if so, whether involvement with the juvenile justice system encourages that process. For this latter consideration, there are two possible comparisons to be made: First, do youths processed in the juvenile system evidence more reform than youths processed in the criminal court? Second, do young offenders who do not come into contact with the justice system (or who experience a less intense intervention) evidence more reform than those who are caught and processed in the juvenile justice system? Obviously, for both of these comparisons, it is important to consider what researchers call *selection factors*—the possibility that youths channeled into the more severe settings (criminal instead of juvenile court or juvenile court instead of no justice system contact) possess characteristics or come from environments that render them less prone to reform in the first place. Several studies that take selection factors into account have been able to shed light on these questions. We review these below.

One of the main criticisms that dogged the juvenile justice system during the 20th century was that it seemed to have failed in its mission to rehabilitate young offenders. Studies consistently observed high rates of recidivism among youths processed in the juvenile court. Even today, many youths involved in the juvenile justice system reoffend—recent reports have estimated the recidivism rate at between 12% and 55% (Snyder & Sickmund, 2006). However, reoffending does not necessarily imply that a youth is incorrigible, nor does it mean that all services provided through the juvenile court are ineffective. In fact, a substantial proportion of adolescents report engaging in some criminal behavior while teenagers, but only a much smaller proportion persist in criminal behavior as adults (e.g., Moffitt, 1993; Piquero, 2008; Shulman, Steinberg, & Piquero, 2013). This has led some theorists to conjecture that engaging in delinquent behavior might be a normal part of adolescent development (Ellis et al., 2012; Moffitt, 1993), although some evidence has suggested that this may only be true for adolescents exposed to less-than-ideal environments (Roisman, Monahan, Campbell, Steinberg, & Cauffman, 2010). Even among individuals convicted of serious offenses as adolescents, researchers have observed high rates of desistance from crime by the early 20s (Monahan, Steinberg, Cauffman, & Mulvey, 2009). Perhaps the strongest evidence of the transitory nature of offending is the famous age–crime curve. Across time and place, it has commonly been observed that arrest rates rise during the adolescence years and fall during early adulthood (Hirschi & Gottfredson, 1983). Thus, the bulk of the evidence suggests that youths who offend during adolescence have a high probability of desisting from crime by the time they reach their early to mid-20s (Farrington, 1986; Jessor & Jessor, 1977; Piquero, Farrington, & Blumstein, 2003), which, in turn, suggests that the vast majority of adolescent offenders are capable of reform.

Whether involvement with the juvenile justice system promotes reform is a separate question, and one that has been fiercely debated. As noted previously, when the juvenile justice system came under fire in the years leading up to *In re Gault* (1967), one of the main criticisms was that it failed to rehabilitate delinquent youths. A widely cited article published in the mid-1970s provided fuel for the critics of the rehabilitative model, concluding that there was no evidence that the juvenile justice system's efforts at rehabilitation worked (Martinson, 1974). Today, disagreement persists as to whether the juvenile court is capable of carrying out its rehabilitative mission. One problem with evaluating the evidence relevant to this question is that the manner of handling juvenile cases and the types of dispositions imposed vary wildly from jurisdiction to jurisdiction (Snyder & Sickmund, 2006). A youth arrested for a common offense such as vandalism could have minimal contact with juvenile justice personnel—perhaps just a single meeting with a probation officer. Alternatively, this youth could receive a disposition from a judge involving detention, close supervision by a probation officer, or both. The effect of involvement with the juvenile court on subsequent offending behavior—and on other developmental outcomes—almost certainly depends on the nature of the youth's juvenile justice experience. The tremendous heterogeneity in this experience makes it hard to draw generalizations about its impact.

Nonetheless one robust pattern that has emerged from longitudinal research on adolescent offenders is that minors whose cases are transferred from juvenile to criminal court tend to have worse outcomes than comparable youths whose cases remain in juvenile court. For example, one study of youths charged with burglary or robbery found that, for those charged with robbery, waiver to criminal court (relative to retention in juvenile court) was associated with higher rates of rearrest and reincarceration (Fagan, 1996). Another set of studies, in which youths processed in criminal or juvenile court were matched on offense and demographic characteristics, found that in five of seven offense categories, criminal court youths were more likely than their juvenile court counterparts to reoffend and be rearrested (Bishop, Frazier, Lanza-Kaduce, & White, 1998; Johnson, Lanza-Kaduce, & Woolard, 2011; Winner, Lanza-Kaduce, Bishop, & Frazier, 1997). Further analysis of follow-up data on these youths indicated that part of the difference between criminal court and juvenile court youths' subsequent recidivism could be explained by juvenile court youths benefiting from a system of graduated sanctions (wherein juveniles receive relatively light sanctions initially, which become harsher if they continue to transgress) that is not available to youths processed in criminal court (Johnson et al., 2011). Beyond the differences in recidivism, another advantage of the juvenile justice system over the adult system is that the former is better positioned to provide developmentally appropriate services, such as therapy and education, which can improve youths' chances of success in other domains of life.

Within the juvenile justice system, many different approaches have been attempted to reform young offenders. Several, such as juvenile boot camps, electronic monitoring, and Scared Straight programs (which expose youths to adult prisoners in an effort to frighten the youths) have been found to have no beneficial and even some detrimental effects on recidivism (MacKenzie & Armstrong, 2004; Petrosino, Turpin-Petrosino, & Finckenauer, 2000; Renzema & Mayo-Wilson, 2005). However, it does not appear to be the case that, as critics once claimed, nothing works. On the contrary, many types of interventions have been found in meta-analytic studies (studies that analyze the effects observed in many individual treatment studies) to be associated with reduced recidivism (e.g., Lipsey & Wilson, 1998). The most promising intervention programs appear to be those that identify youths' criminogenic needs—"malleable risk factors predictive of subsequent criminal conduct such as antisocial attitudes and peer associations, self-control and self-management skills, drug dependencies" (Lipsey, 2009, p. 126)—and respond to these needs with therapeutic services and treatment plans suited to remediating them (Andrews & Bonta, 2006; Andrews et al., 1990; Dowden & Andrews, 1999, 2000; Gendreau, Smith, & French, 2006; Lipsey, 2009; see also Part VII, this handbook).

However, although juvenile court dispositions may reduce the risk of recidivism relative to criminal court sanctions, and some juvenile justice interventions are associated with better outcomes than others, it is not clear that processing a youth in juvenile court is rehabilitative in an absolute sense. In fact, scholars have observed that juvenile court involvement—realitive to no court involvement—might have a negative impact on adolescents' behavior, and they have proffered multiple theories as to why this might be. One theory points to the possibility that adolescents who become involved with the court will come to view themselves as criminals and behave (and be treated) accordingly (labeling theory; H. Becker, 1963; Lemert, 1951; Tannenbaum, 1938). Another theory posits that involvement with the court results in greater contact with other delinquent youths, which leads to youths socializing one another to be more antisocial (deviancy training; Dodge, Dishion, & Lansford, 2006). Beyond the question of whether involvement with the juvenile court makes youth more criminal, it almost certainly has the potential to disrupt youths' lives in ways that reduce their chances for a successful transition to adulthood. For example, juvenile court processing is associated with increased odds of failing to complete high school, which in turn sets off a cascade of consequences adverse to positive life outcomes (e.g., more time spent with other dropouts, difficulty obtaining gainful employment; Sweeten, 2006). Also, the greater supervision incurred by involvement with the court can culminate in additional arrests for minor (even noncriminal) transgressions that violate the terms of probation, thereby leading to more intensive sanctions and even closer supervision—a cycle that can lead to severe sanctions even when the original offense was relatively minor.

Some studies have used experimental designs to test whether juvenile court processing has a beneficial or detrimental effect on recidivism. In these studies, juveniles who are arrested for an offense are randomly assigned to either processing as usual (in the juvenile justice system) or to some kind of diversion program and then followed for a period of time to track reoffending. A meta-analysis of 29 such studies concluded that juvenile court processing had no benefit relative to diversion, and several of the analyses suggested that juvenile court involvement in fact increased recidivism (Petrosino, Turpin-Petrosino, & Guckenburg, 2010).

In two nonexperimental studies that followed samples of male, low socioeconomic status, Canadian adolescents into adulthood, statistical control and matching procedures were used to evaluate the effects of (a) different intensities of juvenile justice involvement and (b) any versus no juvenile court involvement on adult crime (Gatti, Tremblay, & Vitaro, 2009; Petitclerc, Gatti, Vitaro, & Tremblay, 2013). After matching youths on a range of relevant characteristics, including their self-reported offending, these studies found that more intense juvenile court sanctions were associated with greater odds of adult crime (based on official records) and that any contact with the court (vs. none) after arrest as an adolescent was associated with increased odds of adult crime (by a factor of seven in Gatti et al. and a factor of three in Peticlerc et al.). Overall, these studies suggest that processing youths in juvenile court increases the chances of adult criminal behavior.

An interesting question that these studies do not address is whether exposure to any legal processing at all (arrest, probation officer contact, diversion programs) disrupts the tendency of most adolescents to desist from delinquent behavior on their own. One recent analysis of data from a national longitudinal study found that high school students (younger than age 16) who were arrested—even if they were not subsequently processed in court—were much more likely (nearly double the odds) than their nonarrested counterparts to drop out of high school (Sweeten, 2006). (This analysis adjusted for risk factors associated with arrest.) The odds of dropping out were even higher for those processed in court. These findings have important implications for continued offending, because dropping out of school is a major risk factor for recidivism. It is possible, therefore, that adolescent offenders who are arrested—regardless of what happens subsequently—are likely to be slower to desist from criminal behavior than their counterparts whose delinquent acts are undetected or do not lead to an arrest. We are aware of no published study that addresses this question directly. However, if researchers were to find that nonintervention is the best response to adolescent offending, it is unclear how this would influence policy. One option would be to attempt to approximate nonintervention by instructing police officers not to arrest adolescent offenders unless they pose a clear threat to public safety. However, even though the pendulum of public opinion has recently swung away from favoring harsh punishments for juvenile offenders (Nagin, Piquero, Scott, & Steinberg, 2006; Piquero, Cullen, Unnever, Piquero, & Gordon, 2010), it is unlikely that policymakers would be willing to officially endorse a protocol of nonintervention. After all, even if the public and lawmakers embrace the rehabilitative ideal, there remains a strong moral impulse to punish and hold youths responsible for their bad deeds. Critics would complain that a policy of nonintervention, even if it has the consequence of enhancing public safety, sends a message to adolescents that there are no repercussions for their bad deeds. Yet, because of the wide berth given to police in making determinations about whether to arrest a minor caught breaking the law, there may already exist an unregulated policy of nonintervention to juvenile offending under certain circumstances (e.g., if the adolescent behaves respectfully toward the police officer; Allen, 2005) and in certain communities (e.g., suburban neighborhoods; Schulenberg, 2003). Unfortunately, unregulated, discretionary responding to adolescent delinquency provides fertile ground for unequal treatment of youths from different backgrounds and neighborhoods.

Whereas many studies have surveyed the long-term consequences of varying degrees of juvenile justice contact with respect to recidivism (e.g., Gatti et al., 2009; Petitclerc et al., 2013) and, to a lesser extent, educational and occupational outcomes (Bernburg & Krohn, 2003; De Li, 1999; Hirschfield, 2009; Sweeten, 2006), scant research has considered the effects of juvenile justice involvement on psychological development and mental health. Given that adolescence is a critical developmental period for many psychological capacities and social accomplishments—e.g., the formation and deepening of intimate relationships, mental health, identity formation, and various aspects of psychosocial maturity—research is needed to better understand how juvenile justice interventions affect these aspects of youths' lives. Life events (such as incarceration) that disrupt normative development in one or more of these arenas may have significant long-term consequences for adolescents. Indeed, early work in this area has suggested that certain types of legal sanctions can impede the development of psychosocial maturity (Dmitrieva, Monahan, Cauffman, & Steinberg, 2012). Further research on this topic is needed to more fully inform juvenile justice policy.

CONCLUSION

A central question in debates about legal responses to juvenile offending is whether young offenders are children—vulnerable, impulsive, and immature—or adults—autonomous, accountable, and set in their ways. This is a question that lacks a simple answer. At the turn of the 20th century, the prevailing view was that juvenile offenders were children. By the later decades of the century, the pendulum had swung to the other extreme, and a legislative agenda to treat juvenile offenders more like adults followed. At present, thanks to a number of factors, including a drop in juvenile crime and the Supreme Court's attention to developmental science, there has been some retreat from the hardline policies of the 1990s. In the trio of recent cases dealing with the sentencing of youths convicted of the most heinous kinds of crimes, the Supreme Court took the position that juvenile offenders are not adults (*Graham v. Florida*, 2010; *Miller v. Alabama*, 2012; *Roper v. Simmons*, 2005). This is a position that brings American jurisprudence more in line with that of other industrialized nations and more in line with developmental science. Those who study the transition from childhood to adulthood recognize that it is best characterized as gradual, uneven, and dramatically variable from one person to another. There is no one age at which children become adults. Nor is maturity easy to assess. A youth who appears mature and self-possessed under benign circumstances may, compared with the average adult, be more vulnerable to antisocial influence and less capable of self-control in other contexts (Steinberg, 2009).

The degree to which this understanding of human development bears on the question of how to punish to juvenile offenders will vary from one person to another. Those who argue (as Supreme Court Justice Antonin Scalia has) that adolescent offenders know the difference between right and wrong are certainly correct. The capacity to make this distinction develops well before adolescence. Thus, among those for whom the ability to know right from wrong serves as the sole benchmark for judging culpability, arguments rooted in the idea that reduced self-control diminishes criminal responsibility will carry no weight. If, however, one is open to idea that one's criminal responsibility for an act is proportional to one's ability to control one's behavior, then scientific findings about adolescent development become relevant to the evaluation of culpability and to decisions about how to punish younger individuals for their misdeeds. As recognized by the majority of the Supreme Court in *Roper v. Simmons* (2005), *Graham v. Florida* (2010), and *Miller v. Alabama* (2012), research examining developmental change in psychosocial capacities and in the neural mechanisms underlying them provides support for the claim that juvenile offenders, as a class, should be considered less criminally responsible than adults.

Developmental science is relevant to other aspects of the legal response to adolescent offending as well. It tells us, for example, that adolescents (especially those younger than age 16) are likely to lack the cognitive and psychosocial capacities required to participate competently in their own defense or to exercise sound judgment in the context of police questioning or plea bargaining. Scientific findings also tell us that developmental differences between juveniles and adults should be taken into account in determining what sorts of sanctions and programs should be administered to juveniles who are found guilty or adjudicated delinquent. Programs that avoid exposing young offenders to antisocial influences and that help youths to set and pursue adaptive goals are the ones most likely to serve the public good.

At the turn of the 20th century, the lesser blameworthiness of young offenders and their greater capacity for reform were proffered by those who lobbied for the establishment of the juvenile court as a matter of faith or common sense. One hundred years later, the intuitions of those youth advocates are being bolstered by developmental science. We know now that, compared with adults, adolescents are indeed, as Justice Kennedy asserted in *Roper v. Simmons* (2005), more impetuous, more susceptible to outside influences, less formed in their character, and less likely to be deterred by harsh penalties. And although there remains resistance to reappraising youths convicted of terrible crimes as individuals with the potential to reform (Eckholm, 2014), many states have begun to adjust their policies and practices in ways that reflect a scientifically informed conceptualization of adolescence. A growing number of states are scaling back their automatic waiver statutes, disallowing juveniles to waive their rights to counsel, implementing evidence-based rehabilitative programs for adjudicated youths, and diverting nonviolent offenders (and saved monies) into community-based programs (Brown, 2012). These sorts of reforms, which almost certainly lead to better outcomes for youthful offenders, their communities, and taxpayers, underscore the promise of basing juvenile justice policy on sound developmental science.

References

Allen, T. T. (2005). Taking a juvenile into custody: Situational factors that influence police officers' decisions. *Journal of Sociology and Social Welfare, 32*, 121–129.

Andrews, D. A., & Bonta, J. (2006). *The psychology of criminal conduct* (4th ed.). Newark, NJ: LexisNexis/Matthew Bender.

Andrews, D. A., Zinger, I., Hoge, R. D., Bonta, J., Gendreau, P., & Cullen, F. T. (1990). Does correctional treatment work? A clinically relevant and psychologically informed meta-analysis. *Criminology, 28*, 369–404. http://dx.doi.org/10.1111/j.1745-9125.1990.tb01330.x

Arnett, J. (1992). Reckless behavior in adolescence: A developmental perspective. *Developmental Review, 12*, 339–373. http://dx.doi.org/10.1016/0273-2297(92)90013-R

Becker, E. (2001, February 9). As ex-theorist on young "superpredators," Bush aide has regrets. *New York Times*. Retrieved from http://www.nytimes.com/2001/02/09/us/as-ex-theorist-on-young-superpredators-bush-aide-has-regrets.html

Becker, H. (1963). *Outsiders: Studies in the sociology of deviance*. New York, NY: Free Press.

Bellotti v. Baird, 443 U.S. 622 (1979).

Bennett, W. J., DiIulio, J. J., & Walters, J. P. (1996). *Body count: Moral poverty and how to win America's war against crime and drugs*. New York, NY: Simon & Schuster.

Bernburg, J. G., & Krohn, M. D. (2003). Labeling, life chances, and adult crime: The direct and indirect effects of official intervention in adolescence on crime in early adulthood. *Criminology, 41*, 1287–1318. http://dx.doi.org/10.1111/j.1745-9125.2003.tb01020.x

Bishop, D. M., Frazier, C. E., Lanza-Kaduce, L., & White, H. G. (1998). *Juvenile transfers to criminal court study: Phase I final report*. Washington, DC: Office of Juvenile Justice and Delinquency Prevention.

Bonnie, R. J. (1992). The competence of criminal defendants: A theoretical reformulation. *Behavioral Sciences and the Law, 10*, 291–316. http://dx.doi.org/10.1002/bsl.2370100303

Brown, S. A. (2012). *Trends in juvenile justice state legislation 2001–2011*. Washington, DC: National Conference of State Legislatures.

Cauffman, E., Shulman, E. P., Steinberg, L., Claus, E., Banich, M. T., Graham, S., & Woolard, J. (2010). Age differences in affective decision making as indexed by performance on the Iowa Gambling Task. *Developmental Psychology, 46*, 193–207. http://dx.doi.org/10.1037/a0016128

De Li, S. (1999). Legal sanctions and youths' status achievement: A longitudinal study. *Justice Quarterly, 16*, 377–401. http://dx.doi.org/10.1080/07418829900094181

Denver Public Library. (2011). *Manuscript Monday: Benjamin Lindsey* (Western History and Genealogy Blog). Retrieved from http://history.denverlibrary.org/blog/content/manuscript-monday-benjamin-lindsey

DiIulio, J. J. (1995, December 15). Moral poverty. *Chicago Tribune*. Retrieved from http://articles.chicagotribune.com/1995-12-15/news/9512150046_1_crime-talking-bomb

Dmitrieva, J., Monahan, K. C., Cauffman, E., & Steinberg, L. (2012). Arrested development: The effects of incarceration on the development of psychosocial maturity. *Development and Psychopathology, 24*, 1073–1090. http://dx.doi.org/10.1017/S0954579412000545

Dodge, K. A., Dishion, T. J., & Lansford, J. E. (2006). Deviant peer influences in intervention and public policy for youth. *Social Policy Report, 20*, 3–19.

Dowden, C., & Andrews, D. A. (1999). What works for female offenders: A meta-analytic review. *Crime and Delinquency, 45*, 438–452. http://dx.doi.org/10.1177/0011128799045004002

Dowden, C., & Andrews, D. A. (2000). Effective correctional treatment and violent reoffending: A meta-analysis. *Canadian Journal of Criminology, 42*, 449–467.

Dreyer, C. S., & Hart, K. J. (2008). Competence to stand trial-related skills in a sample of urban youth. *American Journal of Forensic Psychology, 26*, 5–23.

Drizin, S. A., & Leo, R. A. (2004). The problem of false confessions in the post-DNA world. *North Carolina Law Review, 82*, 891–1007.

Dusky v. United States, 362 U.S. 402 (1960).

Eckholm, E. (2014, January 20). Juveniles facing lifelong terms despite rulings. *New York Times*. Retrieved from http://www.nytimes.com/2014/01/20/us/juveniles-facing-lifelong-terms-despite-rulings.html

Eddings v. Oklahoma, 455 U.S. 104 (1982).

Ellis, B. J., Del Giudice, M., Dishion, T. J., Figueredo, A. J., Gray, P., Griskevicius, V., . . . Wilson, D. S. (2012). The evolutionary basis of risky adolescent behavior: Implications for science, policy, and practice. *Developmental Psychology*, *48*, 598–623. http://dx.doi.org/10.1037/a0026220

Fagan, J. (1996). The comparative advantages of juvenile versus criminal court sanction on recidivism among adolescent felony offenders. *Law and Policy*, *18*, 77–114. http://dx.doi.org/10.1111/j.1467-9930.1996.tb00165.x

Farrington, D. P. (1986). Age and crime. *Crime and Justice*, *7*, 189–250. http://dx.doi.org/10.1086/449114

Feld, B. C. (2007a). Century of juvenile justice: A work in progress or a revolution that failed? *Northern Kentucky Law Review*, *34*, 189–256.

Feld, B. C. (2007b). Unmitigated punishment: Adolescent criminal responsibility and LWOP sentences. *Journal of Law and Family Studies*, *10*, 11–82.

Figner, B., Mackinlay, R. J., Wilkening, F., & Weber, E. U. (2009). Affective and deliberative processes in risky choice: Age differences in risk taking in the Columbia Card Task. *Journal of Experimental Psychology: Learning, Memory, and Cognition*, *35*, 709–730. http://dx.doi.org/10.1037/a0014983

Fogel, M. H., Schiffman, W., Mumley, D., Tillbrook, C., & Grisso, T. (2013). Ten year research update (2001–2010): Evaluations for competence to stand trial (adjudicative competence). *Behavioral Sciences and the Law*, *31*, 165–191. http://dx.doi.org/10.1002/bsl.2051

Galván, A., & Rahdar, A. (2013). The neurobiological effects of stress on adolescent decision making. *Neuroscience*, *249*, 223–231. http://dx.doi.org/10.1016/j.neuroscience.2012.09.074

Gardner, M., & Steinberg, L. (2005). Peer influence on risk taking, risk preference, and risky decision making in adolescence and adulthood: An experimental study. *Developmental Psychology*, *41*, 625–635. http://dx.doi.org/10.1037/0012-1649.41.4.625

Gatti, U., Tremblay, R. E., & Vitaro, F. (2009). Iatrogenic effect of juvenile justice. *Journal of Child Psychology and Psychiatry, and Allied Disciplines*, *50*, 991–998. http://dx.doi.org/10.1111/j.1469-7610.2008.02057.x

Gendreau, P., Smith, P., & French, S. A. (2006). The theory of effective correctional intervention: Empirical status and future directions. In F. Cullen, J. Wright, & K. Blevins (Eds.), *Advances in criminological theory: Vol. 15. Taking stock: The status of criminological theory* (pp. 419–446). New Brunswick, NJ: Transaction.

Godinez v. Moran, 509 U.S. 389 (1993).

Graham v. Florida, 130 S. Ct. 2011, 560 U.S. 48 (2010).

Gray, J. (1997, May 9). House passes bill to combat juvenile crime. *New York Times*. Retrieved from http://www.nytimes.com/1997/05/09/us/house-passes-bill-to-combat-juvenile-crime.html

Griffin, P. (2008). *Different from adults: An updated analysis of juvenile transfer with recommendations for reform*. Pittsburgh, PA: National Center for Juvenile Justice.

Griffin, P., Addie, S., Adams, B., & Firestine, K. (2011). *Trying juveniles as adults: An analysis of state transfer laws and reporting*. Washington, DC: U.S. Department of Justice, Office of Justice Programs, Office of Juvenile Justice and Delinquency Prevention.

Grisso, T. (1980). Juveniles' capacities to waive Miranda rights: An empirical analysis. *California Law Review*, *68*, 1134–1166. http://dx.doi.org/10.2307/3480263

Grisso, T. (2002). Using what we know about child maltreatment and delinquency. *Children's Services: Social Policy, Research, and Practice*, *5*, 299–305. http://dx.doi.org/10.1207/S15326918CS0504_6

Grisso, T. (2005). *Evaluating juveniles' adjudicative competence: A guide for clinical practice*. Sarasota, FL: Professional Resource Press/Professional Resource Exchange.

Grisso, T., Steinberg, L., Woolard, J., Cauffman, E., Scott, E., Graham, S., . . . Schwartz, R. (2003). Juveniles' competence to stand trial: A comparison of adolescents' and adults' capacities as trial defendants. *Law and Human Behavior*, *27*, 333–363. http://dx.doi.org/10.1023/A:1024065015717

Guggenheim, M., & Hertz, R. (2012). JDB and the maturing of juvenile confession suppression law. *Washington University Journal of Law and Policy*, *38*, 109–176.

Hirschfield, P. (2009). Another way out: The impact of juvenile arrests on high school dropout. *Sociology of Education*, *82*, 368–393. http://dx.doi.org/10.1177/003804070908200404

Hirschi, T., & Gottfredson, M. (1983). Age and the explanation of crime. *American Journal of Sociology*, *89*, 552–584. http://dx.doi.org/10.1086/227905

In re Gault, 387 U.S. 1 (1967).

In re Winship, 397 U.S. 358 (1970).

J.D.B. v. North Carolina, 131 S. Ct. 2394 (2011).

Jessor, R., & Jessor, S. L. (1977). *Problem behavior and psychosocial development: A longitudinal study of youth*. New York, NY: Academic Press.

Johnson, K., Lanza-Kaduce, L., & Woolard, J. (2011). Disregarding graduated treatment: Why transfer aggravates recidivism. *Crime and Delinquency*, *57*, 756–777. http://dx.doi.org/10.1177/0011128708328867

Kassin, S. M. (2008). The psychology of confessions. *Annual Review of Law and Social Science*, *4*, 193–217. http://dx.doi.org/10.1146/annurev.lawsocsci.4.110707.172410

Kassin, S. M., Drizin, S. A., Grisso, T., Gudjonsson, G. H., Leo, R. A., & Redlich, A. D. (2010). Police-induced confessions: Risk factors and recommendations. *Law and Human Behavior*, *34*, 3–38. http://dx.doi.org/10.1007/s10979-009-9188-6

Kent v. United States, 383 U.S. 541 (1966).

Kohlman, A. K. (2012). Kids waive the darndest constitutional rights: The impact of *J.D.B. v. North Carolina* on juvenile interrogation. *American Criminal Law Review*, *49*, 1623–1645.

Kuhn, D. (2009). *Adolescent thinking*. In R. Lerner & L. Steinberg (Eds.), *Handbook of adolescent psychology* (3rd ed., pp. 152–186). Hoboken, NJ: Wiley.

Lemert, E. (1951). *Social pathology*. New York, NY: McGraw-Hill.

Lipsey, M. (2009). The primary factors that characterize effective interventions with juvenile offenders: A meta-analytic review. *Victims and Offenders*, *4*, 124–147.

Lipsey, M. W., & Wilson, D. B. (1998). Effective intervention for serious and violent juvenile offenders: Synthesis of research. In R. Loeber & D. P. Farrington (Eds.), *Serious and violent juvenile offenders* (pp. 313–345). Thousand Oaks, CA: Sage.

Luciana, M., Conklin, H. M., Hooper, C. J., & Yarger, R. S. (2005). The development of nonverbal working memory and executive control processes in adolescents. *Child Development*, *76*, 697–712. http://dx.doi.org/10.1111/j.1467-8624.2005.00872.x

Mack, J. W. (1909). The juvenile court. *Harvard Law Review*, *23*, 104–122. http://dx.doi.org/10.2307/1325042

MacKenzie, D. L., & Armstrong, G. S. (Eds.). (2004). *Correctional boot camps: Military basic training or a model for corrections?* Thousand Oaks, CA: Sage.

Mansnerus, L. (1993, April 4). Kids of the 90's: A bolder breed. *New York Times*. Retrieved from http://www.nytimes.com/1993/04/04/education/kids-of-the-90-s-a-bolder-breed.html

Martinson, R. (1974). What works? Questions and answers about prison reform. *Public Interest*, *35*, 22–54.

McKeiver v. Pennsylvania, 403 U.S. 528 (1971).

Miller v. Alabama, 132 S. Ct. 2455, 567 U.S. (2012).

Moffitt, T. E. (1993). Adolescence-limited and life-course-persistent antisocial behavior: A developmental taxonomy. *Psychological Review*, *100*, 674–701. http://dx.doi.org/10.1037/0033-295X.100.4.674

Monahan, K. C., Steinberg, L., Cauffman, E., & Mulvey, E. P. (2009). Trajectories of antisocial behavior and psychosocial maturity from adolescence to young adulthood. *Developmental Psychology*, *45*, 1654–1668. http://dx.doi.org/10.1037/a0015862

Nagin, D. S., Piquero, A., Scott, E., & Steinberg, L. (2006). Public preferences for rehabilitation versus incarceration of juvenile offenders: Evidence from a contingent valuation survey. *Criminology and Public Policy*, *5*, 627–651. http://dx.doi.org/10.1111/j.1745-9133.2006.00406.x

Office of Juvenile Justice and Delinquency Prevention. (2012). *OJJDP statistical briefing book*. Retrieved from http://www.ojjdp.gov/ojstatbb/structure_process/qa04105.asp

Petitclerc, A., Gatti, U., Vitaro, F., & Tremblay, R. E. (2013). Effects of juvenile court exposure on crime in young adulthood. *Journal of Child Psychology and Psychiatry, and Allied Disciplines*, *54*, 291–297. http://dx.doi.org/10.1111/j.1469-7610.2012.02616.x

Petrosino, A., Turpin-Petrosino, C., & Finckenauer, J. O. (2000). Well–meaning programs can have harmful effects! Lessons from experiments of programs such as Scared Straight. *Crime and Delinquency*, *46*, 354–379. http://dx.doi.org/10.1177/0011128700046003006

Petrosino, A., Turpin-Petrosino, C., & Guckenburg, S. (2010). Formal system processing of juveniles: Effects on delinquency. *Campbell Systematic Reviews*, *1*, 1–88.

Pierce, C. S., & Brodsky, S. L. (2002). Trust and understanding in the attorney-juvenile relationship. *Behavioral Sciences and the Law*, *20*, 89–107. http://dx.doi.org/10.1002/bsl.478

Piquero, A. R. (2008). Taking stock of developmental trajectories of criminal activity over the life course. In A. M. Liberman (Ed.), *The long view of crime: A synthesis of longitudinal research* (pp. 23–78). http://dx.doi.org/10.1007/978-0-387-71165-2_2

Piquero, A. R., Cullen, F. T., Unnever, J. D., Piquero, N. L., & Gordon, J. A. (2010). Never too late: Public optimism about juvenile rehabilitation. *Punishment and Society*, *12*, 187–207. http://dx.doi.org/10.1177/1462474509357379

Piquero, A. R., Farrington, D. P., & Blumstein, A. (2003). The criminal career paradigm. *Crime and Justice*, *30*, 359–506.

Redding, R. E., & Frost, L. E. (2002). Adjudicative competence in the modern juvenile court. *Virginia Journal of Social Policy and the Law*, *9*, 353–410.

Redlich, A. D., Silverman, M., & Steiner, H. (2003). Pre-adjudicative and adjudicative competence in juveniles and young adults. *Behavioral Sciences and the Law*, *21*, 393–410. http://dx.doi.org/10.1002/bsl.543

Regnery, A. S. (1985). Getting away with murder: Why the juvenile justice system needs an overhaul. *Policy Review*, *34*, 65–68.

Renzema, M., & Mayo-Wilson, E. (2005). Can electronic monitoring reduce crime for moderate to high-risk offenders? *Journal of Experimental Criminology*, *1*, 215–237. http://dx.doi.org/10.1007/s11292-005-1615-1

Roisman, G. I., Monahan, K. C., Campbell, S. B., Steinberg, L., & Cauffman, E.; National Institute of Child Health and Human Development Early Child Care Research Network. (2010). Is adolescence-onset antisocial behavior developmentally normative? *Development and Psychopathology*, *22*, 295–311. http://dx.doi.org/10.1017/S0954579410000076

Roper v. Simmons, 543 U.S. 551 (2005).

Schulenberg, J. L. (2003). The social context of police discretion with young offenders: An ecological analysis. *Canadian Journal of Criminology and Criminal Justice*, *45*, 127–158. http://dx.doi.org/10.3138/cjccj.45.2.127

Scott, E., & Grisso, T. (2005). Developmental incompetence, due process, and juvenile justice policy. *North Carolina Law Review*, *83*, 101–147.

Scott, E. S. (2013a). Children are different: Constitutional values and justice policy. *Ohio State Journal of Criminal Law*, *11*, 71–105.

Scott, E. S. (2013b). *Miller vs. Alabama* and the (past and) future of juvenile crime regulation. *Minnesota Journal of Law and Inequality*, *31*, 535–558.

Shulman, E. P., Steinberg, L. D., & Piquero, A. R. (2013). The age-crime curve in adolescence and early adulthood is not due to age differences in economic status. *Journal of Youth and Adolescence*, *42*, 848–860. http://dx.doi.org/10.1007/s10964-013-9950-4

Snyder, H. N., & Sickmund, M. (2006). *Juvenile offenders and victims: 2006 national report*. Washington, DC: U.S. Department of Justice, Office of Justice Programs, Office of Juvenile Justice and Delinquency Prevention.

Stanford v. Kentucky, 492 U.S. 361 (1989).

Stansbury v. California, 511 U.S. 318 (1994).

Steinberg, L. (2008). A social neuroscience perspective on adolescent risk-taking. *Developmental Review*, *28*, 78–106. http://dx.doi.org/10.1016/j.dr.2007.08.002

Steinberg, L. (2009). Should the science of adolescent brain development inform public policy? *American Psychologist*, *64*, 739–750. http://dx.doi.org/10.1037/0003-066X.64.8.739

Steinberg, L. (2013). The influence of neuroscience on U.S. Supreme Court decisions about adolescents' criminal culpability. *Nature Reviews Neuroscience*, *14*, 513–518. http://dx.doi.org/10.1038/nrn3509

Steinberg, L., Albert, D., Cauffman, E., Banich, M., Graham, S., & Woolard, J. (2008). Age differences in sensation seeking and impulsivity as indexed by behavior and self-report: Evidence for a dual systems model. *Developmental Psychology*, *44*, 1764–1778. http://dx.doi.org/10.1037/a0012955

Steinberg, L., Cauffman, E., Woolard, J., Graham, S., & Banich, M. (2009). Are adolescents less mature than adults? Minors' access to abortion, the juvenile death penalty, and the alleged APA "flip-flop." *American Psychologist*, *64*, 583–594. http://dx.doi.org/10.1037/a0014763

Steinberg, L., & Monahan, K. C. (2007). Age differences in resistance to peer influence. *Developmental Psychology*, *43*, 1531–1543. http://dx.doi.org/10.1037/0012-1649.43.6.1531

Steinberg, L., & Scott, E. S. (2003). Less guilty by reason of adolescence: Developmental immaturity, diminished responsibility, and the juvenile death penalty. *American Psychologist*, *58*, 1009–1018. http://dx.doi.org/10.1037/0003-066X.58.12.1009

Sweeten, G. (2006). Who will graduate? Disruption of high school education by arrest and court involvement. *Justice Quarterly*, *23*, 462–480. http://dx.doi.org/10.1080/07418820600985313

Tannenbaum, F. (1938). *Crime and community*. Boston, MA: Ginn.

Thompson v. Oklahoma, 487 U.S. 815 (1988).

U.S. Supreme Court. (2004, October 13). [Transcript of oral argument in *Roper v. Simmons*, No. 03-633]. Retrieved from http://www.supremecourt.gov/oral_arguments/argument_transcripts/03-633.pdf

Viljoen, J. L., Klaver, J., & Roesch, R. (2005). Legal decisions of preadolescent and adolescent defendants: Predictors of confessions, pleas, communication with attorneys, and appeals. *Law and Human Behavior*, *29*, 253–277. http://dx.doi.org/10.1007/s10979-005-3613-2

Warren, J. I., Aaron, J., Ryan, E., Chauhan, P., & DuVal, J. (2003). Correlates of adjudicative competence among psychiatrically impaired juveniles. *Journal of the American Academy of Psychiatry and the Law*, *31*, 299–309.

Winner, L., Lanza-Kaduce, L., Bishop, D. M., & Frazier, C. E. (1997). The transfer of juveniles to criminal court: Reexamining recidivism over the long term. *Crime and Delinquency*, *43*, 548–563. http://dx.doi.org/10.1177/0011128797043004009

CHAPTER 5

ADOLESCENT BRAIN DEVELOPMENT: IMPLICATIONS FOR THE JUVENILE CRIMINAL JUSTICE SYSTEM

Beatriz Luna and Catherine Wright

Recent U.S. Supreme Court opinions regarding extended sentencing for juveniles have made reference to their immaturity on the basis of what any parent knows (*Roper v. Simmons*, 2005) and to evidence from psychology and brain science indicating differences in brain processes underlying control of behavior, making juveniles more vulnerable to impulsivity and risk taking. Society as whole, but parents in particular, recognize the teen years as a period marked by significant changes in behavior, characterized by sensation seeking, defiance, and emotional outbursts. As teens begin to make independent decisions, their choices can, at times, seem ill conceived, putting themselves and others in danger. Teenagers are in the throes of adolescence, the transitional period marked by the beginning of puberty and extending through the late teens and into the early 20s. Recent neuroscience research has provided evidence of specific immaturities in brain processes that offer new insights into possible constraints in decision-making abilities in adolescence. Specifically, advances in noninvasive neuroimaging methods have allowed researchers to quantify changes in brain structure and function throughout adolescence and into adulthood, helping to identify processes that underlie decision making. These findings have implications for juvenile law specific to adolescents as a unique group of individuals that warrant careful interpretation.

Behaviorally, adolescence is a period of heightened propensity for novelty and sensation seeking and is present across cultures and species (Spear, 2010). This increase in sensation seeking is believed to be primarily an adaptive process crucial for gaining skills that support independent trajectories as adults (Casey et al., 2010). Sensation seeking is marked by the pursuit of thrills, adventure, and experience as well as disinhibition and susceptibility to boredom. Sensation seeking, however, can lead to risk-taking behaviors, which can undermine survival. Risk-taking behaviors are defined by having a high-perceived reward value but known potential negative consequences, which are undervalued to pursue thrills. Typical risk-taking behaviors can range from extreme sports to substance abuse and criminal behavior. Research has indicated that adolescents have a heightened sensitivity to the potential rewards of risk taking, as well as increased sensitivity to peer influence (when compared with adults), making them particularly vulnerable to risk taking (Gardner & Steinberg, 2005).

Risk taking involves decision making and planning but, also important, heightened motivation driven by impulsive behavior. During the adolescent period, there is a particular relationship between a newly gained ability to plan and make decisions similar to adults but in the context of still immature impulse control and heightened sensitivity to rewards. These behavioral differences occur in parallel to neurobiological specialization in brain systems that support executive control and motivation. The physical and behavioral distinctions that make adolescents different from adults hold significant implications for the treatment of adolescents in all societal domains. These implications ranging from educational to medical as well as legal. Considering

http://dx.doi.org/10.1037/14643-005
APA Handbook of Psychology and Juvenile Justice, K. Heilbrun (Editor-in-Chief)

the increased risk juveniles face of encountering the legal system as a result of behavioral immaturities, it is critical to understand how legal systems view and treat adolescents and how they incorporate scientific evidence into these legal decisions.

Legal systems typically recognize the adolescent or juvenile period as the stage of development, distinct from adulthood, that ends at age 18, although this threshold can vary from 16 to 21 years depending on location. The law defines juveniles as not yet of an age to be held responsible for criminal acts in the same manner as adults, in great part because of behavioral immaturities. This distinction has often been supported using anecdotal experience with juveniles and intuitive knowledge regarding juveniles' limited understanding of responsible behavior. Within the past decade, however, juvenile law has increasingly looked to scientific findings regarding the differences between adolescents' and adults' brains to make informed, scientifically based legal decisions in cases involving adolescents.

In this chapter, we examine (a) the current evidence regarding structural and functional brain development throughout adolescence that may contribute to sensation seeking at this time and (b) the implications of current neuroscientific evidence for the future of the juvenile justice system, with a particular focus on culpability and rehabilitation.

RELEVANT HISTORY

In order to contextualize the importance of neuroscientific data in its ability to inform the juvenile criminal justice system, we next discuss how behavior within societal norms is perceived during the adolescent period and detail how neuroimaging studies have informed the nature of this behavior in Supreme Court briefs. The adolescent period is perceived to be a unique period of development, with behaviors that undermine survival and that are not guided by sound judgment. In landmark cases reviewed by the U.S. Supreme Court, neuroscientific data were presented within briefs to provide a neurobiological basis for the risk-taking behaviors of juveniles.

Adolescence and Susceptibility to Risk Taking

Adolescence is a period of heightened sensation and novelty seeking (i.e., the propensity to approach novel and varied experiences) that is present across cultures and species (Spear, 2010) and is believed to support the acquisition of skills and experiences that strengthen self-regulation in adulthood and enhance survival (Casey et al., 2010). Yet, increased sensation seeking can also lead to risk taking (i.e., engaging in behaviors with a high perceived reward value but known potential negative consequences), which can undermine survival. Risky choices in adolescence play a primary role in greater mortality during this period as a result of behaviors such as substance abuse, criminal behavior, and unprotected sex (Chambers, Taylor, & Potenza, 2003; Heron, 2012). Developmental theories, including the dual systems theory and the triadic model (Ernst, Pine, & Hardin, 2006; Geier & Luna, 2009; Somerville & Casey, 2010), posit that reward and control processes have different developmental trajectories that result in an imbalance between an immature cognitive executive system and an overactive motivational system during adolescence. Relatedly, adolescence and young adulthood are also characterized by the emergence of major psychiatric illnesses, including anxiety disorders, mood disorders, psychosis, eating disorders, personality disorders, and substance abuse (Kessler et al., 2005; Paus, Keshavan, & Giedd, 2008), underscoring the particular vulnerability during these periods.

Differences between adolescent and adult cognition, emotions, and behavior have been recognized throughout history. Adolescent immaturities have been characterized as both adaptive (in that they encourage young people to acquire independent skills needed for a successful adulthood) and dangerous (in that teenagers are more likely to engage in risky activities such as substance use and delinquency). The characterization of the differences in human brain anatomy and function that underlie these differences, however, has been a more recent phenomenon. Before the technological advances needed for the serial observation of brain changes in living humans, scientists relied on data from animal and postmortem studies to understand the processes underlying brain development. These methods were limited in what they could suggest regarding human behavior, variability between individuals, how individuals change over time, and what factors affect change over time.

Brain Imaging Approaches to Understand the Adolescent Brain

The development of in vivo brain imaging technologies, such as MRI, functional MRI (fMRI), and diffusion tensor imaging, have allowed scientists to map brain activity and structure in living people at different stages of human development and begin to characterize differences between adolescent and adult neurobiology. What makes these methods particularly well suited for developmental studies is that they are noninvasive (no injections or medications), painless, and safe and do not require the use of radiation. These characteristics have allowed for the extensive imaging of the brains of children and adolescents. The harmless nature of these techniques allows researchers to gather many data points from specific individuals over time. Longitudinal studies of large groups of individuals over time, although expensive and time consuming, are the gold standard for characterizing developmental trajectories and understanding variability.

MRI provides noninvasive high-resolution images of different tissues in the human body by placing an individual in a high-strength magnetic field, changing the spin orientation of protons using radio frequency energy, and then measuring the relaxation of these protons to generate an image. The time required for the proton spin orientation to return to the direction of the primary MRI magnetic field differs by tissue type, providing excellent contrast in MRI images to discern gray matter, white matter, cerebrospinal fluid, and oxygenation changes in blood resulting from neuronal activity. Structural MRI studies are predominantly used in developmental studies to characterize changes in the volume of gray and white matter in a variety of brain structures. Gray matter changes are relevant to neural cell processes, whereas white matter changes reflect axonal connections among neurons. fMRI provides a measure of the difference in magnetic susceptibility between oxygenated and deoxygenated blood. When brain regions increase their metabolism during cognition, the delivery of oxygen to activated neurons via hemoglobin can be measured by fMRI, which is referred to as the *blood-oxygen–level dependent contrast*. Diffusion tensor imaging is a popular, diffusion weighted imaging technique that measures the integrity of white matter connectivity by gauging the diffusion of water, which tends to flow parallel to white matter tracts, thereby increasing anisotropy.

These MRI-based technologies have been critical in providing neurobiological evidence associating developmental changes in brain processes with particular adolescent limitations in behavior that have been used to inform legal decision making related to juveniles in the U.S. justice system. Within the past 10 years, there have been three landmark cases involving juveniles in which developmental neuroscience evidence has been cited in briefs and the Court's opinions. We detail these cases in the following section. In each of these cases, briefs submitted to the U.S. Supreme Court cited neuroimaging studies that reported key differences between the adolescent and the adult brain.

Historical Use of Adolescent Brain Research in the Justice System

Roper v. Simmons (2005) was the first Supreme Court case in which *amicus curiae* briefs were submitted citing developmental neuroscience research findings regarding key differences between the adolescent and the adult brain.

The case involved a defendant, Christopher Simmons, 17 years old at the time, who was accused of committing a homicide during a burglary in the state of Missouri. The teenager created a plan to break into the home of Shirley Crook in the middle of the night, tie her up, and throw her off a bridge. Simmons enlisted the help of two friends in executing the plan; however, one of the two younger friends, John Tessmer, backed out. Christopher Simmons and Charles Benjamin followed through with the break-in, bound Crook's limbs, covered her eyes, drove her to a state park, and threw her off a railway bridge.

When the case was brought to court in the state of Missouri, there was an overwhelming amount of evidence suggesting the guilt of Christopher Simmons, including Simmons's own confession, a videotaped reenactment by Simmons at the crime scene, and testimony from Tessmer regarding the premeditated nature of the crime. The jury convicted Simmons of first-degree murder and recommended a death sentence, which was imposed in trial court. Simmons appealed to have the conviction and sentence reconsidered, arguing ineffective assistance of counsel. He claimed that his young age as well as mitigating factors should have been raised during sentencing. Mitigating factors included drug use, mental illness, and physical and emotional abuse at the hands of Simmons's father. The appellate court, however, affirmed Simmons's conviction and sentence, upholding *Stanford v. Kentucky* (1989), a case in which the U.S Supreme Court held that executions of defendants age 16 or 17 were not considered cruel and unusual punishment.

Simmons filed another petition in 2002 for state postconviction relief after the *Atkins v. Virginia* (2002) case, in which the Supreme Court concluded that executing those with intellectual disability constituted cruel and unusual punishment. The state of Missouri appealed to the U.S. Supreme Court in 2004, and the Court agreed to hear the case. The American Psychological Association and the American Medical Association filed separate briefs in Simmons's support, arguing that adolescent defendants warrant exclusion from capital punishment on the grounds that "research shows that adolescent brains are more active in regions related to aggression, anger, and fear, and less active in regions related to impulse control, risk assessment, and moral reasoning than adult brains" (*Roper v. Simmons*, 2005, p. 12). Both briefs cited numerous studies' findings on structural and functional changes to the brain over development and highlighted that the maturation of the brain's executive functions remain incomplete, even in late adolescence (Giedd et al., 1999).

During the hearing, oral arguments focused on the role of the science brief, with 16 of more than 20 questions asked of former Solicitor General Seth Waxman, who argued on behalf of Simmons, relating to the brief (Haider, 2006). Waxman asserted that the cognitive immaturities of juveniles lessen moral culpability, essentially arguing that Simmons's still-developing brain made him less culpable of his crime. *Culpability* describes the degree of one's blameworthiness and is associated with a person's intention to cause harm. If one acts purposely, knowingly, recklessly, or negligently, one is considered culpable and is, therefore, more blameworthy than one who acts unintentionally or under external pressure. The Court held in a 5–4 decision that it was unconstitutional to impose capital punishment for crimes committed by defendants younger than age 18, citing the Eighth Amendment protection against cruel and unusual punishment. Simmons was instead sentenced to life imprisonment without parole, and the death sentences of 72 others who had received capital punishment for crimes committed when younger than age 18 across the country were also changed.

Although Justice Anthony Kennedy did not specifically cite the neuroscience evidence submitted by the American Psychological Association and American Medical Association, the evidence he referred to in his majority opinion drew from the work of neuroscience researchers. He stated that,

> as any parent knows and as the scientific and sociological studies . . . tend to confirm, [a] lack of maturity and an underdeveloped sense of responsibility are found in youth more often than in adults and are more understandable among the young. (*Roper v. Simmons*, 2005, p. 15)

This landmark case was the first to use empirical evidence in place of common sense to draw legal boundaries between adolescents and adults.

The next landmark case heard by the Supreme Court concerning sentencing for juvenile offenders that cited brain research was *Graham v. Florida* (2010), which addressed life without parole for a nonhomicide conviction in a defendant younger than age 18. This case concerned Terrance Graham, who, along with two accomplices, attempted to rob a barbeque restaurant in 2003 at age 16. He was arrested and charged as an adult for armed burglary with assault and battery, a felony charge, as well as attempted armed robbery. Graham pled guilty and received a short sentence and probation. Six months after taking the plea agreement, at age 17,

Graham was arrested again for home invasion robbery. Graham maintained his innocence for the robbery charge but pled guilty to the violation of the terms of his probation. He was adjudicated guilty of his earlier charges, probation was revoked, and he was sentenced to life in prison. Because of the abolition of parole for offenses with a life sentence in Florida in 1995, Graham's sentence became life without the possibility of parole (Ditton & Wilson, 1999). He appealed the sentence under the Eighth Amendment's Cruel and Unusual Punishments Clause, but the state denied relief. Graham then appealed to the U.S. Supreme Court, and the case was argued in 2009.

The American Medical Association, American Psychological Association, National Association of Social Workers, and Mental Health America filed a single *amicus curiae* brief in support of Graham for this case, stating "it is clear that, in late adolescence, important aspects of brain maturation remain incomplete, particularly those involving the brain's executive functions and coordinated activity of regions involved in emotion and cognition" (*Graham v. Florida*, 2010, p. 27). Several of the same neuroscientific studies that were cited in the briefs for *Roper v. Simmons* (2005) were also cited in the brief for *Graham*, although the *Graham* brief also included additional research conducted since the 2005 *Roper* decision. In a 6–3 vote in support of Graham, the Court found that a sentence of life imprisonment without the possibility of parole for nonhomicide offenses is unconstitutional for juveniles. In the majority opinion, Justice Kennedy wrote,

> no recent data provide reason to reconsider the Court's observations in *Roper* about the nature of juveniles. . . . Developments in psychology and brain science continue to show fundamental differences between juvenile and adult minds. For example, parts of the brain involved in behavior control continue to mature through late adolescence. (*Graham v. Florida*, 2010, p. 3)

This was apparently the first time in U.S. history that the Supreme Court cited developmental neuroscience (albeit briefly) in an opinion. In 2012, Graham was resentenced to a 25-year sentence by his original trial judge.

In 2011, the Supreme Court decided the case of *J.D.B. v. North Carolina* (2011), a case related to whether a school-based police questioning of a juvenile constituted a custodial interrogation that required a *Miranda* warning. The Court held that age is relevant when determining police custody for *Miranda* purposes. In reaching this verdict, the court included the recognition of differences between the adolescent and adult brain. This case was the first that referenced the recognition of neurological differences in case law (i.e., *Roper v. Simmons*, 2005) rather than just in science—meaning that in future cases, previous cases can be cited as precedent for neurological differences between adolescents and adults (and accepted as fact) instead of requiring detailed evaluation of the scientific evidence.

The most recent Supreme Court case in which developmental neuroscience findings appeared in a majority opinion was *Miller v. Alabama* (2012). The Court's decision affected two cases, *Jackson v. Hobbs* (2012) and *Miller v. Alabama*, which were argued separately but shared a single Supreme Court opinion. The issue in both cases was whether a mandatory sentence of life without the possibility of parole is constitutional for juveniles convicted of homicide offenses. In the former case, Kuntrell Jackson was one of three teenage boys who walked to a video store in Arkansas in 1999, planning to rob it. Jackson, who was 14 at the time, allegedly stayed outside while one of the other teens entered the store and demanded that the clerk hand over money from the register. When the clerk refused, Jackson entered the store and witnessed his peer shoot the clerk in the face, killing her. The teens did not take anything from the store. Jackson was convicted of capital felony-murder and aggravated robbery. Under Arkansas law at the time of the trial, the judge was barred from considering Jackson's age or other mitigating factors, which included a lifetime of exposure to neglect and violence within his family. Jackson was given a mandatory life sentence without the possibility of parole. After the *Roper v. Simmons* (2005) decision, Jackson filed a writ of habeas corpus to argue that his conviction also violated the Eighth Amendment, but his writ was denied. After being denied an appeal at the state level, the U.S. Supreme Court granted Jackson a hearing in 2011.

The Supreme Court heard *Jackson v. Hobbs* (2012) in tandem with *Miller v. Alabama* (2012), another case in which the defendant was 14 at the time of his crime, was found guilty of homicide, and was sentenced to life without the possibility of parole. Both cases were heard by the Court because of an important distinction between the two cases. In *Jackson*, the youth did not commit the homicide, whereas in the *Miller* case, the defendant, Evan Miller, played a direct role in the murder. The details of the *Miller* case are described below.

On a summer day in 2003, Miller, a 14-year-old boy, entered the trailer of his neighbor, Cole Cannon, with a 16-year-old peer, Colby Smith, in search of drugs and money. Cannon was unconscious at the time the youths entered his home as a result of substance use, but he regained consciousness when the boys returned his wallet to his pocket after taking $300. Cannon attacked Miller, and the two boys struck back with a bat and fists. They covered Cannon's body with a sheet and left the scene. The boys returned shortly after and set fire to the trailer to conceal the crime. Cannon was alive when the fire was set. The jury found Miller guilty of capital murder in the course of arson, and he was given a mandatory sentence of life without parole. Just as Arkansas law barred the judge in Jackson's case from considering his age and mitigating factors, Alabama law disallowed the judge from considering Miller's age and some other mitigating factors, such as physical abuse, neglect, foster care involvement, and substance use beginning at an early age, in determining sentence. Miller appealed his conviction in light of the *Roper v. Simmons* (2005) and *Graham v. Florida* (2010) decisions.

The case was accepted by the Supreme Court and was argued in tandem with *Jackson* in March 2012. The American Psychological Association, American Psychiatric Association, National Association of Social Workers, and Mental Health America submitted a single brief in support of Miller and Jackson. The brief drew heavily on the information and research provided in the *Graham v. Florida* (2010) brief, with the addition of updates to relevant research. It cited several studies that examined the reward circuitry of the adolescent brain, changes in dopamine (DA) transmission, and the development of brain regions and circuitry critical to executive functions such as planning, judgment, impulse control, and decision making. The authors of the brief again suggested that changes in the brain during adolescence provide a physiological basis for the psychosocial immaturity witnessed through adolescent behavior (*Miller v. Alabama*, 2012).

On June 25, 2012, the Court ruled, in a 5–4 opinion, that a mandatory sentence of life without the possibility of parole is unconstitutional for juveniles, including cases involving homicide. The Court devoted an entire paragraph of the majority opinion to neuroscience evidence:

> The evidence presented to us in these cases indicates that the science and social science supporting *Roper*'s and *Graham*'s conclusions have become even stronger. . . . It is increasingly clear that adolescent brains are not yet fully mature in regions and systems related to higher-order executive functions such as impulse control, planning ahead, and risk avoidance. (*Miller v. Alabama*, 2012, p. 9)

This decision was a critical step toward the protection of the rights of juveniles with the support of scientific evidence. However, it does not exclude the possibility of a juvenile being sentenced to life without parole. The ruling simply ensures that the judge or jury, before imposing the harshest possible penalty for a juvenile, must consider mitigating factors.

In the next section, we delve into the details of the most up-to-date research findings regarding the development of the brain throughout adolescence. Changes in brain structure, neurochemistry, and function throughout adolescence and their links to behavioral differences are elucidated. Many of the research findings we describe were referenced in the briefs in the Supreme Court cases of *Roper v. Simmons* (2005), *Graham v. Florida* (2010), and *Miller v. Alabama* (2012).

EVALUATION OF CURRENT NEUROIMAGING EVIDENCE OF ADOLESCENT BRAIN DEVELOPMENT

A growing literature of neuroimaging studies has provided evidence that the brain undergoes substantial reorganization both structurally and functionally during adolescence. These maturational changes occur within and between different brain regions, following distinct timelines through adolescence and into adulthood and having important implications for behavior. To understand morphological and functional changes within the brain, we first provide a basic description of brain components, followed by detailed accounts of the evidence regarding structural, neurochemical, and functional brain maturation.

Basic Brain and Behavior Components

Neurons are the functional cells in the brain that send and receive electrochemical signals throughout the brain for information processing. These electrochemical signals, or action potentials, are projected by way of axons, fibers that extend from the cell bodies of neurons. The electrical signal is transmitted chemically from one neuron to another across a synapse, which is the connecting point between the axon of one neuron and the dendrite of another. The dendrite is a branched projection of a neuron that propagates the received signal. Information is transferred through the release of neurotransmitters at the synapse. Neurotransmitters are endogenous chemicals that activate specific receptors in the membranes of receiving cells.

Specific components of neurons, along with glial cells and blood vessels, make up the brain structure's two tissue components: white matter and gray matter. These components draw their names from the coloration of the brain's interior. Gray matter, or *substantia grisea*, is gray-brown in color and consists of the cell bodies and unmyelinated axons of neurons, dendrites, glial cells, and capillaries. Gray matter makes up the cortical ribbon that surrounds the outer layer of the brain. It is associated with processing and cognition. White matter, or substantia alba, is mainly composed of the myelinated (or insulated) axons of neuronal cells and glial cells. White matter modulates the distribution of electrical signals, which coordinate communication between different brain regions. Both white and gray matter undergo critical changes throughout the period of adolescence. These changes, which include synaptic pruning, myelination, and neurotransmitter availability (described later in this chapter), affect the range of control of behaviors—and as such are relevant to adolescent limitations in decision making.

Voluntary behavior and decision making rely primarily on brain regions that support executive function and motivation. *Executive function* refers to the processes that underlie behaviors that are voluntary and hence planned, in contrast to reflexive behaviors, which are automatic and do not rely on abstraction and planning. The prefrontal cortex is known to play an important role in executive function primarily because of its great connectivity with the rest of the brain, receiving information regarding the environment, and having the ability to influence neural signaling across the brain and especially in brain regions that generate responses (Diamond, 2013). *Motivation* refers to reward and emotional processes that enhance or bias specific responses that increase energy, desire, and the sensation of pleasure. Motivation is primarily linked with the striatum, located in the limbic system, in which the neurotransmitter DA plays a primary role. Developmental studies have focused primarily on the changes to the limbic system and the prefrontal cortex and their associated circuitry as a model for understanding the neural basis of an imbalance between executive and motivational systems in adolescent sensation seeking and risk-taking behavior.

Structural Brain Maturation in Adolescence

Neurons in the brain are formed before birth and persist without replacement (Nowakowski, 2006). However, neuronal structure, its interconnectivity, and the neurochemistry used for information transfer change through adolescence. The gross morphology of the human brain is in place by childhood, with brain weight reaching 95% of a typical adult brain between ages 7 and 11 (Caviness, Kennedy, Bates, & Makris, 1996; Giedd et al., 1996). Specialization of the brain's core morphology, however, continues through adolescence as brain structures adapt and optimize to support specific environmental demands. These maturational changes in brain matter occur in parallel with development of executive functions.

Gray matter changes. Synaptic connections between neurons are the site of information processing in the brain. These connections multiply in the first 2 years of life. Throughout childhood and adolescence, synaptic connections that are used remain, and those that are not used are eliminated, or pruned (Rauschecker & Marler, 1987). Synaptic pruning is thought to be the process that supports specialization of brain processes to environmental demands. The elimination of unused connections and the strengthening of the connections that remain enhance the computational capacity and speed of information processing that support the complex neural processes that support reasoning and decision making.

Synaptic pruning is thought to contribute to the reduction in the thickness of cortical gray matter that is seen over the course of adolescence with MRI (discussed below). Initial morphological studies of postmortem brains found hierarchical pruning throughout the brain. Synaptic connections were found to reach adult levels in the visual cortex by age 7 and in the auditory cortex by age 10, whereas the connections in the prefrontal cortex were found to not reach adult levels until age 16 (Huttenlocher, 1990; Huttenlocher & Dabholkar, 1997). More recent postmortem findings, with substantially larger samples and improved methodologies, have indicated that synaptic pruning continues in the prefrontal cortex throughout the 2nd decade of life (Petanjek et al., 2011), suggesting continued specialization through young adulthood. Petanjek et al. (2011) only looked at prefrontal cortex, but other regions may have similar prolonged specializations.

MRI, which measures gray matter thickness in vivo, indicates that that the total volume of gray matter increases across the cortex before puberty, reaches a peak during the pubertal period, and then declines postpuberty (Giedd et al., 1999). The postpubertal decline varies with respect to brain regions. Specifically, MRI studies have found that areas of the brain in which there is high integration, including prefrontal cortex but also posterior brain regions, have not reached adult levels of thinning in adolescence (Gogtay et al., 2004; see Figure 5.1). For example, the superior temporal cortex, an area supporting social cognitive processes, shows a

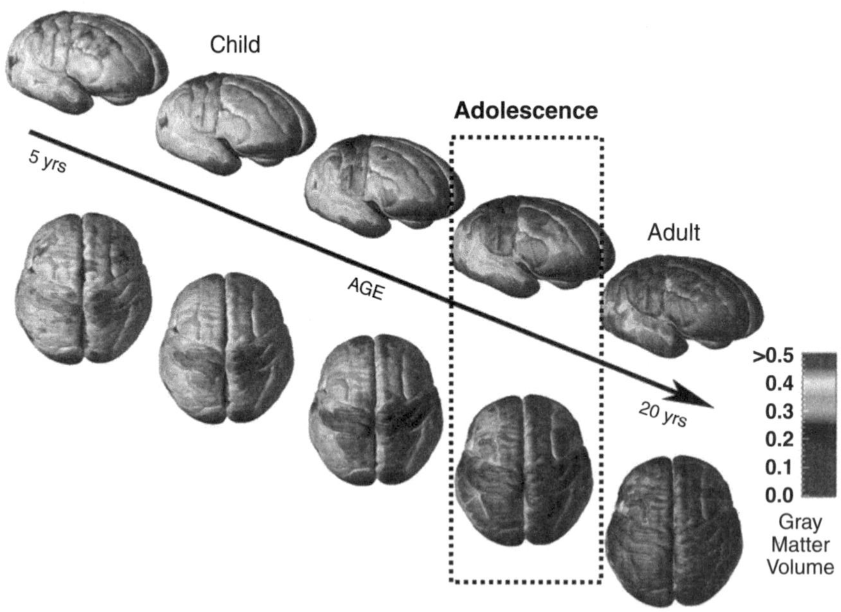

FIGURE 5.1. View of the cortical surface of the brain. Brightness represents degree of thinning of gray matter. Darker gray indicates mature adult levels have been reached. A box surrounding the adolescent stage has been added. From "Dynamic Mapping of Human Cortical Development During Childhood Through Early Adulthood," by N. Gogtay, J. N. Giedd, L. Lusk, K. M. Hayashi, D. Greenstein, A. C. Vaituzis, . . . P. M. Thompson, 2004, *Proceedings of the National Academy of Sciences, 101*, p. 8178. Copyright 2004 National Academy of Sciences. Reprinted with permission.

particular protracted maturation throughout adolescence (Gogtay et al., 2004). MRI studies have also shown that the basal ganglia, a subcortical region that includes areas underlying motivation, also show a protracted development through adolescence (Gogtay et al., 2004; Raznahan et al., 2014; Sowell, Thompson, Holmes, Jernigan, & Toga, 1999; Toga, Thompson, & Sowell, 2006). The continued maturation of cortical and subcortical regions through adolescence indicates important immaturities at this time that are specifically relevant to decision making, especially in emotionally salient situations.

White matter changes. Myelination is the process involving the thickening of the insulation of white matter tracts, significantly increasing the speed of neuronal transmission and improving the fidelity of the neuronal signal. Increased speed of neuronal signaling with improved fidelity supports enhanced communication between distant brain regions that can improve top-down prefrontal executive control of behavior (Goldman-Rakic, Chafee, & Friedman, 1993). Histological studies, which examine cells and tissues by sectioning, staining, and examining under a microscope, have indicated that the visual cortex myelinates within the 1st decade of life, whereas frontal, parietal, and temporal regions of the brain continue to myelinate into the 2nd decade of life (Yakovlev & Lecours, 1967), as does white matter connectivity within subcortical regions (Benes, 1989).

Diffusion tensor imaging studies, which provide an in vivo measure of white matter integrity, have indicated continued maturation through adolescence in tracts that support connectivity across cortical and between cortical and subcortical regions (Asato, Terwilliger, Woo, & Luna, 2010; Eluvathingal, Hasan, Kramer, Fletcher, & Ewing-Cobbs, 2007; Giorgio et al., 2008; Lebel, Walker, Leemans, Phillips, & Beaulieu, 2008; Simmonds, Hallquist, Asato, & Luna, 2014). Longitudinal findings have indicated that the period between childhood and adolescence has significant dynamic growth of white matter integrity throughout the brain, with major white matter tracts (including those that support integration of frontal regions with other cortical and subcortical regions) reaching adult levels by adolescence (Simmonds et al., 2014). Still maturing in adolescence, however, is white matter as it reaches gray matter targets throughout cortical and subcortical regions, attaining maturity in the 2nd decade of life. Last to mature are white tracts that support the integration of prefrontal executive regions relevant to monitoring of performance and emotional (cingulum) and socioemotional (uncinate fasciculus) processing (see Figure 5.2). Paralleling sex differences in pubertal development, the

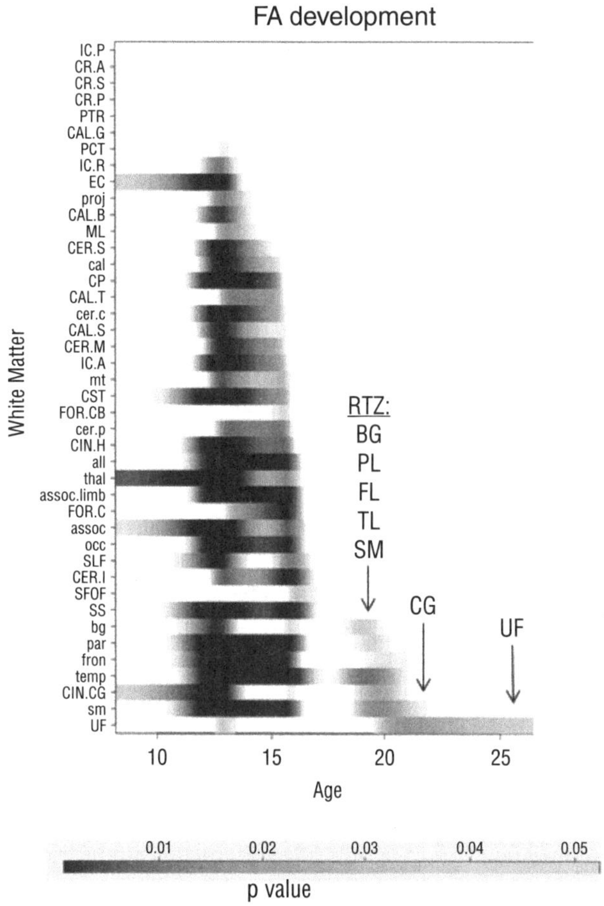

FIGURE 5.2. Timing of the stages of significant growth for white matter tracts and regional terminal zones determined by fractional anisotropy (FA) measures. Heat maps depict stages of significant growth and timing of maturation in white matter development determined by FA measures. Rows are organized by time of maturation in FA, which is defined as the time at which the rate of change was no longer significantly different from the null (p = .05, bootstrap corrected). Different shades represent percentage of change per year. Darker colors represent periods of significant change. Only FA increases with age. RTZ = regional terminal zones; BG = basal ganglia; PL = parietal lobe; FL = frontal lobe; TL = temporal lobe; SM = sensorimotor; CG = cingulum; UF = uncinated fasciculus. Data from Simmonds et al. (2014).

maturation of white matter integrity occurs earlier in females, with males showing a longer trajectory and persistent immaturities throughout adolescence (Asato et al., 2010; Simmonds et al., 2014). Age-related changes in white matter tracts have been found to be positively correlated with developmental improvements in cognitive performance, indicating a strong link between brain changes and behavior (Liston et al., 2006; Nagy, Westerberg, & Klingberg, 2004). These results provide evidence for continued immaturities in white matter connectivity into adolescence, with particular limitations specific to emotional processing continuing to strengthen into adulthood.

Brain maturation has also been found to be influenced by puberty. During puberty, which is the process underlying reproductive maturity, the brain releases increased levels of hormones such as estrogen, testosterone, and gonadotropin-releasing hormone. Exposure to gonadal hormones has been shown to exert unique effects on the brain and behavior processes during adolescence (Sisk & Zehr, 2005). Testosterone and estradiol have been found to be associated with subcortical gray matter volume, including the amygdala, a structure involved in socioemotional processing (Herting et al., 2014). Puberty has also been found to be associated with white matter changes, including frontal regions as well as sex-specific trajectories of maturation (Herting, Maxwell, Irvine, & Nagel, 2012; Raznahan et al., 2010). Effects of puberty on brain maturation provide specificity for unique changes related to adolescence. Similarly, there have been consistent findings indicating an earlier maturation of gray and white matter in females than in males (Lenroot et al., 2007; Simmonds et al., 2014)

Taken together, neuroimaging findings of brain structure have suggested that, during adolescence, brain components that are already in place show continued specialization. We use the term *specialization* to reflect refinement of existing brain processes believed to support an optimal fit with the environment. It is important to note that all structural components are present even in childhood; the process of specialization is one of fine tuning. This suggests that adolescents have access to adult brain systems, but these may be limited in speed and accuracy. For example, gray matter regions that are not fully pruned may be slower and less accurate and have less capacity to process complex demands such as those required of executive function. Similarly, slower and noisier signal transmission in not-fully-myelinated tracts may undermine the ability to integrate information across the brain—such as the ability of prefrontal executive regions to influence response-related regions of the brain in a timely fashion. Regarding adolescent decision making more specifically, brain structural evidence has indicated that the prefrontal cortex and basal ganglia have not reached adult levels of maturation in adolescence, which may contribute to risk-taking behavior. The relative maturational profiles of these two systems may have behavioral implications specific to adolescence, which we discuss further when considering neurochemical and brain functional developmental changes.

Neurochemical changes in adolescence. Paralleling brain structural changes in adolescence are significant changes in the availability of neurotransmitters. Dopamine (DA) is a key neurotransmitter that underlies motivation; as such, it is an integral component of learning, memory, cognition, emotion, and reward processing (Cools, 2008; Schultz, 2002). The neurotransmitter DA regulates emotion and motivation processes through subcortical systems and their influence on prefrontal circuits (Baik, 2013). DA functions through a specialized route called the mesolimbic pathway, starting with the ventral tegmental area deep in the brain where DA cells originate, connecting to limbic regions that support emotion (amygdala), memory (hippocampus), and reward processing (nucleus accumbens in the ventral striatum) and influencing executive function (prefrontal cortex; Chikama, McFarland, Amaral, & Haber, 1997; Di Martino et al., 2008; Fudge, Kunishio, Walsh, Richard, & Haber, 2002; Haber, Kunishio, Mizobuchi, & Lynd-Balta, 1995; Selemon & Goldman-Rakic, 1985). Animal studies as well as human adult neuroimaging and pharmacologic studies have indicated that DA neurons respond to the anticipation, value, and salience of rewards (Cools, 2008; Schultz et al., 2008; Wise, 2004). More important, DA neurons modulate the reciprocal relationship between striatum and prefrontal cortex involved in cognitive control (Cools, 2008). As such, the role of DA in adolescent development has been of great interest (Padmanabhan & Luna, 2014; Spear, 2000; Wahlstrom, Collins, White, & Luciana, 2010), especially the ventral striatum (nucleus accumbens) because of its role in DA processing and reward (Cools, 2008) and because its function can be measured with fMRI (Delgado, 2007). Presently, in vivo neuroimaging methods capable of measuring neurotransmitter function (including DA) such as positron emission tomography are limited in their application to pediatric populations because of the use of radioactive radiotracers and limitations on allowable dosages. Hence, our understanding regarding developmental changes in DA through adolescence comes predominantly from animal models.

Animal studies using rodents and nonhuman primates have shown continued developmental changes to DA neural structure and function in adolescence (Chambers et al., 2003; Spear, 2000; Wahlstrom, Collins, et al., 2010; Wahlstrom, White, & Luciana, 2010). Studies have shown that the aspect of cells receiving neurochemical signaling specialized for DA increases in number in the prefrontal cortex and the striatum during adolescence and then declines into adulthood (Andersen, Thompson, Krenzel, & Teicher, 2002; Lidow & Rakic, 1992; Montague, Lawler, Mailman, & Gilmore, 1999; Seeman et al., 1987). DA activity is also found to peak in subcortical areas and in prefrontal areas during puberty in the animal models (Andersen et al., 2002; Brenhouse, Sonntag, & Andersen, 2008; Goldman-Rakic & Brown, 1982; McCutcheon, White, & Marinelli, 2009).

In humans, postmortem studies have also revealed increased DA innervation in prefrontal cortex in adolescence (Benes, Taylor, & Cunningham, 2000; Lambe, Krimer, & Goldman-Rakic, 2000; Lewis, Melchitzky, & Burgos, 2002; Rosenberg & Lewis, 1994, 1995). These findings are somewhat consistent with one of the only studies to use positron emission tomography with a human developmental sample (Chambers et al., 2003). Research found that DA transmission decreased linearly from ages 10 to 30 in prefrontal regions and the striatum. These results provide suggestive evidence for relative greater DA function during adolescence that may underlie increased motivation during this time of development. These results are somewhat inconsistent with those of some animal studies, however, which have not found evidence for a peak in DA function that is specific to adolescence (e.g., Andersen, Dumont, & Teicher, 1997; Kalsbeek, Voorn, Buijs, Pool, & Uylings, 1988; Lidow & Rakic, 1992; Matthews, Bondi, Torres, & Moghaddam, 2013; Sturman & Moghaddam, 2011). More important, there is a paucity of studies that have related changes in DA to behavior. New studies looking at human models that inform developmental changes in DA in vivo are needed to confirm initial results. The predominance of evidence suggesting a peak in DA expression in adolescence, however, shows that it appears to play an important role in teenagers' increased drive to pursue unfamiliar situations and rewards despite significant risks; its subsequent decrease into adulthood correlates with a decline in risk-taking behaviors (Deakin, Aitken, Robbins, & Sahakian, 2004). In addition to its impact on decision making, DA also supports adaptable learning (Schultz, 2001). With increased DA innervation in the PFC during the adolescent period, teenagers are especially amenable to learning and reward-driven feedback and reinforcement. As such, behaviors during this phase of life may be more highly amenable to treatment and rehabilitation strategies.

Functional Brain Maturation in Adolescence

Developmental changes in brain function are underlaid by the maturation of brain structure and changes in behavior. Regarding adolescence, brain functional studies have focused on changes in brain function supporting cognitive development and reward processing.

Functional brain maturation and executive–cognitive function. As described above, decision making relies on executive function. *Executive function* refers to the ability to voluntarily guide behavior toward a goal in a planned fashion. Essential to executive function are inhibitory control and working memory. Inhibitory control is the ability to voluntarily suppress reflexive or enticing responses that are goal incompatible, and it underlies impulsivity. Crucial to inhibitory control is the ability for "top" executive brain systems to influence "bottom" response systems in the brain. For example, when on a diet one has to suppress the enticing desire to order the hamburger in favor of the salad, which corresponds to the goal of lower caloric intake. Inhibitory control tasks present stimuli that generate reflexive responses that must be ignored to generate a response based on a goal established by an instruction. These tasks probe the integrity of brain systems that support top-down control. Working memory is underlaid by brain processes that maintain the goal that directs voluntary behavior—for example, retaining the goal of wanting to lose weight when ordering a salad instead of a hamburger in a restaurant. Working memory tasks require that responses be guided by a goal that is retained in memory and be able to guide behavior without external stimuli. This may be relevant to juvenile law in that similar systems need to be engaged to sustain goals that support long-term survival while suppressing the desire, which may be more predominant in adolescence, to perform a behavior that generates an immediate result.

Researchers have developed tasks such as the antisaccade and go–no-go tasks that probe the maturation of inhibitory control by measuring a person's capacity to not make a reactive response to a compelling stimulus. In the antisaccade task, subjects are challenged to suppress the reflexive hard-wired response to look at a visual stimulus that appears suddenly on a screen and instead look in the opposite location. In the go–no-go task, after subjects have been asked to respond by button press to a repeated stimuli, they are asked to suppress a response when a specific infrequent stimuli appears. The ability to inhibit a response voluntarily is available in early infancy (Amso & Johnson, 2005). The rate of correct inhibitory responses, however, develops and improves over development, with the ability to control inhibitory responses becoming more consistent in adulthood (Fischer, Biscaldi, & Gezeck, 1997; Luna, Garver, Urban, Lazar, & Sweeney, 2004; Ridderinkhof, Band, & Logan, 1999).

Similar to inhibitory abilities, working memory is available early in life but continues to improve through adolescence (Demetriou, Christou, Spanoudis, & Platsidou, 2002; Luna et al., 2004). Working memory tasks probe subjects' ability to keep a goal in working memory over a delay period, which sometimes includes an interfering stimulus. Findings have indicated that the ability to use working memory precisely and flexibly continues to improve after adolescence (Luna et al., 2004; Sander, Lindenberger, & Werkle-Bergner, 2012; Schleepen & Jonkman, 2009).

The prefrontal cortex plays a crucial role in executive function abilities (Passingham & Sakai, 2004) because it has uniquely distributed connectivity with the rest of brain, including reciprocal interactions within the frontal cortex and with other cortical and subcortical regions. The prefrontal cortex's unique interconnectivity with the rest of the brain allows it to receive and integrate information in addition to the ability to maintain information on line, supporting its role in directing behavior based on working memory. These characteristics make the prefrontal cortex well suited to support volitional planned responses. As delineated above, synaptic pruning proceeds into young adulthood in prefrontal cortex (Petanjek et al., 2011), and white matter connectivity is reaching adult levels by adolescence (Simmonds et al., 2014), indicating continued maturation through adolescence (Olesen, Nagy, Westerberg, & Klingberg, 2003). Although clearly there is continued maturation in prefrontal cortex, it is not clear how these later stages of specialization affect the ability to engage prefrontal cortex during executive tasks. fMRI studies have provided insight into the level of engaging prefrontal cortex for executive function in adolescence.

fMRI studies examining response inhibition and working memory over the course of development have found unique immaturities in adolescents compared with adults. Engagement of prefrontal cortex during working memory tasks are evident by childhood (Nelson et al., 2003; Thomas et al., 1999). Developmental differences in the activity of the prefrontal cortex become evident when the task increases in difficulty, requiring manipulating the information kept on line, response precision, and distractor suppression (Ciesielski, Lesnik, Savoy, Grant, & Ahlfors, 2006; Crone, Wendelken, Donohue, van Leijenhorst, & Bunge, 2006; Geier, Garver, Terwilliger, & Luna, 2009; Klingberg, Forssberg, &

Westerberg, 2002; Olesen, Macoveanu, Tegnér, & Klingberg, 2007; Scherf, Sweeney, & Luna, 2006). Developmental differences in the magnitude of recruitment of critical regions including prefrontal cortex are found in tasks requiring inhibitory control with varied results when cross-sectional designs with different age ranges and tasks are used (Bunge, Dudukovic, Thomason, Vaidya, & Gabrieli, 2002; Crone et al., 2006; Luna et al., 2004; Rubia et al., 2006). In adolescence, the speed with which one engages in inhibitory control has been found to be associated with white matter connectivity between the frontal and subcortical regions (Liston et al., 2006). Recently, a longitudinal study examined age-related trajectories in the recruitment of the extended brain circuitry involved in inhibitory control (Ordaz, Foran, Velanova, & Luna, 2013). fMRI results indicated that regions supporting the generation of a correct inhibitory response did not show changes with age. Prefrontal cortex, however, showed decreased engagement from childhood to adolescence, when it reached adult levels (see Figure 5.3). One region, the anterior cingulate cortex, showed robust increases with age through adolescence that were associated with the ability to generate correct inhibitory responses. The anterior cingulate cortex has been well characterized as monitoring performance and the commission of errors (Botvinick, Nystrom, Fissell, Carter, & Cohen, 1999; Braver, Barch, Gray, Molfese, & Snyder, 2001; Carter et al., 1998). These are particularly important results that suggest that the ability to executively generate an inhibitory response is available by adolescence. What is still immature in adolescence is the ability to supervise responses and integrate error commissions to influence behavior.

Crucial to top-down control of behavior beyond activity in specific regions is the ability for the brain to integrate information across regions. Studies looking at the ability of prefrontal regions to influence other regions of the brain have indicated continued refinements in adolescence (Hwang, Velanova, & Luna, 2010; Stevens, Kiehl, Pearlson, & Calhoun, 2007). Specifically, Hwang et al. (2010) found that by adolescence prefrontal connectivity influencing other regions during an inhibitory control task was present as in adulthood, but there were fewer functional connections and they were weaker than those of adults. To a greater extent, the brain works through intricately organized networks of regions that support unique aspects of behavior (Sporns, 2013). These networks have been identified by classifying regions that show correlated spontaneous signal fluctuations with fMRI while individuals are not engaged in a task (referred to as *rest*).

Research on the development of brain networks has also shown unique developmental differences. A foundational architecture of resting state connectivity that supports integration across the brain has been identified, with regions that act as hubs of communication allowing different networks to integrate (Buckner et al., 2009). Developmental findings

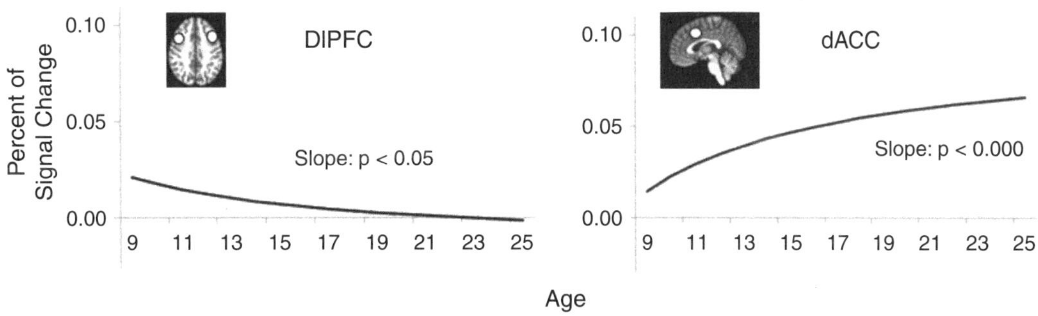

FIGURE 5.3. Mean growth curves of changes in activation in dorsolateral prefrontal cortex (DlPFC) and dorsal anterior cingulate cortex (dACC). DlPFC demonstrates decreased activation with development, reaching adult levels by adolescence, and activation in the dACC shows continued increases through adolescence. From "Longitudinal Growth Curves of Brain Function Underlying Inhibitory Control Through Adolescence," by S. J. Ordaz, W. Foran, K. Velanova, and B. Luna, 2013, *Journal of Neuroscience*, *33*, p. 18118. Copyright 2013 by the Society for Neuroscience. Reprinted with permission.

have indicated that the hub network is established by childhood but that connections between prefrontal hubs to the rest of the brain increase dramatically from childhood to adolescence, when network reaches adult levels that may support the engagement of executive systems by adolescence (Hwang, Velanova, & Luna, 2010). When considering specialized networks, initial findings suggested that short connections gave way to longer connections supporting segregated but integrated networks (Fair et al., 2007), enhancing widely distributed networks that are needed to support complex behavior (Dosenbach et al., 2010). Recent magnetoencephalography and fMRI findings have provided further evidence that throughout adolescence and young adulthood there is increasing integration of brain networks (Schäfer, Morgan, Ye, Taylor, & Doesburg, 2014). Although there is evidence for a linear increase in integration of brain connectivity with age, encephalographic studies have shown that during adolescence there may be a destabilization of integration associated with cognitive performance that may mark a period of reorganization of networks (Uhlhaas et al., 2009).

Taken together, research on changes in brain function underlying cognitive development has suggested that there are specific processes that are still undergoing specialization in adolescence, but there are also many aspects of brain processing that are intact. Behaviorally, adolescents show improved ability to engage core executive systems compared with children but are still not at adult levels. It is important to note that the cognitive abilities are present and available—but what changes behaviorally is the rate of correct responses. The implication is that adolescents can and often do show adult-level executive performance. However, when difficulty is increased, adolescents may be more susceptible to committing errors, which they are limited in their ability to monitor. The fMRI literature has provided evidence for changes in brain function, including recruitment of prefrontal cortex and strengthening of network integration. However, longitudinal findings have indicated that prefrontal function may be at adult levels by adolescence. What may underlie the limitations in the rate of correct executive responses may be specific to limitations in adolescence in the ability to monitor performance and for behavior to be affected by previous errors. That is, the adolescent's ability to direct behavior using executive processes is available, but processes that further support executive performance may be still maturing. In fact, the greatest amount of change in behavior and brain function occurs from childhood to adolescence, when adult levels are often reached. The mature aspects of executive function may afford the adolescent the ability to engage in complex planning of behavior, but the subtle immaturities may undermine the ability to consistently and promptly engage these abilities in decision making especially.

Functional brain maturation and reward processing. Crucial to decision making are motivational factors and their influence on executive function. Given the unique maturational processes occurring during adolescence, including a still-maturing striatum and a peak in DA availability, characterizing brain function during rewards across age has been of special interest. Tasks used to characterize motivation typically measure changes in the ventral striatal function to monetary rewards. The majority of these studies have found that adolescents show increased activation in the ventral striatum compared to adults (Ernst et al., 2006; Galvan et al., 2006; Geier, Terwilliger, Teslovich, Velanova, & Luna, 2010; Padmanabhan, Geier, Ordaz, Teslovich, & Luna, 2011; van Leijenhorst, Gunther Moor, et al., 2010; van Leijenhorst, Zanolie, et al., 2010; see Figure 5.4). When rewards are contingent on cognitive control, increased activity is also found in brain areas that support the response that will gain the reward (Geier et al., 2010; Padmanabhan et al., 2011). However, one reward task generates decreased activity in adolescents compared with adults (Bjork et al., 2004): when they must respond to an abstract stimulus representing a possible reward rather than to a reward cue. This finding may reflect particular sensitivity during adolescence to explicit reward cues. Many of these studies have also reported that in parallel to increased striatal activity in adolescence, there is decreased activity in a region of the prefrontal cortex, the orbitofrontal cortex, that underlies executive aspects of reward assessment (Galvan et al., 2006; Geier et al., 2010;

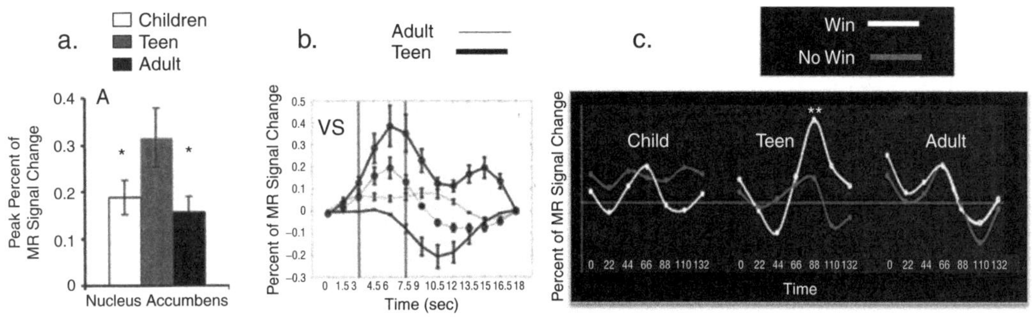

FIGURE 5.4. Studies depicting reward processing changes between adolescents and adults using monetary incentives. Three different independent studies show consistent findings of greater striatal activity in adolescents than in adults. Figure 5.4a is from "Earlier Development of the Accumbens Relative to Orbitofrontal Cortex Might Underlie Risk-Taking Behavior in Adolescents," by A. Galvan, T. A. Hare, C. E. Parra, J. Penn, H. Voss, G. Glover, and B. J. Casey, 2006, *Journal of Neuroscience, 26*, p. 6888. Copyright 2006 by the Society for Neuroscience. Reprinted with permission. Figure 5.4b is from "Immaturities in Reward Processing and Its Influence on Inhibitory Control in Adolescence," by C. F. Geier, R. Terwilliger, T. Teslovich, K. Velanova, and B. Luna, 2010, *Cerebral Cortex, 20*, p. 1622. Copyright 2010 by Oxford University Press. Reprinted with permission. Figure 5.4c is from "What Motivates the Adolescent? Brain Regions Mediating Reward Sensitivity Across Adolescence," by L. van Leijenhorst, K. Zanolie, C. S. Van Meel, P. M. Westenberg, S. A. Rombouts, and E. A. Crone, 2010, *Cerebral Cortex, 20*, p. 65. Copyright 2010 by Oxford University Press. Reprinted with permission.

van Leijenhorst, Zanolie, et al., 2010; see Figure 5.4). Increased activity in the striatum has been found to be associated with increased risk taking in adults (Christopoulos, Tobler, Bossaerts, Dolan, & Schultz, 2009). In adolescents, increased activity in striatum coupled with decreased engagement of prefrontal regions has been found to be associated with self-reported risk taking (Galvan, Hare, Voss, Glover, & Casey, 2007; van Leijenhorst, Crone, & Bunge, 2006). With age, the tendency to choose risky options for a low reward decreases from adolescence to adulthood as prefrontal activation changes (van Leijenhorst, Gunther Moor, et al., 2010), regions that support attention become coupled with reward processing (A. B. Smith, Halari, Giampetro, Brammer, & Rubia, 2011), and circuitry that supports incorporating contextual information increases (Paulsen, Platt, Huettel, & Brannon, 2011). Interestingly, adolescents do not differ from adults in risk assessment and appraisal (Reyna & Brainerd, 2011; Steinberg, 2004) but the ability to readily integrate this information in situations with competing processes, such as in adolescent risk taking, may be limited.

These results provide compelling evidence for a hyperactive reward system during adolescence that may disengage prefrontal executive systems affecting decision making. The connectivity between striatal and prefrontal regions supports top-down executive control of behavior, and the strength of interconnectivity has been associated with the ability to delay reward gratification in development (Christakou, Brammer, & Rubia, 2011). As described earlier, structural changes in white matter (Asato et al., 2010; Lebel et al., 2008; Simmonds et al., 2014) and functional connectivity (Hwang et al., 2010; Stevens et al., 2007) that support prefrontal function increase with age.

The adolescent's readiness to respond to obtain rewards, coupled with the observed hyperactivity of the reward system, may underlie a system prone to impulsive sensation seeking. Immaturities in the ability of adolescents to engage networks that integrate cortical and subcortical regions, such as prefrontal and striatal regions, may limit adolescents' ability to choose rewards that require waiting when given an option to receive immediate rewards (Christakou et al., 2011; Geier & Luna, 2009). Also unique to adolescent reward processing is what constitutes a reward, with novelty seeking and social interactions often taking priority during this life stage (Blakemore, Burnett, & Dahl, 2010).

Taken together, these results suggest that, during adolescence, increased sensitivity to rewards and still strengthening connections between prefrontal and striatal regions may provide a basis for engaging in sensation seeking that in some cases can lead to risk-taking behavior. The interaction between access to adult-level executive function and a reward system that activates to greater levels than that of adults may underlie the ability to make complex plans that are guided by short-term rewards. Although adolescence is a time of increased sensation seeking, most adolescents, however, do not engage in risk-taking behavior. As described earlier, the predisposition for sensation seeking is viewed as an adaptive process to encourage the exploration necessary for a normative transition into adulthood, whereas risk taking is not.

Functional brain maturation and socioemotional cognition. Adolescence is a time of increased socialization, when bonding with peers and potential romantic partners takes priority over established family relationships (Crone & Dahl, 2012; Steinberg, 2008). Social processing is a uniquely complex system that engages several processes ranging from face processing, theory of mind, and emotional processing to social reasoning (Adolphs, 2003). These processes are supported by a widely distributed brain circuitry, including prefrontal and posterior cortical regions, as well as subcortical regions such as the amygdala, that show continued specialization (Blakemore, 2008; M. H. Johnson, Grossmann, & Cohen Kadosh, 2009; A. R. Smith, Chein, & Steinberg, 2013). fMRI studies have found that adolescents struggle more than adults in assessing the intentions of others and in engaging executive control regions to process rejections (Gunther Moor, van Leijenhorst, Rombouts, Crone, & Van der Molen, 2010; Güroğlu, van den Bos, & Crone, 2009). Adolescents also demonstrate increased activation in prefrontal and striatal regions that underlie executive processing of emotions when exposed to emotional stimuli such as emotional faces (Nelson et al., 2003). More important, when in the presence of peers, adolescents demonstrate greater risk taking than adults; such risk taking is modulated by increased activation of reward circuitry (Chein, Albert, O'Brien, Uckert, & Steinberg, 2011), and peer approval engages brain regions involved in action more so than in children and adults (Jones et al., 2014). Adolescents have also been found to be more reactive to threat cues because limbic regions show greater activation to emotional stimuli, especially in males (Dreyfuss et al., 2014). These limitations in socioemotional processing may be associated with the weakened connectivity between prefrontal regions and the amygdala, an area of the limbic system that performs a primary role in the processing of emotional stimuli (Somerville, Jones, & Casey, 2010). Together, these studies have suggested that processing socioemotional stimuli may be more challenging in adolescence, and social dynamics may motivate risk-taking behaviors. Social processing may exert added challenges that may increase demands on the ability to fully engage adult-level prefrontal executive modulation of limbic socioemotional reactivity that may undermine adolescent decision making.

Conclusions. Neuroimaging evidence has suggested continued specialization unique to the adolescent period characterized by continued maturation of prefrontal executive and limbic motivational–emotional processes that may underlie a predisposition for sensation seeking and exploration that could lead to vulnerabilities to risk taking. Initial models proposed that behavior in adolescence is underlaid by limitations in prefrontal control paired with an overactive motivational system (see Figure 5.5). The dual systems model proposes that prefrontal maturation persists longer than that of subcortical regions, resulting in a system that is predominantly driven by motivation, with significant limitations in prefrontal executive control (Casey et al., 2010). The triadic model proposes that limitations in regulatory top-down control, paired with an overactive approach–striatal system and an underactive avoidance–amygdala system, result in the adolescent being driven by rewards (Ernst & Fudge, 2009). In this chapter, we review the recent evidence that leads to a new proposal that builds on the dual systems and triadic models of imbalance in adolescence by proposing

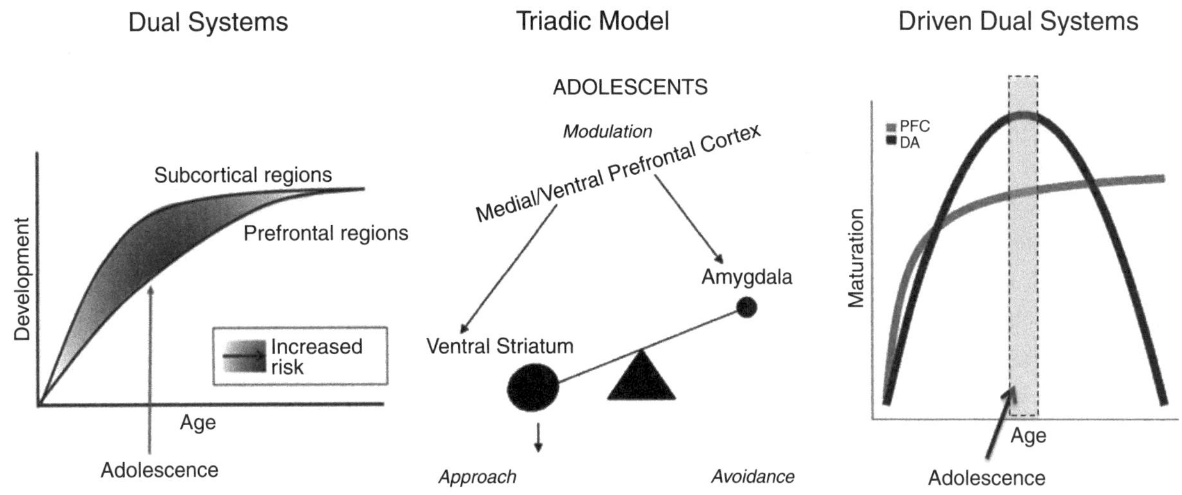

FIGURE 5.5. Models proposing an imbalance between prefrontal executive control and subcortical motivational reactivity in adolescence from the dual systems model, the triadic model, and a newly proposed model, the driven dual systems model. The dual systems model is from "The Storm and Stress of Adolescence: Insights From Human Imaging and Mouse Genetics," by B. J. Casey, R. M. Jones, L. Levita, V. Libby, S. S. Pattwell, E. J. Ruberry, . . . L. H. Somerville, 2010, *Developmental Psychobiology*, 52, p. 226. Copyright 2010 by Wiley. Reprinted with permission. The triadic model is from "A Developmental Neurobiological Model of Motivated Behavior: Anatomy, Connectivity and Ontogeny of the Triadic Nodes," by M. Ernst and J. L. Fudge, 2009, *Neuroscience and Biobehavioral Reviews, 33*, p. 369. Copyright 2009 by Elsevier. Reprinted with permission.

that adult-level prefrontal executive systems are available in adolescence but are slower to integrate and monitor information. In contrast, subcortical limbic processes that support reward–motivation and social–emotional processing undergo more significant changes that may make this system more reactive during adolescence (see Figure 5.5). The implications of this model are that although the limitations in prefrontal systems and overactive motivational systems may enhance impulsivity, it may still support complex planning driven by short-term rewards. Together, these specific maturational trajectories may provide a basis for adolescents to be able to engage complex planning abilities driven by an overactive motivational system that support the adaptive aspect of sensation seeking but may make some adolescents vulnerable to risk-taking behavior. The cases reviewed by the Supreme Court did not reflect the traditional notion of impulsivity, which involves a short time scale reaction; rather, the crimes involved (armed burglary, planned murder) required extensive planning.

Caveats to Interpretation of Neurodevelopmental Evidence

There are important considerations regarding the interpretation of neurodevelopmental findings and their applicability for informing ethical issues that need to be well understood. There are basic limitations to experimental studies in general, and in this area of study in particular, to make conclusive assertions about real differences and to infer causation. The studies reported in this chapter looked at groups of subjects, ranging in size from 10s to 100s, and for the most part included well-adjusted representations of the adolescent population. Most adolescents do not engage in risk taking and even fewer commit crimes, so there is great variability in how possible brain immaturities affect actual risky decision making and criminal activity. Second, brain science provides descriptive and correlational data that do not prove causation. Even studies that have shown associations between changes in brain maturation and risk taking have been correlational in nature and have not spoken to direct causation.

In addition, the results of neuroimaging studies are based on averages of groups of people and may not apply to individuals. Therefore, neuroimaging cannot be used as a predictive or diagnostic tool. It cannot inform us about an individual's guilt or future trajectory. At best, neuroimaging studies have shown the ability to predict brain age in a manner akin to a growth curve (Dosenbach et al., 2010). Because neuroscientific data are highly variable from person to person, neuroimaging does not allow us to designate a threshold separating juvenile decision-making ability from adultlike decision-making ability (Aronson, 2007). The neuroscience data simply describe the average nature of brain development status during adolescence and do not mean that behavior is determined.

IMPLICATIONS

As indicated in the Supreme Court decisions described in this chapter, the understanding of brain immaturities was informative when considering legislation regarding extensive sentencing of adolescents considered as a group with specific characteristics. In these cases, the brain science could answer direct questions regarding if and how the brain during adolescence differs from the brain in adulthood, specifically in its relevance to criminal acts (i.e., prefrontal executive control and limbic motivational processes). The neuroscience evidence bolsters and substantiates what has been known anecdotally and from behavioral psychology research about adolescence; teenagers can be impulsively driven when rewards and emotions are implicated and especially when their friends are involved. This predisposition can increase the risk for some adolescents to become involved in risk taking, whether because of a lower baseline determined by temperament or because particular environmental demands and stress exacerbate this predisposition. What developmental neuroscience contributes to informing the law is specific and limited, but it provides important evidence that must be presented in a responsible manner to be included in the larger discussions that guide legislation. The findings that the adolescent brain system differs from that of adults have specific implications; these implications particularly inform culpability and sentencing.

Implications for Culpability

Immaturities in the brains of teenagers can inform culpability at the time of the offense. The predisposition to impulsivity or risk taking in adolescence due to still-maturing brain processes underlying executive control and motivation can be part of the relevant information about culpability. Adolescents as a group are more prone to being driven by short-term rewards. This predisposition for risk taking can be further exacerbated by the presence of peers. However, it should not be the only or even the primary determinant when assessing an individual's culpability. More important, adolescent brain immaturities should not be interpreted as evidence to exonerate all responsibility, especially considering that not all adolescents commit crimes. The key issue is that the act may have been due, in part, to brain immaturities that enhance risk taking, and that at a later time in life, the decision would not have been made. Although antisocial behavior in childhood and adolescence is predictive of antisocial behavior in adulthood, most adolescents who display delinquent behavior do not persist in their criminal behavior (Thornberry & Krohn, 2001). Brain evidence, however, cannot inform the trajectory of an individual who is predisposed to crime, regardless of age. As a group, adolescents have increased sensitivity to rewards that can lead to risk-taking behaviors; this may play a role in offending for some adolescents who do commit criminal acts.

Implications for Sentencing

Another implication of this developmental neuroscience evidence that adolescent brain processes differ from those of adults is that this period of dynamic change is temporary and driven by specialization of brain systems to adapt to environmental demands. Gray matter is still thinning, in part because of synaptic pruning following a use-it-or-lose-it principle whereby connections that are used become stronger and those that are not are lost. Similarly, connections during development strengthen much like changes after training (Mackey, Miller Singley, & Bunge, 2013; Mackey, Whitaker, & Bunge, 2012).

In addition, DA is critical for learning and habit formation (Wise, 2004), so evidence for a possible increase in DA during adolescence supports a relative enhancement for learning.

As such, there is an aspect of plasticity in brain maturation during adolescence that is qualitatively different from that of the adult, when many of these brain maturational processes have reached stability. One implication is that given the rapid change in brain processes during adolescence, who they will become as adults is not yet clear. A second implication is that proper rehabilitation may be more effective during adolescence than later in life. These implications are important to extended sentences such as the death penalty and life without parole, given that the adolescent may change into a responsible member of society during the transition into adulthood. Crucial during this period is effective rehabilitation and consideration that purely punitive approaches would also influence the trajectory to adulthood. However, individual trajectories are not known, and it could be the case that an individual juvenile might display largely unchanging traits that persist through the life span. Given the lack of knowledge regarding individual trajectories, with most juveniles likely maturing into productive decision makers, periodic assessments of their behavioral maturation would be justified to identify those who have been rehabilitated.

Implications for Adolescent Legal Decision Making

The implications of brain immaturities regarding culpability in criminal acts are also relevant to a teen's ability to make responsible choices. It is important to note that there are important distinctions between committing a criminal act and making responsible choices when given due time to reflect and engage available executive resources. Although both decisions require the ability to exert executive control and modulate emotion, criminal acts are often impulsive, whereas decisions that require reflection for an extended period could be more equivalent to those of adults. Although the prefrontal cortex continues to prune through the 2nd decade of life (Petanjek et al., 2011) and prefrontal gray matter has not reached adult levels (Gogtay et al., 2004), increasing evidence has indicated that its function during executive control and its network connectivity are available at adult levels (Hwang et al., 2013; Ordaz et al., 2013; Simmonds et al., 2014). Despite access to adult-level prefrontal control, its engagement in a controlled fashion may be slower because of immature connectivity. These limitations would affect reactive decisions but could theoretically be accessed at adult levels given time. The implication is that impulsive decisions tap into inherent adolescent immaturities that can lead to risk taking. In contrast, making decisions that demand deliberation and do not have the type of reward contingencies that criminal acts often do could afford the ability to engage available executive systems in a similar manner as adults, especially with the guidance of a responsible adult.

In the cases of juvenile crimes that are well planned (such as in the case of *Roper v. Simmons*, 2005, or school shootings such as Columbine), to the degree that they are not impulsive, it can be argued that immaturities still have an impact on the adolescent's ability to consider long-term consequences. Limitations in executive control and temporal discounting may have undermined the juvenile's ability to understand the nature of the planned act. Juvenile school shooters, for example, appear to not have a plan for actions to take after the crime (they either get caught or terminate their life) and do not appear to have the guidance of adults (parents usually express ignorance of their child's plans) providing adaptive alternatives.

Cautionary Word on the Use of Neuroscience Evidence in the Justice System

It is important to note that brain immaturity is not meant to remove responsibility for decision making. It describes a predisposition but does not determine behavior. Adolescents are in a transitional stage of strengthening the ability to regulate behavior, which is already present but still specializing. These are relevant points given that many adolescents make important decisions, such as those regarding health, and these choices should not be undermined by science indicating a predisposition for being driven by motivation.

The allure of biologically based evidence lends itself to overextended claims. At this time, brain imaging data cannot provide evidence of an individual's guilt or future trajectories. More important, it is not possible to establish causal links for complex behavior such as neuroimaging data and crime. What neuroscience evidence can do is inform how adolescents constitute a special population with respect to culpability and extended sentencing. In regard to culpability, immaturities in the adolescent brain can provide evidence that the defendant may have acted in an impulsive and impassioned manner that might not have occurred had that individual reached full maturity with optimal executive control and dampened motivational reactivity. This evidence, however, should not be primary in determining culpability or be used to exonerate responsibility, given that it is only one piece of a much larger puzzle.

There are justified trepidations about using neuroscience evidence in the legal system before a clear understanding is established of how brain traits relate to real-life decision making (S. B. Johnson, Blum, & Giedd, 2009). At this point, there is little empirical support for a causal relationship between neuromaturational processes and real-world behavior. In addition, research on animals and human studies using simple tasks have borne little resemblance to criminal behavior (Morse, 2006). For example, tasks that investigate inhibitory control, which is used as a proxy for impulsivity, are extremely basic, tapping into the ability to stop a simple impending button press or eye movement to a simple visual stimuli. These concerns are valid. It can be argued, however, that developmental limitations in the core ability of the brain to control behavior assessed with simple tasks reflect an inherent immaturity in the processes that support top-down control of behavior on which more complex behaviors build. Nevertheless, there is accumulating evidence regarding brain development that cannot be dismissed but must be presented in context with an awareness of its limitations. Although the science cannot make direct causal claims regarding juvenile responsibility, it does provide compelling evidence regarding differences in brain status between adolescents and adults that can inform specific aspects of juvenile and criminal law.

References

Adolphs, R. (2003). Is the human amygdala specialized for processing social information? *Annals of the New York Academy of Sciences*, *985*, 326–340. http://dx.doi.org/10.1111/j.1749-6632.2003.tb07091.x

Amso, D., & Johnson, S. P. (2005). Selection and inhibition in infancy: Evidence from the spatial negative priming paradigm. *Cognition*, *95*, B27–B36. http://dx.doi.org/10.1016/j.cognition.2004.08.006

Andersen, S. L., Dumont, N. L., & Teicher, M. H. (1997). Developmental differences in dopamine synthesis inhibition by (+/-)-7-OH-DPAT. *Naunyn-Schmiedeberg's Archives of Pharmacology*, *356*, 173–181. http://dx.doi.org/10.1007/PL00005038

Andersen, S. L., Thompson, A. P., Krenzel, E., & Teicher, M. H. (2002). Pubertal changes in gonadal hormones do not underlie adolescent dopamine receptor overproduction. *Psychoneuroendocrinology*, *27*, 683–691. http://dx.doi.org/10.1016/S0306-4530(01)00069-5

Aronson, J. D. (2007). Brain imaging, culpability and the juvenile death penalty. *Psychology, Public Policy, and Law*, *13*, 115–142. http://dx.doi.org/10.1037/1076-8971.13.2.115

Asato, M. R., Terwilliger, R., Woo, J., & Luna, B. (2010). White matter development in adolescence: A DTI study. *Cerebral Cortex*, *20*, 2122–2131. http://dx.doi.org/10.1093/cercor/bhp282

Atkins v. Virginia, 536 U.S. 304 (2002).

Baik, J.-H. (2013). Dopamine signaling in reward-related behaviors. *Frontiers in Neural Circuits*, *7*, 152. http://dx.doi.org/10.3389/fncir.2013.00152

Benes, F. M. (1989). Myelination of cortical-hippocampal relays during late adolescence. *Schizophrenia Bulletin*, *15*, 585–593. http://dx.doi.org/10.1093/schbul/15.4.585

Benes, F. M., Taylor, J. B., & Cunningham, M. C. (2000). Convergence and plasticity of monoaminergic systems in the medial prefrontal cortex during the postnatal period: Implications for the development of psychopathology. *Cerebral Cortex*, *10*, 1014–1027. http://dx.doi.org/10.1093/cercor/10.10.1014

Bjork, J. M., Knutson, B., Fong, G. W., Caggiano, D. M., Bennett, S. M., & Hommer, D. W. (2004). Incentive-elicited brain activation in adolescents: Similarities and differences from young adults. *Journal of Neuroscience*, *24*, 1793–1802. http://dx.doi.org/10.1523/JNEUROSCI.4862-03.2004

Blakemore, S. J. (2008). The social brain in adolescence. *Nature Reviews Neuroscience*, *9*, 267–277. http://dx.doi.org/10.1038/nrn2353

Blakemore, S. J., Burnett, S., & Dahl, R. E. (2010). The role of puberty in the developing adolescent brain. *Human Brain Mapping*, *31*, 926–933. http://dx.doi.org/10.1002/hbm.21052

Botvinick, M., Nystrom, L. E., Fissell, K., Carter, C. S., & Cohen, J. D. (1999). Conflict monitoring versus selection-for-action in anterior cingulate cortex. *Nature*, *402*, 179–181. http://dx.doi.org/10.1038/46035

Braver, T. S., Barch, D. M., Gray, J. R., Molfese, D. L., & Snyder, A. (2001). Anterior cingulate cortex and response conflict: Effects of frequency, inhibition and errors. *Cerebral Cortex*, *11*, 825–836. http://dx.doi.org/10.1093/cercor/11.9.825

Brenhouse, H. C., Sonntag, K. C., & Andersen, S. L. (2008). Transient D1 dopamine receptor expression on prefrontal cortex projection neurons: Relationship to enhanced motivational salience of drug cues in adolescence. *Journal of Neuroscience*, *28*, 2375–2382. http://dx.doi.org/10.1523/JNEUROSCI.5064-07.2008

Buckner, R. L., Sepulcre, J., Talukdar, T., Krienen, F. M., Liu, H., Hedden, T., . . . Johnson, K. A. (2009). Cortical hubs revealed by intrinsic functional connectivity: Mapping, assessment of stability, and relation to Alzheimer's disease. *Journal of Neuroscience*, *29*, 1860–1873. http://dx.doi.org/10.1523/JNEUROSCI.5062-08.2009

Bunge, S. A., Dudukovic, N. M., Thomason, M. E., Vaidya, C. J., & Gabrieli, J. D. (2002). Immature frontal lobe contributions to cognitive control in children: Evidence from fMRI. *Neuron*, *33*, 301–311. http://dx.doi.org/10.1016/S0896-6273(01)00583-9

Carter, C. S., Braver, T. S., Barch, D. M., Botvinick, M. M., Noll, D., & Cohen, J. D. (1998). Anterior cingulate cortex, error detection, and the online monitoring of performance. *Science*, *280*, 747–749. http://dx.doi.org/10.1126/science.280.5364.747

Casey, B. J., Jones, R. M., Levita, L., Libby, V., Pattwell, S. S., Ruberry, E. J., . . . Somerville, L. H. (2010). The storm and stress of adolescence: Insights from human imaging and mouse genetics. *Developmental Psychobiology*, *52*, 225–235.

Caviness, V. S., Kennedy, D. N., Bates, J. F., & Makris, N. (1996). The developing human brain: A morphometric profile. In R. Thatcher, G. R. Lyon, G. Rumsby, & K. Krasnegor (Eds.), *Developmental neuroimaging: Mapping the development of brain and behavior* (pp. 3–14). New York, NY: Academic Press.

Chambers, R. A., Taylor, J. R., & Potenza, M. N. (2003). Developmental neurocircuitry of motivation in adolescence: A critical period of addiction vulnerability. *American Journal of Psychiatry*, *160*, 1041–1052. http://dx.doi.org/10.1176/appi.ajp.160.6.1041

Chein, J., Albert, D., O'Brien, L., Uckert, K., & Steinberg, L. (2011). Peers increase adolescent risk taking by enhancing activity in the brain's reward circuitry. *Developmental Science*, *14*, F1–F10. http://dx.doi.org/10.1111/j.1467-7687.2010.01035.x

Chikama, M., McFarland, N. R., Amaral, D. G., & Haber, S. N. (1997). Insular cortical projections to functional regions of the striatum correlate with cortical cytoarchitectonic organization in the primate. *Journal of Neuroscience*, *17*, 9686–9705.

Christakou, A., Brammer, M., & Rubia, K. (2011). Maturation of limbic corticostriatal activation and connectivity associated with developmental changes in temporal discounting. *NeuroImage*, *54*, 1344–1354. http://dx.doi.org/10.1016/j.neuroimage.2010.08.067

Christopoulos, G. I., Tobler, P. N., Bossaerts, P., Dolan, R. J., & Schultz, W. (2009). Neural correlates of value, risk, and risk aversion contributing to decision making under risk. *Journal of Neuroscience*, *29*, 12574–12583. http://dx.doi.org/10.1523/JNEUROSCI.2614-09.2009

Ciesielski, K. T., Lesnik, P. G., Savoy, R. L., Grant, E. P., & Ahlfors, S. P. (2006). Developmental neural networks in children performing a categorical *n*-back task. *NeuroImage*, *33*, 980–990. http://dx.doi.org/10.1016/j.neuroimage.2006.07.028

Cools, R. (2008). Role of dopamine in the motivational and cognitive control of behavior. *Neuroscientist*, *14*, 381–395. http://dx.doi.org/10.1177/1073858408317009

Crone, E. A., & Dahl, R. E. (2012). Understanding adolescence as a period of social-affective engagement and goal flexibility. *Nature Reviews Neuroscience*, *13*, 636–650. http://dx.doi.org/10.1038/nrn3313

Crone, E. A., Wendelken, C., Donohue, S., van Leijenhorst, L., & Bunge, S. A. (2006). Neurocognitive development of the ability to manipulate information in working memory. *Proceedings of the National Academy of Sciences, USA*, *103*, 9315–9320. http://dx.doi.org/10.1073/pnas.0510088103

Deakin, J., Aitken, M., Robbins, T., & Sahakian, B. J. (2004). Risk taking during decision-making in normal volunteers changes with age. *Journal of the International Neuropsychological Society*, *10*, 590–598. http://dx.doi.org/10.1017/S1355617704104104

Delgado, M. R. (2007). Reward-related responses in the human striatum. *Annals of the New York Academy of Sciences*, *1104*, 70–88. http://dx.doi.org/10.1196/annals.1390.002

Demetriou, A., Christou, C., Spanoudis, G., & Platsidou, M. (2002). The development of mental processing: Efficiency, working memory, and thinking. *Monographs of the Society for Research in Child Development*, *67*, i–viii.

Diamond, A. (2013). Executive functions. *Annual Review of Psychology*, *64*, 135–168. http://dx.doi.org/10.1146/annurev-psych-113011-143750

Di Martino, A., Scheres, A., Margulies, D. S., Kelly, A. M., Uddin, L. Q., Shehzad, Z., . . . Milham, M. P. (2008). Functional connectivity of human striatum: A resting state fMRI study. *Cerebral Cortex, 18*, 2735–2747. http://dx.doi.org/10.1093/cercor/bhn041

Ditton, P. M., & Wilson. (1999). *Truth in sentencing in state prisons* (Bureau of Justice Statistics Special Report, NCJ 170032). Washington, DC: U.S. Department of Justice, Office of Justice Programs.

Dosenbach, N. U. F., Nardos, B., Cohen, A. L., Fair, D. A., Power, J. D., Church, J. A., . . . Schlaggar, B. L. (2010). Prediction of individual brain maturity using fMRI. *Science, 329*, 1358–1361. http://dx.doi.org/10.1126/science.1194144

Dreyfuss, M., Caudle, K., Drysdale, A. T., Johnston, N. E., Cohen, A. O., Somerville, L. H., . . . Casey, B. J. (2014). Teens impulsively react rather than retreat from threat. *Developmental Neuroscience, 36*, 220–227.

Eluvathingal, T. J., Hasan, K. M., Kramer, L., Fletcher, J. M., & Ewing-Cobbs, L. (2007). Quantitative diffusion tensor tractography of association and projection fibers in normally developing children and adolescents. *Cerebral Cortex, 17*, 2760–2768. http://dx.doi.org/10.1093/cercor/bhm003

Ernst, M., & Fudge, J. L. (2009). A developmental neurobiological model of motivated behavior: Anatomy, connectivity and ontogeny of the triadic nodes. *Neuroscience and Biobehavioral Reviews, 33*, 367–382. http://dx.doi.org/10.1016/j.neubiorev.2008.10.009

Ernst, M., Pine, D. S., & Hardin, M. (2006). Triadic model of the neurobiology of motivated behavior in adolescence. *Psychological Medicine, 36*, 299–312. http://dx.doi.org/10.1017/S0033291705005891

Fair, D. A., Dosenbach, N. U., Church, J. A., Cohen, A. L., Brahmbhatt, S., Miezin, F. M., . . . Schlaggar, B. L. (2007). Development of distinct control networks through segregation and integration. *Proceedings of the National Academy of Sciences, USA, 104*, 13507–13512. http://dx.doi.org/10.1073/pnas.0705843104

Fischer, B., Biscaldi, M., & Gezeck, S. (1997). On the development of voluntary and reflexive components in human saccade generation. *Brain Research, 754*, 285–297. http://dx.doi.org/10.1016/S0006-8993(97)00094-2

Fudge, J. L., Kunishio, K., Walsh, P., Richard, C., & Haber, S. N. (2002). Amygdaloid projections to ventromedial striatal subterritories in the primate. *Neuroscience, 110*, 257–275. http://dx.doi.org/10.1016/S0306-4522(01)00546-2

Galvan, A., Hare, T., Voss, H., Glover, G., & Casey, B. J. (2007). Risk-taking and the adolescent brain: Who is at risk? *Developmental Science, 10*, F8–F14. http://dx.doi.org/10.1111/j.1467-7687.2006.00579.x

Galvan, A., Hare, T. A., Parra, C. E., Penn, J., Voss, H., Glover, G., & Casey, B. J. (2006). Earlier development of the accumbens relative to orbitofrontal cortex might underlie risk-taking behavior in adolescents. *Journal of Neuroscience, 26*, 6885–6892. http://dx.doi.org/10.1523/JNEUROSCI.1062-06.2006

Gardner, M., & Steinberg, L. (2005). Peer influence on risk taking, risk preference, and risky decision making in adolescence and adulthood: An experimental study. *Developmental Psychology, 41*, 625–635. http://dx.doi.org/10.1037/0012-1649.41.4.625

Geier, C., & Luna, B. (2009). The maturation of incentive processing and cognitive control. *Pharmacology, Biochemistry and Behavior, 93*, 212–221. http://dx.doi.org/10.1016/j.pbb.2009.01.021

Geier, C. F., Garver, K., Terwilliger, R., & Luna, B. (2009). Development of working memory maintenance. *Journal of Neurophysiology, 101*, 84–99. http://dx.doi.org/10.1152/jn.90562.2008

Geier, C. F., Terwilliger, R., Teslovich, T., Velanova, K., & Luna, B. (2010). Immaturities in reward processing and its influence on inhibitory control in adolescence. *Cerebral Cortex, 20*, 1613–1629. http://dx.doi.org/10.1093/cercor/bhp225

Giedd, J. N., Blumenthal, J., Jeffries, N. O., Castellanos, F. X., Liu, H., Zijdenbos, A., . . . Rapoport, J. L. (1999). Brain development during childhood and adolescence: A longitudinal MRI study. *Nature Neuroscience, 2*, 861–863. http://dx.doi.org/10.1038/13158

Giedd, J. N., Snell, J. W., Lange, N., Rajapakse, J. C., Casey, B. J., Kozuch, P. L., . . . Rapoport, J. L. (1996). Quantitative magnetic resonance imaging of human brain development: Ages 4-18. *Cerebral Cortex, 6*, 551–559. http://dx.doi.org/10.1093/cercor/6.4.551

Giorgio, A., Watkins, K. E., Douaud, G., James, A. C., James, S., De Stefano, N., . . . Johansen-Berg, H. (2008). Changes in white matter microstructure during adolescence. *NeuroImage, 39*, 52–61. http://dx.doi.org/10.1016/j.neuroimage.2007.07.043

Gogtay, N., Giedd, J. N., Lusk, L., Hayashi, K. M., Greenstein, D., Vaituzis, A. C., . . . Thompson, P. M. (2004). Dynamic mapping of human cortical development during childhood through early adulthood. *Proceedings of the National Academy of Sciences, USA, 101*, 8174–8179. http://dx.doi.org/10.1073/pnas.0402680101

Goldman-Rakic, P. S., & Brown, R. M. (1982). Postnatal development of monoamine content and synthesis in the cerebral cortex of rhesus monkeys. *Developmental Brain Research, 4*, 339–349. http://dx.doi.org/10.1016/0165-3806(82)90146-8

Goldman-Rakic, P. S., Chafee, M., & Friedman, H. (1993). Allocation of function in distributed circuits. In T. Ono, M. Fukuda, L. Squire, M. Raichle, &

D. Perrett (Eds.), *Brain mechanisms of perception and memory: From neuron to behavior* (pp. 445–456). New York, NY: Oxford University Press.

Graham v. Florida, 130 S. Ct. 2011, 560 U.S. 48 (2010).

Gunther Moor, B., van Leijenhorst, L., Rombouts, S. A., Crone, E. A., & Van der Molen, M. W. (2010). Do you like me? Neural correlates of social evaluation and developmental trajectories. *Social Neuroscience*, *5*, 461–482. http://dx.doi.org/10.1080/17470910903526155

Güroğlu, B., van den Bos, W., & Crone, E. A. (2009). Fairness considerations: Increasing understanding of intentionality during adolescence. *Journal of Experimental Child Psychology*, *104*, 398–409. http://dx.doi.org/10.1016/j.jecp.2009.07.002

Haber, S. N., Kunishio, K., Mizobuchi, M., & Lynd-Balta, E. (1995). The orbital and medial prefrontal circuit through the primate basal ganglia. *Journal of Neuroscience*, *15*, 4851–4867.

Haider, A. (2006). Roper v. Simmons: The role of the science brief. *Ohio State Journal of Criminal Law*, *3*, 369–377.

Heron, M. (2012). Deaths: Leading causes for 2008. *National Vital Statistics Reports*, *60*, 1–94.

Herting, M. M., Gautam, P., Spielberg, J. M., Kan, E., Dahl, R. E., & Sowell, E. R. (2014). The role of testosterone and estradiol in brain volume changes across adolescence: A longitudinal structural MRI study. *Human Brain Mapping*, *35*, 5633–5645. http://dx.doi.org/10.1002/hbm.22575

Herting, M. M., Maxwell, E. C., Irvine, C., & Nagel, B. J. (2012). The impact of sex, puberty, and hormones on white matter microstructure in adolescents. *Cerebral Cortex*, 22, 1979–1992. http://dx.doi.org/10.1093/cercor/bhr246

Huttenlocher, P. R. (1990). Morphometric study of human cerebral cortex development. *Neuropsychologia*, *28*, 517–527. http://dx.doi.org/10.1016/0028-3932(90)90031-I

Huttenlocher, P. R., & Dabholkar, A. S. (1997). Regional differences in synaptogenesis in human cerebral cortex. *Journal of Comparative Neurology*, *387*, 167–178. http://dx.doi.org/10.1002/(SICI)1096-9861(19971020)387:2<167::AID-CNE1>3.0.CO;2-Z

Hwang, K., Hallquist, M. N., & Luna, B. (2013). The development of hub architecture in the human functional brain network. *Cerebral Cortex*, *23*, 2380–2393. http://dx.doi.org/10.1093/cercor/bhs227

Hwang, K., Velanova, K., & Luna, B. (2010). Strengthening of top-down frontal cognitive control networks underlying the development of inhibitory control: A functional magnetic resonance imaging effective connectivity study. *Journal of Neuroscience*, *30*, 15535–15545. http://dx.doi.org/10.1523/JNEUROSCI.2825-10.2010

Jackson v. Hobbs, 567 U.S. ____ (2012).

J.D.B. v. North Carolina, 131 S. Ct. 2394 (2011).

Johnson, M. H., Grossmann, T., & Cohen Kadosh, K. (2009). Mapping functional brain development: Building a social brain through interactive specialization. *Developmental Psychology*, *45*, 151–159. http://dx.doi.org/10.1037/a0014548

Johnson, S. B., Blum, R. W., & Giedd, J. N. (2009). Adolescent maturity and the brain: The promise and pitfalls of neuroscience research in adolescent health policy. *Journal of Adolescent Health*, *45*, 216–221. http://dx.doi.org/10.1016/j.jadohealth.2009.05.016

Jones, R. M., Somerville, L. H., Li, J., Ruberry, E. J., Powers, A., Mehta, N., . . . Casey, B. J. (2014). Adolescent-specific patterns of behavior and neural activity during social reinforcement learning. *Cognitive, Affective, and Behavioral Neuroscience*, *14*, 683–697. http://dx.doi.org/10.3758/s13415-014-0257-z

Kalsbeek, A., Voorn, P., Buijs, R. M., Pool, C. W., & Uylings, H. B. (1988). Development of the dopaminergic innervation in the prefrontal cortex of the rat. *Journal of Comparative Neurology*, *269*, 58–72. http://dx.doi.org/10.1002/cne.902690105

Kessler, R. C., Berglund, P., Demler, O., Jin, R., Merikangas, K. R., & Walters, E. E. (2005). Lifetime prevalence and age-of-onset distributions of *DSM–IV* disorders in the National Comorbidity Survey Replication. *Archives of General Psychiatry*, *62*, 593–602. http://dx.doi.org/10.1001/archpsyc.62.6.593

Klingberg, T., Forssberg, H., & Westerberg, H. (2002). Increased brain activity in frontal and parietal cortex underlies the development of visuospatial working memory capacity during childhood. *Journal of Cognitive Neuroscience*, *14*, 1–10.

Lambe, E. K., Krimer, L. S., & Goldman-Rakic, P. S. (2000). Differential postnatal development of catecholamine and serotonin inputs to identified neurons in prefrontal cortex of rhesus monkey. *Journal of Neuroscience*, *20*, 8780–8787.

Lebel, C., Walker, L., Leemans, A., Phillips, L., & Beaulieu, C. (2008). Microstructural maturation of the human brain from childhood to adulthood. *NeuroImage*, *40*, 1044–1055. http://dx.doi.org/10.1016/j.neuroimage.2007.12.053

Lenroot, R. K., Gogtay, N., Greenstein, D. K., Wells, E. M., Wallace, G. L., Clasen, L. S., . . . Giedd, J. N. (2007). Sexual dimorphism of brain developmental trajectories during childhood and adolescence. *NeuroImage*, *36*, 1065–1073. http://dx.doi.org/10.1016/j.neuroimage.2007.03.053

Lewis, D. A., Melchitzky, D. S., & Burgos, G. G. (2002). Specificity in the functional architecture of primate prefrontal cortex. *Journal of Neurocytology, 31*, 265–276. http://dx.doi.org/10.1023/A:1024174026286

Lidow, M. S., & Rakic, P. (1992). Scheduling of monoaminergic neurotransmitter receptor expression in the primate neocortex during postnatal development. *Cerebral Cortex, 2*, 401–416. http://dx.doi.org/10.1093/cercor/2.5.401

Liston, C., Watts, R., Tottenham, N., Davidson, M. C., Niogi, S., Ulug, A. M., & Casey, B. J. (2006). Frontostriatal microstructure modulates efficient recruitment of cognitive control. *Cerebral Cortex, 16*, 553–560. http://dx.doi.org/10.1093/cercor/bhj003

Luna, B., Garver, K. E., Urban, T. A., Lazar, N. A., & Sweeney, J. A. (2004). Maturation of cognitive processes from late childhood to adulthood. *Child Development, 75*, 1357–1372. http://dx.doi.org/10.1111/j.1467-8624.2004.00745.x

Mackey, A. P., Miller Singley, A. T., & Bunge, S. A. (2013). Intensive reasoning training alters patterns of brain connectivity at rest. *Journal of Neuroscience, 33*, 4796–4803. http://dx.doi.org/10.1523/JNEUROSCI.4141-12.2013

Mackey, A. P., Whitaker, K. J., & Bunge, S. A. (2012). Experience-dependent plasticity in white matter microstructure: Reasoning training alters structural connectivity. *Frontiers in Neuroanatomy, 6*, 32. http://dx.doi.org/10.3389/fnana.2012.00032

Matthews, M., Bondi, C., Torres, G., & Moghaddam, B. (2013). Reduced presynaptic dopamine activity in adolescent dorsal striatum. *Neuropsychopharmacology, 38*, 1344–1351. http://dx.doi.org/10.1038/npp.2013.32

McCutcheon, J. E., White, F. J., & Marinelli, M. (2009). Individual differences in dopamine cell neuroadaptations following cocaine self-administration. *Biological Psychiatry, 66*, 801–803. http://dx.doi.org/10.1016/j.biopsych.2009.04.018

Miller v. Alabama, 132 S. Ct. 2455 (2012).

Montague, D. M., Lawler, C. P., Mailman, R. B., & Gilmore, J. H. (1999). Developmental regulation of the dopamine D1 receptor in human caudate and putamen. *Neuropsychopharmacology, 21*, 641–649. http://dx.doi.org/10.1016/S0893-133X(99)00062-7

Morse, S. (2006). Brain overclaim syndrome and criminal responsibility: A diagnostic note. *Ohio State Journal of Criminal Law, 3*, 397–412.

Nagy, Z., Westerberg, H., & Klingberg, T. (2004). Maturation of white matter is associated with the development of cognitive functions during childhood. *Journal of Cognitive Neuroscience, 16*, 1227–1233. http://dx.doi.org/10.1162/0898929041920441

Nelson, E. E., McClure, E. B., Monk, C. S., Zarahn, E., Leibenluft, E., Pine, D. S., & Ernst, M. (2003). Developmental differences in neuronal engagement during implicit encoding of emotional faces: An event-related fMRI study. *Journal of Child Psychology and Psychiatry, and Allied Disciplines, 44*, 1015–1024. http://dx.doi.org/10.1111/1469-7610.00186

Nowakowski, R. S. (2006). Stable neuron numbers from cradle to grave. *Proceedings of the National Academy of Sciences, USA, 103*, 12219–12220. http://dx.doi.org/10.1073/pnas.0605605103

Olesen, P. J., Macoveanu, J., Tegnér, J., & Klingberg, T. (2007). Brain activity related to working memory and distraction in children and adults. *Cerebral Cortex, 17*, 1047–1054. http://dx.doi.org/10.1093/cercor/bhl014

Olesen, P. J., Nagy, Z., Westerberg, H., & Klingberg, T. (2003). Combined analysis of DTI and fMRI data reveals a joint maturation of white and grey matter in a fronto-parietal network. *Cognitive Brain Research, 18*, 48–57. http://dx.doi.org/10.1016/j.cogbrainres.2003.09.003

Ordaz, S. J., Foran, W., Velanova, K., & Luna, B. (2013). Longitudinal growth curves of brain function underlying inhibitory control through adolescence. *Journal of Neuroscience, 33*, 18109–18124. http://dx.doi.org/10.1523/JNEUROSCI.1741-13.2013

Padmanabhan, A., Geier, C. F., Ordaz, S. J., Teslovich, T., & Luna, B. (2011). Developmental changes in brain function underlying the influence of reward processing on inhibitory control. *Developmental Cognitive Neuroscience, 1*, 517–529. http://dx.doi.org/10.1016/j.dcn.2011.06.004

Padmanabhan, A., & Luna, B. (2014). Developmental imaging genetics: Linking dopamine function to adolescent behavior. *Brain and Cognition, 89*, 27–38. http://dx.doi.org/10.1016/j.bandc.2013.09.011

Passingham, D., & Sakai, K. (2004). The prefrontal cortex and working memory: Physiology and brain imaging. *Current Opinion in Neurobiology, 14*, 163–168. http://dx.doi.org/10.1016/j.conb.2004.03.003

Paulsen, D. J., Platt, M. L., Huettel, S. A., & Brannon, E. M. (2011). Decision-making under risk in children, adolescents, and young adults. *Frontier in Psychology, 2*, 72.

Paus, T., Keshavan, M., & Giedd, J. N. (2008). Why do many psychiatric disorders emerge during adolescence? *Nature Reviews Neuroscience, 9*, 947–957.

Petanjek, Z., Judaš, M., Šimić, G., Rašin, M. R., Uylings, H. B. M., Rakic, P., & Kostović, I. (2011). Extraordinary neoteny of synaptic spines in the human prefrontal cortex. *Proceedings of the National*

Academy of Sciences, USA, 108, 13281–13286. http://dx.doi.org/10.1073/pnas.1105108108

Rauschecker, J. P., & Marler, P. (1987). What signals are responsible for synaptic changes in visual cortical plasticity? In J. Ranschecker & P. Marler (Eds.), *Imprinting and cortical plasticity* (pp. 193–200). New York, NY: Wiley.

Raznahan, A., Lee, Y., Stidd, R., Long, R., Greenstein, D., Clasen, L., . . . Giedd, J. N. (2010). Longitudinally mapping the influence of sex and androgen signaling on the dynamics of human cortical maturation in adolescence. *Proceedings of the National Academy of Sciences, USA, 107*, 16988–16993. http://dx.doi.org/10.1073/pnas.1006025107

Raznahan, A., Shaw, P. W., Lerch, J. P., Clasen, L. S., Greenstein, D., Berman, R., . . . Giedd, J. N. (2014). Longitudinal four-dimensional mapping of subcortical anatomy in human development. *Proceedings of the National Academy of Sciences, USA, 111*, 1592–1597. http://dx.doi.org/10.1073/pnas.1316911111

Reyna, V. F., & Brainerd, C. J. (2011). Dual processes in decision making and developmental neuroscience: A fuzzy-trace model. *Developmental Review, 31*, 180–206.

Ridderinkhof, K. R., Band, G. P. H., & Logan, G. D. (1999). A study of adaptive behavior: Effects of age and irrelevant information on the ability to inhibit one's actions. *Acta Psychologica, 101*, 315–337. http://dx.doi.org/10.1016/S0001-6918(99)00010-4

Roper v. Simmons, 543 U.S. 551 (2005).

Rosenberg, D. R., & Lewis, D. A. (1994). Changes in the dopaminergic innervation of monkey prefrontal cortex during late postnatal development: A tyrosine hydroxylase immunohistochemical study. *Biological Psychiatry, 36*, 272–277. http://dx.doi.org/10.1016/0006-3223(94)90610-6

Rosenberg, D. R., & Lewis, D. A. (1995). Postnatal maturation of the dopaminergic innervation of monkey prefrontal and motor cortices: A tyrosine hydroxylase immunohistochemical analysis. *Journal of Comparative Neurology, 358*, 383–400. http://dx.doi.org/10.1002/cne.903580306

Rubia, K., Smith, A. B., Woolley, J., Nosarti, C., Heyman, I., Taylor, E., & Brammer, M. (2006). Progressive increase of frontostriatal brain activation from childhood to adulthood during event-related tasks of cognitive control. *Human Brain Mapping, 27*, 973–993. http://dx.doi.org/10.1002/hbm.20237

Sander, M. C., Lindenberger, U., & Werkle-Bergner, M. (2012). Lifespan age differences in working memory: A two-component framework. *Neuroscience and Biobehavioral Reviews, 36*, 2007–2033. http://dx.doi.org/10.1016/j.neubiorev.2012.06.004

Schäfer, C. B., Morgan, B. R., Ye, A. X., Taylor, M. J., & Doesburg, S. M. (2014). Oscillations, networks, and their development: MEG connectivity changes with age. *Human Brain Mapping, 35*, 5249–5261. http://dx.doi.org/10.1002/hbm.22547

Scherf, K. S., Sweeney, J. A., & Luna, B. (2006). Brain basis of developmental change in visuospatial working memory. *Journal of Cognitive Neuroscience, 18*, 1045–1058. http://dx.doi.org/10.1162/jocn.2006.18.7.1045

Schleepen, T. M., & Jonkman, L. M. (2009). The development of non-spatial working memory capacity during childhood and adolescence and the role of interference control: An N-Back task study. *Developmental Neuropsychology, 35*, 37–56. http://dx.doi.org/10.1080/87565640903325733

Schultz, W. (2001). Reward signaling by dopamine neurons. *Neuroscientist, 7*, 293–302. http://dx.doi.org/10.1177/107385840100700406

Schultz, W. (2002). Getting formal with dopamine and reward. *Neuron, 36*, 241–263. http://dx.doi.org/10.1016/S0896-6273(02)00967-4

Schultz, W., Preuschoff, K., Camerer, C., Hsu, M., Fiorillo, C. D., Tobler, P. N., & Bossaerts, P. (2008). Explicit neural signals reflecting reward uncertainty. *Philosophical Transactions of the Royal Society, Series B: Biological Sciences, 363*, 3801–3811. http://dx.doi.org/10.1098/rstb.2008.0152

Seeman, P., Bzowej, N. H., Guan, H. C., Bergeron, C., Becker, L. E., Reynolds, G. P., . . . Tourtellotte, W. W. (1987). Human brain dopamine receptors in children and aging adults. *Synapse, 1*, 399–404. http://dx.doi.org/10.1002/syn.890010503

Selemon, L. D., & Goldman-Rakic, P. S. (1985). Longitudinal topography and interdigitation of corticostriatal projections in the rhesus monkey. *Journal of Neuroscience, 5*, 776–794.

Simmonds, D. J., Hallquist, M. N., Asato, M., & Luna, B. (2014). Developmental stages and sex differences of white matter and behavioral development through adolescence: A longitudinal diffusion tensor imaging (DTI) study. *NeuroImage, 92*, 356–368. http://dx.doi.org/10.1016/j.neuroimage.2013.12.044

Sisk, C. L., & Zehr, J. L. (2005). Pubertal hormones organize the adolescent brain and behavior. *Frontiers in Neuroendocrinology, 26*, 163–174. http://dx.doi.org/10.1016/j.yfrne.2005.10.003

Smith, A. B., Halari, R., Giampetro, V., Brammer, M., & Rubia, K. (2011). Developmental effects of reward on sustained attention networks. *NeuroImage, 56*, 1693–1704. http://dx.doi.org/10.1016/j.neuroimage.2011.01.072

Smith, A. R., Chein, J., & Steinberg, L. (2013). Impact of socio-emotional context, brain development, and pubertal maturation on adolescent risk-taking. *Hormones and Behavior*, *64*, 323–332. http://dx.doi.org/10.1016/j.yhbeh.2013.03.006

Somerville, L. H., & Casey, B. J. (2010). Developmental neurobiology of cognitive control and motivational systems. *Current Opinion in Neurobiology*, *20*, 236–241. http://dx.doi.org/10.1016/j.conb.2010.01.006

Somerville, L. H., Jones, R. M., & Casey, B. J. (2010). A time of change: Behavioral and neural correlates of adolescent sensitivity to appetitive and aversive environmental cues. *Brain and Cognition*, *72*, 124–133. http://dx.doi.org/10.1016/j.bandc.2009.07.003

Sowell, E. R., Thompson, P. M., Holmes, C. J., Jernigan, T. L., & Toga, A. W. (1999). In vivo evidence for post-adolescent brain maturation in frontal and striatal regions. *Nature Neuroscience*, *2*, 859–861. http://dx.doi.org/10.1038/13154

Spear, L. P. (2000). Neurobehavioral changes in adolescence. *Current Directions in Psychological Science*, *9*, 111–114. http://dx.doi.org/10.1111/1467-8721.00072

Spear, L. P. (2010). *The behavioral neuroscience of adolescence*. New York, NY: Norton.

Sporns, O. (2013). Structure and function of complex brain networks. *Dialogues in Clinical Neuroscience*, *15*, 247–262.

Stanford v. Kentucky, 492 U.S. 361 (1989).

Steinberg, L. (2004). Risk taking in adolescence: What changes, and why? *Annals of the New York Academy of Sciences*, *1021*, 51–58. http://dx.doi.org/10.1196/annals.1308.005

Steinberg, L. (2008). A social neuroscience perspective on adolescent risk-taking. *Developmental Review*, *28*, 78–106. http://dx.doi.org/10.1016/j.dr.2007.08.002

Stevens, M. C., Kiehl, K. A., Pearlson, G. D., & Calhoun, V. D. (2007). Functional neural networks underlying response inhibition in adolescents and adults. *Behavioural Brain Research*, *181*, 12–22. http://dx.doi.org/10.1016/j.bbr.2007.03.023

Sturman, D. A., & Moghaddam, B. (2011). Reduced neuronal inhibition and coordination of adolescent prefrontal cortex during motivated behavior. *Journal of Neuroscience*, *31*, 1471–1478. http://dx.doi.org/10.1523/JNEUROSCI.4210-10.2011

Thomas, K. M., King, S. W., Franzen, P. L., Welsh, T. F., Berkowitz, A. L., Noll, D. C., . . . Casey, B. J. (1999). A developmental functional MRI study of spatial working memory. *NeuroImage*, *10*, 327–338. http://dx.doi.org/10.1006/nimg.1999.0466

Thornberry, T. P., & Krohn, M. D. (2001). The development of delinquency. In S. O. White (Ed.), *Handbook of youth and justice* (pp. 289–305). http://dx.doi.org/10.1007/978-1-4615-1289-9_15

Toga, A. W., Thompson, P. M., & Sowell, E. R. (2006). Mapping brain maturation. *Trends in Neurosciences*, *29*, 148–159. http://dx.doi.org/10.1016/j.tins.2006.01.007

Uhlhaas, P. J., Roux, F., Singer, W., Haenschel, C., Sireteanu, R., & Rodriguez, E. (2009). The development of neural synchrony reflects late maturation and restructuring of functional networks in humans. *Proceedings of the National Academy of Sciences*, *106*, 9866–9871. http://dx.doi.org/10.1073/pnas.0900390106

van Leijenhorst, L., Crone, E. A., & Bunge, S. A. (2006). Neural correlates of developmental differences in risk estimation and feedback processing. *Neuropsychologia*, *44*, 2158–2170. http://dx.doi.org/10.1016/j.neuropsychologia.2006.02.002

van Leijenhorst, L., Gunther Moor, B., Op de Macks, Z. A., Rombouts, S. A., Westenberg, P. M., & Crone, E. A. (2010). Adolescent risky decision-making: Neurocognitive development of reward and control regions. *NeuroImage*, *51*, 345–355. http://dx.doi.org/10.1016/j.neuroimage.2010.02.038

van Leijenhorst, L., Zanolie, K., Van Meel, C. S., Westenberg, P. M., Rombouts, S. A., & Crone, E. A. (2010). What motivates the adolescent? Brain regions mediating reward sensitivity across adolescence. *Cerebral Cortex*, *20*, 61–69. http://dx.doi.org/10.1093/cercor/bhp078

Wahlstrom, D., Collins, P., White, T., & Luciana, M. (2010). Developmental changes in dopamine neurotransmission in adolescence: Behavioral implications and issues in assessment. *Brain and Cognition*, *72*, 146–159. http://dx.doi.org/10.1016/j.bandc.2009.10.013

Wahlstrom, D., White, T., & Luciana, M. (2010). Neurobehavioral evidence for changes in dopamine system activity during adolescence. *Neuroscience and Biobehavioral Reviews*, *34*, 631–648. http://dx.doi.org/10.1016/j.neubiorev.2009.12.007

Wise, R. A. (2004). Dopamine, learning and motivation. *Nature Reviews Neuroscience*, *5*, 483–494. http://dx.doi.org/10.1038/nrn1406

Yakovlev, P. I., & Lecours, A. R. (1967). The myelogenetic cycles of regional maturation of the brain. In A. Minkowski (Ed.), *Regional development of the brain in early life* (pp. 3–70). Oxford, England: Blackwell Scientific.

CHAPTER 6

ADOLESCENT DEVELOPMENT, MENTAL DISORDER, AND DECISION MAKING IN DELINQUENT YOUTHS

Alison G. Nagel, Lucy A. Guarnera, and N. Dickon Reppucci

Adolescence is a unique time of change and challenge, when youths are set with accomplishing a multitude of developmental tasks necessary to transition to successful independent living and adult roles. Adolescents tend to be immature relative to adults in a variety of domains—biological, cognitive, emotional, social—and must undergo significant transformation in these domains before reaching maturity. One notable example (as detailed in Chapter 4, this handbook) concerns juveniles' psychosocial immaturity—that is, deficiencies in youths' social and emotional capacities relative to adults'. For example, adolescents are usually more impulsive, more likely to take risks, and more vulnerable to peer pressure than adults; they also tend to be more susceptible to stress and less able to weigh present benefits in the light of future consequences (Cauffman & Steinberg, 2000; Scott, Reppucci, & Woolard, 1995; Steinberg & Cauffman, 1996). These psychosocial deficiencies, compounded with still-developing cognitive faculties, contribute to adolescents' often immature and short-sighted decision making in a variety of domains, such as engaging in risky sexual practices or reckless driving (Gardner & Steinberg, 2005).

Over the past 20 years, researchers (and, increasingly, the U.S. Supreme Court) have importantly recognized how immature decision making renders adolescents, as a class, more likely to commit delinquent acts, less able to negotiate the demands of the justice system, and more vulnerable in detention facilities (e.g., *Roper v. Simmons*, 2005). In other words, the normal developmental course of adolescent decision making means that youths are both more likely to engage in antisocial behavior and more vulnerable once in contact with the justice system.

If typical adolescents are already at risk for delinquency and involvement with the justice system because of their psychosocial immaturity, youths suffering from mental disorder are particularly vulnerable. Commensurate with the myriad changes that characterize the teenage years, adolescence is also a period of great change in the incidence, manifestation, and consequences of mental disorders. Some mental disorders may develop for the first time in adolescence (e.g., schizophrenia, eating disorders, substance abuse), whereas the presentation or severity of other mental disorders may change as teens face new demands on their capacities (e.g., attention deficit/hyperactivity disorder [ADHD], major depressive disorder). The burden of youths with mental disorders on the juvenile justice system is substantial. As discussed in greater detail later in this chapter, approximately 3 times as many youths in juvenile detention meet the criteria for a mental disorder as compared to community rates (Kazdin, 2000). Regarding mental disability, the average IQ score of youths in detention centers is about 15 points, or 1 standard deviation, lower than the average IQ in the general population (Foley, 2001). Similarly, the proportion of youths in juvenile correctional facilities who were enrolled in special education classes before incarceration is as much as 7 times more than the proportion of youths in the community (Quinn, Rutherford, Leone, Osher, & Poirier, 2005).

http://dx.doi.org/10.1037/14643-006
APA Handbook of Psychology and Juvenile Justice, K. Heilbrun (Editor-in-Chief)

Although there are many potential contributors to this high prevalence of mental disorder among youths detained in the juvenile justice system, an important consideration—and the focus of this chapter—is how mental disorder further impairs adolescents' already immature decision-making capacities. Many mental disorders experienced by adolescents include symptoms (such as impulsivity, aggressiveness, cognitive dulling, and hostile attributions) that have a direct negative effect on youths' decision making. Given the developmental disadvantages faced by all youths, these additional taxes on the decision-making capacities of youth with mental disorders place them at even greater risk for justice involvement (Grisso, 2006). This doubly impaired decision making suggests a dual process, whereby youths with mental disorders are more likely to come into contact with the juvenile justice system and then also more likely to stay involved because of decreased ability to negotiate the demands of the legal system, increased likelihood of secure confinement, increased need for services, and increased likelihood of reoffending.

The question of how best to screen, treat, and manage youths with mental disorders in the juvenile justice system is a pressing one, given the large number of these youths in the system and the special vulnerabilities of this population. The juvenile justice system has always included therapeutic goals, and nowhere are these ideals in sharper focus than in considering detained youths with mental illness (Hafemeister, 2004). These youths touch on the juvenile justice system's dual obligations: the deontic obligation to provide rights and protections to vulnerable populations and the utilitarian obligation to reduce crime and protect the public (Sales & Shuman, 1996). At times, these dual obligations may conflict—for example, when the intensive resources required by severely disturbed delinquent youths divert money and attention away from other crime reduction efforts. However, given the direct contribution that mental disorder may have on youths' delinquency via the pathway of impaired decision making, the deontic and utilitarian obligations of the juvenile justice system may be able to work in tandem: treating youths with mental disorders to alleviate their suffering and thereby simultaneously reducing crime and increasing public safety.

The purpose of this chapter is to provide a developmental perspective on mental disorder among delinquent youths, particularly how these disorders further impair the already immature decision-making capacities of these adolescents. First, to provide a framework for concepts discussed throughout the chapter, we begin with a developmental perspective on mental disorder among juveniles, particularly focusing on continuities and discontinuities with both normal adolescent development and adult psychopathology. Next, we place in context the current challenge of managing youths with mental disorder in the juvenile justice system by providing historical background on relevant legal and public policy changes. Then we discuss current evidence in favor of a pathway of impaired decision making to explain the high prevalence of youths with mental disorders in the juvenile justice system and how the courts generally do not acknowledge such vulnerabilities. Finally, we present best practices for the screening, assessment, and treatment of mentally disordered youths in the juvenile justice system, as well as future directions for research into this significant legal and public health problem.

A DEVELOPMENTAL PERSPECTIVE ON MENTAL DISORDER AMONG ADOLESCENTS

Any discussion of the impact of mental disorder on youths in the criminal justice system must be grounded in an understanding of how mental disorder is defined among youths, as well as how psychopathology emerges and functions in the broader context of adolescent development (Grisso, 2004). Clinical knowledge about adolescent mental disorder can help the juvenile justice system mount an appropriate response to the high rates of youths with mental disorders under its aegis. However, the research into adolescent mental disorder has lagged far behind the research on adult mental disorder, and much remains unknown about the etiology, course, persistence, and consequences of mental disorder among youths (Rutter, 2010). In addition, absurdities and inconsistencies in diagnosis of mental disorder among youths may obscure the scope and nature of the true problem for the juvenile justice system. In this section, we briefly explore how mental disorder is defined in adolescents, how teen psychopathology compares with normal development, and how adolescent mental disorder does or does not persist into adulthood. We also describe prevalence rates of mental disorder in the general adolescent population and juvenile justice system.

Historically, juvenile psychopathology was either ignored or considered merely a downward extension of adult psychopathology (Rutter, 2010). Before the 20th century, adolescent mental disorder did not exist as a psychiatric specialty (Rutter, 2010), and it was not until the 1980s that adolescent psychopathology was considered in the context of the unique changes and vulnerabilities of the developmental period (e.g., Cicchetti, 1984). In contrast to prior theories that saw childhood mental health problems as either irrelevant to or entirely continuous with adult functioning, the new field of developmental psychopathology expected juvenile mental disorder to show both continuity and discontinuity in behavioral variation and developmental course (Rutter, 2013). The American Psychiatric Association's (2013) *Diagnostic and Statistical Manual of Mental Disorders* (5th ed.; *DSM–5*), which is the most widely used classification system for mental disorders in the United States, generally fits adult psychopathology better than adolescent psychopathology because its system of diagnosis does not recognize these continuities and discontinuities inherent in the developmental experience.

Continuity and Discontinuity Between Normal Development and Mental Disorder

When determining how to respond to youths with mental disorders in the juvenile justice system, the system must recognize that significant continuity exists between normal development and mental disorder among adolescents, blurring the lines separating youths with mental disorders from youths without mental disorders. For example, Grisso (2004) discussed what he termed *age relativity*—the concept that almost all problematic behaviors and emotions that might be termed symptoms of a mental disorder are normative at particular points in child development. Therefore, typical (if problematic) youthful traits (such as moodiness, irritability, impulsivity, and separation anxiety) can gradually morph from normative behaviors to pathological symptoms if the child begins to deviate from his or her peers or become maladaptive in the context of the child's developmental period, making the cutoff between normal and pathological unclear (Cicchetti & Rogosch, 2002).

Another important way in which the boundary between youths with and without mental disorder is blurred for the juvenile justice system is the growing recognition that many mental disorders are best conceptualized as dimensional rather than categorical. The *DSM–5* still largely reflects its origins in the neo-Kraepelinian synthesis, which emphasizes finite disease entities with a distinct pattern of prototypical symptoms that individuals must endorse to be labeled as possessing the illness (M. Kendall, 1991). However, consensus is growing that many if not most mental disorders exist along a continuum, rather than as discrete entities (Coghill & Sonuga-Barke, 2012). Even severe psychopathology that had long been assumed to represent a distinct, pathological deviation from normality, such as schizophrenia, appears to have more continuities with typical development than previously thought. For example, research has indicated that psychotic-like experiences, such as hearing voices, are far more common in the general population than previously believed (Laurens, Hobbs, Sunderland, Green, & Mould, 2012).

Even if *DSM–5* disorders were to be considered dimensionally, they would still fail to capture most adolescents' experience of mental illness because of the problem of comorbidity. There is a "ridiculously high rate of co-occurring disorders—supposed 'comorbidity'" (Rutter, 2011, p. 649)—among youths, in which youths meet criteria for two (or more) *DSM–5* disorders simultaneously, such as depression and anxiety (Kovacs, 1990), or ADHD and oppositional defiant disorder (ODD; Barkley, 1990). When comorbidity among adolescents is the norm rather than the exception, this casts doubt on the assertion that the number of distinct mental disorders among youths is finite (M. Kendall,

1991). Youths are much more likely to present with "mixed patterns of symptomatology" (Rutter, 2011, p. 655) that do not fit with the prototype model of categorical diagnosis espoused by the *DSM–5*. Better supported is Grisso's (2004) argument that youths' psychopathology is diffuse and global—consistent with youths' overall immature development—and progresses into more differentiated forms as youths mature. In light of these developmental changes and the astronomically high rates of comorbidity among youths with mental disorders in general, and among juvenile justice populations specifically (near 80%; Shufelt & Cocozza, 2006), it may not be fruitful for the juvenile justice system to classify, treat, or otherwise manage youths with mental disorders on the basis of *DSM–5* diagnosis alone. A focus on symptoms or problems rather than diagnosis seems more supported by the research.

Continuity and Discontinuity Across the Developmental Period

Historically, there has been a divide— among both researchers and mental health institutions—between juvenile psychiatry and adult psychiatry, and this divide has contributed to the failure to understand the natural history of most mental disorders as they progress (or fail to progress) across the developmental period (Duffy & Carlson, 2013). What is known suggests both continuity and discontinuity across the developmental period, with little understanding of why disorders persist into adulthood in some youths but not others. This results in uncertainty about when and for whom aggressive treatment of adolescent mental disorder is warranted. For example, prodromal symptoms (such as cognitive problems and perceptual distortions) in adolescence and early adulthood significantly increase the odds that a youth will go on to develop a full-fledged schizophreniform disorder as an adult (Drake & Lewis, 2005). About 15%–30% of adolescents and young adults presenting with prodromal symptoms transition to a diagnosable psychotic disorder within 1 year—a risk 1,000 times greater than in the general population (Drake & Lewis, 2005). However, these numbers still mean that the majority of prodromal youths will never progress to frank psychosis. Little is known, though, about what differentiates the high-risk prodromal adolescents on a schizophrenic trajectory from those who do not go on to develop the disorder. For the juvenile justice system, this substantial discontinuity suggests that aggressive drug treatment of all youths presenting with psychotic symptoms is likely unwarranted and could induce iatrogenic effects from medication.

This issue becomes even more pointed for the juvenile justice system when thinking about continuity and discontinuity of antisocial behavior. Although early-onset antisocial behavior significantly increases the likelihood that a juvenile will become an antisocial adult, more than 50% of cases of juvenile delinquency do not persist into adulthood (Odgers et al., 2007). Odgers et al. (2007) found that hyperactivity as a child and a positive family history for criminality distinguished the group of antisocial youths who continued on to antisocial behavior as adults, and identification of such moderators is crucial for the juvenile justice system to focus limited resources on the most at-risk youths.

Moreover, findings from the Dunedin longitudinal study of youths have suggested that continuity of mental disorder, when it does occur, may not always be homotypic within a disorder (e.g., depression in adolescence leading to the diagnosis and treatment of depression as an adult; Kim-Cohen et al., 2003). Kim-Cohen et al. (2003) found that although more than 50% of Dunedin participants who were first diagnosed with a mental disorder in their 20s also showed signs of mental disorder in childhood or early adolescence, much of this continuity was heterotypic, in which mental problems earlier in life manifested as dissimilar mental disorders in adulthood. This again supports the contention that children and adolescents experience a general psychopathology that is not yet differentiated into the distinct, persistent forms more common among adults (Rutter, 1994).

More important for the juvenile justice system, the Dunedin longitudinal study revealed that juvenile disruptive behavior disorders—most frequently, ODD and conduct disorder (CD)—were the most common antecedents of adult mental disorder, even if this adult disorder manifested in nondisruptive ways, such as anxiety or eating disorders

(Kim-Cohen et al., 2003). This means that the elevated proportion of youths in the juvenile justice system presenting with disruptive disorders such as ODD or CD (around 50%; Shufelt & Cocozza, 2006) represents a group of individuals distinctly likely to go on to experience other mental disorders as adults; in some, it will manifest in continued disruptive behavior, and in some it will manifest in other ways that require management.

Prevalence Rates of Mental Disorder in the Juvenile Justice System

With this grounding in the limitations of categorical diagnoses for youths and the evidence that not all mental disorders identified in adolescence will manifest as adult problems, we now present data on the prevalence rates of mental disorder for youths in the community versus the juvenile justice system (see Table 6.1).

Although the prevalence rates in Table 6.1 are listed by *DSM–5* diagnosis, we have previously discussed how discrete diagnostic categories may fail to adequately capture youths' dysfunction. In addition, reported prevalence rates vary widely on the basis of the sample in question or the method for defining disorder (e.g., self-report vs. jail staff diagnosis vs. clinician diagnosis). These numbers are further limited in that most prevalence studies fail to adequately consider delinquent female or minority youths. An additional caveat is that diagnoses assigned to detained youths may reflect available treatment space and staff's perceptions of the adolescents in question more than their actual psychiatric symptoms (Warboys & Wilber, 1996).

Although all these conceptual and methodological limitations make the precise numerical prevalence rates uncertain, clearly a huge number of youths in the juvenile justice system have some form of mental problem, both in an absolute sense and in proportion to the number of mentally disordered youths in the community. With these high prevalence rates in mind, Grisso (2004) was quick to emphasize that prevalence rates of any mental disorder, or even prevalence rates of specific disorders, fail to provide information about who requires treatment. The juvenile justice system cannot, and perhaps should not, treat any and every detained youth who presents with any sign of mental disorder, and most youths included in the figures in Table 6.1 do not have a serious mental disorder. In general, serious mental disorders—such as those characterized by psychotic symptoms, extremely disruptive behavior, or tendency toward self-harm—understandably attract the most attention in the juvenile justice system and are the most likely to receive the lion's share of scant treatment

TABLE 6.1

Prevalence of Mental Disorders Among Samples of Detained and Community Adolescents

Mental disorder	Detained samples (%)	Community samples (%)
Anxiety disorders	19–50	2–32
Attention deficit disorders	2–20	1–9
Conduct disorder	32–82	3–7
Intellectual disability	10	3
Mood disorders	9–65	2–14
Posttraumatic stress disorder	5–35	4–6
Psychotic disorders	3–24	0–8
Substance abuse and dependence	46–72	2–11
Any disorder present	67–81	13–28

Note. All estimates are ranges based on current research that differed somewhat in its use of diagnostic categories and used various types of methodology to assess prevalence (including self-report, structured interview, and meta-analyses). Data from Abrantes, Hoffmann, and Anton (2005); Costello, Mustillo, Erkanli, Keeler, and Angold (2003); Fazel, Doll, and Långström (2008); Kelleher et al. (2012); Kilpatrick et al. (2003); Merikangas et al. (2010); Quinn, Rutherford, Leone, Osher, and Poirier (2005); Shufelt and Cocozza (2006).

resources. However, although the minority of youths with serious mental illness may reasonably demand the majority of attention and resources, it is possible that the much larger number of only mildly affected youths may in fact cast a larger shadow over the juvenile justice system. These common and less serious disorders, such as ADHD, depression, and anxiety, likely affect juveniles' propensity for delinquency and their experience in the system in subtler but still profound ways.

The responsibility and capacity of the juvenile justice system to respond to this significant mental health burden is still uncertain. To understand how the system should respond, we must first understand why the prevalence rates of mental disorder among delinquent youths are so high. We present two perspectives that help inform the issue: (a) broader social and historical reasons that contextualize the problem and (b) more individualized, socioclinical reasons that may contribute to this disproportionality.

HISTORICAL AND LEGAL EXPLANATIONS FOR THE HIGH PREVALENCE OF MENTAL DISORDER IN THE JUVENILE JUSTICE SYSTEM

The juvenile justice system has always processed a large number of youths with some sort of mental problem, and it originally saw its goal as explicitly therapeutic. In the 1800s, institutions for "wayward" youths indiscriminately accepted any juvenile who was having or causing problems in the community, and they made no sharp distinction between youths with mental disorder and those who were merely delinquent (see, e.g., Warboys & Wilber, 1996). The modern juvenile justice system, as originally conceived in Chicago in 1899, was still expressly therapeutic, although there was also a focus on crime reduction and public safety via rehabilitating errant youths. Founded on Enlightenment principles emphasizing the impact of environmental influences on human behavior, the early juvenile justice system believed that criminal behavior could be changed by appropriately altering the environment through treatment and intervention. Each young offender was considered individually, with a (purportedly) kindly, paternalistic judge who sought to find the particular cause of the delinquent behavior and was given broad discretion to address the needs he discovered—which included psychological treatment for those youths whose criminal behavior was deemed to spring from mental disturbance (Warboys & Wilber, 1996). Thus, the early juvenile court was often considered a sort of "clinic" for the treatment (psychological and otherwise) of wayward youths, emphasizing the fuzzy border between delinquency and mental disorder from its genesis.

However, even though the juvenile system has always served youths with mental disorder, the proportion of detained youths with mental disorder appears to have increased in the past 20 years (Grisso, 2008). Grisso (2004, 2008) highlighted two important historical and legal changes that have contributed to this trend, increasing the burden of care for youths with mental disorder on the juvenile justice system.

First, in the early years of the juvenile justice system, actors at every stage of the system had broad discretion to divert youths with mental disorder to community treatment and other alternatives. However, the trend since the mid-1980s toward punishment over rehabilitation has reduced this discretion, ensuring that more youths with mental disorders end up in secure facilities (Grisso, 2004, 2008). In response to a national crime wave in the late 1980s, the majority of states initiated harsher policies and punishments across the board. This crime spike also included an increase in juvenile crime, for which juvenile offenders were unfairly pilloried as representing an onslaught of a new breed of "superpredators" who were especially brutal and remorseless (DiIulio, 1995). Thus, almost all states toughened their juvenile statutes in the early 1990s to emphasize public safety over rehabilitation of delinquent youths (Torbet, Gable, & Hurst, 1996). Amendments in the statutes varied from state to state but included provisions such as laws limiting the discretion of a judge to divert a youth with mental disorder from the court system, laws increasing the number of juvenile offenses that must be punished with secure confinement, and laws increasing the length of secure confinement for juvenile offenders

(Torbet et al., 1996). All of these provisions, by making it harder to divert youths with mental disorder from the justice system and increasing the average length of time these youths spent detained, contributed to the increasing mental health burden on the juvenile justice system in the past 20 years (Hafemeister, 2004).

Second, the U.S. economic recession in the early 1990s dramatically reduced the availability of noncorrectional mental health services for juveniles, particularly inpatient beds (Grisso, 2008). A second recession after the housing crisis of 2008 saw massive cuts to non-Medicaid mental health spending across most states, totaling approximately $1.6 billion from 2009 to 2011 (Honberg, Diehl, Kimball, Gruttadaro, & Fitzpatrick, 2011). As a result of these cuts and resulting community and inpatient mental health shortages, the juvenile justice system became an ersatz mental health facility that either provides limited emergency services or simply warehouses youths with mental disorder who have nowhere else to go (U.S. House of Representatives, 2004). For example, a 2003 congressional committee found that almost 15,000 juveniles remained detained in a correctional facility because they could not access community treatment, even though they had no pending charges against them (U.S. House of Representatives, 2004). Indeed, some parents of seriously disturbed youths began to call the police on their own children in an attempt to obtain services (Grisso, 2008). As one juvenile correctional administrator stated, "Understand this and understand it well: when the system is unable to get youth placed in a treatment facility or a mental health facility, they will be placed in a detention facility" (U.S. House of Representatives, 2004, p. 7).

SOCIOCLINICAL EXPLANATIONS FOR THE HIGH PREVALENCE OF MENTAL DISORDER IN THE JUVENILE JUSTICE SYSTEM

These broader historical and cultural changes, particularly of the past 40 years, provide a clear context for understanding how distal ecological influences such as legal reforms and economic pressures contributed to the high prevalence rates of mental disorder among delinquent youths. We now narrow our lens to socioclinical influences more proximal to the adolescents themselves that also help explain the disproportionate number of youths with mental disorder in the juvenile justice system. First, we briefly present evidence suggesting that many of the same sociodemographic factors that contribute to delinquency also pose an elevated risk for mental health problems. Second—and the primary focus of this chapter—we present evidence for a causal link between mental disorder and impaired decision making among delinquent youths, such that mental disorder might further impair the already immature, criminogenic decision making characteristic of adolescents as a class.

Common Causes Model

Adolescents have relatively little control over many aspects of their environment, yet environment is particularly influential on unformed, developing youths relative to adults. In this way, vulnerable youths often experience risk "packages," in which negative environmental and familial influences increase the likelihood that dysfunctional behaviors in a variety of domains will co-occur (Kazdin, 2000). These common causes may contribute to both poor mental health and antisocial behavior. For example, prenatal, perinatal, and neonatal neuropsychological insult—such as maternal drug abuse, poor maternal nutrition, delivery complications, and infant deprivation of nutrition or stimulation—can result in brain damage that contributes to both later mental disorder (e.g., Zornberg, Buka, & Tsuang, 2000) and criminality (likely via executive dysfunction, such as poor planning skills and poor self-control; see, e.g., Moffitt, 1993). In addition, research has supported that family characteristics, such as neglectful parenting styles, parents' marital status, interparental conflict, and maternal depression, are associated with both delinquency (e.g., Hoeve et al., 2008) and development of mental health disorders among youths (e.g., Harold, Osborne, & Conger, 1997).

As another example, living in disadvantaged, high-crime neighborhoods increases the likelihood both that youths will engage in antisocial behavior (e.g., Simcha-Fagan & Schwartz, 1986) and that youths will develop mental problems such as depression, anxiety, ODD, or CD in response to a dangerous, stressful environment (Aneshensel & Sucoff, 1996). In fact, youths moved from high-risk, low-income housing areas into more stable and affluent neighborhoods as a part of a randomized controlled trial reported significantly fewer anxiety and depressive symptoms than those who remained in high-poverty areas (Leventhal & Brooks-Gunn, 2003).

In sum, multiple common causes in youths' development and environment may lead to both delinquency and mental disorder (see Figure 6.1). This packaging of risk factors is another partial explanation for the disproportionately high rates of youths with mental disorder in the juvenile justice system compared with the community.

Decision-Making Pathway Model

An alternative explanation focuses on the pathways through which mental disorder might affect delinquent behavior. Of specific interest is impaired decision making as a result of mental disorder and the subsequent role of this impaired decision making on juvenile justice involvement for youths (see Figure 6.1).

Adolescents fundamentally differ from adults in a variety of important cognitive and psychosocial abilities, including poorer foresight, decreased ability to weigh immediate gains against long-term consequences, and increased sensation seeking and impulsivity (e.g., Steinberg & Cauffman, 1996). Neurobiological findings in recent years have supported these psychological findings. For example, the frontal lobes of the brain play an important role in executive functioning, such as the ability to plan, execute goals, and appropriately manage risk, yet this brain area does not reach full maturity until young adulthood (Mesulam, 2000). Together, these differences amount to a developmental deficit in adolescents' decision-making abilities that may make them more likely to engage in criminal behavior and less culpable for the crimes they commit. For example, teens may be more likely to engage in crimes in a risky, impulsive manner, under the influence of peers, and without the temperance and self-control necessary to weigh the present reward of breaking the law against the future consequences.

The criminal justice system has increasingly come to recognize the legal relevance of these developmental disparities. For example, in *Roper v. Simmons* (2005), the Supreme Court case that

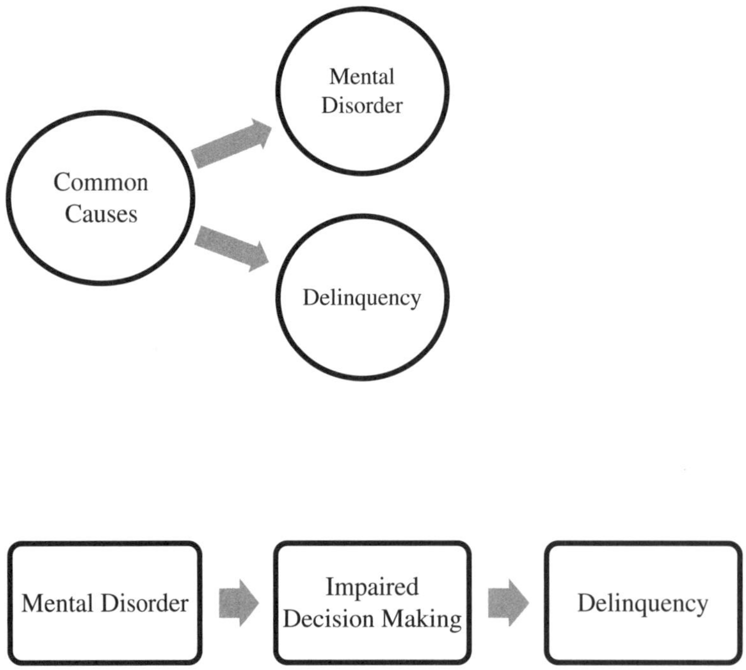

FIGURE 6.1. The common causes model (top) and the decision-making pathway model (bottom).

effectively abolished the death penalty for juveniles, the American Psychological Association filed an influential *amicus* brief that outlined how adolescents' continuing psychosocial maturation and brain development suggest impaired abilities in a variety of legally relevant areas—including decision making—that may make adolescents, as a class, more prone to engage in criminal acts and less culpable for this antisocial behavior.

This argument applies universally to all adolescents, because even typically developing youths experience these developmental deficits in decision making. However, youths in the justice system are not typical; as previously detailed, delinquent youths are approximately 3 times more likely to meet criteria for a mental illness than youths in the community (Kazdin, 2000). Youths with mental disorders are subject to even more pronounced impairment of cognitive and psychosocial capacities than their mentally healthy peers, placing them at increased risk for engaging in impulsive and risky delinquent behavior (and perhaps placing them at greater risk for getting caught; Kazdin, 2000). Mental disorders may have a negative impact on youths' development and cognitive abilities in a variety of ways (Grisso, 2006), and many disorders include symptoms that have clear ties to poor decision making, above and beyond normative adolescent deficits.

Much of the research examining how mental disorder impairs decision making among youths has focused on externalizing disorders, such as ADHD and CD. For instance, when performing the Iowa Gambling Task, a card paradigm that simulates real-world decision making by manipulating the size and frequency of costs and rewards, adolescents with ADHD were more likely than normal controls to make less advantageous card selections as a result of increased hyperactivity and impulsivity (Toplak, Jain, & Tannock, 2005). Furthermore, youths with ADHD seem somewhat blind to the consequences of their decisions, even as the consequences increase in severity, compared with adolescents without ADHD (Luman, Oosterlaan, Knol, & Sergeant, 2008). Not only are youths with ADHD less sensitive to the magnitude of penalties, but they also show less physiological arousal than controls after a high-stakes decision, revealing a blunted sympathetic reaction that suggests difficulty in distinguishing good and bad outcomes (Luman et al., 2008). Thus, youths with ADHD are both more likely to make disadvantageous choices and less likely to perceive the risk of even a highly negative outcome. These findings have clear implications for juvenile justice involvement: Adolescents with ADHD may make riskier choices, increasing the likelihood of being caught engaging in delinquent behavior, and may fail to recognize the seriousness of possible legal consequences.

Similar impairments in decision making have been found among youths with CD, which is characterized by a youth's proclivity to break rules and social norms (Ernst et al., 2003). For example, Fairchild et al. (2009) found that youths with CD are more likely than control subjects to make risky decisions on a gambling task. In addition, youths with CD have been found to have poorer moral reasoning, demonstrating more immature, instrumental judgments about how to behave when faced with moral dilemmas (Stadler et al., 2007). From a neuroscience perspective, youths with CD have reduced functioning in the anterior cingulate cortex, a brain area involved in the cognitive control of behavior and affective reactions to emotional information; this area is important for making thoughtful, nonimpulsive decisions (Sterzer, Stadler, Krebs, Kleinschmidt, & Poustka, 2005). These various findings have suggested that adolescents with CD are more likely to make risky, impulsive decisions as a means to instrumental (as opposed to expressive) ends, which implies a greater likelihood of contact with the juvenile justice system.

This relationship between mental disorder and impaired decision making is not limited to externalizing disorders. In particular, depression is often characterized by low motivation and cognitive distortions (i.e., overly negative automatic thoughts), and these cognitive distortions may impair youths' decision making via impaired reward processing (Kazdin, 2000). For example, research has demonstrated that young boys with depression show lower motivation to obtain a reward, even in optimal low-risk, high-reward conditions (Forbes, Shaw, & Dahl, 2007). The inflexible decision-making strategies displayed by youths with depression may be less sensitive to changes in risk or reward, inhibiting motivation to seek out pleasurable (and prosocial) activities (Forbes et al., 2007). In addition, the automatic negative thoughts of youths with depression make them less likely to choose to make friendship overtures to motivated, prosocial peers and thus more likely to experience peer rejection (Joiner, 2001). Together, these characteristics of youths with depression create a context in which rejection by prosocial peers may lead to greater influence by deviant peers and ensuing delinquency, combined with decreased motivation to seek alternate reinforcing activities.

Youths with posttraumatic stress disorder (PTSD) may also systematically misperceive their environment in meaningful ways that affect decision making, and so PTSD may be another disorder that contributes to delinquency. Research has shown that youths with PTSD are more likely to demonstrate poor restraint and impulse control and so are less likely to suppress aggressive reactions (Steiner, Garcia, & Matthews, 1997). Furthermore, even when in relative safety, youths with PTSD tend to believe that the world is a dangerous place and to perceive neutral stimuli as threatening (Pineles, Shipherd, Mostoufi, Abramovitz, & Yovel, 2009). Research on impaired decision making among individuals with PTSD has demonstrated their difficulty with motivation and reward seeking (Aupperle, Melrose, Stein, & Paulus, 2012), similar to that of youths with depression. Overall, youths with PTSD are more irritable, reckless, and hostile and so are less able to make measured decisions about engagement in violence or other illegal behavior, which may lead to justice involvement.

Aggression, in a more general sense, is an important symptom or consequence of many mental disorders for youths, including ADHD, CD, and PTSD, which have already been discussed. Aggression has been established as a key risk factor for juvenile justice involvement: Aggressive behavior may increase the likelihood that youths are involved in physical altercations that result in arrests, and aggressive behavior toward police officers increases the odds that police will push for continued system involvement or secure detainment (Grisso, 2008; Kazdin, 2000). Aggression is linked to altered decision making in that research has long suggested that aggressive youths are more likely to make hostile attributions in which they interpret ambiguous stimuli as threatening and so feel the need to respond aggressively (Nasby, Hayden, & DePaulo, 1980). Aggressive youths, much more than their nonaggressive peers, are thus required to inhibit strong impulses toward aggression to stay out of trouble, despite perceiving danger and feeling threatened. Adolescents with mental disorder are already doubly taxed when it comes to regulating themselves to make measured decisions, and so youths with mental disorder may be less able to suppress aggressive urges and thus be more likely to engage in antisocial behavior than their peers without mental disorder.

Impaired Decision Making Among Youths With Mental Disorder After System Involvement

We have detailed numerous ways in which youths with mental disorders face added challenges in decision making relative to youths without mental disorders. This impaired decision making may contribute to a greater likelihood of engaging in delinquency and of doing so in an impulsive and risky manner that leads to getting caught and arrested (Kazdin, 2000). Although these vulnerabilities increase the odds that youths will initially come in contact with the juvenile justice system, deficits in decision making among youths with mental disorders also continue to pose problems after system involvement. In this section, we discuss how the juvenile justice system addresses or fails to address the vulnerabilities of youths with mental disorders in terms of (a) legal decision making and (b) treatment while detained.

Impaired legal decision making. Almost no research has specifically investigated how mental disorder may affect youths' decision making within the juvenile justice system. However, an abundance of previous literature has shown the impact of simply being youthful on legal decision making (e.g., Grisso, 2004), and so we can draw some conclusions about how the added challenge of mental disorder might further impair youths in these situations. We discuss adolescents' ability to waive their

Miranda rights as one paradigmatic example (see also Chapter 21, this handbook).

Waiving *Miranda* rights refers to choosing to make a statement to police while in custody, typically during an interrogation, despite the legal protections of the rights to remain silent and have an attorney present during questioning. For any statement to be admissible, *Miranda* must have been waived voluntarily, knowingly, and intelligently; more than 90% of youths waive this right, a higher rate than that for adult defendants (Grisso & Pomicter, 1977). A large body of research has addressed developmental differences in decisions about waiving *Miranda* rights (e.g., Grisso, 1980), and findings have consistently shown that age matters when it comes to *Miranda* comprehension, particularly understanding the implications of the rights. Adolescents younger than age 15 frequently fail to grasp the meaning of *Miranda* warnings, and even older youths are often unable to use the information to make appropriate inferences (Grisso, 2006).

If all adolescents struggle with making the decision to access the rights and protections afforded by *Miranda*, youths with mental disorder may face added challenges. Depending on the circumstances, a youth's mental disorder may call into question the validity of a *Miranda* waiver. However, isolating the contribution of mental disorder to a youth's *Miranda* waiver decision is difficult, because even youth who are mentally healthy often (perhaps foolishly) waive their *Miranda* rights. Yet given struggles with impulsivity, weighing costs against rewards, and restraining impulses (e.g., the impulse to respond to questions posed by police rather than remain silent), youths with mental disorders in the justice system may be most vulnerable to an improper waiver of rights. In addition, the hostility or aggression of some youths with mental disorders may provoke harsher treatment by police during interrogation, and this added pressure might further affect youths' decision to waive *Miranda* rights.

This increased vulnerability of youths with mental disorders regarding waiver of *Miranda* rights similarly affects other decision points throughout the juvenile justice process. For example, questions of a youth's competence to stand trial are further complicated when the offender is not only young but also has a mental disorder. In addition, youths whose mental disorder further impairs their already immature decision making may be less able to weigh the risks and benefits involved in plea bargaining, which is now common in an increasingly adultlike juvenile system. Finally, in a limited number of states, a juvenile delinquent's mental disorder bars him or her from transfer to adult court (Addie, Adams, & Firestine, 2011), and theoretically a transferred youth with mental disorder would receive all the same protections as an adult defendant with mental disorder. However, the increased stress, complexity, and consequences of the adult system would clearly further tax the already impaired decision-making abilities of youths with mental disorder who are transferred to adult court. Because all of these pivotal choice points require a youthful offender to weigh options and make decisions, the court must consider questions of how and when to take into account a youth's mental disorder, what disorders should or should not be heavily weighted, and what obligations exist to respond to youths with mental disorders (Grisso, 2004).

Despite these pressing questions about how the juvenile justice system should acknowledge youths' mental disorder, relatively few legal protections currently exist for youths with mental disorders compared with adults. For example, juvenile courts have been inconsistent on whether youths with mental disorders ought to receive the protection of the insanity defense. The insanity defense acknowledges that an offender's decision-making capacities at the time of the crime were so impaired by mental illness or other serious dysfunction that the offender could not form the requisite criminal intent. The U.S. Supreme Court has never specifically ruled on the juvenile insanity defense, but it has ruled that adults have no constitutional right to an insanity defense (*Delling v. Idaho*, 2012), leaving decisions about both juvenile and adult insanity defense up to the states. Traditionally, the assumption has been that a paternalistic, individualized juvenile system could take a youth's mental disorder into account without formal procedural protections such as the insanity defense, but this may be less true in an increasingly punitive, adultlike juvenile justice system. Currently, only about a dozen states explicitly permit an affirmative insanity defense to be offered in juvenile court, a handful of states specifically deny this protection to youthful offenders, and the majority of states have not yet addressed the issue—leaving juveniles' ability to assert an insanity plea unclear at best (Pollock, 2001).

Among adults, the insanity plea is most often invoked only in cases of severe mental illness (e.g., schizophrenia and other psychotic disorders; Callahan, Steadman, McGreevy, & Robbins, 1991). Given that most psychotic disorders develop in the early 20s, fewer adolescents than adults would meet the standard for the insanity defense even if the legal option were available (Rogers & Myers, 2013). Nevertheless, about 25% of psychotic disorders have their onset in late adolescence (e.g., Kessler et al., 2007), when most youths are still under juvenile court jurisdiction. In addition, even though most delinquent youths with mental disorder present with relatively more minor psychopathology, Grisso (2004) argued that it may be a mistake to use the same legal standards for juveniles as are used for adults. Given that juveniles are already at an inherent disadvantage in terms of psychosocial maturity and decision making, the addition of mental illness (even the less serious forms) may function similarly to more severe psychopathology among adults.

Right to treatment for detained juveniles. To summarize, the legal accommodations for youths with mental disorder as they move through the stages of the juvenile justice system are generally murky at best and absent at worst. This unclear or limited legal response to youths with mental disorder continues with juveniles' right to treatment once detained by the justice system. Hafemeister (2004) pointed out that *right to treatment* is an ambiguous phrase, with many possible definitions of *treatment*—ranging from general rehabilitation for all youths to treatment only of youths with a seriously impairing mental disorder—and these shades of meaning have resulted in a range of responses depending on the historical and legal context.

In the early days of the juvenile justice system, a general right to treatment for all delinquents was assumed, given the therapeutic conception of the juvenile court (Hafemeister, 2004). However, this assumption was strained as the juvenile system became more punitive and adultlike after legal formalization in the 1960s. In addition, a parallel process of widespread deinstitutionalization of adults in the 1970s began the institution-to-prison pipeline, increasing the number of incarcerated individuals with mental disorders (Steadman, Monahan, Duffee, Hartstone, & Robbins, 1984). With an increasing number of incarcerated individuals requiring medical treatment, including mental health treatment, the U.S. Supreme Court ruled definitely on the issue in *Estelle v. Gamble* (1976), holding that the justice system could not deliberately fail to treat a serious need or disorder (which has been interpreted in other cases to include mental disorders). However, despite the increasingly punitive and adultlike legal treatment of youths, the Supreme Court has never ruled specifically on whether the same right to treatment advanced in *Estelle* applies to juveniles in the justice system (Hafemeister, 2004).

Despite the lack of a definitive legal ruling on detained juveniles' right to treatment, beginning in the 1960s and 1970s detained juveniles began filing successful lawsuits against detention facilities because of either poor institutional conditions or lack of services (including inadequate psychiatric or psychological care; Hafemeister, 2004). These early lawsuits, and those continuing to the present, cited various legal bases to support a right to treatment (Hafemeister, 2004), including the Fourteenth Amendment's due process and equal protection provisions as arguments for equal treatment in juvenile facilities. In general, then, legal standards seem to imply that detained juveniles are entitled to at least the level of mental health care mandated for incarcerated adults by law, and some have argued that juveniles ought to receive more care and protections because of their increased vulnerabilities (Hafemeister, 2004; Rogers & Myers, 2013).

However, historically and today, available resources rather than the needs of the child appear to determine what mental health services are offered to youths with mental disorder in the juvenile justice system (Warboys & Wilber, 1996). Such resources are often lacking in an overcrowded and underfunded system. For example, one quarter of juvenile detention facilities holding youths in need of mental health services provide either no services or poor quality services (U.S. House of Representatives, 2004), and three quarters of juvenile detention facilities do not conform to suicide prevention procedures (Coalition for Juvenile Justice, 2000). Although state and federal courts have been prompted to monitor service provision as a result of legal challenges, the courts generally remain reluctant to second guess the decisions of treatment providers or to order treatments that would be unusually expensive (Hafemeister, 2004). Thus, despite a half-century of right-to-treatment jurisprudence, many youths with mental disorders in the juvenile justice system, particularly those manifesting less serious disorders, do not receive treatment because of lack of resources.

BEST PRACTICES FOR YOUTHS WITH MENTAL DISORDERS IN THE JUVENILE JUSTICE SYSTEM

To review, juveniles are afforded some legal right to treatment when in the custody of the juvenile justice system, but the implementation of this treatment in practice is not specified by law and varies widely by jurisdiction according to available resources. To clarify how the juvenile justice system should respond to the substantial burden of youths with mental disorders, researchers and policymakers must turn to available empirical evidence to form the basis of best practice recommendations. In this section, we review best practices in two key domains: (a) identifying and assessing poor mental health among detained juveniles (advances in measurement techniques), and (b) treating youth both in and out of detainment to prevent recidivism and reduce harm to the community (advances in treatment). We also explore recent policies in several states that serve as models for informed change.

Advances in Measurement

Given the large number of youths with mental disorder that come into contact with the justice system, it seems clear that identifying mental health issues early and accurately is an essential first step toward responsiveness (Skowyra & Cocozza, 2007). Only a small minority of youths enter the system with obvious, severe psychopathology (e.g., active psychosis or mania, suicidal behavior), and this minority is likely to attract immediate attention and resources. However, the majority of detained youths with mental disorder have less severe, or at least less prototypically ill, symptomatology. As such, identifying and evaluating this substantial number of less severely ill youths who may still be impaired or in need of treatment is crucial to both protecting adolescents' due process rights and gauging their level of risk to the community. Therefore, advances in measurement are a cornerstone of best practices recommendations.

Measurement refers to both screenings, which are usually brief and administered by nonclinical personnel, and assessments, which are often longer and performed by trained clinicians to provide deeper, more comprehensive information about a youth's mental health (Skowyra & Cocozza, 2007). Screening is most beneficial at youths' initial contact with the juvenile justice system as a form of triage, to identify youths who need immediate treatment and to indicate need for further assessment, which may occur later in the process (Skowyra & Cocozza, 2007). Screening procedures have become more streamlined with advances in empirically supported instrumentation. For example, the Massachusetts Youth Screening Instrument—2 (Grisso & Barnum, 2001), a brief self-report measure, was developed to quickly and efficiently red-flag youths with potential mental health needs.

Increasingly widespread use of screening instruments such as the Massachusetts Youth Screening Instrument—2 in juvenile justice settings has led to benefits for both research and practice. Use of standardized screening instruments across a range of jurisdictions has led to an unprecedented comparability of results, allowing for meta-analyses that can better address questions of race and gender differences in mental disorder among delinquent youths (Vincent, Grisso, Terry, & Banks, 2008). In a more applied sense, several states have passed legislation requiring the use of screening procedures at intake and probation. For example, Connecticut recently mandated that all juvenile probation departments use the Massachusetts Youth Screening Instrument—2 on intake, which ultimately led to important legislative changes to protect youths against later misuse of their personal information (Skowyra & Cocozza, 2007). In sum, screening procedures are being applied more widely and efficiently in an effort to better identify youths with mental health needs, resulting in improved research and needed policy changes.

Youths who are red-flagged with a brief screening instrument may then go on to receive a more thorough mental health assessment to establish both their treatment needs and their level of risk to others. These more formal and valid assessments are beginning to replace the formerly common but highly unreliable practice of ascertaining youths' mental status on the basis of the single criterion of whether they had previously received mental health services (Wasserman, Ko, & McReynolds, 2004). For example, a measure such as the Voice Diagnostic Interview Schedule for Children, which is self-administered on a computer with headphones, presents a reliable and practical method to an adolescent's mental health status while also providing provisional diagnoses and treatment recommendations (Wasserman et al., 2004). Juvenile risk assessment instruments have made similar progress (see Chapter 16, this handbook). A meta-analysis found that currently used instruments predict reoffending in juveniles fairly well and about as well as risk assessments used with adult populations (Schwalbe, 2007). In light of this, the juvenile court has increasingly begun to rely on the results of risk assessment to identify offenders most likely to recidivate (Schwalbe, 2007).

Several states have responded to burgeoning advances in assessment by adopting new policies. For example, Tennessee passed a law in 2009 mandating mental health assessment for any juvenile charged with a crime that would be considered a felony if the accused were an adult (National Conference of State Legislatures, 2011), and Louisiana recently implemented a statewide adoption of a risk assessment instrument for use throughout the juvenile justice system (Mental Health and Juvenile Justice Collaborative for Change, 2014). Overall, the effect of increased use of screening and assessment procedures has allowed for faster and more informed responses to youths with immediate and ongoing mental health needs, including directing youths to an appropriate treatment model.

Advances in Treatment

Treatment models currently used by the juvenile justice system vary widely depending on youths' needs and, more often, on available financial, personnel, and institutional resources in any particular jurisdiction (Oudekerk & Reppucci, 2012; Warboys & Wilber, 1996). Treatment for juvenile offenders with mental disorders has traditionally focused on strategies to reduce recidivism and protect the community, with the underlying assumption that less criminality may also represent improved mental health for youths. To meet these goals and reduce the warehousing of youths with mental illness in the juvenile justice system, two major themes of best practice recommendations have emerged: (a) Increase diversion of low-risk youths away from further system penetration and (b) use empirically supported treatment approaches to improve care and reduce recidivism.

Diversion is designed to provide youths with a range of community-based social and mental health services (with continued oversight by the court) in lieu of further processing within the juvenile justice system (Evans Cuellar, McReynolds, & Wasserman, 2006). Proponents of diversion have argued that the trend of criminalizing the mentally ill will not slow or reverse unless a clear treatment pathway emerges that is distinct from the justice system. Although not all youths are appropriate for diversion, many youths with unmet mental health needs are involved in the system because of minor, nonviolent offenses and may be diverted into community-based mental health services (Skowyra & Cocozza, 2007). Thus, diversion allows access to services while avoiding detention for the adolescent and simultaneously helping to unburden an already overwhelmed juvenile justice system.

One specific form of diversion—specialized mental health courts—has been gaining popularity in many states as an innovative method of addressing concerns about the use of juvenile justice facilities as a conduit to treatment for youths with mental disorders (Skowyra & Cocozza, 2007). Although adult mental health courts are more popular, several states have recently passed legislation to establish juvenile versions. For example, California established the Los Angeles County Juvenile Mental Health Court in 2001, which involves collaboration among the district attorney's office, public defender's office, department of mental health, and probation department. Youths are referred from the juvenile system to the specialized court, where the collaborative team decides whether to accept the case on the basis of the adolescent's level of risk to the community. If the case is accepted, formal punishment is waived in favor of an individualized treatment plan, in which empirically supported treatments are applied in light of the youth's immediate systems of risk and support (Digiovanni, 2002).

Although no efficacy evaluations have examined juvenile mental health courts, findings from the adult literature have shown promising outcomes, including reductions in recidivism and violence and maintenance of gains beyond the length of court supervision (e.g., McNiel & Binder, 2007). Furthermore, evaluations of diversion programs more broadly have shown that community-based treatment approaches are often more effective at reducing recidivism than traditional punitive or deterrence-based tactics (Lipsey, Howell, Kelly, Chapman, & Carver, 2010). Overall, then, best practice recommendations for the juvenile justice system are clear: When possible, youths with mental disorders should be diverted away from further system penetration and into community-based treatment.

Whether adolescents are diverted into community-based services or remain in the juvenile justice system, the best practice is to use evidence-based treatments to address both mental health problems and criminality (Tate, Reppucci, & Mulvey, 1995). Evidence-based treatments—which require research support for efficacious implementation of the treatment in both controlled studies and in real-world situations—are considered the gold standard in mental health. Although the juvenile justice system has traditionally used intuitively appealing but untested treatment approaches with juveniles, harkening back to the days of the paternalistic judge deciding how each wayward youth was best to be reformed, the call for these more rigorously tested practices is growing among policymakers. Indeed, some states are even mandating that only evidence-based programming receive public funding (Skowyra & Cocozza, 2007).

For delinquent youths with mental disorders, particularly those in custody, the two main branches of available treatments are pharmacotherapy (i.e., drug therapy) and psychotherapy (i.e., talk therapy). Research evidence for the use of psychopharmacological approaches has been mixed. Although advances in medication therapies for certain kinds of disorders among adolescents, including ADHD, depression, and anxiety, have had positive results in laboratory settings (Hoagwood, 2005), the effectiveness of medication in everyday practice, with the possibility for human error in both diagnosis and adherence, is less clear (Weisz & Jensen, 1999). In addition, although some smaller studies have supported the use of powerful antipsychotic and mood-stabilizing drugs to reduce aggression among adolescents with CD and related disorders (e.g., Tcheremissine & Lieving, 2006), the long-term safety of such drugs for adolescents is uncertain because few large-scale clinical trials have been conducted among this population. However, certain forms of psychotherapy have substantial evidence supporting their safe and successful use with juvenile delinquents with mental disorders. The best-supported approach for reducing recidivism in this population is cognitive–behavioral therapy, which combines cognitive and behavioral techniques to help youths recognize and solve problems before they escalate, as well as learn to use more effective coping strategies in place of aggression. Multiple studies have spoken to cognitive–behavioral therapy's effectiveness in decreasing youths' risk for future offending (Wilson, Bouffard, & MacKenzie, 2005), particularly youths with anxiety or depressive disorders (e.g., P. C. Kendall, Reber, McLeer, Epps, & Ronan, 1990).

More important, a discussion of mental health treatment for juvenile delinquents would be incomplete without an acknowledgment that mental disorder per se is not the cause of the vast majority of adolescent criminal behavior—even among youths with mental disorders. Although youths with mental disorder are overrepresented in the juvenile system, many of them are not delinquent, and many delinquent youths do not have a mental disorder (Grisso, 2008). Although we have focused primarily on how mental disorder contributes to youths' involvement in the justice system, mental health problems are far from the only, or even the primary, cause of offending; offending youths with and without mental disorder share many of the same causes and motivations for criminal behavior (Oudekerk & Reppucci, 2012). As such, best practice recommendations must account for other criminogenic needs among youths with mental disorders and call for a bigger-picture approach to treatment than individual therapy or medication can provide (see Chapter 23, this handbook). Community-based approaches, those that engage youths in treatment within the ecological context of their everyday lives, answer this call. In fact, community approaches such as multisystemic therapy have been found to be the most cost effective and the most successful at reducing recidivism and improving child welfare among youths with mental disorder (Chapter 25, this handbook; Sexton & Alexander, 2002).

Despite these clear benefits, many jurisdictions fail to implement such programming because community-based services are often complex and require coordination between multiple agencies and treatment providers (Grisso, 2008). Policy changes addressing these real challenges within the community system of care would allow the juvenile justice system to focus more on diverting youths to, and collaborating with, community service providers, rather than trying to manage the tens of thousands of detained youths suffering from mental disorder (Grisso, 2008).

FUTURE RESEARCH DIRECTIONS

The best practice recommendations we have outlined are based on the evidence currently available. However, further research is needed in several broad areas of adolescent mental disorder and delinquency to better inform future clinical approaches, institutional practices, and policy changes.

We began by reviewing evidence suggesting a pathway by which mental disorder may increase the risk of justice involvement for youths via impaired decision making. Emerging research on this topic has provided direct support of a decision-making deficit for youths with externalizing disorders, such as ADHD and CD (Ernst et al., 2003; Toplak et al., 2005), but not specifically among delinquent youths. Also, much of the research supporting this decision-making pathway for other mental disorders is indirect. Although altered reward motivation, hostile attributions, and aggression likely hinder youths' decision-making abilities and have been linked to mental disorder (Grisso, 2008; Nasby et al. 1980), further research is needed to directly examine the role of impaired decision making in delinquent youths with mental disorder.

In addition, virtually no prior research has empirically examined how mental disorder may impair adolescents' decision making in legal contexts. Numerous studies have explored how normative adolescent immaturity may impair legal decision making (e.g., Grisso, 2006), but very little research has explored how mental disorder may exacerbate these deficits. In fact, comparatively little research has explored mental disorder in adolescence at all, relative to the research base for adult mental illness. More research, grounded in a developmental perspective on mental illness, is needed to understand how mental disorder affects an adolescent's ability to engage in legal contexts and to inform the court as to when special protections for such vulnerable youths are warranted (Grisso, 2004). Furthermore, little is known about how mental illness in adolescence may alter the development of decision-making capabilities and what impact this may have on delinquency and recidivism for these youths. Although most delinquent youths tend to desist from crime as they develop into adults (Moffitt, 1993), more research is needed to understand how this trajectory may differ among delinquent youths with mental disorders.

In regard to measurement and treatment, screening procedures would benefit from further research regarding how frequently to screen youths, when screening is most beneficial, and whether or how screening procedures may lead to improved outcomes for youths (Skowyra & Cocozza, 2007). Although the reliability and validity of particular screening measures have been supported by research, less is known about whether these screening procedures actually lead to identified youths being appropriately diverted or provided with effective treatment (Grisso, 2008). In addition, relatively little is known about mental health treatment specifically for detained youths. Currently, most treatment recommendations for youths in detention centers are extrapolated from research examining community samples; research with this particular population is needed to better inform best practices for incarcerated youths (Desai et al., 2006; Oudekerk & Reppucci, 2012).

Last, there is a dearth of research exploring these questions about mental disorder, decision making, and delinquency among female and minority youths. Most of the research cited in this chapter has been conducted on samples of primarily Caucasian, male adolescents. Whether findings from these studies are equally applicable to female and minority youths is unclear because important differences between groups may exist (Grisso, 2004).

For example, prior research has suggested that females in the juvenile justice system display higher rates of severe symptomatology than males (Cauffman, Lexcen, Goldweber, Shulman, & Grisso, 2007). Biological or hormonal differences in how some disorders are expressed in males versus females may be at play in this disparity. Researchers have also proposed a kind of gender paradox, in which female adolescents are generally less likely to commit delinquent acts, be arrested, or be detained than male adolescents; thus, females who are incarcerated represent a considerably more severe subset of delinquents, with more acute symptoms of mental disorder, than their male counterparts, for whom antisocial behavior is more normative (Cauffman et al., 2007). Regardless of why the disparity exists, justice-involved female adolescents are likely to be qualitatively different from their male peers. This casts doubt on the validity of applying the findings and recommendations based on research with male youths to justice-involved female youths (Odgers, Moretti, & Reppucci, 2005).

Similarly, more research is needed to understand how racial, ethnic, or cultural differences may affect treatment recommendations for minority youths with mental disorders. In general, relatively little is known about effective treatments for mental illness among adolescents, and even less is known about the efficacy of existing mental health treatments for youths across racial or ethnic groups or about how to conduct culturally responsive treatments (Gibbs & Huang, 2003). In addition, although some newer research on juvenile justice populations has found small or nonsignificant differences between racial or ethnic groups on mental health symptoms (Vincent et al., 2008), other research has suggested that important racial differences exist in terms of recidivism rates (Wierson & Forehand, 1995) and access to or utilization of treatment services (Rawal, Romansky, Jenuwine, & Lyons, 2004). More research is needed to understand how possible group differences in race or ethnicity may relate to mental health outcomes, recidivism, and treatment recommendations for delinquent youths.

CONCLUSION

The juvenile justice system houses a disproportionate number of youths with mental disorder; some estimates place rates of justice-involved youths with mental disorders at more than 80%, nearly 3 times community rates (Shufelt & Cocozza, 2006). Although many factors likely contribute to this disproportionality, research has suggested that youths with mental disorder experience impaired decision making, above and beyond normative developmental deficits, that serves to make justice involvement more likely and outcomes for youths more precarious. Recommendations for how the system should best handle this vulnerable population are becoming clearer as research in the area grows, although legal ambiguities and resource limitations often prevent best practice recommendations from being carried out. Further research is needed to clarify how the juvenile justice system can best balance its deontic obligation to meet the diverse needs of delinquent youths with mental disorder against its utilitarian obligation to protect the community.

References

Abrantes, A. M., Hoffmann, N. G., & Anton, R. (2005). Prevalence of co-occurring disorders among juveniles committed to detention centers. *International Journal of Offender Therapy and Comparative Criminology*, *49*, 179–193. http://dx.doi.org/10.1177/0306624X04269673

Addie, S., Adams, B., & Firestine, K. (2011). *Trying juveniles as adults: An analysis of state transfer laws and reporting*. Washington, DC: U.S. Department of

Justice, Office of Justice Programs, Office of Juvenile Justice and Delinquency Prevention.

American Psychiatric Association. (2013). *Diagnostic and statistical manual of mental disorders* (5th ed.). Washington, DC: Author.

Aneshensel, C. S., & Sucoff, C. A. (1996). The neighborhood context of adolescent mental health. *Journal of Health and Social Behavior*, *37*, 293–310. http://dx.doi.org/10.2307/2137258

Aupperle, R. L., Melrose, A. J., Stein, M. B., & Paulus, M. P. (2012). Executive function and PTSD: Disengaging from trauma. *Neuropharmacology*, *62*, 686–694. http://dx.doi.org/10.1016/j.neuropharm.2011.02.008

Barkley, R. A. (1990). *Attention-deficit hyperactivity disorder: A handbook for diagnosis and treatment*. New York, NY: Guilford Press.

Callahan, L. A., Steadman, H. J., McGreevy, M. A., & Robbins, P. C. (1991). The volume and characteristics of insanity plea defenses: An eight-state study. *Bulletin of the American Academy of Psychiatry and the Law*, *19*, 331–338.

Cauffman, E., Lexcen, F. J., Goldweber, A., Shulman, E. P., & Grisso, T. (2007). Gender differences in mental health symptoms among delinquent and community youth. *Youth Violence and Juvenile Justice*, *5*, 287–307. http://dx.doi.org/10.1177/1541204007301292

Cauffman, E., & Steinberg, L. (2000). (Im)maturity of judgment in adolescence: Why adolescents may be less culpable than adults. *Behavioral Sciences and the Law*, *18*, 741–760. http://dx.doi.org/10.1002/bsl.416

Cicchetti, D. (1984). The emergence of developmental psychopathology. *Child Development*, *55*, 1–7. http://dx.doi.org/10.2307/1129830

Cicchetti, D., & Rogosch, F. A. (2002). A developmental psychopathology perspective on adolescence. *Journal of Consulting and Clinical Psychology*, *70*, 6–20. http://dx.doi.org/10.1037/0022-006X.70.1.6

Coalition for Juvenile Justice. (2000). *Handle with care: Serving the mental health needs of young offenders*. Washington, DC: Office of Juvenile Justice & Delinquency Prevention.

Coghill, D., & Sonuga-Barke, E. J. (2012). Annual research review: Categories versus dimensions in the classification and conceptualisation of child and adolescent mental disorders—implications of recent empirical study. *Journal of Child Psychology and Psychiatry*, *53*, 469–489. http://dx.doi.org/10.1111/j.1469-7610.2011.02511.x

Costello, E. J., Mustillo, S., Erkanli, A., Keeler, G., & Angold, A. (2003). Prevalence and development of psychiatric disorders in childhood and adolescence. *Archives of General Psychiatry*, *60*, 837–844. http://dx.doi.org/10.1001/archpsyc.60.8.837

Delling v. Idaho, 568 U.S. ___ (2012).

Desai, R. A., Goulet, J. L., Robbins, J., Chapman, J. F., Migdole, S. J., & Hoge, M. A. (2006). Mental health care in juvenile detention facilities: A review. *Journal of the American Academy of Psychiatry and the Law*, *34*, 204–214.

Digiovanni, A. (2002). The Los Angeles County juvenile mental health court: An innovative approach to crime, violence, and delinquency among our youth. *Journal of Juvenile Law*, *23*, 1–14.

DiIulio, J. (1995). The coming of the super-predators. *Weekly Standard*, *1*(11), 23–29.

Drake, R. J., & Lewis, S. W. (2005). Early detection of schizophrenia. *Current Opinion in Psychiatry*, *18*, 147–150. http://dx.doi.org/10.1097/00001504-200503000-00007

Duffy, A., & Carlson, G. A. (2013). How does a developmental perspective inform us about the early natural history of bipolar disorder? *Journal of the Canadian Academy of Child and Adolescent Psychiatry*, *22*, 6–12.

Ernst, M., Grant, S. J., London, E. D., Contoreggi, C. S., Kimes, A. S., & Spurgeon, L. (2003). Decision making in adolescents with behavior disorders and adults with substance abuse. *American Journal of Psychiatry*, *160*, 33–40. http://dx.doi.org/10.1176/appi.ajp.160.1.33

Estelle v. Gamble, 429 U.S. 97 (1976).

Evans Cuellar, A., McReynolds, L. S., & Wasserman, G. A. (2006). A cure for crime: Can mental health treatment diversion reduce crime among youth? *Journal of Policy Analysis and Management*, *25*, 197–214. http://dx.doi.org/10.1002/pam.20162

Fairchild, G., van Goozen, S. H., Stollery, S. J., Aitken, M. R., Savage, J., Moore, S. C., & Goodyer, I. M. (2009). Decision making and executive function in male adolescents with early-onset or adolescence-onset conduct disorder and control subjects. *Biological Psychiatry*, *66*, 162–168. http://dx.doi.org/10.1016/j.biopsych.2009.02.024

Fazel, S., Doll, H., & Långström, N. (2008). Mental disorders among adolescents in juvenile detention and correctional facilities: A systematic review and metaregression analysis of 25 surveys. *Journal of the American Academy of Child and Adolescent Psychiatry*, *47*, 1010–1019.

Foley, R. M. (2001). Academic characteristics of incarcerated youth and correctional educational programs: A literature review. *Journal of Emotional and Behavioral Disorders*, *9*, 248–259. http://dx.doi.org/10.1177/106342660100900405

Forbes, E. E., Shaw, D. S., & Dahl, R. E. (2007). Alterations in reward-related decision making in boys with recent and future depression. *Biological*

Psychiatry, *61*, 633–639. http://dx.doi.org/10.1016/j.biopsych.2006.05.026

Gardner, M., & Steinberg, L. (2005). Peer influence on risk taking, risk preference, and risky decision making in adolescence and adulthood: An experimental study. *Developmental Psychology*, *41*, 625–635. http://dx.doi.org/10.1037/0012-1649.41.4.625

Gibbs, J. T. E., & Huang, L. N. E. (2003). *Children of color: Psychological interventions with culturally diverse youth*. San Francisco, CA: Jossey-Bass.

Grisso, T. (1980). Juveniles' capacities to waive *Miranda* rights: An empirical analysis. *California Law Review*, *68*, 1134–1166. http://dx.doi.org/10.2307/3480263

Grisso, T. (2004). *Double jeopardy: Adolescent offenders with mental disorders*. Chicago, IL: University of Chicago Press.

Grisso, T. (2006). Adolescents' decision making: A developmental perspective on constitutional provisions in delinquency cases. *New England Journal on Criminal and Civil Confinement*, *32*, 3–14.

Grisso, T. (2008). Adolescent offenders with mental disorders. *Future of Children*, *18*, 143–164. http://dx.doi.org/10.1353/foc.0.0016

Grisso, T., & Barnum, R. (2001). *Massachusetts Youth Screening Instrument: Preliminary manual*. Worcester: University of Massachusetts Medical School.

Grisso, T., & Pomicter, C. (1977). Interrogation of juveniles: An empirical study of procedures, safeguards, and rights waiver. *Law and Human Behavior*, *1*, 321–342. http://dx.doi.org/10.1007/BF01048593

Hafemeister, T. L. (2004). Parameters and implementation of a right to mental health treatment for juvenile offenders. *Virginia Journal of Social Policy and the Law*, *12*, 61–139.

Harold, G. T., Osborne, L. N., & Conger, R. D. (1997). Mom and dad are at it again: Adolescent perceptions of marital conflict and adolescent psychological distress. *Developmental Psychology*, *33*, 333–350. http://dx.doi.org/10.1037/0012-1649.33.2.333

Hoagwood, K. E. (2005). Family-based services in children's mental health: A research review and synthesis. *Journal of Child Psychology and Psychiatry*, *46*, 690–713. http://dx.doi.org/10.1111/j.1469-7610.2005.01451.x

Hoeve, M., Blokland, A., Dubas, J. S., Loeber, R., Gerris, J. R., & van der Laan, P. H. (2008). Trajectories of delinquency and parenting styles. *Journal of Abnormal Child Psychology*, *36*, 223–235. http://dx.doi.org/10.1007/s10802-007-9172-x

Honberg, R., Diehl, S., Kimball, A., Gruttadaro, D., & Fitzpatrick, M. (2011). *State mental health cuts: A national crisis*. Washington, DC: National Alliance on Mental Illness.

Joiner, T. E., Jr. (2001). Defensiveness predicts peer rejection of depressed children. *Behaviour Research and Therapy*, *39*, 929–938. http://dx.doi.org/10.1016/S0005-7967(00)00066-8

Kazdin, A. E. (2000). Adolescent development, mental disorders, and decision making of delinquent youths. In T. Grisso & R. G. Schwartz (Eds.), *Youth on trial: A developmental perspective on juvenile justice* (pp. 33–65). Chicago, IL: University of Chicago Press.

Kelleher, I., Connor, D., Clarke, M. C., Devlin, N., Harley, M., & Cannon, M. (2012). Prevalence of psychotic symptoms in childhood and adolescence: A systematic review and meta-analysis of population-based studies. *Psychological Medicine*, *42*, 1857–1863. http://dx.doi.org/10.1017/S0033291711002960

Kendall, M. (1991). The major functional psychoses: Are they independent entities or part of a continuum? Philosophical and conceptual issues underlying the debate. In A. Kerr & H. H. McClelland (Eds.), *Concepts of mental disorder: A continuing debate* (pp. 1–16). London, England: Gaskell.

Kendall, P. C., Reber, M., McLeer, S., Epps, J., & Ronan, K. R. (1990). Cognitive-behavioral treatment of conduct-disordered children. *Cognitive Therapy and Research*, *14*, 279–297. http://dx.doi.org/10.1007/BF01183997

Kessler, R. C., Amminger, G. P., Aguilar-Gaxiola, S., Alonso, J., Lee, S., & Ustün, T. B. (2007). Age of onset of mental disorders: A review of recent literature. *Current Opinion in Psychiatry*, *20*, 359–364. http://dx.doi.org/10.1097/YCO.0b013e32816ebc8c

Kilpatrick, D. G., Ruggiero, K. J., Acierno, R., Saunders, B. E., Resnick, H. S., & Best, C. L. (2003). Violence and risk of PTSD, major depression, substance abuse/dependence, and comorbidity: Results from the National Survey of Adolescents. *Journal of Consulting and Clinical Psychology*, *71*, 692–700. http://dx.doi.org/10.1037/0022-006X.71.4.692

Kim-Cohen, J., Caspi, A., Moffitt, T. E., Harrington, H., Milne, B. J., & Poulton, R. (2003). Prior juvenile diagnoses in adults with mental disorder: Developmental follow-back of a prospective-longitudinal cohort. *Archives of General Psychiatry*, *60*, 709–717. http://dx.doi.org/10.1001/archpsyc.60.7.709

Kovacs, M. (1990). Comorbid anxiety disorders in childhood-onset depressions. In J. Maser & C. Cloninger (Eds.), *Comorbidity of mood and anxiety disorders* (pp. 272–281). Washington, DC: American Psychiatric Press.

Laurens, K. R., Hobbs, M. J., Sunderland, M., Green, M. J., & Mould, G. L. (2012). Psychotic-like experiences in a community sample of 8000 children aged 9 to 11 years: An item response theory analysis. *Psychological Medicine*, *42*, 1495–1506.

Leventhal, T., & Brooks-Gunn, J. (2003). Moving to opportunity: An experimental study of neighborhood effects on mental health. *American Journal of Public Health, 93*, 1576–1582. http://dx.doi.org/10.2105/AJPH.93.9.1576

Lipsey, M. W., Howell, J. C., Kelly, M. R., Chapman, G., & Carver, D. (2010). *Improving the effectiveness of juvenile justice programs*. Washington, DC: Center for Juvenile Justice Reform, Georgetown University.

Luman, M., Oosterlaan, J., Knol, D. L., & Sergeant, J. A. (2008). Decision-making in ADHD: Sensitive to frequency but blind to the magnitude of penalty? *Journal of Child Psychology and Psychiatry, 49*, 712–722. http://dx.doi.org/10.1111/j.1469-7610.2008.01910.x

McNiel, D. E., & Binder, R. L. (2007). Effectiveness of a mental health court in reducing criminal recidivism and violence. *American Journal of Psychiatry, 164*, 1395–1403. http://dx.doi.org/10.1176/appi.ajp.2007.06101664

Mental Health and Juvenile Justice Collaborative for Change. (2014). *Better solutions for youth with mental health needs in the juvenile justice system*. Delmar, NY: National Center for Mental Health and Juvenile Justice.

Merikangas, K. R., He, J. P., Burstein, M., Swanson, S. A., Avenevoli, S., Cui, L., . . . Swendsen, J. (2010). Lifetime prevalence of mental disorders in U.S. adolescents: Results from the National Comorbidity Survey Replication—Adolescent Supplement (NCS-A). *Journal of the American Academy of Child and Adolescent Psychiatry, 49*, 980–989. http://dx.doi.org/10.1016/j.jaac.2010.05.017

Mesulam, M. (2000). Behavioral neuroanatomy: Large scale networks, association cortex, frontal syndromes, the limbic system and hemisphere specialization. In M. Mesulam (Ed.), *Principles of behavioral and cognitive neurology* (pp. 1–120). New York, NY: Oxford University Press.

Moffitt, T. E. (1993). Adolescence-limited and life-course-persistent antisocial behavior: A developmental taxonomy. *Psychological Review, 100*, 674–701. http://dx.doi.org/10.1037/0033-295X.100.4.674

Nasby, W., Hayden, B., & DePaulo, B. M. (1980). Attributional bias among aggressive boys to interpret unambiguous social stimuli as displays of hostility. *Journal of Abnormal Psychology, 89*, 459–468. http://dx.doi.org/10.1037/0021-843X.89.3.459

National Conference of State Legislatures. (2011). *Mental health needs of juvenile offenders: Juvenile justice guidebook for legislators*. Denver, CO: Author.

Odgers, C. L., Milne, B. J., Caspi, A., Crump, R., Poulton, R., & Moffitt, T. E. (2007). Predicting prognosis for the conduct-problem boy: Can family history help? *Journal of the American Academy of Child and Adolescent Psychiatry, 46*, 1240–1249. http://dx.doi.org/10.1097/chi.0b013e31813c6c8d

Odgers, C. L., Moretti, M. M., & Reppucci, N. D. (2005). Examining the science and practice of violence risk assessment with female adolescents. *Law and Human Behavior, 29*, 7–27. http://dx.doi.org/10.1007/s10979-005-1397-z

Oudekerk, B. A., & Reppucci, N. D. (2012). Reducing recidivism on violence among offending youth. In J. A. Dvoskin, J. L. Skeem, R. W. Navaco, & K. S. Douglas (Eds.), *Applying social science to reduce violent offending* (pp. 199–222). New York, NY: Oxford University Press.

Pineles, S. L., Shipherd, J. C., Mostoufi, S. M., Abramovitz, S. M., & Yovel, I. (2009). Attentional biases in PTSD: More evidence for interference. *Behaviour Research and Therapy, 47*, 1050–1057. http://dx.doi.org/10.1016/j.brat.2009.08.001

Pollock, E. S. (2001). Those crazy kids: Providing the insanity defense in juvenile courts. *Minnesota Law Review, 85*, 2041–2080.

Quinn, M. M., Rutherford, R. B., Leone, P. E., Osher, D. M., & Poirier, J. M. (2005). Youth with disabilities in juvenile corrections: A national survey. *Exceptional Children, 71*, 339–345. http://dx.doi.org/10.1177/001440290507100308

Rawal, P., Romansky, J., Jenuwine, M., & Lyons, J. S. (2004). Racial differences in the mental health needs and service utilization of youth in the juvenile justice system. *Journal of Behavioral Health Services and Research, 31*, 242–254. http://dx.doi.org/10.1007/BF02287288

Rogers, J. E., & Myers, W. C. (2013). Commentary: The insanity defense and youths in juvenile court. *Journal of the American Academy of Psychiatry and the Law, 41*, 496–500.

Roper v. Simmons, 543 U.S. 551 (2005).

Rutter, M. (1994). Comorbidity: Meanings and mechanisms. *Clinical Psychology: Science and Practice, 1*, 100–103. http://dx.doi.org/10.1111/j.1468-2850.1994.tb00012.x

Rutter, M. (2010). Child and adolescent psychiatry: Past scientific achievements and challenges for the future. *European Child and Adolescent Psychiatry, 19*, 689–703. http://dx.doi.org/10.1007/s00787-010-0111-y

Rutter, M. (2011). Research review: Child psychiatric diagnosis and classification: Concepts, findings, challenges and potential. *Journal of Child Psychology and Psychiatry, 52*, 647–660. http://dx.doi.org/10.1111/j.1469-7610.2011.02367.x

Rutter, M. (2013). Developmental psychopathology: A paradigm shift or just a relabeling? *Development and Psychopathology, 25*, 1201–1213. http://dx.doi.org/10.1017/S0954579413000564

Sales, B. D., & Shuman, D. W. (1996). The newly emerging mental health law. In B. D. Sales & D. W. Shuman (Eds.), *Law, mental health, and mental disorder* (pp. 2–14). Belmont, CA: Thomson Brooks/Cole.

Schwalbe, C. S. (2007). Risk assessment for juvenile justice: A meta-analysis. *Law and Human Behavior, 31*, 449–462. http://dx.doi.org/10.1007/s10979-006-9071-7

Scott, E. S., Reppucci, N. D., & Woolard, J. L. (1995). Evaluating adolescent decision making in legal contexts. *Law and Human Behavior, 19*, 221–244. http://dx.doi.org/10.1007/BF01501658

Sexton, T. L., & Alexander, J. F. (2002). Family-based empirically supported interventions. *Counseling Psychologist, 30*, 238–261. http://dx.doi.org/10.1177/0011000002302003

Shufelt, J. L., & Cocozza, J. J. (2006). *Youth with mental health disorders in the juvenile justice system: Results from a multi-state prevalence study*. Delmar, NY: National Center for Mental Health and Juvenile Justice.

Simcha-Fagan, O. M., & Schwartz, J. E. (1986). Neighborhood and delinquency: An assessment of contextual effects. *Criminology, 24*, 667–699. http://dx.doi.org/10.1111/j.1745-9125.1986.tb01507.x

Skowyra, K., & Cocozza, J. (2007). *Blueprint for change: A comprehensive model for the identification and treatment of youth with mental health needs in contact with the juvenile justice system*. Delmar, NY: National Center for Mental Health and Juvenile Justice.

Stadler, C., Sterzer, P., Schmeck, K., Krebs, A., Kleinschmidt, A., & Poustka, F. (2007). Reduced anterior cingulate activation in aggressive children and adolescents during affective stimulation: Association with temperament traits. *Journal of Psychiatric Research, 41*, 410–417. http://dx.doi.org/10.1016/j.jpsychires.2006.01.006

Steadman, H. J., Monahan, J., Duffee, B., Hartstone, E., & Robbins, P. C. (1984). The impact of state mental hospital deinstitutionalization on United States prison populations, 1968–1978. *Journal of Criminal Law and Criminology, 75*, 474–490. http://dx.doi.org/10.2307/1143164

Steinberg, L., & Cauffman, E. (1996). Maturity of judgment in adolescence: Psychosocial factors in adolescent decision making. *Law and Human Behavior, 20*, 249–272. http://dx.doi.org/10.1007/BF01499023

Steiner, H., Garcia, I. G., & Matthews, Z. (1997). Posttraumatic stress disorder in incarcerated juvenile delinquents. *Journal of the American Academy of Child and Adolescent Psychiatry, 36*, 357–365. http://dx.doi.org/10.1097/00004583-199703000-00014

Sterzer, P., Stadler, C., Krebs, A., Kleinschmidt, A., & Poustka, F. (2005). Abnormal neural responses to emotional visual stimuli in adolescents with conduct disorder. *Biological Psychiatry, 57*, 7–15. http://dx.doi.org/10.1016/j.biopsych.2004.10.008

Tate, D. C., Reppucci, N. D., & Mulvey, E. P. (1995). Violent juvenile delinquents: Treatment effectiveness and implications for future action. *American Psychologist, 50*, 777–781. http://dx.doi.org/10.1037/0003-066X.50.9.777

Tcheremissine, O. V., & Lieving, L. M. (2006). Pharmacological aspects of the treatment of conduct disorder in children and adolescents. *CNS Drugs, 20*, 549–565. http://dx.doi.org/10.2165/00023210-200620070-00002

Toplak, M. E., Jain, U., & Tannock, R. (2005). Executive and motivational processes in adolescents with attention-deficit-hyperactivity disorder (ADHD). *Behavioral and Brain Functions, 1*, 8–20. http://dx.doi.org/10.1186/1744-9081-1-8

Torbet, P., Gable, R., & Hurst, H. (1996). *State responses to serious and violent juvenile crime: Research report.* http://dx.doi.org/10.1037/e318222004-001

U.S. House of Representatives, Committee on Government Reform—Minority Staff, Special Investigations Division. (2004). *Incarceration of youth who are waiting for community mental health services in the United States*. Washington, DC: U.S. House of Representatives.

Vincent, G. M., Grisso, T., Terry, A., & Banks, S. (2008). Sex and race differences in mental health symptoms in juvenile justice: The MAYSI-2 national meta-analysis. *Journal of the American Academy of Child and Adolescent Psychiatry, 47*, 282–290. http://dx.doi.org/10.1097/CHI.0b013e318160d516

Warboys, L., & Wilber, S. (1996). Mental health issues in juvenile justice. In B. D. Sales & D. W. Shuman (Eds.), *Law, mental health, and mental disorder* (pp. 503–521). Belmont, CA: Thomson Brooks/Cole.

Wasserman, G. A., Ko, S. J., & McReynolds, L. S. (2004, August). Assessing the mental health status of youth in juvenile justice settings. *OJJDP Juvenile Justice Bulletin*, pp. 1–8. http://dx.doi.org/10.1037/e300802005-002

Weisz, J. R., & Jensen, P. S. (1999). Efficacy and effectiveness of child and adolescent psychotherapy and pharmacotherapy. *Mental Health Services Research, 1*, 125–157. http://dx.doi.org/10.1023/A:1022321812352

Wierson, M., & Forehand, R. (1995). Predicting recidivism in juvenile delinquents: The role of mental health diagnoses and the qualification of conclusions by race. *Behaviour Research and Therapy, 33*, 63–67. http://dx.doi.org/10.1016/0005-7967(94)E0001-Y

Wilson, D. B., Bouffard, L. A., & MacKenzie, D. L. (2005). A quantitative review of structured, group-oriented, cognitive-behavioral programs for offenders. *Criminal Justice and Behavior*, *32*, 172–204. http://dx.doi.org/10.1177/0093854804272889

Zornberg, G. L., Buka, S. L., & Tsuang, M. T. (2000). Hypoxic-ischemia-related fetal/neonatal complications and risk of schizophrenia and other nonaffective psychoses: A 19-year longitudinal study. *American Journal of Psychiatry*, *157*, 196–202. http://dx.doi.org/10.1176/appi.ajp.157.2.196

Part IV

PATTERNS OF OFFENDING

CHAPTER 7

SERIOUS QUESTIONS ABOUT SERIOUS JUVENILE OFFENDERS: PATTERNS OF OFFENDING AND OFFENSES

Jennifer L. Woolard and Erika Fountain

Contact with the justice system is a part of adolescence for approximately 1 million youths each year. The Federal Bureau of Investigation (FBI) has reported that people younger than age 18 comprised approximately 10% of all arrests, or more than 1 million charged offenses, in 2012; 3% of arrests were of youths younger than age 15 (FBI, 2013). Youths younger than age 18 were involved in a significant number of arrests for crimes the FBI considers serious, including murder, rape, robbery, and aggravated assault (see Figure 7.1). Male youths younger than age 18 comprised 10.4% (n = 722,855), and female youths younger than age 18 comprised 12% (n = 297,479) of all male and female arrests in 2012, respectively (FBI, 2013). White youths represented the majority of people younger than age 18 arrested for forcible rape, aggravated assault, burglary, larceny or theft, motor vehicle theft, and arson (see Figure 7.2).

These often-cited numbers give an overview of the scope of the problem and emphasize the importance of effective policy and practice responses, but they mask an immense amount of detail. Who are these offenders? Are they first-time offenders or experienced offenders? Will they all continue to commit crime? If so, will their offending escalate? These are important questions that are not addressed by descriptive information about single incidents. In this chapter, we examine some aspects of these questions in greater detail to unpack those numbers and learn more about patterns of offending, particularly among serious offenders. First, we examine how key terms for research and policy on serious offenders and offending patterns are defined and used. Next, we examine relevant methodological choices that undergird the Evaluation of Current Evidence section, a review of key theories and evidence regarding patterns of offending and serious offenders. Finally, we briefly discuss implications for research, policy, and practice.

RELEVANT HISTORY

How is *serious* defined? Is *serious* different from *chronic*? Is *serious* always also *violent?* In the next section, we address these questions of definition.

Fundamentally, we must begin with definitions—political, theoretical, and operational. In some respects, the definition of *serious offenders* is more of a policy concern than an intrinsically developmental or criminological question. However, research terms are important because they set the framework for identifying and understanding causes and consequences, which can both affect and be affected by policy. Policy concerns about who should be worried about (from a public safety perspective) and on whom money should be spent (from a cost–benefit perspective) can shape definitions as well as respond to them.

Moreover, politics and funding opportunities can focus researchers' attention on certain causes to the exclusion of others. As Levine and Levine (1992) argued, in conservative times society tends to focus on intraindividual inadequacies as the root cause of social problems such as juvenile offending, presuming that the environment in which individuals function is adequate. A more situational approach to helping children appears during times of greater reform, assuming that good people are living in poor conditions that can

http://dx.doi.org/10.1037/14643-007
APA Handbook of Psychology and Juvenile Justice, K. Heilbrun (Editor-in-Chief)

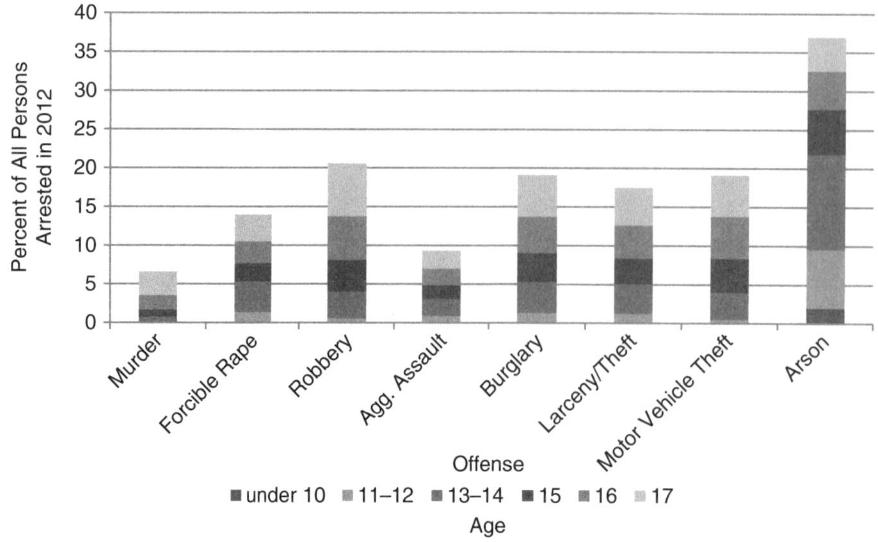

FIGURE 7.1. Percentage of all people arrested in 2012 by offense and age. Data from Federal Bureau of Investigation (2013).

and should be changed. These larger assumptions can in turn affect the types of research questions likely to be funded and the policies that are implemented.

For example, Humphreys and Rappaport (1993) argued that the shift in federal substance abuse funding in the 1980s from community mental health to substance abuse treatment helped spur a corpus of research emphasizing individual risk factors to the detriment of situational and societal factors. The third wave of juvenile justice reform in the 1990s

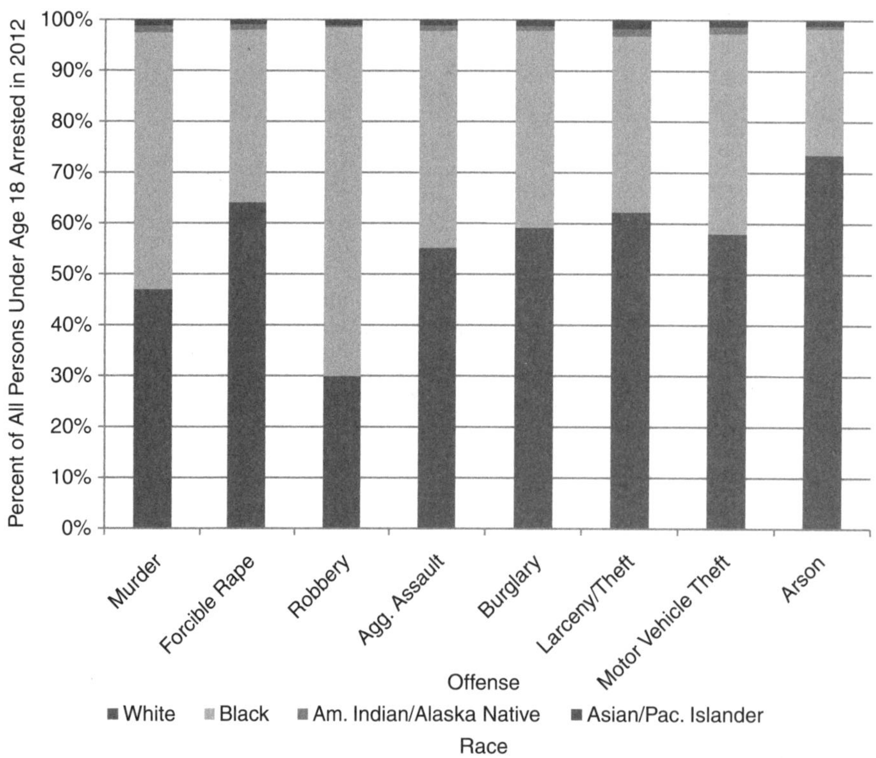

FIGURE 7.2. Percentage of all people younger than age 18 arrested in 2012 by offense and race. Data from Federal Bureau of Investigation (2013).

is a good example of how policy concerns with a coming wave of superpredators—which turned out to be incorrect—helped define what types of offenders were considered serious and how to intervene with them (see, e.g., Zimring, 1998). What some are calling the fourth wave of juvenile justice reform emerged early in the 21st century with a confluence of policy concerns about incarceration costs, program intervention effectiveness, and a growing research corpus taking an ecological approach to understanding adolescent development in legal contexts (e.g., Greenwood, 2006; National Campaign to Reform State Juvenile Justice Systems, 2013).

We start by examining two broad parameters of definitions that undergird policy and research on patterns of juvenile offending—the nature or type of crime and the frequency of crime. Within the nature or type of crime, we examine different categories of offenses as well as type of offending pattern. We then briefly review the advantages and disadvantages of various information sources about offenders and offending.

Nature and Variety of Crime

One fundamental framework for understanding and defining crime is the FBI's Uniform Crime Reporting program and, for greater detail on offenses, the National Incident Based Reporting System. Collecting and aggregating data from law enforcement agencies across the country, the Uniform Crime Reporting program defines serious offenses as Part 1 offenses. Part 1 violent crimes include the use of force or threat of force, and, in descending order of seriousness, these offenses include murder and nonnegligent manslaughter, forcible rape, robbery, and aggravated assault. Part 1 property crimes include burglary, larceny and theft, motor vehicle theft, and arson. Research often follows the broad categorical distinctions of violent and property offenses but varies in the details of what specific offenses are included in these categories and whether they are considered serious.

Serious. Serious violent offenders have captured researchers' attention for quite some time (e.g., Elliott, 1994), but definitions of serious violence vary across studies and sometimes across publications from the same data set. In the Pittsburgh Youth Study (PYS), Loeber, Farrington, Stouthamer-Loeber, and White (2008) defined serious violence as forcible robbery, attacking with intent to injure, sexual coercion, or rape. Some authors have incorporated non–person offenses such as serious property offenses (Baglivio, Jackowski, Greenwald, & Howell, 2014; Loeber, Farrington, Stouthamer-Loeber, & White, 2008) and serious theft (burglary, motor vehicle theft; Rosenfeld, White, & Esbensen, 2012) into a distinct subcategory of their operationalization of serious offending. Loeber et al. (2008) defined serious theft as breaking and entering or auto theft. The Pathways to Desistance Study (Mulvey et al., 2010) sample consisted solely of serious offenders, defined as youths between 14 and 18 years old who were found delinquent (in juvenile court) or guilty (in criminal court) primarily of felonies, including person, property, drug, and weapons offenses.

Violent. Definitions of violent offending often include offenses defined by the FBI Uniform Crime Reporting program as violent (e.g., robbery, aggravated assault, murder, forcible rape) but sometimes include sexual offenses beyond forcible rape (e.g., deviant sexual intercourse, spousal sexual assault; Rosenfeld et al., 2012). In some studies, particularly those that have exclusively focused on childhood or have extended from childhood into adolescence and beyond, antisocial behavior and externalizing behaviors may be used rather than legal definitions, some of which are simply not applicable to young children (Piquero, 2007). Moreover, most operationalizations of violent behavior have not considered the context in which that violence occurs. For example, Tolan (2007) suggested that there are four types of youth violence—situational, relationship, predatory, and pathological. These types blend operationalization with the underlying meaning and causes of violence but are a reminder that it can be difficult to cleanly separate the behavior from its circumstances and meaning.

Specialized. Specialized offending generally describes individuals who show a preference for a particular type of offense, usually illustrated by disproportionate and repeated commitment (Loeber, Farrington, & Jolliffe, 2008). Nieuwbeerta, Blokland, Piquero, and Sweeten (2011) noted that this term has also had multiple operationalizations, including

> the tendency to repeat the same offense type on successive crimes, a relative dominance in a particular offense across some specific period of the career or some specified number of offenses, or the overrepresentation of particular offenses within the careers of certain offenders in contrast to the overall rate of those offenses in the population. (p. 3)

In a specific test of multiple methods to operationalize specialization in the same dataset, Sullivan, McGloin, Ray, and Caudy (2009) concluded that there is no best method for defining or detecting specialization but that methodological choices could vary depending on the theoretical or policy issue in question.

Variety or diversity. Variety scores capture the number of different types of acts or offenses in which an individual engages over a specified time period. What constitutes a type of offense varies by study and publication. For example, the Pathways to Desistance study calculated a total variety score that encompassed all measured crime types as well as two variety subscores: Aggressive Offending and Income Offending (Pathways to Desistance, n.d.).

Frequency of Crime

Even the operationalization of frequency, or number of offenses, can vary depending on whether the denominator is the individual or sample itself or the number of individuals who were actively offending during the time period under study (Piquero, Hawkins, & Kazemian, 2012). Some analyses focus on prevalence (whether a type of offense was ever committed during a specific time period, often a lifetime), and others focus on incidence (the number of times an offense was committed in a given time period such as the past year). Variety scores and frequency scores are usually strongly correlated, but few studies have empirically tested whether and how their patterns covary across time (Brame, Paternoster, & Bushway, 2004; Monahan & Piquero, 2009).

Chronic. Piquero (2014) described the historical consideration of chronicity as concerning those "whose antisocial involvement begins early in the life course, increases in frequency throughout childhood and into adolescence, persists into early adulthood, and desists much later in the life course than more transient offenders" (p. 128). To a certain extent, therefore, chronicity, pattern, and pathway are integral parts of a larger whole; chronicity could be considered a type of pattern. Almost half of juvenile offending has been attributed to chronic offenders (e.g., Savage, 2009), but operationalization of what constitutes a chronic offender or pattern has varied by research team, policymaker, or practitioner. Mears and Cochran (2013) defined chronic offending as a binary measure of whether a youth engaged in any of 17 crimes six or more times. In their study of 5 years of official Florida Department of Juvenile Justice data, Baglivio et al. (2014) distinguished serious, violent, and chronic as separate categories that often co-occurred. They labeled as chronic any offender with at least four official referrals, including misdemeanors and felonies. They noted that previous definitions of chronicity ranged from three to nine events, with events ranging from referrals to adjudications to convictions. Piquero (2007) argued that the field must develop a new definition of chronic that incorporates both time and frequency.

Persistent. *Persistence* generally refers to continued offending over a particular time period, such as adolescence into young adulthood (Piquero, Hawkins, & Kazemian, 2012). Farrington et al. (2008) defined *duration* as the number of years in which offenses occur for each individual and persistence as the continuity of offending across age blocks that distinguish middle and late childhood, early and late adolescence, and early adulthood. Persistent offending does not necessarily require the repetition of similar offenses; instead, it often refers to the simple act of offending itself, irrespective of offense type. For example, Rosenfeld et al.'s (2012) investigation of drug dealers, gang members, murderers, and sex offenders defined persistence as committing an act or behavior in adolescence (ages 13–17) and in young adulthood (ages 18–25); the crimes during these two time periods could differ and still meet their definition of persistence.

Jennings and Reingle (2012) noted that some authors distinguish persistent offenders from chronic offenders on the basis of whether the study design's follow-up period terminated in adolescence (persistent) or continued into adulthood (chronic), presumably allowing for desistance to distinguish nonchronic and chronic offenders. Sometimes chronic is used interchangeably with persistent (e.g., Lussier & Blokland, 2014). Loeber and Farrington (1999) excluded chronicity from their focus on serious violent offenses because definitions of such were not comparable across court, arrest, and self-report data sources.

Theoretical and pragmatic concerns may drive both the conceptualization and the operationalization of each of these offending patterns in any given study design or analysis. Our review here is not meant to undermine conclusions drawn from the literature on offending patterns but instead to emphasize the complexity of pattern definitions and components. This complexity should be considered when evaluating results across different datasets, or even different analyses within a given dataset.

Sources of Information About Crime

The multiple sources of information about youthful offending have contributed complementary information limited by their unique weaknesses (e.g., Krohn, Thornberry, Gibson, & Baldwin, 2010). The FBI Uniform Crime Reporting program exclusively tallies offenses and people known to police. Official reports of arrests, petitions, referrals, convictions, and other justice system processes provide important information about offenses that have come to the attention of authorities but are subject to jurisdictional and individual variation in state and local law enforcement policies, informal and formal processing practices, quality of records and recording practices, and changes in these policies and practices across time (Brame, Fagan, Piquero, Schubert, & Steinberg, 2004; Loftin & McDowall, 2010). Self-report of offending from youths themselves avoids those limitations but engenders several of its own, including limitations of instrument design, sample selection and retention, and response errors (Brame, Fagan, et al., 2004; Krohn et al., 2010). Moreover, violence such as homicide and rape may be disproportionately underreported by offenders themselves (Farrington et al., 2008).

For example, official data may have more consistent definitions within and across jurisdictions for formal crimes, particularly the most serious crimes such as homicide. However, other crimes such as aggravated assault and simple assault can contain a wide range of acts and circumstances; the distinction between *aggravated* and *simple* can vary as a result of a number of factors external to the acts themselves (Zimring, 1998). Self-report data are more likely to focus on antisocial behaviors than on legal definitions of crime to avoid individual misunderstanding or ignorance about the law. Researchers may then determine which acts correspond to legal definitions of delinquency and crime.

Piquero, Hawkins, and Kazemian (2012) noted that a substantial proportion of the research on criminal careers has relied on data from a few longitudinal studies such as the Dunedin study (Moffitt, 1993), the PYS (Loeber, Farrington, Stouthamer-Loeber, & White, 2008), and, more recently, the Pathways to Desistance study (Mulvey et al., 2010). Many of the large longitudinal datasets from which much research on offending patterns has been drawn contain self-report as well as official data and have compared multiple information sources within the same dataset (e.g., Brame, Fagan, et al., 2004; Dunford & Elliott, 1984). In their review of research on youthful violent offending, Piquero, Hawkins, and Kazemian (2012) suggested that self-report and official records have led to some different conclusions. For example, analyses of the PYS found significant differences for prevalence and frequency of offending, but not for average duration of serious careers. The self-reported prevalence of violence and theft was significantly higher than that obtained from arrest records, with the greatest disparity occurring for moderate violence and moderate theft (Loeber, Farrington, Stouthamer-Loeber, & White, 2008). Moreover, this disparity was greater for younger adolescents than for older adolescents. Recent research from the Pathways to Desistance study has suggested that self-report and official data have a moderate positive correlation (overall $r = .23$) across gender, race, and ethnicity in a serious offender sample that included both violent and non-violent offenders (Brame, Fagan, et al., 2004).

Beyond the decisions about definitions and data sources, research on offense patterns has depended on a variety of other methodological choices, including the sample, the outcome period, and the number of patterns identified from the data (Piquero, Hawkins, & Kazemian, 2012; Rosenfeld et al., 2012). For example, Rosenfeld et al. (2012) identified several problems with the definition and use of average age of onset to describe patterns of offending among special categories of serious offenders (e.g., sex and homicide offenders). The average-age-of-onset calculation depends first on the age range of the sample; if the upper range of ages sampled does not extend far enough into adolescence to include those who are considered late onset, the average age might be distorted; that is, younger than it would have been if late-onset adolescents had been included. Cohort and historical factors such as policy changes affecting the nature of surveillance and arrest or cultural changes in the acceptance of certain crimes (e.g., drug use) could affect offending onset. Finally, averages that collapse across racial, ethnic, or gender categories may mask important group differences in initiation and maintenance of offending.

EVALUATION OF CURRENT EVIDENCE

As Farrington (2005) noted, most developmental life course theories attempt to explain "both the development of offenders and the commission of offenses" (p. 3). *Pathways, sequences, trajectories,* and *careers* are all terms used in research on juvenile (and adult) offending and, as with the terms reviewed earlier, can mean different things to different researchers. Loeber and colleagues (Loeber, Farrington, Stouthamer-Loeber, & White, 2008; Loeber, White, & Burke, 2011) used *sequence* to describe the ordering of problem behaviors and *pathway* to describe the same for three or more problem behaviors that escalate in seriousness. In contrast to pathways, they suggested that developmental *trajectories* focus not on this orderly development of specific behaviors within an individual but instead on differentiating groups of individuals for whom a broad class of behaviors such as violence unfolds similarly across time. As such, research on pathways has investigated the sequence of behaviors, often focusing on which sequences lead to escalation toward more serious behaviors and offenses.

Loeber et al. (2011) identified three pathways escalating in seriousness. An authority conflict pathway begins before the teen years with stubborn behaviors that progress to defiance and disobedience and ultimately to authority-avoidant behaviors such as running away. The covert pathway begins before mid-adolescence and has four stages, from minor covert acts (e.g., lying) to property offenses, moderate delinquency, and then serious delinquency. The overt pathway escalates from minor aggression to physical fighting and then to serious violence such as rape. Interestingly, boys could be on more than one pathway simultaneously. A key part of the model's success depends on distinguishing what the authors call experimenters, who may enter a pathway at a later step or not progress to later steps, from persisters, who are likely to follow the full pathway from start to end. Researchers should be interested not only in how far youths progress along these pathways but in their rate of progression, or how quickly they move through the stages (Loeber et al., 2011).

Taking a different approach to understanding patterns of offending, more than 2 decades ago Moffitt (1993) proposed that adolescent offenders follow one of two trajectories, each with their own risk factors, offending patterns, and implications for intervention. The more common trajectory was the adolescent-limited (AL) pattern, in which adolescents engaged in offending during the teen years, primarily precipitated by puberty and maintained during the maturity gap between teens' growing cognitive capacities and their limited social status as not yet adults. Peer contexts that support offending behavior can also contribute to risk for offending in the AL pattern. These youths typically desist from offending as they mature into young adulthood and assume its associated rights and responsibilities without harmful long-term effects as long as they do not experience snares such as criminal records, incarceration, or addiction. Approximately 10% of youths follow what Moffitt termed a life-course-persistent (LCP) trajectory in which offending begins early in life and continues in a stable and escalating pattern into adulthood. She argued that LCP youths experience early neurobiological insults that interact with poor environments such as dysfunctional parenting, dangerous neighborhoods, or poverty to facilitate personality and relationship problems in adolescence that are not easily overcome in later years. Moffitt's original dichotomy of LCP and AL offenders spurred a healthy body of research that has since expanded to other data sets that have identified several other patterns across time, including late starters and desisters (e.g., Bliesener, Beelman, & Stemmler, 2011).

Before examining the data on patterns of offending in greater detail, it would be helpful to list several of what Farrington (2005) described as widely accepted conclusions about juvenile offending, some of which have implications for patterns. Basic information that is consistent across a wide swath of research has included offending onset that peaks between ages 8 and 14, desistance that peaks between ages 20 and 29, and offending prevalence that peaks between ages 15 and 19. Consistent with Moffitt's (1993) typology, Farrington concluded that early-onset age predicts lengthy and frequent offending, with a small proportion of offenders committing a large percentage of crimes. Consistent with Loeber et al.'s (2011) ideas about offending pathways, Farrington argued that the data suggest that different offense types tend to start at different ages. Finally, he suggested that the literature affirms that juvenile offending is versatile and not specialized, with diversification of offending peaking around age 20 and then becoming more specialized among the narrowing group of offenders who persist in adulthood.

Rather than examine persistence and desistance trajectories in great detail (see Chapter 8, this handbook), we highlight research that has examined patterns of trajectories themselves—how trajectories for different types of offending correspond. For example, using the PYS, Lacourse, Dupere, and Loeber (2008) modeled the joint probability of theft and violence trajectories to examine specialization and versatility in offending among two of the PYS cohorts of boys. In both cohorts of youths in the sample, analyses identified no or low (52%–59% of participants) and high declining (5%–10% of participants) trajectories of violence. Other violence trajectories included minor stable (30%; youngest cohort only), moderate declining (35%; oldest cohort only), and late onset (about 10%). Lacourse et al.'s separate analyses of theft also produced no or low (83%, young cohort; 58%, older cohort) and high declining (17%, young cohort; 3%, older cohort) trajectories. The older cohort evidenced two additional trajectories: moderate declining (30%) and late onset (10%). Estimating the probability of joint trajectory membership in the youngest cohort (e.g., no or low trajectory for theft and for violence), Lacourse et al. found that about 60% were low on violence and theft, 22% were only violent, and 20% had declining trajectories for both theft and violence. Approximately one third of the older cohort were low on both violence and theft, 24% had some type of violence trajectory but no theft, and the remainder were late onset (10%), moderate declining (26%), or high declining (7%) for both offense types. In addition to noting that most youths engage in little or no offending over time, Lacourse et al. concluded that serious theft almost always occurs with serious violence, but serious violence occurs without serious theft.

As research accumulates that demonstrates the existence of orderly patterns of offender development and commission of offenses, new questions arise about the heterogeneity and generalizability of both patterns of offenses and trajectories of offending over time across various categories of interest. One approach examines offenders of particular crimes—special groups thought to be qualitatively different from others. These groups include sex offenders, homicide offenders, drug or substance use offenders, gang-involved offenders and, to a certain extent, serious offenders as a whole. Another approach examines whether demographic characteristics such as race, ethnicity, or gender distinguish patterns of offending (DeLisi & Piquero, 2011). Race and gender disparities in the identification, apprehension, and adjudication of youthful offenders create a complicated backdrop for analyses of comparability in offending patterns, particularly those based on official records (e.g., Kempf-Leonard, 2012).

Gender

Although girls consistently represent a small proportion of serious violent offenders, a recurring question in the literature has involved whether boys and girls share similar pathway types and trajectories, particularly for serious and violent offending (Johannson & Kempf-Leonard, 2009). Jones, Brown,

Wanamaker, and Greiner (2014) summarized two approaches—gender neutral and gender responsive. Gender-neutral theorists focus on individual risk factors that predict offending for both boys and girls, with the degree or salience of some factors potentially varying by gender. Gender-responsive or feminist approaches argue that qualitatively different experiences and system or structural factors differentiate pathways for boys and girls. Although this debate extends beyond specific pathway and trajectory analyses (e.g., Woolard, 2012), advances in analytic techniques have enabled more rigorous comparisons of similarities and differences among pathways derived within gender. The major longitudinal data sets vary in their capacity to address gender effects. The PYS focused exclusively on boys but has been analyzed in the companion Pittsburgh Girls Study.

A majority of the literature on gender and delinquency trajectory has found more similarities than differences between females and males, although some assumptions about measurement equivalence across gender may not be appropriate. In one of the few explicit tests of measurement equivalence assumptions, Odgers et al. (2008) first asked whether the Antisocial Conduct Problems scale from the Dunedin study, derived from multiple measures of conduct disorder symptoms, demonstrated measurement invariance across age and gender. The scale operated similarly for males ages 7 to 26, but for females only ages 7 to 15. They concluded that it would be inappropriate to assume that data past age 15 measured the same construct tapped before age 15. As a result, they tested and found equivalence across gender only using data between ages 7 and 15 for boys and girls.

A number of similarities in offending patterns over time for male and female adolescents can be found. In that same study, Odgers et al. (2008) did identify adolescent-onset and LCP pathways in male and female adolescents, but they also found a childhood-limited trajectory. Fontaine, Carbonneau, Vitaro, Barker, and Tremblay (2009) reviewed almost 50 studies and concluded that girls follow multiple trajectories but may be distributed across those trajectories in different proportions than boys. Miller, Malone, and Dodge (2010) examined delinquency trajectories for adolescents in the Fast Track study (Conduct Problems Prevention Research Group, 2002) from 7th through 12th grades, producing four trajectory classes labeled *nonproblem, increasing, desister,* and *chronic*. Although proportions of boys and girls differed across classes, a finding consistent with those of other studies (e.g., Pepler, Jiang, Craig, & Connolly, 2010), both genders appear in all four trajectories. Moreover, gender did not moderate age 19 outcomes of partner violence, depression, risky sexual behavior, or number of pregnancies. Unlike the Miller et al. (2010) study, Pepler et al. (2010) identified five trajectories but found no girls in the chronic group. Although the shape of the low trajectory did not vary by gender, girls in the late-onset group more rapidly increased offending after age 15 than did boys in that same group. Girls in the early-onset and moderate groups increased offending, peaked, and decreased offending at faster rates and earlier than boys.

As previously discussed, trajectories capture patterns of offending over time, often based on variety scores, but do not always capture other offense characteristics (e.g., offense type—violence, property). The Gender and Aggression Project (Oudekerk, Erbacher, & Reppucci, 2012) investigated offending patterns based on lifetime prevalence diversity scores within a sample of high-risk incarcerated females, identifying and replicating a three-class solution describing violent and delinquent, delinquent-only (e.g., drug use, theft), and low-offending girls. These groups differed on a variety of psychopathology, victimization, and family risk factors, with the violent and delinquent group experiencing the greatest risk. Other longitudinal analyses of Gender and Aggression Project data have documented that although serious and diverse delinquent offending was generally stable across adolescence into young adulthood, violence specifically was not (Oudekerk et al., 2012). Adolescent girls who engaged in violence did not mature into seriously violent young adults.

Race/Ethnicity

Any discussion of patterns of offending by race must begin with acknowledgment of the disproportionate minority contact that is prevalent in the U.S. justice system (e.g., Kempf-Leonard, 2007). Although some reductions in disparities at various points in juvenile justice processing have occurred (e.g., Davis & Sorensen, 2013; Mendel, 2009), youth of color remain overrepresented. Piquero (2007) noted the lack of research examining the role of race in trajectories. He pointed out that both the AL and LCP should in theory operate similarly across race, but that offending might be higher among minority youths because they experience a greater number of risk factors by virtue of their social status as minorities.

Sex Offenses

Juveniles who commit sex offenses receive research and policy attention in part because of assumptions about their offending patterns—that they are different from juveniles who commit other types of crimes, that they are likely to recidivate with great frequency, and that they pose ongoing harm to the community that is only partially protected through sex offender registries and other laws (Piquero, Farrington, Jennings, Diamond, & Craig, 2012; Zimring, 2004). A growing body of research, usually focused on the recidivism risk from youths who have already committed a sexual offense, has suggested that sex offenders are not more likely than other offenders to specialize in sex crimes (Piquero, Farrington, et al., 2012; Seto & Lalumière, 2010). Seto and Lalumière (2010) conducted a meta-analysis of 59 studies that compared adolescent sex offenders with other offenders, finding more similarities than differences in risk factors that predict offending. Of particular interest, all 17 relevant studies reported that sexual offenders had a less extensive criminal history, a medium-sized effect. They did not have a significantly earlier age at first justice system contact than other offenders.

A key distinguishing dimension within the group of juvenile sex offenders is age of victim. Recent reviews, operationalizing age of victim as victim age, age difference between offender and victim, or some combination of both, have examined what characteristics might differentially describe the offenses committed by juveniles against children versus same-aged peers. Differences in the specific definitions of children and peers notwithstanding, it appears that juveniles who sexually offend against peers are more likely to use force and victimize female acquaintances or strangers; offenses against children were more likely to target male and female family members (Keelan & Fremouw, 2013). Keelan and Fremouw (2013) could not draw any conclusions about whether the offenses against peers or children predicted different categories of subsequent offending.

Until recently, this focus on recidivism and corresponding risk factors that might differentiate sex offenders made up the bulk of research. Several studies have applied more sophisticated analyses to examine the complexity of offending over time. Lussier, Van Den Berg, Bijleveld, and Hendriks (2012) modeled the trajectories of sexual and nonsexual offending of 498 Dutch juveniles who had committed sexual offenses to test for synchronicity between the two offense types. Analysis of the nonsexual offenses yielded five patterns, with the very-low-rate offender trajectory accounting for more than half of the offenders. The rest followed trajectories described as late starter (21.3%), AL (11%), late bloomer, and high rate (4.2%), the latter of which had the earliest age for first offense and the highest levels of nonsexual offending among all groups. Separate analyses of the sexual offending patterns yielded two trajectories. At 10.4% of the sample, the high-rate slow desisters began offending and peaked before adolescence, then slowly declined well into adulthood. The majority of the youths followed an AL trajectory by beginning their offending later, peaking in early adolescence, and desisting by early young adulthood. Lussier et al. drew three conclusions from the simultaneous analyses of both sexual and non–sexual offending trajectories. Most youths in each of the non–sexual offending trajectories followed the AL sexual offending trajectory. None of the youths in the high-rate non–sexual offending group were also in the high-rate sexual offending group. About one half of the high-rate sexual offenders were in the low-rate non–sexual offending trajectory group. Thus, Lussier et al. concluded that it might be difficult to distinguish the two types of sexual offending during adolescence. Moreover, subsequent analyses have indicated that most juvenile sex offenders do not become adult sex offenders, and most adult sex offenders do not have a juvenile sex offending history (Lussier & Blokland, 2014).

Homicide

A high-profile but low base-rate crime, homicide represented about 1% of all arrests in 2012. Of the more than 14,500 murder offenders, 618, or 4%, were younger than age 18 (FBI, 2013). Of juvenile homicide offenders, 90% were male, 38% were White, and 58% were Black (FBI, 2013). The FBI's Supplementary Homicide Reports provided the foundation for several analyses of homicide offenders including young and older female juvenile offenders (Heide & Sellers, 2014), those who murder siblings (Pecke & Heide, 2012) and parents (Heide, 1993a, 1993b; Heide & Petee, 2007a, 2007b), and those who commit sexual homicides (Chan, Heide, & Myers, 2013; Myers & Chan, 2012).

Although they are mainly descriptive because of the low incidence of these subsets of homicide, most studies have focused on characteristics of victim, offender, and offense, with some suggestion about risk factors. For example, sibling murders tend to be committed by White male teens with guns in situations of sibling conflict (Pecke & Heide, 2012). Few differences were found between offenders who killed a brother versus those who killed a sister, other than the latter were more likely to be female and to kill younger victims. Approximately 20% of 445 sexual homicides—an even rarer crime—committed by juveniles between 1976 and 2005 involved offenders and victims of the same sex; almost all involved male juveniles (Myers & Chan, 2012). About two thirds were committed by 16- to 17-year-olds, and most of the victims were adults.

Loeber et al. (2005) investigated the prevalence and prediction of homicide in multiple reporting sources from the PYS. Of the 1,488 boys, 33 were convicted of homicide during the study period. As in other studies, more than half of the offenses occurred in groups of two or more, and the offenders were mostly African American (85%); because the study period followed youths into young adulthood, age at the time of the offense ranged from 16 to 25. More than 90% of the offenders had a prior violent offense and were more likely than other violent offenders to demonstrate greater risk on predictors such as drug use, gang involvement, poor school performance, and mental health diagnoses. Loeber et al. (2011) indicated that the common history of violence among homicide offenders constitutes a fourth step in their developmental pathways model, with violence a necessary precondition for progression.

Research on recidivism among juvenile homicide offenders has been limited, focused in the United States mainly on youths who commit parricide (killing of a parent). Vries and Liem (2011) examined the population of Dutch juvenile homicide offenders from 1992 to 2007 ($N = 137$), the majority of whom were 16- to 17-year-old boys who offended in groups; the incidents mainly arose from conflictual situations. With an average follow-up period of 8.5 years, almost 60% reoffended postrelease, with an average of 7.5 offenses. Only 3% were involved in another homicide offense. Static risk factors of male gender, low self-control, and criminal history and the dynamic risk factor of delinquent friends and associates predicted recidivism prevalence.

Although they did not focus on intraindividual patterns, Flexon, Stolzenberg, and D'Alessio (2011) examined homicide offending from a different perspective, evaluating the degree to which *Roper v. Simmons*'s (2005) ban on the death penalty for offenses committed by 16- and 17-year-olds affected the homicide rate. Using a multiple time-series design, Flexon et al. tested contradictory theories that the death penalty ban would increase homicides because the deterrent effect was removed and the brutalization theory that the removal of such a punishment would actually reduce the homicide rate. Limitations notwithstanding, they failed to find a statistically significant effect of the *Roper* ban on the homicides reported in the FBI's Supplementary Homicide Report files.

IMPLICATIONS

A number of researchers have identified important research directions in criminal careers research generally and juvenile offending patterns specifically. These directions include a better understanding of co-offending (Goldweber, Dmitrieva, Cauffman, Piquero, & Steinberg, 2011; McGloin & Piquero, 2010) and more information on the number of trajectories and whether they matter (DeLisi & Piquero, 2011), among others. Here we focus on a greater understanding of risk and protective factors, the ecological and situational contexts of offending, and their interaction (DeLisi & Piquero, 2011; Mulvey, 2014).

Defining and describing patterns and pathways does not necessarily identify the causes of those pathways, a task that has brought criminologists, psychologists, and others together (Savage, 2009). Such investigation necessarily requires theories about risk and protective factors, risk mechanisms, and theories about the pathways themselves. Many such theories recognize, if not emphasize, that risk and protective factors occur at multiple ecological levels (e.g., Bronfenbrenner, 1979) and that intra- and extraindividual factors interact with the environment to shape proclivities, behaviors, and institutional responses (Loeber, Farrington, Stouthamer-Loeber, & White, 2008; Woolard, Vidal, & Fountain, 2015). Farrington and Ttofi (2011) distinguished between promotive factors, which predict lower probabilities of offending, and protective factors, which either remove or reduce the effect of risk factors or predict lower offending probability in an otherwise higher risk group. Risk and protective factors from individual and environment can influence the trajectory shape, as can life events and transitions (Farrington, 2005). Across theories about offending, and indeed across developmental research more generally, these factors can be characterized according to proximity, ecological level, and modifiability (Woolard et al., 2015). Proximal factors are more directly close or immediate to youths, and distal factors are more distant or indirect. Those factors can be located on ecological levels ranging from the neurobiological to the societal (e.g., Bronfenbrenner & Ceci, 1994). Theories about patterns of offending also consider the dynamic (or changeable) and static (or constant) nature of risk and protection (e.g., Piquero, 2007).

The literature on risk, protective, and promotive factors is both deep and wide, characteristics that prevent us from completing an adequate review here. Instead, we focus on two relevant aspects of patterns of offending that require additional research: factors that occur at levels larger than the individual and the understudied but important developmental approach to interactions between factors at multiple ecological levels (Mulvey, 2014).

Taking an ecological approach requires examination at levels other than the individual. Although most theoretical frameworks underpinning pathways research recognize and sometimes identify specific risk and protective factors at levels other than the individual level, a significant amount of the empirical work on juvenile offending in psychology appears to have focused on the individual. Indeed, several excellent chapters in this handbook focus on specific individual-level risk factors such as mental illness (Chapter 6), psychopathy (Chapter 10), trauma (Chapter 15), and substance abuse (Chapter 13). This handbook's chapters on the brain (Chapter 5) and human development (Chapter 4) underscore the structural and functional capacities and characteristics of adolescence that are relevant to offending. Without minimizing the importance of individual-level factors, we must also consider those that operate at the family and neighborhood level and beyond and their relation to the determination and replicability of findings on offending patterns (Greenberg, 2010).

Testing a variety of theoretical explanations for the robust relationship between age and crime among a sample of serious violent offenders, for example, Sweeten, Piquero, and Steinberg (2013) found that it could be accounted for by changes in multiple developmental domains across adolescence into young adulthood. They evaluated constructs including social control, social learning and social networks, strain, psychosocial functioning, rational choice, and procedural justice. Once all relevant variables were included, approximately 75% of the variance in the age–crime curve relationship was explained.

Both static and dynamic factors at the family level are important to theories of juvenile offending, but family characteristics and experiences have consistently been associated with offending risk. Structural aspects such as number of children, parents' education level, family composition, and financial security, among others, affect the risk of antisocial behavior (Pagani, 2009). Grigorenko (2012) identified several categories of family-level risk, including child-rearing styles, especially those resulting in abuse and neglect; marital conflicts and family structure; and individual-level characteristics of parents such as psychopathology and substance abuse.

In a specific focus on cultural and national context, Maldonado-Molina, Piquero, Jennings,

Bird, and Canino (2009) examined patterns of offending for samples of Puerto Rican youths in the United States and Puerto Rico. They found differences in the number of trajectories and average level of self-reported delinquency across the two sites. Five trajectories emerged from youths in the Bronx: abstainers (49.1%); initial offending, then no offending (37.4%); low increasing (8.1%); high offending, then no offending (4.2%); and increasing offending (1.3%). The San Juan trajectories included nonoffending (59.3%); very low stable (34.9%); low stable (4.2%); and high offending, then no offending (1.6%). Maldonado-Molina et al. concluded that the nature and role of risk and protective factors operated similarly for both groups; for example, sensation seeking and exposure to violence separated offenders from nonoffenders in both samples. They noted that their data sources limited the capacity to examine more refined characteristics of neighborhoods and communities that might have explanatory power.

Researchers not only need to examine risk and promotive factors at the neighborhood and community levels, but they need to more fully conceptualize and operationalize what the person–environment interaction means. For example, one limitation of the developmental pathways research to date is the need to incorporate the influence of environmental and ecological factors on variability in the rate of progress along such pathways (Loeber et al., 2011). In other words, research must not only identify the influential factors themselves (present or not, predicts or not), but it must also determine whether they might accelerate quantitatively or qualitatively the orderly progression presumed to occur.

Patterns do not and cannot occur in the absence of transactions, or interactions, with a youth's environment (Capaldi & Wiesner, 2009). These interactions include not only risk factors and markers but also the attempts, successful or not, at intervention by a variety of systems, including juvenile justice, mental health, child welfare, education, and others. Patterns also do not occur independently of important developmental changes and milestones. Mulvey (2014) argued that the field must move beyond description of offending patterns to understanding how aspects of development act as moderators and mediators of offending. Developmental turning points, normative and non-normative, can reduce risk and increase the probability of desistance (Bliesener et al., 2011). Not only do psychological factors such as cognition, self-regulation, and psychosocial maturity change across adolescence into young adulthood, but so too do sociological processes (Mulvey, 2014). Key people and institutions in adolescents' lives have changing expectations for what adolescents can and should do. Mulvey (2014) used the example of peer influence to point out that peer importance and influence diminish as adolescents mature into young adults with a stronger sense of their own identity. Individuals simply have fewer opportunities to interact with peers as they move from adolescence into young adulthood. Both diminishing peer influence and decreasing opportunities for peer interaction likely independently and interactively influence patterns of offending.

Best Practice

The implications of research on offending patterns for best practice have already begun to play out in juvenile justice systems across the country. The widespread implementation of the risk–need–responsivity framework (see Chapter 9, this handbook) exemplifies one approach to designing interventions to specifically match a youth's changeable risk factors at a given time, recognizing that those risk factors will probably change over time, whether as a result of intervention or of the lack thereof. The focus on evidence-based practices is important; one can have greater confidence in an intervention strategy that has empirical support for success with youths having particular offending patterns and backgrounds. However, the implementation of effective practices comes with costs that states may not be able to afford. Greenwood and Welsh (2012) highlighted the financial and social capital investments required to change existing juvenile justice and service provider systems, even when the research evidence seems clear. In essence, the will may be present but not the way.

As Lipsey and Howell (2012) pointed out, though, a number of home-grown interventions that do not have the resources for rigorous evaluation studies may still be quite effective for youths with various patterns of offending. Lipsey's (2008) Standardized Program Evaluation Protocol tool is an interesting approach to applying the best research findings to the practicalities of program funding and implementation. The tool provides research-based guidelines with which to classify programs and identify dimensions that are strong versus those that need improvement to increase the likelihood of effective intervention. Combined with the Comprehensive Strategy for Serious, Violent, and Chronic Juvenile Offenders (Howell, 2009; Wilson & Howell, 1993), which emphasizes best practices that include disposition matrices, valid risk assessment tools, and quality assurance procedures, the Standardized Program Evaluation Protocol tool is a promising mechanism by which agencies and service providers can align their work with the latest research findings on risk for offending and effective intervention.

Relevant Policy

Policy can incorporate a more refined approach to identifying, processing, intervening, and evaluating efforts with serious, violent, and chronic offenders. The idea of focusing attention on the identification of and intervention with serious, violent offenders who commit a majority of crime has taken hold in justice policy for quite some time, perhaps best exemplified in the comprehensive strategy recommended by the Office of Juvenile Justice and Delinquency Prevention (Howell, 2009) that has influenced much state-level policy for the past 2 decades. Although there may indeed be a greater bang for the buck in focusing on those offenders who are at risk for engaging in frequent and persistent offending patterns, the assumption by some policymakers that the most extreme sanctions, such as long-term incarceration and transfer to the adult criminal justice system, are necessary and more effective than less severe sanctions is not necessarily accurate (e.g., Loeber & Ahonen, 2012; Loeber & Farrington, 2012; Woolard, Odgers, Lanza-Kaduce, & Daglis, 2005).

Multiple meta-analyses have identified interventions that can be effective with serious, violent offenders (e.g., Lipsey, 2009) and successfully implemented (e.g., Greenwood & Welsh, 2012). Henggeler and Schoenwald (2012) described evidence-based juvenile justice interventions and the types of policies that support those programs, with commentary from several policy stakeholders on the associated challenges and successes of those efforts (e.g., Harvell, 2012; Panzarella, 2012). Baglivio et al. (2014) demonstrated that a combination of risk and protective factors can be used to identify offenders and tailor intervention responses using a risk–need–responsivity framework (see Chapter 10, this handbook).

Translating these research findings on offending patterns into policy changes is a daunting but not insurmountable task for researchers and policymakers. The harsh wave of juvenile justice reform in the 1990s that emphasized determinate sentences and increased use of criminal court processing has begun to give way to a more nuanced approach to recidivism reduction that, when combined with cost-effectiveness arguments, may create the political will and space to modify approaches to protect public safety and reduce recidivism by increasing the likelihood of healthy development, even among serious, violent, and chronic offenders.

References

Baglivio, M. T., Jackowski, K., Greenwald, M. A., & Howell, J. C. (2014). Serious, violent, and chronic juvenile offenders: A statewide analysis of prevalence and prediction of subsequent recidivism using risk and protective factors. *Criminology and Public Policy, 13*, 83–116. http://dx.doi.org/10.1111/1745-9133.12064

Bliesener, T., Beelman, A., & Stemmler, M. (Eds.). (2011). *Antisocial behavior and crime: Contributions of developmental and evaluation research to prevention and intervention*. Cambridge, MA: Hogrefe.

Brame, R., Fagan, J., Piquero, A. R., Schubert, C. A., & Steinberg, L. (2004). Criminal careers of serious delinquents in two cities. *Youth Violence and Juvenile Justice, 2*, 256–272. http://dx.doi.org/10.1177/1541204004265877

Brame, R., Paternoster, R., & Bushway, S. D. (2004). Criminal offending frequency and offense switching. *Journal of Contemporary Criminal Justice, 20*, 201–214. http://dx.doi.org/10.1177/1043986204263779

Bronfenbrenner, U. (1979). *The ecology of human development*. Cambridge, MA: Harvard University Press.

Bronfenbrenner, U., & Ceci, S. J. (1994). Nature–nurture reconceptualized in developmental perspective: A bioecological model. *Psychological Review, 101*, 568–586. http://dx.doi.org/10.1037/0033-295X.101.4.568

Capaldi, D. M., & Wiesner, M. (2009). A dynamic developmental systems approach to understanding offending in early adulthood. In J. Savage (Ed.), *The development of persistent criminality* (pp. 374–388). http://dx.doi.org/10.1093/acprof:oso/9780195310313.003.0018

Chan, H. C., Heide, K. M., & Myers, W. C. (2013). Juvenile and adult offenders arrested for sexual homicide: An analysis of victim-offender relationship and weapon used by race. *Journal of Forensic Sciences, 58*, 85–89. http://dx.doi.org/10.1111/j.1556-4029.2012.02188.x

Conduct Problems Prevention Research Group. (2002). The implementation of the Fast Track program: An example of a large-scale prevention science efficacy trial. *Journal of Abnormal Child Psychology, 30*, 1–17. http://dx.doi.org/10.1023/A:1014292830216

Davis, J., & Sorenson, J. R. (2013). Disproportionate minority confinement of juveniles: A national examination of Black-White disparity in placements, 1997–2006. *Crime and Delinquency, 59*, 115–139. http://dx.doi.org/10.1177/0011128709359653

DeLisi, M., & Piquero, A. R. (2011). New frontiers in criminal careers research, 2000–2011: A state-of-the-art review. *Journal of Criminal Justice, 39*, 289–301. http://dx.doi.org/10.1016/j.jcrimjus.2011.05.001

Dunford, F. W., & Elliott, D. S. (1984). Identifying career offenders using self-reported data. *Journal of Research in Crime and Delinquency, 21*, 57–86. http://dx.doi.org/10.1177/0022427884021001004

Elliott, D. S. (1994). Serious violent offenders: Onset, developmental course, and termination. *Criminology, 32*, 1–21. http://dx.doi.org/10.1111/j.1745-9125.1994.tb01144.x

Farrington, D. P. (2005). Introduction to integrated developmental and life-course theories of offending. In D. P. Farrington (Ed.), *Advances in criminological theory: Vol. 14. Integrated developmental and life course theories of offending* (pp. 1–14). Brunswick, NJ: Transaction.

Farrington, D. P., Loeber, R., & Jolliffe, D. (2008). Comparing arrests and convictions with reported offending. In R. Loeber, D. P. Farrington, M. Stouthamer-Loeber, & H. R. White (Eds.), *Violence and serious theft: Development and prediction from childhood to adulthood* (pp. 105–136). New York, NY: Routledge.

Farrington, D. P., & Ttofi, M. M. (2011). Protective and promotive factors in the development of offending. In T. Bliesener, A. Beelman, & M. Stemmler (Eds.), *Antisocial behavior and crime: Contributions of developmental and evaluation research to prevention and intervention* (pp. 71–88). Cambridge, MA: Hogrefe.

Federal Bureau of Investigation. (2013). *Crime in the United States, 2012*. Retrieved from http://www.fbi.gov/about-us/cjis/ucr/crime-in-the-u.s/2012/crime-in-the-u.s.-2012

Flexon, J. L., Stolzenberg, L., & D'Alessio, S. J. (2011). Cheating the hangman: The effect of the *Roper v. Simmons* decision on homicides committed by juveniles. *Crime and Delinquency, 57*, 928–949. http://dx.doi.org/10.1177/0011128709333726

Fontaine, N., Carbonneau, R., Vitaro, F., Barker, E. D., & Tremblay, R. E. (2009). Research review: A critical review of studies on the developmental trajectories of antisocial behavior in females. *Journal of Child Psychology and Psychiatry, 50*, 363–385. http://dx.doi.org/10.1111/j.1469-7610.2008.01949.x

Goldweber, A., Dmitrieva, J., Cauffman, E., Piquero, A. R., & Steinberg, L. (2011). The development of criminal style in adolescence and young adulthood: Separating the lemmings from the loners. *Journal of Youth and Adolescence, 40*, 332–346. http://dx.doi.org/10.1007/s10964-010-9534-5

Greenberg, D. F. (2010). Longitudinal criminology. *Journal of Quantitative Criminology, 26*, 437–443. http://dx.doi.org/10.1007/s10940-010-9111-9

Greenwood, P. W. (2006). *Changing lives: Delinquency prevention as crime control policy*. Chicago, IL: University of Chicago Press.

Greenwood, P. W., & Welsh, B. C. (2012). Promoting evidence-based practice in delinquency prevention at the state level: Principles, progress, and policy directions. *Criminology and Public Policy, 11*, 493–513. http://dx.doi.org/10.1111/j.1745-9133.2012.00826.x

Grigorenko, E. L. (Ed.). (2012). *Handbook of juvenile forensic psychology and psychiatry*. New York, NY: Springer.

Harvell, S. (2012). Commentary: Supporting evidence-based juvenile justice practice from the top: Progress and possibilities at the federal level. *Social Policy Report, 25*, 21–22.

Heide, K. M. (1993a). Parents who get killed and the children who kill them. *Journal of Interpersonal Violence, 8*, 531–544. http://dx.doi.org/10.1177/088626093008004008

Heide, K. M. (1993b). Weapons used by juveniles and adults to kill parents. *Behavioral Sciences and the Law, 11*, 397–405. http://dx.doi.org/10.1002/bsl.2370110407

Heide, K. M., & Petee, T. A. (2007a). Parricide: An empirical analysis of 24 years of U.S. data. *Journal of Interpersonal Violence, 22*, 1382–1399. http://dx.doi.org/10.1177/0886260507305526

Heide, K. M., & Petee, T. A. (2007b). Weapons used by juveniles and adult offenders in U.S. parricide cases. *Journal of Interpersonal Violence, 22*, 1400–1414. http://dx.doi.org/10.1177/0886260507305528

Heide, K. M., & Sellers, B. G. (2014). Girls arrested for murder: An empirical analysis of 32 years of U.S. data by offender age groups. *Behavioral Sciences and the Law, 32*, 467–482. http://dx.doi.org/10.1002/bsl.2130

Henggeler, S. W., & Schoenwald, S. K. (2012). Evidence based interventions for juvenile offenders and the juvenile justice policies that support them. *Social Policy Report, 25*, 1–20.

Howell, J. C. (2009). *Preventing and reducing juvenile delinquency: A comprehensive framework*. Thousand Oaks, CA: Sage.

Humphreys, K., & Rappaport, J. (1993). From the community mental health movement to the war on drugs: A study in the definition of social problems. *American Psychologist, 48*, 892–901. http://dx.doi.org/10.1037/0003-066X.48.8.892

Jennings, W. G., & Reingle, J. M. (2012). On the number and shape of developmental/life-course violence, aggression, and delinquency trajectories: A state-of-the-art review. *Journal of Criminal Justice, 40*, 472–489. http://dx.doi.org/10.1016/j.jcrimjus.2012.07.001

Johansson, P., & Kempf-Leonard, K. (2009). A gender-specific pathway to serious, violent, and chronic offending? Exploring Howell's risk factors for serious delinquency. *Crime and Delinquency, 55*, 216–240. http://dx.doi.org/10.1177/0011128708330652

Jones, N. J., Brown, S. L., Wanamaker, K. A., & Greiner, L. E. (2014). A quantitative exploration of gendered pathways to crime in a sample of male and female juvenile offenders. *Feminist Criminology, 9*, 113–136. http://dx.doi.org/10.1177/1557085113501850

Keelan, C. M., & Fremouw, W. J. (2013). Child versus peer/adult offenders: A critical review of the juvenile sex offender literature. *Aggression and Violent Behavior, 18*, 732–744. http://dx.doi.org/10.1016/j.avb.2013.07.026

Kempf-Leonard, K. (2007). Minority youths and juvenile justice: Disproportionate minority contact after nearly 20 years of reform efforts. *Youth Violence and Juvenile Justice, 5*, 71–87. http://dx.doi.org/10.1177/1541204006295159

Kempf-Leonard, K. (2012). Race and sex disparity in juvenile justice processing. In E. L. Grigorenko (Ed.), *Handbook of juvenile forensic psychology and psychiatry* (pp. 53–67). http://dx.doi.org/10.1007/978-1-4614-0905-2_4

Krohn, M. D., Thornberry, T. P., Gibson, C. L., & Baldwin, J. M. (2010). The development and impact of self-report measures of crime and delinquency. *Journal of Quantitative Criminology, 26*, 509–525. http://dx.doi.org/10.1007/s10940-010-9119-1

Lacourse, E., Dupere, V., & Loeber, R. (2008). Developmental trajectories of violence and theft. In R. Loeber, D. P. Farrington, Stouthamer-Loeber, & H. R. White (Eds.), *Violence and serious theft: Development and prediction from childhood to adulthood* (pp. 231–268). New York, NY: Routledge.

Levine, M., & Levine, A. (1992). *Helping children: A social history*. New York, NY: Oxford University Press.

Lipsey, M. W. (2008). *The Arizona standardized program evaluation protocol (SPEP) for assessing the effectiveness of programs for juvenile probationers: SPEP ratings and relative recidivism reduction for the initial SPEP sample*. Nashville, TN: Vanderbilt University, Center for Evaluation Research and Methodology.

Lipsey, M. W. (2009). The primary factors that characterize effective interventions with juvenile offenders: A meta-analytic overview. *Victims and Offenders, 4*, 124–147. http://dx.doi.org/10.1080/15564880802612573

Lipsey, M. W., & Howell, J. C. (2012). A broader view of evidence-based programs reveals more options for state juvenile justice systems. *Criminology and Public Policy, 11*, 515–523. http://dx.doi.org/10.1111/j.1745-9133.2012.00827.x

Loeber, R., & Ahonen, L. (2012). What are the policy implications of our knowledge on serious, violent, and chronic offenders? *Criminology and Public Policy, 11*, 117–125.

Loeber, R., & Farrington, D. P. (1999). Major aims of this book. In R. Loeber & D. P. Farrington (Eds.), *Serious and violent juvenile offenders: Risk factors and successful interventions* (pp. 1–12). http://dx.doi.org/10.4135/9781452243740.n1

Loeber, R., & Farrington, D. (Eds.). (2012). *From juvenile delinquency to adult crime: Criminal careers, justice policy, and prevention*. http://dx.doi.org/10.1093/acprof:oso/9780199828166.001.0001

Loeber, R., Farrington, D. P., & Jolliffe, D. (2008). Comparing arrests and convictions with reported offending. In R. Loeber, D. P. Farrington, Stouthamer-Loeber, & H. R. White (Eds.), *Violence and serious theft: Development and prediction from childhood to adulthood* (pp. 105–136). New York, NY: Routledge.

Loeber, R., Farrington, D. P., Stouthamer-Loeber, M., & White, H. R. (Eds.). (2008). *Violence and serious theft: Development and prediction from childhood to adulthood*. New York, NY: Routledge.

Loeber, R., Pardini, D., Homish, D. L., Wei, E. H., Crawford, A. M., Farrington, D. P., . . . Rosenfeld, R. (2005). The prediction of violence and homicide in young men. *Journal of Consulting and Clinical Psychology, 73*, 1074–1088. http://dx.doi.org/10.1037/0022-006X.73.6.1074

Loeber, R., White, H. R., & Burke, J. D. (2011). Developmental sequences and pathways toward serious delinquency and substance use. In T. Bliesener, A. Beelman, M. Stemmler, & M. (Eds.). *Antisocial behavior and crime: Contributions of developmental and evaluation research to prevention and intervention* (pp. 39–52). Cambridge, MA: Hogrefe.

Loftin, C., & McDowall, D. (2010). The use of official records to measure crime and delinquency. *Journal of Quantitative Criminology, 26*, 527–532. http://dx.doi.org/10.1007/s10940-010-9120-8

Lussier, P., & Blokland, A. (2014). The adolescence-adulthood transition and Robin's continuity paradox:

Criminal career patterns of juvenile and adult sex offenders in a prospective longitudinal birth cohort study. *Journal of Criminal Justice, 42*, 153–163. http://dx.doi.org/10.1016/j.jcrimjus.2013.07.004

Lussier, P., Van Den Berg, C., Bijleveld, C., & Hendriks, J. (2012). A developmental taxonomy of juvenile sex offenders for theory, research, and prevention: The adolescent-limited and the high-rate slow desister. *Criminal Justice and Behavior, 39*, 1559–1581. http://dx.doi.org/10.1177/0093854812455739

Maldonado-Molina, M. M., Piquero, A. R., Jennings, W. G., Bird, H., & Canino, G. (2009). Trajectories of delinquency among Puerto Rican children and adolescents at two sites. *Journal of Research in Crime and Delinquency, 46*, 144–181. http://dx.doi.org/10.1177/0022427808330866

McGloin, J. M., & Piquero, A. R. (2010). On the relationship between co-offending network redundancy and offending versatility. *Journal of Research in Crime and Delinquency, 47*, 63–90. http://dx.doi.org/10.1177/0022427809348905

Mears, D. P., & Cochran, J. C. (2013). What is the effect of IQ on offending? *Criminal Justice and Behavior, 40*, 1280–1300. http://dx.doi.org/10.1177/0093854813485736

Mendel, R. A. (2009). *Two decades of JDAI: From demonstration project to national standard.* Retrieved from http://www.aecf.org/resources/two-decades-of-jdai

Miller, S., Malone, P. S., & Dodge, K. A.; Conduct Problems Prevention Research Group. (2010). Developmental trajectories of boys' and girls' delinquency: Sex differences and links to later adolescent outcomes. *Journal of Abnormal Child Psychology, 38*, 1021–1032. http://dx.doi.org/10.1007/s10802-010-9430-1

Moffitt, T. E. (1993). Adolescence-limited and life-course-persistent antisocial behavior: A developmental taxonomy. *Psychological Review, 100*, 674–701. http://dx.doi.org/10.1037/0033-295X.100.4.674

Monahan, K. C., & Piquero, A. R. (2009). Investigating the longitudinal relation between offending frequency and offending variety. *Criminal Justice and Behavior, 36*, 653–673. http://dx.doi.org/10.1177/0093854809335527

Mulvey, E. P. (2014). Using developmental science to reorient our thinking about criminal offending in adolescence. *Journal of Research in Crime and Delinquency, 51*, 467–479.

Mulvey, E. P., Steinberg, L., Piquero, A. R., Besana, M., Fagan, J., Schubert, C., & Cauffman, E. (2010). Trajectories of desistance and continuity in antisocial behavior following court adjudication among serious adolescent offenders. *Development and Psychopathology, 22*, 453–475. http://dx.doi.org/10.1017/S0954579410000179

Myers, W. C., & Chan, H. C. (2012). Juvenile homosexual homicide. *Behavioral Sciences and the Law, 30*, 90–102. http://dx.doi.org/10.1002/bsl.2000

National Campaign to Reform State Juvenile Justice Systems. (2013). *Report on 2013 activities.* Retrieved from http://www.publicinterestprojects.org/wp-content/uploads/2013/09/Report-on-2013-Activities-130912-v2.pdf

Nieuwbeerta, P., Blokland, A., Piquero, A. R., & Sweeten, G. (2011). A life-course analysis of offense specialization across age: Introducing a new method for studying individual specialization over the life course. *Crime and Delinquency, 57*, 3–28. http://dx.doi.org/10.1177/0011128710376336

Odgers, C. L., Moffitt, T. E., Broadbent, J. M., Dickson, N., Hancox, R. J., Harrington, H., . . . Caspi, A. (2008). Female and male antisocial trajectories: From childhood origins to adult outcomes. *Development and Psychopathology, 20*, 673–716. http://dx.doi.org/10.1017/S0954579408000333

Oudekerk, B. A., Erbacher, M. K., & Reppucci, N. D. (2012). A comparison of diversity, frequency, and severity self-reported offending scores among female offending youth. *Psychological Assessment, 24*, 738–750. http://dx.doi.org/10.1037/a0026791

Pagani, L. S. (2009). The influence of family context on the development and persistence of antisocial behavior. In J. Savage (Ed.), *The development of persistent criminality* (pp. 37–53). http://dx.doi.org/10.1093/acprof:oso/9780195310313.003.0002

Panzarella, P. (2012). One state's experience: The perspective of a Connecticut administrator. *Social Policy Report, 25*, 24–25.

Pathways to Desistance. (n.d.). *Pathways codebook.* Retrieved from http://www.pathwaysstudy.pitt.edu/codebook/sro-sb.html

Peck, J. H., & Heide, K. M. (2012). Juvenile involvement in fratricide and sororicide: An empirical analysis of 32 years of U.S. arrest data. *Journal of Family Violence, 27*, 749–760. http://dx.doi.org/10.1007/s10896-012-9456-y

Pepler, D. J., Jiang, D., Craig, W. M., & Connolly, J. (2010). Developmental trajectories of girls' and boys' delinquency and associated problems. *Journal of Abnormal Child Psychology, 38*, 1033–1044. http://dx.doi.org/10.1007/s10802-010-9389-y

Piquero, A. R. (2007). Taking stock of developmental trajectories of criminal activity over the life course. In A. M. Lieberman (Ed.), *The long view of crime: A synthesis of longitudinal research* (pp. 19–75). New York, NY: Springer.

Piquero, A. R. (2014). Moving from description to implementation of evidence-based research findings.

Criminology and Public Policy, 13, 127–134. http://dx.doi.org/10.1111/1745-9133.12065

Piquero, A. R., Farrington, D. P., Jennings, W. G., Diamond, B., & Craig, J. (2012). Sex offenders and sex offending in the Cambridge study in delinquent development: Prevalence, frequency, specialization, recidivism, and (dis)continuity over the life-course. *Journal of Criminal Justice, 35*, 412–426.

Piquero, A. R., Hawkins, J. D., & Kazemian, L. (2012). Criminal career patterns. In R. Loeber & D. P. Farrington (Eds.), *From juvenile delinquency to adult crime* (pp. 14–46). http://dx.doi.org/10.1093/acprof:oso/9780199828166.003.0002

Roper v. Simmons, 543 U.S. 541 (2005).

Rosenfeld, R., White, H. R., & Esbensen, F. A. (2012). Special categories of serious and violent offenders: Drug dealers, gang members, homicide offenders, and sex offenders. In R. Loeber & D. P. Farrington (Eds.), *From juvenile delinquency to adult crime* (pp. 118–149). http://dx.doi.org/10.1093/acprof:oso/9780199828166.003.0005

Savage, J. (2009). Understanding persistent offending: Linking developmental psychology with research on the criminal career. In J. Savage (Ed.), *The development of persistent criminality* (pp. 3–33). http://dx.doi.org/10.1093/acprof:oso/9780195310313.003.0001

Seto, M. C., & Lalumière, M. L. (2010). What is so special about male adolescent sexual offending? A review and test of explanations through meta-analysis. *Psychological Bulletin, 136*, 526–575. http://dx.doi.org/10.1037/a0019700

Sullivan, C. J., McGloin, J. M., Ray, J. V., & Caudy, M. S. (2009). Detecting specialization in offending: Comparing analytic approaches. *Journal of Quantitative Criminology, 25*, 419–441. http://dx.doi.org/10.1007/s10940-009-9074-x

Sweeten, G., Piquero, A. R., & Steinberg, L. (2013). Age and the explanation of crime, revisited. *Journal of Youth and Adolescence, 42*, 921–938. http://dx.doi.org/10.1007/s10964-013-9926-4

Tolan, P. (2007). Understanding violence. In D. J. Flannery, A. T. Vazsonyi, & I. D. Waldman (Eds.), *The Cambridge handbook of violent behavior and aggression* (pp. 5–18). http://dx.doi.org/10.1017/CBO9780511816840.002

Vries, A. M., & Liem, M. (2011). Recidivism of juvenile homicide offenders. *Behavioral Sciences and the Law, 29*, 483–498. http://dx.doi.org/10.1002/bsl.984

Wilson, J. J., & Howell, J. C. (1993). *Comprehensive strategy for serious, violent, and chronic juvenile offenders.* Washington, DC: U.S. Department of Justice, Office of Juvenile Justice and Delinquency Prevention.

Woolard, J. L. (2012). Crossing over: Girls at the intersection of juvenile justice, criminal justice, and child welfare. In S. Miller, L. D. Leve, & P. K. Kerig (Eds.), *Delinquent girls: Contexts, relationships, and adaptations* (pp. 25–39). http://dx.doi.org/10.1007/978-1-4614-0415-6_2

Woolard, J. L., Odgers, C., Lanza-Kaduce, L., & Daglis, H. (2005). Juveniles within adult correctional settings: Legal pathways and developmental considerations. *International Journal of Forensic Mental Health, 4*, 1–18. http://dx.doi.org/10.1080/14999013.2005.10471209

Woolard, J. L., Vidal, S., & Fountain, E. (2015). Juvenile offenders. In B. L. Cutler & P. A. Zapf (Eds.), *APA handbook of forensic psychology: Vol. 2. Criminal investigation, adjudication, and sentencing outcomes* (pp. 33–58). http://dx.doi.org/10.1037/14462-003

Zimring, F. E. (1998). *American youth violence.* New York, NY: Oxford University Press.

Zimring, F. E. (2004). *An American travesty: Legal responses to adolescent sexual offending.* http://dx.doi.org/10.7208/chicago/9780226983592.001.0001

CHAPTER 8

DESISTANCE AND LIFE-COURSE PERSISTENCE: FINDINGS FROM LONGITUDINAL STUDIES USING GROUP-BASED TRAJECTORY MODELING OF ANTISOCIAL BEHAVIOR

Michael A. Russell and Candice L. Odgers

Most children and adolescents engage in some form of antisocial behavior—such as fighting, stealing, vandalism, or delinquency—at some point in their development, but many only do so for a limited period of time. For this majority of youths, involvement in antisocial behavior is typically characterized as transient, infrequent, and of limited severity. A small number of youths remain engaged in antisocial activity across multiple phases of their lives. For these few, antisocial behavior tends to be developmentally persistent, frequent, and of high severity (see Moffitt, 2006, for review). The purpose of this chapter is to review theory and research aimed at understanding these two types of individuals: those who desist and those who persist, respectively, in their antisocial behavior. To this end, we review findings across longitudinal and cohort-sequential studies that used group-based trajectory models to identify heterogeneity in developmental pathways of antisocial behavior, as these methods represent the state of the art in identifying divergent pathways of behavior. We highlight factors commonly associated with persistence and desistance in antisocial behavior as a means of informing theory and future research.

DEFINING DESISTANCE AND PERSISTENCE

The concepts of persistence and desistance are central to the developmental study of antisocial behavior and crime, as is the idea that not all people follow the same antisocial pathway across development. The Robins paradox (Robins, 1978) blends the ideas of persistence and desistance in two simple statements about the development of antisocial behavior: "(1) Adult antisocial behaviour virtually *requires* childhood antisocial behaviour; [and] (2) most antisocial children do *not* become antisocial adults" (p. 611). The first statement reflects the findings that a small group of individuals follows an antisocial trajectory of persistence, showing consistent involvement in antisocial behavior across developmental periods (i.e., from childhood to adulthood), and that most individuals who engage in antisocial behavior as adults began doing so in childhood. The second statement illustrates the point that a larger subgroup of individuals shows a trajectory of desistance—exhibiting antisocial behavior problems at some point but ceasing to show these problems by adulthood. Since Robins' initial writing on this topic, a number of group-based theories of antisocial development have hypothesized the existence of distinct developmental types or pathways that distinguish between those who persist in antisocial behavior across time versus those who exhibit antisocial behavior for a limited time and are expected to desist (see, e.g., Moffitt, 1993; Patterson, DeBaryshe, & Ramsey, 1989; Patterson, Forgatch, Yoerger, & Stoolmiller, 1998; Sampson & Laub, 2005; Tremblay, 2010).

Rather than being static qualities displayed by individuals, persistence and desistance are best

Preparation of this chapter was supported by National Institute on Drug Abuse Awards T32 DA017629 and P50 DA010075. Candice L. Odgers is a William T. Grant Scholar. The content is solely the responsibility of the authors and does not necessarily represent the official views of the National Institute on Drug Abuse or the National Institutes of Health.

http://dx.doi.org/10.1037/14643-008
APA Handbook of Psychology and Juvenile Justice, K. Heilbrun (Editor-in-Chief)

characterized as developmental processes that unfold over time. Desistance and persistence processes for antisocial behavior are hypothesized to operate across the life course, including the emergence and desistance of early- to middle-childhood physical aggression (Tremblay, 2010), childhood- versus adolescent-onset antisocial behavior (Moffitt, 1993; Patterson et al., 1989), and adult crime (Sampson & Laub, 2005). Prospective longitudinal or cohort-sequential studies, which chart the development of individuals' antisocial behaviors across developmental periods, have been essential in characterizing individual trajectories as showing evidence of persistence, desistance, or both. Numerous longitudinal and cohort-sequential studies of antisocial behavior and crime have now been conducted, with many of these following cohorts of individuals into their 20s, 30s, and 40s (e.g., Andersson, Levander, Svensson, & Levander, 2012; Farrington, 2003; Fergusson & Horwood, 2002; Odgers et al., 2008) and, a select few, into their 50s, 60s, and 70s (e.g., Bersani, Nieuwbeerta, & Laub, 2009; Laub & Sampson, 2003). Many of these studies have applied group-based trajectory models (GBTMs) as a means of identifying latent groups of individuals who follow persistent versus desisting trajectories of antisocial behavior (for reviews of these studies, see Jennings & Reingle, 2012; Piquero, 2008; Russell, Robins, & Odgers, 2014). GBTMs are well suited to the study of desistance versus life-course persistence because (a) they provide an empirical means of testing theories about antisocial development; (b) they allow researchers to observe a wide range of changes in antisocial behavior over time, as well as the timing, magnitude, and duration of such changes (Piquero, 2008); and (c) they permit the estimation of groups of individuals who follow divergent pathways of antisocial behavior, which can then be characterized by preexisting, co-occurring, and temporally distal individual, familial, and sociocontextual factors (see Nagin, 1999; Nagin & Odgers, 2010, for reviews and illustrations of GBTMs). For the purposes of this chapter, the desistance descriptor we use includes a wide range of trajectories showing engagement in antisocial behavior for a limited period, followed by eventual desistance. These trajectory groups have been termed *desister–desisting, decreaser–decreasing, childhood limited,* or *adolescence limited* in the original studies cited in this review (see, e.g., Bongers, Koot, Van Der Ende, & Verhulst, 2004; Côté, Vaillancourt, LeBlanc, Nagin, & Tremblay, 2006; Fergusson, Horwood, & Nagin, 2000; Odgers et al., 2008).

This chapter is divided into three sections. In the first section, we review three key theoretical perspectives on antisocial behavior pathways across the life course, beginning with early childhood aggression, transitioning into persistent versus adolescence-limited antisocial behavior, and ending with adult criminality. In the second section, we review empirical studies that used GBTMs to map trajectories of antisocial behavior, illustrating patterns of behavior over time and identifying factors that predict persistence versus desistance in antisocial behavior trajectories. In the third section, we summarize findings from across GBTM applications and discuss avenues for future research.

THEORETICAL PERSPECTIVES ON ANTISOCIAL DEVELOPMENT

Antisocial development is believed to vary markedly across individuals. Theories suggest that antisocial development is composed of a mixture of trajectory groups within the population, some of which show limited involvement and eventual desistance in antisocial behavior and others of which show stability, persistence, and sometimes escalation in antisocial behavior across developmental periods (Loeber & Hay, 1997; Moffitt, 1993; Patterson et al., 1989; Tremblay, 2010). These theories generally agree on two points: (a) that trajectories of persistence and desistance are sustained by the continuous coaction of biological, psychological, and social factors (see, e.g., Bushway, Piquero, Broidy, Cauffman, & Mazerolle, 2001) and (b) that the majority of individuals who show involvement in antisocial behavior will eventually desist (some researchers have suggested that all will desist; see Sampson & Laub, 2005). Here, we review three theoretical perspectives on persistence and desistance in antisocial behavior, each corresponding to a different point in the life course. We do not intend this review of theoretical perspectives to be exhaustive. Rather, we aim to provide three prominent examples of theoretical perspectives offering hypotheses about the prevalence of divergent trajectories of antisocial behavior, as well as the causal mechanisms that support these trajectories across key points in the life course (childhood, adolescence, and adulthood).

Tremblay and Colleagues: The Developmental Origins of Aggression

> Physical aggression is not a behavior children learn, like reading or writing, nor an illness children "catch," like poliomyelitis or smallpox. It is rather a behavior like crying, eating, sleeping, grasping, throwing, and running, which young humans exhibit when the physiological structure is in place, but then learn to control with experience. The learning-to-control process implies regulating one's needs to accommodate those of others, and this process can be labelled "socialization." (Tremblay & Nagin, 2005, p. 95)

Tremblay and Nagin's (2005) statement articulates the following about the origins and expected trajectory of physical aggression, the developmentally earliest form of antisocial behavior. First, at least some aggression is normative, and its onset occurs early in life. Evidence has shown that the majority of children initiate physical aggression between ages 12 and 17 months, with 80% of children engaging in this behavior by 17 months (Tremblay et al., 1999). Second, as children age, they tend to reduce their use of physical aggression. The use of aggression has been shown to peak around ages 2 and 3 as children learn to verbalize and satisfy their needs through more prosocial channels (National Institute of Child Health and Human Development Early Child Care Research Network, 2004; Tremblay, 2002), and the majority of children follow trajectories marked by desistance in aggression as they approach preadolescence (Côté et al., 2006). These findings have led to the assertion that children generally do not learn to use aggression; instead, they learn not to use aggression through a process of socialization from parents, peers, and other adults such as teachers (Tremblay & Nagin, 2005).

In reviews of this literature, Tremblay (1999, 2002, 2010) suggested that *chronic physical aggression,* the term often used to describe the persistent trajectory of aggression, is the result of a socialization failure. That is, the chronically aggressive child, unlike the majority of his or her peers, does not learn the skills necessary to control aggressive urges and resolve social disputes in a nonaggressive manner by the time he or she reaches middle childhood. The proposed causal factors leading to this socialization failure are many but have been generally clustered into three domains (Tremblay, 2002, 2010): (a) individual characteristics (e.g., sex, hyperactivity, cognitive difficulties, oppositionality), (b) physical environmental characteristics (e.g., lead exposure), and (c) social environmental characteristics (e.g., young motherhood, low household income, exposure to school and neighborhood violence). Chronic physical aggression is thought to result from the interaction between individual vulnerabilities and risky physical and social environments. These factors—through biological, psychological, and social mechanisms—increase the risk that the child will not learn to regulate aggressive urges and will instead continue to use aggression well past when his or her peers have learned to control it. The continued and persistent use of aggression by these children fosters a risky lifestyle throughout development and increases their risk of poor outcomes such as school failure, mental and physical health problems, violence, unemployment, and self-harm later in life (Tremblay, 2002).

Moffitt's Dual Taxonomy: Adolescence-Limited Versus Life-Course-Persistent Antisocial Behavior

Moffitt (1993) proposed a dual taxonomy to account for differential patterns in antisocial behavior observed in longitudinal studies covering the period of middle childhood to adulthood. Her dual taxonomy was proposed to account for "[two] incongruous facts about antisocial behavior: (a) it shows impressive continuity with age, but (b) its prevalence changes dramatically over time, increasing almost [ten]fold during adolescence" (p. 674). To account for these seemingly incompatible facts, Moffitt proposed that the aggregate age–crime curve, which suggests that antisocial behavior reaches a peak in adolescence and declines thereafter (see the original age–crime curve by Quetelet, 1833, as cited in Tremblay, 2000), was undergirded by two very different groups of individuals. The first group followed a life-course-persistent (LCP) trajectory, characterized by persistent engagement in antisocial behavior of one form or another all along the life course. The second group followed an adolescence-limited (AL) trajectory, characterized by antisocial behavior that is primarily restricted to the adolescent years.

Apart from showing very different developmental trajectories of antisocial behavior, individuals following each of these pathways were hypothesized to come from very different backgrounds. Children following the LCP pathway were hypothesized to display a confluence of individual vulnerability (e.g., hyperactivity, difficult temperament, low intelligence) and familial–environmental risk (e.g., harsh parental discipline, parental criminality, low socioeconomic status [SES]). This confluence of child vulnerability and contextual risk manifests as a cycle of strained parent–child interactions that serve to generate antisocial behavior in childhood and maintain it during adolescence. The early and persistent expression of antisocial behavior in these individuals is also believed to erode socialization opportunities that typically teach children to use prosocial means of relating to others and solving disputes. As such, individuals following the LCP trajectory tend not to learn the socialization lessons that typically lead to desistance and instead maintain their use of antisocial behavior, in one form or another, through the adolescent years and even into midlife. Moffitt (1993) did not suggest that individuals following the LCP trajectory would necessarily continue their involvement in serious antisocial or criminal behavior in midlife. Rather, she suggested that individuals on the LCP trajectory would continue to engage in diverse forms of antisocial behavior that may or may not come to the attention of police, such as aggression and hostility with coworkers and family members, recklessness, minor or petty theft, and harsh discipline of children. In addition, individuals on the LCP pathway are expected to show mental and physical health problems as well as involvement in social services systems in adulthood (as illustrated by Moffitt, Caspi, Harrington, & Milne, 2002; Odgers et al., 2008).

In contrast, children who follow the AL trajectory were hypothesized to show a more typical pattern of antisocial development: low levels of antisocial behavior in childhood, a large increase during the adolescent years, and a decline during the transition to adulthood (Moffitt, 1993). Moffitt (1993) hypothesized that, compared with children on the LCP trajectory, those on the AL trajectory would come from more normative backgrounds and would therefore not be characterized by significant vulnerability or familial–environmental risk. AL antisocial behavior was driven, Moffitt argued, by the maturity gap that naturally occurs during adolescence, because individuals are biologically adults during this time but do not have the societal rights and privileges awarded to adults. Thus, AL individuals were hypothesized to mimic the behavior of those on the LCP trajectory as a means of asserting their autonomy during the "roleless" years of adolescence. Desistance was hypothesized to occur for these individuals during the transition to adulthood, as they naturally attained the rights and privileges awarded to adults and assumed traditional responsibilities associated with career and family.

Life-Course Desisters? Sampson and Laub's Illustrations of Persistence and Turning Points in Adulthood

Whereas the theories discussed above focus on antisocial behavior and aggression in the normative range, Sampson and Laub's work has drawn from high-risk samples of primarily male delinquents to better understand desistance from involvement in official crime and offending. Sampson and Laub (1993, 2003) contended that desistance is a process observed across all antisocial trajectory pathways, even for individuals on the most persistent pathways. They advanced a theory of social control to explain persistence and desistance in antisocial behavior, emphasizing the role of informal social controls as regulatory agents serving to orient the individual toward societal values and away from criminality (Sampson & Laub, 2005). More important, these informal social controls are age graded, in that they manifest themselves differently across developmental periods. For example, in childhood, informal social controls might include parenting styles and emotional attachment to parents; in adolescence, attachment to school and positive peer groups; in adulthood, marriage, military service, or employment (Sampson & Laub, 2005).

Within this framework, membership in any trajectory group of crime or antisocial behavior is hypothesized to be "continually socially produced over time" (Sampson & Laub, 2005, p. 42). As in other theories, the coaction of both individual agency and social institutions in maintaining persistence as well as generating desistance in antisocial behavior is emphasized. More important, Sampson and Laub suggested that (a) all individuals, even the most persistent offenders, will eventually desist from crime and (b) desistance processes are often initiated by turning points in people's lives, such as the social institutions mentioned previously (i.e., marriage, military service, employment). Key turning points are believed to set in motion a series of events and changes that eventually lead to desistance in antisocial behavior. For example, marriage has been hypothesized to lead to one or more of the following outcomes in the lives of criminal men:

> (1) a "knifing off" of the past from the present; (2) opportunities for investment in new relationships that offer social support, growth, and new social networks; (3) forms of direct and indirect supervision and monitoring of behavior; (4) structured routines that center more on family life and less on unstructured time with peers; and (5) situations that provide an opportunity for identity transformation and that allow for the emergence of a new self or script, what Hill (1971) described as the "movement from a hell-raiser to a family man." (Sampson & Laub, 2005, p. 34)

As an empirical example, Sampson, Laub, and Wimer (2006) examined this issue among the Glueck sample of 500 urban males classified as delinquent in adolescence and followed up through official records through much of their adulthood. Using propensity score and within-person longitudinal models to adjust for the effects of individual and family background factors, Sampson et al. found that being married was associated with a 35% reduction in a man's odds of crime, compared with himself when he was not married. By adjusting for premarriage confounds both explicitly (via propensity scores) and implicitly (via analysis of within-person change), they and others (Bersani, Laub, & Nieuwbeerta, 2009; Burt et al., 2010) have provided powerful illustrations of dynamic factors, or turning points, that may lead to desistance and change in the criminal behaviors of even the most serious offenders.

Summary of Theoretical Perspectives

Although they cover different developmental periods, different segments of the population, and different versions of antisocial outcomes, these theoretical perspectives collectively make the following points about antisocial development. First, as asserted by Moffitt (1993) and Tremblay and Nagin (2005), the normative pathway for children and adolescents is to show some involvement in antisocial behavior followed by eventual desistance. *Normative* in this sense implies that individuals on the desistance trajectory will be both more prevalent and from lower risk backgrounds in comparison with those on a persistently high trajectory. Second, a small percentage of individuals will follow a persistently high trajectory of antisocial behavior, and these individuals will show the greatest levels of both individual and familial–environmental risk. However, as demonstrated by the turning points illustrations, trajectories are likely malleable across the life course, even for the most serious offenders (Sampson & Laub, 2005). Third, desistance and persistence trajectories are generated by developmental processes, which involve the coaction of individual and contextual factors that together either initiate change or maintain persistence in antisocial behavior across development.

EMPIRICAL TRAJECTORY RESULTS

To date, many longitudinal studies have mapped antisocial pathways across development using group-based trajectory modeling. These studies have tested many of the ideas offered in developmental theories of antisocial behavior, such as those reviewed in the previous section. In this section, we review findings from these studies related to the prevalence, etiology, and sequelae of persistence versus desistance trajectories. We begin by reviewing key findings pertaining to individuals following a persistent trajectory, followed by a review of findings regarding those on a desisting trajectory (e.g., decreasing, childhood-limited, and AL pathways).

Persistent Antisocial Trajectories

Prevalence. Studies have identified a subgroup of children who, beginning in early childhood, show high levels of aggression throughout their childhood years (Côté et al., 2006; Côté, Vaillancourt, Barker, Nagin, & Tremblay, 2007; Tremblay et al., 2004). Rather than showing the normative trajectory marked by desistance in the use of aggression with age, these children show persistence in their aggressive behavior across early childhood (Tremblay, 2010). Beginning in early childhood (before age 4), two population-based samples provided estimates of the prevalence of chronic physical aggression. In a sample of 504 children sampled from the province of Quebec, Tremblay et al. (2004) showed that 14% of children followed a high-persistent aggression trajectory between ages 17 and 42 months. Similarly, in a cohort-sequential study of more than 10,000 Canadian youths, Côté et al. (2006) found that 17% followed a trajectory of high stable aggression between the ages of 2 and 11.

Population-based studies examining aggression trajectories beginning in middle childhood and continuing into adolescence have tended to find lower prevalence rates for chronic physical aggression than studies that have included the early childhood years (Bongers et al., 2004; Broidy et al., 2003; Joussemet et al., 2008), with some exceptions (Underwood, Beron, & Rosen, 2009; van Lier, Vitaro, Wanner, Vuijk, & Crijnen, 2005). Broidy et al. (2003) analyzed data from six longitudinal studies of aggression, four of which consisted of population-based samples that collectively spanned ages 6 to 13 across multiple countries, and found that between 7% and 11% of boys and 0% and 10% of girls follow a chronic physical aggression trajectory. Similarly, a longitudinal study of multiple birth cohorts in the Netherlands (the Zuid-Holland study) found that 8% of youths followed a persistent aggressive behavior trajectory from ages 4 to 18 (Bongers et al., 2004). Bongers et al. (2004) called this trajectory group the high decreasers because even though these youths showed evidence of persistence in their aggressive behavior, their levels of aggression tended to decrease with age.

Two population-based studies reported higher rates of persistent antisocial behavior during the childhood-to-adolescence transition. van Lier et al. (2005) found rates that were comparable to those found in studies of early childhood aggression across two population-based samples—289 children in the Netherlands (ages 6–10) and 445 children in Canada (ages 8–12). They found that 17% and 25% of boys followed persistent antisocial trajectories in the Dutch and Canadian samples, respectively, whereas very few girls in the Dutch sample followed a persistent antisocial behavior trajectory (<1%) and no girls in the Canadian sample followed this trajectory. Similarly, Underwood et al. (2009), in their sample of 255 youths from the southern United States, found that 19% followed a persistent physical aggression trajectory from ages 9 to 13.

A handful of population-based studies have examined the development of antisocial behavior across multiple developmental periods. These studies have found small percentages of individuals who engage in antisocial behavior across all assessments. For example, in a sample of 4,572 children of women in the National Longitudinal Survey of Youth, Lahey et al. (2006) found that 7% of children followed an LCP antisocial behavior trajectory from ages 4 to 17. Similarly, in the Dunedin birth cohort of more than 1,000 men and women in New Zealand, Odgers et al. (2008) found that 11% of males followed an LCP trajectory of antisocial behavior between ages 7 and 26. Among females, 8% followed an early-onset persistent trajectory of antisocial behavior between ages 7 and 15. Fergusson and Horwood (2002) found that 9% of males and 2% of females in the Christchurch Longitudinal Study followed a chronic offender pathway from ages 8 to 20.

Many studies have examined antisocial outcomes during the adolescent period only. Similar to studies spanning multiple developmental periods, these population-based adolescent-only studies have provided evidence that a group of individuals shows high and stable levels of antisocial behavior (Barker, Arseneault, Brendgen, Fontaine, & Maughan, 2008; Di Giunta et al., 2010; Jennings,

Higgins, Tewksbury, Gover, & Piquero, 2010; Martino, Ellickson, Klein, McCaffrey, & Edelen, 2008; Pepler, Jiang, Craig, & Connolly, 2008, 2010; Wiesner & Silbereisen, 2003). One study following a representative sample of German adolescents from ages 10 to 17 found that 14% followed a high-level delinquency trajectory (Wiesner & Silbereisen, 2003). Similarly, in a representative sample of Italian adolescents, Di Giunta et al. (2010) found that 16% to 18% followed a high stable aggression trajectory between ages 11 and 14, depending on whether self- or maternal report was used (16% vs. 18%, respectively). In addition, in a representative sample of more than 1,800 South Dakota youths, Martino et al. (2008) found that 17% followed a persistent high aggression trajectory from ages 13 to 18. When official reports of crime are used, the percentage of adolescents showing persistent antisocial behavior becomes much smaller, as evidenced in the Dunedin Longitudinal Study, in which Piquero, Brame, and Moffitt (2005) found that from ages 13 to 17, 1% of males and 0% of females followed a high-rate offending trajectory, as operationalized by officially reported convictions.

Evidence for high stable trajectory groups has also been found in high-risk and all-offender samples (see, e.g., Chung, Hill, Hawkins, Gilchrist, & Nagin, 2002; Connell, Klostermann, & Dishion, 2012; D'Unger, Land, McCall, & Nagin, 1998; Lynne-Landsman, Graber, Nichols, & Botvin, 2011; Marshall, 2005; Miller, Malone, & Dodge, 2010; Monahan, Steinberg, Cauffman, & Mulvey, 2009). Collectively, these studies have shown that even in high-risk samples, heterogeneity in antisocial behavior trajectories exists, and a small group of individuals following a trajectory marked by more severe and persistent antisocial behavior can be identified. For example, in a study of criminal involvement across the life course (the Glueck sample of male offenders), Sampson and Laub (2003) found that 3% of the Glueck men followed a high-rate chronic trajectory of offending. Similarly, in the Dutch Criminal Career and Life Course Study, which followed offenders from ages 12 to 72, Blokland, Nagin, and Nieuwbeerta (2005) found that 2% followed a high-rate persistent offending trajectory. Individuals on the high-rate persistent offending pathway showed the highest rate of offending across all ages and continued their criminal involvement well into their 50s.

Etiology. Recall that children following a persistent trajectory of antisocial behavior have been hypothesized to show high levels of both individual vulnerability (e.g., low verbal intelligence, hyperactivity, and neuropsychological problems) and familial–environmental risk. Research across developmental periods has generally shown this to be the case. Population-based studies including the early childhood years have shown that chronically aggressive children are often characterized by this confluence between individual vulnerability and environmental risk. Côté et al. (2006) found that youths following the high-stable aggression trajectory were more likely to be male and to come from high-risk backgrounds characterized by low income, low maternal education, and harsh parenting. Tremblay et al. (2004) also showed that children on the high-aggression trajectory were more likely to come from high-risk backgrounds, such as those characterized by low income, harsh parenting, and young mothers with a history of antisocial behavior.

Population-based studies beginning after the early childhood years have also supported hypotheses regarding the etiology of persistent antisocial behavior. Findings across these studies have suggested that youths following persistent trajectories of antisocial behavior show evidence of individual vulnerabilities such as low reading ability, low IQ, hyperactivity, oppositionality, and low compliance (Fergusson & Horwood, 2002; Lahey et al., 2006; Odgers et al., 2008), as well as contextual risks such as childhood maltreatment, poverty, parental psychopathology and criminality, family conflict, and low family social support (Fergusson & Horwood, 2002; Maughan, Pickles, Rowe, Costello, & Angold, 2000; Odgers et al., 2008; Wiesner & Windle, 2004).

Outcomes. Youths following a persistent antisocial behavior trajectory within population-based studies tend to exhibit a wide array of poor adolescent and adult outcomes. For example, in their multinational, multicohort study, Broidy et al. (2003) showed that children on a chronic aggression trajectory were significantly more likely to engage in both violent and nonviolent delinquency in adolescence, with these relationships being more consistent for boys than for girls. In their longitudinal study of Italian adolescents, Di Giunta et al. (2010) found that youths following a persistent physical aggression trajectory from ages 11 to 14 were at high risk for both covert and overt antisocial behavior at ages 18 to 19. In the Dunedin birth cohort, Odgers et al. (2008) showed that children on an early-onset persistent trajectory during childhood and adolescence were not only more likely to engage in violence and crime in adulthood (vs. children following a low antisocial trajectory), they were also at the highest risk for mental and physical health problems as well as economic hardship by age 32.

Outcomes for youths on a persistent antisocial behavior trajectory are also poor among high-risk and all-offender samples. In their longitudinal study of high-risk boys, Nagin and Tremblay (1999) showed that children following a chronic aggression trajectory from ages 6 to 15 had the highest likelihood of engaging in serious delinquency and violence at age 17. In the Raising Healthy Children project (20% low-income youths), Harachi et al. (2006) found that children following a persistent aggression trajectory showed the highest levels of substance use, violent behavior, and covert delinquency in ninth grade. In their longitudinal study of high-risk youths (50% low income), Petras et al. (2004) illustrated that boys following a persistent aggression trajectory from first to fifth grade were more likely to be diagnosed with antisocial personality disorder and more likely to have an arrest record in young adulthood than boys on the low trajectory. Schaeffer et al. (2006) extended these analyses to include the girls in the sample and found that girls on the chronic aggression trajectory had the highest rates of antisocial personality disorder and arrest for a violent offense in young adulthood, compared with both the low and the low–moderate aggression trajectory groups. Similarly, in the Fast Track study of children at risk for antisocial behavior problems, Miller et al. (2010) found that youths following a chronic aggression trajectory from ages 12 to 18 showed a higher risk of partner violence and risky sex at age 19 than those following a low aggression trajectory.

Desisting Antisocial Trajectories

Longitudinal studies applying GBTMs to examine antisocial development have identified groups of individuals who could be classified as following a desistance trajectory: showing involvement in antisocial behavior at some point in life, followed by eventual decline and, in some cases, termination of such behavior. In this section, we summarize the prevalence of desistance trajectories across this literature, followed by reviews of the associated etiological factors and outcomes.

Prevalence. In studies that include the first few years of life, the vast majority of children follow a desisting trajectory of antisocial behavior. Côté et al. (2006) found that the majority of children in their sample (52%) followed what they called a moderate desister trajectory, showing a moderate level of aggression in early childhood that subsequently and steadily declined. However, Tremblay et al. (2004) did not find evidence of a desisting aggression group from ages 17 to 42 months in their sample of 504 toddlers.

Studies following individuals from middle childhood into adolescence and beyond have sometimes identified children who follow a trajectory that can be described as childhood limited (e.g., Bongers et al., 2004; Odgers et al., 2008). Youths on a childhood-limited trajectory tend to show moderate to high levels of antisocial behavior during the childhood years, followed by a substantial decrease as they enter subsequent developmental phases, with levels sometimes declining so much that these youths eventually resemble the low antisocial group. In these studies, youths following a childhood-limited trajectory tend to be less prevalent than those following a low trajectory, but more prevalent than youths following an early-onset persistent trajectory. For example, Odgers et al. (2008) reported in their representative cohort study that 24% of boys followed a childhood-limited trajectory from ages 7 to 26, whereas 45% followed a low trajectory and 11% followed an LCP trajectory. Twenty percent of girls followed a childhood-limited trajectory from ages 7 to 15, whereas 55% and 8% followed low and early-onset persistent trajectories, respectively (Odgers et al., 2008). Similarly, Bongers et al. (2004) found that 21% followed a low decreaser trajectory (analogous to childhood limited) from ages 4 to 18, whereas 71% and 8% followed near-zero and high-decreaser trajectories (analogous to early-onset persistent), respectively.

Studies including the adolescent years have tended to find AL trajectories, a class of desistance trajectory whose existence was hypothesized by Moffitt (1993). Recall that individuals following the AL trajectory are expected to show an adolescent onset of their antisocial behavior, followed by desistance during the transition to adulthood. A number of population-based studies have found this pattern (see, e.g., Boers, Reinecke, Seddig, & Mariotti, 2010; D'Unger, Land, & McCall, 2002; Fergusson & Horwood, 2002; Jennings, Maldonado-Molina, Piquero, et al., 2010; Raskin White, Bates, & Buyske, 2001; Xie, Drabick, & Chen, 2011). The strongest examples come from representative cohort studies that have assessed the development of antisocial behavior across childhood into adulthood because these studies are positioned to test for the characteristic adolescent rise in antisocial behavior as well as the adult fall hypothesized in Moffitt's (1993) theory of AL antisocial behavior. For example, in their representative study of 896 individuals in the Christchurch Health and Development Study, Fergusson and Horwood (2002) identified three AL trajectory groups, differing in age of onset but desisting in their offending at the end of the adolescent period. Similarly, in their representative longitudinal sample of 698 males, Raskin White et al. (2001) found that 33% followed an AL trajectory of delinquency from ages 12 to 31.

Some of these studies, however, identified a trajectory that is more accurately described as an adolescent-onset trajectory (see, e.g., Odgers et al., 2008). Those who follow the adolescent-onset trajectory show the characteristic rise in antisocial behavior during mid-adolescence but do not show evidence of complete desistance during and after the transition to adulthood. Although Moffitt (1993) did not explicitly hypothesize a distinct adolescent-onset trajectory, the dual taxonomy did suggest that some individuals following the AL pathway would not desist as a result of snares encountered during their involvement in antisocial behavior (e.g., substance dependence, teenage parenthood, school dropout), which would raise their likelihood of staying involved in antisocial behavior during adulthood.

In addition, many GBTM applications are conducted on longitudinal studies that span multiple years between assessments, raising the possibility that those on the AL pathway are not detected. This may be because GBTMs themselves, without an intensive schedule of assessments, are best positioned to capture long-term and enduring patterns versus transient involvement in antisocial behavior. Therefore, it is possible that many individuals on the AL pathway are not captured by these methods.

Etiology. What characterizes individuals who follow a desisting trajectory of antisocial behavior? Identifying the characteristics of those who desist from involvement in antisocial behavior could help to identify malleable factors for intervention. A number of studies, to be cited in the sections that follow, have measured the individual characteristics and family backgrounds of children who exhibit patterns of desistance in antisocial behavior. Broadly summarized, these studies have suggested that individuals following a desisting trajectory are characterized by higher levels of risk than those who exhibit low or no antisocial behavior across development, but lower levels of risk than those following a persistently high trajectory. Because some studies did not directly contrast the individual and contextual profiles of desistance versus persistence trajectory groups using formal statistical tests, some of the contrasts we describe in this section and in the Outcomes section are based on comparison of descriptive statistics reported in the articles, without formal statistical tests to determine their significance. We describe specific contrasts as significant when statistical tests were provided.

Population-based studies have generally suggested that beginning in childhood, youths on a desistance trajectory show risk profiles that are less severe than those following a persistent trajectory (see, e.g., Côté et al., 2006; Fergusson & Horwood, 2002; Jennings, Maldonado-Molina, Piquero, et al., 2010; Maldonado-Molina, Piquero, Jennings, Bird, & Canino, 2009; Odgers et al., 2008). For example, Côté et al. (2006) reported that children on a desisting trajectory of aggression from ages 2 to 11 were less likely to come from low-income families, were more likely to have mothers who graduated high school, and were more likely to come from homes with less hostile parenting and better family functioning. In the Boricua Youth Study, a longitudinal study of children in the Bronx, New York, and San Juan, Puerto Rico, children who followed a desistance trajectory of delinquency from childhood to early adolescence (ages 5–13) were characterized by significantly lower levels of sensation seeking than children on the persistent delinquency trajectory (Maldonado-Molina et al., 2009; findings refer only to the Bronx sample because no persistent trajectory was found for the San Juan youths).

In the Dunedin birth cohort, both males and females following the childhood-limited trajectory of antisocial behavior were characterized by less individual and contextual risk than their same-sex counterparts following the LCP trajectory. Specifically, children on the childhood-limited trajectory versus the LCP trajectory were less likely to come from low-SES households, experienced less maltreatment, were less likely to have parents with a conviction, and were less likely to have a low IQ and a diagnosis of attention-deficit/hyperactivity disorder (Odgers et al., 2008).

Finally, in the Great Smoky Mountains Study, Maughan et al. (2000) found that youths on a declining versus a persistent trajectory of aggressive conduct problems were significantly less likely to be in poverty, come from a large family, or to experience inadequate parental supervision. Youths following a declining versus a persistent trajectory of nonaggressive conduct problems were also less likely to live in poverty and have inadequate parental supervision.

Population-based studies beginning in adolescence have suggested similar risk patterns for youths following a desisting versus a persisting antisocial behavior pathway. For example, McDermott and Nagin (2001), in their analysis of 835 males from the National Youth Survey, found that individuals following a desisting trajectory of offending from ages 11 to 24 showed greater moral beliefs, spent more time with family, were labeled less negatively by parents, and had fewer delinquent peers than individuals on a persistent trajectory across all ages (all contrasts were significant). However, desisting individuals were classified as showing significantly higher risk on these dimensions than the low offending group. Desisters and persisters did not differ from each other on attachment to convention or likelihood of coming from a two-parent family (McDermott & Nagin, 2001).

Martino et al. (2008), in their representative longitudinal study of 1,877 students followed from ages 13 to 18, showed that White adolescents were significantly less likely to follow a desisting versus persistent aggression trajectory, as were youths with lower academic orientation, whereas being from a two-parent household significantly predicted following a trajectory of desisting versus persistent aggression. Similarly, Raskin White et al. (2001) found that those on an AL versus a persistent trajectory of delinquency differed only in their levels of disinhibition, with youths on the persistent pathway scoring significantly higher than youths on the AL pathway. In their representative sample of 220 adolescents from the Carolina Longitudinal Study, Xie et al. (2011) reported that youths who followed a decreasing aggression trajectory from ages 10 to 18 affiliated with significantly less aggressive and more popular peer groups than youths on the high-aggression trajectory at age 10. In addition, they found that girls following the decreasing aggression trajectory came from families with significantly higher SES than girls on the high aggression pathway. This latter difference was not significant among the boys in the Carolina sample.

Studies of youths in high-risk or all-offender samples, although not informative for desistance etiology, can nonetheless help identify the characteristics of high-risk youths who may eventually desist in their antisocial behavior. In a sample of 284 low-income boys, children following the moderate desistance trajectory of overt antisocial behavior from ages 2 to 8 came from homes with significantly lower levels of maternal depression than children following the persistent trajectory (Shaw, Gilliom, Ingoldsby, & Nagin, 2003). In a follow-up study of these same children, Shaw, Lacourse, and Nagin (2005) found that, compared with children on the persistent conduct problem trajectory, children on the desisting trajectory were less likely to show chronic comorbid hyperactivity and attention problems from ages 2 to 10.

In their longitudinal study of 1,037 high-risk boys followed from ages 6 to 15, Nagin and Tremblay (2001) showed that children on the high declining aggression trajectory were significantly less likely to be born to teenage parents and were also significantly less likely to come from homes characterized by low levels of parental education than children on the persistent aggression trajectory. In addition, children on the moderate declining trajectory showed lower levels of comorbid childhood adjustment problems (such as low IQ, hyperactivity, opposition, and inattention) and higher levels of prosocial behavior than children on the persistent trajectory (Nagin & Tremblay, 2001). In the Cambridge Longitudinal Study of 400 delinquent boys, Nagin and Land (1993) reported that boys following the AL trajectory of offending generally had fewer childhood and adolescent risk markers than boys on the high-rate chronic trajectory, with some exceptions such as increased daring, poor parental supervision, and poor rearing in childhood (ages 8–11).

Some evidence has suggested that in studies of high-risk youths, fewer differences may exist between individuals in desisting versus persistent trajectory groups. For example, Jennings, Maldonado-Molina, and Komro (2010) found that only among girls did a decreasing trajectory of delinquency exist, and girls following the decreasing trajectory were not well distinguished from girls showing high and persistent delinquency from ages 12 to 14. In the Pittsburgh Youth Study of 500 boys (30% high risk), two desisting trajectories of delinquency between the ages of 10 and 19, called the *serious desister* (14% of the sample) and the *moderate desister* (7% of the sample) trajectories, were identified (Hoeve et al., 2008). Serious desisters versus serious persisters showed lower levels of childhood delinquency and experienced lower levels of authoritarian parenting but significantly higher levels of neglectful parenting. Moderate desisters versus minor persisters scored in more problematic directions on some childhood markers (higher authoritarian and neglectful parenting, higher levels of childhood delinquency) but scored in a less problematic direction on family SES (Hoeve et al., 2008).

Outcomes. Do individuals who follow a desisting trajectory represent true recoveries from an otherwise risky trajectory? Population-based studies that have followed desisting youths into late adolescence and adulthood are in the best position to answer this question. Reef, Diamantopoulou, van Meurs, Verhulst, and van der Ende (2011) followed youths from the Zuid-Holland representative developmental study and assessed prevalence of psychiatric disorder by trajectory group. They found that youths who followed the desistance trajectory of aggression (low decreasers) from age 4 to 18 were not at increased risk for psychiatric disorder in adulthood, whereas those who followed the persistent trajectory (high decreasers) were at significantly higher risk for disruptive disorders, which included oppositional defiant disorder, attention deficit/hyperactivity disorder, and antisocial personality disorder, in adulthood. Odgers et al. (2008) assessed outcomes at age 32 across multiple domains for youths in the Dunedin study. They found that children on the childhood-limited trajectory still showed some signs of risk at the age 32 follow-up, but the findings were more pronounced for men than for women. Compared with men on the low conduct problem trajectory, childhood-limited men showed small to medium effect-size differences in violence (Cohen's d = 0.27), mental health problems (d = 0.40), physical health problems (d = 0.37), and economic hardship (d = 0.55) at age 32. For women, effect-size differences were smaller between childhood-limited and low antisocial trajectory groups in age 32 violence (d = 0.23), mental health problems (d = 0.06), physical health problems (d = 0.18), and economic hardship (d = 0.20).

Prospective assessments of desisting youths in high-risk samples have told a similar story—that those following a desisting trajectory tend to fare better than those on a persisting trajectory, but desisting individuals still show evidence of adjustment problems later in life. Shaw, Hyde, and Brennan (2012) found that low-income adolescent boys following a high decreasing versus a high increasing trajectory of delinquency were significantly less likely to meet diagnostic criteria for conduct disorder at age 17. Although a lower percentage of high decreasing versus high increasing youths received court petitions by age 17, the difference between the trajectory groups was not statistically significant, and the rate of court petitions for high decreasing youths remained quite high (60%). In their age 32 follow-up of the Cambridge males, Nagin, Farrington, and Moffitt (1995) found that although AL males fared significantly better than persistent males in work and relationship domains, they continued to abuse substances, get into fights, and commit crime.

SUMMARY AND FUTURE RESEARCH DIRECTIONS

Longitudinal studies using GBTMs have taught us the following about antisocial development. First, involvement in some form of antisocial behavior, followed by desistance in this behavior, is a developmentally normative pattern. This appears to be especially true during early childhood because the vast majority of children follow a desisting pattern of aggression during this time. Throughout childhood and into young adulthood, individuals following a desisting trajectory of antisocial behavior (decreasing, desisting, childhood limited, adolescence limited) tend to be more prevalent than those following a persistently high trajectory and make up a substantial portion of the population (with representative cohort studies identifying as much as 25% of the population as following a childhood-limited course of antisocial behavior; see, e.g., Odgers et al., 2008).

Second, a small percentage of individuals follow a persistently high antisocial trajectory across development. These individuals tend to show the highest levels of antisocial behavior and come from the highest risk backgrounds, showing the greatest levels of individual vulnerability and contextual risk. Individuals on early-onset and persistent pathways of antisocial behavior also show the highest risk for poor outcomes in adulthood across multiple life domains. Elevated risk among those on a persistent pathway of antisocial behavior during the transition to adulthood is found among those whose behavior is characterized by both nonofficial measures of antisocial behavior as well as by more serious markers of criminal involvement.

Third, the backgrounds of individuals following a desistance trajectory tend to be more risky than the backgrounds of those following a low antisocial trajectory, but less risky than those for individuals following a persistent trajectory. This has been shown for nearly all types of desisting trajectories found in population-based studies, including early childhood desisting (Côté et al., 2006), childhood-limited (Odgers et al., 2008), and adolescent-limited trajectory groups (Fergusson & Horwood, 2002). Fourth, although individuals who desist from antisocial behavior show some evidence of recovery from risk in terms of their involvement in antisocial behavior, their recovery appears to be incomplete because they still exhibit some problems with mental and physical health, violence and crime, and socioeconomic hardship in adulthood.

Collectively, the longitudinal studies of antisocial behavior reviewed here suggest the following research directions. First, although many studies have described desistance and persistence trajectories in their samples, only some of these studies have offered direct statistical comparisons between desisting and persisting trajectory groups in terms of their associated etiological factors and outcomes. Additional estimates from representative cohort studies that contain the full range of trajectory groups, risk factors, and observed outcomes for individuals on these divergent pathways are required. Direct comparisons of individuals following these trajectories could offer clues about which factors may best distinguish those on persistent trajectories of antisocial behavior versus those who follow more transient and less consequential trajectories.

Second, studies that combine GBTMs with natural experiments, randomized controlled trials, propensity score matching, and fixed-effects longitudinal regression could help inform theory and research focused on understanding the causes of desistance. Because trajectory modeling of antisocial behavior is often done in naturalistic studies, it is unclear whether the factors associated with the desistance process play a causal role in generating desistence or, conversely, whether unobserved factors are confounding the reported associations. Combining trajectory solutions with propensity score modeling approaches can allow for stronger causal inferences regarding the role of associated factors, or candidate turning points, in generating desistance. For example, Haviland, Nagin, Rosenbaum, and Tremblay (2008) tested the role of joining a gang in future antisocial behavior using a combination of group-based trajectory modeling and propensity score matching. Propensity score matching was used to create balance on covariates associated with the gang-joining event; trajectory solutions were used to match youths on their developmental history of antisocial behavior, which affected both their probability of joining a gang and their subsequent level of antisocial behavior. By comparing youths who joined gangs with youths who followed the same developmental trajectory of antisocial behavior but did not join gangs, Haviland et al. were able isolate the effect of joining gangs on antisocial behavior that could not be easily attributed to other potentially confounding factors or preexisting differences between the groups. Although they used this combination of methods to study factors that may generate antisocial behavior, these same methods could be used to study factors that may generate desistance in antisocial behavior among youths following a persistent antisocial trajectory. Using these methods in nonexperimental studies could inform etiological theory and aid in the development of prevention trials aimed at fostering desistance in antisocial behavior.

Third, although a large body of theory and research has examined how gender, ethnicity, and SES relate to antisocial behavior and crime (see, e.g., Elliott, 1994; Elliott & Ageton, 1980; Schwartz & Milovanovic, 1996), and a body of research is emerging on antisocial development among females versus males (see reviews by Fontaine, Carbonneau, Vitaro, Barker, & Tremblay, 2009; Russell et al., 2014), more research is needed regarding how the intersections of gender, ethnicity, and SES predict differences in the factors associated with desistance versus persistence trajectory membership. Future longitudinal research including sufficient numbers of ethnic minority, low-SES, and female youths will be needed to determine whether the factors associated with desistance differ across the various intersections of gendered, ethnic, and socioeconomic lines.

In sum, most children engage in antisocial behavior at some point during their development. For most, involvement is transient and normative and leaves no lasting mark on adult outcomes or life chances. For the relatively small minority of children who follow a persistently high trajectory of antisocial behavior, the interplay between individual-level and contextual risk serves to both reinforce the negative behaviors and set the stage for a wide range of problems later in life. Even among the most serious offending groups, individuals who exhibit persistently high and stable patterns of antisocial behavior are at heightened risk for poor outcomes compared with their high-risk counterparts exhibiting different patterns of antisocial behavior. We now know a good deal about the developmental patterns, origins, and consequences of persistent antisocial behavior. Future work is required to extend what is known about the desistance process and the factors and turning points that drive individuals away from antisocial behavior and crime across development. Looking forward, it will be important to recognize the ways in which contextual factors and triggers, including features of children's neighborhoods and daily exposures to adversity and violence, influence antisocial behavior across both developmental and momentary timescales.

References

Andersson, F., Levander, S., Svensson, R., & Levander, M. T. (2012). Sex differences in offending trajectories in a Swedish cohort. *Criminal Behaviour and Mental Health, 22*, 108–121. http://dx.doi.org/10.1002/cbm.1822

Barker, E. D., Arseneault, L., Brendgen, M., Fontaine, N., & Maughan, B. (2008). Joint development of bullying and victimization in adolescence: Relations to delinquency and self-harm. *Journal of the American Academy of Child and Adolescent Psychiatry, 47*, 1030–1038.

Bersani, B. E., Laub, J. H., & Nieuwbeerta, P. (2009). Marriage and desistance from crime in the Netherlands: Do gender and socio-historical context matter? *Journal of Quantitative Criminology, 25*, 3–24. http://dx.doi.org/10.1007/s10940-008-9056-4

Bersani, B. E., Nieuwbeerta, P., & Laub, J. H. (2009). Predicting trajectories of offending over the life course: Findings from a Dutch conviction cohort. *Journal of Research in Crime and Delinquency, 46*, 468–494. http://dx.doi.org/10.1177/0022427809341939

Blokland, A. A. J., Nagin, D. S., & Nieuwbeerta, P. (2005). Life span offending trajectories of a Dutch conviction cohort. *Criminology, 43*, 919–954. http://dx.doi.org/10.1111/j.1745-9125.2005.00029.x

Boers, K., Reinecke, J., Seddig, D., & Mariotti, L. (2010). Explaining the development of adolescent violent delinquency. *European Journal of Criminology, 7*, 499–520. http://dx.doi.org/10.1177/1477370810376572

Bongers, I. L., Koot, H. M., Van Der Ende, J., & Verhulst, F. C. (2004). Developmental trajectories of externalizing behaviors in childhood and adolescence. *Child Development, 75*, 1523–1537. http://dx.doi.org/10.1111/j.1467-8624.2004.00755.x

Broidy, L. M., Nagin, D. S., Tremblay, R. E., Bates, J. E., Brame, B., Dodge, K. A., . . . Vitaro, F. (2003). Developmental trajectories of childhood disruptive behaviors and adolescent delinquency: A six-site, cross-national study. *Developmental Psychology, 39*, 222–245. http://dx.doi.org/10.1037/0012-1649.39.2.222

Burt, S. A., Donnellan, M. B., Humbad, M. N., Hicks, B. M., McGue, M., & Iacono, W. G. (2010). Does marriage inhibit antisocial behavior? An examination of selection vs causation via a longitudinal twin design. *Archives of General Psychiatry, 67*, 1309–1315. http://dx.doi.org/10.1001/archgenpsychiatry.2010.159

Bushway, S. D., Piquero, A. R., Broidy, L. M., Cauffman, E., & Mazerolle, P. (2001). An empirical framework for studying desistance as a process. *Criminology, 39*, 491–516. http://dx.doi.org/10.1111/j.1745-9125.2001.tb00931.x

Chung, I.-J., Hill, K. G., Hawkins, J. D., Gilchrist, L. D., & Nagin, D. S. (2002). Childhood predictors of offense trajectories. *Journal of Research in Crime and Delinquency, 39*, 60–90. http://dx.doi.org/10.1177/002242780203900103

Connell, A. M., Klostermann, S., & Dishion, T. J. (2012). Family Check Up effects on adolescent arrest trajectories: Variation by developmental subtype. *Journal of Research on Adolescence, 22*, 367–380. http://dx.doi.org/10.1111/j.1532-7795.2011.00765.x

Côté, S. M., Vaillancourt, T., Barker, E. D., Nagin, D., & Tremblay, R. E. (2007). The joint development of physical and indirect aggression: Predictors of continuity and change during childhood. *Development and Psychopathology, 19*, 37–55. http://dx.doi.org/10.1017/S0954579407070034

Côté, S. M., Vaillancourt, T., LeBlanc, J. C., Nagin, D. S., & Tremblay, R. E. (2006). The development of physical aggression from toddlerhood to pre-adolescence: A nation wide longitudinal study of Canadian children. *Journal of Abnormal Child Psychology, 34*, 68–82. http://dx.doi.org/10.1007/s10802-005-9001-z

Di Giunta, L., Pastorelli, C., Eisenberg, N., Gerbino, M., Castellani, V., & Bombi, A. S. (2010). Developmental trajectories of physical aggression: Prediction of overt and covert antisocial behaviors from self- and mothers' reports. *European Child and Adolescent Psychiatry, 19*, 873–882. http://dx.doi.org/10.1007/s00787-010-0134-4

D'Unger, A., Land, K. C., McCall, P. L., & Nagin, D. S. (1998). How many latent classes of delinquent/criminal careers? Results from mixed Poisson regression analyses. *American Journal of Sociology, 103*, 1593–1630. http://dx.doi.org/10.1086/231402

D'Unger, A. V., Land, K. C., & McCall, P. L. (2002). Sex differences in age patterns of delinquent/criminal careers: Results from Poisson latent class analyses of the Philadelphia cohort study. *Journal of Quantitative Criminology, 18*, 349–375. http://dx.doi.org/10.1023/A:1021117626767

Elliott, D. S. (1994). Serious violent offenders: Onset, developmental course, and termination: The American Society of Criminology 1993 presidential address. *Criminology, 32*, 1–21. http://dx.doi.org/10.1111/j.1745-9125.1994.tb01144.x

Elliott, D. S., & Ageton, S. S. (1980). Reconciling race and class differences in self-reported and official estimates of delinquency. *American Sociological Review, 45*, 95–110. http://dx.doi.org/10.2307/2095245

Farrington, D. P. (2003). Key results from the first 40 years of the Cambridge Study in Delinquent Development. In T. P. Thornberry & M. D. Krohn (Eds.), *Taking stock of delinquency: An overview of findings from contemporary longitudinal studies* (pp. 137–183). http://dx.doi.org/10.1007/0-306-47945-1_5

Fergusson, D. M., & Horwood, L. J. (2002). Male and female offending trajectories. *Development and Psychopathology, 14*, 159–177. http://dx.doi.org/10.1017/S0954579402001098

Fergusson, D. M., Horwood, L. J., & Nagin, D. S. (2000). Offending trajectories in a New Zealand birth cohort. *Criminology, 38*, 525–551. http://dx.doi.org/10.1111/j.1745-9125.2000.tb00898.x

Fontaine, N., Carbonneau, R., Vitaro, F., Barker, E. D., & Tremblay, R. E. (2009). Research review: A critical review of studies on the developmental trajectories of antisocial behavior in females. *Journal of Child Psychology and Psychiatry, 50*, 363–385. http://dx.doi.org/10.1111/j.1469-7610.2008.01949.x

Harachi, T. W., Fleming, C. B., White, H. R., Ensminger, M. E., Abbott, R. D., Catalano, R. F., & Haggerty, K. P. (2006). Aggressive behavior among girls and boys during middle childhood: Predictors and sequelae of trajectory group membership. *Aggressive Behavior, 32*, 279–293. http://dx.doi.org/10.1002/ab.20125

Haviland, A., Nagin, D. S., Rosenbaum, P. R., & Tremblay, R. E. (2008). Combining group-based trajectory modeling and propensity score matching for causal inferences in nonexperimental longitudinal data. *Developmental Psychology, 44*, 422–436. http://dx.doi.org/10.1037/0012-1649.44.2.422

Hoeve, M., Blokland, A., Dubas, J. S., Loeber, R., Gerris, J. R. M., & van der Laan, P. H. (2008). Trajectories of delinquency and parenting styles. *Journal of Abnormal Child Psychology, 36*, 223–235. http://dx.doi.org/10.1007/s10802-007-9172-x

Jennings, W. G., Higgins, G. E., Tewksbury, R., Gover, A. R., & Piquero, A. R. (2010). A longitudinal assessment of the victim-offender overlap. *Journal of Interpersonal Violence, 25*, 2147–2174. http://dx.doi.org/10.1177/0886260509354888

Jennings, W. G., Maldonado-Molina, M. M., & Komro, K. A. (2010). Sex similarities/differences in trajectories of delinquency among urban Chicago youth: The role of delinquent peers. *American Journal of Criminal Justice, 35*, 56–75. http://dx.doi.org/10.1007/s12103-009-9066-2

Jennings, W. G., Maldonado-Molina, M. M., Piquero, A. R., Odgers, C. L., Bird, H., & Canino, G. (2010). Sex differences in trajectories of offending among Puerto Rican youth. *Crime and Delinquency, 56*, 327–357. http://dx.doi.org/10.1177/0011128710372478

Jennings, W. G., & Reingle, J. M. (2012). On the number and shape of developmental/life-course violence, aggression, and delinquency trajectories: A state-of-the-art review. *Journal of Criminal Justice, 40*, 472–489. http://dx.doi.org/10.1016/j.jcrimjus.2012.07.001

Joussemet, M., Vitaro, F., Barker, E. D., Côté, S., Nagin, D. S., Zoccolillo, M., & Tremblay, R. E. (2008). Controlling parenting and physical aggression during elementary school. *Child Development, 79*, 411–425. http://dx.doi.org/10.1111/j.1467-8624.2007.01133.x

Lahey, B. B., Van Hulle, C. A., Waldman, I. D., Rodgers, J. L., D'Onofrio, B. M., Pedlow, S., . . . Keenan, K. (2006). Testing descriptive hypotheses regarding sex differences in the development of conduct problems and delinquency. *Journal of Abnormal Child Psychology, 34*, 730–748. http://dx.doi.org/10.1007/s10802-006-9064-5

Laub, J. H., & Sampson, R. J. (2003). *Shared beginnings, divergent lives: Delinquent boys to age 70*. Cambridge, MA: Harvard University Press.

Loeber, R., & Hay, D. (1997). Key issues in the development of aggression and violence from childhood to early adulthood. *Annual Review of Psychology, 48*, 371–410. http://dx.doi.org/10.1146/annurev.psych.48.1.371

Lynne-Landsman, S. D., Graber, J. A., Nichols, T. R., & Botvin, G. J. (2011). Trajectories of aggression, delinquency, and substance use across middle school among urban, minority adolescents. *Aggressive Behavior, 37*, 161–176. http://dx.doi.org/10.1002/ab.20382

Maldonado-Molina, M. M., Piquero, A. R., Jennings, W. G., Bird, H., & Canino, G. (2009). Trajectories of delinquency among Puerto Rican children and adolescents at two sites. *Journal of Research in Crime and Delinquency, 46*, 144–181. http://dx.doi.org/10.1177/0022427808330866

Marshall, J. (2005). *Juvenile offending trajectories: A South Australian study*. Adelaide, South Australia, Australia: Office of Crime Statistics and Research.

Martino, S. C., Ellickson, P. L., Klein, D. J., McCaffrey, D., & Edelen, M. O. (2008). Multiple trajectories of physical aggression among adolescent boys and girls. *Aggressive Behavior, 34*, 61–75. http://dx.doi.org/10.1002/ab.20215

Maughan, B., Pickles, A., Rowe, R., Costello, E. J., & Angold, A. (2000). Developmental trajectories of aggressive and non-aggressive conduct problems. *Journal of Quantitative Criminology, 16*, 199–221. http://dx.doi.org/10.1023/A:1007516622688

McDermott, S., & Nagin, D. S. (2001). Same or different? Comparing offender groups and covariates over time. *Sociological Methods and Research, 29*, 282–318. http://dx.doi.org/10.1177/0049124101029003002

Miller, S., Malone, P. S., & Dodge, K. A.; Conduct Problems Prevention Research Group. (2010). Developmental trajectories of boys' and girls' delinquency: Sex differences and links to later adolescent outcomes. *Journal of Abnormal Child Psychology, 38*, 1021–1032. http://dx.doi.org/10.1007/s10802-010-9430-1

Moffitt, T. E. (1993). Adolescence-limited and life-course-persistent antisocial behavior: A developmental taxonomy. *Psychological Review, 100*, 674–701. http://dx.doi.org/10.1037/0033-295X.100.4.674

Moffitt, T. E. (2006). Life-course persistent versus adolescence-limited antisocial behavior. In D. Cicchetti & D. J. Cohen (Eds.), *Developmental psychopathology: Vol. 3. Risk, disorder, and adaptation* (2nd ed., pp. 570–598). Hoboken, NJ: Wiley.

Moffitt, T. E., Caspi, A., Harrington, H., & Milne, B. J. (2002). Males on the life-course-persistent and adolescence-limited antisocial pathways: Follow-up at age 26 years. *Development and Psychopathology, 14*, 179–207. http://dx.doi.org/10.1017/S0954579402001104

Monahan, K. C., Steinberg, L., Cauffman, E., & Mulvey, E. P. (2009). Trajectories of antisocial behavior and psychosocial maturity from adolescence to young adulthood. *Developmental Psychology, 45*, 1654–1668. http://dx.doi.org/10.1037/a0015862

Nagin, D., & Tremblay, R. E. (1999). Trajectories of boys' physical aggression, opposition, and hyperactivity on the path to physically violent and nonviolent juvenile delinquency. *Child Development, 70*, 1181–1196. http://dx.doi.org/10.1111/1467-8624.00086

Nagin, D. S. (1999). Analyzing developmental trajectories: A semiparametric, group-based approach. *Psychological Methods, 4*, 139–157. http://dx.doi.org/10.1037/1082-989X.4.2.139

Nagin, D. S., Farrington, D. P., & Moffitt, T. E. (1995). Life-course trajectories of different types of offenders. *Criminology, 33*, 111–139. http://dx.doi.org/10.1111/j.1745-9125.1995.tb01173.x

Nagin, D. S., & Land, K. C. (1993). Age, criminal careers, and population heterogeneity: Specification and estimation of a nonparametric, mixed Poisson model. *Criminology, 31*, 327–362. http://dx.doi.org/10.1111/j.1745-9125.1993.tb01133.x

Nagin, D. S., & Odgers, C. L. (2010). Group-based trajectory modeling in clinical research. *Annual Review of Clinical Psychology, 6*, 109–138. http://dx.doi.org/10.1146/annurev.clinpsy.121208.131413

Nagin, D. S., & Tremblay, R. E. (2001). Parental and early childhood predictors of persistent physical aggression in boys from kindergarten to high school. *Archives of General Psychiatry, 58*, 389–394. http://dx.doi.org/10.1001/archpsyc.58.4.389

National Institute of Child Health and Human Development Early Child Care Research Network. (2004). Trajectories of physical aggression from toddlerhood to middle childhood: Predictors, correlates, and outcomes. *Monographs of the Society for Research in Child Development, 69*, vii, 1–129.

Odgers, C. L., Moffitt, T. E., Broadbent, J. M., Dickson, N., Hancox, R. J., Harrington, H., . . . Caspi, A. (2008). Female and male antisocial trajectories: From childhood origins to adult outcomes. *Development and Psychopathology, 20*, 673–716. http://dx.doi.org/10.1017/S0954579408000333

Patterson, G. R., DeBaryshe, B. D., & Ramsey, E. (1989). A developmental perspective on antisocial behavior. *American Psychologist, 44*, 329–335. http://dx.doi.org/10.1037/0003-066X.44.2.329

Patterson, G. R., Forgatch, M. S., Yoerger, K. L., & Stoolmiller, M. (1998). Variables that initiate and maintain an early-onset trajectory for juvenile offending. *Development and Psychopathology, 10*, 531–547. http://dx.doi.org/10.1017/S0954579498001734

Pepler, D., Jiang, D., Craig, W., & Connolly, J. (2008). Developmental trajectories of bullying and associated factors. *Child Development, 79*, 325–338. http://dx.doi.org/10.1111/j.1467-8624.2007.01128.x

Pepler, D. J., Jiang, D., Craig, W. M., & Connolly, J. (2010). Developmental trajectories of girls' and boys' delinquency and associated problems. *Journal of Abnormal Child Psychology, 38*, 1033–1044. http://dx.doi.org/10.1007/s10802-010-9389-y

Petras, H., Schaeffer, C. M., Ialongo, N., Hubbard, S., Muthén, B., Lambert, S. F., . . . Kellam, S. (2004). When the course of aggressive behavior in childhood does not predict antisocial outcomes in adolescence and young adulthood: An examination of potential explanatory variables. *Development and Psychopathology, 16*, 919–941. http://dx.doi.org/10.1017/S0954579404040076

Piquero, A. R. (2008). Taking stock of developmental trajectories of criminal activity over the life course. In A. M. Liberman (Ed.), *The long view of crime: A synthesis of longitudinal research* (pp. 23–78). http://dx.doi.org/10.1007/978-0-387-71165-2_2

Piquero, A. R., Brame, R., & Moffitt, T. E. (2005). Extending the study of continuity and change: Gender differences in the linkage between adolescent and adult offending. *Journal of Quantitative Criminology, 21*, 219–243. http://dx.doi.org/10.1007/s10940-005-2494-3

Raskin White, H., Bates, M. E., & Buyske, S. (2001). Adolescence-limited versus persistent delinquency: Extending Moffitt's hypothesis into adulthood. *Journal of Abnormal Psychology, 110*, 600–609. http://dx.doi.org/10.1037/0021-843X.110.4.600

Reef, J., Diamantopoulou, S., van Meurs, I., Verhulst, F. C., & van der Ende, J. (2011). Developmental trajectories of child to adolescent externalizing behavior and adult *DSM–IV* disorder: Results of a 24-year longitudinal study. *Social Psychiatry and Psychiatric Epidemiology, 46*, 1233–1241. http://dx.doi.org/10.1007/s00127-010-0297-9

Robins, L. N. (1978). Sturdy childhood predictors of adult antisocial behaviour: Replications from longitudinal studies. *Psychological Medicine, 8*, 611–622. http://dx.doi.org/10.1017/S0033291700018821

Russell, M. A., Robins, S. J., & Odgers, C. L. (2014). Developmental perspectives: Sex differences in antisocial behavior from childhood to adulthood. In R. Gartner & B. McCarthy (Eds.), *Oxford handbook on gender, sex, and crime* (pp. 286–315). Oxford, England: Oxford University Press.

Sampson, R. J., & Laub, J. H. (1993). *Crime in the making: Pathways and turning points through life*. Cambridge, MA: Harvard University Press.

Sampson, R. J., & Laub, J. H. (2003). Life course desisters? Trajectories of crime among delinquent boys followed to age 70. *Criminology, 41*, 555–592. http://dx.doi.org/10.1111/j.1745-9125.2003.tb00997.x

Sampson, R. J., & Laub, J. H. (2005). A life-course view of the development of crime. *Annals of the American Academy of Political and Social Science, 602*, 12–45. http://dx.doi.org/10.1177/0002716205280075

Sampson, R. J., Laub, J. H., & Wimer, C. (2006). Does marriage reduce crime? A counterfactual approach to within-individual causal effects. *Criminology, 44*, 465–508. http://dx.doi.org/10.1111/j.1745-9125.2006.00055.x

Schaeffer, C. M., Petras, H., Ialongo, N., Masyn, K. E., Hubbard, S., Poduska, J., & Kellam, S. (2006). A comparison of girls' and boys' aggressive-disruptive behavior trajectories across elementary school: Prediction to young adult antisocial outcomes. *Journal of Consulting and Clinical Psychology, 74*, 500–510. http://dx.doi.org/10.1037/0022-006X.74.3.500

Schwartz, M. D., & Milovanovic, D. (Eds.). (1996). *Race, gender, and class in criminology: The intersections*. New York, NY: Garland.

Shaw, D. S., Gilliom, M., Ingoldsby, E. M., & Nagin, D. S. (2003). Trajectories leading to school-age conduct problems. *Developmental Psychology, 39*, 189–200. http://dx.doi.org/10.1037/0012-1649.39.2.189

Shaw, D. S., Hyde, L. W., & Brennan, L. M. (2012). Early predictors of boys' antisocial trajectories. *Development and Psychopathology, 24*, 871–888. http://dx.doi.org/10.1017/S0954579412000429

Shaw, D. S., Lacourse, E., & Nagin, D. S. (2005). Developmental trajectories of conduct problems and hyperactivity from ages 2 to 10. *Journal of Child Psychology and Psychiatry, 46*, 931–942. http://dx.doi.org/10.1111/j.1469-7610.2004.00390.x

Tremblay, R. E. (1999). When children's social development fails. In D. P. Keating & C. Hertzman (Eds.), *Developmental health and the wealth of nations: Social, biological, and educational dynamics* (pp. 55–71). New York, NY: Guilford Press.

Tremblay, R. E. (2000). The development of aggressive behaviour during childhood: What have we learned in the past century? *International Journal of Behavioral Development, 24*, 129–141. http://dx.doi.org/10.1080/016502500383232

Tremblay, R. E. (2002). Prevention of injury by early socialization of aggressive behavior. *Injury Prevention, 8*(Suppl. 4), iv17–iv21. http://dx.doi.org/10.1136/ip.8.suppl_4.iv17

Tremblay, R. E. (2010). Developmental origins of disruptive behaviour problems: The "original sin" hypothesis, epigenetics and their consequences for prevention. *Journal of Child Psychology and Psychiatry, 51*, 341–367. http://dx.doi.org/10.1111/j.1469-7610.2010.02211.x

Tremblay, R. E., Japel, C., Perusse, D., McDuff, P., Boivin, M., Zoccolillo, M., & Montplaisir, J. (1999). The search for the age of "onset" of physical aggression: Rousseau and Bandura revisited. *Criminal Behaviour and Mental Health, 9*, 8–23. http://dx.doi.org/10.1002/cbm.288

Tremblay, R. E., & Nagin, D. S. (2005). The developmental origin of physical aggression in humans. In R. E. Tremblay, W. W. Hartup, & J. Archer (Eds.), *Developmental origins of aggression* (pp. 83–106). New York, NY: Guilford Press.

Tremblay, R. E., Nagin, D. S., Séguin, J. R., Zoccolillo, M., Zelazo, P. D., Boivin, M., . . . Japel, C. (2004). Physical aggression during early childhood: Trajectories and predictors. *Pediatrics, 114*, e43–e50. http://dx.doi.org/10.1542/peds.114.1.e43

Underwood, M. K., Beron, K. J., & Rosen, L. H. (2009). Continuity and change in social and physical aggression from middle childhood through early adolescence. *Aggressive Behavior, 35*, 357–375. http://dx.doi.org/10.1002/ab.20313

van Lier, P. A. C., Vitaro, F., Wanner, B., Vuijk, P., & Crijnen, A. A. M. (2005). Gender differences in developmental links among antisocial behavior, friends' antisocial behavior, and peer rejection in childhood: Results from two cultures. *Child Development, 76*, 841–855. http://dx.doi.org/10.1111/j.1467-8624.2005.00881.x

Wiesner, M., & Silbereisen, R. K. (2003). Trajectories of delinquent behaviour in adolescence and their covariates: Relations with initial and time-averaged factors. *Journal of Adolescence, 26*, 753–771. http://dx.doi.org/10.1016/j.adolescence.2003.09.001

Wiesner, M., & Windle, M. (2004). Assessing covariates of adolescent delinquency trajectories: A latent growth mixture modeling approach. *Journal of Youth and Adolescence, 33*, 431–442. http://dx.doi.org/10.1023/B:JOYO.0000037635.06937.13

Xie, H., Drabick, D. A. G., & Chen, D. (2011). Developmental trajectories of aggression from late childhood through adolescence: Similarities and differences across gender. *Aggressive Behavior, 37*, 387–404. http://dx.doi.org/10.1002/ab.20404

Part V

RISK FACTORS FOR OFFENDING

CHAPTER 9

RISK, NEED, AND RESPONSIVITY IN JUVENILES

Robert D. Hoge

The risk–need–responsivity (RNR) model is a framework for analyzing the conditions contributing to criminal behaviors and a guide for assessment and intervention efforts designed to reduce the probability that individuals will engage in these behaviors. The model was originally formulated by Andrews, Bonta, and Hoge (1990) and has undergone significant refinements over the years (Andrews & Bonta, 2010; Andrews, Bonta, & Wormith, 2011; Andrews & Dowden, 2007). Applications to juvenile offenders have been developed by Hoge (2001) and Hoge and Andrews (1996, 2011). The RNR model is built on a general personality and cognitive social learning theory (see Andrews & Bonta, 2010). Applications of the model are most relevant to justice systems embracing both accountability and rehabilitative goals.

KEY CONCEPTS OF THE RISK–NEED–RESPONSIVITY MODEL

The three key concepts of the RNR model are criminogenic risk, criminogenic need, and responsivity.

Criminogenic Risk

Criminogenic risk represents characteristics of youths or their environment associated with criminal activity. In some cases, a risk factor may relate causally to the criminal action. An example would be the case in which a crime is committed in association with negative peers. In this case, the risk factor, antisocial peer associations, is a causal factor. In other cases, the risk factor may simply be a correlate of the criminal activity, with its effect generated through some third variable. Poor parental supervision, for example, is a prominent risk factor, but it is normally not directly related to criminal action. A further distinction is made between static and dynamic risk factors. Static risk factors are those not amenable to change, such as history of criminal activity. Dynamic risk factors are those that can be changed and that, if changed, can potentially reduce the changes of continued criminal activity. Poor parental supervision and negative peer associations are examples. In this chapter, I refer to dynamic risk factors as *need factors*.

The RNR model recognizes eight major risk domains for juveniles:

1. history of conduct disorder or criminal activity;
2. dysfunctional parenting;
3. educational or employment deficiencies;
4. antisocial peer associations;
5. substance abuse;
6. poor use of leisure time;
7. personality or behavior dysfunction; and
8. antisocial attitudes, values, and beliefs.

Research reviewed later in this chapter, in the section Research Evidence Relating to the Risk–Need–Responsivity Model, supports the view that these factors apply across gender and ethnic group memberships.

Other risk factors may also be present and may relate to youths' situation; examples include marital conflict in the family, family economic hardship, or parent's psychiatric disorder. They may also include characteristics of youths such as low intelligence,

http://dx.doi.org/10.1037/14643-009
APA Handbook of Psychology and Juvenile Justice, K. Heilbrun (Editor-in-Chief)

emotional disorder, low self-esteem, or poor personal management skills. These factors are generally less strongly related to the criminal actions, but they may be relevant to case planning. They are referred to as *responsivity factors* and *noncriminogenic need factors* in later discussions.

Criminogenic Need

The second concept in the RNR model—*criminogenic need*—refers to risk factors that can be changed and that, if changed, can reduce the level of risk. As mentioned, some risk factors are static and not subject to change. Most of the others, though, are dynamic risk factors; they can be changed and, if they are, they may have an impact on risk for continued criminal activity. These risk factors are referred to as *need factors* because they represent areas that require attention. For example, replacing criminal attitudes and cognitions with prosocial attitudes can reduce the likelihood of engaging in antisocial activities. Similarly, drawing youths away from antisocial peer associations may reduce risk level. These dynamic risk factors are referred to as *criminogenic need factors*. All of the criminogenic risk domains listed above, except history of conduct disorder or criminal activity, can be considered criminogenic need factors.

Responsivity

The third key concept in the model is *responsivity*. These factors characterize a rather complicated concept that has undergone some transformation since its original formulation. Specific responsivity factors, as distinguished from general responsivity factors, which I discuss later in this section, are characteristics of youths or their circumstances that, although not directly related to the criminal act, may require attention in case planning and management. An example of such a factor is emotional distress. Although the presence of depression or anxiety may not relate directly to the criminal action, it may require attention in treatment planning. There is no point in putting a youth into a substance abuse treatment program without acknowledging that his or her emotional distress might interfere with treatment. Similarly, youths (and their parents) from an oppressed ethnic minority group may require a different approach to intervention. These specific responsivity factors are sometimes referred to as *noncriminogenic needs*. Table 9.1 provides examples of individual, family, and situational responsivity factors.

Motivation or readiness for treatment is an important responsivity factor and merits some special attention. Many youths enter the juvenile justice system without motivation to change attitudes or behaviors; they are simply not ready for any intervention that might be offered to them. Although motivation and readiness may not relate directly to criminal activity, it is a factor that must be taken into account in case planning. There is no point in putting youths directly into an attitude change or substance reduction program unless they have some readiness to address the problem area. In such cases, treatment must first address the motivation issue.

The specific responsivity category also includes strength or protective factors, which are characteristics of a youth or his or her circumstances and can protect against risk or help alleviate the effects of risk. Examples are presented in Exhibit 9.1. A competent and caring parent can, for example, be an important buffer against antisocial peer influences. Similarly, a youth's interest in a sport can be of value in

TABLE 9.1

Examples of Responsivity and Strength Factors

Responsivity factors	Strength factors
Individual	
Depression and anxiety	High self-esteem
Developmental delay	Positive, prosocial attitudes
Poor social skills	Strong academic skills, motivation
Pregnancy issues	Interest in sport, hobby
Poor readiness for treatment or poor motivation	
Family	
History of criminal activity	Competent parents
Emotional distress or psychiatric	Cooperative parents
Marital conflict	Financial stability
Cultural/ethnic	Small family size
Situational	
Problem neighborhood	Good schools
Lack of recreational facilities	Good mental health services
Poor schools	Positive neighborhood
Lack of mental health services	Recreational facilities

Exhibit 9.1
Best-Practice Principles of the Risk–Need–Responsivity Model

Observe risk principle of case planning.
Observe need principle of case planning.
Observe responsivity principle of case planning.
Use standardized, validated assessments.
Deliver services in the community setting.
When institutionalized, provide services to address needs.
Use evidence-based programs.
Provide multimodal services to high-risk cases.
Use quality control procedures.
Select and train staff with care.
Deliver services in a human context.

interventions designed to reduce contact with negative peers and address poor use of leisure time. The RNR model places considerable stress on strengths-based case management practices.

The second aspect of responsivity—general responsivity—refers to features of the intervention or treatment, including such considerations as the nature of the treatment (e.g., behavioral, cognitive, nondirective, psychoanalytic), number of sessions provided, and format (group vs. individual). General responsivity also includes characteristics of the professional delivering the treatment, such as gender, professional background, cultural group membership, and style of interaction. I show below that both specific and general responsivity considerations are relevant because the RNR model stresses the importance of matching characteristics of youths with features of the intervention.

RISK–NEED–RESPONSIVITY PRINCIPLES OF EFFECTIVE PROGRAMMING

The RNR model embraces a number of research and clinically based principles of effective programming (Exhibit 9.1). The first three principles relating to risk, need, and responsivity are considered core principles and (as I show later in this chapter, in the section Research Evidence Relating to the Risk–Need–Responsivity Model) have considerable research support. Some of the other principles of best practice are research based; in other cases, they reflect clinical experience. Relevant research on the principles is discussed in a later section. In the sections that follow, each of the best-practice principles will be discussed. Additional discussions of best practices have been provided by Andrews and Bonta (2010); Guerra, Kim, and Boxer (2008); Guerra and Leaf (2008); and Hoge and Andrews (2010).

Observe the Risk Principle of Case Planning

The risk principle of case planning states that the intensity of treatment provided youths should reflect their risk level. Individuals displaying low levels of risk should receive less intensive services than those displaying higher levels of risk. In fact, in many cases youths displaying very low levels of risk should not be involved in the system at all, provided judicial considerations allow such exclusion. There are two primary reasons for this risk level–service intensity match. First, there is no point in wasting limited resources on youths who do not require them. Intensive and expensive services should be reserved for those with significant risks. Second, involvement with police and the juvenile justice system can have negative consequences (McAra & McVie, 2007; Petitclerc, Gatti, Vitaro, & Tremblay, 2013; Steinberg, Chung, & Little, 2004; Wilson & Hoge, 2013), including the effects of labeling (delinquent, youthful criminal) on academic and employment opportunities as well as the behavioral impact of exposure to antisocial youths. This involvement can be particularly dangerous for lower risk youths, possibly escalating their risk level. Of course, judicial considerations play a role here. Youths who commit serious crimes will necessarily become involved in the system, but involvement for lower risk youths should be reduced to whatever extent possible.

Observe the Need Principle of Case Planning

The need principle of case planning recognizes that interventions should be directed to youths' specific needs. If the criminal activity seems to be primarily related to drug use and the influence of antisocial friends, they should be the targets of service. The RNR model represents, then, a strong argument for individualizing treatment.

Observe the Responsivity Principle of Case Planning

Modes and styles of intervention should match specific responsivity characteristics of the client. To illustrate, a cognitive–behavioral treatment addressing problems of anger management that requires reading complicated material may not be appropriate for a youth with limited reading skills. More generally, youths with limited cognitive capacities may not respond well to programs designed for youths with normal cognitive abilities. As another example, parents from certain minority cultural groups may require a different approach in the interview than parents from the majority culture. Readiness for treatment and strength and protective factors constitute important aspects of specific responsivity and require special attention in case planning.

Use of Standardized, Validated Assessment Procedures

Research reviewed later in this chapter, in the section Implications of the Risk–Need–Responsivity Model for Case Management, supports the superiority of structured and validated actuarial assessment tools relative to clinical or nonvalidated instruments. These instruments should provide for assessments of risk, need, and responsivity.

Dependence on Community-Based Interventions

In general, interventions are more effective when youths remain in the home with treatment interventions offered in the home, school, and community. Youths' risks and needs operate in those environments, and it makes sense to address them there. Youths may make gains in an institutional setting, but they will return to the home, school, and neighborhood, and there is no guarantee that such gains will transfer.

When Institutions Provide Services to Address Needs

When youths are confined to a correctional, mental health, or other residential facility, efforts should be made in those settings to address their criminogenic and noncriminogenic needs. Simple confinement without any effort at treatment is counterproductive.

Dependence on Evidence-Based Programs

Research reviewed later in this chapter, in the section Research Evidence Relating to the Risk–Need–Responsivity Model, has identified a wide range of effective programming to address the needs of juvenile offenders. These programs focus on attitude change, anger management, substance abuse, and parenting. It is noteworthy that most of the evidence-based programs reflect a behavioral, social learning, or cognitive–behavioral strategy. There are, of course, other treatment strategies that may be effective under some circumstances, but because of the strong empirical support for such programs, the RNR model stresses their use.

Use of Multimodal Interventions With Higher Risk Cases

High-risk youths often present with multiple criminogenic and noncriminogenic needs, and they are often related to one another in complex ways. For example, conflicts with a parent may lead to youths' association with an antisocial gang that in turn is associated with substance abuse and criminal activity. Also, the parent may have an emotional disorder that further complicates the parent–youth relationship. Addressing these problems in isolation will probably fail; they have to be addressed in the total context of the risks and needs, which thus explains the success of the various multimodal and wraparound programs.

Attend to Quality Control Issues

The conduct of process and impact evaluation research is critical to the success of programming. It is essential to ensure that programs are being delivered in an effective manner and that programs are having the desired effect. Research (reviewed later) has supported the importance of program integrity in ensuring outcome success.

Select and Train Staff With Care

Although management and supervision are important, the success of interventions directly depends on the competence and commitment of front-line staff. Those individuals who work directly with the family and youths affect the intervention's success or failure. It is important to recognize that working with antisocial and conduct-disordered youths presents special challenges, and it is extremely important to select staff with care and provide them with training and the support that they need to conduct their jobs. Moreover, if the RNR model is being adopted to guide interventions, staff must be educated in the features of that model.

Deliver Services in a Humane Context

The popular view is that youths must be held accountable for their crimes; that accountability, however, should be delivered in a humane and ethical manner that respects the individual. Research cited in the sections that follow has strongly supported the RNR model's assertion that youth-oriented rehabilitative approaches yield much better outcomes, including reduced reoffending levels, than punitive approaches.

RESEARCH EVIDENCE RELATING TO THE RISK–NEED–RESPONSIVITY MODEL

A variety of research areas relate to elements of the RNR model. Of particular importance is research on the validity of the risk factors represented in the model and on the efficacy of the principles of best practice. In this section, I present brief summaries of this research.

Evidence for the Validity of Risk Factors

As discussed earlier, eight major risk factors for youth crime have been identified: history of conduct disorder or criminal activity; family or parent dysfunction; education or employment deficits; antisocial peer associations; substance abuse; poor use of leisure time; dysfunctional personality or behavior traits; and antisocial attitudes, values, and beliefs. Meta-analyses based on research with juveniles have provided considerable support, linking each of these factors to engagement in criminal activities (Cottle, Lee, & Heilbrun, 2001; Farrington, 1998; Heilbrun, Lee, & Cottle, 2005; Loeber & Farrington, 1998, 2000; Vincent, Terry, & Maney, 2009). This research has been conducted with both juveniles and adults. Moreover, composites based on multiple factors from the list have yielded even stronger correlations with criminal outcomes than have individual risk items (see Andrews & Bonta, 2010; Hoge & Andrews, 2011).

Much of the research represented in these meta-analyses has been based on male, North American Caucasian samples. However, evidence has suggested that the same variables constitute risk factors for both males and females and for African American and Aboriginal youths in American and Canadian contexts (Gendreau, Little, & Goggin, 1996; Jung & Rawana, 1999; Redding & Arrigo, 2005; Rowe, Flannery, & Flannery, 1995; Simourd & Andrews, 1994). The pattern of risk factors may differ across groups, but individual items and composites based on the items are significantly predictive for all of these groups. Although extensive research has not been conducted with other minority groups in North America or in other national contexts, clinical experience and some early research have suggested that similar results would be seen (e.g., Chu, Daffern, Thomas, & Lim, 2012; McGrath & Thompson, 2012).

Evidence for the Efficacy of the Risk, Need, and Responsivity Principles of the Risk–Need–Responsivity Model

A number of principles of effective programming were presented earlier; however, the three key principles relate to risk, need, and responsivity. Several investigators have provided narrative reviews and meta-analyses of research conducted on these principles with samples composed of youths and adults (Andrews & Bonta, 2010; Andrews & Dowden, 2007; Andrews, Dowden, & Gendreau, 1999; Andrews, Zinger, et al., 1990; Lipsey, 1995; Smith, Gendreau, & Swartz, 2009). These analyses have provided support for the validity of those principles—adherence to them is associated with decreased reoffending rates. Furthermore, adherence to all three principles has produced the most significant reductions in reoffending. Much of this research has been conducted in North America. However, a recent meta-analysis of European data (Koehler, Losel, Akoensi, & Humphreys, 2013) has supported the efficacy of the RNR model with youthful offenders.

The Andrews et al. (1999; see also Andrews & Bonta, 2010) meta-analysis was particularly thorough. It was based on 374 controlled experimental tests of a variety of interventions conducted with both juvenile and adult offenders. Results revealed the superiority of interventions based on the risk, need, and responsivity principles. Effect sizes reflecting reductions in reoffending were smallest for treatments in which no RNR principles were observed, significantly greater when one principle was represented, even greater when two principles were represented, and largest for treatments in which all three principles were observed. The superiority of programs observing the RNR principles held regardless of whether data were collected in institutional or community settings, although the positive effects were greater in community settings.

The results from research comparing interventions based on punitive strategies (e.g., fines, intensive supervised probation, incarceration, shock incarceration) with those based on rehabilitative principles represented in the RNR model have been particularly striking. The comparisons consistently indicated that appropriate rehabilitative interventions, particularly those observing RNR principles, produce significantly greater reductions in reoffending than those using punitive strategies. In fact, punitive strategies are, on the whole, associated with increased recidivism. For example, the Lipsey (1995) analysis of research with juvenile offenders suggested that two of the popular criminal justice sanctions, shock incarceration and Scared Straight, were associated with the greatest increases in reoffending rates (also see Andrews & Bonta, 2010; Aos, Phipps, Barnoski, & Lieb, 2001).

Evidence for Other Risk–Need–Responsivity Principles of Effective Programming

Some of the other principles of best practice I have described have not been directly tested in research and are based largely on clinical observations, including the principles relating to the importance of careful staff selection and training and the delivery of services in a humane context. Direct support is available in the case of other principles.

The principle stressing the importance of conducting standardized and validated forensic assessments has been emphasized by Grisso (2005), Heilbrun (1997, 2010), Hoge (2008), Hoge and Andrews (1996), Mulvey and Iselin (2008), and Vincent et al. (2009). Research with youths and adults in various contexts has supported the efficacy of standardized actuarial assessments relative to clinical assessments (e.g., Grove, Zald, Lebow, Snitz, & Nelson, 2000; Hilton, Harris, & Rice, 2006).

Although individual strength factors have been explored in relation to reoffending (Werner, 2000), few general empirical tests of the strength principle are available. An exception is the Rennie and Dolan (2010) study, which demonstrated that the presence of strength and protective factors in treatment planning was associated with lower reoffending rates.

Research supporting the principles relating to the relative value of community-based services, attention to criminogenic needs in custody settings, and multidimensional treatments for high-risk youths has been discussed in a number of analyses (Andrews & Bonta, 2010; Guerra et al., 2008; Lipsey & Wilson, 1998). Relevant to the principle emphasizing the use of evidence-based programming is the considerable research attention paid to the efficacy of specific programs (Greenwood, 2005; Guerra et al., 2008; Lipsey & Wilson, 1998). Aggression Replacement Training (Goldstein, 2004), Functional Family Therapy (Sexton & Alexander, 2000), and Multisystemic Therapy (Henggeler, Schoenwald, Borduin, Rowland, & Cunningham, 1998) are just three of numerous programs that have been found to be effective with juvenile offenders. Because so many evidence-based programs reflect behavioral and cognitive–behavioral approaches, the RNR model stresses them as preferred forms of intervention (Andrews & Bonta, 2010; Smith et al., 2009).

The principle relating to quality control has also received considerable support from research conducted in juvenile and adult systems. Studies conducted in a variety of contexts have suggested that program integrity (reflecting careful observance of program specifics and principles) is closely related to program effectiveness (Andrews & Dowden, 2005; Lipsey, 1995).

Cost–Benefit Research on the Risk–Need–Responsivity Model

Considerable efforts are now being made to evaluate programs in monetary terms, which involves attaching a dollar value to the costs of delivering a program and to the program's outcomes. The latter entails estimating, for example, the monetary savings of a particular reduction in reoffending or school dropout rates. Much of this cost–benefit research has been conducted by the Washington State Institute for Public Policy (Aos et al., 2001; Drake, Aos, & Miller, 2009; Welsh et al., 2012). The analyses presented by the institute support two general conclusions. First, punitive sanctions such as incarceration tend to be associated with negative cost–benefit ratios; that is, the monetary costs of the program outweigh the monetary benefits. This likely reflects the fact that these strategies are expensive and not effective in reducing reoffending. More positive rehabilitative programs of the type recommended in the RNR model are generally effective and display positive cost–benefit ratios according to the meta-analyses presented by the institute. Similar results have been obtained by analyses conducted by the Vera Institute of Justice (http://www.vera.org).

Romani, Morgan, Gross, and McDonald (2012) analyzed the cost effectiveness of different approaches to judicial interventions, including approaches incorporating the key RNR principles of risk, need, and responsivity. They reported that appropriate interventions (incorporating RNR principles) were significantly more cost effective than inappropriate interventions (not using RNR principles) and traditional punitive interventions. Mean costs for a 1% reduction in recidivism were as follows: traditional interventions including punitive sanctions, $40.43; inappropriate treatment, $19.67; and appropriate intervention, $2.80. The superiority of appropriate treatment reflects, in part, its relative success in achieving reductions in recidivism and the relatively low cost of the community-based services usually delivered in those programs. The success in reductions in recidivism and relatively low cost are particularly striking in comparison with punitive sanctions.

IMPLICATIONS OF THE RISK–NEED–RESPONSIVITY MODEL FOR CRIMINAL JUSTICE PROCESSING

The RNR model is primarily designed to assist in risk management efforts by estimating youths' risk for continuing antisocial activities and by directing programming to the needs underlying the risk. Various responses to and interventions for antisocial youths are normally delivered by police and the juvenile and criminal justice systems, and it is necessary to consider the relevance of the model for such actions. The discussion in this section reflects the procedures and language used in many North American juvenile justice systems. However, the principles of best practice represented in the RNR model are assumed to have relevance outside those systems as well.

These systems generally embrace several goals:

- Provide the public with protection from crime.
- Ensure victim accountability.
- Hold youths accountable for criminal acts.
- Address youths' rehabilitative needs.

Although the RNR model recognizes the importance of all four goals, it places the emphasis on the fourth goal, enhancing youths' competence by addressing criminogenic and noncriminogenic needs. The assumption is that developing youths' positive competencies will reduce the incidence of future offending as well as address the other goals. Note that the RNR model does not imply that criminal activities on the part of youths should be ignored or that youths should not be held accountable for their crimes. Nor does it suggest that incarceration is never an appropriate disposition. It does imply, however, that actions taken that reflect the principles of the RNR model will be most effective in enhancing youths' competence and reducing the likelihood of continued criminal activity.

At the most fundamental level, the RNR model suggests that prevention resources to address potential risk and need factors should be available for at-risk youths and families even before youths initiate criminal activities. A wide range of evidence-based primary and tertiary prevention strategies are available for implementation in school, mental health, and community settings, and they should be supported (Farrington & Welsh, 2006). The efficacy of many of these prevention programs has also been supported through cost–benefit research (Aos et al., 2001; Drake et al., 2009). Spending money on early interventions can prevent the emergence of very expensive problems later. Ideally, these programs would be based on RNR principles.

A number of responses are available to police, prosecutors, and courts when youths are accused of a crime. These include dismissal, dismissal with warning, precharge diversion, criminal charges, and postcharge, preadjudication diversion programs. They may also involve adjudication to determine guilt or innocence. When a finding of guilt is rendered, disposition decisions must be made, generally at the judge's discretion. Disposition sanctions may include fines, community service orders, probation, or a custody disposition.

The RNR model has implications for the precharge stage of processing, which occurs when youths have been apprehended for a crime but before formal charges are laid. Whether youths are charged with a crime will depend, in part, on the nature of the crime. However, that aside, the risk principle suggests that the intrusive and intensive services provided in the juvenile justice system should be reserved for higher risk cases, and low and moderate risk cases should, whenever possible, be dealt with outside the formal judicial system. This represents an argument for the use of precharge diversion when feasible. The need principle then implies that, whatever diversion option is used, efforts should be made in that system to address any criminogenic or noncriminogenic needs exhibited by youths.

A variety of alternatives are available for precharge interventions, but community-based diversion programs appear to be particularly successful (Wilson & Hoge, 2013). The initial decisions in these programs generally rest with prosecutors, who decide whether youths might be appropriate for diversion. Diversion services are then usually offered by a community organization equipped to deal with youths. Some systems also have diversion systems available after charges and before adjudication. The procedures followed are the same as for the precharge diversion programs. It must be emphasized that the key to the success of diversion programs depends on the delivery of effective services to address youths' needs.

Several options are available to prosecutors after charges: dismissal, referral to a preadjudication diversion program, or proceeding to adjudication. Unless charges are dismissed or there is a referral to another system (e.g., mental health system), the next phase of the process is adjudication, which is designed to decide delinquency (the juvenile court equivalent of a guilty verdict in criminal court). Generally speaking, the RNR model has no relevance at this stage.

A disposition or sentencing phase will normally follow a delinquency finding. The disposition decision will generally rest with the judge, although he or she may be guided by recommendations from a probation officer or other court official. In some cases, disposition decisions are directed or constrained by legal or policy considerations. For example, judges may have limited options in the case of certain types of crime (e.g., gun crimes, sex offenses). The primary consideration in sentencing is generally the severity of the crime (proportionality) and the youth's criminal history. The more severe the crime, the harsher the disposition. However, other considerations may apply, including victim accountability, rehabilitative needs of the youth, or amenability to treatment.

Some fundamental assumptions underlie disposition decisions. One assumption is that some form of punishment is the most appropriate means of holding youths accountable for crimes and the most effective deterrent against continued criminal activity. This assumption accounts for many systems' dependence on punitive sanctions (fines, incarceration, community service orders). However, research and clinical experience have suggested that punishment in itself is not a particularly effective deterrent from criminal activity (Andrews & Bonta, 2010; Bonta & Andrews, 2010; Doob & Webster, 2003; Tonry, 2008). Indeed, meta-analytic results cited earlier in this chapter, in the section Cost–Benefit Research on the Risk–Need–Responsivity Model, have suggested that punitive sanctions, particularly incarceration, are associated with very small declines in reoffending rates and in some cases increased reoffending rates. The cost–benefit research cited earlier has also suggested that this type of option is very expensive.

It follows from the RNR model that the most effective dispositions will be those that observe the risk, need, and responsivity principles. To the extent possible, the intensity of interventions should reflect the youth's risk level, with the more intensive (and expensive) treatments reserved for higher risk cases. Furthermore, whether the youth is assigned probation, custody, boot camp, or any other judicial disposition, the youth's criminogenic and noncriminogenic needs should be identified and interventions provided to address those needs. This position is consistent with the results of the meta-analyses cited earlier comparing rehabilitative interventions based on RNR principles with interventions based on inappropriate services or on punitive sanctions. This position is further illustrated by the finding that boot camps are effective only when rehabilitative services form the core of programming (Bottcher & Ezell, 2005; Kempinin & Kurlychek, 2003). The bottom line is that simply punishing youths without any effort to address the factors underlying their antisocial behavior at best is ineffective and at worst may lead to increased offending.

The importance of targeting youths' criminogenic and noncriminogenic needs through the disposition highlights the importance of the principle relating to the use of standardized and validated assessments at intake. These assessments can help the judge guide the specifics of the disposition as well as treatment within the disposition, whether the disposition involves probation, incarceration, or another intervention. The matching procedure represented in the responsivity principle should also be observed.

Several of the other principles of best practice apply here as well. First, dependence on community-based services is preferable to institution-based residential services. When incarceration is used, programming should be available to address youths' needs. Third, evidence-based programming should be used whenever possible. Finally, a humane and positive approach should be used regardless of disposition. It is important to keep in mind that juvenile justice and correctional systems are dealing with young people, and the ultimate goal is to put them on a path to positive citizenship.

IMPLICATIONS OF THE RISK–NEED–RESPONSIVITY MODEL FOR CASE MANAGEMENT

The RNR model is designed to assist in developing and implementing case plans and management strategies relevant to all stages of intervening with justice-involved youths. Several phases of the process are involved, including assessment, case planning, program delivery, and quality control. These are discussed in turn.

Assessment

The RNR model stresses the importance of conducting standardized assessments of risk, need, and responsivity (Hoge, 1999, 2008; Hoge & Andrews, 1996; Vincent, Guy, & Grisso, 2012). A number of standardized and well-validated measures have been created to evaluate youths' risk for reoffending and to identify their needs (dynamic risk factors). One of these instruments, the Youth Level of Service/Case Management Inventory 2.0 (Hoge & Andrews, 2011), is described for illustrative purposes.

The Youth Level of Service/Case Management Inventory 2.0 is a standardized actuarial measure providing estimates of risk for reoffending and a framework for developing case plans based on a risk–need assessment. The instrument is designed for use by probation officers, social workers, youth workers, and other professionals. It is based on interviews with the youth and with collaterals such as family, teachers, friends, and others and on reviews of file information. It also includes a professional override provision to allow the examiner discretion in identifying level of risk.

Hoge and Andrews (2011) considered several goals in developing the instrument:

- Survey all factors identified in the literature as significantly related to juvenile offending (risk factors and need factors).
- Provide an indication of strength factors within various risk–need areas.
- Provide indications of the presence of other features of the youth and his or her environment relevant to case planning (responsivity and noncriminogenic need factors).
- Incorporate a professional override to allow professional discretion when appropriate.
- Provide a direct link between the identification of risk–need factors and case planning.
- Assist in the detection of changes in risk–need areas.

The instrument is organized in six sections. The first section, Assessment of Risk and Needs, includes 42 items reflecting characteristics of the offender (e.g., "chronic drug use") or his or her circumstances (e.g., "parent provides inadequate supervision") identified in the literature as significant correlates of juvenile offending. These items are divided into the following domains: Prior and Current Offenses/Dispositions, Family Circumstances/Parenting, Education/Employment, Peer Relations, Substance Abuse, Leisure/Recreation, Personality/Behavior, and Attitudes/Orientation. An opportunity is also provided to indicate strength or protective factors in those domains. The measure yields a total score reflecting the overall risk–need level and summary scores for each domain. Normative data are available for comparison purposes. Subsequent sections of the instrument are Summary of Risks and Needs, Assessment of Other Needs and Special Considerations, Professional Override, Contact Level, and Case Management Plan. The latter involves identifying a set of goals reflecting the risk–need assessment and identification of means of achieving those goals.

The inventory can be used as a structured professional judgment procedure or an actuarial procedure. In the latter case, low, moderate, high, and very high ranges for total and subscales are based on empirical data. Risk scores can also be expressed as *T* scores based on normative data. Considerable psychometric research is reported in the user's manual and elsewhere (Hoge, 2005, 2010; Hoge & Andrews, 2011).

Other standardized risk–needs instruments are also available: the Early Assessment of Risk List for Boys (Augimeri, Koegl, Webster, & Levene, 2001), Early Assessment of Risk List for Girls (Levene et al., 2001), Estimate of Sexual Offence Recidivism—2 (Worling & Curwen, 2001), Structured Assessment of Violence Risk in Youth (Borum, Bartel, & Forth, 2005), and the Washington State Juvenile Court Assessment (Barnoski, 2004). Extended discussions of these measures are also available (Borum & Verhaagen, 2006; Grisso, Vincent, & Seagrave, 2005; Hoge, 1999, 2008).

Case Planning

The RNR model identifies a number of critical steps in the case planning process as defined by the principles of best practice:

- Use structured, standardized assessment instruments.
- Observe the risk, need, and responsivity principles.
- Consider youths' developmental level in setting goals.
- Incorporate strength and protective factors.
- Establish a positive relationship with youths.
- Engage youths in the case planning process.
- Use evidence-based interventions.
- Review progress at periodic intervals.

Observing the risk principle means that the extent or intensity of interventions should reflect the overall level of risk–need shown by youths. Cases in which the criminal activity is directly associated with serious drug addiction and association with antisocial gangs will require more intensive and perhaps longer periods of treatment than cases in which youths demonstrate less serious needs. Clinical experience has suggested that interventions are shorter in some cases than they should be. Note also that the best course of action for very low-risk youths is often to simply leave them alone, within the limits required by legal issues. As indicated earlier, there are risks associated with labeling youths as a delinquent and inappropriate placements are sometimes associated with labeling youths as high risk.

Observing the need principle is critical in case planning; programming should focus on the young person's specific needs. If, for example, the criminal activities seem to be particularly associated with antisocial peer associations and drug use, then those should be the primary targets of service. If, however, the criminal activity relates to school failure and poor use of leisure time, these should be the objects of attention. Often multiple needs exist, and it is important to recognize that they may be linked in complex ways. For example, a serious drug use problem may be directly linked with parenting problems. These problems do not exist in isolation and cannot be addressed in isolation. One implication is that it is sometimes necessary to prioritize needs. For example, the parenting issues may have to be addressed before the drug issue can be fully addressed. In higher risk cases in which multiple problems exist, multidimensional or wrap-around programs such as Multisystemic Therapy (Henggeler et al., 1998) may be appropriate, as suggested by the multidimensional programming principle.

A number of aspects of responsivity are important to consider in case planning. Specific responsivity variables include noncriminogenic needs, strength or protective factors, and other features of youths or their environment that may affect an intervention's success or that require attention.

Noncriminogenic factors may need to be addressed. It is not always possible to address needs such as family poverty or marital conflict, but one should at least be aware of these issues. In other cases, there is capacity to address noncriminogenic needs, and they may require direct attention in case planning. For example, the substance abuse problem associated with criminal activities may be associated with depression or anxiety arising from the experience of abuse, and these emotional issues might need to be addressed before the drug abuse problem can be successfully resolved. Simply addressing the drug problem without acknowledging the contributing factors will likely lead to failure. These determinations are part of the process of prioritizing needs.

Considering that youths' developmental level is critical to the success of case planning efforts (Guerra et al., 2008; Hoge, 2010; Steinberg, 2009), it is important to acknowledge that youths exhibit cognitive, moral, emotional, and behavioral limitations affecting their decisions, judgments, and behavior. Many of the traits associated with delinquency (e.g., impulsivity, risk taking, narcissism, peer group influences) simply reflect aspects of adolescents' immaturity. Although it is important to address youths' needs, it is important to do so in a realistic way that considers developmental limitations. Youths have often experienced many failures, and there is no point in setting them up to fail. Careful formulation of short- and long-term goals is important.

Considering readiness for treatment and motivational issues is also critical. As noted earlier, many youths in the system have no interest in changing their attitudes or behaviors, and this lack of motivation must often be addressed before other needs can be met. Valuable guidance in dealing with readiness and motivation can be found in the stages of change (Prochaska, DiClemente, & Norcross, 1992) and motivational interviewing (Miller & Rollnick, 2002) models.

Incorporating strength or protective factors is an important principle of the RNR model. They can be useful in enhancing interventions' effectiveness. Using a positive and cooperative parent who has a good relationship with a youth can, for example, aid in addressing the youth's issues with antisocial peers and poor use of leisure time.

Focusing on positive factors can also assist in forming a relationship with youths. Many of the youths encountered in the juvenile justice system exhibit angry and hostile attitudes and are very challenging to deal with. However, to the extent possible, a positive relationship should be established, and youths should be engaged in the treatment process.

One other RNR principle is relevant: Case plans should incorporate evidence-based programs to the extent they are available. As indicated earlier, many research-supported programs directed toward attitude change, anger management, substance abuse, and education are available and should be considered.

Program Delivery

The RNR model stresses the importance of the staff competence within the delivery system, particularly that of front-line workers in direct contact with youths (Andrews & Bonta, 2010). Several conditions should be observed when implementing the RNR model.

First, the organization's culture should reflect the model's principles, meaning it should have a general commitment to a youth-oriented, rehabilitative focus and adhere to the model's specific principles. This involves having an educational component directed toward all players in the system, including police, attorneys, judges and other court officials, probation officers, correctional officials, and others connected to the system.

Second, professionals in the system should be selected with care and with particular attention to their ability to work with challenging youths. As indicated earlier, initial and continued training should be provided, and this training should focus on the application of the RNR model.

The third condition involves a commitment to continuing quality control efforts. This commitment involves, first, conducting process evaluation studies to ensure that the treatment of clients is consistent with agency policy and that programming is being delivered as intended. Second, the conduct of impact evaluations is essential to determine whether the programming is having the intended effects. These evaluations involve assessing long-term agency goals such as reductions in reoffending and more frequent school completion. It also involves evaluating more short-term effects such as improvement in attitudes, school attendance, or reductions in family conflicts. These evaluations can be conducted internally, but they would ideally be conducted by independent external agencies.

Challenges in Application of the Model

A number of political and economic challenges can be identified in efforts to apply the model in real-world settings. Three sources of political barriers may arise, two external to the juvenile justice system and the other internal.

The first external political barrier derives from policymakers, politicians, and members of the public who reject any rehabilitative goals for the juvenile justice system and feel that punitive strategies represent the only effective means for fighting crime. This position is very common in some settings and makes it difficult to gain support for more rehabilitative approaches. One key mechanism for addressing this barrier is education. Professionals committed to the RNR approach must engage in efforts to educate the public in the research on and clinical support for the rehabilitative approach. Informing the public and policymakers about the cost–benefit advantages of the approach is also necessary, particularly in the case of politicians and other policymakers.

The second external political barrier to implementation of the model derives from the fragmentation often observed in systems serving at-risk families and youths. In many cases, these youths and families are being served by the mental health, school, child protection, and juvenile justice systems. Each system provides unique services, but it is also important that they work together in addressing the family's and youths' needs. Each system will likely have its own assessment procedures, but it is important to have some coordination among them. In fact, in some cases the RNR model has been used satisfactorily in the mental health and education systems as well as in the juvenile justice system, and this might be considered as an option that encourages more cooperative efforts.

The internal political barrier involves resistance within the juvenile justice system to change. Some of this resistance may derive from simple inertia. People often resist any changes to existing policies and procedures. The internal resistance may also derive, however, from rejection of the rehabilitative approach. Just as some members of the general public firmly believe in the efficacy of punitive strategies, so too may police, prosecuting attorneys, judges, probation officers, correctional officers, and other groups. The solution to this problem generally involves leadership from management within the system and the provision of education efforts. Guidelines for implementing RNR principles have been provided by Andrews and Bonta (2010), Hoge and Andrews (2010), and Vincent et al. (2012).

Economic challenges will often arise in efforts to introduce the RNR model into a system. These challenges arise in part from the very common problem that there is never enough money. Most juvenile justice systems are publicly supported, and most are under financial pressure to one degree or another. The challenge may also arise from the perception that creating a rehabilitative system is expensive.

In one sense, this is true. Providing careful monitoring of youths is expensive, and many evidence-based programs are costly. Implementing a program such as Multisystemic Therapy is expensive in terms of hiring qualified professionals and the time they need to devote to individual clients. Substance abuse treatment, anger management, attitude change, and similar programs also require an economic commitment. These perceived costs form the basis for resistance on the part of politicians and policymakers.

Two responses can be made to the economic argument. First, the research reviewed earlier has demonstrated clearly that carefully selected and carefully delivered rehabilitative programs can be effective, particularly in comparison with traditional punitive approaches. Second, these programs, particularly when delivered in community settings, will be less expensive than strategies based on the delivery of police, judicial processing, and correctional placement services. In other words, the cost–benefit ratios of strategies observing RNR principles are much more positive than the traditional alternatives.

LIMITATIONS AND CRITICISMS OF THE RISK–NEED–RESPONSIVITY MODEL

The developers of the RNR model have acknowledged that it is a work in progress. In fact, a number of modifications to the model have appeared over the years in response to research findings and critiques from scholars and practitioners (Andrews & Bonta, 2010; Andrews et al., 2011; Bonta & Andrews, 2010). However, the model's developers have acknowledged that there are areas that require additional attention, and I address some of those areas here.

As I have shown, the best-practice risk, need, and responsivity principles have received considerable research support. However, some gaps remain. One of these relates to the validity of the risk factors identified in the RNR model. Research has been conducted with male and female youths and certain minority groups in the United States and Canada, but more work needs to be done with other cultural/ethnic groups and samples in and outside of North America.

Two other issues related to the risk–need factors require additional attention. First, evidence is available that shows that developmental considerations are important in identifying risk and need (Farrington, 2005; Hoge, 2010; Hoge, Vincent, & Guy, 2012; Vincent & Grisso, 2005), but additional work is needed on the link between age and risk, particularly during the transition years from ages 18 to 22. Second, most of the research has focused on factors associated with the initiation of criminal activity, with less attention given to factors associated with desistance from continued criminal activities (Guerra et al., 2008; Thornberry et al., 2012).

The risk, need, and responsivity principles have received considerable research support. However, the risk principle has received more attention than either the need or the responsivity principle. Vieira, Skilling, and Peterson-Badali's (2009) recent demonstration of a positive relationship between the number of need factors addressed in treatment and declines in reoffending rates illustrates the type of research required to test the need principle.

Exploring the responsivity principle is difficult because the concept covers so much ground. Meta-analytic results discussed earlier in this chapter, in the section Research Evidence Relating to the Risk–Need–Responsivity Model, have shown that programs incorporating responsivity factors into case plans have better outcomes than those that do not. However, more attention is required to individual responsivity factors. For example, more information is needed on the links between responsivity factors such as parent criminal activity, the experience of abuse, and youths' emotional distress on one hand and treatment effectiveness on the other hand. Another issue relating to responsivity concerns motivation and readiness for treatment. Progress has been made in understanding the issue, but practical aids in addressing motivation still need to be developed. The role of strength or protective factors also requires more research. These issues get to the heart of the responsivity principle, which is concerned with the appropriate matching of family and individual characteristics (specific responsivity) and features of treatment (general responsivity). Clearly, more work is required in this area.

This discussion has focused on the need for continued research on aspects of the RNR model. Other criticisms of the model have focused on more fundamental issues. One criticism is that the process of labeling youths as high risk or high need can have unintended and negative consequences. These labels may be used to stigmatize youths or result in placement in an inappropriate treatment program or placement (e.g., custody). However, there is nothing wrong with using labels or diagnoses as long as two conditions are met. First, the label must be meaningful. That condition would seem to be satisfied in the case of the risk–need categorization, which has been defined by research-based criteria—that is, personal characteristics and circumstances have been empirically linked to the likelihood of engaging in antisocial behaviors.

The second condition is that the label or diagnosis be used in an appropriate and ethical manner.

The RNR model includes a built-in guard against inappropriate uses by including a professional override. Final decisions about a youth's risk and need level rest with the professional responsible for decisions about the youth. It must be stressed, however, that precautions regarding use of the label must also rest with the organization providing the services. Safeguards must be in place to ensure that the risk–need assessment is not used in an inappropriate manner.

Another set of criticisms of the RNR model derives in part from advocates of the good lives model (Ward, 2010; Ward & Stewart, 2003; Ward & Willis, 2010) and focuses on the ultimate goal of the RNR strategy. The criticism is that the RNR model focuses too much on addressing youths' criminogenic needs and neglects more basic human needs such as those relating to establishing human relationships, engaging in meaningful work, and pursuing intellectually satisfying goals. The argument is that pursuing these goals will reduce the likelihood of engagement in criminal activities, enhance self-esteem, and lead to general happiness. The good lives model also places considerable stress on youths' motivation and engagement.

Andrews and Bonta (2010) and Andrews et al. (2011) have responded to these criticisms, suggesting that they represent in some respects a misunderstanding of the objectives and procedures of the RNR model. An important assumption of the RNR model is that addressing youths' criminogenic needs will move them from a position that places them at risk for criminal activity toward a more positive lifestyle. Replacing negative parenting and improving relations between youths and their parent, improving youths' school performance and adjustment, steering youths away from antisocial peer associations, addressing substance abuse issues, steering youths from negative to more positive leisure time activities, addressing negative behaviors such as impulsivity and hostility, and replacing negative attitudes and values with positive ones are all associated with reductions in the likelihood that youths will continue to engage in criminal activities. However, these interventions also improve youths' general situation, moving them from a negative adaptation to the world to a positive one and ultimately to higher self-esteem and happiness. This is supported in part by the demonstration that desistance from crime is itself associated with more success in other areas of life (Farrington et al., 2006).

Advocates of the good lives model have stressed the importance of engaging youths in the case planning process and motivating them to make the desired behavioral and attitude changes, and they have suggested that the RNR model neglects these considerations. However, these goals are included in the RNR model. Readiness and motivation are represented as responsivity or noncriminogenic factors, and the model acknowledges that very often these factors must be addressed before criminogenic needs are addressed. A similar point can be made with respect to other noncriminogenic needs such as depression, anxiety, and poor self-esteem. These are important needs and are certainly worthy of attention. However, research reviewed earlier in this chapter, in the section Research Evidence Relating to the Risk–Need–Responsivity Model, has suggested that addressing these needs will not in and of itself reduce youths' risk for criminal activity. If the parenting problem persists, if the youth continues to fail in school and to embrace antisocial attitudes, then the risk of antisocial behavior will continue.

A related criticism of the RNR model is that it does not place enough stress on youths' well-being and happiness. This is inaccurate. The RNR model is designed to be delivered in a humane context, with youths' well-being a prime consideration. This criticism may also be based on a misunderstanding of the link between objective and subjective well-being. What responsible adults view as signs of well-being may not be viewed in the same way by antisocial youths. Youths may not place a high value on a positive relationship with the parent, superior school performance, or engagement in positive leisure activities. They may not contribute to their subjective well-being or happiness. However, youths may derive significant rewards from engaging in criminal behaviors, associating with antisocial peers, and using drugs or alcohol. The RNR model places a great deal of emphasis on shifting youths' reward system from a focus on the rewards available from an antisocial life style and toward more positive sources of reward. This is designed to promote youths' sustained well-being.

FINAL WORDS

It must be acknowledged that the RNR model could be delivered in a negative manner. It could simply involve identifying youths' risk level and needs and placing them in programs designed to address specific needs. However, this is not consistent with the model's underlying philosophy. As discussed throughout this chapter, the model encourages professionals to treat youths in a humane and caring manner. The ultimate goal is to address youths' needs and direct them toward a path leading to a responsible, productive, and happy life.

References

Andrews, D. A., & Bonta, J. (2010). *The psychology of criminal conduct* (5th ed.). New Providence, NJ: Anderson.

Andrews, D. A., Bonta, J., & Hoge, R. D. (1990). Classification for effective rehabilitation: Rediscovering psychology. *Criminal Justice and Behavior, 17*, 19–52. http://dx.doi.org/10.1177/0093854890017001004

Andrews, D. A., Bonta, J., & Wormith, J. S. (2011). The risk-need-responsivity (RNR) model: Does adding the good lives model contribute to effective crime prevention? *Criminal Justice and Behavior, 38*, 735–755. http://dx.doi.org/10.1177/0093854811406356

Andrews, D. A., & Dowden, C. (2005). Managing correctional treatment for reduced recidivism: A meta-analytic review of program integrity. *Legal and Criminological Psychology, 10*, 173–187. http://dx.doi.org/10.1348/135532505X36723

Andrews, D. A., & Dowden, C. (2007). The risk-need-responsivity model of assessment and in prevention and corrections: Crime prevention jurisprudence. *Canadian Journal of Criminology and Criminal Justice, 49*, 439–464. http://dx.doi.org/10.3138/cjccj.49.4.439

Andrews, D. A., Dowden, C., & Gendreau, P. (1999). *Clinically relevant and psychologically informed approaches to reduced reoffending: A meta-analytic study of human services, risk, need, responsivity and other concerns in justice contexts.* Ottawa, Ontario, Canada: Department of Psychology, Carleton University.

Andrews, D. A., Zinger, I., Hoge, R. D., Bonta, J., Gendreau, P., & Cullen, F. T. (1990). Does correctional treatment work? A psychologically informed meta-analysis. *Criminology, 28*, 369–404. http://dx.doi.org/10.1111/j.1745-9125.1990.tb01330.x

Aos, S., Phipps, P., Barnoski, R., & Lieb, R. (2001). *The comparative costs and benefits of programs to reduce crimes.* Olympia: Washington State Institute for Public Policy.

Augimeri, L. K., Koegl, C. J., Webster, C. D., & Levene, K. S. (2001). *Early Assessment Risk List for Boys: EARL-20B Version 2.* Toronto, Ontario, Canada: Earlscourt Child and Family Centre.

Barnoski, R. (2004). *Outcome evaluation of Washington State's research-based programs for juvenile offenders.* Olympia: Washington State Institute for Public Policy.

Bonta, J., & Andrews, D. A. (2010). Viewing offender assessment and rehabilitation through the lens of the risk-need-responsivity model. In J. McDeil, P. Raynor, & C. Trotter (Eds.), *Offender supervision: New directions in theory, research, and practice* (pp. 9–40). New York, NY: Willan.

Borum, R., Bartel, P., & Forth, A. (2005). *Structured Assessment of Violence Risk in Youth (SAVRY).* In T. Grisso, T. Vincent, & D. Seagrave (Eds.), *Mental health screening and assessment in juvenile justice* (pp. 295–310). New York, NY: Guilford Press.

Borum, R., & Verhaagen, D. (2006). *Assessing and managing violence risk in youth.* New York, NY: Guilford Press.

Bottcher, J., & Ezell, M. E. (2005). Examining the effectiveness of boot camps: A randomized experiment with a long-term follow-up. *Journal of Research in Crime and Delinquency, 42*, 309–332. http://dx.doi.org/10.1177/0022427804271918

Chu, M., Daffern, J., Thomas, S., & Lim, J. Y. (2012). Violence risk and gang affiliation in youth offenders: A recidivism study. *Psychology, Crime, and Law, 18*, 299–315. http://dx.doi.org/10.1080/1068316X.2010.481626

Cottle, C., Lee, R. J., & Heilbrun, K. (2001). The prediction of criminal recidivism in juveniles: A meta-analysis. *Criminal Justice and Behavior, 28*, 367–394. http://dx.doi.org/10.1177/0093854801028003005

Doob, A. N., & Webster, C. (2003). Sentence severity and crime: Accepting the null hypothesis. In M. Tonry (Ed.), *Crime and justice: A review of research* (Vol. 39, pp. 143–195). Chicago, IL: University of Chicago Press.

Drake, E. K., Aos, S., & Miller, M. G. (2009). Evidence-based public policy options to reduce crime and criminal justice costs: Implications in Washington State. *Victims and Offenders, 4*, 170–196. http://dx.doi.org/10.1080/15564880802612615

Farrington, D. P. (1998). Predictors, causes and correlates of male youth violence. *Crime and Justice, 24*, 421–475. http://dx.doi.org/10.1086/449284

Farrington, D. P. (2005). *Integrated developmental and life-course theories of offending.* New Brunswick, NJ: Transaction.

Farrington, D. P., Coid, J. W., Harnett, L., Jolliffe, D., Soteriu, N., Turner, R., & West, D. J. (2006). *Criminal careers up to age 50 and life success up to age 48: New findings from the Cambridge study in delinquent development*. London, England: Home Office Research, Development and Statistics Directorate.

Farrington, D. P., & Welsh, B. C. (2006). *Saving children from a life of crime: Early risk factors and effective interventions*. http://dx.doi.org/10.1093/acprof:oso/9780195304091.001.0001

Gendreau, P., Little, T., & Goggin, C. E. (1996). A meta-analysis of the predictors of adult offender recidivism: What works! *Criminology, 34*, 575–608. http://dx.doi.org/10.1111/j.1745-9125.1996.tb01220.x

Goldstein, A. P. (2004). Evaluations of effectiveness. In A. P. Goldstein, R. Nensen, B. Daleflod, & M. Kalt (Eds.), *New perspectives on aggression replacement training* (pp. 230–244). Chichester, England: Wiley.

Greenwood, P. W. (2005). *Changing lives: Delinquency prevention as crime-control policy*. http://dx.doi.org/10.7208/chicago/9780226307237.001.0001

Grisso, T. (2005). Why we need mental health screening and assessment in juvenile justice programs. In T. Grisso, G. Vincent, & D. Seagrave (Eds.), *Mental health screening and assessment in juvenile justice* (pp. 3–21). New York, NY: Guilford Press.

Grisso, T., Vincent, G., & Seagrave, D. (Eds.). (2005). *Mental health screening and assessment in juvenile justice*. New York, NY: Guilford Press.

Grove, W. M., Zald, D. H., Lebow, B. S., Snitz, B. E., & Nelson, C. (2000). Clinical versus mechanical prediction: A meta-analysis. *Psychological Assessment, 12*, 19–30. http://dx.doi.org/10.1037/1040-3590.12.1.19

Guerra, N. G., Kim, T. E., & Boxer, P. (2008). What works: Best practices with juvenile offenders. In R. D. Hoge, N. G. Guerra, & P. Boxer (Eds.), *Treating the juvenile offender* (pp. 79–102). New York, NY: Guilford Press.

Guerra, N. G., & Leaf, C. (2008). Implementing treatment programs in community and institutional settings. In R. D. Hoge, N. G. Guerra, & P. Boxer (Eds.), *Treating the juvenile offender* (pp. 103–126). New York, NY: Guilford Press.

Heilbrun, K. (1997). Prediction versus management models relevant to risk assessment: The importance of legal decision-making context. *Law and Human Behavior, 21*, 347–359. http://dx.doi.org/10.1023/A:1024851017947

Heilbrun, K. (2010). *Violence risk assessment in adults*. New York, NY: Oxford University Press.

Heilbrun, K., Lee, R., & Cottle, C. (2005). Risk factors and intervention outcomes: Meta-analyses of juvenile offending. In K. Heilbrun, N. Goldstein, & R. Redding (Eds.), *Juvenile delinquency: Prevention, assessment and interventions* (pp. 111–133). New York, NY: Oxford University Press.

Henggeler, S. W., Schoenwald, S. K., Borduin, C. M., Rowland, M. D., & Cunningham, P. B. (1998). *Multisystemic treatment of antisocial behavior in children and adolescents*. New York, NY: Guilford Press.

Hilton, Z. N., Harris, G. T., & Rice, R. E. (2006). Sixty-six years of research on the clinical vs. actuarial prediction of violence. *Counseling Psychologist, 34*, 400–409. http://dx.doi.org/10.1177/0011000005285877

Hoge, R. D. (1999). An expanded role for psychological assessments in juvenile justice systems. *Criminal Justice and Behavior, 26*, 251–266. http://dx.doi.org/10.1177/0093854899026002006

Hoge, R. D. (2001). *The juvenile offender: Theory, research, and applications*. http://dx.doi.org/10.1007/978-1-4615-1563-0

Hoge, R. D. (2005). Youth Level of Service/Case Management Inventory. In T. Grisso, T. Vincent, & D. Seagrave (Eds.), *Mental health screening and assessment in juvenile justice* (pp. 283–294). New York, NY: Guilford Press.

Hoge, R. D. (2008). Assessment in juvenile justice systems. In R. D. Hoge, N. G. Guerra, & P. Boxer (Eds.), *Treating the juvenile offender* (pp. 54–75). New York, NY: Guilford Press.

Hoge, R. D. (2010). Developmental perspective on offending. In J. M. Brown & E. A. Campbell (Eds.), *The Cambridge handbook of forensic psychology* (pp. 34–42). http://dx.doi.org/10.1017/CBO9780511730290.004

Hoge, R. D., & Andrews, D. A. (1996). *Assessing the youthful offender: Issues and techniques*. http://dx.doi.org/10.1007/978-1-4757-9296-6

Hoge, R. D., & Andrews, D. A. (2010). *Evaluation of risk for violence in juveniles*. http://dx.doi.org/10.1093/med/9780195370416.001.0001

Hoge, R. D., & Andrews, D. A. (2011). *Youth Level of Service/Case Management Inventory user's manual*. North Tonawanda, NY: Multi-Health Systems.

Hoge, R. D., Vincent, G. M., & Guy, L. S. (2012). Prediction and risk/needs assessment. In R. Loeber & D. P. Farrington (Eds.), *From juvenile delinquency to adult crime* (pp. 50–183). New York, NY: Oxford University Press.

Jung, S., & Rawana, E. P. (1999). Risk and need assessment of juvenile offenders. *Criminal Justice and Behavior, 26*, 69–89. http://dx.doi.org/10.1177/0093854899026001004

Kempinen, C. A., & Kurlychek, M. C. (2003). An outcome evaluation of Pennsylvania's boot camp: Does rehabilitative programming within a disciplinary setting reduce recidivism? *Crime and Delinquency, 49*, 581–602. http://dx.doi.org/10.1177/0011128703252664

Koehler, J. A., Losel, F., Akoensi, T. D., & Humphreys, D. K. (2013). A systematic review and meta-analysis of the effects of young offender treatment programs in Europe. *Journal of Experimental Criminology, 9*, 19–43. http://dx.doi.org/10.1007/s11292-012-9159-7

Levene, K. S., Augimeri, L. K., Pepler, D., Walsh, M., Webster, C. D., & Koegl, C. J. (2001). *Early Assessment Risk List for Girls: EARL-21G Version 1*. Toronto, Ontario, Canada: Earlscourt Child and Family Centre.

Lipsey, M. W. (1995). What do we learn from 400 research studies on the effectiveness of treatment with juvenile delinquents? In J. McGuire (Ed.), *What works: Reducing reoffending* (pp. 63–78). Chichester, England: Wiley.

Lipsey, M. W., & Wilson, D. B. (1998). Effective intervention for serious juvenile offenders: A synthesis of research. In R. Loeber & D. P. Farrington (Eds.), *Serious and violent juvenile offenders: Risk factors and successful interventions* (pp. 313–345). Thousand Oaks, CA: Sage.

Loeber, R., & Farrington, D. P. (Eds.). (1998). *Serious and violent juvenile offenders: Risk factors and successful interventions*. Thousand Oaks, CA: Sage.

Loeber, R., & Farrington, D. P. (2000). Young children who commit crime: Epidemiology, developmental origins, risk factors, early interventions, and policy implications. *Development and Psychopathology, 12*, 737–762. http://dx.doi.org/10.1017/S0954579400004107

McAra, L., & McVie, S. (2007). Youth justice? The impact of system contact on patterns of desistance from offending. *European Journal of Criminology, 4*, 315–345. http://dx.doi.org/10.1177/1477370807077186

McGrath, A. W., & Thompson, A. P. (2012). The relative predictive validity of static and dynamic domain scores in risk-need assessment of juvenile offenders. *Criminal Justice and Behavior, 39*, 250–263. http://dx.doi.org/10.1177/0093854811431917

Miller, W. R., & Rollnick, S. (2002). *Motivational interviewing* (2nd ed.). New York, NY: Guilford Press.

Mulvey, E. P., & Iselin, A.-M. R. (2008). Improving professional judgments of risk and amenability in juvenile justice. *Future of Children, 18*, 35–57. http://dx.doi.org/10.1353/foc.0.0012

Petitclerc, A., Gatti, U., Vitaro, F., & Tremblay, R. E. (2013). Effects of juvenile court exposure on crime in young adulthood. *Journal of Child Psychology and Psychiatry, 54*, 291–297. http://dx.doi.org/10.1111/j.1469-7610.2012.02616.x

Prochaska, J. O., DiClemente, C. C., & Norcross, J. C. (1992). In search of how people change. Applications to addictive behaviors. *American Psychologist, 47*, 1102–1114. http://dx.doi.org/10.1037/0003-066X.47.9.1102

Redding, R. E., & Arrigo, B. (2005). Multicultural perspectives on delinquency among African-American youths: Etiology and intervention. In C. L. Frisby & C. R. Reynolds (Eds.), *A comprehensive handbook of multicultural school psychology* (pp. 710–743). New York, NY: Wiley.

Rennie, C. E., & Dolan, M. C. (2010). The significance of protective factors in the assessment of risk. *Criminal Behaviour and Mental Health, 20*, 8–22. http://dx.doi.org/10.1002/cbm.750

Romani, C. J., Morgan, R. D., Gross, N. R., & McDonald, B. R. (2012). Treating criminal behavior: Is the bang worth the buck? *Psychology, Public Policy, and Law, 18*, 144–165. http://dx.doi.org/10.1037/a0024714

Rowe, D. C., Flannery, A. T., & Flannery, D. J. (1995). Sex differences in crime: Do means and within-sex variation have similar causes? *Journal of Research in Crime and Delinquency, 32*, 84–100. http://dx.doi.org/10.1177/0022427895032001004

Sexton, T. L., & Alexander, J. F. (2000). *Functional family therapy*. Washington, DC: U.S. Department of Justice, Office of Juvenile Justice and Delinquency Prevention, Office of Justice Programs.

Simourd, L., & Andrews, D. A. (1994). Correlates of delinquency: A look at gender differences. *Forum on Corrections Research, 6*, 26–31.

Smith, P. C., Gendreau, P., & Swartz, K. (2009). Validating the principles of effective intervention: A systematic review of the contributions of meta-analysis in the field of corrections. *Victims and Offenders, 4*, 148–169. http://dx.doi.org/10.1080/15564880802612581

Steinberg, L. (2009). Adolescent development and juvenile justice. *Annual Review of Clinical Psychology, 5*, 459–485. http://dx.doi.org/10.1146/annurev.clinpsy.032408.153603

Steinberg, L., Chung, H. L., & Little, M. (2004). Reentry of young offenders from the justice system. *Youth Violence and Juvenile Justice, 2*, 21–38. http://dx.doi.org/10.1177/1541204003260045

Thornberry, T. P., Giordano, P. C., Uggen, C., Matsuda, M., Masten, A. S., Bulten, E., & Donker, A. G. (2012). Explanations for offending. In R. Loeber & D. P. Farrington (Eds.), *From juvenile delinquency to adult crime* (pp. 47–85). New York, NY: Oxford University Press.

Tonry, M. (2008). Learning from the limitations of deterrence research. In M. Tonry (Ed.), *Crime and justice: A review of research* (Vol. 37, pp. 279–311). http://dx.doi.org/10.1086/524825

Vieira, T. A., Skilling, T. A., & Peterson-Badali, M. (2009). Matching court-ordered services with treatment needs: Predicting treatment success with young offenders. *Criminal Justice and Behavior, 36*, 385–401. http://dx.doi.org/10.1177/0093854808331249

Vincent, G., & Grisso, T. (2005). A developmental perspective on adolescent personality, psychopathology, and delinquency. In T. Grisso,

T. Vincent, & D. Seagrave (Eds.), *Mental health screening and assessment in juvenile justice* (pp. 22–43). New York, NY: Guilford Press.

Vincent, G., Guy, L. S., & Grisso, T. (2012). *Risk assessment in juvenile justice: A guidebook for implementation.* Washington, DC: National Juvenile Defender Center.

Vincent, G., Terry, A., & Maney, S. (2009). Risk/needs tools for antisocial behavior and violence among youthful populations. In J. Andrade (Ed.), *Handbook of violence risk assessment and treatment for forensic mental health practitioners* (pp. 337–424). New York, NY: Springer.

Ward, T. (2010). The good lives model of offender rehabilitation: Basic assumptions, aetiological commitments, and practice implications. In F. McNeil, P. Raynor, & C. Trotter (Eds.), *Offender supervision: New directions in theory, research, and practice* (pp. 41–64). New York, NY: Willan.

Ward, T., & Stewart, C. (2003). Criminogenic needs and human needs: A theoretical model. *Psychology, Crime, and Law, 9*, 125–143. http://dx.doi.org/10.1080/1068316031000116247

Ward, T., & Willis, G. (2010). Ethical issues in forensic and correctional research. *Aggression and Violent Behavior, 15*, 399–409. http://dx.doi.org/10.1016/j.avb.2010.07.002

Welsh, B. C., Lipsey, M. W., Rivara, F. P., Hawkins, J. D., Aos, S., & Hollis-Peel, M. E. (2012). Promoting change, changing lives: Effective prevention and intervention to reduce serious offending. In R. Loeber & D. P. Farrington (Eds.), *From juvenile delinquency to adult crime* (pp. 245–277). New York, NY: Oxford.

Werner, E. E. (2000). Protective factors and individual resilience. In J. P. Shonkoff & S. P. Meisels (Eds.), *Handbook of early childhood intervention* (pp. 115–132). http://dx.doi.org/10.1017/CBO9780511529320.008

Wilson, H. A., & Hoge, R. D. (2013). Diverting our attention to what works: Evaluating the effectiveness of a youth diversion program. *Youth Violence and Juvenile Justice, 11*, 313–331. http://dx.doi.org/10.1177/1541204012473132

Worling, J. R., & Curwen, M. A. (2001). *Estimate of Risk of Adolescent Sexual Offense Recidivism (ERASOR).* Toronto, Ontario, Canada: Thistletown Regional Centre.

CHAPTER 10

JUVENILE PSYCHOPATHY: APPROPRIATE AND INAPPROPRIATE USES IN LEGAL PROCEEDINGS

Gina M. Vincent, Eva R. Kimonis, and Alisa Clark

Psychopathy is a personality disorder that involves distinct interpersonal, affective, and behavioral symptoms (Hare, 2003). What distinguishes the psychopathic individual from the broader set of antisocial individuals is a specific symptom pattern that pervades nearly all domains of life. Interpersonally, psychopathic individuals are arrogant and deceitful; affectively, they lack empathy and guilt; behaviorally, they are irresponsible, impulsive, sensation seeking, and prone to delinquency and criminality (Cleckley, 1941/1976). Thus, a psychopathic individual has both the antisocial behavioral problems seen in most serious offenders and a manipulative interpersonal style and callous-unemotional (CU) traits that limit their ability to bond with others. Substantial research with adults, including meta-analytic and longitudinal studies (e.g., Leistico, Salekin, DeCoster, & Rogers, 2008; Salekin, Rogers, & Sewell, 1996) using versions of the Hare Psychopathy Scales,[1] has demonstrated that psychopathy is a strong predictor (with a moderate effect size) of persistent violence and criminal activity.

In the past 15 years, researchers have directed considerable attention to the study and identification of psychopathy among children and adolescents, with essentially two primary interests in mind. First, because psychopathy is a personality disorder in adults, it has been studied and defined in that manner in youths. Symptoms of personality disorders are rigid, inflexible, and maladaptive ways of relating that are stable across time. Therefore, if an individual is a psychopath as an adult, he or she would almost certainly have had psychopathic traits as a child. The impetus for the examination of psychopathy in youths is in this sense (a) to determine its etiology, (b) to identify possible early intervention strategies for the disorder, and (c) to identify the factors that put youths at highest risk for chronic violent behavior.

Second, because of the complications in making personality disorder diagnoses in young people, psychopathy (or, more accurately, psychopathic traits or features) has been described as simply a risk factor that puts young offenders at high risk for displaying psychopathic traits as adults and for reoffending or engaging in violence in the future. In light of the research with adult offenders, it stands to reason that psychopathic traits in youths would be a strong predictor of violence during adolescence. The difference between viewing psychopathy as a risk factor and viewing it as a personality disorder is that a risk factor may be seen as dynamic, whereas personality disorders are static. Psychopathy could be seen as a dynamic risk factor because, among a large percentage of adolescents who exhibit the related behaviors and characteristics, they are of a transitional nature. In this case, the presence of psychopathy would signal a need for intensive intervention (Forth, Kosson, & Hare, 2003).

[1]The Psychopathy Checklist (PCL) and its revised version (PCL–R; Hare, 1991, 2003) and the Psychopathy Checklist: Screening Version (Hart, Hare, & Cox, 1995).

http://dx.doi.org/10.1037/14643-010
APA Handbook of Psychology and Juvenile Justice, K. Heilbrun (Editor-in-Chief)

Regardless of whether psychopathy is seen as a personality disorder or a dynamic risk factor, the psychological construct of psychopathy is of legal relevance for juveniles primarily because of its presumed robust association with serious and violent criminality, which is seen with adult offenders. Indeed, the association among adult offenders is so robust that forensic evaluators should consider psychopathy as a part of any comprehensive assessment of community violence risk when dealing with adults (Hart, 1998; Vincent & Hart, 2012). As such, courts may regard psychopathy as relevant to any decisions with juvenile defendants that involve the protection of public safety (e.g., transfer to adult court or reverse transfer, life without parole sentences, sex offender commitment). Whether these legal uses of juvenile psychopathy can be seen as appropriate rests in part on whether psychopathy (a) can be reliably and accurately assessed in children and adolescents, (b) relates to risk for serious reoffending in young people and over what timeframe, (c) is treatable, and (d) is generally static or dynamic.

In this chapter, we review the current legal uses of juvenile psychopathy and consider whether they are warranted in light of the psychological research evidence. The chapter extends and broadens prior reviews of the research on juvenile psychopathy (Edens, Campbell, & Weir, 2007; Leistico et al., 2008; Lynam & Gudonis, 2005) by including the growing literature on the study of CU traits in children. We conclude with recommendations and precautions for the use of psychopathy in legal settings with adolescent defendants.

DEFINITION OF PSYCHOPATHY

Psychopathy is a multidimensional personality disorder characterized by disturbances in feeling, behaving, and relating to others. Psychopathy has been studied and described as both a dimensional or continuous construct and a binary or taxonic construct (Edens, Marcus, Lilienfeld, & Poythress, 2006; Vasey, Kotov, Frick, & Loney, 2005). Dimensionally, people vary in the presence and severity of psychopathic traits. Sound assessments of psychopathy have continuous scores for the total number of psychopathic traits, as well as continuous scores within each major symptom domain (e.g., interpersonal, affective, and behavioral). The higher the score, the more likely the person is to be aggressive, get in trouble with the law, or have other societal problems. Dichotomously, for adults, assessments of psychopathy (in forensic settings, most commonly the Hare Psychopathy Scales) also have cutoff scores to determine who is and who is not a psychopath. An individual must score relatively high in all the major symptom domains to meet the criteria for psychopathy.

The assessment issues are somewhat different when applied to children and adolescents. The term *callous-unemotional* has been used to describe the affective deficit dimension of psychopathy. The affective dimension of psychopathy was viewed by Cleckley (1941/1976), one of the first prominent clinicians who defined the disorder, as the hallmark of psychopathy. Research on juvenile psychopathy has identified non-normative levels of CU traits as the root of psychopathic tendencies in children and adolescents because these traits can be detected early and have shown robust links to antisocial behavior over time (see Frick, Ray, Thornton, & Kahn, 2014). Children and adolescents with non-normative CU traits possess distinct causal factors leading to their problem behavior and show a distinct pattern of severe, chronic, and aggressive conduct problems (CP) that are resistant to traditional mental health interventions. Youths who exhibit significant and impairing patterns of co-occurring CU traits with CP (symptoms consistent with oppositional defiant disorder or conduct disorder), as opposed to CU traits alone, are at highest risk for developing adult psychopathy (Frick, 1995, 2006; Lynam, 1996).

Based on this body of research, the *Diagnostic and Statistical Manual of Mental Disorders, Fifth Edition* (*DSM–5;* American Psychiatric Association, 2013) integrated CU traits into its criteria for the diagnosis of conduct disorder by including the specifier "with limited prosocial emotions." The specifier is used when a person meeting full diagnostic criteria for conduct disorder persistently (over at least 12 months) exhibits two or more of the following characteristics in multiple relationships or settings:

1. *Lack of remorse or guilt:* Does not feel bad or guilty when he or she does something wrong (except if expressing remorse when caught or facing punishment).
2. *Callous–lack of empathy:* Disregards and is unconcerned about the feelings of others.
3. *Unconcerned about performance:* Does not show concern about poor or problematic performance at school or work or in other important activities.
4. *Shallow or deficient affect:* Does not express feelings or show emotions to others, except in ways that seem shallow or superficial (e.g., can turn emotions on or off quickly) or when they are used for gain (e.g., to manipulate or intimidate others). (American Psychiatric Association, 2013, pp. 549–550)

Studies supporting the development of the *DSM–5* criteria indicated that youths meeting the diagnostic threshold of two or more CU symptoms showed significantly greater impairment on external criteria such as antisocial behavior and aggression than youths with only one or no CU traits. An estimated 12% to 46% (depending on the assessment method) of youths diagnosed with conduct disorder present with non-normative CU traits (Kahn, Frick, Youngstrom, Findling, & Youngstrom, 2012; Pardini, Stepp, Hipwell, Stouthamer-Loeber, & Loeber, 2012; Rowe, Costello, Angold, Copeland, & Maughan, 2010).

RELEVANT HISTORY

The term psychopathy has been used by many different people in many different ways over the years; also, the disorder has had many different names. The modern concept of psychopathy can be traced back to the early 1800s (Arrigo & Shipley, 2001; Berrios, 1996). In the first half of the 20th century, a series of clinical descriptions (e.g., Cleckley, 1941/1976; Karpman, 1961; McCord & McCord, 1956) refined the concept and laid a foundation for subsequent scientific research. The second half of the 20th century saw increasing consensus in clinical descriptions of the disorder but differences in the label. For example, in North America, the primary terms used are *psychopathy, antisocial personality disorder,* and *sociopathy* (or *sociopathic personality disorder*). Outside North America, the term commonly used is *dissocial personality disorder*.

In 1991, Hare produced a manual for the Psychopathy Checklist—Revised (PCL–R) that provided a fairly objective assessment with semistandardized administration procedures and thorough item descriptions with rating schemes for 20 psychopathic traits. With respect to standard psychiatric nosological systems, the *Diagnostic and Statistical Manual of Mental Disorders, Fourth Edition, Text Revision* (*DSM–IV–TR*; American Psychiatric Association, 2000) instead used the term antisocial personality disorder and listed diagnostic criteria that largely emphasized behavioral traits of the disorder. At a conceptual or linguistic level, the various terms are synonyms—they just have different identifiers (or operational definitions) for the same disorder (Vincent & Hart, 2012; Widiger, 2006). Indeed, the *DSM–IV–TR* stated clearly that antisocial personality disorder is “also known as psychopathy or dissocial personality disorder” (American Psychiatric Association, 2000, p. 702). As a result of the vast research and the difficulty in differentiating the severity of problems between males in forensic settings using the criteria for antisocial personality disorder, the PCL–R became the assessment instrument most widely accepted for use in forensic evaluations (Archer, Buffington-Vollum, Stredny, & Handel, 2006). Moreover, it provided researchers with a reliable means of studying the course of the disorder and pattern of violence in adults.

Legal Uses in Adult Criminal Courts

The psycholegal usage of psychopathy in juvenile proceedings has its roots in criminal court. Therefore, it is important to review what has transpired for adult defendants in the criminal courts to set the historical context for current juvenile proceedings. Several surveys of case law have been conducted to examine the use of psychopathy assessments in U.S. courts from 1991 to 2004 (DeMatteo & Edens, 2006; T. Walsh & Walsh, 2006) and from 2005 through 2011 (DeMatteo et al., 2014) and in Canadian courts (Lloyd, Clark, & Forth, 2010; Zinger & Forth, 1998). The use of psychopathy assessments in U.S. court cases has increased considerably over the years. To illustrate, T. Walsh and Walsh (2006) identified 76 cases from 1991 to 2004, 90% of which were from 2000 onward. Since 2005, 348 cases mentioned the PCL–R specifically, with the largest increases in number of mentions in 2010 and 2011 (DeMatteo et al., 2014). Most cases have occurred in state appellate courts.

In adult proceedings, the PCL–R has most commonly been introduced for offenders with a history of violence to determine their risk for violence in the future. According to DeMatteo et al. (2014), the majority of cases using the PCL–R since 2005 have been those with sexually violent predators (62%) and parole hearings (24%). Fortunately, use of the PCL–R for capital sentencing appears to have decreased (only 3.4% of cases since 2005). In *United States v. Taylor* (2004), the Indiana Northern U.S. district court held that admission in a capital trial of a defendant's psychopathy diagnosis to comment on future dangerousness was improper. In sum, the use of psychopathy in criminal court translates to whether to impose long-term incarceration or whether to release an individual into the community.

Among the more recent cases, the majority introduced the PCL–R as one of a number of assessments conducted for a comprehensive risk assessment of the offender (DeMatteo et al., 2014). The most common narrative explanation of PCL–R scores has been dimensional, to establish risk for violence: specifically, labeling the individual as a high or low scorer or as highly likely to reoffend. However, DeMatteo et al. (2014) noted that there are still circumstances in legal cases in which it has been stated inappropriately that high scorers have a particular probability of reoffending (e.g., the defendant is approximately 80% likely to reoffend violently). Conversely, a number of cases (19%) have used the PCL–R diagnostically, stating the offender was or was not a psychopath.

It is unclear from the reviews how often psychopathy has been introduced to restrict access to treatment in adult cases, although there are circumstances in which this has occurred. In the case of *Stanley v. Litscher* (2000), for example, the U.S. Court of Appeals, Seventh Circuit, upheld the Wisconsin Department of Corrections' decision to deny the offender institutional sex offender treatment because he had psychopathy, which traditional treatment programs do not benefit and for which they may in fact be contraindicated. Rarely has the PCL–R been introduced to help establish adjudicative competence or criminal responsibility. Many different courts over the years have decided that psychopathy does not mitigate criminal responsibility (see DeMatteo & Edens, 2006; Lyon & Ogloff, 2000; T. Walsh & Walsh, 2006).

Increasing Interest in Adolescents

Empirical evidence from extensive longitudinal research has established that a small proportion (around 6%) of male delinquents will become chronically antisocial and proceed to commit more than 50% of all crime; these individuals have been termed *chronic offenders* (Farrington, 1995; Farrington & West, 1993; Roberts, Caspi, & Moffitt, 2001). Because the roots of serious offending are found in childhood or adolescence, early identification of chronic offenders has become of increasing interest to the juvenile justice system. Clinicians have more and more frequently been asked to conduct assessments of delinquents' likelihood of future harm to others as a result of the juvenile justice system's obligation to protect public safety (Grisso, 2004). As Grisso (2004) noted, this obligation functions to protect society from the immediate risk of harm from dangerous youths and to reduce recidivism by providing interventions to youths involved with the juvenile justice system.

These assessments can be relevant primarily for two kinds of legal decisions. First, disposition decisions require the court to consider both the most appropriate sanctions and interventions with the best potential for reducing the likelihood of delinquent behaviors in the future. The most dangerous youths should receive the most punitive sanctions and most intensive interventions. Second, transfer decisions designed to waive juveniles to adult court generally require evidence about the youth's likelihood of dangerousness to others, treatment amenability, and level of maturity. If a youth is likely to be dangerous and is likely to be resistant to rehabilitation in the juvenile justice system, transfer to adult court is nearly inevitable.

The consistent themes in both transfer and disposition decisions are dangerousness and treatment needs. Thus, for violence risk assessments forensic evaluators require tools capable of assessing the likelihood of violence in the future, the presence of childhood psychopathology, the relationship between violence and psychopathology, and treatment amenability. In light of the use of psychopathy assessments to help answer these questions in criminal court settings, it is not surprising that forensic evaluators have turned to psychopathy as a model for assessing these issues in adolescent defendants (Vincent, 2006). In fact, use of the term psychopathy in juvenile proceedings dates back to the 1970s (Viljoen, MacDougall, Gagnon, & Douglas, 2010).

EMPIRICAL EVIDENCE AND LEGAL USES OF JUVENILE PSYCHOPATHY

A considerable number of studies have been conducted on psychopathy or psychopathic traits in young people since the late 1990s. We begin this section by reviewing the assessment methods available for both adolescents and children (in which the emphasis is on CU traits) and evidence for the validity of assessments from latent trait statistical analyses and studies of their correlates. Then we cover evidence specific to the questions as to whether juvenile psychopathy has evidence for stability and evidence for use as a risk factor.

Juvenile Psychopathy Assessments

Several instruments have been developed to assess psychopathic traits, or, specifically, the deficient affect dimension (i.e., CU traits), in children or adolescents. These instruments vary in their purpose. Some were designed for clinical use to assist with risk management or to implement early intervention strategies, and others have been used primarily for research, at least for the time being. The assessment methods also vary, ranging from expert clinical rating scales to informant rating scales to self-report scales. Expert clinical rating scales require qualified professionals to make judgments about the presence and severity of symptoms on the basis of examinee interviews and extensive collateral information. Informant rating scales call for ratings of multiple characteristics of an examinee on a Likert-type scale by people associated with the examinee, such as a parent or teacher. Several of these measures are direct downward extensions of the most widely used expert clinical rating scale for adults, the PCL–R (Hare, 2003).

In this section, we provide a brief review of the instruments designed specifically for the purpose of measuring psychopathic traits in youths. Other scales have been created to measure psychopathic traits by using items from youth assessment instruments that were originally designed for different purposes (e.g., general personality inventories, psychiatric symptoms). They include the Modified Childhood Psychopathy Scale (Lynam, 1997), an informant rating scale and self-report inventory derived from the Child Behavior Checklist (Achenbach, 1991) and the common-language version of the California Child Q-Set (Block & Block, 1980); the Psychopathy Content Scale (Murrie & Cornell, 2000), a self-report tool derived from the Millon Adolescent Clinical Inventory; and the NEO Psychopathy Resemblance Index (Lynam & Widiger, 2001), a self-report tool derived from the NEO Personality Inventory. We do not review these scales here.

Expert rating scale: Psychopathy Checklist: Youth Version. The PCL:YV (Forth et al., 2003) is a downward extension of the PCL–R that is used to provide a dimensional assessment of the prototypical psychopath among adolescents ages 12 to 18 years. The PCL:YV can be used for clinical assessments of adolescents. Its authors have specified that the it should be used to identify "youth who represent a more serious management problem within institutions, who need intensive intervention, and who require more resources for risk management in the community" (Forth et al., 2003, p. 17). Like the PCL–R, the PCL:YV is an expert symptom rating scale that defines psychopathy along interpersonal, affective, and behavioral symptom clusters.

PCL:YV assessments are administered through a 60- to 90-minute semistructured interview and a thorough review of collateral information, including psychosocial histories, juvenile offense records, and institutional records at a minimum. It consists of 20 items scored on a 3-point scale (0 = *item does not apply*, 1 = *item applies somewhat*, 2 = *item definitely applies*) on the basis of each symptom's pervasiveness, severity, and chronicity. For the most part, the items do not differ from those of the PCL–R, with the exception of a few items that were adjusted to be developmentally appropriate for youths. These items (e.g., Parasitic Lifestyle, Early Behavioral Problems) were modified to reflect adolescents' experiences and development, including the greater influence of family, peers, and school on their lives. For example, the PCL–R item referring to many short-term marital relationships was revised in the PCL:YV to reflect a general instability in interpersonal relationships.

The PCL:YV normative sample (*N* > 2,000) consisted largely of White boys, primarily from secure custody settings or forensic psychiatric facilities, but it also contained a fair number of African Americans and youths from probation settings. A small proportion of the sample came from community settings; only about 12% of the sample were girls.

In research settings, PCL:YV total scores have demonstrated high interrater reliability (*r*s = .90–.96) and internal consistency regardless of the population tested (i.e., institutional, probation, or community; Forth et al. 2003). Scores are dimensional, meaning that they represent the level or severity of psychopathic traits and can be calculated for both total scores and symptom cluster scores. The PCL:YV cannot be used to make categorical classifications of psychopathy or violence risk on the basis of cutoff scores. Results of confirmatory factor analytic studies (Forth et al., 2003) have suggested that the PCL:YV has two valid test structures: (a) the Hare 20-item, four-factor model consisting of interpersonal, affective, impulsive–behavioral style, and antisocial behavior factors and (b) a 13-item, three-factor model, which includes the same first three factors but eliminates seven items related to specific criminogenic behavior (the antisocial behavior factor).

Consistent with findings from adult psychopathy studies, PCL:YV scores among youths have demonstrated strong associations with symptoms of disruptive behavior disorders (Kosson, Cyterski, Steuerwald, Neumann, & Walker-Matthews, 2002; Rogers, Johansen, Chang, & Salekin, 1997), attention deficit hyperactivity disorder (Forth & Burke, 1998), and substance abuse (Mailloux, Forth, & Kroner, 1997). High-scoring adolescent offenders have also shown anomalies in executive functions related to impulsivity (Roussy & Toupin, 2000).

Informant rating scales and self-report inventories. The PCL:YV was designed for use with adolescents, not children. Two informant rating scales have been designed in an attempt to capture psychopathic traits in children, for whom interviewing strategies and self-reports are not the best approach. Instead, scales such as the Antisocial Process Screening Device (APSD; Frick & Hare, 2001) and the Inventory of Callous-Unemotional Traits (ICU; Frick, 2004; Kimonis et al., 2008) have created paired informant scales for parents and teachers to derive an assessment of psychopathic traits in a child. Both of these scales, as well as the Youth Psychopathic Traits Inventory (YPI; Andershed, Gustafson, Kerr, & Stattin, 2002), are also self-report inventories for use with adolescents. Self-report inventories were developed for examining psychopathic traits in adolescents because they require less time and training than the PCL:YV. At present, these scales are typically used for research purposes and not for clinical practice, although research into practical applications is underway.

Antisocial Process Screening Device. The APSD (Frick & Hare, 2001) is a 20-item informant rating scale (parent, teacher) designed to measure the CU, narcissism, and impulsivity dimensions of psychopathy in children ages 6 to 13. Like the PCL:YV, it also has a manual and is commercially available for clinical purposes. When available, parent and teacher ratings are combined, using the higher score on each item for a multi-informant assessment. The APSD is a dimensional rating scale designed for early identification so that preventive measures can be taken before tendencies lead to crime and other destructive behaviors. Like the PCL:YV, the APSD was patterned after the PCL–R, with 20 items rated on the same 3-point scale. Frick and Hare (2001) adapted each PCL–R item into an analogous behavioral rating item that was more applicable to children. Items are phrased as statements, which requires informants to rate the presence of psychopathic traits, such as whether the child's emotions seem shallow and whether the child seems to keep the same friends.

Confirmatory factor analytic findings have suggested that the APSD fits two valid test structures: (a) a two-factor model consisting of a CU factor and a second factor reflecting narcissistic traits and CP and (b) a three-factor model that divides narcissistic traits and impulsivity or CP into separate dimensions (Frick, Bodin, & Barry, 2000). APSD scores represent the level of psychopathic traits displayed by the child and should not be used to make categorical diagnoses of psychopathy on the basis of a cutoff score. Factor scores have demonstrated fair to good internal consistency (Frick & Hare, 2001). Correlations between parent and teacher ratings range from .26 to .40 (Frick, Lilienfeld, Ellis, Loney, & Silverthorn, 1999), which seems quite low but is consistent with common childhood emotional and behavioral problems (Youngstrom, Loeber, & Stouthamer-Loeber, 2000).

The APSD normative sample consisted of 1,120 elementary school children from the third, fourth, sixth, and seventh grades. Validation studies extended its use to children referred to outpatient mental health clinics in which some samples were 50% female (Frick, Barry, & Bodin, 2000; Frick, Bodin, & Barry, 2000). There is some evidence that APSD scores do not differ significantly between gender groups (Frick, O'Brien, Wootton, & McBurnett, 1994) but may vary according to ethnicity (Frick et al., 1999). The APSD detects a subtype of children with severe conduct disorder and low susceptibility to anxiety, and the factors have different correlates implying assessments of distinct traits; the CU factor is associated with cognitive and emotional deficits and the impulsivity factor with behavioral dysregulation (Pardini, Lochman, & Frick, 2003). APSD scores are also associated with symptoms of behavioral disorders and attention deficit hyperactivity disorder (Barry et al., 2000; Frick et al., 1994).

Self-Report Antisocial Process Screening Device. The Self-Report Antisocial Process Screening Device (APSD–SR; Frick & Hare, 2001; Muñoz & Frick, 2007) is a modification of the informant-rated APSD, which is designed to assess psychopathic traits as reported by the adolescent. APSD items were rewritten in the first person for adolescents to rate their own behaviors (Frick, Bodin, & Barry, 2000). According to confirmatory factor analytic studies, the APSD–SR taps three factors—Narcissism, Impulsivity, and CU traits (Vitacco, Rogers, & Neumann, 2003).

Across a total of 13 studies, the internal consistency of total scores ranges from moderate to good. The internal consistency is adequate for the Narcissism and Impulsivity scales, but marginal to poor for the CU scale (Muñoz & Frick, 2007; Poythress, Skeem, & Lilienfeld, 2006; Vaughn & Howard, 2005). APSD–SR scores are moderately correlated with parent ratings on the APSD, moderately stable across a 4-year period, and show the expected associations with measures of antisocial behavior (Frick, Kimonis, Dandreaux, & Farell, 2003; Muñoz & Frick, 2007). Studies of the APSD–SR have primarily used justice-involved adolescent samples with fairly equal numbers of boys and girls (Caputo, Frick, & Brodsky, 1999; Silverthorn, Frick, & Reynolds, 2001). There is some evidence that the APSD–SR designates a more serious type of juvenile offender with a high frequency of violent acts (Kruh, Frick, & Clements, 2005) and impaired emotional processing (Loney, Frick, Clements, Ellis, & Kerlin, 2003).

Youth Psychopathic Traits Inventory. The YPI (Andershed et al., 2002) is a 50-item self-report tool designed to measure psychopathic traits in community-based adolescents ages 12 to 18 years. The YPI was based on the three-factor model of psychopathy by excluding items related to criminogenic behaviors to be consistent with Cooke and Michie's (2001) view that psychopathy consists of three symptom dimensions related to personality deviance (Andershed et al., 2002). Individual items are rated on a 4-point scale and aggregated into one of 10 subscales (i.e., Dishonest Charm, Grandiosity, Lying, Manipulation, Remorselessness, Callousness, Unemotionality, Impulsivity, Irresponsibility, and Thrill-Seeking). These scales each map onto one of three domains: interpersonal (grandiose–manipulative), affective (callous-unemotional), and lifestyle–behavioral (impulsive–irresponsible), which are moderately to strongly correlated ($rs = .58$–$.64$, all $ps < .001$; Cauffman, Kimonis, Dmitrieva, & Monahan, 2009). The 10 scales ($\alpha s = .60$–$.91$), three domains, and YPI total score ($\alpha = .93$) demonstrate adequate to excellent internal consistency ($\alpha s = .73$–$.91$; Cauffman et al., 2009).

Using a sample of adolescent offenders, Skeem and Cauffman (2003) reported that YPI scores had good test–retest reliability, sound concurrent validity as indicated by correlations with PCL:YV scores and measures of anxiety, and predictive validity for self-reported institutional misbehaviors over a 1-month period. Comparisons between the YPI and PCL:YV have suggested that the two measures are moderately correlated ($rs = .24–.35$, $p < .001$; Cauffman et al., 2009; Skeem & Cauffman, 2003). YPI and PCL:YV factor scores are also moderately correlated ($rs = .30–.51$; Andershed, Hodgins, & Tengström, 2007). For both girls and boys, some evidence has shown that the impulsive–irresponsible dimension is related to increased drug and alcohol use (Hillege, Das, & de Ruiter, 2010).

Inventory of Callous-Unemotional Traits. The ICU (Frick, 2004) is a 24-item questionnaire designed to provide a comprehensive assessment of the shallow–deficient affect dimension of psychopathy that can be used in both offender and nonoffender samples. The scale has five versions: youth self-report, parent report, teacher report, and preschool versions of the parent- and teacher-report versions. The ICU is particularly useful when access to detailed file information is not available or if time and resources are limited. The ICU provides one of the most comprehensive measures of CU traits currently available (Frick, 2009). It taps three meaningful dimensions of CU traits in nonreferred (Essau, Sasagawa, & Frick, 2006; Fanti, Frick, & Georgiou, 2009) and detained or incarcerated (Kimonis et al., 2008) samples: uncaring, callousness, and unemotional.

The ICU was developed to overcome some of the APSD's psychometric limitations (e.g., a small number of items assessing CU traits, items with limited response options, and low internal consistency in many samples; Poythress et al., 2006). The ICU took the four items from the APSD that loaded most consistently on a CU factor in both community and clinic-referred samples (Frick, Bodin, & Barry, 2000) and added more, created an even number of positively and negatively worded variants, and expanded the response options to four (ranging from 0 [*not at all true*] to 3 [*definitely true*]). ICU scores show acceptable internal consistency and are associated with important outcomes across a wide range of ages, gender, types of samples (community and incarcerated youths), and different language translations (e.g., Byrd, Kahn, & Pardini, 2013; Ezpeleta, de la Osa, Granero, Penelo, & Domènech, 2013; Fanti et al., 2009; Kimonis et al., 2008).

Several studies have supported the construct validity of ICU scores for identifying both community and incarcerated youths at risk for severe current and future impairment (e.g., Frick, Bodin, & Barry, 2000; Kimonis et al., 2008; Roose, Bijttebier, Decoene, Claes, & Frick, 2010). Youths with a high ICU total score are more likely to have CP and delinquency, offense histories, aggression, sensation seeking, and susceptibility to boredom (Essau et al., 2006; Fanti et al., 2009). With respect to the ICU's subscales, the Uncaring factor is linked to delinquency and emotional deficits, and both the Uncaring and Callousness factors are associated with aggression (Essau et al., 2006; Fanti et al., 2009; Kimonis et al., 2008). In contrast, the Unemotional factor has not demonstrated consistent or robust correlations with external correlates, which is one criticism of the ICU. The affective deficit in psychopathy appears specific to experiencing certain emotions, such as sadness and fear (Pardini et al., 2003; Stevens, Charman, & Blair, 2001), and the ICU's Unemotional subscale items may not adequately capture this level of specificity.

Item response theory methods have been used to develop a short version of the ICU's parent-report version (S. W. Hawes et al., 2014). This short version uses 12 of the original 24 items that load onto two factors, Callous and Uncaring. In one study, scores on this version of the ICU demonstrated adequate test–retest reliability, good internal consistency, and good discrimination across the CU latent trait continuum. They also correlated with measures of theoretically meaningful constructs (S. W. Hawes et al., 2014). However, the majority of ICU items designed to measure the shallow–deficient affect dimension were dropped from this scale.

The ICU was one of two measures of CU traits used to develop the potential symptom criteria sets for the *DSM–5* (see Frick & Moffitt, 2010). The four-item criteria set ultimately adopted by the *DSM–5* (reviewed earlier in this chapter) was developed by identifying items that consistently loaded on the CU dimension of the APSD in community and clinic-referred samples (Frick, Bodin, & Barry, 2000). However, results of a confirmatory factor analysis of the ICU in four cross-national samples were used to develop a second nine-item set that was also tested for inclusion in the *DSM–5* (Essau et al., 2006; Fanti et al., 2009; Kimonis et al., 2008; Roose et al., 2010). Item response theory results suggested that the four-item criteria set from the self-report ICU represented the construct of CU traits well, supporting its inclusion in the *DSM–5* (Kimonis, Bagner, Linares, Blake, & Rodriguez, 2014; Kimonis, Fanti, et al., 2014). Approximating symptom presence from ICU items using a more stringent method (i.e., taking only the most extreme responses on the Likert scale) best identified community adolescents who were highly antisocial, whereas a more lenient method (i.e., taking the higher two responses out of four) best distinguished more antisocial incarcerated youths.

Do the Assessments Identify a Unique Syndrome?

To investigate the question of whether psychopathy can be identified as a distinct syndrome, we briefly review the evidence that assessments of juvenile psychopathy correlate with other variables in a manner that distinguishes them from other youths with conduct disorder (i.e., construct validity). The Juvenile Psychopathy Assessments section indicated that many of the tools correlate in the expected direction but are not synonymous with symptoms of other behavioral disorders. In addition, assessments of child and adolescent psychopathic traits are associated with dispositional and contextual factors, psychophysiological responses, and genetics that are distinct from those of other youths with conduct disorder who do not have CU traits.

Dispositional differences.

Cognitive–affective deficits. Conduct-disordered children and adolescents with CU traits show deficits in processing negative emotional stimuli and, even more specifically, deficits in their reactivity to signals of fear and distress in others. Studies using the APSD have indicated that this is evidenced by their reduced autonomic responses to others' distress (Blair, 1999), reduced recognition of fearful and sad facial expressions (Blair, Colledge, Murray, & Mitchell, 2001; Stevens et al., 2001), reduced responsiveness to fearful vocal tones (Blair, Budhani, Colledge, & Scott, 2005), reduced focus on the eye region of the face when processing fearful expressions (Dadds, El Masry, Wimalaweera, & Guastella, 2008), and reduced attentional orienting to others' distress cues (Kimonis, Frick, Fazekas, & Loney, 2006). Studies with the ICU have reported that it also correlates with laboratory indices of constricted emotion (Essau et al., 2006; Kimonis et al., 2008; Roose et al., 2010). These differences in emotional processing may be apparent very early in life. To illustrate, 5-year-old children ($N = 178$) with high levels of parent-reported CU traits and symptoms of oppositional defiant disorder were rated as less soothable and showed less negative reactivity to a parental face showing no emotion than did those with symptoms of oppositional defiant disorder but without a CU presentation (Willoughby, Waschbusch, Moore, & Propper, 2011).

Conduct-disordered children and adolescents with psychopathic traits also show a distinct pattern of emotional learning with respect to reinforcement and punishment. They have lower levels of fear and anxiety than conduct-disordered youths without psychopathic traits when processing punishment cues, especially when controlling for co-occurring impulsivity or delinquent behavior (Frick et al., 2014). They perform poorly in learning tasks that require them to stop a previously rewarded response after that response becomes more associated with punishment (Fisher & Blair, 1998; O'Brien & Frick, 1996). They also show impairments in reversal learning, which involves learning to reverse a response associated with a reward after a change in the reinforcement contingency (Blair, Colledge, & Mitchell, 2001; Budhani & Blair, 2005). These studies have suggested that youths with psychopathic traits are not simply unresponsive to punishment, they specifically have difficulties changing a response that was previously rewarded, even in the face of punishment (Budhani & Blair, 2005).

These youths also tend to have cognitive–affective deficits related to aggression. They expect more instrumental gain (e.g., obtaining goods or social goals) from their aggressive actions with peers than do other conduct-disordered youths without CU traits (Pardini et al., 2003). Adolescents with psychopathic traits endorse more deviant values and goals in social situations than youths with conduct disorder alone. Such deviance includes viewing aggression as an acceptable means to obtain goals, blaming others for their misbehavior, and emphasizing the importance of dominance in social conflicts (Chabrol, van Leeuwen, Rodgers, & Gibbs, 2011; Pardini et al., 2003; Stickle, Kirkpatrick, & Brush, 2009).

Attachment difficulties. Several studies have reported an association between CU traits and disorganized attachment styles (Bohlin, Eninger, Brocki, & Thorell, 2012; Fite, Greening, & Stoppelbein, 2008; Pasalich, Dadds, Hawes, & Brennan, 2011). In one study, Dadds, Jambrak, Pasalich, Hawes, and Brennan (2011) reported that children with high levels of CU traits made less eye contact with parents in free play and "emotional talk" scenarios than conduct-disordered youths without CU traits. In a second study, Dadds, Cauchi, Wimalaweera, Hawes, and Brennan (2012) found that children with delinquent behavior and CU traits showed lower levels of physical and verbal affection and made less eye contact with mothers during a task in which the mother said she loved the child and showed affection than did delinquent children without CU traits. PCL:YV scores in adolescents are also related to poor interpersonal relations and parental attachment (Kosson et al., 2002).

Contextual differences.

Peer factors. Adolescents high on psychopathic traits may be more likely to commit crimes in groups than those low on psychopathic traits, and they show the highest level of association with delinquent and antisocial peers (Goldweber, Dmitrieva, Cauffman, Piquero, & Steinberg, 2011; Muñoz, Frick, Kimonis, & Aucoin, 2008; Pardini & Loeber, 2008). Muñoz, Kerr, and Besic (2008), using a large population-based sample ($N = 667$) of adolescents (ages 12–15), found that those with CU traits had as many friends as other adolescents; however, their friendships were less stable and were perceived as more conflicted. Similarly, community boys and girls scoring high on CU traits and CP reported having friends, but their friends tended to be more delinquent than the friends of youths with CU traits or CP alone (Kimonis, Frick, & Barry, 2004). Adolescents with CU traits also seem to be less influenced by peer delinquency than delinquent adolescents without CU traits, although their delinquent behaviors strongly influence their peers (Kerr, Van Zalk, & Stattin, 2012).

Parenting factors. One of the most robust findings in the field is that harsh, inconsistent, and coercive parental discipline is more highly associated with the CP of youths low on CU traits than it is with the CP of youths high on these traits (e.g., Edens, Skopp, & Cahill, 2008; Pasalich et al., 2011; Wootton, Frick, Shelton, & Silverthorn, 1997; Yeh, Chen, Raine, Baker, & Jacobson, 2011). However, dysfunctional parenting practices are directly related to CU and psychopathic traits themselves (Barker, Oliver, Viding, Salekin, & Maughan, 2011; Waller et al., 2012), as is childhood maltreatment (see Farrington, Ullrich, & Salekin, 2010). For example, in a prospective longitudinal study of a large population-based sample ($N = 7{,}000$), harsh parenting of children at age 4 significantly predicted CU traits in these children at age 13, accounting for 10% and 14% of the variance in these traits in boys and girls, respectively (Barker et al., 2011). However, the direction of influence between parenting practices and CU traits is unclear. In the few longitudinal studies that have examined bidirectional effects, CU traits have been more predictive of changes in parenting over time than parenting has been of changes in CU traits (D. J. Hawes, Dadds, Frost, & Hasking, 2011; Muñoz, Pakalniskiene, & Frick, 2011).

In contrast, low warmth in parenting appears to be more highly associated with the delinquent behaviors of youths with psychopathic traits than with the behaviors of youths without these traits (Kimonis, Cross, Howard, & Donoghue, 2013; Pasalich et al., 2011). Pardini, Lochman, and Powell (2007) found that children exposed to warm and involved parenting showed a reduction in CU traits 1 year later. Thus, warm and involved parenting may provide a buffer against the development of CU and psychopathic traits, particularly among children with risky, fearless temperaments.

Psychophysiological differences. Research on psychophysiological correlates of psychopathic traits has suggested that these children and adolescents show blunted emotional reactivity to certain types of stimuli. For example, youths with delinquent behavior and CU traits showed a lower magnitude of heart rate change to emotionally evocative films than conduct-disordered youths without psychopathic traits (Anastassiou-Hadjicharalambous & Warden, 2008; de Wied, van Boxtel, Matthys, & Meeus, 2012). Adolescents with psychopathic traits showed reduced skin conductance reactivity when anticipating aversive stimuli (Fung et al., 2005; Isen et al., 2010) and abnormal event-related potentials to stimuli of others in pain (Cheng, Hung, & Decety, 2012). Moreover, among a sample of detained adolescent boys, psychopathic traits were negatively related to skin conductance reactivity when responding to peer provocation (Kimonis et al., 2008).

Genetic differences. The genetic influence on antisocial behaviors among youths is greater for those with high levels of psychopathic traits than among those low on such traits (Larsson, Andershed, & Lichtenstein, 2006; Taylor, Loney, Bobadilla, Iacono, & McGue, 2003). The most direct support has come from a large twin study of 7-year-old children that reported that the heritability of antisocial behaviors for children high on CU traits was more than twice as great (.81) as that for children low on CU traits (.30; Viding, Blair, Moffitt, & Plomin, 2005). Differences in heritability could not be attributed to the severity of CP or to levels of impulsivity–hyperactivity (Viding et al., 2005; Viding, Jones, Frick, Moffitt, & Plomin, 2008).

A particularly promising area of research is that investigating potential genetic polymorphisms associated with psychopathic traits. Fowler et al. (2009) reported that, among adolescents (ages 12–19) with childhood attention deficit hyperactivity disorder, those either possessing a low-activity monoamine oxidase-a receptor allele, homozygous for the low-activity serotonin transporter allele, or with the high-activity catechol-o-methyltransferase Val/Val genotype, demonstrated significantly higher levels of psychopathic traits than youths without these polymorphisms.

Also, in a study of 162 children and adolescents (ages 6–16), CU traits were associated with two polymorphisms on the oxytocin receptor gene (Beitchman et al., 2012). Specifically, CU traits were associated with the haplotypes consisting of the OXTR_rs237885 A allele and OXTR_rs2268493es A allele. However, conclusions about potential genetic polymorphisms that may be related to the development of psychopathic traits would be premature because this research is still in its infancy.

Summary: Psychopathy assessment and correlates. Reliability and concurrent validity studies from cross-sectional research have suggested that it is possible to assess traits phenotypically similar to adult psychopathy among youths. Such traits relate to a number of negative outcomes in the expected direction and do so with good interrater reliability. Youth psychopathy measures differ in their intended purpose and practical application. The preferred measures for clinical practice with adolescents ages 12 to 18 years are the PCL:YV and ICU and (when a parent or teacher informant is available) the APSD and ICU (informant scale versions). For example, the *DSM–5* CU criteria explicitly recognize the importance of carefully considering multiple sources of information from people who have known the individual for a significant period of time (American Psychiatric Association, 2013). Most of the instruments (with the exception of the ICU) examine the whole construct of psychopathy by including overconfident interpersonal, callous affective, and impulsive behavioral features and contain multiple symptom indicators related to each of these traits. With the exception of the PCL:YV (four-facet model only), the assessments deemphasize specific criminogenic behaviors, focusing more on the key three facets or factors of psychopathy that define personality deviance.

Most instruments have been validated on youth samples that were reasonably distributed across ages and settings (e.g., secure custody, community). The PCL:YV has high interrater reliability in research settings, and most other measures have fair to moderate item reliability and sound factor structures. Each of the instruments has research evidence indicating moderate to strong correlations with future aggression or reoffending, although evidence is most limited for the YPI. Finally, most of the instruments have evidence for concurrent validity with other features that should relate to psychopathy, such as interpersonal problems, difficulties processing emotion, and deficient psychophysiological responses.

Though the research is promising, these tools still have a number of limitations. First, the extent to which the self-report measures should be used in clinical practice remains unclear. In general, the use of tools using only self-report to assess psychopathy is problematic for a number of reasons (including an inability to detect deception) and depends somewhat on the self-awareness of examinees (which is particularly problematic in a child sample; Hemphill & Hart, 2002). However, among adolescents, the measurement of CU traits specifically might be more reliable using self-report or interview measures than caregiver informant measures, which appear to be biased (Fink, Tant, Tremba, & Kiehl, 2012). The validity of self-report measures of psychopathic and other personality traits tends to increase with age, and the validity of parent and teacher reports tends to decrease from childhood to adolescence (Frick, Barry, & Kamphaus, 2010).

Second, although research in the area has greatly increased in the past few years, important questions remain about the use of psychopathy assessments with girls. Most tools lack adequate normative samples for this population. In addition, their generalizability has not been thoroughly tested, although testing has been better for the APSD and ICU than for other measures.

Recently, rigorous analyses of gender differences on the PCL:YV using item response theory methods have shed some light on this issue. Item response theory is a statistical approach that permits an assessment of the unique characteristics of each item of an instrument across the continuum of a latent trait. In this case, the latent trait is thought to be psychopathic personality disorder. Item response theory advances knowledge about the items comprising an instrument by permitting an examination of (a) what level of latent trait (in this case, psychopathy) is necessary for each symptom (item) to become apparent (i.e., difficulty), (b) how well each item discriminates between individuals at all levels of the latent trait (i.e., discrimination), and, depending on the type of study conducted, (c) whether scales are comparable in how they measure symptoms along the latent trait.

Item response theory analyses of the PCL–R normative sample of adults identified significant gender bias, particularly for many of the behavioral items, which were less relevant indicators of psychopathy among women than among men (Bolt, Hare, Vitale, & Newman, 2004). For girls, Dillard, Salekin, Barker, and Grimes (2013) identified gender-related measurement bias on items of the self-report APSD and PCL:YV, including different levels of discrimination and difficulty for affective items. On average, PCL:YV items were more discriminating along levels of the latent trait for boys than for girls. Gender differences were similar for the APSD. Dillard et al. also found some important differences between the APSD and the PCL:YV in the measurement of psychopathy. For example, the PCL:YV was more effective in measuring affective deficits, and the APSD was more effective in assessing impulsivity.

Third, youth psychopathy assessments are not diagnostic tools. None of the instruments reviewed have established cutoffs for categorical decisions about who is and who is not a psychopath. Indeed, as the authors of the PCL:YV explicitly stated, "It is inappropriate for clinicians or other professionals to label a youth as a psychopath" (Forth et al., 2003, p. 17). One important issue is that, because psychopathy is a personality disorder, one would need evidence that scores are relatively stable over time and definitely into adulthood. Although it was not a study of stability per se, an item response theory study comparing PCL:YV scores in a sample of youthful offenders with PCL–R scores in a sample of adult offenders provided relevant data. Vincent (2002) found that most items, with the exception of the affective deficit items, did not have the same level of discrimination in relation to the latent trait (psychopathy) for adolescents and adults. Specifically, the behavioral items were far less discriminating and characteristic of the disorder among adolescents than among adults. In other words, youths could score higher on the behavioral features than adults without its indicating the presence of an actual psychopathic syndrome. With respect to the interpersonal items, youths had to be at very high levels of the latent trait for most of these symptoms to become apparent. This study provides evidence that some symptoms of the disorder manifest differently in adolescents than in adults.

A final issue that highlights the reason these tools cannot be used diagnostically is the lack of overlap across measures. For example, the APSD–SR has low diagnostic efficiency with respect to the PCL:YV and is not significantly correlated with PCL:YV scores among young adolescent offenders ages 14 to 16 years (Lee, Vincent, Hart, & Corrado, 2003; Vitacco et al., 2003). In an examination of the YPI, PCL:YV, and NEO Psychopathy Resemblance Index, Cauffman et al. (2009) reported that although the instruments significantly correlated with each other (*rs* = .26–.36), their correspondence in the identification of psychopathy was poor; one measure might designate an individual as high, but the other two measures would not. Similar results were reported by Fink et al. (2012) when comparing the self-report and parent-report APSD, the self-report and parent-report ICU, and the YPI with the PCL:YV.

Legal Uses of Psychopathy With Adolescent Offenders

One of the more publicized juvenile cases in the past decade in which assessments of psychopathy were used was in New Mexico in 2006. Cody Posey was being considered for transfer to adult court for killing his family in 2004 at age 14. Posey was a "cold-blooded killer" with psychopathic traits (Romo, 2010). The defense attorney argued that Posey was not a psychopath but a teen traumatized by years of physical and psychological abuse that began when he was 18 months old.

Two clinicians on opposing sides conducted the PCL:YV to provide recommendations regarding transfer. The evaluator for the prosecution gave Posey a score of 19 and stated that the average child in the community receives a score of 3.2 (Grinberg, 2006). This testimony resulted in news reports containing statements such as "Posey scores high on psychopath test" (Romo, 2006). The evaluator for the defense assigned a score of 11 and noted that this score was below average. In addition to other problems with the use of the PCL:YV in this case, it is notable that scores from the opposing clinicians were 8 points apart, which is far from the standard error of measurement. Furthermore, a score of 19 is considered moderate, and it does not indicate a diagnosis or classification of psychopathy. The expert for the prosecution compared Posey's PCL:YV score with the mean for community samples (suggesting Posey scored high), whereas the expert for the defense compared his score with the mean for justice-involved youths (suggesting his score was low).

Viljoen et al. (2010) searched U.S. and Canadian legal databases for cases involving adolescent offenders and psychopathy from the 1970s to 2008. They identified 111 cases, most of which involved male defendants who violently offended at an average age of 16 years. Major increases occurred in cases introducing psychopathy from 1990 onward (when assessment measures became available), with considerably more cases in Canada than in the United States. The majority of adolescent cases that mentioned psychopathy or psychopathic traits involved transfer to or from adult court (66% of all Canadian cases and 40% of U.S. cases), followed by sentencing (33.8% of Canadian cases and 25% of U.S. cases). A few of the U.S. cases also related to confessions, adjudicative competence, insanity, or sex offender commitment (*n* = 15).

Only 25% of the total cases mentioned how psychopathy was assessed, with the majority of those using a version of the PCL (*n* = 18). Eight cases used the Minnesota Multiphasic Personality Inventory—Adolescent (Hathaway & McKinley, 1989), and many evaluators mentioned they did not use any assessment tool. The failure to use any of the newer youth psychopathy assessment tools is not surprising, given when many of these cases occurred. In roughly 90% of the evaluations, examiners described psychopathy dimensionally—referring to the presence or absence of psychopathic features. Many of these cases described developmental barriers to diagnosing youths as psychopaths. Conversely, in about 10% of cases psychopathy was described diagnostically regardless of whether developmental cautions were noted. An example provided by Viljoen et al. (2010) was *In the matter of N.B.P.* (1998), in which the judge stated, "This young man is society's worst nightmare. But for his age the diagnosis would be that he is a psychopath." In this case, the evaluator described criteria from the *Diagnostic and Statistical Manual of Mental Disorders, Third Edition, Revised* (American Psychiatric Association, 1987), indicating that diagnoses of personality disorder should not be made before age 18. However, he also described these criteria as arbitrary and added that he did not expect the defendant to change much.

The most common statements in these cases from clinicians or the court regarding the use of psychopathy were made with respect to decisions about whether the defendant was (a) amenable to treatment (approximately 25%) or (b) a risk for future violence or reoffending (approximately 12%–15%). With respect to treatment amenability, in 32 cases the youth was judged (by clinicians or the court) to be difficult to treat because of the presence of psychopathy or psychopathic features (Viljoen et al., 2010). Generally, evaluators took the stance that if the youth was high in psychopathic traits or considered a psychopath, then the youth could not benefit from treatment or be cured.

Alternatively, in one case (*R. v. W.[M.B.]*, 2008), the clinicians argued that because the youth was high in psychopathic features, intensive treatment from highly qualified professionals was important (Viljoen et al., 2010). In eight cases, the absence of psychopathy or psychopathic features led to judgments that the defendants were amenable to treatment. With respect to risk, most of the cases asserted that the youth was a high risk to reoffend because of psychopathy or psychopathic features, and a handful of cases actually claimed the risk was long term. In approximately 20% of cases, the use of psychopathy in sentencing was challenged, often by mentioning developmental complications with juvenile psychopathy assessment. The judges referred to psychopathy in their opinions in about one third of the court cases.

We conducted a LexisNexis search for U.S. State Supreme Court or Court of Appeals cases that involved the concept of psychopathy for an adolescent defendant since the review by Viljoen et al. (2010). There were a few cases from 2009 onward. For example, in *Conley v. Indiana* (2012), the Indiana Supreme Court ruled that the trial court did not err by allowing a state expert to testify that 17.5-year-old Conley, convicted of killing his 10-year-old brother, had traits of a person with a diagnosis of psychopathy. In part, the ruling was upheld because the expert was merely rebutting testimony from the defense expert, who stated that the defendant did not fit the psychotic personality. Conley's sentence of life without parole was upheld. In another example, in 2012 the Appellate Court of Illinois upheld a trial court's decision for mandatory consecutive sentencing for Nichols, who was automatically transferred to adult court for aggravated criminal sexual assault at age 15 (*Illinois v. Nichols,* 2012). The decision was due, in part, to the evaluator's conclusion that Nichols was a moderate risk to reoffend on the basis of his young age and potential for psychopathy.

In 2011, the Supreme Court of Idaho affirmed a trial court's life sentence for a 16-year-old convicted of murdering his mother (*Idaho v. Windom,* 2011), stating there was no error in the finding that the defendant represented an unreasonable risk of future dangerous behavior. In this case, experts and counselors were split as to whether the juvenile was psychopathic or psychotic. In the case of *South Carolina v. Stanko* (2013), the State Supreme Court upheld the conviction (denying the insanity defense) for murder and robbery. The forensic expert did not use the term psychopathy specifically but referred to the defendant as having a severe personality disorder characterized by narcissism, repeated antisocial behavior, and no conscience.

Empirical Evidence Pertaining to Psychopathy in Youths

Reviews of legal cases have indicated that the primary uses of juvenile psychopathy have been to determine risk for violence and reoffending and to make decisions concerning treatment amenability. According to the review by Viljoen et al. (2010), these issues have often been described in ways that are static or relatively hopeless (e.g., a high scorer presents a long-term risk of reoffending or psychopaths are untreatable), which would be more consistent with the research reported with adults. Less commonly, clinicians in these cases have described psychopathy in a manner that implies it is more dynamic in nature, by acknowledging the transitional nature of characteristics and behavior during adolescence. Evaluators have described juvenile psychopathy as both a continuous trait (having psychopathic features at varying levels) and as a taxonic personality disorder. Thus, the scientific evidence that is relevant to use of psychopathy in the courtroom relates to (a) whether psychopathy can be described as a stable disorder in youths, (b) the ability of juvenile psychopathy assessments to predict reoffending or aggression, and (c) the association between psychopathic traits and treatment for youths.

Stability of juvenile psychopathy assessments. An important question concerns the stability of juvenile psychopathy over time. Several scholars have argued that the malleability of the presence and expression of symptoms of psychopathology across the early stages of development makes it unclear whether psychopathy can be identified in children and adolescents (Edens, Skeem, Cruise, & Cauffman, 2001; Hart, Watt, & Vincent, 2002; Seagrave & Grisso, 2002). In the past decade, research has attempted to address the issue of stability specifically.

Some studies have spoken to the stability of traits from childhood to adolescence. One study that used a population-based sample (*N* = 7,000) indicated that fearless temperament at age 2 predicted both CU traits and antisocial behavior at age 13 (Barker et al., 2011). In a shorter prospective study of children in which assessments were repeated over time, Frick, Kimonis, et al. (2003) reported that CU traits were relatively stable for school-age children, with a stability estimate (intraclass correlation coefficient) for parent-report ratings on the APSD of .93 across all 4 years. Stability was lower for youth self-report (intraclass correlation coefficient = .79). Although sample stability estimates were very good, only 30% of the children rated as high in CU traits on the first assessment stayed high at all three time points, whereas 59% of youths who were rated low in CU traits at the first assessment stayed low at all three time points.

In another study of juvenile offenders, Lee, Klaver, Hart, Moretti, and Douglas (2009) examined the stability of scores on both the self-reported APSD and the PCL:YV after 6 months (raters for the Time 2 PCL:YV assessment were instructed to rate items on the basis of the past 6 months only). Overall, these authors reported moderate to high stability for total scores. However, deeper examination of the change in PCL:YV scores indicated that only 34% of young offenders had stable scores across the 6 months and that a remarkable 50% had a substantial decrease in scores after 6 months. The decrease was most common among younger adolescents in the sample, and the CU traits factor was the least stable.

The stability of psychopathic traits from childhood or adolescence into adulthood has also proven to be only modest. Parent and teacher ratings of interpersonal callousness among children ages 7 to 12 predicted psychopathy ratings in the same youths at ages 18 to 19 (Burke, Loeber, & Lahey, 2007). Longitudinal studies examining measurement invariance in measures of interpersonal callousness or psychopathic features indicated that the same construct was being assessed in a similar way over a 6-year period from late adolescence to young adulthood (Loney, Taylor, Butler, & Iacono, 2007). However, one longitudinal study found that, of the juveniles who scored in the top 20% on a measure of psychopathic traits at age 13, the vast majority (86%) did not score above a diagnostic threshold on the short version of the PCL as adults 11 years later (Lynam, Caspi, Moffitt, Loeber, & Stouthamer-Loeber, 2007). The fact that 14% continued to score high as adults, though, makes this construct more stable than other youth disorders (see the next section).

Summary: Stability of traits. On the surface, the few studies that have examined the stability of psychopathic features by using measures over time have indicated high stability based on intraclass correlation coefficients. These stability estimates differ somewhat depending on the method used, with generally lower stability for self-report than parent-report measures or the PCL:YV. However, deeper examination has indicated that most of the stability comes from the subset of youths who start out scoring low in psychopathic features, and the general stability during a particular developmental stage (childhood or adolescence) is around 30%. The study by Lynam et al. (2007) indicated that scores may be stable for an even smaller proportion of youths (14%) when extending into young adulthood.

These findings are not surprising given the stability of most forms of childhood psychopathology in general (Mash & Dozois, 2003). Childhood disorders can arise early in life and remit altogether as a result of developmental processes (Cicchetti & Cohen, 1995). Moreover, children may express symptoms indicative of psychopathology at some point in their development because of normal variations in functioning (Cicchetti & Rogosch, 1996). With respect to psychopathy, these symptoms may include extreme impulsivity, irresponsibility, need for stimulation, and other characteristics that would be abnormal in adults. Moreover, the reliability of symptom assessments with young people is complicated by heterotypic continuity, meaning symptoms rarely manifest in the same manner across time (Cicchetti & Cohen, 1995; Cicchetti & Rogosch, 1996). For example, chronic defiance in early childhood could manifest as major rule violations in later childhood or adolescence.

Although psychopathic traits appear relatively stable compared with other areas of childhood psychopathology, this is only because most childhood disorders are highly unstable from childhood to adulthood. With respect to psychopathic traits, the proportion of high scorers who will remain higher scorers, even over just one developmental period, is only 30% (see Frick, Kimonis, et al., 2003), meaning that if clinicians were to generate diagnoses for youths who might initially be assessed as high scorers, they would be incorrect more often than they would be correct (i.e., high rate of false positives). Alternatively, the diagnosis could be made in youths, but only if it is described as dynamic and reassessed at regular intervals.

One possible explanation for the lack of stability and divergent findings from different assessment tools may be the existence of variants of psychopathy. Most theories concerning psychopathy subtypes center on differentiating between two types: primary and secondary (e.g., Karpman, 1948; Lykken, 1957; Mealey, 1995; Porter, 1996). Secondary psychopathy is thought to be acquired through environmental insult; parental abuse, rejection, or overindulgence; and other traumatic experiences (Porter, 1996). Karpman (1948) described this as a "psychopathic façade" (p. 523). Primary psychopathy is thought to result from an innate lack of conscience.

Several theorists posited that secondary psychopaths may be more aggressive and violent than primary psychopaths (Blackburn, 1987; Karpman, 1948, 1955; Lykken, 1995; Mealey, 1995). B. M. Hicks et al. (2004) found that high-anxious adult secondary variants—labeled *aggressive psychopaths*—had more extensive histories of violence and criminality and displayed greater aggression, reactive hostility, and impulsivity. Research conducted with juvenile offenders indicated that 92% of secondary variants committed institutional violence over a 2-year time period compared with 69.4% of primary variants (Kimonis, Skeem, Cauffman, & Dmitrieva, 2011).

Juvenile Psychopathy as a Risk Factor for Violence or Reoffending

The second area of psychopathy research that becomes relevant is studies that examined the association between measures of juvenile psychopathic or CU traits and future offending. Research has been conducted on a range of issues pertaining to juvenile psychopathic traits and offending; including retrospective and prospective studies of repeat offending with children and adolescents and analyses of their patterns of offending (e.g., institutional violence, types of violence).

Patterns of offending.

Adolescent studies. Similar to research findings with adults, there is good evidence that delinquent adolescents scoring high on the PCL:YV have a specific and severe pattern of offending. These findings are most pronounced for incarcerated adolescent boys. High PCL:YV scorers are most likely to have a history of frequent and violent offending that begins at a younger age than that of other offenders (Brandt, Kennedy, Patrick, & Curtin, 1997; Corrado, Vincent, Hart, & Cohen, 2004; Toupin, Mercier, Déry, Côté, & Hodgins, 1996). Both PCL:YV studies (Forth, Hart, & Hare, 1990; M. M. Hicks, Rogers, &

Cashel, 2000) and APSD–SR studies have found that high scorers show severe patterns of institutional misconduct, violence, and program noncompliance (Falkenbach, Polythress, & Heide, 2003; Murrie, Cornell, Kaplan, McConville, & Levy-Elkon, 2004). Evidence has shown that the commission of violent crimes increases from early adolescence to early adulthood (ages 19–21) for relatively psychopathic adolescents and decreases for less psychopathic adolescents (Forth & Burke, 1998). In contrast, the rates of nonviolent crime increase for adolescent offenders scoring both high and low on the PCL:YV.

Not only are high-scoring adolescents more likely to be violent than are other delinquent youths, the nature of their violence also differs. The interpersonal and affective dimensions of psychopathy measures are associated with instrumental violence (Kennealy, Skeem, Walters, & Camp, 2010; Vitacco & Kosson, 2010; Z. Walsh, Swogger, & Kosson, 2009), meaning violence committed for personal gain (e.g., status, money). Youths with CP and CU traits tend to expect more instrumental gain from their aggressive actions with peers than do those with CP alone (Pardini et al., 2003). They also engage in proactive aggression in the form of bullying. Although bullying can also involve reactive aggression (committed out of anger or for other emotional reasons), it has been described as a form of proactive aggression that involves achieving dominance over peers through intimidation to "construct, promote and/or reinforce [a] grandiose self-image" (Washburn, McMahon, King, Reinecke, & Silver, 2004, p. 256). Using a longitudinal study design, Fanti and Kimonis (2012) found that adolescents (N = 1,416) with CP and CU traits were at greater risk for engaging in bullying behaviors across development than youths exhibiting low or moderate levels of CU traits or CP alone.

Child studies. In studies of children ages 6 to 13, the presence of non-normative levels of CU traits has predicted a severe, stable, and aggressive pattern of behavior among youths showing severe early CP (Kahn et al., 2012; McMahon, Witkiewitz, & Kotler, 2010; Rowe et al., 2010). Several studies have reported strong associations between the informant rating version of the APSD and number of conduct problems, aggression, and delinquency in the past or currently (Caputo et al., 1999; Christian, Frick, Hill, Tyler, & Frazer, 1997; Wootton et al., 1997), although the majority have been cross-sectional studies. In addition, as with adolescents, children with CP and CU traits may have a predilection for instrumental violence. They view aggression as an acceptable means of obtaining their goals.

Moreover, a study of a community sample found that children with both CU traits and CP (as measured by the APSD) had higher rates of instrumental aggression than those with CP alone over a 1-year follow-up period (Frick, Cornell, Barry, Bodin, & Dane, 2003). Children with CP and CU traits have also shown a more severe and pervasive pattern of proactive aggression than those with CP alone (Flight & Forth, 2007; Frick, Cornell, et al., 2003; Kruh et al., 2005). For example, Viding, Simmonds, Petrides, and Frederickson (2009) found that the combination of CP and CU traits predicted greater rates of bullying than either condition alone among a large (N = 704) sample of youths in later childhood (11- to 13-year-olds). CU traits contributed to the statistical prediction of peer-reported bullying beyond the variance accounted for by CP.

Prediction of reoffending.

Adolescent studies. Results with respect to prediction of delinquent behavior, recidivism, or violence have been somewhat varied, depending on the instrument used. Of the juvenile psychopathy assessment tools available, the PCL:YV has been the most extensively studied with respect to recidivism, lending itself to meta-analytic studies. A meta-analysis of PCL:YV total scores yielded medium effect sizes (using the mean weighted r) for general recidivism (r = .26) across 20 unique samples and violent recidivism (r = .23) across 14 samples (Edens et al., 2007). The average follow-up period across the studies was 32 months, with the longest being 10 years. The association between PCL:YV total scores and reoffending was significantly smaller for girls than for boys. Parsing the PCL:YV into factors indicated that Factor 2 (the lifestyle and antisocial behavioral features) scores were more strongly related to general and violent recidivism than the Factor 1 (the interpersonal and affective features) scores.

An updated meta-analysis of 28 recidivism studies that included the PCL:YV found similar results. Olver, Stockdale, and Wormith (2009) reported the PCL:YV yielded moderate effect sizes for general (mean weighted $r = .28$) and violent ($r = .25$) recidivism. The PCL:YV's effect sizes were comparable to those of comprehensive youth risk assessment tools (e.g., the Youth Level of Service/Case Management Inventory and the Structured Assessment of Violence Risk for Youth), which include some psychopathic features (e.g., CU) in addition to a number of other risk factors. Beyond a greater likelihood of reoffending, other studies have found that those who score high on the PCL:YV also reoffend sooner after release from an institution than do other offenders (Corrado et al., 2004; Gretton, McBride, Hare, O'Shaughnessy, & Kumka, 2001).

Fewer studies are available for self-report adolescent psychopathy measures, although two studies have examined the predictive accuracy of the YPI specifically. In one study, Colins, Vermeiren, De Bolle, and Broekaert (2012) conducted a 2- to 4-year follow-up of official recidivism using a sample of 223 detained male juvenile offenders. Generally, YPI total scores did not significantly predict recidivism after controlling for the youths' offending history. In another study, Cauffman et al. (2009) found that YPI total scores significantly predicted self-reported offending at 36 months. They also predicted self-reported aggression, but only for short-term follow-ups (i.e., 6 and 12 months). In a study of the self- and parent-report APSD in a group of adolescent offenders, Falkenbach et al. (2003) found significant correlations with rearrest over a 1-year period. Subsequently, Boccaccini et al. (2007) found weak correlations between APSD–SR scores and rearrest 1 year later. Other researchers have found that the APSD–SR correlated with official charges and convictions 1 year later, but not after taking other risk factors into account (Douglas, Epstein, & Poythress, 2008).

Child studies. Far fewer prospective studies of psychopathy-related assessments have been conducted with children. The advantage of the child studies that do exist, however, is that they have tended to study associations with aggression or delinquency on the basis of the presence of symptom clusters (i.e., co-occurring CP and CU traits) rather than continuous scores alone. For example, one study using the informant-rated APSD found that children with co-occurring CP and CU traits had higher rates of self-reported delinquency, CP, and parent-reported police contacts every year for 4 years into early adolescence (Frick, Stickle, Dandreaux, Farrell, & Kimonis, 2005). Half of the sample was female, but predictive validity estimates were not reported separately for girls.

Child studies have provided significant support for the predictive utility of CU traits, even after controlling for behavioral risk factors (Loeber et al., 2005; Stickle et al., 2009). In a recent and very pertinent study of a large high-risk sample of seventh graders ($N = 754$), McMahon et al. (2010) reported that CU traits, measured using the parent-report version of the APSD, significantly predicted delinquent behavior 2 years later (e.g., self-reported delinquent behavior and juvenile arrests during early adolescence) and young adult outcomes measured 1 year after high school (e.g., adult arrests and symptoms of antisocial personality disorder). The combination of conduct disorder symptoms and CU traits had the best predictive accuracy for all of these negative outcomes relative to symptoms of conduct disorder, attention deficit hyperactivity disorder, oppositional defiant disorder, or CU traits alone. Similarly, Byrd, Loeber, and Pardini (2012) reported that parent- and teacher-rated CU traits at age 7 predicted criminal behavior at age 25 among a sample of boys ($N = 503$), even after controlling for childhood oppositional defiant disorder, conduct disorder, and attention-deficit/hyperactivity disorder .

Adolescent and child studies. Most studies included in the meta-analyses reviewed were limited to official records to define recidivism, which could underestimate the frequency and severity of repeat offending. This issue is particularly problematic in the case of reconviction, which is especially vulnerable to selection bias (Edens et al., 2007). For example, Cauffman et al. (2009) found that the PCL:YV did not predict self-reported reoffending or aggression in a large sample of serious juvenile offenders over a period of 3 years. The PCL:YV did, however, predict both outcomes after 6-month and 12-month follow-ups, but this prediction was accounted for by the antisocial behavioral items.

More recently, a major meta-analysis of 60 samples spanning ages 9 to 18 years has spoken to this issue. The meta-analysis expanded prior work by including studies using any child or adolescent psychopathy measure that also (a) was cross-sectional in addition to longitudinal and (b) included self-reported delinquency from community samples in addition to official records of recidivism from offender samples (Asscher et al., 2011). The majority of the studies used the PCL:YV, followed by the YPI, APSD, and ICU. Three studies used a version of the Child Psychopathy Screen. Two studies included measures that were not designed to assess psychopathy (i.e., the Global Risk Assessment Device and the California Child Q-Set). *Delinquency* was defined as self-reported or informant-reported illegal acts and official acts, and *recidivism* was defined as official records of new charges or convictions only in offender samples. However, the distinction between these two outcomes was difficult to discern. Psychopathy scores moderately predicted delinquency ($r = .23$), general recidivism ($r = .21$), and violent recidivism ($r = .22$). Effect sizes had considerable heterogeneity, however.

For example, clinical assessments of psychopathy had significantly stronger effects than self-report measures. This was especially true when predicting general recidivism, for which the effect size for the PCL was .25, compared with .12 for other measures. Effect sizes were also larger when self-reports or informant reports of the outcome were used instead of official records. Surprisingly, Asscher et al. (2011) found no significant moderating effects for gender, indicating that the measures performed equally well for both boys and girls. Separate examinations of the three main symptom clusters of psychopathy, which the authors referred to as narcissism, CU, and impulsive–delinquent behavior, consistent with APSD factor terminology, indicated that each dimension moderately predicted recidivism.

Summary: Prediction of reoffending or violence. Aside from the PCL:YV, little support has been found for the use of any other juvenile psychopathy measure to assess risk of future reoffending or violence. Although numerous prediction studies have indicated that the PCL:YV has a moderate effect size with respect to reoffending, these interpretations have several cautions.

First, according to the meta-analyses and other studies (e.g., Vincent, Odgers, McCormick, & Corrado, 2008), there is minimal evidence to suggest that the tool predicts reoffending well in samples of girls. An exception may be the Asscher et al. (2011) meta-analysis, which found that gender did not moderate the relation between psychopathy and reoffending; however, the moderating effect did approach significance, and it was not reported separately for the PCL:YV. Second, there is minimal evidence that the PCL:YV predicts sexual reoffending as confirmed by the meta-analyses described earlier. Effect sizes have been extremely low. Third, juvenile psychopathy measures have rarely been rigorously scrutinized by considering whether they provide incremental validity over other youth violence risk factors (e.g., age of onset, number of prior offenses). Studies that have examined this issue have suggested that the PCL:YV has little to no incremental validity (Douglas et al., 2008).

Fourth, most adolescent studies and meta-analyses have examined PCL:YV scores or psychopathy features (factors or facet score) separately, as opposed to examining the presence of an actual syndrome with all the symptom clusters present, which may be a more powerful predictor. This point is crucial. As Vincent (2006) argued, if measures of psychopathy merely predict recidivism among youths on the basis of dimensions related to criminogenic or impulsive behavior, one must seriously question whether a coherent syndrome, or even just its unique interpersonal and unemotional symptoms, operates for youths similarly to adults. For example, Vincent, Vitacco, Grisso, and Corrado (2003) found that a cluster of adolescent offenders scoring high on each of the interpersonal, affective, and lifestyle behavioral factors of the PCL:YV were much more likely to recidivate violently (50%), and did so sooner after release (after an average of 14 months), than adolescents with behavioral features alone (27% recidivated after an average of 18 months). Corrado et al. (2004) examined the incremental validity of the factors included in the three-factor model (interpersonal, affective, and lifestyle behavioral) and their interactions. They reported that the prediction of any form of recidivism, and of violent recidivism specifically, could be attributed to the interaction of all three factors, thought to be more representative of an underlying psychopathy syndrome. Studies conducted with child samples have supported the utility of this approach by consistently finding that the combination of CP and CU traits is associated with a very different pattern of aggression and offending than either symptom cluster alone.

Last, and probably most important in light of the use of the PCL:YV in court settings, most studies have spanned follow-up periods of 1 to 3 years and have rarely tracked reoffending into later adulthood. In one notable exception, a 12-year follow-up study of 126 juveniles (average age around 15 years) found that PCL:YV total scores and all facet scores except the interpersonal facet, were correlated with increased numbers of violent and other types of convictions into young adulthood (age 23; Dyck, Campbell, Schmidt, & Wershler, 2013). Examination of the patterns of offending showed that a moderate psychopathy group was reconvicted in every follow-up year at essentially the same rate as the high psychopathy group, although the high psychopathy group was more diverse in its type of offenses. Moreover, there was a general decline in reconvictions into young adulthood (age 23) for all youths regardless of their PCL:YV score, indicating that all young offenders displayed a higher level of criminal activity during adolescence than in adulthood. This may also be an indication that psychopathic traits can change over time for many youths and, therefore, reduce the predictive power. A few caveats are necessary. First, the high scorers were identified by a score of only 21.09 or higher (of a possible score of 34 because behavioral items were removed), indicating that the sample was generally not very high on psychopathy. Second, Dyck et al. (2013) were unable to examine trends in reconviction by type of crime.

Juvenile Psychopathy and Amenability to Treatment

A few studies have suggested that psychopathic adult offenders do not benefit from treatment and may even get worse (e.g., Ogloff, Wong, & Greenwood, 1990). However, others have successfully argued that these studies were riddled with methodological flaws (Salekin, Worley, & Grimes, 2010; Skeem, Monahan, & Mulvey, 2002). The case law seems to have extended the findings of poor treatment outcomes downward to youths. Some limited evidence has shown that this may be the case. For example, a prospective study reported noncompliance with institutional programming among adolescents scoring high on the PCL:YV (Rogers et al., 1997). CU and psychopathic traits have also proven useful in identifying youths with conduct disorder who benefit less from traditional behavioral interventions (Frick et al., 2014).

Treatment outcomes: Antisocial behavior. The current state of research has suggested that children and adolescents with CU or psychopathic traits can benefit from psychosocial treatment. Research has suggested that these youths require more intensive, comprehensive, and specialized interventions that are tailored to their unique emotional, cognitive, and motivational styles (Frick, 2012; Kimonis, Pardini, Pasalich, & McMahon, 2014). For example, in a study of 177 clinic-referred children, those with CU traits who received an individualized and comprehensive modular intervention—involving medication for attention-deficit/hyperactivity disorder, cognitive–behavioral treatment, parent management training, school-based contingency management, family therapy, peer relationship development, and crisis management—showed rates of improvement similar to those of children with conduct disorder but without CU (Kolko & Pardini, 2010).

Similarly, incarcerated adolescent offenders with high PCL:YV scores treated with an intensive intervention were less likely to recidivate over a 2-year follow-up period than were a matched group of high scorers who underwent a standard treatment program in the same correctional facility (Caldwell, Skeem, Salekin, & van Rybroek, 2006). The intervention used reward-oriented contingency management strategies that targeted the self-interests of the adolescent and also taught empathy skills. Despite these promising findings, other studies examining multimodal interventions, such as Multisystemic Therapy, have reported that treatment effects were poorer for youths with psychopathic traits (Manders, Deković, Asscher, van der Laan, & Prins, 2013; Stadler, Kröger, Clement, & Grasmann, 2012).

Parent management training interventions are among the best-supported treatments for antisocial behaviors in youths (Brestan & Eyberg, 1998; Comer, Chow, Chan, Cooper-Vince, & Wilson, 2013). This is because failures in parental socialization of children are a central component of many theories developed to explain the etiology of childhood antisocial behaviors (e.g., Patterson, 1982). However, as mentioned previously, the role of parenting in the development of these behaviors among youths with psychopathic traits is less clear (e.g., Wootton et al., 1997). As such, several studies have reported that traditional parent management training interventions are less effective at treating the CP of children with CU traits than that of children without these traits. For example, parent–child interaction therapy (Zisser & Eyberg, 2010) effectively reduced CP to below clinically significant levels in a sample of very young developmentally delayed children with CU features (mean age = 3.87 years), albeit not to the same levels as children low on these traits (Kimonis, Bagner, et al., 2014). Similarly, D. J. Hawes and Dadds (2005) found that parents of oppositional boys (mean age = 6.29 years) with high levels of CU traits were more likely to rate the discipline component (i.e., time out) of a manualized parent management training as ineffective in reducing their child's CP during treatment relative to parents of children without CU traits (see also D. J. Hawes, Dadds, Brennan, Rhodes, & Cauchi, 2013).

In a sample of school-age children (7–12 years) with attention deficit hyperactivity disorder in a summer treatment program, Waschbusch, Carrey, Willoughby, King, and Andrade (2007) found that those with CP and CU traits showed less improvement after behavior therapy than those with CP alone. Children high on CU traits were also observed to be less compliant with the discipline (i.e., time out) component of the intervention (Haas et al., 2011). Another study of justice-involved adolescents (11–17 years) found that those scoring high on CU traits were more likely to engage in violent behavior during the course of functional family therapy and demonstrated lower youth- and parent-reported perceptions of improvement (White, Frick, Lawing, & Bauer, 2012). They also showed the highest levels of CP, aggression, and emotional symptoms before treatment, which were significantly reduced but remained higher than those of youths with low CU traits after treatment. More important, these behavioral programs rely on punishment-induced arousal to change antisocial behaviors, a strategy that is likely to be poorly effective for punishment-insensitive youths with CU or psychopathic traits.

Components of parent management training that focus on the use of reward-based techniques are effective in reducing behavioral problems in youths with CU traits. To illustrate, D. J. Hawes and Dadds (2005) found that CU traits were not significantly associated with parents' perceptions of the ineffectiveness of reward-based strategies, as they were for time out. This research has suggested that existing empirically supported interventions for behavioral problems may be adapted or modified to better fit the individualized needs of children with CU traits by emphasizing reward-based strategies. Along these lines, maternal support or responsiveness and secure parent–child attachment are important protective factors against the development of antisocial behaviors generally that may be particularly relevant to the development of CU traits or psychopathy specifically (Shaw, Gilliom, Ingoldsby, & Nagin, 2003). Parenting styles promoting greater attachment security—that is, sensitive responding to the child's emotions, parental warmth—are believed to be critical to socializing and fostering conscience development among children with the fearless and uninhibited temperament believed to underlie CU or psychopathic traits and also to reducing the risk of further development of these traits (Kochanska, 1997).

Treatment outcomes: Psychopathic traits. Notwithstanding their reduced effectiveness for treating CP in children with psychopathic traits, parent management training interventions appear to improve psychopathic traits themselves, with medium to large effect sizes reported. For example, one randomized controlled trial found that children (ages 4–9 years) diagnosed with oppositional defiant disorder or conduct disorder and recruited from domestic violence shelters whose mothers received parent management training and supportive therapy exhibited greater reductions in psychopathic traits than those who received services as usual in the community (McDonald, Dodson, Rosenfield, & Jouriles, 2011). Furthermore, improvements in mothers' harsh and inconsistent parenting partly accounted for reductions in levels of CU traits.

Similarly, D. J. Hawes and Dadds (2007) found lower levels of CU traits at 6 months posttreatment for a subset of their 2005 study sample. A randomized controlled trial of Israeli children (2.6–5 years old) with significant behavioral problems that incorporated strategies for improving aspects of the parent–child relationship (e.g., warmth, communication skills) in a parent management training program and mandated participation by both parents as well as addressing coparenting found improvements in their CU traits posttreatment compared with controls (Somech & Elizur, 2012). Taken together, these findings suggest that traditional parent management training interventions delivered in the context of a warm and supportive parent–child relationship may prevent or ameliorate the development of CU traits (Pasalich et al., 2011).

Summary: Treatment amenability. The field has made significant advances in the treatment of youths with CU or psychopathic traits since the first published study in 2005 (D. J. Hawes & Dadds, 2005). However, the current literature on interventions for youths with psychopathic traits also has several gaps in knowledge and limitations that can be informed by future research. First, a minority of studies have focused on adolescent or incarcerated populations specifically. Incarcerated youths present a unique treatment challenge because their psychopathic traits are modestly associated with treatment noncompliance, poor attendance, and dropout (see Salekin, 2010, for a review). Other areas of concern for therapists treating incarcerated adolescents with psychopathic traits are their poor motivation to change, manipulation and deceit, and inability to form lasting attachments or experience deep emotions.

Second, previously tested interventions for antisocial youths with CU or psychopathic traits are generally limited in that they fail to address core deficits in emotional reactivity and understanding of others' distress cues, which are believed to interfere with moral development and also distinguish these youths from others with antisocial behaviors (Blair, 1999). One line of study has attributed poor emotion recognition to problematic allocation of attention to critically salient environmental cues: failing to focus on the eye region of the face when processing fearful expressions as determined by eye tracking (Dadds et al., 2008). When youths with CU traits were instructed to attend to the eyes of stimulus faces, their deficits in fear recognition ameliorated, suggesting that altering the attentional focus of children with CU traits may, at least temporarily, modify impairments in emotion recognition (Dadds et al., 2006, 2008). Whether such changes will affect CU traits and antisocial behaviors is an empirical question, because there is no longitudinal evidence to suggest that eye-gaze deficits are associated with the stability of CU traits or antisocial behaviors over time. However, in a randomized controlled trial of mostly male youths referred for emotional and behavioral problems (ages 6–16 years), those with elevated CU traits showed significant improvements in affective empathy and CP after a computerized emotional recognition training that involved studying images of various human emotional expressions and then discussing them with parents during homework activities (i.e., MindReading) compared with a treatment-as-usual parent management training intervention (Dadds et al., 2012). It is important to note, however, that positive changes in the antisocial behaviors of children high on CU traits could not be attributed to improvements in emotion recognition and affective empathy. Nonetheless, these findings highlight the promising potential of empirically based adjunctive interventions to address core emotional deficiencies in antisocial children with CU traits.

Third, no treatment studies, or randomized controlled trials in particular, have explicitly targeted children with co-occurring antisocial behaviors and CU–psychopathic traits. A rich body of basic science findings has the potential to inform the development of novel targeted behavioral, cognitive, and biological interventions for children with CU–psychopathic traits, which are critically needed to address the unique cognitive–affective deficits that are believed to contribute to their poor moral socialization. Furthermore, more longitudinal studies are needed to establish whether reported improvements in treatment outcomes persist across extended periods of time.

Ethical Issues

Although no research has directly tested the effects of the label *CU traits,* there is an empirical literature on the negative effects of the use of the term psychopathy when applied to children and adolescents (for a review, see Murrie, Boccaccini, McCoy, & Cornell, 2007). To summarize, the findings have indicated that the term psychopathy affects decision making by professionals (e.g., clinicians' estimation of treatability), but it does not have any more negative effects than using the term *conduct disorder*. Thus, it appears that any term used to describe individuals with antisocial behavior or traits will gain a negative connotation. Also, as noted earlier, previous attempts to capture CU traits in the *DSM* used the term *undersocialized* to minimize the potentially stigmatizing effects of the label. It is not clear, however, that this term has any less negative connotation, and its lack of clarity led to considerable variability in how the construct was conceptualized and assessed by researchers and clinicians.

IMPLICATIONS AND RECOMMENDATIONS

In *Graham v. Florida* (2010), the U.S. Supreme Court held that sentences of life without parole were unconstitutional for juvenile offenders convicted of any crime other than murder. In 2012, the U.S. Supreme Court ruled in *Miller v. Alabama* that, in the case of murder, a mandatory sentence of life without parole was unconstitutional. The implications of these decisions are that criminal courts nationwide will be asked to weigh the potentially mitigating factors of young people's lesser maturity in cases eligible for a sentence of life without parole. In addition, the rulings potentially bring into question the prior sentencing decisions for many offenders currently serving sentences of life without parole for acts committed as juveniles. The temptation for forensic evaluators and courts to use juvenile psychopathy assessments in decisions regarding life without parole is undeniable.

Several implications can be drawn from the literature regarding the use of psychopathy measures with adolescent offenders. We list these implications and provide some recommendations for use of psychopathy measures in the courtroom.

- The PCL:YV and other psychopathy measures are not diagnostic tools. These tools do not have established valid cutoffs for making categorical decisions about who is or is not a psychopath. The research to date has not established a sufficiently high level of stability of traits in those scoring as high in psychopathy to warrant testimony about whether a youth has psychopathic personality disorder. Until that time, it is still most appropriate to communicate that a youth has psychopathic traits or psychopathic features. Practically speaking, use of assessments of these traits in childhood and adolescence to predict who would be psychopathic as adults would lead to a large number of false-positive predictions. However, research on stigma has indicated that these labels may not have any more effect on jurors than labels such as conduct disorder.
- High PCL:YV scores compel a conclusion of high risk for serious and imminent reoffending over short periods of time spanning 1 to 3 years. Other psychopathy measures have yet to achieve the level of evidence (see Asscher et al., 2011) that would warrant their use in court-ordered evaluations of risk for violence and reoffending.
- Among high scorers, psychopathic features should be seen as dynamic; however, among those who score low on psychopathy, there is more evidence to suggest that the absence of psychopathy features will remain stable. We recommend that forensic clinicians conducting these assessments acknowledge the developmental considerations, particularly the malleability of traits, when identifying a high scorer from the assessment results, for example,

> the offender scored in the high range on the PCL:YV with all major features of psychopathy present. These traits appear

to be stable into adulthood in roughly 20% of youth. Currently, the developmental complications do not permit us to accurately determine whether this offender will be one of those individuals for whom traits are stable.

- With a few notable exceptions, little research has examined whether measures of juvenile psychopathy accurately predict long-term recidivism among adolescent offenders. Research from the Pathways to Desistance Study of felony juvenile offenders has indicated that no set of risk factors predicted which juvenile offenders would continue to offend chronically versus desist their offending (Mulvey et al., 2010). Therefore, clinicians do not have reliable methods to identify youths who have embarked on the type of long-range, violent criminal career that is particularly important in adult transfer cases and life without parole sentences (Grisso, 2010). Among the few studies that used some form of psychopathy measure and tracked youths into adulthood, the time period was typically into very early adulthood (up to about age 24) when most adolescent offenders will still be offending or just beginning to desist (see, e.g., Roberts et al., 2001). We should note, however, that one secondary data analysis study of PCL short version scores may speak to this issue. Piquero, Jennings, and Barnes (2012) analyzed data from the Cambridge Study in Delinquent Development community sample. They found that PCL short version assessments conducted with men in the sample at age 48 were the strongest predictors of whether they were on the chronic offender trajectory. This version of the PCL had incremental validity over a number of childhood risk factors. This is a promising line of research, but until it is demonstrated prospectively from juvenile psychopathy assessments, it does not warrant conclusions regarding lifetime offending in court.
- Given that adolescence is a time of extreme developmental change, high-risk youths should routinely be reassessed for risk and psychopathic characteristics to determine whether maturation attenuates risk.
- There is no evidence that youths with psychopathic features are incapable of benefiting from treatment or that treatment is contraindicated. Children and adolescents with psychopathic traits present a particular treatment challenge because of their poor response to traditional treatments administered in mental health or juvenile justice settings. However, scholars who extended the construct of psychopathy from adults to youths did so, in large part, because they believed that intervention would be more effective in the earlier, more malleable years of life (Frick, 1998; Frick & Marsee, 2006; Frick & White, 2008; Lynam & Gudonis, 2005). Consistent with this prediction, the research is encouraging in suggesting that treatment outcomes may be improved by intensively targeting the specific needs and deficits of children and adolescents with CU–psychopathic traits. This may be accomplished by (a) emphasizing reward-oriented approaches that target youths' self-interests to modify behaviors rather than relying on punishment-related arousal, (b) strengthening the parent–child relationship (i.e., warmth, mutual responsiveness); (c) prescribing stimulant medication when there is comorbid attention-deficit/hyperactivity disorder; and (d) focusing on enhancing empathy and emotional responsiveness in the child.

Future research is needed in the following areas to help answer some of the remaining questions:

- To determine whether juvenile psychopathy is a predictor of chronic offending behavior from early adolescence onward, studies are needed that examine the predictive accuracy of measures into late adulthood. These studies would need to establish that long-range offending can be attributed to the presence of the primary symptom clusters of psychopathy (CU plus conduct disorder) as opposed to the impulsive behavioral features alone.
- Child and adolescent psychopathy measures should be tested to determine their ability to assess changes in risk and psychopathic features over time.

- There is a strong need for future intervention research focused on adolescent and incarcerated populations that examines long-term outcomes for youths with CU–psychopathic traits relative to youths without these features.
- Knowledge gained from research on psychopathy subtypes or variants has suggested that apparent psychopathic traits may signal greater risk for severe antisocial, aggressive, and violent behavior when they co-occur with emotional instability, anxiety, and distress than when they appear alone (Kimonis et al., 2011). If the goal is to decrease violence, the secondary variant is the most appropriate group to target with intervention efforts. Fostering particular optimism for reducing violence among youths with psychopathic traits, secondary variants were found to be less psychosocially mature and manifested greater change in violent behavior—but not in PCL:YV scores—over a 2-year period compared with those primary variants. Future controlled treatment studies are needed to address the validity of Karpman's (1948) claim that secondary variants "are amenable to psychotherapeutic treatment and therefore offer a far more hopeful outlook than is currently given to the [primary] psychopathic cases" (p. 533). Research into differences in treatment amenability and outcomes between juvenile psychopathy variants is essential. Research is also needed regarding whether targeted treatments—for example, using evidence-based cognitive–behavioral treatments to address pathological anxiety or traumatic experiences in secondary variants—are supported for juvenile psychopathy variants.

CONCLUSIONS

In conclusion, there is evidence from case law that the concept of psychopathy is used in juvenile cases to argue for or against adult transfer or harsher sentencing. In light of the Supreme Court's decision in *Miller v. Alabama* (2012), we expect an upsurge of youth cases in which courts will be seeking experts' opinions about the necessity of a life without parole sentence to protect public safety. Our analysis of the research suggests that there is currently no evidence that juvenile psychopathy assessments can be used to discriminate youths who will continue to offend violently well into their adult years from youths who will desist in early adulthood. Indeed, there is currently no compelling evidence that any assessment tool or single risk factor can effectively discriminate these groups of youths. Instead, psychopathic traits in adolescence should be seen as a risk factor that will be dynamic for the majority of youths and, if present, marks the need for intensive treatment and a high likelihood for serious reoffending over a period of as long as 3 years. The only assessment tools that have achieved a significant level of evidence to warrant use in a forensic assessment are the PCL:YV and the APSD, which must be conducted by appropriately trained evaluators. The ideal scenario would be to reform juvenile sentencing laws for the most severe crimes in a manner that is commensurate with youth development and the limits of risk assessment by imposing shorter mandatory incarceration with the opportunity for parole when findings from reassessments are positive.

References

Achenbach, T. M. (1991). *Manual for the Child Behavior Checklist and 1991 Profile.* Burlington: University of Vermont, Department of Psychiatry.

American Psychiatric Association. (1987). *Diagnostic and statistical manual of mental disorders* (3rd ed., rev.). Washington, DC: Author.

American Psychiatric Association. (2000). *Diagnostic and statistical manual of mental disorders* (4th ed., text rev.). Washington, DC: Author.

American Psychiatric Association. (2013). *Diagnostic and statistical manual of mental disorders* (5th ed.). Arlington, VA: Author.

Anastassiou-Hadjicharalambous, X., & Warden, D. (2008). Physiologically-indexed and self-perceived affective empathy in conduct-disordered children high and low on callous-unemotional traits. *Child Psychiatry and Human Development, 39,* 503–517. http://dx.doi.org/10.1007/s10578-008-0104-y

Andershed, H., Hodgins, S., & Tengström, A. (2007). Convergent validity of the Youth Psychopathic Traits Inventory (YPI) association with the Psychopathy Checklist: Youth Version (PCL:

YV). *Assessment, 14*, 144–154. http://dx.doi.org/10.1177/1073191106298286

Andershed, H. A., Gustafson, S. B., Kerr, M., & Stattin, H. (2002). The usefulness of self-reported psychopathy-like traits in the study of antisocial behaviour among non-referred adolescents. *European Journal of Personality, 16*, 383–402. http://dx.doi.org/10.1002/per.455

Archer, R. P., Buffington-Vollum, J. K., Stredny, R. V., & Handel, R. W. (2006). A survey of psychological test use patterns among forensic psychologists. *Journal of Personality Assessment, 87*, 84–94. http://dx.doi.org/10.1207/s15327752jpa8701_07

Arrigo, B. A., & Shipley, S. (2001). The confusion over psychopathy: I. Historical considerations. *International Journal of Offender Therapy and Comparative Criminology, 45*, 325–344. http://dx.doi.org/10.1177/0306624X01453005

Asscher, J. J., van Vugt, E. S., Stams, G. J., Deković, M., Eichelsheim, V. I., & Yousfi, S. (2011). The relationship between juvenile psychopathic traits, delinquency and (violent) recidivism: A meta-analysis. *Journal of Child Psychology and Psychiatry, 52*, 1134–1143. http://dx.doi.org/10.1111/j.1469-7610.2011.02412.x

Barker, E. D., Oliver, B. R., Viding, E., Salekin, R. T., & Maughan, B. (2011). The impact of prenatal maternal risk, fearless temperament, and early parenting on adolescent callous-unemotional traits: A 14-year longitudinal investigation. *Journal of Child Psychology and Psychiatry, 52*, 878–888. http://dx.doi.org/10.1111/j.1469-7610.2011.02397.x

Barry, C. T., Frick, P. J., DeShazo, T. M., McCoy, M. G., Ellis, M., & Loney, B. R. (2000). The importance of callous-unemotional traits for extending the concept of psychopathy to children. *Journal of Abnormal Psychology, 109*, 335–340. http://dx.doi.org/10.1037/0021-843X.109.2.335

Beitchman, J. H., Zai, C. C., Muir, K., Berall, L., Nowrouzi, B., Choi, E., & Kennedy, J. L. (2012). Childhood aggression, callous-unemotional traits and oxytocin genes. *European Child and Adolescent Psychiatry, 21*, 125–132. http://dx.doi.org/10.1007/s00787-012-0240-6

Berrios, G. E. (1996). *The history of mental symptoms: Descriptive psychopathology since the nineteenth century*. New York, NY: Cambridge University Press.

Blackburn, R. (1987). Two scales for the assessment of personality disorder in antisocial populations. *Personality and Individual Differences, 8*, 81–93.

Blair, R. J. R. (1999). Responsiveness to distress cues in the child with psychopathic tendencies. *Personality and Individual Differences, 27*, 135–145. http://dx.doi.org/10.1016/S0191-8869(98)00231-1

Blair, R. J. R., Budhani, S., Colledge, E., & Scott, S. (2005). Deafness to fear in boys with psychopathic tendencies. *Journal of Child Psychology and Psychiatry, 46*, 327–336. http://dx.doi.org/10.1111/j.1469-7610.2004.00356.x

Blair, R. J. R., Colledge, E., & Mitchell, D. G. V. (2001). Somatic markers and response reversal: Is there orbitofrontal cortex dysfunction in boys with psychopathic tendencies? *Journal of Abnormal Child Psychology, 29*, 499–511. http://dx.doi.org/10.1023/A:1012277125119

Blair, R. J. R., Colledge, E., Murray, L., & Mitchell, D. G. V. (2001). A selective impairment in the processing of sad and fearful expressions in children with psychopathic tendencies. *Journal of Abnormal Child Psychology, 29*, 491–498. http://dx.doi.org/10.1023/A:1012225108281

Block, J., & Block, J. H. (1980). *The California Child Q-Set*. Palo Alto, CA: Consulting Psychologists Press.

Boccaccini, M. T., Epstein, M., Poythress, N., Douglas, K. S., Campbell, J., Gardner, G., & Falkenbach, D. (2007). Self-report measures of child and adolescent psychopathy as predictors of offending in four samples of justice-involved youth. *Assessment, 14*, 361–374. http://dx.doi.org/10.1177/1073191107303569

Bohlin, G., Eninger, L., Brocki, K. C., & Thorell, L. B. (2012). Disorganized attachment and inhibitory capacity: Predicting externalizing problem behaviors. *Journal of Abnormal Child Psychology, 40*, 449–458. http://dx.doi.org/10.1007/s10802-011-9574-7

Bolt, D. M., Hare, R. D., Vitale, J. E., & Newman, J. P. (2004). A multigroup item response theory analysis of the Psychopathy Checklist—Revised. *Psychological Assessment, 16*, 155–168. http://dx.doi.org/10.1037/1040-3590.16.2.155

Brandt, J. R., Kennedy, W. A., Patrick, C. J., & Curtin, J. J. (1997). Assessment of psychopathy in a population of incarcerated adolescent offenders. *Psychological Assessment, 9*, 429–435. http://dx.doi.org/10.1037/1040-3590.9.4.429

Brestan, E. V., & Eyberg, S. M. (1998). Effective psychosocial treatments of conduct-disordered children and adolescents: 29 years, 82 studies, and 5,272 kids. *Journal of Clinical Child Psychology, 27*, 180–189. http://dx.doi.org/10.1207/s15374424jccp2702_5

Budhani, S., & Blair, R. J. R. (2005). Response reversal and children with psychopathic tendencies: Success is a function of salience of contingency change. *Journal of Child Psychology and Psychiatry, 46*, 972–981. http://dx.doi.org/10.1111/j.1469-7610.2004.00398.x

Burke, J. D., Loeber, R., & Lahey, B. B. (2007). Adolescent conduct disorder and interpersonal callousness as predictors of psychopathy in young adults. *Journal of*

Clinical Child and Adolescent Psychology, 36, 334–346. http://dx.doi.org/10.1080/15374410701444223

Byrd, A. L., Kahn, R. E., & Pardini, D. A. (2013). A validation of the Inventory of Callous-Unemotional Traits in a community sample of young adult males. *Journal of Psychopathology and Behavioral Assessment, 35*, 20–34. http://dx.doi.org/10.1007/s10862-012-9315-4

Byrd, A. L., Loeber, R., & Pardini, D. A. (2012). Understanding desisting and persisting forms of delinquency: The unique contributions of disruptive behavior disorders and interpersonal callousness. *Journal of Child Psychology and Psychiatry, 53*, 371–380. http://dx.doi.org/10.1111/j.1469-7610.2011.02504.x

Caldwell, M., Skeem, J., Salekin, R., & van Rybroek, G. (2006). Treatment response of adolescent offenders with psychopathy features: A 2-year follow-up. *Criminal Justice and Behavior, 33*, 571–596. http://dx.doi.org/10.1177/0093854806288176

Caputo, A. A., Frick, P. J., & Brodsky, S. L. (1999). Family violence and juvenile sex offending: The potential mediating role of psychopathic traits and negative attitudes toward women. *Criminal Justice and Behavior, 26*, 338–356. http://dx.doi.org/10.1177/0093854899026003004

Cauffman, E., Kimonis, E. R., Dmitrieva, J., & Monahan, K. C. (2009). A multimethod assessment of juvenile psychopathy: Comparing the predictive utility of the PCL:YV, YPI, and NEO PRI. *Psychological Assessment, 21*, 528–542. http://dx.doi.org/10.1037/a0017367

Chabrol, H., van Leeuwen, N., Rodgers, R. F., & Gibbs, J. C. (2011). Relations between self-serving cognitive distortions, psychopathic traits, and antisocial behavior in a non-clinical sample of adolescents. *Personality and Individual Differences, 51*, 887–892. http://dx.doi.org/10.1016/j.paid.2011.07.008

Cheng, Y., Hung, A. Y., & Decety, J. (2012). Dissociation between affective sharing and emotion understanding in juvenile psychopaths. *Development and Psychopathology, 24*, 623–636. http://dx.doi.org/10.1017/S095457941200020X

Christian, R. E., Frick, P. J., Hill, N. L., Tyler, L., & Frazer, D. R. (1997). Psychopathy and conduct problems in children: II. Implications for subtyping children with conduct problems. *Journal of the American Academy of Child and Adolescent Psychiatry, 36*, 233–241. http://dx.doi.org/10.1097/00004583-199702000-00014

Cicchetti, D., & Cohen, D. (1995). *Developmental psychopathology: Vol. 2. Risk, disorder, and adaptation.* New York, NY: Wiley.

Cicchetti, D., & Rogosch, F. A. (1996). Equifinality and multifinality in developmental psychopathology. *Development and Psychopathology, 8*, 597–600. http://dx.doi.org/10.1017/S0954579400007318

Cleckley, H. (1976). *The mask of sanity*. St. Louis, MO: Mosby. (Original work published 1941)

Colins, O. F., Vermeiren, R., De Bolle, M., & Broekaert, E. (2012). Self-reported psychopathic-like traits as predictors of recidivism in detained male adolescents. *Criminal Justice and Behavior, 39*, 1421–1435. http://dx.doi.org/10.1177/0093854812456526

Comer, J. S., Chow, C., Chan, P. T., Cooper-Vince, C., & Wilson, L. A. (2013). Psychosocial treatment efficacy for disruptive behavior problems in very young children: A meta-analytic examination. *Journal of the American Academy of Child and Adolescent Psychiatry, 52*, 26–36. http://dx.doi.org/10.1016/j.jaac.2012.10.001

Conley v. Indiana, 972 N. E. 2d 864 (2012)

Cooke, D. J., & Michie, C. (2001). Refining the construct of psychopathy: Towards a hierarchical model. *Psychological Assessment, 13*, 171–188. http://dx.doi.org/10.1037/1040-3590.13.2.171

Corrado, R. R., Vincent, G. M., Hart, S. D., & Cohen, I. M. (2004). Predictive validity of the Psychopathy Checklist: Youth Version for general and violent recidivism. *Behavioral Sciences and the Law, 22*, 5–22. http://dx.doi.org/10.1002/bsl.574

Dadds, M. R., Cauchi, A. J., Wimalaweera, S., Hawes, D. J., & Brennan, J. (2012). Outcomes, moderators, and mediators of empathic-emotion recognition training for complex conduct problems in childhood. *Psychiatry Research, 199*, 201–207. http://dx.doi.org/10.1016/j.psychres.2012.04.033

Dadds, M. R., El Masry, Y., Wimalaweera, S., & Guastella, A. J. (2008). Reduced eye gaze explains "fear blindness" in childhood psychopathic traits. *Journal of the American Academy of Child and Adolescent Psychiatry, 47*, 455–463. http://dx.doi.org/10.1097/CHI.0b013e31816407f1

Dadds, M. R., Jambrak, J., Pasalich, D., Hawes, D. J., & Brennan, J. (2011). Impaired attention to the eyes of attachment figures and the developmental origins of psychopathy. *Journal of Child Psychology and Psychiatry, 52*, 238–245. http://dx.doi.org/10.1111/j.1469-7610.2010.02323.x

Dadds, M. R., Perry, Y., Hawes, D. J., Merz, S., Riddell, A. C., Haines, D. J., . . . Abeygunawardane, A. I. (2006). Attention to the eyes and fear-recognition deficits in child psychopathy. *British Journal of Psychiatry, 189*, 280–281. http://dx.doi.org/10.1192/bjp.bp.105.018150

DeMatteo, D., & Edens, J. F. (2006). The role and relevance of the Psychopathy Checklist—Revised in court: A case law survey of US courts (1991–2004). *Psychology, Public Policy, and Law, 12*, 214–241. http://dx.doi.org/10.1037/1076-8971.12.2.214

DeMatteo, D., Edens, J. F., Galloway, M., Cox, J., Smith, S. T., & Formon, D. (2014). The role and reliability of the Psychopathy Checklist—Revised in U.S. sexually violent predator evaluations: A case law survey. *Law and Human Behavior, 38*, 248–255. http://dx.doi.org/10.1037/lhb0000059

de Wied, M., van Boxtel, A., Matthys, W., & Meeus, W. (2012). Verbal, facial and autonomic responses to empathy-eliciting film clips by disruptive male adolescents with high versus low callous-unemotional traits. *Journal of Abnormal Child Psychology, 40*, 211–223. http://dx.doi.org/10.1007/s10802-011-9557-8

Dillard, C. L., Salekin, R. T., Barker, E. D., & Grimes, R. D. (2013). Psychopathy in adolescent offenders: an item response theory study of the Antisocial Process Screening Device-Self Report and the Psychopathy Checklist: Youth Version. *Personality Disorders: Theory, Research, and Treatment, 4*, 101–120. http://dx.doi.org/10.1037/a0028439

Douglas, K. S., Epstein, M. E., & Poythress, N. G. (2008). Criminal recidivism among juvenile offenders: Testing the incremental and predictive validity of three measures of psychopathic features. *Law and Human Behavior, 32*, 423–438. http://dx.doi.org/10.1007/s10979-007-9114-8

Dyck, H. L., Campbell, M., Schmidt, F., & Wershler, J. L. (2013). Youth psychopathic traits and their impact on long-term criminal offending trajectories. *Youth Violence and Juvenile Justice, 11*, 230–248.

Edens, J. F., Campbell, J. S., & Weir, J. M. (2007). Youth psychopathy and criminal recidivism: A meta-analysis of the Psychopathy Checklist measures. *Law and Human Behavior, 31*, 53–75. http://dx.doi.org/10.1007/s10979-006-9019-y

Edens, J. F., Marcus, D. K., Lilienfeld, S. O., & Poythress, N. G., Jr. (2006). Psychopathic, not psychopath: Taxometric evidence for the dimensional structure of psychopathy. *Journal of Abnormal Psychology, 115*, 131–144. http://dx.doi.org/10.1037/0021-843X.115.1.131

Edens, J. F., Skeem, J. L., Cruise, K. R., & Cauffman, E. (2001). Assessment of "juvenile psychopathy" and its association with violence: A critical review. *Behavioral Sciences and the Law, 19*, 53–80. http://dx.doi.org/10.1002/bsl.425

Edens, J. F., Skopp, N. A., & Cahill, M. A. (2008). Psychopathic features moderate the relationship between harsh and inconsistent parental discipline and adolescent antisocial behavior. *Journal of Clinical Child and Adolescent Psychology, 37*, 472–476. http://dx.doi.org/10.1080/15374410801955938

Essau, C. A., Sasagawa, S., & Frick, P. J. (2006). Callous-unemotional traits in a community sample of adolescents. *Assessment, 13*, 454–469. http://dx.doi.org/10.1177/1073191106287354

Ezpeleta, L., de la Osa, N., Granero, R., Penelo, E., & Domènech, J. M. (2013). Inventory of callous-unemotional traits in a community sample of preschoolers. *Journal of Clinical Child and Adolescent Psychology, 42*, 91–105. http://dx.doi.org/10.1080/15374416.2012.734221

Falkenbach, D. M., Poythress, N. G., & Heide, K. M. (2003). Psychopathic features in a juvenile diversion population: Reliability and predictive validity of two self-report measures. *Behavioral Sciences and the Law, 21*, 787–805. http://dx.doi.org/10.1002/bsl.562

Fanti, K. A., Frick, P. J., & Georgiou, S. (2009). Linking callous un-emotional traits to instrumental traits and non-instrumental forms of aggression. *Journal of Psychopathology and Behavioral Assessment, 31*, 285–298. http://dx.doi.org/10.1007/s10862-008-9111-3

Fanti, K. A., & Kimonis, E. R. (2012). Bullying and victimization: The role of conduct problems and psychopathic traits. *Journal of Research on Adolescence, 22*, 617–631. http://dx.doi.org/10.1111/j.1532-7795.2012.00809.x

Farrington, D. P. (1995). The Twelfth Jack Tizard Memorial Lecture—The development of offending and antisocial behaviour from childhood: Key findings from the Cambridge Study in Delinquent Development. *Journal of Child Psychology and Psychiatry, 36*, 929–964. http://dx.doi.org/10.1111/j.1469-7610.1995.tb01342.x

Farrington, D. P., Ullrich, S., & Salekin, R. T. (2010). Environmental influences on child and adolescent psychopathy. In R. T. Salekin & D. R. Lynam (Eds.), *Handbook of child and adolescent psychopathy* (pp. 202–230). New York, NY: Guilford Press.

Farrington, D. P., & West, D. J. (1993). Criminal, penal and life histories of chronic offenders: Risk and protective factors and early identification. *Criminal Behaviour and Mental Health, 3*, 492–523.

Fink, B. C., Tant, A. S., Tremba, K., & Kiehl, K. A. (2012). Assessment of psychopathic traits in an incarcerated adolescent sample: A methodological comparison. *Journal of Abnormal Child Psychology, 40*, 971–986. http://dx.doi.org/10.1007/s10802-012-9614-y

Fisher, L., & Blair, R. J. R. (1998). Cognitive impairment and its relationship to psychopathic tendencies in children with emotional and behavioral difficulties. *Journal of Abnormal Child Psychology, 26*, 511–519. http://dx.doi.org/10.1023/A:1022655919743

Fite, P. J., Greening, L., & Stoppelbein, L. (2008). Relation between parenting stress and psychopathic traits among children. *Behavioral Sciences and the Law, 26*, 239–248. http://dx.doi.org/10.1002/bsl.803

Flight, J. I., & Forth, A. E. (2007). Instrumentally violent youths: The roles of psychopathic traits, empathy, and attachment. *Criminal Justice and Behavior, 34*, 739–751. http://dx.doi.org/10.1177/0093854807299462

Forth, A. E., & Burke, H. (1998). Psychopathy in adolescence: Assessment, violence, and developmental precursors. In D. J. Cooke, A. E. Forth, & R. D. Hare (Eds.), *Psychopathy: Theory, research and implications for society* (pp. 205–229). http://dx.doi.org/10.1007/978-94-011-3965-6_10

Forth, A. E., Hart, S. D., & Hare, R. D. (1990). Assessment of psychopathy in male young offenders. *Psychological Assessment, 2*, 342–344. http://dx.doi.org/10.1037/1040-3590.2.3.342

Forth, A. E., Kosson, D. S., & Hare, R. D. (2003). *Hare Psychopathy Checklist: Youth version.* Toronto, Ontario, Canada: Multi-Health Systems.

Fowler, T., Langley, K., Rice, F., Whittinger, N., Ross, K., van Goozen, S., . . . Thapar, A. (2009). Psychopathy traits in adolescents with childhood attention-deficit hyperactivity disorder. *British Journal of Psychiatry, 194*, 62–67. http://dx.doi.org/10.1192/bjp.bp.107.046870

Frick, P. J. (1995). Callous-unemotional traits and conduct problems: A two-factor model of psychopathy in children. *Issues in Criminological and Legal Psychology, 24*, 47–51.

Frick, P. J. (1998). *Conduct disorders and severe antisocial behavior.* http://dx.doi.org/10.1007/978-1-4615-5343-4

Frick, P. J. (2004). *The Inventory of Callous-Unemotional Traits.* Unpublished rating scale.

Frick, P. J. (2006). Developmental pathways to conduct disorder. *Child and Adolescent Psychiatric Clinics of North America, 15*, 311–331. http://dx.doi.org/10.1016/j.chc.2005.11.003

Frick, P. J. (2009). Extending the construct of psychopathy to youth: Implications for understanding, diagnosing, and treating antisocial children and adolescents. *Canadian Psychiatric Association Journal, 54*, 803–812.

Frick, P. J. (2012). Developmental pathways to conduct disorder: Implications for future directions in research, assessment, and treatment. *Journal of Clinical Child and Adolescent Psychology, 41*, 378–389. http://dx.doi.org/10.1080/15374416.2012.664815

Frick, P. J., Barry, C. T., & Bodin, S. D. (2000). Applying the concept of psychopathy to children: Implications for the assessment of antisocial youth. In C. B. Gacono (Ed.), *The clinical and forensic assessment of psychopathy: A practitioner's guide* (pp. 3–24). Mahwah, NJ: Erlbaum.

Frick, P. J., Barry, C. T., & Kamphaus, R. W. (2010). *Clinical assessment of children's personality and behavior.* http://dx.doi.org/10.1007/978-1-4419-0641-0

Frick, P. J., Bodin, S. D., & Barry, C. T. (2000). Psychopathic traits and conduct problems in community and clinic-referred samples of children: Further development of the psychopathy screening device. *Psychological Assessment, 12*, 382–393. http://dx.doi.org/10.1037/1040-3590.12.4.382

Frick, P. J., Cornell, A. H., Barry, C. T., Bodin, S. D., & Dane, H. E. (2003). Callous-unemotional traits and conduct problems in the prediction of conduct problem severity, aggression, and self-report of delinquency. *Journal of Abnormal Child Psychology, 31*, 457–470. http://dx.doi.org/10.1023/A:1023899703866

Frick, P. J., & Hare, R. D. (2001). *The Antisocial Process Screening Device.* Toronto, Ontario, Canada: Multi-Health Systems.

Frick, P. J., Kimonis, E. R., Dandreaux, D. M., & Farell, J. M. (2003). The 4 year stability of psychopathic traits in non-referred youth. *Behavioral Sciences and the Law, 21*, 713–736. http://dx.doi.org/10.1002/bsl.568

Frick, P. J., Lilienfeld, S. O., Ellis, M., Loney, B., & Silverthorn, P. (1999). The association between anxiety and psychopathy dimensions in children. *Journal of Abnormal Child Psychology, 27*, 383–392. http://dx.doi.org/10.1023/A:1021928018403

Frick, P. J., & Marsee, M. A. (2006). Psychopathy and developmental pathways to antisocial behavior in youth. In C. J. Patrick (Ed.), *Handbook of psychopathy* (pp. 353–374). New York, NY: Guilford Press.

Frick, P. J., & Moffitt, T. E. (2010). *A proposal to the DSM–V Childhood Disorders and the ADHD and Disruptive Behavior Disorders Work Groups to include a specifier to the diagnosis of conduct disorder based on the presence of callous-unemotional traits.* Washington, DC: American Psychiatric Association. Retrieved from http://www.dsm5.org/Proposal%20Revision%20Attachments/Proposal%20for%20Callous%20and%20Unemotional%20Specifier%20of%20Conduct%20Disorder.pdf

Frick, P. J., O'Brien, B. S., Wootton, J. M., & McBurnett, K. (1994). Psychopathy and conduct problems in children. *Journal of Abnormal Psychology, 103*, 700–707. http://dx.doi.org/10.1037/0021-843X.103.4.700

Frick, P. J., Ray, J. V., Thornton, L. C., & Kahn, R. E. (2014). Can callous-unemotional traits enhance the understanding, diagnosis, and treatment of serious conduct problems in children and adolescents? A comprehensive review. *Psychological Bulletin, 140*, 1–57. doi:1037/a0033076

Frick, P. J., Stickle, T. R., Dandreaux, D. M., Farrell, J. M., & Kimonis, E. R. (2005). Callous-unemotional traits in predicting the severity and stability of conduct problems and delinquency. *Journal of*

Abnormal Child Psychology, 33, 471–487. http://dx.doi.org/10.1007/s10648-005-5728-9

Frick, P. J., & White, S. F. (2008). Research review: The importance of callous-unemotional traits for the development of aggressive and antisocial behavior. *Journal of Child Psychology and Psychiatry, 49*, 359–375. http://dx.doi.org/10.1111/j.1469-7610.2007.01862.x

Fung, M. T., Raine, A., Loeber, R., Lynam, D. R., Steinhauer, S. R., Venables, P. H., & Stouthamer-Loeber, M. (2005). Reduced electrodermal activity in psychopathy-prone adolescents. *Journal of Abnormal Psychology, 114*, 187–196. http://dx.doi.org/10.1037/0021-843X.114.2.187

Goldweber, A., Dmitrieva, J., Cauffman, E., Piquero, A. R., & Steinberg, L. (2011). The development of criminal style in adolescence and young adulthood: Separating the lemmings from the loners. *Journal of Youth and Adolescence, 40*, 332–346. http://dx.doi.org/10.1007/s10964-010-9534-5

Graham v. Florida, 130 S. Ct. 2011 (2010).

Gretton, H. M., McBride, M., Hare, R. D., O'Shaughnessy, R., & Kumka, G. (2001). Psychopathy and recidivism in adolescent sex offenders. *Criminal Justice and Behavior, 28*, 427–449. http://dx.doi.org/10.1177/009385480102800403

Grinberg, E. (2006). *Psychiatrist: Teen knew killing his family was wrong*. Retrieved from http://www.courttv.com/trials/posey/013106_ctv.html

Grisso, T. (2004). *Double jeopardy*. New York, NY: Guilford Press.

Grisso, T. (2010). Guidance for improving forensic reports: A review of common errors. *Open Access Journal of Forensic Psychology, 2*, 102–115.

Haas, S. M., Waschbusch, D. A., Pelham, W. E., Jr., King, S., Andrade, B. F., & Carrey, N. J. (2011). Treatment response in CP/ADHD children with callous/unemotional traits. *Journal of Abnormal Child Psychology, 39*, 541–552. http://dx.doi.org/10.1007/s10802-010-9480-4

Hare, R. D. (1991). *The Hare Psychopathy Checklist*. Toronto, Ontario, Canada: Multi-Health Systems.

Hare, R. D. (2003). *The Hare Psychopathy Checklist—Revised*. Toronto, Ontario, Canada: Multi-Health Systems.

Hart, S. D. (1998). The role of psychopathy in assessing risk for violence: Conceptual and methodological issues. *Legal and Criminological Psychology, 3*, 121–140. http://dx.doi.org/10.1111/j.2044-8333.1998.tb00354.x

Hart, S. D., Hare, R. D., & Cox, D. N. (1995). *The Hare Psychopathy Checklist: Screening Version (PCL: SV)*. Toronto, Ontario, Canada: Multi-Health Systems.

Hart, S. D., Watt, K. A., & Vincent, G. M. (2002). Commentary on Seagrave and Grisso: Impressions of the state of the art. *Law and Human Behavior, 26*, 241–245. http://dx.doi.org/10.1023/A:1014648227688

Hathaway, S. R., & McKinley, J. C. (1989). *Minnesota Multiphasic Personality Inventory—2: Manual for administration and scoring*. Minneapolis: University of Minnesota Press.

Hawes, D. J., & Dadds, M. R. (2005). The treatment of conduct problems in children with callous-unemotional traits. *Journal of Consulting and Clinical Psychology, 73*, 737–741. http://dx.doi.org/10.1037/0022-006X.73.4.737

Hawes, D. J., & Dadds, M. R. (2007). Stability and malleability of callous-unemotional traits during treatment for childhood conduct problems. *Journal of Clinical Child and Adolescent Psychology, 36*, 347–355. http://dx.doi.org/10.1080/15374410701444298

Hawes, D. J., Dadds, M. R., Brennan, J., Rhodes, T., & Cauchi, A. (2013). Revisiting the treatment of conduct problems in children with callous-unemotional traits. *Australian and New Zealand Journal of Psychiatry, 47*, 646–653. http://dx.doi.org/10.1177/0004867413484092

Hawes, D. J., Dadds, M. R., Frost, A. D., & Hasking, P. A. (2011). Do childhood callous-unemotional traits drive change in parenting practices? *Journal of Clinical Child and Adolescent Psychology, 40*, 507–518. http://dx.doi.org/10.1080/15374416.2011.581624

Hawes, S. W., Byrd, A. L., Henderson, C. E., Gazda, R. L., Burke, J. D., Loeber, R., & Pardini, D. A. (2014). Refining the parent-reported Inventory of Callous-Unemotional Traits in boys with conduct problems. *Psychological Assessment, 26*, 256–266. http://dx.doi.org/10.1037/a0034718

Hemphill, J. F., & Hart, S. D. (2002). Treatment of psychopathic personality disorder. In E. Blauuw & L. Sheridan (Eds.), *Psychopaths: Current international perspectives* (pp. 159–174). Amsterdam, the Netherlands: Elsevier.

Hicks, B. M., Markon, K. E., Patrick, C. J., Krueger, R. F., & Newman, J. P. (2004). Identifying psychopathy subtypes on the basis of personality structure. *Psychological Assessment, 16*, 276–288. http://dx.doi.org/10.1037/1040-3590.16.3.276

Hicks, M. M., Rogers, R., & Cashel, M. (2000). Predictions of violent and total infractions among institutionalized male juvenile offenders. *Journal of the American Academy of Psychiatry and the Law, 28*, 183–190.

Hillege, S., Das, J., & de Ruiter, C. (2010). The Youth Psychopathic Traits Inventory: Psychometric properties and its relation to substance use and interpersonal style in a Dutch sample of non-referred adolescents. *Journal of Adolescence, 33*, 83–91. http://dx.doi.org/10.1016/j.adolescence.2009.05.006

Idaho v. Windom, 150 Idaho 873, 253 P. 3d 310 (2011).

Illinois v. Nichols, 964 N. E. 2d 1190 (2012).

In the matter of N.B.P. (1998), 230 A. R. 195 (Prov. Ct.) (WL Canada).

Isen, J., Raine, A., Baker, L., Dawson, M., Bezdjian, S., & Lozano, D. I. (2010). Sex-specific association between psychopathic traits and electrodermal reactivity in children. *Journal of Abnormal Psychology, 119*, 216–225. http://dx.doi.org/10.1037/a0017777

Kahn, R. E., Frick, P. J., Youngstrom, E., Findling, R. L., & Youngstrom, J. K. (2012). The effects of including a callous-unemotional specifier for the diagnosis of conduct disorder. *Journal of Child Psychology and Psychiatry, 53*, 271–282. http://dx.doi.org/10.1111/j.1469-7610.2011.02463.x

Karpman, B. (1948). The myth of the psychopathic personality. *American Journal of Psychiatry, 104*, 523–534. http://dx.doi.org/10.1176/appi.ajp.104.9.523

Karpman, B. (1955). Criminal psychodynamics: A platform. *Archives of Criminal Psychodynamics, 1*, 3–100.

Karpman, S. B. (1961). Personality patterns. *Georgetown Medical Bulletin, 14*, 294–297.

Kennealy, P. J., Skeem, J. L., Walters, G. D., & Camp, J. (2010). Do core interpersonal and affective traits of PCL-R psychopathy interact with antisocial behavior and disinhibition to predict violence? *Psychological Assessment, 22*, 569–580. http://dx.doi.org/10.1037/a0019618

Kerr, M., Van Zalk, M., & Stattin, H. (2012). Psychopathic traits moderate peer influence on adolescent delinquency. *Journal of Child Psychology and Psychiatry, 53*, 826–835. http://dx.doi.org/10.1111/j.1469-7610.2011.02492.x

Kimonis, E. R., Bagner, D. M., Linares, D., Blake, C. A., & Rodriguez, G. (2014). Parent training outcomes among young children with callous-unemotional conduct problems with or at-risk for developmental delay. *Journal of Child and Family Studies, 23*, 437–448. http://dx.doi.org/10.1007/s10826-013-9756-8

Kimonis, E. R., Cross, B., Howard, A., & Donoghue, K. (2013). Maternal care, maltreatment and callous-unemotional traits among urban male juvenile offenders. *Journal of Youth and Adolescence, 42*, 165–177. http://dx.doi.org/10.1007/s10964-012-9820-5

Kimonis, E. R., Fanti, K. A., Goldweber, A., Marsee, M. A., Frick, P. J., & Cauffman, E. (2014). Callous-unemotional traits in incarcerated adolescents. *Psychological Assessment, 26*, 227–237. http://dx.doi.org/10.1037/a0034585

Kimonis, E. R., Frick, P. J., & Barry, C. (2004). Callous-unemotional traits and delinquent peer affiliation. *Journal of Consulting and Clinical Psychology, 72*, 956–966. http://dx.doi.org/10.1037/0022-006X.72.6.956

Kimonis, E. R., Frick, P. J., Fazekas, H., & Loney, B. R. (2006). Psychopathy, aggression, and the processing of emotional stimuli in non-referred girls and boys. *Behavioral Sciences and the Law, 24*, 21–37. http://dx.doi.org/10.1002/bsl.668

Kimonis, E. R., Frick, P. J., Skeem, J. L., Marsee, M. A., Cruise, K., Muñoz, L. C., . . . Morris, A. S. (2008). Assessing callous-unemotional traits in adolescent offenders: Validation of the Inventory of Callous-Unemotional Traits. *International Journal of Law and Psychiatry, 31*, 241–252. http://dx.doi.org/10.1016/j.ijlp.2008.04.002

Kimonis, E. R., Pardini, D., Pasalich, D., & McMahon, R. (2014). Callous and unemotional specifier for conduct disorder. In G. O. Gabbard (Ed.), *Gabbard's treatments of psychiatric disorders* (5th ed.). Arlington, VA: American Psychiatric Publishing.

Kimonis, E. R., Skeem, J. L., Cauffman, E., & Dmitrieva, J. (2011). Are secondary variants of juvenile psychopathy more reactively violent and less psychosocially mature than primary variants? *Law and Human Behavior, 35*, 381–391. http://dx.doi.org/10.1007/s10979-010-9243-3

Kochanska, G. (1997). Multiple pathways to conscience for children with different temperaments: From toddlerhood to age 5. *Developmental Psychology, 33*, 228–240. http://dx.doi.org/10.1037/0012-1649.33.2.228

Kolko, D. J., & Pardini, D. A. (2010). ODD dimensions, ADHD, and callous-unemotional traits as predictors of treatment response in children with disruptive behavior disorders. *Journal of Abnormal Psychology, 119*, 713–725. http://dx.doi.org/10.1037/a0020910

Kosson, D. S., Cyterski, T. D., Steuerwald, B. L., Neumann, C. S., & Walker-Matthews, S. (2002). The reliability and validity of the Psychopathy Checklist: Youth Version (PCL:YV) in nonincarcerated adolescent males. *Psychological Assessment, 14*, 97–109. http://dx.doi.org/10.1037/1040-3590.14.1.97

Kruh, I. P., Frick, P. J., & Clements, C. B. (2005). Historical and personality correlates to the violence patterns of juveniles tried as adults. *Criminal Justice and Behavior, 32*, 69–96. http://dx.doi.org/10.1177/0093854804270629

Larsson, H., Andershed, H., & Lichtenstein, P. (2006). A genetic factor explains most of the variation in the psychopathic personality. *Journal of Abnormal Psychology, 115*, 221–230. http://dx.doi.org/10.1037/0021-843X.115.2.221

Lee, Z., Klaver, J. R., Hart, S. D., Moretti, M. M., & Douglas, K. S. (2009). Short-term stability of psychopathic traits in adolescent offenders. *Journal of Clinical Child and Adolescent Psychology, 38*, 595–605. http://dx.doi.org/10.1080/15374410903103536

Lee, Z., Vincent, G. M., Hart, S. D., & Corrado, R. R. (2003). The validity of the Antisocial Process Screening Device as a self-report measure of psychopathy in adolescent offenders. *Behavioral Sciences and the Law, 21*, 771–786. http://dx.doi.org/10.1002/bsl.561

Leistico, A. M. R., Salekin, R. T., DeCoster, J., & Rogers, R. (2008). A large-scale meta-analysis relating the Hare measures of psychopathy to antisocial conduct. *Law and Human Behavior, 32*, 28–45. http://dx.doi.org/10.1007/s10979-007-9096-6

Lloyd, C. D., Clark, H. J., & Forth, A. E. (2010). Psychopathy, expert testimony, and indeterminate sentences: Exploring the relationship between Psychopathy Checklist—Revised testimony and trial outcome in Canada. *Legal and Criminological Psychology, 15*, 323–339. http://dx.doi.org/10.1348/135532509X468432

Loeber, R., Pardini, D., Homish, D. L., Wei, E. H., Crawford, A. M., Farrington, D. P., . . . Rosenfeld, R. (2005). The prediction of violence and homicide in young men. *Journal of Consulting and Clinical Psychology, 73*, 1074–1088. http://dx.doi.org/10.1037/0022-006X.73.6.1074

Loney, B. R., Frick, P. J., Clements, C. B., Ellis, M. L., & Kerlin, K. (2003). Callous-unemotional traits, impulsivity, and emotional processing in adolescents with antisocial behavior problems. *Journal of Clinical Child and Adolescent Psychiatry, 32*, 66–80. http://dx.doi.org/10.1207/S15374424JCCP3201_07

Loney, B. R., Taylor, J., Butler, M. A., & Iacono, W. G. (2007). Adolescent psychopathy features: 6-year temporal stability and the prediction of externalizing symptoms during the transition to adulthood. *Aggressive Behavior, 33*, 242–252. http://dx.doi.org/10.1002/ab.20184

Lykken, D. T. (1957). A study of anxiety in the sociopathic personality. *Journal of Abnormal and Social Psychology, 55*, 6–10. http://dx.doi.org/10.1037/h0047232

Lykken, D. T. (1995). *The antisocial personalities*. Hillsdale, NJ: Erlbaum.

Lynam, D. R. (1996). Early identification of chronic offenders: Who is the fledgling psychopath? *Psychological Bulletin, 120*, 209–234. http://dx.doi.org/10.1037/0033-2909.120.2.209

Lynam, D. R. (1997). Pursuing the psychopath: Capturing the fledgling psychopath in a nomological net. *Journal of Abnormal Psychology, 106*, 425–438. http://dx.doi.org/10.1037/0021-843X.106.3.425

Lynam, D. R., Caspi, A., Moffitt, T. E., Loeber, R., & Stouthamer-Loeber, M. (2007). Longitudinal evidence that psychopathy scores in early adolescence predict adult psychopathy. *Journal of Abnormal Psychology, 116*, 155–165. http://dx.doi.org/10.1037/0021-843X.116.1.155

Lynam, D. R., & Gudonis, L. (2005). The development of psychopathy. *Annual Review of Clinical Psychology, 1*, 381–407. http://dx.doi.org/10.1146/annurev.clinpsy.1.102803.144019

Lynam, D. R., & Widiger, T. A. (2001). Using the five-factor model to represent the *DSM–IV* personality disorders: An expert consensus approach. *Journal of Abnormal Psychology, 110*, 401–412. http://dx.doi.org/10.1037/0021-843X.110.3.401

Lyon, D. R., & Ogloff, J. R. P. (2000). Legal and ethical issues in psychopathy assessment. In C. Gacono (Ed.), *The clinical and forensic assessment of psychopathy: A practitioner's guide* (pp. 139–173). Mahwah, NJ: Erlbaum.

Mailloux, D. L., Forth, A. E., & Kroner, D. G. (1997). Psychopathy and substance use in adolescent male offenders. *Psychological Reports, 81*, 529–530.

Manders, W. A., Deković, M., Asscher, J. J., van der Laan, P. H., & Prins, P. J. (2013). Psychopathy as predictor and moderator of multisystemic therapy outcomes among adolescents treated for antisocial behavior. *Journal of Abnormal Child Psychology, 41*, 1121–1132. http://dx.doi.org/10.1007/s10802-013-9749-5

Mash, E. J., & Dozois, D. J. A. (2003). Child psychopathology: A developmental-systems perspective. In E. J. Mash & R. A. Barkley (Eds.), *Child psychopathology* (2nd ed., pp. 3–71). New York, NY: Guilford Press.

McCord, W. M., & McCord, J. (1956). *Psychopathy and delinquency*. New York, NY: Grune & Stratton.

McDonald, R., Dodson, M. C., Rosenfield, D., & Jouriles, E. N. (2011). Effects of a parenting intervention on features of psychopathy in children. *Journal of Abnormal Child Psychology, 39*, 1013–1023. http://dx.doi.org/10.1007/s10802-011-9512-8

McMahon, R. J., Witkiewitz, K., & Kotler, J. S.; Conduct Problems Prevention Research Group. (2010). Predictive validity of callous-unemotional traits measured in early adolescence with respect to multiple antisocial outcomes. *Journal of Abnormal Psychology, 119*, 752–763. http://dx.doi.org/10.1037/a0020796

Mealey, L. (1995). The sociobiology of sociopathy: An integrated evolutionary model. *Behavioral and Brain Sciences, 18*, 523–541. http://dx.doi.org/10.1017/S0140525X00039595

Miller v. Alabama, 132 S. Ct. 2455 (2012)

Mulvey, E. P., Steinberg, L., Piquero, A. R., Besana, M., Fagan, J., Schubert, C., & Cauffman, E. (2010).

Trajectories of desistance and continuity in antisocial behavior following court adjudication among serious adolescent offenders. *Development and Psychopathology, 22*, 453–475. http://dx.doi.org/10.1017/S0954579410000179

Muñoz, L. C., & Frick, P. J. (2007). The reliability, stability, and predictive utility of the self-report version of the Antisocial Process Screening Device. *Scandinavian Journal of Psychology, 48*, 299–312. http://dx.doi.org/10.1111/j.1467-9450.2007.00560.x

Muñoz, L. C., Frick, P. J., Kimonis, E. R., & Aucoin, K. J. (2008). Types of aggression, responsiveness to provocation, and callous-unemotional traits in detained adolescents. *Journal of Abnormal Child Psychology, 36*, 15–28. http://dx.doi.org/10.1007/s10802-007-9137-0

Muñoz, L. C., Kerr, M., & Besic, N. (2008). The peer relationships of youths with psychopathic personality traits: A matter of perspective. *Criminal Justice and Behavior, 35*, 212–227. http://dx.doi.org/10.1177/0093854807310159

Muñoz, L. C., Pakalniskiene, V., & Frick, P. J. (2011). Parental monitoring and youth behavior problems: Moderation by callous-unemotional traits over time. *European Child and Adolescent Psychiatry, 20*, 261–269. http://dx.doi.org/10.1007/s00787-011-0172-6

Murrie, D. C., Boccaccini, M. T., McCoy, W., & Cornell, D. G. (2007). Diagnostic labeling in juvenile court: How do descriptions of psychopathy and conduct disorder influence judges? *Journal of Clinical Child and Adolescent Psychology, 36*, 228–241. http://dx.doi.org/10.1080/15374410701279602

Murrie, D. C., & Cornell, D. G. (2000). The Millon Adolescent Clinical Inventory and psychopathy. *Journal of Personality Assessment, 75*, 110–125. http://dx.doi.org/10.1207/S15327752JPA7501_8

Murrie, D. C., Cornell, D. G., Kaplan, S., McConville, D., & Levy-Elkon, A. (2004). Psychopathy scores and violence among juvenile offenders: A multi-measure study. *Behavioral Sciences and the Law, 22*, 49–67. http://dx.doi.org/10.1002/bsl.573

O'Brien, B. S., & Frick, P. J. (1996). Reward dominance: Associations with anxiety, conduct problems, and psychopathy in children. *Journal of Abnormal Child Psychology, 24*, 223–240. http://dx.doi.org/10.1007/BF01441486

Ogloff, J. R., Wong, S., & Greenwood, A. (1990). Treating criminal psychopaths in a therapeutic community program. *Behavioral Sciences and the Law, 8*, 181–190. http://dx.doi.org/10.1002/bsl.2370080210

Olver, M. E., Stockdale, K. C., & Wormith, J. S. (2009). Risk assessment with young offenders: A meta-analysis of three assessment measures. *Criminal Justice and Behavior, 36*, 329–353. http://dx.doi.org/10.1177/0093854809331457

Pardini, D., Stepp, S., Hipwell, A., Stouthamer-Loeber, M., & Loeber, R. (2012). The clinical utility of the proposed *DSM–5* callous-unemotional subtype of conduct disorder in young girls. *Journal of the American Academy of Child and Adolescent Psychiatry, 51*, 62–73.e4. http://dx.doi.org/10.1016/j.jaac.2011.10.005

Pardini, D. A., Lochman, J. E., & Frick, P. J. (2003). Callous/unemotional traits and social-cognitive processes in adjudicated youths. *Journal of the American Academy of Child and Adolescent Psychiatry, 42*, 364–371. http://dx.doi.org/10.1097/00004583-200303000-00018

Pardini, D. A., Lochman, J. E., & Powell, N. (2007). The development of callous-unemotional traits and antisocial behavior in children: Are there shared and/or unique predictors? *Journal of Clinical Child and Adolescent Psychology, 36*, 319–333. http://dx.doi.org/10.1080/15374410701444215

Pardini, D. A., & Loeber, R. (2008). Interpersonal callousness trajectories across adolescence: Early social influences and adult outcomes. *Criminal Justice and Behavior, 35*, 173–196. http://dx.doi.org/10.1177/0093854807310157

Pasalich, D. S., Dadds, M. R., Hawes, D. J., & Brennan, J. (2011). Do callous-unemotional traits moderate the relative importance of parental coercion versus warmth in child conduct problems? An observational study. *Journal of Child Psychology and Psychiatry, 52*, 1308–1315. http://dx.doi.org/10.1111/j.1469-7610.2011.02435.x

Patterson, G. R. (1982). *Coercive family process*. Eugene, OR: Castalia.

Piquero, A. R., Jennings, W. G., & Barnes, J. C. (2012). Violence in criminal careers: A review of the literature from a developmental life-course perspective. *Aggression and Violent Behavior, 17*, 171–179. http://dx.doi.org/10.1016/j.avb.2012.02.008

Porter, S. (1996). Without conscience or without active conscience? The etiology of psychopathy revisited. *Aggression and Violent Behavior, 1*, 179–189. http://dx.doi.org/10.1016/1359-1789(95)00010-0

Poythress, N. G., Skeem, J. L., & Lilienfeld, S. O. (2006). Associations among early abuse, dissociation, and psychopathy in an offender sample. *Journal of Abnormal Psychology, 115*, 288–297. http://dx.doi.org/10.1037/0021-843X.115.2.288

Roberts, B. W., Caspi, A., & Moffitt, T. E. (2001). The kids are alright: Growth and stability in personality development from adolescence to adulthood. *Journal of Personality and Social Psychology, 81*, 670–683. http://dx.doi.org/10.1037/0022-3514.81.4.670

Rogers, R., Johansen, J., Chang, J. J., & Salekin, R. T. (1997). Predictors of adolescent psychopathy: Oppositional and conduct-disordered symptoms.

Journal of the American Academy of Psychiatry and the Law, 25, 261–271.

Romo, R. (2006, February 1). Posey scored high on psychopath test. *Albuquerque Journal*. Retrieved from http://abqjournal.com/news/state/429395nm02-01-06.htm

Romo, R. (2010, October 10). Posey released from custody. *Albuquerque Journal*. Retrieved from http://www.abqjournal.com/news/state/10235632state10-10-10.htm

Roose, A., Bijttebier, P., Decoene, S., Claes, L., & Frick, P. J. (2010). Assessing the affective features of psychopathy in adolescence: A further validation of the Inventory of Callous and Unemotional Traits. *Assessment, 17*, 44–57. http://dx.doi.org/10.1177/1073191109344153

Roussy, S., & Toupin, J. (2000). Behavioral inhibition deficits in juvenile psychopaths. *Aggressive Behavior, 26*, 413–424. http://dx.doi.org/10.1002/1098-2337(200011)26:6%3C413::AID-AB1%3E3.0.CO;2-Q

Rowe, R., Costello, E. J., Angold, A., Copeland, W. E., & Maughan, B. (2010). Developmental pathways in oppositional defiant disorder and conduct disorder. *Journal of Abnormal Psychology, 119*, 726–738. http://dx.doi.org/10.1037/a0020798

R. v. W. (M. B.), 2008 ABPC 12, [2008] A. W. L. D. 1391 (WL Canada).

Salekin, R. T. (2010). Treatment of child and adolescent psychopathy: Focusing on change. In R. T. Salekin & D. R. Lynam (Eds.), *Handbook of child and adolescent psychopathy* (pp. 343–373). New York, NY: Guilford Press.

Salekin, R. T., Rogers, R., & Sewell, K. W. (1996). A review and meta-analysis of the Psychopathy Checklist and Psychopathy Checklist—Revised: Predictive validity of dangerousness. *Clinical Psychology: Science and Practice, 3*, 203–215. http://dx.doi.org/10.1111/j.1468-2850.1996.tb00071.x

Salekin, R. T., Worley, C., & Grimes, R. D. (2010). Treatment of psychopathy: A review and brief introduction to the mental model approach for psychopathy. *Behavioral Sciences and the Law, 28*, 235–266. http://dx.doi.org/10.1002/bsl.928

Seagrave, D., & Grisso, T. (2002). Adolescent development and the measurement of juvenile psychopathy. *Law and Human Behavior, 26*, 219–239. http://dx.doi.org/10.1023/A:1014696110850

Shaw, D. S., Gilliom, M., Ingoldsby, E. M., & Nagin, D. S. (2003). Trajectories leading to school-age conduct problems. *Developmental Psychology, 39*, 189–200. http://dx.doi.org/10.1037/0012-1649.39.2.189

Silverthorn, P., Frick, P. J., & Reynolds, R. (2001). Timing of onset and correlates of severe conduct problems in adjudicated girls and boys. *Journal of Psychopathology and Behavioral Assessment, 23*, 171–181. http://dx.doi.org/10.1023/A:1010917304587

Skeem, J. L., & Cauffman, E. (2003). Views of the downward extension: Comparing the youth version of the Psychopathy Checklist with the Youth Psychopathic Traits Inventory. *Behavioral Sciences and the Law, 21*, 737–770. http://dx.doi.org/10.1002/bsl.563

Skeem, J. L., Monahan, J., & Mulvey, E. P. (2002). Psychopathy, treatment involvement, and subsequent violence among civil psychiatric patients. *Law and Human Behavior, 26*, 577–603. http://dx.doi.org/10.1023/A:1020993916404

Somech, L. Y., & Elizur, Y. (2012). Promoting self-regulation and cooperation in pre-kindergarten children with conduct problems: A randomized controlled trial. *Journal of the American Academy of Child and Adolescent Psychiatry, 51*, 412–422. http://dx.doi.org/10.1016/j.jaac.2012.01.019

South Carolina v. Stanko, 402 S. C. 252, 741 S. E. 2d 708 (2013).

Stadler, C., Kröger, A., Clement, H., & Grasmann, D. (2012). Aggressive behavior disorders: Efficacy of an intensive therapeutic treatment program VIA. *Kindheit und Entwicklung, 21*, 103–113. http://dx.doi.org/10.1026/0942-5403/a000076

Stanley v. Litscher, Wis. App. 213 F. 3d 340 (2000).

Stevens, D., Charman, T., & Blair, R. J. R. (2001). Recognition of emotion in facial expressions and vocal tones in children with psychopathic tendencies. *Journal of Genetic Psychology: Research and Theory on Human Development, 162*, 201–211. http://dx.doi.org/10.1080/00221320109597961

Stickle, T. R., Kirkpatrick, N. M., & Brush, L. N. (2009). Callous-unemotional traits and social information processing: Multiple risk-factor models for understanding aggressive behavior in antisocial youth. *Law and Human Behavior, 33*, 515–529. http://dx.doi.org/10.1007/s10979-008-9171-7

Taylor, J., Loney, B. R., Bobadilla, L., Iacono, W. G., & McGue, M. (2003). Genetic and environmental influences on psychopathy trait dimensions in a community sample of male twins. *Journal of Abnormal Child Psychology, 31*, 633–645. http://dx.doi.org/10.1023/A:1026262207449

Toupin, J., Mercier, H., Déry, M., Côté, G., & Hodgins, S. (1996). Validity of the PCL-R for adolescents. In D. J. Cooke, A. E. Forth, J. P. Newman, & R. D. Hare (Eds.), *Issues in criminological and legal psychology: Vol. 24. International perspectives on psychopathy* (pp. 143–145). Leicester, England: British Psychological Society.

United States v. Taylor, 320 F. Supp. 2d 790 (N. D. Ind. 2004).

Vasey, M. W., Kotov, R., Frick, P. J., & Loney, B. R. (2005). The latent structure of psychopathy in youth: A taxometric investigation. *Journal of Abnormal Child Psychology, 33*, 411–429. http://dx.doi.org/10.1007/s10802-005-5723-1

Vaughn, M. G., & Howard, M. O. (2005). Self-report measures of juvenile psychopathic personality traits: A comparative review. *Journal of Emotional and Behavioral Disorders, 13*, 152–162. http://dx.doi.org/10.1177/10634266050130030301

Viding, E., Blair, R. J. R., Moffitt, T. E., & Plomin, R. (2005). Evidence for substantial genetic risk for psychopathy in 7-year-olds. *Journal of Child Psychology and Psychiatry, 46*, 592–597. http://dx.doi.org/10.1111/j.1469-7610.2004.00393.x

Viding, E., Jones, A. P., Paul, J. F., Moffitt, T. E., & Plomin, R. (2008). Heritability of antisocial behaviour at 9: Do callous-unemotional traits matter? *Developmental Science, 11*, 17–22. http://dx.doi.org/10.1111/j.1467-7687.2007.00648.x

Viding, E., Simmonds, E., Petrides, K. V., & Frederickson, N. (2009). The contribution of callous-unemotional traits and conduct problems to bullying in early adolescence. *Journal of Child Psychology and Psychiatry, 50*, 471–481. http://dx.doi.org/10.1111/j.1469-7610.2008.02012.x

Viljoen, J. L., MacDougall, E. A. M., Gagnon, N. C., & Douglas, K. S. (2010). Psychopathy evidence in legal proceedings involving adolescent offenders. *Psychology, Public Policy, and Law, 16*, 254–283. http://dx.doi.org/10.1037/a0019649

Vincent, G. M. (2002). *The legitimacy of psychopathy assessments in young offenders: Contributions of item response theory* (Unpublished doctoral dissertation). Simon Fraser University, Burnaby, British Columbia, Canada.

Vincent, G. M. (2006). Psychopathy and violence risk assessment in youth. *Child and Adolescent Psychiatric Clinics of North America, 15*, 407–428. http://dx.doi.org/10.1016/j.chc.2005.12.001

Vincent, G. M., & Hart, S. D. (2012). Legal uses and assessment of psychopathy. In D. Faust (Ed), *Coping with psychiatry and psychological testimony* (6th ed., pp. 563–586). New York, NY: Oxford University Press.

Vincent, G. M., Odgers, C. L., McCormick, A. V., & Corrado, R. R. (2008). The PCL: YV and recidivism in male and female juveniles: A follow-up into young adulthood. *International Journal of Law and Psychiatry, 31*, 287–296. http://dx.doi.org/10.1016/j.ijlp.2008.04.012

Vincent, G. M., Vitacco, M. J., Grisso, T., & Corrado, R. R. (2003). Subtypes of adolescent offenders: Affective traits and antisocial behavior patterns. *Behavioral Sciences and the Law, 21*, 695–712. http://dx.doi.org/10.1002/bsl.556

Vitacco, M. J., & Kosson, D. S. (2010). Understanding psychopathy through an evaluation of interpersonal behavior: Testing the factor structure of the interpersonal measure of psychopathy in a large sample of jail detainees. *Psychological Assessment, 22*, 638–649. http://dx.doi.org/10.1037/a0019780

Vitacco, M. J., Rogers, R., & Neumann, C. S. (2003). The Antisocial Process Screening Device: An examination of its construct and criterion-related validity. *Assessment, 10*, 143–150. http://dx.doi.org/10.1177/1073191103010002005

Waller, R., Gardner, F., Hyde, L. W., Shaw, D. S., Dishion, T. J., & Wilson, M. N. (2012). Do harsh and positive parenting predict parent reports of deceitful-callous behavior in early childhood? *Journal of Child Psychology and Psychiatry, 53*, 946–953. http://dx.doi.org/10.1111/j.1469-7610.2012.02550.x

Walsh, T., & Walsh, Z. (2006). The evidentiary introduction of Psychopathy Checklist—Revised assessed psychopathy in U.S. courts: Extent and appropriateness. *Law and Human Behavior, 30*, 493–507. http://dx.doi.org/10.1007/s10979-006-9042-z

Walsh, Z., Swogger, M. T., & Kosson, D. S. (2009). Psychopathy and instrumental violence: Facet level relationships. *Journal of Personality Disorders, 23*, 416–424. http://dx.doi.org/10.1521/pedi.2009.23.4.416

Waschbusch, D. A., Carrey, N. J., Willoughby, M. T., King, S., & Andrade, B. F. (2007). Effects of methylphenidate and behavior modification on the social and academic behavior of children with disruptive behavior disorders: The moderating role of callous/unemotional traits. *Journal of Clinical Child and Adolescent Psychology, 36*, 629–644. http://dx.doi.org/10.1080/15374410701662766

Washburn, J. J., McMahon, S. D., King, C. A., Reinecke, M. A., & Silver, C. (2004). Narcissistic features in young adolescents: Relations to aggression and internalizing symptoms. *Journal of Youth and Adolescence, 33*, 247–260. http://dx.doi.org/10.1023/B:JOYO.0000025323.94929.d9

White, S. F., Frick, P. J., Lawing, K., & Bauer, D. (2012). Callous-unemotional traits and response to functional family therapy in adolescent offenders. *Behavioral Sciences and the Law, 31*, 271–285. http://dx.doi.org/10.1002/bsl. 2041.

Widiger, T. A. (2006). Psychopathy and *DSM–IV* psychopathology. In C. J. Patrick (Ed.), *Handbook of psychopathy* (pp. 156–171). New York, NY: Guilford Press.

Willoughby, M. T., Waschbusch, D. A., Moore, G. A., & Propper, C. B. (2011). Using the ASEBA to screen for callous unemotional traits in early childhood: Factor structure, temporal stability, and utility. *Journal of Psychopathology and Behavioral Assessment, 33*, 19–30. http://dx.doi.org/10.1007/s10862-010-9195-4

Wootton, J. M., Frick, P. J., Shelton, K. K., & Silverthorn, P. (1997). Ineffective parenting and childhood conduct problems: The moderating role of callous-unemotional traits. *Journal of Consulting and Clinical Psychology, 65*, 301–308. http://dx.doi.org/10.1037/0022-006X.65.2.292.b

Yeh, M. T., Chen, P., Raine, A., Baker, L. A., & Jacobson, K. C. (2011). Child psychopathic traits moderate relationships between parental affect and child aggression. *Journal of the American Academy of Child and Adolescent Psychiatry, 50*, 1054–1064. http://dx.doi.org/10.1016/j.jaac.2011.06.013

Youngstrom, E., Loeber, R., & Stouthamer-Loeber, M. (2000). Patterns and correlates of agreement between parent, teacher, and male adolescent ratings of externalizing and internalizing problems. *Journal of Consulting and Clinical Psychology, 68*, 1038–1050. http://dx.doi.org/10.1037/0022-006X.68.6.1038

Zinger, I., & Forth, A. E. (1998). Psychopathy and Canadian criminal proceedings: The potential for human rights abuses. *Canadian Journal of Criminology, 40*, 237–276.

Zisser, A., & Eyberg, S. M. (2010). Parent-child interaction therapy and the treatment of disruptive behavior disorders. In J. R. Weisz & A. E. Kazdin (Eds.), *Evidence-based psychotherapies for children and adolescents* (2nd ed., pp. 179–193). New York, NY: Guilford Press.

CHAPTER 11

SCHOOL-BASED RISK FACTORS, BULLYING, AND THREAT ASSESSMENT

Dewey Cornell and Anna Heilbrun

Schools are the primary setting outside the home in which children encounter the rules of society and experience a formal system of consequences for their misbehavior. School authorities are often the first to apply labels to children, such as *oppositional* or *defiant*. It is not surprising, then, that schools may be the first place in which children are identified as at risk for criminal offending. Indeed, there are few serious juvenile offenders whose school histories do not reflect patterns of aggressive and defiant behavior at school. Thus, it might be said that criminal careers begin at school. In an era of community-focused interventions, it is inevitable that both prevention and rehabilitation of juvenile delinquency will increasingly involve schools. Accordingly, in this chapter we consider school-based risk factors such as bullying and school-based threat assessment as a strategy for appraising and reducing risk.

Longitudinal studies have identified both academic and behavioral problems at school as risk factors for delinquency and young adult offending. A wide variety of school-based indicators, such as reading problems, poor grades, weak achievement test performance, teacher ratings of misbehavior, school suspension, truancy, and dropout are associated with juvenile offending (Lösel, Bottoms, & Farrington, 2012; Moffitt, 1990). A school disengagement warning index for 8th and 9th grade used five risk indicators obtained from school records: low score on one or more standardized tests, absence for 20% or more of school days, failing one or more core subjects, school suspension, and grade retention (Henry, Knight, & Thornberry, 2012). The index predicted school dropout, which in turn served as a mediator of serious violent crime, arrest, and drug and alcohol use. These findings are compatible with those of a longitudinal study that identified emotional and behavioral engagement in school as a predictor of both school misconduct and general delinquency (Hirschfield & Gasper, 2011).

School adjustment has also been used to assess recidivism and violence risk in juvenile offenders (Conroy, 2012). School behavior problems and low achievement are commonly recognized risk factors, whereas good adjustment to school can be a protective factor. For example, the Structured Assessment of Violence Risk in Youth (Borum, Bartel, & Forth, 2003) identifies poor school achievement and low interest or commitment to school as two of its 24 risk factors, whereas strong commitment to school is one of six protective factors. Another example is the Positive Achievement Change Tool (Baglivio & Jackowski, 2013), which scores both school history and current school status as predictors of juvenile offending.

The association between school problems and antisocial behavior makes sense in light of the prevalence of neuropsychological deficits among delinquent youths. As Moffitt observed (1993), antisocial behavior is strongly associated with deficits in verbal intelligence and executive functioning, including problems with attention and impulse control. Longitudinal findings from the Pittsburgh Youth Study indicated that both low intelligence and cognitive impulsivity at ages 12 to 13 were associated with criminal offending during

http://dx.doi.org/10.1037/14643-011
APA Handbook of Psychology and Juvenile Justice, K. Heilbrun (Editor-in-Chief)

adolescence (Loeber et al., 2012). These kinds of deficits can impair school performance and make school a highly frustrating environment.

Adolescents' psychosocial immaturity can also contribute to difficulties in school performance. Key elements of psychosocial maturity include risk perception, temporal orientation, and susceptibility to peer and adult influence (Steinberg & Scott, 2003). Adolescents are less likely than adults to appreciate the consequences of their actions (Grisso et al., 2003), and these developmental limitations have neurological underpinnings. The prefrontal cortex, which controls planning, executive functioning, logical reasoning, and impulse control, develops over the course of adolescence through synaptic pruning and myelination that continues into the mid-20s (Steinberg, 2010).

In light of the link between cognitive impairment and delinquency, it is not surprising that incarcerated youths have a high incidence of education-related disabilities. A national survey reported that 33.4% of youths in state juvenile corrections systems had formally identified disabilities, compared with just 8.8% in the general population (Quinn, Rutherford, Leone, Osher, & Poirier, 2005). The most commonly identified disabilities in this study, using the classifications of the Individuals With Disabilities Education Act of 1990, were specific emotional disturbance (47.7%), specific learning disabilities (38.6%), mental retardation (9.7%), and other health impairments (a category that includes attention deficit hyperactivity disorder; 2.9%). As noted by Quinn et al. (2005), the overrepresentation of youths with disabilities in the correctional population may have multiple explanations. Individuals with disabilities may have deficits in impulse control, anger, and judgment that lead them to delinquent behavior such as fighting and stealing. Alternatively, disabilities may simply predispose some youths to school failure and dropout, which in turn may place them at risk for delinquency because they lack more positive alternatives.

Although school-related problems are widely recognized as a risk factor for juvenile offending, there is little evidence regarding their sensitivity and specificity. A history of school problems alone would not be sufficient evidence of risk for juvenile offending. Most students with learning problems do not become juvenile offenders and, similarly, many students engage in some degree of misbehavior at school that does not evolve into a broader pattern of delinquency or juvenile offending.

Questions about the persistence or continuity of childhood misbehavior and aggression have been intensively examined for several decades (Van Domburgh, Loeber, Bezemer, Stallings, & Stouthamer-Loeber, 2009). Moffit (1993) proposed a distinction between life-course persistent offenders and adolescent-limited offenders, hypothesizing that youths in the latter category desist from offending by the time they reach adulthood. Although estimates vary, 70% to 80% of juvenile offenders are considered to be adolescent limited (Heilbrun, Goldstein, & Redding, 2005). Furthermore, an estimated 8% to 10% of repeat offenders are responsible for between 60% and 80% of serious or violent offenses committed by juveniles (Henggeler & Sheidow, 2012).

The distinction between persistent and desisting patterns of offending is compelling, and certainly the predominant pattern among adolescents is for declining levels of both school misbehavior and community offending (Mulvey, 2011). However, some authorities have questioned whether the distinction between early-onset and adolescence-onset delinquency is taxonomic (Van Domburgh et al., 2009). An alternative view is that the distinction is really a continuum that can be explained by the severity of neuropsychological problems or interactions with environmental adversity (e.g., poverty, child abuse, exposure to trauma; Fairchild, van Goozen, Calder, & Goodyer, 2013). Studies have found that adolescence-onset delinquents continue to engage in rule breaking and experience mental health problems in adulthood at higher levels than adult controls (e.g., Odgers et al., 2007). All of these findings underscore the need for individualized assessment that recognizes the variety of pathways and outcomes associated with school adjustment problems.

BULLYING AS A RISK FACTOR

Bullying has become widely recognized as one of the most pervasive behavior problems in school

(Swearer, Espelage, Vaillancourt, & Hymel, 2010). Although bullying certainly occurs outside of school, it has been studied most extensively in school settings, and its negative impact on student adjustment and learning has stimulated the development of numerous school-based intervention programs (Ttofi & Farrington, 2009). International studies have documented that bullying and bullying victimization are common experiences for youths of all ages and across diverse cultures and societies (Craig et al., 2009).

Bullying can be defined as the repeated humiliation or injury of a weaker person (Cornell & Cole, 2012; Olweus, 1991). Bullying can be carried out directly or indirectly in a wide variety of forms, often classified as physical, verbal, or social–relational. Direct bullying through physical injury or threat of physical injury is the iconic form of bullying, but verbal bullying in the form of teasing and name calling is the most commonly reported experience of bullying. Social or relational bullying is an indirect form of bullying that involves the use of ostracism and rumors to damage someone's reputation and friendships.

Cyberbullying is a relatively new form of bullying that involves the use of information technologies such as Internet postings and cell phone messages to embarrass or insult someone. Cyberbullying has received a great deal of media attention, but most studies have found that it is less common than traditional bullying and usually co-occurs with other forms of bullying (Lovegrove & Cornell, 2014; Price, Chin, Higa-McMillan, Kim, & Frueh, 2013).

Bullying is often confused with more general forms of peer aggression such as teasing, arguing, and fighting (Cornell & Cole, 2012; Green, Felix, Sharkey, Furlong, & Kras, 2013). The concept of bullying is intended to identify a particularly troubling form of peer aggression in which an identifiable victim is subject to repeated and intentional harm by a dominant aggressor (Olweus, 1991). The three characteristics that distinguish bullying from other forms of peer conflict are that it is an intentional effort to harm someone, occurs repeatedly, and involves a power imbalance in which the aggressor has dominance over the victim (Cornell & Cole, 2012; Gladden, Vivolo-Kantor, Hamburger, & Lumpkin, 2014; Green et al., 2013). The presence of a power imbalance between aggressor and victim is the most distinctive quality of bullying, but it is also the most difficult to assess. Many studies of bullying fail to make this distinction, so they may inflate the prevalence of bullying with other forms of peer aggression (Cornell & Cole, 2012; Green et al., 2013).

Prevalence of Bullying

Self-report surveys have provided a range of estimates of the prevalence of bullying. Results from the National Crime Victimization Study indicated that 28% of students ages 12 to 18 report being bullied at school during the school year (Robers, Kemp, & Truman, 2013). According to the Youth Risk Behavior Survey, 20% of female and 18% of male high school students reported being bullied on school property in the past 12 months (Centers for Disease Control and Prevention, 2014). However, surveys relying on single questions about bullying may underestimate the prevalence of bullying in comparison with multiple-item scales that ask about a variety of bullying behaviors (Esbensen & Carson, 2009). A nationally representative sample using multiple items yielded prevalence rates of approximately 13% for physical bullying, 37% for verbal bullying, 41% for social or relational bullying, and 10% for cyberbullying at least once in the past 2 months (Wang, Iannotti, & Nansel, 2009). The widespread perception that bullying has increased is likely due to greater public awareness and news reports of bullying, because the available data have indicated no change or a slight decrease in bullying over the past decade (Molcho et al., 2009; Robers et al., 2013).

Victims of Bullying

Bullying is regarded as a major health risk that is associated with a host of negative outcomes (Swearer et al., 2010). Bullying victimization has been associated with the development of chronic anxiety, depression, psychosomatic problems, and social adjustment difficulties (Carlisle & Rofes, 2007; Espelage, Low, & De la Rue, 2012; Gini & Pozzoli, 2009; Ttofi, Farrington, Lösel, & Loeber, 2011). Bullying has been linked to suicidal behavior, although this connection is likely moderated by preexisting mental health conditions such as depression (Copeland, Wolke, Angold, & Costello, 2013). In some cases, bullying can be regarded as a stressful life event that triggers a depressive episode (Hanish et al., 2013; Holma, Holma, Melartin, & Isometsä, 2010). Longitudinal studies have indicated that the negative effects of bullying persist into late adolescence and adulthood (Sourander et al., 2007). A meta-analysis of 18 longitudinal studies found that internalizing problems are both antecedents to and consequences of bullying (Reijntjes, Kamphuuis, Prinzie, & Telch, 2010).

Bullying also affects academic achievement. Victims of bullying become disengaged in learning and avoid school because they feel unsafe (Card & Hodges, 2010; Holt & Espelage, 2007). Their school performance and grades decline (Juvonen, Wang, & Espinoza, 2011; Nakamoto & Schwartz, 2010). On a schoolwide level, schools with a higher prevalence of teasing and bullying have lower student engagement (Mehta, Cornell, Fan, & Gregory, 2013), lower passing rates on state-mandated achievement testing (Lacey & Cornell, 2013), and higher dropout rates (Cornell, Gregory, Huang, & Fan, 2013).

Although there is no profile of a victim of bullying, some of the most reliable predictors of bully victimization include poor social competence, low self-esteem, and low peer status (Cook, Williams, Guerra, Kim, & Sadek, 2010). Certain subgroups of students are more vulnerable to being bullied. Students with disabilities are much more likely to be victims (and perpetrators) of bullying than students without disabilities (Rose, Espelage, Aragon, & Elliott, 2011). Students who identify as lesbian, gay, bisexual, or transgender are frequently targets of bullying and harassment (Coker, Austin, & Schuster, 2010). This victimization helps explain why these students are more likely to be truant from school and report higher levels of internalizing symptoms, such as depression, anxiety, and suicidal ideation, than their heterosexual peers (Robinson & Espelage, 2012). Other target characteristics might be height, weight, or physical appearance that distinguish a student from peers. Some youths may be targeted out of jealousy because of desirable characteristics such as academic aptitude or popularity.

Legal Ramifications of Bullying

In 2010, the U.S. Department of Education (USDOE; 2010) sent a "Dear Colleague" letter to state departments of education and local school districts advising them that many forms of bullying constitute violations of federal antidiscrimination laws and that schools must take prompt and effective steps to prevent and eliminate harassment. Whereas bullying is a general concept not defined in federal law, harassment is a well-established legal construct in civil rights law. *Harassment* refers to any unwelcome aggressive actions, and certain forms of harassment constitute civil rights violations. As the Dear Colleague letter advised, bullying of an individual on the basis of race, color, national origin, sex, or disability can be a civil rights violation if it is so severe, pervasive, or persistent that it interferes with a student's ability to benefit from the school's services, activities, or opportunities (USDOE, 2010). Furthermore, when a student who is being bullied is also identified as a victim of a federal civil rights violation, the school has more than an obligation to stop the violation. The USDOE (2010) indicated that schools must "eliminate any hostile environment and its effects" as well as take steps to "prevent the harassment from recurring" (pp. 2–3).

The USDOE (2010) cited several relevant statutes: Title VI of the Civil Rights Act of 1964 prohibits discrimination based on race, color, or national origin; Title IX of the Education Amendments of 1972 prohibits discrimination on the basis of sex; and both Section 504 of the Rehabilitation Act of 1973 and Title II of the Americans With Disabilities Act of 1990 prohibit discrimination on the basis of disability. These laws have the effect of protecting students from discriminatory actions that deprive them of their right to a free and appropriate public education, a concept articulated in the Education for All Handicapped Children Act of 1975 (also known as Public Law 94–142) and revised in the Individuals With Disabilities Education Act of 1990.

The relevance of Title IX to peer bullying and harassment was established in a 1999 U.S. Supreme Court decision, *Davis v. Monroe County Board of Education* (1999). In this case, a fifth-grade girl was repeatedly harassed by a male classmate who made sexually suggestive statements and touched her inappropriately. During months of harassment, the girl became depressed and suicidal, did not want to go to school, and made poorer grades. Eventually the parents went to the police and pressed charges that led to a conviction for sexual battery. The parents then sued school authorities. In a landmark decision, the Supreme Court ruled that school authorities could be held liable under Title IX on the basis of the provision that "no person shall, on the basis of sex, be excluded from participation in, be denied the benefits of, or be subjected to discrimination under any education program or activity receiving Federal financial assistance" (Title IX, 1972, section 1681[a]).

Subsequent cases have applied the *Davis v. Monroe* (1999) decision. For example, in *Scruggs v. Meriden Board of Education* (2005), the school system was found liable when a 12-year-old boy killed himself after years of physical and verbal bullying about personal characteristics linked to his learning disability. This case prompted the Connecticut legislature to pass antibullying legislation (Connecticut Commission on Children, n.d.).

In another case (*Shore Regional High School Board of Education v. P.S.*, 2004), a boy who was receiving special education services for emotional disturbance was bullied because of his perceived girlish appearance and called names such as *gay* and *faggot*. The school district's failure to stop the bullying was considered to be denial of his right to a free and appropriate public education under the Individuals With Disabilities Education Act (1990).

Before 1999, no states had laws regarding bullying, but the issue of bullying came to the forefront after the 1999 shooting at Columbine High School, which was perpetrated by two students who claimed to have been victims of bullying (Alley & Limber, 2009). Within 8 years, 30 states had enacted bullying laws, and by 2012 every state but Montana had adopted a bullying law (Sacco, Silbaugh, Corredor, Casey, & Dohert, 2012). Most state laws present a definition of bullying and provide varying degrees of guidance for their state department of education and local school systems to address it. In some cases, the state laws are notably prescriptive, such as the New Jersey Anti-Bullying Bill of Rights Act (Cerf, Hespe, Gantwerk, Martz, & Vermeire, 2010). This bill requires that all schools have a plan to address bullying and train all teachers and administrators to identify and respond to bullying. New Jersey also requires every public school, including higher education institutions, to conduct investigations and report all cases of bullying or teasing to the state within a strict timeframe.

Bullying Perpetration

On anonymous surveys, many students admit to bullying their peers. A nationally representative survey of students in Grades 6 to 10 found that the prevalence of bullying others at least once in the past 2 months was 13% for physical bullying, 37% for verbal bullying, 27% for social bullying, and 8% for cyberbullying (Wang et al., 2009). These estimates do not distinguish students who bullied someone just once from those who engage in repeated bullying or those who target one peer versus those who bully multiple students. Chan (2006) reported one of the few studies to identify victims and bullies by name. This study allowed him to determine that a relatively small percentage (12%) of students, termed *serial bullies*, were responsible for 69% of victims. Serial bullies were more likely than other bullies to engage in physical bullying. In one exceptional case, a single 13-year-old boy was identified as the bully by 15 victims, nine of whom reported a physical assault. One victim reported more than 30 physical assaults and more than 100 verbal attacks in the past 4 weeks. These findings demonstrate the need to assess the severity of a student's bullying.

A meta-analysis of 153 studies found that externalizing behaviors were the strongest predictors of bullying (Cook et al., 2010). Other robust predictors were low academic performance, poor social competence, and normative beliefs about others that reflected low empathy and rationalizations for harming others. Bullies were more likely than other students to have family problems and higher community crime. A study of 1,416 Greek Cypriot adolescents found that a history of conduct problems, callous–unemotional traits associated with psychopathy, narcissism, and impulsivity were predictive of bullying 1 year later (Fanti & Kimonis, 2013). However, some studies have identified more positive characteristics associated with bullying.

A study of middle-school students found that bullies were among the most popular students in the school, receiving an average of 21 peer nominations for popularity compared with 13 for students uninvolved in bullying and four for victims (Thunfors & Cornell, 2008).

Arnocky and Vaillancourt (2012) presented an evolutionary perspective on bullying as a social dominance strategy to defeat same-sex rivals and gain social status with the opposite sex. They examined bullying and dating status in a group of 350 adolescents (Grades 6–9) over a 1-year period. As predicted, indirect aggression (social bullying) was predictive of having a dating partner 1 year later for both boys and girls. Contrary to Arnocky and Vaillancourt's hypothesis, physical bullying was negatively rather than positively associated with dating status for boys and unrelated to dating status for girls. However, self-reported peer victimization was associated with not having a dating partner 1 year later.

Bullying Outcome Studies

Bullying perpetration predicts a host of negative outcomes, including delinquency, drug use, and physical aggression (Bender & Lösel, 2011; Hemphill et al., 2011), and has been extensively linked to adult criminality. A meta-analysis of 28 longitudinal studies found that school bullies were significantly more likely than noninvolved students (odds ratio = 2.50) to commit criminal offenses as young adults (Ttofi et al., 2011). For example, a prospective, nationwide birth cohort study of 5,351 Finnish children born in 1981 found a strong association between bullying by boys at age 8 and adult crime at age 23 to 26 years (Sourander et al., 2011). The study collected informant data from parents, teachers, and children on patterns of bullying at age 8 and followed up with data from the National Police Registry at ages 23 to 26 years. Although all three informant reports predicted adult crime, teacher reports of bullying were the strongest predictor of adult criminality. Frequent bullying was more highly predictive of adult violence.

Bully-Victims

Students who both engage in bullying and are victims of bullying are referred to as *bully-victims* (Olweus, 1991). The prevalence of students who identify themselves as both bullies and victims is 5% for physical bullying, 20% for verbal bullying, 17% for social–relational bullying, and 5% for cyberbullying (Wang et al., 2009). There is consistent evidence that bully-victims have problems with self-image, social competence, and both externalizing and internalizing behaviors (Cook et al., 2010). Bully-victims tend to be low on measures of self-control (Higgins, Jennings, Tewksbury, & Gibson, 2009) and high on aggressive impulsivity (O'Brennan, Bradshaw, & Sawyer, 2009).

Effectiveness of Bullying Prevention Programs

There is a worldwide literature on bullying prevention programs dating back to the early 1980s when Dan Olweus (1991) directed a seminal nationwide program in Norway. The Olweus Bullying Prevention Program (Hazelden Foundation, 2014) is the most influential program in the field and has been widely implemented in the United States. School-based bullying prevention programs based on this model emphasize a schoolwide approach. They typically involve staff training in identifying and responding to bullying, the establishment of school rules against bullying, and classroom meetings and lessons intended to convince students not to bully others or allow their peers to engage in bullying. They also rely on student self-report questionnaires to measure the extent of bullying and assess program effects.

The effectiveness of school bullying prevention programs has been subject to debate. Although the initial reports of the Olweus program showed a 50% drop in victimization and other positive effects in Norway, the program's results in other nations have been mixed, and no other programs have achieved the level of success reported in Norway. A meta-analysis of 44 program evaluations found a wide range of outcomes, including a handful with negative effects, but on average, antibullying programs decreased bullying by 20% to 23% and victimization by 17% to 20% (Ttofi & Farrington, 2009). The most intensive programs were the most effective, which is noteworthy because there are many brief and untested programs marketed to schools that school authorities would be well advised to avoid.

Many school-based programs designed to reduce student aggression or improve student behavior generally are not focused specifically on bullying. Meta-analyses have consistently shown that there are numerous effective programs with moderate to strong effects (Wilson & Lipsey, 2007; Wilson, Lipsey, & Derzon, 2003). These programs range from parent training and family counseling to cognitive–behavioral therapy and academic tutoring. Evidence-based programs have been identified by several authorities (e.g., Center for the Study and Prevention of Violence, 2014; Substance Abuse and Mental Health Services Administration, 2014).

PREVALENCE OF SCHOOL VIOLENCE

Youth violence in the United States is not a new problem, but a recurrent one that has long captured public attention (Crews & Counts, 1997). For example, a 1975 Senate report (Bayh, 1975) received national attention when it asserted that homicide, rape, and robbery were soaring in schools. These preliminary findings were not substantiated. In 1995, a political scientist raised a false alarm that a wave of young "super-predators" would soon engulf the nation in juvenile crime (DiIulio, 1995). On the contrary, juvenile violence plummeted rather than soared, and the super-predator theory was declared a myth (Cornell, 2006; Zimring, 1998). Highly publicized school shootings such as those at Columbine High School in 1999, a Pennsylvania Amish school in 2006, and Sandy Hook Elementary School in 2012 also generated widespread perceptions of an epidemic of school violence that were not substantiated by crime records.

Forensic clinicians should be leery of news reports claiming that school shootings are increasing because such reports tend to be based on selective counts of events over short intervals that reflect little more than random fluctuations in crime. For example, after the 2006 shooting at a Pennsylvania Amish school, ABC News reported that there had been 25 shootings "at or near schools" in the first month of school and that there was a "disturbing new trend of adults killing children in schools" (Thomas, 2006, p.1). On further investigation, these shootings turned out to include news reports compiled by a school security company that included incidents that had little to do with schools, such as a shooting in the same neighborhood as a school and a midnight shooting in an urban school parking lot. One of the shootings involved an intoxicated man who was arrested for firing an air rifle at ducks on a school athletic field.

In the months after the Sandy Hook Elementary School shooting, all 50 states passed school safety legislation (Armario, 2013). These school safety initiatives included school security measures, proposals to arm teachers with firearms, security video cameras, metal detectors, and intruder alarms (Armario, 2013; Healy, 2013). These actions reflected the widespread perception that schools were not safe, but it is critical to temper such perceptions with reliable evidence (Cornell, 2006). Studies have consistently found that base rates for serious violent crime are very low in schools. In the 2010 to 2011 school year, there were 25 school-associated homicides or suicides, which is approximately one death for every 3.5 million students enrolled (Robers et al., 2013). An analysis of crime data from the Federal Bureau of Investigation's National Incident Based Reporting System found that homicides at schools accounted for only 0.3% of total homicide incidents and 0.8% of all multiple-casualty homicides (Nekvasil, Cornell, & Huang, in press). The majority of youth homicides occurred in residences (53%), followed by roads (23%) and parking lots or garages (6%).

Another way to place school violence in perspective is to consider the number of school homicides relative to the total number of schools in the United States. With an average of 21 student homicides per year across 125,000 schools, the average U.S. school can expect a student to be murdered approximately every 6,000 years (Borum, Cornell, Modzeleski, & Jimerson, 2010). This approximation does not include homicides of nonstudents or attempted homicides; nevertheless, such figures should raise caution among school authorities about the need to fortify schools against homicidal assaults. The likelihood of homicidal assault is far greater in other locations such as restaurants, shopping centers, and residences (Nekvasil et al., in press).

Contrary to public perception, violent crime in schools has declined over the past 2 decades. The National Crime Victimization Survey (NCVS) provides annual estimates of the rate of violent crime based on interviews with representative samples of the general population, including 12- to 18-year-olds. By recording the locations in which the crimes took place, the NCVS can provide estimates of violent crime in schools. One strength of the NCVS system is that it includes crimes that might not have been reported to the police or registered in school records. As a result, NCVS data should be more complete than police or school records. According to the NCVS report prepared for education authorities, serious violent crime (robbery, forcible rape, and aggravated assault) peaked at a rate of 22.1 per 1,000 students in 1992 and fell to 3.5 per 1,000 by 2011 (Robers et al., 2013).

Although serious violent crime is low in schools, rates of less serious forms of aggression, such as fighting, are relatively higher. Sixteen percent of boys and 8% of girls in Grades 9 to 12 reported involvement in a physical fight at school at least once during the previous 12 months (Robers et al., 2013). This count of fights is based on self-report, so the definition of a fight and the severity of the altercation are not standardized.

SCHOOL-TO-PRISON PIPELINE

Concern over school violence propelled the federal government to enact the Improving America's Schools Act of 1994, which required states to pass legislation mandating schools to expel for at least 1 year any student found with a firearm at school. Although the federal law permitted school authorities to make exceptions in extenuating circumstances, state laws and local school policies were often less flexible. Moreover, school authorities extended zero tolerance for firearms into a general philosophy of school discipline that applied to other weapons, drugs, fighting, and other infractions. Under zero tolerance, students could be automatically suspended even if the violation was accidental or posed no serious threat to others. For example, students have been suspended for misbehavior such as pointing their fingers like a gun or pretending to shoot someone with a pencil (Rubinkam, 2013).

Many education authorities have criticized zero tolerance practices as fueling a nationwide increase in school suspensions (Losen & Martinez, 2013). There is considerable evidence that school suspension does not achieve its stated objectives of reforming misbehaving students or deterring other students from breaking school rules (American Psychological Association Zero Tolerance Task Force, 2008). A longitudinal study following 1 million Texas students from Grades 6 through 12 found that suspensions did not have a positive impact on students and instead increased the likelihood of school failure, dropout, and juvenile court involvement (Fabelo et al., 2011). Likewise, schools with high suspension rates have lower graduation rates than other schools, even after controlling for differences in school demographics (Lee, Cornell, Gregory, & Fan, 2011; Losen & Martinez, 2013).

An important question is whether the link between suspension and juvenile offending reflects the continuity and persistence of a student's underlying disposition to misbehave—or indicates that the school disciplinary system itself has a detrimental impact that contributes to a downward spiral into delinquency. Many child advocates have charged that the school discipline system facilitates rather than deters the development of juvenile offending and have labeled this process the *school-to-prison pipeline* (Losen & Martinez, 2013). Suspension rates are highest for minority students (especially Black and Hispanic students) and consist largely of minor infractions such as dress code violations and disruptive behavior (Fabelo et al., 2011; Gregory & Weinstein, 2008; Skiba et al., 2011). Several studies have found that Black students are more likely than White students to be suspended for more subjective and less serious offenses (Bradshaw, Mitchell, O'Brennan, & Leaf, 2010; Fabelo et al., 2011; Skiba & Rausch, 2006).

In its 2014 "Dear Colleague" letter, the U.S. Department of Justice and USDOE (2014) jointly called on school authorities to examine the problem of student discipline practices that discriminate on the basis of race, color, or national origin. They cited the federal Civil Rights Data Collection program that found that Black students were more than 3 times as likely as White students to be expelled or suspended. The letter acknowledged that disparities in student discipline rates could be due to many different factors, but that research indicated that racial disparities cannot be explained by more frequent or more serious misbehavior by minority students. The federal initiative also called for reconsideration of zero tolerance policies and the creation of positive school climates that use less punitive and more constructive approaches to discipline.

School systems in Baltimore, Maryland; Chicago, Illinois; and Denver, Colorado, among others, have started to move away from zero tolerance and reliance on school suspension. Schools in Broward County, Florida, eliminated zero tolerance policies and reported a subsequent 41% reduction in school-based arrests (Alvarez, 2013). Los Angeles, California, school police ceased issuing citations to truant students and began referring them for educational counseling and other services (Watanabe, 2012).

THREAT ASSESSMENT

Although school shootings are statistically rare, their impact is profound; many authorities in education and law enforcement have investigated the problem in search of preventive measures. In its study of school shootings, the U.S. Secret Service observed that more than three quarters of the student perpetrators had communicated to someone, usually a friend or classmate, that they intended to carry out an attack at school (Vossekuil, Fein, Reddy, Borum, & Modzeleski, 2002). In more than two thirds of cases, the boys felt bullied or harassed by others. Similarly, a Federal Bureau of Investigation study noted the frequent leakage of violent intentions in the communications of students before they carried out school shootings (O'Toole, 2000). These observations supported the conclusion that school authorities should focus on the identification and investigation of student threats as a violence prevention strategy (Vossekuil et al., 2002).

Although threat assessment was an unfamiliar concept to most educators and mental health professionals at the time, it has become widely recognized as a valuable strategy for preventing acts of targeted violence such as those seen in mass shootings in schools and colleges, business places, and other settings. The term *behavioral threat assessment* is sometimes used to distinguish this process from a physical assessment of a facility's vulnerability to attack. Threat assessment is used by the U.S. Secret Service, the U.S. State Department, and the U.S. Marshal Service to protect federal officials and is a recommended practice for the prevention of workplace violence (American Psychological Association, 2013; Pollard, Nolan, & Deisinger, 2012).

Threat assessment is a form of risk assessment that is conducted when someone threatens to commit a violent act or engages in threatening behavior. A threat may be directly communicated to an intended victim or it may be indirectly communicated to a third party. Threats can be quite explicit, or they may be vague statements that imply an intention to harm someone. Usually there is a specific target or intended victim, but some threats are more diffuse, such as a threat to carry out a mass shooting with no specific victims. Threats are not always verbal and might be reflected in behavior that suggests that someone intends to commit a violent act. Whenever someone is concerned that a person intends to harm others, a threat assessment can investigate and determine whether a threat exists and then identify appropriate steps on the basis of the seriousness of the threat.

Threat assessments are best conducted by multidisciplinary teams that can provide the breadth of perspective and access to resources that are often needed. Mental health professionals play a central role in threat assessment because of their expertise in psychological assessment, diagnosis, and behavioral interventions. However, law enforcement professionals may be needed to investigate possible criminal behavior, consider legal issues, and address security concerns. When threat assessments are conducted in an institutional setting such as a school, university, or business, it is important to have administrators on the team who have the authority to represent institutional needs as well as take appropriate administrative actions. An important strategic virtue of a school-based threat assessment team is its ability to receive and integrate information from multiple sources.

Because threat assessment is fundamentally a problem-solving initiative, it is essential to evaluate the threatening situation from multiple perspectives and to consider alternative hypotheses that can be critically analyzed and carefully considered before reaching conclusions and making decisions. Once decisions about the seriousness of a threat are made, it is also important to have as many resources available to the team as possible in order to develop the most effective and practical plans for intervention.

Individuals who conduct threat assessments on their own will typically have more limited information and fewer resources available to them. They will inevitably have the difficult task of persuading others in authority to accept their judgment and to take the actions they recommend. It is best to have institutional representatives and onsite professionals engaged in the threat assessment process so the team can build the consensus necessary for a plan to be carried out effectively.

Typically, threat assessment teams do not want individuals such as students or teachers to make their own determination of whether someone is dangerous because that is a difficult judgment that should be left to the team. Often an individual's observations might not raise serious concerns by themselves but, combined with observations from other sources, could indicate to a threat assessment team that a potentially dangerous situation merits investigation. For example, in the case of the Virginia Tech shooting, multiple faculty members had concerns about Seung-Hui Cho's classroom behavior and violent writings, and other university authorities had concerns about his mental health and his social interactions, but no one party had access to all of this information (Virginia Tech Review Panel, 2007).

The outcome period for a threat assessment is much shorter than for other risk assessments, such as those conducted when there are questions about releasing someone from a psychiatric or correctional institution. Traditional risk assessments are often open ended in determining whether someone is likely to commit any kind of violent act at any time in the future, and individuals are classified according to their level of risk. In contrast, threat assessments are concerned with whether someone currently poses a risk of carrying out a specific attack in the near future. (In some respects, the imminence of a threat is similar to the immediacy of harm posed by individuals being considered for civil commitment, but threat assessments are not bound by the requirement that the individual meet criteria for a serious mental illness.) Threat assessments focus on the individual's readiness, motivation, and intention to commit a specific act of violence. Accordingly, they examine current behavior, such as whether the individual has engaged in planning or preparation to carry out the threatened attack, and they place great emphasis on situational factors, such as the degree of support available to the individual and whether the individual is under stress that might increase the risk of violence.

The concept of threat assessment has evolved to include not only the identification and assessment of threats, but the management of people who have made threats (Borum et al., 2010; Heilbrun, Dvoskin, & Heilbrun, 2009). People usually make a threat because they are frustrated by a problem or conflict, and one effective violence prevention strategy is to resolve that difficulty and eliminate the motivation for violence. Accordingly, the threat assessment team may attempt to resolve a threat by addressing an underlying problem or conflict. For this reason, threat assessment can be regarded as a problem-oriented approach to violence prevention. Threat assessment teams function as consultants who help school authorities solve problems before they escalate into violence.

Whereas traditional risk assessment attempts to predict whether someone will engage in violence, other approaches to risk assessment (including threat assessment) are concerned with managing and reducing risk as well as appraising the level of such risk (Otto & Douglas, 2010). There is a common misconception that prevention is not possible without accurate prediction, but the public health model of prevention has demonstrated otherwise. For example, it is not possible to predict accurately who will be killed in a motor vehicle accident, but preventive actions aimed at the general population, such as use of seat belts, driver training, and speed limits, have demonstrated benefits.

Similarly, it is not possible to predict accurately who will die from lung cancer, but programs designed to reduce risk factors such as active and passive smoking have reduced the death rate. A threat assessment can prevent violence by helping individuals resolve problems and conflicts that stimulated their threatening behavior. Even if the individual does not currently pose a threat (i.e., is not actively planning or preparing to carry out an attack), an effort to address the underlying conflict or problem can prevent the situation from escalating. The provision of threat assessment services on a large scale can have a preventive effect on the population served even if it is not possible to predict which individuals might actually have carried out a threat.

Some authorities have asserted that threat assessment is a dynamic process that should be distinguished from prediction-oriented risk assessment (Reddy et al., 2001). The dynamic and interactive nature of threat assessment makes using risk scores, a staple of traditional risk assessment, questionable. Risk scores are static indicators used to assess a person's level of risk for committing a violent act in the future, but such scores are not practical when it comes to immediate efforts to prevent violence. Much of the research literature is concerned with identifying a fixed set of predictors that can be measured in a sample of subjects, ignoring individual variation and idiosyncratic factors. This simplification is necessary for statistical analyses, but unrealistic for prevention purposes because it ignores potentially important information that is specific to the individual case. For this reason, professional judgment is an essential component of risk management (Borum et al., 2003).

One of the first reports of a threat assessment model in schools was the Dallas Threat of Violence Risk Assessment (Van Dyke & Schroeder, 2006) developed in the Dallas, Texas school system. It consists of 19 risk factors derived from a review of literature on risk factors for violence. Each item is rated as *low* (1), *medium* (2), or *high* (3) and then summed into a total risk score in which scores lower than 9 are considered low risk and scores higher than 14 are considered high risk. A structured system such as this one is appealing, but the authors cautioned that the scoring system and cutoff points were "arbitrarily chosen by the committee without empirical validation" (Van Dyke & Schroeder, 2006, p. 608).

There are two problems with using standardized risk assessment instruments that produce a score or classification to predict whether a student will commit a violent act. First, because severe acts of violence in schools are extremely rare, they present a classic low base-rate problem for prediction (Heilbrun et al., 2009). When the base rate for a behavior is extremely low, it becomes extraordinarily difficult for any assessment procedure to generate a prediction that is more accurate than chance. Consider the hypothetical example that there are 10 schools that experience a shooting in 1 year in a population of 100,000 schools; the base rate for school shootings would be 10 divided by 100,000, or .0001. This means that 99.99% of schools will not have a shooting; therefore, a predictive instrument could be 99.99% accurate simply by predicting that no school will have a shooting. It seems unrealistic to expect that any assessment instrument could be more accurate than this chance level.

Risk instruments rely on a checklist or profile of characteristics, such as having a history of prior violence, being a victim of bullying, and being preoccupied with violent video games. It is possible to construct lists of characteristics that seem compelling but that are still too general to be useful for prediction purposes. Critics have pointed out that profiles or lists of warning signs typically contain indicators that are too broad to be useful in identifying violent individuals and will generate a high rate of false-positive identifications (Sewell & Mendelsohn, 2000). As the Federal Bureau of Investigation's profiling experts concluded, "Trying to draw up a catalogue or 'checklist' of warning signs to detect a potential school shooter can be shortsighted, even dangerous. Such lists, publicized by the media, can end up unfairly labeling many nonviolent students as potentially dangerous" (O'Toole, 2000, p. 2).

A second problem is that the risk of violence is more situational and transitory than risk scores imply (Borum et al., 2003). Risk scores, as well as ordinal classifications of risk (e.g., high, medium, low) are static designations that ignore the variability in youth behavior and adolescents' responsiveness to their immediate environment. Even an aggressive youth is low risk when supervised and feeling calm but much more dangerous when angry, intoxicated, or surrounded by peers who encourage aggressive behavior. A student's level of risk rises when he or she moves from a supervised classroom into the hallway between classes, and again when he or she leaves school in the afternoon. Risk is not a fixed quality; rather, it fluctuates over time and across situations.

Within the risk assessment literature, there has been a robust debate about the use of actuarial measures that rely on objectives scores and minimize the use of professional judgment versus measures that attempt to inform and enhance professional judgment, often referred to as *structured professional judgment measures* (Childs, Frick, Ryals, Lingonblad, & Villio, 2014; Otto & Douglas, 2010). Although a comprehensive review of this literature is beyond the scope of this chapter, the threat assessment model described in this chapter emphasizes the use of structured professional judgment.

VIRGINIA STUDENT THREAT ASSESSMENT GUIDELINES

The reports by the Federal Bureau of Investigation (O'Toole, 2000) and the Secret Service and USDOE (Fein et al., 2002) made strong arguments for a threat assessment approach, but there was no established model for schools to use. In response, the Virginia Youth Violence Project at the University of Virginia's Curry School of Education developed and field tested a student threat assessment model for schools. The model was intended to provide school authorities with a standard and systematic approach for responding to student threats of violence. In 2002, the threat assessment guidelines were formulated, reviewed by a board of national experts in psychology and risk assessment, and field tested in 35 Virginia schools for 1 year. The guidelines were refined and then published in a 145-page manual, *Guidelines for Responding to Student Threats of Violence* (Cornell & Sheras, 2006).

Threat Assessment Team

Threat assessments using the Virginia guidelines are conducted by an interdisciplinary team, which includes representatives from administration, mental health, and law enforcement. The team leader is typically an administrator (principal or assistant principal) who has responsibility for student discipline and safety. The leader or another designated team member typically begins the threat assessment process with a triage evaluation to determine the seriousness of the threat. As described below, a transient threat is quickly and easily resolved, whereas a substantive threat engages more team members in a full-scale assessment and intervention.

The law enforcement representative for the team is usually a school resource officer or another police officer who is available to work with the school. The school resource officer can advise the team whether a student's behavior has violated the law and can conduct a criminal investigation and take appropriate action in the most serious cases. The resource officer's everyday role is to be a member of the school community who encourages law-abiding behavior and establishes positive relationships with students. School resource officers can take a preventive approach to crime by identifying potentially volatile conflicts between students or groups of students.

Depending on the school's staffing pattern, a threat assessment team should include one or more mental health professionals (e.g., school psychologist, counselor, social worker). A mental health professional may be involved at multiple stages in a threat assessment. In the most common, transient cases that, by definition, do not involve serious, substantive threats, the mental health professional may work in tandem with the team leader to interview witnesses and clarify that the identified student does not pose a threat of violence. Many student threats are simply figures of speech or expressions of anger that can be easily resolved.

In the most serious cases, a school psychologist or another suitably qualified mental health professional member conducts a mental health evaluation of the student. These evaluations have two main objectives. The first objective is to screen the student for mental health problems that demand immediate attention, such as psychotic symptoms or suicidality. The second objective is to assess why the student made the threat and to provide recommendations for dealing with the problem or conflict that stimulated the threatening behavior.

Mental health professionals may also conduct interventions such as counseling a distressed student or resolving conflicts between students. There is a large body of evidence that school-based interventions can reduce aggressive behavior (Wilson & Lipsey, 2007). As noted above, there are several comprehensive lists of evidence-based programs, such as the National Registry of Evidence-Based Programs and Practices (Substance Abuse and Mental Health Services Administration, 2014) and Blueprints for Healthy Youth Development (Center for the Study and Prevention of Violence, 2014), in areas such as social competence training, cognitive–behavioral counseling to improve social interaction and problem-solving skills, and conflict resolution programs. In all cases, follow-up monitoring should ensure that a plan is working.

A school-based team is preferable to an external team for multiple reasons. First, a threat assessment requires an immediate response. School authorities cannot wait for a team of outside experts to begin an investigation. In some school systems, students have been suspended from school for weeks awaiting evaluations by external teams. Second, threat assessment requires careful consideration of contextual and situational factors that are familiar to school staff but not to outsiders. Third, most student threats are not serious enough to warrant the use of an outside team. Many cases involve rash or foolish statements that can be quickly resolved by a school administrator or counselor. Finally, threat assessment should not be limited to an initial assessment but should involve an ongoing process of intervention and reassessment. An effective threat assessment team will implement a response to a serious threat that is intended to reduce the risk of violence and will continue to monitor the student's status. Nevertheless, in a complicated case involving a serious threat of violence, the school-based team may want to draw on the expertise of outside mental health experts and other resources in the community.

Steps in a Threat Assessment

Threat assessment teams using the Virginia model follow a seven-step decision tree (see Figure 11.1). One goal of the Virginia guidelines is to be flexible and efficient so that less serious cases can be readily resolved. The first three steps of the assessment are a triage phase to determine whether the case can be quickly and easily resolved as a transient threat or will require more extensive evaluation and intervention as a substantive threat. In the easiest cases, a threat can be resolved the same day, but more complex cases may involve a comprehensive assessment of the student, interviews with witnesses, meetings with parents, and the formulation of an intervention plan.

The team leader usually begins by interviewing the student who made the threat with a standard set of questions that can be adapted to the specific situation. The interviewer is concerned with determining the context in which the threat was made and what the student meant and intended in making the threat. The team leader or other team members also interview witnesses to the threat and make notes on a standard form.

At Step 2, the team must distinguish between serious threats that pose a continuing risk or danger to others and those that are not serious because they can be quickly resolved and do not pose a continuing risk. Less serious threats are termed *transient threats*, which can be readily identified as expressions of anger or frustration, or perhaps inappropriate attempts at humor. These threats are described as transient because they dissipate when the student has time to reflect on the meaning of what he or she has said. The most important characteristic of a transient threat is that the student does not have a sustained intent to harm someone.

If a threat is judged to be transient, it is resolved at Step 3 without further assessment. The student may receive a reprimand or other disciplinary consequence, but the team is not compelled to take protective action because the threat is not serious. Ideally, the student will apologize and explain or make amends for his or her behavior.

Any threat that cannot be resolved as transient is regarded as a substantive threat. A threat is substantive because it involves a sustained intent to harm someone beyond the immediate incident during which the threat was made. Substantive threats may be identified by several features that are regarded as presumptive, but not necessary or sufficient,

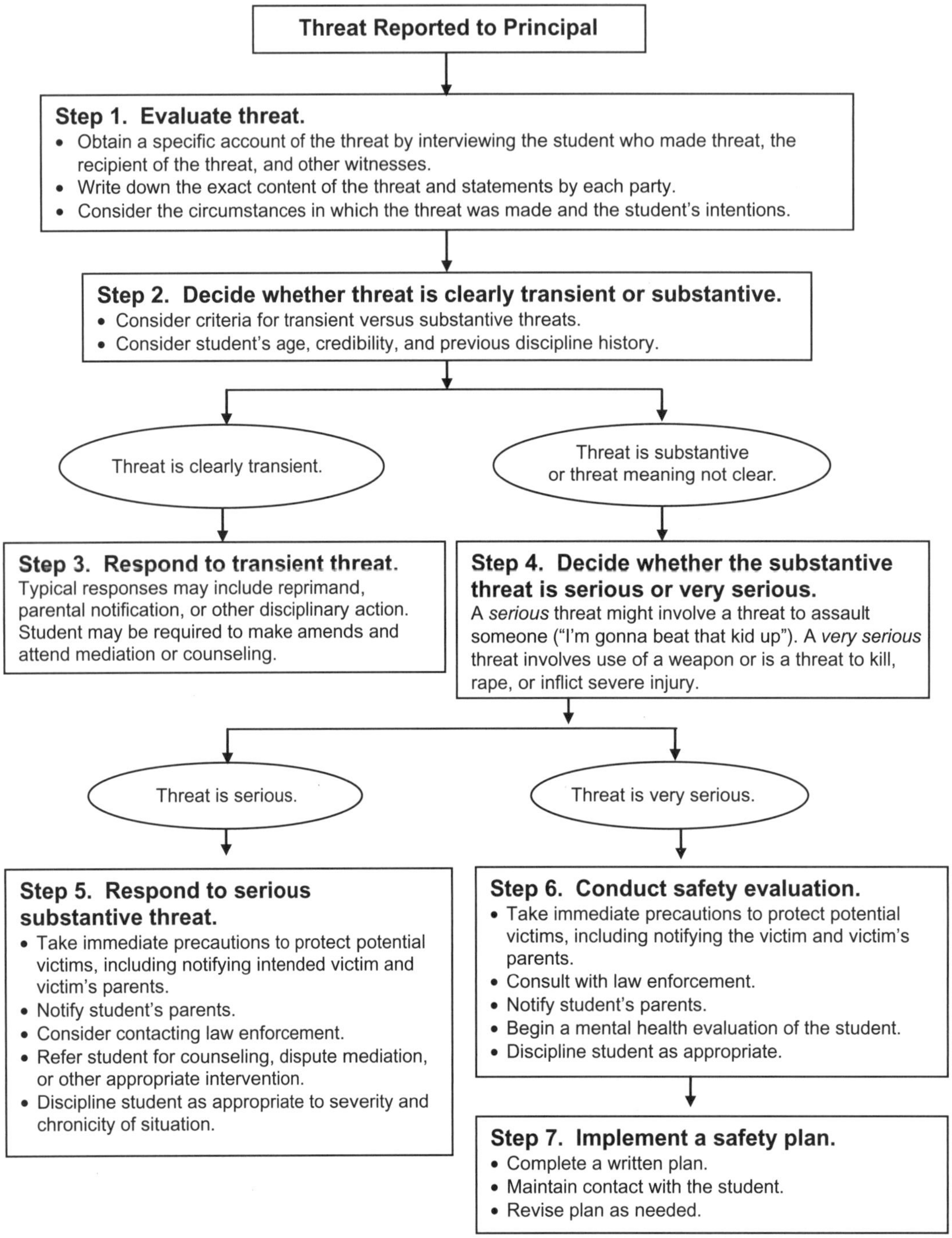

FIGURE 11.1. Decision tree for student threat assessment. *From Guidelines for Responding to Student Threats of Violence* (p. 16), by D. Cornell and P. Sheras, 2006, Longmont, CO: Sopris West. Copyright 2006 by Dewey Cornell. Reprinted with permission.

indicators. Some examples of these indicators include the following:

- The threat includes plausible details, such as a specific victim, time, place, and method of assault.
- The threat involves planning and preparation, including efforts to recruit accomplices or to invite an audience.
- There is physical evidence of intent to carry out the threat, such as a weapon, bomb materials, map, or written plan.

Although the presence of one or more of these features may lead the school administrator to presume the threat is substantive, none is an absolute indicator. In each case, the team must consider the total circumstances and make reasoned judgments based on all available information. The team should consider the student's age and capabilities, mental health status, prior history of violent behavior, and other relevant factors. The guidelines assist the team in its investigation, but do not provide a prescription or formula.

At Step 4, a substantive threat is classified as serious or very serious on the basis of the intended severity of injury. A threat to hit or fight someone is classified as a serious substantive threat. A threat to kill, sexually assault, or severely injure someone is classified as very serious. A threat involving the use of a weapon is generally considered a threat to severely injure, but teams must always use their judgment. For example, if a student threatens to shoot someone with a water pistol, it would not make sense to treat such a threat as very serious.

Step 5 is the final step for serious substantive threats. The team responds to a serious substantive threat by taking action to prevent the threat from being carried out. Immediate protective actions include cautioning the student about the consequences of carrying out the threat, providing supervision so that the threat is not carried out at school, and contacting the student's parents (or adult caretakers) so that they can assume responsibility after school. A team member should also meet with the intended victim of the threat, both in an effort to resolve the underlying dispute or problem and to warn the intended victim. If the intended victim is a student, that student's parents should be contacted as well. For serious substantive threats, threat assessment ends here.

Step 6 is the response to a very serious substantive threat. The team takes protective actions and warns potential victims as in Step 5, but they also take some additional actions. Typically, a mental health professional such as a school psychologist will conduct a mental health evaluation of the student with two goals. The first goal is to assess the student's mental state and need for immediate mental health services. For example, does the student have delusional ideas that could motivate aggressive action? Is the student so depressed or suicidal that he or she might take desperate action without concern for the consequences? In such cases, the team seeks immediate treatment from available community resources. A second goal of the mental health evaluation is to identify the reasons for the threat and recommend strategies addressing the problem or conflict underlying the threat. For example, is the student a victim of bullying or involved in some other peer conflict?

During the course of the mental health evaluation, the student may be suspended from school on a short-term basis. Although the use of suspension in response to a threat is generally discouraged, a brief suspension is an appropriate safety precaution until the team can complete its evaluation in very serious substantive cases. There is both the risk that the student may engage in aggressive behavior at school and the risk that others in the school might react to the student. Almost invariably, other students in a school learn that a classmate has made a threat, and their responses to this student may range from being supportive to being antagonistic. Many school authorities have raised concern that a student who makes a threat may provoke anger and thoughts of retaliatory aggression among some classmates.

Suspensions do not guarantee the safety of the school, and in several school shootings, the student had been suspended from school before the attack. Suspensions must be carefully considered because they may add stress to the situation and leave the student unsupervised outside of school. Threat assessment teams always make safety their first priority and must weigh the pros and cons of school suspension or any other action they consider taking.

At the same time as the mental health evaluation is being performed, the school resource officer may conduct a law enforcement investigation to determine appropriate legal action. The officer may conduct a search for weapons, interview witnesses, and generally look for evidence that the student was engaged in planning and preparing to carry out the threat. In the most severe cases, the student may be arrested and charged with an offense. The officer's presence in the school and involvement in the threat assessment process also helps to reassure the school community and provide a sense of safety and security.

At Step 7, the team synthesizes its findings into a written safety plan. The plan may include a combination of mental health and counseling recommendations, findings from the law enforcement investigation, and disciplinary consequences. The safety plan is designed both to protect potential victims and to address the educational needs of the student who made the threat. These plans vary widely according to the circumstances of each case. A key feature of any plan is that it is oriented toward resolving the problem or conflict that stimulated the threatening behavior. Threats can be symptoms of a problem that a student is unable to resolve, such as bullying or conflict with peers, or perhaps academic difficulties in school. In many cases, the student struggles with depression and suicidal feelings. An effective plan will take a comprehensive, problem-solving approach.

Safety plans will include provisions for monitoring the student over a reasonable period of time to make sure that the plan is working. For example, a team member might be in regular contact with a student for several months to assess how things are going and whether efforts to address a problem with bullying have been successful. If the student has been referred for counseling or mental health services, there should be a provision to share information about the student's attendance and progress. For students who are receiving special education services, changes may be made in the student's Individualized Education Program (a U.S. federal requirement for students with disabilities). An Individualized Education Program might include behavior support plans to help a student deal with anger or interpersonal conflict or improve social skills.

When a student is returning to school, a reentry plan might be appropriate. Students who know about the threat may have anxiety (or anger) in reaction to a classmate returning to school after a threat. It may be appropriate to meet with potentially affected classmates and their parents to pave the way for the student's successful return. As part of this process, the team might request permission from the student's parents to share a limited amount of information with the affected parties. In some cases, students have made apologies as part of their return-to-school plan.

RESEARCH ON THE VIRGINIA STUDENT THREAT ASSESSMENT GUIDELINES

The Virginia Student Threat Assessment Guidelines were developed in 2002 (Cornell & Sheras, 2006), and it is the only threat assessment program recognized as an evidence-based practice (National Registry of Evidence-Based Programs and Practices, 2013). In this section, we summarize a series of studies conducted over a 10-year period.

One key feature of the threat assessment approach is training school-based multidisciplinary teams to take a flexible but systematic and investigative approach to evaluating student threats rather than pursue a more rigid zero tolerance approach that does not consider the context and meaning of the student's behavior. Several studies have shown that staff training in the Virginia guidelines has a substantial effect on the attitudes and knowledge of school personnel across disciplines (Allen, Cornell, Lorek, & Sheras, 2008; Cornell, Allen, & Fan, 2012; Cornell, Gregory, & Fan, 2011; Cornell, Sheras, Gregory, & Fan, 2009; Cornell et al., 2004; Strong & Cornell, 2008). After training, school personnel showed a decrease in fears of school violence and a shift in attitudes consistent with a threat assessment perspective. For example, they were willing to adopt a problem-solving approach to student conflicts and reduced their endorsement of a zero tolerance approach. These changes were observed across groups of school principals, psychologists, counselors, social workers, and school-based police officers.

Two year-long field tests demonstrated that school-based teams could conduct threat assessments in a safe and efficient manner and that almost all students would be able to return to school without long-term suspension (Cornell et al., 2004; Strong & Cornell, 2008). The first field test of the Virginia guidelines involved school-based teams in 35 public schools that investigated 188 student threats over 1 school year (Cornell et al., 2004). Most of the cases (70%) were resolved as transient threats through an explanation or apology accompanied by counseling services and relatively minor disciplinary consequences. The remaining 30% were substantive threats that required protective action and the development of plans to address the underlying conflicts or problems that drove the students to make the threats. Nearly all students were able to return to their original schools, and only three students were given long-term suspensions. Follow-up interviews with school principals the next year indicated that none of the threats were carried out. Although it is possible that some students engaged in fights that were never disclosed to school authorities, school administrators were reasonably confident that the more serious threats of killing, shooting, and stabbing were not carried out.

The second field test (Strong & Cornell, 2008) was conducted in a large urban school district using a centralized threat assessment team. Two hundred nine cases were referred for assessment by school principals, including 109 threats to kill, shoot, or stab someone. The threat assessment team developed an individualized plan for each case, typically involving a combination of counseling to resolve interpersonal conflicts or disputes, various forms of mental health services, and academic assistance. Almost all of the students were able to return to school or transfer to an alternative school. Only five students were not recommended for return to school (i.e., expelled). The study also found evidence of improved student behavior, with a 55% reduction in disciplinary referrals for the students who made threats and subsequently returned to school. As in the first field test, school authorities reported that none of the threats were carried out.

Subsequently, four controlled studies found strong support for the Virginia guidelines. The first controlled study was a retrospective assessment of school climate in a statewide sample of 95 high schools using the Virginia guidelines, 131 schools using locally developed procedures, and 54 schools not using a threat assessment approach (Cornell et al., 2009). Students in schools using the Virginia guidelines reported a consistently more favorable school climate than students in the other two groups of schools. The students in the schools using the Virginia guidelines reported less bullying in the previous 30 days, greater willingness to seek help for bullying and threats of violence, and more positive perceptions of the school climate than students in either of the other two groups of schools. Students in schools using the Virginia guidelines were more likely to report that school staff members treated students with fairness and respect and were concerned about bullying and attempted to stop it. School records also showed that schools using the Virginia guidelines had approximately one third fewer long-term suspensions than schools in the other two groups.

An important limitation of the Cornell et al. (2009) high school study was that there was no pre–post assessment of schools before and after the schools adopted the threat assessment model. To remedy this limitation, a quasi-experimental study examined school discipline records for a group of 23 high schools for the year before and the year after implementation of the Virginia guidelines and compared them with those of a control group of 26 high schools not using the guidelines (Cornell et al., 2011). Schools using the Virginia guidelines showed a 52% reduction in long-term suspensions and a 79% reduction in bullying infractions from the pretraining year to the posttraining year, in contrast to schools in the control group, which showed little change. These findings could not be attributed to differences in school enrollment size, proportion of minority students, or proportion of students eligible for a free or reduced-price meal, which were statistically controlled.

A third study was a randomized controlled study of threat assessment in elementary, middle, and high schools (Cornell et al., 2012). In this study, a single school system agreed that 20 of its 40 schools could be randomly assigned to receive threat assessment training, and the other 20 schools delayed training for 1 year and served as a control group. During 1 school year, 201 students (100 in intervention schools and 101 in control schools) were identified as making threats of violence. The critical issue was how school authorities responded to these threats and the extent to which they relied on school exclusionary consequences. The Virginia guidelines were designed to produce three outcomes that were assessed in this study: (a) use of counseling and mental health services to resolve conflicts; (b) involvement of parents in response to threats; and (c) return of students to school without long-term suspensions or alternative school placements.

For each hypothesized outcome, a series of logistic regression analyses compared the intervention and control students after controlling for the effects of demographic variables (student gender, school level, and race) and threat severity. Students in schools using the Virginia guidelines were approximately 4 times as likely than control students to receive counseling services and 2.5 times as likely to have the benefit of a parent conference than students in the control group. Students in the control group were about 3 times as likely to receive long-term suspension and 8 times as likely to receive an alternative school placement than students in the intervention group (for more information, see Cornell et al., 2012).

A fourth study examined suspension rates in secondary schools across the state of Virginia that had adopted the Virginia guidelines (Cornell & Lovegrove, in press). Among Virginia's 663 secondary schools (middle, high, or combined schools), the 398 schools that used the Virginia guidelines recorded 15% fewer short-term suspensions and 25% fewer long-term suspensions per year than the other 265 schools. This study was particularly concerned with the racial disparity between Black and White students because Black students across all schools were twice as likely as White students to be suspended from school. Notably, short-term and long-term suspension rates were lower for both White and Black students in schools using the Virginia guidelines, and the lower rate for Black students substantially reduced the racial disparity in long-term suspensions.

SUMMARY

In conclusion, schools are critical settings that can increase or reduce risk for juvenile offending. School adjustment in both academic and behavioral domains provides important information about a child's developmental course, and the emergence of serious and repeated misbehavior at school can foreshadow the development of antisocial behavior patterns. Bullying has been identified as an especially pervasive and pernicious problem in school that is associated with negative outcomes for both victims and perpetrators.

Concerns about school violence have been shaped by high-profile shootings that are statistically rare but prominent in public consciousness. A resultant zero tolerance philosophy of school discipline has contributed to a substantial increase in the use of school suspension and expulsion. However, this policy has shown no beneficial impact on students or schools and has had well-documented negative consequences, such as the disproportionate punishment of minority students. More broadly, the use of school suspension has received criticism because of evidence from multiple large-scale studies that it increases the risk of school failure, dropout, and juvenile offending, and such punitive disciplinary policies have been termed the school-to-prison pipeline.

Threat assessment offers a flexible, individualized alternative to zero tolerance policies. Using threat assessment allows students to remain in school without suspension. Much more research on threat assessment, as well as other school safety and violence prevention strategies, is needed. In their analysis of school safety research, Astor, Guerra, and Van Acker (2010) called for more research on the impact of school discipline and supervisory practices on school safety conditions and emphasized the need for empirical research specifically concerned with aggression and violence in school contexts. They emphasized the need to move the field toward evidence-based programs that function as effectively in practice as they do in efficacy studies.

References

Allen, K., Cornell, D., Lorek, E., & Sheras, P. (2008). Response of school personnel to student threat assessment training. *School Effectiveness and School Improvement*, *19*, 319–332. http://dx.doi.org/10.1080/09243450802332184

Alley, R., & Limber, S. P. (2009). Legal issues for school personnel. In S. M. Swearer, D. L. Espelage, & S. A. Napolitano (Eds.), *Bullying prevention and intervention: Realistic strategies for schools* (pp. 53–73). New York, NY: Guilford Press.

Alvarez, L. (2013, December 2). Seeing the toll, schools revise zero tolerance. *New York Times*. Retrieved from http://www.nytimes.com/2013/12/03/education/seeing-the-toll-schools-revisit-zero-tolerance.html

American Psychological Association. (2013). *Gun violence: Prediction, prevention, and policy.*

Retrieved from http://www.apa.org/pubs/info/reports/gun-violence-prevention.aspx

American Psychological Association Zero Tolerance Task Force (2008). Are zero tolerance policies effective in the schools? An evidentiary review and recommendations. *American Psychologist, 63*, 852–862. http://dx.doi.org/10.1037/0003-066X.63.9.852

Americans With Disabilities Act of 1990, Pub. L. No. 101-336, 104 Stat. 327 (1991).

Armario, C. (2013, August 24). More schools provide armed security after Newton. *Washington Post*. Retrieved from http://articles.washingtonpost.com/2013-08-24/politics/41442731_1_school-resource-officer-sandy-hook-elementary-school-school-safety-legislation

Arnocky, S., & Vaillancourt, T. (2012). A multi-informant longitudinal study on the relationship between aggression, peer victimization, and dating status in adolescence. *Evolutionary Psychology, 10*, 253–270.

Astor, R., Guerra, N., & Van Acker, R. (2010). How can we improve school safety research? *Educational Researcher, 39*, 69–78. http://dx.doi.org/10.3102/0013189X09357619

Baglivio, M. T., & Jackowski, K. (2013). Examining the validity of a juvenile offending risk assessment instrument across gender and race/ethnicity. *Youth Violence and Juvenile Justice, 11*, 26–43. http://dx.doi.org/10.1177/1541204012440107

Bayh, B. (1975). *Our nation's schools—A report card: "A" in school violence and vandalism. Preliminary report of the Subcommittee to Investigate Juvenile Delinquency, based on investigations, 1971–1975*. Washington, DC: Senate Committee on the Judiciary. (ERIC Document Reproduction Service No. ED104006)

Bender, D., & Lösel, F. (2011). Bullying at school as a predictor of delinquency, violence and other anti-social behaviour in adulthood. *Criminal Behaviour and Mental Health, 21*, 99–106. http://dx.doi.org/10.1002/cbm.799

Borum, R., Bartel, P., & Forth, A. (2003). *Structured Assessment of Violence Risk in Youth (SAVRY)*. Lutz, FL: Psychological Assessment Resources.

Borum, R., Cornell, D., Modzeleski, W., & Jimerson, S. R. (2010). What can be done about school shootings? A review of the evidence. *Educational Researcher, 39*, 27–37. http://dx.doi.org/10.3102/0013189X09357620

Bradshaw, C. P., Mitchell, M. M., O'Brennan, L. M., & Leaf, P. J. (2010). Multilevel exploration of factors contributing to the overrepresentation of Black students in office disciplinary referrals. *Journal of Educational Psychology, 102*, 508–520. http://dx.doi.org/10.1037/a0018450

Card, N., & Hodges, E. (2010). It takes two to fight in school, too: A social relations model of the psychometric properties and relative variance of dyadic aggression and victimization in middle school. *Social Development, 19*, 447–469. http://dx.doi.org/10.1111/j.1467-9507.2009.00562.x

Carlisle, N., & Rofes, E. (2007). School bullying: Do adult survivors perceive long-term effects? *Traumatology, 13*, 16–26. http://dx.doi.org/10.1177/1534765607299911

Center for the Study and Prevention of Violence. (2014). *Blueprints for healthy youth development*. Retrieved from http://www.blueprintsprograms.com

Centers for Disease Control and Prevention. (2014). *Youth Risk Behavior Surveillance System (YRBSS)*. Retrieved from http://www.cdc.gov/healthyyouth/yrbs/index.htm

Cerf, C., Hespe, D., Gantwerk, B., Martz, S., & Vermeire, G. (2010). *Guidance for schools on implementing the Anti-Bullying Bill of Rights Act*. Trenton: New Jersey Department of Education.

Chan, J. H. F. (2006). Systemic patterns in bullying and victimization. *School Psychology International, 27*, 352–369. http://dx.doi.org/10.1177/0143034306067289

Childs, K., Frick, P. J., Ryals, Jr., J. S., Lingonblad, A., & Villio, M. J. (2014). A comparison of empirically based and structured professional judgment estimation of risk using the Structured Assessment of Violence Risk in Youth. *Youth Violence and Juvenile Justice, 12*, 40–57. http://dx.doi.org/1177/1541204013480368

Civil Rights Act of 1964, Pub. L. 88-352, 78 Stat. 241, 42 U.S.C. §§ 1981–2000.

Coker, T. R., Austin, S. B., & Schuster, M. A. (2010). The health and health care of lesbian, gay, and bisexual adolescents. *Annual Review of Public Health, 31*, 457–477. http://dx.doi.org/10.1146/annurev.publhealth.012809.103636

Connecticut Commission on Children. (n.d.). *Bullying*. Retrieved from http://www.cga.ct.gov/coc/bullying.htm

Conroy, M. A. (2012). Assessing juveniles for risk of violence. In E. L. Grigorenko (Ed.), *Handbook of juvenile forensic psychology and psychiatry* (pp. 227–238). http://dx.doi.org/10.1007/978-1-4614-0905-2_15

Cook, C. R., Williams, K. R., Guerra, N. G., Kim, T. E., & Sadek, S. (2010). Predictors of bullying and victimization in childhood and adolescence: A meta-analytic investigation. *School Psychology Quarterly, 25*, 65–83. http://dx.doi.org/10.1037/a0020149

Copeland, W., Wolke, D., Angold, A., & Costello, E. (2013). Adult psychiatric outcomes of bullying and being bullied by peers in childhood and adolescence. *JAMA Psychiatry*, *70*, 419–426.

Cornell, D. (2006). *School violence: Fears versus facts.* Mahwah, NJ: Erlbaum.

Cornell, D., Allen, K., & Fan, X. (2012). A randomized controlled study of the Virginia Student Threat Assessment Guidelines in Grades K-12. *School Psychology Review*, *41*, 100–115.

Cornell, D., & Cole, J. (2012). Assessment of bullying. In S. R. Jimerson, A. B. Nickerson, M. J. Mayer, & M. J. Furlong (Eds.), *The handbook of school violence and school safety: International research and practice* (2nd ed., pp. 289–303). New York, NY: Routledge.

Cornell, D., Gregory, A., & Fan, X. (2011). Reductions in long-term suspensions following adoption of the Virginia Student Threat Assessment Guidelines. *NASSP Bulletin*, *95*, 175–194.

Cornell, D., Gregory, A., Huang, F., & Fan, X. (2013). Perceived prevalence of teasing and bullying predicts high school dropout rates. *Journal of Educational Psychology*, *105*, 138–149. http://dx.doi.org/10.1037/a0030416

Cornell, D., & Lovegrove, P. (in press). Student threat assessment as method for reducing student suspensions. In D. Losen (Ed.), *Closing the school discipline gap: Research for policymakers.* New York, NY: Teachers College Press.

Cornell, D., & Sheras, P. (2006). *Guidelines for responding to student threats of violence.* Longmont, CO: Sopris West.

Cornell, D., Sheras, P., Gregory, A., & Fan, X. (2009). A retrospective study of school safety conditions in high schools using the Virginia Threat Assessment Guidelines versus alternative approaches. *School Psychology Quarterly*, *24*, 119–129. http://dx.doi.org/10.1037/a0016182

Cornell, D., Sheras, P., Kaplan, S., McConville, D., Douglass, J., Elkon, A., . . . Cole, J. (2004). Guidelines for student threat assessment: Field-test findings. *School Psychology Review*, *33*, 527–546.

Craig, W., Harel-Fisch, Y., Fogel-Grinvald, H., Dostaler, S., Hetland, J., Simons-Morton, B., . . . Pickett, W.; HBSC Violence & Injuries Prevention Focus Group & the HBSC Bullying Writing Group. (2009). A cross-national profile of bullying and victimization among adolescents in 40 countries. *International Journal of Public Health*, *54*(Suppl. 2), 216–224. http://dx.doi.org/10.1007/s00038-009-5413-9

Crews, G. A., & Counts, M. R. (1997). *The evolution of school disturbance in America.* Westport, CT: Praeger.

Davis v. Monroe County Board of Education, 526 U.S. 629 (1999).

DiIulio, J. J., Jr. (1995, November 27). The coming of the super-predators. *Weekly Standard*, *1*(11), 23–28.

Education for All Handicapped Children Act of 1975, Pub. L. 94-142.

Esbensen, F., & Carson, D. C. (2009). Consequences of being bullied: Results from a longitudinal assessment of bullying victimization in a multisite sample of American students. *Youth and Society*, *41*, 209–233. http://dx.doi.org/10.1177/0044118X09351067

Espelage, D., Low, S., & De La Rue, L. (2012). Relations between peer victimization subtypes, family violence, and psychological outcomes during early adolescence. *Psychology of Violence*, 2, 313–324. http://dx.doi.org/10.1037/a0027386

Fabelo, T., Thompson, M. D., Plotkin, M., Carmichael, D., Marchbanks, M. P., & Booth, E. A. (2011). *Breaking schools' rules: A statewide study of how school discipline relates to students' success and juvenile justice involvement.* New York, NY: Council of State Governments Justice Center.

Fairchild, G., van Goozen, S. H. M., Calder, A. J., & Goodyer, I. M. (2013). Research review: Evaluating and reformulating the developmental taxonomic theory of antisocial behaviour. *Journal of Child Psychology and Psychiatry*, *54*, 924–940. http://dx.doi.org/10.1111/jcpp.12102

Fanti, K., & Kimonis, E. (2013). Dimensions of juvenile psychopathy distinguish "bullies," "bully-victims," and "victims." *Psychology of Violence*, *3*, 396–409. http://dx.doi.org/10.1037/a0033951

Fein, R., Vossekuil, B., Pollack, W., Borum, R., Modzeleski, W., & Reddy, M. (2002). *Threat assessment in schools: A guide to managing threatening situations and to creating safe school climates.* Washington, DC: U.S. Secret Service and Department of Education.

Gini, G., & Pozzoli, T. (2009). Association between bullying and psychosomatic problems: A meta-analysis. *Pediatrics*, *123*, 1059–1065. http://dx.doi.org/10.1542/peds.2008-1215

Gladden, R. M., Vivolo-Kantor, A. M., Hamburger, M. E., & Lumpkin, C. D. (2014). *Bullying surveillance among youths: Uniform definitions for public health and recommended data elements, Version 1.0.* Atlanta, GA: National Center for Injury Prevention and Control, Centers for Disease Control and Prevention, and U.S. Department of Education.

Green, J. G., Felix, E. D., Sharkey, J. D., Furlong, M. J., & Kras, J. E. (2013). Identifying bully victims: Definitional versus behavioral approaches. *Psychological Assessment*, *25*, 651–657. http://dx.doi.org/10.1037/a0031248

Gregory, A., & Weinstein, R. S. (2008). The discipline gap and African Americans: Defiance or cooperation in the high school classroom. *Journal of School Psychology*, *46*, 455–475. http://dx.doi.org/10.1016/j.jsp.2007.09.001

Grisso, T., Steinberg, L., Woolard, J., Cauffman, E., Scott, E., Graham, S., . . . Schwartz, R. (2003). Juveniles' competence to stand trial: A comparison of adolescents' and adults' capacities as trial defendants. *Law and Human Behavior*, *27*, 333–363. http://dx.doi.org/10.1023/A:1024065015717

Hanish, L. D., Bradshaw, C. P., Espelage, D. L., Rodkin, P. C., Swearer, S. M., & Horne, A. (2013). Looking forward toward the future of bullying research: Recommendations for research and funding priorities. *Journal of School Violence*, *12*, 283–295. http://dx.doi.org/10.1080/15388220.2013.788449

Hazelden Foundation. (2014). *Violence prevention works! Safer schools, safer communities*. Retrieved http://www.violencepreventionworks.org/public/index.page

Healy, J. (2013, September 2). National gun debate hits close to home in Colorado recall vote. *New York Times*. Retrieved from http://www.nytimes.com/2013/09/03/us/national-debate-on-gun-control-hits-home-in-colorado-recall.html

Heilbrun, K., Dvoskin, J., & Heilbrun, A. (2009). Toward preventing future tragedies: Mass killings on college campuses, public health, and threat/risk assessment. *Psychological Injury and Law*, *2*, 93–99. http://dx.doi.org/10.1007/s12207-009-9040-9

Heilbrun, K., Goldstein, N. E. S., & Redding, R. (2005). *Juvenile delinquency: Prevention, assessment, and intervention*. New York, NY: Oxford University Press.

Hemphill, S. A., Kotevski, A., Herrenkohl, T. I., Bond, L., Kim, M. J., Toumbourou, J. W., & Catalano, R. F. (2011). Longitudinal consequences of adolescent bullying perpetration and victimisation: A study of students in Victoria, Australia. *Criminal Behaviour and Mental Health*, *21*, 107–116. http://dx.doi.org/10.1002/cbm.802

Henggeler, S. W., & Sheidow, A. J. (2012). Empirically supported family-based treatments for conduct disorder and delinquency in adolescents. *Journal of Marital and Family Therapy*, *38*, 30–58. http://dx.doi.org/10.1111/j.1752-0606.2011.00244.x

Henry, K. L., Knight, K. E., & Thornberry, T. P. (2012). School disengagement as a predictor of dropout, delinquency, and problem substance use during adolescence and early adulthood. *Journal of Youth and Adolescence*, *41*, 156–166. http://dx.doi.org/10.1007/s10964-011-9665-3

Higgins, G., Jennings, W., Tewksbury, R., & Gibson, C. (2009). Exploring the link between low self-control and violent victimization trajectories in adolescents. *Criminal Justice and Behavior*, *36*, 1070–1084. http://dx.doi.org/10.1177/0093854809344046

Hirschfield, P. J., & Gasper, J. (2011). The relationship between school engagement and delinquency in late childhood and early adolescence. *Journal of Youth and Adolescence*, *40*, 3–22. http://dx.doi.org/10.1007/s10964-010-9579-5

Holma, I. A., Holma, K. M., Melartin, T. K., & Isometsä, E. T. (2010). Treatment attitudes and adherence of psychiatric patients with major depressive disorder: A five-year prospective study. *Journal of Affective Disorders*, *127*, 102–112. http://dx.doi.org/10.1016/j.jad.2010.04.022

Holt, M. K., & Espelage, D. L. (2007). Perceived social support among bullies, victims, and bully-victims. *Journal of Youth and Adolescence*, *36*, 984–994. http://dx.doi.org/10.1007/s10964-006-9153-3

Improving America's Schools Act of 1994, Pub. L. 103-382, 108 Stat. 3518.

Individuals With Disabilities Education Act of 1990, Pub. L. 101-476.

Juvonen, J., Wang, Y., & Espinoza, G. (2011). Bullying experiences and compromised academic performance across middle school grades. *Journal of Early Adolescence*, *31*, 152–173. http://dx.doi.org/10.1177/0272431610379415

Lacey, A., & Cornell, D. (2013). The impact of bullying climate on schoolwide academic performance. *Journal of Applied School Psychology*, *29*, 262–283.

Lee, T., Cornell, D., Gregory, A., & Fan, X. (2011). High suspension schools and dropout rates for Black and White students. *Education and Treatment of Children*, *34*, 167–192.

Loeber, R., Menting, B., Lynam, D., Moffitt, T., Stouthamer-Loeber, M., Stallings, R., . . . Pardini, D. (2012). Findings from the Pittsburgh Youth Study: Cognitive impulsivity and intelligence as predictors of the age-crime curve. *Journal of the American Academy of Child and Adolescent Psychiatry*, *51*, 1135–1149.

Lösel, F., Bottoms, A., & Farrington, D. P. (2012). *Young adult offenders: Lost in transition?* New York, NY: Routledge.

Losen, D. J., & Martinez, T. E. (2013). *Out of school and off track: The overuse of suspensions in American middle and high schools*. Los Angeles, CA: UCLA Center for Civil Rights Remedies at The Civil Rights Project.

Lovegrove, P. J., & Cornell, D. G. (2014). Patterns of bullying and victimization associated with other problem behaviors among high school students: A conditional latent class approach. *Journal of Crime and Justice*, *37*, 5–22. http://dx.doi.org/10.1080/0735648X.2013.832475

Mehta, S., Cornell, D., Fan, X., & Gregory, A. (2013). Bullying climate and school engagement in ninth grade students. *Journal of School Health*, *83*, 45–52.

Moffitt, T. E. (1990). Juvenile delinquency and attention deficit disorder: Boys' developmental trajectories from age 3 to age 15. *Child Development*, *61*, 893–910.

Moffitt, T. E. (1993). Adolescence-limited and life course-persistent antisocial behavior. *Psychological Review*, *100*, 674–701. http://dx.doi.org/10.1037/0033-295X.100.4.674

Molcho, M., Craig, W., Due, P., Pickett, W., Harel-Fisch, Y., & Overpeck, M.; HBSC Bullying Writing Group. (2009). Cross-national time trends in bullying behaviour 1994–2006: Findings from Europe and North America. *International Journal of Public Health*, *54*(Suppl. 2), 225–234. http://dx.doi.org/10.1007/s00038-009-5414-8

Mulvey, E. P. (2011). *Highlights from pathways to desistance: A longitudinal study of serious adolescent offenders*. Washington, DC: Office of Juvenile Justice and Delinquency Prevention, U.S. Department of Justice.

Nakamoto, J., & Schwartz, D. (2010). Is peer victimization associated with academic achievement? A meta-analytic review. *Social Development*, *19*, 221–242.

National Registry of Evidence-Based Programs and Practices. (2013). *Virginia student threat assessment guidelines*. Retrieved from http://www.nrepp.samhsa.gov/ViewIntervention.aspx?id=263

Nekvasil, E. K., Cornell, D. G., & Huang, F. L. (in press). Prevalence and offense characteristics of multiple casualty homicides: Is school fortification needed? *Psychology of Violence*.

O'Brennan, L., Bradshaw, C., & Sawyer, A. (2009). Examining development differences in the social-emotional problems among frequent bullies, victims, and bully/victims. *Psychology in the Schools*, *46*, 100–115.

Odgers, C., Caspi, A., Broadbent, J. M., Dickson, N., Hancox, B., Harrington, H., . . . Moffitt, T. E. (2007). Conduct problems subtypes in males predict differential adult health burden. *Archives of General Psychiatry*, *64*, 476–484.

Olweus, D. (1991). Bully/victim problems among school children: Basic facts and effects of a school based intervention program. In D. Peper & K. Rubin (Eds.), *The development and treatment of childhood aggression* (pp. 411–448). Hillsdale, NJ: Erlbaum.

O'Toole, M. E. (2000). *The school shooter: A threat assessment perspective*. Retrieved from http://www.fbi.gov/stats-services/publications/school-shooter

Otto, R., & Douglas, K. (Eds.). (2010). *Handbook of violence risk assessment*. New York, NY: Routledge.

Pollard, J., Nolan, J., & Deisinger, E. (2012). The practice of campus-based threat assessment: An overview. *Journal of College Student Psychotherapy*, 26, 263–276. http://dx.doi.org/10.1080/87568225.2012.711142

Price, M., Chin, M. A., Higa-McMillan, C., Kim, S., & Frueh, B. C. (2013). Prevalence and internalizing problems of ethnoracially diverse victims of traditional and cyber bullying. *School Mental Health*, *5*, 183–191.

Quinn, M. M., Rutherford, R. B., Leone, P. E., Osher, D. M., & Poirer, J. M. (2005). Youth with disabilities in juvenile corrections: A national survey. *Exceptional Children*, *71*, 339–345.

Reddy, M., Borum, R., Berglund, J., Vossekuil, B., Fein, R., & Modzeleski, W. (2001). Evaluating risk for targeted violence in schools: Comparing risk assessment, threat assessment, and other approaches. *Psychology in the Schools*, *38*, 157–172.

Rehabilitation Act of 1973, Pub. L. 93-112, 29 U.S.C. §§ 701–796.

Reijntjes, A., Kamphuuis, J. H., Prinzie, P., & Telch, M. J. (2010). Peer victimization and internalizing problems in children: A meta-analysis of longitudinal studies. *Child Abuse and Neglect*, *34*, 244–252.

Robers, S., Kemp, J., & Truman, J. (2013). *Indicators of school crime and safety: 2012* (NCES 2013-036/NCJ 241446). Washington, DC: National Center for Education Statistics, U.S. Department of Education, and Bureau of Justice Statistics, Office of Justice Programs, U.S. Department of Justice.

Robinson, J., & Espelage, D. (2012). Bullying explains only part of LGBTQ-heterosexual risk disparities: Implications for policy and practice. *Educational Research*, *41*, 309–319.

Rose, C., Espelage, D., Aragon, S., & Elliott, J. (2011). Bullying and victimization among students in special education and general education curricula. *Exceptionality Education International*, *21*(2–3), 2–14.

Rubinkam, M. (2013). Kids' recent school suspensions renew debate over zero tolerance. *Huffington Post*. Retrieved from http://www.huffingtonpost.com/2013/02/19/kids-school-suspensions_n_2717996.html

Sacco, D. T., Silbaugh, K., Corredor, F., Casey, J., & Dohert, D. (2012). *An overview of state anti-bullying legislation and other related laws*. Retrieved from http://cyber.law.harvard.edu/files/State_Anti_bullying_Legislation_Overview_0.pdf

Scruggs v. Meriden Board of Education, 2005 WL 2072312 (D. Conn. Aug. 26, 2005).

Sewell, K., & Mendelsohn, M. (2000). Profiling potentially violent youth: Statistical and conceptual problems. *Children's Services: Social Policy, Research, and Practice*, *3*, 147–169.

Shore Regional High School Board of Education v. P.S., 41 IDELR 234, 381 F.3d 194 (3d Cir. 2004).

Skiba, R., Horner, R., Chung, C., Rausch, M., May, S., & Tobin, T. (2011). Race is not neutral: A national investigation of African American and Latino disproportionality in school discipline. *School Psychology Review*, *40*, 85–107.

Skiba, R. J., & Rausch, M. K. (2006). Zero tolerance, suspension, and expulsion: Questions of equity and effectiveness. In C. M. Evertson & C. S. Weinstein (Eds.), *Handbook of classroom management: Research, practice, and contemporary issues* (pp. 1063–1089). Mahwah, NJ: Erlbaum.

Sourander, A., Elonheimo, H., Niemela, S., Nuutila, A., Helenius, H., Sillanmaki, L., . . . Almquist, F. (2007). Who is at greatest risk of adverse long-term outcomes? The Finnish From a Boy to a Man Study. *Academy of Child and Adolescent Psychiatry*, *46*, 1148–1161.

Sourander, A., Klomek, A. B., Kumpulainen, K., Puustjärvi, A., Elonheimo, H., Ristkari, T., . . . Ronning, J. A. (2011). Bullying at age eight and criminality in adulthood: Findings from the Finnish Nationwide 1981 Birth Cohort Study. *Social Psychiatry and Psychiatric Epidemiology*, *46*, 1211–1219. http://dx.doi.org/10.1007/s00127-010-0292-1

Steinberg, L. (2010). A dual systems model of adolescent risk-taking. *Developmental Psychobiology*, *52*, 216–224.

Steinberg, L., & Scott, E. (2003). Less guilty by reason of adolescence: Developmental immaturity, diminished responsibility, and the juvenile death penalty. *American Psychologist*, *58*, 1009–1018.

Strong, K., & Cornell, D. (2008). Student threat assessment in Memphis City Schools: A descriptive report. *Behavioral Disorders*, *34*, 42–54.

Substance Abuse and Mental Health Services Administration. (2014). NREPP: SAMHSA's National Registry of Evidence-based Programs and Practices. Retrieved from http://nrepp.samhsa.gov/index.aspx

Swearer, S. M., Espelage, D. L., Vaillancourt, T., & Hymel, S. (2010). What can be done about school bullying? Linking research to educational practice. *Educational Researcher*, *39*, 38–47. http://dx.doi.org/10.3102/0013189X09357622

Thomas, P. (2006, October 3). Why the spike in school shootings? *ABC News*. Retrieved from http://abcnews.go.com/GMA/story?id=2521025

Thunfors, P., & Cornell, D. (2008). The popularity of middle school bullies. *Journal of School Violence*, *7*, 65–82.

Title IX, Education Amendments of 1972, 20 U.S.C. §§ 1681–1688.

Ttofi, M. M., & Farrington, D. P. (2009). What works in preventing bullying: Effective elements of anti-bullying programmes. *Journal of Aggression, Conflict and Peace Research*, *1*, 13–24.

Ttofi, M. M., Farrington, D. P., Lösel, F., & Loeber, R. (2011). The predictive efficiency of school bullying versus later offending: A systematic/meta-analytic review of longitudinal studies. *Journal of Experimental Criminology*, *7*, 27–56.

U.S. Department of Education, Office for Civil Rights (2010). *Dear colleague letter: Harassment and bullying*. Retrieved from http://www2.ed.gov/about/offices/list/ocr/letters/colleague-201010.pdf

U.S. Department of Justice & U.S. Department of Education (2014). *Dear colleague letter on the nondiscriminatory administration of school discipline*. Retrieved from http://www2.ed.gov/about/offices/list/ocr/letters/colleague-201401-title-vi.pdf

Van Domburgh, L., Loeber, R., Bezemer, D., Stallings, R., & Stouthamer-Loeber, M. (2009). Childhood predictors of desistance and level of persistence in offending in early onset offenders. *Journal of Abnormal Child Psychology*, *37*, 967–980.

Van Dyke, R., & Schroeder, J. (2006). Implementation of the Dallas Threat of Violence Risk Assessment. In S. R. Jimerson & M. J. Furlong (Eds.) *Handbook of school violence and school safety: From research to practice* (pp. 603–616). Mahwah, NJ: Erlbaum.

Virginia Tech Review Panel. (2007). *Mass shootings at Virginia Tech, April 16, 2007*. Retrieved from http://www.vtreviewpanel.org/report/index.html

Vossekuil, B., Fein, R., Reddy, M., Borum, R., & Modzeleski, W. (2002). *The final report and findings of the Safe School Initiative: Implications for the prevention of school attacks in the United States*. Washington, DC: U.S. Secret Service and U.S. Department of Education.

Wang, J., Iannotti, R. J., & Nansel, T. R. (2009). School bullying among adolescents in the United States: Physical, verbal, relational, and cyber. *Journal of Adolescent Health*, *45*, 368–375.

Watanabe, T. (2012, September 3). L. A. schools moving away from zero tolerance policies. *Los Angeles Times*. Retrieved from http://articles.latimes.com/2012/sep/03/local/la-me-citations-20120904

Wilson, S. J., & Lipsey, M. W. (2007). School-based interventions for aggressive and disruptive behavior: Update of a meta-analysis. *American Journal of Preventive Medicine*, *33*, 130–143. http://dx.doi.org/10.1016/j.amepre.2007.04.01

Wilson, S. J., Lipsey, M. W., & Derzon, J. H. (2003). The effects of school-based intervention programs on aggressive behavior: A meta-analysis. *Journal of Consulting and Clinical Psychology*, *71*, 136–149.

Zimring, F. (1998). *American youth violence*. New York, NY: Oxford University Press.

CHAPTER 12

DISRUPTING THE SCHOOL-TO-PRISON PIPELINE: STRATEGIES TO REDUCE THE RISK OF SCHOOL-BASED ZERO TOLERANCE POLICIES RESULTING IN JUVENILE JUSTICE INVOLVEMENT

Brian P. Daly, Aimee K. Hildenbrand, Emily Haney-Caron, Naomi E. S. Goldstein, Meghann Galloway, and David DeMatteo

Youth violence in the school setting is considered a major public health issue, given its negative impact on youths' physical and psychosocial well-being. Although longitudinal data have indicated that the prevalence of school violence has decreased in recent decades (Eaton et al., 2012), violence still exists at significant rates in schools. For instance, 12% of a nationally representative sample of youths in high schools reported having been in a physical fight on school property during the previous 12 months, and approximately 6% of this sample did not attend school at least 1 day in the past month because they felt unsafe in or on the way to school (Eaton et al., 2012). Findings from a recent national survey revealed that nearly 7% of high school students were threatened or injured with a weapon on school property at least once in the past year (National Center for Injury Prevention and Control, 2013). Students exposed to school violence are at increased risk for mental health problems such as depression, anxiety, traumatic stress symptoms, suicidal behavior, and substance use problems (Flannery, Wester, & Singer, 2004). Exposure to school violence also interferes with youths' academic success, thereby hindering their ability to lead productive lives and posing a serious challenge to society as a whole.

Beyond the deleterious consequences for victims and perpetrators of school violence, the problem of how best to address youth violence in schools extends to groups (educators, administrators, caregivers, health professionals), systems (schools, criminal justice), and the larger community. All of these stakeholders have grappled with the complex challenges around developing strategies to reduce school violence. A school disciplinary approach known as zero tolerance, aimed at preventing violence and other misconduct, gained momentum in the mid- to late 1990s and has subsequently been used by many schools across the country. Some common outcomes of this policy, such as expulsion and long-term suspension from school, are associated with negative academic, social, emotional, and behavioral consequences for youths (American Psychological Association [APA] Zero Tolerance Task Force, 2008). The impact of zero tolerance policies is not restricted to individual students and schools; it also extends to the juvenile justice system.

Although schools have widely used zero tolerance policies for the past 3 decades, only recently

http://dx.doi.org/10.1037/14643-012
APA Handbook of Psychology and Juvenile Justice, K. Heilbrun (Editor-in-Chief)

have the mainstream media and federal agencies called for a reexamination of these policies. For example, a recent op-ed by the editorial board of the *New York Times* suggested that zero tolerance policies be reconsidered ("Zero Tolerance, Reconsidered," 2014). In addition, the administration of President Barack Obama, in combination with the U.S. Department of Justice and the U.S. Department of Education, released guidelines for reforming zero tolerance policies in the school setting (U.S. Department of Education, 2012). Given these recent shifts in public policy, the timing is right to critically examine the connection between zero tolerance policies and juvenile justice involvement and suggest alternative strategies for reducing the school-to-prison pipeline.

In this chapter, we briefly review the historical context and philosophy behind the use of zero tolerance policies in school settings. Next, we describe the stage–environment fit theory and examine how the negative effects of zero tolerance policies applied in the school setting are better understood within this social and developmental framework. We then detail the evidence regarding key assumptions of the zero tolerance approach and describe how these policies have contributed to the school-to-prison pipeline. We also describe the use of zero tolerance policies for discipline in juvenile correctional facilities and probation cases. Finally, we propose several strategies to reduce the risk of these policies' resulting in juvenile justice involvement.

DEFINITION OF ZERO TOLERANCE

Zero tolerance has been defined in various ways. For instance, it has been described as a policy approach that mandates "the application of predetermined consequences, most often severe and punitive in nature, that are intended to be applied regardless of the gravity of behavior, mitigating circumstances, or situational context" (APA Zero Tolerance Task Force, 2008, p. 852). When applied to educational settings, zero tolerance has been defined as "a general school discipline policy that responds with similar punishments to both nonviolent behaviors that are perceived to be disruptive and weapons and drug related infractions of school discipline codes" (Robbins, 2008, p. 5). Another definition of zero tolerance suggests that it is a policy characterized by significant penalties for all major and minor violations of an established disciplinary code (Skiba, 2010). Unfortunately, the lack of a universally accepted definition of zero tolerance has confounded attempts to accurately estimate the frequency of enforcement of such policies.

Definitional challenges notwithstanding, the prevalence rates of enactment of these policies in U.S. schools appear high (APA Zero Tolerance Task Force, 2008). Most schools reserve this approach for severe offenses; however, many incidents have been documented in which students were suspended or expelled for relatively inconsequential infractions, such as the possession of squirt guns and plastic knives brought in lunch boxes to cut food (Skiba, 2010). In Los Angeles, for example, suspensions affected more than one third of the students in a single year; in Florida, 20,000 students were referred to the Department of Juvenile Justice in a single year (González, 2012). In Texas, even elementary school students are commonly given misdemeanor tickets for school disruption (Fowler, 2011). Indeed, the majority of arrests of preteens occur in schools (Thurau & Wald, 2010). Thus, it has been argued that zero tolerance has essentially become public policy for school discipline (Stader, 2004). Several critical questions remain, though, regarding whether these policies are applied fairly and whether they effectively reduce negative behaviors in school settings and potentially prevent involvement with the juvenile justice system.

HISTORICAL CONTEXT OF ZERO TOLERANCE POLICIES

The roots of zero tolerance date back to the 1980s, when local and national efforts in the United States to combat drugs—the "war on drugs"—led to the development of zero tolerance as an approach to drug enforcement (APA Zero Tolerance Task Force, 2008; Teske, 2011). In the early 1990s, schools responded to the increasing incidence of student-to-student violence on school grounds by adopting zero tolerance as a discipline strategy (APA Zero Tolerance Task Force, 2008). The Gun-Free Schools

Act of 1994 gave states financial incentives to implement zero tolerance policies in their schools. For schools to receive federal funding, this legislation requires them to expel for at least 1 calendar year and refer to the criminal justice or juvenile delinquency system any student who brings a firearm or weapon to school. The Gun-Free Schools Act allows states to define *weapon* and to reduce the punishment at the discretion of the highest school administrator on a case-by-case basis. However, many states have broadly construed what constitutes a weapon and eliminated the individual assessment in favor of more rigid and universal punishment (Cerrone, 1999). Notably, the Gun-Free Schools Act remains the only federal law that mandates specific disciplinary consequences for negative student behavior.

The federal government has also passed several other forms of legislation to address the problem of violence in schools, including Goals 2000 (U.S. Department of Education, 1993), the Safe Schools/ Healthy Start Initiative (U.S. Department of Education, 2001), and the No Child Left Behind Act of 2001 (NCLB). In particular, NCLB aimed to improve and maintain teacher quality, increase academic achievement, and ensure accountability for states and districts in meeting these goals. A key component of the accountability requirements established by NCLB is the requirement for states to periodically test students in reading, mathematics, and science and to publish these test results for public consumption. Subsequently, standardized test results in combination with student achievement, school attendance, and graduation rates are used to determine whether a school is making adequate yearly progress. If annual yearly progress is not achieved, schools and districts can incur various penalties, ranging from warnings to corrective actions (e.g., replacing school staff, implementing a new curriculum) and restructuring (i.e., school taken over by the state educational agency). As a result, schools face enormous pressure to meet standards for annual yearly progress under NCLB. Given that poor academic performance and behavioral misconduct are strongly associated (McLeod, Uemura, & Rohrman, 2012), some have argued that schools have incentives to use zero tolerance approaches to expel problematic or misbehaving students, thereby excluding their standardized test scores from annual yearly progress determination (Klehr, 2009). In this way, NCLB may have unintentionally promoted the continued and broadened application of zero tolerance policies in schools.

Finally, school shootings also played a prominent role in encouraging schools to use zero tolerance policies. In particular, the tragic events at Columbine High School in 1999 focused the public's attention on school violence. The fear engendered by this and other school shootings inflated public perceptions of school danger (Borum, Cornell, Modzeleski, & Jimerson, 2010). For instance, a Gallup poll conducted shortly after Columbine found that approximately two thirds of Americans believed that a similar school shooting was somewhat or very likely to occur in their neighborhood (Saad, 1999). These concerns persisted, with 71% of parents reporting that Columbine had changed their view of how safe their children were at school 1 year later (Nagy & Danitz, 2000). Hence, school shootings significantly influenced the national discourse around student safety and helped to drive the continuing expansion of zero tolerance policies in schools.

Since the introduction of zero tolerance policies in schools, many states and local school districts have broadened this disciplinary approach beyond weapons to address other misconduct including alcohol, drugs, and fighting (Zweifler & De Beers, 2002). Consequently, the number of students arrested and referred to juvenile court for school infractions increased considerably after zero tolerance policies were instituted in schools, a trend known as the school-to-prison pipeline (Wald & Losen, 2003). In fact, 41 states require schools to report students to law enforcement for various infractions that take place on school grounds (González, 2012). Findings from a national survey of schools during the 2009 to 2010 school year revealed that approximately 3 million students were suspended out of school, 108,000 students were expelled, and more than 240,000 students were referred to law enforcement (U.S. Department of Education, Office of Civil Rights, 2008). Evidence has also indicated that referrals to juvenile courts from school systems have increased markedly even as the number of serious problems in schools has remained constant (González, 2012). Some (e.g., Tuzzolo & Hewitt, 2006–2007) have attributed the rising rate in the juvenile prison population to the more punitive disciplinary practices in school settings rather than to any real increase in behavioral problems among today's youths.

PHILOSOPHY OF ZERO TOLERANCE POLICIES

Zero tolerance policies are based on the assumption that removing students with disruptive behavior will effectively deter others from similar disruptive conduct, creating a safe environment conducive to learning (Skiba, 2010). This approach also posits that predetermined, mandated punishments increase the consistency of school discipline and thereby help students feel safer at school (APA Zero Tolerance Task Force, 2008). Moreover, this philosophy is steeped in the belief that school violence rates are increasing and necessitate direct, compelling disciplinary strategies (APA Zero Tolerance Task Force, 2008). In response, many school districts have implemented zero tolerance policies in an attempt to reduce school violence. Critics of this strategy, however, have suggested that this disciplinary policy fails to consider typical behaviors associated with normal adolescent development (Skiba & Rausch, 2006).

STAGE–ENVIRONMENT FIT THEORY

The stage–environment fit (SEF) theory posits that the characteristics and quality of opportunities present in home and school environments directly influence positive (e.g., prosocial behavior, academic motivation) or negative (e.g., lower self-efficacy) changes as determined by their match (or mismatch) with adolescents' developmental needs (Eccles et al., 1993). For example, when home and school environments developmentally match adolescents' emerging skills and needs, SEF theory predicts that adolescents are more likely to demonstrate positive outcomes. Alternatively, when home and school environments are not responsive to adolescents' developing capabilities and needs, a mismatch between the adolescent and the environment occurs such that adolescents are more likely to demonstrate difficulties (Roeser, 2005). Because school serves as a prominent social environment for adolescents, SEF theory has been advanced as a model to explain variability in school-related outcomes (e.g., behavior, academic achievement) for youths (Eccles, Early, Frasier, Belansky, & McCarthy, 1997). Specifically, this perspective postulates that adolescents are more likely to demonstrate positive adaptation, prosocial behaviors, and academic success when their developmental needs are aligned with responsive and supportive structures and policies in the school environment (Eccles & Midgley, 1989; Eccles et al., 1993; Midgley, Feldlaufer, & Eccles, 1989). However, divergence between the opportunities and structure provided in school and youths' developmental needs is likely to result in maladaptive behaviors (e.g., youth aggression), which then increase the risk of negative outcomes, such as suspension and expulsion (Eccles et al., 1993).

EVIDENCE REGARDING THE KEY ASSUMPTIONS OF ZERO TOLERANCE POLICIES

Several of the assumptions underlying zero tolerance have not received empirical support. For instance, a key supposition of zero tolerance is that providing consequences to students with disruptive behavior will deter these students from engaging in similar conduct in the future. However, findings from one survey indicated that 30% to 50% of students who were suspended continued to engage in disruptive behavior in school (Costenbader & Markson, 1994). In addition, out-of-school suspension actually predicts higher rates of future misconduct and suspension (Costenbader & Markson, 1998; Raffaele-Mendez, 2003; Tobin, Sugai, & Colvin, 1996). Students who are suspended or expelled are also less likely to succeed academically (Raffaele-Mendez, 2003), are more likely to drop out or fail to graduate on time (Bowditch, 1993), and are at increased risk of juvenile detention (Skiba et al., 2003). Moreover, school suspension increases the risk of antisocial and delinquent behaviors (Teske, 2011). Research has also demonstrated that school attendance is a protective factor against delinquent conduct (U.S. Department of Health and Human Services, 2001) and, thus, suspension and expulsion of students may be counterproductive to the goal of deterring future misconduct (Teske, 2011).

According to the SEF perspective, school disciplinary policies such as zero tolerance that are considered to be developmentally regressive, overly punitive, uncaring, and nonresponsive to the emerging capabilities and needs of youths increase the risk that adolescents will experience behavioral difficulties in that environment (Battistich & Hom, 1997; Eccles & Midgley, 1989; Eccles et al., 1993; Midgley et al., 1989). In essence, one of the biggest problems with zero tolerance is that it places strict limits on autonomy during a time when facilitating autonomy is particularly important for adolescent development. Consequently, it has been argued that if youths' behavior reflects normal immaturity and does not pose a serious threat to their own safety or that of others, the long-term negative consequences of sanctions frequently associated with zero tolerance (e.g., suspension and expulsion) may be unwarranted and counterproductive (APA Zero Tolerance Task Force, 2008; Teske, 2011) and may interfere with the normal desistance of aggression and other problem behaviors (e.g., Ayres et al., 1999). As such, policymakers and school officials should not overlook the potential iatrogenic effect of zero tolerance policies.

The second major assumption of zero tolerance policies is that removal of disruptive students leads to a safer and more productive learning environment for the school's general student body. Despite intuitive appeal, a thorough search of the empirical literature did not produce any research findings supporting the claim that zero tolerance policies are effective in reducing violent and other delinquent behaviors in schools. On the contrary, data have suggested that schools that expel students for relatively minor behavioral infractions—and schools with higher suspension and expulsion rates—have other negative outcomes that include lower satisfaction ratings for school climate, school connectedness, and governance structures (Bickel & Qualls, 1980; Wu, Pink, Crain, & Moles, 1982).

From the SEF perspective, the negative impact of zero tolerance is felt more acutely by students who are most in need of support, because they are also those most likely to be punished. For this reason, the SEF framework suggests that these policies fail to promote school safety because their punitive nature and, often, indiscriminate application criminalizes normative, developmentally appropriate adolescent behavior (Skiba & Rausch, 2006). For example, certain minor disciplinary violations (e.g., pushing, tripping, slapping, screaming) are expected given adolescents' relatively imprudent decision-making skills, poor judgment, limited capacity for emotion regulation, and overall psychosocial immaturity. However, when zero tolerance is applied to these minor disciplinary violations, students are often subject to substantial disciplinary sanctions that are so severe in nature (e.g., expulsion, police involvement) that they provide no opportunities for learning and future behavior change. As such, when school discipline practices unnecessarily remove students from their classroom or school, an opportunity may be missed to promote adolescents' developing capabilities and needs.

Zero tolerance advocates have also contended that applying predetermined consequences for all violations of a disciplinary code enhances the consistency of institutional discipline, removes subjective influences from disciplinary decisions, and ensures fairer treatment of students traditionally overrepresented in school disciplinary cases (Casella, 2003). However, a robust literature has suggested that school discipline approaches are frequently used in a discriminatory fashion. Students of color (i.e., African American and Hispanic or Latino) receive harsh discipline, such as suspensions and expulsions, at disproportionately high rates (APA Zero Tolerance Task Force, 2008). For example, although African American youths make up only 16% of public school enrollment, these students account for 42% of multiple suspensions (U.S. Department of Education, Office of Civil Rights, 2014). From 2002 to 2007, the expulsion rate increased 33% for African American students and 6% for Hispanic students but decreased 2% for White, non-Hispanic students (Advancement Project, 2010). In addition, African American students were 2.6 times more likely to be suspended and 3.5 times more likely to be expelled than White, non-Hispanic students (Wald & Losen, 2003). Moreover, African American male students receive harsher punishments than do their White, non-Hispanic peers for similar behaviors (Archer, 2009; Kim, 2009).

There is no evidence to suggest, however, that African American students demonstrate higher rates of disruption that would warrant higher rates of zero tolerance discipline, nor is this overrepresentation explained entirely by poverty (APA Zero Tolerance Task Force, 2008). Instead, it has been suggested that minority students are the most likely to suffer the negative consequences of zero tolerance because they are disciplined more harshly for less severe violations (McFadden, Marsh, Price, & Hwang, 1992; Skiba, Michael, Nardo, & Peterson, 2002). A report by the APA Zero Tolerance Task Force (2008) noted that disproportionate rates of suspension for minority students in schools were associated with racial and ethnic disparities in juvenile justice settings, providing further support for the school-to-prison pipeline. Notably, though, no studies have examined whether zero tolerance policies are more prevalent in schools with large minority populations; instead, extant research has attributed this disparity to school officials' referral bias (Skiba et al., 2002).

In the context of the SEF framework, these findings are concerning given that adolescents' perceptions of teacher fairness are associated with positive adolescent development (Resnick et al., 1997; Wentzel, 2002). In addition, students who perceive their school to be overly reliant on suspension and punitive punishment practices have also reported more negative perceptions of school climate and strained relationships with adults in the school, factors considered key to promoting school success (Comer & Poussaint, 1992). Moreover, greater use of school suspension and expulsion has been associated with poorer schoolwide academic performance, even when controlling for key demographic indicators such as socioeconomic status (Raffaele-Mendez, 2003; Skiba & Rausch, 2006). Instead of the school environment serving as a match with students' developmental needs for autonomy by providing a supportive, equitable, and responsive disciplinary structure, students in zero tolerance schools may experience school as hostile and alienating, thereby diminishing their attachment to school—a key determinant of prosocial behavior and academic achievement (Skiba & Peterson, 2000). Some scholars have therefore suggested that zero tolerance policies may lead to negative academic and mental health outcomes by increasing student alienation, anxiety, and rejection and by interrupting or breaking healthy bonds with adults (Comer & Poussaint, 1992; Reynolds & Kamphaus, 2004).

ZERO TOLERANCE AS A RISK FACTOR FOR OFFENDING AND THE SCHOOL-TO-PRISON PIPELINE

Some advocates of the zero tolerance approach have also argued that it is an appropriate solution to youth violence, given the states' moral and legal responsibility to ensure the safety and welfare of children (Bogos, 1996). Similarly, others have argued that even the most trivial threat of violence must be taken seriously because students who make jokes about violence may still intend to commit it (Gagliardi, 2001). However, these arguments often fail to consider that when zero tolerance policies are applied to youths, there is potential for increased school-based arrests, referrals to alternative schools, and referrals to law enforcement. In fact, some zero tolerance policies mandate school officials to refer students to law enforcement for infractions that were previously handled by school administrators (Wald & Losen, 2003). These policies are counterproductive to community safety because they often result in increased crime and poorer educational outcomes among those who are punished.

Overly punitive school disciplinary policies, especially those that result in suspension or expulsion, often have the effect of removing students from educational institutions and funneling them into juvenile and correctional facilities. Although only 2% of students who had no school disciplinary action came into contact with the juvenile justice system, approximately 50% of students who were disciplined 11 or more times had some contact with the juvenile justice system (Council of State Governments, 2011). Research has demonstrated that students suspended or expelled for a discretionary violation (e.g., disobedience, classroom disruption, insubordination) were nearly 3 times as likely to be involved with the juvenile justice system the following year as their peers, even when considering individual student and campus characteristics (Council of State Governments, 2011). Another study found that 61% of youths in custody reported having been expelled or suspended during the year before juvenile detention, an expulsion and suspension rate substantially higher than the 8% in the general population (Sedlak & McPherson, 2010). This is particularly concerning considering the overrepresentation of students with disabilities, particularly those who have been diagnosed with either an emotional or a behavior disorder, and students of color in both school disciplinary reports and criminal justice facilities (Rivkin, 2009; U.S. Department of Education, 2014).

As zero tolerance policies were gaining momentum, schools also saw the introduction of police on campus (also called school resource officers, or SROs). In the presence of SROs, students who engaged in behavioral disruptions or infractions were increasingly referred to juvenile courts. For example, when SROs were first introduced into Clayton County, Georgia, in 1994, the school system saw a 1,248% increase in law enforcement referrals (Teske & Huff, 2011). In 1999, the U.S. Department of Justice implemented the Community Oriented Policing Services in Schools program, which resulted in the hiring of more than 6,500 new SROs (Curtis, 2010). A study conducted in 2010 found that school referrals to juvenile courts in West Virginia specifically had increased approximately 30% over the past 10 years, and Missouri demonstrated an approximately 50% increase during the same period of time (Krezmien, Leone, & Achilles, 2006).

Not only do zero tolerance policies increase the likelihood that children will become justice involved, but they may also compromise the opportunity for these youths to return to school on release, diminishing their chances of success postrelease and making recidivism much more likely. This is especially concerning given that youths who attend school regularly after release from the juvenile justice system are substantially less likely to be rearrested in the 24 months after release and, if rearrested, tend to commit significantly less serious crimes than do youths who do not return to school (Blomberg, Bales, Mann, Piquero, & Berk, 2011). In general, the school-to-prison pipeline created by zero tolerance policies places students on a pathway into the juvenile justice system and then, in some cases, diminishes their chances of success postrelease. Notably, youths prosecuted for a first offense are more likely to recidivate than those not prosecuted. This risk is particularly pronounced for youths prosecuted for status offenses and misdemeanors (Barrett, Katsiyannis, & Zhang, 2010), which make up a large proportion of youth cases triggered by zero tolerance policies. Overall, intervention by the juvenile justice system is associated with an increased likelihood of adult involvement in the criminal justice system (Gatti, Tremblay, & Vitaro, 2009), even when controlling for educational attainment and employment (Bernburg & Krohn, 2003). Zero tolerance policies, therefore, may both prevent at-risk students from receiving needed education and treatment and also increase their risk for engaging in future criminal behavior.

Racial and ethnic disparities within the juvenile justice system mirror those found in school discipline. African American students are 300% more likely to be suspended or expelled than White students and represent 31% of school-related arrests (U.S. Department of Education, Office of Civil Rights, 2014). Similarly, one study found that African American and Latino youths were 6 and 3 times more likely to be incarcerated, respectively, than their White, non-Hispanic counterparts for the same offenses (Poe-Yamagata & Jones, 2000). Although youths with minority racial and ethnic backgrounds make up approximately one third of the adolescent population, individuals from these groups represent two thirds of all juvenile detainees in secure facilities (Poe-Yamagata & Jones, 2000).

Juvenile involvement in the justice system can have broader negative effects, as well. Depending on the jurisdiction and the nature of the charges, a juvenile adjudication may result in the youth's entire family being removed from public housing

(UNC Center for Civil Rights, n.d.). The expungement process is not automatic in most states, even for youths who have no further involvement with the juvenile or criminal justice system. Consequently, a single juvenile justice involvement resulting from school referral under zero tolerance policies has a negative impact on both future employment and access to public benefits into adulthood (UNC Center for Civil Rights, n.d.) and can limit a youth's ability to join the military or pursue higher education (Juvenile Law Center, 2011). In addition, placement in juvenile justice facilities is associated with short- and long-term negative impacts on mental health functioning, which can serve as risk factors for delinquency (Goldstein, Olubadewo, Redding, & Lexcen, 2005).

ZERO TOLERANCE WITHIN JUVENILE JUSTICE

Although the literature on zero tolerance has focused almost exclusively on policies within schools, analogous policies seem to exist within juvenile justice settings. To the best of our knowledge, there is no literature or empirical research on zero tolerance within the juvenile justice system. However, on the basis of our experience, zero tolerance policies exist at many juvenile justice facilities. Although the specifics of these zero tolerance policies tend to vary dramatically by site, their intention seems to be fairly consistent across facilities, and they closely mirror the philosophy of school-based zero tolerance policies. As with school-based zero tolerance policies, juvenile justice facilities—in attempts to deter future negative behaviors and create safer environments—have established policies to remove disruptive youths by transferring them from less to more secure facilities or by removing them from the general population if they are already in the most restrictive settings. As with school-based zero tolerance policies, these juvenile justice regulations tend to specify sets of specific behaviors that trigger predetermined consequences, often severely punitive and usually applied without considering mitigation or context.

Across juvenile justice facilities, a number of behaviors may result in zero tolerance–like outcomes, including use of substances, verbal aggression, physical violence, and possession of a weapon or a weapon analog (i.e., anything that could be used as a weapon, such as a branch found outside or a pen carved to a sharp point). In our experience, fighting commonly triggers a zero tolerance consequence for both participants, without consideration of whether one was a victim, whether the perpetrator was threatened into action, or whether mental health factors played a role. Consequences of such behaviors may include isolation, additional charges, or other severe sanctions, which have both proximal and distal consequences for youths. For instance, isolation has been associated with exacerbating mental health symptoms and increasing the risk of substance use and suicidal behavior, and additional charges may limit youths' abilities to access educational resources and future vocational opportunities (Hayes, 2009).

ZERO TOLERANCE AND JUVENILE PROBATION

Probation is the most common disposition for most juveniles found delinquent; in 2009, one third of all delinquency cases resulted in probation, involving half a million youths in the United States (Livsey, 2012). When evaluating youths' compliance and progress, juvenile probation has historically used a zero tolerance approach that philosophically parallels that of zero tolerance policies in schools. For instance, probation officers—who are on the front lines and have more contact with the juveniles than do judges—may adopt a zero tolerance approach and refer youths for a probation violation hearing on the basis of minor deviations from probation requirements. Although judges have enormous discretion in handling the probation cases over which they preside (Steinhart, 1999), the structure of probation mandates full compliance—youths must fully comply with all probation requirements or risk revocation of probation and placement in a residential juvenile justice facility (Steinhart, 1999). Some judges recognize effort and improvement, but many take a zero tolerance approach to probation (Steinhart, 1999). For example, a juvenile with a probation condition requiring perfect school attendance may improve (say, from 1 day per week to 3 days per week) and have this be interpreted as reflecting positive effort or be seen as insufficient, resulting in probation revocation and placement.

Notably, the majority of juveniles on probation do not fully comply with all probation requirements, which for some youths may include as many as 13 distinct requirements and can include such stipulations as mandatory school attendance, drug screens, curfew, or community service (NeMoyer et al., 2014). In one jurisdiction, 52% of juveniles on probation failed to meet all of their probation requirements at least once, and 48% of juveniles on probation had probation revoked at least one time (NeMoyer et al., 2014). Given the large number of juveniles on probation, zero tolerance approaches to probation may place many of these youths at substantial risk of residential placement. The Office of Juvenile Justice and Delinquency Prevention estimated that of more than 100,000 youths in custody, 58% were probation or parole violators (Sedlak & Bruce, 2010), and 28% of detained youths were placed in detention because of a status offense or technical violation such as truancy, curfew violation, house arrest, or electronic monitoring violation (Mendel, 2009). This is not surprising, given that 40 states sanction at least some juvenile probation violators with detention (National Center for Juvenile Justice, 2006).

Across jurisdictions, probation orders often contain zero tolerance language, either explicitly indicating that there will be zero tolerance for violation of a condition or specifying detention as the immediate consequence of a condition violation (Harms, 2012). Compounding the issue, time in detention then functions as an additional risk factor for these already high-risk youths, decreasing high school graduation and employment rates and increasing rates of drug and alcohol abuse and recidivism (Mendel, 2009). When a zero tolerance approach to probation is used, a youth's risk of violence or recidivism may not be considered in the decision to place a probation violator in juvenile detention, even in jurisdictions that otherwise use risk assessment tools (Steinhart, 1999). Youths on probation, therefore, may not benefit from a risk–need–responsivity approach, even when this approach forms the basis of other phases (e.g., detention decision, postadjudication placement decision, community-based program referrals) of the jurisdiction's juvenile justice process, because the consequence is determined solely on the basis of the infraction rather than the characteristics of the particular youth. Youths who are at low risk for serious criminal activity or for community violence may still engage in relatively minor infractions, especially status offenses (e.g., truancy, curfew violations), while on probation. However, youths at a higher risk for serious criminal activity or risk to the community may be comparably likely to commit minor probation infractions. If even minor infractions are met with placement in detention, no attempt is made to distinguish between low-risk and high-risk youths and to provide the appropriate level of services to each.

The risk–need–responsivity approach to juvenile justice highlights the importance of evaluating an offender's risk, targeting treatment to address the offender's individual needs, and considering the offender's strengths to match interventions to the individual (Bonta & Andrews, 2007). Applying the risk–need–responsivity model to treating justice-involved youths leads to reduced recidivism (Dowden & Andrews, 2003), even when less intensive intervention is provided (Vincent, Guy, Gershenson, & McCabe, 2012)—a benefit lost to youths placed on probation when a zero tolerance approach is used.

REDUCING ZERO TOLERANCE PRACTICES IN THE EDUCATIONAL SYSTEM

Although evidence supporting the use of zero tolerance policies in the educational system is lacking, many school districts continue to implement these punitive policies for both minor and major behavioral offenses committed by students (APA Zero Tolerance Task Force, 2008). The challenge of effectively addressing youth violence in schools and preventing the school-to-prison pipeline is obviously complex and requires multipronged, systemic, and sustained efforts by students, parents, teachers, administrators, communities, and society. It is worth noting that some strategies (e.g., use of metal detectors or other security measures) currently used in schools lack data to support their effectiveness and may even be counterproductive by having a negative impact on students' perception of safety (Hankin, Hertz, & Simon, 2011). Other strategies (e.g., youth mentoring, antitruancy programs) may be considered promising and seem intuitive, but the results of the program evaluations are uneven (DuBois, Portillo, Rhodes, Silverthorn, & Valentine, 2011). Fortunately, many alternative strategies to zero tolerance can help reduce youth aggression, maintain and enhance safety in the school setting, and provide appropriate and normative responses to misbehavior (Cornell, Sheras, Gregory, & Fan, 2009). Because schools and school systems vary widely in their needs and resources, in the following section we provide a brief review of different strategies (prevention, intervention, policy changes) that can be used at various levels (student, classroom, schoolwide) within school systems.

Violence Prevention Programs

One promising strategy to reduce the use of zero tolerance policies by both administrators and SROs in school settings is to deliver prevention programming at the student level that directly addresses the correlates and instances of aggressive and disruptive behavior that often trigger these policies. Violence prevention programs seek to remediate risk factors associated with youth violence (poor decision making, lack of empathy, negative attitudes about self and others), as well as directly address many forms of violence, including bullying, aggressive classroom behavior, weapon carrying, or organized gang activity. Many school-based, evidence-based universal and secondary violence prevention programs are available. Descriptions and evaluations of these programs can be found at (a) the Substance Abuse and Mental Health Services Administration website (http://www.nrepp.samhsa.gov/Bullying.aspx) and (b) the website of the Blueprints for Violence Prevention Program at the Center for the Study and Prevention of Violence, Institute of Behavioral Science, University of Colorado at Buffalo (http://www.blueprintsprograms.com). We briefly describe two programs to give the reader a better sense of the evidence behind these types of programs.

The Second Step program, designed for use with preschoolers through junior high students (ages 5–12 years), is delivered in classrooms and focuses on reducing impulsive and aggressive behaviors by promoting self-reflection, emotional awareness, and problem-solving skills (Committee for Children, 1997). In the first randomized controlled trial of the Second Step program, children in the intervention classrooms demonstrated lower levels of aggression and more instances of prosocial behavior 2 weeks after completing the curriculum than did students in the control classroom (Grossman et al., 1997). Findings from a study with elementary school students revealed significant reductions in aggression and gains in positive student behavior for students in the intervention group compared with peers in the control group (Frey, Nolen, Edstrom, & Hirschstein, 2005). In another study that assessed teacher ratings and included urban African American children, participants in the program demonstrated improved prosocial behaviors at the completion of the program; however, there were no significant changes in aggression and impulsivity (McMahon & Washburn, 2003). In a randomized controlled trial of middle schools, the schools that received Second Step programming demonstrated significant student-reported decreases in involvement in physical aggression relative to the control schools (Espelage, Low, Polanin, & Brown, 2013).

Similarly, the Providing Alternative Thinking Strategies program (Kusche & Greenberg, 1994) is a classroom-based intervention designed for kindergarten through 5th graders (ages 5–11 years). This program is administered by trained teachers or school counselors and is designed to promote social and emotional competence while also reducing behavior problems, such as aggression and disruptive behavior. Instructional methods include group discussion, role playing, art activities, stories, and educational games (Greenberg, Kusche, & Mihalic, 2002). Results from an intervention study of second and third graders revealed stronger gains in social problem solving and emotional understanding for those who participated in Providing Alternative Thinking Strategies than for those students in the control group (Greenberg & Kusche, 1997). A longitudinal analysis of children in Grades 1 through 3 revealed positive effects of the Providing Alternative Thinking Strategies curriculum via reductions in student aggression and increases in prosocial behavior (Bierman et al., 2010). A recent randomized controlled trial conducted by independent researchers replicated these earlier findings with results demonstrating teacher-reported reductions in student aggression, conduct problems, and disruptive classroom behavior among students who participated in the program (Crean & Johnson, 2013).

Schoolwide Disciplinary Strategies

Schools face a difficult challenge in balancing multiple priorities—the need to protect the safety and security of all students, an approach to discipline that is proportionally responsive but not overly punitive, and a setting that encourages learning. To achieve a balance, many schools have recently moved toward a graduated schoolwide positive disciplinary approach that emphasizes keeping youths in school rather than pushing them out. These graduated approaches are designed to foster safe and supportive schools that promote students' academic, social, and behavioral success. They tend to involve policy changes in which school systems revise their codes of discipline; rather than indicating zero tolerance for specific behaviors, these newer policies emphasize responsivity to individual students' needs, introduction of schoolwide prevention and intervention programming, or both.

Promising reforms for school disciplinary practices include academic interventions for students struggling or at risk of dropping out, a discipline code that uses graduated and restorative responses and prevents students from being suspended for minor behavioral infractions, and counseling for students already displaying behavioral problems (Morgan, Salomon, Plotkin, & Cohen, 2014; U.S. Department of Education, 2014). Additional strategies that target improvements to school climate include increased teacher training for managing student behavior, a collaborative problem-solving approach to school safety, and early warning systems that identify students in need of behavioral support (Morgan et al., 2014; U.S. Department of Education, 2014).

Positive behavioral supports and social skills training programs can also be used in a schoolwide approach or with students who already display emotional or behavioral problems, social skills deficits, or both. These approaches seek to improve school climate, use graduated and fair disciplinary strategies, and increase parent and community involvement. An evidence-based example of a schoolwide disciplinary approach is Positive Behavior Interventions and Support, a comprehensive, multitiered universal prevention and intervention program that focuses on providing behavioral support to students and consultation support to teachers (Bradshaw, Mitchell, & Leaf, 2010). Research findings have indicated that Positive Behavior Interventions and Support is effective in decreasing rates of office referrals, suspensions, and expulsions and improving student ratings of school climate (Metzler, Biglan, Rusby, & Sprague, 2001). In addition, children in schools with Positive Behavior Interventions and Support systems are 33% less likely to receive an office discipline referral than are children in comparison schools (Bradshaw, Waasdorp, & Leaf, 2012).

REDUCING ZERO TOLERANCE POLICIES IN THE JUVENILE JUSTICE SYSTEM

In juvenile justice settings, when punishment is used alone as a single strategy to modify behavior, youths are at increased risk of reoffending (Andrews, Bonta, & Wormith, 2006; Lowenkamp & Latessa, 2004). Rather than imposing a severe penalty for low-risk youths, consideration should be given to the use of graduated sanctions. Graduated sanctions have been shown to lead to lower recidivism rates into adulthood when properly administered (Johnson, Lanza-Kaduce, & Woolard, 2011). For these sanctions to be effective, they should be individualized and predictably escalate in severity, proportionate to the severity of a youth's behavior (Cooley, 2011). It is this predictable and proportionate increase in punishment that most clearly separates graduated sanctions from zero tolerance policies. Rather than immediately receiving severe punishment for infractions, juveniles should initially receive the most lenient of punishments designated for the specific infraction.

Probation approaches exist along a continuum, from zero tolerance to graduated response. With zero tolerance, noncompliance with a probation requirement automatically results in a sanction—potentially revocation of probation and facility placement. With graduated responding, planned and proportional sanctions and incentives are systematically administered based on (non)performance of behaviors related to probation requirements. In a graduated response approach, a behavior that would be considered a violation of probation under a zero tolerance policy could actually be viewed as partial fulfillment of a probation condition, progress that is deemed worthy of reinforcement. Rather than sanctioning the previously truant youth for attending school only 3 days per week (as one would under a zero tolerance policy), the student should be reinforced for this initial improvement from attending only 2 days per week. Beyond the theoretical distinction of conceptualizing a specific behavior as a violation under zero tolerance or as improved compliance under graduated response, the response to this behavior should be guided by empirically established methods of promoting behavior change: Rewarding improved attendance is a more effective intervention strategy (Epstein & Sheldon, 2002).

Although some scholars (Gendreau, 1996; Wodahl, Garland, Culhane, & McCarty, 2011) have suggested that incentives are more effective than sanctions in shaping behavior and should be used in a 4:1 ratio for individuals involved with the justice system, graduated response approaches also recognize that sanctions—including serious sanctions—are needed at times, particularly when youths are at high risk of violence and recidivism and have committed severe violations of conditions. When sanctions are deemed necessary for probation violations, alternatives to detention should be used when appropriate (Center for Children's Law & Policy, 2012). Alternatives such as intensive home supervision, electronic monitoring, day and evening reporting, or weekend detention allow youths to continue attending school, maintain family involvement, work, continue to engage with prosocial peers, and avoid antisocial peers in detention centers—each of which is associated with decreased risk of future offending (Lowenkamp & Latessa, 2004). Such an approach also allows youths the opportunity to receive incentivizes for progress toward meeting probation requirements, which fosters further improvement (Center for Children's Law and Policy, 2012).

Promisingly, many jurisdictions (e.g., Berks County, Pennsylvania; Philadelphia, Pennsylvania; Washington, DC; many counties in central and eastern Oregon) are now moving toward developing graduated response approaches that emphasize improvement rather than complete fulfillment of requirements, particularly in the early stages of a youth's probation term. Risk of residential detention or placement—and the associated negative consequences of increased recidivism and poor educational and employment outcomes (Mendel, 2009)—may be reduced as juvenile probation systems shift from zero tolerance to graduated response approaches.

COLLABORATIVE APPROACHES TO DISRUPTING THE SCHOOL-TO-PRISON PIPELINE

Although the educational and judicial systems can implement their own setting-based changes to reduce the use of zero tolerance policies, a collaborative approach across multiple systems has the potential to effectively narrow the school-to-prison pipeline. Collaborative efforts to this effect are ongoing in several jurisdictions, involving cross-system agreement and coordination by such entities as the police department, juvenile court system, district attorneys' and public defenders' offices, departments of human services and behavioral health, school districts, university partners, and other community stakeholders. For example, in Philadelphia, Pennsylvania, the Philadelphia Police Department—in collaboration with the Philadelphia School District, Philadelphia Department of Human Services, Philadelphia District Attorney's Office, Philadelphia Family Court, and other stakeholders—initiated the Police School Diversion Program in May 2014. This program seeks to divert low-risk youths from arrest and juvenile justice involvement to community-based prevention services without removing them from the school setting. The program targets youths ages 10 and older (10 is the minimum age at which a child can be considered delinquent under Pennsylvania's Juvenile Act) who have no previous juvenile or criminal justice record and who have committed a summary offense or misdemeanor delinquent act on school property. Under previous district and school police policies and practices, these students would typically have been arrested.

With the Police School Diversion Program, if a police officer is called to a school for an alleged incident, the officer appraises the student's eligibility through a review of school and delinquency records as well as interviews with youths, school personnel, and other parties involved in the incident. If eligible for the program, the youth is not arrested. Instead, the youth is referred to the diversion program, and a Philadelphia Department of Human Services social worker conducts a home visit with the youth and family within the next 72 hours. During this home visit, the social worker educates the student and family about the collateral consequences of juvenile justice system involvement and refers them to the nearest community-based Intensive Prevention Services program. Individualized services for youths and families can include a wide range of programming, such as academic support, individual and group mental health treatment, substance use services, recreational and vocational programming, community service, mentoring, and family counseling and support. In addition, diversion program personnel communicate with the SROs to address issues at school (e.g., bullying) that may affect the student's behavior. Evaluation of individual, school, and systemwide outcomes is in progress.

Another effort to disrupt the school-to-prison pathway was developed in Clayton County, Georgia, via a cooperative agreement initiated by Juvenile Court Judge Steven Teske involving a partnership among the juvenile justice system, law enforcement, the local school system, and social service groups. Clayton County's model involves an early warning system in which misdemeanor delinquent acts (e.g., fighting, disorderly conduct, disrupting the school) do not trigger official complaints. The exception to this policy is when a student commits a third or subsequent similar act during the school year. In these cases, the student is referred to a mediation or school conflict training program. It is noteworthy that this policy also mandates that elementary school students are fully prohibited from being referred to law enforcement for any misdemeanor delinquent act. Initial results from this collaborative approach revealed reduced out-of-school suspensions and school referrals (Teske, 2011). In addition, graduation rates improved by 20% and delinquent felony rates decreased by nearly 50% (Teske, 2011).

CONCLUSION

Youth violence in the school setting is a serious concern for students, parents, teachers, administrators, and policymakers. One of the primary approaches used to deter youth violence—zero tolerance policies—continues to be enforced in many school districts and juvenile justice systems despite the lack of evidence of their effectiveness. Indeed, the extant literature has indicated that enforcement of zero tolerance policies may actually result in a range of counterproductive outcomes, such as students feeling less safe in school, less favorable ratings of school climate, and poorer schoolwide academic performance. Moreover, the evidence is clear that students from minority backgrounds are disproportionately suspended and expelled as a result of zero tolerance policies. Negative consequences also occur outside of the school setting because students expelled as a result of zero tolerance policies are at increased risk for entering the juvenile justice system and never returning to school.

Many effective and promising alternatives to zero tolerance in the school setting are available. They include research-based strategies that deter youth violence in schools and promote positive youth outcomes (e.g., violence prevention programming, social skills training and positive behavior supports, and schoolwide disciplinary approaches). Notably, these programs can be implemented at the individual, group, school, or district level, and there is some evidence that they reduce risk of later involvement with the juvenile justice system.

The use of a graduated sanctions approach to discipline in the juvenile justice system represents a promising strategy to address ongoing delinquent behavior and deter future misbehavior. To enhance this approach, it is recommended that juvenile justice personnel use a broader graduated response model—an approach intended to shape behavior through planned and proportionate use of sanctions and incentives. Moreover, when juvenile justice system involvement is unavoidable, officials should consider ways to keep kids in school and out of residential facilities by using alternative programming such as intensive home supervision, electronic monitoring, day and evening reporting, or weekend detention. Considering various models of student discipline underscores the promise of early warning systems, diversionary programs, and partnership between various groups and systems. Finally, stakeholders must advocate for legislation that is in students' best interest by supporting discipline programs that are fair, equitable, and research based and produce the most positive outcomes.

Although the topics reviewed in this chapter have received significant attention in the research literature, few studies have rigorously evaluated the impact of zero tolerance on youth violence and the school-to-prison pipeline. One of the challenges in conducting this research is the variability in how zero tolerance policies are implemented. For example, some schools use a strict interpretation of zero tolerance, whereby minor and major infractions are cause for suspension and expulsion; others using zero tolerance nonetheless use a graduated system in which administrators attempt to match the consequence to the seriousness of the offense (Skiba & Peterson, 2000). Such challenges have limited researchers' ability to systematically collect data on the trajectory of zero tolerance practices over the past 2 decades. Areas that are ripe for investigation include in-depth study of important factors that drive zero tolerance policies, such as structure, environment, systems, and culture.

For example, researchers could critically evaluate whether zero tolerance policies are influenced by limited school district resources (e.g., funding, infrastructure) in developing and maintaining programs that respond to youths with disciplinary challenges. The relationship between school environment factors, such as school climate and connectedness, and disciplinary practices, such as suspension and expulsion, has received some attention in the literature (Orpinas & Horne, 2006; Stinchcomb, Bazemore, & Rienstenberg, 2006). However, more study is needed given the importance of these variables in promoting school safety and reducing violence (Gottfredson, Gottfredson, Payne, & Gottfredson, 2005). There is a compelling need to study how systems factors, such as professional developmental and teacher preparation programs in schools, are related to the implementation of zero tolerance practices. Cultural factors, including student and family culture, professional culture, and community and political culture, also warrant more rigorous investigation. It is important to note the relative absence of evidence-based programs specifically designed for students in high schools; this also represents an important area for future research. Furthermore, policymakers, school districts, police departments, and juvenile justice personnel have begun to recognize the negative aspects of zero tolerance policies and their unintended effects on the school-to-prison pipeline. As such, these key stakeholders are beginning to develop and implement alternative approaches to school discipline in individual jurisdictions. These new approaches must be evaluated in terms of their individual and system-level effects on youth well-being, school retention and performance, school safety, and recidivism. If these new models receive empirical support, those seeking to replace zero tolerance policies with more effective practices will have evidence-based alternatives from which to draw.

References

Advancement Project. (2010). *Test, punish, and push out: How "zero tolerance" and high stakes testing policies funnel youth into the school-to-prison pipeline.* Washington, DC: Author.

American Psychological Association Zero Tolerance Task Force. (2008). Are zero tolerance policies effective in the schools? An evidentiary review and recommendations. *American Psychologist, 63,* 852–862. http://dx.doi.org/10.1037/0003-066X.63.9.852

Andrews, D. A., Bonta, J., & Wormith, S. J. (2006). The recent past and near future of risk/need assessment. *Crime and Delinquency, 52,* 7–27. http://dx.doi.org/10.1177/0011128705281756

Archer, D. N. (2009). Introduction: Challenging the school-to-prison pipeline. *New York Law School Law Review*, *54*, 867–872.

Ayres, C. D., Williams, J. H., Hawkins, J. D., Peterson, P. L., Catalano, R. F., & Abbott, R. D. (1999). Assessing correlates of onset, escalation, deescalation, and desistance of delinquent behavior. *Journal of Quantitative Criminology*, *15*, 277–306. http://dx.doi.org/10.1023/A:1007576431270

Barrett, D. E., Katsiyannis, A., & Zhang, D. (2010). Predictors of offense severity, adjudication, incarceration, and repeat referrals for juvenile offenders: A multicohort replication study. *Remedial and Special Education*, *31*, 261–275. http://dx.doi.org/10.1177/0741932509355990

Battistich, V., & Hom, A. (1997). The relationship between students' sense of their school as a community and their involvement in problem behaviors. *American Journal of Public Health*, *87*, 1997–2001. http://dx.doi.org/10.2105/AJPH.87.12.1997

Bernburg, J. G., & Krohn, M. D. (2003). Labeling, life chances, and adult crime: The direct and indirect effects of official intervention in adolescence on crime in early adulthood. *Criminology*, *41*, 1287–1318. http://dx.doi.org/10.1111/j.1745-9125.2003.tb01020.x

Bickel, F., & Qualls, R. (1980). The impact of school climate on suspension rates in the Jefferson County Public Schools. *Urban Review*, *12*, 79–86. http://dx.doi.org/10.1007/BF02009317

Bierman, K. L., Coie, J. D., Dodge, K. A., Greenberg, M. T., Lochman, J. E., McMahon, R. J., & Pinderhughes, E. (2010). The effects of a multiyear universal social–emotional learning program: The role of student and school characteristics. *Journal of Consulting and Clinical Psychology*, *78*, 156–168. http://dx.doi.org/10.1037/a0018607

Blomberg, T. G., Bales, W. D., Mann, K., Piquero, A. R., & Berk, R. A. (2011). Incarceration, education and transition from delinquency. *Journal of Criminal Justice*, *39*, 355–365. http://dx.doi.org/10.1016/j.jcrimjus.2011.04.003

Bogos, P. M. (1996). Expelled. No excuses. No exceptions. Michigan's zero-tolerance policy in response to school violence: M.C.L.A. Section 380.1311. *University of Detroit Mercy Law Review*, *74*, 357–388.

Bonta, J., & Andrews, D. A. (2007). Risk-need-responsivity model for offender assessment and rehabilitation. *Rehabilitation*, *6*, 1–22.

Borum, R., Cornell, D., Modzeleski, W., & Jimerson, S. R. (2010). What can be done about school shootings? A review of the evidence. *Educational Researcher*, *39*, 27–37. http://dx.doi.org/10.3102/0013189X09357620

Bowditch, C. (1993). Getting rid of troublemakers: High school disciplinary procedures and the production of dropouts. *Social Problems*, *40*, 493–509. http://dx.doi.org/10.2307/3096864

Bradshaw, C. P., Mitchell, M. M., & Leaf, P. J. (2010). Examining the effects of schoolwide positive behavioral interventions and supports on student outcomes: Results from a randomized controlled effectiveness trial in elementary schools. *Journal of Positive Behavior Interventions*, *12*, 133–148. http://dx.doi.org/10.1177/1098300709334798

Bradshaw, C. P., Waasdorp, T. E., & Leaf, P. J. (2012). Effects of school-wide positive behavioral interventions and supports on child behavior problems. *Pediatrics*, *130*, e1136–e1145. http://dx.doi.org/10.1542/peds.2012-0243

Casella, R. (2003). Zero tolerance policy in schools: Rationale, consequences, and alternatives. *Teachers College Record*, *105*, 872–892. http://dx.doi.org/10.1111/1467-9620.00271

Center for Children's Law and Policy. (2012). *Developing a system of graduated responses for youth supervised by the juvenile justice system*. Washington, DC: Author.

Cerrone, K. M. (1999). Gun-free school zones: Zero-tolerance takes aim at due process. *Pace Law Review*, *20*, 131–188.

Comer, J., & Poussaint, A. (1992). *Raising Black children: Two leading psychiatrists confront the educational, social, and emotional problems facing Black children*. New York, NY: Plume.

Committee for Children. (1997). *Second Step: A violence prevention curriculum—Middle school/junior high*. Seattle, WA: Committee for Children.

Cooley, V. A. (2011). Community-based sanctions for juvenile offenders: Issues in policy implementation. *Criminal Justice Policy Review*, *22*, 65–89. http://dx.doi.org/10.1177/0887403410369826

Cornell, D., Sheras, P., Gregory, A., & Fan, X. (2009). A retrospective study of school safety conditions in high schools using the Virginia Threat Assessment guidelines versus alternative approaches. *School Psychology Quarterly*, *24*, 119–129. http://dx.doi.org/10.1037/a0016182

Costenbader, V., & Markson, S. (1994). School suspension: A survey of current policies and practices. *NASSP Bulletin*, *78*, 103–107. http://dx.doi.org/10.1177/019263659407856420

Costenbader, V., & Markson, S. (1998). School suspension: A study with secondary school students. *Journal of School Psychology*, *36*, 59–82. http://dx.doi.org/10.1016/S0022-4405(97)00050-2

Council of State Governments. (2011). *Breaking schools' rules: A statewide study of how school discipline relates to students' success and juvenile justice involvement*.

Retrieved from http://csgjusticecenter.org/youth/breaking-schools-rules-report

Crean, H. F., & Johnson, D. B. (2013). Promoting Alternative Thinking Strategies (PATHS) and elementary school aged children's aggression: Results from a cluster randomized trial. *American Journal of Community Psychology*, *52*, 56–72. http://dx.doi.org/10.1007/s10464-013-9576-4

Curtis, A. J. (2010). Tracing the school-to-prison pipeline from zero-tolerance policies to juvenile justice dispositions. *Georgetown Law Journal*, *102*, 1251–1277.

Dowden, C., & Andrews, D. A. (2003). Does family intervention work for delinquents? Results of a meta-analysis. *Canadian Journal of Criminology and Criminal Justice*, *45*, 327–342. http://dx.doi.org/10.3138/cjccj.45.3.327

DuBois, D. L., Portillo, N., Rhodes, J. E., Silverthorn, N., & Valentine, J. C. (2011). How effective are mentoring programs for youth? A systematic assessment of the evidence. *Psychological Science in the Public Interest*, *12*, 57–91. http://dx.doi.org/10.1177/1529100611414806

Eaton, D. K., Kann, L., Kinchen, S., Shanklin, S., Flint, K. H., Hawkins, J., . . . Wechsler, H. (2012). Youth risk behavior surveillance—United States, 2011. *Morbidity and Mortality Weekly Report Surveillance Summaries*, *61*(SS4), 1–162.

Eccles, J. S., Early, D., Frasier, K., Belansky, E., & McCarthy, K. (1997). The relation of connection, regulation, and support for autonomy to adolescents' functioning. *Journal of Adolescent Research*, *12*, 263–286. http://dx.doi.org/10.1177/0743554897122007

Eccles, J. S., & Midgley, C. (1989). Stage-environment fit: Developmentally appropriate classrooms for early adolescents. In R. E. Ames & C. Ames (Eds.), *The development of achievement motivation* (pp. 283–331). Greenwich, CT: JAI Press.

Eccles, J. S., Midgley, C., Wigfield, A., Buchanan, C. M., Reuman, D., Flanagan, C., & Mac Iver, D. M. (1993). Development during adolescence: The impact of stage-environment fit on young adolescents' experiences in schools and in families. *American Psychologist*, *48*, 90–101. http://dx.doi.org/10.1037/0003-066X.48.2.90

Epstein, J. L., & Sheldon, S. B. (2002). Present and accounted for: Improving student attendance through family and community involvement. *Journal of Educational Research*, *95*, 308–318. http://dx.doi.org/10.1080/00220670209596604

Espelage, D. L., Low, S., Polanin, J. R., & Brown, E. C. (2013). The impact of a middle school program to reduce aggression, victimization, and sexual violence. *Journal of Adolescent Health*, *53*, 180–186. http://dx.doi.org/10.1016/j.jadohealth.2013.02.021

Flannery, D. J., Wester, K. L., & Singer, M. I. (2004). Impact of exposure to violence in school on child and adolescent mental health and behavior. *Journal of Community Psychology*, *32*, 559–573. http://dx.doi.org/10.1002/jcop.20019

Fowler, D. (2011). School discipline feeds the "pipeline to prison." *Phi Delta Kappan*, *93*, 14–19. http://dx.doi.org/10.1177/003172171109300204

Frey, K. S., Nolen, S. B., Edstrom, L. V. S., & Hirschstein, M. K. (2005). Effects of a school-based social–emotional competence program: Linking children's goals, attributions, and behavior. *Journal of Applied Developmental Psychology*, *26*, 171–200. http://dx.doi.org/10.1016/j.appdev.2004.12.002

Gagliardi, V. A. (2001). In defense of zero tolerance. *New Jersey Law Journal*, *164*, 1–5.

Gatti, U., Tremblay, R. E., & Vitaro, F. (2009). Iatrogenic effect of juvenile justice. *Journal of Child Psychology and Psychiatry*, *50*, 991–998. http://dx.doi.org/10.1111/j.1469 7610.2008.02057.x

Gendreau, P. (1996). The principles of effective intervention with offenders. In A. Harland (Ed.), *Choosing correctional options that work* (pp. 117–130). Thousand Oaks, CA: Sage.

Goldstein, N. E. S., Olubadewo, S., Redding, R., & Lexcen, F. (2005). Mental health disorders: The neglected risk factor in juvenile delinquency. In K. S. Heilbrun, N. E. S. Goldstein, & R. E. Redding (Eds.), *Juvenile delinquency: Prevention, assessment, and intervention* (pp. 85–110). New York, NY: Oxford University Press.

González, T. (2012). Keeping kids in schools: Restorative justice, punitive discipline, and the school to prison pipeline. *Journal of Law and Education*, *41*, 281–335.

Gottfredson, G. D., Gottfredson, D. C., Payne, A. A., & Gottfredson, N. C. (2005). School climate predictors of school disorder: Results from the national study of delinquency prevention in schools. *Journal of Research in Crime and Delinquency*, *42*, 412–444. http://dx.doi.org/10.1177/0022427804271931

Greenberg, M. T., & Kusche, C. A. (1997, April). *Improving children's emotion regulation and social competence: The effects of the PATHS curriculum.* Paper presented at the meeting of the Society for Research in Child Development, Washington, DC.

Greenberg, M. T., Kusche, C. A., & Mihalic, S. F. (2002). *Blueprints for violence prevention, Book 10: Promoting alternative thinking strategies (PATHS)*. Boulder, CO: Center for the Study and Prevention of Violence.

Grossman, D. C., Neckerman, H. J., Koepsell, T. D., Liu, P. Y., Asher, K. N., Beland, K., . . . Rivara, F. P. (1997). Effectiveness of a violence prevention curriculum among children in elementary school: A randomized controlled trial. *JAMA*,

277, 1605–1611. http://dx.doi.org/10.1001/jama.1997.03540440039030

Gun-Free Schools Act of 1994, Pub. L. 103–227, § 1031 *et seq.*, 108 Stat. 270 (1994).

Hankin, A., Hertz, M., & Simon, T. (2011). Impacts of metal detector use in schools: Insights from 15 years of research. *Journal of School Health, 81*, 100–106. http://dx.doi.org/10.1111/j.1746-1561.2010.00566.x

Harms, R. J. (2012). *Detention for probation violators: Characteristics of youth locked up for violating probation* (Unpublished master's thesis). Wichita, KS: Wichita State University.

Hayes, L. M. (2009). Juvenile suicide in confinement—Findings from the first national survey. *Suicide and Life-Threatening Behavior, 39*, 353–363. http://dx.doi.org/10.1521/suli.2009.39.4.353

Johnson, K., Lanza-Kaduce, L., & Woolard, J. (2011). Disregarding graduated treatment: Why transfer aggravates recidivism. *Crime and Delinquency, 57*, 756–777. http://dx.doi.org/10.1177/0011128708328867

Juvenile Law Center. (2011). *Collateral consequences of delinquency*. Retrieved from http://jlc.org/current-initiatives/improving-outcomes-court-involved-youth/collateral-consequences-delinquency

Kim, C. Y. (2009). Procedures for public law remediation in school-to-prison pipeline litigation: Lessons learned from Antoine v. Winner School District. *New York Law School Law Review, 54*, 955–974.

Klehr, D. G. (2009). Addressing the unintended consequences of No Child Left Behind and zero tolerance: Better strategies for safe schools and successful students. *Georgetown Journal on Poverty Law and Policy, 16*, 585–610.

Krezmien, M. P., Leone, P. E., & Achilles, G. M. (2006). Suspension, race and disability: Analysis of state-wide practices and reporting. *Journal of Emotional and Behavioral Disorders, 14*, 217–226. http://dx.doi.org/10.1177/10634266060140040501

Kusche, C. A., & Greenberg, M. T. (1994). *The PATHS curriculum*. Seattle, WA: Developmental Research and Programs.

Livsey, S. (2012). *Juvenile delinquency probation caseload, 2009* (Juvenile Offenders and Victims National Report Series fact sheet). Washington, DC: Office of Juvenile Justice and Delinquency Prevention.

Lowenkamp, C. T., & Latessa, E. J. (2004). Understanding the risk principle: How and why correctional interventions can harm low-risk offenders. *Topics in Community Corrections*, 3–8.

McFadden, A. C., Marsh, G. E., Price, B. J., & Hwang, Y. (1992). A study of race and gender bias in the punishment of school children. *Education and Treatment of Children, 15*, 140–146.

McLeod, J. D., Uemura, R., & Rohrman, S. (2012). Adolescent mental health, behavior problems, and academic achievement. *Journal of Health and Social Behavior, 53*, 482–497. http://dx.doi.org/10.1177/0022146512462888

McMahon, S. D., & Washburn, J. J. (2003). Violence prevention: An evaluation of program effects with urban African-American students. *Journal of Primary Prevention, 24*, 43–62. http://dx.doi.org/10.1023/A:1025075617356

Mendel, R. A. (2009). *Two decades of JDAI: A progress report*. Retrieved from http://www.aecf.org/resources/two-decades-of-jdai

Metzler, C. W., Biglan, A., Rusby, J. C., & Sprague, J. R. (2001). Evaluation of a comprehensive behavior management program to improve school-wide positive behavior support. *Education and Treatment of Children, 24*, 448–479.

Midgley, C., Feldlaufer, H., & Eccles, J. S. (1989). Change in teacher efficacy and student self- and task-related beliefs in mathematics during the transition to junior high school. *Journal of Educational Psychology, 81*, 247–258. http://dx.doi.org/10.1037/0022-0663.81.2.247

Morgan, E., Salomon, N., Plotkin, M., & Cohen, R. (2014). *The school discipline consensus report: Strategies from the field to keep students engaged in school and out of the juvenile justice system*. New York, NY: Council of State Governments Justice Center.

Nagy, J., & Danitz, T. (2000). *Parental fears heightened by Columbine, poll shows*. Retrieved from http://www.stateline.org/live/ViewPage.action?siteNodeId=136&languageId=1&contentId=13994

National Center for Injury Prevention and Control. (2013). *Understanding school violence: Fact sheet, 2013*. Atlanta, GA: Centers for Disease Control and Prevention.

National Center for Juvenile Justice. (2006). *State juvenile justice profiles*. Pittsburgh, PA: Author.

NeMoyer, A., Goldstein, N. E., McKitten, R. L., Prelic, A., Ebbecke, J., Foster, E., & Burkard, C. (2014). Predictors of juveniles' noncompliance with probation requirements. *Law and Human Behavior, 38*, 580–591.

No Child Left Behind Act of 2001, Pub. L. 107-110, 20 U.S.C. §§ 6301–8962 (2001).

Orpinas, P., & Horne, A. M. (2006). School social competence development and bullying prevention model: The school. In P. Orpinas & A. M. Horne (Eds.), *Bullying prevention: Creating a positive school climate and developing social competence* (pp. 79–105). http://dx.doi.org/10.1037/11330-004

Poe-Yamagata, E., & Jones, M. (2000). *And justice for some: Differential treatment of minority youth in the justice system*. Washington, DC: Building Blocks for Youth.

Raffaele Mendez, L. M. (2003). Predictors of suspension and negative school outcomes: A longitudinal investigation. *New Directions for Youth Development, 2003*, 17–33. http://dx.doi.org/10.1002/yd.52

Resnick, M. D., Bearman, P. S., Blum, R. W., Bauman, K. E., Harris, K. M., Jones, J., . . . Udry, J. R. (1997). Protecting adolescents from harm: Findings from the National Longitudinal Study on Adolescent Health. *JAMA, 278*, 823–832. http://dx.doi.org/10.1001/jama.1997.03550100049038

Reynolds, C. R., & Kamphaus, R. W. (2004). *Behavior assessment system for children* (2nd ed.). Circle Pines, MN: American Guidance Service.

Rivkin, D. H. (2009). Decriminalizing students with disabilities. *New York Law School Law Review, 54*, 909–952.

Robbins, C. (2008). *Expelling hope: The assault on youth and the militarization of schooling*. Albany, NY: SUNY Press.

Roeser, R. (2005). Stage-environment fit theory. In C. Fisher & R. Lerner (Eds.), *Encyclopedia of applied developmental science* (pp. 1056–1061). http://dx.doi.org/10.4135/9781412950565.n403

Saad, L. (1999). *Public views Littleton tragedy as sign of deeper problems in country*. Washington, DC: Gallup.

Sedlak, A., & McPherson, K. (2010). Youth's needs and services. *FBI Law Enforcement Bulletin, 79*, 22.

Sedlak, A. J., & Bruce, C. (2010). *Youth's characteristics and backgrounds: Findings from the survey of youth in residential placement* (Juvenile Justice Bulletin). Washington, DC: Office of Juvenile Justice and Delinquency Prevention.

Skiba, R. (2010). Zero tolerance and alternative discipline strategies. *Communique, 39*. Retrieved from http://www.nasponline.org/publications/cq/index.aspx?vol=39&issue=1

Skiba, R., Michael, R. S., Nardo, A. C., & Peterson, R. L. (2002). The color of discipline: Sources of racial and gender disproportionality in school punishment. *Urban Review, 34*, 317–342. http://dx.doi.org/10.1023/A:1021320817372

Skiba, R., & Rausch, M. K. (2006). Zero tolerance, suspension, and expulsion: Questions of equity and effectiveness. In C. M. Evertson & C. S. Weinstein (Eds.), *Handbook of classroom management: Research, practice, and contemporary issues* (pp. 1063–1089). Mahwah, NJ: Erlbaum.

Skiba, R., Simmons, A., Staudinger, L., Rausch, M., Dow, G., & Feggins, R. (2003, May). *Consistent removal: Contributions of school discipline to the school-prison pipeline*. Paper presented at the School to Prison Pipeline Conference, Cambridge, MA.

Skiba, R. J., & Peterson, R. L. (2000). School discipline at a crossroads: From zero tolerance to early response. *Exceptional Children, 66*, 335–346.

Stader, D. L. (2004). Zero tolerance as public policy: The good, the bad, and the ugly. *Clearing House: A Journal of Educational Strategies, Issues and Ideas, 78*, 62–66. http://dx.doi.org/10.3200/TCHS.78.2.62-66

Steinhart, D. (1999). *Special detention cases: Strategies for handling difficult populations* (Pathways to Juvenile Detention Reform No. 9). Baltimore, MD: Annie E. Casey Foundation.

Stinchcomb, J. B., Bazemore, G., & Rienstenberg, N. (2006). Beyond zero tolerance: Restoring justice in secondary schools. *Youth Violence and Juvenile Justice, 4*, 123–147. http://dx.doi.org/10.1177/1541204006286287

Teske, S. C. (2011). A study of zero tolerance policies in schools: A multi-integrated systems approach to improve outcomes for adolescents. *Journal of Child and Adolescent Psychiatric Nursing, 24*, 88–97. http://dx.doi.org/10.1111/j.1744-6171.2011.00273.x

Teske, S. C., & Huff, J. B. (2011, Winter). When did making adults mad become a crime? The court's role in dismantling the school-to-prison pipeline. *Juvenile and Family Justice Today*, pp. 14–16.

Thurau, L. H., & Wald, J. (2010). Controlling partners: When law enforcement meets discipline in public schools. *New York Law School Law Review, 54*, 977–1020.

Tobin, T., Sugai, G., & Colvin, G. (1996). Patterns in middle school discipline records. *Journal of Emotional and Behavioral Disorders, 4*, 82–94. http://dx.doi.org/10.1177/106342669600400203

Tuzzolo, E., & Hewitt, D. T. (2006–2007). Rebuilding inequality: The re-emergence of the school-to-prison pipeline in New Orleans. *High School Journal, 90*, 59–68. http://dx.doi.org/10.1353/hsj.2007.0009

UNC Center for Civil Rights. (n.d.). *Juvenile delinquency adjudication, collateral consequences, and expungement of juvenile records: A survey of law and policy in Delaware, Virginia, North Carolina and Florida*. Retrieved from http://www.law.unc.edu/documents/civilrights/centerforcivilrightsexpungementreport.pdf

U.S. Department of Education. (1993). *Goals 2000: Educate America Act*. Washington, DC: U.S. Government Printing Office.

U.S. Department of Education. (2001). *Safe Schools Healthy Students initiative*. Washington, DC: Author.

U.S. Department of Education. (2012). *Testimony of Deborah Delisle, assistant secretary, Office of Elementary and Secondary Education*. Washington, DC: Author.

U.S. Department of Education. (2014). *Guiding principles: A resource guide for improving school climate and discipline*. Washington, DC: Author.

U.S. Department of Education, Office of Civil Rights. (2008). *2006 data collection*. Retrieved from http://www.ocrdata.ed.gov/ocr2006rv30

U.S. Department of Education, Office of Civil Rights. (2014). *Civil rights data collection: Data snapshot: School discipline* (Issue Brief No. 1). Washington, DC: Author.

U.S. Department of Health and Human Services. (2001). *Youth violence: A report of the Surgeon General*. Retrieved from http://www.surgeongeneral.gov/library/youthviolence/toc.html

Vincent, G. M., Guy, L. S., Gershenson, B. G., & McCabe, P. (2012). Does risk assessment make a difference? Results of implementing the SAVRY in juvenile probation. *Behavioral Sciences and the Law*, *30*, 384–405. http://dx.doi.org/10.1002/bsl.2014

Wald, J., & Losen, D. J. (2003). Defining and redirecting a school-to-prison pipeline. *New Directions for Youth Development*, *99*, 9–15.

Wentzel, K. R. (2002). Are effective teachers like good parents? Teaching styles and student adjustment in early adolescence. *Child Development*, *73*, 287–301. http://dx.doi.org/10.1111/1467-8624.00406

Wodahl, E. J., Garland, B., Culhane, S. E., & McCarty, W. P. (2011). Utilizing behavioral interventions to improve supervision outcomes in community-based corrections. *Criminal Justice and Behavior*, *38*, 386–405. http://dx.doi.org/10.1177/0093854810397866

Wu, S. C., Pink, W. T., Crain, R. L., & Moles, O. (1982). Student suspension: A critical reappraisal. *Urban Review*, *14*, 245–303. http://dx.doi.org/10.1007/BF02171974

Zero tolerance, reconsidered. (2014, January 5). *New York Times*, p. A18.

Zweifler, R., & De Beers, J. (2002). The children left behind: How zero tolerance impacts our most vulnerable youth. *Michigan Journal of Race and Law*, *8*, 191–220.

CHAPTER 13

SUBSTANCE USE AND SUBSTANCE USE DISORDERS AS RISK FACTORS FOR JUVENILE OFFENDING

Laurie Chassin, Andre D. Mansion, Brandon Nichter, and Danielle Pandika

Substance use and substance use disorders are highly prevalent in the juvenile justice system and represent important risk factors for both the onset and the maintenance of juvenile offending. Indeed, of the 1.6 million juvenile arrests in 2010, almost 17% resulted from substance use–related crimes, including drug abuse violations (e.g., selling, manufacturing, or possessing drugs; 10.4%), driving under the influence (0.74%), liquor law violations (5.8%), and drunkenness (0.78%; Office of Juvenile Justice and Delinquency Prevention, 2014). In addition, substance use increases the likelihood for other, nondrug offending in adolescence (D'Amico, Edelen, Miles, & Morral, 2008; Johnston, O'Malley, Bachman, & Schulenberg, 2005). Furthermore, juvenile offenders with persistent substance use or substance use disorders have been shown to have more frequent correctional stays and to stay longer in these correctional settings than do their non–substance-using peers (Anderson, Ramo, Cummins, & Brown, 2010). Aside from the implications of substance use for offending behavior, substance use and substance use disorders create risk for a broad range of other negative outcomes for adolescent offenders.

Conversely, substance use disorder treatment and recovery in adolescent offenders have both been associated with numerous positive outcomes in both the short and the long term (Anderson et al., 2010; Dennis, Foss, & Scott, 2007; Laudet, Morgen, & White, 2006). These outcomes include reductions in drug and alcohol use (Chassin, Knight, Vargas-Chanes, Losoya, & Naranjo, 2009), decreased delinquent behavior in adolescence (Hser et al., 2001), and decreased criminal behavior in adulthood (Dennis et al., 2007). Therefore, although substance use and substance use disorders are risk factors for the onset and maintenance of offending, recovery from substance use disorders or reductions in substance use are important factors in desistence from criminal behavior.

The strong relations among substance use, substance use disorders, and offending careers illustrate the importance of addressing substance use and substance use disorders in the juvenile justice system. Our goal in this chapter is to describe the empirical literature on substance use and substance use disorders as risk factors for juvenile offending. First, we review the empirical literature on the epidemiology of substance use and substance use disorders among juvenile offenders. We then examine the role of substance use and substance use disorders in juvenile offending, describing multiple theoretical models that are not mutually exclusive. Finally, we describe the broader negative consequences of substance use involvement for adolescent offenders and conclude the chapter with implications of the empirical literature for policy in the juvenile justice system.

EPIDEMIOLOGY: PREVALENCE AND DEMOGRAPHIC CORRELATES OF SUBSTANCE USE DISORDERS AND SUBSTANCE USE AMONG JUVENILE OFFENDERS

Adolescents who come in contact with the juvenile justice system have a much higher rate of substance use disorders than adolescents in the general

http://dx.doi.org/10.1037/14643-013
APA Handbook of Psychology and Juvenile Justice, K. Heilbrun (Editor-in-Chief)

population (Teplin, Abram, McClelland, Dulcan, & Mericle, 2002). In the general population, the lifetime prevalence of substance use disorder in adolescence is approximately 11.4% (Merikangas et al., 2010). However, juvenile offender samples show rates of substance use disorder ranging from 25% to 55%, depending on the study (Washburn et al., 2008; Wasserman, McReynolds, Ko, Katz, & Carpenter, 2005). Although there is wide variation across different juvenile offender samples, all of these rates are substantially higher than those found in the general U.S. adolescent population, and they suggest that substance use disorders are a significant problem for adolescent offenders.

Table 13.1 summarizes findings concerning the prevalence of clinically diagnosable substance use disorders among juvenile justice samples and illustrates the wide variability in prevalence. There are several reasons for the observed discrepancies in prevalence rates. Most obviously, study samples varied in gender and race/ethnicity, as well as in the diagnostic criteria that were used. For example, female adolescents generally have substance use disorders at rates lower than those of male adolescents (Merikangas et al., 2010), yet offender samples frequently contain few female participants (see, e.g., Teplin et al., 2002). Moreover, in the general adolescent population, rates of substance use disorders differ as a function of race/ethnicity (Merikangas et al., 2010), and study samples of juvenile offenders vary in their race/ethnic composition. Also, different diagnostic systems provide different prevalence rates. For example, studies that use diagnostic criteria from the *Diagnostic and Statistical Manual of Mental Disorders, Third Edition, Revised* tend to produce a higher prevalence of substance use disorders than do those that use criteria from the *Diagnostic and Statistical Manual of Mental Disorders, Fourth Edition* (Schuckit et al., 1994).

The prevalence of substance use disorders in the juvenile justice system also differs depending on the point in the juvenile justice process at which participants are assessed (Shufelt & Cocozza, 2006; Teplin et al., 2002), which likely reflects differing characteristics of offenders at different points in the process (e.g., differences in age, crime severity, number of prior arrests). Offenders who make it to the disposition phase (the equivalent of sentencing in the adult criminal system) are often older, have committed more serious crimes, and have come in contact with the juvenile system more times than those who do not proceed past arrest. This may help to explain why Wasserman et al. (2005) found lower rates of substance use disorders in their sample, who were assessed immediately after arrest, whereas studies that assessed adolescents while they were in long-term correctional facilities observed higher rates (see, e.g., Robertson, Dill, Husain, & Undesser, 2004).

Despite these many methodological differences, when taken together, these studies allow general conclusions to be made about substance use disorders in the juvenile justice system. First, as stated earlier, juvenile offenders have a higher rate of substance use disorders than adolescents in the general population. Second, cannabis and alcohol use disorders are the most commonly diagnosed substance use disorders (Teplin et al., 2002; Washburn et al., 2008; Wasserman et al., 2005). This is also true of the general adolescent population, although alcohol disorders are more common than cannabis disorders in the general adolescent population (Stinson, Ruan, Pickering, & Grant, 2006; Wittchen et al., 2007). The difference between alcohol and cannabis use prevalence rates may be due to the fact that African Americans are more likely to use cannabis than alcohol, and African Americans are overrepresented in the juvenile justice system (Teplin et al., 2002). Third, rates of substance use disorders differ by race/ethnicity. Non-Hispanic Caucasian adolescents have the highest rate of substance use disorders, African Americans have the lowest rate of substance use disorders, and Hispanics fall somewhere in between (Chassin, Piquero, Losoya, Mansion, & Schubert, 2013; Teplin et al., 2002). This is also true in the general adolescent population (Merikangas et al., 2010).

Finally, girls have alcohol and marijuana use disorders at lower rates than boys (Karnik et al., 2009) but are significantly more likely than boys to have other illicit drug use disorders (Karnik et al., 2009; Kim & Fendrich, 2002; Teplin et al., 2002; Wasserman et al., 2005). The gender differences observed in the juvenile justice system have also been observed for illicit drug use in the general

TABLE 13.1

Summary of Prevalence Rates of Substance Use Disorders Among Multiple Juvenile Offender Samples

Authors	Mean age (years)	*N*	Gender	Population	Legal status	Assessment	Prevalence (%) Any SUD	AUD	CUD	Other SUD	Time frame
Teplin et al. (2002)	14.9	1,829	Male (90%) & female	Detainees & offenders sentenced ≥ 30 days	Juvenile/adult	DISC 2.3 (*DSM–III–R*)					Past 6 months
Male							50.7	25.9	44.8	2.4	
Female							46.8	26.5	40.5	6.9	
Washburn et al. (2008)	15.7	275	Male (92.3%) & female	Youths processed in adult criminal court	Adult	DISC 2.3 (*DSM–III–R*)					
Asian American							49.1	24.6	44.4	0.5	
Non-Hispanic Caucasian							62.6	30.1	53.8	21.1	
Hispanic							55.4	30.8	45.4	6.0	
Wasserman et al. (2005)	14.7	991	Male (80.0%) & female	Recipients of referral for formal court action	Juvenile	Voice DISC–IV (*DSM–IV*)	55.0	29	49	2.0	Past 6 months
Mulvey et al. (2004)	16.0	1302	Male (86.4%) & female	Serious juvenile offenders (drug crime cap of 15%)	Juvenile/adult	CIDI (*DSM–III–R*)					Past month
Male							26.3	Abuse, 7.3; dependence, 3.0	Abuse, 9.9; dependence, 13.2	Abuse, 2.8; dependence, 3.3	
Female							22.0	Abuse, 5.4; dependence, 3.5	Abuse, 8.1; dependence, 11.3	Abuse, 3.8; dependence, 4.9	
Robertson et al. (2004)	15.3	482	Male (64.3%) & female	Youths in long-term juvenile correctional facilities & detainees	Juvenile	APS (*DSM–IV*)					Past year
Male							36.3	—	—	—	
Female							34.9	—	—	—	

Note. SUD = substance use disorder; alcohol use disorder; CUD = cannabis use disorder; DISC = Diagnostic Interview Schedule for Children; *DSM–III–R* = *Diagnostic and Statistical Manual of Mental Disorders, Third Edition, Revised*; *DSM–IV* = *Diagnostic and Statistical Manual of Mental Disorders, Fourth Edition*; CIDI = Composite International Diagnostic Interview; APS = Adolescent Psychopathology Scale; Drug Use Disorder.

adolescent population (Johnston, O'Malley, Bachman, & Schulenberg, 2013; Latimer, Stone, Voight, Winters, & August, 2002). Although the reasons for this finding are unclear, several hypotheses may explain this phenomenon. One hypothesis is that females are more likely than males to take stimulant medication as a way to control their weight (Kloos, Weller, Chan, & Weller, 2009). Another hypothesis is that girls' increased likelihood of trauma and a history of abuse leads them to use more potent drugs to cope with the symptoms of their traumatic experiences (Stevens, Murphy, & McKnight, 2003). Finally, young females may have relationships with males who are several years older, which may give them increased access to harder drugs compared with young males (Stevens, Estrada, Murphy, McKnight, & Tims, 2004). However, current research has not fully explained the reasons for the increased prevalence of illicit drug use among female adolescents compared with male adolescents.

The prevalence of clinical substance use disorders does not fully capture adolescent offenders' rates of substance use. Not surprisingly, juvenile offenders also show higher rates of substance use than do their peers in the general population. For example, in a sample of serious juvenile offenders between ages 14 and 17 years, 80% of adolescents reported using alcohol in their lifetime and 40% reported using alcohol within 6 months before their arrest (Mulvey, Schubert, & Chassin, 2010). In another sample of incarcerated youths, 30.2% of adolescents reported being heavy users of alcohol (defined as 100 or more lifetime use occasions; Freedenthal, Vaughn, Jenson, & Howard, 2007). In a study of juvenile probationers ages 14 to 18, approximately 70% of participants used alcohol and 42% said they almost always or always got drunk (Feldstein Ewing, Venner, Mead, & Bryan, 2011).

These levels of alcohol use are higher than levels of use in the general population. In the general population, 52.1% of 15-year-olds reported using alcohol in their lifetime and 33.5% reported being drunk in their lifetime (Johnston et al., 2013). McCurley and Snyder (2008) found even lower rates of alcohol use in the general population of adolescents, with only 23% of all adolescents ages 12 to 17 reporting drinking alcohol within the past year.

Tobacco use is an often overlooked form of substance use that is also prevalent in the juvenile justice system. Cigarette smoking is particularly important because it is the largest single preventable cause of death and disability in the United States (Centers for Disease Control and Prevention, 2008; Mokdad, Marks, Stroup, & Gerberding, 2004). In a sample of incarcerated juveniles, 58.3% were found to be heavy smokers (Freedenthal et al., 2007). In a sample of probationers, 70% reported smoking cigarettes; the average number of cigarettes smoked per day was four to six (Feldstein Ewing et al., 2011). However, only about 25.7% of 15-year-olds in the general population reported ever smoking cigarettes in their lifetime, and only 4.4% reported smoking cigarettes daily (Johnston et al., 2013).

Marijuana use is also higher in the juvenile justice population than in the general population. In a sample of serious juvenile offenders, 85% reported using marijuana at some point in their lifetime and 57% reported marijuana use in the past 6 months before their arrest (Mulvey et al., 2010). In another sample of incarcerated youths, 60% were heavy users of marijuana (Freedenthal et al., 2007), and in a sample of probationers, 70% had used marijuana within the past 6 months before being assessed (48% of them smoked marijuana every day during that time period; Feldstein Ewing et al., 2011). However, in the general population, between 32% and 36% of 15-year-olds reported marijuana use in their lifetime (Johnston et al., 2013; McCurley & Snyder, 2008).

There is also more use of illegal drugs other than marijuana in the juvenile justice population. In a sample of serious juvenile offenders, the use of other illicit drugs ranged from 4% (amyl nitrate odorizers) to more than 25% (hallucinogens), with drugs such as cocaine, sedatives, and stimulants falling somewhere in between (Mulvey et al., 2010). Among probationers, 29% endorsed hard drug use, including ecstasy (19%), mushrooms (15%), and crack cocaine (12%; Feldstein Ewing et al., 2011). These rates are higher than those in the general population, in which 5.7% of adolescents admit to using ecstasy within their lifetime by age 15, and even fewer (3.3%) report using cocaine (Johnston et al., 2013). In addition, at the time of arrest, 53.9% of adolescents tested positive for some type of drug

(National Center on Addiction and Substance Abuse at Columbia University, 2004). Overall, these rates show that substance use is widespread among juvenile offenders.

Finally, another indicator of the extent of drug involvement among juvenile offenders is the prevalence of drug-related juvenile arrests. Drug-related arrests (e.g., drug sales and possession) showed a steady increase after the initiation of President Nixon's War on Drugs in 1971, with arrest rates for drug-related offenses for juveniles increasing 66% between 1986 and 2006 (Snyder & Sickmund, 2006). However, since 2007 drug-related arrests among U.S. youth have decreased (Office of Juvenile Justice and Delinquency Prevention, 2014). This decrease in drug-related arrests may be due to the general decrease in youth arrests in the past few years, but it may also be influenced by reforms stemming from the failure of the War on Drugs, as well as the changing trends in drug crime attitudes and policies across the United States (Global Commission on Drug Policy, 2011). For example, the Obama administration's view that "we cannot arrest our way out of our nation's drug problem" led to new strategies in combating the sales and use of drugs (Kerlikowske, 2012). These strategies included the passage of the Fair Sentencing Act of 2010 (reducing the extent of the sentencing disparity between powder and crack cocaine) and the implementation of the Second Chance Act of 2007 (providing resources for evidence-based approaches to reducing crimes; Office of National Drug Control Policy, 2013). In addition, laws at the state level, such as the legalization of recreational marijuana use in Washington and Colorado, as well as the decriminalization of marijuana possession in California, have resulted in fewer drug-related arrests and a decrease in arrests overall. For example, California's 2011 marijuana law reform resulting from the passage of Senate Bill 1449 to the California Health and Safety Code downgraded most simple marijuana possessions from an arresting offense to a citation. By 2012, youth marijuana possession arrests in California were reduced by 61% (Males, 2012). These examples show that both state and federal policies have a substantial impact on the prevalence of substance use–related arrests in the juvenile justice system.

In summary, although substance use and substance use disorder prevalence rates may be affected by demographic characteristics, the diagnostic measures used, and the stage of the juvenile justice system process at which adolescents were assessed, it is clear that substance use and substance use disorders are highly prevalent among juvenile offenders. In addition, changes in laws clearly affect prevalence rates of substance use and substance use disorders in the juvenile justice system. Therefore, the continued monitoring of epidemiological data on these phenomena is important in assessing both the extent of treatment needs and the impact of changing public policies.

MODELS OF THE RELATION BETWEEN SUBSTANCE USE AND ADOLESCENT OFFENDING

The epidemiological data described above show a clear relation between substance use and juvenile offending. Indeed, this is one of the most consistent and robust findings in the fields of criminology and public health (Loeber & Farrington, 2000; Teplin et al., 2002). More important, this relation is not simply due to the fact that substance use itself is an illegal behavior and therefore by definition substance use and delinquency are related (Mulvey et al., 2010; Phillips, 2012). For example, previous evidence has indicated that the associations between adolescent substance use and substance use disorders and offending are strong even after drug-related offenses are removed from measures of offending (Mulvey et al., 2010).

Although the co-occurrence of adolescent substance use and criminal offending has been well established, the mechanisms that explain their association remain unclear (Becker et al., 2012; D'Amico et al., 2008; Mason & Windle, 2002). Research has yielded evidence for several possible models explaining the relations between these behaviors: (a) Early substance use has a causal effect that increases later delinquency; (b) early delinquency has a causal effect that leads to later substance use; (c) bidirectional relations between delinquency and substance use exist such that they are mutually reinforcing; and (d) substance use and delinquency

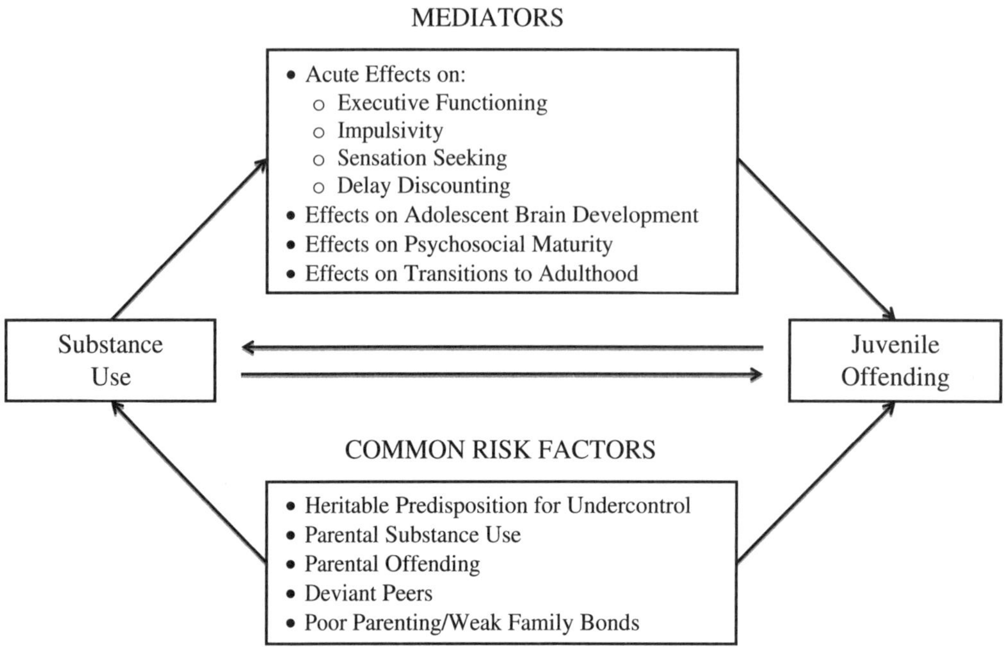

FIGURE 13.1. Mediators and common risk factors between substance use and juvenile offending.

stem from similar etiological factors and may even be different age-varying manifestations of a common predisposition toward externalizing behavior (see Figure 13.1). More important, these different mechanisms are not mutually exclusive, and multiple pathways likely explain this association.

Results from numerous longitudinal studies of community samples have provided evidence that substance use is a prospective predictor of the onset of juvenile delinquency as measured by self-reported offending (Bui, Ellickson, & Bell, 2000; Loeber & Farrington, 2000; Maldonado-Molina, Reingle, & Jennings, 2011; Weiner, Sussman, Sun, & Dent, 2005). Both alcohol and illicit drug use have been shown to increase youths' risk for violent offending (Ellickson & McGuigan, 2000; Fergusson, Lynskey, & Horwood, 1996; Maldonado-Molina et al., 2011; Plüddemann, Flisher, McKetin, Parry, & Lombard, 2010) as well for other forms of criminal behavior, such as theft and vandalism (Barnes, Welte, & Hoffman, 2002; Fergusson et al., 1996; French & Maclean, 2006). In general, alcohol consumption has been the strongest and most consistent predictor of delinquency among adolescents (Dawkins, 1997; Komro et al., 1999; Maldonado-Molina et al., 2011; Parker & Auerhahn, 1998). Indeed, multiple indices of alcohol use, including age of first use, frequency of drinking, and average alcohol consumption, have been found to be robust predictors of juvenile offending, accounting for anywhere between 2% and 25% of total variance in predicting delinquent behavior (Barnes et al., 2002; Baskin-Sommers & Sommers, 2006; French & Maclean, 2006; S. A. Gruber & Yurgelun-Todd, 1996; Neal & Fromme, 2007; Resnick, Ireland, & Borowsky, 2004).

For example, Peleg-Oren et al. (2009) found that youths who initiated alcohol use before age 13 had nearly 3 times greater odds of engaging in serious violent offending at Grade 12 (e.g., carrying a handgun to school) than did youths who initiated alcohol use after age 13 and 5 times greater odds relative to nondrinking adolescents. Similarly, a prospective study using data from the National Longitudinal Study of Adolescent Health (Add Health) found that adolescents who engaged in early alcohol use were nearly 1.5 times more likely to engage in subsequent violent offending than youths who did not consume alcohol (Maldonado-Molina et al., 2011). Moreover, Baskin-Sommers and Sommers (2006) found that adolescents were 14 times more likely to commit assault while using alcohol than those who did not drink. Thus, although most alcohol-using youths will not commit crimes, early alcohol use is a consistent risk factor of moderate to strong effect size (French & Maclean, 2006; E. Gruber, DiClemente, Anderson, & Lodico, 1996).

Although alcohol use is a consistent risk factor for juvenile offending, several potential confounds suggest the need for caution about the interpretability of such findings. First, most previous studies in the literature have not statistically controlled for concurrent illicit drug use, and therefore it is possible that other substance use may in fact be driving or contributing to the association (e.g., Baskin-Sommers & Sommers, 2006; Peleg-Oren et al., 2009). Moreover, given the low base rates of illicit drug use (other than marijuana use) compared with alcohol use, the stronger prediction of delinquency from alcohol use than illegal drug use may be a statistical artifact caused by the fact that illegal drug use is a poorly distributed, zero-inflated predictor variable.

Nonetheless, considerable evidence has also shown that illicit drug use prospectively predicts the onset of non–substance-related delinquency among adolescents (Derzon & Lipsey, 1999; Ellickson & McGuigan, 2000; Resnick et al., 2004). For example, in a longitudinal study of high school students and dropouts from California and Oregon, Ellickson and McGuigan (2000) found that adolescents who engaged in any illicit drug use in Grade 7 were significantly more likely to commit acts of predatory violence in Grade 12 than those who did not consume drugs. Although previous literature has established a link between several illicit drugs and juvenile delinquency, marijuana and psychostimulants (e.g., cocaine, methamphetamine) are the most consistently strong predictors overall (Dukarm, Byrd, Auinger, & Weitzman, 1996; Ford, 2005; Plüddemann et al., 2010; Resnick et al., 2004).

For example, Plüddemann et al. (2010) found that adolescents who self-reported past-year methamphetamine use were nearly twice as likely to report delinquent or serious acts of aggression as abstainers. However, as noted earlier, alcohol and illicit drug use frequently co-occur among youths, and most research on juvenile delinquency to date has not attempted to disaggregate the effects of specific substances (Ellickson & McGuigan, 2000; Weiner et al., 2005). Indeed, a comprehensive review using urinalysis found that 54% of juvenile offenders tested positive for illicit drugs at the time of arrest, and 38% of the same teens were also found to be under the influence of alcohol (National Center on Addiction and Substance Abuse at Columbia University, 2004). The issue of polysubstance use among juvenile delinquents is of particular public health importance because this population is at significantly higher risk for violent offending relative to teens who only consume alcohol (Swahn & Donovan, 2004).

More generally, multiple aspects of substance use trajectories, including age of onset, escalation, and persistence, have been found to be important factors in predicting the onset and course of juvenile delinquency. First, evidence has indicated that the earlier the age of onset of any type of substance use, the greater the odds that an adolescent will engage in severe and chronic offending (Loeber & Farrington, 2000). Second, evidence has suggested that periods of escalation of substance use are associated with subsequent increases in serious violence and other offending behavior (Huizinga, Loeber, & Thornberry, 1993; Neal & Fromme, 2007). Third, youths who engage in persistent substance use throughout adolescence are more likely to be violent offenders (Ellickson, Saner, & McGuigan, 1997). Moreover, persistent substance use is also associated with increased probability of reoffending and reentry into the juvenile court system among prior juvenile offenders (Chassin, 2008).

EXPLAINING THE EFFECTS OF SUBSTANCE USE ON OFFENDING

Substance use can influence the risk for offending through multiple pathways, with both acute and chronic use contributing to effects that range from neural to developmental levels. These various pathways are not necessarily mutually exclusive or direct, further highlighting the complex mechanisms linking adolescent substance use with juvenile offending.

Acute Effects of Substance Use

Several mechanisms are theorized to explain why substance use would increase the likelihood of future offending (Goldstein, 2003; Hoaken & Stewart, 2003; Parker & Auerhahn, 1998; see Figure 13.1). First, psychopharmacological models posit that the acute effects of ingesting substances may cause individuals to act violently or engage in other delinquent acts in part because of diminished cognitive control, increased physiological excitation, or both (Goldstein, 2003). For example, these models hold that acute substance use may have a direct pharmacological effect on the prefrontal cortex and other brain regions thought to be responsible for regulating cognitive and behavioral responses over behavior (Abernathy, Chandler, & Woodward, 2010; Boles & Miotto, 2003; Friedman, 1998; Wagner, 1996).

A large literature has examined the acute effects of alcohol and drug consumption in laboratory studies of animals and adult human participants. Although a complete review of this extensive literature is beyond the scope of this chapter, in this section we illustrate some of the acute psychopharmacological effects by which alcohol, marijuana, and psychostimulants may increase youths' likelihood for later offending, given that these three substances represent the most consistent predictors of juvenile offending.

A wealth of laboratory studies with adult participants have demonstrated that consumption of alcohol, marijuana, and psychostimulants impairs cognitive functioning that is central to the maintenance of inhibitory control over behavior (Abroms, Gottlob, & Fillmore, 2006; Field, Wiers, Christiansen, Fillmore, & Verster, 2010; Fillmore & Rush, 2002; Garavan, Kaufman, & Hester, 2008; S. A. Gruber & Yurgelun-Todd, 2005; Weafer & Fillmore, 2008). More specifically, each of these substances has been found to disrupt higher order cognitive abilities that underlie executive functioning. Although multiple definitions of executive functioning exist (Barkley, 1997), overlapping definitions suggest that executive functioning can be broadly conceptualized as a set of mental processes responsible for self-regulation of one's own thoughts and goal-oriented actions (Borkowski & Burke, 1996; Lehto, Juujärvi, Kooistra, & Pulkkinen, 2003). Measurement batteries of executive functioning generally include multiple measures of cognitive capacities, including inhibitory control, planning, working memory, abstract reasoning, cognitive flexibility, and behavior monitoring, among other related processes (Barkley, 1997). A large body of studies have indicated that poor executive functioning is linked to increased aggression and criminal behavior (as reviewed in Brower & Price, 2001; Moffitt, 1993; Morgan & Lilienfeld, 2000; Paschall & Fishbein, 2002).

There are several reasons why diminished executive functioning caused by acute intoxication may lead youths to be more at risk for criminal offending. First, decreased behavioral inhibition paired with heightened impulsivity may cause youths to exhibit risk-taking behavior without consideration of the potential longer term consequences (Moffitt, 1993). Second, youths may turn to violent behavior as the default method for navigating difficult environments as a result of poor ability to actively monitor behavior and respond appropriately in different social contexts (Hancock, Tapscott, & Hoaken, 2010). Finally, diminished ability to engage in abstract reasoning and planning may lead to a lack of problem-solving skills and reflection on the ethics of engaging in certain criminal acts.

The impairing effects of intoxication on executive functioning may be particularly detrimental for juvenile offenders, who often have preexisting executive functioning and neuropsychological deficits relative to the general population (Lahey & Waldman, 2003; Moffitt, 1993). Indeed, evidence has suggested that antisocial youths frequently show neuropsychological deficits including verbal and executive functioning compared with controls matched on age, IQ, and socioeconomic status (Giancola, Mezzich, & Tarter, 1998; Moffitt, 1993; Morgan & Lilienfeld, 2000). Some evidence has also suggested that early deficits in executive functioning among antisocial youths may subsequently predict later offending behavior (Moffitt, Lynam, & Silva, 1994; Nigg & Huang-Pollock, 2003). For example, in a birth cohort study of 13- to 18-year-old youths, Moffitt et al. (1994) found that poor executive functioning scores before age 13 significantly predicted the early onset of serious delinquent behavior.

In fact, accumulating evidence has supported the contention that executive functioning may mediate the association between substance use and aggressive behavior (Dawe, Davis, Lapworth, & McKetin, 2009; Denson, DeWall, & Finkel, 2012; Giancola, 2000; Hoaken, Giancola, & Pihl, 1998) and that this mechanism may be particularly strong for alcohol consumption (Giancola, 2000; Hoaken & Stewart, 2003). For example, Giancola (2000) proposed a conceptual framework in which alcohol consumption disrupts executive functioning, resulting in a diminished focus on future goal-oriented behavior and greater concern with short-term gratification. This focus on short-term gratification results in increased aggression, particularly in circumstances of provocation (Giancola, 2000) and in increased offending more generally.

The acute effects of consumption of alcohol or drugs may also increase adolescents' risk for offending by increasing sensation-seeking behavior (Zuckerman, 1994). This is especially true for acute alcohol intoxication, which causes increases in novel experience seeking as well as heightened behavioral disinhibition toward risk behavior (Hittner & Swickert, 2006; Neal & Fromme, 2007; Roberti, 2004). Furthermore, findings from laboratory studies have indicated that alcohol (de Wit, Crean, & Richards, 2000; Reed, Levin, & Evans, 2012; Reynolds, Richards, & de Wit, 2006), marijuana (McDonald, Schleifer, Richards, & de Wit, 2003), and cocaine (Dawe et al., 2009; Fillmore & Rush, 2002) elicit pharmacological effects that decrease inhibitory cognitive control and increase behavioral measures of impulsive behavior.

In studying the acute effects of alcohol and drug consumption, one important outcome relevant to juvenile offending is delay discounting (Nagin & Pogarsky, 2004; Richards, Zhang, Mitchell, & de Wit, 1999; Steinberg et al., 2009). *Delay discounting* refers to an individual's preference for the delivery of a small immediate award over a larger delayed reward (Petry, 2001). Findings from numerous studies using samples of adolescent and adult substance users have suggested that heavy marijuana, cocaine, and alcohol use may be associated with more rapidly discounted delay of rewards (see Reynolds, 2006, for a review). For example, Field, Christiansen, Cole, and Goudie (2007) found that heavy-drinking adolescents showed more rapid discounting of delayed hypothetical monetary and alcohol-related rewards than light drinkers. Likewise, Coffey, Veit, Wolfe, Cini, and Patton (2003) found that actively dependent cocaine and crack users discounted monetary rewards at a more pronounced rate than did non–drug-using matched controls.

Other research has examined the acute effects of alcohol and illicit drug use on delay discounting among nondependent substance-using participants (MacKillop et al., 2011; Reynolds, 2006). A comprehensive review by Reynolds (2006) found mixed evidence for the acute effects of alcohol for increasing delay discounting depending on whether a real-time or questionnaire-based measure was used to assess delay discounting. To this end, it has been suggested that certain measures of delay discounting may be more sensitive than others to the acute effects of alcohol (Reynolds, 2006; Reynolds & Schiffbauer, 2004). Reynolds et al. (2006) examined the effects of acute alcohol intoxication on two measures of delay discounting and three measures of risk-taking propensity, including (a) a questionnaire-based measure of delay discounting, (b) an experiential discounting task, (c) a balloon analogue risk task, (d) a stop task, and (e) a go–no-go task. Results indicated that acute alcohol intoxication increased risk-taking behavior only on the experiential discounting task and stop task.

Although the evidence regarding the acute effects of substance use on delay discounting is mixed, existing findings have nonetheless suggested that both acute and more chronic substance use may cause adolescents to increase the value they place on immediate rewards, which may in turn heighten the probability of risk-taking behavior and delinquency while ignoring potential longer term negative consequences (Field et al., 2007; Kollins, 2003; Reynolds, 2006).

In addition, findings from experimental studies have demonstrated that under high provocation, alcohol and psychostimulant consumption may exacerbate aggressive behavior (Lau, Pihl, & Peterson, 1995; McKetin, McLaren, Ridell, & Robins, 2006; Parrott & Giancola, 2006). Indeed, several avenues of evidence have suggested that substance use intoxication may escalate situations from a low level of conflict to more serious physical aggression

(Brunelle, Brochu, & Cousineau, 2000; Mason & Windle, 2002). For example, a host of laboratory studies have demonstrated that aggression is exacerbated in conditions in which participants are under high provocation while under the influence of alcohol (Giancola, 2002; Giancola et al., 2002; Lau et al., 1995).

Although most of the human data on acute substance use effects have come from laboratory studies with adult participants, some informative findings have also come from studies using ecological momentary assessment (EMA), which yield support for this psychopharmacological explanation of delinquency. EMA is a research method that involves repeated collection of within-individual data typically many times per day in the natural environment in attempt to sample real-world experiences (Shiffman, Stone, & Hufford, 2008). This methodology is useful for separating within-person effects from between-person effects. Between-subject designs that compare substance-using and non–substance-using adolescents are confounded by shared risk factors between criminality and substance use. However, within-subject designs such as EMA control for these differences and allow the researcher to determine whether given individuals tend to engage in more delinquent behavior on the days on which they consume more substances (Shiffman et al., 2008).

For example, Neal and Fromme (2007) used EMA to examine the association between alcohol intoxication and different behavioral risks in a sample of 1st-year college students who self-reported behavior using daily diaries each day for 30 days. Findings revealed that alcohol use was globally related to nine of 10 risk-taking behaviors (e.g., vandalism, perpetrating sexual coercion, aggressive behavior). Furthermore, significant event-level associations were found between alcohol use and risk behavior, such that behavioral risks were more likely to occur on days when alcohol was consumed and risk increased as a function of the individual's intoxication level. These findings are significant because they demonstrate the direct intraindividual effects of acute alcohol consumption in promoting multiple delinquent behaviors. However, although EMA studies shed light on the complex nature by which substance use may heighten risk for delinquent behavior, few studies to date have used this this method with adolescent samples; this is an important priority for future research.

In summary, laboratory studies of animal and human participants, as well as some EMA data, have suggested that acute substance use intoxication may cause loss of cognitive control, increased delay discounting and impulsivity, and heightened behavioral disinhibition. In turn, these effects may lead to an increased risk for adolescent criminal offending.

Effects of Chronic Substance Use on Adolescent Brain Development and Psychosocial Maturity

In addition to acute intoxication, more chronic exposure to alcohol or drugs may have effects on the developing adolescent brain that influence risk for juvenile offending. Typical adolescent neurobiological development is characterized by structural and functional brain changes that optimize neural efficiency and eventually contribute to mature behavior. On the neural level, weak or less-used neural connections are pruned away during adolescence, and increased myelination of the remaining neurons improves the speed of neural communication (Jacobus & Tapert, 2013; Wetherill, Squeglia, Yang, & Tapert, 2013). However, this process of neural refinement does not occur uniformly throughout the brain. Rather, protracted maturation of brain regions important to higher order executive cognitive functioning is characteristic of adolescent brain development (Jacobus & Tapert, 2013). Specifically, the prefrontal cortex continues to develop throughout adolescence, which may thus account for the reduced cognitive control typically demonstrated as impulsivity in youths (Casey, Jones, & Hare, 2008).

In contrast to the gradual maturation of cognitive control, changes in dopamine autoreceptor density occur early in adolescence. These structural changes may result in dopamine activity increasing and peaking at this stage of development (Galvan, 2010; Steinberg, 2008). The neurotransmitter dopamine plays a pivotal role in the neural reward system, resulting in increased reward seeking and sensation seeking during adolescence. It is this temporal gap between the early dopaminergic development of reward seeking and the protracted development of cognitive control that has been proposed to underlie the risk-taking behavior definitive of adolescence (Steinberg, 2008).

A growing body of literature has indicated that exposing the developing adolescent brain to substances can disrupt these normative processes, resulting in structural and functional effects that may manifest as executive function deficits. These deficits, in turn, may translate into maladaptive behavior that perpetuates substance use and encourages juvenile offending over time. Much of this evidence comes from an extensive animal literature on the effects of periadolescent substance use on the brain, which is beyond the scope of this chapter (see Smith, 2003; Spear, 2011).

In human adolescents, emerging functional MRI research has indicated that adolescent substance use may impair the development of brain systems underlying cognitive control, thereby increasing the risk for offending. For example, Medina, Nagel, and Tapert (2010) found evidence of the deleterious structural and functional impact of adolescent substance use on neurocognitive abilities important in self-control and future planning. After a month of abstinence, adolescents who used marijuana possessed significantly greater cerebellar vermis volumes than non–marijuana users, indicating significantly stunted or deficient synaptic pruning. In addition, greater vermis volume was related to poorer executive functioning, including inhibition and planning (Medina et al., 2010). Adolescent marijuana use has thus been linked to structural, neurological, and executive cognitive control deficits that may contribute to poor decision making and less inhibition of impulsive behavior, which might result in increased offending. However, because these data are cross-sectional, it is unclear whether these structural deficits were present before marijuana use. The differences found between marijuana users and nonusers may reflect preexisting vulnerabilities to initiate use rather than the effects of substance exposure. Longitudinal data are necessary to rule out this possibility.

Wetherill et al. (2013) used such a longitudinal design to identify the effects of adolescent substance use on neural activity by comparing functional MRI data from alcohol-abstinent youths performing a go–no-go inhibition task with functional MRI data from those same youths 6 months later. They found a significant Time × Drinking Status interaction, whereby adolescents who transitioned from abstinence to heavy drinking demonstrated increased blood-oxygen-level–dependent activation from baseline to follow-up task performance compared with continuous nonusers who demonstrated the decreased activation reflective of developing neural efficiency. Although performance on the inhibition task was comparable between groups, imaging data suggested that, compared with abstainers, youths who began drinking heavily required more neural activity, or more neural effort, to achieve inhibition. This differential neural activity between users and nonusers was distinct from preonset differences that placed adolescents at risk for transitioning to heavy drinking. At-risk future users had less activation during the go–no-go task before use and required significantly greater activation after substance exposure. These longitudinal data therefore demonstrate that the inefficient neural activity found in substance users did not exist before initiation and is markedly distinct from preonset vulnerabilities (Wetherill et al., 2013).

Paralleling the effects of adolescent substance use on brain development, some evidence has shown that consuming substances as an adolescent can inhibit the development of psychosocial maturity among juvenile offenders, and this research may help to account for the relation between substance use and adolescent offending. Steinberg and Cauffman (1996) conceptualized psychosocial maturity as a broad collection of qualities or dispositions, including responsibility, temperance, and perspective taking, that improve significantly between adolescence and early adulthood. Deficits in psychosocial maturity—lacking future orientation, impulse control, and responsibility for one's actions—may render an adolescent more prone to offending. For example, stunted impulse control combined with an inability to evaluate future consequences may lead a youth to engage in risk-taking behavior in general and offending behavior in particular. Indeed, a significant link has been found between psychosocial maturity and trajectories of antisocial and delinquent behavior, with those on a persistently antisocial trajectory exhibiting lower initial levels of psychosocial maturity (Monahan, Steinberg, Cauffman, & Mulvey, 2009).

In their longitudinal study, Chassin et al. (2010) demonstrated that among male adolescent offenders, levels of marijuana and alcohol use were not only inversely related to psychosocial maturity but actually prospectively predicted lowered future maturity levels. That is, individuals who reported elevated levels of marijuana and alcohol use demonstrated a decline in psychosocial maturity 6 months later. However, this change was temporary, in that those who reported a decrease in substance use also demonstrated an increase in maturity 6 months later (Chassin et al., 2010). Thus, whether chronic substance use would result in more permanent deficits in psychosocial maturity is unclear.

In summary, adolescent substance use may disrupt normative neural development such that brain structures and functions important in cognitive control are significantly altered. These neural changes may compromise inhibition and planning abilities, thus increasing risk of juvenile offending. Psychosocial maturity is also deficient in adolescents after regular substance use, additionally contributing to increased risk for offending. However, much of this literature is limited by cross-sectional designs. Although there is some longitudinal support, additional prospective research is necessary to gauge the duration of adolescent substance use effects and to confirm that any structural or functional differences in youths' brains resulted from substance exposure and did not exist before use. Additional research is necessary to determine the average duration and necessary dose that is needed to produce neural effects of substance use in adolescence. Future research is also necessary to tease out the specific brain regions and functions altered by substances and whether these effects are age and substance specific.

Financial and Social Effects of Adolescent Substance Use on Juvenile Offending

Substance use can also increase juvenile offending because it creates a need for income, and some youths may commit criminal acts as a functional means to obtain that goal (Goldstein, 2003; Seddon, 2006). Prior studies of illicit drug users have reported that gaining income to purchase drugs is one of the most prevalent self-reported reasons for engaging in predatory crime (Goldstein, 2003; Inciardi, 1990; Romero-Daza, Weeks, & Singer, 2003).

Furthermore, within samples of offenders, higher rates of theft have been found during periods of drug addiction compared with nonaddiction (Chaiken & Chaiken, 1990). In addition to increasing financial motives, substance use can also heighten the likelihood of later juvenile offending by placing the adolescent in high-risk social situations in which criminal offending may occur (Goldstein, 2003). For example, substance use usually occurs in peer contexts, and most juvenile offending also occurs with peers (Chung & Steinberg, 2006; Monahan et al., 2009). Moreover, because of peer selection effects, these peers are themselves more likely to use substances and engage in other illegal behaviors (Ennett et al., 2006; Weerman, 2011).

Substance Use Effects on the Transition to Adulthood

In addition to these mechanisms, substance use can cause the maintenance of or increase in offending by restricting adolescents' opportunities to succeed in more prosocial domains such as school, work, and prosocial relationships. Put another way, substance use may lead an adolescent to be less successful in transitioning to adulthood, thereby reducing the likelihood of desistance from offending (Mulvey et al., 2004).

As mentioned earlier, substance use can have lasting effects on cognitive function and psychosocial maturity that may leave an adolescent ill equipped to perform well in school or to maintain responsibilities necessary for gaining other life opportunities such as employment. Indeed, adolescent substance users show poor academic achievement and increased school dropout and are more likely to be unemployed as adults (Bryant, Schulenberg, O'Malley, Bachman, & Johnston, 2003; Fergusson & Boden, 2008; Patton et al., 2007). In addition, adolescent substance users are less likely to have satisfying romantic relationships in young adulthood (Fergusson & Boden, 2008; Patton et al., 2007)—another important aspect of adult life.

The effects of romantic relationships on juvenile offending are complex because a partner who also uses substances or is delinquent will not foster prosocial behavior.

For example, Fleming, White, and Catalano (2010) found that although romantic relationship quality was high, substance-using young adults demonstrated greater substance use when in a relationship with partners who also used. This finding highlights an important caveat in studying at-risk adolescents' transition into the adult role of romantic partner. Although entering a serious romantic relationship can significantly reduce substance use (Fleming et al., 2010) and offending (Theobald & Farrington, 2009), if the partner engages in maladaptive behavior, the relationship may instead exacerbate substance use and discourage prosocial development.

To the extent that adolescent substance users are less likely to successfully occupy adult roles, they will be less likely to desist from offending. Incompatibility between offending and the demands of adult roles has been associated with desistance from offending (Laub & Sampson, 1993; Mulvey et al., 2004). Therefore, substance use may limit opportunities to move away from offending by impairing an adolescent's ability to acquire these important adult roles.

Finally, adolescent substance use may increase offending because it impedes the normal development of coping skills. According to Baumrind and Moselle (1985), social competence and coping skills are developed through engagement with normative developmental challenges that gradually move an adolescent away from the security and attachment of childhood toward competent independent functioning. Substances may offer an alternative method of coping with these life challenges through self-medication rather than by developing effective coping. This dysfunctional coping limits adolescents' growth and ability to handle more adult responsibilities (Baumrind & Moselle, 1985).

Summary

In summary, acute and chronic substance use increase the risk for juvenile offending through multiple, but not necessarily mutually exclusive, pathways. Adolescent substance use may have acute pharmacological effects that impair cognitive functioning and increase sensation seeking, thereby increasing a youth's chance of risk taking or escalating social situations into aggressive behavior. Substance use may have structural and functional effects on the adolescent brain that increase risk for offending via deficient neurocognitive functions important in self-control and decision making. Substance use is also a costly behavior that may motivate youths to obtain funds through illegal means. It may also act to increase juvenile offending by inhibiting the development of mature coping strategies and the transition into adult roles that move an individual away from offending.

Despite ample support for the effects of substance use on offending, the current literature has several limitations in terms of identifying the underlying mechanisms. For ethical reasons, laboratory-based investigations of the acute effects of substances on cognitive function are limited to adults or animal studies. The EMA design is an alternative method that is well suited to determining whether acute intoxication results in comparable cognitive deficits in teens. However, there is currently almost no EMA research on the relation between adolescent substance use and offending. Such research may be difficult to conduct because of barriers to self-reporting illegal behavior, but it remains a potentially valuable future direction. As recommended earlier, longitudinal research is also needed to explore the long-term effects of chronic substance use on the developing adolescent brain. Additional research is needed to clarify whether the effect of substance use on brain functioning and on psychosocial maturity is dose dependent, and substance specific, and to determine the persistence of this effect. Recently, a large research investment has been made in answering these and other questions surrounding the effects of substance use on the adolescent brain through the National Consortium on Alcohol and Neurodevelopment in Adolescence, which is a national, multisite collaboration aimed at exploring the structural and functional effects of alcohol on the adolescent brain through advanced imaging techniques.

EFFECTS OF OFFENDING BEHAVIORS ON ADOLESCENT SUBSTANCE USE AND RECIPROCAL EFFECTS

Although there is consistent evidence that substance use prospectively predicts later juvenile offending, there is also evidence for a reverse direction of effect such that early delinquency and conduct problems are associated with the development of subsequent substance use (Doherty, Green, & Ensminger, 2008; Mason, Hitchings, & Spoth, 2007; van den Bree & Pickworth, 2005). This reverse direction of effect has been shown among serious juvenile offenders (Chaiken & Chaiken, 1990; Huizinga et al., 1993) as well as general community samples (Becker et al., 2012; Doherty et al., 2008; Mason et al., 2007; van den Bree & Pickworth, 2005). Indeed, the presence of early conduct problems is one of the most robust predictors of adolescent substance use and early-onset substance use disorders (Disney, Elkins, McGue, & Iacono, 1999; Elkins, McGue, & Iacono, 2007; Iacono, Carlson, Taylor, Elkins, & McGue, 1999). The prevailing explanation for this direction of effect is that juvenile offending is often perpetrated in peer contexts and affiliation with antisocial peers provides both opportunity and encouragement for substance use behavior (Dishion, Capaldi, Spracklen, & Li, 1995; Snyder & Sickmund, 1999; Wikstrom & Loeber, 2000).

Given the evidence both for the effects of substance use on later offending and for the effects of early conduct problems on later substance use, it is not surprising that a growing body of evidence has also suggested that the relation between substance use and offending is reciprocal and mutually reinforcing (Becker et al., 2012; D'Amico et al., 2008; Ford, 2005; Xue, Zimmerman, & Cunningham, 2009). According to this model, bidirectional relations exist between each behavior that encourages the other over time (Becker et al., 2012; D'Amico et al., 2008). For example, D'Amico et al. (2008) conducted a cross-lagged panel study with a sample of high-risk juvenile delinquents ages 13 to 17 from the California juvenile probation system. Results demonstrated that across three types of delinquent behavior (property, interpersonal, and drug-related offenses), substance use predicted delinquency, and one form of delinquency, interpersonal crime, predicted substance use across all three types. That is, consistent bidirectional effects were found that were temporally stable over time, suggesting that each behavior might foster the other (D'Amico et al., 2008). Similarly, in a study of high-school-aged African American youths, Xue et al. (2009) found that early alcohol use significantly predicted violent behavior (e.g., using a weapon) later in adolescence, and early violence predicted subsequent frequency of alcohol use. These results suggest that the presence of each of these behaviors may increase the likelihood of the other occurring over time.

SHARED RISK FACTORS AND THE EXTERNALIZING SPECTRUM

Finally, rather than resulting from bidirectional causal influence, it is also possible that the relation between juvenile offending and adolescent substance use reflects the effects of shared underlying risk factors (see Figure 13.1). Indeed, both outcomes may actually be age-varying manifestations of a single externalizing spectrum (Young et al., 2009). Longitudinal twin studies have provided support for a heritable, general externalizing liability related to both substance misuse and conduct disorder (Hicks, Krueger, Iacono, McGue, & Patrick, 2004; Young, Stallings, Corley, Krauter, & Hewitt, 2000). Therefore, the frequent co-occurrence of juvenile offending and substance use may be driven by the same propensity for behavioral disinhibition that underlies such externalizing spectrum disorders. Young et al. (2009) found that the structure of behavioral disinhibition changed significantly between ages 12 and 17 in a community sample of twin pairs. At age 12, attention deficit hyperactivity disorder and conduct disorder largely accounted for behavioral disinhibition, and at age 17 the structure had changed such that attention deficit hyperactivity disorder, conduct disorder, substance use, and novelty seeking were more equal in their relation to behavioral disinhibition.

In short, conduct problems account for more variance in disinhibition in early adolescence, and substance use has increasing weight in later adolescence (Young et al., 2009). Furthermore, manifestations of the externalizing spectrum at earlier developmental stages cumulatively influence its manifestation in adolescence (Beauchaine & McNulty, 2013). Thus, the precise form of behavioral disinhibition is developmentally linked. Substance use and offending may not be apparent until adolescence allows independence from adult supervision and access to substances (Patterson, 1993; Young et al., 2009). Additional genetic and shared environmental factors may further differentiate the specific form of externalizing vulnerability (e.g., using marijuana vs. stealing) that an at-risk youth may exhibit (Hicks, Schalet, Malone, Iacono, & McGue, 2011).

In addition to a heritable predisposition for behavioral undercontrol as a common risk factor underlying both substance use and juvenile offending, there are environmental risk factors that are common to both juvenile offending and substance use that might account for their co-occurrence. Adolescents whose parents have substance use disorder are themselves more likely to use and misuse substances, and they are also more likely to be juvenile offenders (S. M. King et al., 2009; Marmorstein, Iacono, & McGue, 2009). Similarly, adolescents with an antisocial parent are more likely to both use substances and engage in criminal behavior (Murray, Loeber, & Pardini, 2012; Roettger, Swisher, Kuhl, & Chavez, 2011). This intergenerational transmission may reflect heritable pathways, but it may also result from the influence of poor parenting. Not only do antisocial and substance-abusing parents provide low levels of support, control, and monitoring (Chassin, Pillow, Curran, Molina, & Barrera, 1993; Coley, Carrano, & Lewin-Bizan, 2011), but adolescents with elevated levels of behavioral undercontrol (impulsivity, sensation seeking) are also likely to evoke poor parenting (Marceau et al., 2013; Mezzich et al., 2007; Narusyte et al. 2011).

Deviant peers are another shared risk factor for both juvenile offending and substance use and are particularly important during adolescence (Monahan, Rhew, Hawkins, & Brown, 2014; Simons-Morton, Haynie, Crump, Eitel, & Saylor, 2001; Steinberg, 2008). Among a community sample of youths evaluated annually for 5 years, Monahan et al. (2014) found that having more substance-using or delinquent peers increased the likelihood of adolescents engaging in both behaviors, thus highlighting the influence of maladaptive peer behavior on the co-occurrence of juvenile offending and substance use.

Finally, families that are characterized by poor monitoring and weak family bonds increase adolescents' experimentation with substances (Ford, 2005; Steinberg, Fletcher, & Darling, 1994) and their delinquent behavior (Henneberger, Durkee, Truong, Atkins, & Tolan, 2013; Hussong, Zucker, Wong, Fitzgerald, & Puttler, 2005). Indeed, affiliation with deviant peers actually mediates the relation between poor parenting and both adolescent substance use and offending. Among a sample of adolescent male offenders, less effective parenting behavior (e.g., less warmth, monitoring, or knowledge) was related to increased affiliation with deviant peers and, consequently, to elevated levels of juvenile offending (Chung & Steinberg, 2006). A similar relation between low parental monitoring, deviant peer affiliation, and adolescent substance use was found in a community sample (Malone & Lansford, 2010).

In summary, the relation between juvenile offending and substance use can be linked to dynamic, shared risk factors that range from heritable liability to a youth's interpersonal environment. To some extent, both offending and substance use may be the adolescent-stage manifestations of a single, heritable externalizing spectrum. The impulsivity and novelty seeking that characterize those with externalizing liability may evoke poor parenting and also increase the selection of deviant peers. Taken together, these findings lend support for a common set of risk factors underlying both adolescent substance use and offending.

BROADER CONSEQUENCES OF SUBSTANCE USE FOR JUVENILE OFFENDERS

For juvenile offenders, criminal offending is not the only undesirable outcome to result from substance use. Rather, substance use has been linked to a variety of adverse life outcomes. First, substance use has been shown to increase risky sexual behavior, resulting in heightened vulnerability to HIV and other sexually transmitted diseases. Juvenile offenders who use substances are more likely to have multiple sexual partners and not to use condoms (Teplin et al., 2002). Indeed, juvenile offenders with substance use disorders have been shown to be more likely to engage in risky sexual behaviors than those with other clinical mental health disorders (Teplin et al., 2002). Furthermore, alcohol use increases instances of sexual assault when the offender or the victim has engaged in alcohol use (Hingson, Heeren, Winter, & Wechsler, 2005).

Second, as described earlier, substance use is related to adverse educational and developmental outcomes later in life (Giancola et al., 1998; Jacobus & Tapert, 2013; K. M. King, Meehan, Trim, & Chassin, 2006; Morgan & Lilienfeld, 2000; Wetherill et al., 2013). Even when controlling for other risk factors, such as parental alcoholism and maternal monitoring, substance use has been shown to decrease the likelihood of college degree completion (for drug use, but not alcohol use), which in turn leads to less positive educational and occupational outcomes later in life (K. M. King et al., 2006). Third, substance use and substance use disorders are related to early mortality and other negative health effects among juvenile offenders (Chassin et al., 2013; Teplin et al., 2002). The link between adolescent substance use and early mortality is expressed through multiple pathways, such as overdose (Coffey et al., 2003), suicide (Windle, 1992), lethal violence (Mclaughlin, Daniel, & Joost, 2000), and impaired driving (Hingson, Heeren, Zakocs, Winter, & Wechsler, 2003). Finally, in the long term, elevated rates of cigarette smoking create significant risk for premature mortality and morbidity.

IMPLICATIONS FOR POLICY IN THE JUVENILE JUSTICE SYSTEM

The data reviewed in this chapter have important implications for policy in the juvenile justice system, as well as government policy at both the state and the federal level. Both the high prevalence of substance disorders among adolescent offenders and the relation between substance use involvement and the onset and maintenance of juvenile offending suggest the importance of (a) appropriate screening for and assessment of substance use disorders, (b) the availability of substance use treatment, (c) substance use treatment that is evidence based and efficacious, and (d) aftercare for continued desistance.

Access to treatment for substance use disorders is important for adolescents in general, but it is especially important among juvenile offenders because of the relation between substance use and continued offending. However, the first step in treating substance use disorders is correctly identifying them in adolescents who come in contact with the juvenile justice system. Juvenile justice settings need to use empirically validated screening and in-depth assessments to identify adolescents who are in need of substance use treatment (National Institute on Drug Abuse [NIDA], 2014). Screening should take place for every juvenile who enters the juvenile justice system, and it should take place as early in the process as possible because the average length of stay in a juvenile facility can be as short as 5 months (Gallagher & Dobrin, 2006; NIDA, 2014).

Once substance use has been properly identified, the juvenile justice system should begin to treat adolescents who have substance use disorders. Failure to treat substance use disorders in this population results in poorer adjustment during and after confinement and interferes with the justice system's mission of rehabilitation (Belenko, 2002; Dennis, Scott, Funk, & Foss, 2005; Hser et al., 2001; Randall & Cunningham, 2003). Promoting recovery from substance use disorders should be a priority for the juvenile justice system because chronic substance use problems are related to continuous offending (Cottle, Lee, & Heilbrun, 2001; D'Amico et al., 2008; Hussong, Curran, Moffitt, Caspi, & Carrig, 2004; Stouthamer-Loeber, Wei, Loeber, & Masten, 2004). Treatment literature has shown that substance use services are effective in both the recovery from substance use disorders and in reducing reoffending (Behnken, Arredondo, & Packman, 2009; Chassin et al., 2009; Farabee, Shen, Hser, Grella, & Anglin, 2001; Lipsey, 2009).

The juvenile justice system is now the largest publicly funded source of substance use treatment in the United States (Garland et al., 2001; NIDA, 2014). However, even within the juvenile justice system, adolescent substance use disorders are undertreated (Garland et al., 2005; Grisso, 2008; Hazen, Hough, Landsverk, & Wood, 2004). For example, Johnson et al. (2004) found that only 48% of adolescents in need of alcohol and drug treatment received some form of substance abuse treatment service. Mulvey, Schubert, and Chung (2007) showed similar rates of treatment, with about 44% of youths in need of alcohol and drug use treatment receiving the appropriate services. Further exacerbating this problem is a lack of community intervention resources for substance use and the tendency for the juvenile justice system and drug treatment agencies not to collaborate well with professional service providers to provide the proper type of treatment (Nissen, Butts, Merrigan, & Kraft, 2006). Moreover, given the connection between substance use and cigarette smoking (Dani & Harris, 2005), a focus on smoking cessation should not be overlooked. Smoking cessation is important for overall health (Taylor, Hasselblad, Henley, Thun, & Sloan, 2002). Moreover, evidence has suggested that smoking cessation does not compromise, and may even enhance, long-term sobriety from alcohol and other illicit drugs (Prochaska, Delucchi, & Hall, 2004; Sullivan & Covey, 2002).

In addition to the lack of substance use treatment in general, there is also a lack of evidence-based substance use treatment in the juvenile justice system (Henggeler et al., 2006; McLellan, Carise, & Kleber, 2003; NIDA, 2014). Given that numerous outcome studies have shown the effectiveness of various types of substance use disorder treatments for adolescents (see, e.g., multisystemic therapy; Henggeler, Clingempeel, Brondino, & Pickrel, 2002; NIDA, 2014; see also Chapters 23–28, this handbook), the lack of use of evidence-based treatments is alarming. However, state and federal governments are becoming aware of the necessity of offering evidence-based treatments for mental health and substance use disorders (Glisson & Schoenwald, 2005; Mitchell, Wilson, & MacKenzie, 2007). For example, several states (including Connecticut, Oregon, and Washington) have passed legislation requiring that empirically based treatment methods be used in the juvenile justice system (Glisson & Schoenwald, 2005).

In addition, the U.S. Congress created the Residential Substance Abuse Treatment Program to address the limitations of existing substance use disorder treatment programs (Bureau of Justice Assistance, 2005). However, despite recognition of this problem, widespread implementation of evidence-based treatments has still been unsuccessful in the juvenile justice system (Glisson & Schoenwald, 2005; for further discussion of treatments and interventions, see Chapters 24–29, this handbook).

Furthermore, substance use and substance use disorders are often thought of as acute conditions, curable through one treatment episode, rather than as a more chronic condition that may require continuing care (McLellan, Lewis, O'Brien, & Kleber, 2000; Watkins, Pincus, Tanielian, & Lloyd, 2003). However, successful recovery from drug and alcohol addiction is often achieved after multiple unsuccessful attempts and relapses. Relapse rates among adolescents have been shown to be as high as 66% within 6 months of receipt of substance use disorder treatment (Cornelius et al., 2003). Therefore, substance use disorders may warrant continued care and attention from the juvenile justice system (NIDA, 2014).

Research has suggested that some type of posttreatment program can be beneficial, even as long as 6 months after discharge (McLellan et al., 1996). Posttreatment monitoring (including even brief contact; Stout, Rubin, Zwick, Zywaiak, & Bellino, 1999) and contingency management (Stitzer & Petry, 2006) have shown the ability to support abstinence and avert relapse. Aftercare is especially important in the juvenile justice system because adolescents released from custody are most likely to be placed back in their home communities with the same risk factors that may have initially led to substance use and substance use disorders.

The need for aftercare for substance use also suggests the need for changes to juvenile justice policies concerning health insurance termination. For example, although many adolescents in the custody of the juvenile justice system are covered under Medicaid or the Children's Health Insurance Plan, this coverage stops as soon as the adolescent becomes incarcerated (Cuellar & Cheema, 2012), which in most cases means that their current insurance is terminated. This becomes a problem when the adolescent is released back into the community because reinstating insurance after returning to the community can be very difficult and can take as long as 90 days (Evans Cuellar, Kelleher, Rolls, & Pajer, 2005; National Conference of State Legislatures, 2010). However, federal regulations do not require states to terminate Medicaid enrollment, and instead give states the option to suspend eligibility for the duration of the adolescent's incarceration (National Conference of State Legislatures, 2010). If states adopted this type of policy, it would make it easier for adolescents to return to care after their release and therefore allow them to continue to receive the substance use disorder care that they require. The provisions of the Patient Protection and Affordable Care Act make substance use treatment an essential benefit, which may increase access to substance use treatment for adolescents with insurance coverage. Other options available to the states include continuous eligibility (in which eligibility is guaranteed for 12 months regardless of status changes) or presumptive eligibility (in which eligibility is assumed, and the process can be simplified to afford quicker access to care; National Conference of State Legislatures, 2010).

In addition, states may increase the availability of substance use disorder treatment by increasing Medicaid and Children's Health Insurance Plan outreach and enrollment efforts for juveniles who have been recently released from incarceration (Cueller & Cheema, 2012). States can also designate providers who treat substance use disorders as qualified entities under Medicaid, which allows for temporary eligibility pending the final eligibility determination (Cueller & Cheema, 2012). This way, substance use disorder treatment would not lapse while the juvenile is awaiting the eligibility decision. Finally, both states and juvenile justice facilities could invest in reentry programs that provide services aimed at reintegrating juveniles with substance use disorders into the community. These programs could provide substance use services and long-term care after release from incarceration.

CONCLUSION

As shown in this chapter, substance use and substance use disorders are a substantial risk factor for juvenile offending. Substance use and substance use disorders are highly prevalent among juvenile offenders, and they increase the likelihood that adolescent offending will become persistent and chronic rather than desist. Moreover, substance use and substance use disorders create risk for a broad range of negative outcomes among juvenile offenders, including risk for premature mortality and significant threats to physical health.

As clearly demonstrated in the research reviewed in this chapter, substance use, substance use disorders, and juvenile offending are closely linked and show bidirectional relations over time. Substance use disorders and offending may even represent age-varying manifestations of a common, heritable externalizing spectrum, with other common risk factors including parental and peer substance use and antisociality as well as poor parenting behavior. The effects of adolescent substance use may increase offending through multiple mechanisms, including (a) acute effects on executive functioning, cognitive control, delay discounting, and sensation seeking; (b) effects on the developing adolescent brain that impair cognitive functioning, self-regulation, and reward sensitivity; (c) social effects that place adolescents in peer contexts that make offending more likely; and (d) cumulative effects that impair the transition to adulthood, including the failure to develop mature coping strategies and the inability to successfully occupy adult roles.

These multiple and substantial risks of adolescent substance use have important implications for research and policy in the juvenile justice system. In terms of research, a better understanding is needed of the acute and chronic effects of substance use on cognitive functioning, self-regulation, and reward sensitivity, including the extent to which these effects are age specific to adolescent exposure and the extent to which the effects are or are not reversible with the reduction or cessation of substance use. A need also exists for continuing epidemiological research that monitors changes in substance use and substance use–related effects in relation to changes in state law and justice policies. Finally, research is needed on how to increase the adoption and high-quality implementation of evidence-based substance use treatment.

In terms of juvenile justice system policy, there is a need for increased provision of evidence-based treatment and improved mechanisms to provide (and to fund) continuing care after release. Continuing efforts to prevent justice system involvement and to provide treatment in community settings are also important. Given that the juvenile justice system is currently the largest publicly-funded adolescent drug treatment system in the United States, it is important both to improve these treatment services and to provide access to alternative, affordable treatment outside of the justice system. Juvenile justice policy would benefit from adopting a developmental perspective that applies research advances in understanding adolescent biopsychosocial development and the ways in which such development is affected by the acute and chronic effects of substance use. This approach has the potential both to inform juvenile justice policy and to reduce the harmful effects of adolescent substance use for adolescents in general and juvenile offenders in particular.

References

Abernathy, K., Chandler, L. J., & Woodward, J. J. (2010). Alcohol and the prefrontal cortex. *International Review of Neurobiology*, *91*, 289–320. http://dx.doi.org/10.1016/S0074-7742(10)91009-X

Abroms, B. D., Gottlob, L. R., & Fillmore, M. T. (2006). Alcohol effects on inhibitory control of attention: Distinguishing between intentional and automatic mechanisms. *Psychopharmacology*, *188*, 324–334. http://dx.doi.org/10.1007/s00213-006-0524-y

Anderson, K. G., Ramo, D. E., Cummins, K. M., & Brown, S. A. (2010). Alcohol and drug involvement after adolescent treatment and functioning during emerging adulthood. *Drug and Alcohol Dependence*, *107*, 171–181. http://dx.doi.org/10.1016/j.drugalcdep.2009.10.005

Barkley, R. A. (1997). Behavioral inhibition, sustained attention, and executive functions: Constructing a unifying theory of ADHD. *Psychological Bulletin*, *121*, 65–94. http://dx.doi.org/10.1037/0033-2909.121.1.65

Barnes, G. M., Welte, J. W., & Hoffman, J. H. (2002). Relationship of alcohol use to delinquency and illicit drug use in adolescents: Gender, age, and racial/ethnic differences. *Journal of Drug Issues*, *32*, 153–178. http://dx.doi.org/10.1177/002204260203200107

Baskin-Sommers, A., & Sommers, I. (2006). The co-occurrence of substance use and high-risk behaviors. *Journal of Adolescent Health*, *38*, 609–611. http://dx.doi.org/10.1016/j.jadohealth.2005.07.010

Baumrind, D., & Moselle, K. A. (1985). A development perspective on adolescent drug abuse. *Advances in Alcohol and Substance Abuse*, *4*, 41–66. http://dx.doi.org/10.1300/J251v04n03_03

Beauchaine, T. P., & McNulty, T. (2013). Comorbidities and continuities as ontogenic processes: Toward a developmental spectrum model of externalizing psychopathology. *Development and Psychopathology*, *25*, 1505–1528. http://dx.doi.org/10.1017/S0954579413000746

Becker, S. J., Nargiso, J. E., Wolff, J. C., Uhl, K. M., Simon, V. A., Spirito, A., & Prinstein, M. J. (2012). Temporal relationship between substance use and delinquent behavior among young psychiatrically hospitalized adolescents. *Journal of Substance Abuse Treatment*, *43*, 251–259. http://dx.doi.org/10.1016/j.jsat.2011.11.005

Behnken, M. P., Arredondo, D. E., & Packman, W. L. (2009). Reduction in recidivism in a juvenile mental health court: A pre-and post-treatment outcome study. *Juvenile and Family Court Journal*, *60*, 23–44. http://dx.doi.org/10.1111/j.1755-6988.2009.01030.x

Belenko, S. (2002). The challenges of conducting research in drug treatment court settings. *Substance Use and Misuse*, *37*, 1635–1664. http://dx.doi.org/10.1081/JA-120014425

Boles, S. M., & Miotto, K. (2003). Substance abuse and violence: A review of the literature. *Aggression and Violent Behavior*, *8*, 155–174. http://dx.doi.org/10.1016/S1359-1789(01)00057-X

Borkowski, J. G., & Burke, J. E. (1996). Theories, models, and measurements of executive functioning: An information processing perspective. In G. R. Lyon & N. A. Krasnegor (Eds.), *Attention, memory, and executive function* (pp. 235–261). Baltimore, MD: Paul H. Brookes.

Brower, M. C., & Price, B. H. (2001). Neuropsychiatry of frontal lobe dysfunction in violent and criminal behaviour: A critical review. *Journal of Neurology, Neurosurgery, and Psychiatry*, *71*, 720–726. http://dx.doi.org/10.1136/jnnp.71.6.720

Brunelle, N., Brochu, S., & Cousineau, M. M. (2000). Drug-crime relations among drug-consuming juvenile delinquents: A tripartite model and more. *Contemporary Drug Problems*, *27*, 835–866.

Bryant, A. L., Schulenberg, J. E., O'Malley, P. M., Bachman, J. G., & Johnston, L. D. (2003). How academic achievement, attitudes, and behaviors relate to the course of substance use during adolescence: A 6-year, multiwave national longitudinal study. *Journal of Research on Adolescence*, *13*, 361–397. http://dx.doi.org/10.1111/1532-7795.1303005

Bui, K. V. T., Ellickson, P. L., & Bell, R. M. (2000). Cross-lagged relationships among adolescent problem drug use, delinquent behavior, and emotional distress. *Journal of Drug Issues*, *30*, 283–303.

Bureau of Justice Assistance. (2005). *Residential substance abuse treatment for state prisoners (RSAT) program*. Washington, DC: Author.

California Health and Safety Code, § 11357.

Casey, B. J., Jones, R. M., & Hare, T. A. (2008). The adolescent brain. *Annals of the New York Academy of Sciences*, *1124*, 111–126. http://dx.doi.org/10.1196/annals.1440.010

Centers for Disease Control and Prevention. (2008). Smoking-attributable mortality, years of potential life lost, and productivity losses—United States, 2000–2004. *Morbidity and Mortality Weekly Report*, *57*, 1226–1228.

Chaiken, J. M., & Chaiken, M. R. (1990). Drugs and predatory crime. In M. Tonry & J. G. Wilson (Eds.), *Drugs and crime* (pp. 203–239). Washington, DC: University of Chicago Press.

Chassin, L. (2008). Juvenile justice and substance use. *Future of Children*, *18*, 165–183. http://dx.doi.org/10.1353/foc.0.0017

Chassin, L., Dmitrieva, J., Modecki, K., Steinberg, L., Cauffman, E., Piquero, A. R., . . . Losoya, S. H. (2010). Does adolescent alcohol and marijuana use predict suppressed growth in psychosocial maturity among male juvenile offenders? *Psychology of Addictive Behaviors*, *24*, 48–60. http://dx.doi.org/10.1037/a0017692

Chassin, L., Knight, G., Vargas-Chanes, D., Losoya, S. H., & Naranjo, D. (2009). Substance use treatment outcomes in a sample of male serious juvenile offenders. *Journal of Substance Abuse Treatment*, *36*, 183–194. http://dx.doi.org/10.1016/j.jsat.2008.06.001

Chassin, L., Pillow, D. R., Curran, P. J., Molina, B. S., & Barrera, M., Jr. (1993). Relation of parental alcoholism to early adolescent substance use: A test of three mediating mechanisms. *Journal of Abnormal Psychology*, *102*, 3–19. http://dx.doi.org/10.1037/0021-843X.102.1.3

Chassin, L., Piquero, A. R., Losoya, S. H., Mansion, A. D., & Schubert, C. A. (2013). Joint consideration of distal and proximal predictors of premature mortality among serious juvenile offenders. *Journal of Adolescent Health*, *52*, 689–696. http://dx.doi.org/10.1016/j.jadohealth.2012.11.018

Chung, H. L., & Steinberg, L. (2006). Relations between neighborhood factors, parenting behaviors, peer deviance, and delinquency among serious juvenile offenders. *Developmental Psychology*, *42*, 319–331. http://dx.doi.org/10.1037/0012-1649.42.2.319

Coffey, C., Veit, F., Wolfe, R., Cini, E., & Patton, G. C. (2003). Mortality in young offenders: Retrospective cohort study. *BMJ*, *326*, 1064–1068. http://dx.doi.org/10.1136/bmj.326.7398.1064

Coley, R. L., Carrano, J., & Lewin-Bizan, S. (2011). Unpacking links between fathers' antisocial behaviors and children's behavior problems: Direct, indirect, and interactive effects. *Journal of Abnormal Child Psychology*, *39*, 791–804. http://dx.doi.org/10.1007/s10802-011-9496-4

Cornelius, J. R., Maisto, S. A., Pollock, N. K., Martin, C. S., Salloum, I. M., Lynch, K. G., & Clark, D. B. (2003). Rapid relapse generally follows treatment for substance use disorders among adolescents. *Addictive Behaviors*, *28*, 381–386. http://dx.doi.org/10.1016/S0306-4603(01)00247-7

Cottle, C. C., Lee, R. J., & Heilbrun, K. (2001). The prediction of criminal recidivism in juveniles: A meta-analysis. *Criminal Justice and Behavior*, *28*, 367–394. http://dx.doi.org/10.1177/0093854801028003005

Cuellar, A. E., & Cheema, J. (2012). As roughly 700,000 prisoners are released annually, about half will gain health coverage and care under federal laws. *Health Affairs*, *31*, 931–938. http://dx.doi.org/10.1377/hlthaff.2011.0501

D'Amico, E. J., Edelen, M. O., Miles, J. N., & Morral, A. R. (2008). The longitudinal association between substance use and delinquency among high-risk youth. *Drug and Alcohol Dependence*, *93*, 85–92. http://dx.doi.org/10.1016/j.drugalcdep.2007.09.006

Dani, J. A., & Harris, R. A. (2005). Nicotine addiction and comorbidity with alcohol abuse and mental illness. *Nature Neuroscience*, *8*, 1465–1470. http://dx.doi.org/10.1038/nn1580

Dawe, S., Davis, P., Lapworth, K., & McKetin, R. (2009). Mechanisms underlying aggressive and hostile behavior in amphetamine users. *Current Opinion in Psychiatry*, 22, 269–273. http://dx.doi.org/10.1097/YCO.0b013e32832a1dd4

Dawkins, M. P. (1997). Drug use and violent crime among adolescents. *Adolescence*, *32*, 395–405.

Dennis, M. L., Foss, M. A., & Scott, C. K. (2007). An eight-year perspective on the relationship between the duration of abstinence and other aspects of recovery. *Evaluation Review*, *31*, 585–612. http://dx.doi.org/10.1177/0193841X07307771

Dennis, M. L., Scott, C. K., Funk, R., & Foss, M. A. (2005). The duration and correlates of addiction and treatment careers. *Journal of Substance Abuse Treatment*, *28*(Suppl. 1), S51–S62. http://dx.doi.org/10.1016/j.jsat.2004.10.013

Denson, T. F., DeWall, C. N., & Finkel, E. J. (2012). Self-control and aggression. *Current Directions in Psychological Science*, *21*, 20–25. http://dx.doi.org/10.1177/0963721411429451

Derzon, J. H., & Lipsey, M. W. (1999). A synthesis of the relationship of marijuana use with delinquent and problem behaviors. *School Psychology International*, *20*, 57–68. http://dx.doi.org/10.1177/0143034399201005

de Wit, H., Crean, J., & Richards, J. B. (2000). Effects of d-amphetamine and ethanol on a measure of behavioral inhibition in humans. *Behavioral Neuroscience*, *114*, 830–837. http://dx.doi.org/10.1037/0735-7044.114.4.830

Dishion, T. J., Capaldi, D., Spracklen, K. M., & Li, F. (1995). Peer ecology of male adolescent drug use. *Development and Psychopathology*, *7*, 803–824. http://dx.doi.org/10.1017/S0954579400006854

Disney, E. R., Elkins, I. J., McGue, M., & Iacono, W. G. (1999). Effects of ADHD, conduct disorder, and gender on substance use and abuse in adolescence. *American Journal of Psychiatry*, *156*, 1515–1521.

Doherty, E. E., Green, K. M., & Ensminger, M. E. (2008). Investigating the long-term influence of adolescent delinquency on drug use initiation. *Drug and Alcohol Dependence*, *93*, 72–84. http://dx.doi.org/10.1016/j.drugalcdep.2007.08.018

Dukarm, C. P., Byrd, R. S., Auinger, P., & Weitzman, M. (1996). Illicit substance use, gender, and the risk of violent behavior among adolescents. *Archives of Pediatrics and Adolescent Medicine*, *150*, 797–801. http://dx.doi.org/10.1001/archpedi.1996.02170330023004

Elkins, I. J., McGue, M., & Iacono, W. G. (2007). Prospective effects of attention-deficit/hyperactivity disorder, conduct disorder, and sex on adolescent substance use and abuse. *Archives of General Psychiatry*, *64*, 1145–1152. http://dx.doi.org/10.1001/archpsyc.64.10.1145

Ellickson, P., Saner, H., & McGuigan, K. A. (1997). Profiles of violent youth: Substance use and other concurrent problems. *American Journal of Public Health*, *87*, 985–991. http://dx.doi.org/10.2105/AJPH.87.6.985

Ellickson, P. L., & McGuigan, K. A. (2000). Early predictors of adolescent violence. *American Journal of Public Health*, *90*, 566–572. http://dx.doi.org/10.2105/AJPH.90.4.566

Ennett, S. T., Bauman, K. E., Hussong, A., Faris, R., Foshee, V. A., Cai, L., & DuRant, R. H. (2006). The peer context of adolescent substance use: Findings from social network analysis. *Journal of Research on Adolescence*, *16*, 159–186. http://dx.doi.org/10.1111/j.1532-7795.2006.00127.x

Evans Cuellar, A., Kelleher, K. J., Rolls, J. A., & Pajer, K. (2005). Medicaid insurance policy for youths involved in the criminal justice system. *American Journal of Public Health*, *95*, 1707–1711. http://dx.doi.org/10.2105/AJPH.2004.056259

Fair Sentencing Act of 2010, Pub. L. 111–220, 124 Stat. 2372 (2010).

Farabee, D., Shen, H., Hser, Y. I., Grella, C. E., & Anglin, M. D. (2001). The effect of drug treatment on criminal behavior among adolescents in DATOS-A. *Journal of Adolescent Research*, *16*, 679–696. http://dx.doi.org/10.1177/0743558401166009

Feldstein Ewing, S. W., Venner, K. L., Mead, H. K., & Bryan, A. D. (2011). Exploring racial/ethnic differences in substance use: A preliminary theory-based investigation with juvenile justice-involved youth. *BMC Pediatrics*, *11*, 71–81. http://dx.doi.org/10.1186/1471-2431-11-71

Fergusson, D. M., & Boden, J. M. (2008). Cannabis use and later life outcomes. *Addiction*, *103*, 969–976. http://dx.doi.org/10.1111/j.1360-0443.2008.02221.x

Fergusson, D. M., Lynskey, M. T., & Horwood, L. J. (1996). Alcohol misuse and juvenile offending in adolescence. *Addiction*, *91*, 483–494. http://dx.doi.org/10.1111/j.1360-0443.1996.tb02302.x

Field, M., Christiansen, P., Cole, J., & Goudie, A. (2007). Delay discounting and the alcohol Stroop in heavy drinking adolescents. *Addiction*, *102*, 579–586. http://dx.doi.org/10.1111/j.1360-0443.2007.01743.x

Field, M., Wiers, R. W., Christiansen, P., Fillmore, M. T., & Verster, J. C. (2010). Acute alcohol effects on inhibitory control and implicit cognition: Implications for loss of control over drinking. *Alcoholism: Clinical and Experimental Research*, *34*, 1346–1352.

Fillmore, M. T., & Rush, C. R. (2002). Impaired inhibitory control of behavior in chronic cocaine users. *Drug and Alcohol Dependence*, *66*, 265–273. http://dx.doi.org/10.1016/S0376-8716(01)00206-X

Fleming, C. B., White, H. R., & Catalano, R. F. (2010). Romantic relationships and substance use in early adulthood: An examination of the influences of relationship type, partner substance use, and relationship quality. *Journal of Health and Social Behavior*, *51*, 153–167. http://dx.doi.org/10.1177/0022146510368930

Ford, J. A. (2005). Substance use, the social bond, and delinquency. *Sociological Inquiry*, *75*, 109–128. http://dx.doi.org/10.1111/j.1475-682X.2005.00114.x

Freedenthal, S., Vaughn, M. G., Jenson, J. M., & Howard, M. O. (2007). Inhalant use and suicidality among incarcerated youth. *Drug and Alcohol Dependence*, *90*, 81–88. http://dx.doi.org/10.1016/j.drugalcdep.2007.02.021

French, M. T., & Maclean, J. C. (2006). Underage alcohol use, delinquency, and criminal activity. *Health Economics*, *15*, 1261–1281. http://dx.doi.org/10.1002/hec.1126

Friedman, A. S. (1998). Substance use/abuse as a predictor to illegal and violent behavior: A review of the relevant literature. *Aggression and Violent Behavior, 3*, 339–355. http://dx.doi.org/10.1016/S1359-1789(97)00012-8

Gallagher, C. A., & Dobrin, A. (2006). Deaths in juvenile justice residential facilities. *Journal of Adolescent Health, 38*, 662–668. http://dx.doi.org/10.1016/j.jadohealth.2005.01.002

Galvan, A. (2010). Adolescent development of the reward system. *Frontiers in Human Neuroscience, 4*, 6.

Garavan, H., Kaufman, J. N., & Hester, R. (2008). Acute effects of cocaine on the neurobiology of cognitive control. *Philosophical Transactions of the Royal Society of London, Series B: Biological Sciences, 363*, 3267–3276. http://dx.doi.org/10.1098/rstb.2008.0106

Garland, A. F., Hough, R. L., McCabe, K. M., Yeh, M., Wood, P. A., & Aarons, G. A. (2001). Prevalence of psychiatric disorders in youths across five sectors of care. *Journal of the American Academy of Child and Adolescent Psychiatry, 40*, 409–418. http://dx.doi.org/10.1097/00004583-200104000-00009

Garland, A. F., Lau, A. S., Yeh, M., McCabe, K. M., Hough, R. L., & Landsverk, J. A. (2005). Racial and ethnic differences in utilization of mental health services among high-risk youths. *American Journal of Psychiatry, 162*, 1336–1343. http://dx.doi.org/10.1176/appi.ajp.162.7.1336

Giancola, P. R. (2000). Executive functioning: A conceptual framework for alcohol-related aggression. *Experimental and Clinical Psychopharmacology, 8*, 576–597. http://dx.doi.org/10.1037/1064-1297.8.4.576

Giancola, P. R. (2002). Alcohol-related aggression in men and women: The influence of dispositional aggressivity. *Journal of Studies on Alcohol, 63*, 696–708.

Giancola, P. R., Helton, E. L., Osborne, A. B., Terry, M. K., Fuss, A. M., & Westerfield, J. A. (2002). The effects of alcohol and provocation on aggressive behavior in men and women. *Journal of Studies on Alcohol, 63*, 64–73.

Giancola, P. R., Mezzich, A. C., & Tarter, R. E. (1998). Executive cognitive functioning, temperament, and antisocial behavior in conduct-disordered adolescent females. *Journal of Abnormal Psychology, 107*, 629–641. http://dx.doi.org/10.1037/0021-843X.107.4.629

Glisson, C., & Schoenwald, S. K. (2005). The ARC organizational and community intervention strategy for implementing evidence-based children's mental health treatments. *Mental Health Services Research, 7*, 243–259. http://dx.doi.org/10.1007/s11020-005-7456-1

Global Commission on Drug Policy. (2011). *War on drugs: Report of the Global Commission on Drug Policy*. Washington, DC: Author.

Goldstein, P. (2003). The drugs/violence nexus: A tripartite conceptual framework. In A. Bean (Ed.), *Crime: Critical concepts in sociology* (96–109). New York, NY: Routledge.

Grisso, T. (2008). Adolescent offenders with mental disorders. *Future of Children, 18*, 143–164. http://dx.doi.org/10.1353/foc.0.0016

Gruber, E., DiClemente, R. J., Anderson, M. M., & Lodico, M. (1996). Early drinking onset and its association with alcohol use and problem behavior in late adolescence. *Preventive Medicine, 25*, 293–300. http://dx.doi.org/10.1006/pmed.1996.0059

Gruber, S. A., & Yurgelun-Todd, D. A. (2005). Neuroimaging of marijuana smokers during inhibitory processing: A pilot investigation. *Cognitive Brain Research, 23*, 107–118. http://dx.doi.org/10.1016/j.cogbrainres.2005.02.016

Hancock, M., Tapscott, J. L., & Hoaken, P. N. (2010). Role of executive dysfunction in predicting frequency and severity of violence. *Aggressive Behavior, 36*, 338–349.

Hazen, A. L., Hough, R. L., Landsverk, J. A., & Wood, P. A. (2004). Use of mental health services by youths in public sectors of care. *Mental Health Services Research, 6*, 213–226. http://dx.doi.org/10.1023/B:MHSR.0000044747.54525.36

Henggeler, S. W., Clingempeel, W. G., Brondino, M. J., & Pickrel, S. G. (2002). Four-year follow-up of multisystemic therapy with substance-abusing and substance-dependent juvenile offenders. *Journal of the American Academy of Child and Adolescent Psychiatry, 41*, 868–874. http://dx.doi.org/10.1097/00004583-200207000-00021

Henggeler, S. W., Halliday-Boykins, C. A., Cunningham, P. B., Randall, J., Shapiro, S. B., & Chapman, J. E. (2006). Juvenile drug court: Enhancing outcomes by integrating evidence-based treatments. *Journal of Consulting and Clinical Psychology, 74*, 42–54. http://dx.doi.org/10.1037/0022-006X.74.1.42

Henneberger, A. K., Durkee, M. I., Truong, N., Atkins, A., & Tolan, P. H. (2013). The longitudinal relationship between peer violence and popularity and delinquency in adolescent boys: Examining effects by family functioning. *Journal of Youth and Adolescence, 42*, 1651–1660. http://dx.doi.org/10.1007/s10964-012-9859-3

Hicks, B. M., Krueger, R. F., Iacono, W. G., McGue, M., & Patrick, C. J. (2004). Family transmission and heritability of externalizing disorders: A twin-family study. *Archives of General Psychiatry, 61*, 922–928. http://dx.doi.org/10.1001/archpsyc.61.9.922

Hicks, B. M., Schalet, B. D., Malone, S. M., Iacono, W. G., & McGue, M. (2011). Psychometric and genetic architecture of substance use disorder and behavioral disinhibition measures for gene association studies. *Behavior Genetics*, *41*, 459–475. http://dx.doi.org/10.1007/s10519-010-9417-2

Hingson, R., Heeren, T., Winter, M., & Wechsler, H. (2005). Magnitude of alcohol-related mortality and morbidity among U.S. college students ages 18–24: Changes from 1998 to 2001. *Annual Review of Public Health*, *26*, 259–279. http://dx.doi.org/10.1146/annurev.publhealth.26.021304.144652

Hingson, R., Heeren, T., Zakocs, R., Winter, M., & Wechsler, H. (2003). Age of first intoxication, heavy drinking, driving after drinking and risk of unintentional injury among U.S. college students. *Journal of Studies on Alcohol*, *64*, 23–31.

Hittner, J. B., & Swickert, R. (2006). Sensation seeking and alcohol use: A meta-analytic review. *Addictive Behaviors*, *31*, 1383–1401. http://dx.doi.org/10.1016/j.addbeh.2005.11.004

Hoaken, P. N., Giancola, P. R., & Pihl, R. O. (1998). Executive cognitive functions as mediators of alcohol-related aggression. *Alcohol and Alcoholism*, *33*, 47–54. http://dx.doi.org/10.1093/oxfordjournals.alcalc.a008347

Hoaken, P. N., & Stewart, S. H. (2003). Drugs of abuse and the elicitation of human aggressive behavior. *Addictive Behaviors*, *28*, 1533–1554. http://dx.doi.org/10.1016/j.addbeh.2003.08.033

Hser, Y. I., Grella, C. E., Hubbard, R. L., Hsieh, S. C., Fletcher, B. W., Brown, B. S., & Anglin, M. D. (2001). An evaluation of drug treatments for adolescents in 4 US cities. *Archives of General Psychiatry*, *58*, 689–695. http://dx.doi.org/10.1001/archpsyc.58.7.689

Huizinga, D., Loeber, R., & Thornberry, T. P. (1993). Longitudinal study of delinquency, drug use, sexual activity, and pregnancy among children and youth in three cities. *Public Health Reports*, *108*(Suppl. 1), 90–96.

Hussong, A. M., Curran, P. J., Moffitt, T. E., Caspi, A., & Carrig, M. M. (2004). Substance abuse hinders desistance in young adults' antisocial behavior. *Development and Psychopathology*, *16*, 1029–1046. http://dx.doi.org/10.1017/S095457940404012X

Hussong, A. M., Zucker, R. A., Wong, M. M., Fitzgerald, H. E., & Puttler, L. I. (2005). Social competence in children of alcoholic parents over time. *Developmental Psychology*, *41*, 747–759. http://dx.doi.org/10.1037/0012-1649.41.5.747

Iacono, W. G., Carlson, S. R., Taylor, J., Elkins, I. J., & McGue, M. (1999). Behavioral disinhibition and the development of substance-use disorders: Findings from the Minnesota Twin Family Study. *Development and Psychopathology*, *11*, 869–900. http://dx.doi.org/10.1017/S0954579499002369

Inciardi, J. A. (1990). The crack-violence connection within a population of hard-core adolescent offenders. In M. De La Rosa, E. Y. Lambert, & B. Gropper (Eds.), *Drugs and violence: Causes, correlates, and consequences* (NIDA Research Monograph No. 103, pp. 90–111). Washington, DC: National Institute on Drug Abuse.

Jacobus, J., & Tapert, S. F. (2013). Neurotoxic effects of alcohol in adolescence. *Annual Review of Clinical Psychology*, *9*, 703–721. http://dx.doi.org/10.1146/annurev-clinpsy-050212-185610

Johnson, T. P., Cho, Y. I., Fendrich, M., Graf, I., Kelly-Wilson, L., & Pickup, L. (2004). Treatment need and utilization among youth entering the juvenile corrections system. *Journal of Substance Abuse Treatment*, *26*, 117–128. http://dx.doi.org/10.1016/S0740-5472(03)00164-8

Johnston, L. D., O'Malley, P. M., Bachman, J. G., & Schulenberg, J. E. (2005). *Monitoring the Future national results on adolescent drug use: Overview of key findings, 2004* (NIH Publication No. 05–5726). Bethesda, MD: National Institute on Drug Abuse.

Johnston, L. D., O'Malley, P. M., Bachman, J. G., & Schulenberg, J. E. (2013). *Monitoring the Future national results on drug use: 2012 overview, key findings on adolescent drug use*. Ann Arbor: University of Michigan, Institute for Social Research.

Karnik, N. S., Soller, M., Redlich, A., Silverman, M., Kraemer, H. C., Haapanen, R., & Steiner, H. (2009). Prevalence of and gender differences in psychiatric disorders among juvenile delinquents incarcerated for nine months. *Psychiatric Services*, *60*, 838–841. http://dx.doi.org/10.1176/appi.ps.60.6.838

Kerlikowske, G. (2012, November). *Address to National Harm Reduction Conference*. Speech presented at the Ninth National Harm Reduction Conference, Portland, OR.

Kim, J. Y. S., & Fendrich, M. (2002). Gender differences in juvenile arrestees' drug use, self-reported dependence, and perceived need for treatment. *Psychiatric Services*, *53*, 70–75. http://dx.doi.org/10.1176/appi.ps.53.1.70

King, K. M., Meehan, B. T., Trim, R. S., & Chassin, L. (2006). Marker or mediator? The effects of adolescent substance use on young adult educational attainment. *Addiction*, *101*, 1730–1740. http://dx.doi.org/10.1111/j.1360-0443.2006.01507.x

King, S. M., Keyes, M., Malone, S. M., Elkins, I., Legrand, L. N., Iacono, W. G., & McGue, M. (2009). Parental alcohol dependence and the transmission of adolescent behavioral disinhibition: A study of adoptive and non-adoptive families. *Addiction*, *104*, 578–586. http://dx.doi.org/10.1111/j.1360-0443.2008.02469.x

Kloos, A., Weller, R. A., Chan, R., & Weller, E. B. (2009). Gender differences in adolescent substance abuse.

Current Psychiatry Reports, *11*, 120–126. http://dx.doi.org/10.1007/s11920-009-0019-8

Kollins, S. H. (2003). Delay discounting is associated with substance use in college students. *Addictive Behaviors*, *28*, 1167–1173. http://dx.doi.org/10.1016/S0306-4603(02)00220-4

Komro, K. A., Williams, C. L., Forster, J. L., Perry, C. L., Farbakhsh, K., & Stigler, M. H. (1999). The relationship between adolescent alcohol use and delinquent and violent behaviors. *Journal of Child and Adolescent Substance Abuse*, *9*, 13–28. http://dx.doi.org/10.1300/J029v09n02_02

Lahey, B. B., & Waldman, I. D. (2003). A developmental propensity model of the origins of conduct problems during childhood and adolescence. In B. B. Lahey, T. E. Moffit, & A. Caspi (Eds.), *Causes of conduct disorder and juvenile delinquency* (pp. 76–117) New York, NY: Guilford Press.

Latimer, W. W., Stone, A. L., Voight, A., Winters, K. C., & August, G. J. (2002). Gender differences in psychiatric comorbidity among adolescents with substance use disorders. *Experimental and Clinical Psychopharmacology*, *10*, 310–315. http://dx.doi.org/10.1037/1064-1297.10.3.310

Lau, M. A., Pihl, R. O., & Peterson, J. B. (1995). Provocation, acute alcohol intoxication, cognitive performance, and aggression. *Journal of Abnormal Psychology*, *104*, 150–155. http://dx.doi.org/10.1037/0021-843X.104.1.150

Laub, J. H., & Sampson, R. J. (1993). Turning points in the life course: Why change matters to the study of crime. *Criminology*, *31*, 301–325. http://dx.doi.org/10.1111/j.1745-9125.1993.tb01132.x

Laudet, A. B., Morgen, K., & White, W. L. (2006). The role of social supports, spirituality, religiousness, life meaning and affiliation with 12-step fellowships in quality of life satisfaction among individuals in recovery from alcohol and drug problems. *Alcoholism Treatment Quarterly*, *24*, 33–73. http://dx.doi.org/10.1300/J020v24n01_04

Lehto, J. E., Juujärvi, P., Kooistra, L., & Pulkkinen, L. (2003). Dimensions of executive functioning: Evidence from children. *British Journal of Developmental Psychology*, *21*, 59–80. http://dx.doi.org/10.1348/026151003321164627

Lipsey, M. W. (2009). The primary factors that characterize effective interventions with juvenile offenders: A meta-analytic overview. *Victims and Offenders*, *4*, 124–147. http://dx.doi.org/10.1080/15564880802612573

Loeber, R., & Farrington, D. P. (2000). Young children who commit crime: Epidemiology, developmental origins, risk factors, early interventions, and policy implications. *Development and Psychopathology*, *12*, 737–762. http://dx.doi.org/10.1017/S0954579400004107

MacKillop, J., Amlung, M. T., Few, L. R., Ray, L. A., Sweet, L. H., & Munafò, M. R. (2011). Delayed reward discounting and addictive behavior: A meta-analysis. *Psychopharmacology*, *216*, 305–321. http://dx.doi.org/10.1007/s00213-011-2229-0

Maldonado-Molina, M. M., Reingle, J. M., & Jennings, W. G. (2011). Does alcohol use predict violent behaviors? The relationship between alcohol use and violence in a nationally representative longitudinal sample. *Youth Violence and Juvenile Justice*, *9*, 99–111. http://dx.doi.org/10.1177/1541204010384492

Males, M. (2012). *California youth crime plunges to all-time low*. San Francisco, CA: Center on Juvenile and Criminal Justice.

Malone, P. S., & Lansford, J. E. (2010). *A dynamic cascade model of the development of substance-use onset*. New York, NY: Wiley.

Marceau, K., Horwitz, B. N., Narusyte, J., Ganiban, J. M., Spotts, E. L., Reiss, D., & Neiderhiser, J. M. (2013). Gene-environment correlation underlying the association between parental negativity and adolescent externalizing problems. *Child Development*, *84*, 2031–2046. http://dx.doi.org/10.1111/cdev.12094

Marmorstein, N. R., Iacono, W. G., & McGue, M. (2009). Alcohol and illicit drug dependence among parents: Associations with offspring externalizing disorders. *Psychological Medicine*, *39*, 149–155. http://dx.doi.org/10.1017/S0033291708003085

Mason, W. A., Hitchings, J. E., & Spoth, R. L. (2007). Emergence of delinquency and depressed mood throughout adolescence as predictors of late adolescent problem substance use. *Psychology of Addictive Behaviors*, *21*, 13–24. http://dx.doi.org/10.1037/0893-164X.21.1.13

Mason, W. A., & Windle, M. (2002). Reciprocal relations between adolescent substance use and delinquency: A longitudinal latent variable analysis. *Journal of Abnormal Psychology*, *111*, 63–76. http://dx.doi.org/10.1037/0021-843X.111.1.63

McCurley, C., & Snyder, H. N. (2008). *Co-occurrence of substance use behaviors in youth*. http://dx.doi.org/10.1037/e531112008-001

McDonald, J., Schleifer, L., Richards, J. B., & de Wit, H. (2003). Effects of THC on behavioral measures of impulsivity in humans. *Neuropsychopharmacology*, *28*, 1356–1365. http://dx.doi.org/10.1038/sj.npp.1300176

McKetin, R., McLaren, J., Ridell, S., & Robins, L. (2006). *The relationship between methamphetamine use and violent behavior*. Sydney, Australia: Crime and Justice Bulletin, NSW Bureau of Crime Statistics and Research.

Mclaughlin, C. R., Daniel, J., & Joost, T. F. (2000). The relationship between substance use, drug selling, and lethal violence in 25 juvenile murderers. *Journal of Forensic Sciences*, *45*, 349–353.

McLellan, A. T., Carise, D., & Kleber, H. D. (2003). Can the national addiction treatment infrastructure support the public's demand for quality care? *Journal of Substance Abuse Treatment*, *25*, 117–121. http://dx.doi.org/10.1016/S0740-5472(03)00156-9

McLellan, A. T., Lewis, D. C., O'Brien, C. P., & Kleber, H. D. (2000). Drug dependence, a chronic medical illness: Implications for treatment, insurance, and outcomes evaluation. *JAMA*, *284*, 1689–1695. http://dx.doi.org/10.1001/jama.284.13.1689

McLellan, A. T., Woody, G. E., Metzger, D., McKay, J., Durrell, J., Alterman, A. I., & O'Brien, C. P. (1996). Evaluating the effectiveness of addiction treatments: Reasonable expectations, appropriate comparisons. *Milbank Quarterly*, *74*, 51–85. http://dx.doi.org/10.2307/3350433

Medina, K. L., Nagel, B. J., & Tapert, S. F. (2010). Abnormal cerebellar morphometry in abstinent adolescent marijuana users. *Psychiatry Research: Neuroimaging*, *182*, 152–159. http://dx.doi.org/10.1016/j.pscychresns.2009.12.004

Merikangas, K. R., He, J. P., Burstein, M., Swanson, S. A., Avenevoli, S., Cui, L., . . . Swendsen, J. (2010). Lifetime prevalence of mental disorders in U.S. adolescents: Results from the National Comorbidity Survey Replication—Adolescent Supplement (NCS-A). *Journal of the American Academy of Child and Adolescent Psychiatry*, *49*, 980–989. http://dx.doi.org/10.1016/j.jaac.2010.05.017

Mezzich, A. C., Tarter, R. E., Kirisci, L., Feske, U., Day, B. S., & Gao, Z. (2007). Reciprocal influence of parent discipline and child's behavior on risk for substance use disorder: A nine-year prospective study. *American Journal of Drug and Alcohol Abuse*, *33*, 851–867. http://dx.doi.org/10.1080/00952990701653842

Mitchell, O., Wilson, D. B., & MacKenzie, D. L. (2007). Does incarceration-based drug treatment reduce recidivism? A meta-analytic synthesis of the research. *Journal of Experimental Criminology*, *3*, 353–375. http://dx.doi.org/10.1007/s11292-007-9040-2

Moffitt, T. E. (1993). The neuropsychology of conduct disorder. *Development and Psychopathology*, *5*, 135–151. http://dx.doi.org/10.1017/S0954579400004302

Moffitt, T. E., Lynam, D. R., & Silva, P. A. (1994). Neuropsychological tests predicting persistent male delinquency. *Criminology*, *32*, 277–300. http://dx.doi.org/10.1111/j.1745-9125.1994.tb01155.x

Mokdad, A. H., Marks, J. S., Stroup, D. F., & Gerberding, J. L. (2004). Actual causes of death in the United States, 2000. *JAMA*, *291*, 1238–1245. http://dx.doi.org/10.1001/jama.291.10.1238

Monahan, K. C., Rhew, I. C., Hawkins, J. D., & Brown, E. C. (2014). Adolescent pathways to co-occurring problem behavior: The effects of peer delinquency and peer substance use. *Journal of Research on Adolescence*, *24*, 630–645. http://dx.doi.org/10.1111/jora.12053

Monahan, K. C., Steinberg, L., Cauffman, E., & Mulvey, E. P. (2009). Trajectories of antisocial behavior and psychosocial maturity from adolescence to young adulthood. *Developmental Psychology*, *45*, 1654–1668. http://dx.doi.org/10.1037/a0015862

Morgan, A. B., & Lilienfeld, S. O. (2000). A meta-analytic review of the relation between antisocial behavior and neuropsychological measures of executive function. *Clinical Psychology Review*, *20*, 113–136. http://dx.doi.org/10.1016/S0272-7358(98)00096-8

Mulvey, E. P., Schubert, C. A., & Chassin, L. (2010). *Substance use and offending in serious adolescent offenders*. Washington, DC: U.S. Department of Justice, Office of Justice Programs, Office of Juvenile Justice and Delinquency Prevention.

Mulvey, E. P., Schubert, C. A., & Chung, H. L. (2007). Service use after court involvement in a sample of serious adolescent offenders. *Children and Youth Services Review*, *29*, 518–544. http://dx.doi.org/10.1016/j.childyouth.2006.10.006

Mulvey, E. P., Steinberg, L., Fagan, J., Cauffman, E., Piquero, A. R., Chassin, L., . . . Losoya, S. H. (2004). Theory and research on desistance from antisocial activity among serious adolescent offenders. *Youth Violence and Juvenile Justice*, *2*, 213–236. http://dx.doi.org/10.1177/1541204004265864

Murray, J., Loeber, R., & Pardini, D. (2012). Parental involvement in the criminal justice system and the development of youth theft, marijuana use, depression, and poor academic performance. *Criminology*, *50*, 255–302. http://dx.doi.org/10.1111/j.1745-9125.2011.00257.x

Nagin, D. S., & Pogarsky, G. (2004). Time and punishment: Delayed consequences and criminal behavior. *Journal of Quantitative Criminology*, *20*, 295–317. http://dx.doi.org/10.1007/s10940-004-5866-1

Narusyte, J., Neiderhiser, J. M., Andershed, A. K., D'Onofrio, B. M., Reiss, D., Spotts, E., . . . Lichtenstein, P. (2011). Parental criticism and externalizing behavior problems in adolescents: The role of environment and genotype-environment correlation. *Journal of Abnormal Psychology*, *120*, 365–376. http://dx.doi.org/10.1037/a0021815

National Center on Addiction and Substance Abuse at Columbia University. (2004). *CASA analysis of the arrestee drug abuse monitoring program (ADAM) 2000* [Data file]. Washington, DC: U.S. Department of

Justice, Office of Justice Programs, National Institute of Justice.

National Conference of State Legislatures. (2010). *Medicaid for juvenile justice–involved children*. Retrieved from http://www.ncsl.org/documents/cj/jjguidebook-medicaid.pdf

National Institute on Drug Abuse. (2014). *Principles of adolescent substance use disorder treatment: A research-based guide*. Retrieved from http://www.drugabuse.gov/publications/principles-adolescent-substance-use-disorder-treatment-research-based-guide

Neal, D. J., & Fromme, K. (2007). Event-level covariation of alcohol intoxication and behavioral risks during the first year of college. *Journal of Consulting and Clinical Psychology*, *75*, 294–306. http://dx.doi.org/10.1037/0022-006X.75.2.294

Nigg, J. T., & Huang-Pollock, C. L. (2003). An early-onset model of the role of executive functions and intelligence in conduct disorder/delinquency. In B. B. Lahey, T. E. Moffitt, & A. Caspi (Eds.), *Causes of conduct disorder and juvenile delinquency* (pp. 227–253). New York, NY: Guilford Press.

Nissen, L. B., Butts, J. A., Merrigan, D., & Kraft, M. K. (2006). The RWJF Reclaiming Futures Initiative: Improving substance abuse interventions for justice-involved youths. *Juvenile and Family Court Journal*, *57*, 39–51. http://dx.doi.org/10.1111/j.1755-6988.2006.tb00130.x

Office of Juvenile Justice and Delinquency Prevention. (2014). *Statistical briefing book*. Retrieved from http://www.ojjdp.gov/ojstatbb/crime/JAR_Display.asp?ID=qa05200

Office of National Drug Control Policy. (2013). *National drug control strategy*. Retrieved from http://www.whitehouse.gov/sites/default/files/ndcs_2013.pdf

Parker, R. N., & Auerhahn, K. (1998). Alcohol, drugs, and violence. *Annual Review of Sociology*, *24*, 291–311. http://dx.doi.org/10.1146/annurev.soc.24.1.291

Parrott, D. J., & Giancola, P. R. (2006). The effect of past-year heavy drinking on alcohol-related aggression. *Journal of Studies on Alcohol and Drugs*, *67*, 122–130.

Paschall, M. J., & Fishbein, D. H. (2002). Executive cognitive functioning and aggression: A public health perspective. *Aggression and Violent Behavior*, *7*, 215–235. http://dx.doi.org/10.1016/S1359-1789(00)00044-6

Patient Protection and Affordable Care Act, Pub. L. 111-148, 42 U.S.C. §§ 18001–18121 (2010).

Patterson, G. R. (1993). Orderly change in a stable world: The antisocial trait as a chimera. *Journal of Consulting and Clinical Psychology*, *61*, 911–919. http://dx.doi.org/10.1037/0022-006X.61.6.911

Patton, G. C., Coffey, C., Lynskey, M. T., Reid, S., Hemphill, S., Carlin, J. B., & Hall, W. (2007). Trajectories of adolescent alcohol and cannabis use into young adulthood. *Addiction*, *102*, 607–615. http://dx.doi.org/10.1111/j.1360-0443.2006.01728.x

Peleg-Oren, N., Saint-Jean, G., Cardenas, G. A., Tammara, H., & Pierre, C. (2009). Drinking alcohol before age 13 and negative outcomes in late adolescence. *Alcoholism: Clinical and Experimental Research*, *33*, 1966–1972. http://dx.doi.org/10.1111/j.1530-0277.2009.01035.x

Petry, N. M. (2001). Delay discounting of money and alcohol in actively using alcoholics, currently abstinent alcoholics, and controls. *Psychopharmacology*, *154*, 243–250. http://dx.doi.org/10.1007/s002130000638

Phillips, M. D. (2012). Assessing the impact of drug use and drug selling on violent offending in a panel of delinquent youth. *Journal of Drug Issues*, *42*, 298–316. http://dx.doi.org/10.1177/0022042612456017

Plüddemann, A., Flisher, A. J., McKetin, R., Parry, C., & Lombard, C. (2010). Methamphetamine use, aggressive behavior and other mental health issues among high-school students in Cape Town, South Africa. *Drug and Alcohol Dependence*, *109*, 14–19. http://dx.doi.org/10.1016/j.drugalcdep.2009.11.021

Prochaska, J. J., Delucchi, K., & Hall, S. M. (2004). A meta-analysis of smoking cessation interventions with individuals in substance abuse treatment or recovery. *Journal of Consulting and Clinical Psychology*, *72*, 1144–1156. http://dx.doi.org/10.1037/0022-006X.72.6.1144

Randall, J., & Cunningham, P. B. (2003). Multisystemic therapy: A treatment for violent substance-abusing and substance-dependent juvenile offenders. *Addictive Behaviors*, *28*, 1731–1739. http://dx.doi.org/10.1016/j.addbeh.2003.08.045

Reed, S. C., Levin, F. R., & Evans, S. M. (2012). Alcohol increases impulsivity and abuse liability in heavy drinking women. *Experimental and Clinical Psychopharmacology*, *20*, 454–465. http://dx.doi.org/10.1037/a0029087

Resnick, M. D., Ireland, M., & Borowsky, I. (2004). Youth violence perpetration: What protects? What predicts? Findings from the National Longitudinal Study of Adolescent Health. *Journal of Adolescent Health*, *35*, 424e1–10.

Reynolds, B. (2006). A review of delay-discounting research with humans: Relations to drug use and gambling. *Behavioural Pharmacology*, *17*, 651–667. http://dx.doi.org/10.1097/FBP.0b013e3280115f99

Reynolds, B., Richards, J. B., & de Wit, H. (2006). Acute-alcohol effects on the experiential discounting task (EDT) and a question-based measure of delay discounting. *Pharmacology, Biochemistry and*

Behavior, 83, 194–202. http://dx.doi.org/10.1016/j.pbb.2006.01.007

Reynolds, B., & Schiffbauer, R. (2004). Measuring state changes in human delay discounting: An experiential discounting task. *Behavioural Processes*, *67*, 343–356. http://dx.doi.org/10.1016/j.beproc.2004.06.003

Richards, J. B., Zhang, L., Mitchell, S. H., & de Wit, H. (1999). Delay or probability discounting in a model of impulsive behavior: Effect of alcohol. *Journal of the Experimental Analysis of Behavior*, *71*, 121–143. http://dx.doi.org/10.1901/jeab.1999.71-121

Roberti, J. W. (2004). A review of behavioral and biological correlates of sensation seeking. *Journal of Research in Personality*, *38*, 256–279. http://dx.doi.org/10.1016/S0092-6566(03)00067-9

Robertson, A. A., Dill, P. L., Husain, J., & Undesser, C. (2004). Prevalence of mental illness and substance abuse disorders among incarcerated juvenile offenders in Mississippi. *Child Psychiatry and Human Development*, *35*, 55–74. http://dx.doi.org/10.1023/B:CHUD.0000039320.40382.91

Roettger, M. E., Swisher, R. R., Kuhl, D. C., & Chavez, J. (2011). Paternal incarceration and trajectories of marijuana and other illegal drug use from adolescence into young adulthood: Evidence from longitudinal panels of males and females in the United States. *Addiction*, *106*, 121–132. http://dx.doi.org/10.1111/j.1360-0443.2010.03110.x

Romero-Daza, N., Weeks, M., & Singer, M. (2003). "Nobody gives a damn if I live or die": Violence, drugs, and street-level prostitution in inner-city Hartford, Connecticut. *Medical Anthropology*, *22*, 233–259. http://dx.doi.org/10.1080/01459740306770

Schuckit, M. A., Hesselbrock, V., Tipp, J., Anthenelli, R., Bucholz, K., & Radziminski, S.; Collaborative Study on the Genetics of Alcoholism. (1994). A comparison of *DSM–III–R*, *DSM–IV*, and *ICD–10* substance use disorders diagnoses in 1922 men and women subjects in the COGA study. *Addiction*, *89*, 1629–1638. http://dx.doi.org/10.1111/j.1360-0443.1994.tb03764.x

Second Change Act of 2007, Pub. L. 110–199, 122 Stat. 657 (2007).

Seddon, T. (2006). Drugs, crime and social exclusion: Social context and social theory in British drugs–crime research. *British Journal of Criminology*, *46*, 680–703. http://dx.doi.org/10.1093/bjc/azi079

Shiffman, S., Stone, A. A., & Hufford, M. R. (2008). Ecological momentary assessment. *Annual Review of Clinical Psychology*, *4*, 1–32. http://dx.doi.org/10.1146/annurev.clinpsy.3.022806.091415

Shufelt, J. L., & Cocozza, J. J. (2006). *Youth with mental health disorders in the juvenile justice system: Results from a multi-state prevalence study* (Research and Program Brief). Delmar, NY: National Center for Mental Health and Juvenile Justice.

Simons-Morton, B., Haynie, D. L., Crump, A. D., Eitel, S. P., & Saylor, K. E. (2001). Peer and parent influences on smoking and drinking among early adolescents. *Health Education and Behavior*, *28*, 95–107. http://dx.doi.org/10.1177/109019810102800109

Smith, R. F. (2003). Animal models of periadolescent substance abuse. *Neurotoxicology and Teratology*, *25*, 291–301. http://dx.doi.org/10.1016/S0892-0362(02)00349-5

Snyder, H., & Sickmund, M. (1999). *Juvenile offenders and victims: 1999 national report*. Washington, DC: Office of Juvenile Justice and Delinquency Prevention.

Snyder, H. N., & Sickmund, M. (2006). *Juvenile offenders and victims: 2006 national report*. Washington, DC: Office of Juvenile Justice and Delinquency Prevention.

Spear, L. P. (2011). Adolescent neurobehavioral characteristics, alcohol sensitivities, and intake: Setting the stage for alcohol use disorders? *Child Development Perspectives*, *5*, 231–238. http://dx.doi.org/10.1111/j.1750-8606.2011.00182.x

Steinberg, L. (2008). A social neuroscience perspective on adolescent risk taking. *Developmental Review*, *28*, 78–106. http://dx.doi.org/10.1016/j.dr.2007.08.002

Steinberg, L., & Cauffman, E. (1996). Maturity of judgment in adolescence: Psychosocial factors in adolescent decision making. *Law and Human Behavior*, *20*, 249–272. http://dx.doi.org/10.1007/BF01499023

Steinberg, L., Fletcher, A., & Darling, N. (1994). Parental monitoring and peer influences on adolescent substance use. *Pediatrics*, *93*, 1060–1064.

Steinberg, L., Graham, S., O'Brien, L., Woolard, J., Cauffman, E., & Banich, M. (2009). Age differences in future orientation and delay discounting. *Child Development*, *80*, 28–44. http://dx.doi.org/10.1111/j.1467-8624.2008.01244.x

Stevens, S. J., Estrada, B., Murphy, B. S., McKnight, K. M., & Tims, F. (2004). Gender difference in substance use, mental health, and criminal justice involvement of adolescents at treatment entry and at three, six, 12 and 30 month follow-up. *Journal of Psychoactive Drugs*, *36*, 13–25. http://dx.doi.org/10.1080/02791072.2004.10399720

Stevens, S. J., Murphy, B. S., & McKnight, K. (2003). Traumatic stress and gender differences in relationship to substance abuse, mental health, physical health, and HIV risk behavior in a sample of adolescents enrolled in drug treatment. *Child Maltreatment*, *8*, 46–57. http://dx.doi.org/10.1177/1077559502239611

Stinson, F. S., Ruan, W. J., Pickering, R., & Grant, B. F. (2006). Cannabis use disorders in the USA: Prevalence, correlates and co-morbidity. *Psychological Medicine*, *36*, 1447–1460. http://dx.doi.org/10.1017/S0033291706008361

Stitzer, M., & Petry, N. (2006). Contingency management for treatment of substance abuse. *Annual Review of Clinical Psychology*, *2*, 411–434. http://dx.doi.org/10.1146/annurev.clinpsy.2.022305.095219

Stout, R. L., Rubin, A., Zwick, W., Zywiak, W., & Bellino, L. (1999). Optimizing the cost-effectiveness of alcohol treatment: A rationale for extended case monitoring. *Addictive Behaviors*, *24*, 17–35. http://dx.doi.org/10.1016/S0306-4603(98)00029-X

Stouthamer-Loeber, M., Wei, E., Loeber, R., & Masten, A. S. (2004). Desistance from persistent serious delinquency in the transition to adulthood. *Development and Psychopathology*, *16*, 897–918. http://dx.doi.org/10.1017/S0954579404040064

Sullivan, M. A., & Covey, L. S. (2002). Nicotine dependence: The role for antidepressants and anxiolytics. *Current Opinion in Investigational Drugs (London, England: 2000)*, *3*, 262–271.

Swahn, M. H., & Donovan, J. E. (2004). Correlates and predictors of violent behavior among adolescent drinkers. *Journal of Adolescent Health*, *34*, 480–492. http://dx.doi.org/10.1016/j.jadohealth.2003.08.018

Taylor, D. H., Hasselblad, V., Henley, S. J., Thun, M. J., & Sloan, F. A. (2002). Benefits of smoking cessation for longevity. *American Journal of Public Health*, *92*, 990–996.

Teplin, L. A., Abram, K. M., McClelland, G. M., Dulcan, M. K., & Mericle, A. A. (2002). Psychiatric disorders in youth in juvenile detention. *Archives of General Psychiatry*, *59*, 1133–1143. http://dx.doi.org/10.1001/archpsyc.59.12.1133

Theobald, D., & Farrington, D. P. (2009). Effects of getting married on offending results from a prospective longitudinal survey of males. *European Journal of Criminology*, *6*, 496–516. http://dx.doi.org/10.1177/1477370809341226

van den Bree, M. B., & Pickworth, W. B. (2005). Risk factors predicting changes in marijuana involvement in teenagers. *Archives of General Psychiatry*, *62*, 311–319. http://dx.doi.org/10.1001/archpsyc.62.3.311

Wagner, E. F. (1996). Substance use and violent behavior in adolescence. *Aggression and Violent Behavior*, *1*, 375–387. http://dx.doi.org/10.1016/S1359-1789(96)00008-0

Washburn, J. J., Teplin, L. A., Voss, L. S., Simon, C. D., Abram, K. M., & McClelland, G. M. (2008). Psychiatric disorders among detained youths: A comparison of youths processed in juvenile court and adult criminal court. *Psychiatric Services*, *59*, 965–973. http://dx.doi.org/10.1176/appi.ps.59.9.965

Wasserman, G. A., McReynolds, L. S., Ko, S. J., Katz, L. M., & Carpenter, J. R. (2005). Gender differences in psychiatric disorders at juvenile probation intake. *American Journal of Public Health*, *95*, 131–137. http://dx.doi.org/10.2105/AJPH.2003.024737

Watkins, K., Pincus, H. A., Tanielian, T. L., & Lloyd, J. (2003). Using the chronic care model to improve treatment of alcohol use disorders in primary care settings. *Journal of Studies on Alcohol and Drugs*, *64*, 209–218.

Weafer, J., & Fillmore, M. T. (2008). Individual differences in acute alcohol impairment of inhibitory control predict ad libitum alcohol consumption. *Psychopharmacology*, *201*, 315–324. http://dx.doi.org/10.1007/s00213-008-1284-7

Weerman, F. M. (2011). Delinquent peers in context: A longitudinal-network analysis of selection and influence effects. *Criminology*, *49*, 253–286. http://dx.doi.org/10.1111/j.1745-9125.2010.00223.x

Weiner, M. D., Sussman, S., Sun, P., & Dent, C. (2005). Explaining the link between violence perpetration, victimization and drug use. *Addictive Behaviors*, *30*, 1261–1266. http://dx.doi.org/10.1016/j.addbeh.2004.12.007

Wetherill, R. R., Squeglia, L. M., Yang, T. T., & Tapert, S. F. (2013). A longitudinal examination of adolescent response inhibition: Neural differences before and after the initiation of heavy drinking. *Psychopharmacology*, *230*, 663–671. http://dx.doi.org/10.1007/s00213-013-3198-2

Wikstrom, P. O. H., & Loeber, R. (2000). Do disadvantaged neighborhoods cause well-adjusted children to become adolescent delinquents? A study of male juvenile serious offending, individual risk, and protective factors, and neighborhood context. *Criminology*, *38*, 1109–1142. http://dx.doi.org/10.1111/j.1745-9125.2000.tb01416.x

Windle, M. (1992). A longitudinal study of stress buffering for adolescent problem behaviors. *Developmental Psychology*, *28*, 522–530. http://dx.doi.org/10.1037/0012-1649.28.3.522

Wittchen, H. U., Fröhlich, C., Behrendt, S., Günther, A., Rehm, J., Zimmermann, P., . . . Perkonigg, A. (2007). Cannabis use and cannabis use disorders and their relationship to mental disorders: A 10-year prospective-longitudinal community study in adolescents. *Drug and Alcohol Dependence*, *88*(Suppl. 1), S60–S70. http://dx.doi.org/10.1016/j.drugalcdep.2006.12.013

Xue, Y., Zimmerman, M. A., & Cunningham, R. (2009). Relationship between alcohol use and violent behavior among urban African American youths from adolescence to emerging adulthood:

A longitudinal study. *American Journal of Public Health*, *99*, 2041–2048. http://dx.doi.org/10.2105/AJPH.2008.147827

Young, S. E., Friedman, N. P., Miyake, A., Willcutt, E. G., Corley, R. P., Haberstick, B. C., & Hewitt, J. K. (2009). Behavioral disinhibition: Liability for externalizing spectrum disorders and its genetic and environmental relation to response inhibition across adolescence. *Journal of Abnormal Psychology*, *118*, 117–130. http://dx.doi.org/10.1037/a0014657

Young, S. E., Stallings, M. C., Corley, R. P., Krauter, K. S., & Hewitt, J. K. (2000). Genetic and environmental influences on behavioral disinhibition. *American Journal of Medical Genetics*, *96*, 684–695. http://dx.doi.org/10.1002/1096-8628(20001009)96:5<684::AID-AJMG16>3.0.CO;2-G

Zuckerman, M. (1994). *Behavioral expressions and biosocial bases of sensation seeking*. New York, NY: Cambridge University Press.

CHAPTER 14

GANGS

Wesley G. Jennings and Jennifer M. Reingle Gonzalez

Gang membership is one of the most well-known correlates of offending, and this relationship has been documented for nearly a century. Despite this considerable amount of research, the linkages between gang membership and offending (and victimization, to a lesser extent) have been described as complex. We begin this chapter by discussing the definitional–conceptual and measurement discrepancies regarding how to best measure gang membership and reviewing the previous research on the prevalence of gangs. We follow this discussion with a summary of the prevalence of gang membership across gender and race/ethnicity with a focus on the similarities and differences in gang membership across these important demographic variables. Next, we separately consider the association between gang membership and violent offending and violent victimization. We then proceed with a considerable amount of discussion of the prevailing theoretical explanations for why individuals join gangs and why gang membership is a risk factor for offending (and victimization). Finally, we conclude the chapter with a review of the prevention and intervention efforts that have been undertaken to address gang problems, with a particular focus on highlighting some of the successes of these strategies.

CONCEPTUAL DEBATE: WHAT IS A GANG?

In an attempt to measure the correlates and effects of gang membership, a number of definitions have been proposed to measure the construct. Gang members have been distinguished from other peer groups on the basis of their (a) participation in criminal behavior; (b) shared identity; and (c) naming, symbols, colors, or other means of distinguishing themselves and their territory from other groups (Esbensen, 2000; Spergel, 1993; Spergel et al., 1994; White, 2002). A commonly used definition proposed by Klein, Weerman, and Thornberry (2006) described gangs as "any durable, street-oriented youth group whose involvement in illegal activity is part of their group identity" (p. 414). However, this type of definition did not exist previously, because earlier gang researchers had not focused on the illegal and violent behavior that is typically associated with gang membership as it is examined today.

For example, Thrasher (1963) proposed a definition that continually influences how gang membership is measured today. In this work, Thrasher suggested that to be characterized as a gang, a group of adolescents must (a) have organization and a sense of solidarity distinguishing them from mobs, (b) be responsive to outside threats, (c) create a self-identity, and (d) identify and defend a territory. Later, Klein (1971) argued that illegal activity should be added to this list of requirements. Specifically, Klein proposed that gang members are a group of adolescents (generally younger than age 18) who are (a) perceived to be a "distinct aggregation" by peers in their community, (b) self-identify as a group (and often have a name), and (c) report involvement in delinquency to the extent that neighborhood residents become unhappy and law enforcement becomes involved. Participation in illegal activities as a necessary factor for gang

http://dx.doi.org/10.1037/14643-014
APA Handbook of Psychology and Juvenile Justice, K. Heilbrun (Editor-in-Chief)

membership remains an issue for debate (Esbensen et al., 2010; Spergel, 1993; Spergel et al., 1994; White, 2002).

MEASUREMENT DEBATE: HOW DO YOU MEASURE GANG MEMBERSHIP?

Many definitions have been used to measure gang membership. Many surveys will simply ask, "Are you a member of a named gang?" or "Do you belong to a gang?" with follow-up items including gang names and characteristics (Ball & Curry, 1995). Others have built on this definition and categorized gang members on the basis of self-reported gang membership and self-proclaimed involvement of the gang in illegal activities (Huizinga, Loeber, & Thornberry, 1995). Although these questions incorporate self-identifying measures of gang membership, they do not evaluate the violent behavior that is often closely linked with gang membership.

Some surveys of adolescent youths, including Monitoring the Future (Johnston, O'Malley, Bachman, & Schulenberg, 2010) and the National Longitudinal Survey of Adolescent Health (K. M. Harris et al., 2009), have measured gang membership as participation in a group fight, a measure of assault that has been associated with gang membership. Other surveys, including the National Youth Survey (Elliott, 1984), have used a similar construct of gang fight. There is some evidence that the distinction between group fighting and gang fighting may produce different results and prevalence estimates (Esbensen, Winfree, He, & Taylor, 2001; Menard & Elliott, 1993).

Differences in the operationalization of gang membership will lead to differences in prevalence estimates; however, whether these differences in prevalence are due to differences in actual gang membership or in the internal validity of the gang membership construct may not be clear. For example, in three urban communities (Seattle, WA; Rochester, NY; and Denver, CO), drastically different prevalence rates were estimated. In Seattle, Hill, Lui, and Hawkins (2001) found 15.3% of their sample to be self-reported gang members. In Rochester, Thornberry (1998) found that more than 30% of the high-risk sample were self-reported gang members. However, in Denver, Huizinga et al. (1995) found that 15% of adolescents surveyed were gang members, requiring self-identification as a gang member as well as participation in illegal activities. Using the measure of group fighting as an indicator of gang membership, the National Longitudinal Study of Adolescent Health reported that rates of group fighting varied from 19.9% (Wave I, age 16) to 4.0% (Wave IV, age 26; K. M. Harris et al., 2009).

Whether these differences were due to community-level differences, sampling, sample characteristics, time, or measurement of the gang membership construct was not clear. To address this issue, Esbensen et al. (2001) categorized gang members (e.g., wannabe, former, and active) on the basis of adolescents' responses to a number of gang-related items. For example, gang members were classified as to whether they were currently or had previously been a gang member; whether their gang engaged in illegal or delinquent activity; whether their gang was organized; and whether their gang had initiation rites, symbols or colors, and organized leaders (Esbensen et al., 2001). These categories produced substantial differences in the prevalence estimates that were derived as a result (2%–17% of the sample would be categorized as gang members). In addition, Winfree, Fuller, Vigil, and Mays (1992) found that the less restrictive definition of gang member (e.g., self-identified) explained more variance in gang-related crime and predicted gang-related crime more strongly than the more restrictive definition (e.g., initiation rites, symbols, and colors). Overall, there is some disagreement and discrepancy in how gang membership has been operationalized, and these differences may have a substantial impact on estimates of prevalence and effect sizes.

PREVALENCE OF GANGS

During the past decade, the United States has witnessed a dramatic increase in gang membership among adolescents and young adults. According to a national survey of law enforcement agencies in 2008, approximately 32.4% (or 3,330) of all cities cited a problem with gang activity within their jurisdiction (Egley, Howell, & Moore, 2010). These figures translate to 774,000 gang members and

27,900 active gangs in 2008, a 15% increase from 2002 (Egley et al., 2010). The estimated number of gangs and gang members peaked in 1996 and declined until 2001, according to National Youth Gang Center reports (Egley & O'Donnell, 2008). Since 2001, the estimated number of gangs and gang members has steadily increased (Egley & O'Donnell, 2008). Considering that these numbers are derived from police encounters with gangs and their members, the actual numbers are assumed to be substantially higher when undetected gang activities are considered.

The prevalence of gang membership varies substantially on the basis of population and geographical location. School-based surveys of gang membership have generally reported prevalence estimates of 10% to 15% (Esbensen, Peterson, Taylor, & Freng, 2010; K. M. Harris et al., 2009; Hill et al., 2001). However, the Rochester Youth Development Study (Thornberry, 1998), for example, found that nearly 30% of the adolescent population qualified as gang members in Rochester, New York. Urban locations have more gang members than rural locations (Esbensen et al., 2010), although gang membership is not limited to inner-city neighborhoods.

Despite the fact that gang members account for a small proportion of the adolescent population, they account for the majority of violent and delinquent activities (Farrington & Loeber, 2000; Hill et al., 2001). The literature has suggested that adolescents who join gangs are more likely to be violent, and engage in delinquent acts more frequently, than non–gang members (Stretesky & Pogrebin, 2007; Thornberry, 1998). According to Thornberry (1998), the Rochester Youth Development Study reported that although less than one third of the population were members of gangs, this group of adolescents was responsible for as much as 80% of the delinquent behavior of the entire sample. Specifically, compared with non–gang members, gang members were responsible for 86% of serious delinquent acts, 69% of violent delinquency, and 70% of drug sales (Thornberry, 1998). Similarly, Hill et al. (2001) reported that gang members are more than 10 times as likely than non–gang members to rob others, five times more likely to sell drugs, four times more likely to be arrested and engage in felony theft, three times more likely to be involved in breaking and entering and assault, and two times more likely to use marijuana and binge drink than non–gang members.

GENDER DIFFERENCES IN GANG MEMBERSHIP

The vast majority of research on gangs has been conducted with boys because they comprise the majority of gang members in the United States. Surveys of law enforcement have estimated that more than 90% of gang members are boys (Curry, Ball, & Fox, 1994; Egley & Ritz, 2006; Huff, 1998). Specifically, Curry et al. (1994) conducted a study of 61 police departments in 79 cities nationwide and found that only 4% of gang members were girls. However, self-report surveys of girls have revealed that more girls are members of gangs than law enforcement data project. Self-reports among high-risk samples of adolescents living in impoverished conditions have indicated that nearly 31% of all gang members are girls (Bjerregaard & Smith, 1993). Even general population samples of adolescents have indicated that girls are more involved in gang activity than expected, with prevalence estimates ranging from 21% to 46% (Cohen, Williams, Bekelman, & Crosse, 1995; Esbensen & Huizinga, 1993; K. M. Harris et al., 2009). According to a multisite national gang prevention intervention conducted by Esbensen et al. (2010), girls represented one third of gang members; however, only 6% of girls in the study reported gang membership (compared with 12% of boys). These findings provide some evidence that boys are twice as likely to be involved in gangs as girls.

There is evidence that girls' duration of gang membership is shorter than boys'. Many intervention studies have found that self-reported gang membership among girls (and boys) decreases with age (Esbensen & Huizinga, 1993; Thornberry, Krohn, Lizotte, & Chard-Wierschem, 1993). Other survey data have supported this claim, because girls appear to be most active in gangs between the ages of 13 and 16 (Esbensen et al., 2010; K. M. Harris et al., 2009; M. G. Harris, 1994; Moore & Hagedorn, 1996). Overall, it is clear that the prevalence and duration of gang membership differ by gender.

There also appear to be gender differences in violence participation within gangs. Boys are generally more violent within gangs, but girls who are members of gangs are more violent than non–gang member boys (Bjerregaard & Smith, 1993; Huizinga, 1997). Boys in gangs are responsible for most homicides and use firearms more frequently than girls, and girls are more active in other types of violence (including hitting someone, participating in group fights, and general and serious violence) and use other types of weapons (such as knives and razors; Campbell, 1991; Esbensen et al., 2010; W. B. Miller, 2001). The composition of the gang may also alter girls' behavior within the gang. Using Gang Resistance Education and Training (GREAT) data, Esbensen et al. (2010) found that girls who were members of gangs consisting of mostly boys had higher rates of violence than boys in boy-only gangs. Overall, the evidence on gender differences suggests that girls are active gang members, and their violent behavior within gangs is different from boys' behavior.

RACIAL/ETHNIC DIFFERENCES IN GANG MEMBERSHIP

The majority of gang members self-identify as African American or Hispanic, and these racial/ethnic disparities in gang membership differ between self-report data sources and official records (Hill et al., 2001; Huff, 1998). More specifically, some evidence has shown that African American youths underreport their gang membership status in self-report surveys (Farrington, Loeber, & Stouthamer-Loeber, 2003). Official records have suggested that African Americans and Hispanics are the groups most present in gangs (Elliott & Ageton, 1980; Walker, Spohn, & DeLone, 2006); however, these reports may be problematic because some evidence exists that law enforcement may systematically target African Americans and Hispanics more than Whites (Smith & Alpert, 2007). Despite the potential for overrepresentation of racial and ethnic minorities in official records, some similarities between self-reports and official records remain.

For instance, both self-report methods and official records agree that membership in predominantly Hispanic gangs has been on the rise (Howell & Moore, 2010), and substantial evidence has shown that the risk factors for Hispanic gang membership are different than those for membership in predominantly Caucasian or African American gangs (Curry & Spergel, 1992; Freng & Esbensen, 2007; Knox, McCurrie, Laskey, & Tromanheuser, 1996). For example, social control and street socialization (e.g., family, peer, school, and law enforcement characteristics) were important predictors for African Americans and Hispanics, whereas ecological and economic stress variables (including parental education, cultural identity, and social isolation) were more significant predictors of gang membership for Whites (Freng & Esbensen, 2007). In addition, Hispanics and African Americans with lower commitment to school, fewer positive attitudes toward law enforcement, and higher levels of street socialization were more likely to report gang membership (Freng & Esbensen, 2007).

In an attempt to explain racial/ethnic differences in violent behavior, McNulty and Bellair (2003) found that gang membership explained a large proportion of the ethnic differences in serious violence (McNulty & Bellair, 2003), and the variables explaining violence differed by ethnic group. Specifically, community disadvantage explained most of the variance in violence among African Americans, and gang membership explained violence among Hispanics (McNulty & Bellair, 2003). In this study (using a nationally representative, school-based sampling design), Hispanics reported the second highest levels of gang involvement (10%), next to Native Americans (12%). Overall, there appear to be differences in the causes of violence by ethnicity. Gang membership may play a role in violence, although this role may differ by racial/ethnic group.

Preliminary evidence has also indicated that violent behavior by gangs varies by the racial or ethnic composition of the gang. Although most studies of gangs have been conducted with racially or ethnically homogeneous gangs, the few studies that compare violence by race/ethnicity have tended to report differences in violent behavior (Curry & Spergel, 1992; Esbensen et al., 2010; Lyons, Henggeller, & Hall, 1992). For instance, Lyons et al. (1992) found that Hispanic gang members had lower rates of violent behavior than Whites, and Curry and Spergel (1992) found that African Americans engaged in criminal activity more frequently than Hispanics. More recently, Esbensen et al. (2010) found that there were few differences in violent offending by race/ethnicity but that White gang members were less likely to be involved in group fights than African Americans. Overall, there is no consensus in the literature as to whether racial or ethnic differences in gang violence exist, but it does appear that African Americans in gangs are at the greatest risk for violent behavior, followed by Whites and Hispanics.

GANG MEMBERSHIP AS A RISK FACTOR FOR VIOLENCE

Gang membership is a serious risk factor for violent delinquency and many other high-risk behaviors (Knox et al., 1996; Thornberry, Huizinga, & Loeber, 1995). Gangs are responsible for a disproportionate amount of criminal behavior, although not all of this criminal behavior includes violence (Esbensen et al., 2010; Thornberry & Burch, 1997). The majority of these nonviolent offenses include drug-related crimes, such as the sale and possession of drugs and drug paraphernalia (Block & Block, 1995).

Although many gangs do engage in violent behavior, violence is not inherent in all gangs (Howell, 1998; J. Miller, 1998). Some gangs specialize in drug trafficking and dealing, other gangs focus on violence, and some gangs are involved in multiple types of criminal behavior (Howell, 1998; J. Miller, 1998; Spergel, Wa, & Sosa, 2005d). However, the overwhelming majority of gang members participate in and are at risk for violence, drug use and drug dealing, and criminal activity.

Compared with non–gang members, gang members have higher rates of violent offending. For example, gang members reported significantly higher levels of general delinquency, index offenses, aggression, and school delinquency (e.g., hit a teacher or strong-armed students) than non–gang members (Egley & Ritz, 2006; Lyons et al., 1992; Taylor, Peterson, Esbensen, & Freng, 2007). According to Esbensen et al. (2010), gang members are more likely than non–gang members to hit (78% vs. 44%) and rob (26% vs. 3%), attack others with a weapon (47% vs. 9%), participate in group fighting (79% vs. 11%), and have shot at somebody (30% vs. 2%). Within gender groups, both boys and girls who were involved in gangs were approximately 3 times more likely to be involved in general violence and serious violence than non–gang members (Esbensen et al., 2010). Given this evidence, it appears that gang members are much more likely to be involved in violent behavior than non–gang members. Furthermore, the high rates of violence that frequently emerge from delinquent gangs highlight the need for prevention efforts to reduce the negative consequences associated with violent delinquency.

RISK AND PROTECTIVE FACTORS FOR GANG MEMBERSHIP

Several risk and protective factors for gang membership have emerged from the etiological literature, and these factors are similar to those that put adolescents at risk for violent delinquency generally. At the community level, availability of marijuana, lower levels of neighborhood attachment, and higher crime rates appear to increase the risk for gang membership (Herrenkohl et al., 2000; Hill, Howell, Hawkins, & Battin-Pearson, 1999). Family and peer-level variables also play an important role in gang membership, including growing up in a single-parent household, having parents who foster attitudes favorable to violent behavior, having siblings who engage in antisocial behavior, having violent friends, increased family conflict, lack of parental warmth, and peer pressure to join gangs (Herrenkohl et al., 2000; Hill et al., 1999; Walker-Barnes & Mason, 2001).

Individual-level risk factors tend to be the strongest correlates of gang membership among adolescents. Variables that have been demonstrated to increase the risk of gang membership include previous marijuana and other drug use, participation in violent behavior, hyperactivity, rejection of conventional values, poor refusal skills, and early onset of alcohol consumption (Herrenkohl et al., 2000; Hill et al., 1999; Walker-Barnes & Mason, 2001). Overall, youths who were exposed to risk factors at multiple levels were most likely to be gang members (Herrenkohl et al., 2000; Hill et al., 1999).

GANG MEMBERSHIP AS A RISK FACTOR FOR VIOLENT VICTIMIZATION

Gang membership is generally, and almost exclusively, focused on in the literature as a risk factor for offending. Despite this reality, researchers in the past decade or so have become increasingly more focused on the effect of gang membership on violent victimization (Gibson, Swatt, Miller, Jennings, & Gover, 2012). By and large, these recent studies have demonstrated an association between gang membership and violent victimization (Curry, Decker, & Egley, 2002; Decker, Katz, & Webb, 2008; Fox, Lane, & Akers, 2013; Gover, Jennings, & Tewksbury, 2009; Katz, Maguire, & Choate, 2011; Savitz, Rosen, & Lalli, 1980; Spano, Freilich, & Bolland, 2008; Taylor, Freng, Esbensen, & Peterson, 2008; Taylor et al., 2007). Having said this, the majority of these studies have relied on cross-sectional research designs, so investigators are unable to make a definitive statement regarding the potential causal linkage between joining a gang and being violently victimized as a result.

In recognition of this limitation, Gibson, Miller, Jennings, Swatt, and Gover (2009) performed a methodologically rigorous assessment of the relationship between gang membership and violent victimization using data from the GREAT program and applying propensity score matching methods. Their results suggested that there was an observable effect of joining a gang on the likelihood of being violently victimized, although this effect was no longer observed once gang members were matched with non–gang members who resembled gang members across a host of relevant risk factors. This finding led Gibson et al. to conclude that the relationship between gang membership and violent victimization may not necessarily be causal. Rather, this relationship appeared to be spurious because it could be explained by accounting for a number of confounding influences that are related to both joining a gang and risk for violent victimization. In a replication attempt, DeLisi, Barnes, Beaver, and Gibson (2009) analyzed a similar research question but with a different dataset (the National Longitudinal Study of Adolescent Health) and looked at violent victimization frequency rather than violent victimization prevalence. In contrast to Gibson et al.'s (2009) results, DeLisi et al. (2009) found that after adjusting for a number of potentially relevant confounds, the effect of joining a gang on violent victimization persisted, although it was substantively diminished.

Taken together, the results from this emerging body of research have indicated that gang membership may be relevant as a risk factor for violent victimization, but this relationship may be complex, precluding more definitive statements regarding causality until more studies are conducted using rigorous and longitudinal designs, which are better designed to answer this type of research question. Nevertheless, Gibson et al. (2012) provided a list of important recommendations for gang researchers to consider if they are interested in studying the linkage between gangs and violent victimization:

1. Pay attention to the fluidity of gang membership over time, and the impact that transitioning in and out of gangs may have on violent victimization risk.
2. Determine the extent to which the effect of gang membership on violent victimization may be conditional on unique developmental trajectories of offending and/or victimization.
3. Consider alternative definitions of gang membership beyond a mere dichotomous measure (yes/no). Measurement should take into account the organizational structure and/or the role of the individual within the gang.
4. Assess whether or not gang membership has similar or differential effects on violent victimization prevalence and violent victimization frequency.
5. Continue to apply methodologically rigorous empirical designs such as propensity score matching methods when examining the relationship between gang membership and violent victimization.
6. Analyze the relationship between gang membership and violent victimization using high-risk samples.

THEORETICAL EXPLANATIONS OF GANG MEMBERSHIP

Several theoretical foundations provide insight into to why adolescents engage in violent behavior. We review four prevailing criminological theories because they are complementary and examine behavior at different contextual levels. First, social learning theory, proposed by Akers (1973) as a merger of Sutherland and Bandura's learning theories, suggests that individuals engage in deviant behavior because their social group does so, and the deviant behavior is reinforced. Under this theoretical framework, young people do not understand deviance to be overwhelmingly harmful to themselves or others, and they are taught how to engage in illegal activity through their peer group (Akers, 1973). Second, social bond theory, proposed by Hirschi (1969), explains that adolescents are deviant because their bonds to conventional society are weak, and the individual has little motivation to adhere to social norms.

Finally, Shaw and McKay (1942) proposed a macro-level theory of social disorganization using data from Chicago, Illinois. They found that most crime took place in the "zone of transition," or an area densely populated with immigrants and transients, with high levels of poverty, and characterized by a high number of single-parent homes and high ethnic diversity. We discuss each of these theories in detail in the following sections.

Social Learning Theory

Social learning theory has been applied to studies of gang membership and delinquency. Specifically, it has been hypothesized that the constructs of differential association (e.g., having a delinquent peer group, adult approval of delinquency), social reinforcers (e.g., peers' and parents' reactions to violence), neutralization of the delinquent behavior, and positive attitudes toward gangs tend to increase gang membership and violent behavior (Esbensen & Deschenes, 1998; Winfree, Backström, & Mays, 1994). Each of these constructs additively contributes to the likelihood of delinquent and gang-related behavior.

Social learning theory posits that individuals learn to engage in criminal behavior by observing those around them (Akers, 1973). The social learning theoretical framework was derived from theories by Bandura (operant conditioning; Bandura, 1971) and consists of four central components: excess of definitions favorable to criminality, association with deviant peers, reinforcement of criminal behavior, and imitation. When these elements are combined, an individual is more likely to engage in deviant or criminal behavior.

For each additional element of social learning to which an individual is exposed, the greater the risk of violence is (Akers, 1973). First, individuals will be at increased risk for deviant behavior if they believe that such behavior is not intrinsically harmful to themselves or others and if the deviance will benefit them in some way. This would be considered a definition favorable to criminality or deviance. When the definitions favorable to violence outweigh the definitions unfavorable to violence, the likelihood that individuals will engage in violence is increased. Second, in agreement with Sutherland (1947), Akers (1973) suggested that association with deviant peers increases the likelihood of deviance. The theory of differential association suggests that criminal behavior is learned via social interaction with others, because the social environment and values gained from relations with deviant peers and family members would affect individuals' criminal behavior (Sutherland, 1947).

Sutherland (1947) used nine propositions to explain his theory. He believed that criminal or deviant behavior is learned through interaction with others in personal groups and that the learning of criminal behavior requires the learning of criminal techniques, attitudes, rationalizations, and motives. In addition, Sutherland stated that to become a criminal, one must learn to view the law negatively and have a deficiency in definitions favorable to law-abiding behavior. His final propositions state that criminal behavior is learned in the same way as any other type of behavior and it is not explained by general needs and values (Sutherland, 1947). Burgess and Akers (1966) revised Sutherland's list of propositions, or principles, in the following manner:

1. Criminal behavior is learned according to the principles of operant conditioning (reformulation of Sutherland's principles 1 and 8).

2. Criminal behavior is learned both in nonsocial situations that are reinforcing or discriminative and through that social interaction in which the behavior of other persons is reinforcing or discriminative for criminal behavior (reformulation of Sutherland's principle 2).
3. The principal part of the learning of criminal behavior occurs in those groups that comprise the individual's major source of reinforcements (reformulation of Sutherland's principle 3).
4. The learning of criminal behavior, including specific techniques, attitudes, and avoidance procedures, is a function of the effective and available reinforcers, and the existing reinforcement contingencies (reformulation of Sutherland's principle 4).
5. The specific class of behaviors which are learned and their frequency of occurrence are a function of the reinforcers which are effective and available, and the rules or norms by which these reinforcers are applied (reformulation of Sutherland's principle 5).
6. Criminal behavior is a function of norms which are discriminative for criminal behavior, the learning of which takes place when such behavior is more highly reinforced than noncriminal behavior (reformulation of Sutherland's principle 6).
7. The strength of criminal behavior is a direct function of the amount, frequency, and probability of its reinforcement (reformulation of Sutherland's principle 7). (pp. 132–145)

In addition to differential association and definitions favorable to deviance, Akers (1973) suggested that reinforcement of deviance and imitation are important in predicting deviant behavior. When relatively minor deviant behaviors are positively reinforced by others, it is likely that more frequent and perhaps more severe deviant behaviors will result. It is important to note that all relationships are not created equally under this theory, because longer relationships and those who became acquainted early in life are more influential in their reinforcement of deviant behavior. Finally, deviant behavior may be learned through mimicry of social circle members (Akers, 1973). Akers' (1973) theory highlights the role of the peer group and early relationships in explaining why individuals engage in gang-related delinquent activities.

Social Bond Theory

Hirschi's (1969) social bond theory has frequently been applied to studies of gangs, gang membership, and violent delinquency (Bjerregaard & Smith, 1993; Blum, Ireland, & Blum, 2003; Booth, Farrell, & Varano, 2008). Social bond variables including school success (Bjerregaard & Smith, 1993; Blum et al., 2003), high levels of parental attachment (Blum et al., 2003; Booth et al., 2008), belief in traditional norms (Booth et al., 2008), and involvement in prosocial activities (Blum et al., 2003; Booth et al., 2008) are protective from participation in delinquency and gang violence. According to this theoretical framework, the absence of any construct (attachment, commitment, involvement, or belief) puts an adolescent at risk for delinquency, violence, and gang membership (Hirschi, 1969).

Social bond theory asserts that criminal behavior results from weak bonds to conventional society. The four main domains are attachment (an individual's ability to identify with others and maintain their support), involvement (participation in conventional activities), belief (a person's acceptance of society's conventional values), and commitment (dedication to conventional behavior; Hirschi, 1969). According to Hirschi (1969), the more people are attached to other members of conventional society, the more they will seek their support and adhere to positive social norms.

These four domains, or elements, all contribute additively to the likelihood of deviant behavior. People who are more committed to conventional activities are less likely to engage in deviant behavior. For instance, conventional activities may include attending college or having a job in the community. Participation in these activities invests the individual in the well-being of the community and decreases the likelihood of deviant behavior. In addition, committed individuals have more to lose if they are caught engaging in deviant behavior, further reducing their likelihood of deviance. Involved people participate in many conventional activities, and they are generally considered to be too busy to engage in deviant behavior.

Finally, people who believe in the conventional norms and values of society are less likely to be delinquent because they are more likely to adhere to these norms. In comparison, those who do not believe in the norms of conventional society are more likely to be deviant because they do not endorse the values and norms of society. Weaknesses in any one of these domains increase the likelihood of deviant and criminal behavior.

Moffitt's Life-Course Perspective

Many studies have supported the existence of the age–crime curve (Farrington, 1986), which displays the population-level trajectory of crime trends across the life course. Moffitt's (1993) taxonomy of crime applies a developmental perspective to criminal behavior, focusing on the decrease in criminality and delinquency as adolescents age. This perspective reflects the decline in most types of criminal behavior with age and considers that most offenders discontinue their delinquent behavior early in life. Moffitt's (1993) taxonomy suggests that gang members comprise many of the life-course-persistent offenders, or the small group who continues to engage in delinquency and violence throughout adulthood.

Moffitt (1993, 2003) offered her dual taxonomy of criminal behavior, recognizing life-course persistent offenders and adolescence-limited offenders as distinct in their reasons for engaging in crime. She argued that life-course-persistent offenders (or those who engage in criminal behavior for the majority of their lifetime) begin life with differences in neurological functioning and have early behavioral problems (Moffitt, 2003). These children may have been abused or neglected and often exhibit antisocial behavior (Moffitt, 2003). They often come from poorly functioning families, do poorly in school, and associate with other criminal or deviant peers (Moffitt, 1993). They are also more likely to be raised in neglected, low-income neighborhoods and to have parents with antisocial tendencies or below-average cognitive abilities. These environments increase the likelihood that the child's genetic predispositions to violence will surface, and antisocial behavior will prevail (Moffitt, 1993).

Criminal behavior in life-course-persistent offenders begins early and continues throughout life. A cycle of cumulative disadvantage entrenches them in the criminal world. Furthermore, these individuals have few law-abiding friends (because of their antisocial behavior) and do poorly in school. Outside of school, they engage in delinquent and, later, criminal behavior. This lifestyle is very difficult for the individual to break away from because the individual has very few conventional ties (Moffitt, 1993). Gradually throughout childhood and adolescence, the individual begins to identify him- or herself as criminal (Moffitt, 1993). As a result, life-course-persistent offenders exhibit "contemporary continuity," meaning that they bring the same deviant traits that they exhibited as adolescents to adulthood and act in a similar manner. At this point in time, any major turning points (or pathways away from crime, such as marriage or higher education) are likely to be bypassed (Moffitt, 1993). After all pathways out of delinquency are no longer available, life-course-persistent offenders are embedded in their deviant lifestyle for the majority of their lives.

The other path of offending that Moffitt (1993) described in her taxonomy is the adolescent-limited type. Unlike life-course-persistent offenders, adolescent-limited offenders have normal childhoods, begin engaging in criminal behavior later in life (usually between ages 15 and 17), and terminate their illegal behavior shortly after initiating it (usually by age 19; Moffitt, 1993). Adolescent-limited offenders are often tempted to engage in criminal acts because of the maturity gap: Young people feel biologically and socially mature, but they are not legally allowed to be independent or given adult freedoms (Moffitt, 1993). They want to engage in deviant, dangerous, or other behaviors to defy their parents and appear mature.

To this end, adolescent-limited offenders briefly (and sporadically) model the life-course-persistent offenders in their criminal behavior. A short time later, adolescent-limited offenders return to their law-abiding lives because the risks of criminal behavior are far too severe. These individuals are likely to go to college or obtain a good job; therefore, the costs of criminal behavior are far higher for this group than the life-course-persistent offenders. These adolescent-limited offenders recognize the potential consequences of getting caught and discontinue any criminal behavior early in life (Moffitt, 1993).

Social Disorganization Theory

Shaw and McKay's (1942) theory of social disorganization has been applied to gang violence and delinquency because many studies have reported a clustering of high homicide rates, gang violence, and gang activity in general in the urban centers of U.S. cities (Curry & Spergel, 1988; Kawachi, Kennedy, & Wilkinson, 1999). Specifically, Shaw and McKay (1942) believed that residents in cohesive communities have more control over youths in their neighborhoods and could therefore prevent any behavior that would set the context for gang violence (e.g., supervise leisure-time activities, challenge youths who appear to be behaving inappropriately, etc.; Kawachi et al., 1999). This neighborhood-level theory of violence highlights the role of the community in violence, delinquency, and gang prevention.

Social disorganization theory is primarily based on the work of Shaw and McKay (1942) in Chicago, Illinois. In their classic study, they analyzed concentric zones radiating from the city center of Chicago to determine how crime is distributed and identify the characteristics of high-crime neighborhoods. They found that most crime took place in the zone of transition, or the impoverished area densely populated with immigrants and transients and characterized by a high number of single-parent homes and high ethnic diversity. They also noted that the crime rate stayed the same over time, despite the constant flow of people to and from the city. These zones of transition harbor social disorganization, and low levels of social organization in these communities facilitate crime. The major factors in defining an area as socially disorganized include concentration of poverty, population density, high mobility rates, and ethnic heterogeneity.

Shaw and McKay (1942) maintained that the characteristics of the community, rather than the individuals within that community, are what facilitate crime. For example, transient individuals are unlikely to watch over their neighbor's property, or even care who their neighbors are. Therefore, a neighbor would never know whether someone is stealing a car out of the driveway because they do not know who resides in that particular home. Suburban areas have these types of neighborly ties, and neighbors would recognize when someone (or something) does not belong. Using the framework provided by social disorganization theory, the lack of neighborly recognition is one of the reasons why crime is higher in transient, disorganized communities.

Sampson, Raudenbush, and Earls (1997) further elaborated on this aspect of social disorganization in defining the collective efficacy of communities. Collective efficacy is the ability of a neighborhood to come together to reduce criminal or disorderly behavior. Cohesive suburban neighborhoods are very likely to do this; when there is some sort of problem within the community, they organize themselves and remedy it. Alternatively, urban, disadvantaged, disorganized neighborhoods are not likely to have such a mechanism in place to filter out criminal behavior among residents. This lack of social control in a community allows crime and gang involvement to multiply.

Generally, crime flourishes in these inner-city communities simply because the community cannot control it (Shaw & McKay, 1942). Disorganized neighborhoods cannot control children or their behavior because familial control is minimal (both parents or single parents are constantly working to pay bills or may be involved in illegal behaviors themselves), and children are frequently left to care for themselves. This may allow them to engage in illegal activities with other children in the same situation and be drawn to gangs. Residents have little stake in their community because they will be relocating as soon as they have the means to do so. The culmination of all of these factors allows certain neighborhoods to remain disorganized for generation after generation. To summarize, the structural characteristics of the community (poverty, population density, mobility, and ethnic heterogeneity) lead to constant social disorganization and a persistent delinquent subculture that is consistently engaged in criminal behavior, and this delinquent subculture can be manifested in the form of gangs.

All of these theoretical perspectives come together to explain delinquency and gang membership among adolescents. Social learning theory highlights how the various elements of the social learning process (definitions, differential association, differential reinforcement, and imitation) influence gang membership and related violence. Social bond theory describes risk factors at the individual level (e.g., commitment to school, education, family, and peers; attachment to parents; involvement in prosocial extracurricular activities) for gang membership and delinquency. Moffitt's (1993, 2003) life-course perspective contributes multilevel risk factors that are highly influential early in life (e.g., genetic composition, characteristics of the family, neighborhood, peer delinquency) and describes how the presence of these characteristics will play a large role in whether an adolescent becomes a life-course-persistent offender or an adolescent-limited offender. Social disorganization considers the external influence of the communities in which adolescents reside and how the community influences delinquent behavior and gang membership. These theoretical perspectives provide the context for gang and delinquency prevention and intervention efforts.

GANG PREVENTION AND INTERVENTION

Many gang prevention programs have been implemented in the United States in an attempt to reduce gang membership and, by extension, violent delinquency. Although one recent meta-analysis (Fisher, Gardner, & Montgomery, 2008) has documented that there have been no randomized controlled trials of gang prevention interventions, there is some evidence that many of these programs have had success in preventing gang membership among adolescents. Some of the more prominent examples (e.g., multisite interventions with large, diverse samples of adolescents) of school- and community-based gang prevention programs are discussed below.

Community-Based Gang Prevention Programs

Chicago Area Project. The Chicago Area Project was one of the first gang and violence prevention programs to be developed in the United States (Kobrin, 1959). The theory behind the Chicago Area Project lies in the work of Shaw and McKay (1942), who hypothesized that the constant influx of poor people to the center city of Chicago produced an environment in which crime was easily learned and diffused among youths. The program used local residents to organize the community and identify youths who were at high risk for violence. These youths were then targeted for youth welfare activities while receiving the support of the local community. The hiring of local workers was instrumental to the project because the local workers did not have communication barriers between them and other local residents, they knew their neighborhoods better than project staff did, and they had direct access to delinquent youths. To prevent street gangs, targeted programs included specific supervision plans once an adolescent was involved in the justice system. Boys were also sent to reformatories, informal treatment groups were held, and recreational activities as alternatives to gang membership were provided to boys (e.g., recreation, summer camps, physical maintenance). These interventions were not constant across neighborhoods, and most components of the Chicago Area Project were not directly evaluated for their effectiveness in preventing gang membership and violence.

Community-Wide Approach to Gang Prevention, Intervention, and Suppression (Office of Juvenile Justice and Delinquency Prevention [OJJDP]). The Community-Wide Approach to Gang Prevention, Intervention and Suppression (Spergel, Wa, & Sosa, 2005a, 2005b, 2005c, 2005d) was a multisite community mobilization program to reduce gang violence in five cities in the western United States (Bloomington–Normal, IL; San Antonio, TX; Mesa, AZ; Tucson, AZ; Riverside, CA). The prevention model was based on five tenets: community mobilization, provision of social opportunities, suppression of gangs, organizational development and change, and social intervention (Spergel et al., 2005a, 2005b, 2005c, 2005d). Multiple agencies were involved in the intervention, including a street team, grassroots groups, employment and training agencies, schools, and the criminal justice system. As a part of the intervention, youth outreach services were provided to gang members, schools maintained a controversial zero tolerance policy for gang behaviors, and youths who were involved in gangs were referred to alternative schools at which they were able to receive counseling and mediation to reduce attachment to the gang. Job opportunities were also available for youths involved in gangs, and case workers met with youths approximately three times per month.

Specific program implementation differed by city; therefore, each of these cities was evaluated independently. In three of the project sites (San Antonio, Bloomington–Normal, Mesa), the program did not appear to be successful in reducing arrests of program youths, and differences between treatment and comparison groups were similar in their rates of gang membership at posttest (Spergel et al., 2005a, 2005b, 2005c, 2005d, 2005e). However, some of the more positive outcomes of the project were significantly different for the treatment group and the controls (e.g., property crime, drug arrests) at some sites. In Mesa, participation in the program reduced violent arrests and total arrests; however, there was no change in gang membership between groups. The two locations that were successful in reducing violence or arrest outcomes, Mesa and Tucson, were more likely to implement several components of the OJJDP Comprehensive Gang Program Model (community mobilization, social services provision, case management, grassroots campaigns against gangs, community-oriented policing, counseling, etc.). The less successful cities, Bloomington, Riverside, and San Antonio, did not follow the OJJDP model, invested few police resources, or failed to interest the community in the program.

Little Village Project. The Little Village Project is a multicomponent approach to gang violence prevention in Chicago, Illinois (Spergel & Grossman, 1997). This project includes a team of probation officers, police officers, community youths, and a community mobilization team that seek to (a) involve local citizens and former gang youths; (b) provide better jobs, special education, and training programs to meet the needs of low-income youths; (c) provide outreach to at-risk youths at the ecological level via social interventions; (d) suppress gang activity and promote positive communication with at-risk youths in gangs; and (e) target at-risk youths with gang-specific prevention activities. During the evaluation of this project, 200 active gang members were targeted over a period of 4 years. Initially, the intervention did not appear to significantly reduce arrests for violence; however, the community's perception of gang violence and gang property crime among residents was significantly reduced (Spergel & Grossman, 1997).

Dallas Anti-Gang Initiative. The Dallas Anti-Gang Initiative was first implemented in 1996 to reduce gang-related violence in five neighborhoods of Dallas, Texas (Fritsch, Caeti, & Taylor, 1999). These five areas were selected because of a high rate of gang activity in the past year. This police-based intervention funded gang unit officers and interactive community police officers to develop innovative strategies for gang violence enforcement across the targeted neighborhoods, including curfew enforcement, aggressive truancy enforcement, and saturation patrol (e.g., an increased number of patrol officers in a targeted region). Teams of officers were dedicated to the implementation of these strategies. This evaluation provides a different approach to gang prevention through reactive techniques, and the evaluation process was more rigorous than many school- and community-based evaluation designs in gang prevention research. Program evaluation results reported that the truancy enforcement and aggressive curfew enforcement resulted in reduced gang violence, and the saturation police patrol did not (Fritsch et al., 1999).

Neutral Zone. Neutral Zone was created in 1992 in Mountlake Terrace, Washington, and it sought to reduce the number of youths on the streets at night (between 10:00 p.m. and 2:00 a.m.; Thurman, Giacomazzi, Reisig, & Mueller, 1996). The Neutral Zone was a physical location where youths could participate in recreational activities, participate in projects to enhance job skills, and have access to positive mentors and appropriate role models. These locations were generally located in elementary schools and were available to youths during times of high crime activity (e.g., late at night). Programs included sports, movies, music, free food, counseling, and job preparation services in addition to occupying youths' free time. The program has since been expanded to more than 10 locations in the state of Washington. Qualitative reports and trends in arrests by police have suggested that this program has been successful at keeping youths off the street at night during high-crime hours (Thurman et al., 1996).

School-Based Gang Prevention Programs

Gang Resistance Education and Training. GREAT is a school-based gang membership prevention program originally developed in Phoenix, Arizona (Esbensen & Osgood, 1999). The pilot program was expanded in 1995 to include 11 locations nationwide (Kansas City, MO; Las Cruces, NM; Milwaukee, WI; Omaha, NE; Orlando, FL; Philadelphia, PA; Phoenix, AZ; Pocatello, ID; Providence, RI; Torrance, CA; and Will County, IL). The research design sampled at the school level, and students within the schools were not randomized to treatment condition. The sampling design was intended to oversample African American, Hispanic, and White youths (Esbensen et al., 2010).

The GREAT program includes 9 weeks of skills training, including conflict resolution, cultural sensitivity, and education regarding the negative aspects of gang membership (Esbensen & Osgood, 1999). Weekly lessons implemented by police officers were conducted for 9 weeks when students were in seventh grade, and pretests and posttests were administered to evaluate changes in behavior and attitude after participation in the program. Follow-up tests were administered when youths were in eighth grade, 1 year after participating in the intervention. The program was universally administered to students, meaning that a student did not need to be at risk for gang membership to participate (Esbensen & Osgood, 1999).

The final sample included 5,935 eighth-grade students from 315 classrooms in 42 schools across the United States. Although these schools and students were not selected randomly to participate in the intervention, Esbensen and Osgood (1999) suggested that participants represent a variety of community types (urban, rural, suburban), racial/ethnic compositions, and gang activity in the surrounding city. Students who participated in the program appeared to engage in more prosocial activities and have more prosocial attitudes than comparison youths (Esbensen & Osgood, 1999). More recent evaluations have shown that lagged program effects are present because participants appeared to be less violent 2 years later (Esbensen, Freng, Taylor, Peterson, & Osgood, 2002).

Violence Intervention and Prevention Team. The Violence Intervention and Prevention Team began as a small ($N = 48$), school-based gang prevention program targeted at middle-school students who were at high risk for violence (Rothman et al., 2010). It was established in 2005 and continued with different cohorts of participants through 2008 in two middle schools in Boston, Massachusetts. In the program, counselors trained students in conflict resolution, provided referrals to community-based violence prevention programs, provided tutoring and job placement, and organized visits to colleges. Participants were referred to the program by guidance counselors and teachers. Only adolescents who were deemed to be motivated to attend (e.g., nominated themselves for participation in the program) were invited to participate in this efficacy trial of the Violence Intervention and Prevention Team intervention. Once accepted into the program, participants took a nonviolence pledge and were formally inducted. Qualitative results showed that the 48 initial participants were motivated to contemplate college attendance, and some students reported fewer arguments as a result of conflict resolution training. As of 2009, more than 400 students had been members of the Violence Intervention and Prevention Team program (Rothman et al., 2010).

Overall, there are few school-based gang prevention programs, and the extant programs have largely not been rigorously evaluated. Community-based programs are more common, yet the evaluations of these programs lack methodological rigor to some extent as well. Nevertheless, it appears that participation in these programs can reduce adolescents' risk of violence and gang membership.

CONCLUSION

In this chapter, we discussed how the issue of gang membership is complex etiologically and detailed several theoretical and empirical examples of why youths join gangs, why adolescents remain in gangs, the negative effects of gang membership, and gender and racial/ethnic differences in gang membership. We also discussed the difficulty in studying gangs, because the conceptualization and measurement of gang membership can vary substantially, affecting prevalence rates and the validity of the gang construct. A thorough understanding of how gangs should be most accurately defined, as well as an understanding of the joining process and desistence from gangs, is necessary before effective prevention programs and policies may be developed, although some prevention and intervention efforts reviewed in this chapter seem promising.

Overall, the research has suggested that gangs are a complex problem that cannot be remedied with broad-sweeping policies. Reduction of gangs in a community requires teamwork and collaboration by citizens, the police department, social and medical services, and policymakers. Together, the community must identify gangs as a problem and, rather than seek to punish gang members, they should serve to systematically identify members and provide them with the tools and services they need to desist from the gang.

Future research on this topic should identify which community-based prevention models are best suited to different types of communities (e.g., urban, rural, even jails and prisons) and gangs (e.g., predominantly Hispanic, African American, or regional gangs). Gang prevention and intervention programs have been limited in their scope of testing, and these interventions could benefit from broader use. In addition, the use of and collaboration with public health departments may be a direction for future research and program development because the crime and violence associated with gangs and gang membership constitute a serious public health hazard. In summary, gang membership is not an easy problem to solve, and multidimensional, cross-discipline collaborations are required to improve community safety by reducing the presence of gangs.

References

Akers, R. (1973). *Deviant behavior: A social learning approach*. Belmont, CA: Wadsworth.

Ball, R. A., & Curry, G. D. (1995). The logic of definition in criminology: Purposes and methods for defining gangs. *Criminology*, *33*, 225–245. http://dx.doi.org/10.1111/j.1745-9125.1995.tb01177.x

Bandura, A. (1971). *Social learning theory*. New York, NY: General Learning Press.

Bjerregaard, B., & Smith, C. (1993). Gender differences in gang participation, delinquency, and substance use. *Journal of Quantitative Criminology*, *9*, 329–355. http://dx.doi.org/10.1007/BF01064108

Block, C. R., & Block, R. (1995). Street gang crime in Chicago. In J. Miller, C. Maxson, & M. Klein (Eds.), *The modern gang reader* (2nd ed., pp. 186–199). Los Angeles, CA: Roxbury.

Blum, J., Ireland, M., & Blum, R. W. (2003). Gender differences in juvenile violence: A report from Add Health. *Journal of Adolescent Health*, *32*, 234–240. http://dx.doi.org/10.1016/S1054-139X(02)00448-2

Booth, J. A., Farrell, A., & Varano, S. P. (2008). Social control, serious delinquency, and risky behavior: A gendered analysis. *Crime and Delinquency*, *54*, 423–456. http://dx.doi.org/10.1177/0011128707306121

Burgess, R. L., & Akers, R. L. (1966). A differential association-reinforcement theory of criminal behavior. *Social Problems*, *14*, 128–147. http://dx.doi.org/10.2307/798612

Campbell, A. (1991). *The girls in the gang* (2nd ed.). Cambridge, MA: Basil Blackwell.

Cohen, M. I., Williams, K., Bekelman, A. M., & Crosse, S. (1995). Evaluation of the National Youth Gang Drug Prevention Program. In J. Miller, C. Maxson, & M. Klein (Eds.), *Modern gang reader* (pp. 266–275). Los Angeles, CA: Roxbury.

Curry, G. D., Ball, R. A., & Fox, R. J. (1994). *Gang crime and law enforcement recordkeeping* (NIJ Research In Brief No. 148345). Washington, DC: U.S. Department of Justice, Office of Justice Programs, National Institute of Justice.

Curry, G. D., Decker, S., & Egley, A., Jr. (2002). Gang involvement and delinquency in a middle school population. *Justice Quarterly*, *19*, 275–292. http://dx.doi.org/10.1080/07418820200095241

Curry, G. D., & Spergel, I. A. (1988). Gang homicide, delinquency, and community. *Criminology*, *26*, 381–406. http://dx.doi.org/10.1111/j.1745-9125.1988.tb00847.x

Curry, G. D., & Spergel, I. A. (1992). Gang involvement and delinquency among Hispanic and African-American adolescent males. *Journal of Research in Crime and Delinquency*, *29*, 273–291. http://dx.doi.org/10.1177/0022427892029003002

Decker, S., Katz, C., & Webb, V. (2008). Understanding the black box of gang organization: Implications for involvement in violent crime, drug sales, and violent victimization. *Crime and Delinquency*, *54*, 153–172. http://dx.doi.org/10.1177/0011128706296664

DeLisi, M., Barnes, J. C., Beaver, K. M., & Gibson, C. L. (2009). Delinquent gangs and adolescent victimization revisited: A propensity score matching approach. *Criminal Justice and Behavior*, *36*, 808–823. http://dx.doi.org/10.1177/0093854809337703

Egley, A., Howell, J. C., & Moore, J. P. (2010). *Highlights of the 2008 national youth gang survey* (OJJDP Fact Sheet). Washington, DC: U.S. Department of Justice, Office of Juvenile Justice and Delinquency Prevention.

Egley, A., & O'Donnell, C. E. (2008). *Highlights from the 2006 national youth gang survey* (OJJDP Fact Sheet). http://dx.doi.org/10.1037/e511822008-001

Egley, A., & Ritz, C. E. (2006). *Highlights of the 2004 national youth gang survey* (OJJDP Fact Sheet). http://dx.doi.org/10.1037/e453512008-001

Elliott, D. (1984). *National Youth Survey, Wave VI, 1983* (ICPSR 9948). Ann Arbor, MI: Inter-University Consortium for Political and Social Research.

Elliott, D., & Ageton, S. S. (1980). Reconciling race and class differences in self-reported and official estimates of delinquency. *American Sociological Review*, *45*, 95–110. http://dx.doi.org/10.2307/2095245

Esbensen, F.-A. (2000). *Preventing adolescent gang involvement* (Juvenile Justice Bulletin). Washington, DC: U.S. Department of Justice, Office of Juvenile Justice and Delinquency Prevention.

Esbensen, F.-A., & Deschenes, E. P. (1998). A multisite examination of youth gang membership: Does gender matter? *Criminology*, *36*, 799–828. http://dx.doi.org/10.1111/j.1745-9125.1998.tb01266.x

Esbensen, F.-A., Freng, A., Taylor, T. J., Peterson, D., & Osgood, D. W. (2002). National evaluation of the Gang Resistance Education and Training (GREAT) program. In S. Decker & W. Reed (Eds.), *Responding to gangs: Evaluation and research* (pp. 139–167). Washington, DC: U.S. Department of Justice.

Esbensen, F.-A., & Huizinga, D. (1993). Gangs, drugs, and delinquency in a survey of urban youth. *Criminology*, *31*, 565–589. http://dx.doi.org/10.1111/j.1745-9125.1993.tb01142.x

Esbensen, F.-A., & Osgood, D. W. (1999). Gang Resistance Education and Training (GREAT): Results from a national evaluation. *Journal of Research in Crime and Delinquency*, *36*, 194–225. http://dx.doi.org/10.1177/0022427899036002004

Esbensen, F.-A., Peterson, D., Taylor, T. J., & Freng, A. (2010). *Youth violence: Sex and race differences in offending, victimization, and gang membership*. Philadelphia, PA: Temple University Press.

Esbensen, F.-A., Winfree, L. T., He, N., & Taylor, T. J. (2001). Youth gangs and definition issues: When is a gang a gang, and why does it matter? *Crime and Delinquency*, *47*, 105–130. http://dx.doi.org/10.1177/0011128701047001005

Farrington, D. P. (1986). Age and crime. *Crime and Justice*, *7*, 189–250. http://dx.doi.org/10.1086/449114

Farrington, D. P., & Loeber, R. (2000). Epidemiology of juvenile violence. *Child and Adolescent Psychiatric Clinics of North America*, *9*, 733–748.

Farrington, D. P., Loeber, R., & Stouthamer-Loeber, M. (2003). How can the relationship between race and violence be explained? In D. Hawkins (Ed.), *Violent crime: Assessing race and ethnic differences* (pp. 213–237). http://dx.doi.org/10.1017/CBO9780511499456.014

Fisher, H., Gardner, F., & Montgomery, P. (2008). Cognitive-behavioral interventions for preventing youth gang involvement for children and young people. *Cochrane Database of Systematic Reviews, 2008*, CD007008).

Fox, K. A., Lane, J., & Akers, R. L. (2013). Understanding gang membership and crime victimization among jail inmates: Testing the effects of self-control. *Crime and Delinquency*, *59*, 764–787.

Freng, A., & Esbensen, F. (2007). Race and gang affiliation: An examination of multiple marginality. *Justice Quarterly*, *24*, 600–628. http://dx.doi.org/10.1080/07418820701717136

Fritsch, E. J., Caeti, T. J., & Taylor, R. W. (1999). Gang suppression through saturation patrol, aggressive curfew, and truancy enforcement: A quasi-experimental test of the Dallas anti-gang initiative. *Crime and Delinquency*, *45*, 122–139. http://dx.doi.org/10.1177/0011128799045001007

Gibson, C., Swatt, M., Miller, J. M., Jennings, W. G., & Gover, A. (2012). The causal relationship between gang joining and violent victimization: A critical review and directions for future research. *Journal of Criminal Justice*, *40*, 490–501. http://dx.doi.org/10.1016/j.jcrimjus.2012.08.001

Gibson, C. L., Miller, J. M., Jennings, W. G., Swatt, M. L., & Gover, A. (2009). Using propensity score matching to understand the relationship between gang members and violent victimization: A research note. *Justice Quarterly*, *26*, 625–643. http://dx.doi.org/10.1080/07418820802593345

Gover, A. R., Jennings, W. G., & Tewksbury, R. (2009). Adolescent male and female gang members' experiences of violent victimization, dating violence, and sexual assault. *American Journal of Criminal Justice*, *34*, 103–115. http://dx.doi.org/10.1007/s12103-008-9053-z

Harris, K. M., Halpern, C., Whitsel, E., Hussey, J., Tabor, J., Entzel, P., & Udry, J. (2009). The National

Longitudinal Study of Adolescent Health: Research design. Retrieved from http://www.cpc.unc.edu/projects/addhealth/design

Harris, M. G. (1994). Cholas, Mexican-American girls, and gangs. *Sex Roles, 30*, 289–301. http://dx.doi.org/10.1007/BF01420995

Herrenkohl, T. I., Maguin, E., Hill, K. G., Hawkins, J. D., Abbott, R. D., & Catalano, R. F. (2000). Developmental risk factors for youth violence. *Journal of Adolescent Health, 26*, 176–186. http://dx.doi.org/10.1016/S1054-139X(99)00065-8

Hill, K. G., Howell, J. C., Hawkins, J. D., & Battin-Pearson, S. R. (1999). Childhood risk factors for adolescent gang membership: Results from the Seattle social development project. *Journal of Research in Crime and Delinquency, 36*, 300–322. http://dx.doi.org/10.1177/0022427899036003003

Hill, K. G., Lui, C., & Hawkins, J. D. (2001). *Early precursors of gang membership: A study of Seattle youth*. Washington, DC: U.S. Department of Justice, Office of Juvenile Justice and Delinquency Prevention.

Hirschi, T. (1969). *Causes of delinquency*. Berkeley: University of California Press.

Howell, J. C. (1998, August). Youth gangs: An overview. *Juvenile Justice Bulletin*, pp. 1–20.

Howell, J. C., & Moore, J. P. (2010). *History of street gangs in the United States* (National Gang Center Bulletin No. 4). Washington, DC: U.S. Department of Justice, Office of Juvenile Justice and Delinquency Prevention.

Huff, C. R. (1998). *Comparing the criminal behavior of youth gangs and at-risk youth* (Research in Brief). Washington, DC: National Institutes of Justice.

Huizinga, D. (1997, February). *Gangs and the volume of crime*. Paper presented at the annual meeting of the Western Society of Criminology, Honolulu, Hawaii.

Huizinga, D., Loeber, R., & Thornberry, T. P. (1995). *Recent findings from the program of research on the causes and correlates of delinquency*. Washington, DC: National Institutes of Justice.

Johnston, L. D., O'Malley, P. M., Bachman, J. G., & Schulenberg, J. E. (2010). *Monitoring the Future: National results on adolescent drug use—Overview of key findings, 2009*. Bethesda, MD: National Institutes of Drug Abuse.

Katz, C. M., Maguire, E. R., & Choate, D. (2011). A cross-national comparison of gangs in the United States and Trinidad and Tobago. *International Criminal Justice Review, 21*, 243–262. http://dx.doi.org/10.1177/1057567711417179

Kawachi, I., Kennedy, B. P., & Wilkinson, R. G. (1999). Crime: Social disorganization and relative deprivation. *Social Science and Medicine, 48*, 719–731. http://dx.doi.org/10.1016/S0277-9536(98)00400-6

Klein, M. W. (1971). *Street gangs and street workers*. Englewood Cliffs, NJ: Prentice Hall.

Klein, M. W., Weerman, F. M., & Thornberry, T. P. (2006). Street gang violence in Europe. *European Journal of Criminology, 3*, 413–437. http://dx.doi.org/10.1177/1477370806067911

Knox, G. W., McCurrie, T. F., Laskey, J. A., & Tromanheuser, E. D. (1996). National law enforcement gang analysis survey, 1996: A research report from the National Gang Crime Research Center. *Journal of Gang Research, 3*, 41–55.

Kobrin, S. (1959). The Chicago area project—A 25-year assessment. *Annals of the American Academy of Political and Social Science, 322*, 19–29. http://dx.doi.org/10.1177/000271625932200104

Lyons, J., Henggeller, S., & Hall, J. A. (1992). The family relations, peer associations, and criminal activities of Caucasians and Hispanic-American gang members. *Journal of Child Psychology and Psychiatry, and Allied Disciplines, 20*, 439–449.

McNulty, T. L., & Bellair, P. E. (2003). Explaining racial and ethnic differences in serious adolescent violent behavior. *Criminology, 41*, 709–747. http://dx.doi.org/10.1111/j.1745-9125.2003.tb01002.x

Menard, S., & Elliott, D. S. (1993). Data set comparability and short-term trends in crime and delinquency. *Journal of Criminal Justice, 21*, 433–445. http://dx.doi.org/10.1016/0047-2352(93)90030-Q

Miller, J. (1998). Gender and victimization risk among young women in gangs. *Journal of Research in Crime and Delinquency, 35*, 429–453. http://dx.doi.org/10.1177/0022427898035004004

Miller, W. B. (2001). *The growth of youth gang problems in the United States: 1970–1988*. Washington, DC: U.S. Department of Justice, Office of Juvenile Justice and Delinquency Prevention.

Moffitt, T. E. (1993). The neuropsychology of conduct disorder. *Development and Psychopathology, 5*, 135–151. http://dx.doi.org/10.1017/S0954579400004302

Moffitt, T. E. (2003). Pathways in the life course to crime. In F. T. Cullen, R. Agnew, & P. Wilcox (Eds.), *Criminological theory past to present: Essential readings* (pp. 450–469). Los Angeles, CA: Roxbury.

Moore, J. W., & Hagedorn, J. M. (1996). What happens to girls in the gang? In C. Huff (Ed.), *Gangs in America* (2nd ed., pp. 205–218). Thousand Oaks, CA: Sage.

Rothman, E. F., Ireland, C., Curry, L., Polanco, A., Baughman, A., & Thompson, D. (2010). The Violence Intervention and Prevention team (VIP):

Results of an action research evaluation. *Progress in Community Health Partnerships: Research, Education, and Action*, 4, 181–188. http://dx.doi.org/10.1353/cpr.2010.0000

Sampson, R. J., Raudenbush, S. W., & Earls, F. (1997). Neighborhoods and violent crime: A multilevel study of collective efficacy. *Science*, 227, 918–924. http://dx.doi.org/10.1126/science.277.5328.918

Savitz, L., Rosen, L., & Lalli, M. (1980). Delinquency and gang membership as related to victimization. *Victimology*, 5, 152–160.

Shaw, C. R., & McKay, H. D. (1942). *Juvenile delinquency and urban areas*. Chicago, IL: University of Chicago Press.

Smith, M. R., & Alpert, G. P. (2007). Explaining police bias: A theory of social conditioning and illusory correlation. *Criminal Justice and Behavior*, 34, 1262–1283. http://dx.doi.org/10.1177/0093854807304484

Spano, R., Freilich, J. D., & Bolland, J. (2008). Gang membership, gun carrying, and employment: Applying routine activities theory to explain violent victimization among inner city, minority youth living in extreme poverty. *Justice Quarterly*, 25, 381–410. http://dx.doi.org/10.1080/07418820802024911

Spergel, I. A. (1993). *Gang suppression and intervention: An assessment*. Washington, DC: U.S. Department of Justice, Office of Juvenile Justice and Delinquency Prevention.

Spergel, I. A., Chance, R., Ehrensaft, K., Regulus, T., Kane, C., Laseter, R., . . . Oh, S. (1994). *Gang suppression and intervention: Community models, research summary*. Retrieved from http://www.ncjrs.gov/pdffiles/gangcorr.pdf

Spergel, I. A., & Grossman, S. F. (1997). The Little Village Project: A community approach to the gang problem. *Social Work*, 42, 456–470. http://dx.doi.org/10.1093/sw/42.5.456

Spergel, I. A., Wa, K. M., & Sosa, R. V. (2005a). *Evaluation of the Bloomington–Normal comprehensive gang prevention program* (Report No. 209186). Washington, DC: U.S. Department of Justice.

Spergel, I. A., Wa, K. M., & Sosa, R. V. (2005b). *Evaluation of the Mesa gang intervention program* (Report No. 209187). Washington, DC: U.S. Department of Justice.

Spergel, I. A., Wa, K. M., & Sosa, R. V. (2005c). *Evaluation of the Riverside comprehensive community-wide approach to gang prevention, intervention, and suppression* (Report No. 209188). Washington, DC: U.S. Department of Justice.

Spergel, I. A., Wa, K. M., & Sosa, R. V. (2005d). *Evaluation of the San Antonio comprehensive community-wide approach to gang prevention, intervention and suppression program* (Report No. 209189). Washington, DC: U.S. Department of Justice.

Spergel, I. A., Wa, K. M., & Sosa, R. V. (2005e). *Evaluation of the Tucson comprehensive community-wide approach to gang prevention, intervention and suppression program* (Report No. 209189). Washington, D. C.: U.S. Department of Justice.

Stretesky, P. B., & Pogrebin, M. R. (2007). Gang-related gun violence: Socialization, identity, and self. *Journal of Contemporary Ethnography*, 36, 85–114. http://dx.doi.org/10.1177/0891241606287416

Sutherland, E. H. (1997). *Principles of criminology*. Philadelphia, PA: Lippincott.

Taylor, T. J., Freng, A., Esbensen, F. A., & Peterson, D. (2008). Youth gang membership and serious violent victimization: The importance of lifestyles and routine activities. *Journal of Interpersonal Violence*, 23, 1441–1464. http://dx.doi.org/10.1177/0886260508314306

Taylor, T. J., Peterson, D., Esbensen, F., & Freng, A. (2007). Gang membership as a risk factor for violent victimization. *Journal of Research in Crime and Delinquency*, 44, 351–380. http://dx.doi.org/10.1177/0022427807305845

Thornberry, T. (1998). Membership in youth gangs and involvement in serious and violent offending. In R. Loeber & D. Farrington (Eds.), *From serious and violent juvenile offenders: Risk factors and successful interventions* (pp. 147–166). Thousand Oaks, CA: Sage.

Thornberry, T., & Burch, J. (1997, June). Gang members and delinquent behavior. *Juvenile Justice Bulletin*, pp. 1–6.

Thornberry, T. P., Huizinga, D., & Loeber, R. (1995). The prevention of serious delinquency and violence: Implications from the program of research on the causes and correlates of delinquency. In J. Howell, B. Krisberg, J. Hawkins, & J. Wilson (Eds.), *Sourcebook on serious, violent, and chronic juvenile offenders* (pp. 213–237). Thousand Oaks, CA: Sage.

Thornberry, T. P., Krohn, M. D., Lizotte, A. J., & Chard-Wierschem, D. (1993). The role of juvenile gangs in facilitating delinquent behavior. *Journal of Research in Crime and Delinquency*, 30, 55–87. http://dx.doi.org/10.1177/0022427893030001005

Thrasher, F. M. (1963). *The gang*. Chicago, IL: University of Chicago Press.

Thurman, Q. C., Giacomazzi, A. L., Reisig, M. D., & Mueller, D. G. (1996). Community-based gang prevention and intervention: An evaluation of the neutral zone. *Crime and Delinquency*, 42, 279–295. http://dx.doi.org/10.1177/0011128796042002009

Walker, S., Spohn, C., & DeLone, M. (2006). *The color of justice*. Belmont, CA: Wadsworth.

Walker-Barnes, C. J., & Mason, C. A. (2001). Perceptions of risk factors for female gang involvement among African-American and Hispanic women. *Youth and Society*, *32*, 303–336. http://dx.doi.org/10.1177/0044118X01032003002

White, R. (2002). *Understanding youth gangs*. Canberra, Australia: Australian Institute of Criminology.

Winfree, L. T., Backström, T. V., & Mays, G. L. (1994). Social learning theory, self-reported delinquency, and youth gangs: A new twist on a general theory of crime and delinquency. *Youth and Society*, *26*, 147–177. http://dx.doi.org/10.1177/0044118X94026002001

Winfree, L. T., Fuller, K., Vigil, T., & Mays, G. L. (1992). The definition and measurement of "gang status": Policy implications for juvenile justice. *Juvenile and Family Court Journal*, *43*, 29–37. http://dx.doi.org/10.1111/j.1755-6988.1992.tb00717.x

CHAPTER 15

TRAUMA, ADVERSE EXPERIENCE, AND OFFENDING

Amanda D. Zelechoski

The number of incarcerated individuals with a history of traumatic exposure is disproportionately high and increasingly concerning, given the associated consequences. The relationship between trauma exposure and chronic and severe negative outcomes is well established and includes physical problems (D'Andrea, Sharma, Zelechoski, & Spinazzola, 2011), psychological issues (Abram et al., 2013), addiction (Grella, Stein, & Greenwell, 2005), educational and employment problems (Perkins & Graham-Bermann, 2012), and chronic risk-related behaviors (Felitti et al., 1998). Youths involved with the juvenile justice system represent one of the most complexly and pervasively traumatized populations (Abram et al., 2013). Yet this group has only relatively recently begun to garner attention, both in the research literature and with respect to clinical practice and public policy efforts. As Ford, Chapman, Hawke, and Albert (2007) noted, until recently, "juvenile justice systems have not routinely responded to the trauma histories of youth who come into contact with their system" (p. 3). Accordingly, the question remains: Is there a relationship between a history of traumatic exposure or adverse experience and subsequent delinquency and, if so, should the juvenile justice system be addressing that relationship?

In this chapter, I address the question of whether and to what extent a relationship exists between a history of traumatic exposure and juvenile offending behavior. First, I present a historical context for the trauma–delinquency relationship, in which I review early theoretical foundations and empirical examinations of the link as well as limitations to those initial understandings. Second, I discuss the current state of the issue, considering the underlying foundation for a relationship between trauma and offending, the evidence demonstrating and refuting a relationship, contributory and intervening factors that expound the nature of the relationship, and whether trauma history influences juveniles' risk for offending. Finally, in the last section I present practice-, policy-, and research-related implications and discuss future directions for consideration in each of these domains.

RELEVANT HISTORY OF TRAUMA, ADVERSE EXPERIENCE, AND OFFENDING

Empirical interest in identifying whether a link exists between early victimization and future delinquent behavior dates back to the early 1960s (Maschi, Bradley, & Morgen, 2008). According to Schwartz, Rendon, and Hsieh (1994), the publication of *The Battered Child Syndrome* (Kempe, Silverman, Steele, Droegemueller, & Silver, 1962) initiated much of the dialogue, followed by the emergence of the cycle of violence theory (Curtis, 1963), which helped the notion gain traction. Now, a half century later, numerous studies have been conducted to investigate the nature and prevalence of the trauma–delinquency link—if, in fact, such a link exists. Much of this research has suggested that abused children often go on to engage in problem behavior; whether the relationship between these factors is associative or causal continues to be examined and debated.

I acknowledge the invaluable research assistance of Mary Bentley throughout the preparation of this chapter.

http://dx.doi.org/10.1037/14643-015
APA Handbook of Psychology and Juvenile Justice, K. Heilbrun (Editor-in-Chief)

Many of the early studies yielded results supporting a relationship between childhood maltreatment and future violent behavior (e.g., Fagen, Hansen, & Jang, 1983; Falshaw, Browne, & Hollin, 1996; Kaufman & Zigler, 1987; Widom, 1989a) but were criticized for research design and methodological flaws (Maschi et al., 2008; Schwartz et al., 1994; Widom, 1989a, 1989b). The primary methodological issues included the lack of baseline data and absence of control groups, use of primarily self-report and archival data collection methods, and small or unrepresentative samples (Schwartz et al., 1994; Widom, 1989a, 1989b). Maschi et al. (2008) also noted the heavy reliance on male samples and a general failure to examine mediating factors in the relationship between trauma exposure and offending.

Perhaps one of the biggest challenges to date in synthesizing this body of research is the widespread inconsistency in defining the measured constructs, which applies to definitions of traumatic exposure as well as definitions of offending behavior. Traumatic exposure in previous research has been inconsistently operationalized as abuse (i.e., physical and sexual, and sometimes emotional), as maltreatment (i.e., some or all types of abuse and neglect), as inclusive of additional traumatic experiences (e.g., natural disasters, car accidents, witnessing domestic or community violence), as encompassing subjective experiences of trauma (e.g., thought self or close other was going to be hurt or killed), as unverifiable potentially traumatic experiences, and as broadly inclusive of any adverse experiences or life stressors (e.g., peer rejection, parental divorce, transition to new school). Widom (1989b, as cited in Schwartz et al., 1994) highlighted additional discrepancies in

> definitions of abuse (ranging from mild physical punishment to extreme physical violence); forms of abuse studied (physical, sexual, and neglect); sources of abuse (parents, caregivers, family members), number of abuse episodes, and whether the abuse was validated by an external source. (p. 643)

The field also has a long history of divergence as to what constitutes the variable of interest—trauma history, posttraumatic stress symptoms, posttraumatic stress disorder (PTSD) diagnosis, or some combination of these factors.

Similar inconsistencies exist in how offending is operationalized, ranging on a continuum of antisocial behavior from measurement of at-risk or problem behaviors and attitudes to actual arrests and, ultimately, to adjudicated offenses. Additional variation is related to whether an offending outcome variable is further classified according to violent versus nonviolent offending, inclusion or exclusion of status offenses (e.g., truancy, violating curfew, running away), and self-reported illegal behavior versus adjudicated offenses.

These substantial and frequent definitional discrepancies have made comparison across the earlier studies difficult at best and perhaps impossible, inappropriate, or misleading at worst, as some have cautioned (Schwartz et al., 1994; Widom, 1989a, 1989b). Historically, these and other methodological inconsistencies led to substantial disagreement within the field, with some commentators indicating that the research regarding a trauma–delinquency relationship was inconclusive (e.g., Doerner, 1987; Schwartz et al., 1994; Zingraff, Leiter, Myers, & Johnsen, 1993), and others describing a robust and well-established relationship (e.g., Maschi et al., 2008; Stewart, Livingston, & Dennison, 2008).

From a public policy perspective, Schwartz et al. (1994) provided some historical context related to the impact of these early studies. Citing transcripts from hearings between 1983 and 1993 of the U.S. Senate Subcommittees on Juvenile Justice, Human Resources, and Select Education, they referenced several instances of congressional testimony by senators, scholars, and clinicians attesting to an unequivocal causal link between child abuse and subsequent juvenile delinquency and lamented, "It seems that federal agencies have accepted this maltreatment/delinquency relationship at face value" (p. 641). At that time, they called for a shift in focus to delinquency prevention, noting that

> The federal Office of Juvenile Justice and Delinquency Prevention (OJJDP) is responsible for providing policy and leadership in juvenile justice. The office

> has been in existence since 1974, but during its 20-year history, prevention activities have not been a major priority. Consequently, relatively little of OJJDP's national discretionary funds has been allocated to delinquency prevention research and demonstrations. (Schwartz et al., 1994, p. 650)

In the past 20 years, substantial federal funding and targeted initiatives have specifically focused not only on recognizing but also addressing the unique needs of traumatized youths in the juvenile justice system. For example, the U.S. Congress established the National Child Traumatic Stress Network in 2000, under the purview of the U.S. Department of Health and Human Services's Substance Abuse and Mental Health Services Administration. Among many National Child Traumatic Stress Network initiatives is a subsection focused on trauma in the juvenile justice system, which has published numerous resources for judges, attorneys, and mental health and juvenile justice professionals focused on working with juvenile justice–involved traumatized youths (National Child Traumatic Stress Network, n.d.).

Similarly, the Substance Abuse and Mental Health Services Administration (2011) identified trauma and justice as one of its primary strategic initiatives in its most recent strategic plan. It has also established the National Center for Trauma-Informed Care (Substance Abuse and Mental Health Services Administration, n.d.), which is a technical assistance center, and its Federal Partners Committee on Women and Trauma (2013) recently published a report on trauma-informed approaches across a variety of settings, including criminal and juvenile justice, that represented one of the "largest interagency collaborations in federal government history" (National Association of State Mental Health Program Directors, n.d., para. 1). The Office of Juvenile Justice and Delinquency Prevention (2012, 2014) has also continued to emphasize its long-standing objective to address trauma and violence exposure in delinquency prevention efforts. Given this considerable public health and policy focus on the relationship between trauma and juvenile offending, it is important to evaluate the current state of the research on whether and to what extent an empirical relationship exists.

CURRENT STATE OF TRAUMA, ADVERSE EXPERIENCE, AND OFFENDING

In the last 50 years, substantial research and policy efforts have aimed to address the question of whether a relationship exists between traumatic exposure and offending behavior in youth. This empirical work and its subsequent applications provide an important foundation for unpacking questions about the existence of a trauma–delinquency relationship, as well as the nature and extent of that relationship.

Why Would We Expect a Relationship?

Numerous psychological, sociological, and criminological theoretical perspectives have been advanced to explain the emergence of delinquent behavior and, more specifically, the relationship between a history of traumatic experiences and subsequent problem behavior. These perspectives include theories on applications of information processing (Crick & Dodge, 1994; Dodge, 1980), social learning (Akers, 1998; Bandura, 1986), general strain (Agnew, 1992), social control (Gottfredson & Hirschi, 1990; Hirschi, 1969), dual taxonomy (Moffitt, 1993), life course (Sampson & Laub, 1993), social disorganization (Figueira-McDonough, 1991; Sampson & Groves, 1989; Shaw & McKay, 1942), and feminist pathways (Belknap & Holsinger, 2006).

In addition to the seemingly strong theoretical foundation for a relationship between traumatic exposure and juvenile delinquency, a wide body of relevant empirical research has supported this relationship. However, Bender (2010) recently noted that although the field has "made great strides in confirming the existence and strength of the maltreatment-delinquency relationship," there is a "divergence of related research into two bodies of literature that have developed independent of one another" (p. 467): child welfare research and juvenile justice research. Much research has been conducted on the consequences of trauma and adverse experience, as well as on predictors and risk factors for delinquency; however, despite the obvious and sizable overlap, there appears to have been little integration of the findings and implications (Bender, 2010).

Is There a Relationship Between Trauma and Offending?

Perhaps the most widely cited, relatively recent epidemiological examination of the prevalence of trauma exposure in a detained juvenile population is the study conducted by Abram et al. (2004). In that study, 898 arrested and newly detained youths participated in a comprehensive diagnostic interview. They inquired about eight specific trauma types (i.e., perceived impending harm to self or a family member, physical assault, sexual assault, threatened with a weapon, bad accident, natural disaster, exposure to violence, and exposure to deceased bodies), and the results indicated that 92.5% of youths had experienced at least one trauma and 84% had experienced more than one. Notably, more than half of the youths in that sample had been exposed six or more times, with a mean of 14.6 traumatic incidents over the course of their lives. The three most frequently reported trauma types were "having seen or heard someone get hurt very badly or be killed," "having been threatened with a weapon," and "being in a situation where you thought you or someone close to you was going to be hurt very badly or die" (Abram et al., 2004, pp. 405–406).

More recently, findings from the National Child Traumatic Stress Network Core Data Set (Dierkhising et al., 2013) described trauma histories among youths ($N = 658$) who had been referred for trauma-focused treatment and reported recent involvement with the juvenile justice system. That study examined the prevalence of 19 different trauma types, including exposures that were classified as less severe life stressors or adverse experiences in other studies (e.g., community violence, domestic violence, impaired caregiver). Findings yielded an average of 4.9 different trauma types, with the most frequent being loss and bereavement (61.2%), followed by impaired caregiver (51.7%), domestic violence (51.6%), emotional abuse or psychological maltreatment (49.4%), physical maltreatment or abuse (38.6%), and community violence (34%; Dierkhising et al., 2013).

Given that trauma has been operationally defined and measured in vastly disparate ways throughout the empirical literature, as discussed above, it is important to consider studies that have evaluated the prevalence of other life stressors or adverse experiences among juvenile justice–involved youths. Often, the assessment of trauma exposure in children and adolescents focuses primarily on child maltreatment, specifically on physical and sexual abuse. However, other studies have broadened their definitions of trauma to include adverse experiences such as exposure to community violence, traumatic loss, peer rejection, parental separation or divorce, domestic violence, moving to a new school or home, and other potentially traumatic experiences (see, e.g., Costello, Erkanli, Fairbank, & Angold, 2002; Eitle & Turner, 2002; Hoffman & Cerbone, 1999; Maschi et al., 2008; Riggs Romaine, Sevin Goldstein, Hunt, & DeMatteo, 2011). Research examining these types of adverse experience has generally found a significant link between juvenile justice involvement and stressful life events (e.g., Hoffman & Cerbone, 1999; Maschi et al., 2008). Accordingly, Maschi et al. (2008) noted the importance of recognizing that "traumatic experiences that place youth at risk for juvenile delinquency may range from minor to serious and occur in the home and/or the community" (p. 152).

In terms of PTSD diagnosis, Abram et al. (2004) found that only 11.2% of detained youths met the criteria for PTSD, which was surprising given that more than 90% of their sample reported at least one prior trauma exposure. In addition, most youths (88%) reported that their worst precipitating trauma had occurred within the previous 2 years. No significant difference was found between male and female youths in PTSD diagnosis, but Abram et al. noted that "although male detainees were significantly more likely than female detainees to have experienced trauma, female detainees were as likely to have PTSD as were male detainees" (p. 408). They suggested that these discrepancies may be attributable to their measurement methods (i.e., only one screening questionnaire, measurement primarily focused on only the worst trauma experience, lack of anonymity in interview participation, and the possibility of an alternative diagnosis accounting for

PTSD-related symptoms) or to an insufficient understanding of factors that promote resilience to developing PTSD among trauma-exposed youths.

In the aforementioned National Child Traumatic Stress Network study, Dierkhising et al. (2013) reported that 23.6% of juvenile justice–involved youths met symptom criteria for a PTSD diagnosis and underscored that "many youth who do not meet criteria for a diagnosis of PTSD are still experiencing clinically significant post-traumatic stress symptoms within individual symptom clusters" (p. 9). Specifically, using the PTSD symptom clusters identified in the *Diagnostic and Statistical Manual of Mental Disorders, Fourth Edition, Text Revision* (American Psychiatric Association, 2000), 71.8% of youths fell in the clinically significant range for Criterion B (reexperiencing), 53.2% for Criterion C (avoidance), and 80.6% for Criterion D (hyperarousal; Dierkhising et al., 2013).

The findings from these large-scale studies, and from numerous smaller studies, suggest that there is clearly a relationship between a history of traumatic exposure and involvement with the juvenile justice system, even considering the differences in how traumatic exposure is defined and measured. However, the current understanding of the nature of this relationship warrants closer examination, because empirical understanding has evolved since many of the previously discussed early studies.

What Is the Nature of the Relationship Between Trauma and Offending?

The recent prevalence estimates presented above seem to clearly establish the existence of a relationship between history of traumatic exposure and involvement with the juvenile justice system. The nature of that relationship may still be unclear and is undoubtedly complex; however, the past several decades have produced a wide body of pertinent empirical research, examining the relationship from innovative and multidisciplinary perspectives, using a variety of methodological and definitional approaches. In this section, I review recent trends in the empirical literature, particularly as they relate to factors and considerations that help to unravel the trauma–delinquency association.

Demographic factors.

Gender. Gender differences in trauma exposure, posttraumatic stress symptoms, and delinquent behavior patterns are now well established. With respect to history of traumatic exposure, most studies have found gender-based patterns, particularly related to specific types of traumatic or adverse experiences. Some studies have found higher rates of overall trauma exposure for males than for females (e.g., Abram et al., 2004, with 93.2% of males and 84.0% of females reporting exposure), but most studies have found higher overall exposure rates among female juvenile justice–involved youths (e.g., Ford, Hartman, Hawke, & Chapman, 2008; Kerig & Becker, 2012). Regarding specific types of traumatic exposure, female juvenile justice–involved youths tend to report higher rates of abuse, sexual assault victimization, and polyvictimization (i.e., multiple types of trauma; Abram et al., 2004; Dierkhising et al., 2013; Ford et al., 2008; Kerig & Becker, 2012), whereas male juvenile justice–involved youths tend to report higher rates of witnessing violence (Cauffman, Feldman, Waterman, & Steiner, 1998; Kerig & Becker, 2010; Kerig, Ward, Vanderzee, & Arnzen Moeddel, 2009), experiencing physical assaults (Lawyer, Ruggiero, Resnick, Kilpatrick, & Saunders, 2006; Yoshinaga, Kadomoto, Otani, Sasaki, & Kato, 2004), and being in serious accidents (Abram et al., 2004).

With respect to PTSD diagnosis and symptoms, Kerig and Becker (2012) reviewed 19 studies that included gender-specific analyses and highlighted prevalence discrepancies, with some studies finding no significant gender differences in PTSD prevalence among delinquent youths (e.g., Abram et al., 2004; Ford, Chapman, Mack, & Pearson, 2006; McCabe, Lansing, Garland, & Hough, 2002) and other studies finding significant gender differences (e.g., Cauffman et al., 1998; Kerig & Becker, 2010; Kerig et al., 2009; Wood, Foy, Layne, Pynoos, & James, 2002). Most of the research they reviewed found that juvenile justice system–involved girls are more likely than boys to meet diagnostic criteria for PTSD, and they attributed the substantial discrepancy in prevalence rates across studies (e.g., 7%–75% among delinquent females) to inconsistencies in construct definition and measurement (Kerig & Becker, 2012). More recent research has confirmed higher rates of PTSD among juvenile justice–involved females (Dierkhising et al., 2013).

In addition to gender differences in trauma exposure and PTSD diagnosis, Bender (2010) highlighted the differences between males' tendency to respond to maltreatment in more externalizing ways and females' tendency to respond in more internalizing ways and emphasized:

> Not only do female offenders report more victimization than male offenders, but they report more extreme victimization and more repeat victimization experiences (Wood et al., 2002). In fact, female offenders are significantly more likely than males to report that victimization was a key factor leading to their offending (Belknap & Holsinger, 2006). The differential impact of, and responses to, maltreatment suggest that males' and females' pathways from maltreatment to delinquency are likely to be significantly different (pp. 466–467).

If traumatic experience plays a significant role in these pathways, Kerig and Becker (2012) suggested that it may be a function of how posttraumatic stress manifests differently for boys and girls. Specifically, girls are more likely to experience interpersonal trauma (e.g., be victimized by family members), which in turn increases their risk of status offenses (e.g., running away, truancy) perhaps to escape from the abusive situation or internalized behaviors. In contrast, boys are more likely to react aggressively or engage in high-risk, externalized behaviors in response to common stressors, such as witnessing domestic or community violence.

Age. Another important demographic factor to consider is the youth's age, both at the time of traumatic exposure and at first offense. It is well established that early victimization or traumatic exposure increases an individual's likelihood of subsequent victimization (e.g., Finkelhor, Ormrod, & Turner, 2007; Tyler, Hoyt, & Whitbeck, 2000) and that early onset of delinquent behavior is robustly predictive of chronic delinquency (Moffitt, 1993, 2003). What is not as widely understood is the relationship between age at traumatic exposure and the emergence of delinquent behavior. Not surprisingly, given the importance of timing in developmental course, recent research has suggested that juvenile justice system–involved youths are generally exposed to trauma early in life (before age 5) and experience high rates of subsequent victimization (Dierkhising et al., 2013) and that this early traumatic exposure is predictive of their subsequent delinquent involvement (Maschi, 2006). In addition, although a relationship between earlier traumatic exposure and subsequent offending behavior would be expected, findings have also suggested that more juvenile justice–involved youths who are older (age 14 years or older) report trauma exposure than do justice-involved youths who are younger (ages 10–13 years; Abram et al., 2004). In addition, maltreatment experienced later in childhood or adolescence increases the risk of juvenile justice involvement (Bright & Jonson-Reid, 2008; Stewart, Dennison, & Waterson, 2001; Stewart et al., 2008; Thornberry, Ireland, & Smith, 2001), and a relatively high proportion of juvenile justice-involved youths experience additional maltreatment subsequent to first arrest (Huang, Ryan, & Herz, 2012).

Race/ethnicity. Given the vast overrepresentation of youths of color in both the child welfare and the juvenile justice systems (Ryan, Herz, Hernandez, & Marshall, 2007), one would expect that patterns in the trauma–delinquency relationship would differ across racial groups. Abram et al. (2004) did not find any significant race-related differences in trauma prevalence rates or PTSD diagnosis. They did, however, find differences related to the types of trauma exposure reported by delinquent youths: White males were more likely than African American males to have experienced physical assault, as were Hispanic females relative to African American females; African American males were more likely to have witnessed violence than White males.

Other studies have reported higher rates of polyvictimization among White and African American youths than among Hispanic youths (Ford, Grasso, Hawke, & Chapman, 2013). Given these and other inconsistent findings, the role of race/ethnicity in the relationship between trauma exposure and delinquency remains unclear. It is widely accepted, however, that the juvenile justice system needs to satisfactorily address the issue of disproportionate minority contact, ideally from a trauma-informed perspective (Lacey, 2013).

Trauma type. Little discussion has yet been devoted to the cumulative versus differential effects (Maschi, 2006) of various types of adverse and traumatic experiences on delinquent behavior. Not surprisingly, childhood exposure to more and varied types of trauma is generally predictive of worse outcomes (Boyer, Hallion, Hammell, & Button, 2009; Ford et al., 2013; Maschi et al., 2008). In addition, delinquent youths who are exposed to multiple types of potentially traumatic events are more likely to have clinically significant levels of PTSD symptoms than are delinquent youths with only a single traumatic exposure (Abram et al., 2004; Ford et al., 2008; Stimmel, Cruise, Ford, & Weiss, 2013).

With respect to the relationship between trauma exposure type and offending behaviors, there is limited available research and somewhat contradictory findings (Mallett, Stoddard Dare, & Seck, 2009). Some research has suggested a robust relationship between delinquency and prior physical abuse and neglect, but not between delinquency and sexual abuse (Egeland, Yates, Appleyard, & van Dulmen, 2002; Fagan, 2005). Other studies have suggested a stronger link between exposure to violence and subsequent violent offenses, as compared with property offenses (Maschi, 2006; Maschi et al., 2008). Additional findings have highlighted the impact of exposure to what may be considered more minor adverse experiences (e.g., parental separation, death of a family member) on propensity to engage in delinquent behavior (Hoffman & Cerbone, 1999), although that relationship is typically mediated by other factors (e.g., anger, deviant peer association; Maschi et al., 2008). Although there seem to be numerous potential pathways, the relationship between trauma and subsequent offending appears to differ on the basis of trauma type and the nature of the delinquent behavior, with the type of trauma exposure often closely mirroring the type of subsequent offense (Maschi, 2006).

Co-occurrence with other risk factors. In addition to considering the role played by demographic factors in the trauma–delinquency relationship, it is important to consider other frequently co-occurring factors that may contribute to traumatized youths' elevated risk of offending. These are factors that have been established as both consequences of trauma exposure and risk factors for delinquent behavior (Bender, 2010). They include running away and homelessness, poverty (Bright & Jonson-Reid, 2008), weapon carrying (Vaughn, Howard, & Harper-Chang, 2006), substance abuse (see Chapter 12, this handbook), school problems and bullying (see Chapter 11, this handbook), and association with delinquent peers and gangs (see Chapter 13, this handbook).

In addition, the co-occurrence of trauma exposure and mental health symptoms, psychiatric disorders, or both put maltreated youths at even higher risk of offending behavior (King et al., 2011; Mallett et al., 2009; Rosenberg et al., 2014). Also relevant are personality-related constructs, such as juvenile psychopathy or callous–unemotional traits (see Chapter 10, this handbook), given the growing body of research examining the relationship between trauma exposure and psychopathy (Krischer & Sevecke, 2008; Tatar, Cauffman, Kimonis, & Skeem, 2012). The presence of one or more of these co-occurring factors puts traumatized youths at increased risk for both subsequent victimization and participation in delinquent behavior—and may even play a mediating role in the trauma–delinquency relationship, along with other potential mediators discussed in the next section.

Potentially mediating considerations. Understanding the relationship between trauma, adverse experience, and offending behavior necessarily warrants consideration of intervening mechanisms that may better explain or account for that relationship. A number of mediating factors have been examined, including attachment disruption, emotional dysregulation, cognitive processes or deficits, and the degree to which protective factors were present.

One of the most widely recognized consequences of childhood maltreatment is the disruption in attachment to consistent and supportive caregivers, which often results in the development of disorganized or insecure attachment patterns (Lyons-Ruth, 1996). This attachment disruption can result in a number of developmental deficits, including inappropriate interpersonal interactions, lack of boundaries, difficulty trusting others, and an inability to consider multiple perspectives (Cook et al., 2005). The extremely high prevalence of placement instability for traumatized youths removed from the home after maltreatment results in attachment disruptions that, in turn, increase the risk of delinquency (Ryan & Testa, 2005). Moreover, child maltreatment tends to increase during times of transition in the child's life (e.g., between schools or grade levels, between foster home placements), which further hinders the development of secure and consistent attachment relationships (Stewart et al., 2008). Given the long-term ramifications of chronic and pervasive attachment disruption, it is not surprising that attachment disruption appears to play an intervening or explanatory role in the trauma–delinquency relationship (Anderson, Holmes, & Ostresh, 1999).

Another potentially mediating factor is affect regulation among traumatized youths. Traumatic exposure appears to have a profound impact on a child's subsequent ability to maintain homeostasis, or effectively modulate physiological and emotional arousal levels (Cook et al., 2005; van der Kolk & Fisler, 1994). This lack of self-regulatory capacity is particularly evident among traumatized youths involved with the juvenile justice system (Ford, 2005; Ford & Blaustein, 2013). It might be understood in the context of their adaptive need to constantly maintain a "survival-oriented preoccupation with detecting and surviving threats" (Pine, 2007, as cited in Ford, Chapman, Connor, & Cruise, 2012, p. 696). Ford et al. (2012) identified the following specific self-regulatory deficits resulting from complex trauma exposure: "(a) attention and learning; (b) sensorimotor functions; (c) working (short-term processing), declarative (verbal) and narrative (autobiographical) memory; and (d) emotion regulation and social relatedness (attachment)" (p. 696). As several studies have demonstrated (e.g., Ford, 2005; Ford et al., 2006; Maschi et al., 2008), it is perhaps these and related deficiencies in self-regulation that account for the relationship between trauma exposure and delinquent behavior. Specifically,

> when exposed to trauma or mistreatment, a youth may cope by resorting to indifference, defiance, or aggression as self-protective reactions. In these cases, risk taking, breaking rules, fighting back, and hurting others who are perceived to be powerful or vulnerable may become a way to survive emotionally or literally. It is often these behaviors that bring youth into the juvenile justice system. (Ford et al., 2007, p. 3)

In addition to emotional dysregulation, cognitive and information processing factors have also been considered as potential mediators in the relationship between trauma and delinquency. For example, Shahinfar, Kupersmidt, and Matza (2001) examined several elements of the social information processing model of children's social adjustment (Dodge, 1980) in incarcerated adolescents, namely endorsement of aggressive beliefs, causal attributions, social goals, and perceived outcomes of aggression. Exposure to violence significantly predicted incarcerated youths' social information processing patterns, which has important implications for a potential pathway by which violence-exposed youths engage in offending behavior (Shahinfar et al., 2001). Specifically, patterns in cognitive processing appeared to play a mediating role between community violence exposure and subsequent aggressive behavior in that study. Other studies have yielded similar results, suggesting that problematic cognitive processes, such as misinterpreting social cues (Baer & Maschi, 2003) or demonstrating a lack of future orientation (Allwood, Baetz, DeMarco, & Bell, 2012; Allwood & Bell, 2008), play an intermediary role between trauma exposure and offending (Dierkhising et al., 2013).

Posttraumatic stress symptoms may also play a mediating role between trauma (or adverse experience) and delinquent behavior. The research on this point is mixed, though, with some studies demonstrating that posttraumatic stress or PTSD diagnosis at least partially accounts for the relationship between being victimized and offending behavior (e.g., Kerig et al., 2009; Stimmel et al., 2013), and other studies not finding that PTSD played a significant mediating role (e.g., Ford, Elhai, Connor, & Frueh, 2010). Other research has suggested that the mediating mechanism between trauma and delinquency may be a broader construct, such as negative affect (e.g., Maschi et al., 2008), or a more specific and nuanced process, such as emotional numbing (Kerig, Bennett, Thompson, & Becker, 2012, p. 273).

An additional potentially intervening factor between trauma exposure and delinquency is the presence of protective factors (Brown, Henggeler, Brondino, & Pickrel, 1999). Frequently cited protective factors include intelligence, supportive family, strong peer relationships, and school and community attachment (Hawkins, Catalano, & Miller, 1992). Less commonly cited protective factors include parental divorce (found to be protective when compared with youth from never-married families; Stoddard Dare & Mallett, 2009), parental monitoring (Griffin, Botvin, Scheier, Diaz, & Miller, 2000), and high levels of resiliency (Rosenberg et al., 2014).

Dispositional variation. One of the more recent questions being examined in the literature is the degree to which traumatized youths may be treated differently at various stages of involvement with the child welfare and juvenile justice systems. This differential treatment could be beneficial if, for example, traumatized youths are identified early in the adjudication process and provided with appropriate trauma-informed intervention as a means of diversion. In such a case, a history of traumatic exposure may even serve as a protective factor by decreasing youths' likelihood of future delinquent involvement after appropriate intervention (Mallett et al., 2009). Unfortunately, this approach appears to be the exception rather than the rule.

More often, it appears that youths with a history of traumatic exposure become further entrenched in the criminal justice system over the course of their lives than do their nontraumatized peers (Grella et al., 2005), which raises several questions related to how and why this variability in dispositional decisions and outcomes occurs. Espinosa, Sorensen, and Lopez (2013) examined this phenomenon, with particular attention to whether gender differences existed in juvenile placement trends and whether a history of traumatic exposure influenced the removal of juveniles from the home. In their assessment of more than 30,000 juvenile justice–involved youths, they found that a history of traumatic experiences was the most significant predictor of restrictive (vs. nonrestrictive) placement, regardless of gender, which suggests that previous traumatic exposure "influenced how deeply juveniles penetrated the system" (p. 1824).

Similarly, Ryan et al. (2007) found an apparent bias in disposition decisions between crossover youths (i.e., youths simultaneously involved with the child welfare and juvenile justice systems) and non–crossover youths, with crossover youths more likely to be ordered to an out-of-home or correctional placement rather than to probation. Given that youths are involved with the child welfare system as the result of substantial family dysfunction of some sort, dependency classification is often used as a proxy for presumed traumatic exposure (i.e., maltreatment or neglect). Accordingly, these findings and similarly observed discrepancies in case disposition and subsequent placement decisions for dependent youths (e.g., Conger & Ross, 2001; Stevenson, 2009) raise the question of why this apparent dispositional bias exists and how it affects traumatized youths' risk of subsequent offending.

One potential explanation for the dispositional variation is the degree to which the legal decision maker perceives a history of traumatic exposure as increasing or decreasing an individual's risk for reoffending. Because research has repeatedly demonstrated a pattern of harsher sanctions for individuals perceived to be less amenable to treatment or rehabilitation (Albonetti & Hepburn, 1996; Riggs Romaine et al., 2011), it is not surprising that maltreated children are often considered more likely to recidivate as a result of their complex treatment and rehabilitation needs (Cottle, Lee, & Heilbrun, 2001; Huang et al., 2012).

Another potential explanation for the differential treatment of traumatized youths at various stages of the adjudication process is that law enforcement and judicial officers simply have no safe or appropriate alternative placement option other than a juvenile justice facility. This may be the case if, for example, there is no legal guardian to whom police could release a dependent youth from secure detention, which would also make it unlikely that probation would be a viable option, given the youth's placement instability (Ryan et al., 2007). Unfortunately, inadequate alternatives often mean secure placement that could exacerbate the youth's trauma symptoms and risk for future offending (Espinosa et al., 2013; Ford et al., 2007).

Is Trauma a Risk Factor for Offending?

The available research seems to support a relationship between trauma exposure and juvenile offending, even as the precise nature of that relationship is disentangled. However, does current or previous trauma or adverse experience increase a juvenile's risk for offending? Establishing an unequivocally causal relationship between trauma exposure and delinquent behavior may not be possible using current methodological and data-analytic strategies, given the typical co-occurrence of trauma exposure and numerous other established risk factors. However, the extant research reviewed in this chapter provides compelling empirical support for consideration of a juvenile's differential and cumulative trauma history in the overall weighing of relative risk (see Chapter 16, this handbook). Despite substantial evidence that traumatized youths are at increased risk of engaging in delinquent behavior (Bender, 2010), it is also critical to consider that the majority of maltreated children do not engage in offending behavior (Stewart et al., 2008).

IMPLICATIONS FOR PRACTICE, POLICY, AND RESEARCH

Perhaps one of the most significant outcomes to emerge from the examination of the trauma–delinquency link is the increasing emphasis on trauma-informed approaches to juvenile justice, both in practice and in policy (see Chapter 24, this handbook). This has not always been the case. As Ford et al. (2007) noted, "It has only been within the past decade, as the collective knowledge base on youth exposure to psychological trauma has grown, that there has been a push to improve the juvenile justice system's response to traumatized youth" (p. 3). Targeted efforts to identify and address the impact of trauma and adverse experience on delinquent youths have resulted in a growing body of promising and best practices related to various stages of the juvenile justice system (Askew, 2013). I review policy and practice implications for each of these stages below.

Prevention

In 1994, Schwartz et al. noted, with respect to prevention efforts,

> although it is true that child abuse prevention and treatment programs are desperately needed, policymakers, child welfare professionals, child advocates, and the public should be cautioned to lower their expectations about the impact these interventions can be expected to have on future delinquent behavior, particularly violence. (p. 650)

It appears that some aspects of Schwartz et al.'s concerns may have been somewhat premature, given the lack of empirical evaluation of the effectiveness of trauma-specific prevention and intervention efforts at that time. As discussed in the beginning of this chapter, in the 2 decades since the publication of those cautionary statements, numerous resources and policy efforts have been directed toward preventing child maltreatment, reducing juvenile offending, and diverting youths from the criminal justice system (e.g., Centers for Disease Control and Prevention, n.d.), all while adopting an increasingly developmentally sensitive approach to juvenile justice (Bonnie, Johnson, Chemers, & Schuck, 2013). Certainly, when considering youths with a history of traumatic exposure or child welfare system involvement, effective and targeted prevention efforts are key to minimizing the likelihood of subsequent delinquent behavior (see Chapter 3, this handbook).

Assessment

The findings related to the screening and assessment of exposure to traumatic or adverse experiences among juvenile justice–involved youths are disparate.

Discrepancies in whether and to what extent trauma history is assessed span from the preadjudication (e.g., Riggs Romaine et al., 2011) through the post-adjudication (e.g., Maschi & Schwalbe, 2012) phases of juvenile justice involvement. Even if history of traumatic exposure is assessed, there are substantial differences in measurement approach and process. For example, how trauma history is defined and measured, whether the assessment includes trauma exposure and posttraumatic stress symptoms, and the degree to which trauma-related mental health diagnoses are considered all vary significantly across jurisdictions as well as across child welfare and juvenile justice agencies (Murray, Glaser, & Calhoun, 2013). Others have also emphasized the importance of including cognitive deficits or proclivities (e.g., hostile attribution, lack of empathy, poor problem-solving skills) in the assessment of traumatized youths, given their relevance to risk-related behaviors (Baer & Maschi, 2003).

Another important consideration more recently emphasized in the literature is the lack of validity and reliability in diagnosing trauma-related disorders in juvenile justice settings, given the inconsistency in screening and assessment procedures (Abram et al., 2004). Trauma and adverse experiences are vastly underreported, with respect to both youths' self-reports and official child welfare and court records (Swahn et al., 2006). However, when youths' histories of traumatic exposure have been thoroughly assessed and documented, more effective, trauma-informed intervention approaches can be implemented—often with considerable success (Ford & Hawke, 2012). For example, in one study, probation officers' awareness of a youth's history of traumatic exposure had a direct impact on whether a rehabilitative versus punitive strategy was used (Maschi & Schwalbe, 2012).

In addition to adequately assessing history of traumatic exposure, the diagnostic appropriateness of PTSD for these youths has been questioned, given the high prevalence of youths with clinically elevated posttraumatic stress symptoms that are just below diagnostic thresholds (Dierkhising et al., 2013), as well as the failure of PTSD diagnostic criteria to account for the developmental and symptomatic complexities of children with chronic and pervasive trauma exposure (D'Andrea, Ford, Stolbach, Spinazzola, & van der Kolk, 2012; Kisiel et al., 2014; van der Kolk, 2005). Because inaccurate or inadequate diagnoses can directly affect conceptualization of a youth's level of risk and subsequent placement, this issue has significant practical implications related to determining youths' treatment needs and amenability.

Intervention

Until recently, very few trauma-focused interventions were being used in juvenile justice facilities (Bender, 2010; Ford et al., 2007). Indeed, a 2002 Child Welfare League of America report indicated that fewer than 10% of juvenile justice agencies had implemented trauma-specific programming or established partnerships with other agencies to do so. Given the high prevalence of trauma exposure in the juvenile justice population and the associated risk for reoffending, the importance of implementing trauma-informed interventions within juvenile justice settings cannot be overstated (Askew, 2013).

This approach does not come without challenges, particularly those related to insufficient mental health staffing and concerns that intentionally addressing youths' trauma histories and symptoms will exacerbate emotional and behavioral problems (Ford & Hawke, 2012). However, increasing empirical evidence has shown that incorporating trauma-informed strategies into residential treatment and juvenile justice facilities actually reduces critical incidents (e.g., incidences of restraint and seclusion) within the facility (Askew, 2013; Ford & Blaustein, 2013; Zelechoski et al., 2013), as well as recidivism postrelease (Ford & Hawke, 2012). Many aspects of juvenile justice settings can be triggering for traumatized youth, and they often exacerbate existing mental health and posttraumatic stress symptoms (Askew, 2013; Espinosa et al., 2013; Ford & Blaustein, 2013). However, promising empirical trends demonstrate increasing support for the risk reduction benefits of trauma-informed juvenile justice systems (see Chapters 24 and 26, this handbook).

Legal and Procedural Considerations

Although there is not a substantial body of case law or legal scholarship specifically related to the links among trauma, adverse experience, and juvenile offending, some relevant considerations have emerged throughout the juvenile adjudication process. First, one area of scholarly disagreement is whether youths' history of traumatic exposure should be considered in juvenile justice proceedings and, if so, whether it functions more in mitigation or aggravation. Empirical research seems mixed on this issue (Caldwell, 2012; Stevenson, 2009), with some studies demonstrating the mitigating role played by the presence of trauma exposure (e.g., Lynch & Haney, 2000) and others demonstrating the tendency of trauma history to raise additional risk-related concerns, in effect, acting as an aggravating factor (e.g., Grisso, Tomkins, & Casey, 1988; Riggs Romaine et al., 2011; Sanborn, 1996).

A second area of consideration related to legal ramifications for traumatized youths is the dispositional variation discussed above. Specifically, additional logistical or practical barriers may exist for traumatized youths, such as exclusion of traditional probation as an option because of the youth's transitions between foster homes—meaning that no feasible or stable supervisory arrangement exists in the home (Ryan et al., 2007). Additional procedural issues related to increasing youths' risk of offending include determining what constitutes "cruel and unusual punishment" for traumatized youth (Levick, Feierman, Messenheimer Kelley, Goldstein, & Mordecai, 2012) and the effects of juvenile justice facility procedures, such as strip searches, on traumatized youth (Feierman & Shah, 2007).

Implications for Future Research

Perhaps the most significant implication to emerge from this synthesis of the research on the relationship among trauma, adverse experience, and offending is that researchers still have much to disentangle. Research, practice, and public policy have increasingly emphasized the importance of considering the role of trauma in juvenile risk considerations. Yet close examination of this link has been relatively recent, particularly as it involves using more sophisticated data-analytic and modeling techniques. Although substantial empirical literature related to additive and potentially intervening risk factors was discussed in this chapter, further research is needed to better understand the nature and various manifestations of the trauma–delinquency relationship. Future research should also address the definitional and methodological inconsistencies discussed above, particularly with respect to making distinctions among trauma history, trauma-related symptoms, and PTSD or related diagnoses and their differential and cumulative risks for offending. As Quas, Bottoms, and Nunez (2002) noted,

> mischaracterizing the links between maltreatment and delinquency as predictive in a practical legal sense could lead to perceptions that youth with past histories of child maltreatment are inevitably persistent offenders who should receive the harsher punishments. This, Grisso notes, would contribute to the final victimization of the victims of childhood maltreatment. (p. 247)

Continuing to understand the relationship among trauma, adverse experience, and offending allows us to better rehabilitate juvenile justice–involved youths and, ultimately, to prevent their criminal justice system involvement altogether.

References

Abram, K. M., Teplin, L. A., Charles, D. R., Longworth, S. L., McClelland, G. M., & Dulcan, M. K. (2004). Posttraumatic stress disorder and trauma in youth in juvenile detention. *Archives of General Psychiatry*, *61*, 403–410. http://dx.doi.org/10.1001/archpsyc.61.4.403

Abram, K. M., Teplin, L. A., King, D. C., Longworth, S. L., Emanuel, K. M., Romero, E. G., & Olson, N. D. (2013). *PTSD, trauma, and comorbid psychiatric disorders in detained youth* (Juvenile Justice Bulletin). Washington, DC: U.S. Department of Justice, Office of Justice Programs, Office of Juvenile Justice and Delinquency Prevention.

Agnew, R. (1992). Foundation for a general strain theory of crime and delinquency. *Criminology*, *30*, 47–88. http://dx.doi.org/10.1111/j.1745-9125.1992.tb01093.x

Akers, R. (1998). *Social learning and social structure: A general theory of crime and deviance*. Boston, MA: Northeastern University Press.

Albonetti, C., & Hepburn, J. (1996). Prosecutorial discretion to defer criminalization: The effects of defendant's ascribed and achieved status characteristics. *Journal of Quantitative Criminology*, *12*, 63–81. http://dx.doi.org/10.1007/BF02354471

Allwood, M. A., Baetz, C., DeMarco, S., & Bell, D. J. (2012). Depressive symptoms, including lack of future orientation, as mediators in the relationship between adverse life events and delinquent behaviors. *Journal of Child and Adolescent Trauma*, *5*, 114–128. http://dx.doi.org/10.1080/19361521.2012.671795

Allwood, M. A., & Bell, D. J. (2008). A preliminary examination of emotional and cognitive mediators in the relations between violence exposure and violent behaviors in youth. *Journal of Community Psychology*, *36*, 989–1007. http://dx.doi.org/10.1002/jcop.20277

American Psychiatric Association. (2000). *Diagnostic and statistical manual of mental disorders* (4th ed., text revision). Washington, DC: Author.

Anderson, B., Holmes, M. D., & Ostresh, E. (1999). Male and female delinquents' attachments and effects of attachments on severity of self-reported delinquency. *Criminal Justice and Behavior*, *26*, 435–452. http://dx.doi.org/10.1177/0093854899026004002

Askew, W. (2013). Keeping promises to preserve promise: The necessity of committing to a rehabilitation model in the juvenile justice system. *Georgetown Journal of Law and Public Policy*, *20*, 373–395.

Baer, J., & Maschi, T. (2003). Random acts of delinquency: Trauma and self-destructiveness in juvenile offenders. *Child and Adolescent Social Work Journal*, *20*, 85–98. http://dx.doi.org/10.1023/A:1022812630174

Bandura, A. (1986). *Social foundations of thought and action: A social cognitive theory*. Englewood Cliffs, NJ: Prentice Hall.

Belknap, J., & Holsinger, K. (2006). The gendered nature of risk factors for delinquency. *Feminist Criminology*, *1*, 48–71. http://dx.doi.org/10.1177/1557085105282897

Bender, K. (2010). Why do some maltreated youth become juvenile offenders? A call for further investigation and adaptation of youth services. *Children and Youth Services Review*, *32*, 466–473. http://dx.doi.org/10.1016/j.childyouth.2009.10.022

Bonnie, R. J., Johnson, R. L., Chemers, B. M., & Schuck, J. A.; Committee on Assessing Juvenile Justice Reform, Committee on Law and Justice, Division of Behavioral and Social Sciences and Education, National Research Council (Eds.). (2013). *Reforming juvenile justice: A developmental approach*. Washington, DC: National Academies Press.

Boyer, S. N., Hallion, L. S., Hammell, C. L., & Button, S. (2009). Trauma as a predictive indicator of clinical outcome in residential treatment. *Residential Treatment for Children and Youth*, *26*, 92–104. http://dx.doi.org/10.1080/08865710902872978

Bright, C. L., & Jonson-Reid, M. (2008). Onset of juvenile court involvement: Exploring gender-specific associations with maltreatment and poverty. *Children and Youth Services Review*, *30*, 914–927. http://dx.doi.org/10.1016/j.childyouth.2007.11.015

Brown, T. L., Henggeler, S. W., Brondino, M. J., & Pickrel, S. G. (1999). Trauma exposure, protective factors, and mental health functioning of substance-abusing and dependent juvenile offenders. *Journal of Emotional and Behavioral Disorders*, *7*, 94–102. http://dx.doi.org/10.1177/106342669900700204

Caldwell, B. (2012). Appealing to empathy: Counsel's obligation to present mitigating evidence for juveniles in adult court. *Maine Law Review*, *64*, 391–423.

Cauffman, E., Feldman, S., Waterman, J., & Steiner, H. (1998). Posttraumatic stress disorder among female juvenile offenders. *Journal of the American Academy of Child and Adolescent Psychiatry*, *37*, 1209–1216. http://dx.doi.org/10.1097/00004583-199811000-00022

Centers for Disease Control and Prevention. (n.d.). *Child maltreatment: Prevention strategies*. Retrieved from http://www.cdc.gov/violenceprevention/childmaltreatment/prevention.html

Child Welfare League of America. (2002). *Juvenile justice report: Raising the level of awareness between child maltreatment and juvenile delinquency: Results of an online survey*. Arlington, VA: Author.

Conger, D., & Ross, T. (2001). *Reducing the foster care bias in juvenile detention decisions: The impact of Project Confirm*. New York, NY: Vera Institute of Justice.

Cook, A., Spinazzola, J., Ford, J., Lanktree, C., Blaustein, M., Cloitre, M., . . . van der Kolk, B. (2005). Complex trauma in children and adolescents. *Psychiatric Annals*, *35*, 390–398.

Costello, E. J., Erkanli, A., Fairbank, J. A., & Angold, A. (2002). The prevalence of potentially traumatic events in childhood and adolescence. *Journal of Traumatic Stress*, *15*, 99–112. http://dx.doi.org/10.1023/A:1014851823163

Cottle, C. C., Lee, R. J., & Heilbrun, K. (2001). The prediction of criminal recidivism in juveniles: A meta-analysis. *Criminal Justice and Behavior*, *28*, 367–394. http://dx.doi.org/10.1177/0093854801028003005

Crick, N. R., & Dodge, K. A. (1994). A review and reformulation of social information-processing mechanisms in children's social adjustment. *Psychological Bulletin*, *115*, 74–101. http://dx.doi.org/10.1037/0033-2909.115.1.74

Curtis, G. C. (1963). Violence breeds violence—Perhaps? *American Journal of Psychiatry*, *120*, 386–387.

D'Andrea, W., Ford, J., Stolbach, B., Spinazzola, J., & van der Kolk, B. A. (2012). Understanding interpersonal trauma in children: Why we need a developmentally appropriate trauma diagnosis. *American Journal of Orthopsychiatry*, *82*, 187–200. http://dx.doi.org/10.1111/j.1939-0025.2012.01154.x

D'Andrea, W., Sharma, R., Zelechoski, A. D., & Spinazzola, J. (2011). Physical health problems after single trauma exposure: When stress takes root in the body. *Journal of the American Psychiatric Nurses Association*, *17*, 378–392. http://dx.doi.org/10.1177/1078390311425187

Dierkhising, C. B., Ko, S. J., Woods-Jaeger, B., Briggs, E. C., Lee, R., & Pynoos, R. S. (2013). Trauma histories among justice-involved youth: Findings from the National Child Traumatic Stress Network. *European Journal of Psychotraumatology*, *4*, 1–12. http://dx.doi.org/10.3402/ejpt.v4i0.20274

Dodge, K. A. (1980). Social cognition and children's aggressive behavior. *Child Development*, *51*, 162–170. http://dx.doi.org/10.2307/1129603

Doerner, W. G. (1987). Child maltreatment seriousness and juvenile delinquency. *Youth and Society*, *19*, 197–224. http://dx.doi.org/10.1177/0044118X87019002006

Egeland, B., Yates, T., Appleyard, K., & van Dulmen, M. (2002). The long-term consequences of maltreatment in the early years: A developmental pathway model to antisocial behavior. *Children's Services*, *5*, 249–260. http://dx.doi.org/10.1207/S15326918CS0504_2

Eitle, D., & Turner, R. J. (2002). Exposure to community violence and young adult crime: The effects of witnessing violence, traumatic victimization, and other stressful life events. *Journal of Research in Crime and Delinquency*, *39*, 214–237. http://dx.doi.org/10.1177/002242780203900204

Espinosa, E. M., Sorensen, J. R., & Lopez, M. A. (2013). Youth pathways to placement: The influence of gender, mental health need and trauma on confinement in the juvenile justice system. *Journal of Youth and Adolescence*, *42*, 1824–1836. http://dx.doi.org/10.1007/s10964-013-9981-x

Fagan, A. A. (2005). The relationship between adolescent physical abuse and criminal offending: Support for an enduring and generalized cycle of violence. *Journal of Family Violence*, *20*, 279–290. http://dx.doi.org/10.1007/s10896-005-6604-7

Fagen, J., Hansen, D. V., & Jang, M. (1983). Profiles of chronically violent delinquents: Empirical test of an integrated theory. In J. Kleugel (Ed.), *Evaluating juvenile justice* (pp. 91–119). Beverly Hills, CA: Sage.

Falshaw, L., Browne, K. D., & Hollin, C. R. (1996). Victim to offender: A review. *Aggression and Violent Behavior*, *1*, 389–404. http://dx.doi.org/10.1016/S1359-1789(96)00005-5

Federal Partners Committee on Women and Trauma. (2013). *Trauma-informed approaches: Federal activities and initiatives* (2nd report). Retrieved from http://www.nasmhpd.org/docs/Women%20and%20Trauma/2013FederalPartnersReportFinal.pdf

Feierman, J. R., & Shah, R. S. (2007). Protecting personhood: Legal strategies to combat the use of strip searches on youth in detention. *Rutgers Law Review*, *60*, 67–103.

Felitti, V. J., Anda, R. F., Nordenberg, D., Williamson, D. F., Spitz, A. M., Edwards, V., . . . Marks, J. S. (1998). Relationship of childhood abuse and household dysfunction to many of the leading causes of death in adults: The Adverse Childhood Experiences (ACE) Study. *American Journal of Preventive Medicine*, *14*, 245–258. http://dx.doi.org/10.1016/S0749-3797(98)00017-8

Figueira-McDonough, J. (1991). Community structure and delinquency: A typology. *Social Service Review*, *65*, 68–91. http://dx.doi.org/10.1086/603817

Finkelhor, D., Ormrod, R. K., & Turner, H. A. (2007). Re-victimization patterns in a national longitudinal sample of children and youth. *Child Abuse and Neglect*, *31*, 479–502. http://dx.doi.org/10.1016/j.chiabu.2006.03.012

Ford, J. D. (2005). Implications for psychiatric treatment of altered neurobiology, affect regulation and information processing after child maltreatment. *Psychiatric Annals*, *35*, 410–419.

Ford, J. D., & Blaustein, M. E. (2013). Systemic self-regulation: A framework for trauma-informed services in residential juvenile justice programs. *Journal of Family Violence*, *28*, 665–677. http://dx.doi.org/10.1007/s10896-013-9538-5

Ford, J. D., Chapman, J., Connor, D. F., & Cruise, K. C. (2012). Complex trauma and aggression in secure juvenile justice settings. *Criminal Justice and Behavior*, *39*, 694–724. http://dx.doi.org/10.1177/0093854812436957

Ford, J. D., Chapman, J., Mack, J. M., & Pearson, G. (2006). Pathways from traumatic child victimization to delinquency: Implications for juvenile and permanency court proceedings and decisions. *Juvenile and Family Court Journal*, *57*, 13–26. http://dx.doi.org/10.1111/j.1755-6988.2006.tb00111.x

Ford, J. D., Chapman, J. F., Hawke, J., & Albert, D. (2007). *Trauma among youth in the juvenile justice system: Critical issues and new directions* (Research and Program Brief). Delmar, NY: National Center for Mental Health and Juvenile Justice.

Ford, J. D., Elhai, J. D., Connor, D. F., & Frueh, B. C. (2010). Poly-victimization and risk of posttraumatic, depressive, and substance abuse disorders and involvement in delinquency in a national sample of adolescents. *Journal of Adolescent Health*, *46*,

545–552. http://dx.doi.org/10.1016/j.jadohealth.2009.11.212

Ford, J. D., Grasso, D. J., Hawke, J., & Chapman, J. F. (2013). Poly-victimization among juvenile justice-involved youths. *Child Abuse and Neglect*, *37*, 788–800. http://dx.doi.org/10.1016/j.chiabu.2013.01.005

Ford, J. D., Hartman, J. K., Hawke, J., & Chapman, J. F. (2008). Traumatic victimization, post-traumatic stress disorder, suicidal ideation, and substance abuse risk among juvenile justice-involved youth. *Journal of Child and Adolescent Trauma*, *1*, 75–92. http://dx.doi.org/10.1080/19361520801934456

Ford, J. D., & Hawke, J. (2012). Trauma affect regulation psychoeducation group and milieu intervention outcomes in juvenile detention facilities. *Journal of Aggression, Maltreatment, and Trauma*, *21*, 365–384. http://dx.doi.org/10.1080/10926771.2012.673538

Gottfredson, M., & Hirschi, T. (1990). *A general theory of crime*. Stanford, CA: Stanford University Press.

Grella, C. E., Stein, J. A., & Greenwell, L. (2005). Associations among childhood trauma, adolescent problem behaviors, and adverse adult outcomes in substance-abusing women offenders. *Psychology of Addictive Behaviors*, *19*, 43–53. http://dx.doi.org/10.1037/0893-164X.19.1.43

Griffin, K. W., Botvin, G. J., Scheier, L. M., Diaz, T., & Miller, N. L. (2000). Parenting practices as predictors of substance use, delinquency, and aggression among urban minority youth: Moderating effects of family structure and gender. *Psychology of Addictive Behaviors*, *14*, 174–184. http://dx.doi.org/10.1037/0893-164X.14.2.174

Grisso, T., Tomkins, A., & Casey, P. (1988). Psychosocial concepts in juvenile law. *Law and Human Behavior*, *12*, 403–437. http://dx.doi.org/10.1007/BF01044626

Hawkins, J. D., Catalano, R. F., & Miller, J. Y. (1992). Risk and protective factors for alcohol and other drug problems in adolescence and early adulthood: Implications for substance abuse prevention. *Psychological Bulletin*, *112*, 64–105. http://dx.doi.org/10.1037/0033-2909.112.1.64

Hirschi, T. (1969). *Causes of delinquency*. Berkeley: University of California Press.

Hoffmann, J. P., & Cerbone, F. G. (1999). Stressful life events and delinquency escalation in early adolescence. *Criminology*, *37*, 343–374. http://dx.doi.org/10.1111/j.1745-9125.1999.tb00489.x

Huang, H., Ryan, J. P., & Herz, D. (2012). The journey of dually-involved youth: The description and prediction of rereporting and recidivism. *Children and Youth Services Review*, *34*, 254–260. http://dx.doi.org/10.1016/j.childyouth.2011.10.021

Kaufman, J., & Zigler, E. (1987). Do abused children become abusive parents? *American Journal of Orthopsychiatry*, *57*, 186–192. http://dx.doi.org/10.1111/j.1939-0025.1987.tb03528.x

Kempe, C. H., Silverman, F. N., Steele, B. F., Droegemueller, W., & Silver, H. K. (1962). The battered-child syndrome. *JAMA*, *181*, 17–24. http://dx.doi.org/10.1001/jama.1962.03050270019004

Kerig, P. K., & Becker, S. P. (2010). From internalizing to externalizing: Theoretical models of the processes linking PTSD to juvenile delinquency. In S. J. Egan (Ed.), *Post-traumatic stress disorder (PTSD): Causes, symptoms, and treatment* (pp. 33–78). Hauppauge, NY: Nova Science.

Kerig, P. K., & Becker, S. P. (2012). Trauma and girls' delinquency. In S. Miller, L. D. Leve, & P. K. Kerig (Eds.), *Delinquent girls: Contexts, relationships, and adaptation* (pp. 119–140). New York, NY: Springer.

Kerig, P. K., Bennett, D. C., Thompson, M., & Becker, S. P. (2012). "Nothing really matters": Emotional numbing as a link between trauma exposure and callousness in delinquent youth. *Journal of Traumatic Stress*, *25*, 272–279. http://dx.doi.org/10.1002/jts.21700

Kerig, P. K., Ward, R. M., Vanderzee, K. L., & Arnzen Moeddel, M. (2009). Posttraumatic stress as a mediator of the relationship between trauma and mental health problems among juvenile delinquents. *Journal of Youth and Adolescence*, *38*, 1214–1225. http://dx.doi.org/10.1007/s10964-008-9332-5

King, D. C., Abram, K. M., Romero, E. G., Washburn, J. J., Welty, L. J., & Teplin, L. A. (2011). Childhood maltreatment and psychiatric disorders among detained youths. *Psychiatric Services*, *62*, 1430–1438. http://dx.doi.org/10.1176/appi.ps.004412010

Kisiel, C. L., Fehrenbach, T., Torgersen, E., Stolbach, B., McClelland, G., Griffin, G., & Burkman, K. (2014). Constellations of interpersonal trauma and symptoms in child welfare: Implications for a developmental trauma framework. *Journal of Family Violence*, *29*, 1–14. http://dx.doi.org/10.1007/s10896-013-9559-0

Krischer, M. K., & Sevecke, K. (2008). Early traumatization and psychopathy in female and male juvenile offenders. *International Journal of Law and Psychiatry*, *31*, 253–262. http://dx.doi.org/10.1016/j.ijlp.2008.04.008

Lacey, C. (2013). *Racial disparities and the juvenile justice system: A legacy of trauma*. Los Angeles, CA: National Center for Child Traumatic Stress.

Lawyer, S. R., Ruggiero, K. J., Resnick, H. S., Kilpatrick, D. G., & Saunders, B. E. (2006). Mental health correlates of the victim-perpetrator relationship among interpersonally victimized adolescents. *Journal of Interpersonal Violence*, *21*, 1333–1353. http://dx.doi.org/10.1177/0886260506291654

Levick, M., Feierman, J., Messenheimer Kelley, S., Goldstein, N. E. S., & Mordecai, K. (2012). The eighth amendment evolves: Defining cruel and unusual punishment through the lens of childhood and adolescence. *University of Pennsylvania Journal of Law and Social Change*, *15*, 285–321.

Lynch, M., & Haney, C. (2000). Discrimination and instructional comprehension: Guided discretion, racial bias, and the death penalty. *Law and Human Behavior*, *24*, 337–358. http://dx.doi.org/10.1023/A:1005588221761

Lyons-Ruth, K. (1996). Attachment relationships among children with aggressive behavior problems: The role of disorganized early attachment patterns. *Journal of Consulting and Clinical Psychology*, *64*, 64–73. http://dx.doi.org/10.1037/0022-006X.64.1.64

Mallett, C. A., Stoddard Dare, P., & Seck, M. M. (2009). Predicting juvenile delinquency: The nexus of childhood maltreatment, depression and bipolar disorder. *Criminal Behaviour and Mental Health*, *19*, 235–246. http://dx.doi.org/10.1002/cbm.737

Maschi, T. (2006). Unraveling the link between trauma and male delinquency: The cumulative versus differential risk perspectives. *Social Work*, *51*, 59–70. http://dx.doi.org/10.1093/sw/51.1.59

Maschi, T., Bradley, C. A., & Morgen, K. (2008). Unraveling the link between trauma and delinquency. *Youth Violence and Juvenile Justice*, *6*, 136–157. http://dx.doi.org/10.1177/1541204007305527

Maschi, T., & Schwalbe, C. S. (2012). Unraveling probation officers' practices with youths with histories of trauma and stressful life events. *Social Work Research*, *36*, 21–30. http://dx.doi.org/10.1093/swr/svs007

McCabe, K. M., Lansing, A. E., Garland, A., & Hough, R. (2002). Gender differences in psychopathology, functional impairment, and familial risk factors among adjudicated delinquents. *Journal of the American Academy of Child and Adolescent Psychiatry*, *41*, 860–867. http://dx.doi.org/10.1097/00004583-200207000-00020

Moffitt, T. E. (1993). Adolescence-limited and life-course-persistent antisocial behavior: A developmental taxonomy. *Psychological Review*, *100*, 674–701. http://dx.doi.org/10.1037/0033-295X.100.4.674

Moffitt, T. E. (2003). Life-course persistent and adolescent-limited antisocial behavior: A 10-year research review and a research agenda. In B. B. Lahey, T. E. Moffitt, & A. Caspi (Eds.), *Causes of conduct disorder and juvenile delinquency* (pp. 49–75). New York, NY: Guilford Press.

Murray, H., Glaser, B., & Calhoun, G. (2013). Using the MMPI-A in identifying trauma symptoms among juvenile offenders. *Journal of Forensic Psychiatry and Psychology*, *24*, 337–352. http://dx.doi.org/10.1080/14789949.2013.795600

National Association of State Mental Health Program Directors. (n.d.). *Federal partners Committee on Women and Trauma report*. Retrieved from http://www.nasmhpd.org/Publications/Women_and_Trauma.aspx

National Child Traumatic Stress Network. (n.d.). *Juvenile justice system*. Retrieved from http://www.nctsnet.org/resources/topics/juvenile-justice-system

Office of Juvenile Justice and Delinquency Prevention. (2012). *Report of the Attorney General's National Task Force on Children Exposed to Violence*. Retrieved from http://www.justice.gov/defendingchildhood/cev-rpt-full.pdf

Office of Juvenile Justice and Delinquency Prevention. (2014). *E-News: Administrator Listenbee op-ed addressed tribal children's exposure to violence*. Retrieved from http://www.ojjdp.gov/enews/14juvjust/140203.html

Perkins, S., & Graham-Bermann, S. (2012). Violence exposure and the development of school-related functioning: Mental health, neurocognition, and learning. *Aggression and Violent Behavior*, *17*, 89–98. http://dx.doi.org/10.1016/j.avb.2011.10.001

Quas, J. A., Bottoms, B. L., & Nunez, N. (2002). Child maltreatment and delinquency: Framing issues of causation and consequence. *Children's Services: Social Policy, Research, and Practice*, *5*, 245–248. http://dx.doi.org/10.1207/S15326918CS0504_1

Riggs Romaine, C. L., Sevin Goldstein, N. E., Hunt, E., & DeMatteo, D. (2011). Traumatic experiences and juvenile amenability: The role of trauma in forensic evaluations and judicial decision making. *Child and Youth Care Forum*, *40*, 363–380. http://dx.doi.org/10.1007/s10566-010-9132-4

Rosenberg, H. J., Vance, J. E., Rosenberg, S. D., Wolford, G. L., Ashley, S. W., & Howard, M. L. (2014). Trauma exposure, psychiatric disorders, and resiliency in juvenile-justice-involved youth. *Psychological Trauma: Theory, Research, Practice, and Policy*, *6*, 430–437.

Ryan, J. P., Herz, D., Hernandez, P. M., & Marshall, J. (2007). Maltreatment and delinquency: Investigating child welfare bias in juvenile justice processing. *Children and Youth Services Review*, *29*, 1035–1050. http://dx.doi.org/10.1016/j.childyouth.2007.04.002

Ryan, J. P., & Testa, M. F. (2005). Child maltreatment and juvenile delinquency: Investigating the role of placement and placement instability. *Children and Youth Services Review*, *27*, 227–249. http://dx.doi.org/10.1016/j.childyouth.2004.05.007

Sampson, R. J., & Groves, W. B. (1989). Community structure and crime: Testing social-disorganization theory. *American Journal of Sociology*, *94*, 774–802. http://dx.doi.org/10.1086/229068

Sampson, R. J., & Laub, J. H. (1993). *Crime in the making*. Cambridge, MA: Harvard University Press.

Sanborn, J. B., Jr. (1996). Factors perceived to affect delinquent dispositions in juvenile court: Putting the sentencing decisions into context. *Crime and Delinquency*, *42*, 99–113. http://dx.doi.org/10.1177/0011128796042001006

Schwartz, I. M., Rendon, J. A., & Hsieh, C. M. (1994). Is child maltreatment a leading cause of delinquency? *Child Welfare*, *73*, 639–655.

Shahinfar, A., Kupersmidt, J. B., & Matza, L. S. (2001). The relation between exposure to violence and social information processing among incarcerated adolescents. *Journal of Abnormal Psychology*, *110*, 136–141. http://dx.doi.org/10.1037/0021-843X.110.1.136

Shaw, C., & McKay, H. (1942). *Juvenile delinquency and urban areas*. Chicago, IL: University of Chicago Press.

Stevenson, M. C. (2009). Perceptions of juveniles who were abused as children. *Journal of Aggression, Maltreatment and Trauma*, *18*, 331–349. http://dx.doi.org/10.1080/10926770902901428

Stewart, A., Livingston, M., & Dennison, S. (2008). Transitions and turning points: Examining the links between child maltreatment and juvenile offending. *Child Abuse and Neglect*, *32*, 51–66. http://dx.doi.org/10.1016/j.chiabu.2007.04.011

Stewart, A. L., Dennison, S., & Waterson, E. (2001). *Pathways from child maltreatment to juvenile offending* (Trends and Issues Paper No. 241). Griffith, Australian Capital Territory, Australia: Australian Institute of Criminology.

Stimmel, M. A., Cruise, K. R., Ford, J. D., & Weiss, R. A. (2013). Trauma exposure, posttraumatic stress disorder symptomatology, and aggression in male juvenile offenders. *Psychological Trauma: Theory, Research, Practice, and Policy*, *5*, 1–8.

Stoddard Dare, P., & Mallett, C. A. (2009). Parental divorce: A protection from later delinquency for maltreated children. *Journal of Divorce and Remarriage*, *50*, 388–399. http://dx.doi.org/10.1080/10502550902766498

Substance Abuse and Mental Health Services Administration. (2011). *Leading change: A plan for SAMHSA's roles and actions 2011–2014* (HHS Publication No. [SMA] 11-4629). Rockville, MD: Author.

Substance Abuse and Mental Health Services Administration. (n.d.). *Welcome to the National Center for Trauma-Informed Care*. Retrieved from http://www.samhsa.gov/nctic

Swahn, M. H., Whitaker, D. J., Pippen, C. B., Leeb, R. T., Teplin, L. A., Abram, K. M., & McClelland, G. M. (2006). Concordance between self-reported maltreatment and court records of abuse or neglect among high-risk youths. *American Journal of Public Health*, *96*, 1849–1853. http://dx.doi.org/10.2105/AJPH.2004.058230

Tatar, J. R., Cauffman, E., Kimonis, E. R., & Skeem, J. L. (2012). Victimization history and posttraumatic stress: An analysis of psychopathy variants in male juvenile offenders. *Journal of Child and Adolescent Trauma*, *5*, 102–113. http://dx.doi.org/10.1080/19361521.2012.671794

Thornberry, T. P., Ireland, T. O., & Smith, C. A. (2001). The importance of timing: The varying impact of childhood and adolescent maltreatment on multiple problem outcomes. *Development and Psychopathology*, *13*, 957–979.

Tyler, K. A., Hoyt, D. R., & Whitbeck, L. B. (2000). The effects of early sexual abuse on later sexual victimization among female homeless and runaway adolescents. *Journal of Interpersonal Violence*, *15*, 235–250. http://dx.doi.org/10.1177/088626000015003001

van der Kolk, B. A. (2005). Developmental trauma disorder: Toward a rational diagnosis for children with complex trauma histories. *Psychiatric Annals*, *35*, 401–408.

van der Kolk, B. A., & Fisler, R. E. (1994). Childhood abuse and neglect and loss of self-regulation. *Bulletin of the Menninger Clinic*, *58*, 145–168.

Vaughn, M. G., Howard, M. O., & Harper-Chang, L. (2006). Do prior trauma and victimization predict weapon carrying among delinquent youth? *Youth Violence and Juvenile Justice*, *4*, 314–327. http://dx.doi.org/10.1177/1541204006292665

Widom, C. S. (1989a). The cycle of violence. *Science*, *244*, 160–166. http://dx.doi.org/10.1126/science.2704995

Widom, C. S. (1989b). Does violence beget violence? A critical examination of the literature. *Psychological Bulletin*, *106*, 3–28. http://dx.doi.org/10.1037/0033-2909.106.1.3

Wood, J., Foy, D. W., Layne, C., Pynoos, R., & James, C. B. (2002). An examination of the relationships between violence exposure, posttraumatic stress symptomatology, and delinquent activity: An "ecopathological" model of delinquent behavior among incarcerated adolescents. *Journal of Aggression, Maltreatment and Trauma*, *6*, 127–147. http://dx.doi.org/10.1300/J146v06n01_07

Yoshinaga, C., Kadomoto, I., Otani, T., Sasaki, T., & Kato, N. (2004). Prevalence of post-traumatic stress disorder in incarcerated juvenile delinquents in Japan. *Psychiatry and Clinical Neurosciences*,

58, 383–388. http://dx.doi.org/10.1111/j.1440-1819.2004.01272.x

Zelechoski, A., Sharma, R., Beserra, K., Miguel, J., DeMarco, M., & Spinazzola, J. (2013). Traumatized youth in residential treatment settings: Prevalence, clinical presentation, treatment, and policy implications. *Journal of Family Violence*, *28*, 639–652. http://dx.doi.org/10.1007/s10896-013-9534-9

Zingraff, M. T., Leiter, J., Myers, K. A., & Johnsen, M. C. (1993). Child maltreatment and youthful problem behavior. *Criminology*, *31*, 173–202. http://dx.doi.org/10.1111/j.1745-9125.1993.tb01127.x

Part VI

FORENSIC ASSESSMENT

CHAPTER 16

FORENSIC ASSESSMENT OF JUVENILES

Kirk Heilbrun and Benjamin Locklair

Psychological evaluations regarding adolescents under the jurisdiction of the juvenile system provide important information to the courts and attorneys about relevant issues such as reoffense risk, rehabilitation needs and amenability, and sophistication–maturity. In this chapter, we summarize important developments in the forensic assessment of juveniles, summarize relevant developments in law and science, provide an overview of the process with applicable foundational principles of forensic assessment, and describe the implications for research, policy, and practice.

IMPORTANT DEVELOPMENTS IN JUVENILE FORENSIC ASSESSMENT

The first juvenile court, developed in Chicago in 1889, represented a rehabilitation-focused response to the more explicitly punitive goal of the criminal justice system. The evolution of the process of juvenile forensic assessment changed substantially beginning in the 1960s with the greater prioritization of procedural rights of juveniles recognized in *Kent v. United States* (1966) and *In re Gault* (1967). These cases were an early harbinger of the importance of having goals such as public safety and sophistication–maturity to accompany the explicitly rehabilitative domain of treatment amenability in juvenile decision making. It was also an assertion that juveniles, although protected by greater procedural rights after these decisions, would not always be assumed to be good or appropriate candidates for rehabilitation.

This trend expanded in the 1970s as the fields of medical and behavioral sciences began to develop approaches to forensic assessment that focus on the legal standard and the functional–legal capacities associated with such a standard. One example of this trend in the criminal justice area involved the development of checklists to assist in the assessment of a defendant's competence to stand trial (see, e.g., Lipsitt, Lelos, & McGarry, 1971).

The measurement of risk and criminogenic needs, both relevant to many kinds of legal decisions involving juveniles, was promoted with the development of risk–need–responsivity theory (Andrews, Bonta, & Hoge, 1990; see Chapter 9, this handbook). This theory called for the measurement of reoffense risk and the application of the risk principle (higher risk individuals need more intensive treatment and monitoring), the needs principle (identified deficits should be criminogenic, or relevant to reoffense risk, so that interventions can be most effectively targeted), and the responsivity principle (interventions should be generally consistent with approaches that are empirically supported and specifically applicable to this individual). The risk–need–responsivity theory was also the basis for the development of a specialized measure of risk, need, and responsivity for juveniles (the Youth Level of Service/Case Management Inventory; Hoge & Andrews, 2002), which was followed by the development of another such risk–needs measure (the Structured Assessment of Violence Risk in Youth; Borum, Bartels, & Forth, 2005).

The 1990s witnessed an expansion of semistructured and specialized measures to assist evaluators in providing relevant and empirically supported assessment. Although no specialized

http://dx.doi.org/10.1037/14643-016
APA Handbook of Psychology and Juvenile Justice, K. Heilbrun (Editor-in-Chief)

measure was developed for juvenile competence to proceed, a semistructured approach guiding such evaluations became available (Grisso, 1998). The MacArthur Network of Adolescent Development and Juvenile Justice provided a programmatic examination of the relationship between human development and issues such as competence to stand trial (Grisso et al., 2003) and culpability (Steinberg & Scott, 2003).

By 2000, the process of the forensic assessment of juveniles had matured, with relevant science and applicable law pointing to areas in which the potential for empirically supported assessment was enhanced. The question of psychosocial maturity could be evaluated with a greater empirical foundation, much of it provided by the MacArthur adolescent network. Issues such as competence, Miranda waiver capacity, risk, treatment needs, and treatment responsivity also had a stronger theoretical and empirical base. Before turning to these areas, however, we provide an overview of the nature of juvenile forensic assessment using broad foundational principles of forensic mental health assessment (FMHA; Heilbrun, 2001; Heilbrun, Grisso, & Goldstein, 2009).

HISTORICAL PRESUMPTIONS OF JUVENILE CRIMINAL INCAPACITY: THE INFANCY DEFENSE

Although the juvenile court is a relatively recent innovation, U.S. law and the English common law from which it was originally derived have long supported the notion that youth is relevant to how at least some defendants ought to be treated. Conviction of any criminal defense requires that the state independently prove the existence of two elements: *actus reus*, which is the specific wrongful act the law prohibits, and *mens rea*, which is the state of mind (such as intentionality or recklessness) that distinguishes a criminal offense from an accident. As early as the 14th century, English common law considered children younger than age 7 years to be incapable of forming *mens rea*, and legal thinking at the time considered it unlikely that children so young would be deterred by the threat of punishment. Extreme youth, or infancy, thus became an affirmative defense to criminal prosecution that has endured to the present day (LaFave, 2007, § 9.6).

The intervening centuries have both expanded and refined the infancy defense. Although some variation exists across states, children younger than age 7 generally cannot be convicted of crimes because they are presumed to lack the capacity to form *mens rea*, and this presumption is not rebuttable. Children older than age 14, however, are presumed to have this capacity. Absent a showing that some special circumstance causes the child to lack capacity, these youths who are age 14 years and older can be convicted of crimes. Children between 7 and 14 are still presumed to lack capacity for criminal offending, but this presumption can be rebutted by evidence showing that the child's mental state is sufficiently like that of an adult's to sustain a finding of *mens rea* and therefore criminal culpability (LaFave, 2007). The infancy defense, both historically and contemporaneously, can be understood as a legal recognition of the psychological differences between adults and children. In more recent years, however, and particularly after the enhanced emphasis on procedural protections for juveniles resulting from *Kent v. United States* (1966) and *In re Gault* (1967), courts have been confronted with developmental differences that must be balanced against such procedural protections.

CONTEXTS OF JUVENILE FORENSIC MENTAL HEALTH ASSESSMENT

There are a number of legal questions that are the focus of juvenile forensic assessments. We address these questions of legal context in the sections that follow.

Miranda Waiver

Differences between adults and children become salient even during the investigation stage of a criminal or juvenile proceeding, often before the filing of charges or the involvement of any judicial officer (see Chapter 21, this handbook). In *Miranda v. Arizona* (1966), the U.S. Supreme Court held that the Fifth Amendment privilege against compelled self-incrimination and the Sixth Amendment right to counsel, applied together, entailed a number of other rights, which attach at the time a person is subjected to custodial interrogation by the police: (a) to be informed of the right to remain silent, (b) to be warned that any statements one makes can be used in court, (c) to be informed of the right to counsel before and during any interrogation, and (d) to be informed that a lawyer will be appointed if the defendant cannot afford one. This decision led police agencies across the country to formalize statements of these rights, commonly called *Miranda* warnings, to be read to suspects in advance of any custodial interrogation.

There are serious doubts, however, about how effectively these warnings serve to increase juveniles' understanding of these rights or the likely consequences of waiving them. Even when *Miranda* warnings are adapted for use with a juvenile population, they are typically lengthy and written at a higher reading level than many juveniles can comprehend (Rogers et al., 2012). In addition, children might feel compelled to answer questions from authority figures such as police regardless of whether they have been arrested or otherwise formally placed in custody of the police, as the Supreme Court recently acknowledged in *J.D.B. v. North Carolina* (2011). Juvenile waivers of *Miranda* rights are thus potentially problematic for two primary reasons: (a) The juvenile may not understand the rights waived and (b) the juvenile may have a limited capacity to refrain from answering questions while in custodial interrogation.

Competence to Stand Trial

Competence to stand trial[1] is another area in which the relevant legal standards require different treatment for juveniles and adults (see Chapter 22, this handbook). In *Dusky v. United States* (1960), the U.S. Supreme Court laid out the basic test for competence to stand trial: The defendant must "possess sufficient present ability to consult with his lawyer with a reasonable degree of rational understanding and a rational as well as factual understanding of the proceedings against him" (p. 240). Although the Supreme Court declined to extend the requirements of *Dusky* to proceedings in juvenile courts (see *McKeiver v. Pennsylvania*, 1971), most states have nevertheless adopted standards for juvenile competence to stand trial. These standards tend to focus on the same considerations as adult standards (functional–legal capacities specific to clinical symptoms and competence to stand trial), with little regard for how juveniles' immaturity may affect their capability to effectively protect their own interests in the context of a delinquency or criminal proceeding (O'Donnell & Gross, 2012). Only four states (Arizona, Arkansas, Georgia, and Louisiana) have adopted statutes that recognize developmental immaturity as a potential basis for a finding of incompetence (Bryant, Matthews, & Wilhelmsen, 2013). Strong evidence suggests, however, that age is a powerful predictor of juveniles' abilities related to competence to stand trial in criminal court as assessed by specialized instruments and that juveniles' IQ interacts with age to produce wide variability in ability scores for competency-related constructs (Grisso et al., 2003).

Diversion

Specialty courts and other programs centering on diversion from standard prosecution have proliferated in U.S. jurisdictions during the past 2 decades. Similar diversion programs have begun to emerge for juveniles; juvenile drug and mental health courts, in particular, have become more prevalent in recent years (Schwalbe, Gearing, MacKenzie, Brewer, & Ibrahim, 2012). There has also been interest in programs that promote the deinstitutionalization of juveniles adjudicated delinquent, in a parallel to jail diversion and other community-based programs. Characteristics of individual juveniles, including their age and sophistication–maturity, are relevant to their prospects for placement and success in these diversion programs, and as such the juvenile forensic evaluator can be of service to courts in helping to identify those youths who could benefit most from these alternatives to standard delinquency proceedings.

Waiver and Reverse Waiver

With the "get tough" era that began in the early 1990s, it has become increasingly common for

[1]This form of competence has been more aptly termed *competence to proceed*, or *adjudicatory competence* (see Bonnie, 1992), in recognition of the reality that most criminal cases are not adjudicated at trial. We retain the historical usage because it is so widely recognized but agree that it does not capture the nature of the adjudicatory process.

juveniles to face charges in criminal court as though they were adults. When the juvenile court has initial jurisdiction, this requires a motion for waiver (also called *transfer*) to criminal court, typically filed by the prosecution and subject to approval by the court. In states allowing prosecutorial discretion for the initial filing of charges, a prosecutor may file charges in criminal court when the youth meets enumerated criteria for age and offense type. When allowable under relevant jurisdiction statutes, the defendant may petition for reverse waiver or decertification—a transfer of jurisdiction from criminal court back to juvenile court (Salekin, Rogers, & Ustad, 2001). Although determinations of waiver or reverse waiver are typically appealable, it is unusual for the initial decision to be reversed, and some legal commentators have expressed concern that the potential arbitrariness of this determination may rise to the level of a denial of due process (Jacobs, 2013).

Whether waiver to an adult court is appropriate in a particular case typically depends on a broad best-interests inquiry, balancing the characteristics of the juvenile defendant against the community's interest in effective punishment and public safety. Those characteristics of the individual defendant that courts typically consider in waiver proceedings are the juvenile's dangerousness (best translated as risk of further offending or other harm to others), sophistication–maturity, and amenability to treatment (with the identification of appropriate rehabilitative needs in the area of risk factors for offending as well as other areas constituting a useful framework in which to consider such amenability; Chen & Salekin, 2012). These functional–legal capacities are discussed in more detail subsequently in this chapter. For the purpose of waiver, though, defendants who are higher risk, more sophisticated or mature, and less amenable to treatment are considered less appropriate for retention within or return to the juvenile court system.

Postadjudication Disposition

Once an adjudication of delinquency has been made (the analogue of a conviction in criminal court), the court must determine the appropriate postadjudication disposition for the juvenile. Although some states have implemented sentencing guidelines for juveniles, juvenile courts generally remain free to exercise considerable discretion in the dispositions they impose. A court may dismiss the case before it, impose probation with a variety of conditions, or commit the juvenile to the custody of a correctional facility or treatment program. In keeping with the general orientation toward rehabilitation in juvenile courts, these dispositions are often selected keeping in mind the individual characteristics and treatment needs of the juvenile in question (Hoge, 2012).

Although the factors relevant to waiver (most frequently sophistication–maturity, treatment amenability, and risk) are also pertinent to disposition decisions, disposition planning is largely focused on treatment and public safety. As such, a comprehensive assessment of a juvenile's intellectual, academic, and vocational skills can be used to improve outcomes after disposition (Hecker & Steinberg, 2002). Likewise, signs of mental health difficulties may indicate a need for specific kinds of mental health treatment as part of the disposition. Although mental health professionals do not routinely participate in disposition planning, there are circumstances in which a court might request a mental health professional's input. In addition, specialized FMHA instruments such as the Youth Level of Service/Case Management Inventory are often a valuable source of information in disposition planning.

Postsentence Civil Commitment

Juveniles convicted of sexual offenses may also face the prospect of indefinite postsentence civil commitment under one of the sexually violent predator statutes that have proliferated within the past 20 years. The U.S. Supreme Court held in *Kansas v. Hendricks* (1997) that it is not a violation of the right to due process to confine people with a "mental abnormality" or "personality disorder" (p. 346) that predisposes them to commit sexually violent offenses using postsentence civil commitment, despite their having served the full sentence for the crime of which they were convicted. Although it was a Kansas statute that was under review in *Hendricks*, other states have adopted statutes that are fundamentally similar both in structure and in effect. Typically, the statutes authorize indefinite commitment for sex offenders who have a mental disease or disorder that makes it sufficiently likely that they will commit further sexual offenses that they are to be considered a threat to public safety. A finding that an adult or juvenile is appropriate for indefinite commitment under *Hendricks*-style sexually violent predator statutes, then, is informed by FMHA in two respects. First, it requires a finding of a mental disease or defect; second, it requires information about the likely future risk of the person to be committed. In some states, juvenile sex offenders may be subject to civil commitment when they age out of juvenile court jurisdiction if they are still believed to present a threat to public safety (Caldwell, 2010).

FUNCTIONAL–LEGAL CAPACITIES IN JUVENILE FORENSIC MENTAL HEALTH ASSESSMENT

There are several functional–legal capacities that recur across different legal questions for juvenile forensic assessment. We describe them in the sections that follow.

Public Safety and Risk

The functional–legal capacities that are evaluated in forensic assessment of juveniles have a certain amount of overlap with those that are relevant with adults. One area in which juvenile FMHA is substantially similar to adult FMHA is that of public safety and risk, which in legal contexts is sometimes cited as "dangerousness." This is a dichotomous, aggregated legal construct in which an individual "(a) has a sufficient number and type of risk factors to (b) make the likelihood acceptably high that (c) harm of a sufficient seriousness will be caused by the individual's behavior" (Heilbrun, 2009, p. 8). Because of the imprecision of these components, intermixing of the evaluator's personal values may occur. Partly for this reason, the field has over the past 2 decades moved away from assessing dangerousness in favor of risk assessment. Risk assessment is a more targeted and value-neutral practice that seeks to determine (a) risk of what outcome, (b) risk at what level, and (c) the applicable risk factors (Heilbrun, 2009).

A frequent outcome of interest in juvenile risk assessment contexts is risk of interpersonal violence. A number of risk factors have been identified for a juvenile's risk for serious or violent criminal offending. These factors include history of aggressive conduct; dysfunctional family dynamics or parenting; antisocial peer-group associations; dysfunctional behavior and personality traits; and antisocial attitudes, values, and beliefs (Hoge & Andrews, 2010). Forensic evaluators can assess each of these constructs to inform courts about the nature and extent of the risk posed by a given juvenile, but it is important to note that whether a juvenile presents an unacceptable risk to public safety is a legal, not empirical, question. Moreover, it is a question for which the answer depends in part on the personal values of the legal decision maker (i.e., how much risk to public safety is too much?).

Sophistication–Maturity

Sophistication or maturity is a functional–legal capacity that is frequently of interest in juvenile contexts, particularly in waiver and reverse waiver proceedings. The essential question in an evaluation of sophistication–maturity involves how much the juvenile's alleged offending behavior and lifestyle resemble that of an adult. Early attempts to describe the sophistication–maturity construct on the basis of the reasoning explained in juvenile court opinions were largely unsuccessful, but later studies of juvenile judges' concerns in this domain identified a number of relevant factors: (a) the extent to which the juvenile's criminal behaviors are becoming more advanced or sophisticated; (b) the juvenile's ability to form the intent to criminally offend; (c) the juvenile's social maturity or sophistication, to the extent that it relates to the ability to understand and conform to social norms; and (d) the juvenile's cognitive capacities in terms of the ability to delay gratification or use alternative strategies to attain gratification (Grisso, 2013; Salekin, Yff, Neumann, Leistico, & Zalot, 2002).

Amenability to Treatment

In a variety of juvenile justice contexts, the legal decision maker's impression of the juvenile's prospects for responding favorably to treatment and rehabilitation interventions is important to the outcome of the juvenile's case. Juveniles who are more amenable to treatment are generally viewed as more appropriate for placement in less restrictive settings and also as more likely to be retained within the juvenile justice system. In a survey of juvenile court judges, Salekin et al. (2002) identified a number of broad domains considered by judges in the context of treatment amenability. These domains include (a) responsibility and motivation to change, (b) consideration for and tolerance of others, (c) the cooperation of the juvenile's family, and (d) the extent to which the juvenile exhibits appropriate conduct in court and other prosocial behaviors. Considerations relevant to a juvenile's amenability to treatment extend beyond the characteristics of the juvenile. For example, amenability to treatment depends on the youth's needs, the type of treatment that is avail able under the auspices of the particular juvenile jurisdiction, and the amount of time that the juvenile court can retain jurisdiction over the juvenile in question (Grisso, 2013).

LANDMARKS IN U.S. SUPREME COURT JUVENILE JURISPRUDENCE

In the 1960s, the U.S. Supreme Court issued two decisions—*Kent v. United States* (1966) and *In re Gault* (1967)—that substantially changed juvenile court proceedings across the country. Before these decisions, juvenile courts were broadly empowered under a *parens patriae* scheme to make decisions in the best interests of the juveniles before them. Because these courts considered their mission to be far more rehabilitative than punitive, and because their proceedings were not formally criminal, juvenile proceedings lacked the procedural and substantive constitutional safeguards afforded to adult criminal defendants. This approach to juvenile justice often had the unfortunate effect of subjecting delinquent youths to prolonged deprivations of liberty through commitment to juvenile justice facilities, as well as protracted separation from their families—decisions made with only very limited due process protections.

In many ways *Kent v. United States* (1966) and *In re Gault* (1967) opened the door for forensic evaluators to become involved in the juvenile court. It is important to note, however, that the Supreme Court has never held that juveniles are entitled to all of the same protections as adult defendants; on the contrary, the Court has stated that there would be little reason for a juvenile court to exist if that were so (see *McKeiver v. Pennsylvania*, 1971).

Subsequently, the Supreme Court has incorporated much of the behavioral science research on human development in the context of Eighth Amendment analysis on imposing certain severe punishments on juveniles. In the first of these cases, *Stanford v. Kentucky* (1989), the Supreme Court considered and ultimately rejected the imposition of the death penalty for offenders who are younger than 16 at the time of the offense. The court revisited the issue of juvenile eligibility for the death penalty in *Roper v. Simmons* (2005), holding that the imposition of the death penalty for offenders younger than age 18 at the time of the offense was cruel and unusual—and thus unconstitutional under the Eighth Amendment—thereby eliminating capital punishment as a penalty for any juvenile offender. Next, in *Graham v. Florida* (2010), the Court held that a sentence of life imprisonment without parole was unconstitutional under the Eighth Amendment for individuals younger than age 18 committing offenses other than homicide. Most recently, in *Miller v. Alabama* (2012), the Court held that mandatory life sentences without parole for offenders younger than age 18 at the time of the offense were also inconsistent with the Eight Amendment prohibition of cruel and unusual punishment. The Supreme Court has thus gradually proscribed the application of the most severe forms of criminal punishment to individuals who are younger than age 18 when they commit an offense.

These decisions are noteworthy in both their reasoning and their impact. The Court made clear that much of the justification for limiting the most severe criminal sanctions to adults involved the developmental differences between adults and juveniles. In *Roper v. Simmons* (2005), consistent with its previous death penalty jurisprudence, the Court stressed that the death penalty was to be reserved for only the most blameworthy offenders. *Roper* went on to cite behavioral scientific evidence that suggested the following differences relevant to blameworthiness between juveniles and adults: (a) "a lack of maturity and an underdeveloped sense of responsibility," (b) greater susceptibility to outside influences such as peer pressure, and (c) character that is less well formed (*Roper v. Simmons*, 2005, p. 570). These three factors, under the Court's reasoning, made the imposition of the death penalty on juveniles disproportionate to their blameworthiness and thus unconstitutional. The Court further also relied on these three factors in its subsequent opinions in *Graham v. Florida* (2010) and *Miller v. Alabama* (2012), applying them to find lesser blameworthiness in juveniles who would have received a mandatory life sentence if convicted for a homicide or a nonhomicide offense. The Court also applied these developmental considerations to its reasoning regarding how adolescents might interpret the nature of custodial interrogation (*J.D.B. v. North Carolina*, 2011).

These decisions are also remarkable for their absence of emphasis on individualized inquiry into the extent to which they apply to any particular juvenile. In *Roper v. Simmons* (2005), the Court acknowledged that the age of 18 is somewhat arbitrary, noting that "the qualities that distinguish juveniles from adults do not disappear when an individual turns eighteen" (p. 574). The adoption of this bright-line rule eliminates the need to involve forensic mental health experts in making individualized applications of the death penalty to juveniles.

SCIENTIFIC DEVELOPMENTS RELEVANT TO JUVENILE FORENSIC MENTAL HEALTH ASSESSMENT

There have been important scientific advances in our understanding of risk assessment and human development relevant to juveniles. We discuss them in the sections that follow.

Human Development

The developmental differences between youths and adults are a primary justification for the existence of a separate juvenile court. As such, understanding these differences and the process of human development is relevant to legal decision making about juvenile offenders, particularly when the juvenile's sophistication or maturity is a relevant factor (see Chapter 4, this handbook, for a fuller discussion). Chapter 5 of this handbook details recent findings about the development of the human brain, which have recently become of particular interest to legal scholars and judges, including members of the U.S. Supreme Court. Chapter 6 of this handbook contains a discussion of findings about the intersection among human development, mental disorder, and decision making among justice-involved juveniles. This section of the handbook contains fuller discussions of the process of evaluating developmental progress in the context of sophistication–maturity assessment (see Chapter 19).

Patterns of Offending

Researchers, practitioners, and legal professionals have all sought to better understand the question of whether juvenile offenders are likely to continue their offending behaviors after they have matured into adults—and whether there is a reliable way to determine which individuals are likely to do so, which has obvious implications for how the criminal justice system and the juvenile court should dispose of their cases. Chapter 7 of this handbook reviews findings concerning typical or characteristic patterns of offending among youths. Chapter 8 of this handbook contains a full discussion of desistence versus life-course persistence in juvenile offending—that is, whether juvenile offenders are likely to continue offending in adulthood.

Juvenile Risk Assessment

Risk assessment often informs disposition planning, as well as placement and release decision making, and is valuable whenever public safety is explicitly a consideration. Generally, courts prefer to impose stricter or more intensive placement or supervision schemes on juveniles who present higher risk. Accordingly, such risk assessment should be a part of juvenile evaluations of transfer, reverse transfer, and commitment. Part V of this handbook contains a review of risk factors for juveniles, including psychopathy (Chapter 10), substance abuse (Chapter 13), gangs (Chapter 14) and trauma (Chapter 15), as well as detailing efforts to create an overarching model for delinquent behavior in juveniles (the risk–needs–responsivity model, Chapter 9). The handbook also contains a fuller discussion of the process of evaluating risk in juveniles (see Chapter 17).

Psychological Tests in Juvenile Forensic Mental Health Assessment

When called on to assist a legal decision maker, psychologists often turn to assessment instruments that are commonly used in clinical practice, which has a number of advantages—good psychological tests are extensively validated and normed, and they are well established in the field. In a forensic setting, however, clinicians must sometimes use these instruments in a different way or with a heightened awareness of their strengths and limitations. Chapter 20 (this handbook) discusses the details of using clinical instruments in forensic settings generally. Other chapters in Part VI of this handbook discuss the use of clinical instruments in specific forensic assessment contexts, including risk (Chapter 17); treatment needs and amenability (Chapter 18); sophistication–maturity (Chapter 19); transfer, waiver, and commitment (Chapter 21); *Miranda* waiver (Chapter 22); and competence to stand trial (Chapter 23).

Specialized Instruments in Juvenile Forensic Mental Health Assessment

The increasing demand for FMHA has driven the development of psychological assessments whose specific purpose is to be used in a forensic context. Although the development of a tool specifically for juvenile FMHA has lagged somewhat behind that for adults, some such measures have been derived and validated. Other chapters in this handbook discuss the use of specialized forensic instruments in contexts such as risk (Chapter 17); treatment needs and amenability (Chapter 18); sophistication–maturity (Chapter 18); transfer, waiver, and commitment (Chapter 21); *Miranda* waiver (Chapter 22); and competence to stand trial (Chapter 23).

Interventions and Their Effectiveness

One important goal of the juvenile system is to connect justice-involved juveniles to services and resources that can improve their overall well-being and reduce their likelihood for further justice involvement. In keeping with this goal, a number of interventions have been developed to address the specific criminogenic and noncriminogenic needs of juvenile offenders. These interventions are discussed further in this handbook in the context of demonstrated effectiveness and cost-effectiveness. Details are discussed concerning risk reduction interventions (Chapter 24), trauma-informed interventions for juveniles generally (Chapter 25) and for young men of color especially (Chapter 27), community-based interventions (Chapter 26), residential interventions (Chapter 28), and interventions for juveniles involved in sexual offending (Chapter 29).

PRINCIPLES OF FORENSIC MENTAL HEALTH ASSESSMENT WITH APPLICABILITY TO JUVENILES

In discussing the forensic assessment of juveniles provided for courts and attorneys by mental health professionals, it is important to describe how such evaluations can be guided by broad, foundational principles of FMHA. It is also important to consider how such principles may differ when applied to juveniles. Differences may result from various influences, including the developmental level of those evaluated, the distinctive aspects of the juvenile court system, and the availability of specialized, empirically supported measures that provide relevant information.

In this section, we begin with foundational principles of FMHA (Heilbrun, 2001) that have more recently been revised and updated (Heilbrun et al., 2009). We consider each of these principles as they apply to juvenile forensic evaluations (see Table 16.1). In this way, we offer an overview of the best-practice approaches to juvenile evaluation that provide a foundation for the forensic assessment of juveniles. In subsequent sections of this chapter, we elaborate on the relevant law and research.

These principles have been described both generally and with respect to specific cases. In the area of specific cases, they are further detailed in the following sequence: preparation, data collection, data interpretation, written communication, and expert testimony. As may be seen from reviewing

TABLE 16.1

Expanded Principles of Forensic Mental Health Assessment Applied to Juveniles

FMHA principle	Juvenile application
Generally	
1. Be aware of the important differences between clinical and forensic domains.	1. Similar. There is somewhat more overlap between clinical and forensic domains with youths than with adults, given the rehabilitative focus of the juvenile system.
2. Obtain appropriate education, training, and experience in one's area of forensic specialization.	2. Similar. Also need to have specific training and experience with youths.
3. Be familiar with the relevant legal, ethical, scientific, and practice literatures pertaining to FMHA.	3. Same.
4. Be guided by honesty and striving for impartiality, actively disclosing the limitations on as well as the support for one's opinions.	4. Same.
5. Control potential evaluator bias in general by monitoring case selection, continuing education, and consultation with knowledgeable colleagues.	5. Same.
6. Be familiar with specific aspects of the legal system, particularly communication, discovery, deposition, and testimony.	6. Same.
7. Do not become adversarial, but present and defend your opinions effectively.	7. Similar. Those presenting expert testimony should be prepared for more active questioning by the judge and more relaxed procedural rules relative to criminal court.
In specific cases: Preparation	
8. Identify relevant forensic issues.	8. Same.
9. Accept referrals only within area of expertise.	9. Same.
10. Decline the referral when evaluator impartiality is unlikely.	10. Same.
11. Clarify the evaluator's role with the attorney.	11. Same.
12. Clarify financial arrangements.	12. Same.
13. Obtain appropriate authorization.	13. Same.
14. Avoid playing the dual roles of therapist and forensic evaluator.	14. Same.
15. Determine the particular role to be played within forensic assessment if the referral is accepted.	15. Same.
16. Select the most appropriate model to guide data gathering, interpretation, and communication.	16. Models including a description of *clinical condition* should be broadened to include developmental maturity and age-appropriate clinical and educational functioning.
In specific cases: Data collection	
17. Use multiple sources of information for each area being assessed. Review the available background information and actively seek important missing elements.	17. Same.
18. Use relevance and reliability (validity) as guides for seeking information and selecting data sources.	18. Same.
19. Obtain relevant historical information.	19. Same.
20. Assess clinical characteristics in relevant, reliable, and valid ways.	20. Similar. *Clinical* should be defined to include developmentally appropriate clinical and behavioral functioning.
21. Assess legally relevant behavior.	21. Same.
22. Ensure that conditions for evaluation are quiet, private, and distraction free.	22. Same.
23. Provide appropriate notification of purpose and obtain appropriate authorization before beginning.	23. Same.
24. Determine whether the individual understands the purpose of the evaluation and the associated limits on confidentiality.	24. Similar. Expectations for understanding should be developmentally appropriate.
In specific cases: Data interpretation	
25. Use third-party information in assessing response style.	25. Same.
26. Use testing when indicated in assessing response style.	26. Same.

(*continues*)

TABLE 16.1 (*Continued*)

Expanded Principles of Forensic Mental Health Assessment Applied to Juveniles

27. Use case-specific (idiographic) evidence in assessing clinical condition, functional abilities, and causal connection.	27. Same.
28. Use nomothetic evidence in assessing clinical condition, functional abilities, and causal connection.	28. Same.
29. Use scientific reasoning in assessing causal connection between clinical condition, functional abilities, and causal connection.	29. Same.
30. Carefully consider whether to answer the ultimate legal question. If it is answered, it should be in the context of a thorough evaluation, clearly describing data and reasoning, and with the clear recognition that this question is in the domain of the legal decision maker.	30. Similar. There may be particular interest on the part of the juvenile judge in having the expert directly answer the ultimate legal question, so the expert should be prepared to carefully consider the request to do so.
31. Describe findings and limits so that they need change little under cross examination.	31. Same.
In specific cases: Written communication	
32. Attribute information to sources.	32. Same.
33. Use plain language; avoid technical jargon.	33. Same.
34. Write report in sections, according to model and procedures.	34. Same.
In specific cases: Expert testimony	
35. Base testimony on the results of the properly performed FMHA.	35. Same.
36. Prepare.	36. Same.
37. Communicate effectively.	37. Same.
38. Control the message. Strive to obtain, retain, and regain control over the meaning and impact of what is presented in expert testimony.	38. Similar. If there is more direct responding to questions posed by the judge, however, such questions should be assumed to be inquisitorial rather than adversarial—and controlling the meaning of responses becomes less important.

Note. FMHA = forensic mental health assessment. From *Foundations of Forensic Mental Health Assessment* (pp. 86–90), by K. Heilbrun, T. Grisso, and A. Goldstein, 2009, New York, NY: Oxford University Press. Copyright 2009 by Oxford University Press. Adapted with permission.

Table 16.1, 30 of the 38 principles appear to apply comparably to the assessment of juveniles, and the remaining eight require minor changes but are largely similar. It would seem, therefore, that the use of these foundational FMHA principles is a reasonable way to describe the more specific component of forensic assessment involving juveniles.

Juvenile Application of Forensic Mental Health Assessment Principles Generally

A major theme involving broad FMHA principles involves recognizing the specialized nature of evaluations conducted for courts and attorneys by mental health professionals. To the extent that clinical services involve diagnosis and other assessment for treatment-planning purposes, and the delivery of such treatment services, they are distinct from forensic services, which involve gathering information for legal decision-making purposes. There are some areas of overlap, of course, particularly when the legal question is directly related to the presence of a clinical disorder (e.g., the mental disease or defect that is part of the criteria for civil commitment or insanity) or the likely response to intervention (e.g., treatment needs and amenability as part of the criteria for juvenile transfer or reverse waiver). Given the greater rehabilitative focus of the juvenile system, it is likely that questions concerning treatment are more often specified within the legal questions being considered. It is important to note that treatment, when delivered in a juvenile or criminal justice context, emphasizes public safety to a much greater extent than does clinical treatment provided in a nonjustice context. In addition to improved functioning in symptom remission and deficit improvement, such treatment in justice-related contexts focuses on improving deficits in risk-relevant areas such as family, school, peers, substance abuse, and criminogenic thinking with the goal of reducing the individual's risk of reoffending.

Having the education, training, and experience sufficient to yield expertise in any kind of specialized forensic assessment applies similarly to juvenile forensic evaluations. It has been recommended that mental health professionals conducting forensic evaluations have both foundational training in mental health (e.g., MD plus psychiatric residency; PhD in clinical, counseling, or school psychology, including an accredited clinical internship) and specific training and experience in forensic assessment, with a specialty reflected by at least 25% of a clinician's caseload involving forensic work (Heilbrun, 2001). The 25% is somewhat arbitrary; it is more important that it be a significant part of the professional's training and ongoing experience. An additional consideration applies with working with juveniles: Medical and mental health training in either psychiatry or psychology does not necessarily include substantial work with children and adolescents or a focus on the scientific and professional aspects of human development. Both are important in providing services to adolescents.

Four general, foundational principles seem to apply comparably to forensic assessment with juveniles as to that with other populations: (a) familiarity with the relevant legal, ethical, scientific, and practice literatures; (b) honesty and striving for impartiality on the part of the examiner; (c) controlling evaluator bias; and (d) familiarity with specific aspects of the legal system. Four major sources of authority are relevant in forensic assessment: law (statutes, case law, and administrative code), ethics (ethics codes and more specialized ethical guidelines), science (empirical studies, reviews, and meta-analyses on relevant points), and practice (miscellaneous descriptive and prescriptive works regarding good practice; Melton, Petrila, Poythress, & Slobogin, 2007). These domains remain constant across different kinds of forensic evaluations, although the specific content of each changes depending on the characteristics of the evaluee and the referral questions. We advocate that forensic assessments of juveniles be legally relevant, ethically sensitive, scientifically based, and within the bounds of good practice (see Heilbrun et al., 2009; Melton et al., 2007), so it is clearly important for the examiner to be informed in each of these areas.

Impartiality is an important consideration whenever a mental health professional is conducting a forensic evaluation of a juvenile. Such evaluations may be requested by the juvenile's attorney or ordered by the court; under both circumstances, it is important for the evaluator to strive to be as honest, accurate, fair, and unbiased as possible and seems comparably applicable to both juvenile evaluations and other kinds of forensic assessments. It does not necessarily include the distinct role of consultant to one of the parties in the proceeding (Otto, Goldstein, & Heilbrun, in press), but it does apply to the kind of juvenile evaluations described in this chapter.

Achieving reasonable impartiality and honesty across cases requires controlling both case-specific and more general forms of bias. It is certainly as important to control bias in juvenile contexts as in adult contexts. Potentially biasing influence may result from influences that are financial (e.g., accepting a fee contingent on the case's outcome; accepting a fee with the understanding that payment is contingent on the contents of the report or testimony), personal (e.g., the belief that juvenile offenders need only clinical treatment to reform; the conviction that juvenile offenders are hardened young adults with stable personalities and propensities; having a personal relationship with the youth), or professional (e.g., having a current treatment relationship with the youth). Controlling such bias in specific cases can be as straightforward as ensuring that one's professional conduct is consistent with applicable general ethical standards (American Psychological Association, 2010) and more specific forensic ethical guidelines (American Psychological Association, 2013). Across a broader range of cases, the relevant questions are somewhat different. Is there a discernable pattern of accepting and declining referrals associated with cases from the defense and the prosecution, respectively? Is there a very high percentage of cases in which (whatever the source of the referral) the evaluator reports findings that are favorable to the retaining party? The latter was proposed by Colbach (1981), who called it the "integrity quotient." Because the actual proportion of cases in which favorable findings are reported depends on the proportion of cases in which favorable findings actually exist, the specific value of this fraction is always unknown. However, evaluators who nearly always report findings favoring the retaining party should consider the possibility of bias in favor of the referral source.

Next among the general principles, it is important to be familiar with various aspects of the legal system. These range from the process of conducting an evaluation and conveying the results to provision of testimony in a deposition, hearing, or trial and ongoing communication with relevant parties concerning the findings, the report, and possible testimony. It is important to have such familiarity with the juvenile and the criminal system, if conducting evaluations in both, and to have sufficient familiarity with the distinctive aspects of the juvenile system to provide effective services in the role of juvenile forensic evaluator.

Finally, it is important to be an effective advocate for one's opinion but to avoid becoming argumentative, unbalanced, or otherwise drawn into the adversarial aspect of the U.S. legal process. This can be challenging. Particularly when the examiner is careful to provide a thorough, unbiased, fair appraisal of the juvenile, some information will exist that is inconsistent with the examiner's ultimate conclusions. In reaching conclusions, forensic evaluators seek to identify stable patterns through multiple sources of converging data, but there will always be some data inconsistent with these broader patterns. The examiner should not yield to the temptation to underreport some of these inconsistent aspects or to place more weight than is indicated on the data that do support the examiner's conclusions. Even when the report conveys this information in a careful and fair way, a rigorous cross-examination may create the urge to respond to challenge by distorting one's data. Fortunately, it is possible to be clear and effective as an expert without engaging in such distortion, but it requires a recognition of the nature of this process and a willingness to master the stylistic as well as the substantive aspects of expert testimony (Brodsky, 1991, 1999, 2004, 2013).

Juvenile Application of Forensic Mental Health Assessment Principles in Specific Cases

Preparation. The next nine foundational principles move from general background to specific cases. These principles are as follows:

1. Identify relevant forensic issues.
2. Accept referrals only within one's area of expertise.
3. Decline the referral when evaluator impartiality is unlikely.
4. Clarify the evaluator's role with the attorney.
5. Clarify financial arrangements.
6. Obtain appropriate authorization.
7. Avoid playing the dual roles of therapist and forensic evaluator.
8. Determine the particular role to be played within forensic assessment if the referral is accepted.
9. Select the most appropriate model to guide data gathering, interpretation, and communication.

In most respects, these principles seem to apply to juvenile forensic assessments with little elaboration or modification.

Relevant forensic issues are the functional–legal capacities and propensities that are included within the broader legal question. They involve the capacity to think or behave in a certain way—areas in which mental health professionals have particular expertise. For example, consider the legal question of transfer from juvenile to criminal court. Among the criteria identified by some jurisdictions as guiding the transfer decision are public safety, treatment amenability, sophistication–maturity, and whether the transfer would be in the public interest. The first question is which of these criteria should be excluded from consideration for the evaluation because it involves something for which mental health professionals have no particular expertise. This would be the matter of whether the transfer is in the public interest, because that is a public policy issue, not a clinical or scientific one. Next, a consideration of public safety would suggest that the juvenile's risk of reoffending is a relevant issue for evaluation. That would mean that the appraisal of a juvenile's risk for reoffending (Hoge & Andrews, 2010) would be a central aspect of the evaluation. In a similar vein, the questions of treatment amenability and sophistication–maturity (Salekin, 2008) would be considered relevant forensic issues to be evaluated as part of the assessment.

As part of being informed about law, science, ethics, and practice, it is important to have specific expertise sufficient to apply this information. This expertise involves not only foundational training in clinical and scientific areas, but experience with individuals in the particular population being evaluated. If the examiner has specific training and experience with adolescents and has applied that training in the context of forensic assessments, then that satisfies the fundamental need for specialization noted in this principle. It is less important that there be primary specialization (Heilbrun, 2001; Melton et al., 2007), as long as the examiner is familiar with the important considerations; can apply the relevant scientific, developmental, and clinical knowledge; and can use specialized measures when relevant and available.

The importance of impartiality was addressed earlier in this chapter and elsewhere (Otto et al., in press). When some significant influence could affect the examiner's attempt to be thorough, accurate, and balanced in the collection and interpretation of relevant information, it is best to simply decline the referral. Such influences may arise from different sources—values, personal or professional relationships, or financial considerations—but when they exist, they should be acknowledged and the referral declined. Related to the possibility of bias stemming from financial influences, the evaluator should clarify what payment will be provided for the evaluation services and how it will be provided. When the examiner is in the role of evaluator and this service might result in the submission of a report and the provision of expert testimony, then any arrangement in which the provision or amount of payment is contingent on the evaluation's findings or the case's outcome is unacceptable (American Psychological Association, 2013). Rather, payment should be commensurate with the time necessary to provide the evaluation, unless the initial agreement by both parties results in the understanding that there will be a maximum amount beyond which the examiner will not bill. Evaluations with a significant pro bono component fall into this category; the agreement to conduct an evaluation for a total fee (or at an hourly rate) that is substantially less than usual for the examiner does not constitute a biasing influence as long as it reflects the initial agreement.

The sources of authorization to conduct a forensic evaluation with juveniles are quite similar to those with other populations. An assessment may be ordered by the court or requested by the juvenile's attorney; either is sufficient to allow the examiner to conduct the forensic assessment. A question may arise about whether the juvenile, as a minor, needs the permission of a parent or guardian if the evaluation has been requested by the defense attorney (and would, therefore, require the evaluee's informed consent to proceed). Certainly, the juvenile must agree before participating in any evaluation that is not ordered by the court. However, such agreement by a minor is regarded as assent rather than consent, and additional authorization is needed under such circumstances (particularly when the individual's capacity to provide informed assent are limited). Such additional authorization could be requested from the parent or guardian in the form of permission for the evaluation. However, this may be impractical when the parent or guardian is unavailable. For most juvenile evaluations requested by the defense attorney, it appears both legally and ethically sufficient to have the attorney provide permission for such evaluation if the attorney deems it to be in the best interest of the client's defense. Minimal risk is incurred by using the paper-and-pencil and interview techniques that are used for most evaluations. In a few cases, however—when an evaluator uses techniques that are unconventional and more invasive (e.g., brain imaging, sodium amytal)—the evaluator may need additional authorization in the form of permission of the attorney, permission of the parent or guardian, and assent of the youth (Melton et al., 2007).

The next consideration involves roles. As with forensic assessments with other populations, juvenile forensic evaluations should not be provided by a professional who is also treating the evaluee. One possible exception involves a program in which juveniles are being treated for restoration of competence to stand trial and must be evaluated as part of such treatment to determine whether they appear to have been restored. This exception aside, the principle that treatment and forensic assessment roles remain distinct applies to juveniles in the same way as it does to other populations undergoing forensic assessment. It is, of course, possible for a mental health professional or a behavioral scientist to play a role other than that of evaluator in a juvenile's case. Two other such roles include consultant and expert on the state of the science or practice (Otto et al., in press).

As a consultant, the professional might engage in any number of activities intended to assist counsel (e.g., review of the literature; review of the reports of experts retained by opposing counsel and preparation of the attorney to cross-examine such an expert; identification of appropriate placements for the juvenile). In the role of expert on the state of the science or practice, the professional would identify and describe relevant research, approaches to evaluation, practice guidelines, and similar information that is relevant to the immediate case in general but not sufficient to yield a specific opinion about this individual. It is important to be aware of the different possible roles within a given case and to identify the one that is played and retained throughout the case.

The final preparation principle involves using a model to guide data gathering, interpretation, and communication. Two models are broadly applicable in forensic assessment: those of Morse (1978) and of Grisso (1986, 2003). The Morse model calls for the gathering of clinical information as one of three components (clinical functioning, functional–legal capacities, and causal connection). If used with juveniles, it would be necessary to define *clinical* as including developmental maturity and more developmentally relevant functioning in educational, family, and peer areas as well as psychopathology. The Grisso model does not specifically cite clinical condition among its components, so it could be applied to juvenile evaluations without this kind of modification.

Data collection. The next eight foundational principles arise in the course of gathering information as part of the evaluation:

1. Use multiple sources for each area and actively seek missing elements.
2. Use relevance and reliability (validity) as guides for seeking information and selecting data sources.
3. Obtain relevant historical information.
4. Assess clinical characteristics in relevant, reliable, and valid ways.
5. Assess legally relevant behavior.
6. Ensure that conditions for evaluation are quiet, private, and distraction free.
7. Provide appropriate notification of purpose and obtain appropriate authorization before beginning.
8. Determine whether the individual understands the purpose of the evaluation and the associated limits on confidentiality.

Five of these principles (1–3, 5, and 6) appear to apply to juvenile evaluations without change, whereas defining clinical characteristics, providing notification of purpose and obtaining appropriate authorization, and determining whether the individual has understood the notification of purpose require some adjustment to account for age and developmental considerations.

Forensic evaluations require multiple sources of information. Self-report may be inaccurate in some cases when the individual deliberately distorts such information, but it should be assumed that the accuracy of self-report should in all cases be checked by appraising its consistency with information from other sources (Melton et al., 2007). Three important domains of information are self-report, testing and specialized measures, and records and third-party interviews. Juvenile evaluations, although limited in the second domain to measures that have been validated with adolescents, should nonetheless incorporate information from all three domains. The decision about which tests and specialized measures to consider is informed by available data on validity and reliability, but the focus of forensic evaluations is somewhat different than that of conventional clinical assessments. Because public safety (reoffense risk assessment) and treatment amenability (likely response to interventions addressing both offense risk and prosocial behavioral effectiveness) are the primary considerations in such assessments, the selection of tests and specialized measures should also be influenced by the relevance of such measures to reoffense risk assessment and this kind of treatment amenability.

As forensic evaluations proceed, the foundational principles suggest that history, clinical characteristics, and functional–legal capacities are the important broad domains to consider. With some modification, these apply reasonably well to the forensic evaluation of juveniles. History is important, particularly in the areas of prior juvenile involvement (including placements), school, family, and mental health. Legally relevant behavior is identified from the applicable legal question and its components that can be appraised by a mental health professional. The term clinical should be defined with juveniles in a way that is developmentally appropriate; this involves attention to dysfunction in the areas of school and family as well as the presence of symptoms (considered broadly to include milder disorders such as attention deficit hyperactivity disorder and learning disabilities).

Evaluation conditions—quiet, privacy, and freedom from distraction—are as important in evaluating juveniles as they are with any other population. It is important to begin the evaluation with a notification of purpose (if the evaluation is court ordered and the youth has no legal right to decline to participate) or the request for informed consent (if the evaluation is referred by the attorney and the youth can legally decline). Because youths younger than age 18 cannot provide informed consent for most important life decisions—youth assent plus parental or guardian permission is needed instead—any request for informed consent must be reconceptualized somewhat. The juvenile's agreement (assent) to participate, combined with the attorney's permission (implicit in the request for evaluation), suffices for decisions related to the juvenile's legal defense, unless there is a very strong basis for doubting the capacity of the youth to provide informed assent.

Data interpretation. The area of data interpretation has seven foundational principles. Six of them appear to apply in juvenile evaluations without change:

1. Use third-party information in assessing response style.
2. Use testing when indicated in assessing response style.
3. Use case-specific (idiographic) evidence in assessing clinical condition, functional abilities, and causal connection.
4. Use nomothetic evidence in assessing clinical condition, functional abilities, and causal connection.
5. Use scientific reasoning in assessing causal connection between clinical condition and functional abilities.
6. Describe findings and limits so that they need change little under cross-examination.

Because Principles 3, 4, and 5 refer to clinical condition, it is worth reiterating that clinical should be defined in a way that is developmentally appropriate.

The principle that does need minor adjustment involves determining whether to answer the ultimate legal question directly. We are not aware of empirical data on the question of whether juvenile judges request ultimate-issue opinions more frequently than do criminal court judges. Anecdotally, it is our impression that they do, consistent with an inclination to be more active in directly questioning expert witnesses. If so, then examiners who provide forensic assessments of juveniles and do not routinely provide a direct answer to the ultimate legal question before the court will confront this issue more frequently.

Written communication. Three foundational principles apply to report writing:

1. Attribute information to sources.
2. Use plain language and avoid technical jargon.
3. Write report in sections, according to model and procedures.

All three appear to apply to juvenile assessment in the same way that they are more broadly applicable.

Expert testimony. The first foundational principle in this area involves an accumulation of previous principles. By basing testimony solidly on the results of the forensic assessment communicated in the report, the examiner offers substantively strong information concerning the relevant issues before the court. However, testimony in an adversarial context requires more than substantively strong information to be effective; the expert must also convey this information in a style that is clear, credible, and balanced and that holds up to challenge. Two of the remaining principles—prepare and communicate effectively—seem to apply to juvenile forensic assessment as well as to forensic assessment with any other population. None of these three principles, therefore, needs alteration in their application to juvenile forensic work. The final principle, involving controlling the message during testimony, does need minor modification, however. If there is a greater tendency for juvenile hearings to be inquisitorial rather than adversarial, then experts will be responding to questions posed directly by judges without the assumption that such questioning is adversarial. It becomes less about controlling the message, therefore, and more about answering questions clearly and in sufficient detail.

IMPLICATIONS FOR RESEARCH, POLICY, AND PRACTICE

This chapter has addressed broad and foundational issues relevant to the forensic assessment of juveniles. Implications for research, policy, and practice that are particular to the more specific legal questions and their associated scientific support are discussed in the other chapters in Part VI of this handbook. However, implications are raised by the broad focus of this chapter, to which we now turn.

Research

Consistent with the contemporary emphasis on empirically supported assessment and interventions in a broad array of human services, we strongly emphasize the importance of providing juvenile FMHA that is empirically driven and scientifically supported. Toward that end, we identify the following as questions in particular need of further research.

First, to what extent do those who request and use juvenile FMHA demand assessments that are relevant and empirically supported? When a judge orders the assessment of a juvenile to help inform a legal decision on Miranda waiver capacity, competence to stand trial, commitment, or transfer, is there a reasonable expectation that the resulting evaluation will incorporate up-to-date scientific evidence in addressing legally relevant capacities? This question involves the perceptions of judges, attorneys, and others who are involved in requesting and using juvenile FMHA. Measuring such perceptions on a widespread basis, across jurisdictions and disciplines, would probably be straightforward to design and deliver; achieving a sufficiently high response rate to generalize findings, however, would be challenging.

Second and relatedly, to what extent are those conducting juvenile FMHA providing reports that are legally relevant and scientifically respectable? The limited evidence to date in this area (Christy, Douglas, Otto, & Petrila, 2004; Hecker & Steinberg, 2002; Sanschagrin, 2005) does not suggest optimism on this point. However, this handful of studies was conducted about a decade ago. Research using large, multijurisdiction samples would be useful in providing a contemporary answer to this question.

Third, how do we weigh the potentially competing values of longer duration, greater thoroughness, and longer reports against efficiency and cost effectiveness? Although some might argue that legally relevant and scientifically driven juvenile FMHA represents an unaffordable luxury in a world of limited resources, there is research evidence that might inform this debate. By quantifying perceptions of overall report quality as applied to reports requiring varying amounts of time to complete, including all elements of the evaluation and report writing (e.g., 1 hour, 5 hours, 10 hours, 20 hours), we might hypothesize a curve plotting the relationship between time (on the *x*-axis) and quality (on the *y*-axis) of the shape shown in Figure 16.1.

If this were accurate, it would have three meanings. First, a minimum amount of time must be invested for any evaluation to yield meaningful results. Second, a sharp increase in the perception of quality and utility results from relatively modest

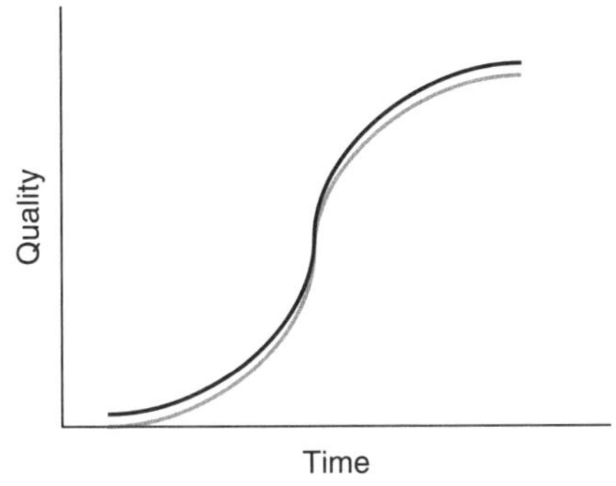

FIGURE 16.1. Hypothesized relationship between time devoted to and quality of forensic mental health assessment.

commensurate increases in time (e.g., the 3-hour difference associated with an increase from 2.5 to 5.5 hours). Finally, a level of time commitment exists beyond which the returns of increased quality rapidly diminish. Conducting research that would test this hypothesis, perhaps identifying the lower and upper thresholds for the time needed to produce good evaluations, would encourage courts to focus on identifying an acceptable level of quality and making the investment of resources necessary to produce such results. Depending on the complexity of the referral questions, the amount of time might vary, but it is hypothesized that the shape of the curve would remain constant across different types of evaluations.

Policy

The advances in FMHA described in this chapter, and in other chapters in this handbook, clearly have implications for informing those who make policy and others who implement it. One relevant question involves how such information should best be conveyed. Although edited books provide a good platform for acknowledged experts to summarize particular content areas, such books may not be the most efficient way to reach policymakers. However, there are particular conclusions to be drawn from this chapter that are important to disseminate widely if forensic evaluations of juveniles are to improve: the importance of structure, the necessity of legal relevance, the use of validated measures (particularly those developed specifically for application to the legal question at hand), the employment of multiple sources of information, the impartial interpretation of findings, and the communication of results in such a way that allows those reading (or hearing) them to understand the basis for such conclusions. Such dissemination should include venues that are specific to those who make policy (e.g., congressional fellows and legislative staffers) and implement it (e.g., judicial conferences, attorney continuing education).

There are also high-quality training curricula produced by respected organizations (e.g., the MacArthur/Juvenile Law Center/American Bar Association curriculum on adolescent development and juvenile evaluations; see Chapter 30, this handbook) that convey similar conclusions but whose primary developers are legal experts. Also, the development and regular updating of best-practice standards by national organizations in law, behavioral science, and medicine can serve as guides to those outside these professions who are engaged in the development or implementation of legal policy relevant to juvenile evaluations.

Practice

The first implication for practice relates directly to the research question posed earlier: To what extent are professionals conducting FMHAs providing reports and testimony that are legally relevant, scientifically supported, and consistent with the principles described in this chapter? Assuming that improvement is still needed, it is useful to consider this chapter as offering foundational information relevant to the training of child and adolescent psychologists and psychiatrists, forensic psychologists and psychiatrists, forensic social workers, forensic nurses, parole and probation officers, and any others who might be involved in providing information to the juvenile courts in this context. Such training might be provided at levels ranging from graduate to internship and from residency to fellowship and during continuing education.

The practice standards that could be developed by national organizations (e.g., American Bar Association, American Psychological Association, American Psychiatric Association) and specialty national organizations (e.g., American Psychology-Law Society, American Academy of Psychiatry and Law,

National Association of Forensic Social Workers) have the potential for significant impact on individuals within those organizations. Such standards must be developed in their specific application to juveniles, however, and they must be updated regularly. Some progress has been made in the development of such standards, but not specifically with respect to juvenile FMHA.

The importance of structure and access to relevant best-practice guidelines raises a related issue involving implementation. The technological advances in the past 2 decades—particularly in the availability of the Internet as an information repository and tools (e.g., smartphones, tablets) for accessing it—have been staggering. The extent to which these advances have been implemented into practice seems minimal, however. Using this technology to enhance the structure, legal relevance, and scientific basis for juvenile FMHA offers enormous potential for creating change and making improvements that are both needed and potentially transformative.

References

American Psychological Association. (2010). *Ethical principles of psychologists and code of conduct.* Retrieved from http://www.apa.org/ethics/code/index.aspx

American Psychological Association. (2013). *Specialty guidelines for forensic psychology.* Retrieved from http://www.apa.org/practice/guidelines/forensic-psychology.aspx

Andrews, D., Bonta, J., & Hoge, R. (1990). Classification for effective rehabilitation: Rediscovering psychology. *Criminal Justice and Behavior, 17,* 19–52. http://dx.doi.org/10.1177/0093854890017001004

Bonnie, R. (1992). The competence of criminal defendants: A theoretical reformulation. *Behavioral Sciences and the Law, 10,* 291–316. http://dx.doi.org/10.1002/bsl.2370100303

Borum, R., Bartels, P., & Forth, A. (2005). *Structured Assessment of Violence Risk in Youth.* Lutz, FL: Psychological Assessment Resources.

Brodsky, S. (1991). *Testifying in court: Guidelines and maxims for the expert witness.* Washington, DC: American Psychological Association.

Brodsky, S. (1999). *The expert expert witness: More maxims and guidelines for testifying in court.* Washington, DC: American Psychological Association.

Brodsky, S. (2004). *Coping with cross-examination and other pathways to effective testimony.* http://dx.doi.org/10.1037/10748-000

Brodsky, S. (2013). *Testifying in court: Guidelines and maxims for the expert witness* (2nd ed.). http://dx.doi.org/10.1037/14037-000

Bryant, A., Matthews, G., & Wilhelmsen, B. (2013). Assessing the legitimacy of competence to stand trial in the juvenile court: The practice of CST with and without statutory law. *Criminal Justice Policy Review.* Advance online publication. http://dx.doi.org/10.1177/0887403413515999

Caldwell, M. F. (2010). Study characteristics and recidivism base rates in juvenile sex offender recidivism. *International Journal of Offender Therapy and Comparative Criminology, 54,* 197–212. http://dx.doi.org/10.1177/0306624X08330016

Chen, D. R., & Salekin, R. T. (2012). Transfer to adult court: Enhancing clinical forensic evaluations and informing policy. In E. L. Grigorenko (Ed.), *Handbook of juvenile forensic psychology and psychiatry* (pp. 105–125). http://dx.doi.org/10.1007/978-1-4614-0905-2_8

Christy, A., Douglas, K., Otto, R., & Petrila, J. (2004). Juveniles evaluated incompetent to proceed: Characteristics and quality of mental health professionals' evaluations. *Professional Psychology: Research and Practice, 35,* 380–388. http://dx.doi.org/10.1037/0735-7028.35.4.380

Colbach, E. M. (1981). Integrity checks on the witness stand. *Bulletin of the American Academy of Psychiatry and the Law, 9,* 285–288.

Dusky v. United States, 362 U.S. 402 (1960).

Graham v. Florida, 130 S. Ct. 2011 (2010).

Grisso, T. (1986). *Evaluating competencies: Forensic assessments and instruments.* http://dx.doi.org/10.1007/978-1-4899-5046-8

Grisso, T. (1998). *Forensic evaluation of juveniles.* Sarasota, FL: Professional Resource Press.

Grisso, T. (2003). *Evaluating competencies: Forensic assessments and instruments* (2nd ed.). New York, NY: Kluwer Academic/Plenum.

Grisso, T. (2013). *Forensic evaluation of juveniles* (2nd ed.). Sarasota, FL: Professional Resource Press.

Grisso, T., Steinberg, L., Woolard, J., Cauffman, E., Scott, E., Graham, S., . . . Schwartz, R. (2003). Juveniles' competence to stand trial: A comparison of adolescents' and adults' capacities as trial defendants. *Law and Human Behavior, 27,* 333–363. http://dx.doi.org/10.1023/A:1024065015717

Hecker, T., & Steinberg, L. (2002). Psychological evaluation at juvenile court disposition. *Professional Psychology: Research and Practice, 33,* 300–306. http://dx.doi.org/10.1037/0735-7028.33.3.300

Heilbrun, K. (2001). *Principles of forensic mental health assessment*. New York, NY: Kluwer Academic/Plenum.

Heilbrun, K. (2009). *Evaluation for risk of violence in adults*. http://dx.doi.org/10.1093/med/9780195369816.001.0001

Heilbrun, K., Grisso, T., & Goldstein, A. (2009). *Foundations of forensic mental health assessment*. New York, NY: Oxford University Press.

Hoge, R., & Andrews, D. (2002). *The Youth Level of Service/Case Management Inventory*. Toronto, Ontario, Canada: Multi-Health Systems.

Hoge, R., & Andrews, D. (2010). *Evaluation for risk of violence in juveniles*. http://dx.doi.org/10.1093/med/9780195370416.001.0001

Hoge, R. D. (2012). Forensic assessment of juveniles: Practice and legal considerations. *Criminal Justice and Behavior, 39*, 1255–1270. http://dx.doi.org/10.1177/0093854812444024

In re Gault, 387 U.S. 1 (1967).

Jacobs, R. (2013). Waiving goodbye to due process: The juvenile waiver system. *Cardozo Journal of Law and Gender, 19*, 989–1017.

J.D.B. v. North Carolina, 131 S. Ct. 2394 (2011).

Kansas v. Hendricks, 521 U.S. 346 (1997).

Kent v. United States, 383 U.S. 541 (1966).

LaFave, W. R. (2007). *Criminal law* (3rd ed.). Eagan, MN: Thomson/West.

Lipsitt, P. D., Lelos, D., & McGarry, A. L. (1971). Competency for trial: A screening instrument. *American Journal of Psychiatry, 128*, 105–109.

McKeiver v. Pennsylvania, 403 U.S. 528 (1971).

Melton, G., Petrila, J., Poythress, N., & Slobogin, C. (2007). *Psychological evaluations for the court: A handbook for mental health professionals and lawyers* (3rd ed.). New York, NY: Guilford Press.

Miller v. Alabama, 132 S. Ct. 2455 (2012).

Miranda v. Arizona, 384 U.S. 436 (1966).

Morse, S. (1978). Crazy behavior, morals, and science: An analysis of mental health law. *Southern California Law Review, 51*, 527–654.

O'Donnell, P. C., & Gross, B. (2012). Developmental incompetence to stand trial in juvenile courts. *Journal of Forensic Sciences, 57*, 989–996. http://dx.doi.org/10.1111/j.1556-4029.2012.02093.x

Otto, R. K., Goldstein, A., & Heilbrun, K. (in press). *Ethics and forensic psychological assessment*. New York, NY: Kluwer.

Rogers, R., Blackwood, H. L., Fiduccia, C. E., Steadham, J. A., Drogin, E. Y., & Rogstad, J. E. (2012). Juvenile *Miranda* warnings: Perfunctory rituals or procedural safeguards? *Criminal Justice and Behavior, 39*, 229–249. http://dx.doi.org/10.1177/0093854811431934

Roper v. Simmons, 543 U.S. 551 (2005).

Salekin, R. (2008). Risk-Sophistication-Treatment Inventory (RSTI). In B. Cutler (Ed.), *Encyclopedia of psychology and law* (pp. 702–704). http://dx.doi.org/10.4135/9781412963848

Salekin, R. T., Rogers, R., & Ustad, K. (2001). Juvenile waiver to adult criminal court: Prototypes for dangerousness, sophistication-maturity, and amenability to treatment. *Psychology, Public Policy, and Law, 7*, 381–408. http://dx.doi.org/10.1037/1076-8971.7.2.381

Salekin, R. T., Yff, R. M. A., Neumann, C. S., Leistico, A. R., & Zalot, A. A. (2002). Juvenile transfer to adult courts: A look at the prototypes for dangerousness, sophistication-maturity, and amenability to treatment through a legal lens. *Psychology, Public Policy, and Law, 8*, 373–410. http://dx.doi.org/10.1037/1076-8971.8.4.373

Sanschagrin, K. (2005). *The quality of forensic mental health assessments of juvenile offenders* (Doctoral dissertation). Retrieved from http://idea.library.drexel.edu/bitstreat/1860/658/1/Sanschagrin_Kimberly.pdf

Schwalbe, C. S., Gearing, R. E., MacKenzie, M. J., Brewer, K. B., & Ibrahim, R. (2012). A meta-analysis of experimental studies of diversion programs for juvenile offenders. *Clinical Psychology Review, 32*, 26–33. http://dx.doi.org/10.1016/j.cpr.2011.10.002

Stanford v. Kentucky, 462 U.S. 361 (1989).

Steinberg, L., & Scott, E. S. (2003). Less guilty by reason of adolescence: Developmental immaturity, diminished responsibility, and the juvenile death penalty. *American Psychologist, 58*, 1009–1018. http://dx.doi.org/10.1037/0003-066X.58.12.1009

CHAPTER 17

RISK ASSESSMENT WITH JUVENILES

David DeMatteo, Melinda Wolbransky, and Casey LaDuke

The practice of violence risk assessment with adults is well supported by a large and growing body of empirical research (see Heilbrun, 2009; Heilbrun, Yasuhara, & Shah, 2010, for reviews). Relevant research conducted over the past several decades has, among other accomplishments, identified risk factors and protective factors, developed frameworks for approaching risk assessment and management (e.g., risk–need–responsivity), and developed several instruments that can reliably predict risk for future offending (general, violent, sexual). Moreover, various researchers and scholars have developed best-practice guidelines for conducting risk assessments, and the empirical and practice literatures provide considerable guidance to forensic practitioners who conduct violence risk assessments with adults.

In contrast, risk assessment with adolescents has received less attention from researchers and policymakers. To be clear, research on juvenile risk assessment has increased considerably over the past 15 years, and the research literature contains several examples of well-conducted cross-sectional risk assessment studies, longitudinal studies that examine risk trajectory, and studies validating various risk assessment instruments designed for use with adolescents. A more recent contribution to the juvenile risk assessment literature is meta-analyses examining the predictive and incremental validity of risk assessment instruments. This research certainly represents progress, but knowledge of best practices when it comes to assessing a juvenile's risk of future delinquent or violent behavior is still somewhat limited. As such, practitioners who work with adolescents—and policymakers who develop relevant policy—are at a disadvantage.

Despite incomplete (albeit developing) knowledge of juvenile risk assessment, evaluations of a juvenile's likelihood of engaging in delinquent or violent acts are being conducted in a variety of settings and at various stages of the juvenile adjudication process with increasing frequency (Hoge & Andrews, 2010a). For example, risk assessments with juveniles are being conducted in schools, inpatient mental health facilities, community treatment centers, juvenile detention centers, and other forensic settings (see Hoge & Andrews, 2010a). Focusing on the forensic arena, evaluations of a juvenile's risk may be conducted at the precharge stage (e.g., to determine the appropriateness of offering admission to a juvenile diversion program in which an adolescent is not charged with an offense and instead is directed toward a specific intervention), the postcharge but preadjudication stage (e.g., decisions relating to transfer to and from the adult system, preadjudication detention, and preadjudication diversion), and the disposition stage (e.g., decisions regarding the appropriateness of probation vs. detention or incarceration). The legal system has come to rely on assessments of a juvenile's risk in a variety of contexts, and the results of these assessments can have important consequences for the juvenile.

In this chapter, we provide a concise overview of juvenile risk assessment. We begin by presenting a brief history of juvenile risk assessment, with a particular focus on the development of the field of juvenile risk assessment, an examination of relevant

http://dx.doi.org/10.1037/14643-017
APA Handbook of Psychology and Juvenile Justice, K. Heilbrun (Editor-in-Chief)

foundational trends, and the regulation of juvenile risk assessment. Next, we focus on current empirical research regarding juvenile risk assessment, including discussions of models of juvenile risk assessment, empirically supported risk and protective factors, and the predictive and incremental validity of juvenile risk assessment measures. Finally, we discuss implications for practice, policy, and research, with a discussion focused on conducting juvenile risk assessments and future directions for research and policy.

RELEVANT HISTORY OF JUVENILE RISK ASSESSMENT

Juvenile risk assessment and management was developed using the framework of adult risk assessment and applying research specific to juvenile crime. In this section, we briefly review general developments in risk assessment, the U.S. juvenile justice system, and theoretical and empirical investigations around criminal behavior in juvenile populations that had a bearing on the eventual emergence of juvenile risk assessment. We then review the more recent history of juvenile risk assessment per se and follow with a discussion of foundational trends in the practice and regulation of risk assessment with justice-involved youths.

Development of Juvenile Risk Assessment

Juvenile risk assessment is a relatively recent development in forensic mental health assessment. Contemporary juvenile risk assessment reflects the convergence of trends in the judicial treatment of juveniles in the United States, developments within violence risk assessment generally, and the scientific investigation of juveniles who commit crime. These foundational developments are discussed before we elaborate on the development of contemporary juvenile risk assessment.

Historical development of the U.S. juvenile justice system. The roots of the juvenile justice system in the United States stem from legal scholarship in Great Britain, where lawyers in the mid-18th century began distinguishing between "infants" of age 7 and younger and adults of age 14 and older (American Bar Association, 2007). The more contemporary history of the U.S. juvenile justice system effectively began in 1899, followed by a slow evolution from retributive justice to a focus on rehabilitation for justice-involved juveniles.

Before 1899, adult and juvenile offenders were under the custody of the same criminal justice system. Although the adult and juvenile systems were structurally similar, there was an inherent and frequent assumption in the adult system that immaturity might mitigate responsibility on the basis of a defense of "infancy," which was usually delineated as ages 7 to 10 years, depending on the jurisdiction (Melton, Petrila, Poythress, & Slobogin, 2007). Responding to a growing systemic interest in rehabilitative justice, the court systems in Chicago and Denver established the country's first juvenile courts (Chapman, 2012; Hoge & Andrews, 2010a). These early juvenile courts were based on the progressive view that juvenile offenders were less culpable for their crimes than their adult counterparts because of sociodevelopmental factors (e.g., poverty, parental neglect) and were more malleable and amenable to rehabilitation (see Mack, 1909; Redding, Sevin Goldstein, & Heilbrun, 2005). Procedural changes were adopted in this new system so juvenile court judges could inquire further into the character of the juvenile offender to determine his or her fitness for rehabilitation (Chapman, 2012). Judges were tasked with identifying the underlying causes of the delinquent behavior and then tailoring interventions for the juvenile offender that would be offered in community settings by mental health providers and social workers (Mack, 1909; Redding et al., 2005). The establishment of juvenile courts marked a philosophical and procedural paradigm shift away from punitive justice and toward rehabilitative justice for juvenile offenders.

The development of juvenile courts over the next 25 years was rapid, but the goals of the system were not fully realized. By 1925, 48 states had established distinct juvenile justice systems (Coalition for Juvenile Justice, 1998), but they had done so with limited input from the mental health community (e.g., only 7% of juvenile courts had a mental health clinic by 1922) and in a climate of growing legal criticism (U.S. Department of Labor, 1922). Critics assailed the juvenile court model, citing two major concerns (Fox, 1970; Redding et al., 2005). First, critics argued that the informal and nonadversarial process in juvenile court afforded fewer due process protections than the adult system, resulting in many juveniles being found delinquent without sufficient evidence, based on judges' broad adjudicatory and dispositional authority. Second, critics contended that the system relied on for community rehabilitation was either not established or not forthcoming, resulting in the de facto incarceration of juveniles for indeterminate periods of time. As summarized by U.S. Supreme Court Justice Abe Fortas, "The child received the worst of both worlds. . . . He gets neither the protection afforded to adults, nor the solicitous care and regenerative treatment postulated for children" (*In re Gault*, 1967, p. 18). The juvenile court system appeared to be falling short of its procedural and rehabilitative goals.

Several subsequent judicial decisions had profound impacts on the juvenile justice system. A series of cases from the U.S. Supreme Court—*Kent v. United States* (1966), *In re Gault* (1967), and *In re Winship* (1970)—effectively established full due process protections within juvenile courts (except for the right to trial by jury; see *McKeiver v. Pennsylvania*, 1971). These decisions benefited youths in the juvenile justice system by ensuring court findings were based on the nature of the offense rather than judges' perceptions of rehabilitative needs, and they also allowed for shorter and more rehabilitative dispositions (Scott, 2000). As these Supreme Court cases were being decided, however, several authoritative reports reinforced the continued concerns about the effectiveness of the juvenile justice system. The President's Commission on Law Enforcement and Administration of Justice (1967) stated that juvenile courts were ineffective in rehabilitating offenders and reducing recidivism, and a review of program evaluations in the fields of juvenile and criminal justice famously concluded that nothing works (Martinson, 1974). The juvenile justice system, thus, continued to develop in an environment of political and professional pressure.

The 1980s saw added societal pressure on the juvenile justice system, which led to a reversion toward punitive justice. The number of juveniles arrested for violent crimes increased substantially between 1980 and 1984 (Hoge & Andrews, 2010a; Redding et al., 2005). In part because of increasingly negative portrayals of the juvenile violence "epidemic" by the media and politicians, public perceptions at the time tended to overestimate rates of crime among youths and resulted in calls for more punitive responses to juvenile crime (see Warr, 2007). In response to these concomitant factors, policymakers and voters at the state and federal levels began to enact laws designed to "get tough" on juvenile crime (see Beresford, 2000). The growing consensus among these groups was that juvenile offenders' culpability for their crimes was comparable to that of adults, juvenile courts were too lenient, rehabilitation efforts were ineffective, serious offenders were beyond rehabilitation, and incarceration was needed to protect public safety (Redding et al., 2005). Encapsulating the punitive zeal behind this countermovement, in 1997 Congressman Bill McCollum famously announced, "In America today, no population poses a greater threat to public safety than juvenile criminals" (Redding et al., 2005, p. 6).

Contemporary juvenile justice represents a balance between punitive and rehabilitative justice. Despite some calls to abolish the system altogether, juvenile courts currently strive to integrate accountability and punishment with treatment and rehabilitation (Tate & Redding, 2005; Wilson & Howell, 1995). Although states show considerable variability in juvenile justice laws and practices, the most common approach appears to be delivery of rehabilitative interventions within the context of legal processing and supervision, with the recognition that the management of juvenile offenders ultimately depends on providing them with the resources to lead prosocial lives (Hoge & Andrews, 2010a). Among the most frequently asked questions within contemporary juvenile justice are those related to risk and risk reduction: What is the likelihood a juvenile defendant will commit future delinquent acts, and how can this risk be reduced through rehabilitative intervention (Conroy & Murrie, 2007; Schwalbe, 2007)? It is within this legal framework that juvenile risk assessment has developed.

History of violence risk assessment with juveniles. Rehabilitative justice has withstood the press of punitive sentiment largely because of a developing understanding of what works in juvenile offender rehabilitation (Henggeler, Cunningham, Pickrel, Schoenwald, & Brondino, 1996). Program evaluation continues to support the ideology that rehabilitation can be successful with juvenile offenders, including youths adjudicated delinquent of violent offenses (Lipsey, 1995; Lipsey & Wilson, 1998; see Redding et al., 2005). Moreover, mounting empirical evidence continues to elucidate the historical, personal, and contextual factors that serve to increase or decrease a juvenile's likelihood of performing delinquent and violent behavior. The clinical practice of juvenile risk assessment and management has developed to address the question of risk and to offer actionable recommendations on how to reduce the likelihood of such risk. Juvenile risk assessment has been a relatively recent development, using the framework of adult risk assessment and applying research specific to juvenile offending. We briefly discuss both of these areas—violence risk assessment in adults and research on juvenile offending—before we offer a more focused discussion of juvenile risk assessment.

Violence risk assessment with adults. Contemporary violence risk assessment is the result of centuries of clinical experience and decades of empirical investigation. A complete review of this history is beyond the scope of this chapter, and interested readers are referred to several historical and contemporary works for further information (see Grisso, 2013; Heilbrun, 2009; Melton et al., 2007; Monahan, 1981, 1984; Singh, 2012). One important trend in the development of violence risk assessment is the transition from unstructured clinical judgment to actuarial measures in the mid-20th century and then to structured professional judgment paradigms beginning in the 1990s. The advent of empirically derived risk assessment techniques and measures led not only to increased predictive accuracy in the practice of risk assessment, but also to a renewed interest in investigating the nature and quality of factors related to antisocial and violent behavior across a variety of offender populations (discussed further in the next section).

The early 2000s saw a broadening of violence risk assessment to include both estimations of the likelihood that an individual would exhibit antisocial and violent behavior (risk assessment) and the provision of specific treatment recommendations aimed at reducing this likelihood (risk management; Douglas, Ogloff, & Hart, 2003; Douglas & Skeem, 2005; Heilbrun, 2003; see also Heilbrun, 1997). This broadened focus can be seen not only in the practice of violence risk assessment generally, but in more recent editions of the most widely used actuarial (Level of Service/Case Management Inventory; Andrews, Bonta, & Wormith, 2004) and structured professional judgment (Historical Clinical Risk Management–20, Version 3; Douglas, Hart, Webster, & Belfrage, 2013) measures. The most recent trend in violence risk assessment appears to involve the understanding of protective factors that reduce an individual's risk of violence (DeMatteo & Marczyk, 2005; Rogers, 2000). The research regarding protective factors for violence is currently limited, but much of the work that has been done has been in the context of juvenile offenders (Conroy, 2012).

Theoretical and empirical investigation of crime by juveniles. It has long been held that aggressive behavior among children and adolescents is common, normative, and multidetermined (Grisso, 2013). Research regarding the multiple pathways to delinquent behavior and the many types of delinquent youths extends back to the first juvenile court in 1899 (Healy, 1915), and these developmental trends and typologies have been continuously supported and elaborated over the subsequent 116 years (see Quay & Peterson, 1987, for one seminal typology). Hoge and Andrews (2010a) nicely summarized the empirical consensus regarding violence among juveniles. As they noted, the majority of children and adolescents are responsible and law-abiding individuals, and risk-taking and minor criminal behaviors are considered normative in this population (Hoge & Andrews, 2010a; see Williams, Tuthill, & Lio, 2008). A small number of juveniles engage in violence, which is usually less serious in nature and does not continue. Indeed, in relation to their proportion in the population, adolescents are responsible for more illegal and harmful behavior than are adults (Grisso, 2013). A still smaller number of juveniles engage in more serious acts of violence, but, again, this behavior does not usually continue. In fact, one of the best-documented findings regarding delinquency is its time-limited nature, with both the severity and the frequency of antisocial and violent behaviors decreasing with age (Gottfredson & Hirschi, 1990; Moffitt, 1993). Thus, only a small minority of juveniles commit violent behaviors that are serious, continuing, and escalating.

The traditional theories of juvenile violence—including classical, biological, psychodynamic, social learning, control, and economic–sociological theories (Hoge & Andrews, 2010a)—have given way to contemporary theories that seek to integrate ecological and developmental models that focus on specific risk (and, more recently, protective) factors that are empirically associated with violent behavior (see Compas, Hinden, & Gerhardt, 1995; DeMatteo & Marczyk, 2005; Guerra, Williams, Tolan, & Modecki, 2008; Jessor, Van den Bos, Vanderryn, Costa, & Turbin, 1995). Overall, this research has supported the proposition that "'delinquent' is not a type of juvenile, and 'aggression' does not define a homogenous category of adolescents" (Grisso, 2013, p. 148).

Another line of research has attempted to track and explain trends in the rates of violence among juveniles in the United States. As previously noted, the number of juveniles arrested for violent crime increased significantly between 1980 and 1984 (Hoge & Andrews, 2010a; Redding et al., 2005). This peak in arrests has since been declining for both Caucasian and African American males—especially between 1992 and 2003 (Hoge & Andrews, 2010a)—but arrests have been increasing among females (Puzzanchara & Hockenberry, 2013). The explanations for these trends are contentious and complex, and they include changes in population demographics, economic conditions, and juvenile justice policies resulting from political reaction to public perception (or misperception) about crime rates (Hoge & Andrews, 2010a; Redding et al., 2005). Regardless of the reasoning behind these trends and the opinions held by the general public, juvenile crime rates have declined in recent years, high-profile incidents propagated through media exposure do not represent juvenile crime generally, and the public does not appear to favor punitive justice for juvenile offenders at the expense of rehabilitation (Redding et al., 2005). This research has been seminal not only for juvenile justice policy but also for the development of juvenile violence risk assessment.

Development of juvenile risk assessment. Violence risk assessment specific to juvenile offenders is a relatively recent trend in forensic mental health assessment that has developed substantively over the past 15 years (Grisso, 2003, 2013; Hoge & Andrews, 2010a). Before these recent developments in juvenile risk assessment, "the best that clinicians could do in juvenile risk assessment was to attend to empirically based risk factors during their interviews and other data collection methods" (Grisso, 2013, p. 144). Beginning primarily in the 1990s, however, a number of studies systematically investigated the risk factors for juvenile offending (e.g., Hawkins et al., 1998; Hoge & Andrews, 1996). The field quickly capitalized on this research by developing several semistructured interview paradigms, checklists, and rating instruments (Hoge & Andrews, 2010a), with the first widely implemented risk assessment tool specific to juvenile populations published several years later (see Schwalbe, 2007, for a review).

Several standardized non–risk assessment measures have since been developed or refined to make them more relevant to assessing juvenile risk (i.e., the Minnesota Multiphasic Personality Inventory—Adolescent [Butcher et al., 1992], Psychopathy Checklist: Youth Version [PCL:YV; Forth, Kosson, & Hare, 2003]). Standardized measures specific to juvenile violence risk also continue to be developed and refined, including measures to assess violence risk generally (Structured Assessment of Violence Risk in Youth [SAVRY; Borum, Bartel, & Forth, 2006], Youth Level of Service/Case Management Inventory 2.0 [YLS/CMI 2.0; Hoge & Andrews, 2010b]), gender-specific risk of violence for young boys (Early Assessment Risk List for Boys, Version 2; Augimeri, Koegel, Webster, & Levene, 2001) and girls (Early Assessment Risk List for Girls, Version 1 Consultation Edition; Levene et al., 2001), and sexual violence, either as add-on factors (Worling & Langstrom, 2006) or within specific instruments (Estimate of Risk of Adolescent Sexual Offense Recidivism [Worling & Curwen, 2001], Juvenile Sex Offender Assessment Protocol—II [J-SOAP–II; Prentky & Righthand, 2003], Juvenile Sexual Offense Recidivism Risk Assessment Tool—II [Epperson, Ralston, Fowers, DeWitt, & Gore, 2006]). For more specific information, readers are referred to the professional manuals for these measures and more generally to several recent reviews (Grisso, 2013; Hoge & Andrews, 2010a; Otto & Douglas, 2010; Vincent, Terry, & Maney, 2009).

Foundational Trends in Juvenile Risk Assessment

The foundation of contemporary juvenile risk assessment rests on the evolution of the juvenile justice system, the development of violence risk assessment generally, and research specific to juvenile offenders and offending. As the juvenile justice system sought to balance the ideals of rehabilitation with the push for punitive justice, the estimation of future risk among justice-involved youths and the ability to provide tailored and evidence-based targets for intervention became central concerns in juvenile courts. Today, juvenile courts frequently seek risk–needs assessments to help inform legal decisions regarding pre- and postcharge diversion, transfer to and waiver from adult court, disposition decisions, and appropriate sentences.

Capitalizing on decades of research enhancing violence risk assessment in adults and more recent research on the factors associated with increased risk for continued antisocial behavior, forensic mental health researchers and clinicians sought to provide evidence for these legal questions by developing more structured clinical procedures and specialized measures specifically designed for use with juveniles. These techniques and measures have continued to develop in line with current trends in the field. Contemporary juvenile risk assessment has thus adapted to incorporate structured and evidence-based risk and protective factors shown to influence a juvenile's likelihood of future violence, with the dual goals of estimating a juvenile's likelihood of future risk and providing recommendations for risk management.

Regulation of Juvenile Risk Assessment

There is both legislative and professional regulation of juvenile risk assessment in some jurisdictions. Though several judicial decisions impose some general guidelines on the treatment of juvenile defendants in the United States—particularly concerning due process (e.g., *In re Gault*, 1967; *Kent v. United States*, 1966; *McKeiver v. Pennsylvania*, 1971) and punitive limits (*Roper v. Simmons*, 2005, prohibiting the execution of juvenile offenders; *Graham v. Florida*, 2010, holding that juveniles cannot be sentenced to life without parole for nonhomicide crimes; *Miller v. Alabama*, 2012, holding that juveniles cannot receive a mandatory sentence of life without parole for homicide crimes)—there is no case law that is directly relevant to juvenile risk assessment (Hoge & Andrews, 2010a). The treatment of justice-involved youths rests largely with state statutes regulating relevant legal processing. As noted previously, states show considerable variability in juvenile justice laws and practices. Most jurisdictions have established procedures to protect juvenile defendants' rights generally, and some have included specific efforts to address youths' risks and needs when determining delinquency dispositions. The guidance regarding risk–need assessment is limited aside from referral to the adult judicial or mental health system, and even here states show considerable latitude (Grisso, 2013; Hoge & Andrews, 2010a). Mental health professionals involved in juvenile risk assessment are strongly advised to familiarize themselves with the relevant statutes regulating juvenile justice (if any) in their jurisdiction of practice.

The professional regulation of juvenile risk assessment incorporates ethical guidance and evolving best practices elaborated in authoritative texts. The *Ethical Principles of Psychologists and Code of Conduct* (American Psychological Association, 2010) and *Specialty Guidelines for Forensic Psychology* (American Psychological Association, 2013) provide professional guidance regarding informed consent, assessment procedures, and responding to immediate threats of violence, all of which might be particularly relevant to juvenile risk assessment. Moreover, several of the sources referenced throughout this chapter provide authoritative guidance in assessing violence risk and risk management among juvenile defendants, particularly Grisso (2013) and Hoge and Andrews (2010a). Mental health professionals involved in juvenile risk assessment are strongly advised to familiarize themselves with the relevant jurisdictional statutes, as well as the ethical and professional literatures involving the clinical assessment of juveniles generally and the assessment of violence risk among juvenile populations specifically.

CURRENT STATE OF JUVENILE RISK ASSESSMENT

As we have reviewed, risk assessment specific to justice-involved youths is a relatively recent trend in forensic mental health assessment that has developed substantially over the past 15 years (Grisso, 2003, 2013; Hoge & Andrews, 2010a). Empirical research has greatly assisted in the identification of specific risk and protective factors and in the subsequent development of evidence-based, youth-specific risk assessment instruments. Forensic mental health professionals involved in the evaluation and management of justice-involved youths should be guided by such research when choosing risk assessment instruments and offering risk-related recommendations. Furthermore, it is imperative that both legal decision makers and policymakers in the juvenile justice system are appropriately informed and subsequently guided by the empirical evidence underlying juvenile risk assessment. Although relevant case law is limited, numerous states have developed, adopted, and implemented evidence-based risk assessment and risk management instruments. After reviewing the available research regarding juvenile risk assessment and recent standards and procedures affecting assessment practice, we explore possible areas of improvement with regard to current juvenile risk assessment and offer recommendations relevant to future research, policy, and practice.

Empirical Research Regarding Juvenile Risk Assessment

The general rehabilitative approach underlying the juvenile justice system, and specific legal decisions (e.g., disposition, transfer to adult court) and policy considerations (e.g., potential threat to the community), requires the integration of risk assessment into juvenile justice decisions. In fact, more than 85% of courts use formal risk assessment at some point during the juvenile court process (Schwalbe, 2008). Juvenile risk assessments provide an estimation of the likelihood that a youth will engage in delinquent behavior (i.e., risk prediction), and when risk assessments include dynamic risk factors and protective factors, they also facilitate intervention planning (i.e., risk management). Both risk prediction and management are relevant to juvenile risk assessment (Heilbrun, 2001). Research has identified empirically supported risk and protective factors, allowed for the development of standardized and empirically supported risk assessment instruments, and evaluated the utility of risk assessment instruments when used for assessment and management purposes.

Models of juvenile risk assessment. Juvenile risk assessment is based in theory on risk factors primarily related to adult risk. Traditionally, risk factors have been classified into two categories: static and dynamic. Static risk factors are historical and not subject to change (e.g., age at first arrest, history of abuse). Dynamic risk factors, by contrast, are those that can change over time or with successful intervention (e.g., impulsivity, substance use); when changed, dynamic factors may reduce the risk of future offending. Numerous models are grounded in a multidimensional psychosocial framework (e.g., Bronfenbrenner, 1979; Monahan et al., 2001), attempting to categorize risk and protective factors by domain (e.g., individual factors, family-related factors, school-related factors, contextual factors) and account for the complex interactions among these categories. Furthermore, general developmental research has established the importance of taking adolescent-specific developmental factors into account when evaluating and estimating future risk (Hoge & Andrews, 2010a).

The risk–need–responsivity (RNR) model is an empirically validated approach to risk assessment (Andrews & Bonta, 2010a, 2010b; see Chapter 9, this handbook). This model integrates a psychological and developmental understanding of antisocial behavior with the identification of youths' multidimensional criminogenic risks and needs, and it encourages the use of evidence-based practices and strength-based interventions. The RNR model evaluates both static and dynamic risk factors associated with increased likelihood of future offending. The dynamic factors, often referred to as *criminogenic needs*, are those associated with increased risk and are therefore the targets of intervention. *Responsivity* refers to the nature and context of the intervention and to specific youth characteristics that may affect the outcome of intervention efforts. Empirical evaluation research has supported the value of the RNR framework with youths (Andrews & Bonta, 2010b; Lipsey, 2009).

Empirically validated risk factors. The current practice of conducting juvenile risk assessment has been standardized and evidence based through the identification of risk and protective factors found to be associated with the likelihood of general, violent, or sexual recidivism. Evaluation of these factors enhances the assessment's predictive ability and provides data for targeted and effective treatment. The body of empirical research regarding juvenile risk factors is considerable (see Borum & Verhaagen, 2006, for a thorough review of risk factors), with some concomitant advances in empirical understanding of need and responsivity factors (Hoge & Andrews, 2010a; Thornberry & Krohn, 2003). However, no single factor or group of risk factors will predict future behavior with an extremely high degree of accuracy. What follows is a review of risk factors empirically related to future delinquent behaviors, and these risk factors form the foundation of evidence-based risk assessment.

Specific risk factors. Consistent with the notion that past behavior is the best indicator of future behavior, a history of aggressive and delinquent behavior is strongly associated with future recidivism. Specifically, the predictive validity of age of first contact with the law or age of first adjudication has been firmly established (Cottle, Lee, & Heilbrun, 2001; Hawkins et al., 1998; Hoge, 2013). The earlier a youth becomes involved in aggressive or antisocial behavior, the more likely it is that such aggression will continue beyond adolescence (Moffitt, 2003). There appear to be differences in future aggressive behavior between youths who engage in violence before age 9, or between ages 10 and 12, and youths whose first violent act is after age 13, with earlier age of onset associated with increased likelihood of aggression (Borum & Verhaagen, 2006). Other factors associated with future risk of general offending include number of previous arrests, commitments and out-of-home placements, recency and length of prior commitments, seriousness of prior offenses, and prior substance use (Cottle et al., 2001; DeMatteo & Marczyk, 2005; Hoge, 2013; Lipsey & Derzon, 1998).

Individual personality and behavioral characteristics, including antisocial attitudes and beliefs, lack of empathy, and aspects of psychosocial maturity (e.g., low self-control, sensation seeking, susceptibility to peer pressure), have also been associated with general and violent reoffending (Cottle et al., 2001; Hawkins et al., 1998; Mulvey et al., 2010). Recent research has also focused on the construct of psychopathy and its relationship to predicting future delinquent behavior, with mixed results (see DeMatteo, Edens, & Hart, 2010; see Chapter 10, this handbook). Given the high rates of traumatic exposure in juvenile offender populations (Abram et al., 2013), it is not surprising that previous physical or sexual abuse is associated with general and violent reoffending (Cottle et al., 2001; Ford, Elhai, Connor, & Freuh, 2010; Resnick, Ireland, & Borowsky, 2004; see Chapter 15, this handbook). The presence of mental health disorders, symptoms, or previous treatment (e.g., posttraumatic stress disorder, depression, attention-deficit/hyperactivity disorder) appear related—albeit indirectly—to antisocial behavior (U.S. Department of Health and Human Services, 2001). Recent research has suggested that the presence of internalizing problems is associated with an increased likelihood of late onset offending (after age 21; Zara & Farrington, 2013). This finding supports the inclusion of mental health symptoms as targets of youth intervention and a means of prevention.

Other factors that have consistently emerged as being strongly associated with future risk include poor school achievement, dysfunctional parenting, antisocial peers, and unstructured leisure time (Hoge, 2013), as well as poor academic performance or failure and frequent absences (Hawkins et al., 2000; Hoge, 2013; Lipsey & Derzon, 1998; Resnick et al., 2004). As with aggressive behaviors, poor school achievement is more indicative of antisocial behavior when indicators are evident early. Dysfunctional parenting relates to delinquency in various ways. Antisocial parents may model delinquent or criminal behaviors (Lipsey & Derzon, 1998), absent or limited parenting is associated with youth conduct problems (Cottle et al., 2001; Wasserman et al., 2003), and family conflict—particularly child abuse—is a significant predictor of delinquent behavior (Cottle et al., 2001).

Peer influence has a significant impact on all adolescents, and negative peer influence, through associations with delinquent youths or negative peer relationships, is strongly associated with youths' antisocial behavior (Hawkins et al., 1998; Hoge, 2013). Last, low socioeconomic status has been shown to predict future antisocial or violent behavior (Lipsey & Derzon, 1998; Loeber, Farrington, Stouthamer-Loeber, Moffitt, & Caspi, 1998). One hypothesis relating to low socioeconomic status is that youths raised in low-income households are not afforded structured prosocial leisure time—a commonly found protective factor—thereby resulting in unstructured leisure time and an increased likelihood of future offending.

Research has strongly supported the identification of risk and protective factors as necessary to juvenile risk assessment. However, a more recent focus has been on the relationship between the criminogenic needs and protective factors (particularly those that are treatment related) and youths' future risk. When a causal relationship exists (as opposed to a simple association), it follows that addressing risk factors and enhancing protective factors will lead to a reduction in risk. As such, the identification and evaluation of this relationship will help guide both treatment recommendations and, more important, the utility of such treatment in actually reducing future risk (Skeem & Monahan, 2011). To this end, more recent advances have been made in understanding the extent to which protective factors relate to future risk and recidivism (e.g., van der Put, van der Laan, Stams, Dekovic, & Hoeve, 2011).

Understanding risk factors within a developmental and gender-specific framework. Determining the presence of risk factors will not sufficiently estimate the likelihood of future risk. The impact of specific risk and protective factors varies greatly depending on the context in which they appear. It is therefore important to consider gender and developmental context when estimating likelihood of future risk. These considerations also relate to the predictive validity of risk assessment instruments because the presence of certain youth characteristics may moderate an instrument's predictive validity (as discussed below).

Most important, juvenile risk assessment must account for the nature of the population being assessed (i.e., juveniles), which raises two considerations. First, the most reliable factors associated with future risk are past behaviors. Youths have a limited pool of past behavior from which to draw (Mulvey, 2005). Estimations of future behavior must account for this limited data set and adjust accordingly (e.g., limiting the time frame of estimation; Zara & Farrington, 2013).

Second, the identified risk factors must be considered within a developmental context. Justice-involved youths are experiencing (or entering) the period of adolescence, which is a transformative period of growth (Steinberg, 2009). The biological, psychosocial, and cognitive changes evident throughout adolescence make it difficult to know whether a given risk factor is related to an individual's innate characteristics or simply developmentally driven (and often developmentally appropriate). For example, younger adolescents may exhibit more risk factors, whereas older adolescents may present with comparatively more protective factors (van der Put et al., 2011). Juvenile risk assessment must therefore include an evaluation of whether the identified risk factors are developmentally appropriate and whether such factors will change (or can be changed) over time. The prevalence and influence of specific risk factors on future offending may also vary with age, with both risk and protective factors showing stronger relationships with younger adolescents' recidivism (van der Put et al., 2011).

As previously noted, most delinquent behavior desists with age, leaving a small minority of juveniles who commit serious, continuing, and escalating violence (Hoge & Andrews, 2010a). In fact, only 5% to 10% of justice-involved youths go on to become chronic or life-course-persistent offenders (Moffitt, 2003). In other words, only a small subset of juvenile offenders will engage in aggressive or antisocial behavior into adulthood (Borum & Verhaagen, 2006). It is significantly more common for youths to exhibit an adolescence-limited pattern, in which antisocial behavior desists during the late adolescent and early adult years. This remains true even when youths exhibiting identified risk factors are considered at high risk for future offending; a high-risk designation during adolescence does not necessarily mean youths will be chronic or life-course-persistent offenders (Mulvey et al., 2010).

Given the rise in females' delinquent behavior (Pepler & Craig, 2005) and empirical support for gender differences in developmental and delinquent trajectories (Moretti, Odgers, & Jackson, 2004), a recent focus has been on gender-specific risk–needs assessment and intervention. Risk factors strongly associated with future aggressive and delinquent behavior appear to generalize across gender and ethnicity, although the dynamics of their functioning may vary across groups (Hoge, 2013). Female juvenile offenders have often experienced disproportionately high rates of previous victimization and abuse, particularly sexual abuse (Abram et al., 2013; Begle et al., 2011; Herrera & McCloskey, 2001), although the precise relationship between abusive history and delinquent behaviors remains unclear. Justice-involved female youths also exhibit differences in mental health symptoms, self-injurious behaviors, and parental and family dysfunction relative to their male counterparts (Cauffman, Lexcen, Goldweber, Shulman, & Grisso, 2007; Gammelgård, Weizmann-Henelius, Koivisto, Eronen, & Kaltiala-Heino, 2012; Gavazzi, Yarcheck, & Chesney-Lind, 2006; Odgers, Moretti, & Reppucci, 2005). Evaluating gender-specific risk through the use of standardized risk assessment instruments is discussed below.

Prevalence and predictive validity of empirically supported juvenile risk assessment instruments. Several standardized, empirically supported instruments available in varying formats have been created to assist with the evaluation of juvenile risk assessment. Dating back to Meehl's (1954) review, these tools have traditionally been divided into two categories: unstructured clinical judgment and actuarial measures. Whereas clinical judgment is more likely to be based on information specific to the individual youth, actuarial measures provide risk estimates based on relevant, known group data. This division has spawned controversy in the field, particularly with regard to whether group data can inform individual risk assessment (i.e., the utility of pure actuarial instruments). Nonetheless, it has generally been agreed that unstructured clinical judgment is a less accurate predictor than actuarial risk assessment (Schwalbe, 2008).

More recent discussion has focused on the utility of merging both clinical and actuarial methods, resulting in the development of structured professional judgment (SPJ) and the push for evidence-based practice procedures. Clinicians using SPJ are guided and informed by a structured interview or checklist based on empirical considerations of risk (Hoge, 2013). Newer thinking about risk assessment instruments has suggested that instead of separating instruments using a strict trichotomy (i.e., clinical judgment vs. actuarial vs. SPJ), they should be placed along a continuum (see Skeem & Monahan, 2011).

Prevalence. The use of risk assessment within the juvenile justice system more than doubled between 1990 and 2003 (see Schwalbe, 2007). Today, numerous juvenile risk assessment instruments are available that have varying levels of empirical support. Many of these instruments were mentioned earlier, and thorough reviews are available (see Grisso, 2013; Grisso, Vincent, & Seagrave, 2005; Hoge & Andrews, 2010a; Otto & Douglas, 2010; Vincent et al., 2009). However, little research has looked at the acceptability and frequency of usage of juvenile risk instruments when conducting forensic mental health assessments. Research has supported the use of specialized risk assessment instruments when evaluating risk for violence and sexual violence among adults (see Archer, Buffington-Vollum, Stredny, & Handel, 2006; Lally, 2003; Tolman & Mullendore, 2003), but similar prevalence data for the use of juvenile risk assessment instruments do not exist.

Given the absence of comparable juvenile data, to evaluate prevalence we turn to the available juvenile risk assessment research and the implementation of juvenile risk assessment instruments in state systems. Three of the most widely studied instruments used to evaluate future risk of general offending include the PCL:YV (Forth et al., 2003), SAVRY (Borum et al., 2006; Borum, Lodewijks, Bartel, & Forth, 2010), and YLS/CMI 2.0 (Hoge & Andrews, 2010b; see, e.g., Olver, Stockdale, & Wormith, 2009). Many states have created, adopted, or implemented structured juvenile risk tools to be used within the juvenile justice system when risk assessments are completed by system personnel (e.g., case managers, probation officers). Although some states have developed jurisdictional-specific tools (e.g., the Washington State Juvenile Court Assessment; Barnoski, 2004), other states have adopted previously validated risk assessment instruments (e.g., Connecticut and Louisiana: SAVRY). Funded by the MacArthur Foundation's Model for Change, Vincent, Guy, and Grisso (2012) evaluated the implementation and utility of evidence-based risk assessment instruments in probation. Findings supported state adoption of the SAVRY and YLS/CMI, showing changes in perceptions of risk, future risk estimates, and system utilization of services (Vincent, Guy, & Grisso, 2012; see also Vincent, Guy, Fusco, & Gershenson, 2012; Vincent, Paiva-Salisbury, Cook, Guy, & Perrault, 2012).

Predictive and incremental validity. The utility of juvenile risk assessment instruments is largely based on their predictive validity, or the accuracy of their risk estimate determination. Incremental validity, or whether an instrument increases the predictive validity of other tools, is another important and relatively recent consideration when comparing the use of different risk assessment instruments (Hunsley, 2003; Welsh, Schmidt, McKinnon, Chattha, & Meyers, 2008).

Risk assessment based on unstructured clinical judgment has consistently exhibited poor interrater reliability and limited predictive validity, particularly compared with other risk assessment instrument methods (Andrews, Bonta, & Wormith, 2006; Hanson & Morton-Bourgon, 2009), and both structured clinical judgment and pure actuarial assessment instruments provide more valid estimates of risk than unstructured clinical judgment (Hoge, 2013). Furthermore, recent empirical findings have suggested there may not be a difference in predictive or incremental validity between structured clinical judgment and pure actuarial assessment instruments (Olver et al., 2009; Schwalbe, 2008). Both structured clinical judgment and clinically adjusted actuarial measures appear to have comparable interrater reliability, which suggests that judgment-based instruments rooted in empirically supported risk factors provide a reliable framework for juvenile risk assessment (Vincent, Guy, & Grisso, 2012). However, the predictive validity of risk assessment instruments may be affected when they are used by untrained evaluators or those who do not follow standardized procedures (Vincent, Guy, Fusco, & Gersenson, 2012).

Several recent meta-analyses have evaluated the predictive and incremental validity of risk assessment instruments, with findings suggesting that empirically supported tools effectively predict risk. Olver et al. (2009) evaluated three commonly used instruments—the PCL:YV, SAVRY, and YLS/CMI—and found that all three measures were equally significant predictors of general, nonviolent, and violent reoffending. Although the YLS/CMI appears to have incremental validity over the PCL:YV (Viljoen, Elkovitch, Scalora, & Ullman, 2009), the PCL:YV may not add incremental validity over the YLS/CMI or SAVRY (Viljoen et al., 2009; Welsh et al., 2008). Unlike the SAVRY and YLS/CMI, the PCL:YV was not developed for assessing risk. Moreover, given the possible stigmatization of the psychopathy label, using the PCL:YV may have unintended negative consequences.

Jurisdictional-specific risk assessment instruments have also found some empirical support. The Washington State Juvenile Court Assessment (Barnoski, 2004) is a comprehensive SPJ measure that also includes a screening component, and research has supported its predictive validity (Barnoski & Markhussen, 2005). Other states have modeled risk assessment tools after the Washington State Juvenile Court Assessment, including the Positive Achievement Change Tool (Baglivio & Jackowski, 2013), implemented in Florida for case management, and the Youth Assessment and Screening Instrument (Orbis Partners, 2007), which is currently used in New York State to predict recidivism and guide case management. North Carolina has also developed a risk assessment screening instrument (the North Carolina Assessment of Risk), and research has yielded mixed support for its predictive validity across subgroups (Schwalbe, Fraser, Day, & Cooley, 2006).

Research has been inconclusive about whether there is currently a risk assessment instrument that accurately predicts juvenile sexual reoffending (Olver et al., 2009; Viljoen et al., 2009). Viljoen et al. (2008, 2009) examined risk assessment instruments with male youths who had previously committed sexual offenses, concluding that none of the instruments they evaluated significantly predicted sexual reoffending. This included instruments designed or previously found to predict general recidivism (i.e., PCL:YL, SAVRY, YLS/CMI) and those designed to predict sexual recidivism among adults (i.e., Estimate of Risk of Adolescent Sexual Offense Recidivism, J-SOAP–II, Juvenile Sexual Offense Recidivism Risk Assessment Tool—II, Static-99). Conversely, the YLS/CMI (total score and professional rating), PCL:YV, SAVRY, and J-SOAP–II have been shown to significantly predict nonsexual offending in this population (Viljoen et al., 2008, 2009). Consistent with the notion that juvenile risk assessment must evaluate adolescents' particular developmental considerations, the J-SOAP–II and SAVRY more accurately predicted violent reoffending among youths ages 15 and older than among younger adolescents (Viljoen et al., 2008). Given the relatively little research that has examined sexual reoffending among adolescents, additional research is clearly needed.

Research evaluating the predictive validity of risk assessment instruments when used with female adolescents is limited because of the relatively low base rates of female offending and the recent emergence of female-specific research among adolescents (Odgers et al., 2005). Nonetheless, research indicating differences in risk and protective factors among male and female justice-involved youths (e.g., previous sexual violence) has suggested that gender-sensitive risk assessments are necessary (Emeka & Sorensen, 2009). Two gender-specific SPJ risk assessments are designed for use with adolescents—the Early Assessment Risk List for Boys, Version 2 (Augimeri et al., 2001) and the Early Assessment Risk List for Girls, Version 1 Consultation Edition (Levene et al., 2001). Both have shown good interrater reliability and predictive validity, but their utility is limited because they were designed to be used with youths younger than age 12 (Augimeri, Enebrink, Walsh, & Jiang, 2010). A recent meta-analysis found that the use of non–gender-specific risk assessment instruments "leads to risk classifications with similar levels of predictive validity for male and female offenders" (Schwalbe, 2008, p. 1377).

Legal Decisions, Standards, and Procedures Affecting Juvenile Risk Assessment

As previously noted, there does not appear to be any statutory or case law specifically regulating how mental health professionals conduct juvenile risk assessments. Nonetheless, legislative and judicial guidance may exist for legal issues generally, adult risk assessment, and the growing systematic use of juvenile risk assessments within the justice system. Obviously, juvenile risk assessment used in legal contexts must comport with constitutional standards of equal protection and due process, meaning that considering race, ethnicity, or religion as factors in estimating likelihood of future risk would come under a strict scrutiny analysis because those are protected characteristics. Although equal protection and due process considerations are, technically, only relevant to government decision making (i.e., judicial and legislative determinations), both independent mental health practitioners and juvenile court system personnel should refrain from making unsupported decisions on the basis of these characteristics. Evidence-based risk assessment easily ensures that estimations comply with constitutional standards because neither race/ethnicity nor religion has independently been found to significantly predict future delinquent behavior.

There may be an emerging trend in states to require the use of specific risk assessment instruments when evaluating justice-involved adolescents and adults (Skeem & Monahan, 2011). This trend would be consistent with the U.S. Office of Juvenile

Justice and Delinquency Prevention's recommendation to use actuarial prediction instruments or risk assessment to create more equitable disposition decisions (Howell, 2003). As previously noted, some states have already developed jurisdiction-specific instruments, and other states have implemented policies requiring the internal systematic use of risk assessment instruments (Vincent, Guy, & Grisso, 2012), including standardized, evidence-based instruments (i.e., SAVRY and YLS/CMI). States should be sure to validate the use of home-grown risk assessment instruments with justice-involved youths in their states before requiring implementation, especially when adopting instruments developed in other states.

IMPLICATIONS FOR PRACTICE, POLICY, AND RESEARCH

As the preceding sections illustrate, conducting juvenile risk assessments requires consideration of multiple factors. Fortunately, the research base is growing, and practitioners who conduct juvenile risk assessments can look to the literature for emerging guidance. In this section, we discuss the process of conducting juvenile risk assessments, with a particular focus on current best practices.

Conducting Juvenile Risk Assessments

Forensic mental health professionals conducting juvenile risk assessments should be guided by general principles of forensic mental health assessment, empirical research underlying juvenile risk assessment and estimation, jurisdiction-specific legal regulations, and applicable ethical guidelines. Juvenile risk assessment evaluations should comport with the field's standards of practice, including being driven by the legal question, using multiple sources of data, and integrating standardized and empirically supported assessment instruments (Heilbrun, 2001; Heilbrun, Grisso, & Goldstein, 2009). Furthermore, such evaluations should be evidence based; evaluators should select appropriate risk assessment instruments and reach valid estimates of risk. Depending on the nature and context of the evaluation, making recommendations designed to reduce risk may also be indicated. As stated in a recent publication by Zara and Farrington (2013):

> From a public policy perspective if assessment of risk of future antisocial onset is not based on research findings it is unsound and fallacious; if it does not inform clinicians it is impractical; if it falls outside the range of application it is unhelpful; if it is not tailored to the individual's criminogenic needs it is unethical. (p. 246)

This statement effectively highlights the considerations that are most relevant to conducting juvenile risk assessments.

Selection of a juvenile risk assessment tool. The risk assessment instrument should be chosen on the basis of the nature of the evaluation (i.e., legal question) and the specific individual being assessed. This is particularly important given previous research suggesting limited differences in predictive validity between structured juvenile risk assessment instruments (i.e., SPJ vs. actuarial instruments; Olver et al., 2009). However, structured assessment tools—either SPJ or actuarial—consistently produce more accurate estimates of risk than unstructured clinical judgment. Best practice, therefore, suggests that mental health professionals use an SPJ or actuarial measure (Andrews & Bonta, 2010a), and the SAVRY and YLS/CMI appear to have the most support for accurately estimating future risk among adolescents.

Depending on the nature of the evaluation, either a brief screening tool or a comprehensive instrument may be appropriate. Brief tools are generally short and provide initial risk-relevant information by grouping youths into low-, moderate-, or high-risk categories. However, they are limited in that they do not consider a broad range of risk factors, may not consider need or responsivity factors, and tend to only accurately identify those who are high risk. Furthermore, evaluators should choose a measure with sound psychometric properties that specifically relate to the individual being assessed, including age, gender, race/ethnicity, and placement in the adjudication process. Last, because instruments most accurately predict the specific type of offending they were designed to assess (i.e., general, violent, or sexual offending), use of the measures should be limited to such predictions unless subsequent empirical evidence has suggested otherwise (Hanson & Morton-Bourgon, 2009; Olver et al., 2009).

Making risk estimations and recommendations. Estimates of future risk should not simply be rooted in whether specific factors are present; rather, risk estimates must also consider how empirical research has suggested such factors are (or are not) related to future risk. Furthermore, consideration must be given to relevant broad-based factors shown to affect justice-involved youths' likelihood of future risk (Mulvey, 2005). These factors include context-specific behaviors, the time frame under consideration, and developmental considerations specific to the age of the adolescent. To ensure this occurs, estimates of risk and related recommendations should not be driven solely by results of the risk assessment; instead, consistent with accepted principles of forensic mental health assessment, juvenile risk determinations should result from integration across multiple sources of data (see Heilbrun, 2001). This is particularly important given findings that demonstrate that risk assessment instruments evidence low to moderate predictive accuracy. Last, risk reduction recommendations should be based on the presence of dynamic risk factors, or criminogenic needs, and protective factors as they relate to the adolescent's developmental process. This is especially useful with youths identified as low risk because strengthening protective factors may, in turn, strengthen resiliency to delinquent behavior (see Pollard, Hawkins, & Arthur, 1999).

Limitations to Current Understanding of Juvenile Risk Assessment

As noted throughout this chapter, knowledge of juvenile risk assessments is somewhat limited. One limitation to juvenile risk assessment, or risk assessment in general, is that the accuracy of prediction naturally decreases over time (Zara & Farrington, 2013). It is important that risk estimations accurately reflect this by specifying the time frame within which the estimation applies. Longitudinal and prospective studies have evaluated the short- and long-term predictive validity of risk assessment instruments, and tools should be chosen on the basis of this research. Furthermore, there is a dearth of research examining the predictive validity of risk assessment instruments among female adolescents and specific ethnic groups (Olver et al., 2009). Finally, the incorporation of criminogenic needs and protective factors continues to improve the utility of juvenile risk assessments. However, research linking risk estimation with subsequent treatment and disposition decisions is needed. For example, although low-risk and moderate-risk groups may respond to prevention programs, high-risk groups may benefit most from intense treatment, consistent with RNR principles and related research (Andrews & Bonta, 2010a).

Future Directions in Research and Policy

Given that the field of juvenile risk assessment is relatively young, further research is needed to better understand the complexity of juvenile risk assessment. Specific risk factors appear firmly rooted in empirical data. However, developmental and contextual influences on empirically supported risk factors should be further examined; with this understanding, evaluation and modification of risk assessment instruments may be necessary. Current juvenile risk assessment instruments, particularly the SAVRY and YLS/CMI, significantly assist with estimating future risk, but continuing to incorporate research on developmental, contextual, and protective factors may further improve the incremental validity of existing tools. As discussed previously, two additional areas in need of further research are gender differences in risk estimation and estimating risk of future sexual offending.

Furthermore, the breadth of research on violent juvenile offenders is limited. This is particularly important in the area of transfer laws because one of the underlying justifications is selective incapacitation, or incarcerating the most serious offenders to reduce the opportunity of reoffending, thereby increasing public safety. Research should continue to examine the predictive validity of measures in terms of violent juvenile offenders, including the use of age and offense type as automatic transfer criteria to adult court. Such results, or lack thereof, should be incorporated into related policy and law. For example, on the basis of current knowledge, blended sentencing has been suggested as a more evidence-based alternative to automatic transfer laws (see Mulvey, 2005).

It is difficult to discuss juvenile risk assessment without also discussing prevention and risk reduction. Andrews and Bonta (2010a) supported the "never too early" approach to prevention. Simply measuring and identifying youths who may exhibit a high risk of future delinquent behaviors neglects the opportunity to inform intervention and sustain prevention. Communicating risk in a way that includes preventive- and intervention-focused explanations and related recommendations could lead to the implementation of timely and effective interventions.

The juvenile justice system should continue developing policy and procedure around the implementation of evidence-based risk assessment (Crime and Justice Institute at Community Resources for Justice, 2009). These practices should further juvenile justice objectives, such as increasing public safety by reducing future reoffending and improving adolescents' quality of life. Support for the standardized use of risk assessment instruments and procedures, particularly when based on the RNR framework, already exists—and best practices suggest that systems using standardized procedures are more effective than those using clinical procedures (Andrews & Bonta, 2010a; Andrews, Bonta, & Wormith, 2011). There is, however, a continued need to evaluate the effectiveness of juvenile risk assessment on both individual and systematic levels to ensure ongoing evidence-based policy change.

CONCLUSION

Assessments of juveniles' propensity for delinquent and violent behaviors are becoming a foundational part of the juvenile justice system. These risk assessments are now being conducted at various stages of the adjudication process, and they (ideally) function to improve the decisions of those who work with justice-involved youths. In this chapter, we summarized the development of juvenile risk assessment and current knowledge regarding juvenile risk assessment, with a focus on the many considerations that are relevant when conducting juvenile risk assessments. The recommendations highlighted in this chapter were derived from a synthesis of the available practice-relevant literature and were offered to assist evaluators who work with justice-involved youths.

References

Abram, K. M., Teplin, L. A., King, D. C., Longworth, S. L., Emanuel, K. M., Romero, E. G., . . . Olson, N. D. (2013). *PTSD, trauma, and comorbid psychiatric disorders in detained youth* (Juvenile Justice Bulletin). Washington, DC: U.S. Department of Justice, Office of Justice Programs, Office of Juvenile Justice and Delinquency Prevention.

American Bar Association. (2007). *Dialogue on youth and justice: Part 1. The history of juvenile justice.* Chicago, IL: Author. Retrieved from http://www.abanet.org/publiced/features/DYJfull.pdf

American Psychological Association. (2010). *Ethical principles of psychologists and code of conduct (2002, Amended June 1, 2010).* Retrieved from http://www.apa.org/ethics/code/index.aspx

American Psychological Association. (2013). Specialty guidelines for forensic psychology. *American Psychologist, 68,* 7–19. http://dx.doi.org/10.1037/a0029889

Andrews, D. A., & Bonta, J. (2010a). *The psychology of criminal conduct* (5th ed.). Cincinnati, OH: Anderson.

Andrews, D. A., & Bonta, J. (2010b). Rehabilitating criminal justice policy and practice. *Psychology, Public Policy, and Law, 16,* 39–55. http://dx.doi.org/10.1037/a0018362

Andrews, D. A., Bonta, J., & Wormith, S. J. (2004). *The Level of Service/Case Management Inventory (LS/CMI): User's manual.* Toronto, Ontario, Canada: Multi-Health Systems.

Andrews, D. A., Bonta, J., & Wormith, S. J. (2006). The recent past and near future of risk and/or need assessment. *Crime and Delinquency, 52,* 7–27. http://dx.doi.org/10.1177/0011128705281756

Andrews, D. A., Bonta, J., & Wormith, S. J. (2011). The risk/need/responsivity (RNR) model: Does adding the good lives model contribute to effective crime prevention? *Criminal Justice and Behavior, 38,* 735–755. http://dx.doi.org/10.1177/0093854811406356

Archer, R. P., Buffington-Vollum, J. K., Stredny, R. V., & Handel, R. W. (2006). A survey of psychological test use patterns among forensic psychologists. *Journal of Personality Assessment, 87,* 84–94. http://dx.doi.org/10.1207/s15327752jpa8701_07

Augimeri, L. K., Enebrink, P., Walsh, M., & Jiang, D. (2010). Gender-specific childhood risk assessment tools. In R. K. Otto & K. S. Douglas (Eds.), *Handbook of violence risk assessment* (pp. 43–62). New York, NY: Routledge.

Augimeri, L. K., Koegel, C. J., Webster, C. D., & Levene, K. S. (2001). *Early Assessment Risk List for Boys: EARL-20B,*

Version 2. Toronto, Ontario, Canada: Earlscourt Child and Family Centre.

Baglivio, M. T., & Jackowski, K. (2013). Examining the validity of a juvenile offending risk assessment instrument across gender and race/ethnicity. *Youth Violence and Juvenile Justice, 11*, 26–43. http://dx.doi.org/10.1177/1541204012440107

Barnoski, R. (2004). *Assessing risk for re-offense: Validating the Washington State Juvenile Court Assessment*. Retrieved from http://www.wsipp.wa.gov/ReportFile/869

Barnoski, R., & Markhussen, S. (2005). Washington State Juvenile Court Assessment. In T. Grisso, T. Vincent, & D. Seagrave (Eds.), *Mental health screening and assessment in juvenile justice* (pp. 271–282). New York, NY: Guilford Press.

Begle, A. M., Hanson, R. F., Danielson, C. K., McCart, M. R., Ruggiero, K. J., Amstadter, A. B., . . . Kilpatrick, D. G. (2011). Longitudinal pathways of victimization, substance use, and delinquency: Findings from the National Survey of Adolescents. *Addictive Behaviors, 36*, 682–689. http://dx.doi.org/10.1016/j.addbeh.2010.12.026

Beresford, L. (2000). Is lowering the age at which juveniles can be transferred to adult criminal court the answer to juvenile crime? A state-by-state assessment. *San Diego Law Review, 37*, 783–851.

Borum, R., Bartel, P., & Forth, A. (2006). *Manual for the Structured Assessment for Violence Risk in Youth (SAVRY)*. Odessa, FL: Psychological Assessment Resources.

Borum, R., Lodewijks, H., Bartel, P. A., & Forth, A. E. (2010). Structured Assessment of Violence Risk in Youth (SAVRY). In R. K. Otto & K. S. Douglas (Eds.), *Handbook of violence risk assessment* (pp. 63–79). New York, NY: Routledge.

Borum, R., & Verhaagen, D. (2006). *Assessing and managing violence risk in juveniles*. New York, NY: Guilford Press.

Bronfenbrenner, U. (1979). *The ecology of human development: Experiments by nature and design*. Cambridge, MA: Harvard University Press.

Butcher, J. N., Williams, C. L., Graham, J. R., Archer, R. P., Tellegen, A., Ben-Porath, Y. S., & Kaemmer, B. (1992). *Minnesota Multiphasic Personality Inventory—Adolescent Version (MMPI–A): Manual for administration, scoring and interpretation*. Minneapolis: University of Minnesota Press.

Cauffman, E., Lexcen, F. J., Goldweber, A., Shulman, E. P., & Grisso, T. (2007). Gender differences in mental health symptoms among delinquent and community youth. *Youth Violence and Juvenile Justice, 5*, 287–307. http://dx.doi.org/10.1177/1541204007301292

Chapman, J. F. (2012). The juvenile forensic court clinic in theory and practice. In E. L. Grigorenko (Ed.), *Handbook of juvenile forensic psychology and psychiatry* (pp. 201–214). http://dx.doi.org/10.1007/978-1-4614-0905-2_13

Coalition for Juvenile Justice. (1998). *A celebration or a wake? The juvenile court after 100 years*. Washington, DC: Author.

Compas, B. E., Hinden, B. R., & Gerhardt, C. A. (1995). Adolescent development: Pathways and processes of risk and resilience. *Annual Review of Psychology, 46*, 265–293. http://dx.doi.org/10.1146/annurev.ps.46.020195.001405

Conroy, M. A. (2012). Assessing juveniles for risk of violence. In E. L. Grigorenko (Ed.), *Handbook of juvenile forensic psychology and psychiatry* (pp. 227–239). http://dx.doi.org/10.1007/978-1-4614-0905-2_15

Conroy, M. A., & Murrie, D. C. (2007). *Forensic assessment of violence risk: A guide for risk assessment and risk management*. http://dx.doi.org/10.1002/9781118269671

Cottle, C., Lee, J., & Heilbrun, K. (2001). The prediction of criminal recidivism in juveniles. *Criminal Justice and Behavior, 28*, 367–394. http://dx.doi.org/10.1177/0093854801028003005

Crime and Justice Institute at Community Resources for Justice. (2009). *Implementing evidence-based policy and practice in community corrections* (2nd ed.). Washington, DC: National Institute of Corrections.

DeMatteo, D., Edens, J. F., & Hart, A. (2010). The use of measures of psychopathy in violence risk assessment. In R. K. Otto & K. S. Douglas (Eds.), *Handbook of violence risk assessment* (pp. 19–40). New York, NY: Routledge.

DeMatteo, D., & Marczyk, G. (2005). Risk factors, protective factors, and the prevention of antisocial behavior among juveniles. In K. Heilbrun, N. E. Sevin Goldstein, & R. E. Redding (Eds.), *Juvenile delinquency: Prevention, assessment, and intervention* (pp. 19–44). New York, NY: Oxford University Press.

Douglas, K. S., Hart, S. D., Webster, C. D., & Belfrage, H. (2013). *HCR-20V3: Assessing risk of violence—User guide*. Burnaby, British Columbia, Canada: Mental Health, Law, and Policy Institute, Simon Fraser University.

Douglas, K. S., Ogloff, J. R. P., & Hart, S. D. (2003). Evaluation of a model of violence risk assessment among forensic psychiatric patients. *Psychiatric Services, 54*, 1372–1379. http://dx.doi.org/10.1176/appi.ps.54.10.1372

Douglas, K. S., & Skeem, J. L. (2005). Violence risk assessment: Getting specific about being dynamic. *Psychology, Public Policy, and Law, 11*, 347–383. http://dx.doi.org/10.1037/1076-8971.11.3.347

Emeka, T. Q., & Sorensen, J. R. (2009). Female juvenile risk: Is there a need for gendered assessment instruments? *Youth Violence and Juvenile Justice*, *7*, 313–330. http://dx.doi.org/10.1177/1541204009334083

Epperson, D. L., Ralston, C. A., Fowers, D., DeWitt, J., & Gore, K. S. (2006). Actuarial risk assessment with juveniles who sexually offend: Development of the Juvenile Sexual Offense Recidivism Risk Assessment Tool-II (JSORRAT-II). In D. S. Prescott (Ed.), *Risk assessment of youth who have sexually abused: Theory, controversy, and emerging strategies* (pp. 118–169). Oklahoma City, OK: Woods & Barnes.

Ford, J. D., Elhai, J. D., Connor, D. F., & Frueh, B. C. (2010). Poly-victimization and risk of posttraumatic, depressive, and substance use disorders and involvement in delinquency in a national sample of adolescents. *Journal of Adolescent Health*, *46*, 545–552. http://dx.doi.org/10.1016/j.jadohealth.2009.11.212

Forth, A., Kosson, D., & Hare, R. (2003). *The Hare Psychopathy Checklist: Youth Version, Technical manual*. North Tonawanda, NY: Multi-Health Systems.

Fox, S. (1970). Juvenile justice reform: An historical perspective. *Stanford Law Review*, *22*, 1187–1239. http://dx.doi.org/10.2307/1227960

Gammelgård, M., Weizmann-Henelius, G., Koivisto, A., Eronen, M., & Kaltiala-Heino, R. (2012). Gender differences in violence risk profiles. *Journal of Forensic Psychiatry and Psychology*, *23*, 76–94. http://dx.doi.org/10.1080/14789949.2011.639898

Gavazzi, S. M., Yarcheck, C. M., & Chesney-Lind, M. (2006). Global risk indicators and the role of gender in a juvenile detention sample. *Criminal Justice and Behavior*, *33*, 597–612. http://dx.doi.org/10.1177/0093854806288184

Gottfredson, M., & Hirschi, T. (1990). *A general theory of crime*. Stanford, CA: Stanford University Press.

Graham v. Florida, 130 S. Ct. 2011 (2010).

Grisso, T. (2003). *Evaluating competencies: Forensic assessment and instruments* (2nd ed.). New York, NY: Kluwer Academic/Plenum.

Grisso, T. (2013). *Forensic evaluations of juveniles* (2nd ed.). Sarasota, FL: Professional Resource Press.

Grisso, T., Vincent, G. M., & Seagrave, D. (Eds.). (2005). *Mental health screening and assessment for juvenile justice*. New York, NY: Guilford Press.

Guerra, N. G., Williams, K. R., Tolan, P. H., & Modecki, K. L. (2008). Theoretical and research advances in understanding the causes of juvenile offending. In R. D. Hoge, N. G. Guerra, & P. Boxer (Eds.), *Treating the juvenile offender* (pp. 33–53). New York, NY: Guilford Press.

Hanson, R. K., & Morton-Bourgon, K. E. (2009). The accuracy of recidivism risk assessments for sexual offenders: A meta-analysis of 118 prediction studies. *Psychological Assessment*, *21*, 1–21. http://dx.doi.org/10.1037/a0014421

Hawkins, J. D., Herrenkohl, T. I., Farrington, D. P., Brewer, D., Catalano, R. F., & Harachi, T. W. (1998). A review of predictors of youth violence. In R. Loeber & D. P. Farrington (Eds.), *Serious and violent juvenile offenders: Risk factors and successful interventions* (pp. 106–146). Thousand Oaks, CA: Sage.

Hawkins, J. D., Herrenkohl, T. I., Farrington, D. P., Brewer, D., Catalano, R. F., Harachi, T. W., & Cothern, L. (2000). *Predictors of youth violence* (Juvenile Justice Bulletin). Washington, DC: U.S. Department of Justice, Office of Justice Programs, Office of Juvenile Justice and Delinquency Prevention.

Healy, W. (1915). *The individual delinquent: A textbook of diagnosis and prognosis for all concerned in understanding offenders*. Boston, MA: Little, Brown.

Heilbrun, K. (1997). Prediction versus management models relevant to risk assessment: The importance of legal decision-making context. *Law and Human Behavior*, *21*, 347–359. http://dx.doi.org/10.1023/A:1024851017947

Heilbrun, K. (2001). *Principles of forensic mental health assessment*. New York, NY: Kluwer Academic/Plenum.

Heilbrun, K. (2003). From risk assessment to risk management. In D. Carson & R. Bull (Eds.), *Handbook of psychology in legal contexts* (2nd ed., pp. 127–142). Chichester, England: Wiley.

Heilbrun, K. (2009). *Evaluation for risk of violence in adults*. New York, NY: Oxford University Press. http://dx.doi.org/10.1093/med/9780195369816.001.0001

Heilbrun, K., Grisso, T., & Goldstein, A. M. (2009). *Foundations of forensic mental health assessment*. New York, NY: Oxford University Press.

Heilbrun, K., Yasuhara, K., & Shah, S. (2010). Violence risk assessment tools: Overview and critical analysis. In R. K. Otto & K. S. Douglas (Eds.), *Handbook of violence risk assessment* (pp. 1–17). New York, NY: Routledge/Taylor & Francis.

Henggeler, S. W., Cunningham, P. B., Pickrel, S. G., Schoenwald, S. K., & Brondino, M. J. (1996). Multisystemic therapy: An effective violence prevention approach for serious juvenile offenders. *Journal of Adolescence*, *19*, 47–61. http://dx.doi.org/10.1006/jado.1996.0005

Herrera, V. M., & McCloskey, L. A. (2001). Gender differences in the risk for delinquency among youth exposed to family violence. *Child Abuse and Neglect*, *25*, 1037–1051. http://dx.doi.org/10.1016/S0145-2134(01)00255-1

Hoge, R. D. (2013). Evaluation of juveniles' risks and needs. In R. Roesch & P. A. Zapf (Eds.), *Forensic assessment in criminal and civil law* (pp. 237–248). New York, NY: Oxford University Press.

Hoge, R. D., & Andrews, D. A. (1996). *Assessing the youthful offender: Issues and techniques*. New York, NY: Plenum. http://dx.doi.org/10.1007/978-1-4757-9296-6

Hoge, R. D., & Andrews, D. A. (2010a). *Evaluation for risk of violence in juveniles*. New York, NY: Oxford University Press. http://dx.doi.org/10.1093/med/9780195370416.001.0001

Hoge, R. D., & Andrews, D. A. (2010b). *Youth Level of Service/Case Management Inventory 2.0 (YLS/CMI) users' manual*. North Tonawanda, NY: Multi-Health Systems.

Howell, J. C. (2003). *Preventing and reducing juvenile delinquency: A comprehensive framework*. Thousand Oaks, CA: Sage.

Hunsley, J. (2003). Introduction to the special section on incremental validity and utility in clinical assessment. *Psychological Assessment*, *15*, 443–445. http://dx.doi.org/10.1037/1040-3590.15.4.443

In re Gault, 387 U.S. 1 (1967).

In re Winship, 397 U.S. 358 (1970).

Jessor, R., Van Den Bos, J., Vanderryn, J., Costa, F., & Turbin, M. (1995). Protective factors in adolescent problem behaviour: Moderator effects and developmental change. *Developmental Psychology*, *31*, 923–933. http://dx.doi.org/10.1037/0012-1649.31.6.923

Kent v. United States, 383 U.S. 541 (1966).

Lally, S. J. (2003). What tests are acceptable for use in forensic evaluations? A survey of experts. *Professional Psychology: Research and Practice*, *34*, 491–498. http://dx.doi.org/10.1037/0735-7028.34.5.491

Levene, K. S., Augimeri, L. K., Pepler, D. J., Walsh, M., Webster, C. D., & Koegel, C. J. (2001). *Early Assessment Risk List for Girls: EARL-21G, Version 1 Consultation edition*. Toronto, Ontario, Canada: Earlscourt Child and Family Centre.

Lipsey, M. W. (1995). What do we learn from 400 research studies on the effectiveness of treatment with juvenile delinquents? In J. McGuire (Ed.), *What works? Reducing reoffending* (pp. 313–345). New York, NY: Wiley.

Lipsey, M. W. (2009). The primary factors that characterize effective interventions with juvenile offenders: A meta-analytic overview. *Victims and Offenders*, *4*, 124–147. http://dx.doi.org/10.1080/15564880802612573

Lipsey, M. W., & Derzon, J. H. (1998). Predictors of violent or serious delinquency in adolescence and early adulthood. In R. Loeber & D. P. Farrington (Eds.), *Serious and violent juvenile offenders: Risk factors and successful interventions* (pp. 86–105). Thousand Oaks, CA: Sage.

Lipsey, M. W., & Wilson, D. B. (1998). Effective interventions with serious juvenile offenders: A synthesis of research. In R. Loeber & D. Farrington (Eds.), *Serious and violent juvenile offenders: Risk factors and successful interventions* (pp. 313–345). Thousand Oaks, CA: Sage.

Loeber, R., Farrington, D. P., Stouthamer-Loeber, M., Moffitt, T. E., & Caspi, A. (1998). The development of male offending: Key findings from the first decade of the Pittsburgh Youth Study. *Studies on Crime and Crime Prevention*, *7*, 141–171.

Mack, J. W. (1909). The juvenile court. *Harvard Law Review*, *23*, 104–122. http://dx.doi.org/10.2307/1325042

Martinson, R. (1974). What works? Questions and answers about prison reform. *Public Interest*, *35*, 22–54.

McKeiver v. Pennsylvania, 403 U.S. 528 (1971).

Meehl, P. E. (1954). *Clinical versus statistical prediction: A theoretical analysis and a review of the evidence*. Minneapolis: University of Minnesota Press. http://dx.doi.org/10.1037/11281-000

Melton, G. B., Petrila, J., Poythress, N. G., & Slobogin, C. (2007). *Psychological evaluations for the courts: A handbook for mental health professionals and lawyers* (3rd ed.). New York, NY: Guilford Press.

Miller v. Alabama, 132 S. Ct. 2455 (2012).

Moffitt, T. E. (1993). Adolescence-limited and life-course-persistent antisocial behavior: A developmental taxonomy. *Psychological Review*, *100*, 674–701. http://dx.doi.org/10.1037/0033-295X.100.4.674

Moffitt, T. E. (2003). Life-course persistent and adolescent-limited antisocial behavior: A 10-year research review and a research agenda. In B. B. Lahey, T. E. Moffitt, & A. Caspi (Eds.), *Causes of conduct disorder and juvenile delinquency* (pp. 49–75). New York, NY: Guilford Press.

Monahan, J. (1981). *The clinical prediction of violence behavior*. Rockville, MD: U.S. Department of Health and Human Services.

Monahan, J. (1984). The prediction of violent behavior: Toward a second generation of theory and policy. *American Journal of Psychiatry*, *141*, 10–15.

Monahan, J., Steadman, H. J., Silver, E., Appelbaum, P. S., Robbins, P. C., Mulvey, E. P., . . . Banks, S. (2001). *Rethinking risk assessment: The MacArthur Study of Mental Disorders and Violence*. New York, NY: Oxford University Press.

Moretti, M., Odgers, C., & Jackson, M. (Eds.). (2004). *Girls and aggression: Contributing factors and intervention principles*. http://dx.doi.org/10.1007/978-1-4419-8985-7

Mulvey, E. (2005). Risk assessment in juvenile justice policy and practice. In K. Heilbrun, N. E. S. Goldstein, & R. E. Redding (Eds.), *Juvenile delinquency: Prevention, assessment, and intervention* (pp. 209–231). New York, NY: Oxford University Press.

Mulvey, E. P., Steinberg, L., Piquero, A. R., Besana, M., Fagan, J., Schubert, C., & Cauffman, E. (2010). Trajectories of desistance and continuity in antisocial behavior following court adjudication among serious adolescent offenders. *Development and Psychopathology*, *22*, 453–475. http://dx.doi.org/10.1017/S0954579410000179

Odgers, C. L., Moretti, M. M., & Reppucci, N. D. (2005). Examining the science and practice of violence risk assessment with female adolescents. *Law and Human Behavior*, *29*, 7–27. http://dx.doi.org/10.1007/s10979-005-1397-z

Olver, M. E., Stockdale, K. C., & Wormith, J. S. (2009). Risk assessment with young offenders: A meta-analysis of three assessment measures. *Criminal Justice and Behavior*, *36*, 329–353. http://dx.doi.org/10.1177/0093854809331457

Orbis Partners. (2007). *Long-term validation of the Youth Assessment and Screening Instrument (YASI) in New York state juvenile probation*. Ottawa, Ontario, Canada: Author.

Otto, R. K., & Douglas, K. S. (Eds.). (2010). *Handbook of violence risk assessment*. New York, NY: Routledge/Taylor & Francis.

Pepler, D. J., & Craig, W. (2005). Aggressive girls on troubled trajectories: A developmental perspective. In D. J. Pepler, K. C. Madsen, C. Webster, & K. S. Levene (Eds.), *The development and treatment of girlhood aggression* (pp. 3–28). Mahwah, NJ: Erlbaum.

Pollard, J. A., Hawkins, J. D., & Arthur, M. W. (1999). Risk and protection: Are both necessary to understand diverse behavioral outcomes in adolescence? *Social Work Research*, *23*, 145–158. http://dx.doi.org/10.1093/swr/23.3.145

Prentky, R., & Righthand, S. (2003). *Juvenile Sex Offender Protocol—II (J-SOAP–II) manual*. Washington, DC: U.S. Department of Justice, Office of Justice Programs, Office of Juvenile Justice and Delinquency Prevention.

President's Commission on Law Enforcement and Administration of Justice. (1967). *The challenge of crime in a free society*. Washington, DC: U.S. Government Printing Office.

Puzzanchara, C., & Hockenberry, S. (2013). *Juvenile court statistics 2010*. Pittsburgh, PA: National Center for Juvenile Justice.

Quay, H. C., & Peterson, D. R. (1987). *Manual for the Revised Behavior Problem Checklist*. Miami, FL: University of Miami.

Redding, R. E., Sevin Goldstein, N. E., & Heilbrun, K. (2005). Juvenile delinquency: Past and present. In K. Heilbrun, N. E. Sevin Goldstein, & R. E. Redding (Eds.), *Juvenile delinquency: Prevention, assessment, and intervention* (pp. 3–18). New York, NY: Oxford University Press.

Resnick, M. D., Ireland, M., & Borowsky, I. (2004). Youth violence perpetration: What protects? What predicts? Findings from the National Longitudinal Study of Adolescent Health. *Journal of Adolescent Health*, *35*, 424.e1–424.e10. http://dx.doi.org/10.1016/j.jadohealth.2004.01.011

Rogers, R. (2000). The uncritical acceptance of risk assessment in forensic practice. *Law and Human Behavior*, *24*, 595–605. http://dx.doi.org/10.1023/A:1005575113507

Roper v. Simmons, 543 U.S. 551 (2005).

Schwalbe, C. S. (2007). Risk assessment for juvenile justice: A meta-analysis. *Law and Human Behavior*, *31*, 449–462. http://dx.doi.org/10.1007/s10979-006-9071-7

Schwalbe, C. S. (2008). Strengthening the integration of actuarial risk assessment with clinical judgment in an evidence based practice framework. *Children and Youth Services Review*, *30*, 1458–1464. http://dx.doi.org/10.1016/j.childyouth.2007.11.021

Schwalbe, C. S., Fraser, M. W., Day, S. H., & Cooley, V. (2006). Classifying offenders according to risk of recidivism: Predictive validity, race/ethnicity, and gender. *Criminal Justice and Behavior*, *33*, 305–324. http://dx.doi.org/10.1177/0093854806286451

Scott, E. S. (2000). The legal construction of adolescence. *Hofstra Law Review*, *29*, 547–598.

Singh, J. P. (2012). The history, development, and testing of forensic risk assessment tools. In E. L. Grigorenko (Ed.), *Handbook of juvenile forensic psychology and psychiatry* (pp. 215–225). http://dx.doi.org/10.1007/978-1-4614-0905-2_14

Skeem, J. L., & Monahan, J. (2011). Current directions in violence risk assessment. *Current Directions in Psychological Science*, *20*, 38–42. http://dx.doi.org/10.1177/0963721410397271

Steinberg, L. (2009). Adolescent development and juvenile justice. *Annual Review of Clinical Psychology*, *5*, 459–485. http://dx.doi.org/10.1146/annurev.clinpsy.032408.153603

Tate, D. C., & Redding, R. E. (2005). Mental health and rehabilitative services in juvenile justice: System reforms and innovative approaches. In K. Heilbrun, N. E. Sevin Goldstein, & R. E. Redding (Eds.), *Juvenile delinquency: Prevention, assessment, and intervention* (pp. 134–160). New York, NY: Oxford University Press.

Thornberry, T. P., & Krohn, M. D. (2003). *Taking stock of delinquency: An overview of findings from contemporary longitudinal studies*. New York, NY: Kluwer/Plenum Academic.

Tolman, A. O., & Mullendore, K. B. (2003). Risk evaluations for the courts: Is service quality a function of specialization? *Professional Psychology: Research and Practice*, *34*, 225–232.

U.S. Department of Health and Human Services. (2001). *Youth violence: A report of the surgeon general*. Retrieved from http://www.surgeongeneral.gov/library/youthviolence/toc.html

U.S. Department of Labor, Children's Bureau. (1922). *Proceedings of the conference on juvenile-court standards* (Bureau Publication No. 97). Washington, DC: Author.

van der Put, C. E., van der Laan, P., Stams, G., Dekovic, M., & Hoeve, M. (2011). Promotive factors during adolescence: Are there changes in impact and prevalence during adolescence and how does this relate to risk factors? *International Journal of Child, Youth and Family Studies*, 2, 119–141.

Viljoen, J. L., Elkovitch, N., Scalora, M. J., & Ullman, D. (2009). Assessment of reoffense risk adolescents who have committed sexual offenses. *Criminal Justice and Behavior*, *36*, 981–1000.

Viljoen, J. L., Scalora, M., Cuadra, L., Bader, S., Chavez, V., Ullman, D., & Lawrence, L. (2008). Assessing risk for violence in adolescents who have sexually offended: A comparison of the J-SOAP-II, J-SORRAT-II, and SAVRY. *Criminal Justice and Behavior*, *35*, 5–23. http://dx.doi.org/10.1177/0093854807307521

Vincent, G. M., Guy, L. S., Fusco, S. L., & Gershenson, B. G. (2012). Field reliability of the SAVRY with juvenile probation officers: Implications for training. *Law and Human Behavior*, *36*, 225–236. http://dx.doi.org/10.1037/h0093974

Vincent, G. M., Guy, L. S., & Grisso, T. (2012). *Risk assessment in juvenile justice: A guidebook for implementation*. Retrieved from http://njjn.org/uploads/digital-library/Risk_Assessment_in_Juvenile_Justice_A_Guidebook_for_Implementation.pdf

Vincent, G. M., Paiva-Salisbury, M. L., Cook, N. E., Guy, L. S., & Perrault, R. T. (2012). Impact of risk/needs assessment on juvenile probation officers' decision making: Importance of implementation. *Psychology, Public Policy, and Law*, *18*, 549–576. http://dx.doi.org/10.1037/a0027186

Vincent, G. M., Terry, A., & Maney, S. (2009). Risk/needs tools for antisocial behavior and violence among youthful populations. In J. Andrade (Ed.), *Handbook of violence risk assessment and treatment: New approaches for forensic mental health practitioners* (pp. 377–423). New York, NY: Springer.

Warr, M. (2007). Violence and culture in the United States. In D. J. Flannery, A. T. Vazsonyi, & I. D. Waldman (Eds.), *The Cambridge handbook of violent behavior and aggression* (pp. 571–582). http://dx.doi.org/10.1017/CBO9780511816840.030

Wasserman, G. A., Keenan, K., Tremblay, R. E., Cole, J. D., Herrenkohl, T. I., Loeber, R., & Petechuk, D. (2003). *Risk and protective factors of child delinquency* (Child Delinquency Bulletin Series). Washington, DC: U.S. Department of Justice, Office of Justice Programs, Office of Juvenile Justice and Delinquency Prevention.

Welsh, J. L., Schmidt, F., McKinnon, L., Chattha, H. K., & Meyers, J. R. (2008). A comparative study of adolescent risk assessment instruments: Predictive and incremental validity. *Assessment*, *15*, 104–115. http://dx.doi.org/10.1177/1073191107307966

Williams, K. R., Tuthill, L., & Lio, S. (2008). A portrait of juvenile offending in the United States. In R. D. Hoge, N. G. Guerra, & P. Boxer (Eds.), *Treating the juvenile offender* (pp. 15–32). New York, NY: Guilford Press.

Wilson, J. J., & Howell, J. C. (1995). *Comprehensive strategy for serious, violent, and chronic juvenile offenders*. Washington, DC: U.S. Department of Justice, Office of Justice Programs, Office of Juvenile Justice and Delinquency Prevention.

Worling, J. R., & Curwen, T. (2001). The Estimate of Risk of Adolescent Sexual Offense Recidivism (ERASOR, Version 2). In M. C. Calder (Ed.), *Juveniles and children who sexually abuse: Frameworks for assessment* (pp. 372–397). Lyme Regis, England: Russell House.

Worling, J. R., & Langstrom, N. (2006). Risk of sexual recidivism in adolescents who offend sexually: Correlates and assessment. In H. E. Barbaree & W. L. Marshall (Eds.), *The juvenile sex offender* (2nd ed., pp. 219–247). New York, NY: Guilford Press.

Zara, G., & Farrington, D. P. (2013). Assessment of risk for juvenile compares with adult criminal onset: Implications for policy, prevention, and intervention. *Psychology, Public Policy, and Law*, *19*, 235–249. http://dx.doi.org/10.1037/a0029050

CHAPTER 18

DISTINGUISHING AND ASSESSING TREATMENT NEEDS AND AMENABILITY TO REHABILITATION

Robert T. Kinscherff

In this chapter, I review approaches to the forensic mental health assessment of juvenile defendants' treatment needs and amenability to rehabilitation. Prognostications about a youth's amenability to rehabilitation can no longer shape a decision about execution because the death penalty for capital offenses committed while a juvenile was declared unconstitutional in 2005. Recent U.S. Supreme Court cases have, however, focused renewed attention on the developmental characteristics of juveniles and their potential for rehabilitation in both homicide and nonhomicide cases.

The highest stakes cases are compelling and complex; but even seemingly minor first-offense cases can be deceptive, and seemingly routine decisions made in these cases may have major consequences later. For example, a minor or first offender who fails out of an improper or inadequate intervention may later find this failure cited as a reason for being treated more harshly or tried as an adult for subsequent offenses. In other cases, a court may have to determine whether the prospects of rehabilitation are sufficient with community probation or whether the balance of public safety needs and rehabilitative prospects warrants a term of juvenile incarceration or secure treatment after commitment to a juvenile justice authority. In still other cases, a judicial determination of amenability to rehabilitation may shape whether a youth is prosecuted in juvenile court or criminal court or whether a convicted youth remains in the community on probation (juvenile or criminal) or is remanded to a juvenile justice or criminal justice authority for incarceration.

Mental health professionals are often called on to address the amenability of youths to treatment or rehabilitation. Their contributions to these determinations by courts and juvenile justice authorities can have life-changing consequences for young people, even in seemingly routine cases. This chapter provides relevant information for mental health professionals, clinical administrators, policymakers, criminal justice professionals, and legal professionals who encounter these issues professionally, as well as those who use this information as part of their education or training.

Professionals conducting these assessments should consider whether they have the training and experience required to provide these assessments because a general familiarity with adolescents and clinical work with adolescents are ordinarily insufficient (see Chapter 31, this handbook). To conduct competent evaluations of treatment needs and amenability to rehabilitation, professionals should be well informed about research in domains relevant to these youths, including different developmental trajectories found among youths engaging in antisocial behavior, socioeconomic and clinical characteristics, clinical and specialized forensic assessment tools, risk and treatment readiness assessments, positive youth development, trauma-informed approaches, evidence-based interventions for behavioral health disorders, and evidence-based interventions specifically for youths with delinquent misconduct.

In addition, professionals must be familiar with local court practices because jurisdictions vary widely in the specific framework of law and

http://dx.doi.org/10.1037/14643-018
APA Handbook of Psychology and Juvenile Justice, K. Heilbrun (Editor-in-Chief)

procedure applied to cases in which amenability to rehabilitation is an issue. Familiarity with practices and available resources in the community and juvenile justice system (and, on occasion, in the adult correctional system) is also required. For example, in jurisdictions in which the court considers whether the juvenile defendant is amenable to rehabilitation in the juvenile justice system, it is important to know precisely what interventions and supports are available and (at times) the competence with which they are delivered and the outcomes the juvenile justice system has had with similarly situated youths.

HISTORY OF REHABILITATION FOR JUVENILES

Anglo-American law has a long history of youths being considered different for the purposes of crime and punishment. Dattilio and Fromm (2011) noted that during the reign of the 10th-century Anglo-Saxon king Aethelstan, a youth younger than age 15 would not be executed for robbery unless he resisted arrest or fled, nor could the youth be imprisoned if the family could ensure his future good conduct. In the United States, this perception of youths as different from adults and with meaningful potential for rehabilitation contributed to reforms over time that included the juvenile courts created in Chicago (1899) and Boston (1906) that rapidly expanded across the United States in the early 20th century.

Kent v. United States (1966) was the first juvenile case decided by the Supreme Court, and it focused on the "special rights and immunities" (p. 556) lost if a child was transferred and tried as an adult. The subsequent landmark case of *In re Gault* (1967) instituted procedural reforms intended to protect the rights of court-involved youths but did not signal a challenge to their capacity for rehabilitation. The predominant discourse until the last 2 decades of the 20th century accepted that, compared with adults who engage in criminal behavior, youths are developmentally immature and more subject to negative influences. As a result, youths have been viewed as less morally culpable and more amenable to interventions that promote positive development while also protecting the public by reducing recidivism.

Still, from the very beginning, juvenile justice reformers "remained skeptical as to whether this separate [juvenile justice] system could effectively deal with all juvenile offenders," skepticism that "led to the early development of transfer as a safety valve" (Martin, 1992, pp. 66–67) to move at least some juvenile cases for trial to criminal court on the basis of a determination of probable cause of having committed the alleged offense and the youth's potential amenability to treatment. During the 1980s and early 1990s, a rising rate of violent juvenile crimes and particularly homicides led to the public perception of youth crime as being out of control. The media presented predictions of a rising generation of violent juvenile "superpredators," rhetoric laced with slogans such as "old enough to do the crime, old enough to do the time," and a thinly veiled racial discourse largely identifying youths of color as the superpredators.[1] By the early years of the 21st century, 47 states and the District of Columbia had made it easier to prosecute and punish youths as adults. Ironically, these reforms occurred although rates of violent crime by juveniles had been sharply dropping since the mid-1990s.

This drop in both violent and nonviolent crime cannot be attributed to more punitive approaches toward juvenile offenders adopted by many states. In fact, it became increasingly clear that treating juveniles as adults resulted in higher recidivism rates among youths and had, at best, an equivocal deterrent effect on crime by youths (Redding, 2008). Possible reasons offered for the poorer recidivism outcomes of youths dealt with as adults have included (a) a selection process resulting in more intractably antisocial youths being diverted for adult criminal prosecution, (b) the impact of stigma and labeling of youths tried as adults, (c) a sense of resentment and injustice on

[1]Contemporary media scholars Gilliam and Iyengar (1998) observed, "Of course, the clear but unspoken subtext of the superpredator thesis is that a disproportionate number of criminal youth are from racial minority groups. To be sure, minority youth offenders are arrested for violent crimes at rates exceeding their population sizes. But those who analyze the role of TV news—as we do—find that the overwhelming focus on violent crime adds to this distortion because the dominant message is consistent with the widely held public perception that young people of color commit violent crime" (para. 2).

the part of youths transferred for adult prosecution that worked against rehabilitation, (d) the consequences of forced interactions between youths and older and more antisocial criminals during terms of incarceration, and (e) the relative paucity of rehabilitative focus and family intervention and supports for youths handled in the criminal justice rather than the juvenile justice system.

Several developments in the early 21st century prompted renewed debate about the proper balance of rehabilitation and punishment for court-involved youths. First, the emerging neuroscience regarding adolescent brain development, along with research on the developmental (emotional, social, behavioral, cognitive) manifestations of adolescent developmental immaturity (L. Steinberg & Scott, 2003), had tremendous legal and policy impact.

Second, research described the robust phenomenon of desistence from misconduct even for youths with a history of chronic or violent delinquency on entering early adulthood (Mulvey et al., 2004).[2]

Third, the social mechanisms by which a cradle-to-prison pipeline resulted in disproportionate contact and confinement of youths of color, especially impoverished youths of color, in the juvenile and criminal justice systems received increasing recognition (Children's Defense Fund, 2007).

Fourth, concerns increased that juvenile justice was becoming more and more a de facto juvenile forensic mental health system largely populated by youths with behavioral health, cognitive, and trauma-related needs. Research consistently found that some 65% to 75% of youths involved in the juvenile justice system had a diagnosable behavioral health disorder (mental health, substance use, or both), with almost 66% of youths having one or more diagnosable disorders other than a disruptive behavior disorder such as conduct disorder (Shufelt & Cocozza, 2006; Teplin, Abram, McClellan, Dulcan, & Mericle, 2002; Wasserman, McReynolds, Schwalbe, Keating, & Jones, 2010) and most youths with mental disorders also presenting with a co-occurring substance use disorder. Youths in the juvenile justice system also have significant rates of cognitive and learning disabilities (Quinn, Rutherford, Leone, Osher, & Poirier, 2005).[3] Not surprisingly, they also have high rates of psychological trauma (Abram et al., 2004; National Child Traumatic Stress Network, 2008[4]) arising from adverse childhood experiences and exposures to chronic toxic stressors now recognized to significantly elevate risks for poorer developmental, social, legal, and health outcomes (Anda et al., 2006; Teicher, Andersen, Polcari, Anderson, & Navalta, 2002). Exposure to adverse experiences, trauma, and chronic toxic stress are associated in complex ways with behaviors that contribute to risks for delinquent misconduct (Kerig & Becker, 2010) and conduct disorder (Koenen et al., 2005).

These developments prompted major philanthropic foundation initiatives.[5] Shifts in federal juvenile justice policy began to generate a change in policy and practice because states increasingly concluded that existing juvenile justice systems were expensive and ineffective—possibly even counterproductive—but that increasing the number of youths subjected to the adult criminal justice system was also counterproductive. Emerging strategies emphasized diversion from unwarranted penetration into the juvenile justice system, reducing disproportionate minority contact and confinement, developing restorative justice alternatives, lowering juvenile detention and commitments and incarcerations, identifying and meeting behavioral health needs,

[2]Mulvey et al. found that some 5% to 6% of delinquent offenders persist into adulthood with significant criminal misconduct.

[3]Prevalence data for cognitive and learning disabilities are provided later. Shandra and Hogan (2012) noted that research has reported higher delinquency rates among youths with disabilities but cautioned that research is only now beginning to distinguish rates among youths with different types of disabilities. Their research has found no differences in delinquency rates among U.S. youths with and without disabilities with the exception of two subgroups with higher rates and a subgroup (with chronic or sensory disabilities) with lower rates of property offenses. Youths with disabilities are disproportionately represented among youths in juvenile justice facilities and programs.

[4]The National Child Traumatic Stress Network (2008) study found that more than 50% of youths in the juvenile justice system have had trauma exposures and that more than 30% of them had developed at least some trauma symptoms; Abram et al. (2004) found that 92.5% of youths in an urban juvenile detention center had experienced at least one traumatic event ($M = 14.6$, $Mdn = 6$), with 11.2% meeting criteria for PTSD in the previous year.

[5]Highly visible major national initiatives included those by the John D. and Catherine T. MacArthur Foundation (Models for Change) and the Annie E. Casey Foundation (Juvenile Detention Alternatives Initiatives).

developing special sessions such as juvenile drug courts, and using trauma-informed care models (Mahoney, Ford, Ko, & Siegfried, 2004).

In 2005, the U.S. Supreme Court revisited the capacities for rehabilitation of juveniles convicted of murder, their moral culpability, the limits of prognostication about youths' rehabilitation, and evolving standards of decency about punishing youths. The majority opinion in *Roper v. Simmons* (2005) pointed to developmental immaturity, adolescent brain development, susceptibility to negative influences, and the still-forming character of juveniles as among the reasons to categorically bar the execution of people younger than age 18 for capital crimes. The Supreme Court subsequently relied on the reasoning in *Roper* to bar imposition of life without possibility of parole for nonhomicide crimes committed by juveniles in *Graham v. Florida* (2010) and then to bar sentencing schemes imposing mandatory life imprisonment without the possibility of parole on juveniles even for homicides in *Miller v. Alabama* (2012).

Before *Roper v. Simmons* (2005; execution), *Graham v. Florida* (2010; lifetime incarceration for a nonhomicide) and *Miller v. Alabama* (2012; mandatory lifetime incarceration for a homicide), the law created one group of youths for whom the issue of rehabilitative potential was irrelevant. Whether the sentence was execution or life without possibility of parole, the nature of the sentence meant certain incarceration until death. Since *Miller*, a court must hold a postconviction sentencing hearing for youths convicted of homicide.[6] A youth's potential for rehabilitation is critical at sentencing because *Miller* still permits lifetime incarceration after the hearing as long as there is one meaningful opportunity to demonstrate that the youth has achieved rehabilitation, even if that opportunity is decades in the future.[7]

Currently, issues regarding amenability to rehabilitation or treatment arise in differing legal contexts. As indicated earlier, it is critical that professionals be familiar with legal standards, rules, and procedures governing the cases in which they are involved; the availability and quality of recommended services and interventions; and research regarding desistence from delinquent misconduct and factors tending to sustain it into adulthood. These cases may include the following:

- *Juvenile court*: In these cases, the youth is unquestionably within the jurisdiction of the juvenile court. Issues of rehabilitation are most likely to bear on decisions about probation, commitment to a juvenile justice authority, or release on juvenile parole or conditional liberty.
- *Transfer or waiver from juvenile court (judicial waiver)*: These cases originate in juvenile court but may be transferred for adult criminal prosecution on the basis of the nature of the charges or the juvenile court's determination on the basis of statutory or case law factors.
- *Jurisdictional determination by prosecution (prosecutorial waiver)*: In these jurisdictions, the prosecution has authority under certain circumstances to proceed by indictment or otherwise to move the case from juvenile court to criminal court.
- *Reverse transfer or waiver from criminal court*: These cases originate in criminal court but may be subject to transfer to juvenile court on the basis of statutory or case law factors. As with cases originating in juvenile court, professionals must be familiar with factors enumerated in case law or statute and frame the forensic mental health evaluation accordingly.
- *Statutory criminal jurisdiction (or legislative waiver)*: These cases come before the criminal court and will remain there, most commonly because of statutes that enumerate serious crimes and an age range that defines which crimes allegedly committed by youths of specific ages will trigger criminal prosecution. *Roper v. Simmons* (2005) precluded execution of juveniles, *Graham v. Florida* (2010) precluded life without possibility

[6]The *Miller* decision did not provide clear guidance to states about what a meaningful opportunity would be nor about whether the decision could or should be applied retroactively to the approximately 2,000 people in the United States previously sentenced under the now-barred mandatory sentencing schemes. In December 2013, the Massachusetts Supreme Judicial Court held that the *Miller* case applied retroactively and cases would be reviewed by the state parole board.

[7]Many states have resisted the implication of *Miller* that youthful homicide offenders should be treated differently than adults by attempting to impose minimum mandatory sentences of 3 or more decades before the convicted youths receives the meaningful opportunity to make the case for rehabilitation and release that *Miller* requires (Eckholm, 2014).

of parole for nonhomicide crimes, and *Miller v. Alabama* (2012) precluded mandatory life without possibility of parole.

Factors to be considered when making transfer–waiver or dispositional–sentencing decisions vary by jurisdiction but commonly include factors such as (a) age and maturity of the juvenile, (b) cognitive capacities and any mental illness, (c) the nature and circumstances of the offense, (d) the role of the juvenile in the offense, (e) prior offense history and degree of criminal involvement or sophistication, (f) responses to previous interventions, (g) availability of services and interventions through the juvenile justice system, (h) the amenability of the youth to rehabilitation as a juvenile, and (i) the timeframe available for rehabilitative efforts in the juvenile justice system. This list is not exhaustive nor does it track individual variation across jurisdictions, so evaluators should be familiar with the specific factors relevant to the case and be sure to specifically address any factor that is subject to clinical information, analysis, or opinion.[8]

DISTINGUISHING REHABILITATION AND TREATMENT

The terms *rehabilitation* and *treatment* are sometimes used interchangeably regarding youths with juvenile justice involvement. This interchangeable use is reflected in statutes and case law and in discussions of youths by clinical, legal, and other professionals. Failure to consistently distinguish between rehabilitation and treatment has led to (a) a blurring of roles between juvenile justice and clinical professionals, (b) inconsistencies in distinguishing between behavioral health conditions (mental health disorders and substance use disorders) that are the traditional domain of clinical professionals and delinquent socialization processes and cognitions (attitudes, values, and beliefs) that are the traditional domain of juvenile justice professionals, and (c) unnecessary confusion and tension regarding whether juvenile justice should focus on accountability or on clinical care and treatment.

For the purposes of this chapter, the concept of rehabilitation is broader than the concept of treatment.[9] Rehabilitation broadly encompasses domains—social (family, peers, community), educational, vocational, recreational, health and behavioral health, community, and other—supporting a youth's ability to productively live without criminal recidivism. Psychotherapeutic treatments, psychoeducational interventions, psychiatric medications, and other clinical interventions are often supportive or even critical elements in the rehabilitation of a juvenile but commonly do not encompass the multiple domains of a youth's functioning in the way that empirically supported interventions increasingly tend to do in specifically targeting delinquent misconduct to reduce recidivism.

Rehabilitation may rely on treatment efforts but will typically address multiple domains. Notably, the most effective treatments for youths at risk of involvement with the juvenile justice system or in violent acts likely to prompt prosecution as adults are increasingly those that focus specifically on factors associated with recidivism while vigorously intervening with families, schools, peers, and communities (see Chapters 24–29, this handbook). In short, the key outcome for rehabilitation is reduced delinquent recidivism, and the key outcome for most clinical treatments is reduction of clinically impairing symptoms (such as symptoms of posttraumatic stress disorder [PTSD] or depression) or manifestations of enduring disorders (such as learning disabilities or developmental disorders) that complicate or compromise functioning and normative youth development.

Assessments of amenability to rehabilitation should attend to several areas (Kinscherff, 2006):

- Assessments of youths involved with the juvenile justice system are most relevant when they specifically address rehabilitation, particularly

[8]Some factors may be outside of the purview of clinical expertise such as (a) the "prospective merit of the complaint" (likelihood that the charges would lead to conviction) or (b) "the desirability of trial and disposition of the entire offense in one court if the minor's associates in the alleged offense were adults who will be charged with a crime" (New Hampshire, 2010).

[9]In addition, rehabilitation implies that the individual is being restored to some previous and more preferable state. However, youths are developmentally works in progress, and rehabilitation efforts for some youths consist of the process of helping them establish—perhaps for the first time—more positive developmental pathways than they previously have had during childhood and adolescence.

when they link case-specific factors contributing to delinquent misconduct to the features of recommended interventions that reduce recidivism risk. Assessment should consider the youth's individual characteristics, the nature of any diagnosis or condition with which the youth presents and research regarding the youth's prognosis with a properly matched intervention, the nature of the treatment or intervention available, and the psychosocial context in which the treatment or intervention will take place.[10]

- The actual availability of recommended services or interventions must be considered, as well as their adequacy (discussed below), because rehabilitation cannot occur if the recommended services cannot be accessed. The law in some jurisdictions specifically requires that services or interventions be accessible through the local juvenile justice system. If optimal services or interventions cannot be accessed or do not use empirically supported or best-practices approaches, the evaluator must nonetheless (a) articulate what the optimal services and interventions would be and why and (b) provide an assessment as to whether and how the services or interventions that are actually available are likely to contribute to rehabilitation. When a significant gap exists between what is optimal and what is available that bears on the likelihood of rehabilitation, the evaluator describes what, if any, administrative or other mechanisms might be used to secure access to the optimal and recommended services or interventions. Consideration must also be given to the duration of the anticipated treatment or intervention and whether it can be accomplished while the youth is under the supervision of the court or a juvenile or adult correctional authority.
- Practitioners must have solid clinical skills specifically with youths, but practitioners in this context must also be very familiar with research regarding developmental psychopathology, trajectories of delinquent misconduct, and the psychiatric and cognitive impairments commonly found among delinquent populations.
- Special populations call for specialized training, experience, and skills. Populations requiring additional training, experience, and familiarity with research include juvenile sexual offenders; youths with psychopathic traits; gang-involved youths; youths with significant learning and intellectual disabilities; trafficked youths; youths on the autism spectrum; immigrant and refugee populations; lesbian, gay, bisexual, transgender, and questioning youths; and culturally and linguistically diverse populations. Most research and juvenile justice practice involves male adolescents, and practitioners should maintain familiarity with research and practice guidance involving female and preteen offenders.
- Practitioners in this context must also be familiar with research and forensic mental health practice regarding clinical assessments, the efficacy of treatment of behavioral health conditions commonly found among youths involved with the juvenile justice system, specialized interventions specifically targeting the reduction of recidivism risks (rehabilitation), and the use of standard behavioral health treatments as adjunct or supportive interventions with the specialized interventions.
- Professionals assessing amenability to rehabilitation must be familiar with relevant law, policies, and practices of the specific juvenile justice system in which they are providing services as well as the clinical and other relevant resources accessible through that system.

STANDARD AND SPECIALIZED TREATMENT OR INTERVENTIONS

Persons in court settings or working with court-involved youth often focus on interventions intended to foster rehabilitation. However, it is important to distinguish between treatment and rehabilitation and to rigorously consider how interventions align with alleviating risk factors or serve to support protective factors. Standard behavioral health interventions may or may not contribute to rehabilitation, and

[10]Salekin, Rogers, and Ustad (2001; Salekin, Yff, Neumann, Leistico, & Zalot, 2002) observed that elements considered in the juvenile justice context commonly include youths' motivation to engage in treatment; acknowledgment of their own difficulties; anxiety, guilt, and remorse regarding offending; expectation that treatment or intervention would be helpful; and a stable and supporting parent–caretaker environment.

professionals should consider treatment matching issues that include specialized, evidence-based interventions for delinquent misconduct.

Distinguishing Standard From Specialized Treatment or Interventions

For purposes of this chapter, *standard behavioral treatment or interventions*[11] refers to clinical interventions that focus on diagnosable conditions such as are found in formal diagnostic systems[12] or are otherwise subject to research-based clinical descriptions such as complex developmental trauma (van der Kolk, 2005) or psychopathy in childhood and adolescence (Salekin, 2006). Assessments of the need for and type of behavioral health intervention and the interventions themselves are typically provided or supervised by professionals with special training in mental health who are licensed to provide behavioral health care.

Also for purposes of this chapter, standard behavioral health treatments are those ordinarily intended for clinical care whether or not the youth is engaging in significant misconduct or is court involved for this misconduct. These treatments include interventions that can range from supportive counseling, psychiatric medications, and various psychotherapies (individual, group, family) to empirically supported treatments for mood, anxiety, neurodevelopmental, trauma or stressor-related, substance use, and other disorders.

Specialized evidence-based treatments specifically target risk factors and criminogenic needs associated with disruptive and illegal misconduct. These factors include affiliation with delinquent peers; adequacy of adult supervision; school engagement and attendance; substance abuse; family dysfunction; and attitudes, values, and beliefs that maintain misconduct. Reducing misconduct that can contribute to court involvement (school disruption, truancy) or that has already done so (delinquent offenses) and reducing any new arrests (lowering recidivism) are explicit goals of these kinds of specialized interventions.

Several empirically supported specialized treatments exist for youths roughly between the ages of 12 and 17 with significantly disruptive or delinquent misconduct (Eyberg, Nelson, & Boggs, 2008; see also Chapters 23–28, this handbook).[13] Although some of these specialized treatments focus on skill building and self-regulation with individual youths, others conceptualize youths as functioning within a social ecology consisting of broader systems (e.g., families, peers, schools, communities) and focus instead on the interactions among these social-ecological domains. Ironically, although youths are generally held accountable as individuals for purposes of prosecution and sanction, these specialized treatments expand accountability beyond youths to systems shaping youths' functioning and potential. This is reflected in their incorporation of nonclinical interventions, such as educational advocacy, provision of vocational supports, facilitating positive leisure and recreational activities, or providing outreach and tracking services, as part of an overall treatment strategy in individual cases.

Reflecting this social-ecological perspective, researchers and policymakers have increasingly argued for an emphasis on fostering positive youth development by involving youths with social resources that facilitate safety and healthy development while discouraging unsafe or harmful behaviors as a strategy for delinquency prevention. Positive youth development approaches have also been advocated for the majority of court-involved youths with first or minor offenses (Butts, Mayer, & Ruth, 2005) or in support of community reentry when youths have been removed from the community for secure treatment or incarceration. This approach

[11]The terms *treatment* and *behavioral health interventions* are often used interchangeably in this chapter. The periodic use of *behavioral health* is intended as a reminder that both mental disorders and substance use disorders are included when considering treatments and interventions, particularly given the high rates of co-occurring disorders among youths involved with the juvenile justice system. At times, *intervention* is used to characterize measures that support the goal of rehabilitation but are not ordinarily considered clinical behavioral health interventions.

[12]Examples of these diagnostic systems are the *International Classification of Diseases* system of the World Health Organization or the *Diagnostic and Statistical Manual of Mental Disorders* system promulgated by the American Psychiatric Association.

[13]The following have been identified as empirically supported treatments for youths with misconduct that could trigger or has triggered court involvement: functional family therapy, group assertiveness training, multidimensional treatment foster care, multisystemic therapy, the rational–emotive mental health program, Parent Management Training—Oregon, anger control training, and problem-solving skills training.

reinforces the tendency of specialized treatments focusing on rehabilitation to also use measures to establish or return delinquent youths to a more normative developmental pathway by identifying and supporting strengths and resiliencies as well as addressing risk and criminogenic factors.

Youths meeting criteria for conduct disorder pose an interesting challenge because the criteria for this diagnosis are mostly behaviors that could result in arrest.[14] Oddly, the criteria serving as symptoms for the purposes of this diagnosis are also grounds for prosecution—some of them potentially triggering prosecution as an adult. This overlap between clinical and legal domains also exists for youths diagnosed with a substance use disorder as defined by the *Diagnostic and Statistical Manual of Mental Disorders, Fifth Edition* (*DSM–5*; American Psychiatric Association, 2013) because their possession or distribution of alcohol and other substances may also result in charges.

Two Goals of Standard Behavioral Health Interventions in Rehabilitation

Conceptually, the use of standard behavioral health interventions in the juvenile justice context can be considered as having two distinguishable goals. One goal is to address treatable disorders (such as depression, attention-deficit/hyperactivity disorder [ADHD], or PTSD) or to remediate or compensate as much as possible for enduring conditions (such as intellectual disability, learning disability, impairment resulting from fetal alcohol exposure) that complicate or compromise normative development. Effective treatment of an identified condition may help resolve symptoms or support better functioning but have little, if any, impact on misconduct. For example, for a youth presenting with moderate depression but severe conduct disorder, effective treatment of the depression may simply result in this youth having a brighter mood and better concentration while engaging in serious misconduct. It may be necessary to treat the depression so that the youth can be motivated to change, but it would be unreasonable to expect that treating the depression would resolve the delinquent behavior.

A second goal of standard behavioral health interventions can be as an adjunctive support or component of a treatment using a specialized empirically based treatment explicitly targeting delinquent misconduct. For example, specialized interventions such as multisystemic therapy or functional family therapy may in individual cases benefit from a standard behavioral health intervention. Sometimes the standard intervention is required before and then consistently during the specialized intervention, such as when a youth presents with an emerging psychotic disorder or bipolar disorder. Sometimes the standard intervention is required at least for a time to maintain a youth's stability during the course of a specialized intervention, such as when a youth has an episode of depression or a substance abuse relapse.

Particularly with conduct disorder, mental health professionals will need to consider what in addition to bad behavior may be present in a given case. Conduct disorder (Connor, Ford, Albert, & Doerfler, 2007; Nock, Kazdin, Hiripi, & Kessler, 2006) and substance use disorders (Chan, Dennis, & Funk, 2008) have significant rates of comorbid conditions and are commonly comorbid with each other (Armstrong & Costello, 2002). Differential diagnosis among conditions commonly found in court-involved youths such as conduct disorder, ADHD, major depressive disorder, PTSD and other trauma- and stress-related disorders, bipolar disorder (and presumably, *DSM–5*'s temper dysregulation disorder), and substance use disorders is very challenging, and evaluators will need to work carefully to identify potential comorbid conditions warranting specific intervention.

One way of conceiving of conduct disorder and substance use disorder is that each represents a

[14]The criteria for conduct disorder in *DSM–5* are essentially unchanged from those of the fourth edition, text revision, but for the inclusion of a specifier to describe people who have a callous–unemotional interpersonal style. The criteria reflect aggression toward people and animals, destruction of property, deceitfulness and theft, and serious violations of rules. Except for the serious violations of rules (which could be status offenses), the criteria reflect behavior that could be prosecuted, and many of them could be charged as felonies (e.g., rape, arson, armed robbery, aggravated assault, breaking and entering) and potentially prompt prosecution as an adult in many states. Because three criteria must have been met in the previous 12 months with at least one met within the past 6 months, conduct disorder may be regarded as reflecting diverse and serious delinquent misconduct for which the youth may or may not have been formally charged.

common behavioral outcome at a particular time in a youth's life that can potentially reflect many developmental pathways toward significant misconduct and substance abuse. Sometimes, it is only the severe misconduct or the abuse of substances that youths diagnosed with conduct disorder or a substance use disorder have in common. In every other respect relevant to understanding their developmental pathways, current functioning, role of delinquent misconduct and substance use in their lives, and amenability to standard clinical intervention or, more broadly, for rehabilitation, they may be very different from each other. Rendering a diagnosis will not be particularly informative without going well beyond the diagnostic criteria to articulate an individualized and developmentally informed pathway describing in detail how a particular youth came to warrant one or both of these diagnoses. Only then will it be possible to consider what constellation of standard and specialized behavioral health interventions might be recommended and what role each would play in achieving rehabilitation.

In practice, in assessing the potential role to be played by standard treatments in contributing to rehabilitation, evaluators should consider the caution that "evidence is building that efforts to identify and promote empirically supported treatments (ESTs) have had minimal impact on the practice of front-line practitioners" (Stewart & Chambless, 2010, p. 73). As a result, an assessment of amenability to rehabilitation must take into account (a) the possible presence of a condition warranting a standard treatment intervention; (b) what, if any, links there are between an identified condition and a youth's misconduct; and (c) the adequacy of the available adjunctive clinical intervention. A key factor in considering the adequacy of an intervention is whether it is empirically supported. This is particularly important in circumstances in which a youth's failure to respond to an adjunctive treatment may have significant legal consequences should the youth be designated a treatment failure or should the treatment fail to support a specialized intervention in which the youth is concurrently enrolled. Assessment of the adequacy of an available adjunctive standard intervention that would be part of an evaluation of amenability to rehabilitation or interventional planning will require the forensic evaluator to know what treatment modalities will be used and the empirical support for their use for the identified conditions.

Relationship Between Standard and Specialized Treatments in Rehabilitation

Youths involved with the juvenile justice system are disproportionately likely to present with mental health disorders, substance use disorders,[15] federally defined severe emotional disturbance, learning disabilities, intellectual disabilities,[16] and other diagnosable or functional (such as complex developmental trauma) conditions. The prevalence of trauma-related diagnosable disorders and trauma-related functional impairments that do not meet formal diagnostic criteria is also very high among juvenile justice populations. Notably, although trauma and exposure to adverse childhood experiences is associated with a range of risky behaviors,[17] except for conditions that are also legal misconduct (such as conduct disorders largely defined by illegal conduct and substance use disorders in which even possession of a substance may be a delinquent offense), most youths with these conditions do not engage in significant or persisting misconduct likely to trigger deep penetration into the juvenile justice system.

However, among court-involved youths any of these conditions may be linked in complex ways with delinquent misconduct. As a result, assessment of rehabilitation must include a detailed analysis of the relationship between any diagnosed or functionally described clinical condition and misconduct

[15]Many youths (65%–70%) have at least one diagnosable behavioral health condition, and 20% to 25% have serious emotional issues (Shufelt & Cocozza, 2006; Teplin, Abram, McClelland, Dulcan, & Mericle, 2002; Wasserman, McReynolds, Lucas, Fisher, & Santos, 2002).

[16]One national survey (Quinn et al., 2005) of youths' needs in juvenile justice correctional custody found that, among agencies responding, 47.7% of youths met disability criteria for emotional disturbance, 38.6% had specific learning disabilities, and 9.7% were diagnosed with mental retardation. The term *mental retardation* has been replaced with the term *intellectual disability*.

[17]Exposure to adverse childhood experiences correlated with increased likelihood of risky behaviors includes unsafe sexual practices, alcohol abuse, smoking, illegal substance use, self-harm, school underachievement or failure, and failures on conditional supervision such as juvenile probation.

that has or could[18] result in juvenile justice involvement. In individual cases in which there is a behavioral health (mental health disorder, substance use disorder), cognitive (learning disability, intellectual disability), or other clinically impairing condition, it is essential to consider a range of potential links between the clinical condition and the delinquent misconduct.

Using violence risk as an example, professionals should consider whether the clinical condition reflects the following:

- *Direct contribution to the violent misconduct*: Some examples are a youth with no prior history of aggressive behavior who becomes assaultive, but only after becoming depressed with an uncharacteristic and marked irritability that seems to be driving the assaults; a youth who, after being raped, becomes extremely hypervigilant and intensely emotionally reactive in a manner seeming to drive threatened and actual aggression toward people the youth (mis)perceives as potentially threatening; a youth addicted to heroin who robs at people knifepoint to get cash for drug purchases but who had little or no prior history of initiating overt aggression before addiction; and a youth diagnosed with conduct disorder who was raised in a family who inculcated in the youth attitudes, values, and beliefs that predispose him or her to instrumental use of threatened or actual use of violence to achieve material, sexual, and interpersonal goals.
- *Indirect contribution to an associated violence risk factor*: Some examples are a youth with PTSD who self-medicates with increasing levels of alcohol consumption that at times results in disinhibition, confrontation, and initiation of fights; a youth whose autism spectrum disorder contributes to social misperceptions and interactions that lead him or her into situations in which he or she is highly frustrated and impulsively physically strikes out at others; a youth whose autism spectrum disorder prompts bullying by peers that becomes increasingly persistent and so severe that he or she gradually becomes intensely desperate and considers violent retribution to stop the bullying; a youth whose parents find him or her so disagreeable because of oppositional and defiant features that they have burned out on trying to enforce limits or supervise him or her, resulting in the youth's drift to unsupervised affiliation with violent delinquent peers; and a youth whose unrecognized learning disability and academic struggles contribute to disengagement from school, increasing truancy, and an affiliation with youths involved in daytime burglaries when they are not in school.
- *Direct contribution to suppressing violence risk*: Some examples include a gang-involved youth who becomes depressed, hypervigilant, and avoidant after witnessing the violent death of a peer and so no longer leaves his or her house and whose isolation has cut him or her off from gang involved peers and a youth whose self-medication with marijuana blunts his or her otherwise heightened emotional reactivity and irritability.
- *Indirect contribution to suppression of a violence risk factor*: An example is a youth whose depression or other condition prompts a supportive response by parents or others, who then take steps to initiate clinical care or put other stabilizing supports into place that lead the youth to again engage in school, stop carrying a weapon, and shift his or her affiliations to a more positive peer group.

At times, treating a disorder or needs arising from enduring conditions with a standard clinical response will be sufficient to diminish or even eliminate delinquent misconduct. Consider a youth who does not have a significant history of aggression but who has begun to hit others as he or she becomes depressed, with a clinical picture of marked irritability and demoralization. Effective treatment of the depression will reduce irritability and restore the youth's ability to care about the consequences of his or her conduct for him- or herself and others. The assaultive behavior leading to the youth's arrest may

[18]Some youths are legally charged with misconduct that does not reflect their actual misconduct. For example, a youth may be charged with drug possession or a misdemeanor charge while actually frequently engaging in conduct that could be charged as felonies, or a youth may be charged with a felony for a single and atypical act.

well achieve rehabilitation by restoring the youth to his or her functional and developmental baseline.

Sometimes addressing a disorder or enduring condition with a standard clinical response is necessary but foreseeably insufficient to achieve rehabilitation solely. For example, a youth with a history of significant aggression with onset as a preschooler may become even more aggressive should she or he, like the youth above, suffer from a depression characterized by marked irritability and demoralization. Effective individual treatment of the depression would restore the youth's previous baseline of significant aggression, but it would not be reasonable to expect that it alone would result in rehabilitation. Similarly, academic adjustments after identification of a learning disability alone are unlikely to result in the rehabilitation of a youth who is gang involved and derives significant satisfaction and peer status from that affiliation. In each of these cases, intervention focusing on risks and criminogenic needs (such as family dysfunction, affiliating with delinquent peers, school engagement) would likely be required to reduce the baseline of aggressive behaviors.

In some situations, providing standard clinical care may help the youth be a more successful delinquent or actually increase public safety risk. An example of the former is a youth with untreated ADHD who has been raised in a family of car thieves but is referred for treatment as a condition of probation as part of a plea negotiation in which his car theft was characterized as impulsive. Effective treatment may make the youth more attentive and less impulsive—and thus less likely to be caught—when effectively treated for the ADHD.

Situations also occur in which addressing a disorder with standard clinical care is a helpful or essential support for the success of specialized treatments to diminish delinquent misconduct. For example, treating psychosis or symptoms of emerging bipolar disorder is likely to be a necessary component of successful specialized treatment and nonclinical interventions such as probation. A standard clinical response is also warranted to maintain functioning of a youth during a course of specialized interventions such as when a youth becomes depressed or has a substance abuse relapse.

FORENSICALLY DEFENSIBLE APPROACHES TO EVALUATION OF AMENABILITY TO REHABILITATION

Forensic evaluators assessing a juvenile's amenability to rehabilitation must be particularly attentive to the methods relied upon in generating information that is sufficiently scientifically reliable to be admitted into evidence in a legal proceeding. In the sections that follow, I describe issues to be considered, content that may warrant inclusion, and assessment tools that may be informative in conducting forensically defensible evaluations.

Establishing the Referral Question

The evaluator should establish whether amenability to rehabilitation (or, in alternative language, amenability to treatment) is an explicit legal factor in the case referred for evaluation. If so, the evaluator should determine whether there are specific factors the court must weigh in coming to a decision about amenability. This is especially important in cases involving transfer, waiver, or reverse waiver between juvenile and criminal court or when the case involves an aid in sentencing that might include a post–*Miller v. Alabama* (2012) disposition hearing about potential life without possibility of parole for a capital offense committed as a juvenile.

Most commonly, the questions are simply "What needs to be done so this youth does not reoffend and what is the likelihood that these measures would work?" and "What is the likelihood that the recommended interventions or supports can be put into place and maintained long enough to achieve the goal of rehabilitation?" In most cases, assessment of amenability to rehabilitation involves an explicit or implicit assessment of recidivism risk—especially when violent or sexual offenses are involved. In any event, clarity regarding the referral question and any specific legal criteria involved will bear directly on the methods relied on in answering the referral question.

Grisso (1998) has offered a useful framework for structuring evaluations of amenability to rehabilitation by posing four key assessment questions:

1. What are the youth's important characteristics?
2. What must change?

3. What modes of intervention could accomplish the rehabilitation objective?
4. What is the likelihood of change given the relevant interventions?

In applying this framework, it is essential that evaluators consistently attend to specific links among (a) the youth's characteristics and functioning and the developmental pathway shaping the youth's current presentation, (b) the charged offenses and possibly also other misconduct that has not been charged, (c) research-based risk or criminogenic needs, (d) protective or resiliency factors, (e) any specific characteristics of the individual youth relevant to treatment matching and prognosis,[19] and (f) the specific standard treatments and specialized interventions available and their prognoses for the features of the youth most relevant to the offense and potential recidivism.

Establishing the Client of the Evaluation

The client of the evaluation must be confidently established before initiating the evaluation because it may have a bearing on what concerns prompted the referral, what evaluation methods might be most relevant, rules regarding confidentiality or privilege, and the informed consents required. The identified client will ordinarily be the court or defense counsel, although at times professionals may be retained by the prosecution or by juvenile justice authorities. Any limits on confidentiality or testimonial privilege, including mandated reporting requirements, must be clarified before initiating the evaluation.[20]

Considering the Timing of the Evaluation

Evaluators should consider whether the referral is made before a legal finding of fact (admission to sufficient facts or adjudication) or after a legal finding of fact. If a transfer or waiver decision is to be made before admission or adjudication of the alleged offense, the evaluator should clarify how he or she will proceed and the impact this will have on the evaluation. For example, in a case in which the charge is serious and the defendant denies involvement in the crime, the evaluator should clarify whether he or she will assume the facts as alleged, ignore the alleged offense and write a report based on the history and collateral information unrelated to the offense, or write a report that considers amenability to rehabilitation for both scenarios (the youth did commit the act as alleged or the youth did not). If evaluation is requested after an admission or legal finding of fact, the evaluator is entitled to rely on the official version but may have to consider what (if any) weight to assign continued denial of an offense after adjudication and the empirical basis on which that weight is assigned.

Selecting the Method of Evaluation

A best-practices approach to assessment of amenability to rehabilitation increasingly precludes sole reliance on clinical interview and unstructured clinical decision making. This is particularly the case if relying solely on clinical interview with only the juvenile defendant, but it also holds when the evaluator has information from collateral sources. The vagaries of unstructured clinical judgment (including in diagnosis, violence and sex offender risk assessment, prognosis for treatments) increasingly argue for careful attention to measures that structure and support the information gathering and professional decision making of even the most experienced forensic mental health professionals.

In all cases, but especially in cases such as those determining whether a youth is prosecuted in juvenile court or as an adult or in a post–*Miller v. Alabama* (2012) proceeding in which a court may impose a lifetime incarceration, evaluators have an obligation to rely on forensically defensible evaluation methods. These methods typically include

[19]For example, a youth with significant auditory processing deficits may not fare well in a group treatment model, one with intellectual disabilities may not benefit from a treatment that does not take this disability into account, or a youth with untreated PTSD may require prior or concurrent treatment of the PTSD to help him or her accommodate to a juvenile secure treatment facility that he or she experiences as unsafe and triggering.

[20]See, for example, *Elijah W. v. Superior Court of Los Angeles County* (2013), in which the attorney–client privilege for a juvenile defendant was held to overcome the duty of a licensed mental health professional retained by defense counsel to comply with mandated reporting of child abuse or neglect. In many jurisdictions, it is not clear whether as a matter of law attorney–client privilege or the mandated reporting requirements of licensed mental health professionals prevail. Professionals in a forensic context should ascertain what rules govern in their own jurisdiction or, in the absence of clear legal guidance, disclose to the identified client their own practice, especially if retained by defense counsel.

multiple sources and approaches to information gathering[21] and analysis. This is done to safeguard against the well-known unreliability of unstructured clinical judgment (e.g., in diagnosis, risk assessment, intervention matching, outcome prediction) and the scientific limits of offering longer term prognostications about a youth's amenability to rehabilitation. The emergence in recent years of tools to inform clinical assessment, risk assessment, treatment readiness, and other domains has increasingly called for their routine incorporation in forensic assessment. However, evaluators must be aware of the limits of even best-practices methods in yielding reliable science-based prognostications about long-term rehabilitation outcomes. Indeed, given these limits on reliable prediction in individual cases, professionals willing to offer a confident forensic opinion about a youth's rehabilitation outcome over a span of many years may so outstrip the available science[22] that doing so rises to the level of highly questionable professional practice and a potential major ethical violation (Kinscherff & Grisso, 2013).[23]

Evaluations of amenability to rehabilitation commonly include (a) identification of historical (static) risk and protective factors contributing to the delinquent misconduct; (b) identification of dynamic factors (e.g., contextual, clinical, interpersonal, familial, attitudinal, social) contributing to incidents of delinquent misconduct, especially if they are targets for rehabilitative interventions; (c) identification of protective or other positive youth development assets that may be engaged in the service of rehabilitation; and (d) an opinion regarding the prospects for successful rehabilitative interventions, including standard and specialized behavioral health interventions that may be components of a plan of rehabilitation.

However information may be organized for purposes of a written report, the evaluation ordinarily includes attention to the following to create the foundation for inferences, opinions, and recommendations relevant to the specific factors to be considered by the legal decision maker (e.g., court, juvenile parole authority) or otherwise important to communicate:

- Developmental history and description of the youth's developmental pathway to current presentation and functioning (prenatal and early development and temperament, especially regarding callous–unemotional traits or high levels of stimulation seeking or risk taking; developmental delays or disabilities; early learning skills; peer relations and affiliations; interests and competencies; onset and pattern of behavioral disturbances, including overt and covert misconduct; and other pathways of developmental psychopathology or resiliencies).
- Medical and behavioral mental health (including behavioral health difficulties and interventions; temperamental or clinical conditions relevant to disinhibition and impaired executive functioning; history of clinical care; and history of any potential developmental insults such as head injuries, exposures to lead or other toxins, intrauterine substance exposures, or maternal distress or injury during pregnancy).
- Cognitive capacities (intellectual capacities, learning disabilities or areas of relative strength or learning vulnerability, optimal learning style, and preferred areas of interest).

[21]These approaches can include (a) interviews with the juvenile and family or caretakers; (b) information from probation, school, clinical care providers, facilities at which the youth has been detained or treated, or others; (c) review of relevant police reports, crime scene analyses, autopsy reports, witness or victim statements, or other information that can help provide an understanding of the alleged or adjudicated offense; (d) review of relevant educational, clinical, social service, child protection, or other records; (e) validated tools for clinical assessment, risk assessment, risk–needs–responsivity profile, or other relevant domain; (f) measures to become familiar with the services available through the juvenile justice system; and (g) potentially informational contacts with defense counsel and prosecutor. Information gathering may also include reviewing websites visited; social media exchanges; computer files and activities; cell phone information; and inquiries into movies, videogames, music, and other entertainment activities by the youth.

[22]For example, "even high scores on the PCL:YV do not mean that a youth *will* be violent in the future . . . [although a high score] places the adolescent at a higher risk for violence *over a relatively short time period* [italics added]" (Vitacco & Salekin, 2013, p. 81).

[23]Kinscherff and Grisso (2013) observed that "ethical challenges arise from the sharp limits of existing science in predicting in individual cases whether the juvenile defendant can or will be rehabilitated. Indeed, given the evidence of a broad trend of self-desistance of criminal misconduct among even serious juvenile offenders, it would be difficult to confidently anticipate on the basis of existing research which individual juvenile defendants would *fail* to follow this trend" (p. 75).

- Family history and functioning[24] (including parent–child interactions, separations and losses, discipline, mental health history, criminal justice history, intimate partner violence history, child maltreatment history, substance use history, and current family relationships and functioning).
- Educational history (including disciplinary history, school engagement, special educational needs, learning disabilities, and areas of relative achievement and challenge).
- Social and peer functioning (including history of engagement in community activities, history of peer relationships, any affiliations with problematic peers or peer groups,[25] and preferred activities when with peers).
- Cultural affiliation and adaptation factors (including history of immigration, dislocations and relocations, nature and degree of assimilation into specific groups,[26] languages, and any generational tensions over assimilation).
- History of exposure to adverse childhood experiences (significant or toxic stresses)[27] and experiences resulting in posttraumatic symptoms (e.g., PTSD) or posttraumatic adaptations (including either subsequent resiliencies or manifestations of a developmental or complex trauma condition that is not readily summed up in *DSM–5* diagnostic categories).
- History of behavioral health needs, services received, and outcomes from past and any current standard behavioral health treatments, including those for substance abuse, psychiatric disorder, medical condition, or other condition.
- History of rule breaking and illegal misconduct (onset; pattern; persistence; and manifestation across time, relationships, and environments); responses intended to address misconduct and the outcomes of these interventions; responses to any specialized interventions including recidivism risks among its targets; and responses to efforts by parents, school, police, and courts to set limits on misconduct.
- History of interventions and their outcomes (including degree of engagement, individual strengths or complications to intervention, assessment of why past interventions succeeded or failed, assessment of response to usual deterrents to misconduct, attitudes toward any successful or failed past interventions, current attitudes toward most likely interventions).
- Summary of the youth's developmental trajectory and key historical and current factors, including any factors specified by case law or statute (e.g., youth sophistication or maturity, history of misconduct, history of previous interventions).
- Assessment of relevant risks (e.g., violence, sexual offense, nonviolent offenses) based on interview, collateral information, and specialized assessment tools.
- Assessment of recidivism risk for the charged behavior and, if clinically relevant and legally permissible, for other significant misconduct with a description of with whom the youth is being compared in terms of risk (e.g., all youths, all delinquent youths, or some subgroup of delinquent youths, such as those who have been charged with specific offenses or have failed on community-based supervision for prior offenses).
- Level of containment required for public or youth safety and to ensure implementation of interventions and specific indicators recommended for increasing or decreasing the level of containment or monitoring.
- Consideration of potential criminogenic or iatrogenic consequences of the various options before the legal decision maker that may complicate or compromise efforts at rehabilitation.

[24]Family factors associated with recidivism risk include low parental emotional warmth, parental criminal history or antisocial behavior, erratic parental responses to misconduct, and parental absence.

[25]Factors associated with peer groups that have been linked to recidivism risk include peer deviance, peer rejection, and peer group novelty-seeking and risk-taking behaviors.

[26]These factors may overlap but include these kinds of groupings: origin groups (e.g., ethnic or linguistic groups of origin), organizational (e.g., religious, military, corporate, professional, or occupational), and affiliative (e.g., political, ideological, and organized around common interests or activities).

[27]Evaluators will need to be familiar with the literature on long-term and neurodevelopmental outcomes associated with exposure to adverse childhood experiences (Anda et al., 2006; Bremner, 2003; Perry, 2001).

- Availability of recommended standard treatments and specialized interventions, including (a) whether the recommended interventions are available through the juvenile justice system or, if not, through identifiable mechanisms; (b) the quality of the recommended services if they are available, or consideration of the nature and quality of alternative services if the recommended services are not available, and assessment of whether the recommended or alternative services can realistically meet the needs of the youth across one or multiple domains; and (c) whether conditions or circumstances that complicate rehabilitation efforts (e.g., psychiatric or cognitive impairment, family hostility) can be addressed sufficiently so that interventions can still succeed.

It is beyond the scope of this chapter to comprehensively review screening and assessment tools that can be used by trained practitioners when conducting assessments of amenability to rehabilitation.[28] However, a nonexhaustive list of psychological tests and assessment tools—chosen on the basis of empirical support for their intended purpose or otherwise consistent with best-practice approaches—would include the following:

- *Clinical and personality instruments*: Minnesota Multiphasic Personality Inventory—Adolescent version (Butcher et al., 1992), Millon Adolescent Clinical Inventory (Millon, Millon, Davis, & Grossman, 2006), and the Child Behavior Checklist/6–18 (Achenbach, 2001).
- *Risk and risk–needs assessment instruments*: Youth Level of Service/Case Management Inventory (Hoge, Andrews, & Leschied, 2002) and Global Risk Assessment Device (Gavazzi et al., 2003).
- *Global needs screening or assessment*: Massachusetts Youth Screening Instrument—Version 2 (Grisso & Barnum, 2006) and Problem Oriented Screening Instrument for Teenagers (Rahdert, 1991).
- *Level of maturity, risk to others, amenability to rehabilitation*: Risk-Sophistication-Treatment Inventory (Salekin, 2004).
- *Child and youth psychopathy and antisocial traits:*[29] Hare Psychopathy Checklist—Youth Version (Forth, Kosson, & Hare, 2003), Antisocial Process Screening Device (Frick & Hare, 2001), and Childhood Psychopathy Scale (Lynam et al., 2005).
- *Youth violence risk assessment tools*: Structured Assessment of Violence Risk in Youth (Borum, 2002). Screening tools in several domains (e.g., attitudes, psychosocial factors, behavior) can also be found in *Measuring Violence-Related Attitudes, Beliefs, and Behaviors Among Youths: A Compendium of Assessment Tools* (Dahlberg, Toal, & Behrens, 1998).
- *Substance abuse instruments*: Adolescent Chemical Dependency Inventory—Corrections Version II (Behavior Data Systems, 2004) and Comprehensive Addiction Severity Index for Adolescents (Meyers, McLellan, Jaeger, & Pettinati, 1995).
- *Trauma screening tools*: Clinician-Administered PTSD Scale for Children and Adolescents (Nader et al., 1996), UCLA PTSD Reaction Index (A. M. Steinberg, Brymer, Decker, & Pynoos, 2004), and the Trauma Symptom Checklist for Children (Briere, 1996). The screening for adverse childhood experiences used in the Adverse Childhood Experiences study (Centers for Disease Control and Prevention, 2014; Felitti et al., 1998) may be useful because of research linking them to a range of poorer outcomes in adulthood and adolescents (Edwards et al., 2005) and emerging research finding disproportionately high adverse childhood experience exposures among youths in juvenile justice who are likely to fail probation and penetrate the juvenile justice system (Mosher & Olds, 2013).
- *Youth resilience screen*: Child and Health Youth Resilience Measure (Liebenberg, Ungar, & LeBlanc, 2013).

[28]Brumbaugh, Walters, and Winterfield (2009) have offered a thorough review of the suitability of specific assessment tools for delinquent girls.

[29]Evaluators inquiring after traits consistent with emerging psychopathy or enduring antisocial orientation must ensure that they are adequately familiar with the research, controversies, and communication strategies involved when attributing psychopathic traits or antisocial orientation in a forensic mental health context.

Whatever the methods of data gathering, it is essential that attention be given to the specific links among (a) the youth's characteristics and functioning currently and as a product of an articulated developmental pathway; (b) the charged misconduct and potential misconduct that has not resulted in formal charges; (c) the risk and protective factors, criminogenic needs, resiliency resources, and individual characteristics of the youth that provide a context for understanding the misconduct; and (d) the specific modalities and prognoses of recommended standard and specialized interventions, including the empirical support for the utility of the recommended interventions.

In considering recommendations to match standard or specialized interventions to the needs of individual youths, the evaluator should consider that,

> juvenile delinquency treatment programs that include family intervention and multisystemic and cognitive-behavioral therapies, and which concentrate on factors which reinforce delinquency (e.g., drugs, alcohol, deviant peers, etc.) show greater success as a more stable adaptation of the adolescents and a lower recidivism rate is concerned. (Cécile & Born, 2009, p. 1218)[30]

Although public safety interests or disposition or sentencing schemes may call for a term of facility-based containment and intervention, evaluators should take into account the possibility of inadvertent reinforcement of delinquent attitudes and behavior by means such as forced affiliation with delinquent peers or, if sentenced to a term in an adult correctional facility, adult criminals. In short, evaluators should consider the potential iatrogenic effects of particular treatment or dispositional options and weigh them in communicating recommendations in the case.

EMERGING ISSUES AND IMPLICATIONS

The following are developing areas of research and practice with bearing on assessment of amenability to rehabilitation. Practitioners should continue to keep abreast of these areas and their potential implications for conceptualizing and assessing amenability to rehabilitation in individual cases.

- *Adolescent brain development*: This area is receiving increasing attention from policymakers and the public. The basic brain science regarding key mechanisms of brain development during adolescence is no longer controversial science, but significant challenges remain in considering what it means for understanding adolescence and for understanding individual adolescents and its implications for public policy. Practitioners should familiarize themselves with the key findings of the science but carefully consider the complexities of their implications (L. Steinberg, 2009) for public policy and professional practice in individual cases, especially given the additionally complicating overlay of disproportionate exposure to adverse childhood experiences among youths who penetrate the juvenile justice system or may be tried and sentenced as adults.
- *Desistance of delinquent misconduct*: This is a complex but important area of research describing (a) the general trend toward desistance of delinquent misconduct among adolescents as they enter early adulthood or (b) the relative rates of desistance among youths engaging in particular kinds of misconduct such as juvenile sexual offenses. This research poses challenges for assessment of rehabilitation for juveniles because practitioners are often being asked to "predict against the tide" of a general trend of desisting behavior as youths grow into young adulthood (general delinquency) or within a group whose base rate of recidivism is very low (sexual offense recidivism among juvenile sexual offenders). Research is emerging regarding subgroups of serious juvenile offenders (Mulder, Brand, Bullens, & Van Marle, 2010) and prediction of outcomes for youths transferred to adult court (Schubert et al., 2010), but it can currently provide only broad guidance for prognostications

[30]Standard treatments or counseling approaches that do not specifically take into account risk–need–responsivity profiles of individual youths, programs such as juvenile boot camps that rely largely on negative reinforcement strategies, and nonspecific activities such as wilderness challenge programs or vocational training are largely ineffective in reducing delinquent misconduct and may inadvertently reinforce such behavior.

about rehabilitation outcomes in individual cases. These challenges argue for routine use of research-based structured clinical judgment tools rather than unstructured clinical judgment.

- *Research regarding resiliencies and adolescent development*: L. Steinberg (2009) observed that a tension can be perceived between the model of vulnerability implicit in an adolescent brain development perspective and a strengths-based model reflected in positive youth development approaches. These need not be in opposition to a broad developmental perspective and, for purposes of assessment of amenability to rehabilitation, it is important to identify the resiliencies and positive youth development strengths and needs of individual youths.
- *Research regarding youths with psychopathic traits*: The past 2 decades have seen increasing research and applied practice for assessment and intervention with youths with traits (callous, unemotional) and behaviors (early-onset persisting rule breaking and aggression) that may signal a developmental pathway toward adult psychopathy. Once thought to be virtually intractable to treatment, further research on developmental pathways toward adult psychopathy, development of measures sensitive to interventions,[31] and efforts to develop specific interventions for youths with conduct problems who also have interpersonal callous traits have led to specialized interventions warranting greater prognostic optimism (Caldwell, Skeem, Salekin, & Van Rybroek, 2006; Salekin, Tippey, & Allen, 2012). Practitioners need to be meticulously research based, thoughtful, and measured when using assessment measures and reporting their results in terms of psychopathy given the potential impact on judicial (Jones & Cauffman, 2008) and clinical (Rockett, Murrie, & Boccacini, 2007) decision making.

In summary, practitioners can provide legal decision makers with relevant information, education, and clinical or forensic opinion that can substantively inform determinations of a youth's needs in support of rehabilitation and the likelihood of rehabilitative success. That being said, practitioners assessing amenability to rehabilitation have an obligation to remain within the limits of the existing science. It is important to incorporate best practices, including tools to facilitate (a) structured professional judgment, (b) thoughtful and research-informed prognostications about rehabilitation in individual cases, and (c) attention to how assessment results are communicated to courts or other legal decision makers. Practitioners in this area assume considerable responsibility for competent professional practice and deeply meaningful ethical obligations whether offering recommendations about conditions of probation for a low-level or first offender or rendering forensic opinions regarding amenability to rehabilitation when possible trial as an adult is at stake or when involved in post–*Miller v. Alabama* (2012) dispositions in which a lifetime of incarceration is a potential outcome.

References

Abram, K. M., Teplin, L. A., Charles, D. R., Longworth, S. L., McClelland, G. M., & Dulcan, M. K. (2004). Posttraumatic stress disorder and trauma in youth in juvenile detention. *Archives of General Psychiatry, 61*, 403–410. http://dx.doi.org/10.1001/archpsyc.61.4.403

Achenbach, T. (2001). *Manual for the Child Behavior Checklist/6–18*. Burlington: University of Vermont, Department of Psychiatry.

American Psychiatric Association. (2013). *Diagnostic and statistical manual of mental disorders* (5th ed.) Arlington, VA: American Psychiatric Publishing.

Anda, R. F., Felitti, V. J., Bremner, J. D., Walker, J. D., Whitfield, C., Perry, B. D., . . . Giles, W. H. (2006). The enduring effects of abuse and related adverse experiences in childhood. *European Archives of Psychiatry and Clinical Neuroscience, 256*, 174–186. http://dx.doi.org/10.1007/s00406-005-0624-4

Armstrong, T. D., & Costello, E. J. (2002). Community studies on adolescent substance use, abuse, or dependence and psychiatric comorbidity. *Journal of Consulting and Clinical Psychology, 70*, 1224–1239. http://dx.doi.org/10.1037/0022-006X.70.6.1224

Behavior Data Systems. (2004). *Adolescent Chemical Dependency Inventory—Corrections Version II*. Phoenix, AZ: Professional On-Line Testing Solutions.

[31]An example of such a measure is the Treatment Amenability scale of the Risk-Sophistication-Treatment Inventory Self Report (Iselin & Salekin, 2008).

Borum, R. (2002). *Structured Assessment of Violence Risk in Youth*. Lutz, FL: Psychological Assessment Resources.

Bremner, J. D. (2003). Long-term effects of childhood abuse on brain and neurobiology. *Child and Adolescent Psychiatric Clinics of North America, 12*, 271–292. http://dx.doi.org/10.1016/S1056-4993(02)00098-6

Briere, J. (1996). *Trauma Symptom Checklist for Children (TSCC) professional manual*. Odessa, FL: Psychological Assessment Resources.

Brumbaugh, S., Walters, J. L. H., & Winfield, L. A. (2009). *Suitability of assessment instruments for delinquent girls*. Washington, DC: U.S. Department of Justice, Office of Juvenile Justice and Delinquency Prevention, Girls Study Group. Retrieved from http://www.ojp.usdoj.gov/ojjdp

Butcher, J., Williams, C., Graham, J., Archer, R., Tellegen, R., Ben-Porath, Y., & Kaemmer, B. (1992). *MMPI-A: Manual for administration, scoring and interpretation*. Minneapolis: University of Minnesota Press.

Butts, J., Mayer, S., & Ruth, R. (2005). *Focusing juvenile justice on positive youth development* (Chapin Hall Center for Children: Issue Brief No. 105). Chicago, IL: University of Chicago.

Caldwell, M., Skeem, J., Salekin, R., & Van Rybroek, G. (2006). Treatment response of adolescent offenders with psychopathy features: A 2-year follow-up. *Criminal Justice and Behavior, 33*, 571–596. http://dx.doi.org/10.1177/0093854806288176

Cécile, M., & Born, M. (2009). Intervention in juvenile delinquency: Danger of iatrogenic effects? *Children and Youth Services Review, 31*, 1217–1221. http://dx.doi.org/10.1016/j.childyouth.2009.05.015

Centers for Disease Control and Prevention. (2014). *Injury prevention and control: Division of Violence Prevention*. Retrieved from http://www.cdc.gov/ace

Chan, Y. F., Dennis, M. L., & Funk, R. R. (2008). Prevalence and comorbidity of major internalizing and externalizing problems among adolescents and adults presenting to substance abuse treatment. *Journal of Substance Abuse Treatment, 34*, 14–24. http://dx.doi.org/10.1016/j.jsat.2006.12.031

Children's Defense Fund. (2007). *The cradle to prison pipeline*. Retrieved from http://www.childrensdefense.org/child-research-data-publications/data/cradle-prison-pipeline-report-2007-full-highres.html

Connor, D. F., Ford, J. D., Albert, D. B., & Doerfler, L. A. (2007). Conduct disorder subtype and comorbidity. *Annals of Clinical Psychiatry, 19*, 161–168. http://dx.doi.org/10.1080/10401230701465269

Dahlberg, L. L., Toal, S. B., & Behrens, C. B. (Eds.). (1998). *Measuring violence-related attitudes, beliefs, and behaviors among youths: A compendium of assessment tools*. Atlanta, GA: Centers for Disease Control and Prevention, National Center for Injury Prevention and Control, Division of Violence Prevention.

Dattilio, F. M., & Fromm, L. (2011). Juvenile delinquency and decertification. In E. Y. Drogin, F. M. Dattilio, R. L. Sadoff, & T. G. Gutheil (Eds.), *Handbook of forensic assessment: Psychological and psychiatric perspectives* (pp. 227–253). Hoboken, NJ: Wiley. http://dx.doi.org/10.1002/9781118093399.ch11

Eckholm, E. (2014, January 19). Juveniles facing lifelong terms despite rulings. *New York Times*. Retrieved from http://www.nytimes.com/2014/01/20/us/juveniles-facing-lifelong-terms-despite-rulings.html

Edwards, V. J., Anda, R. F., Dube, S. R., Dong, M., Chapman, D. F., & Felitti, V. J. (2005). The wide-ranging health consequences of adverse childhood experiences. In K. A. Kendall-Tackett & S. M. Giacomoni (Eds.), *Child Victimization: Maltreatment, Bullying and Dating Violence, Prevention and Intervention* (pp. 8-1–8-9). Kingston, NJ: Civic Research Institute.

Elijah W. v. Superior Court, 216 Cal. App. 4th 140, 156 Cal. Rptr. 3d 592 (2013).

Eyberg, S. M., Nelson, M. M., & Boggs, S. R. (2008). Evidence-based psychosocial treatments for children and adolescents with disruptive behavior. *Journal of Clinical Child and Adolescent Psychology, 37*, 215–237. http://dx.doi.org/10.1080/15374410701820117

Felitti, V. J., Anda, R. F., Nordenberg, D., Williamson, D. F., Spitz, A. M., Edwards, V., . . . Marks, J. S. (1998). Relationship of childhood abuse and household dysfunction to many of the leading causes of death in adults: The Adverse Childhood Experiences (ACE) Study. *American Journal of Preventive Medicine, 14*, 245–258. http://dx.doi.org/10.1016/S0749-3797(98)00017-8

Forth, A. E., Kosson, D. S., & Hare, R. D. (2003). *The Hare Psychopathy Checklist—Youth Version* (PCLR-YV). Toronto, Ontario, Canada: Multi-Health Systems.

Frick, P., & Hare, R. D. (2001). *The Antisocial Process Screening Device*. Toronto, Ontario, Canada: Multi-Health Systems.

Gavazzi, S. M., Slade, D., Buettner, C. K., Partridge, C., Yarcheck, C. M., & Andrews, D. W. (2003). Toward conceptual development and empirical measurement of global risk indicators in the lives of court-involved youth. *Psychological Reports, 92*, 599–615. http://dx.doi.org/10.2466/pr0.2003.92.2.599

Gilliam, F. D., & Iyengar, S. (1998). *The superpredator script*. Retrieved from http://www.nieman.harvard.edu/reports/article/102293/The-Superpredator-Script.aspx

Graham v. Florida, 560 U.S. 48 (2010).

Grisso, T. J. (1998). *Forensic evaluations of juveniles*. Sarasota, FL: Professional Resource Press.

Grisso, T. J., & Barnum, R. (2006). *Massachusetts Youth Screening Instrument (MAYSI-2): User's manual and technical report*. Sarasota, FL: Professional Resource Press.

Hoge, R. D., Andrews, D. A., & Leschied, A. W. (2002). *The Youth Level of Service/Case Management Inventory*. Toronto, Ontario, Canada: Multi-Health Systems.

In re Gault, 387 U.S. 1 (1967).

Iselin, A. M., & Salekin, R. T. (2008). *Risk-Sophistication-Treatment Inventory—Self Report*. Unpublished test, University of Alabama, Department of Psychology.

Jones, S., & Cauffman, E. (2008). Juvenile psychopathy and judicial decision making: An empirical analysis of an ethical dilemma. *Behavioral Sciences & the Law, 26*, 151–165. http://dx.doi.org/10.1002/bsl.792

Kent v. United States, 383 U.S. 541 (1966).

Kerig, P. K., & Becker, S. P. (2010). From internalizing to externalizing: Theoretical models of the processes linking PTSD to juvenile delinquency. In S. J. Egan (Ed.), *Posttraumatic stress disorder (PTSD): Causes, symptoms and treatment* (pp. 33–78). Hauppauge, NY: Nova Science.

Kinscherff, R. T. (2006). Forensic assessment of amenability to rehabilitation in juvenile delinquency. In G. P. Koocher & S. N. Sparta (Eds.), *Forensic assessment of children and adolescents* (pp. 311–329). New York, NY: Oxford University Press.

Kinscherff, R. T., & Grisso, T. J. (2013). Human rights violations and Standard 1.02: Intersections with human rights law and applications in juvenile capital cases. *Ethics & Behavior, 23*, 71–76. http://dx.doi.org/10.1080/10508422.2013.757963

Koenen, K. C., Fu, Q. J., Lyons, M. J., Toomey, R., Goldberg, J., Eisen, S. A., . . . Tsuang, M. (2005). Juvenile conduct disorder as a risk factor for trauma exposure and posttraumatic stress disorder. *Journal of Traumatic Stress, 18*, 23–32. http://dx.doi.org/10.1002/jts.20010

Liebenberg, L., Ungar, M., & LeBlanc, J. C. (2013). The CYRM-12: A brief measure of resilience. *Canadian Journal of Public Health, 104*, e131–e135.

Lynam, D. R., Caspi, A., Moffitt, T. E., Raine, A., Loeber, R., & Stouthamer-Loeber, M. (2005). Adolescent psychopathy and the Big Five: Results from two samples. *Journal of Abnormal Child Psychology, 33*, 431–443. http://dx.doi.org/10.1007/s10648-005-5724-0

Mahoney, K., Ford, J. D., Ko, S. J., & Siegfried, C. B. (2004). *Trauma-focused interventions for youth in the juvenile justice system*. Retrieved from https://www.ncjrs.gov/App/Publications/abstract.aspx?ID=265700

Martin, G. A. (1992). The delinquent and the juvenile court: Is there still a place for rehabilitation? *University of Connecticut Law Review, 25*, 57–88.

Meyers, K., McLellan, A. T., Jaeger, J. L., & Pettinati, H. M. (1995). The development of the Comprehensive Addiction Severity Index for Adolescents (CASI-A): An interview for assessing multiple problems of adolescents. *Journal of Substance Abuse Treatment, 12*, 181–193. http://dx.doi.org/10.1016/0740-5472(95)00009-T

Miller v. Alabama, 132 S. Ct. 2455 (2012).

Millon, T., Millon, C., Davis, R., & Grossman, S. (2006). *MCMI-III manual* (3rd ed.). Minneapolis, MN: Pearson Education.

Mosher, C., & Olds, A. (2013). *Adverse childhood experiences in a sample of Clark County juvenile probationers*. Unpublished document, Washington State University, Vancouver. Retrieved from http://www.ccyj.org/WSU%20Trauma%20Study%20n40.doc

Mulder, E., Brand, E., Bullens, R., & Van Marle, H. (2010). A classification of risk factors in serious juvenile offenders and the relation between patterns of risk factors and recidivism. *Criminal Behaviour and Mental Health, 20*, 23–38. http://dx.doi.org/10.1002/cbm.754

Mulvey, E. P., Steinberg, L., Fagan, J., Cauffman, E., Piquero, A. R., Chassin, L., . . . Losoya, S. H. (2004). Theory and research on desistance from antisocial activity among serious adolescent offenders. *Youth Violence and Juvenile Justice, 2*, 213–236. http://dx.doi.org/10.1177/1541204004265864

Nader, K., Kriegler, J. A., Blake, D. D., Pynoos, R. S., Newman, E., & Weather, F. W. (1996). *Clinician Administered PTSD Scale, Child and Adolescent Version*. White River Junction, VT: National Center for PTSD.

National Child Traumatic Stress Network. (2008). *Judges and child trauma: Findings from the National Traumatic Stress Network/National Council of Juvenile and Family Court Judges Focus Groups* (Service Systems Brief, Vol. 2, No. 2). Los Angeles, CA: Author.

New Hampshire, Title XII, RSA 169-B:24 transfer to Superior Court. (2010).

Nock, M. K., Kazdin, A. E., Hiripi, E., & Kessler, R. C. (2006). Prevalence, subtypes, and correlates of *DSM–IV* conduct disorder in the National Comorbidity Survey Replication. *Psychological Medicine, 36*, 699–710. http://dx.doi.org/10.1017/S0033291706007082

Perry, B. D. (2001). The neurodevelopmental impact of violence in childhood. In D. Schetky & E. P. Benedek (Eds.), *Textbook of child and adolescent forensic psychiatry* (pp. 221–238). Washington, DC: American Psychiatric Publishing.

Quinn, M. M., Rutherford, R. B., Leone, P. E., Osher, D. M., & Poirier, J. M. (2005). Youth with disabilities in juvenile corrections: A national survey. *Exceptional Children, 71*, 339–345. http://dx.doi.org/10.1177/001440290507100308

Rahdert, E. R. (1991). *The Adolescent Assessment/Referral System manual*. Bethesda, MD: Pacific Institute for Research and Evaluation.

Redding, R. E. (2008). *Juvenile transfer laws: An effective deterrent to delinquency?* Washington, DC: U.S. Department of Justice, Office of Juvenile Justice and Delinquency Prevention.

Rockett, J. L., Murrie, D. C., & Boccacini, M. T. (2007). Diagnostic labeling in juvenile justice settings: Do psychopathy and conduct disorder findings influence clinicians? *Psychological Services, 4*, 107–122. http://dx.doi.org/10.1037/1541-1559.4.2.107

Roper v. Simmons, 543 U.S. 551 (2005).

Salekin, R. T. (2004). *Risk-Sophistication-Treatment Inventory (RSTI) professional manual*. Odessa, FL: Psychological Assessment Resources.

Salekin, R. T. (2006). Psychopathy in children and adolescents: Key issues in conceptualization and assessment. In C. J. Patrick (Ed.), *Handbook of psychopathy* (pp. 389–414). New York, NY: Guilford Press.

Salekin, R. T., Rogers, R., & Ustad, K. L. (2001). Juvenile waiver to adult criminal courts: Prototypes for dangerousness, sophistication-maturity, and amenability to treatment. *Psychology, Public Policy, and Law, 7*, 381–408. http://dx.doi.org/10.1037/1076-8971.7.2.381

Salekin, R. T., Tippey, J. G., & Allen, A. D. (2012). Treatment of conduct problem youth with interpersonal callous traits using mental models: Measurement of risk and change. *Behavioral Sciences & the Law, 30*, 470–486. http://dx.doi.org/10.1002/bsl.2025

Salekin, R. T., Yff, R. A., Neumann, C. S., Leistico, A. R., & Zalot, A. A. (2002). Juvenile transfer to adult courts: A look at the prototypes for dangerousness, sophistication-maturity, and amenability to treatment through a legal lens. *Psychology, Public Policy, and Law, 8*, 373–410. http://dx.doi.org/10.1037/1076-8971.8.4.373

Schubert, C. A., Mulvey, E. P., Loughran, T. A., Fagan, J., Chassin, L. A., Piquero, A. R., . . . Cauffman, E. (2010). Predicting outcomes for youth transferred to adult court. *Law and Human Behavior, 34*, 460–475. http://dx.doi.org/10.1007/s10979-009-9209-5

Shandra, C. L., & Hogan, D. P. (2012). Delinquency among adolescents with disabilities. *Child Indicators Research, 5*, 771–788.

Shufelt, J., & Cocozza, J. (2006). *Youth with mental health disorders in the juvenile justice system: Results from a multi-state prevalence study*. Delmar, NY: National Center for Mental Health and Juvenile Justice.

Steinberg, A. M., Brymer, M., Decker, K., & Pynoos, R. S. (2004). The University of California at Los Angeles posttraumatic stress disorder reaction index. *Current Psychiatry Reports, 6*, 96–100. http://dx.doi.org/10.1007/s11920-004-0048-2

Steinberg, L. (2009). Should the science of adolescent brain development inform public policy? *American Psychologist, 64*, 739–750. http://dx.doi.org/10.1037/0003-066X.64.8.739

Steinberg, L., & Scott, E. S. (2003). Less guilty by reason of adolescence: Developmental immaturity, diminished responsibility, and the juvenile death penalty. *American Psychologist, 58*, 1009–1018. http://dx.doi.org/10.1037/0003-066X.58.12.1009

Stewart, R. E., & Chambless, D. L. (2010). Interesting practitioners in training in empirically supported treatments: Research reviews versus case studies. *Journal of Clinical Psychology, 66*, 73–95.

Teicher, M. H., Andersen, S. L., Polcari, A., Anderson, C. M., & Navalta, C. P. (2002). Developmental neurobiology of childhood stress and trauma. *Psychiatric Clinics of North America, 25*, 397–426, vii–viii. http://dx.doi.org/10.1016/S0193-953X(01)00003-X

Teplin, L. A., Abram, K. M., McClelland, G. M., Dulcan, M. K., & Mericle, A. A. (2002). Psychiatric disorders in youth in juvenile detention. *Archives of General Psychiatry, 59*, 1133–1143. http://dx.doi.org/10.1001/archpsyc.59.12.1133

van der Kolk, B. A. (2005). Developmental trauma disorder. *Psychiatric Annals, 35*, 401–408.

Vitacco, M., & Salekin, R. T. (2013). Adolescent psychopathy and the law. In K. A. Kiehl & W. P. Sinnott-Armstrong (Eds.), *Handbook of psychopathy and law* (pp. 78–89). New York, NY: Oxford University Press.

Wasserman, G. A., McReynolds, L. S., Lucas, C. P., Fisher, P., & Santos, L. (2002). The Voice DISC-IV with incarcerated male youths: Prevalence of disorder. *Journal of the American Academy of Child & Adolescent Psychiatry, 41*, 314–321. http://dx.doi.org/10.1097/00004583-200203000-00011

Wasserman, G. A., McReynolds, L. S., Schwalbe, C. S., Keating, J. M., & Jones, S. A. (2010). Psychiatric disorder, comorbidity, and suicidal behavior in juvenile justice youth. *Criminal Justice and Behavior, 37*, 1361–1376. http://dx.doi.org/10.1177/0093854810382751

CHAPTER 19

DEVELOPMENTAL MATURITY AND SOPHISTICATION–MATURITY: LEARNING MORE ABOUT ITS PURPOSE AND ASSESSMENT

Randall T. Salekin, Emily A. M. MacDougall, and Natalie A. Harrison

Key legal cases transpiring over the past decade have highlighted the importance of developmental maturity and its role in the juvenile and adult legal systems. Specifically, in *Roper v. Simmons* (2005), the death penalty was removed as an option for juvenile offenders, in part because of concerns regarding adolescents' developmental maturity. Similarly, in *Graham v. Florida* (2010), life without parole for nonhomicide cases was eliminated, and in *Miller v. Alabama* (2012), mandatory life without parole for homicide cases was eliminated. These latter decisions stemmed from concerns related to developmental maturity. Landmark legal cases have changed the way in which juvenile offenders are handled in the U.S. legal system and have underscored the importance of developmental maturity. Despite the centrality of this construct, considerable confusion still exists regarding the meaning of developmental maturity as it pertains to adolescents and the law.

Our aim in this chapter is to further illuminate the understanding of developmental maturity. To meet this goal, several questions need to be answered:

1. When is developmental maturity relevant, and what is its purpose?
2. What are the defining features of developmental maturity?
3. What instrumentation is available to measure developmental maturity?
4. What is the best timing for the assessment of developmental maturity?
5. What is the future of the developmental maturity assessment?

With these questions in mind, we had five primary aims. First, we begin with a brief history of the relevance of the developmental maturity concept, highlighting its significance from the initiation of the juvenile justice system to its present-day purpose. In this section, we also discuss the term *developmental maturity* as a general construct and then delineate how the construct applies to the law and becomes the term *sophistication–maturity*. Second, we review information pertaining to the defining features and structure of the developmental maturity concept. Third, we discuss the measurement of developmental maturity. Fourth, we cover the important issue of the timing of testing for the assessment of developmental maturity. Finally, we highlight the need for future work in this area. In the section below, we begin with a discussion of the historical relevance of the developmental maturity concept.

HISTORICAL RELEVANCE OF DEVELOPMENTAL MATURITY

The juvenile justice system was founded on the belief that youths lacked developmental maturity and full criminal intent and that children should be rehabilitated because they are still in their formative years, with their life chances still intact (Chen & Salekin, 2012; Sacks & Reader, 1992; Schetky & Benedek, 1980, 1985, 1992; Scott & Grisso, 1997). Despite the rehabilitative focus of the juvenile justice

http://dx.doi.org/10.1037/14643-019
APA Handbook of Psychology and Juvenile Justice, K. Heilbrun (Editor-in-Chief)

system, the courts have always recognized that some youths have greater levels of maturity than others. In fact, since the inception of the juvenile justice system there has always been an option for removing from the justice system those youths who were viewed as hardened, chronic, or sophisticated. In *Kent v. United States* (1966), Supreme Court Justice Abe Fortas observed that developmental maturity ought to be considered along with risk and amenability to treatment when deciding whether to transfer young people to adult court. Since this Supreme Court ruling, developmental maturity, along with risk and amenability, has been explicitly listed in numerous state statutes for transfer.

The relevance of the developmental maturity construct appears to be interpretable at three levels. First, developmental maturity is relevant on a very broad level when considering the maturity differences between adolescents and adults who come into contact with the law. The relevance of developmental maturity here is to recognize that adolescents are less mature than adults and to provide a developmentally sensitive system that allows for prosocial growth. Second, as seen in the cases of *Roper v. Simmons* (2005), *Graham v. Florida* (2010), and *Miller v. Alabama* (2012), the contribution of developmental maturity is also to create fairness in the legal and decision-making process and to reduce punishment for juvenile offenders. Third, developmental maturity is relevant when the juvenile court is making disposition recommendations, including the potential for transfer. This is when "mature" participants can be waived to adult court. These perspectives reflect the notion that adolescents as a group are less mature than adults while simultaneously acknowledging the considerable variability in adolescent developmental maturity.

Although the relevance of juvenile maturity is rather clear, what is less clear is the specific connection between developmental maturity and culpability (see Fischer, Stein, & Heikkinen, 2009; Grisso & Vierling, 1978; *Hodgson v. Minnesota*, 1990; *Roper v. Simmons*, 2005). In two Supreme Court cases (*Hodgson v. Minnesota*, 1990; *Roper v. Simmons*, 2005), two different pictures of adolescents were painted regarding adolescent decision making—one that described the mature adolescent decision maker and the other that described the immature adolescent decision maker.

The two perspectives raise a number of questions. What is developmental maturity? To what degree do young people possess it? What level of developmental maturity is needed to navigate early life effectively while holding tightly to one's moral compass? In terms of research, this latter question has been queried for many years but perhaps most vigorously over the past decade (e.g., Fischer et al., 2009; Steinberg, Cauffman, Woolard, Graham, & Banich, 2009). We cannot fully answer this complex question in a single chapter. Instead, for the purposes of this chapter, we assume that adolescents as a class possess some maturity and rely on the same theory presented in *Hodgson v. Minnesota* (1990) to support this notion. However, this assumption is made with the caveat that additional factors (e.g., psychopathology) explain the variance in youth developmental maturity delineated above. In terms of the final legal decision, the law typically determines what quantity, or level, of developmental maturity is required for various decisions, although psychology may be able to facilitate these decisions and help shape policy in the future, making the conversation and research regarding developmental maturity a worthy pursuit.

One final critical issue in discussing the relevance of developmental maturity is the relevance of sophistication–maturity, which is not to be mistaken for developmental maturity. Although up to this point we have used the term developmental maturity, the term sophistication–maturity has commonly been used in legal contexts as a psycholegal concept. This raises the question of the relevance of sophistication–maturity. Does sophistication–maturity sufficiently vary from developmental maturity, or is it the same thing? From our reading of the literature, the answer to this query is that it does vary and it is, indeed, different. However, we should note that sophistication–maturity can be interpreted in several ways. First, some legal scholars refer to sophistication–maturity to signify the sophisticated adolescent offender. This type of adolescent offender breaks the law knowingly and with some complexity (e.g., involved in the planning and execution of the crime). Second, others have used the term to reflect the two sides of the maturity coin—namely, criminal sophistication and prosocial behavior. Developmental maturity, however, simply reflects the maturity of an adolescent, over time, irrespective of the adolescent's potential involvement with the law. For the purposes of this chapter, we use the term developmental maturity or maturity because research on this topic (e.g., Salekin, Yff, Neumann, Leistico, & Zalot, 2002) has suggested that a third variable (criminal identity or thinking or, e.g., psychopathy) moderates developmental maturity to make this version of maturity criminal sophistication versus prosocial maturity.

In summary, the concept of developmental maturity is highly relevant to young people involved with the legal system. For example, developmental maturity is considered pertinent when deciding on appropriate treatment programs for youths, when considering the risk a youth may pose or be exposed to in certain treatment facilities, and when examining treatment outcome in which maturity such as perspective taking and emotional regulation is expected to change.

Developmental maturity's relevance is at a heightened level when considering transfer and sentencing in adult courts. So important is the construct of developmental maturity that it is likely also applicable in an even larger number of other legal issues and areas in juvenile and adult courts. In fact, it is difficult to imagine that developmental maturity is not considered at every level of juvenile justice decision making, including decisions regarding Miranda, competence, eyewitness testimony, dependency cases, and other child-related legal issues. Although the relevance and purpose of developmental maturity have been increasingly well articulated, the defining features of the construct have, unfortunately, not always been clear.

DEFINING FEATURES OF DEVELOPMENTAL MATURITY

Some researchers have considered delinquent behavior to be a normative component of adolescent development, with delinquency part of the defining criteria for maturity and adolescence. Specifically, adolescence often includes raging hormones, pimples, numerous embarrassing moments, and law violation. Under this argument, delinquency should not be a common feature of childhood or adulthood but rather a common feature of adolescence that ceases naturally through the process of maturation (Baumrind, 1987; Moffitt, 1993; Scott & Grisso, 1997). Moffitt (1993) proposed a maturity gap thesis that states that there are two distinct categories of juveniles who demonstrate offending behavior: life course persistent and adolescent limited. The life-course-persistent category includes individuals who demonstrate various antisocial behaviors at every life stage because of a pathological personality that stems from childhood neuropsychological problems and a criminogenic environment. In contrast, a larger group of individuals lie within the adolescent-limited category; these youths commit antisocial behavior solely during adolescence. The adolescent-limited trajectory thus suggests that delinquency during adolescence is normal, resulting from a maturation process that encourages adolescents to demonstrate antisocial behavior in adaptive ways (Moffitt, 1993). According to this thesis, most offending does not persist past adolescence, and not all adolescents will commit antisocial behavior.

However, not all youths who are categorized into the two groups follow the expected trajectories. That is, research has shown that many adolescent-limited offenders continue on with their criminal activity well into adulthood. Similarly, many chronic offenders (early starters) desist in adolescence or early adulthood. These recent findings have raised some concerns regarding the accuracy of large-scale class distinctions (e.g., adolescent limited vs. life course persistent, or even adolescent vs. adult). More important, Moffitt (1993; Jennings & Reingle, 2012; Piquero & Moffitt, 2010) acknowledged that several proposed factors, some of which hint at developmental maturity, may protect against delinquent behavior. These factors include delayed puberty, access to roles that are respected by adults, environments that limit learning about delinquency, and personal characteristics. These factors align with the earlier views noted by G. Stanley Hall (1904) and more modern views delineated by Kazdin (2000), which outline a more nuanced perspective regarding developmental maturity in adolescence. Below, we review several contemporary definitions of maturity as they pertain to the law.

Specific Definitions of Developmental Maturity

The law is not always clear when it comes to defining concepts used in rendering legal decisions. Psychology and psychiatry have also not perfected their science in arriving at precise definitions of various concepts, as can be seen in the numerous versions of the *Diagnostic and Statistical Manual of Mental Disorders* and the *International Classification of Diseases*, with the fifth edition of the former recently having been released (American Psychiatric Association, 2013) and 11th version of the latter on the horizon. Some thoughtful attempts to define maturity in the psychological literature have since been used to consider maturity within the law. We cover three major attempts, which include both rational and empirical development efforts, in the paragraphs below.

Greenberger and Sørenson (1974): Psychosocial maturity. One psychological framework developed in the early 1970s attempted to understand the relationship between maturity and juvenile offending by referring to youths' psychosocial maturity, or challenges faced by youths as they develop into successful adults (Greenberger & Sørenson, 1974). According to Greenberger and Sørensen (1974), psychosocial maturity is made up of (a) individual adequacy, (b) interpersonal adequacy, and (c) social adequacy. Individual adequacy was described as being composed of self-reliance, identity, and work orientation. Interpersonal adequacy consisted of communication skills, what the authors referred to as "enlightened trust," and knowledge of major roles (e.g., role-appropriate behavior). Social adequacy contains social commitment, openness to sociopolitical change, and tolerance of individuals and cultural differences.

Greenberger and Sørensen's (1974) outline of maturity offers an excellent description of maturity; in many respects, however, some of its components (e.g., social maturity) do not easily apply to justice-involved youths and may also be difficult to fully apply in juvenile justice settings because youths who are in contact with the law automatically score low on social aspects of the maturity scale. Within the Greenberger and Sørensen model are numerous subfactors such as social commitment, openness to sociopolitical change, and tolerance of individual and cultural differences that would be more applicable to developmental maturity in prosocial youths but not antisocial youths. Such items might be appropriate to consider as intervention targets.

Important to the theory, however, is the notion of judgment. Specifically, according to Greenberger and Sørensen (1974), psychosocial immaturity in adolescents typically presents as misguided judgment, or an inability to make decisions based on their own inclinations and principles. Since Greenberger and Sorensen initially outlined their psychosocial maturity model, several researchers have attempted to further refine the concept of maturity of judgment as it pertains to adolescent judgment (Reppucci, 1999; Scott, Reppucci, & Woolard, 1995; Steinberg & Cauffman, 1996). One theory postulates that various social and environmental factors contribute to a youth's inability to make a mature judgment—specifically, decreased risk perception, poor future-time perspective, and increased peer influence (Scott et al., 1995). Another theory similarly postulated that several factors contribute to maturity of judgment, including responsibility, temperance, and perspective (Steinberg & Cauffman, 1996). We provide an overview of this model next.

Steinberg and Cauffman (1996). Steinberg and Cauffman (1996) built on the work of Greenberger and Sørenson (1974) and Scott et al. (1995). Their article focused on the maturity of judgment, examining theory and research on three aspects of mature judgment termed (a) responsibility, (b) temperance, and (c) perspective. *Responsibility* was defined as healthy autonomy, self-reliance, and clarity of identity. *Temperance* was defined as the ability to limit impulsivity and avoid the extremes in decision making and to evaluate a situation thoroughly before acting, including seeking advice from adults when appropriate. *Perspective* was defined as being able to acknowledge the complexity of a situation and to frame a specific decision within a larger context. According to Steinberg and Cauffman, these dispositions comprise the attitudes most often associated with mature decision making in the literature on adolescent psychological development (cf. Greenberger & Sørensen, 1974; Irwin & Millstein, 1992). Although maturity of judgment is an important concept to investigate when examining developmental maturity, it should be noted that the act of mature judgment is an outcome that is produced by those who are developmentally mature (those high in developmental maturity could also make poor decisions, but such decisions would likely be less frequent). For this reason, it continues to be important to examine the concept of developmental maturity as a psychological concept rather than solely on the behavior it produces.

As with adults, adolescents' judgment could well be sound most of the time, but a set of circumstances, such as being late for a planned event, might cause an adolescent to speed excessively and be ticketed for his or her violation or, worse, drive home drunk and crash into another motorist. Similar examples could be raised with adults. For example, after working late an adult might decide to drive excessively fast to arrive on time to his or her daughter's dance recital, potentially hitting and even injuring another motorist. These examples illustrate how examination of the concept of developmental maturity may be different than judgment. Thus, it is necessary to underscore the importance of considering the frequency of good and bad decision making on the basis of autonomy, cognition, and emotion regulation skills.

Factor-Analytic and Prototype Studies

Grisso, Tomkins, and Casey (1988) conducted one of the earliest studies on the psychosocial concepts in juvenile law. Specifically, they attempted to clarify the types of information about juveniles and their families that are relevant for three types of juvenile decisions: the pretrial detention of juveniles, their transfer for trial in criminal court, and disposition decisions after delinquency adjudication. With regard to developmental maturity, their factor-analytic study produced items that included sophistication, maturity, adultlike physical characteristics, self-reliance, cool and composed, and knowledge of the street (street survival). Although the first two items do not add much to the defining feature of maturity, the last three do because they reflect autonomy, effective decision making (in the streets), and emotion regulation. This definition provided by court personnel removed the element of prosocial development from their view of maturity, perhaps because prosocial development is absent or limited in some justice-involved youths or may be viewed as irrelevant. Thus, the juvenile court appeared to be interested in a maturity that applied to youths in the legal system that did not necessarily pertain to prosocial functioning but rather to whether the young person was a mature participant at the time of the offense and at the time of assessment, regardless of his or her antisocial versus prosocial path.

Building on the work of Grisso et al. (1988), Salekin, Rogers, and Ustad (2001) provided additional empirical data on the core criteria that underpin the developmental maturity construct by using prototypical analysis studies (e.g., Salekin, 2002a, 2002b; Salekin et al., 2002). Prototypical analysis studies offer one way to clarify vague constructs. Rosch (1978), in his seminal monograph, outlined the importance and methodology for prototype research. Specifically, Rosch offered, for example, color as one way to illustrate the ways in which prototype studies can determine the most representative or prototypical color. As Rosch put it, there are numerous versions of the color green, yet through prototype research the most typical green can be determined. This is true for physical objects as well, such as bicycles, and mental or psychological concepts, such as developmental maturity. Thus, prototypical analysis provides key information on the items that experts believe are most central, core, or primary to the concept. By identifying the clearest case of a construct, individuals can eventually be assessed on the prototype (Broughton, 1990; Broughton, Boyes, & Mitchell, 1993; Broughton, Trapnell, & Boyes, 1991).

In two separate studies, Salekin and colleagues examined the prototypical characteristics of developmental maturity (Salekin, Rogers, & Ustad, 2001; Salekin et al., 2002). First, psychologists (n = 244) from the Society of Clinical Child and Adolescent Psychology (Division 53) of the American Psychological Association were asked to rate the core characteristics of developmental maturity. In addition, forensic diplomates ($n = 75$) were asked to provide prototypical ratings of juveniles whom they had evaluated and who were subsequently transferred to adult court. Through this investigation, the participating experts helped the researchers identify core characteristics that were associated with developmental maturity, as well as characteristics that were prototypical of youths transferred to adult courts.

In a second prototypical analytic study, Salekin et al. (2002) asked juvenile court judges from the National Council of Juvenile and Family Court Judges to provide their perspective regarding the core criteria for developmental maturity in adolescents. Using mean ratings and the use of exploratory and confirmatory factor-analytic procedures, they reported that three factors for developmental maturity emerged and best fit the data: (a) autonomy, (b) cognitive skills, and (c) emotional skills. The items that made up each of the factors are seen in Exhibit 19.1.

Interestingly, some of the characteristics that were considered part of the criminal sophistication component of maturity (e.g., having criminal sophistication, capable of planned and premeditated crime, able to get others to do what they want, outwardly conforming but manipulative) fit better with a Risk for Dangerousness superordinate factor. Thus, in the confirmatory factor-analytic analyses, the only way to achieve adequate model fit was to have sophistication–maturity load on the Risk for Dangerousness factor. This was true for both the judge sample and the clinical child psychologist sample. In this way, criminal sophistication appeared within the realm of risk, or between risk and developmental maturity, where it is a mix of risk items and sophistication–maturity items that likely highly overlap with one another. Conceptually, this may also mean that some additional factor, such as psychopathy or criminal thinking patterns, moderates developmental maturity (Salekin, Rogers, & Ustad, 2001; Salekin et al., 2002). Further evidence regarding this perspective can also be seen in the Grisso et al. (1988) study, in which items such as "hard-core criminal personality" loaded on an Antisocial factor that tapped "prior contacts with the law." This factor appeared to reflect the chronicity of antisocial behavior, suggesting a more seasoned offender.

Exhibit 19.1
Core Characteristics of Developmental Maturity

Autonomy
- Able to resist pressures from others
- Internal locus of control
- Maintains convictions even when criticized
- Resourceful
- Absence of excessive need for social validation
- Clarity of self-concept
- Consideration of life goals
- High self esteem
- Open to periods of reevaluation and incorporation
- Aware of personal strengths and weaknesses

Cognitive capacities
- Able to think abstractly
- Ability to identify alternative actions and consequences
- Has the ability to switch goals
- Has future time perspective (projects)
- Goal-setting behaviors
- Engages in cost–benefit analysis
- Deals with others' feelings effectively
- Ability to analyze and understand relations
- Makes clear requests

Emotional skills
- Clear about values and priorities
- Psychological insight
- Aware of mood and thoughts about mood
- Develops realistic expectations of self
- Is able to consult others for advice
- Knows and manages own feelings well
- Delays gratification in pursuit of goals
- Able to cope with frustrations
- Generally open to change
- Intentionality and acts with competence and persistence
- Able to regulate emotions

Taken together, the studies from Greenberger and Sørensen (1974), Grisso et al. (1988), Steinberg and Cauffman (1996), and Salekin and colleagues (Salekin, 2002c; Salekin, Rogers, & Ustad, 2001) have provided further clarity on the concept of developmental maturity, suggesting that three factors—Autonomy, Cognitive Skills, and Emotional Skills—best capture, and thus underpin, developmental maturity. To illustrate the convergence of the models, it can be seen that the Steinberg and Cauffman model (a theoretical three-factor model) maps onto the empirically derived trifactor model for developmental maturity yielded in the Salekin et al. studies (e.g., Salekin et al., 2002). Specifically, these facets can be mapped onto the trifactor model of maturity, with the Salekin model's autonomy being similar to the Steinberg and Cauffman model's responsibility. The Salekin model's cognitive capacities would be similar to the Steinberg model's perspective. Finally, the Salekin model's emotion regulation skills would be similar to the Steinberg and Cauffman model's temperance component. These factors also loosely align with Greenberger and Sørensen, but to a lesser degree because of the inclusion of the Prosocial scale and items that make up the third factor of the Greenberger and Sørensen model (see Table 19.1).

The close alignment of these three models shows the considerable convergence between the important constructs that underpin developmental maturity. Moreover, Steinberg and Cauffman's (1996) model originated from a review of theory (top-down) whereas the trifactor model derived from investigations in Salekin's laboratory was obtained through empirical research (bottom-up) and the use of expert raters, giving the model even further credence. Because the concepts offer greater clarity to clinicians and court personnel, they are likely to better inform juvenile disposition and transfer evaluations, thereby addressing some of the concerns raised by Johnson Niarhos and Routh (1992), Provorse and Sarata (1989), and Hecker and Steinberg (2002) to the effect that psychologists were not addressing pertinent questions, primarily because they were not assessing pertinent constructs. Although both sets of terms would be useful for the courts, the terms *autonomy*, *cognitive capacities*, and *emotion regulation* might be most easily understood across a range of professionals.

BIOLOGICAL ASPECTS OF MATURITY: WHAT IS KNOWN, AND HOW MUCH MATURITY IS NEEDED?

With respect to the physiology of maturity, we now know that the myelination and pruning process has an impact on developmental maturity. Considerable research has shown that youths continue to develop myelin sheaths for brain neurons and that the myelinated neurons in the brain increase from childhood until roughly age 26 years (Giedd, 2004; Paus, 2005). Research has also shown that a pruning process occurs whereby neurons are pruned back over the developmental years. This process also facilitates decision making and forethought (Giedd, 2004; Gogtay et al., 2004; Paus, 2005). In fact, the pruning process is thought to play a major role in the development, shaping, and sculpting of neural circuits.

Although age and maturation are related, there is clearly variation in youths' developmental maturity. Some adolescents during this period are highly creative, engage in student government, and become competent musicians and athletes. Other youths embrace reading and scholastics and the arts. These examples suggest that adolescence, as a class, is not synonymous with poor judgment in a real-world environment. Adolescents take many different life paths, with some showing autonomy, integrity, emotion regulation, and increasingly sound decision

TABLE 19.1

Developmental Maturity: Converging Top-Down and Bottom-Up Models

Greenberger & Sørensen (1974)	Salekin (2001, 2002c; bottom-up development)	Steinberg and Cauffman (1996; top-down development)
Individual adequacy	Autonomy	Responsibility
Interpersonal adequacy	Cognitive capacities	Perspective
Social adequacy	Emotion regulation skills	Temperance

Note. Adapted from *Forensic Evaluation and Treatment of Juveniles: Innovation and Best Practice* (p. 82), by R. T. Salekin, 2015, Washington, DC: American Psychological Association. Copyright 2015 by the American Psychological Association.

making and others making less sound, and sometimes impulsive, decisions for a host of reasons.

Developmental maturity can also be impaired by many of the deficits that are often seen in juvenile offender populations, including family dysfunction, learning deficits, mental illness, and poverty. This makes the inclusion of other relevant factors besides age important in the consideration of developmental maturity, and it likely makes the discussion of biology and maturity much more nuanced and complex. Moreover, the development of maturity may well have to do with the many new neural connections that occur daily—and it is particularly influenced by whether the structures of the brain are healthily developed, or underdeveloped, for one's age (Salekin, 2015).

Variations in developmental maturity may be related to the socioemotional learning that occurs over early child and adolescent development. Therefore, issues such as sustained attention and conscientiousness, warmth, kindness, and cooperation are factors that can likely be trained into youth to enhance brain development and subsequent decision making and improve levels of developmental maturity (Giedd et al., 1999, 2011; Gogtay et al., 2004; Lebel & Beaulieu, 2011), further highlighting the importance of indexing developmental maturity in youths.

The research foundation and theory regarding developmental maturity would suggest that mental health professionals should consider issues such as moral reasoning and the development of conscience. These are factors that could well be enhanced by building traits such as consideration, warmth, and kindness. The extent to which young people develop in a social versus antisocial manner may have to do with the emotional valence of some of the neural connections that consequently affect their decision making. Thus, in terms of understanding the young person's level of developmental maturity, it can be helpful to assess the level of correspondence between the young person's level of moral development and his or her behavior.

Fried and Reppucci (2001) conducted a study that shed further light on this perspective. Specifically, they reviewed maturity of judgment factors: temporal perspective, peer influence, and risk perception. They found that detained youths were more likely to think of the future-oriented consequences (i.e., take perspective) of engaging in a delinquent act than were nondetained youths and were also less likely to anticipate pressure from their friends than were nondetained youths. Furthermore, Fried and Reppucci found some age-based effects for temporal perspective, peer influence, and risk perception, in which younger and older adolescents on a U-shaped age continuum displayed greater maturity than those in the middle of the continuum (see also Mulvey & Peeples, 1996).

Research has also shown that psychosocial development may increase an adolescent's risk for offending (Chung, Little, & Steinberg, 2005). Indeed, maturity factors have been found to have an impact on antisocial decision making, including an adolescent's proclivity to sell or use illegal drugs and commit minor delinquent acts (Barnes & Beaver, 2010; Cauffman & Steinberg, 2000; Little & Steinberg, 2006). Moreover, specific maturity variables are linked to predicting delinquency; one study has suggested that temperance significantly predicted violent, nonviolent, and total delinquent behavior among boys (Cruise et al., 2008). In this study, *temperance* referred to the ability to control impulsivity and think before acting. However, temperance is likely predictive of both positive and negative outcomes depending on environment.

With the removal of prosocial items (e.g., social commitment) and items related to work or family functioning as well as sociopolitical view, the description of maturity for the law may be somewhat less based on what young people are specifically doing and more on how they are doing it (regulated and thoughtful actions). Thus, with a definition of developmental maturity that is based on autonomy, cognitive skills, and emotion skills, it is not required that one focus on whether the behavior is prosocial or antisocial at any particular time. Rather, the law is more likely interested in this issue of regulation and the extent to which youths thought about their actions before engaging in them. With greater clarity regarding the juvenile justice system's conception of developmental maturity, the question is raised,

What measures are available to tap developmental maturity?

MEASUREMENT OF DEVELOPMENTAL MATURITY

In the following sections, we cover several self-report measures that have been developed for the assessment of developmental maturity. In addition, we review the Risk–Sophistication–Treatment Inventory (RSTI; Salekin, 2004) interview and rating scale on the basis of developmental maturity measures.

Self-Report Measures of Developmental Maturity

Within the empirical literature, some commonly used measures of developmental maturity and maturity of judgment among adolescent offenders are the Psychosocial Maturity Inventory Form D (PSMI; Greenberger, Josselson, Knerr, & Knerr, 1975), the Weinberger Adjustment Inventory (WAI; Weinberger & Schwartz, 1990), the Consideration of Future Consequences Scale (CFCS; Strathman, Gleicher, Boninger, & Edwards; 1994), the Stanford Time Perspective Inventory (STPI; Zimbardo, 1990), and the Criminal Decision Making Questionnaire (Goldberg, 2007). These measures, although they attempt to tap aspects of developmental maturity, are different in some regard, and careful examination of the item content, factors assessed, and psychometric properties offered is essential before using such measures in the assessment. These measures are covered in some detail below.

The PSMI is a 30-item self-report inventory that assesses various dimensions of personal responsibility on a 4-point Likert scale (ranging from 1 = *strongly agree* to 4 = *strongly disagree*). These dimensions are self-reliance (i.e., feelings of internal control and the ability to make decisions without extreme reliance on others), identity (i.e., self-esteem, clarity of the self, and consideration of life goals), and work orientation (i.e., pride in the successful completion of tasks). This measure has some similarities and overlaps with the constructs of developmental maturity mentioned above. Work orientation, however, is more likely to be endorsed by youths from prosocial backgrounds. Research has shown the measure to be reliable and valid in some studies (e.g., Cauffman & Steinberg, 2000; Colwell et al., 2005).

Several studies have used the PSMI Personal Responsibility subscale to measure the maturity of judgment Responsibility factor (Cauffman & Steinberg, 2000; Colwell et al., 2005; Cruise et al., 2008; Modecki, 2008). Other PSMI subscales (namely the Identity and Self-Reliance subscales) have been used to examine autonomy, one of four maturational dispositions that include future orientation (Little & Steinberg, 2006). Another study viewed responsibility as being composed of two components: personal responsibility as measured by the PSMI scale and resistance to peer influence as measured by the Resistance to Peer Influence (RPI; Monahan, Steinberg, Cauffman, & Mulvey, 2009; Steinberg & Monahan, 2007).

Resistance to peer influence has also been individually examined as a maturational disposition via the RPI (Little & Steinberg, 2006). The RPI includes 10 items that assess the degree to which adolescents act autonomously while interacting with peers. Participants choose one of two conflicting statements that most closely characterizes their behavior, then rate the degree to which the statement is accurate on a 4-point scale (ranging from 1 [*really false*] to 4 [*really true*]). According to the literature, the RPI appears to have shown reliability and validity (Steinberg & Monahan, 2007).

The WAI is another commonly used self-report measure developed to assess self-restraint and emotional distress. Items are presented on a 5-point Likert-type scale (ranging from 1 = *almost never* to 5 = *almost always*) and make up two superordinate dimensions, subjective experience of distress and self-restraint. The self-restraint dimension is further broken down into four scales: Impulse Control, Suppression of Aggression, Consideration of Others, and Temperance. Concurrent and predictive validities for the WAI have been established by both cross-sectional and longitudinal research (Feldman & Weinberger, 1994; Weinberger, 1996, 1998; Weinberger & Gomes, 1995). This scale's content does not map well onto the developmental maturity concepts outlined by prototypical analysis studies.

Instead, many of the items are reflective of antisocial behavior and control. Thus, this scale would likely overlap with antisocial and risk scales.

However, to examine the maturity of judgment Temperance factor, studies have both averaged and independently analyzed scores from the WAI's Suppression of Aggression and Impulse Control subscales (Cauffman & Steinberg, 2000; Colwell et al., 2005; Cruise et al., 2008; Little & Steinberg, 2006; Modecki, 2008; Monahan et al., 2009). Several of the same studies that used the WAI subscales to examine temperance also averaged scores across the WAI Consideration of Others subscale and the CFCS to measure perspective (Cauffman & Steinberg, 2000; Colwell et al., 2005; Cruise et al., 2008; Modecki, 2008). Monahan et al. (2009) chose to evaluate perspective using the CFCS independently. Researchers have combined the WAI with other measures or avoided using it altogether, suggesting that it may not tap developmental maturity as clearly as such other maturity measures.

The CFCS is a 12-item questionnaire that assesses individuals' ability to consider the immediate versus distant consequences of actions and allow such perceived outcomes to influence their behavior. Examinees respond on a 5-point Likert-type scale (ranging from 1 = *extremely characteristic* to 5 = *extremely uncharacteristic*). Low CFCS scores are associated with placing a greater emphasis on immediate needs and concerns, and high CFCS scores are associated with consideration of distant goals and consequences. There is some support for the CFCS's adequate internal consistency and test–retest reliability (Petrocelli, 2003; Strathman et al., 1994). Furthermore, in some studies, the CFCS is correlated with other measures of future orientation, such as the STPI (Zimbardo, 1990).

The STPI is a 56-item measure examining the inclination of an individual to attend to long-range consequences (e.g., "When I want to achieve something, I set goals and consider specific means for reaching those goals"). The questionnaire contains five subscales: Future, Present-Fatalistic, Past-Positive, Present-Hedonistic, and Past-Negative. Various studies have supported this measure's reliability and validity for the assessment of temporal perspective through experimental research (Zimbardo & Boyd, 1999). Fried and Reppucci (2001) examined temporal perspective using this measure.

The 15-item Future Outlook Inventory is another measure of maturity of judgment factors. It was developed by Cauffman and Woolard (1999), using items from the Life Orientation Task (Scheier & Carver, 1985), Zimbardo's (1990) STPI, and the CFCS. Subjects taking the Future Outlook Inventory indicate the degree to which each statement reflects how they usually are (e.g., "I will keep working at difficult, boring tasks if I know they will help me get ahead later"). Each statement is ranked on a scale ranging from 1 to 4 (1 = *never true*; 4 = *always true*), on which higher scores demonstrate a greater degree of future consideration and planning. This inventory has been used to examine both future orientation and perspective in adolescent offenders (Little & Steinberg, 2006; Monahan et al., 2009).

Finally, the RSTI Self-Report (RSTI–SR) is a newly developed self-report scale that includes a Developmental Maturity scale. The Developmental Maturity scale has three clusters: autonomy, cognitive skills, and emotion regulation–skills. The items are rated on a 3-point scale (0 = *no*, 1 = *some*, 2 = *yes*). The RSTI–SR has been shown to have reliability and validity in previous studies (Ang, Salekin, Sellbom, & Lee, 2014; Lee, Salekin, & Iselin, 2010; Salekin, Tippey, & Allen, 2012).

The aforementioned measures are self-report instruments of developmental maturity that appear to be effective at measuring some aspects of developmental maturity or behaviors that would be related to maturity (e.g., ability to resist peer influence). Table 19.2 provides information on the degree to which the measures tap autonomy, cognitive skills, and emotional skills. In addition, information on reliability and validity is provided for each of the measures. To our knowledge, the vast majority of these measures have been used exclusively in research. Thus, one should be cautious when examining the measures to see whether they have sound reliability and good validity data and that they have been used with the population of interest. This information should then guide clinicians in the determination of whether the measure

TABLE 19.2

Self-Report Measures for Developmental Maturity or Aspects of Maturity

Measure	Brief description	Subscales	Psychometric properties	Correspondence with prototypical studies
CDMQ (Goldberg, 2007)	Criminal thinking scale	None	Not known	Fit with criminal sophistication
CFCS (Strathman, Gleicher, Boninger, & Edwards, 1994)	12-item self-report questionnaire	None	Acceptable reliability and validity (Strathman et al., 1994)	Partial cognitive skills; emotional skills are tied to delay of gratification
FOI (Cauffman & Woolard, 1999)	15-item measure measuring how well adolescents weigh long- and short-term goals, using items from the Life Orientation Task (Scheier & Carver, 1985), the Zimbardo Time Perspective Scale (Zimbardo & Boyd, 1999), and the CFCS (Strathman et al., 1994)	None	Unpublished test	Partial cognitive skills, focusing solely on future consideration and planning
PSMI (Greenberger, Josselson, Knerr, & Knerr, 1975)	30-item self-report inventory of psychosocial maturity	Three subscales including Self-Reliance, Identity, and Work Orientation	Acceptable psychometric properties, including good internal consistency and validity (Greenberger & Bond, 1976)	Partial (2 of 3), in terms of autonomy and cognitive skills; emotional skills are not adequately assessed because the items are tied to prosocial activities
ZTPI (Zimbardo, 1990)	56-item self-report measuring an individual's inclination to attend to long-rage consequences	Five subscales including Past-Negative, Present-Hedonistic, Future, Past-Positive, and Present-Fatalistic	Acceptable internal and test–retest reliability; correlational and experimental research has demonstrated convergent, discriminant, and predictive validity (Zimbardo & Boyd, 1999)	Partial cognitive skills, autonomy, and, to a smaller extent, emotional skills; all items solely focus on attitudes about time and life as related to cognitive skills, autonomy, and emotional skills
RPI (Steinberg & Monahan, 2007)	10-item self-report measure of resistance to peer influence	None	Adequate reliability and good validity (Steinberg & Monahan, 2007)	Partial emotional skills, but tied specifically to peer influence
RSTI–SR (Salekin & Iselin, 2010)	74-item self-report inventory that includes a measure of developmental maturity	Three scales including Risk, Developmental Maturity, and Treatment Amenability; within the Developmental Maturity scale are 3 subscales: Autonomy, Cognitive Skills, and Emotion Regulation	Very good reliability and validity; appears to be sensitive to change following psychological therapy (Salekin et al., 2012)	Full coverage; measure is designed to tap autonomy, cognitive skills, and emotional skills

(*continues*)

TABLE 19.2 (*Continued*)

Self-Report Measures for Developmental Maturity or Aspects of Maturity

Measure	Brief description	Subscales	Psychometric properties	Correspondence with prototypical studies
WAI Self Restraint subscale (Weinberger, & Schwartz, 1990)	30-item self-report subscale used to assess socioemotional development	Within the Self-Restraint subscale, four superordinate subscales: Impulse Control, Suppression of Aggression, Consideration of Others, and Responsibility	Adequate internal consistency and convergent and discriminant validity have been established (Feldman & Weinberger, 1994; Weinberger, 1996), in addition to concurrent and predictive validity (e.g., Weinberger & Gomes, 1995)	Partial, in terms of cognitive skills and emotional skills; partial autonomy that is mainly tied to responsibility

Note. CDMQ = Criminal Decision Making Questionnaire; CFCS = Consideration of Future Consequences Scale; FOI = Future Outlook Inventory; PSMI = Psychosocial Maturity Inventory Form D; ZTPI = Zimbardo Time Perspective Scale; RPI = Resist Peer Influence; RSTI–SR; Risk–Sophistication–Treatment Inventory Self-Report; WAI = Weinberger Adjustment Inventory. Adapted from *Forensic Evaluation and Treatment of Juveniles: Innovation and Best Practice* (p. 146), by R. T. Salekin, 2015, Washington, DC: American Psychological Association. Copyright 2015 by the American Psychological Association.

is appropriate for use. Although the preceding paragraphs covered the important topic of self-report measures of developmental maturity, next we discuss the RSTI, which is an interview rating-based scale that provides for the assessment of developmental maturity.

Interview-Based Measure for Developmental Maturity: The Risk–Sophistication–Treatment Inventory

Developmental maturity is a complicated construct because it consists of elements of maturity that may influence both prosocial and antisocial behavior—and both sets of behaviors can be moderated by developmental maturity. The law occasionally needs to differentiate maturity that acts as a protective factor (e.g., engaging in prosocial activities, taking responsibility for actions) from maturity that aids in criminal involvement (e.g., well-planned and premeditated criminal acts).

The RSTI (Salekin, 2004) was created for the assessment of juveniles who come into contact with the law at the juvenile level and are being considered for disposition decision making or transfer. The RSTI consists of 45 items, 15 of which are developmental maturity items. To accurately and reliably code the RSTI items, the RSTI is accompanied by a semistructured interview that was developed to assist in the process of gathering pertinent information. The interview structure consists of general questions regarding background and primary questions, with follow-up probes, regarding risk for dangerousness, developmental maturity, and treatment amenability. Information from the interview protocol, as well as collateral information from the youth's criminal file, guardians, and other relevant sources, is interpreted and coded onto the 45-item rating form. Clinical raters score items using detailed criteria provided in item descriptors, and each item score is based on a 3-point scale, with 0 denoting the absence of the characteristic or ability, 1 suggesting subclinical or moderate presence of the characteristic or ability, and 2 denoting the presence of the characteristic or ability. Specific rating criteria vary and are outlined for each item in the RSTI manual.

The Developmental Maturity scale is structurally underpinned by three subscales that are referred to as Autonomy, Cognitive Skills, and Emotional Skills. To help address the young person's functioning, separate Risk and Amenability subscales were included. They provide information regarding an adolescent's risk and likelihood of change through psychological therapy in juvenile justice settings. Clinicians, aside from assessing developmental maturity, can use the Developmental Maturity scale to indicate whether the youth's decision making seems to be primarily used for prosocial versus criminological purposes.

Because of the complexity of rating developmental maturity, the RSTI was designed to provide mental health professionals with a structured empirical base to aid in assessing developmental maturity and also to aid in writing psychological reports for justice-involved youths that may inform general disposition or transfer decisions. With regard to the latter, it should be noted that the RSTI allows for proper interpretation and application of the *Kent v. United States* (1966) transfer criteria of risk of dangerousness, developmental maturity, and amenability to treatment that can be of use to a wide range of professionals, including child and adolescent forensic psychologists, juvenile court judges, and parole officers (Leistico & Salekin, 2003; Salekin, 2004).

A normative sample of 690 juvenile cases was used to assess the psychometric properties of the RSTI. The findings reflected good to excellent interrater reliability for each of the scales (Risk, $\alpha = .94$; Sophistication–Maturity, $\alpha = .74$; Treatment Amenability, $\alpha = .91$; interclass correlations of $\alpha = .6$ for the Criminal Sophistication subscale). Leistico and Salekin (2003) also established convergent validity via significant relationships between each cluster and important defining factors. Risk was related to younger age at criminal onset, violent crimes, and both violent and nonviolent symptoms of conduct disorder. Furthermore, Sophistication–Maturity and the Criminal Sophistication subscale correlated with nonviolent offenses; Treatment Amenability was related to older age at criminal onset and negatively correlated with conduct disorder symptoms. Perhaps most important, youths transferred to adult court had higher mean Risk and Developmental Maturity scores and lower mean Treatment Amenability scores, than youths who remained in juvenile court, suggesting that the measure has good predictive validity (Leistico & Salekin, 2003).

Many of these findings were replicated in a Canadian sample of 74 youth cases of manslaughter or murder to code the RSTI (Spice, Viljoen, Gretton, & Roesch, 2010). Spice et al. (2010) found good interrater reliability (Risk, intraclass correlation [ICC] = .68; Developmental Maturity, ICC = .60; Treatment Amenability, ICC = .72). Moreover, Spice et al. found good to excellent internal consistency within each cluster (Risk, $\alpha = .77$; Developmental Maturity, $\alpha = .69$; Treatment Amenability, $\alpha = .87$). Treatment Amenability and Developmental Maturity related to older age at first arrest and fewer conduct disorder symptoms. Moreover, risk was again related to younger age at first arrest and more violent and nonviolent conduct disorder symptoms.

Criminal sophistication was positively related to risk scales on another juvenile risk assessment, the Structured Assessment of Violence Risk in Youth (Borum, Lodewijks, Bartel, & Forth, 2010), and negatively related to its treatment amenability and protective factors. Risk and criminal sophistication were also positively correlated with psychologists' and psychiatrists' judgments of risk and negatively associated with opinions of treatment amenability. In contrast, treatment amenability was positively related to judgments of amenability to treatment and negatively related to risk. Of the 74 youths examined, 40 were transferred to adult court, and transfer decisions concerning those youths were significantly associated with higher rates of risk and criminal sophistication, and lower rates of treatment amenability, than for youths with juvenile sentences or no sentence. It is important to note that criminal sophistication, but not developmental maturity, was predictive of transfer to adult court in this sample. This finding suggests that transfer decisions were based on how youths used maturity (prosocial vs. antisocial).

Given that the measure was normed in an offender population, scores denote the youth's standing among other adolescent offenders, not adolescents in general. Youths are considered to have scores in the low offender range if their *t* scores on a given scale or subscale are 40 or below, or within or below the 24th percentile of a cluster. In contrast, if youths demonstrate scale *t* scores of 60 or more, or cluster percentiles of 75% or more, they are considered to be in a high offender range. It is important to note that scores in the high offender range indicate a reversed prediction in comparison to the dangerousness scale, in that youths high on treatment amenability may benefit more from psychological interventions than other young offenders (Salekin, 2004).

The utility of the RSTI has also been examined through an international lens. One review of the juvenile justice system in Victoria, Australia, suggested that the RSTI might be of use in transfer decisions within the Australian system. In Victoria, youthful offenders between the ages of 18 and 21 can be referred back to the juvenile system from the adult system if certain criteria are met (e.g., requiring confinement to a facility, appearing to be amenable to treatment, showing a lack of maturity, or the possibility that they would incur undesirable influence within the adult prison system). These requirements correspond closely to Ewing's (1990) requirements of risk of dangerousness, treatment amenability, and developmental maturity. However, Luebbers and Ogloff (2011) cautioned that because the RSTI was normed with a majority African American and Anglo American sample in Alabama, it may not be applicable to the majority indigenous population of the Australian juvenile system. This being said, Spice et al.'s (2010) Canadian sample was largely composed of aboriginal or mixed Caucasian and aboriginal youths (35.1% and 12.2%, respectively), and they found that RSTI was a good predictor of transfer to adult court in the Canadian juvenile justice system. Furthermore, after controlling for age, offense severity, and number of prior convictions, criminal sophistication still significantly related to transfer to adult court, and the other scales approached significance (Spice et al., 2010). More recently, Gillen, MacDougall, Salekin, and Forth (in press) have shown that a shorter version of the RSTI, the RSTI—Abbreviated (RSTI–A), is a reliable and valid tool to use with juvenile offenders. These findings suggest that the RSTI can be applied to a diverse population of juveniles, but independent research investigating the RSTI's reliability and validity will further benefit our understanding of its utility within diverse international samples.

The RSTI has also been used to measure increments of improvements in developmental maturity and treatment amenability after a 12-week treatment protocol. The treatment consisted of leading a group of approximately 12 youths at a time in discussion of brain development, decision making, the utility of positive emotions, and how to increase positive emotion. Another important aspect of the intervention was creating mental models, which consisted of setting goals, planning incremental steps to attain the goals, and enacting the steps throughout the week. The treatment resulted in improvements in the juveniles' treatment amenability scores such that they demonstrated modest improvement in awareness of problems, motivation to change, and consideration and tolerance of others (Salekin et al., 2012). Also noted were improvements in developmental maturity.

Timing: When to Assess Developmental Maturity

Grisso (2013) noted that developmental maturity is not about the person's mental state at the time of the crime. He also stated, "It is not the clinician's role—and arguably not the court's objective in a waiver hearing—to form an opinion as to whether the youth could grasp the nature of what he or she was doing at the time of the alleged offense" (p. 248). However, many recent studies on adolescent decision making in the context of the law address this very issue (e.g., culpability). That is, scholarly articles and research studies on developmental maturity pertain to youth decision making as it relates to their ability to make sound judgments at the time of the offense. For this reason, it may be of particular interest to appraise developmental maturity at the time of the alleged offense for justice-involved youths.

It is our belief that clinicians will want to assess developmental maturity at both the time of the evaluation and around the time of the alleged offense. Both can be helpful. Assessing maturity only at the time of the evaluation could be misleading because such maturity scores may have been different (e.g., lower) when the offense was committed. However, appraising maturity only at the time of the offense might exclude valuable information relevant to risk and treatment amenability (*Graham v. Florida*, 2010; *Miller v. Alabama*, 2012; *Roper v. Simmons*, 2005). Thus, assessment of maturity that is relevant to mental state at the time of the offense would be important to assess. When the evaluation is conducted shortly after the alleged offense, then it is likely that a single appraisal of maturity would suffice due to its proximity to the offense.

CONCLUSION AND FUTURE DIRECTIONS

Developmental maturity has been described by some as the factor about which child forensic clinicians may offer the courts the most useful information (Ewing, 1990; Salekin, 2015). We very much agree with this sentiment. According to Salekin (2015), developmental maturity is a set of adolescent characteristics involving autonomous, cognitive, and emotional factors. These factors have been further defined as including an internal locus of control, forethought, planning, and emotional regulation that can manifest prosocially or in criminological ways. Greater involvement in advanced criminality, premeditation of actions, and understanding of behavior norms are some ways in which maturity can manifest in an antisocial manner. Such a youth might try to coach others into delinquency or even become involved in gang activity. Alternately, maturity can also manifest itself prosocially through increased reading and writing, concentrating on earning good grades in school, and performing well in music (e.g., playing the piano), at a sport (e.g., playing hockey or basketball), and in hobbies (e.g., collecting stamps, visiting museums).

Youths appear to have varying levels of maturity and varying ways in which they can display maturity (or immaturity). Fortunately, research has converged, at least preliminarily, on a set of defining features for maturity. The field is also fortunate in that a number of self-report measures have now been developed to measure developmental maturity or components of developmental maturity. These include the PMI, the Criminal Decision Making Questionnaire, CFCS, Future Outlook Inventory, PSMI, STPI, RPI, STPI, WAI, and RSTI–SR. However, clinicians will want to be cognizant of which factor is being tapped with the measure they choose. In addition, the RSTI's interview-based rating scale can be used in the assessment of developmental maturity to shed further light on a young person's level of developmental maturity. This latter method is best practice in cases in which developmental maturity is pertinent.

Although this chapter presented information on the relevance of assessing maturity as well as the measures used to assess developmental maturity, much research remains to be conducted regarding the developmental maturity construct. First, prosocial maturity is an excellent set of traits to have early in life when this maturity translates into prosocial behavior. With such maturity, youths can gain a sense of control, further develop their identities, better forecast behavior, avoid hazards, and regulate their emotions so that they can navigate life and have healthy self-esteem and accumulate important life successes. Increasingly autonomous youths might display their developmental maturity in terms of school performance, work, and healthy peer relationships. Specifically, a young person might earn good grades (honor roll), work a job (cutting grass), and then eventually experience increased self-confidence and feelings of accomplishment from those experiences. Such a young person may also develop feelings for the community and want to be part of it. That some youths possess some of these characteristics suggests that developmental maturity can be cultivated and even taught to adolescents, and much more research is needed on this topic—especially as it pertains to justice-involved youths. The social aspect of developmental maturity should also become a part of training programs. Thus, social commitment, openness to sociopolitical change, warmth, and kindness, as noted by Greenberger and Sørensen in 1974, could all be targets of an intervention and taught to youths during the earliest years of development and even to those entering juvenile facilities.

Assessment technology is another area for future research. Although numerous self-reports are available, few assess all three aspects of developmental maturity. We do not know much about how these scales perform in clinical settings, although some of the research on them has shown that they have been somewhat effective in research settings, whereas the results have been more equivocal in others. We have initiated work with the RSTI–SR in both research and clinical settings to help shore up this gap in the literature and the gap in measurement technology for adolescent offenders. In addition, we are piloting the RSTI–A to determine whether a shorter interview will allow us to continue to assess the important construct of developmental maturity in an effective but also time-efficient way. One study has already shown support for the RSTI–A (Gillen et al., in press). More research is needed on the change sensitivity of developmental maturity measures, because if the expectation is that maturity is dynamic, then there should be some manner in which to detect such change.

Much research seems to be ongoing regarding the brains of adolescents as pertains to their mature decision making. Future research could work to determine what the signature neural track in the brain is for mature judgment. This research might eventually reduce the need for psychological measures, especially if functional MRI scans become more affordable. We suspect developmental maturity involves, in part, greater neural tracts from the amygdala to the prefrontal cortex, but other areas across the brain and concentrated connections in the prefrontal cortex may be responsible for mature decision making. Fortunately, the brain is malleable; it is possible that these traits can be built on, highlighting the importance of attempting to "train in" maturity (see Salekin, 2015).

More research is also needed on developmental maturity and the way in which psychopathology affects that developmental maturity. Attention-deficit/hyperactivity disorder appears to be one disorder that may demonstrate how a psychopathology could affect decision making. We imagine depression and other disorders might also affect development and shape maturity in different directions. One also presumes that youths with higher levels of maturity might be more amenable to treatment because those with greater cognitive skills, emotion regulation, and clearer identity are likely to benefit from psychotherapy and reach their treatment goals (Garfield, 1994; Salekin, Rogers, & Ustad, 2001; Taylor, Pham, Rivkin, & Armor, 1998). More research is needed on this topic. With regard to this aspect, individuals who demonstrate autonomy, initiative, industry, identity, and integrity may make smoother transitions and quicker gains in psychotherapy (Salekin, Rogers, & Machin, 2001).

Much remains to be learned regarding the impact of transfers to adult court on adolescents' trajectories for growth and development. Researchers in juvenile forensic psychology have voiced concern that youths sentenced to serve time in adult correctional facilities may incur harm or become developmentally stunted in their capacity for psychosocial maturity (Steinberg, Chung, & Little, 2004; Woolard, Odgers, Lanza-Kaduce, & Daglis, 2005). These claims require further study. However, secure facilities halt youthful exploration and experimentation, run the risk of halting healthy development of self-identity, autonomy, friendships, and intimate relationships.

Woolard et al. (2005) have suggested that prisons should have appropriate knowledge on adolescent health and development to ensure that youths are provided with the nutrients that they need during this important life stage of physical and mental growth. Moreover, given the impact of prosocial adult support on healthy adolescent development, correctional staff can facilitate positive relationships by allowing youths more regular contact with family members. Finally, until adult facilities are better equipped to handle juvenile offenders, it may be beneficial to house juvenile offenders in juvenile facilities during their adolescent years (until age 18), so that they will be more likely to receive developmentally appropriate treatment and education, after which they can be transferred to an adult facility if it is deemed necessary .

Further efforts are also needed to communicate the meaning of developmental maturity and its underlying factors to the broader community. Specifically, clinicians and researchers could assist in training attorneys, judges, and mental health professionals in the concept of developmental maturity to overcome issues regarding the defining features of the construct as well as issues regarding how it should be tested (i.e., the measures used) and when it should be assessed (one vs. two time points). Moreover, researchers could report to judges on data related to developmental maturity and publish information on the construct in psychology and law journals. Greater collaboration among all parties involved in disposition and transfer decisions may aid in creating cohesive definitions of the important factors involved in decisions, thus increasing the likelihood that juvenile court judges and officials will make informed decisions regarding juvenile offenders that are in the best interest of both youths and the greater society.

Researchers have come a long way in understanding the role that maturity plays in juvenile delinquency and how it can be effectively measured and applied to both disposition and transfer decisions. Yet, a substantial amount of knowledge remains to be uncovered, and it is our hope that further research efforts will be devoted to better understanding developmental maturity. We also hope that through research, scholarly writings, and practice that courts will be better informed about developmental maturity. Finally, we hope that developmental maturity will be promoted and trained in youths so that crimes driven in part by developmental immaturity will be greatly reduced.

References

American Psychiatric Association. (2013). *Diagnostic and statistical manual of mental disorders* (5th ed.). Arlington, VA: Author.

Ang, X., Salekin, R. T., Sellbom, M., & Lee, Z. (2014, March). *Assessment of sophistication–maturity with the Risk–Sophistication–Treatment Inventory—Self-Report (RSTI–SR)*. Poster presented at the American Psychology–Law Society Conference, New Orleans, LA.

Barnes, J. C., & Beaver, K. M. (2010). An empirical examination of adolescence-limited offending: A direct test of Moffitt's maturity gap thesis. *Journal of Criminal Justice*, *38*, 1176–1185.

Baumrind, D. (1987). A developmental perspective on adolescent risk taking in contemporary America. *New Directions for Child and Adolescent Development*, *1987*, 93–125. http://dx.doi.org/10.1002/cd.23219873706

Borum, R., Lodewijks, H., Bartel, P. A., & Forth, A. E. (2010). Structured Assessment of Violence Risk in Youth (SAVRY). In R. K. Otto & K. S. Douglas (Eds.), *Handbook of violence risk assessment* (pp. 63–79). New York, NY: Routledge.

Broughton, R. (1990). The prototype concept in personality assessment. *Canadian Psychology*, *31*, 26–37. http://dx.doi.org/10.1037/h0078928

Broughton, R., Boyes, M. C., & Mitchell, J. (1993). DIStance-from-the-PROtotype (DISPRO) personality assessment for children. *Journal of Research in Personality*, *60*, 32–47. http://dx.doi.org/10.1016/0092-6566(91)90022-I

Broughton, R., Trapnell, P. D., & Boyes, M. C. (1991). Classifying personality types with occupational prototypes. *Journal of Research in Personality*, *25*, 302–321. http://dx.doi.org/10.1016/0092-6566(91)90022-I

Cauffman, E., & Steinberg, L. (2000). (Im)maturity of judgment in adolescence: Why adolescents may be less culpable than adults. *Behavioral Sciences and the Law*, *18*, 741–760. http://dx.doi.org/10.1002/bsl.416

Cauffman, E., & Woolard, J. (1999). *The Future Outlook Inventory*. Unpublished manuscript.

Chen, D. R., & Salekin, R. T. (2012). Juvenile transfer: Enhancing clinical evaluations and informing policy. In E. L. Grigorenko (Ed.), *Handbook of forensic psychology and psychiatry* (pp. 105–125). http://dx.doi.org/10.1007/978-1-4614-0905-2_8

Chung, H. L., Little, M., & Steinberg, L. (2005). The transition to adulthood for adolescents in the juvenile justice system: A developmental perspective. In C. Flanagan, G. R. Ruth, D. W. Osgood, & E. M. Foster (Eds.), *On your own without a net: The transition to adulthood for vulnerable populations* (pp. 68–91). Chicago, IL: University of Chicago Press.

Colwell, L. H., Cruise, K. R., Guy, L. S., McCoy, W. K., Fernandez, K., & Ross, H. H. (2005). The influence of psychosocial maturity on male juvenile offenders' comprehension and understanding of the *Miranda* warning. *Journal of the American Academy of Psychiatry and the Law*, *33*, 444–454.

Cruise, K. R., Fernandez, K., McCoy, W. K., Guy, L. S., Colwell, L. H., & Douglas, T. R. (2008). The influence of psychosocial maturity on adolescent offenders' delinquent behavior. *Youth Violence and Juvenile Justice*, *6*, 178–194. http://dx.doi.org/10.1177/1541204007313229

Ewing, C. P. (1990). Juveniles or adults? Forensic assessment of juveniles considered for trial in criminal court. *Forensic Reports*, *3*, 3–13.

Feldman, S. S., & Weinberger, D. A. (1994). Self-restraint as a mediator of family influences on boys' delinquent behavior: A longitudinal study. *Child Development*, *65*, 195–211. http://dx.doi.org/10.2307/1131375

Fischer, K. W., Stein, Z., & Heikkinen, K. (2009). Narrow assessments misrepresent development and misguide policy: Comment on Steinberg, Cauffman,

Woolard, Graham, and Banich (2009). *American Psychologist*, *64*, 595–600. http://dx.doi.org/10.1037/a0017105

Fried, C. S., & Reppucci, N. D. (2001). Criminal decision making: The development of adolescent judgment, criminal responsibility, and culpability. *Law and Human Behavior*, *25*, 45–61. http://dx.doi.org/10.1023/A:1005639909226

Garfield, S. L. (1994). Eclecticism and integration in psychotherapy: Developments and issues. *Clinical Psychology: Science and Practice*, *1*, 123–137. http://dx.doi.org/10.1111/j.1468-2850.1994.tb00015.x

Giedd, J. N. (2004). Structural magnetic resonance imaging of the adolescent brain. *Annals of the New York Academy of Sciences*, *1021*, 77–85. http://dx.doi.org/10.1196/annals.1308.009

Giedd, J. N., Blumenthal, J., Jeffries, N. O., Castellanos, F. X., Liu, H., Zijdenbos, A., . . . Rapoport, J. L. (1999). Brain development during childhood and adolescence: A longitudinal MRI study. *Nature Neuroscience*, *2*, 861–863. http://dx.doi.org/10.1038/13158

Giedd, J. N., Raznahan, A., Lee, N. R., Weddle, C., Liverpool, M., Stockman, M., & Lalonde, F. (2011). Structural brain magnetic resonance imaging of typically developing children and adolescents. In E. Amsel & J. G. Smetana (Eds.), *Adolescent vulnerabilities and opportunities: Developmental and constructivist perspectives* (pp. 23–40). http://dx.doi.org/10.1017/CBO9781139042819.004

Gillen, C., MacDougall, E. A. M., Salekin, R. T., & Forth, A. E. (in press). The validity of the Risk–Sophistication–Treatment Inventory—Abbreviated (RSTI–A): Initial evidence in support of a measure designed for juvenile evaluations. *Psychology, Public Policy, and Law*.

Gogtay, N., Giedd, J. N., Lusk, L., Hayashi, K. M., Greenstein, D., Vaituzis, A. C., . . . Thompson, P. M. (2004). Dynamic mapping of human cortical development during childhood through early adulthood. *Proceedings of the National Academy of Sciences, USA*, *101*, 8174–8179. http://dx.doi.org/10.1073/pnas.0402680101

Goldberg, J. H. (2007). Worldview of high-risk juvenile delinquents: Relationship to decisions to shoot. *Criminal Justice and Behavior*, *34*, 846–861. http://dx.doi.org/10.1177/0093854807299413

Graham v. Florida, 130 S. Ct. 2011 (2010).

Greenberger, E., & Bond, L. (1976). *Technical manual for the Psychosocial Maturity Inventory*. Unpublished manuscript, Program in Social Ecology, University of California, Irvine.

Greenberger, E., Josselson, R., Knerr, C., & Knerr, B. (1975). The measurement and structure of psychosocial maturity. *Journal of Youth and Adolescence*, *4*, 127–143. http://dx.doi.org/10.1007/BF01537437

Greenberger, E., & Sørensen, A. B. (1974). Toward a concept of psychosocial maturity. *Journal of Youth and Adolescence*, *3*, 329–358. http://dx.doi.org/10.1007/BF02214746

Grisso, T. (2013). *Forensic evaluation of juveniles* (2nd ed.). Sarasota, FL: Professional Resource Press.

Grisso, T., Tomkins, A., & Casey, P. (1988). Psychosocial concepts in juvenile law. *Law and Human Behavior*, *12*, 403–437. http://dx.doi.org/10.1007/BF01044626

Grisso, T., & Vierling, L. (1978). Minors' consent to treatment: A developmental perspective. *Professional Psychology: Research and Practice*, *9*, 412–427. http://dx.doi.org/10.1037/0735-7028.9.3.412

Hall, G. S. (1904). *Adolescence: Its psychology and its relations to physiology, anthropology, sociology, sex, crime, religion, and education: Vols. I & II*. New York, NY: Appleton.

Hecker, T., & Steinberg, L. (2002). Psychological evaluation at juvenile court disposition. *Professional Psychology: Research and Practice*, *33*, 300–306.

Hodgson v. Minnesota, 497 U.S. 417 (1990).

Irwin, C., & Millstein, S. (1992). Risk-taking behaviors and biopsychosocial development during adolescence. In E. Susman, L. Feagans, & W. Ray (Eds.), *Emotion, cognition, and development in children and adolescents* (pp. 75–102). Hillsdale, NJ: Erlbaum.

Jennings, W. G., & Reingle, J. M. (2012). On the number and shape of developmental/life-course violence, aggression, and delinquency trajectories: A state-of-the-art review. *Journal of Criminal Justice*, *40*, 472–489. http://dx.doi.org/10.1016/j.jcrimjus.2012.07.001

Johnson Niarhos, F., & Routh, D. K. (1992). The role of clinical assessment in the juvenile court: Predictors of juvenile dispositions and recidivism. *Journal of Clinical Child Psychology*, *2*, 151–159. http://dx.doi.org/10.1207/s15374424jccp2102_7

Kazdin, A. E. (2000). *Psychotherapy for children and adolescents: Directions for research and practice*. New York, NY: Oxford University Press.

Kent v. United States, 383 U.S. 541 (1966).

Lebel, C., & Beaulieu, C. (2011). Longitudinal development of human brain wiring continues from childhood into adulthood. *Journal of Neuroscience*, *31*, 10937–10947. http://dx.doi.org/10.1523/JNEUROSCI.5302-10.2011

Lee, Z., Salekin, R. T., & Iselin, A. M. (2010). Psychopathic traits in youth: Is there evidence for primary and secondary subtypes? *Journal of Abnormal Child Psychology*, *38*, 381–393. http://dx.doi.org/10.1007/s10802-009-9372-7

Leistico, A. R., & Salekin, R. T. (2003). Testing the reliability and validity of the Risk, Sophistication–Maturity, and Treatment Amenability Instrument (RST-i). *International Journal of Forensic Mental Health Services*, *2*, 101–117. http://dx.doi.org/10.1080/14999013.2003.10471182

Little, M., & Steinberg, L. (2006). Psychosocial correlates of adolescent drug dealing in the inner city: Potential roles of opportunity, conventional commitments, and maturity. *Journal of Research in Crime and Delinquency*, *43*, 357–386. http://dx.doi.org/10.1177/0022427806291260

Luebbers, S., & Ogloff, J. R. P. (2011). "Boys will be boys" or budding criminal: Differentiating youthful offenders. *Psychiatry, Psychology and Law*, *18*, 557–572. http://dx.doi.org/10.1080/13218719.2010.501779

Miller v. Alabama, 132 S. Ct. 2455 (2012).

Modecki, K. L. (2008). Addressing gaps in the maturity of judgment literature: Age differences and delinquency. *Law and Human Behavior*, *32*, 78–91. http://dx.doi.org/10.1007/s10979-007-9087-7

Moffitt, T. E. (1993). Adolescent limited and life-course-persistent antisocial behavior: A developmental taxonomy. *Psychological Review*, *100*, 674–701. http://dx.doi.org/10.1037/0033-295X.100.4.674

Monahan, K. C., Steinberg, L., Cauffman, E., & Mulvey, E. P. (2009). Trajectories of antisocial behavior and psychosocial maturity from adolescence to young adulthood. *Developmental Psychology*, *45*, 1654–1668. http://dx.doi.org/10.1037/a0015862

Mulvey, E. P., & Peeples, F. L. (1996). Are disturbed and normal adolescents equally competent to make decisions about mental health treatments? *Law and Human Behavior*, *20*, 273–287. http://dx.doi.org/10.1007/BF01499024

Paus, T. (2005). Mapping brain maturation and cognitive development during adolescence. *Trends in Cognitive Sciences*, *9*, 60–68. http://dx.doi.org/10.1016/j.tics.2004.12.008

Petrocelli, J. V. (2003). Factor validation of the Consideration of Future Consequences Scale: Evidence for a short version. *Journal of Social Psychology*, *143*, 405–413. http://dx.doi.org/10.1080/00224540309598453

Piquero, A., & Moffitt, T. E. (2010). Life-course-persistent and adolescence-limited offending. In J. Adler (Ed.), *Forensic psychology debates, concepts, and practice* (2nd ed., pp. 201–222). Devon, England: Willan Publishing.

Provorse, D., & Sarata, B. (1989). The social psychology of juvenile court judges in rural communities. *Journal of Rural Community Psychology*, *10*, 3–15.

Reppucci, N. D. (1999). Adolescent development and juvenile justice. *American Journal of Community Psychology*, *27*, 307–326. http://dx.doi.org/10.1023/A:1022277809281

Roper v. Simmons, 543 U.S. 551 (2005).

Rosch, E. (1978). Principles of categorization. In E. Rosch & B. B. Lloyd (Eds.), *Cognition and categorization* (pp. 27–48). Hillsdale, NJ: Erlbaum.

Sacks, H., & Reader, W. (1992). History of the juvenile court. In M. G. Kalogerakis (Ed.), *Handbook of psychiatric practice in the juvenile court* (pp. 5–11). Washington, DC: American Psychiatric Association.

Salekin, R. T. (2002a). Clinical evaluation of youth considered for transfer to adult criminal court: Refining practice and directions for science. *Journal of Forensic Psychology Practice*, *2*, 55–72. http://dx.doi.org/10.1300/J158v02n01_03

Salekin, R. T. (2002b). Juvenile transfer to adult court: How can developmental and child psychology inform policy decision making? In B. L. Bottoms, M. B. Kovera, & B. D. McAuliff (Eds.), *Children, social science, and U.S. law* (pp. 203–232). New York, NY: Cambridge University Press.

Salekin, R. T. (2002c). Psychopathy and therapeutic pessimism: Clinical lore or clinical reality? *Clinical Psychology Review*, *22*, 79–112. http://dx.doi.org/10.1016/S0272-7358(01)00083-6

Salekin, R. T. (2004). *The Risk–Sophistication–Treatment Inventory: Professional manual*. Lutz, FL: Psychological Assessment Resources.

Salekin, R. T. (2015). *Forensic evaluation and treatment of juveniles: Innovation and best practice*. Washington, DC: American Psychological Association.

Salekin, R. T., & Iselin, A. M. (2010). *The Risk–Sophistication–Treatment Inventory—Self-Report*. Unpublished manuscript.

Salekin, R. T., Rogers, R., & Machin, D. (2001). Psychopathy in youth: Pursuing diagnostic clarity. *Journal of Youth and Adolescence*, *30*, 173–195. http://dx.doi.org/10.1023/A:1010393708227

Salekin, R. T., Rogers, R., & Ustad, K. L. (2001). Juvenile waiver to adult criminal courts: Prototypes for dangerousness, sophistication–maturity, and amenability to treatment. *Psychology, Public Policy, and Law*, *7*, 381–408. http://dx.doi.org/10.1037/1076-8971.7.2.381

Salekin, R. T., Tippey, J. G., & Allen, A. D. (2012). Treatment of conduct problem youth with interpersonal callous traits using mental models: Measurement of risk and change. *Behavioral Sciences and the Law*, *30*, 470–486.

Salekin, R. T., Yff, R., Neumann, C. S., Leistico, A.-M., & Zalot, A. A. (2002). Juvenile transfer to adult court: A look at the prototypes for dangerousness, sophistication–maturity, and amenability to treatment through a legal lens. *Psychology, Public Policy, and Law*, *8*, 373–410.

Scheier, M. F., & Carver, C. S. (1985). Optimism, coping, and health: Assessment and implications of generalized outcome expectancies. *Health Psychology*, *4*, 219–247.

Schetky, D., & Benedek, E. (Eds.). (1980). *Child psychiatry and the law*. New York, NY: Brunner/Mazel.

Schetky, D., & Benedek, E. (Eds.). (1985). *Emerging issues in child psychiatry and the law*. New York, NY: Brunner/Mazel.

Schetky, D., & Benedek, E. (Eds.). (1992). *Clinical handbook of child psychiatry and the law*. Baltimore, MD: Williams & Wilkins.

Scott, E., & Grisso, T. (1997). The evolution of adolescence: A developmental perspective on juvenile justice reform. *Journal of Criminal Law and Criminology*, *88*, 137–189. http://dx.doi.org/10.2307/1144076

Scott, E., Reppucci, N., & Woolard, J. (1995). Evaluating adolescent decision-making in legal contexts. *Law and Human Behavior*, *19*, 221–244. http://dx.doi.org/10.1007/BF01501658

Spice, A., Viljoen, J. L., Gretton, H. M., & Roesch, R. (2010). Psychological assessment for adult sentencing of juvenile offenders: An evaluation of the RSTI and the SAVRY. *International Journal of Forensic Mental Health*, *9*, 124–137. http://dx.doi.org/10.1080/14999013.2010.501846

Steinberg, L., & Cauffman, E. (1996). Maturity of judgment in adolescence: Psychosocial factors in adolescent decision making. *Law and Human Behavior*, *20*, 249–272. http://dx.doi.org/10.1007/BF01499023

Steinberg, L., Cauffman, E., Woolard, J., Graham, S., & Banich, M. (2009). Are adolescents less mature than adults? Minors' access to abortion, the juvenile death penalty, and the alleged APA "flip-flop." *American Psychologist*, *64*, 583–594. http://dx.doi.org/10.1037/a0014763

Steinberg, L., Chung, H. L., & Little, M. (2004). Reentry of young offenders from the justice system: A developmental perspective. *Youth Violence and Juvenile Justice*, *2*, 21–38. http://dx.doi.org/10.1177/1541204003260045

Steinberg, L., & Monahan, K. C. (2007). Age differences in resistance to peer influence. *Developmental Psychology*, *43*, 1531–1543. http://dx.doi.org/10.1037/0012-1649.43.6.1531

Strathman, A., Gleicher, F., Boninger, D. S., & Edwards, C. S. (1994). The consideration of future consequences: Weighing immediate and distant outcomes of behavior. *Journal of Personality and Social Psychology*, *66*, 742–752. http://dx.doi.org/10.1037/0022-3514.66.4.742

Taylor, S. E., Pham, L. B., Rivkin, I. D., & Armor, D. A. (1998). Harnessing the imagination. Mental simulation, self-regulation, and coping. *American Psychologist*, *53*, 429–439. http://dx.doi.org/10.1037/0003-066X.53.4.429

Weinberger, D. A. (1996). Distorted self-perceptions: Divergent self-reports as statistical outliers in the multimethod assessment of children's social-emotional adjustment. *Journal of Personality Assessment*, *66*, 126–143. http://dx.doi.org/10.1207/s15327752jpa6601_10

Weinberger, D. A. (1998). Defenses, personality structure, and development: Integrating psychodynamic theory into a typology approach to personality. *Journal of Personality*, *66*, 1061–1080. http://dx.doi.org/10.1111/1467-6494.00042

Weinberger, D. A., & Gomes, M. E. (1995). Changes in daily mood and self-restraint among undercontrolled preadolescents: A time-series analysis of "acting out." *Journal of the American Academy of Child and Adolescent Psychiatry*, *34*, 1473–1482. http://dx.doi.org/10.1097/00004583-199511000-00014

Weinberger, D. A., & Schwartz, G. E. (1990). Distress and restraint as superordinate dimensions of self-reported adjustment: A typological perspective. *Journal of Personality*, *58*, 381–417. http://dx.doi.org/10.1111/j.1467-6494.1990.tb00235.x

Woolard, J. L., Odgers, C., Lanza-Kaduce, L., & Daglis, H. (2005). Juveniles within adult correctional settings: Legal pathways and developmental considerations. *International Journal of Forensic Mental Health*, *4*, 1–18. http://dx.doi.org/10.1080/14999013.2005.10471209

Zimbardo, P. G. (1990, August). *Strategies for coping with social traps: Time perspectives influences*. Paper presented at the 98th Annual Meeting of the American Psychological Association, Boston, MA.

Zimbardo, P. G., & Boyd, J. N. (1999). Putting time in perspective: A valid, reliable individual-differences metric. *Journal of Personality and Social Psychology*, *77*, 1271–1288. http://dx.doi.org/10.1037/0022-3514.77.6.1271

CHAPTER 20

FORENSIC USES OF CLINICAL ASSESSMENT INSTRUMENTS

Robert P. Archer and Linda J. Baum

Juvenile delinquency continues to be a significant concern in the United States. In 2009, 1.9 million juveniles were arrested (Office of Juvenile Justice and Delinquency Prevention, 2011), and in 2010, more than 1.3 million delinquency cases were addressed in juvenile courts in the United States (Office of Juvenile Justice and Delinquency Prevention, 2013). Although approximately 200,000 individuals younger than age 18 are processed in the adult justice system per year (Annie E. Casey Foundation, 2009), the vast majority of juveniles will be processed through a juvenile and domestic relations court rather than an adult criminal court. The juvenile justice system was created as a quasi-judicial system, differing from the adult justice system. Although these two systems have several differences, one distinction is the primary emphasis on the rehabilitation of delinquent juveniles, as opposed to the punishment of guilty men and women. Specifically, although culpability and public safety remain primary concerns, the rehabilitative potential of the juvenile is also particularly relevant to the course of action taken by the juvenile court (Melton, Petrila, Poythress, & Slobogin, 2007).

Although rehabilitation efforts in the justice system have a variety of targets, mental health treatment is one key area of focus. Indeed, mental health has been cited by Grisso (2005) as the most important issue for the juvenile detention population; he reported that approximately two thirds of the children involved in the justice system have been diagnosed with one or more psychiatric disorders. Indeed, research has shown that psychiatric problems are more common among detained youths than in the general population (Fazel, Doll, & Långström, 2008). These mental health problems affect a variety of areas in the criminal justice domain. For instance, although the causes of the commission of crime are multifactorial, the occurrence of psychological conditions within the delinquent population appears to be a relevant variable (Rosenblatt, Rosenblatt, & Biggs, 2000; Vander Stoep, Evens, & Taub, 1997). Adolescents adjudicated delinquent have identified psychological conditions as causal in the commission of crimes (Horstkötter, Berghmans, de Ruiter, Krumeich, & de Wert, 2012). In addition, research has indicated that mental health difficulties have been linked to misconduct among adolescents during their placement in detention (Blackburn & Trulson, 2010; McDougall, Campbell, & Santor, 2013). Such misconduct can lead to additional punitive measures and may negatively affect the juvenile's ability to receive rehabilitative services (Blackburn & Trulson, 2010). Untreated mental health conditions may also contribute to recidivism after detention.

Mental health problems continue for many youths after they leave detention (Harrington et al., 2005; Teplin, Welty, Abram, Dulcan, & Washburn, 2012), and a variety of mental health issues have been shown to affect juveniles' functioning after their return to the community. For example, juveniles with a substance use disorder are at greater risk for engaging in recidivism involving serious offenses (e.g., Hoeve, McReynolds, Wasserman, & McMillan, 2013). Conduct disorder has similarly been found to be related to an increased recidivism risk

http://dx.doi.org/10.1037/14643-020
APA Handbook of Psychology and Juvenile Justice, K. Heilbrun (Editor-in-Chief)

(e.g., Mallett, Fukushima, Stoddard-Dare, & Quinn, 2013). Therefore, adequate psychiatric treatment for the youthful offender is often crucial to the rehabilitation process. However, individual treatment needs vary extensively across those adjudicated delinquent (Grisso, 2005), and assessment of needs on a case-by-case basis allows for more adequate individualized care as well as an appropriate allocation of limited mental health resources.

Given the pervasive problem of psychopathology among adolescents in the juvenile justice system, appropriate assessment is critical to determining the unique needs of these juveniles and to offering them the most appropriate interventions. R. P. Archer, Stredny, and Wheeler (2013) have described different kinds of assessment tools used in justice settings: specialized forensic assessment instruments and traditional clinical assessment instruments. Although several assessment instruments have been specifically designed for use in juvenile justice settings, the most widely used is the Massachusetts Youth Screening Instrument, Second Version (MAYSI–2; Grisso & Barnum, 2006). This 52-item self-report questionnaire has been adopted across 34 states as of 2004 (Grisso & Quinlan, 2005) as a screening measure to identify emerging mental health needs among adolescents in detention facilities. The MAYSI–2 provides a basic assessment of alcohol and drug use problems, depression and suicidal ideation, and exposure to traumatic experiences, for instance. Unique among forensic assessment instruments for adolescents, the MAYSI–2 has been the subject of extensive reliability and validity investigations (see Grisso & Quinlan, 2005). As is often the case in the area of forensic assessment, the remaining forensic instruments created for adolescents are few in number and tend to be less well validated. Otto, Greenstein, Johnson, and Friedman (1992), for example, have indicated that the ability to treat justice-involved youths has been limited by inadequate instruments with poor or unknown psychometrics.

R. P. Archer et al. (2013) have noted that in addition to limited reliability and validity data available for most forensic instruments, other disadvantages have been identified for specialized forensic assessment instruments. The applicability of specialized tests, for example, may be limited by their specificity. For example, tests designed to evaluate adolescents' ability to waive their *Miranda* rights or their competency to stand trial may be limited by the variability found across states in statutes defining these issues. There are also numerous specific legal issues for which there are no specialized forensic assessment instruments currently available. Moreover, specialized forensic assessment instruments are by their very nature tightly focused and do not usually provide sufficient data to permit a broader and more contextual understanding of the adolescent's overall psychological functioning. Although forensic assessment instruments have an important role to play in the evaluation of adolescents in the juvenile justice system, the role of traditional clinical assessment instruments will also continue to be crucial for the foreseeable future.

In contrast to more narrowly focused forensic instruments, traditional clinical assessment instruments address the widest range of uses and typically have superior psychometric properties and a stronger research basis than forensic assessment instruments. R. P. Archer et al. (2013) recently discussed the advantages and limitations of the use of clinical assessment instruments in forensic applications. For example, traditional clinical tests, including objective personality tests such as the Minnesota Multiphasic Personality Inventory (MMPI) and cognitive tests such as the Wechsler intelligence scales, have the ability to provide a broad understanding of the individual's intellectual, emotional, and personality functioning. Moreover, instruments such as the MMPI contain validity scales that are an important source of information in evaluating an individual's tendency to respond in a defensive manner or in a manner that overreports the individual's actual level of symptomatology. Traditional clinical assessment tests also typically have more extensive research bases and better established psychometric properties than forensic assessment instruments, enhancing the usefulness of the conclusions reached on the basis of these former instruments in the courtroom setting. Finally, the broader scope of traditional clinical assessment instruments helps to generate hypotheses for further evaluation beyond the specific issues that more typically serve as the focus of forensic assessment instruments.

Clinical assessment instruments, however, are also subject to a number of inherent difficulties associated with using tests developed for the assessment of general clinical populations in a criminal justice system context. For example, clinical assessment instruments have typically been developed to yield traditional diagnoses and to assist in treatment planning in inpatient and outpatient mental health settings. Moreover, few clinical assessment instruments have been developed with appropriate forensic norms or comparison groups. Therefore, test results from traditional instruments are often difficult to interpret in the context of a forensic population. Furthermore, although traditional assessment instruments often have a large research base, the subset of literature based on forensic applications is often much smaller for these instruments. Finally, the results from traditional clinical assessments often cannot be used to directly address specific legal issues, and the users of clinical assessment tools should not attempt to address specific questions that are beyond the scope of the instrument. For example, traditional clinical tests are typically of limited value in attempting to reconstruct an individual's mental state at the time of the commission of a crime and become increasingly more limited in this regard as the period of time between the commission of the crime and the assessment increases.

Despite substantive limitations, most forensic psychologists believe that traditional psychological assessment instruments play an important role in providing additional sources of information in the psychological evaluation of individuals in forensic settings when combined with collateral interviews, record reviews, and other sources of information (e.g., R. P. Archer et al., 2013; Heilbrun, Marczyk, & DeMatteo, 2002). Indeed, surveys of psychological test use patterns among forensic psychologists have demonstrated that traditional clinical assessment instruments dominate assessments conducted in this area (e.g., R. P. Archer, Buffington-Vollum, Stredny, & Handel, 2006; R. P. Archer et al., 2013). In this chapter, therefore, we focus on the uses of traditional clinical assessment instruments in juvenile justice settings.

FREQUENTLY USED ASSESSMENT MEASURES

Self-report personality instruments are less frequently used in the juvenile population, in contrast to the adult population, because a number of developmental concerns may limit their utility with adolescents. For instance, younger individuals may have difficulty in engaging in accurate self-assessment because of a limited cognitive ability to understand and report on psychological aspects of their functioning. Accurate self-report is also compromised when an adolescent's reading level or reading comprehension does not permit adequate understanding of the vocabulary used in a test. Despite these limitations, adolescents have important insights regarding their functioning that can be obtained through standardized assessment procedures. Therefore, assessments created specifically for juvenile populations, which consider the issues of reading ability and cognitive development, can contribute significantly to the evaluation of psychological functioning. In addition, a means of circumventing literacy and cognitive concerns is to use an adult informant report in which an adolescent's functioning is assessed by a parent, caregiver, or teacher.

In 2000, R. P. Archer and Newsom surveyed 346 practitioners to determine their frequency of use of standardized assessments in juvenile forensic-related evaluations. Results indicated that the top four instruments used were (in descending order of frequency) the Minnesota Multiphasic Personality Inventory—Adolescent (MMPI–A; Butcher et al., 1992), the Parenting Stress Index (PSI; Abidin, 1995), the Child Behavior Checklist (CBCL; Achenbach, 1991), and the Millon Adolescent Clinical Inventory (MACI; Millon, 1993). We review these instruments in detail in the remainder of this chapter, along with the Personality Assessment Instrument—Adolescent (PAI–A; Morey, 2007), an adaptation of the PAI for adolescent respondents that holds substantial potential but was developed too recently (i.e., 2007) to be included in the Archer and Newsom survey.

Minnesota Multiphasic Personality Inventory—Adolescent

The MMPI (Hathaway & McKinley, 1943) has a long history of use in the assessment of adolescents (e.g., R. P. Archer, 1987; Hathaway & Monachesi, 1963; Marks, Seeman, & Haller, 1974), which includes its use in juvenile justice settings in the early 1940s (Capwell, 1945a, 1945b). However, because the MMPI was created primarily for use with adults, its use with adolescents required substantial normative and interpretive adjustments for this younger age group (e.g., R. P. Archer, 1984, 1987). Although a survey of psychologists found that the original MMPI was the most widely used objective assessment tool for use with adolescents (R. P. Archer, Maruish, Imhof, & Piotrowski, 1991), a revised version of the instrument created specifically for use with adolescents was a substantial improvement in terms of simplifying and standardizing the use of this instrument with adolescents (R. P. Archer, 2005).

The MMPI–A (Butcher et al., 1992) was developed as a self-report measure of psychopathology for adolescents ages 14 through 18, inclusive. However, applications of the MMPI–A have been used with adolescents as young as age 12 (R. P. Archer & Krishnamurthy, 2002; Janus, de Groot, & Toepfer, 1998) who had the necessary cognitive and reading ability to accurately complete the MMPI–A item pool. As noted in the MMPI–A manual (Butcher et al., 1992), 18-year-olds may be evaluated with the MMPI–A if they are living with their parents in a dependent environment. In contrast, 18-year-olds who are living independently are better suited for the administration of the MMPI–2.

The test consists of 478 items that are answered using a true–false response format and scored on a wide range of scales. It is created around 10 basic clinical scales, the same scales that served as the basis for clinical measurement on the MMPI. These clinical scales are Hypochondriasis, Depression, Hysteria, Psychopathic Deviate, Masculinity/Femininity, Paranoia, Psychasthenia, Schizophrenia, Hypomania, and Social Introversion. The current form of the test also contains seven validity scales that assess for random responding, overreporting, and underreporting. In addition, the test has 15 content scales that measure a wide variety of internalizing and externalizing forms of symptomatology, and 31 content component scales developed to identify meaningful clusters of items within 13 of the 15 MMPI–A content scales. Also, the MMPI–A contains six supplementary scales that include three scales related to substance abuse, as well as the Anxiety, Repression, and Immaturity scales. Finally, the MMPI–A includes the Personality Psychopathology Five scales, developed to measure personality domains including Aggression, Psychoticism, and Disconstraint. Although most of these scales (i.e., the clinical, content, and supplementary scales) were available at the time of the test release in 1992, other scales (i.e., the Personality Psychopathology Five scales and the content component scales) were developed later and added to the standard test scoring and interpretation process in the MMPI–A's more recent manual supplement (Ben-Porath, Graham, Archer, Tellegen, & Kaemmer, 2006).

The MMPI–A was developed to evaluate adolescents who are experiencing, or suspected of experiencing, some type of psychopathology. The MMPI–A has two major functions in the assessment of adolescent psychopathology. First, it provides the ability to objectively evaluate and describe an adolescent's level of functioning in relation to selective standardized dimensions of psychopathology reflected in the MMPI–A scales. A clinician might use the MMPI–A, for example, to evaluate the degree to which an adolescent's psychological functioning deviates substantively from that typically reported by normal adolescents. In this type of application, the clinician compares the adolescent's test scores with those obtained from the 1,620 adolescents in the MMPI–A normative sample. If the adolescent exhibits clinical levels of psychopathology on the MMPI–A, the clinician may consult the extensive clinical literature on the MMPI and MMPI–A to find the most appropriate descriptors relevant to that adolescent's psychiatric condition (e.g., R. P. Archer, 2005; R. P. Archer & Krishnamurthy, 2002; Williams & Butcher, 2011). These descriptors have been established on the basis of research with adolescents in a variety of clinical, medical, and forensic settings.

A second function involves the repeated use of the MMPI–A with an adolescent. Ongoing assessment over time can provide clinicians with a means of assessing longitudinal changes in psychopathology. When used in this manner, repeated administrations of the MMPI–A provide the ability to assess temporal changes in psychopathology, a particularly important issue during adolescence in which rapid changes occur in personality and psychopathology (e.g., R. P. Archer, 2005). In addition, when the MMPI–A is administered at various points in the treatment process, test findings can provide clinicians with a sensitive index of therapeutic change.

An important strength of the MMPI–A is its use with demographically diverse populations. The original version of the MMPI was translated into a wide variety of foreign languages, facilitating an impressive amount of research on cross-cultural applications of this instrument. The MMPI–A has followed in this same tradition, and a Spanish version is available for use in the United States and another for use in Mexico, along with translations into Dutch-Flemish, French, and Italian (R. P. Archer, 2005).

The psychometric properties of the MMPI–A are reported in the test manual (Butcher et al., 1992), as well as a variety of other sources (e.g., Ben-Porath et al., 2006). The normative sample consisted of 805 boys and 815 girls between the ages of 14 and 18 (with a mean age of 15 years). Data collection efforts occurred in eight states (Minnesota, Ohio, California, Virginia, Pennsylvania, New York, North Carolina, and Washington) to ensure adequate geographical representation of the sample (R. P. Archer, 2005). Test–retest reliability coefficients ranged from .65 to .84 for the clinical scales, .62 to .82 for the content scales, and .47 to .81 for the supplementary scales. Internal consistency alpha coefficient values ranged from .35 to .91 (M = .68) for the clinical scales, .55 to .89 (M = .76) for the content scales, and .44 to .92 (M = .68) for the supplementary scales, across samples of boys and girls in normative and clinical settings. More recent summaries of MMPI–A reliability and validity data have been provided in Williams and Butcher (2011) and Graham (2011).

A substantial amount of research has been conducted with the MMPI–A across a variety of settings. Baum, Archer, Forbey, and Handel (2009) provided a review of this literature and found 267 citations for the MMPI–A between 1992 and 2007 (108 of which referred to dissertations). An update to this review for this chapter indicated that 55 additional references (23 of which were dissertations) are available in the PsycINFO database related to material appearing between 2008 and 2012. Baum et al. (2009) found that the publications focused on a variety of topic areas, including the factor structure of the instrument, the utility of the validity scales in detecting invalid profiles, and the use of the test with specific populations such as students, medical patients, and ethnically diverse groups. In addition, five publications (as well as 25 dissertations) referenced the use of the MMPI–A as an external criterion in the evaluation of other instruments, supporting the notion that the MMPI–A has been sufficiently validated to serve as a criterion variable for new measures.

Baum et al.'s (2009) review of the MMPI–A literature indicated that 28 books, chapters, and articles focused on test use in a forensic context. Of those additional works published between 2008 and 2012, 17 referred to the forensic use of the MMPI–A, more than half of which (11) were from dissertation abstracts. It appears that research on the use of the MMPI–A continues to grow and that interest in applications of the instrument to juvenile justice populations remains an important focus of test use. Baum et al. (2009) found that the MMPI–A has received more research attention with adolescents in forensic settings than any other objective personality assessment instrument.

Research on the MMPI–A in juvenile justice settings has been varied, reflecting its continued use with a variety of forensic populations. Baum et al. (2009) provided comparison data for adolescents evaluated in juvenile justice settings, including scale-level mean scores. In addition, their review of the research indicated that MMPI–A scale scores have been significantly associated with a variety of external criteria (i.e., Cashel, Rogers, Sewell, & Holliman, 1998; Hicks, Rogers, & Cashel, 2000; Toyer & Weed, 1998). For instance, the use of the MMPI–A to assess substance use in juvenile correctional settings has been supported in the research literature (Stein & Graham, 2001, 2005). A substantial body of research, spanning 6 decades, has also supported the ability of the MMPI and MMPI–A to discriminate delinquents from nondelinquents (e.g., R. P. Archer, Bolinskey, Morton, & Farris, 2003; Capwell, 1945a, 1945b; Katz & Marquette, 1996; Peña, Megargee, & Brody, 1996). Research has also examined MMPI–A scale scores across juveniles presenting with varying types of criminal offenses (Freeman, Dexter-Mazza, & Hoffman, 2005; Glaser, Calhoun, & Petrocelli, 2002; Losada-Paisey, 1998; Parker, Morton, Lingefelt, & Johnson, 2005). The samples in published research have been diverse and have included adolescents in correctional placements (i.e., Cashel, Ovaert, & Holliman, 2000; Stein & Graham, 1999), male and female adolescents adjudicated delinquent (i.e., Fabry, Bertinetti, & Guzman-Cavazos, 2011; Gumbiner, Arriaga, & Stevens, 1999; Morton, Farris, & Brenowitz, 2002), predispositional adolescents (Handel, Archer, Elkins, Mason, & Simonds-Bisbee, 2011), and male sexual offenders (Freeman et al., 2005; Losada-Paisey, 1998). Research addressing civil forensic evaluation with the MMPI–A (e.g., custody evaluations or personal injury litigation) has been much more limited. Among the few investigations in this latter area is that of Perfect, Tharinger, Keith, and Lyle-Lahroud (2011), who used the MMPI–A in the assessment of a Child Protective Services sample.

Pennuto and Archer (2008) conducted research to evaluate the frequency with which the MMPI–A has been noted in documented legal cases. They conducted a comprehensive search for the MMPI–A in the Westlaw database. Westlaw is an online searchable legal database that contains references for a variety of materials including administrative codes, statutes (federal and state), and case law. Pennuto and Archer found eight legal cases reporting the use of the MMPI–A. These cases addressed a range of issues, including competency to stand trial, transfer to adult status, sentencing mitigation factors, and child custody recommendations. An updated search of the Westlaw database through 2012 conducted for this chapter provided citations for five additional cases in which the MMPI–A had been used and presented in court. These newer cases pertained to legal issues of transfer to adult status, eligibility for social security disability benefits, and eligibility for special education services.

Although the psychometric properties and documented usage in legal cases constitute strengths of the MMPI–A, its limitations in forensic settings have also been noted. R. P. Archer and Handel (2013) observed that research on the MMPI–A in juvenile justice settings remains limited, in comparison with that performed with clinical samples, and its application in forensic settings is clearly an extension of the test beyond typical clinical applications. In addition, the MMPI–A assesses current states of psychological functioning that may not be directly relevant to many legal questions that are focused on questions of past or future behavior. Finally, R. P. Archer and Handel (2013) noted that its reading level, which is conservatively estimated at sixth grade, may be too high for many justice-involved youths, who frequently present with academic problems including reading disabilities.

At the time of the writing of this chapter, the MMPI–A–Restructured Form (MMPI–A–RF; R. P. Archer, Handel, Ben-Porath, & Tellegen, 2015) was being developed as the newest member of the MMPI family of instruments. The MMPI–A–RF is a 241-item test derived from the 478-item pool of the MMPI–A. R. P. Archer et al. (2015) used the MMPI–2–RF by Tellegen and Ben-Porath (2008) as a template for the MMPI–A–RF's scale organization, with appropriate modifications for the unique characteristics of adolescents. The MMPI–A–RF is the result of a multiyear project with the goal of representing the clinical content of the MMPI items in a group of psychometrically sound and comprehensive contemporary personality and psychopathology constructs. As a by-product of this revision, the MMPI–A–RF has about 50% fewer items, a potential advantage in terms of ease of administration to adolescents in the juvenile justice system. Although research on the MMPI–A–RF is not yet available, this new instrument may provide an important resource to clinicians and adolescents in forensic settings in the future.

Parenting Stress Index, Fourth Edition

The PSI (Abidin, 1983) was created in 1983 and is now in its fourth edition (the PSI–4). This measure was created as a self-report measure of parental stress, assessing a variety of factors that contribute to stress, including parental factors, child characteristics, and environmental stressors. The test items were created on the basis of Abidin and Burke's (1978) model for dysfunctional parenting, combined with clinician and parent reports and a review of the research literature (Abidin, Flens, & Austin, 2006). The PSI–4 (Abidin, 2012) consists of 120 items through which a parent evaluates his or her current functioning, as well as aspects of his or her child's behavior (ages 1 month–12 years) that contribute to experienced stress. Each item is answered on a 5-point Likert scale ranging from *strongly agree* to *strongly disagree*. Individual items are scored to yield scores on scales grouped in three domains (i.e., Child, and Parent, which are combined to form a Total Stress scale) and 13 subscale scores. The Child domain consists of six subscales: Distractibility/Hyperactivity, Adaptability, Reinforces Parent, Demandingness, Mood, and Acceptability. The Parent domain includes seven subscales, Competence, Isolation, Attachment, Health, Role Restriction, Depression, and Spouse/Parenting Partner Relationship. The Total Stress scale provides a measure of environmental contributors to stress within the parent–child relationship. The PSI–4 also includes one validity scale, Defensive Responding, which provides a measure of defensiveness on the part of the parent respondent. Although the PSI–4 provides a means of evaluating children, an upward extension of the PSI for adolescents is also available, the Stress Index for Parents of Adolescents (Sheras, Abidin, & Konold, 1998).

The PSI was originally designed for use as a screening instrument in pediatric medical settings to evaluate the stress level present in the parenting system. The PSI was created on the basis of the view that parents generally act as buffers for their children and that their effectiveness in this role is potentially decreased as parenting stress increases (Abidin, Austin, & Flens, 2013). Abidin et al. (2013) noted that Abidin (1983) postulated that the best predictor of dysfunctional parenting is the total level of parenting stress and that a portion of this stress may be related to parent–child transactions. Abidin et al. proposed that the PSI–4 has three primary uses: for screening and triage of large populations, as a first-gate intake measure to determine the need for further psychological services, and as part of an individual clinical assessment. In the forensic context, Abidin et al. noted that the PSI has a unique potential to contribute to psychological testing in custody evaluations because the variables included in the PSI are similar to variables noted in statutory factors in most U.S. states regarding custody issues (i.e., child's developmental status, child's adjustment and psychological functioning, quality of the parent–child relationship, and nature and degree of support between the parents in their parenting responsibilities). Moreover, they observed that researchers have repeatedly identified the role of stress and parental coping ability as important factors in determining the adjustment of children to separation and divorce.

The normative data for the PSI–4 are based on a sample of 534 mothers and 522 fathers who matched the demographic composition of the 2007 U.S. Census. Internal consistency reliability coefficients for the Child subscales range from .78 to .88, and test–retest reliability coefficients range from .69 to .91. Validation studies have been conducted internationally, including among Chinese (Chan, 1994), Canadian (Lacharité, Ethier, & Piché, 1992), Portuguese (Abidin & Santos, 2003), and Dutch (De Brock, Vermulist, Gerris, & Abidin, 1992) samples. Abidin et al. (2013) reported that there are currently 42 official foreign-language translations of the PSI. Overall, the instrument has substantial support for its construct and predictive validity, as well as for the robustness of the PSI factor structure (Abidin et al., 2006, 2013).

Abidin (2013) provided a comprehensive reference list for the test, which consists of 649 citations. Although not all of these references refer to published material or the assessment of children or adolescents, four are listed under the topic of forensic and three are listed as related to child custody. Although two articles are also included under the topic of incarceration, these studies used samples of incarcerated mothers rather than adolescents. Published work on the PSI in child custody evaluations has addressed the test's high frequency of use in these evaluations (Bow & Quinnell, 2002; Quinnell & Bow, 2001). Similarly, research on the PSI in the forensic context has addressed the frequency of its use in forensic evaluations (Abidin et al., 2013), as well as how the test can most appropriately be used in testimony and in reports provided to the court (Bow & Quinnell, 2002; Harnett, 2007; Ireland, 2008).

We conducted a search of all state and federal cases in Westlaw for the terms *PSI* and *Parenting Stress Index*. Results indicated 49 cases referencing the PSI, the majority of which addressed issues of child custody or the termination of parental rights. One case in which the PSI was discussed involved a petition for a protection order for a child by her mother (*Shereen Jaouni v. Said Samir Ibrahim Salah*, 2012). The applicability of the PSI constructs in child custody evaluations has led to its frequent use in forensic evaluations involving child custody.

The PSI has frequently been included in evaluations for child custody and presented as evidence in court proceedings. This, combined with the support for the PSI in the research literature, led Abidin et al. (2006) to propose that the PSI can likely meet the standards for admissibility set forth in *Daubert v. Merrell Dow Pharmaceuticals* (1993). However, research supporting the use of the PSI beyond custody issues has been limited. Furthermore, although some preliminary data have been provided as norms for a child custody sample (Abidin et al., 2006), these data are limited ($N = 214$) and may not suffice for routine forensic evaluation. In addition, the PSI is limited to children (ages 12 and younger), whereas adolescents require the use of the Stress Index for Parents of Adolescents, which has produced a more limited research literature. However, the extent of international work with the test does make it accessible to a wider range of parents.

Abidin et al. (2013) emphasized the use of the PSI and the Stress Index for Parents of Adolescents as a means of generating hypotheses to identify salient issues in custody cases when combined with other important sources of data concerning parent and child functioning. They proposed that the PSI–4 provides an important contribution in this context because of the equal proportions of male and female respondents in the normative sample. They also noted that a custody litigant normative sample is currently under development for the PSI–4 (Abidin et al., 2013).

Child Behavior Checklist

The CBCL is a part of the Achenbach System of Empirically Based Assessment (ASEBA; Achenbach & Rescorla, 2001). This measure allows for parental ratings of 118 items referencing behaviors and emotional functioning for youths ages 6 to 18 years, inclusive. Test items were obtained from the clinical literature as well as from surveys of mental health professionals and parents describing the child's behavior over the past 6 months. Responses are provided on a 3-point scale ranging from *not true* to *often true*. Factor analysis was used in the test development process to create one total score, in addition to two broadband scales and eight syndrome scales. The broadband scores assess externalizing and internalizing behaviors as well as a Total Problems scale, which incorporates the total scores of the following eight syndrome scales: Withdrawn/Depressed, Anxious/Depressed, Somatic Complaints, Social Problems, Thought Problems, Attention Problems, Aggressive Behavior, and Rule-Breaking Behavior. An additional 20 open-ended items are used to assess social functioning. The social functioning items yield three social competence scales: Activities, School, and Social.

The CBCL was updated, including new norms, in 2001. The update also included an additional scale set (the *Diagnostic and Statistical Manual of Mental Disorders* [*DSM*]-oriented scales)—Affective Problems, Anxiety Problems, Somatic Problems, Attention-Deficit/Hyperactivity Problems, Oppositional Defiant Problems, and Conduct Problems—that focuses on psychological diagnoses. For the development of these scales, international experts were asked to review CBCL test items to determine their applicability to psychiatric diagnoses found in the *DSM* (Achenbach & Rescorla, 2013). These scales were created using the criteria of the *DSM*'s fourth edition, but an update based on the fifth-edition criteria is anticipated (Achenbach & Rescorla, 2013).

Psychometric properties for the CBCL presented in the test manual support the instrument's reliability and validity (see Achenbach & Rescorla, 2013). The normative sample consisted of 1,753 children, with a roughly equal gender distribution. The majority of the normative sample was Caucasian (60%), and the sampling method used ensured representation consistent with the U.S. population in terms of geographic region (40 states and the District of Columbia were represented), socioeconomic status, ethnicity, and urbanization. Mean test–retest reliability correlation coefficients for the scale sets range from .88 (for the *DSM*-oriented scales) to .94 (for the Total Problems scale). Mean Cronbach's alpha internal consistency reliability values range from .82 (for the *DSM*-oriented scales) to .97 (for the Total Problems scale). Evidence for the CBCL's construct, concurrent, and predictive validity is also provided in the test manual through presentation of the relationships between test scores and a variety of assessment instruments, extratest correlates, and relevant outcomes.

Research on the CBCL has been extensive. Berube and Achenbach (2005) reported that the ASEBA has been included in more than 5,000 publications, and Achenbach and Rescorla (2013) described more than 8,000 publications. Although the CBCL has a significant base of research support and is a frequently used test in juvenile justice settings (R. P. Archer & Newsom, 2000), it appears that research on the instrument's utility specific to justice settings has been more limited. However, the available research has supported its ability to assess symptom characteristics in probated youths (Cashel, 2003) and incarcerated youths (Atkins et al., 1999; Dolan & Rennie, 2007; Forehand, Frame, Wierson, Armistead, & Kempton, 1991; Goethals, Willigenburg, Buitelaar, & Van Marle, 2008), as well as factors related to risk for violence (Gammelgård, Koisisto, Eronen, & Kaltiala-Heino, 2010; Jiang, Walsh, & Augimeri, 2011). Several of these studies used the CBCL as a criterion measure to evaluate the psychometric properties of other instruments in forensic settings.

A substantial amount of cross-cultural and cross-national research has been focused on the CBCL. For example, the CBCL has been used to assess severity of conduct disorder in a sample of Israeli boys adjudicated delinquent ($N = 16$) referred by correctional services (Golubchik, Mozes, Maayan, & Weizman, 2009) as well as oppositional defiant disorder symptoms in a sample of 1,031 Swiss children and adolescents (Aebi, Plattner, Metzke, Bessler, & Steinhausen, 2013). Research has also been conducted with U.K. (Dolan & Rennie, 2007) and Dutch (Goethals et al., 2008) samples. This research has generally supported the CBCL's concurrent and predictive validity for assessing delinquent behaviors in international delinquent samples.

As with the other measures discussed, the CBCL has been cited in a number of legal cases. A review of Westlaw for the terms *Child Behavior Checklist* and *CBCL* yielded seven references to the CBCL. Although the majority of these cases focused on eligibility for special education services, the CBCL was also discussed in the context of child custody evaluations and eligibility evaluations for Supplemental Security Income benefits. This review of U.S. federal and state legal cases within Westlaw likely represents only a fraction of the times in which assessment data have actually been presented in the legal context. The majority of child cases are adjudicated in domestic relations courts rather than criminal courts. Because domestic relations courts do not routinely produce written opinions of court proceedings, it is difficult to know how frequently such test data are actually presented in juvenile court proceedings.

The frequency with which the CBCL is used within juvenile justice may be attributable to its numerous strengths. Achenbach and Rescorla (2013) cited ease of use and cost-effectiveness as major strengths of the ASEBA family of instruments (including the CBCL) in forensic settings. The checklist format of the test, in addition to the low required reading level (fifth grade), makes it easy for most parents to use. In addition, the CBCL has been translated into more than 90 languages, and multicultural norms are available (Achenbach & Rescorla, 2013). Therefore, the test can be used with a wide variety of children who may come into contact with the justice system. However, Achenbach and Rescorla (2013) also acknowledged that although a broad overview of functioning can be obtained from the CBCL, a more comprehensive evaluation would likely be needed in the forensic context; therefore, the use of this test should be supplemented with other test data and sources of information. The CBCL is not limited to providing the perspective of child functioning from a single parent, and it can also be used to obtain cross-informant data with the use of other measures within the ASEBA (such as the self-report form [Achenbach & Rescorla, 2001] or teacher report [Achenbach & Rescorla, 2001]). This ability to compare various sources of information on a child's functioning is an important strength of the measure. Achenbach and Rescorla (2013) also noted that in child custody evaluations, the ASEBA family of instruments can be used to assess parents (Adult Behavior Checklist) as well as children (CBCL).

Millon Adolescent Clinical Inventory

The MACI (Millon, 1993) was released in 1993 as a complement to the Millon Adolescent Personality Inventory (Millon, Green, & Meagher, 1982). The MACI was specifically designed to evaluate adolescents with clinical symptoms, whereas the Millon Adolescent Personality Inventory was normed on adolescents in settings in which clinical problems were not assumed to be present. The MACI also serves as an adolescent counterpart to the Millon Clinical Multiaxial Inventory—III (Millon, 1997) used to evaluate adults. These tests were all created on the basis of Millon's theory of personality and on *DSM* criteria. The MACI consists of 160 items that are endorsed as true or false and scored on 31 scales in four domains: Modifying Indices, Personality Patterns scales, Expressed Concerns scales, and Clinical Syndrome scales. The Modifying Indices are consistent with those on the adult version of the test (i.e., Disclosure, Desirability, Debasement, and Reliability). Personality patterns assessed on the MACI are Introversive, Inhibited, Doleful, Submissive, Dramatizing, Egotistic, Unruly, Forceful, Conforming, Oppositional, Self-Demeaning, and Borderline Tendency. The Expressed Concerns scales are Identity Confusion, Self-Devaluation, Body Disapproval, Sexual Discomfort, Peer Insecurity, Social Insensitivity, Family Discord, and Childhood Abuse. Clinical concerns are assessed with the Eating Dysfunctions, Substance-Abuse Proneness, Delinquent Predisposition, Impulsive Propensity, Anxious Feelings, Depressive Affect, and Suicidal Tendency scales. With the Modifying Indices, the MACI can address not only personality characteristics and psychopathological symptomatology, but also the potential for response bias, the latter of which is particularly critical in the forensic context. In addition, the MACI, similar to the Millon Clinical Multiaxial Inventory—III, uses base-rate scores that provide the individual's score in relation to the frequency of the problem or symptom in clinical populations.

Millon (1993) provided information regarding the normative population and psychometric properties of the MACI in the test manual. The development sample consisted of 313 males and 266 females, ages 13 to 19. The majority of the normative sample was Caucasian (79%). Two additional samples ($N = 139$ and $N = 194$) were used in cross-validation and were also primarily Caucasian (83% and 74%, respectively). Internal consistency reliability coefficients range from .73 to .90 ($M = .80$) for the Personality Patterns scales, from .69 to .91 ($M = .80$) for the Expressed Concerns scales, and from .75 to .89 ($M = .83$) for the Clinical Syndromes scales. Three- to seven-day test–retest reliability coefficients range from .63 to .88 ($M = .79$) for the Personality Pattern scales, .57 to .89 ($M = .79$) for the Expressed Concerns scales, and .78 to .91 ($M = .83$) for the Clinical Syndrome scales. Correlations were calculated between the MACI and the Beck scales, Eating Disorder Inventory–2, and the Problem Oriented Screening Instrument for Teenagers to provide evidence for the instrument's validity.

Baum et al. (2009) provided a review of the MACI literature available between 1993 and 2007 and found 84 citations for the MACI (36 of which referred to dissertations). Of these works, 16 books, chapters, and articles, as well as 17 dissertations, focused on the use of the MACI in a forensic context. An updated search in PsycINFO (through 2012) yielded 37 additional citations (9 of which were dissertations), with 15 focused on forensic samples. This research base placed the MACI as second only to the MMPI–A among objective personality inventories used in forensic assessments.

The MACI is frequently used in the juvenile justice system (Baum et al., 2009; Salekin, Leistico, Schrum, & Mullins, 2005), and research on the instrument in this context has been broad and varied. Samples have included males in detention (Glaser, Calhoun, Petrocelli, Bates, & Owens-Hennick, 2005), incarcerated males and females (Loper, Hoffschmidt, & Ash, 2001; Murrie, Cornell, Kaplan, McConville, & Levy-Elkon, 2004), and male sexual offenders (Glowacz & Born, 2013; W. A. Kennedy, Licht, & Caminez, 2004; Oxnam & Vess, 2008). Research has addressed characteristics of the test such as its factor structure in a juvenile offender sample (Salekin, 2002) and the ability to create new scales from the MACI item pool (Salekin, Ziegler, Larrea, Anthony, & Bennett, 2003). Research has also been used to differentiate offender groups. For instance, T. D. Kennedy, Burnett, and Edmonds (2011) compared violent offenders ($n = 64$) with nonviolent offenders

($n = 31$) and found that Inhibition, Oppositional, and Peer Insecurity scale scores were significantly related to offender status. Glaser et al. (2005) concluded that Doleful, Self-Demeaning, Self-Devaluation, Depressive Affect, and Suicidal Tendency scale scores differed between groups of somatizing ($n = 32$) and nonsomatizing ($n = 51$) adolescents adjudicated delinquent. Also, in both studies, the inclusion of MACI scales in predictive models was useful in determining class membership. A discriminant model using MACI scales has also been found to be effective in identifying male adjudicated offenders who were violent toward staff (Caggiano, 2000).

A review of the Westlaw database conducted for this chapter for the terms *MACI* and *Millon Adolescent Clinical Inventory* yielded 10 references. The MACI appears to have been used in a variety of forensic evaluations. Adult transfer was most often the legal issue being addressed in cases in which the MACI was administered (four cases); however, cases also addressed eligibility for special education services, commitment, juvenile placement, eligibility for Supplemental Security Income benefits, and petition to change plea.

A common theme noted for all the instruments reviewed in this chapter is the importance of the interpretive test results with other sources of information, particularly in forensic evaluations. Salekin et al. (2005) noted, for example, that the greatest utility of the MACI occurs in its role as part of a comprehensive evaluation process identifying areas of strengths and deficits for adolescents. However, Salekin et al. have also noted several weaknesses of the measure. For instance, the MACI research base is limited in terms of the effects of demographic variables such as ethnicity, gender, and age on MACI scale scores. In addition, empirical evidence for the effectiveness of the MACI validity scales in detecting inaccurate responding has been quite limited.

Personality Assessment Inventory—Adolescent

Although not included as a frequently used instrument in the survey by R. P. Archer and Newsom (2000), the PAI–A (Morey, 2007) has the potential to play an important role in the assessment of justice-involved youths. Although the adult version, the Personality Assessment Inventory (PAI; Morey, 1997), has received substantial research attention and the forensic applications of this test were recently reviewed by Morey and Meyer (2013), the use of the PAI–A to evaluate adolescents in forensic settings has been subject to few investigations to date.

The PAI–A is considered an important broadband measure of personality that incorporated advances in test construction methods along with measurement of areas of functioning not assessed by other adolescent personality measures (Krishnamurthy, 2010), such as factors related to treatment considerations. Released in 2007, the test was designed to assess adolescents ages 12 to 18. Morey and Meyer (2013) noted that because the items and scales designed for the PAI–A were intended to parallel those of the PAI, the scoring and interpretation of both tests are similar. The PAI–A contains 264 items that are endorsed by means of a 4-point response format ranging from *not at all true* to *very true*. Items are scored and used to create *T*-score scale scores on four scale sets: Validity scales, Clinical scales, Treatment Consideration scales, and Interpersonal scales. Four Validity scales are used to assess inconsistent responding as well as positive and negative impression management. Eleven Clinical scales address somatic concerns, anxiety and anxiety-related disorders, depression and mania, paranoia, schizophrenia, features of borderline personality disorder, antisocial behavior, and drug and alcohol use problems. Nine of the scales are also each broken down into three subscales that assess specific facets of the overall clinical concern (substance use scales do not have associated subscales). The five Treatment Consideration scales are Aggression, Suicidal Ideation, Stress, Nonsupport, and Treatment Rejection, with only the Aggression scale containing subscales. Two Interpersonal scales—Dominance and Warmth—are also included that are derived from Leary's (1957) interpersonal circumplex model.

As described in the PAI–A manual (Morey, 2007), the test used data gathered from a census-matched community sample of 707 12- to 18-year-olds and a clinical sample of 1,160 adolescents predominantly from outpatient mental health settings. PAI–A scores are based on linear *T*-scores calculated in reference to the 707 adolescents in the community sample. The average internal consistencies for the PAI–A substantive scales were .79 and .80 for the community and clinical samples, respectively. The average test–retest reliability coefficient for the substantive scales across an 18-day retest interval was .78. The PAI–A was evaluated in terms of concurrent validity against a number of external criteria measures, including the MMPI–A.

The research on the usage and utility of the instrument with forensic and juvenile justice samples has been scant. Cashel, Schember, Goodman, and Reed (2006) reported mean scale scores for a sample of incarcerated adolescent girls. They also found that Aggression scale scores were related to previous violent offenses and disciplinary infractions, and scores on the Suicide scale were related to suicide attempts and referrals in a juvenile detention sample. Given the support that has been found for the use of the adult version of the instrument in forensic settings (Douglas, Hart, & Kropp, 2001; Morey & Meyer, 2013), the PAI–A has the potential to become a useful instrument in juvenile forensic evaluations pending the outcome of future PAI–A research in this area.

IMPLICATIONS FOR BEST PRACTICE

Treatment of the mental health problems of adolescents is critical to addressing their psychiatric needs and reducing their risk for recidivism. Although treatment has been shown to be effective for youths in the juvenile justice system (e.g., Caldwell, Skeem, Salekin, & Van Rybroek, 2006), adequate assessment is necessary to ensure that the most appropriate services are provided, leading to optimal treatment outcomes (e.g., Simpson, Frick, Kahn, & Evans, 2013). Using psychological assessment tools to target treatment needs could lead not only to improved outcomes for justice-involved youths but also to a cost savings for the already burdened justice system (see Foster & Jones, 2006; Welsh & Farrington, 2000).

Unfortunately, the criminal justice system varies widely from state to state, and often within districts or counties within states, in the adequacy of psychological evaluation and treatment services. Every state has a juvenile justice system that is designed to respond to juvenile offenders in a manner that is consistent with the state statutes within that state (R. P. Archer, 2005), but many states have inadequate resources directed to serving the mental health needs of youths in their systems. Assessment-based options for addressing juvenile delinquency, which will promote the intended focus of the juvenile courts on rehabilitation of children and adolescents, are needed. This approach may allow for a greater allocation of resources to be directed toward effective interventions for mental health problems.

IMPLICATIONS FOR RELEVANT POLICY

Epidemiological studies of psychiatric disorders among youths within the juvenile justice system have consistently shown that roughly 40% to 60% of this population meet the criteria for one or more psychiatric diagnoses, even when conduct disorder and substance abuse disorders are excluded (e.g., Teplin, Abram, McClelland, Dulcan, & Mericle, 2002). Although the MAYSI–2 has served a very important role as a standardized screening measure used in numerous juvenile justice systems across the United States, similar development of a more comprehensive psychological evaluation system for adolescents found in need of treatment services has been largely unaddressed. Standardization of a comprehensive evaluation system, including standards for what types of information and test results are most useful in identifying treatment needs for this population, diversion of lower risk offenders, and reduction of recidivism, is a crucial area for policy development.

FUTURE RESEARCH DIRECTIONS

Much research remains to be done on the use of traditional assessment instruments with adolescents in juvenile justice settings. Although a substantial amount of research has been accomplished with the MMPI–A in forensic settings, considerably less has been amassed with the MACI, and very little research is available on new instruments such as the PAI–A. This research is critical because the forensic use of these instruments differs from their typical clinical applications in mental health treatment settings in a number of important ways. As a consequence, normative expectations, correlate patterns, and the potential effects of demographic variables such as gender or ethnic background may be substantially different for these instruments in forensic settings. Therefore, it may not be possible to generalize findings for the MMPI–A, for example, on the basis of investigations of psychopathology among adolescents in traditional clinical settings to applications of this instrument in the assessment of juveniles adjudicated delinquent. Careful research in forensic settings is necessary to establish the meaning of test score results in forensic populations. In this regard, psychological testing is often used at a variety of points in the juvenile justice system, including detention placement, preadjudication, postadjudication, and during correctional placement. Samples derived from these various stages in the justice system should be obtained to determine not only whether the characteristics of these samples differ in important ways, but also the unique contributions that assessment can make at each step of the juvenile justice process.

Future research should also focus on the potential effects of demographic variables such as gender, race, ethnicity, and age in terms of test results and treatment outcomes. For instance, although some research has been focused on the female juvenile offender population (e.g., Vinet & Banares, 2009), the majority of research studies have focused on male adolescents, and the needs of juvenile female offenders have typically been overlooked (Bergsmann, 1989). Research data have indicated, however, that female offenders account for increasingly larger proportions of adolescents in juvenile justice systems (Snyder & Sickmund, 2006). In addition, more research is needed on the potential effects of race and ethnicity on psychological assessment findings in forensic settings. Racial disparities within the juvenile justice system have been widely documented, including the high proportion of African American youths within the juvenile justice system (e.g., Puzzanchera, 2013). Although a substantial amount of research has focused on the potential effects of race and ethnicity on adult versions of traditional test instruments (e.g., Choca, Shanley, Peterson, & Van Denburg, 1990; Monnot, Quirk, Hoerger, & Brewer, 2009), much less research is available on this issue with adolescents.

Another important area of research that would facilitate the use of traditional assessment instruments with adolescents and in juvenile justice settings involves the development of appropriate comparison normative groups for these instruments in specific forensic settings. For example, the development of forensic norms that has been proposed for the PSI–4 should greatly enhance the use of this instrument for custody evaluation purposes. Similarly, the recent report of MMPI–2–RF scale *T*-score mean values by E. M. Archer, Hagan, Mason, Handel, and Archer (2012) should be extended to provide similar research findings for the MMPI–A in varied adolescent forensic settings. These types of research investigations would provide invaluable data concerning the extent to which findings for traditional clinical instruments in clinical settings may be generalizable to forensic settings, and what test characteristics may be uniquely related to the use of these instruments in forensic settings.

In addition, research is needed that addresses the effectiveness of traditional assessment instruments in facilitating the optimal placement of adolescents in detention and correctional facilities. Adequate placement in correctional settings allows for adequate management of detainees as well as improved utilization of services (Megargee, 1997). Megargee (1977) empirically developed a MMPI-based system for adult classification that has frequently been used. This classification method allows criminal offenders to be placed into nine distinct groups on the basis of their MMPI profiles. This system has been investigated in a wide variety of criminal justice settings including corrections, probation, and parole and has proved useful in identifying the optimal placement and treatment program on the basis of the MMPI and MMPI–2 type of offender. Megargee, Carbonell, Bohn, and Sliger (2001), for example, described the use of this profile classification system with adult criminal offenders on the basis of MMPI–2 results. The utility of a similar classification system for use with juveniles, however, has received very limited examination. For example, Dillon (2011) found that a modification of the Megargee classification system for the MMPI–2 could be usefully extended to the MMPI–A, but this method has not been subject to further investigation in the research literature. Similarly, Taylor, Kemper, Loney, and Kistner (2009) examined the potential utility of the MACI in the classification and placement of adolescents in the juvenile justice system, but much more research is needed to fully explore this issue.

CONCLUSION

We reviewed the use of several traditional assessment instruments, the MMPI–A, MACI, PSI, and CBCL, in terms of their use with adolescents in the juvenile justice system. In addition, we briefly discussed two newer instruments—the PAI–A and MMPI–A–RF—in terms of their potential applicability to the evaluation of adolescents in forensic settings.

Although forensic psychologists (e.g., R. P. Archer & Newsom, 2000) frequently use traditional clinical assessment tools, it is clear that the increased use of assessment is needed in the juvenile justice system (Grisso, 2005). Ongoing efforts are recommended within both the justice system and the academic community. Standards for addressing the mental health needs of juveniles involved with the legal system should be proposed, evaluated, and established. Given the limited resources available in many jurisdictions, the most effective use of psychological assessment with the juvenile justice population should be determined so that the many juveniles with mental health difficulties will have access to appropriate assessment and treatment.

References

Abidin, R., Flens, J. R., & Austin, W. G. (2006). The Parenting Stress Index. In R. Archer (Ed.), *Forensic uses of clinical assessment instruments* (pp. 297–328). Mahwah, NJ: Erlbaum.

Abidin, R. R. (1983). *Parenting Stress Index manual*. Charlottesville, VA: Pediatric Psychology Press.

Abidin, R. R. (1995). *Parenting Stress Index* (3rd ed.). Odessa, FL: Psychological Assessment Resources.

Abidin, R. R. (2012). *PSI–4 professional manual*. Lutz, FL: Psychological Assessment Resources.

Abidin, R. R. (2013). *Bibliography for the Parenting Stress Index*. Retrieved from http://www4.parinc.com

Abidin, R. R., Austin, W. G., & Flens, J. R. (2013). The forensic uses and limitations of the Parenting Stress Index. In R. P. Archer & E. M. A. Wheeler (Eds.), *Forensic uses of clinical assessment instruments* (2nd ed., pp. 346–379). New York, NY: Routledge.

Abidin, R. R., & Burke, W. T. (1978). *Parenting Stress Index—Draft manual*. Unpublished manuscript, University of Virginia, Department of Foundations of Education.

Abidin, R. R., & Santos, S. V. (2003). *Indice de Stress Parental Portuguese*. Lisbon, Portugal: CEGOC-TEA.

Achenbach, T. M. (1991). *Integrative guide for the 1991 CBCL/4–18, YSR, and TRF Profiles*. Burlington: University of Vermont, Department of Psychiatry.

Achenbach, T. M., & Rescorla, L. A. (2001). *Manual for the ASEBA school age forms and profile*. Burlington: University of Vermont.

Achenbach, T. M., & Rescorla, L. A. (2013). The Achenbach System of Empirically Based Assessment (ASEBA): Applications in forensic contexts. In R. Archer & E. M. A. Wheeler (Eds.), *Forensic uses of clinical assessment instruments* (2nd ed., pp. 311–345). New York, NY: Routledge.

Aebi, M., Plattner, B., Metzke, C. W., Bessler, C., & Steinhausen, H. C. (2013). Parent- and self-reported dimensions of oppositionality in youth: Construct validity, concurrent validity, and the prediction of criminal outcomes in adulthood. *Journal of Child Psychology and Psychiatry*, *54*, 941–949. http://dx.doi.org/10.1111/jcpp.12039

Annie E. Casey Foundation. (2009). *Reform the nation's juvenile justice system*. Retrieved from http://www.aecf.org/~/media/PublicationFiles/Juvenile_Justice_issuebrief3.pdf

Archer, E. M., Hagan, L. D., Mason, J., Handel, R., & Archer, R. P. (2012). MMPI–2–RF characteristics of custody evaluation litigants. *Assessment*, *19*, 14–20. http://dx.doi.org/10.1177/1073191110397469

Archer, R. P. (1984). Use of the MMPI with adolescents: A review of salient issues. *Clinical Psychology Review*, *4*, 241–251. http://dx.doi.org/10.1016/0272-7358(84)90002-3

Archer, R. P. (1987). *Using the MMPI with adolescents*. Hillsdale, NJ: Erlbaum.

Archer, R. P. (2005). *MMPI–A: Assessing adolescent psychopathology* (3rd ed.). Mahwah, NJ: Erlbaum.

Archer, R. P., Bolinskey, P. K., Morton, T. L., & Farris, K. L. (2003). MMPI–A characteristics of male adolescents in juvenile justice and clinical treatment settings. *Assessment*, *10*, 400–410. http://dx.doi.org/10.1177/1073191103256128

Archer, R. P., Buffington-Vollum, J. K., Stredny, R. V., & Handel, R. W. (2006). A survey of psychological test use patterns among forensic psychologists. *Journal of Personality Assessment*, *87*, 84–94. http://dx.doi.org/10.1207/s15327752jpa8701_07

Archer, R. P., & Handel, R. W. (2013). The Minnesota Multiphasic Personality Inventory—Adolescent. In R. P. Archer & E. M. A. Wheeler (Eds.), *Forensic uses of clinical assessment instruments* (2nd ed., pp. 63–107). New York, NY: Routledge.

Archer, R. P., Handel, R. W., Ben-Porath, Y. S., & Tellegen, A. (2015). *Minnesota Multiphasic Personality Inventory—Adolescent—Restructured Form*

(MMPI–A–RF): Manual for administration, scoring, and interpretation. Manuscript in preparation.

Archer, R. P., & Krishnamurthy, R. (2002). *Essentials of MMPI–A assessment*. New York, NY: Wiley.

Archer, R. P., Maruish, M., Imhof, E. A., & Piotrowski, C. (1991). Psychological test usage with adolescent clients: 1990 survey findings. *Professional Psychology: Research and Practice*, *22*, 247–252. http://dx.doi.org/10.1037/0735-7028.22.3.247

Archer, R. P., & Newsom, C. R. (2000). Psychological test usage with adolescent clients: Survey update. *Assessment*, *7*, 227–235. http://dx.doi.org/10.1177/107319110000700303

Archer, R. P., Stredny, R., & Wheeler, E. M. A. (2013). Introduction to forensic uses of clinical assessment instruments. In R. P. Archer & E. M. A. Wheeler (Eds.), *Forensic uses of clinical assessment instruments* (2nd ed., pp. 1–20). New York, NY: Routledge.

Atkins, D. L., Pumariega, A. J., Rogers, K., Montgomery, L., Nybro, C., Jeffers, G., & Sease, F. (1999). Mental health and incarcerated youth. I: Prevalence and nature of psychopathology. *Journal of Child and Family Studies*, *8*, 193–204. http://dx.doi.org/10.1023/A:1022040018365

Baum, L. J., Archer, R. P., Forbey, J. D., & Handel, R. W. (2009). A review of the Minnesota Multiphasic Personality Inventory—Adolescent (MMPI–A) and the Millon Adolescent Clinical Inventory (MACI) with an emphasis on juvenile justice samples. *Assessment*, *16*, 384–400. http://dx.doi.org/10.1177/1073191109338264

Ben-Porath, Y. S., Graham, J. R., Archer, R. P., Tellegen, A., & Kaemmer, B. (2006). *Supplement to the MMPI–A manual for administration, scoring, and interpretation: The Content Component Scales, the Personality Psychopathology Five (PSY5) Scales, and the Critical Items*. Minneapolis: University of Minnesota Press.

Bergsmann, I. R. (1989). The forgotten few: Juvenile female offenders. *Federal Probation*, *53*, 73–78.

Berube, R. L., & Achenbach, T. M. (2005). *Bibliography of published studies using the Achenbach System of Empirically Based Assessment (ASEBA): 2005 edition*. Burlington: University of Vermont, Research Center for Children, Youth, and Families.

Blackburn, A. G., & Trulson, C. R. (2010). Sugar and spice and everything nice? Exploring institutional misconduct among serious and violent female delinquents. *Journal of Criminal Justice*, *38*, 1132–1140. http://dx.doi.org/10.1016/j.jcrimjus.2010.09.001

Bow, J. N., & Quinnell, F. A. (2002). A critical review of child custody evaluation reports. *Family Court Review*, *40*, 164–176. http://dx.doi.org/10.1111/j.174-1617.2002.tb00827.x

Butcher, J. N., Williams, C. L., Graham, J. R., Archer, R. P., Tellegen, A., Ben-Porath, Y. S., . . . Kaemmer, B. (1992). *Minnesota Multiphasic Personality Inventory—Adolescent (MMPI–A): Manual for administration, scoring, and interpretation*. Minneapolis: University of Minnesota Press.

Caggiano, A. D. (2000). Identifying violent-towards-staff juvenile delinquents via the Millon Adolescent Clinical Inventory and neuropsychological measures. *Journal of Offender Rehabilitation*, *32*, 147–165. http://dx.doi.org/10.1300/J076v32n01_06

Caldwell, M., Skeem, J., Salekin, R., & Van Rybroek, G. (2006). Treatment response of adolescent offenders with psychopathy features. *Criminal Justice and Behavior*, *33*, 571–596. http://dx.doi.org/10.1177/0093854806288176

Capwell, D. F. (1945a). Personality patterns of adolescent girls: I. Girls who show improvement in IQ. *Journal of Applied Psychology*, *29*, 212–228. http://dx.doi.org/10.1037/h0062853

Capwell, D. F. (1945b). Personality patterns of adolescent girls: II. Delinquents and nondelinquents. *Journal of Applied Psychology*, *29*, 289–297. http://dx.doi.org/10.1037/h0054701

Cashel, M. L. (2003). Validity of self-reports of delinquency and socio-emotional functioning among youth on probation. *Journal of Offender Rehabilitation*, *37*, 11–23. http://dx.doi.org/10.1300/J076v37n01_02

Cashel, M. L., Ovaert, L., & Holliman, N. G. (2000). Evaluating PTSD in incarcerated male juveniles with the MMPI–A: An exploratory analysis. *Journal of Clinical Psychology*, *56*, 1535–1549. http://dx.doi.org/10.1002/1097-4679(200012)56:12<1535::AID-5>3.0.CO;2-8

Cashel, M. L., Rogers, R., Sewell, K. W., & Holliman, N. B. (1998). Preliminary validation of the MMPI–A for a male delinquent sample: An investigation of clinical correlates and discriminant validity. *Journal of Personality Assessment*, *71*, 49–69. http://dx.doi.org/10.1207/s15327752jpa7101_4

Cashel, M. L., Schember, J., Goodman, C., & Reed, P. (2006, March). *Concurrent and predictive validity of the PAI–A for incarcerated female adolescents: Strategies for risk assessment*. Paper presented at the Annual Meeting of the Society for Personality Assessment, San Diego, CA.

Chan, Y. C. (1994). Parenting stress and social support of mothers who physically abuse their children in Hong Kong. *Child Abuse and Neglect*, *18*, 261–269. http://dx.doi.org/10.1016/0145-2134(94)90110-4

Choca, J. P., Shanley, L. A., Peterson, C. A., & Van Denburg, E. (1990). Racial bias and the MCMI. *Journal of Personality Assessment*, *54*, 479–490. http://dx.doi.org/10.1207/s15327752jpa5403&4_5

Daubert v. Merrell Dow Pharmaceuticals, Inc., 590 U.S. 579 (1993).

De Brock, A. J., Vermulist, A. A., Gerris, J. R., & Abidin, R. R. (1992). *Nijmeese Ouderlijke Stress Index*. Lisse, the Netherlands: Swets & Zeitlinger.

Dillon, J. A. (2011). The applicability of the Megargee classification system for the MMPI–A. *Dissertation Abstracts International: Section B. Sciences and Engineering, 72,* 2433.

Dolan, M. C., & Rennie, C. E. (2007). The relationship between psychopathic traits measured by the Youth Psychopathic Trait Inventory and psychopathology in a UK sample of conduct disordered boys. *Journal of Adolescence, 30,* 601–611. http://dx.doi.org/10.1016/j.adolescence.2006.07.002

Douglas, K. A., Hart, S. D., & Kropp, P. R. (2001). Validity of the Personality Assessment Inventory for forensic assessments. *International Journal of Offender Therapy and Comparative Criminology, 45,* 183–197. http://dx.doi.org/10.1177/0306624X01452005

Fabry, J. J., Bertinetti, J. F., & Guzman-Cavazos, L. (2011). Characteristics of juvenile offenders with invalid and valid MMPI–A profiles. *Psychological Reports, 108,* 908–918. http://dx.doi.org/10.2466/03.09.16.28.PR0.108.3.908-918

Fazel, S., Doll, H., & Långström, N. (2008). Mental disorders among adolescents in juvenile detention and correctional facilities: A systematic review and metaregression analysis of 25 surveys. *Journal of the American Academy of Child and Adolescent Psychiatry, 47,* 1010–1019.

Forehand, R., Frame, C. L., Wierson, M., Armistead, L., & Kempton, T. (1991). Assessment of incarcerated juvenile delinquents: Agreement across raters and approaches to psychopathology. *Journal of Psychopathology and Behavioral Assessment, 13,* 17–25. http://dx.doi.org/10.1007/BF00960736

Foster, E. M., & Jones, D.; Conduct Problems Prevention Research Group. (2006). Can a costly intervention be cost-effective? An analysis of violence prevention. *Archives of General Psychiatry, 63,* 1284–1291. http://dx.doi.org/10.1001/archpsyc.63.11.1284

Freeman, K. A., Dexter-Mazza, E. T., & Hoffman, K. C. (2005). Comparing personality characteristics of juvenile sex offenders and non-sex offending delinquent peers: A preliminary investigation. *Sexual Abuse: A Journal of Research and Treatment, 17,* 3–12.

Gammelgård, M., Koisisto, A., Eronen, M., & Kaltiala-Heino, R. (2010). Violence risk and psychopathology in institutionalized adolescents. *Journal of Forensic Psychiatry and Psychology, 21,* 933–949. http://dx.doi.org/10.1080/14789949.2010.504857

Glaser, B. A., Calhoun, G. B., & Petrocelli, J. V. (2002). Personality characteristics of male juvenile offenders by adjudicated offenses as indicated by the MMPI–A. *Criminal Justice and Behavior, 29,* 183–201. http://dx.doi.org/10.1177/0093854802029002004

Glaser, B. A., Calhoun, G. B., Petrocelli, J. V., Bates, J. M., & Owens-Hennick, L. A. (2005). Depression and somatic complaints among male juvenile offenders: Differentiating somatizers from non-somatizers with the Millon Adolescent Clinical Inventory (MACI). *Journal of Forensic Psychiatry and Psychology, 16,* 566–576. http://dx.doi.org/10.1080/14789940500098558

Glowacz, F., & Born, M. (2013). Do adolescent child abusers, peer abusers, and non-sex offenders have different personality profiles? *European Child and Adolescent Psychiatry, 22,* 117–125. http://dx.doi.org/10.1007/s00787-012-0333-2

Goethals, K., Willigenburg, L., Buitelaar, J., & Van Marle, H. (2008). Behaviour problems in childhood and adolescence in psychotic offenders: An exploratory study. *Criminal Behaviour and Mental Health, 18,* 153–165. http://dx.doi.org/10.1002/cbm.688

Golubchik, P., Mozes, T., Maayan, R., & Weizman, A. (2009). Neurosteroid blood levels in delinquent adolescent boys with conduct disorder. *European Neuropsychopharmacology, 19,* 49–52. http://dx.doi.org/10.1016/j.euroneuro.2008.08.008

Graham, J. R. (2011). *MMPI–2: Assessing personality and psychopathology* (5th ed.). New York, NY: Oxford University Press.

Grisso, T. (2005). Why we need mental health screening and assessment in juvenile justice programs. In T. Grisso, G. Vincent, & D. Seagrave (Eds.), *Mental health screening and assessment in juvenile justice* (pp. 3–21). New York, NY: Guilford Press.

Grisso, T., & Barnum, R. (2006). *Massachusetts Youth Screening Instrument Version 2: User's manual and technical report* (rev. ed.). Sarasota, FL: Professional Resource Press.

Grisso, T., & Quinlan, J. C. (2005). Massachusetts Youth Screening Instrument—Version 2. In T. Grisso, G. Vincent, & D. Seagrave (Eds.), *Mental health screening and assessment in juvenile justice* (pp. 99–111). New York, NY: Guilford Press.

Gumbiner, J., Arriaga, T., & Stevens, A. (1999). Comparison of MMPI–A, Marks and Briggs, and MMPI–2 norms for juvenile delinquents. *Psychological Reports, 84,* 761–766. http://dx.doi.org/10.2466/pr0.1999.84.3.761

Handel, R. W., Archer, R. P., Elkins, D. E., Mason, J. A., & Simonds-Bisbee, E. C. (2011). Psychometric properties of the Minnesota Multiphasic Personality Inventory—Adolescent (MMPI–A) Clinical, Content, and Supplementary scales in a forensic sample. *Journal of Personality Assessment, 93,* 566–581. http://dx.doi.org/10.1080/00223891.2011.608752

Harnett, P. H. (2007). A procedure for assessing parents' capacity for change in child protection cases. *Children and Youth Services Review*, *29*, 1179–1188. http://dx.doi.org/10.1016/j.childyouth.2007.04.005

Harrington, R. C., Kroll, L., Rothwell, J., McCarthy, K., Bradley, D., & Bailey, S. (2005). Psychosocial needs of boys in secure care for serious or persistent offending. *Journal of Child Psychology and Psychiatry*, *46*, 859–866. http://dx.doi.org/10.1111/j.1469-7610.2004.00388.x

Hathaway, S. R., & McKinley, J. C. (1943). *The Minnesota Multiphasic Personality Inventory* (rev. ed.). Minneapolis: University of Minnesota Press.

Hathaway, S. R., & Monachesi, E. D. (1963). *Adolescent personality and behavior: MMPI patterns of normal, delinquent, dropout, and other outcomes*. Minneapolis: University of Minnesota Press.

Heilbrun, K., Marczyk, G. R., & DeMatteo, D. (2002). *Forensic mental health assessment: A casebook*. New York, NY: Oxford University Press.

Hicks, M. M., Rogers, R., & Cashel, M. (2000). Predictions of violent and total infractions among institutionalized male juvenile offenders. *Journal of the American Academy of Psychiatry and the Law*, *28*, 183–190.

Hoeve, M., McReynolds, L. S., Wasserman, G. A., & McMillan, C. (2013). The influence of mental health disorders on severity of reoffending in juveniles. *Criminal Justice and Behavior*, *40*, 289–301. http://dx.doi.org/10.1177/0093854812459639

Horstkötter, D., Berghmans, R., de Ruiter, C., Krumeich, A., & de Wert, G. (2012). "We are also normal humans, you know?" Views and attitudes of juvenile delinquents on antisocial behavior, neurobiology and prevention. *International Journal of Law and Psychiatry*, *35*, 289–297. http://dx.doi.org/10.1016/j.ijlp.2012.04.006

Ireland, J. L. (2008). Psychologists as witnesses: Background and good practice in the delivery of evidence. *Educational Psychology in Practice*, *24*, 115–127. http://dx.doi.org/10.1080/02667360802019172

Janus, M.-D., de Groot, C., & Toepfer, S. M. (1998). The MMPI–A and 13-year-old inpatients: How young is too young? *Assessment*, *5*, 321–332. http://dx.doi.org/10.1177/107319119800500402

Jiang, D., Walsh, M., & Augimeri, L. K. (2011). The linkage between childhood bullying behaviour and future offending. *Criminal Behaviour and Mental Health*, *21*, 128–135. http://dx.doi.org/10.1002/cbm.803

Katz, R. C., & Marquette, J. (1996). Psychosocial characteristics of young violent offenders: A comparative study. *Criminal Behaviour and Mental Health*, *6*, 339–348. http://dx.doi.org/10.1002/cbm.120

Kennedy, T. D., Burnett, K. F., & Edmonds, W. A. (2011). Intellectual, behavioral, and personality correlates of violent vs. non-violent juvenile offenders. *Aggressive Behavior*, *37*, 315–325. http://dx.doi.org/10.1002/ab.20393

Kennedy, W. A., Licht, M. H., & Caminez, M. (2004). False positives among adolescent sex offenders: Concurrent and predictive validity of the Millon Adolescent Clinical Inventory. *Journal of Offender Rehabilitation*, *39*, 1–13. http://dx.doi.org/10.1300/J076v39n04_01

Krishnamurthy, R. (2010). Assessment of adolescents using the PAI–A. In M. Blais, M. Baity, & C. J. Hopwood (Eds.), *Clinical applications of the Personality Assessment Inventory* (pp. 55–76). New York, NY: Routledge.

Lacharité, C., Ethier, L., & Piché, C. (1992). Le stress parental chez les mères d'enfants d'âge préscolaire: Validation et normes québécoises pour l'Inventaire de Stress Parental [Parental stress of mothers with preschool children: Quebec validation and norms for the Parental Stress Inventory]. *Sante Mentale au Quebec*, *17*, 183–203. http://dx.doi.org/10.7202/502077ar

Leary, T. (1957). *Interpersonal diagnosis of personality*. New York, NY: Ronald Press.

Loper, A. B., Hoffschmidt, S. J., & Ash, E. (2001). Personality features and characteristics of violent events committed by juvenile offenders. *Behavioral Sciences and the Law*, *19*, 81–96. http://dx.doi.org/10.1002/bsl.424

Losada-Paisey, G. (1998). Use of the MMPI–A to assess personality of juvenile male delinquents who are sex offenders and nonsex offenders. *Psychological Reports*, *83*, 115–122. http://dx.doi.org/10.2466/pr0.1998.83.1.115

Mallett, C. A., Fukushima, M., Stoddard-Dare, P., & Quinn, L. (2013). Factors related to recidivism for youthful offenders. *Criminal Justice Studies: A Critical Journal of Crime, Law and Society*, *26*, 84–98.

Marks, P. A., Seeman, W., & Haller, D. L. (1974). *The actuarial use of the MMPI with adolescents and adults*. Baltimore, MD: Williams & Wilkins.

McDougall, A., Campbell, M. A., & Santor, D. A. (2013). Institutional offense patterns in adolescent offenders: The role of antisocial and mental health indicators. *Youth Violence and Juvenile Justice*, *11*, 99–114. http://dx.doi.org/10.1177/1541204012457960

Megargee, E. I. (1977). A new classification system for criminal offenders [Special issue]. *Criminal Justice and Behavior*, *4*(2). http://dx.doi.org/10.1177/009385487700400201

Megargee, E. I. (1997). Using the Megargee MMPI-based classification system with the MMPI–2s of female prison inmates. *Psychological Assessment*, *9*, 75–82. http://dx.doi.org/10.1037/1040-3590.9.2.75

Megargee, E. I., Carbonell, J. L., Bohn, M. J., Jr., & Sliger, G. L. (2001). *Classifying criminal offenders with the MMPI–2: The Megargee System*. Minneapolis: University of Minnesota Press.

Melton, G. B., Petrila, J., Poythress, N. G., & Slobogin, C. (2007). *Psychological evaluations for the courts: A handbook for mental health professionals and lawyers* (3rd ed.). New York, NY: Guilford Press.

Millon, T. (1993). *Millon Adolescent Clinical Inventory: Manual*. Bloomington, MN: NCS Pearson.

Millon, T. (1997). *Millon Clinical Multiaxial Inventory—III: manual* (2nd ed.). Minneapolis, MN: Pearson Assessments.

Millon, T., Green, C. J., & Meagher, R. B., Jr. (1982). *Millon Adolescent Personality Inventory manual*. Minneapolis, MN: National Computer Systems.

Monnot, M. J., Quirk, S. W., Hoerger, M., & Brewer, L. (2009). Racial bias in personality assessment: Using the MMPI–2 to predict psychiatric diagnoses of African American and Caucasian chemical dependency inpatients. *Psychological Assessment*, *21*, 137–151. http://dx.doi.org/10.1037/a0015316

Morey, L. C. (1997). *Personality Assessment Inventory professional manual* (2nd ed.). Lutz, FL: Psychological Assessment Resources.

Morey, L. C. (2007). *Personality Assessment Inventory—Adolescent professional manual*. Lutz, FL: Psychological Assessment Resources.

Morey, L. C., & Meyer, J. K. (2013). The Personality Assessment Inventory. In R. P. Archer & E. M. A. Wheeler (Eds.), *Forensic uses of clinical assessment instruments* (2nd ed., pp. 140–174). New York, NY: Routledge.

Morton, T. L., Farris, K. L., & Brenowitz, L. H. (2002). MMPI–A scores and high points of male juvenile delinquents: Scales 4, 5, and 6 as markers of juvenile delinquency. *Psychological Assessment*, *14*, 311–319. http://dx.doi.org/10.1037/1040-3590.14.3.311

Murrie, D. C., Cornell, D. G., Kaplan, S., McConville, D., & Levy-Elkon, A. (2004). Psychopathy scores and violence among juvenile offenders: A multi-measure study. *Behavioral Sciences and the Law*, *22*, 49–67. http://dx.doi.org/10.1002/bsl.573

Office of Juvenile Justice and Delinquency Prevention. (2011). *Juvenile arrests, 2009*. Retrieved from http://www.ojjdp.gov/ojstatbb/publications/StatBB.asp

Office of Juvenile Justice and Delinquency Prevention. (2013). *Easy access to juvenile court statistics: 1985–2010*. Retrieved from http://www.ojjdp.gov/ojstatbb/ezajcs

Otto, R., Greenstein, J., Johnson, M., & Friedman, R. (1992). Prevalence of mental disorders among youth in the juvenile justice system. In J. J. Cocozza (Ed.), *Responding to the mental health needs among youth in the juvenile justice system* (pp. 7–48). Seattle, WA: National Coalition for the Mentally Ill in the Criminal Justice System.

Oxnam, P., & Vess, J. (2008). A typology of adolescent sexual offenders: Millon Adolescent Clinical Inventory profiles, developmental factors, and offence characteristics. *Journal of Forensic Psychiatry and Psychology*, *19*, 228–242. http://dx.doi.org/10.1080/14789940701694452

Parker, J. A., Morton, T. L., Lingefelt, M. E., & Johnson, K. S. (2005). Predictors of serious and violent offending by adjudicated male adolescents. *North American Journal of Psychology*, *7*, 407–417.

Peña, L. M., Megargee, E. I., & Brody, E. (1996). MMPI–A patterns of male juvenile delinquents. *Psychological Assessment*, *8*, 388–397. http://dx.doi.org/10.1037/1040-3590.8.4.388

Pennuto, T. O., & Archer, R. P. (2008). MMPI–A forensic case studies: Uses in documented court decisions. *Journal of Personality Assessment*, *90*, 215–226. http://dx.doi.org/10.1080/00223890701884897

Perfect, M. M., Tharinger, D. J., Keith, T. Z., & Lyle-Lahroud, T. (2011). Relations between Minnesota Multiphasic Personality Inventory–A scales and Rorschach variables with the scope and severity of maltreatment among adolescents. *Journal of Personality Assessment*, *93*, 582–591. http://dx.doi.org/10.1080/00223891.2011.608754

Puzzanchera, C. (2013, December). *Juvenile arrests, 2010*. Retrieved from http://www.ncjj.org/Publication/Juvenile-Arrests-2010.aspx

Quinnell, F. A., & Bow, J. N. (2001). Psychological tests used in child custody evaluations. *Behavioral Sciences and the Law*, *19*, 491–501. http://dx.doi.org/10.1002/bsl.452

Rosenblatt, J. A., Rosenblatt, A., & Biggs, E. E. (2000). Criminal behavior and emotional disorder: Comparing youth served by the mental health and juvenile justice systems. *Journal of Behavioral Health Services and Research*, *27*, 227–237. http://dx.doi.org/10.1007/BF02287315

Salekin, R. T. (2002). Factor analysis of the Millon Adolescent Clinical Inventory in a juvenile offender population: Implications for treatment. *Journal of Offender Rehabilitation*, *34*, 15–29. http://dx.doi.org/10.1300/J076v34n03_02

Salekin, R. T., Leistico, A. R., Schrum, C. L., & Mullins, J. (2005). Millon Adolescent Clinical Inventory. In T. Grisso, G. Vincent, & D. Seagrave (Eds.), *Mental health screening and assessment in juvenile justice* (pp. 253–264). New York, NY: Guilford Press.

Salekin, R. T., Ziegler, T. A., Larrea, M. A., Anthony, V. L., & Bennett, A. D. (2003). Predicting dangerousness with two Millon Adolescent Clinical Inventory psychopathy scales: The importance of egocentric and callous traits. *Journal of Personality Assessment*, *80*, 154–163. http://dx.doi.org/10.1207/S15327752JPA8002_04

Sheras, P. L., Abidin, R. R., & Konold, T. R. (1998). *Stress Index for Parents of Adolescents*. Odessa, FL: Psychological Assessment Resources.

Shereen Jaouni v. Said Samir Ibrahim Salah, No. 0168-11-4, No. 0378-11-4, 2012 Va. App. LEXIS 15 (Va. Ct. App. January 24, 2012).

Simpson, T. P., Frick, P. J., Kahn, R. E., & Evans, L. J. (2013). Therapeutic alliance in justice-involved adolescents undergoing mental health treatment: The role of callous-unemotional traits. *International Journal of Forensic Mental Health*, *12*, 83–92. http://dx.doi.org/10.1080/14999013.2013.787559

Snyder, H. N., & Sickmund, M. (2006). *Juvenile offenders and victims: 2006 national report*. Pittsburgh, PA: National Center for Juvenile Justice.

Stein, L. A. R., & Graham, J. R. (1999). Detecting fake good MMPI–A profiles in a correctional facility. *Psychological Assessment*, *11*, 386–395. http://dx.doi.org/10.1037/1040-3590.11.3.386

Stein, L. A. R., & Graham, J. R. (2001). Use of the MMPI–A to detect substance abuse in a juvenile correctional setting. *Journal of Personality Assessment*, *77*, 508–523. http://dx.doi.org/10.1207/S15327752JPA7703_10

Stein, L. A. R., & Graham, J. R. (2005). Ability of substance abusers to escape detection on the Minnesota Multiphasic Personality Inventory—Adolescent (MMPI–A) in a juvenile correctional facility. *Assessment*, *12*, 28–39. http://dx.doi.org/10.1177/1073191104270838

Taylor, J., Kemper, T. S., Loney, B., & Kistner, J. A. (2009). Recidivism in subgroups of severe male juvenile offenders. *Psychology, Crime, and Law*, *15*, 395–408. http://dx.doi.org/10.1080/10683160802275805

Tellegen, A., & Ben-Porath, Y. S. (2008). *Minnesota Multiphasic Personality Inventory-2 Restructured Form (MMPI–2–RF) technical manual*. Minneapolis: University of Minnesota Press.

Teplin, L. A., Abram, K. M., McClelland, G. M., Dulcan, M. K., & Mericle, A. A. (2002). Psychiatric disorders in youth in juvenile detention. *Archives of General Psychiatry*, *59*, 1133–1143. http://dx.doi.org/10.1001/archpsyc.59.12.1133

Teplin, L. A., Welty, L. J., Abram, K. M., Dulcan, M. K., & Washburn, J. J. (2012). Prevalence and persistence of psychiatric disorders in youth after detention: A prospective longitudinal study. *Archives of General Psychiatry*, *69*, 1031–1043. http://dx.doi.org/10.1001/archgenpsychiatry.2011.2062

Toyer, E. A., & Weed, N. C. (1998). Concurrent validity of the MMPI–A in a counseling program for juvenile offenders. *Journal of Clinical Psychology*, *54*, 395–399. http://dx.doi.org/10.1002/(SICI)1097-4679(199806)54:4<395::AID-JCLP1>3.0.CO;2-N

Vander Stoep, A., Evens, C. C., & Taub, J. (1997). Risk of juvenile justice systems referral among children in a public mental health system. *Journal of Mental Health Administration*, *24*, 428–442.

Vinet, E., & Banares, P. A. (2009). Personality characterization of female juvenile offenders: A comparative study. *Paidéia*, *19*, 143–152.

Welsh, B. C., & Farrington, D. P. (2000). Correctional intervention programs and cost-benefit analysis. *Criminal Justice and Behavior*, *27*, 115–133. http://dx.doi.org/10.1177/0093854800027001007

Williams, C. L., & Butcher, J. N. (2011). *A beginner's guide to the MMPI–A*. Washington, DC: American Psychological Association.

CHAPTER 21

TRANSFER AND COMMITMENT OF YOUTH IN THE UNITED STATES: LAW, POLICY, AND FORENSIC PRACTICE

Kimberly Larson and Thomas Grisso

In this chapter, we discuss two reasons why juvenile courts request evaluations related to the disposition of juvenile cases: commitment and transfer to criminal court. The discussion focuses especially on the ways in which the juvenile and criminal justice systems can overlap as systems attempt to balance public safety with a desire to treat youths according to their unique developmental needs. We begin by discussing the history and foundations of the juvenile justice system, including both transfer and potential punishments juveniles have faced historically and those they face today. We outline the standards and mechanisms used for both transfer and commitment, as well as the historical context for change to these processes. A particular emphasis is placed on the factors most relevant for juvenile forensic evaluators and the associated empirical research. We then explore whether transfer and commitment are accomplishing their stated purposes, address the potential collateral consequences of decisions to transfer or remove a juvenile's liberty, and point out where inequity exists in our system. Finally, we make suggestions for research and practice, as well as potential policy changes, on the basis of the evidence reviewed.

As we review these matters, it is important to keep in mind the justification and purpose for criminal systems and punishment. Society determines the appropriate action to be taken by the state if one is accused or convicted of an offense that violates agreed-on rules or social compacts. Without understanding and identifying the purposes and goals that underlie those decisions, the administration of such a system can be incoherent, inconsistent, and ineffective. To create sound law and policy, one must be aware of, and examine, what one hopes to achieve.

The United States leads the world in the punishment of its citizens, making it particularly important to examine its rationales and understand that the decisions made reflect the society's values. Multiple underlying purposes can be competing, and one may take precedence over others as historical context influences goals. The purposes or goals of justice systems are usually divided into four categories: retribution, deterrence, incapacitation, and rehabilitation. *Retribution* seeks to punish the individual for his or her wrongdoing and pursue justice for the victims and the individual's violation of the social compact of societal rules prohibiting that action. Restitution to victims is sometimes subsumed within this category or separated out as its own category. *Deterrence* can be general or specific. General deterrence embodies the idea that others will be stopped from committing similar offenses by seeing another punished for it. Specific deterrence implies that this particular individual will not commit future offenses for fear of being punished again. *Incapacitation* of offenders refers to incarcerating them or otherwise keeping them away from society so that they may not harm others for the duration of their sentence. Finally, the goal of *rehabilitation* is to use the state's police power to help individuals avoid future offenses and perhaps improve their lives. For example, a system might provide education or job skills so that offenders can be productive members of society upon their release from jail or prison (Demleitner, Berman, Miller, & Wright, 2013).

http://dx.doi.org/10.1037/14643-021
APA Handbook of Psychology and Juvenile Justice, K. Heilbrun (Editor-in-Chief)

In the United States, as in any society, overlaid on these general principles are the limits imposed by its particular legal system. These limits may affect the ability to accomplish some or all of these goals. For example, constitutional prohibitions against cruel and unusual punishment and the requirement of proportionality to the act committed and the individual's associated intent may limit retributive goals. Legislation may proscribe sentencing procedures that limit the length of incapacitation within a set range. These legal variations may implicitly or explicitly result in one theory of punishment becoming more dominant, pushing others into the background.

FOUNDATIONS OF JUVENILE COURTS IN THE UNITED STATES

Before social reform movements that led to the creation of the juvenile courts in the late 1800s, juveniles were generally treated similarly to adults with regard to criminal offenses. Youths younger than age 7 could be charged, but could assert an "infancy" defense, contending legal incompetence and the inability to form the intent to commit the crime alleged (Dressler, 1999). For those between ages 7 and 14, there was a rebuttable presumption of lack of capacity. Youthfulness did not enter into consideration for those older than 14. They were subject to the same sentencing as adults and, if incarcerated, sent to the same facilities as adults (Stapleton & Teitelbaum, 1972).

Social reformers wanted to change this system (Mack, 1909). They believed that juveniles were still developing and thus more capable of change than their adult counterparts. Reformers attributed delinquency to poverty and environmental sources rather than simply to individual causes. Using the *parens patriae* powers of the state, they sought to aid rather than punish youths (Garner, 1999). They envisioned a separate system that would provide assessment and individualized treatment and would be civil rather than criminal in nature, resulting in decreased stigma.[1] Because this new juvenile system would be rehabilitative, reformers thought the same procedural protections afforded adults were unnecessary (Stapleton & Teitelbaum, 1972). If the juvenile system was to protect rather than punish the child, the trappings and formalities of the adult court would restrict the ability of the court to accomplish its rehabilitative goals (Larson, 2003).

Foundations of Transfer and Commitment of Youths

Both commitment and transfer of juveniles were possible even at the juvenile court's inception. Commitment is the curtailment or removal of an individual's liberty, often through confinement in a secure institution. With regard to commitment determinations, juvenile judges had more latitude to fashion a disposition with more available treatment-based options than were available in the adult system. These sanctions ranged from less restrictive means, such as release into the community with probation conditions, to the removal of a youth's liberty. In the latter case, youths could be committed or incapacitated. In the early 19th century, secure youth facilities were known as houses of refuge. As these facilities began to face the same problems of overcrowding and abuses seen in adult correctional facilities, new institutions were opened. These new facilities, often called training schools, reform schools, or industrial schools, still sometimes retain these names but are more often simply known today as youth correctional institutions.

Transfer is a pretrial mechanism that allows youths to be moved from the jurisdiction of the juvenile court to the jurisdiction of the criminal court. Once the decision is made to hear the case in adult court, the youth is subject to the same criminal statutory scheme and punishments that apply to adult offenders (Grisso & Schwartz, 2000). Early in the history of the juvenile court, transfer was reserved for only the most severe offenses committed by older juveniles. In the early 1900s, few youths were transferred for adjudication as adults. Most of those youths were 16- to 17-year-olds who were charged with serious offenses. Until the 1970s,

[1]With the creation of the juvenile system came a separate set of terms aimed at reducing the stigma associated with justice system involvement. For example, youths were not found guilty or not guilty; they were delinquent or not delinquent. Instead of being incarcerated, they were committed to a youth facility.

most cases were transferred according to judicial discretion. Early on, the rationale for transfer was that a particular youth would have a negative impact on efforts to rehabilitate other youths if he or she remained in the juvenile system. In the 1990s, fueled by media portrayals of the emergence of juvenile "superpredators," transfer became more common. Legislatures responded to the fear of the spike in juvenile crime in the 1980s and 1990s by changing statutory schemes to allow more youths to be transferred for more crimes at younger ages. States also began to add additional mechanisms to accomplish transfer (reviewed in detail later in this chapter; Griffin, Addie, Adams, & Firestine, 2011).

Decline of the Juvenile System and Recognition of Youths' Legal Rights

Some have argued that the juvenile system's laudable goals never came to fruition (Ryerson, 1978). Others have pointed to a lack of resources combined with the burgeoning caseload of the juvenile courts to explain the downturn of the juvenile courts (Besharov, 1974; Krisberg & Austin, 1993). Either way, by the 1960s the U.S. Supreme Court began to take a close look at the juvenile system. Beginning with *Kent v. United States* (1966) and *In re Gault* (1967), and continuing with their progeny, the Supreme Court recognized that youths were receiving the worst of both worlds—harsh punishments rather than rehabilitative opportunities and none of the due process protections afforded in the adult criminal system. The Court held that youths were entitled to procedural protections, including the right to notice of the charges, the right to counsel, the right to confront and cross-examine witnesses against them, and the privilege against self-incrimination. More importantly, the Court also outlined factors to guide transfer decisions. Commonly referred to as the *Kent* factors, they include (a) seriousness of the offense and risk to public safety; (b) violence or premeditation; (c) whether it was an offense against a person or property; (d) merit of the complaint and strength of the case; (e) whether codefendants were adults who would be tried in District Court and desirability of trial of entire case in one court; (f) sophistication and maturity of the youth, including home, environmental situation, emotional attitude, and pattern of living; (g) prior offense history; and (h) the probability that the youth could be treated or rehabilitated using the services available to the juvenile court (*Kent v. United States*, 1966).

Since *Kent v. United States* (1966) and *In re Gault* (1967), the Court has affirmed that youth are entitled to the use of the "beyond a reasonable doubt" standard (*In re Winship*, 1970, p. 368) and held that juvenile adjudication constitutes jeopardy within the meaning of the Fifth Amendment because the trier of fact hears facts and evidence. Thus, subsequent criminal charges arising out of the same incident would constitute double jeopardy (*Breed v. Jones*, 1975). The Court has declined to require jury trials in juvenile proceedings, however, stating that it would increase the formality of proceedings too much, resulting in a decrease in the flexibility needed to accomplish its goals (*McKeiver v. Pennsylvania*, 1971). Nonetheless, regardless of the causes of the perceived failures of the juvenile system, rehabilitative ideals are still cited as the foundation of the juvenile justice system, and youths are entitled to due process rights similar to those of their adult counterparts.[2]

Recent Supreme Court Developments Affecting Conceptualizations of Adolescence

More recently, the Supreme Court granted *certiorari* and heard a line of landmark cases that have influenced the law's conceptualization of adolescence. Akin to the Court's Eighth Amendment jurisprudence that "death is different," this recent line of cases appears to demonstrate that the Court recognizes that adolescence is different. It is important to note that the Supreme Court's understanding of adolescence and youthfulness was shaped in part by the extant body of psychological research (reviewed in more detail below) demonstrating how adolescents are different from adults in their decision making. Forensic experts in juvenile cases will want to be knowledgeable about this recent body of jurisprudence and its

[2]The Supreme Court did not require juvenile courts to hold jury trials. However, this serves as the "constitutional floor." States may provide more protection, and a handful of states allow juvenile court jury trials (e.g., Massachusetts).

ramifications for legal interpretations regarding the unique characteristics of youths.

Beginning with *Roper v. Simmons* (2005),[3] in which the Court held that those younger than age 18 could not be subject to the death penalty, the Court recognized that, based on both social science research and common sense, youths differed from adults in important ways that had implications for adjudication. The Court cited three broad categories of divergence between the two groups: (a) a "lack of maturity and an underdeveloped sense of responsibility" (*Roper v. Simmons*, 2005, p. 569); (b) "juveniles have less control, or less experience with control, over their own environment. . . . [As] legal minors, . . . juveniles lack the freedom that adults have to extricate themselves from a criminogenic setting"; and (c) "that the character of a juvenile is not as well formed as that of an adult" (*Roper v. Simmons*, 2005, p. 570). The Court explained,

> The differences between juvenile and adult offenders are too marked and well understood to risk allowing a youthful person to receive the death penalty despite insufficient culpability. An unacceptable likelihood exists that the brutality or cold-blooded nature of any particular crime would overpower mitigating arguments based on youth as a matter of course, even where the juvenile offender's objective immaturity, vulnerability, and lack of true depravity should require a sentence less severe than death. . . . These differences render suspect any conclusion that a juvenile falls among the worst offenders. (*Roper v. Simmons*, 2005, p. 573)

Juveniles' susceptibility to immature and irresponsible behavior means "their irresponsible conduct is not as morally reprehensible as that of an adult" (*Roper v. Simmons*, 2005, p. 570). Six years later, in the *Miranda v. Arizona* (1966) context, the Court again held that the "reasonable person under the circumstances" test must be adjusted to account for developmental differences. In *J.D.B. v. North Carolina* (2011), the Court asked whether a juvenile's age should be accounted for when determining whether the youth felt he or she could leave an interrogation for the purposes of the Court's analysis of custodial status according to the standards set out in *Miranda* and expounded on through its later jurisprudence (e.g., *Berghuis v. Thompkins*, 2010). The Court held in the affirmative, stating that youthfulness is one factor that must be considered by courts in this calculation—in essence creating a "reasonable juvenile under the circumstances" standard.

In 2010, the Court squarely took up the question of whether youths could be subject to life without parole (LWOP) for nonhomicide offenses, deciding that youthful factors should exclude them from LWOP (*Graham v. Florida*, 2010). Relying in part on research presented by both the American Medical Association and the American Psychological Association, the Court stated that "developments in psychology and brain science continue to show fundamental differences between the juvenile and adult minds" (*Graham v. Florida*, 2010, p. 13). *Graham*, however, left open the question of whether juveniles who committed homicide offenses were also excluded from LWOP.

In the consolidated cases of *E.J.M. v. State* (2004) and *Jackson v. State* (2004), just 2 years after *Graham*, the Court again examined juvenile LWOP, this time addressing homicide offenses (*Miller v. Alabama*, 2012). Ultimately, the Court held that mandatory LWOP sentences for homicide offenses committed by juveniles were unconstitutional. The Court stated that imposing a mandatory sentence with no meaningful opportunity to obtain release did not take into account age and other mitigating factors unique to youths. Thus, if a youth could demonstrate increased maturity, growth, and rehabilitation, he or she should not by rule be locked away without at least some hope for future release. Although the full import of this decision is currently being determined by legislative and court action nationally, it is clear that the Court has continued its line of jurisprudence recognizing the importance of youthfulness in legal decision making (Larson, DiCataldo, & Kinscherff, 2013).

[3]Notably, approximately 15 years before *Roper* the Supreme Court faced the question of whether it was permissible to execute those who had committed a capital offense at age 16 or 17, finding that it was acceptable under the evolving standards of decency standard at that time and was not cruel and unusual punishment under the Eighth Amendment (*Stanford v. Kentucky*, 1989).

Standards and Mechanisms for Transfer and Commitment

Every state currently allows for transfer and commitment of youths, but they differ regarding which youth, under what conditions, who makes the determination, and what criteria are used (Griffin et al., 2011). Judges make determinations regarding commitment of youths, and they may or may not be steered by guidelines. Sentencing guidelines are a grid that provides a range for length of sentence available to the court. The ranges are based on current offense type and prior offense history. They sometimes incorporate age as a consideration. In some states in which the sentence is judicially determined, the judge may commit the juvenile to the youth authority, who then perform an evaluation to determine placement. Little is known about how judges weigh the various options in commitment decisions. However, factors considered in their decision making may involve social and moral issues, appropriately judged solely by legal criteria and societal mores such as prior offense history, seriousness of the offense, or whether the offense was against people or property. Forensic evaluators, however, can provide input on issues such as the youth's age and level of maturity, the nature of the offense in relation to the youth's level of risk to the community, placement options, appropriate services available at each placement, and the youth's likelihood of success. Given the variability among states, forensic evaluators should know the governing law in their jurisdiction.

Decisions regarding transfer are much more varied regarding who holds the decision-making power and the structure guiding the process. Three common ways that youths end up in adult courts are by statutory exclusion, judicial waiver, and prosecutorial discretion (Sickmund, 2003). The U.S. Department of Justice reports that statutory exclusion is the most commonly used method of transfer, with 41.6% of all juvenile transfers occurring via this mechanism (Griffin et al., 2011). Also known as statutory waiver, this mechanism legislatively removes discretion regarding transfer. Youths who are of a certain age and charged with certain types of offenses are sent straight to adult court. In some states, there is no method of review; in others, youths may be evaluated to determine reverse waiver or decertification, that is, whether the youth's case should be adjudicated in juvenile court.

In prosecutorial waiver (also known as direct file or prosecutorial discretion), the prosecutor determines whether the youth should remain in juvenile court or be tried in criminal court. This discretion is not without limits. Generally, only older youths who are charged with specific categories of offenses can be considered. In some states, there is no method of review of the prosecutor's determination and the entrance of discretion into the decision can result in disparate decisions across similar cases or offenders (discussed further later in this chapter).

Today, judicial waiver most closely approximates the transfer procedure as it existed at the inception of the juvenile courts, but the stated rationale has changed. The rationale is now more public safety oriented than in the past, with less focus on the protection of other youths in the juvenile system. Today, under the standards set in *Kent v. United States* (1966), the court must also state the reasons or factors it considered in its transfer decision.[4]

Judicial waiver can be divided into three subtypes. In discretionary judicial waiver, the court must hold a hearing and must consider certain factors. This procedure allows the judge the greatest amount of latitude in fashioning individualized treatment of each youth. Some states limit the judge's discretion through statutorily enumerated factors that must be considered in the judge's decision. Other states use presumptive waivers in which juveniles older than a certain age charged with certain offenses face a presumption that they are not amenable to rehabilitation. The juvenile bears the burden and must overcome this presumption to remain in juvenile court. Mandatory judicial waivers are more akin to statutory exclusions. Although the judge still holds a hearing, the court's role is much more limited. The judge must determine whether certain criteria are met (e.g., the juvenile is older

[4]The three most common factors relevant for forensic evaluators are risk or dangerousness, amenability to treatment, and sophistication or maturity of the youth.

than a particular age, charged with a certain offense, and probable cause exists to believe the youth committed the offense). If the conditions are met, the case is transferred to criminal court.

Blended sentencing laws and youthful offender programs provide additional mechanisms by which youths can overlap the juvenile and adult systems. These policies and programs attempt to balance individualization and rehabilitative goals with public safety. Blended sentencing laws generally expand the sentencing options for juvenile or criminal court judges, allowing them to sentence juveniles to some combination of juvenile and adult consequences. If a judge believes a youth is particularly amenable to treatment and should have one more chance, he or she can send the youth to a youthful offender program, which is sometimes referred to as an intermediate system or middle system. Such programs may be contained within the adult corrections system but follow more treatment-oriented philosophies. However, as the names *intermediate system* and *middle system* imply, through use of both juvenile and adult system resources, youthful offender programs seek to incorporate rehabilitation while protecting the public.

There are three types of blended sentencing laws: inclusive, exclusive, and contiguous. Two detailed reviews are available (Cheeseman, 2011; Snyder & Sickmund, 2006). The most common blended sentences are the inclusive blends. The court with jurisdiction (either juvenile or criminal) sentences the juvenile to both juvenile and adult sanctions. The adult sentence is suspended as long as the juvenile successfully completes the juvenile program and does not commit any new offenses. These types of sentences are imposed to increase compliance with a program and to deter future criminal activity; they are allowed in 16 states (11 juvenile inclusive and 5 criminal inclusive).

The second most common type of blended sentences are the exclusive blends. Under these sentencing schemes, the court of jurisdiction is allowed to impose either juvenile or adult sanctions. This model expands the sentencing options for both juvenile and criminal courts such that either can impose a more rehabilitative or retributive sentence as they deem appropriate. Nine states have this type of sentencing scheme (one juvenile exclusive and eight criminal exclusive).

Finally, five states follow the contiguous model of blended sentencing. Under this model, juvenile judges can sentence a juvenile to a longer sentence than would typically be allowed under the state's juvenile statutes. The juvenile is initially committed to a juvenile facility and may be transferred to an adult facility at a later date. On reaching the typical statutory maximum age of jurisdiction, the juvenile court decides whether the juvenile should serve the remainder of the sentence in an adult facility. In general, blended sentencing increases judges' discretion, allowing them to sentence juveniles who are convicted in one type of court (either juvenile or criminal) to sentences that are typically only available in the other type of court.

Although the compromises sought by blended sentencing may be appealing, the constitutionality of such sentences could be questioned. In the line of sentencing cases involving adult defendants, the Supreme Court considered the question of whether a fact that increases a penalty above the statutorily delineated maximum can be determined by a judge or must be found by a jury (*Apprendi v. New Jersey*, 2000) The Court in *Apprendi* held any facts that increase a penalty beyond the statutory maximum must be found by a jury. *Blakely v. Washington* (2004) defined the key term *statutory maximum*. The Court held the statutory maximum is the highest penalty the judge can impose without any additional facts. Judges exceed their authority if they increase a penalty that was not based on the jury's findings alone (*Blakely v. Washington*, 2004).

In blended sentencing schemes, the judge can impose juvenile and adult sentences or punishments. The addition of this adult penalty enhances the sentencing authority of the court and also exposes the youth to a variety of concomitant additional risks collateral to adult sentences (discussed in more detail below), calling into question the constitutionality of blended sentencing under this body of Supreme Court sentencing jurisprudence. However, one could also argue that the differences between juvenile and adult courts make this line of Supreme Court cases inapplicable. In particular, following the Supreme Court's holding in *McKeiver v.*

Pennsylvania (1971), most states do not allow jury trials in juvenile proceedings.

FORENSIC EVALUATIONS FOR COMMITMENT AND TRANSFER OF YOUTHS

The courts regularly call on forensic evaluators to assist in answering questions regarding the commitment and transfer of youths. In practice, many of the factors enumerated in the *Kent v. United States* (1966) criteria are reflected in a variety of types of juvenile forensic assessments. Evaluators may find significant overlap in the types of factors one might assess in opining about the appropriateness of transfer to adult court or reverse waiver to juvenile court, whether to commit a youth to a juvenile justice authority or sentence him or her to a term of incarceration in an adult correctional facility, or even in considering the more recent issues expounded in *Miller v. Alabama* (2012) for consideration regarding juvenile LWOP. Across contexts and legal issues, whether in case law or legislatively enumerated, similar questions can be grouped, and several common factors emerge. In particular, forensic evaluators can provide expertise in three areas: (a) danger or risk, (b) amenability to treatment given available resources, and (c) the sophistication or maturity of the youth. Each of these factors has been the subject of entire chapters and, indeed, even books. We provide broad contours below, but readers are directed to discussions in specific chapters of this handbook devoted to each topic as well as references provided here for fuller discussion.

Danger and Risk of Recidivism

Over the past 40 years, the field of risk assessment has advanced substantially from the common practice of using highly unreliable clinical judgment alone to make dichotomous dangerous versus not-dangerous categorizations. Practice has evolved to include the use of standardized methods with greatly enhanced understanding of the subtleties of this multiply-determined construct. Assessment of risk is now understood not to be a prediction of future dangerousness but instead an estimation of the likelihood that an individual will engage in a specific behavior given a specific set of circumstances.

Good risk assessment practices involve the use of standardized methods that are empirically validated, incorporating factors that have been demonstrated to be associated with risk across multiple research studies, and using tools validated for a specific situation and population. Assessments incorporate not only risk factors but areas in which interventions are needed and consider areas of possible resiliency that might mitigate against future risk of harm or continued criminal engagement (Borum, Bartel, & Forth, 2006). Moreover, they must take into account special types of risk or categories of individuals and consider the impact of developmental status on risk assessment (Larson & Kinscherff, 2014). Clinicians may use the same underlying basic theories and approaches, but they understand that assessment of risk is a person–situation analysis that considers both individual characteristics and context.

Methodology is similar in commitment and transfer cases, but the questions posed in a transfer decision differ from those posed in decisions regarding placement (Grisso, 2013). The difference in legal context alters the objectives of the evaluation. In the commitment context, the question is whether the youth's risk is such that his or her liberty should be curtailed to protect the public. In other words, it involves a description and comparison of the likelihood of the youth's risk under varying sets of circumstances created by the various dispositional options available to the juvenile court. This type of evaluation calls for a shorter term evaluation of risk than those involved in the transfer context. The evaluator must consider the contexts or situations in which a youth may be placed given the various options available to the court. Each type of placement can influence the likelihood of a youth exhibiting aggression.

In the transfer or waiver context, courts ask whether this youth is of such high risk now that he or she could pose a danger in the juvenile system and whether the youth's risk will likely continue into early adulthood, such that he or she should be treated as an adult for the purposes of his or her adjudication. The clinician should, therefore, assess the youth's likely response to rehabilitation in the juvenile system in the time left within the court's jurisdiction, but he or she will also need to examine risk further into the future. Compared with commitment context, transfer asks for longer term assessment of risk and about much more serious types of risk. The further into the future one is asked to assess the likelihood of risk, the less effective or accurate are current methodologies and tools. This decrease is particularly important with youths who are constantly developing and changing, giving risk assessments an even shorter shelf life.

Evaluators should start from the baseline that most youths will desist from offending behavior. Even among those who have committed violent acts, there is a low likelihood of continuing violence in adulthood (Elliott, Huizinga, & Morse, 1986; Moffitt, 1993). Starting from this premise, evaluators should use empirically based factors and tools to assess risk. Evaluators should be knowledgeable about the literature on risk factors and examine factors such as past behavior, substance abuse, peer groups, community and family influences, stressors, personality characteristics, and mental health issues. The assessment may need to take into account case-specific factors or necessary adjustments for special populations. For example, males are more likely to engage in delinquent behaviors than females and have been the subject of more empirical research. Risk factors applicable to males may not apply to females or may need to be weighed differently. One must also consider the type of risk being assessed. For example, if the case involves a sex offense, then the evaluator must consider the specialized literature on this type of risk (DiCataldo, 2009).

Evaluators should also be well versed in the types of tools available to assess factors empirically shown to be related to risk and the approaches on which they are based. Examples of well-studied and commonly used instruments include actuarial tools such as the Youth Level of Service/Case Management Inventory (Hoge & Andrews, 2010), as well as those that are based on structured professional judgment such as the Structured Assessment of Violence Risk in Youth (Borum et al., 2006). Actuarial tools use validated factors to arrive at a score that classifies a youth as high, moderate, or low risk. Structured professional judgment tools use validated factors as categories of information to be collected by the examiner but allow the examiner to arrive at a judgment about level of risk that does not rely on a formula. The two approaches have been found to be of equal value in estimating the likelihood of recidivism, but the structured professional judgment approach tends to be more responsive to changes in likelihood of recidivism when a youth is reassessed in the future (Vincent, Terry, & Maney, 2009).

Amenability to Treatment and Relation to Resources Available

In line with its rehabilitative foundation, juvenile courts are interested in what can be done in providing services to change a youth, as well as the youth's ability to be changed and likely response to any interventions available in the juvenile system. Research-validated methods for formulating such recommendations are not available. However, clinicians can rely on theory and personal expertise and knowledge of the system to assist the court (Grisso, 2013).

Issues of treatment amenability are of interest to the court in both transfer and commitment decisions. In both, courts ask amenability-related questions focused on improving youth functioning, decreasing risk of future criminal involvement, and promoting public safety. In the transfer context, amenability is raised before adjudication because the court must determine whether the youth is most appropriate for the juvenile or adult system. The inquiry focuses on the characteristics of the youth that call for intervention, and whether these interventions are likely to be successful or are available within the jurisdiction in which the question is raised (Grisso, 2013). In commitment cases, the primary focus is learning about the youth and his or her needs. Those needs can then be matched with that jurisdiction's available services. Where no service exists, the court can sometimes look outside the jurisdiction for the needed service. The court will also have questions regarding the level of security a youth may require.

Forensic evaluators should examine the characteristics of a particular youth, which of these are appropriate targets for intervention, the interventions that meet the youth's needs that are available, and the likelihood that the plan will succeed

(Grisso, 2013). Important domains of youth functioning include the youth's physical and mental health, both historically and currently; intellectual capacities and school performance; information about the youth's family and its functioning; and other relevant information related to the child's social history. The report should discuss the youth's behavior (including misbehavior in school and delinquent acts) and personality and any clinical diagnostic impressions formed. More importantly, research has demonstrated that the presence of mental health issues in juvenile justice populations is significant. Some studies have estimated that as many as two thirds of youths meet criteria for at least one diagnosis, with many meeting criteria for two or more (Cocozza & Skowyra, 2000; Teplin, Abram, McClelland, Dulcan, & Mericle, 2002). Notably, this means that although many youths will meet criteria for conduct disorder, it is important to look further. About 80% of youths who meet criteria for conduct disorder also meet criteria for another mental health diagnosis (Grisso, 2004). Issues related to mood such as depression and anxiety disorders such as posttraumatic stress disorder are frequently seen in juvenile justice–involved youths. Attention-deficit/hyperactivity disorder and substance abuse or dependence are also very commonly diagnosed (Schufelt & Cocozza, 2006).

Courts often seek information about remorsefulness, but forensic examiners should tread carefully because this can be a particularly difficult construct to address. Currently available tools do not directly tap this construct, and preadjudication questioning about remorse may violate youths' Fifth Amendment rights (Heilbrun, Shah, Foster, Keesler, & Brooks, 2014). Furthermore, youths have the potential and motivation to express remorse when none is present, but they can also be inhibited from expressing it or potentially appear to lack remorse when it is present because of other developmental factors (Grisso, 2013).

Past treatment and rehabilitation efforts should be carefully described because courts often use such information in deciding whether a youth can be rehabilitated. In assessing amenability, descriptions of past treatment are also important, but evaluators should be careful to collect detailed information. Some youths may never have had access to treatment. Others will have multiple recorded past treatment attempts. Both treatment successes and failures should be scrutinized, and evaluators should describe each intervention and its outcome. Treatment failures should not automatically be equated with youth lack of investment or effort (Grisso, 2013). The examiner should look for detail regarding the type, quality, and design of the treatment. Moreover, evaluators should consider whether the treatment provided was a match for this youth's needs during the particular developmental stage it was provided. Questions might include whether the intervention was well implemented (including what services were planned compared with what was actually received), how they were provided and by whom, and whether intervening or superseding events occurred that may have interfered with success. Finally, it is also important to look for treatment successes and the conditions surrounding improvements. What worked or has not worked can be clues used to design future services.

One must identify the areas that, with intervention, are likely to decrease future risk of delinquency or future harm, increase the youth's functioning, or both. The enumerated areas can then be matched to approaches to address them. Notably, this involves not only knowing what interventions are best suited to addressing the problem, but the quality of those interventions and which interventions are available to the court. A court is not assisted by a list of suggestions that are not among the options available to it, and options will vary from state to state (and even within states).

In fashioning a plan, clinicians should note two important legal trends or concepts: (a) requirements to provide services in the least restrictive alternative and (b) diversion programs aimed at decreasing juvenile justice contact. The youth's liberty should only be curtailed as much as is required to protect the public and rehabilitate the youth. For example, given equivalent services, a community-based service is preferable unless the juvenile's security needs dictate otherwise. Relatedly, the juvenile justice system has moved toward diverting youth to decrease their juvenile justice system involvement and exposure and minimize removal of their liberty though efforts such as the Juvenile Detention Alternatives Initiative.

Legal system constraints can create difficult transfer decisions in some cases. The upper age limit of the juvenile court varies among states. For example, if a state's limit was 18 and the juvenile was 16, the youth would only remain within the court's jurisdiction or power for 2 more years. The clinician may think the youth would be assisted by the types of services available to the court, but not within the remaining 2 years. The upper jurisdictional limit of the court could result in the court leaning toward a decision involving transfer, for instance. As discussed earlier, mechanisms such as blended sentencing have evolved in some states to attempt to address such issues. Clinicians must be familiar with the upper jurisdictional age limit and legal mechanisms (e.g., blended sentencing, youthful offender programs) available in their state.

Sophistication and Maturity

The juvenile justice system is based on two assumptions: (a) Youths are less capable of mature judgment than adults, making them less culpable for offenses they commit, and (b) they are more amenable to treatment than their adult counterparts (Scott & Grisso, 1998). A youth who is less mature may therefore be seen as more appropriate to remain in the juvenile system, which can provide individualized treatment to account for the youth's unique developmental characteristics.

Both transfer and commitment determinations may also consider whether a juvenile is psychologically mature enough to be considered culpable for his or her actions. Both will also likely involve the examination of the whether the youth's offenses have become more "adultlike" (i.e., whether the youth's offenses have become too repetitive or whether the youth is solidly committed to a criminal culture), such that he or she is unlikely to desist from such behavior and continue criminal patterns. In the transfer determination, those who are more adultlike will be seen as appropriately handled in criminal court because they are less likely to change and more likely to continue their criminality into adulthood. For commitment purposes, more sophisticated youths may be seen as having higher security needs, whereas immature youths may not be appropriate for secure treatment facilities. However, if the crime is serious enough, maturity and its relationship to culpability may become secondary considerations to safety and security.

The age of majority is typically sometime between the 18th and 21st birthday, depending on the state. The cutoff for the age of majority is based on social convention rather than any empirical evidence. The extant body of developmental and psychological research, however, supports the ideas put forth by the creators of the juvenile system—youths differ from adults in important ways. Their still-developing capacities have been well documented through behavioral research and, more recently, through the use of technology such as functional MRI. Youths mature on different trajectories and complete various maturational stages at different times—many after the arbitrary legal age cutoff for adulthood.

Changes during adolescence, including the development of psychosocial maturity, can affect decision making. Compared with most adults, adolescents are more impulsive, less future oriented, weigh risks differently, and are more susceptible to the influences of others such as peers (Scott & Steinberg, 2008). Adolescents, for example, are less likely to consider the long-term consequences of their actions (Cauffman et al., 2007). They have difficulty taking the perspective of others and are still developing capacities for impulse control (Steinberg & Scott, 2003), which can put them at greater risk for reoffending (Little & Steinberg, 2006). Although juveniles may recognize that certain aspects of their behavior are problematic, they are likely to engage in these behaviors if they do not perceive immediate negative consequences. Rather than considering the potential long-term consequences of their behavior, they are likely to give more weight to their own curiosity and peer approval. Moreover, some behaviors that are considered delinquent, criminal, or both are common and normative in adolescents; adolescents engage in these behaviors to determine their role and test boundaries in the adult world (Cauffman, Steinberg, & Piquero, 2005). The frequency of many of these behaviors peaks in mid-adolescence, then decreases into young adulthood.

By measuring psychosocial maturity, clinicians are able to assess a range of psychological and social factors that can affect the quality of a juvenile's decision making. Psychosocial maturity might be better than simply using age as a proxy to measure whether young people are functioning at an adult level. Evaluators will want to look not only at the youth's age in examinations of sophistication and maturity, but also at each of these developmental factors, providing the court with information about the youth's maturational level with regard to each and explaining their potential impact on the youth's behavior.

Clinicians can use methods developed by developmental psychologists to examine developmental maturity or immaturity. Well-developed tools are available to tap into constructs such as intellectual and cognitive ability, capacity for emotional control, and development of social skills. Newer tools are exploring youths' decisional capacities in relation to blameworthiness and abilities related to competence to stand trial. One relatively recently developed instrument that holds particular promise in the transfer context is the Risk Sophistication Treatment Inventory (Salekin, Salekin, Clements, & Leistico, 2005). This tool assesses not only psychosocial maturity but also risk and amenability to treatment. Within the domain of psychosocial maturity, it structures the collection of data on three dimensions: autonomy or self-directedness, cognitive capacities such as the ability to think and plan ahead, and emotional development, including concepts such as impulse control.

THE NATIONAL LANDSCAPE: RATES OF TRANSFER AND COMMITMENT OF YOUTHS IN THE UNITED STATES

Seemingly in contrast to the psychological research and recent Supreme Court decisions (discussed earlier), youths continue to be transferred and committed at high rates. Although rates of youth crime peaked in 1994 and then steadily declined, thousands of youths are transferred to criminal court each year (Griffin et al., 2011). Under the expanded mechanisms outlined earlier, transfer during the 1990s changed from being an infrequently used remedy to one used much more frequently, with some states allowing multiple mechanisms for transfer. Transfer was no longer reserved for the worst cases.

In approximately 45 states, judicial discretion can be used to transfer a youth to adult court. Prosecutors have discretion to make this determination in another 15 states (Griffin et al., 2011). Legislative changes also allow for youths to be transferred at younger ages for wider varieties of offenses. In fact, in at least four states there is no age below which youths cannot be transferred. In three states, 10-year-olds are eligible for transfer, with one state having no restrictions on the type of criminal offense charged. In three additional states, 13-year-olds may be transferred for any offense, and six more states allow this at age 14. Some states specify a certain group of offenses for which younger youths may be transferred, with 10-year-olds qualifying in one state, 13-year-olds in three states, and 14-year-olds in 13 states. Transfer-eligible offenses can include nonviolent felonies, drug charges, and in some states property offenses (Hoeffel, 2013).

Some research has shown evidence of state attempts to reverse this trend, decreasing the use of transfer. Between 2005 and 2010, legislation in 10 states made it more likely that youths would remain in the juvenile system, three states changed their laws to decrease the number of older youths who would be automatically sent to the adult system, and four states passed legislation changing their mandatory minimum sentences to account for developmental factors (Campaign for Youth Justice, 2011). From 2011 to 2013, this pattern continued with an additional four, 12, and 11 states passing these types of legislation, respectively (Campaign for Youth Justice, 2013).

In comparison to other countries, the United States' policies appear far more punitive with regard to sentencing and incarceration of juveniles (Annie E. Casey Foundation, 2013). The numbers of committed youths in the United States exploded between 1985 and 2000, nearly doubling (National Juvenile Justice Network & Texas Public Policy Institute, 2011). Youth confinement by all accounts appears to have peaked and be on the decline. Some reports have shown an apex in 1995 with 107,637 confined on an average day (Annie E. Casey Foundation, 2013), and others have argued that this peak did not occur until 2000 (National Juvenile Justice Network & Texas Public Policy Institute, 2011). Nonetheless, reliance on incapacitation may be reversing (Kids Count Data Center, 2014). An examination of 2010 data demonstrated a 39% decrease in incarceration of juveniles since 2000 (National Juvenile Justice Network & Texas Public Policy Institute, 2011). Similarly, other studies have shown that, since 1995, confinement of youths has decreased from 381 per 100,000 youths to 225 per 100,000 youths (Annie E. Casey Foundation, 2013). California, Connecticut, Illinois, Ohio, Mississippi, New York, Texas, Washington, and Wisconsin have been singled out for their particularly strong results in their efforts at reducing youth incarceration.

National decline in youth confinement has been attributed to factors such as efforts to close or decrease facilities available to confine youths and requiring intake procedures designed to decrease use of incapacitation, increased use of evidence-based alternatives to incarceration, efforts to interrupt the school-to-prison pipeline, and decreased use of incarceration for minor offenses, especially through special prearraignment diversion programs (National Juvenile Justice Network & Texas Public Policy Institute, 2011). Between 2005 and 2010, four states passed legislation to decrease the use of adult correctional facilities for youths (Campaign for Youth Justice, 2011). From 2011 to 2013, another 11 states passed such legislation (Campaign for Youth Justice, 2013).

Nearly 40% of youths are committed for nonviolent, low-level infractions, including technical violations of probation conditions and status offenses (Annie E. Casey Foundation, 2013; Justice Policy Institute, 2009; Sickmund, Sladky, Kang, & Puzzanchera, 2008), indicating an area in which continued efforts at reduction of use of confinement may be warranted. Others have argued that reduction of commitment of youths also makes fiscal sense. Holding a youth in secure state-funded facilities after adjudication costs an average of $240.99 per day, resulting in each state spending approximately $5.7 billion per year (Justice Policy Institute, 2009).

Are the Stated Goals Being Accomplished?

Given the continued use of both transfer and commitment of youth, it is important to examine whether the stated goals of these policies are being accomplished. In the case of the juvenile system, those goals focus on rehabilitation, and thus reduction in recidivism. In addition, given that rehabilitation is not the sole focus of the legal system, it is logical to examine the other historically cited purposes of punishment (incapacitation, deterrence, and retribution).

Transfer. On the issue of transfer, several comprehensive reviews have found mixed results (e.g., Redding, 2010). The impacts of transfer are not likely to be rehabilitative (Bishop, Frazier, Lanza-Kaduce, & Winner, 1996; Jensen & Metsger, 1994; Fagan, 1996; Winner, Lanza-Kaduce, Bishop, & Frazier, 1997). Retributive and incapacitation goals are likely being accomplished when youths are transferred because more serious penalties may be imposed, including longer periods of incarceration. Transfer policies, however, are primarily designed to accomplish general or specific deterrence (Redding, 2010).

The creation of transfer legislation was predicated on the idea that the risk of facing adjudication in adult court would have a deterrent impact on youths. Research on the topic has called into question whether this goal is being accomplished. Large-scale studies on specific deterrence have shown that transfer may actually have the opposite effect. Not only are juveniles not deterred by the fact that they could face more adultlike penalties, it appears that transfer laws may actually increase recidivism (Bishop et al., 1996; Fagan, 1996; Lanza-Kaduce, Lane, Bishop, & Frazier, 2005; Myers, 2001, 2003). This is particularly true for youths who were tried for similar violent offenses in adult court instead of juvenile court. For this group, adult court prosecution created the greatest risk of continuing to offend into adulthood (Scott, 2000). Similarly, the bulk of the extant research has shown no general deterrent effect (Fagan, Kupchik, & Lieberman, 2003; Jensen & Metsger, 1994; Winner et al., 1997).

Commitment. Incarceration or commitment accomplishes incapacitation by restricting the liberty of the individual. Overall, removal of liberty is likely experienced as retributive. Deterrence and rehabilitation are probably less likely to be outcomes of incapacitation or commitment (Bishop et al., 1996; Fagan, 1996; Jensen & Metsger, 1994; Winner et al., 1997). Rehabilitative efforts may, however, succeed under the right conditions.

If simply separated from society, individuals are also deprived of any support systems, and their educational and vocational skills are often left deficient. Their social skills and other abilities are also likely to be negatively affected, and they will face multiple challenges on release, with little equipping them to meet those challenges. Statistics demonstrating that long-term incarceration alone has not been proven to be an effective method of rehabilitation are probably not surprising under such conditions. With appropriate intervention, however, the picture improves (Cullen, 2005; Greenwood, 2006; Lipsey, Howell, Kelly, Chapman, & Carver, 2010; Palmer, 1975, 1978, 1983, 1992, 1996).

Although many expressed doubt during the 1970s about whether rehabilitative programming worked, more recent treatment advances have led to better outcomes. Forensic mental health experts might consider one of their functions to be educating the court about these improvements from the times of the "nothing works" doctrine (Lipton, Martinson, & Wilks, 1975; Martinson, 1974) to discussions of what works, including best practices and evidence-based practices (Cullen & Sundt, 2003; Henninger, Cubellis, & Butts, 2013; Latessa, Cullen, & Gendreau, 2002; MacKenzie, 2000; Sherman, 1998). Research has shown that if programs are well designed and well implemented, rehabilitative programming while incarcerated can be at least moderately effective (Cullen, 2005; Greenwood, 2006; Lipsey et al., 2010; Palmer, 1975, 1978, 1983, 1992, 1996). Such programming must be tailored to the needs of the individual and his or her learning style to obtain moderate effects (Lipsey et al., 2010; National Research Council, 2013; Walker, Trupin, & Hansen, 2013). Attention must be paid to reentry planning early on in an individual's incapacitation. A sound reentry plan incorporates family and marshals community supports such as faith-based community organizations, as well as services offered through state agencies or nonprofit organizations. A written plan that provides daily structure and addresses individual needs on release such as substance abuse and mental health services, housing, vocational needs (to create stable employment), and development of a structure of social support will decrease the individual's likelihood of reentering the criminal justice system.

A growing research base and the legal trend toward the least restrictive alternative have indicated that community programming should be used whenever security needs allow. Some programs have demonstrated reductions in recidivism as high as 22% (e.g., multidimensional treatment foster care). Others have demonstrated more modest impacts, but have still demonstrated improvement, including use of restorative justice with low-risk offenders (8.7%) and aggression replacement training (7.3%). At the same time, some well-established evidence-based treatments such as multisystemic therapy or functional family therapy may save money and increase public safety (Justice Policy Institute, 2009), showing a savings of $13 for public safety for every dollar spent and 15.9% and 10.5% reductions in recidivism, respectively (Andrews et al., 1990; Justice Policy Institute, 2009).

Collateral Consequences

Opinions differ regarding the consequences of transfer and commitment for youths. One could argue that youths whose cases are heard by criminal court judges accustomed to hearing far more serious incidents may see their offenses as less serious than a similarly situated juvenile court judge. Others have argued that if it is the youth's first adult charge, the judge may also be more likely to be lenient. Similarly, some have attributed the decrease in youth crime from 1994 to 2004, which has since held steady at these lower levels, to the implementation and effectiveness of transfer policies. However, most believe commitment and transfer have a negative impact on juveniles, and the bulk of the research has pointed to their deleterious impacts on youth development (see, e.g., Austin, Johnson, & Weitzer, 2005; Cocozza & Skowyra, 2000; Teplin, 2001).

By virtue of being transferred to adult court, youths may experience a variety of short-term and long-term impacts. For these youths, their developmental trajectory is interrupted; family relationships and connections to ongoing, existing services are also disrupted. These youths may end up being excluded from their school, resulting in poorer educational achievement. They are processed in the adult court and at risk for longer periods of incarceration. Once transferred for one case, in some states the individual will be tried in the adult system for any future cases under "once an adult, always an adult" provisions. They lose the confidentiality of the juvenile system, in which it is afforded through closed procedures and the potential to have records sealed or expunged to decrease the impact of individuals' youthful indiscretions on their adult lives, which is particularly important given that the vast majority of youths will desist from delinquency after adolescence (Moffit, 1993).

If incarcerated, juveniles may be housed in adult facilities and possibly have some contact with adult offenders. Adult facilities often have fewer rehabilitative resources available. In adult facilities, youths may be in fear of being or actually be victimized by adult inmates, leading to increased anxiety and depression. Justice-involved youths are also at increased risk for exacerbation of preexisting mental illness because of these stresses, with some studies showing that 30% to 70% of this population meet criteria for at least one mental illness (Austin et al., 2005; Cocozza & Skowyra, 2000; Teplin, 2001). Incarceration in an adult facility may also have more extreme criminogenic effects. For example, youths may learn more about how to commit crimes.

On release, these youths are subject to more collateral consequences than youths adjudicated in the juvenile system. They are subject to a different type of stigma and even loss of rights. Their adult record can have deleterious impacts on their ability to find employment or adequate housing. They may be ineligible for financial aid, making college or other higher education a financial impossibility. Individuals who are unable to support themselves may be more likely to return to commission of crime. In fact, studies have shown that youths processed in the adult system are more likely to recidivate (Bishop et al., 1996; Fagan, 1996; Lanza-Kaduce et al., 2005; Myers, 2001, 2003). They may lose the right to vote, hold office, join the military, and sit on a jury.

Inequality in the Transfer and Commitment of Youths and Efforts to Remove Bias

The juvenile system has an inherent tension between the desire for individualized treatment, which requires judicial discretion to individualize legal responses to youths' offending, and the fact that allowing discretion introduces the potential for human bias. Factors outside of awareness (e.g., socioeconomic status, race, ethnicity, gender, age) can influence one's judgment. Police, prosecutors, defense attorneys, judges, and other legal actors are human—subject to the same biases as everyone else (De La Fuente, De La Fuente, & Garcia, 2003; Hahn & Clayton, 1996; Jones & Kaplan, 2003; Warling, 2001; Warling & Peterson-Badali, 2003). Bias can result in the justice system acting as a funnel at each decision point. Some groups are pushed deeper into the system at points such as arrest, decision to charge, or sentencing, and others are systematically and disproportionately treated more leniently.

Racial disparities have probably been the most thoroughly studied (Jones & Kaplan, 2003) and have been documented at all points of the system. Transfer and commitment involving incarceration are no exception. Research using national samples has demonstrated that youths of color are transferred to adult court in higher proportions than their representation in the general population (Soler, 2010). For example, Black youths charged with a drug offense are 40% more likely to be tried in criminal court than their White counterparts (Juszkiewicz, 2007).

Youths of color (including Latinos, Native Americans, Asians, Pacific Islanders, and African Americans) are also punished more harshly, including increased risk of incarceration and longer sentences. They are estimated to make up 35% of the U.S. population, but 58% of those sentenced to adult correctional facilities (Hoytt, Schiraldi, Smith, & Zeidenberg, 2001; Piquero, 2008). Studies specifically examining Black youths have found that they are more likely to be incarcerated, especially if sentenced in adult court (Kupchik, 2006). Youths of color are disadvantaged when racial groups are compared on rates of receipt of probation versus incarceration. Blacks were 3 times more likely, and Latinos 2 times more likely, than Whites to be incarcerated rather than placed on probation (McNulty, 1996). Black and Latino youths have been shown to receive longer sentences (61 and 112 days longer than Whites, respectively).

Research has shown that other characteristics such as attractiveness (De La Fuente et al., 2003), age (Warling, 2001), socioeconomic status, ethnicity, religion, and gender (Hahn & Clayton, 1996) can also have an impact on decision making about youths. Studies examining the relation of age and sentencing showed that it did not affect whether an individual was found guilty, but mock jurors gave younger individuals shorter sentences (Warling, 2001; Warling & Peterson-Badali, 2003). Moreover, in studies conducted before *Roper v. Simmons* (2005), older hypothetical defendants in a vignette were more likely to be treated more harshly, receiving the death penalty (Crosby, Britner, Preston, Jodl, & Portwood, 1995). Ghetti and Redlich (2001) found that younger individuals were perceived as less culpable, although this did not result in shorter sentences.

The impact of gender on treatment within the justice system is less clear. Research can generally be divided into one of three categories: (a) research that provides evidence of more lenient treatment for females (e.g., Pearson, 1997); (b) research that provides evidence of harsher treatment on the basis of gender (Simon & Ahn-Redding, 2005); and (c) research that has found no effect (Simon & Sharma, 1979). Findings of more lenient treatment have been supported by theories such as the fact that males treat females less harshly due to chivalry, women's perceived naiveté compared with men, or for family reasons such as the fact that they have small children with no one else to care for them (e.g., Julian, 1993; Pearson, 1997). Proponents of the idea that women are treated more harshly focus on the violation of social norms of femininity (Chesney-Lind, 1997; Ghali & Chesney-Lind, 1986; Simon & Ahn-Redding, 2005; Temen, 1973).

That disparities exist in how various groups are treated in the juvenile justice system is known, but what accounts for this? Several hypotheses have been proposed to explain these differences, including race differences in offending, selection bias based on race/ethnicity, cumulative disadvantage, and implicit bias. With regard to whether actual differences in offending may exist among racial groups, the picture is complex, with research being mixed and explanations for such effects being controversial (Burt, Simons, & Gibbons, 2012).

Systemic mechanisms to combat or remove bias have been tested, including both bottom-up and top-down approaches. One of the most important efforts to legislate change was the Juvenile Justice and Delinquency Prevention Act, which was first passed in 1974. Disparate minority contact was added during its 1989 reauthorization. Using the federal government's Spending Clause powers, the legislation requires states to comply with certain mandates or risk losing their formula grant funding. Although only advisory, sentencing guidelines aim to decrease inequities. Sentencing guidelines give a range of potential penalties based on past criminal history and type of offense. In this way, a judge's discretion is limited, and bias is reduced.

Others have tested more direct interventions (e.g., prevention programs aimed at increasing protective factors, addressing educational deficits, and addressing substance use or abuse). Others have created educational and training programs to increase awareness among system stakeholders about unconscious bias or cultural competency (Leiber & Rodriguez, 2011). The John D. and Catherine T. MacArthur Foundation, Annie E. Casey Foundation, Haywood Burns Institute, and the Office of Juvenile Justice and Delinquency Prevention have promoted the use of standardized detention screening instruments that decrease the risk of biased discretion. Others have recommended services aimed at the specific needs of at-risk youths to prevent them from entering the justice system, as well as intervention programs to address those who are already system involved (Leiber & Peck, 2012) rather than attempting to change systems themselves.

Reducing discretion, however, also decreases the ability to individualize the treatment of juveniles. If no discretion is afforded judges or prosecutors, they are unable to account for particularly salient details of a case that might indicate a certain juvenile would be better served through means other than those proscribed by statute. Some have argued that when discretion is entirely removed (e.g., through statutory exclusion), some mechanism for review of that decision should exist. Because discretion gives great power to individual actors in the system, the question of who should be allowed to have such discretion is also controversial. If discretion is allowed with some groups, similar questions arise regarding when it is most beneficial to allow discretion more generally. The following discussion takes up these questions, making suggestions for policy changes that might be considered.

IMPLICATIONS FOR FORENSIC MENTAL HEALTH EXAMINERS

Although research continues to guide improvements in this area, practitioners should be clear about and acknowledge the limitations of the extant body of knowledge and any associated methods. Experts should be aware of the literature, tools, and best practices for each area of evaluation and use caution to avoid overstepping their bounds and going beyond the limits of the state of the science. The literature and the ability to validly and reliably measure psychological constructs related to transfer and commitment varies, with some having more robust research bases than others. For example, the literature regarding risk assessment has evolved through several generations, and clinicians' ability to assess various types of risk, across different spans of time, and for different purposes has been honed, even within the past decade. In contrast, although understanding of the concept of immaturity has been thoroughly researched, conceptualizations differ, and clinicians' ability to measure the construct is presently more limited.

Clinical evaluations are further complicated in some instances by the unique characteristics of youths as well as the limitations of the legal system. The ongoing development and maturational processes youths are undergoing at a critical stage in their lives can affect assessments of constructs important to both transfer and commitment decisions. For example, developmental processes render the shelf life of assessments relatively short. Such assessments possibly tell one little to nothing about the youth after a delay in proceedings of some months or years. Furthermore, in some cases examiners may not be able to obtain information that might change their assessment. Collateral information can ameliorate this issue in some cases. However, if a state limits the information available about an offense or the youth does not want to discuss the alleged offense, the evaluator could be missing important information, resulting in a different assessment. Evaluators should be current about such issues and be sure to clearly communicate them to the courts.

Some might argue that youths have reason to dissimulate or malinger during transfer or commitment evaluations. In other words, youths may try to appear more impaired than their actual level of ability so that they can remain in the juvenile system or perhaps receive a different placement. For example, they may believe that if they appear to have a more serious mental illness or intellectual disability, they will be sent to a treatment facility rather than committed to a secure facility run by the youth authority. However, interview strategies and assessment instruments are available to clinicians to assist in determining whether a youth is attempting to malinger, exaggerate, or suppress such symptoms (McCann, 1998; Rogers, Hinds, & Sewell, 1996; Rogers, Sewell, & Gillard, 2010).

IMPLICATIONS FOR POLICY

Policymakers working toward reform of transfer laws must gain clarity about the true purposes or goals of their system. As noted earlier, research has demonstrated that some purposes of transfer and commitment are met, and others are not. Clarification of goals should guide policy change. For example, wanting to transfer only those who are adultlike versus wanting youths to receive adultlike punishments would guide one toward very different legislative solutions. Other important issues that must be considered are who, if anyone, is most appropriately given discretion to transfer youths and under what conditions—and the potential impact of that discretion. In the commitment context, policymakers should examine and clarify the true goals in this area, which appear to have become muddled over time. Systems wanting to shift back toward more rehabilitative goals should, for example, consider the evidence of success of community alternatives.

The body of psychological research outlined earlier with regard to the differences between youths and adults, along with the Supreme Court cases outlined, appears to point to the need for reforms that recognize the unique developmental status of youths. Moreover, the line of Supreme Court cases calls for individualized treatment of youths. Some current mechanisms of transfer, such as statutory exclusion, would seem to be contrary to these tenets. Nonetheless, our discussion of the impacts of discretion and its role in creating potential disparities cautions against going too far toward unfettered discretion for either judges or prosecutors. Thus, it appears that the system is faced with the difficult challenge of reforming laws to increase consistency and fairness while maintaining individualized treatment.

When considering reforms, policymakers should examine the potential benefits and detriments of each type of transfer mechanism and the data supporting each contention. Those arguing for increased use of judicial discretion point to the fact that a judge's role is more in line with this type of decision making. Implementation of this policy would require commitment of more resources but could potentially save in the long run if it reduced negative collateral consequences. Furthermore, unlike prosecutorial discretion, juvenile judges must at least make findings and provide rationales for their decision. On balance, an increase in judicial discretion could also mean an increase in arbitrariness of decisions if there is no mechanism for reining in or guiding these decisions.

Prosecutorial transfer places much discretion in the hands of one individual whose role may be more in line with the interests of the victim and the state and is also subject to political pressures in his or her decisions. Such decisions are not appealable and, unlike the courts, they provide no explanation for their decision-making process. Prosecutors' discretion also has the same inherent risks of arbitrariness if unguided. However, the breadth of prosecutorial discretion is widely accepted in other areas. Continuing to look at the growing body of data will be important in weighing this mechanism because current research has shown a lack of deterrent value, potential increase in recidivism, and contribution to disparate minority representation in the justice system.

Legislative waiver decreases discretion and potential arbitrariness of decisions while saving resources by being more efficient in requiring fewer hearings. However, it abandons the individualization on which the juvenile system is predicated, and it has been shown to lack the deterrent impact on youth that spurred its creation initially. Arbitrarily drawing lines regarding certain offenses at certain ages is also out of line with current developmental literature and recent Supreme Court cases recognizing the need for individualized decisions for youths because of their unique developmental characteristics.

Blended sentencing attempts to protect society and continue to enforce get-tough policies while balancing the desire to maintain the goals of continuing to treat youths differently than adults and make efforts toward their rehabilitation. It may also create an incentive for youths to comply with treatment efforts. However, the law is unsettled with regard to the constitutionality of this system under the *Blakely v. Washington* (2004) and *Apprendi v. New Jersey* (2000) line of cases.

Perhaps one way to accomplish the needed reform of transfer laws may be to emulate the Supreme Court's jurisprudence in the death penalty arena. In the mid-1970s, when faced with similar doubts as to the fairness of jury discretion, the Court effectively placed a moratorium on the death penalty until a solution could be found. Through a number of cases, states tested the constitutionality of their proposed statutes. In the end, the Court allowed schemes that took all mitigating evidence into account and also guided discretion with enumerated factors that had to be considered, thus increasing consistency and fairness by providing structure for the decision while maintaining individualized treatment.

Another implication of the developmental research demonstrating the differences of youths is that they are likely at higher risk of not being competent to stand trial than their adult counterparts. In the adult system, youths must make more complex decisions at a time when both behavioral and brain research has shown that their developmental status and factors impede their decision-making abilities. States might consider requiring that youths' competence-related abilities be more closely examined on transfer, given their increased risk.

Policymakers should consider who should conduct transfer and commitment evaluations. If performed in the adult system, an adult-trained clinician would likely complete the forensic evaluation. Juvenile forensic evaluation is a specialized practice requiring training and a background in the assessment of children and adolescents. An adult clinician, no matter how highly skilled, could miss or misinterpret developmental factors affecting competence-related abilities. In fact, an adult clinician conducting such evaluations could be considered to be practicing unethically outside the bounds of his or her competence under the *Ethical Principles of Psychologists and Code of Conduct* (American Psychological Association, 2010). Thus, policy reforms might require a child and adolescent forensic clinician to conduct the evaluation before adjudication in the adult system.

Finally, policy should emulate and build on the successes of programs such as the Juvenile Detention Alternatives Initiative and the MacArthur Foundation's Models for Change initiative. Policymakers should learn about newer alternatives and treatments that can make secure detention less necessary. Especially given the potential negative collateral consequences outlined earlier, decreasing youths' system contact should be prioritized. Confinement should be reserved only for those serious offenders who significantly threaten public safety, especially because in many cases decreased incarceration saves public funds without compromising public safety.

References

American Psychological Association. (2010). *Ethical principles of psychologists and code of conduct (2002, Amended June 1, 2010)*. Retrieved from http://www.apa.org/ethics/code/index.aspx

Andrews, D. A., Zinger, I., Hoge, R. D., Bonta, J., Gendreau, P., & Cullen, F. R. (1990). Does correctional treatment work? A clinically relevant and psychologically informed meta-analysis. *Criminology, 28*, 369–404. http://dx.doi.org/10.1111/j.1745-9125.1990.tb01330.x

Annie E. Casey Foundation. (2013). *Reducing youth incarceration in the United States*. Retrieved from http://www.aecf.org/resources/reducing-youth-incarceration-in-the-united-states

Apprendi v. New Jersey, 530 U.S. 466 (2000).

Austin, J., Johnson, K. D., & Weitzer, R. (2005). *Alternatives to the secure detention and confinement of juvenile offenders* (Juvenile Justice Bulletin). Retrieved from http://www.ncjrs.gov/pdffiles1/ojjdp/208804.pdf

Berghuis v. Thompkins, 560 U.S. 370 (2010).

Besharov, D. J. (1974). *Juvenile justice advocacy: Practice in a unique court*. New York, NY: Practicing Law Institute.

Bishop, D. M., Frazier, C. E., Lanza-Kaduce, L., & Winner, L. (1996). The transfer of juveniles to criminal court: Does it make a difference? *Crime and Delinquency, 42*, 171–191. http://dx.doi.org/10.1177/0011128796042002001

Blakely v. Washington, 542 U.S. 296 (2004).

Borum, R., Bartel, P., & Forth, A. (2006). *Manual for the Structured Assessment for Violence Risk in Youth (SAVRY)*. Odessa, FL: Psychological Assessment Resources.

Breed v. Jones, 421 U.S. 519 (1975).

Burt, C. H., Simons, R. L., & Gibbons, F. X. (2012). Racial discrimination, ethnic-racial socialization, and crime: A micro-sociological model of risk and resilience. *American Sociological Review, 77*, 648–677. http://dx.doi.org/10.1177/0003122412448648

Campaign for Youth Justice. (2011). *New report highlights state legislative changes and reform efforts over the last five years*. Retrieved from http://www.campaignforyouthjustice.org/documents/CFYJ_State_Trends_Report.pdf

Campaign for Youth Justice. (2013). *State trends—Legislative victories from 2011–2013: Removing youth from the adult criminal justice system*. Retrieved from http://www.campaignforyouthjustice.org/documents/ST2013.pdf

Cauffman, E., Piquero, A. R., Kimonis, E., Steinberg, L., Chassin, L., & Fagan, J. (2007). Legal, individual, and environmental predictors of court disposition in a sample of serious adolescent offenders. *Law and Human Behavior, 31*, 519–535. http://dx.doi.org/10.1007/s10979-006-9076-2

Cauffman, E., Steinberg, L., & Piquero, A. (2005). Psychological, neuropsychological, and psychophysiological correlates of serious antisocial behavior in adolescence. *Criminology, 43*, 133–176. http://dx.doi.org/10.1111/j.0011-1348.2005.00005.x

Cheeseman, F. (2011). *A decade of NCSC research on blended sentencing of juvenile offenders*. Williamsburg, VA: National Center for State Courts. Retrieved from http://www.ncsc.org/sitecore/content/microsites/future-trends-2011/home/Special-Programs/4-4-Blended-Sentencing-of-Juvenile-Offenders.aspx

Chesney-Lind, M. (1997). *The female offender: Girls, women, and crime*. Thousand Oaks, CA: Sage.

Cocozza, J., & Skowyra, K. (2000). Youth with mental health disorders: Issues and emerging responses. *Office of Juvenile Justice and Delinquency Prevention Journal*, 7, 3–13.

Crosby, C. A., Britner, P. A., Jodl, K. M., & Portwood, S. G. (1995). Juvenile death penalty and the Eighth Amendment: An empirical investigation of societal consensus and proportionality. *Law and Human Behavior*, *19*, 245–261. http://dx.doi.org/10.1007/BF01501659

Cullen, F. (2005). The twelve people who saved rehabilitation: How the science of criminology made a difference. *Criminology*, *43*, 1–42. http://dx.doi.org/10.1111/j.0011-1348.2005.00001.x

Cullen, F., & Sundt, J. (2003). Reaction essay: Reaffirming evidence-based corrections. *Criminology and Public Policy*, 2, 353–358. http://dx.doi.org/10.1111/j.1745-9133.2003.tb00131.x

De La Fuente, L., De La Fuente, E. I., & Garcia, J. (2003). Effects of pretrial juror bias, strength of evidence, and deliberation process on juror decisions: New validity evidence of the juror bias scale scores. *Psychology, Crime, and Law*, *9*, 197–209. http://dx.doi.org/10.1080/1068316031000116283

Demleitner, N., Berman, D., Miller, M., & Wright, R. (2013). *Sentencing law and policy: Cases, statutes, and guidelines* (3rd ed.). New York, NY: Aspen.

DiCataldo, F. (2009). *The perversion of youth: Controversies in the assessment and treatment of juvenile sex offenders*. New York, NY: New York University Press.

Dressler, J. (1999). *Cases and materials on criminal law* (2nd ed.). Eagan, MN: West Group.

E.J.M. v. State, 928 So. 2d 1077, 1081 (Ala. Crim. App. 2004).

Elliott, D. S., Huizinga, D., & Morse, B. (1986). Self-reported violent offending: A descriptive analysis of juvenile violent offenders and their offending careers. *Journal of Interpersonal Violence*, *4*, 472–514. http://dx.doi.org/10.1177/088626086001004006

Fagan, J. A. (1996). The comparative advantage of juvenile versus criminal court sanctions on recidivism among adolescent felony offenders. *Law and Policy*, *18*, 77–114. http://dx.doi.org/10.1111/j.1467-9930.1996.tb00165.x

Fagan, J., Kupchik, A., & Lieberman, A. (2003). *Be careful what you wish for: The comparative impacts of juvenile versus criminal court sanctions on recidivism among adolescent felony offenders* (Public Law Research Paper No. 03-61). New York, NY: Columbia University Law School.

Garner, B. A. (Ed.-in-Chief). (1999). *Black's Law Dictionary* (7th ed.). St. Paul, MN: West Group.

Ghali, M., & Chesney-Lind, M. (1986). Gender bias and the criminal justice system: An empirical investigation. *Sociology and Social Research*, *70*, 164–171.

Ghetti, S., & Redlich, A. D. (2001). Reactions to youth crime: Perceptions of accountability and competence. *Behavioral Sciences and the Law*, *19*, 33–52. http://dx.doi.org/10.1002/bsl.426

Graham v. Florida, 560 U.S. 48 (2010).

Greenwood, P. (2006). *Changing lives: Delinquency prevention and crime control policy*. Chicago, IL: University of Chicago Press.

Griffin, P., Addie, S., Adams, B., & Firestine, K. (2011). *Trying juveniles as adults: An analysis of state transfer laws and reporting* (Juvenile Offenders and Victims National Report Series). Washington, DC: U.S. Department of Justice, Office of Justice Programs, Office of Juvenile Justice and Delinquency Prevention. Retrieved from https://www.ncjrs.gov/pdffiles1/ojjdp/232434.pdf

Grisso, T. (2004). *Double jeopardy: Adolescent offenders with mental disorders* (2nd ed.). Chicago, IL: University Press of Chicago.

Grisso, T. (2013). *Forensic evaluation of juveniles*. Sarasota, FL: Professional Resource Press.

Grisso, T., & Schwartz, R. (Eds.). (2000). *Youth on trial: A developmental perspective on juvenile justice*. Chicago: University of Chicago Press.

Hahn, P. W., & Clayton, S. D. (1996). The effects of attorney presentation style, attorney gender, and juror gender on juror decisions. *Law and Human Behavior*, *20*, 533–554. http://dx.doi.org/10.1007/BF01499040

Heilbrun, K., Shah, S., Foster, E., Keesler, M., & Brooks, S. (2014). Empathy, acceptance of responsibility, and compelled testimony in juvenile transfer hearings: Legal context and empirical evidence. *Court Review*, *50*, 21–31.

Henninger, A., Cubellis, M., & Butts, J. A. (2013). *Evidence based*. New York: City University of New York, John Jay College of Criminal Justice, Research and Evaluation Center.

Hoeffel, J. C. (2013). The jurisprudence of death and youth: Now the twain should meet. *Texas Tech Law Review*, *46*, 29–70.

Hoge, R., & Andrews, D. (2010). Youth Level of Service Case Management Inventory. In R. Otto & K. Douglas

(Eds.), *Handbook of violence risk assessment* (pp. 81–95). New York, NY: Taylor & Francis.

Hoytt, E., Schiraldi, V., Smith, B. V., & Ziedenberg, J. (2001). *Pathways to juvenile detention reform. 8: Reducing racial disparities in juvenile detention*. Baltimore, MD: Annie E. Casey Foundation.

In re Gault, 387 U.S. 1 (1967).

In re Winship, 397 U.S. 358 (1970).

Jackson v. State, 359 Ark. 87, 89, 194 S. W. 3d 757, 759 (2004)

J.D.B. v. North Carolina, 131 S. Ct. 2394 (2011).

Jensen, E. L., & Metsger, L. K. (1994). A test of the deterrent effect of legislative waiver on violent juvenile crime. *Crime and Delinquency*, *40*, 96–104. http://dx.doi.org/10.1177/0011128794040001007

Jones, C. S., & Kaplan, M. F. (2003). The effects of racially stereotypical crimes on juror decision-making and information-processing strategies. *Basic and Applied Social Psychology*, *25*, 1–13. http://dx.doi.org/10.1207/S15324834BASP2501_1

Julian, F. H. (1993). Gender and crime: Different sex, different treatment? In C. C. Culliver (Ed.), *Female criminality: The state of the art* (pp. 343–362). New York, NY: Garland.

Justice Policy Institute. (2009). *The costs of confinement: Why good juvenile justice policies make good fiscal sense*. Retrieved from http://www.justicepolicy.org/images/upload/09_05_rep_costsofconfinement_jj_ps.pdf

Juszkiewicz, J. (2007). *To punish a few: Too many youth caught in the net of adult prosecution*. Retrieved from http://www.campaignforyouthjustice.org/documents/to_punish_a_few_final.pdf

Juvenile Justice and Delinquency Prevention Act of 1974, Pub. L. No. 93-415, § 223(a)(22).

Kent v. United States, 383 U.S. 541 (1966).

Kids Count Data Center. (2014). *Youth residing in juvenile detention, correctional, and/or residential facilities*. Retrieved from http://datacenter.kidscount.org/data/tables/42-youth-residing-in-juvenile-detention-correctional-and-or-residential-facilities

Krisberg, B., & Austin, J. F. (1993). *Reinventing juvenile justice*. http://dx.doi.org/10.4135/9781483326450

Kupchik, A. (2006). The decision to incarcerate in juvenile and criminal courts. *Criminal Justice Review*, *31*, 309–336. http://dx.doi.org/10.1177/0734016806295584

Lanza-Kaduce, L., Lane, J., Bishop, D. M., & Frazier, C. E. (2005). Juvenile offenders and adult felony recidivism: The impact of transfer. *Journal of Criminal Justice*, *28*, 59–77.

Larson, K. (2003). Improving the "Kangaroo courts": A proposal for reform in evaluating juveniles waiver of Miranda. *Villanova Law Review*, *48*, 629–666.

Larson, K., DiCataldo, F., & Kinscherff, R. (2013). *Miller v. Alabama*: Implications for forensic mental health assessment at the intersection of social science and the law. *New England Journal on Criminal and Civil Confinement*, *39*, 319–345.

Larson, K., & Kinscherff, R. (2014). Ethical considerations and professional posture in working with violent offenders. In C. Pietz & C. Mattson (Eds.), *Violent offenders: Understanding and assessment* (pp. 474–502). New York, NY: Oxford University Press.

Latessa, E. J., Cullen, F. T., & Gendreau, P. (2002). Beyond correctional quackery: Professionalism and the possibility of effective treatment. *Federal Probation*, *66*, 43–49.

Leiber, M., & Rodriguez, N. (2011). The implementation of the Disproportionate Minority Confinement/Contact (DMC) Mandate: A failure or success? *Race and Justice*, *1*, 103–124. http://dx.doi.org/10.1177/2153368710377614

Leiber, M. J., & Peck, J. H. (2012). Probation violations and juvenile justice decision making: Implications for Blacks and Hispanics. *Youth Violence and Juvenile Justice*, *11*, 60–78. http://dx.doi.org/10.1177/1541204012447960

Lipsey, M. W., Howell, J. C., Kelly, M. R., Chapman, C., & Carver, D. (2010). *Improving the effectiveness of juvenile justice programs: A new perspective on evidence-based practice*. Washington, DC: Center for Juvenile Justice Reform. Retrieved from http://www.modelsforchange.net/publications/284

Lipton, D., Martinson, R., & Wilks, J. (1975). *The effectiveness of correctional treatment: A survey of treatment evaluation studies*. New York, NY: Praeger.

Little, M., & Steinberg, L. (2006). Psychosocial correlates of adolescent drug dealing in the inner city: Potential roles of opportunity, conventional commitments, and maturity. *Journal of Research in Crime and Delinquency*, *43*, 357–386. http://dx.doi.org/10.1177/0022427806291260

Mack, J. (1909). The juvenile court. *Harvard Law Review*, *23*, 104–122. http://dx.doi.org/10.2307/1325042

MacKenzie, D. L. (2000). Evidence-based corrections: Identifying what works. *Crime and Delinquency*, *46*, 457–471. http://dx.doi.org/10.1177/0011128700046004003

Martinson, R. (1974). What works? Questions and answers about prison reform. *Public Interest*, *35*, 22–54.

McCann, J. (1998). *Malingering and deception in adolescents: Assessing credibility in clinical and forensic settings*. http://dx.doi.org/10.1037/10249-000

McKeiver v. Pennsylvania, 403 U.S. 528 (1971).

McNulty, E. (1996). The transfer of juvenile offenders to adult court: Panacea or problem? *Law and Policy*, *18*, 61–75. http://dx.doi.org/10.1111/j.1467-9930.1996.tb00164.x

Miller v. Alabama, 132 S. Ct. 2455 (2012).

Miranda v. Arizona, 384 U.S. 436 (1966).

Moffitt, T. (1993). Adolescence-limited and life-course-persistent antisocial behavior: A developmental taxonomy. *Psychological Review*, *100*, 674–701. http://dx.doi.org/10.1037/0033-295X.100.4.674

Myers, D. L. (2001). *Excluding violent youths from juvenile court: The effectiveness of legislative waiver*. New York, NY: LFB Scholarly.

Myers, D. L. (2003). The recidivism of violent youths in juvenile and adult court: A consideration of selection bias. *Youth Violence and Juvenile Justice*, *1*, 79–101. http://dx.doi.org/10.1177/1541204002238365

National Juvenile Justice Network and Texas Public Policy Institute. (2011). *The comeback states: Reducing youth incarceration in the United States*. Retrieved from http://www.njjn.org/uploads/digital-library/Comeback-States-Report_FINAL.pdf

National Research Council. (2013). *Reforming juvenile justice: A developmental approach*. Washington, DC: National Academies Press.

Palmer, T. (1975). Martinson revisited. *Journal of Research in Crime and Delinquency*, *12*, 133–152. http://dx.doi.org/10.1177/002242787501200206

Palmer, T. (1978). *Correctional intervention and research: Current issues and future prospects*. Lexington, MA: Lexington Books.

Palmer, T. (1983). The "effectiveness" issue today: An overview. *Federal Probation*, *46*, 3–10.

Palmer, T. (1992). *The re-emergence of correctional intervention*. http://dx.doi.org/10.4135/9781483326009

Palmer, T. (1996). Programmatic and nonprogrammatic aspects of successful interventions. In A. T. Harland (Ed.), *Choosing correctional options that work: Defining the demand and evaluating the supply* (pp. 131–182). Thousand Oaks, CA: Sage.

Pearson, P. (1997). *When she was bad*. New York, NY: Viking.

Piquero, A. (2008). Disproportionate minority contact. *Future of Children*, *18*, 59–79. Retrieved from http://files.eric.ed.gov/fulltext/EJ815073.pdf

Redding, R. E. (2010). *Juvenile transfer laws: An effective deterrent to delinquency?* Washington, DC: U.S. Department of Justice, Office of Justice Programs, Office of Juvenile Justice and Delinquency Prevention.

Rogers, R., Hinds, J. D., & Sewell, K. W. (1996). Feigning psychopathology among adolescent offenders: Validation of the SIRS, MMPI-A, and SIMS. *Journal of Personality Assessment*, *67*, 244–257. http://dx.doi.org/10.1207/s15327752jpa6702_2

Rogers, D., Sewell, K., & Gillard, N. (2010). *Structured Interview of Reported Symptoms-2*. Lutz, FL: Psychological Assessment Resources.

Roper v. Simmons, 543 U.S. 551 (2005).

Ryerson, E. (1978). *The best-laid plans: America's juvenile court experiment*. New York, NY: Hill & Wang.

Salekin, R., Salekin, K., Clements, C., & Leistico, A. (2005). Risk-Sophistication-Treatment Inventory. In T. Grisso, G. Vincent, & D. Seagrave (Eds.), *Mental health screening and assessment in juvenile justice* (pp. 341–356). New York, NY: Guilford Press.

Schufelt, C., & Cocozza, J. (2006). *Youth with mental health disorders in the juvenile justice system: Results from a multi-state prevalence study* (National Center for Mental Health and Juvenile Justice Research and Program Brief). Retrieved from http://www.unicef.org/tdad/usmentalhealthprevalence06(3).pdf

Scott, E. S. (2000). The legal construction of adolescence. *Hofstra Law Review*, *29*, 547–588.

Scott, E. S., & Grisso, T. (1998). The evolution of adolescence: A developmental perspective on juvenile justice reform. *Journal of Criminal Law and Criminology*, *88*, 137–189. http://dx.doi.org/10.2307/1144076

Scott, E. S., & Steinberg, L. (2008). Adolescent development and the regulation of youth crime. *Future of Children*, *18*, 15–33. Retrieved from http://files.eric.ed.gov/fulltext/EJ815071.pdf

Sherman, L. W. (1998). *Evidence-based policing*. Washington, DC: Police Foundation.

Sickmund, M. (2003). *Juveniles in court* (Juvenile Offenders and Victims National Report Series). Washington, DC: U.S. Department of Justice, Office of Justice Programs, Office of Juvenile Justice and Delinquency Prevention. Retrieved from https://www.ncjrs.gov/pdffiles1/ojjdp/195420.pdf

Sickmund, M., Sladky, T. J., Kang, W., & Puzzanchera, C. (2008). *Easy access to the census of juveniles in residential placement*. Washington, DC: U.S. Department of Justice, Office of Justice Programs, Office of Juvenile Justice and Delinquency Prevention. Retrieved from http://ojjdp.ncjrs.gov/ojstatbb/ezacjrp/asp/display.asp

Simon, R., & Sharma, N. (1979). Women and crime: Does the American experience generalize. In F. Alder and R. Simon (Eds.), *Criminology of deviant women* (pp. 391–400). Boston, MA: Houghton Mifflin.

Simon, R. J., & Ahn-Redding, H. (2005). *The crimes women commit and the punishments they receive* (3rd ed.). Oxford, England: Lexington.

Snyder, H. N., & Sickmund, M. (2006). *Juvenile offenders and victims: 2006 national report*. Washington, DC: U.S. Department of Justice, Office of Justice Programs, Office of Juvenile Justice and Delinquency Prevention.

Soler, M. (2010). Missed opportunity: Waiver, race, data, and policy reform. *Louisiana Law Review, 71*, 17–33.

Stanford v. Kentucky, 492 U.S. 361 (1989).

Stapleton, W. V., & Teitelbaum, L. E. (1972). *In defense of youth: A study of the role of counsel in American juvenile courts*. New York, NY: Russell Sage Foundation.

Steinberg, L., & Scott, E. S. (2003). Less guilty by reason of adolescence: Developmental immaturity, diminished responsibility, and the juvenile death penalty. *American Psychologist, 58*, 1009–1018. http://dx.doi.org/10.1037/0003-066X.58.12.1009

Temen, L. (1973). Discriminatory sentencing of women offenders. *Criminal Law Review, 11*.

Teplin, L. (2001). Assessing alcohol, drug, and mental disorders in juvenile detainees. ODJJP Fact Sheet. Retrieved from http://www.ncjrs.gov/pdffiles1/ojjdp/fs200102.pdf

Teplin, L. A., Abram, K. M., McClelland, G. M., Dulcan, M. K., & Mericle, A. A. (2002). Psychiatric disorders in youth in juvenile detention. *Archives of General Psychiatry, 59*, 1133–1143. http://dx.doi.org/10.1001/archpsyc.59.12.1133

Vincent, G., Terry, A., & Maney, S. (2009). Risk needs tools for antisocial behavior and violence among youthful populations. In J. Andrade (Ed.), *Handbook of violence risk assessment and treatment: New approaches for forensic mental health practitioners* (pp. 377–423). New York, NY: Springer.

Walker, S. C., Trupin, E., & Hansen, J. (2013). *A toolkit for applying the cultural enhancement model to evidence-based practice*. Seattle: University of Washington, Division of Public Behavioral Health & Justice Policy, & the John D. and Catherine T. MacArthur Foundation Models for Change Initiative. Retrieved from http://www.modelsforchange.net/publications/476

Warling, D., & Peterson-Badali, M. (2003). The verdict on jury trials for juveniles: The effects of defendant's age on trial outcomes. *Behavioral Sciences and the Law, 21*, 63–82. http://dx.doi.org/10.1002/bsl.517

Warling, D. L. (2001). *Are juveniles getting a fair trial? The jury is still out* (Unpublished doctoral dissertation). University of Toronto, Toronto, Ontario, Canada.

Winner, L., Lanza-Kaduce, L., Bishop, D. M., & Frazier, C. E. (1997). The transfer of juveniles to criminal court: Reexamining recidivism over the long term. *Crime and Delinquency, 43*, 548–563. http://dx.doi.org/10.1177/0011128797043004009

CHAPTER 22

EVALUATION OF *MIRANDA* WAIVER CAPACITY

Naomi E. S. Goldstein, Sharon Messenheimer Kelley, Lindsey Peterson, Leah Brogan, Heather Zelle, and Christina Riggs Romaine

In the U.S. legal system, two of the most fundamental due process protections are the right against self-incrimination and the right to counsel. Described in the Fifth and Sixth Amendments, respectively, these rights provide the foundation for an individual's protections against unfair criminal prosecution. For juveniles, these protections are, arguably, even more important than they are for adult defendants because, as evidence reviewed in this chapter shows, juveniles are developmentally disadvantaged during interactions with representatives of the legal system. The *Miranda* warnings provide suspects with basic information about these two fundamental rights and were designed as a protective mechanism for suspects during custodial interrogations.

Although *Miranda* warnings are part of U.S. vernacular, the significance of the U.S. Supreme Court's holding in *Miranda v. Arizona* (1966) is often overlooked. Under most circumstances, individuals are presumed to know the law and are required to invoke their rights without assistance. In *Miranda v. Arizona*, however, the Court recognized that the coercive nature of custodial interrogations places individuals at risk of forfeiting their right against self-incrimination. The Court's decision required police to inform suspects of their rights as a prerequisite to using suspects' statements against them at trial.

Despite their importance, the right against self-incrimination and the right to an attorney can be waived. Valid waivers must meet certain legal requirements—they must be made knowingly, intelligently, and voluntarily. When questions are raised about a defendant's *Miranda* waiver and admissibility of subsequent statements, forensic mental health professionals may provide information to assist the court in determining the waiver's validity.

The *Miranda* decision has a number of implications for law, policy, and psychological study and practice. In this chapter, we review the history and meaning of the *Miranda* decision, the current status of the law surrounding *Miranda*, and empirical evidence about how well juveniles comprehend the *Miranda* warnings. We then review the process of conducting forensic mental health evaluations of juvenile defendants' capacities to have waived *Miranda* rights during custodial interrogations.

RELEVANT HISTORY

The central issue in the *Miranda v. Arizona* (1966) decision, and the fundamental judicial determination that rests on forensic psychologists' evaluations of *Miranda* waiver capacity, is the admissibility of confessions. Decades before *Miranda*, the U.S. Supreme Court held that the Due Process Clause of the Fourteenth Amendment ("nor shall any State deprive any person of life, liberty, or property, without due process of law") governed the admissibility of confession evidence (*Brown v. Mississippi*, 1936). Thus, confessions extracted through coercion, whether physical (*Brown v. Mississippi*, 1936) or mental (*Blackburn v. Alabama*, 1960; *Haynes v. Washington*, 1963), could not be admitted into evidence. Nevertheless, lengthy and otherwise coercive interrogation practices continued, and law

http://dx.doi.org/10.1037/14643-022
APA Handbook of Psychology and Juvenile Justice, K. Heilbrun (Editor-in-Chief)

enforcement officers were left without clear indicators of whether particular confessions would be admissible in criminal proceedings.

In 1966, the U.S. Supreme Court resolved four criminal appeals, consolidated under one case: *Miranda v. Arizona*. In each case, suspects had been interrogated at length without being informed of their right to remain silent or their right to counsel. Despite a common perception that the core holding concerned the famous *Miranda* warnings, the case actually had three holdings, all of equal importance (Schulhofer, 1987). First, the Court held that informal pressure to speak in an interrogation setting can constitute compulsion within the meaning of the Fifth Amendment (i.e., "nor shall [any person] be compelled in any criminal case to be a witness against himself"). Second, the Court held that this compulsion exists in any custodial questioning. The third holding contained the actual warnings; the Court held that to "dispel the compulsion inherent in custodial settings," law enforcement officials needed to use certain devices designed to protect the suspect (*Miranda v. Arizona*, 1966, p. 458). The protective device recommended by the Court consisted of a set of warnings, hundreds of versions of which are commonly used today (Rogers, Hazelwood, Sewell, Harrison, & Shuman, 2008).

Thus, the holding in *Miranda v. Arizona* (1966) required law enforcement, during custodial interrogations, to inform suspects of their rights as a prerequisite to using their statements against them at trial. Without evidence that a suspect had been informed of these warnings and validly waived them, inculpatory statements cannot be introduced against a defendant at trial as part of the prosecution's case-in-chief. Although the Court has been flexible with respect to the specific language used to communicate suspects' rights (e.g., *California v. Prysock*, 1981; *Florida v. Powell*, 2010), it articulated that suspects must be informed of "the right to remain silent, that any statement he does make may be used as evidence against him, and that he has a right to the presence of an attorney, either retained or appointed" (*Miranda v. Arizona*, 1966, p. 444). The Court also stated that suspects have the ability to assert their rights at any time during an interrogation. On the basis of the language of the *Miranda* decision, it is somewhat unclear whether suspects need to be informed of their ability to assert rights at any time. In the Court's first recitation of the warnings, only the first four elements were included. In the second (and final) discussion of the warnings, the first four warnings were followed by the statement "Opportunity to exercise these rights must be afforded to him throughout the interrogation" (*Miranda v. Arizona*, 1966, p. 479). Currently, approximately 80% of jurisdictions include some version of this right as the fifth component of the *Miranda* warnings (Rogers, Hazelwood, Sewell, Shuman, & Blackwood, 2008).

Parallel Protections for Juvenile Suspects

The line of cases just described specifically referenced adult suspects. However, a nearly contemporaneous line of cases also emerged as the Supreme Court began to address the rights of juvenile suspects. Early on, the Court recognized juveniles' vulnerability during interrogations. In *Haley v. Ohio* (1948), police had arrested and questioned the defendant, a 15-year-old boy, about the murder of a confectionary store owner. Officers interrogated the boy overnight in relays of one or two at a time. At 5:00 a.m., the defendant confessed. Justice Douglas, writing for a plurality, held that admitting the defendant's confession was a due process violation. He noted that the Court needed to use special care in evaluating the voluntariness of a juvenile's confession and that the defendant's age, nature of the questioning, absence of a friend or lawyer, and police officers' apparent disregard of his rights indicated that the defendant's due process rights had been violated (*Haley v. Oho*, 1948). Notably, the Court was unwilling to accept the State's argument that the confession was obtained legitimately because the defendant had been advised of his constitutional rights. Justice Douglas wrote, "That assumes, however, that a boy of fifteen, without aid of counsel, would have a full appreciation of that advice and that on the facts of this record he had a freedom of choice. We cannot indulge those assumptions" (*Haley v. Oho*, 1948, p. 601).

The Court's cautious evaluation of juvenile confessions resurfaced in *Gallegos v. Colorado* (1962). The defendant in *Gallegos* was a 14-year-old boy, arrested in connection with an assault and robbery and subsequently charged with first-degree murder. The Court quoted at length from *Haley* and, ultimately, held that the defendant's confession was obtained in violation of due process. The Court emphasized that the defendant's youth, in conjunction with the absence of adult protection, indicated that the defendant would be unlikely to understand or assert his constitutional rights.

Haley v. Ohio (1948) and *Gallegos v. Colorado* (1962) laid a foundation for the Court's decision in *In re Gault* (1967), decided 1 year after *Miranda*. In *Gault*, the Court considered the case of a 15-year-old boy who had been found delinquent of making a lewd phone call and subsequently sentenced to a juvenile facility until he was 18. Several due process protections, standard in adult court, were notably absent. The Court's holding specifically extended these due process protections to juvenile proceedings: notice of charges, right to counsel, the rights of confrontation and cross-examination, the right against self-incrimination, and the right to appellate review (but not the right to a jury trial). Therefore, *Gault* extended the *Miranda* warnings, articulated 1 year earlier, to the interrogations of juveniles.

When Does *Miranda* Apply?

Although the *Miranda v. Arizona* (1966) holdings, in part, protect suspects from the coercion inherent in custodial interrogation, the warnings were also intended to allow interrogations to proceed (Schulhofer, 1987). In *Michigan v. Tucker* (1974), Justice Rehnquist wrote that the warnings should "help police officers conduct interrogations without facing continued risk that valuable evidence [will] be lost" (p. 443). Thus, in an important way, the *Miranda* decision was intended to simplify elements of criminal investigations by making it clear to police when they could interrogate a suspect and reasonably expect to use inculpatory evidence against him or her at trial.

With the practical side of *Miranda v. Arizona* (1966) in mind, it should be noted that the *Miranda* decision did not create a procedural rule that police must follow (i.e., that police officers must read suspects their *Miranda* rights before questioning). Instead, *Miranda* created a rule of admissibility: A suspect's statements cannot be admitted into evidence against him or her if the suspect was not informed of his or her *Miranda* rights. Moreover, the holdings in *Miranda* do not apply to every interaction between an individual and law enforcement. For the *Miranda* warnings to govern admissibility of an individual's inculpatory statement, that person must be in police custody and that person must be interrogated. In other words, *Miranda* only applies in cases of custodial interrogation.

The *Miranda v. Arizona* (1966) Court provided a brief definition of this term. "By custodial interrogation, we mean questioning initiated by law enforcement officers after a person has been taken into custody or otherwise deprived of his freedom of action in any significant way" (*Miranda v. Arizona*, 1966, p. 444). In *Thompson v. Keohane* (1995), the Court subsequently clarified the custody inquiry: "Two discrete inquiries are essential to the determination: first, what were the circumstances surrounding the interrogation; and second, given those circumstances, would a reasonable person have felt he or she was at liberty to terminate the interrogation and leave" (p. 112). Thus, custody is based on an objective evaluation of how a "reasonable person" would have felt under the circumstances specific to the interrogation that took place.

Miranda Waivers

Despite their importance, *Miranda* rights can be, and frequently are, waived by suspects (Kassin et al., 2007). To be accepted by courts, *Miranda* waivers must meet certain requirements. In *Miranda v. Arizona* (1966), the Court indicated that the "defendant may waive effectuation of these rights, provided the waiver is made voluntarily, knowingly, and intelligently" (p. 444). Thus, *knowing, intelligent*, and *voluntary* constitute the three requirements of a valid *Miranda* waiver. The Court briefly enumerated these requirements in the decision itself and elaborated on the elements of a knowing, intelligent, and voluntary waiver in later cases. In essence, the knowing and intelligent elements refer to a suspect's ability to comprehend his or her rights and the implications of surrendering them; voluntariness refers to the suspect's decision to waive his or her rights free from police coercion (e.g., *Colorado v. Connelly*, 1986; *Moran v. Burbine*, 1986; *Oregon v. Elstad*, 1985).

The knowing and intelligent components of a valid waiver are frequently discussed together, because they both reference the basic concept of rights comprehension. However, it is noteworthy that the Court used both knowing and intelligent to describe *Miranda* waivers. Although some readers may (correctly) observe that many Supreme Court opinions tend toward the verbose, it is unlikely that the Court, in this context, used two words to convey one meaning. When the knowing and intelligent components are disaggregated, *knowing* is used to convey a basic understanding of one's rights, and *intelligent* references one's ability to apply the rights to one's own situation and appreciate the significance of waiving those rights (e.g., *People v. Lara*, 1967). Despite these comprehension requirements, in later cases the Court stated that suspects do not need complete appreciation of every possible consequence of waiving their rights (e.g., *Colorado v. Spring*, 1987; *Oregon v. Elstad*, 1985). Some states have interpreted these cases to require only a basic understanding of the *Miranda* rights to satisfy the knowing and intelligent requirement (see, e.g., *Illinois v. Young*, 2006; *People v. Cheatham*, 1996), and others have taken an intermediate approach, requiring not only basic understanding, but also a somewhat more complex appreciation of the consequences of waiving one's rights (e.g., *People v. Al-Yousif*, 2002; *State v. Bushey*, 1982). The Court has never issued a dispositive ruling on this subject; however, the language of its decisions implies that the Court requires a basic appreciation of rights without requiring a suspect to appreciate every possible consequence of waiving his or her rights.

The voluntariness component of *Miranda* waivers is more circumscribed than the knowing and intelligent components as a result of the holding in *Colorado v. Connelly* (1986). In this case, the defendant approached an off-duty police officer and spontaneously confessed to a murder. Although a psychiatrist later testified that Connelly had schizophrenia and experienced command hallucinations ordering him to confess to the murder or commit suicide, the Court determined that his confession was, nevertheless, voluntary. The Court held that "coercive police activity is a necessary predicate to the finding that a confession is not 'voluntary'" (*Colorado v. Connelly*, 1986, p. 167). Therefore, the Court effectively foreclosed broader, more philosophical discussions about a suspect's free will or choice by limiting the voluntariness inquiry to police overreaching. Notably, police deception (e.g., lying to suspects about the evidence against them) does not constitute coercion (see *Frazier v. Cupp*, 1969). Other interrogation tactics, such as inducing guilt and empathy for the victim; emphasizing the suspect's need to show remorse to appear favorable to the prosecutor, judge, or jury; or promising to communicate information about a suspect's cooperation to the prosecutor are typically considered legally permissible when determining the voluntariness of a *Miranda* waiver (see *Frazier v. Cupp*, 1969; *Haynes v. Washington*, 1963; *Schneckloth v. Bustamonte*, 1973).

Judicial Evaluations of *Miranda* Waivers

Courts evaluate the validity of *Miranda* waivers by considering the totality of the circumstances around the waiver. Before the *Miranda* decision, courts had evaluated the voluntariness and admissibility of confessions using the totality-of-the-circumstances approach (e.g., *Blackburn v. Alabama*, 1960; *Haynes v. Washington*, 1963; *Johnson v. Zerbst*, 1938; *Spano v. New York*, 1958). Under this approach, a multitude of factors were considered, including characteristics of the suspect and factors specific to his or her interrogation. Thus, the totality of the circumstances is best described as a case-by-case approach in which no one factor necessarily validates or invalidates a *Miranda* waiver (A. M. Goldstein & Goldstein, 2010). In *Fare v. Michael C.* (1979), the Supreme Court clarified that the totality-of-the-circumstances approach should be used to evaluate juveniles' *Miranda* waivers. The Court specified that the approach requires inquiry into "all the circumstances surrounding the interrogation," including the juvenile's "age, experience, education, background, and intelligence, and whether he has the capacity to understand the warnings given to him, the nature of his Fifth Amendment rights, and the consequences of waiving those rights" (*Fare v. Michael*, 1979, p. 725).

Over time and across cases, several common totality factors have emerged. These factors include age, intelligence, comprehension of rights, whether the juvenile was given an opportunity to consult with an interested adult, methods used in interrogation, length of interrogation, and prior experience with the police or the juvenile justice system (e.g., *A.M. v. Butler*, 2004; *West v. United States*, 1968). However, this list is not exhaustive; states are free to consider other factors or require consideration of specific factors (King, 2006).

Despite the fact that the totality approach is used in the overwhelming majority of jurisdictions, it has certain limitations. One frequently cited problem with this approach is that it leaves law enforcement officers without clear guidance that can be applied in an interrogation context (Feld, 1984). Because the totality analysis is implemented after the interrogation, waiver, and confession have taken place, interrogating officers cannot guarantee that a waiver is valid or that a confession is voluntary. Commentators have also noted that the totality approach gives trial courts a significant amount of discretion—and that such an approach leaves judges without clear indicators of invalid waivers or inadmissible confessions. As a result, certain commentators have observed that juveniles' confessions are only excluded in egregious cases (Drizin & Luloff, 2007).

Notwithstanding the documented shortcomings of a totality-of-the-circumstances analysis, it remains relevant and is used in most jurisdictions. Proponents of the totality approach have noted that it is more consistent with the adversarial system than bright-line tests because it allows judges to consider evidence offered by both the prosecution and the defense (e.g., Huang, 2000). Some supporters of this approach (e.g., Milhizer, 2008) have argued that the totality approach leads to more reliable determinations of valid waivers and voluntary confessions than bright-line tests: "Reliability is a multifaceted, fact-dependent judgment that is not susceptible to bright-line rules or tests" (p. 51).

Role of Psychology in *Miranda* Warnings and Waivers

Thus far, we have covered the law surrounding *Miranda* warnings and waivers. In this section, we address the role of psychology in this area of law and set the stage for a more complete discussion of how forensic mental health professionals conduct evaluations of *Miranda* waiver capacity.

One of the earliest applications of psychology to this particular area of law was Grisso's (1981) effort to describe, empirically, the nature of juveniles' *Miranda* comprehension. Accomplishing this larger goal required two interrelated and important prerequisites. First, the legal terms knowing and intelligent needed to be transformed into useful psychological constructs. Second, a method was needed to assess those two constructs.

Grisso (1981) translated the legal constructs of knowing and intelligent into separate psychological constructs. The term knowing was conceptualized as "understanding"—that is, a person's basic understanding of the rights' meanings. The term intelligent was interpreted as "appreciation," or the extent to which a person can apply the rights to his or her own situation and grasp the consequences of waiving or asserting those rights. Grisso (1998) did not address voluntariness because the courts had ruled that the presence of coercion was a factual matter, rather than a psychological one. Nonetheless, forensic mental health experts address voluntariness by considering totality-of-the-circumstances factors that may increase or decrease an individual's susceptibility to police coercion, if factual evidence establishes its presence (A. M. Goldstein & Goldstein, 2010; Melton, Petrila, Poythress, & Slobogin, 2007).

In the 1970s, Grisso initiated research on suspects' capacities to validly waive *Miranda* rights. He created the Instruments for Assessing Understanding and Appreciation of *Miranda* Rights as a standardized research instrument for evaluating juveniles' capacities to understand and appreciate *Miranda* warnings and the consequences of waiving their rights (A. M. Goldstein & Goldstein, 2010).

With a functional translation of the cognitively based legal requirements into psychological constructs and an assessment tool designed to evaluate information about those constructs, research on juveniles' understanding and appreciation of their rights could proceed. Grisso's (1981) research yielded a number of important findings with respect to juveniles' abilities in an absolute sense (i.e., compared with the set of required abilities), as well as in a relative sense (i.e., compared with a typical suspect or defendant; A. M. Goldstein & Goldstein, 2010).

Age and IQ emerged as robust predictors of *Miranda* comprehension, with younger individuals (i.e., those age 13 years and younger) and those with lower IQ scores (i.e., 70 and below) demonstrating poorer *Miranda* comprehension than older individuals and those with IQ scores above 70. Age was strongly related to *Miranda* understanding through middle adolescence and appeared to plateau around ages 14 to 15. Between the ages of 14 and 16, IQ emerged as a more powerful influence on *Miranda* comprehension and a better predictor of deficits in juveniles' *Miranda* understanding relative to that of adults. Moreover, youths younger than age 16 demonstrated significant deficits in appreciation of the right to silence and right to counsel compared with adults (Grisso, 1981). For example, nearly one third of youths believed that the public defender only works in the interests of the innocent, and a similar proportion believed that a judge could revoke an individual's right to silence. In summary, Grisso's (1981) results suggested that youths' inferior understanding and appreciation of their *Miranda* rights diminished their capacity to offer knowing and intelligent waivers of their rights.

Given juveniles' difficulties with *Miranda* comprehension, some have questioned whether a simplified version of the warnings would facilitate understanding and appreciation (Ferguson & Douglas, 1970; Helms, 2003). It would seem that sentences that are easier to read and require less skill to be understood should be better comprehended. However, youths' understanding and appreciation did not differ when they were presented with simpler and more complex versions of the *Miranda* warnings (Ferguson & Douglas, 1970; N. E. S. Goldstein, Messenheimer, Riggs Romaine, & Zelle, 2012). Such findings have generated suggestions that *Miranda* comprehension may be a conceptual ability and not primarily based on the linguistic properties of the warnings (N. E. S. Goldstein, Condie, Kalbeitzer, Osman, & Geier, 2003; N. E. S. Goldstein, Messenheimer, et al., 2012). However, the linguistic complexity of the warnings adds a layer of complication to juveniles' *Miranda* comprehension, even when juvenile-specific versions of the warnings are available. When juvenile-specific and general (i.e., intended for use with adult suspects or both juvenile and adult suspects) versions of the warnings have been compared, juvenile versions tend to be more complicated, with longer warnings, higher reading levels, and lower reading ease scores (Helms, 2007; Kahn, Zapf, & Cooper, 2006; Rogers, Blackwood, et al., 2012; Rogers, Hazelwood, Sewell, Shuman, & Blackwood, 2008).

Empirical examinations of juveniles' *Miranda* comprehension laid the foundation for forensic mental health assessment in this arena. After their development for research purposes, Grisso's (1981) instruments were widely incorporated into forensic evaluations of defendants' capacities to have understood and appreciated their *Miranda* rights during interrogation (Archer, Buffington-Vollum, Stredny, & Handel, 2006; Lally, 2003; Ryba, Brodsky, & Schlosberg, 2007). In contrast to unstructured interviews in which forensic mental health professionals determined, independently, which questions to ask to gather information relevant to a waiver's validity, Grisso's instruments offered a standardized method of evaluating a defendant's understanding and appreciation of *Miranda* rights. In 1998, Grisso enhanced the credibility and admissibility of his instruments by publishing them, along with their psychometric properties, based on data collected in an extensive study of justice-involved youths and adults as well as a community sample of adults (N. E. S. Goldstein, Zelle, & Grisso, 2014). Before N. E. S. Goldstein, Zelle, and Grisso's (2012) revisions of the instruments (discussed below) and later release of Rogers, Sewell, Drogin, and Fiduccia's (2012) measures, Grisso's (1981, 1998) instruments were the only standardized tool to offer forensic evaluators specific information about the degree and type of cognitive abilities required to comprehend *Miranda* warnings and associated rights (N. E. S. Goldstein et al., 2014).

CURRENT EVENTS IN THE LAW AND PSYCHOLOGY OF *MIRANDA*

Several developments have occurred in the legal and psychological landscapes surrounding *Miranda v. Arizona* (1966). In the section that follows, we review recent legal decisions that have affected *Miranda* jurisprudence and, potentially, forensic evaluations of *Miranda* waiver capacity. Subsequently, we provide an overview of advances in psychology's understanding of adolescent development, particularly with respect to neuropsychological development and the emerging construct of developmental immaturity. Then we describe recent empirical evidence about juveniles' *Miranda* comprehension and the different types of policies that have been implemented to attempt to protect juveniles during the interrogation process, given concerns about their *Miranda* comprehension abilities. Finally, we discuss current best practices for evaluating *Miranda* comprehension and describe the specialized forensic assessment instruments available for this purpose.

Recent *Miranda* Case Law

In the decades since *Miranda v. Arizona* (1966), the decision has been met with some criticism and resistance (e.g., Cassell, 2011). The cornerstone of legal resistance to the *Miranda* decision was a federal statute, 18 U.S.C. § 3501. The statute made decisions about the admissibility of confessions in federal courts turn solely on whether the confession was offered voluntarily, thereby "overruling" the Supreme Court's decision and returning evaluations of confessions to the pre-*Miranda* voluntariness test. In 2000, the Supreme Court addressed a challenge to this statute in *Dickerson v. United States* (2000) and held that "*Miranda* announced a constitutional rule that Congress may not supersede legislatively" (p. 444).

Thus, it appears that *Miranda v. Arizona* (1966) is here to stay. Since the *Dickerson v. United States* (2000) decision, the Supreme Court has taken multiple opportunities to clarify and elaborate on the precise meaning of *Miranda* and the limits of that decision. In the past 5 years, the Court has addressed issues such as using a defendant's silence in a noncustodial interrogation against him at trial (*Salinas v. Texas*, 2013) and nuances in the *Miranda* custody analysis (*Howes v. Fields*, 2012; *Maryland v. Shatzer*, 2010). The Court further clarified that it would not scrutinize the language used to convey the *Miranda* warnings (*Florida v. Powell*, 2010) and that law enforcement could use post-*Miranda* behavior that is inconsistent with a prior invocation of *Miranda* as an implicit waiver of rights (*Berghuis v. Thompkins*, 2010).

Notably, the Supreme Court also recently addressed how the legal definition of custody, one of the prerequisites for *Miranda v. Arizona* (1966), should apply to juveniles. In 2011, the Court heard arguments in *J.D.B. v. North Carolina*. The factual question in the case was whether a seventh-grade student, questioned by police in school, was in custody for the purposes of *Miranda*. The broader issue was whether law enforcement officers should consider the age of a child when deciding whether he or she is in police custody. J.D.B. had been removed from his afternoon class by a uniformed police officer and escorted to a conference room where an investigator, assistant principal, and administrative intern were present. The conference room door was closed, and J.D.B. was questioned by the investigator for 30 to 45 minutes without the opportunity to speak with his legal guardian and without receiving the *Miranda* warnings.

In the *J.D.B. v. North Carolina* (2011) decision, the Court reaffirmed the objective nature of the *Miranda v. Arizona* (1966) custody analysis: Given the totality of the circumstances surrounding an interrogation, would "a reasonable person have felt he or she was at liberty to terminate the interrogation and leave" (*J.D.B. v. North Carolina*, 2011, p. 2407, citing *Thompson v. Keohane*, 1995)? The Court also made a number of observations it believed to be consistent with the objective nature of the analysis. Its first observation was that the "law has historically reflected the . . . assumption that children characteristically lack the capacity to exercise mature judgment and possess only an incomplete ability to understand the world around them" (*J.D.B. v. North Carolina*, 2011, p. 2403). The Court also noted that a "reasonable child subjected to police questioning will sometimes feel pressured to submit when a reasonable adult would feel free to go" (*J.D.B. v. North Carolina*, 2011, p. 2403). Ultimately, the Court held that the age of a child, when either known to police at the time of questioning or "objectively apparent to a reasonable officer," is relevant to the *Miranda* custody analysis (*J.D.B. v. North Carolina*, 2011, p. 2406). The Court cautioned, however, that age would not necessarily be a significant factor in every case.

In sum, the Court reaffirmed its commitment to the core holdings in *Miranda v. Arizona* (1966).

At the same time, recent cases have endeavored to provide greater clarity about the precise contours of *Miranda*. With *J.D.B. v. North Carolina* (2011), the Court also required law enforcement to be more attentive to a juvenile's age when determining whether *Miranda* applies.

Advances in Understanding Adolescent Development

The past 2 decades have yielded an abundance of information about adolescents' neurological, cognitive, and social development. We briefly review that information below, particularly as it may relate to adolescents' abilities to understand and appreciate the *Miranda* warnings' meaning and function during interrogations.

Neurological development. Emerging evidence has indicated that the human brain continues to develop well into the 3rd decade of life. Longitudinal imaging studies have revealed that the frontal lobes are both structurally immature and less active during adolescence (Gogtay et al., 2004; Rubia et al., 2000). Simultaneously, the limbic system, which is generally regarded as the socio-emotional center of the brain, is particularly active (Rubia et al., 2000). These developing systems interact as the underdeveloped frontal lobes receive and modulate synaptic transmissions from the highly active limbic system, making the adolescent brain particularly vulnerable to social and emotional cues in decision making and impulsive behavior (Albert & Steinberg, 2011). In addition, the dopaminergic system, which plays an important role in processing rewards, is restructured during adolescence (Steinberg, 2010). The system's projections to the mesolimbic area and prefrontal cortex increase during mid- and late adolescence and then decline. These changes may lead to the increase in reward-seeking behavior observed among adolescents and may increase the reinforcing properties of situations or individuals.

Cognitive and social development. Adolescents are qualitatively different from adults in their cognitive and social functioning; the term *developmental immaturity* is used here to describe these differences. Developmental immaturity refers to the changes that occur during the transition from adolescence to adulthood across four dimensions: independent functioning, decision making, emotional regulation, and general cognitive processing (Kemp, 2010). Independent functioning refers to both one's self-reliance (i.e., the ability to make autonomous decisions) and self-concept (i.e., clarity of values, recognizing personal strengths and weaknesses; Cauffman & Steinberg, 2000; Kemp, 2010). Adolescents often struggle to make decisions that are independent of authority figures or friends and that are consistent with their personal values. In the context of decision making, adolescents are heavily influenced by social and emotional factors and are more likely to engage in sensation- and reward-seeking behaviors (Cauffman & Steinberg, 2000; Steinberg, 2010). Emotion regulation also develops throughout adolescence and into adulthood, meaning that adolescents are less able to recognize and express their feelings, manage their emotions, or cope with undesirable feelings (Kemp, 2010). Finally, cognitive functioning continues to improve into adulthood; thus, adolescents are still developing in domains such as reasoning, memory, processing speed, and verbal fluency (Klaczynski, 2001; Levin et al., 1991).

Implications for juveniles' *Miranda* waiver capacity. These neurologically based age differences in cognitive, social, emotional, and behavioral functioning are important in the context of *Miranda* comprehension for three reasons. First, cognitive abilities influence core *Miranda* comprehension skills such as vocabulary, verbal fluency, and memory (e.g., Levin et al., 1991). Second, the fact that *Miranda* comprehension may be, in part, a conceptual skill also suggests that adults may be better suited to understand and appreciate these rights, because adults' reasoning abilities can be more abstract (Baird & Fugelsang, 2004). Finally, although features of developmental immaturity, such as limited independent functioning and emotion regulation, do not appear to affect *Miranda* comprehension per se, they can influence adolescents' abilities to understand and reason about novel information in a demanding situation such as an interrogation. For example, time-pressured decision making; the absence of consultation with an informed, objective adult; and heightened emotional arousal all detract from an adolescent's ability to engage in rational decision making (Steinberg, Cauffman, Woolard, Graham, & Banich, 2009).

Therefore, even if a particular adolescent understood her or his *Miranda* rights, the combination of underdeveloped independent functioning, poor emotion regulation abilities, and the pressure exerted by police officers could potentially interfere with the adolescent's ability to appreciate how those rights could benefit her or him and the consequences of waiving those rights. These factors could also make the adolescent more likely to comply with a police officer's explicit or implicit requests to waive his or her rights and provide inculpatory information.

Recent Evidence about Juveniles' *Miranda* Comprehension

Empirical research over the past 40 years has revealed consistent deficits in juveniles' *Miranda* comprehension. Many juveniles continue to struggle with conceptualizing the rights to silence and counsel, the cornerstones of the *Miranda* warnings (N. E. S. Goldstein et al., 2003). One of the foundations of juveniles' poor *Miranda* comprehension may be their fundamental misunderstanding of what rights are; many juveniles define *right* as an opportunity, a choice, or something they are permitted to do instead of as an entitlement. Thus, many juveniles believe that individuals, such as judges, can revoke their rights (N. E. S. Goldstein et al., 2003; Grisso, 1997).

For instance, Peterson-Badali, Abramovitch, Koegl, and Ruck (1999) found that 36% of the juveniles who waived their right to silence or to speak with a parent during an actual interrogation reported believing that they had to waive those rights. Juveniles also frequently misunderstand the role that defense attorneys play in the justice system. Many have reported the belief that a defense attorney plays a fact-finding role and would report inculpatory information to the judge; others have indicated that lawyers are only available to protect the innocent (Abramovitch, Peterson-Badali, & Rohan, 1995; N. E. S. Goldstein et al., 2003; Grisso, 1997). In one sample of youths who had been interrogated by police, 76% did not believe that they had access to a lawyer even though they remembered the police telling them that they had the right to "retain and instruct counsel without delay" (Peterson-Badali et al., 1999, p. 459).

Juveniles demonstrate deficits in the appreciation domain as well, meaning that they may not be able to apply the *Miranda* rights to their own situations or to recognize the consequences of waiving or asserting their rights. For example, one fundamental implication of waiving *Miranda* rights is that police probably will begin or continue an interrogation, seeking a confession or other inculpatory information, and many youths fail to appreciate this consequence (Abramovitch, Higgins-Biss, & Biss, 1993). In the right-to-counsel sphere, many juveniles fail to appreciate how the concepts of confidentiality and privilege apply to the attorney–client relationship. For instance, nearly three quarters (72%) of youths in one study thought the lawyer could relate information to the police, 70% believed the lawyer could report information to the judge, and 84% believed the lawyer could share information with their parents (Peterson-Badali, Abramovitch, & Duda, 1997).

Public Policy on Interrogations of Juveniles

Most of the empirical research reviewed thus far has focused on the nature of juveniles' deficits in *Miranda* comprehension and the disadvantages they have during interrogations. In light of these problems, public policy developments in this area have focused on ways of enhancing juveniles' abilities and protecting them during interactions with police. In this section, we review policies that have been adopted by states or proposed by advocates, including interested-adult rules and the growing trend of recording interrogations.

Interested-adult rules. The notion of an interested adult to protect juveniles during interrogations dates as far back as the Supreme Court's decision in *Haley v. Ohio* (1948), when the Court observed the absence of a friend or counsel during the juvenile suspect's interrogation. Since then, certain states have adopted per se rules requiring the presence of an interested adult during the interrogation of juveniles younger than a certain age. Seven states have created presumptions that juveniles younger than a certain age cannot waive these rights without consulting with a parent or legal guardian; seven others require a parent or legal guardian's presence during the interrogation of juveniles younger than a certain age (King, 2006). These decisions are sometimes the result of legislation and, less frequently, created by case law (King, 2006). Even in states that have not established per se rules regarding an interested adult, courts rely heavily on the presence or absence of an interested adult in the totality analysis (e.g., *A.M. v. Butler*, 2004; *West v. United States*, 1968).

Interested-adult rules certainly have intuitive appeal, and a number of legal scholars have called for these rules to be implemented on a wider basis (e.g., Huang, 2000; McGuire, 2000). Judges and legal advocates appear to assume that parents will explain the *Miranda* rights to their children and act as legal advocates (e.g., *Commonwealth v. A Juvenile*, 1983). Empirical psychological research, however, has identified some meaningful differences between the theory and practice of interested-adult rules.

The first problem with an interested-adult rule is its assumption that parents have the ability to explain the *Miranda* rights to their children. Research, however, has shown that many adults show poor *Miranda* comprehension themselves. Grisso (1981) found that approximately 23% of his adult sample displayed inadequate *Miranda* comprehension, and fewer than 50% provided an adequate definition of the word *right*. A further problem is that parents frequently do not act as legal advocates for their children (Grisso, 1981). In some instances, parents do not speak with their children at all when given opportunities by police (Grisso & Ring, 1979). When they do speak with their children, parents often direct them to waive their rights and cooperate with police, and they sometimes go so far as to pressure them to confess (Grisso, 1981; Grisso & Ring, 1979). Instead of seeing this evidence as a potential problem with parental presence during interrogations, at least one court has expressed approval of this moral, as opposed to legal, advice (*Anglin v. State*, 1972).

Even if one assumes that parents possess adequate comprehension of *Miranda*, are capable of and willing to explain the meaning of those rights to their children, and actually provide useful legal advice, legal commentators have noted that police are often instructed in how to marginalize parents during interrogations (Drizin & Luloff, 2007). Conflicts of interest can also arise when parents are involved in the interrogations of their children, particularly in domestic violence cases or when the parent is the guilty party (Drizin & Luloff, 2007). In sum, there are a wide variety of reasons why an interested adult may not be able to assist a juvenile during an interrogation and several other reasons why the adult could fail to serve the intended protective function, increasing the probability of a youth's *Miranda* waiver.

Recording interrogations. Advocates and scholars have also promoted efforts to require law enforcement to record interrogations of juveniles (e.g., Kassin et al., 2010; Schlam, 1995). Proponents have argued that video recordings can depict interrogations more accurately than can testimony from either juvenile defendants or police officers and therefore can assist courts in understanding the precise circumstances surrounding juveniles' waivers and admissions. One legal commentator observed that recording interrogations offers a cost-effective and feasible compromise to less practical proposals, such as requiring on-call attorneys for juvenile suspects or requiring a blanket exclusion of juvenile confessions (Schlam, 1995). Additional benefits of videotaping interrogations include reducing frivolous claims of police misconduct and detecting potential false confessions (Kassin et al., 2010; Schlam, 1995).

Through state court decisions or legislative action, 13 jurisdictions require recording of interrogations in at least some circumstances: Alaska, Illinois, Indiana, Maine, Maryland, Massachusetts, Minnesota, Nebraska, New Mexico, New Jersey, Wisconsin, North Carolina, and the District of Columbia (Taslitz, 2012). Surveys of police and sheriffs' offices have revealed that the practice is increasingly common and has been voluntarily adopted by a number of law enforcement agencies in jurisdictions that do not require it (Kassin et al., 2010).

Evaluating Juveniles' *Miranda* Comprehension

Within the context of forensic mental health assessments, identifying convergent information from a variety of sources helps evaluators draw reliable conclusions (Heilbrun, DeMatteo, Brooks Holliday, & LaDuke, 2014; Heilbrun, Marczyk, & DeMatteo, 2002). Therefore, forensic mental health evaluations, regardless of the specific issue, should include information drawn from various sources, including a review of records, a clinical interview, and data gathered from relevant measures.

Record review. Because a focused evaluation will provide the most relevant and material information for the issue at hand while still protecting the privacy of interested parties, the records obtained should include only those that can provide meaningful information for the evaluation of *Miranda* waiver capacity. This means that evaluators should avoid a blanket request for all records. Instead, evaluators should seek to identify and collect those records that are most likely to aid in answering the referral question.

With regard to *Miranda* waiver capacity, evaluators should attempt to collect and review any records that specifically involve the interrogation process in the case and the actual version of the *Miranda* rights administered by police. This latter step is particularly important because the forensic mental health expert must question the defendant about the actual rights administered, not a generic version of the rights (A. M. Goldstein & Goldstein, 2010). If available, evaluators should obtain copies of the signed *Miranda* waiver form, any documents that describe the interrogation or waiver process, and any recordings that involve administration of the *Miranda* warnings, rights waivers, or the interrogation (A. M. Goldstein & Goldstein, 2010; Oberlander & Goldstein, 2001). Finally, although a signed copy or transcript of the defendant's confession may be available, the forensic mental health expert must determine whether it is relevant to the evaluation. If it contains information related to the interrogation process or rights waiver, it may be of great value to the evaluation. However, unless the transcript provides such information or the validity or trustworthiness of the defendant's statement is being questioned, the confession is not relevant to an evaluation of the defendant's *Miranda* waiver capacity, and experts should generally avoid questioning the defendant about details of the crime (A. M. Goldstein & Goldstein, 2010).

In addition to the documents that directly involve the *Miranda* waiver process, evaluators should try to obtain other records that summarize information related to the ability to understand and appreciate the *Miranda* warnings. Such records may include previous psychological assessment data (e.g., IQ scores, educational achievement scores), school records, prior juvenile or criminal justice records, employment records, medical records, and mental health records (A. M. Goldstein & Goldstein, 2010; Oberlander & Goldstein, 2001). Finally, third-party interviews with people familiar with the defendant may help the forensic mental health expert evaluate the reliability of the defendant's assertions about his or her own history or conditions that may have affected his or her *Miranda* waiver capacity (A. M. Goldstein & Goldstein, 2010).

Interview. Before initiating the interview, the evaluator should obtain informed consent from the defendant. This process, while sounding deceptively simple, has a number of complexities with respect to both juveniles and evaluations of *Miranda* waiver capacity. First, when evaluating a juvenile, unless the evaluation was court ordered, consent should be sought from either the parent or legal guardian or the referring defense attorney. Then, regardless of whether the evaluation is the result of a referral or court order, the evaluator should seek the youth's assent. Generally, this means that the evaluator will explain the nature and purpose of the evaluation and the limits of confidentiality, in language that is developmentally appropriate, and then ask the youth to paraphrase the information that was provided (A. M. Goldstein & Goldstein, 2010). The evaluator should anticipate that informed assent will be difficult to obtain because of both (a) developmental limitations that will affect any juvenile's ability to assent to a forensic evaluation and (b) the potential impairments that prompted the referral for the evaluation (A. M. Goldstein & Goldstein, 2010). Therefore, the evaluator should be prepared to explain and reexplain the required information and document the defendant's responses (A. M. Goldstein & Goldstein, 2010). However, with these explanations, the evaluator should take care not to educate the defendant about information that would contaminate the *Miranda* waiver evaluation—for instance, by directly defining the word *right*.

During the interview, the evaluator gathers data about how the *Miranda* warnings were understood at the time of arrest (Frumkin, 2000; Grisso, 1981). It is important to identify this specific time frame because how the warnings are understood at the current time—the time of the evaluation—is not the most important issue. The way a juvenile understands the warnings at the time of evaluation may be different from the way he or she understood the warnings at the time of arrest for a variety of reasons, including maturation associated with the passing of time; changes in mental status; or more recent interactions with police, attorneys, and other individuals throughout the course of proceedings that may have included explanations of rights or identification of consequences of talking with others about the legal case (A. M. Goldstein & Goldstein, 2010). Therefore, it is important to focus primarily on the time of the waiver and interrogation.

The interview should be designed to gather data about a variety of functional domains that may have affected capacity to provide a valid *Miranda* waiver. Areas of importance include background data and psychological functioning. Background data often include information about education, medical health, vocational history, substance use, prior arrest history, and family (including family mental health and cognitive functioning; Frumkin, 2000; A. M. Goldstein & Goldstein, 2010; Oberlander, 1998).

In addition to these domains, the evaluator should (a) obtain the juvenile's account of the arrest and events surrounding administration of the warnings and the rights waiver, (b) assess comprehension of the warnings, and (c) gauge the juvenile's reaction to being interrogated (A. M. Goldstein & Goldstein, 2010; Oberlander & Goldstein, 2001). As part of the interview and assessment of comprehension, the evaluator may choose to conduct a semistructured clinical interview and use the warnings as worded in the jurisdiction in which the arrest occurred. Evaluators may use a semistructured interview by asking the juvenile to paraphrase the warnings and identify any words he or she does not understand (Frumkin, 2000; Grisso, 1998; Oberlander & Goldstein, 2001). In some cases, evaluators may choose to combine this approach with a structured assessment, described below, by using a semistructured interview to gauge a juvenile's comprehension of the specific warnings provided by police and by administering a structured, specialized measure to compare the juvenile's comprehension with a designated standard. Evaluators must be cognizant of the implications of how they choose to order the semistructured interview and structured assessment. Although conducting the semistructured interview may seem to flow naturally from the clinical interview in which the evaluator gathers background information, this approach may contaminate the psychometrically sound data offered by a structured assessment by providing the defendant with information about his or her *Miranda* rights. The manual for structured *Miranda* assessment instruments states that the instruments should be administered "prior to any discussion or testing that may inform an examinee about the meaning of the *Miranda* warnings" (N. E. S. Goldstein et al., 2014, p. 26).

Assessment. *Miranda* waiver evaluations should include administration of traditional clinical assessment tools (e.g., measures of cognitive ability, academic achievement, personality), as well as administration of forensic mental health tools specific to the legal question of juveniles' capacities to have waived rights during police questioning. To determine which traditional assessment tools should be administered in a *Miranda* waiver evaluation, the evaluator must identify the totality-of-the-circumstance factors that may be relevant to the specific case. Most *Miranda* waiver evaluations include instruments that measure cognitive functioning (e.g., Wechsler Intelligence Scale for Children—Fourth Edition; Wechsler, 2003) and academic achievement (e.g., Wide Range Achievement Test 4

[Wilkinson & Robertson, 2006] and Wechsler Individual Achievement Test—Third Edition [Breaux, 2009]) because these instruments measure abilities that are directly implicated in providing a knowing and intelligent waiver. If mental illness is present, measures should be used to evaluate deficits, particularly those that may have an impact on understanding and appreciation of rights or susceptibility to coercion if it occurred. If a history of impairments or symptoms is well documented (e.g., intellectual disability via school-based IQ testing and individualized education programs), specific tests may be unnecessary to evaluate their existence, and the forensic evaluator can, instead, merely emphasize the link (or lack thereof) between established impairments and the youth's comprehension or susceptibility to coercion that may have occurred (Oberlander & Goldstein, 2001).

In addition to administering traditional assessment measures as part of the evaluation, specialized tools are available that can provide rich data on youths' functioning (Heilbrun et al., 2002, 2014). More important, these instruments can provide both qualitative data about the nature of a youth's specific deficits and quantitative data to identify the extent of deficits and to compare a defendant's scores with those of normative groups. In terms of juvenile *Miranda* waiver evaluations, this means that the evaluator can specifically assess a defendant's understanding and appreciation of the rights to silence and legal counsel and obtain descriptive information about how the rights are understood by the youthful defendant. Such specialized forensic assessment tools also generate instrument scores that can be compared with a normative group, such as same-aged peers, adults in criminal court (if the youth's case is under the jurisdiction of criminal court), or youths of similar intelligence.

Specialized instruments. Instruments for Assessing Understanding and Appreciation of *Miranda* Rights. Grisso's (1981) Instruments for Assessing Understanding and Appreciation of *Miranda* Rights were the first standardized tools to evaluate a defendant's cognitive capacities related to the knowing and intelligent requirements of a valid rights waiver (Grisso, 1998).

Four component measures make up Grisso's (1981) Instruments for Assessing Understanding and Appreciation of *Miranda* Rights: the Comprehension of *Miranda* Rights (CMR), Comprehension of *Miranda* Rights—Recognition (CMR–R), Comprehension of *Miranda* Vocabulary (CMV), and Function of Rights in Interrogation (FRI). The CMR and CMV measure a juvenile's verbal expressive abilities by requiring the examinee to, respectively, paraphrase each *Miranda* warning and define six words that frequently appear in *Miranda* warnings. The CMR–R requires the examinee to identify, rather than verbally express, similarities and differences between sets of preconstructed sentences and specified *Miranda* warning statements. The fourth component measure, the FRI, uses picture stimuli, accompanied by brief vignettes, to assess appreciation of *Miranda* warnings, specifically of the adversarial nature of interrogation (NI subscale), the function of and right to legal counsel (RC subscale), and the right to silence (RS subscale; Grisso, 1998).

Grisso (1998) reported excellent test–retest reliability for the CMR using a juvenile-only sample and sound interrater reliability for the CMR, CMV, and FRI using a mixed adult and juvenile sample. Colwell et al. (2005) later reexamined the psychometric properties with a sample of 85 male and female juvenile offenders and calculated both Cronbach's alphas and intraclass correlation coefficients for the CMR, CMV, and FRI, reporting adequate internal consistency and interrater reliability across all three instruments in their sample. Both Grisso and Colwell et al. established construct validity for the instruments via their associations with IQ and age. Regarding concurrent validity, Grisso (1998) found that instruments assessing the same construct (i.e., understanding) demonstrated greater associations with each other than with instruments assessing different constructs (i.e., appreciation, IQ). Specifically, the CMR, CMR–R, and CMV demonstrated stronger correlations with each other than they did with the FRI or with IQ.

Miranda Rights Comprehension Instruments. The *Miranda* Rights Comprehension Instruments (MRCI; N. E. S. Goldstein, Zelle & Grisso, 2012) are the revised version of Grisso's (1981)

Instruments for Assessing Understanding and Appreciation of *Miranda* Rights. N. E. S. Goldstein et al., (2014) updated Grisso's (1981) original instruments for the following purposes: (a) to simplify the language so that the instruments would better generalize across jurisdictions; (b) to include a fifth right, frequently included in contemporary *Miranda* warnings, that acknowledges the suspect's privilege to assert rights at any time; (c) to generate modern normative data to maintain the instruments' applicability in clinical and research settings; and (d) to update the psychometric properties using modern data and statistical methodology. With these revisions and updates, the MRCI better parallel the current legal standard of *Miranda* comprehension and serve as an important component of evaluating the cognitive capacities associated with the knowing and intelligent requirements of a valid *Miranda* waiver.

Like Grisso's (1981) original instruments, the MRCI assess an individual's understanding and appreciation of the warnings. The MRCI consist of four distinct instruments, each measuring capacities central to the knowing and intelligent requirements of a valid waiver. Each instrument generates a total score, but instrument scores are not totaled to produce one overall MRCI score because each instrument provides a different type of information related to *Miranda* waiver capacities. As with Grisso's (1981) original instruments, score interpretation involves examining patterns of responses, both qualitatively (i.e., specific areas of accurate and inaccurate understanding) and quantitatively (i.e., comparison with normative age group and IQ data), across the four measures (A. M. Goldstein & Goldstein, 2010). The four component instruments are as follows:

1. Comprehension of *Miranda* Rights—II (CMR–II) evaluates an examinee's understanding of the *Miranda* warnings by asking the examinee to paraphrase each of the five *Miranda* warning statements contained in the instrument. Examiners read each warning aloud and simultaneously show it, in written form, to the examinee. Responses are rated as reflecting adequate (2 points), questionable (1 point), or inadequate (0 points) understanding of each warning, and total CMR–II scores can range from 0 to 10. The CMR–II demonstrated moderate internal consistency and test–retest reliability, excellent interrater reliability, and moderate construct validity and convergent validity with justice-involved and community youths (N. E. S. Goldstein et al., 2011, 2014).
2. Comprehension of *Miranda* Rights—Recognition—II (CMR–R–II) evaluates an examinee's understanding of the *Miranda* warnings by differentiating between correct and incorrect interpretations of each warning. The examiner reads aloud a written warning that is also shown to the examinee. The examiner then reads three other statements, and the examinee must identify whether each statement has the same meaning as the warning initially presented. Correct responses receive 1 point, and incorrect responses receive 0 points. Total CMR–R–II scores can range from 0 to 15. The CMR–R–II demonstrated moderate internal consistency and test–retest reliability, as well as moderate construct validity and convergent validity, with justice-involved and community youth samples (N. E. S. Goldstein et al., 2011, 2014).
3. Function of Rights in Interrogation (FRI) evaluates an examinee's appreciation of *Miranda* rights in the context of police interrogations, as well as their implications for later legal proceedings. The FRI is composed of three subscales: Nature of Interrogation (i.e., risks associated with interrogation), Right to Counsel (i.e., purpose of legal counsel), and Right to Silence (i.e., safeguards to the right to silence and role of confessions). The examiner presents four pictures, coupled with brief vignettes related to the interrogation process, and asks a total of 15 questions. The scoring process and criteria (i.e., adequate, questionable, and inadequate responses) parallel those of the CMR–II. Subscale and total scores are calculated for the FRI, with subscale scores ranging from 0 to 10 and total scores ranging from 0 to 30. The FRI demonstrated adequate to moderate subscale and moderate total internal consistency, moderate to excellent subscale and total interrater reliability, and moderate subscale and total

test–retest reliability. Moreover, the FRI demonstrated adequate construct validity and adequate to moderate convergent validity with justice-involved and community youths (N. E. S. Goldstein et al., 2011; N. E. S. Goldstein, Zelle, & Grisso, 2012).

4. Comprehension of *Miranda* Vocabulary—II (CMV–II) evaluates an examinee's ability to define 16 words frequently appearing in *Miranda* warnings. The examiner reads the word aloud, uses it in a sentence, repeats the word, and then asks the examinee to define the word. Similar to the CMR–II and FRI, each response is assigned a score ranging from 0 to 2. Total scores on the CMV–II can range from 0 to 32. The CMV–II demonstrated good to excellent internal consistency and test–retest reliability, excellent interrater reliability, and moderate construct validity and convergent validity with justice-involved and community youths (N. E. S. Goldstein et al., 2011, 2014).

The psychometric properties of the MRCI, based on data gathered from multiple juvenile samples, closely mirror the psychometric properties of Grisso's original instruments (N. E. S. Goldstein et al., 2011). The MRCI have demonstrated moderate internal consistency. All of the instruments have shown excellent interrater reliability and moderate to strong stability over time. Finally, psychometric analyses revealed the MRCI's concurrent (i.e., correlations with age and IQ) and convergent (i.e., cross-test comparisons between MRCI component measures) validity.

Interpreting patterns in an individual's performance on these instruments can be done both quantitatively and qualitatively. Quantitative interpretation involves comparing an individual's scores with those of normative samples, such as those of same-aged youths or those with similar IQ scores. For example, an examiner may choose to compare a 13-year-old's CMR–II score with that of the average 13-year-old involved with the juvenile justice system to reveal similarities or differences in extent of understanding. Alternatively, if this youth's case is under the jurisdiction of criminal court, the evaluator might compare the youth's performance on the CMR–II with that of adult offenders to demonstrate differences between the juvenile defendant's understanding and that of the typical adult in the criminal justice system (A. M. Goldstein & Goldstein, 2010; Grisso, 1981).

Qualitative interpretation involves evaluating the individual's performance across the component instruments, and courts may be interested in learning about a youth's specific understanding and appreciation of the individual rights to silence and counsel. For instance, the evaluator may present and explain the defendant's misinterpretation of the right to silence on the CMR–II (e.g., "You can't speak until they tell you to") by describing the definition of right on the CMV–II (e.g., "Something you are allowed to do") and its implications for appreciation on the FRI item asking about what should happen if a judge learns that a youth suspect would not speak to police (e.g., "He will get in trouble and go to jail"). More important, the examiner should highlight consistency and inconsistency across instruments, as well as accurate and inaccurate appreciation of rights. Interpreting an individual's performance both quantitatively and qualitatively assists the examiner in clearly communicating the defendant's understanding and appreciation of *Miranda* warnings within the context of interrogations (N. E. S. Goldstein et al., 2014; Grisso, 1998).

As with any forensic assessment measure (Heilbrun, 2001), MRCI scores cannot provide determinations of waiver validity because that is a legal decision to be made by the courts. However, quantitative and qualitative data from the MRCI can be used to structure a forensic mental health expert's report or testimony to inform the court about key totality-of-circumstances factors closely related to a suspect's *Miranda* waiver capacities (A. M. Goldstein & Goldstein, 2010).

Standardized Assessment of *Miranda* Abilities. Rogers, Sewell, et al. (2012) developed the Standardized Assessment of *Miranda* Abilities (SAMA) with the goal of making *Miranda* assessments "more accurate, systematic, and informed by domain-specific information" (p. 13). Similar to Grisso's (1998) and N. E. S. Goldstein, Zelle, and Grisso's (2012) instruments, the SAMA follows a legal–empirical–forensic model (Rogers, Sewell, et al., 2012). However, the SAMA differs from these instruments by incorporating case-specific details into the administration and interpretation of the component measures (Rogers, Sewell, et al., 2012). The SAMA consists of five composite measures, each of which evaluates a *Miranda* comprehension construct through semistructured interviewing, true–false questions, and free recall and interpretation (Rogers, Sewell, et al., 2012). The five composite measures are as follows:

1. The *Miranda* Quiz evaluates potential common misconceptions about the *Miranda* warnings through a 25-item true–false quiz (Rogers, Sewell, et al., 2012). According to the SAMA manual (Rogers, Sewell, et al., 2012), primary items demonstrated low to moderate test–retest reliability and moderate to strong discriminant validity for *Miranda*-related abilities. The *Miranda* Quiz Primary Item Total evidenced adequate test–retest reliability, solid convergent validity with cognitive abilities, and moderate to large discriminant validity with intelligence and *Miranda*-relevant abilities (e.g., *Miranda* vocabulary, comprehension, and reasoning; Rogers, Sewell, et al., 2012). Very good content validity was reported for the *Miranda* Quiz (Rogers, Sewell, et al., 2012).
2. The *Miranda* Reasoning Measure is a semi-structured measure designed to evaluate an examinee's recall of his or her considerations in determining whether to waive or exercise the rights to silence and counsel at the time of initial advisement (Rogers, Sewell, et al., 2012). The manual indicated excellent interrater reliability for the *Miranda* Reasoning Measure; appreciable convergent validity for exercise items but weaker convergent validity for waive items; and moderate to high discriminant validity for both exercise and waive items (Rogers, Sewell, et al., 2012).
3. The *Miranda* Comprehension Template is an individualized tool that summarizes case-specific details (i.e., modality in which rights were administered, format of warnings, elapsed time between advisement and waiver) and evaluates the examinee's paraphrasing of the specific warnings used at the time of interrogation to identify possible deficits in an examinee's *Miranda* comprehension at the time of actual advisement (Rogers, Sewell, et al., 2012). Reliability and validity estimates are not available for the *Miranda* Comprehension Template because it is considered to be "a template and not a measure with formal validation" (Rogers, Sewell, et al., 2012, p. 79).
4. The *Miranda* Acquiescence Questionnaire assesses acquiescence and legally relevant beliefs via oppositely worded pairs of questions (Rogers, Sewell, et al., 2012). According to the SAMA manual (Rogers, Sewell, et al., 2012), the *Miranda* Acquiescence Questionnaire has low interitem consistency because of the breadth and inconsistency of its content, as expected. Modest convergent validity and small to large effect sizes for discriminant validity were reported for the Congruent Content and Acquiescence subscales, with good content validity but negligible convergent validity and small to moderate effect sizes for discriminant validity for the Nay-Saying subscale (Rogers, Sewell, et al., 2012).
5. The *Miranda* Vocabulary Scale measures an examinee's capacity to appropriately define 36 *Miranda*-related words. Feigned cognitive impairment may be indicated when a pattern of stronger performance on more difficult items emerges (Rogers, Sewell, et al., 2012). According to the SAMA manual (Rogers, Sewell, et al., 2012), the *Miranda* Vocabulary Scale demonstrated significant internal consistency, very high interrater reliability, and low-moderate to moderate test–retest reliability at the item and scale levels (Rogers, Sewell, et al., 2012). Moreover, strong construct validity and modest to extremely large effect sizes for discriminant validity were reported for the *Miranda* Vocabulary Scale (Rogers, Sewell, et al., 2012).

Evaluating response style and effort. Because defendants may be motivated to present with deficits in their understanding and appreciation of *Miranda* rights, evaluators must consider the possibility that a given defendant is malingering. Defendants may present with exaggeration of cognitive deficits as a result of reduced effort on assessments; they may fake the presence or embellish the severity of symptoms, or both. Evaluators can assess distortions and malingering through multiple avenues: comparing the information provided by the defendant with that obtained from collateral sources (e.g., records and third-party interviews), evaluating the consistency of the information provided by the defendant, administering objective tests in relevant domains (such as those described above), and administering tests that specifically evaluate feigned cognitive or mental health impairments (A. M. Goldstein & Goldstein, 2010).

Notably, although a number of stand-alone malingering measures have not been normed with children and adolescents, several instruments in other domains include embedded measures of effort and response style that can be used to evaluate the possibility of malingering (e.g., reliable digit span on the Wechsler Intelligence Scale for Children—Fourth Edition; validity scales on the Minnesota Multiphasic Personality Inventory—Adolescent [Butcher et al., 1992] and Personality Assessment Inventory—Adolescent [Morey, 2007]).

Communication of findings. Finally, all the data gathered must be synthesized, interpreted, and communicated in a clear and concise manner. The two primary avenues for communication of findings are written reports and courtroom testimony. There are excellent references for both general principles of written reports and oral testimony (e.g., Heilbrun, 2001) and issues specific to evaluations of *Miranda* waiver capacity (e.g., A. M. Goldstein & Goldstein, 2010). Notably, evaluators should be aware that providing descriptions of any deficits and each of their relationships to *Miranda* comprehension can help illustrate the impact of these totality-of-circumstances factors. When qualitative information is presented in conjunction with quantitative data, statistically relevant information becomes more easily digestible for readers (Oberlander & Goldstein, 2001). When writing reports and providing testimony, it is important to keep the intended audience in mind—reports will be read by a legal audience, not by individuals well versed in technical psychological terminology or statistics. Therefore, brief, descriptive, and clear communication is valued.

IMPLICATIONS

Forensic mental health evaluators who receive a referral regarding a juvenile's capacity to have waived *Miranda* rights should consider a number of issues before accepting the case and while completing the evaluation.

Best Practices

In addition to the steps involved in conducting an evaluation of *Miranda* waiver capacity, discussed above, other focal issues include the evaluator's competence to conduct the evaluation and accurate interpretation of results.

First, the evaluator must be competent to conduct this type of forensic mental health assessment. Competence of the evaluator is multifaceted, but it is substantially informed by relevant professional ethical guidelines. For psychologists, the two primary ethical references are the *Ethical Principles of Psychologists and Code of Conduct* (Ethics Code) of the American Psychological Association (2010) and the *Specialty Guidelines for Forensic Psychology* (American Psychological Association, 2013).
The latter is an aspirational model that applies the Ethics Code to forensic situations. The Ethics Code specifies that competence is based on "education, training, supervised experience, consultation, study, or professional experience" (Section 2.01). Moreover, psychologists assuming forensic roles must "become reasonably familiar with the judicial or administrative rules governing their roles" (Section 2.01[f]). Similarly, the *Specialty Guidelines for Forensic Psychology* describes the various bases of competence as well as requirements specific to knowledge of the legal system and legal rights of individuals (Section 2.04) and knowledge of the scientific foundations for opinions and testimony (Section 2.05). Professional competence in the context of *Miranda* waiver evaluations requires familiarity with core *Miranda* case law; jurisdiction-specific standards relevant to *Miranda* waivers; how to gather relevant data to answer the referral question, including administration of general and specialized assessment

instruments; and factors unique to adolescence that can affect a juvenile's comprehension of *Miranda* rights and susceptibility to police coercion.

Important best-practice issues also concern how evaluators synthesize and interpret all of the data they collect from record reviews, interviews with third parties, interviews with the defendant, and results from testing. Evaluators should use scientific reasoning (i.e., hypothesis testing) to establish links between the defendant's abilities and clinical condition and the functional legal capacities required under the law (Heilbrun, 2001). In the context of *Miranda* evaluations, the defendant's clinical condition should be connected to her or his ability to make a knowing, intelligent, and voluntary waiver of her or his *Miranda* rights (A. M. Goldstein & Goldstein, 2010). A. M. Goldstein and Goldstein (2010) articulated several hypotheses that evaluators might consider in these evaluations, including the following:

- The defendant was capable of waiving all of the *Miranda* rights, consistent with the knowing and intelligent legal requirements.
- The defendant did not understand (in part or in full) one or more of the *Miranda* rights.
- The defendant understood the basic meaning of all of his *Miranda* rights but failed to appreciate the role of the lawyer as advocate for the suspect. (p. 151)

The expert should carefully review all of the data, including contradictory data, to determine which hypotheses should be rejected or accepted as the forensic evaluator's opinion (A. M. Goldstein & Goldstein, 2010).

New Policy Developments

Perhaps the most notable policy development in the area of *Miranda* waivers and admissibility of confessions involves the blended line between school and police. Over the past several years, there have been increases in the number of school-based police officers, schools' adoption of zero tolerance policies, and the impact of both of these developments on the school-to-prison pipeline (American Psychological Association Zero Tolerance Task Force, 2008). In the context of evaluations of *Miranda* waiver capacity, the most relevant aspect of these policies is school-based questioning and interrogation. As addressed in the *J.D.B. v. North Carolina* (2011) decision described earlier, law enforcement and school personnel may not be cognizant of the ways in which a juvenile's age, the school venue, and the presence of adults from varied settings (e.g., police department, school administration) can interact to influence the *Miranda* custody analysis; they may also be unaware of how the stress of such a situation could affect a youth's capacities to understand and appreciate his or her *Miranda* rights.

Research Directions

Given juveniles' difficulties with *Miranda* comprehension, at least some of which likely stem from developmental immaturity factors that are not immediately modifiable, future research should explore whether environmental variables can enhance juveniles' abilities. For instance, separate from assessing the impact of reading grade and reading ease levels on *Miranda* comprehension, it would be valuable to explore whether *Miranda* understanding and appreciation could be improved by providing explanations of rights within *Miranda* warnings. Similarly, there is a dearth of research on how the delivery of the *Miranda* warnings (e.g., format: oral, written, oral and written; speed) affects juveniles' *Miranda* comprehension and whether the presence of legal advocates could enhance juveniles' understanding and appreciation of their rights. Limited research has been conducted on the effects of school-based educational programs on improving adolescents' *Miranda* comprehension (Kalbeitzer, 2008; Tapp & Levine, 1977), and future research could examine such programming in greater depth and with youths at elevated risk of justice system involvement.

Moreover, as *Miranda* case law develops, it will be important to identify and clarify how judicially identified factors affect comprehension. Because the totality-of-the-circumstances analysis is a flexible approach guided by the particular circumstances of a suspect's interrogation, researchers should be attuned to factors discussed in legal opinions about juveniles' *Miranda* waivers and be prepared to investigate the empirical foundations of these factors. To a certain extent, it also remains unclear when developments in case law need to be incorporated into forensic evaluations of *Miranda* waiver capacity. For example, the Supreme Court recently held that, although invocations of *Miranda* rights must be explicit, waivers of *Miranda* rights can be implicit—indicated merely by responding to police questions (*Berghuis v. Thompkins*, 2010). The practical implications of this decision have yet to be identified—specifically, whether evaluations of capacity to have waived *Miranda* should assess a defendant's understanding and appreciation of these functional aspects of *Miranda*. In other words, was the defendant aware that she or he needed to explicitly state that she or he was invoking the right to silence and that she or he was waiving that right by speaking with police, even if the defendant had previously asserted the rights to silence and counsel? When such new case law emerges, surveys of forensic mental health professionals may provide data about when and how to incorporate policy into practice.

References

Abramovitch, R., Higgins-Biss, K. L., & Biss, S. R. (1993). Young persons' comprehension of waivers in criminal proceedings. *Canadian Journal of Criminology*, *35*, 309–322.

Abramovitch, R., Peterson-Badali, M., & Rohan, M. (1995). Young people's understanding and assertion of their rights to silence and legal counsel. *Canadian Journal of Criminology*, *37*, 1–18.

Albert, D., & Steinberg, L. (2011). Judgment and decision making in adolescence. *Journal of Research on Adolescence*, *21*, 211–224. http://dx.doi.org/10.1111/j.1532-7795.2010.00724.x

A.M. v. Butler, 360 F.3d 787 (7th Cir. 2004).

American Psychological Association. (2010). *Ethical principles of psychologists and code of conduct (2002, Amended June 1, 2010)*. Retrieved from http://www.apa.org/ethics/code/index.aspx

American Psychological Association. (2013). Specialty guidelines for forensic psychology. *American Psychologist*, *68*, 7–19. http://dx.doi.org/10.1037/a0029889

American Psychological Association Zero Tolerance Task Force. (2008). Are zero tolerance policies effective in the schools? An evidentiary review and recommendations. *American Psychologist*, *63*, 852–862. http://dx.doi.org/10.1037/0003-066X.63.9.852

Anglin v. State, 259 So. 2d 752 (Fla. Ct. App. 1972).

Archer, R. P., Buffington-Vollum, J. K., Stredny, R. V., & Handel, R. W. (2006). A survey of psychological test use patterns among forensic psychologists. *Journal of Personality Assessment*, *87*, 84–94. http://dx.doi.org/10.1207/s15327752jpa8701_07

Baird, A. A., & Fugelsang, J. A. (2004). The emergence of consequential thought: Evidence from neuroscience. *Philosophical Transactions of the Royal Society B: Biological Sciences*, *359*, 1797–1804. http://dx.doi.org/10.1098/rstb.2004.1549

Berghuis v. Thompkins, 560 U.S. 370 (2010).

Blackburn v. Alabama, 361 U.S. 199 (1960).

Breaux, K. C. (2009). *Wechsler Individual Achievement Test—Third edition technical manual*. San Antonio, TX: NCS Pearson.

Brown v. Mississippi, 297 U.S. 278 (1936).

Butcher, J. N., Williams, C. L., Graham, J. R., Archer, R. P., Tellegen, A., Ben-Porath, Y. S., & Kaemmer, B. (1992). *Minnesota Multiphasic Personality Inventory-A (MMPI-A): Manual for administration, scoring and interpretation*. Minneapolis: University of Minnesota Press.

California v. Prysock, 453 U.S. 355 (1981).

Cassell, P. G. (2011). Freeing the guilty without protecting the innocent: Some skeptical observations on proposed new "innocence" procedures. *New York Law School Law Review*, *56*, 1063–1096.

Cauffman, E., & Steinberg, L. (2000). (Im)maturity of judgment in adolescence: Why adolescents may be less culpable than adults. *Behavioral Sciences and the Law*, *18*, 741–760. http://dx.doi.org/10.1002/bsl.416

Colorado v. Connelly, 479 U.S. 157 (1986).

Colorado v. Spring, 479 U.S. 564 (1987).

Colwell, L. H., Cruise, K. R., Guy, L. S., McCoy, W. K., Fernandez, K., & Ross, H. H. (2005). The influence of psychosocial maturity on male juvenile offenders' comprehension and understanding of the *Miranda* warning. *Journal of the American Academy of Psychiatry and the Law*, *33*, 444–454.

Commonwealth v. A Juvenile, 389 Mass. 128 (1983).

Dickerson v. United States, 530 U.S. 428 (2000).

Drizin, S. A., & Luloff, G. (2007). Are juvenile courts a breeding ground for wrongful convictions? *Northern Kentucky Law Review*, *34*, 257–322.

Fare v. Michael C., 442 U.S. 707 (1979).

Feld, B. C. (1984). Criminalizing juvenile justice: Rules of procedure for the juvenile court. *Minnesota Law Review*, *69*, 141–276.

Ferguson, A. B., & Douglas, A. C. (1970). A study of juvenile waiver. *San Diego Law Review*, *7*, 39–54.

Florida v. Powell, 559 U.S. 50 (2010).

Frazier v. Cupp, 394 U.S. 731 (1969).

Frumkin, I. B. (2000). Competency to waive *Miranda* rights: Clinical and legal issues. *Mental and Physical Disability Law Reporter, 24*, 326–331.

Gallegos v. Colorado, 370 U.S. 49 (1962).

Gogtay, N., Sporn, A., Clasen, L. S., Nugent, T. F., III, Greenstein, D., Nicolson, R., . . . Rapoport, J. L. (2004). Comparison of progressive cortical gray matter loss in childhood-onset schizophrenia with that in childhood-onset atypical psychoses. *Archives of General Psychiatry, 61*, 17–22. http://dx.doi.org/10.1001/archpsyc.61.1.17

Goldstein, A. M., & Goldstein, N. E. S. (2010). *Evaluating capacity to waive* Miranda *rights*. http://dx.doi.org/10.1093/med/9780195366174.001.0001

Goldstein, N. E. S., Condie, L. O., Kalbeitzer, R., Osman, D., & Geier, J. L. (2003). Juvenile offenders' *Miranda* rights comprehension and self-reported likelihood of offering false confessions. *Assessment, 10*, 359–369. http://dx.doi.org/10.1177/1073191103259535

Goldstein, N. E. S., Messenheimer, S., Riggs Romaine, C., & Zelle, H. (2012). Impact of juvenile suspects' linguistic abilities on *Miranda* understanding and appreciation. In P. Tiersma & L. Solan (Eds.), *Oxford handbook on language and law* (pp. 299–311). New York, NY: Oxford University Press.

Goldstein, N. E. S., Romaine, C. L., Zelle, H., Kalbeitzer, R., Mesiarik, C., & Wolbransky, M. (2011). Psychometric properties of the *Miranda Rights Comprehension Instruments* with a juvenile justice sample. *Assessment, 18*, 428–441. http://dx.doi.org/10.1177/1073191111400280

Goldstein, N. E. S., Zelle, H., & Grisso, T. (2012). *Miranda Rights Comprehension Instruments: MRCI*. Sarasota, FL: Professional Resource Press.

Goldstein, N. E. S., Zelle, H., & Grisso, T. (2014). *Miranda Rights Comprehension Instruments (MRCI): Manual for juvenile and adult evaluations*. Sarasota, FL: Professional Resource Press.

Grisso, T. (1981). *Juvenile's waiver of rights: Legal and psychological competence*. http://dx.doi.org/10.1007/978-1-4684-3815-4

Grisso, T. (1997). The competence of adolescents as trial defendants. *Psychology, Public Policy, and Law, 3*, 3–32. http://dx.doi.org/10.1037/1076-8971.3.1.3

Grisso, T. (1998). *Instruments for assessing understanding and appreciation of* Miranda *rights*. Sarasota, FL: Professional Resource Press.

Grisso, T., & Ring, M. (1979). Parents' attitudes toward juveniles' rights in interrogation. *Criminal Justice and Behavior, 6*, 211–226. http://dx.doi.org/10.1177/009385487900600301

Haley v. Ohio, 332 U.S. 596 (1948).

Haynes v. Washington, 373 U.S. 503 (1963).

Heilbrun, K. (2001). *Principles of forensic mental health assessment*. New York, NY: Kluwer Academic/Plenum.

Heilbrun, K., DeMatteo, D., Brooks Holliday, S., & LaDuke, C. (Eds.). (2014). *Forensic mental health assessment: A casebook* (2nd ed.). New York, NY: Oxford University Press.

Heilbrun, K., Marczyk, G. R., & DeMatteo, D. (2002). *Forensic mental health assessment: A casebook*. New York, NY: Oxford University Press.

Helms, J. L. (2003). Analysis of *Miranda* reading across jurisdictions: Implications for evaluating waiver competency. *Journal of Forensic Psychology Practice, 3*, 25–37.

Helms, J. L. (2007). Analysis of the components of the *Miranda* warnings. *Journal of Forensic Psychology Practice, 7*, 59–76. http://dx.doi.org/10.1300/J158v07n03_03

Howes v. Fields, 132 S. Ct. 1181 (2012).

Huang, D. T. (2000). Less unequal footing: State court's per se rules for juvenile waivers during interrogations and the case for their implementation. *Cornell Law Review, 86*, 437–477.

Illinois v. Young, 850 N.E. 2d 284 (Ill. Ct. App. 2006).

In re Gault, 387 U.S. 1 (1967).

J.D.B. v. North Carolina, 131 S. Ct. 2394 (2011).

Johnson v. Zerbst, 304 U.S. 458 (1938).

Kahn, R., Zapf, P. A., & Cooper, V. G. (2006). Readability of *Miranda* warnings and waivers: Implications for evaluating *Miranda* comprehension. *Law and Psychology Review, 30*, 119–142.

Kalbeitzer, R. (2008). *Evaluating legal learning: The effects of time and development on adolescents' understanding of legal rights* (Doctoral dissertation). Retrieved from http://hdl.handle.net/1860/2833

Kassin, S. M., Drizin, S. A., Grisso, T., Gudjonsson, G. H., Leo, R. A., & Redlich, A. D. (2010). Police-induced confessions: Risk factors and recommendations. *Law and Human Behavior, 34*, 3–38. http://dx.doi.org/10.1007/s10979-009-9188-6

Kassin, S. M., Leo, R. A., Meissner, C. A., Richman, K. D., Colwell, L. H., Leach, A. M., & La Fon, D. (2007). Police interviewing and interrogation: A self-report survey of police practices and beliefs. *Law and Human Behavior, 31*, 381–400. http://dx.doi.org/10.1007/s10979-006-9073-5

Kemp, K. (2010). *Characteristics of developmental immaturity: A cross-disciplinary survey of psychologists* (Doctoral dissertation). Retrieved from http://hdl.handle.net/1860/3490

King, K. J. (2006). Waiving childhood goodbye: How juvenile courts fail to protect children from unknowing, unintelligent, and involuntary waivers of *Miranda* rights. *Wisconsin Law Review, 2006*, 431–477.

Klaczynski, P. A. (2001). Analytic and heuristic processing influences on adolescent reasoning and decision-making. *Child Development*, *72*, 844–861. http://dx.doi.org/10.1111/1467-8624.00319

Lally, S. J. (2003). What tests are acceptable for use in forensic evaluations? A survey of experts. *Professional Psychology: Research and Practice*, *34*, 491–498. http://dx.doi.org/10.1037/0735-7028.34.5.491

Levin, H. S., Culhane, K. A., Hartmann, J., Evankovich, K., Mattson, A. J., Harward, H., . . . Fletcher, J. M. (1991). Developmental changes in performance on tests of purported frontal lobe functioning. *Developmental Neuropsychology*, *7*, 377–395. http://dx.doi.org/10.1080/87565649109540499

Maryland v. Shatzer, 559 U.S. 98 (2010).

McGuire, J. (2000). Can the criminal law ever be therapeutic? *Behavioral Sciences and the Law*, *18*, 413–426. http://dx.doi.org/10.1002/1099-0798(2000)18:4<413::AID-BSL365>3.0.CO;2-H

Melton, G. B., Petrila, J., Poythress, N. G., & Slobogin, C. (2007). *Psychological evaluation for the courts: A handbook for mental health professionals and lawyers* (3rd ed.). New York, NY: Guilford Press.

Michigan v. Tucker, 417 U.S. 433 (1974).

Milhizer, E. R. (2008). Confessions after *Connelly*: An evidentiary solution for excluding unreliable confessions. *Temple Law Review*, *81*, 1–66.

Miranda v. Arizona, 384 U.S. 436 (1966).

Moran v. Burbine, 475 U.S. 412 (1986).

Morey, L. C. (2007). *Personality Assessment Inventory—Adolescent: Professional manual*. Odessa, FL: Psychological Assessment Resources.

Oberlander, L. B. (1998). *Miranda* comprehension and confessional competence. *Expert Opinion*, *2*, 11–12.

Oberlander, L. B., & Goldstein, N. E. (2001). A review and update on the practice of evaluating *Miranda* comprehension. *Behavioral Sciences and the Law*, *19*, 453–471. http://dx.doi.org/10.1002/bsl.453

Oregon v. Elstad, 470 U.S. 298 (1985).

People v. Al-Yousif, 49 P.3d 1165 (Colo. 2002).

People v. Cheatham, 551 N.W.2d 355 (Mich. 1996).

People v. Lara, 432 P.2d 202 (Cal. 1967).

Peterson-Badali, M., Abramovitch, R., & Duda, J. (1997). Young children's legal knowledge and reasoning ability. *Canadian Journal of Criminology*, *39*, 145–170.

Peterson-Badali, M., Abramovitch, R., Koegl, C. J., & Ruck, M. D. (1999). Young people's experience of the Canadian youth justice system: Interacting with police and legal counsel. *Behavioral Sciences and the Law*, *17*, 455–465. http://dx.doi.org/10.1002/(SICI)1099-0798(199910/12)17:4<455::AID-BSL358>3.0.CO;2-R

Rogers, R., Blackwood, H. L., Fiduccia, C. E., Steadham, J. A., Drogin, E. Y., & Rogstad, J. E. (2012). Juvenile *Miranda* warnings: Perfunctory rituals or procedural safeguards? *Criminal Justice and Behavior*, *39*, 229–249. http://dx.doi.org/10.1177/0093854811431934

Rogers, R., Hazelwood, L. L., Sewell, K. W., Harrison, K. S., & Shuman, D. W. (2008). The language of *Miranda* warnings in American jurisdictions: A replication and vocabulary analysis. *Law and Human Behavior*, *32*, 124–136. http://dx.doi.org/10.1007/s10979-007-9091-y

Rogers, R., Hazelwood, L. L., Sewell, K. W., Shuman, D. W., & Blackwood, H. L. (2008). The comprehensibility and content of juvenile *Miranda* warnings. *Psychology, Public Policy, and Law*, *14*, 63–87. http://dx.doi.org/10.1037/a0013102

Rogers, R., Sewell, K. W., Drogin, E. Y., & Fiduccia, C. E. (2012). *Standardized Assessment of Miranda Abilities (SAMA) professional manual*. Lutz, FL: Psychological Assessment Resources.

Rubia, K., Overmeyer, S., Taylor, E., Brammer, M., Williams, S. C., Simmons, A., . . . Bullmore, E. T. (2000). Functional frontalisation with age: Mapping neurodevelopmental trajectories with fMRI. *Neuroscience and Biobehavioral Reviews*, *24*, 13–19. http://dx.doi.org/10.1016/S0149-7634(99)00055-X

Ryba, N. L., Brodsky, S. L., & Schlosberg, A. (2007). Evaluations of capacity to waive *Miranda* rights: A survey of practitioners' use of the Grisso instruments. *Assessment*, *14*, 300–309. http://dx.doi.org/10.1177/1073191110730284

Salinas v. Texas, 133 S. Ct. 2174 (2013).

Schlam, L. (1995). Police interrogation of children and state constitutions: Why not videotape the MTV generation? *University of Toledo Law Review*, *26*, 901–935.

Schneckloth v. Bustamonte, 412 U.S. 218 (1973).

Schulhofer, S. J. (1987). Reconsidering *Miranda*. *University of Chicago Law Review*, *54*, 435–461. http://dx.doi.org/10.2307/1599796

Spano v. New York, 360 U.S. 315 (1958).

State v. Bushey, 453 A.2d 1265 (N.H. 1982).

Steinberg, L. (2010). A dual systems model of adolescent risk-taking. *Developmental Psychobiology*, *52*, 216–224.

Steinberg, L., Cauffman, E., Woolard, J., Graham, S., & Banich, M. (2009). Are adolescents less mature than adults? Minors' access to abortion, the juvenile death penalty, and the alleged APA "flip-flop." *American*

Psychologist, 64, 583–594. http://dx.doi.org/10.1037/a0014763

Tapp, J. L., & Levine, F. J. (1977). *Law, justice, and the individual in society: Psychological and legal issues.* New York, NY: Holt, Rinehart & Winston.

Taslitz, A. E. (2012). High expectations and some wounded hopes: The policy and politics of a uniform statute on videotaping custodial interrogations. *Northwestern Journal of Law and Social Policy*, *7*, 400–454.

Thompson v. Keohane, 516 U.S. 99 (1995).

Wechsler, D. (2003). *Wechsler Intelligence Scale for Children—Fourth Edition (WISC–IV)*. San Antonio, TX: Psychological Corporation.

West v. United States, 399 F.2d 467 (5th Cir. 1968).

Wilkinson, G. S., & Robertson, G. J. (2006). *Wide Range Achievement Test (WRAT) 4*. Lutz, FL: Psychological Assessment Resources.

CHAPTER 23

EVALUATION AND RESTORATION OF COMPETENCY TO STAND TRIAL

Janet I. Warren, Shelly L. Jackson, and Jessica Jones Coburn

The right to be competent to stand trial has a rich history that has evolved through legal doctrine identified in 14th-century common law (Blackstone Commentaries), through protections identified in the U.S. Constitution (Sixth and Fourteenth Amendments), and further elucidated in U.S. Supreme Court decisions (*Drope v. Missouri*, 1975; *Dusky v. United States*, 1960), and emergent state law (e.g., Va. Code § 16.1-356). The constitutional basis for adjudicative competence derives from the Due Process Clause of the U.S. Constitution, which requires that an accused person not be deprived of life, liberty, or property without due process of law. With this protection comes the implicit assumption that the individual must have the requisite ability to exercise the rights afforded to him or her for such rights to be of intrinsic value to the individual and to society.

Adjudicative competency or competency to stand trial is a functional assessment that addresses capacities rather than knowledge, is contextual in nature, and is calibrated according to the complexity of the legal situation facing each defendant (Christy, Douglas, Otto, & Petrila, 2004; Mossman et al., 2007; Zapf & Roesch, 2006). The test for competence was articulated in *Dusky v. United States* (1960), ruling that the defendant had to have and be able to demonstrate "sufficient present ability to consult with his lawyer with a reasonable degree of rational understanding" and a "rational as well as factual understanding of the proceedings against him" (p. 402). *Dusky* has been interpreted to include three elements: a factual understanding (i.e., the defendant understands the role of legal personnel, procedures, and terms), a rational understanding (i.e., the defendant has the ability to apply that information without distortions created by mental illness or developmental immaturity to his or her own situation), and the ability to assist counsel (i.e., the defendant understands the privileged nature of the relationship, communicates facts of the case to the attorney, understands and responds to attorney's inquiries, and collaborates with the attorney in developing a defense). The *Dusky* decision has been further interpreted to include the ability to reason about decisions and to waive counsel, prompting the U.S. Supreme Court to opine that "the competence that is required of a defendant seeking to waive his right to counsel is the competence to waive the right, not the competence to represent himself" (*Godinez v. Moran*, 1993, p. 399). While these deliberations were under way by the Supreme Court, Bonnie (1992) offered a related reconceptualization of the standard for competency to stand trial that he called *adjudicative competency*. This term is now used broadly to refer to competency to stand trial so as to better capture the legal decisional requirements of the majority of defendants who never proceed to trial but rather find resolution of their charges through a plea bargain.

Historically, adjudicative competence was relevant only in criminal court. The juvenile justice system was predicated on the legal doctrine of *parens patriae*, or guardianship of youth, which derived inclusively from their less mature and more vulnerable condition as children. Consequently, the juvenile justice system was designed and implemented to address therapeutic and rehabilitative goals rather than to serve a

http://dx.doi.org/10.1037/14643-023
APA Handbook of Psychology and Juvenile Justice, K. Heilbrun (Editor-in-Chief)

deterrent or punitive function as seen in criminal court. Concern over an absence of constitutional protections for youths in the juvenile justice system, however, emerged as the juvenile justice system became more adversarial, beginning in the 1960s.

In *Kent v. United States* (1966), Justice Fortas observed when considering the transfer of Morris Kent to criminal court that "there may be grounds for concern that the child receives the worst of both worlds: that he gets neither the protections accorded to adults nor the solicitous care and regenerative treatment postulated for children" (p. 556). A year later, when considering the due process rights of Gerald Gault, Justice Fortas commented, "Neither the Fourteenth Amendment nor the Bill of Rights is for adults alone" (*In re Gault*, 1967, p. 13). On the basis of this edict, the Court concluded that juveniles subject to delinquency hearings were entitled to notice of the charges against them, the right to legal counsel, the right against self-incrimination, and the right to confront and cross-examine witnesses. In 1970, the court determined in *In re Winship* (1970) that every element of an offense had to be proven beyond a reasonable doubt, thereby vacating the previous standard of a preponderance of the evidence and further accentuating issues of guilt and punishment in juvenile court.

Although these decisions helped to change the landscape of juvenile court, as of yet the U.S. Supreme Court has not ruled on whether juveniles must be competent to proceed to trial (Felthous, 2011; Redding & Frost, 2001; Soulier, 2012; Soulier & Scott, 2010) nor on whether and how *Dusky v. United States* (1960) applies to juveniles (Bonnie & Grisso, 2000; Soulier, 2012). Consequently, there is no single, recognized standard for juvenile competency to participate in a delinquency proceeding (Soulier & Scott, 2010). Furthermore, states vary in whether and how they address juvenile adjudicative competence (Larson & Grisso, 2011; O'Donnell & Gross, 2012; Sanborn, 2009). Nonetheless, perhaps out of concern for or as a strategy to help youths, defense attorneys are increasingly raising the issue of adjudicative competency in juvenile court (Kruh & Grisso, 2009; Larson & Grisso, 2011; Soulier, 2012; Soulier & Scott, 2010).

Although juvenile competency is less settled in the legislative arena, a comprehensive body of research on the clinical and developmental differences in juvenile adjudicative competence has emerged (Fogel, Schiffman, Mumley, Tillbrook, & Grisso, 2013). Two bodies of research, one that has considered chronological age and the other focused on developmental maturity (i.e., incomplete development in one or more domains—neurological, social, emotional—that manifests in functional limitations relative to a specified comparison group; see Grisso, 2005), have converged in recent years, yielding a growing consensus that there are few meaningful differences between older adolescents and adults in their cognitive abilities to reason logically about moral, social, and interpersonal matters (Cauffman & Steinberg, 2000; Furby & Beyth-Marom, 1992; Sarkar, 2011; E. S. Scott, Reppucci, & Woolard, 1995; Soulier, 2012; Steinberg, 2007; Steinberg et al., 2009).

In contrast, *reasoning*—the "cognitive capacities to process information" (Grisso, 2000, p. 157)—and *judgment*—the "processes of attaching differential importance to various possible consequences of decisions" (Grisso, 2000, p. 159)—are two integrative functions that are developmentally and age specific. These two functions are central to legal decisional capacity and are pivotal in understanding why adolescents do not reach the same decisions as adults (Bonnie & Scott, 2013; Cauffman & Steinberg, 2012; Grisso, 2000). Furthermore, they help to explain why other aspects of psychosocial development, such as emotion regulation (Mayzer, Bradley, Rusinko, & Ertelt, 2009), can tax the decision-making abilities of children and adolescents, particularly when they are faced with high-stress and complex situations (Redlich, 2007).

It is against this backdrop that a juvenile's adjudicative competence is evaluated and the juvenile, if deemed incompetent by the court, is ordered into restoration services. These topics are addressed in the remainder of this chapter.

RAISING THE ISSUE OF ADJUDICATIVE COMPETENCE IN JUVENILE COURT

In most jurisdictions, any member of the court has the option of raising the issue of juvenile competency: the prosecutor, the defense attorney, the judge, or the guardian ad litem (Larson & Grisso, 2011; Viljoen,

McLachlan, Wingrove, & Penner, 2010). However, defense attorneys are the primary source for recognizing competence concerns and in the majority of instances bear the burden of proving incompetence when the issue is contested (Redding, 2002).

Viljoen et al. (2010) conducted the only study estimating the percentage of cases in which juvenile competency is raised. In a survey of 214 defense attorneys affiliated with the National Association of Counsel for Children and Youth or the National Juvenile Defender Center, attorneys indicated that they had concern about competency in approximately 10% of their clients. However, only 53% of defense attorneys indicated that they actually sought a competency evaluation when they had such concerns.

Scholars (Jackson, Warren, & Jones Coburn, 2014; Varela, Boccaccini, Gonzalez, Gharagozloo, & Johnson, 2011; Viljoen et al., 2010) have identified several barriers to raising the issue of competency: Some of the offenses are minor; the youth or parents did not want a competency evaluation; a competency evaluation would delay proceedings; the youth or parents believe that the youth is likely to be found competent anyway; the legal standards are insufficiently clear to know when a juvenile competency evaluation should be requested; the desire to avoid the stigma associated with a competency evaluation; some attorneys continue to believe that competence is less relevant in juvenile court; and finally, some judges are characterized as having a resistant attitude to this issue as identified by the defense bar. In addition, high caseloads and limited training in recognizing competency-related issues are also cited as reasons why the issue of adjudicative competency is raised relatively infrequently in juvenile court (Viljoen et al., 2010).

These barriers are used to call for more adequate training and reasonable levels of compensation for attorneys representing youths in juvenile court (Burrell, Kendrick, & Blalock, 2008). Research has suggested that sufficient training affects the outcome of the competency evaluations that are conducted and presented to the court. Finkle, Kurth, Cadle, and Mullan (2009) found that referring defendants to a specialized mental health court increased the finding of incompetency from 43% in the 1st year of the program to 72% by the 3rd year. Grisso (2004) echoed these sentiments, asserting that perhaps the primary obligation owed to delinquent youths is ensuring them access to well-trained and experienced defense attorneys.

In criminal court, the *Pate v. Robinson* (1966) and *Drope v. Missouri* (1975) decisions mandated that if there is a genuine concern, the issue of competence must be raised. This mandate is less clear in juvenile court. In making recommendations for California's handling of juvenile competence, Burrell et al. (2008) recommended that states clearly delineate procedures for raising the issue of competence. Soulier (2012) has suggested four conditions that should prompt inquiry into a juvenile's competence to stand trial: age 12 or younger; prior diagnosis of or treatment for a mental illness or mental retardation; borderline level of intellectual functioning or a record of learning disability; and pretrial observations by others that suggest deficits in memory, attention, or appreciation of reality.

This list is supported by a surprisingly small body of research. The few studies that have compared juveniles referred for a competency evaluation with those not referred have found that incompetent youths tend to be younger (Baerger, Griffin, Lyons, & Simmons, 2003; Cowden & McKee, 1995; Kruh, Sullivan Ellis, Lexcen, & McClellan, 2006; McKee, 1998; McKee & Shea, 1999), have more severe clinical diagnoses or a history of mental health treatment (Baerger et al., 2003; Cowden & McKee, 1995; Kruh et al., 2006), have a history of special education (Baerger et al., 2003; Cowden & McKee, 1995; Kruh et al., 2006), and have lower intellectual functioning (Kruh et al., 2006; McKee & Shea, 1999). Research has indicated that in practice, defense attorneys are more likely to raise the issue of competency when the youth is younger, has been charged with a serious offense, and has demonstrated more extensive legal deficits (Viljoen et al., 2010). However, defense attorneys are less likely to raise the issue of competency solely for the reason of developmental immaturity (Viljoen et al., 2010).

Role of Defense Attorneys

Defense attorneys representing juveniles may have a particularly difficult task because their training has often not encompassed the experiences that are unique to representing children and adolescents in juvenile court (Birckhead, 2010; Frost & Volenik,

2004). Interviewing and collaborating with children and adolescents can prove far more challenging than an inexperienced attorney might anticipate. Defense attorneys are also trained to rely on their client's expressed interest rather than on their best interest, a principle that can be complex in its implementation when working with a vulnerable latency-aged child or a recalcitrant teenager. The degree to which a child age 8 or 9 years can appropriately exercise his or her decisional autonomy in an age-appropriate manner can make this aspect of representation complex and is rather fluidly composed of providing information, seeking to advocate for a child, and listening authentically to the child's preferences and wishes concerning the development of the case. There is currently no privilege that protects parents from having to testify to information provided to them by their child, as exists between a husband and wife, and the defense attorney must therefore also serve a communicative role to and with the parents (this information simply becoming hearsay if conveyed to the parents by a third party such as the attorney) to protect the child from this type of potentially damaging disclosure.

Judicial Responsibility for Referring Juveniles for a Competency Evaluation

Once the issue of competence has been raised, the judge is responsible for referring a juvenile for an adjudicative competency evaluation (Finkle et al., 2009; Viljoen & Roesch, 2005). The proceedings are then stayed until an evaluation can be completed and the judge makes a determination concerning competency (Soulier, 2012). *Pate v. Robinson* (1966) held that the trial court has a duty to order a competency evaluation whenever there is a bona fide question about the defendant's ability to proceed (Finkle et al., 2009), although there is no U.S. Supreme Court guidance on this issue in the context of juvenile court.

JUVENILE EVALUATOR QUALIFICATIONS AND TRAINING

The emergence of juvenile competency law has by its very nature created the need for juvenile forensic evaluators who are qualified to offer informed opinions to the court, both when the issue is first raised and after the remediation efforts have been completed. Perhaps the longest standing training for this type of forensic activity is based at the University of Virginia, where the Institute of Law, Psychiatry, and Public Policy initiated a 6-day training program in 2001 shortly after the juvenile competency laws were implemented on July 1, 1999. The structure of this training built on the 5-day adult forensic training program that had been offered by the Institute of Law, Psychiatry, and Public Policy since 1981 on contract with the Virginia Department of Behavioral Health and Disability Services. The statutes used for ordering the adult and juvenile assessments of competency (and sanity) in the case of criminal court contain explicit language requiring that all forensic evaluators who conduct mental health assessments in the Commonwealth of Virginia must have completed a forensic training program recognized and approved by the Commissioner of Mental Health. To attend the basic juvenile forensic training program, the applicants must demonstrate at least 2 years of previous experience working in a mental health or residential setting with children and adolescents.

The 6-day juvenile training program was designed to capture the distinct processes that characterize the forensic evaluation of children and adolescents. Lectures offered by a multidisciplinary faculty are both generic regarding the methods of conducting any type of forensic assessment and specific to juvenile topics, including the juvenile justice system, juvenile competency laws in Virginia, research on juvenile competency, developmental issues pertinent to adjudicative competency, psychiatric conditions common to children and adolescents, neurobiological development, clinical issues unique to juvenile defendants, malingering, transfer, expert testimony, and report writing. Cases are also presented of youths ages 8 to 17 years to engender a discussion of the calibration issues that can be particularly complex when working with individuals younger than age 18 years. After the completion of the program, all attendees are required to complete a multiple-choice open manual exam and submit a work product of a juvenile competency evaluation that is reviewed by faculty before their names are posted to the expert directory maintained by the Institute of Law, Psychiatry, and Public Policy for use by Virginia courts.

Recently, Heilbrun and DeMatteo (2012) attempted to address the issue of establishing professional standards for conducting juvenile forensic mental health assessments. They argued that a juvenile forensic evaluator needs to possess a range of skills that combine experience in working with children and adolescents with knowledge of specific aspects of the legal system—including communication, discovery, deposition, and testimony—particularly those that uniquely apply to the juvenile system (e.g., shorter timeframes for completing evaluations, less formal rules of evidence, interjection of judge's questions during testimony). They, along with other authors, emphasized the importance of training in human development and the ways in which developmental changes may affect legal decisional capacities (see, e.g., Ferguson, Jimenez, & Jackson, 2010; Grisso, 2005; Grisso et al., 2003; Heilbrun & DeMatteo, 2012; Soulier, 2012); the importance of acquiring skill in assessing clinical characteristics of youths, taking into account the instability in personal characteristics during adolescence; and the importance of understanding fully the differences between juveniles and adults who have mental illness and mental retardation. These are differences that can be expected to play a significant role in their understanding of the legal process (Ferguson et al., 2010). Generally, researchers have argued that specialized juvenile forensic training is required to obtain greater consistency and quality across evaluators. However, the more stringent the professional requirements, the more difficulty a state may face in finding qualified evaluators (Larson & Grisso, 2011). Regardless, mental health clinicians are urged to decline a referral when they do not possess the requisite qualifications (Heilbrun & DeMatteo, 2012).

One issue that has created a considerable amount of debate and controversy, particularly in the juvenile arena, involves the professional credentials that are required to be recognized by statute or administrative edict as qualified to conduct juvenile adjudicative competency assessments. Some states such as Virginia, Michigan, Arizona, and Florida have either explicitly included licensed clinical social workers, licensed professional counselors, and licensed marriage and family therapists in their statutes or stated more generically that the evaluations will be performed by mental health experts. Alternatively, states such as Arkansas, Kansas, Minnesota, Ohio, and Idaho require that the evaluations be conducted only by clinical psychologists and psychiatrists. Those who advocate for licensed master's-level mental health providers being included in the pool of evaluators (e.g., Siegel, 2008) have pointed to their broad experience in providing mental health services to youths in community mental health, educational, residential, and detention settings; their skills in working with youths in a family context; their availability in more rural areas in which clinical psychologists and psychiatrists are sparse; and their demonstrated abilities when provided comprehensive training on juvenile competency issues. In contrast, advocates who argue for the exclusion of master's-level evaluators point to the psychological testing that can be relevant either directly or through reference to earlier reports; the more nuanced clinical skills required to diagnose children and adolescents accurately; the importance of medication management in understanding some aspects of disruptive behavior by youths; the complexity of neurobiological and behavioral research that is central to understanding juvenile competency; and the perceived higher status that accrues in the court when the assessment is conducted by doctorally or medically trained professionals.

The experience of each state in developing a juvenile forensic service delivery system, compounded by the lobbying efforts of different professional groups, will undoubtedly continue to affect this national debate and the decisions made in response to it over the next decade. Our experience in Virginia, however, has demonstrated over the past 15 years that it is the quality of training and the mentorship that follows that determines the quality of the assessment, report writing, and testimony rather than the professional qualifications of the licensed mental health provider.

JUVENILE COMPETENCY EVALUATION

Evaluations of competence to stand trial are the most common forensic mental health evaluations conducted in the United States for both juveniles (Bonnie & Grisso, 2000) and adults (Melton, Petrila, Poythress, & Slobogin, 2007), with the number of competency evaluations conducted nationally each year widely cited as an estimated 60,000 (Bonnie & Grisso, 2000). The standard set out in *Dusky v. United States* (1960) has generally been adopted in the juvenile statutes that have arisen across the country. Specifically, *Dusky* asserted, "the test must be whether [the defendant] has sufficient present ability to consult with his attorney with a reasonable degree of rational understanding and a rational as well as factual understanding of the proceedings against him" (p. 402).

Although relatively brief in content, this standard contains a number of conceptual components or features that are central to the associated forensic assessment. First, it identifies two prongs that are relevant to the assessment, one being an understanding of the legal process and the respective roles of the various participants and the other being the ability of the defendant to consult and collaborate with counsel in determining the nature of the defense and the role that the juvenile will play in presenting it. Second, the standard underscores that these abilities are being assessed as they are presently demonstrated, leaving the door open for this competence state to fluctuate over time given changes in mental state, levels of maturity, and situational factors that can often affect the functioning and experience of children and adolescents more extensively than in adults.

Third, the *Dusky* standard references the capacity of youths and not the state of knowledge that is manifest at the time of the assessment. This component of the *Dusky* standard is particularly relevant to youths who might, because of their more limited experience, possess a more limited understanding of the court process. It also underscores the importance of trying to educate the youth during a competency evaluation to assess whether the youth is able to understand and apply new legal information to his or her emerging legal situation. Fourth, the standard addresses the need for a factual as well as rational understanding of these different dimensions of the standard. This distinction is often explained in terms of the youth's ability to both offer a rote definition of various legal terms and apply legal constructs to their own legal situation. It is this need to extrapolate abstract ideas that most directly relates to the importance of developmental considerations in the assessment of juvenile competency because many youths younger than a certain age will be developmentally limited in their levels of abstract thinking and their attendant ability to apply legal constructs to their own situation (Grisso, 2005).

Fifth, in integrating these many considerations into the assessment and the resulting conclusion, it is important to make reference to the requirement that the different capacities identified by *Dusky v. United States* (1960) are required to a reasonable degree but not an impeccable degree of understanding. This component of the standard is often expressed in the assertion that the standard for competency is not particularly high and varies according to the complexity and seriousness of the legal context that is facing the juvenile. In 1974, the Group for the Advancement of Psychiatry cautioned that a list of competency inquiries was meant only to indicate areas of inquiry and should not leave the impression that "enormous legal sophistication is required of both psychiatrist or defendant" (Melton et al., 2007, p. 128). Finally, the assessment of adjudicative competency is functional and not based on any specific psychiatric, intellectual, or developmental deficit. Recently, R. D. Hoge (2012) emphasized that the mere presence of age, mental illness, mental retardation, or developmental immaturity does not equate with or automatically constitute incompetency, asserting that the evaluation must demonstrate the specific functional deficits that link to the *Dusky* standard and prevent the youth from adequately understanding and participating in the legal process.

Time Constraints

Tension exists between the needs of evaluators for sufficient time to gather relevant collateral information and the needs of the courts to have a speedy trial (Larson & Grisso, 2011). A competency evaluation extends the time that the juvenile is in the pretrial legal process, and therefore states limit the amount of time permitted to conduct a juvenile competency evaluation and submit a written report to the court, typically ranging from 10 to 45 days (Larson & Grisso, 2011). Virginia statute (Va. Code §16.1 356), for example, requires that all collateral information must be provided to the evaluator within 96 hours of the issuance of the court order and that the evaluator must submit the competency report to the court no longer than 14 days after the receipt of all required information. Larson and Grisso (2011) similarly recommended 2 weeks after the court order to complete the evaluation.

Location of the Evaluation

In recent decades, states have adopted the least restrictive alternative (i.e., least restrictive setting possible), which permits competency evaluations to be performed in the evaluator's office (i.e., in the community) or in pretrial detention centers (Larson & Grisso, 2011). However, youths hospitalized for a psychiatric illness may have their competency evaluated while residing in a secure setting. For example, one Virginia statute (Va. Code §16.1.356) explicitly states that the evaluation of each youth shall be conducted on an outpatient basis at a community services board or behavioral health authority, juvenile detention home, or juvenile justice facility unless the court specifically finds that the results of the outpatient competency evaluation indicate that hospitalization of the juvenile is necessary or the juvenile is currently hospitalized in a juvenile hospital. This hospitalization option is used sparingly, primarily in cases in which the initial evaluation suggests malingering, indicating a need for further observation and assessment.

Right to Avoid Self-Incrimination

The competency evaluation cannot violate the defendant's Fifth Amendment right to avoid self-incrimination. During a competency evaluation, youths are asked to recite the events that led up to their arrest; consequently, important evidentiary information is often obtained during the evaluation. To protect against this type of disclosure, some states include Fifth Amendment language in their statutory code, and others include it in the model court order that is used in ordering the evaluation by the court. One example of this language states that

> No statement or disclosure by the juvenile relating to the alleged offense made during a competency evaluation ordered pursuant to Va. Code §16.1-356 or services offered according to Va. Code §16.1-356 may be used against the juvenile at the adjudication or disposition hearing as evidence or as the basis for such evidence. (Virginia Code 16.1-360)

These same protections are integral to the provision of restoration services after a determination of incompetency because the youth is often inclined to discuss the offense with the remediation service provider who works with the juvenile multiple times a week, often over a 2- to 3-month period.

Right to Counsel

Larson and Grisso (2011) noted that youths can undergo a competency evaluation in the absence of counsel if this stage of the adjudication is determined not to be a "critical stage" (p. 49) of the adjudication. However, citing a statute from the Louisiana state code (Louisiana Laws, 2005), Larson and Grisso recommended that when a question of competency is raised no further steps in the delinquency proceeding occur until counsel has been appointed and the youth has been determined competent to proceed. Whether to submit to an evaluation may have important implications for the outcome of the case, and therefore youths should be able to consult with their attorney about this issue. Melton et al. (2007) addressed this issue in the criminal context and suggested that professional guidelines and the American Bar Association's (1982) Criminal Justice Mental Health Standards agree that a clinician asked to evaluate a defendant acquires an ethical responsibility to ascertain whether the defendant is represented by counsel and, if this is not the case, to defer the evaluation until one has been obtained.

PROCESS OF CONDUCTING THE JUVENILE COMPETENCE EVALUATION

The majority of evaluations of adjudicative competency are conducted on a court order and therefore do not technically require the assent of the youth or the consent of a parent or guardian. Ethical considerations, however, require that the evaluating clinician make a bona fide effort to inform the youth of the parameters of the evaluation, its purpose and nature, and the limits to confidentiality that are intrinsic to it. Many clinicians also proceed by obtaining not only the assent of the youth (Soulier, 2012), but also the consent of the juvenile's parent or guardian. The inclusion of the parent or guardian may lengthen the preparation time that precedes the evaluation but is viewed by many as integral in ensuring their cooperation with and contribution to the evaluation process and their involvement with services should the youth be determined incompetent to stand trial.

Before completing the assessment, clinicians are advised to speak with the referring party to determine the reasons and behavior that led to the initiation of a competency assessment. The referring party will most often be the defense attorney, because defense counsel is expected to have had the most contact with the juvenile at this point in the adjudication process and is singularly involved in a privileged, ongoing relationship with the youth. Often by statute or practice standards, the referring party is also responsible for collecting and providing to the evaluating clinician the background collateral information that can be central to understanding the youth's prior mental health treatment, educational and psychological testing, and involvement in special education services. With youths in particular it is essential that this background material be obtained, because it is often difficult to accurately identify certain mental disorders, assess the significance or applicability of medication compliance to the impairments being observed, and determine the long-standing nature and seriousness of particular disorders without this type of documentation and review. In cases in which the attorneys are lax in providing this information, it falls to the evaluating clinician to seek this information avidly in the context of the time limits that are generally associated with competency assessments in juvenile court.

Soulier (2012) outlined the six components of a competency evaluation: assessment of mental disorder or intellectual disability; assessment of functional abilities for adjudicative competence; assessment of developmental status; linkage of deficits to functional abilities for adjudicative competence; an opinion of competence; and the potential for remediation or restoration when the youth is opined to be incompetent. Each of these components requires the integration of clinical observation with the assessment of functional capacities, considering the legal context of the assessment and the developmental maturity of the juvenile as applied to a reasonable standard of observed capacity and the ability of the youth to remedy deficits in knowledge through simple interactions with counsel. The synthesis that is required to adequately consider all of these elements simultaneously underscores the importance of professional training to ensure calibration between different evaluators working in a single forensic system.

The role of psychological testing in competency evaluations is somewhat controversial, with psychologists possibly exaggerating its importance to an assessment that is functional in nature and for which rather extensive testing appears to be the norm rather than the exception. In a small number of instances, however, further intellectual or neuropsychological testing may be warranted, particularly when the diagnosis is unclear and there is no consistent history to point toward an underlying pathology. In cases in which malingering is suspected, the clinician may also want to use certain tests to help provide more objective evidence of a response style that seems inauthentic (e.g., the Test of Memory Malingering [Teichner & Wagner, 2004], the Test of Malingered Incompetence [Colwell, Colwell, Perry, Wasieleski, & Billings, 2008], and possibly the Structured Interview of Reported Symptoms [Heilbronner, 2011] with older youths). However, as observed by Melton et al. (2007), routine administration of psychological tests often is not a cost efficient way of gathering information that is directly relevant to competency assessments.

In contrast, structured instruments designed specifically to assist with the competency assessment can serve a useful function in standardizing assessments across clinicians and in assisting in capturing all of the relevant information as part of their evaluation (Kruh & Grisso, 2009; Mayzer et al., 2009; O'Donnell & Gross, 2012). The most common tests used in the field at this time include the MacArthur Competence Assessment Tool—Criminal Adjudication (S. K. Hoge et al., 1997), the Fitness Interview Test—Revised (Viljoen, Vincent, & Roesch, 2006), the Georgia Court Competency Test—Mississippi State Hospital Revision (Nicholson, Briggs, & Robertson,

1988), the Competence Screening Test (Lipsitt, Lelos, & McGarry, 1971), the Competency Assessment for Standing Trial for Defendants With Mental Retardation (Everington & Luckasson, 1992), and the Evaluation of Competency to Stand Trial—Revised (Rogers, Grandjean, Tillbrook, Vitacco, & Sewell, 2001). However, none of these instruments were designed for or normed on juvenile samples (Ferguson et al., 2010; Fogel et al., 2013; O'Donnell & Gross, 2012; Soulier, 2012), and many were designed before the research on the relevance of developmental immaturity to adjudicative competency in juveniles.

The Juvenile Adjudicative Competence Interview (Grisso, 2005) has served an instrumental role in explaining the process of the evaluation to new evaluators, in ensuring that the relevant legal inquiries have been made, and in integrating psychopathy and developmental issues into a coherent opinion concerning the functional, causal, and contextual considerations that underlie competency. With the advent of new competency laws, it has served an essential function in guiding the field and providing some standardization across evaluators and states. Its use as a quasi-quantitative instrument with the counting of correct answers is a misuse of the measure, however. The Juvenile Adjudicative Competence Interview is not normed, prompting scholars to call for new measures of juvenile competency designed to detect deficits in competence-related abilities associated with psychosocial or cognitive immaturity and to assess malingering (Ferguson et al., 2010; Fogel et al., 2013; Heilbrun & DeMatteo, 2012; Poythress, Lexcen, Grisso, & Steinberg, 2006; Soulier, 2012; Viljoen, Penner, & Roesch, 2012).

The legal questions that need to be addressed in a competency assessment have been identified by many legal scholars, forensic clinicians, and forensic researchers (Grisso, 2005; Larson & Grisso, 2011; Melton et al., 2007). Soulier (2012) has succinctly suggested that an adjudicative competence evaluation should assess the juvenile's factual and rational understanding of the court proceeding by discussing (a) the alleged criminal offense, including its relative seriousness and the potential penalties; (b) the roles of all of the participants in a trial, including the prosecutor, defense attorney, judge, and witnesses; (c) the basic purpose of a trial and the adversarial nature of court procedures; (d) the implications, drawbacks, and benefits of a plea bargain; (e) the trial-related rights, including the right to deny an offense and the avoidance of self-incrimination; and (f) the reasoning a juvenile would use if faced with common legal choices and options such as a plea bargain. In assessing the youth's ability to assist counsel, Soulier suggests that the evaluator should discuss (a) the name, purpose, and relationship of a defense attorney; (b) the level of motivation to help and trust a defense attorney; (c) the youth's ability to communicate, understand, and retain information; (d) the youth's ability to process and respond rationally to new information; (e) the youth's ability to articulate facts pertaining to the alleged offense; (f) the youth's ability to maintain proper courtroom behavior; and (g) the strengths and weaknesses of a potential trial.

It is still unclear to what extent juvenile competency evaluators actually assess maturity and address it directly in their reports to the court (Cox, Goldstein, Dolores, Zelechoski, & Messenheimer, 2012). The rather severe intellectual deficits and significant mental illnesses found among many youths who are adjudicated incompetent suggest that developmental considerations may be overshadowed by the intellectual deficits and clinical symptoms found among this population of youths. The research that has been conducted on this topic has identified many relevant developmental constructs, however, including autonomy, temperance, perspective, developmental stage, judgment, reasoning and decision-making ability, future orientation, risk perception, peer influences, the influence of the parental relationship, and suggestibility and compliance with others (Larson & Grisso, 2011; Soulier, 2012).

The challenge in juvenile competency assessments involves contextualizing these more subtle influences in the context of rather severe psychopathology and significant intellectual disability according to a legal standard that is rather low in its demands for defendant capacities. However, as noted by Viljoen and Wingrove (2007), judges seem poised to consider immaturity in their deliberation of competency, thus obliging evaluators to consider these influences carefully and to educate the court about them when relevant to the opinion being offered by the expert.

This, however, can prove difficult when the very environment in juvenile court is responsive to the immaturity of its constituents, making it necessary to identify specific deficits with a specific impact on the legal decisional capacity of a specific youth. It is also possible that the relatively low standard captured by the competency doctrine makes these developmental issues less compelling in relationship to the significant psychiatric and intellectual deficits that are identified in many youths referred for competency evaluations.

Feigning Incompetency

The assessment of malingering is an important consideration in forensic assessments. Youths are also possibly more proficient than adults in passing on information, particularly in detention settings, that can educate and inform other youths as to the nature of the competency assessment and the significant impact it can have on their legal situation should they be found incompetent to stand trial. As in other assessments, malingering is best assessed using information elicited from multiple sources to look for inconsistency, obtaining mental health and educational records to help in assessing an inexplicable deterioration in functioning, and in some instances arranging for an inpatient assessment to provide 24-hour observation of a youth over a period of multiple days. Despite this being a necessary consideration in all forensic evaluations, clinicians seem overly hesitant about identifying malingering, particularly when they are evaluating a child or adolescent. This propensity is further aggravated by some efforts to turn competency assessments into a question-and-answer session with no effort to explore behaviors and abilities outside the assessment context. As indicated above, some instruments can be used to help assess malingering, but an effective approach to identifying malingering is (a) to carefully observe behavior while exploring different topics, over a number of sessions, and view it in the context of behavior manifested in all other aspects of the juvenile's life and (b) to consider the youth's history from multiple sources indicating whether the observed deficits have been seen by others, and over what period of time, and identify any inconsistency between such history and the current presentation.

Evaluator's Opinion

States differ in whether they explicitly require (or permit) the evaluator to offer a conclusion or "ultimate opinion" concerning the juvenile's competence to stand trial (Larson & Grisso, 2011). Because competency is by definition a legal determination, some believe the judge should make an adjudication of competency assisted by a description of the defendant's impairments contained in the evaluation report (Tillbrook, Mumley, & Grisso, 2003). Alternatively, proponents of the inclusion of an ultimate legal opinion assert that judges are aided by and often desire the opinions of highly qualified evaluators and remain free to disagree with the evaluator's opinion (Redding, Floyd, & Hawk, 2001; Rogers & Ewing, 2003). The *Specialty Guidelines for Forensic Psychology* (American Psychological Association, 2013) do not provide direct guidance regarding answering the ultimate legal question in an evaluation report. One reasonable alternative to providing an ultimate opinion involves offering conclusions that directly address the different components of the *Dusky v. United States* (1960) standard but that do not include a definite opinion about the defendant's trial competency. This position does not overstep the expertise and role of the evaluator and conveys respect for the decision-making autonomy of the court.

Regardless of the inclusion of ultimate or penultimate language in a competency report, the opinion section should serve as an amalgamation of the report that educates the reader and furthers the reader's appreciation of this youth and his or her unique legal situation. This integration should assimilate diverse behavioral, clinical, and developmental factors with a functional assessment of capacities and skills, calibrating this information according to the different components of the *Dusky v. United States* (1960) standard. Often included in this section will be an assessment of whether a predicate condition is present (e.g., intellectual disability, mental illness); the different cognitive, emotional, and behavioral ways in which these impairments manifest and affect specific legal decisional capacities (e.g., lack of knowledge, concrete thinking, flawed decision making, poor impulse control); and the specific ways in which these impairments will adversely affect the juvenile's understanding and effective participation in his or her trial or other aspects of the legal process (O'Donnell & Gross, 2012). This type of synthesis remains integral to a high-quality report because it provides both the defense and the prosecution the richest opportunity to argue the issue of competency in contested cases before the court. This position has recently been articulated by Rotter and Greenspan (2011), who urged the field to move beyond binary competence and include the complex interplay between symptoms and fitness-related capacities that may be related to adjudicative competence.

Options for Opinions

On the basis of due consideration of the evidence presented to the court, the judge can determine that the youth is competent, incompetent but amendable to restoration services, or incompetent and unrestorable. If a defendant is adjudicated competent, the case proceeds to trial or alternative disposition. Of cases referred for a competency evaluation, relatively few (14%–18%) are found incompetent (Cowden & McKee, 1995; McKee, 1998; McKee & Shea, 1999). However, if the youth is determined to be incompetent but likely restorable, the youth will be ordered into restoration services, usually with the requirement of a regular schedule of review of the youth's progress and status. When the court decides that the youth is unrestorable, most courts (guided by applicable statutes) may order restoration services for a relatively brief trial period or grant a motion to have the charges dismissed.

Predictions of Restorability

The U.S. Supreme Court ruled in *Jackson v. Indiana* (1972) that a defendant cannot be held for longer than the reasonable time necessary to determine whether there is substantial probability that he or she will attain competency in the foreseeable future. Because of this legal constraint, evaluators are often required to predict an adult defendant's probability of regaining competency at the time of the initial evaluation (Advokat, Guidry, Burnett, Manguno-Mire, & Thompson, 2012; Mossman, 2007; Warren, Chauhan, Kois, Dibble, & Knighton, 2013; Zapf & Roesch, 2011). This requirement is being extrapolated to the juvenile context; it is good practice to include this information in the report to better inform the court at the time of the first competency hearing.

Despite this requirement, most studies have suggested that clinicians' ability to predict competency restoration among adults is limited (Advokat et al., 2012; Zapf & Roesch, 2011), and there is no comparable research regarding juveniles. However, it is unlikely that these predictions would be more accurate in the juvenile context, given the added complexity of the developmental issues at play among youths. Research by D. R. Morris and DeYoung (2012) has indicated that service providers were able to predict 6-month competency status using data obtained at the 3-month postrestoration review with adults, suggesting that the quality of the predictions improve with time and observation—and that by the 3-month mark, clinicians have well-informed and increasingly accurate opinions of the remediation effort's outcome.

Incompetent but Restorable

If the youth is deemed amenable to remediation services, the evaluator is further asked to comment on the type of services he or she believes would best facilitate the remediation of the youth. Ideally, these recommendations are specific to each of the barriers that have been identified and together describe the best possibility of facilitating the restoration attainment of each individual youth. Common interventions include psychiatric assessment and medication management, intensive case management, psycholegal education, medical treatment, the use of an interpreter or more culturally pertinent interventions, the provision of assistive devices such as glasses or a hearing aid, or other interventions such as neuropsychological testing that might help to further the restoration counselor's understanding of the competency-related deficits that are being addressed.

To some extent, these recommendations help the judge to understand the process that will be required to remediate the youth while also offering an intervention baseline to assist providers who are court ordered to deliver remediation services to the youth after an adjudication of incompetency. In developing these laws, however, it has been noted that recommending generic mental health could undermine the specificity of a competency restoration program—and encourage attorneys and families to seek a finding of incompetency as a viable back door for attaining treatment for a child in need of broader clinical services.

Unrestorably Incompetent

There is no consensus in the literature as to when a defendant should be determined to be unrestorably incompetent. The American Academy of Psychiatry and Law practice guidelines (Mossman et al., 2007) recommend that evaluators indicate whether a defendant has a treatable or untreatable condition interfering with competence. Parker (2012) warned, however, that a court might consider any probability greater than zero sufficiently substantial to justify attempted remediation services.

The U.S. Supreme Court has left it to the states to determine disposition with a defendant who is not able to attain competency (Parker, 2012; Zapf & Roesch, 2011). Virginia is one of the few states to provide explicit statutory guidance regarding the timelines and steps that can be used when diverting an unrestorable youth from the juvenile justice system (Va. Code § 16.1-358). States generally have two options if a youth is unrestorable: The charges may be dropped or the case dismissed with or without prejudice (Larson & Grisso, 2011; Soulier & Scott, 2010; Viljoen & Grisso, 2007).

In Virginia, the court is also afforded the right to issue a Child In Need of Services petition that allows it to maintain some degree of supervisory authority over the juvenile even after his or her involvement in the delinquency system has ended. Nevertheless, the reality of having to dismiss charges despite what may have been a serious and potentially dangerous crime can prompt concerns about a poor evaluation leading to a miscarriage of justice or, alternatively, an accurate assessment posing a threat to public safety when a violent but impaired youth is released back to the community without any further supervision or containment by the court (Viljoen & Grisso, 2007).

Lack of Consistency Among Evaluators and Across Jurisdictions

Lack of consistency among evaluators regarding juvenile competence has plagued the field and results at least in part from the different methods used by evaluators (Fogel et al., 2013; Mayzer et al., 2009), confounded by a lack of consensus on standards of practice for the juvenile court (Heilbrun & DeMatteo, 2012; Rogers & Cruise, 1998). In the context of adults, Murrie, Boccaccini, Zapf, Warren, and Henderson (2008) argued that although competency determinations are dichotomous, the capacities underlying competency may be dimensional—and that clinicians may draw the distinction between competent and incompetent at different places within the midrange, accounting for different outcomes.

The lack of well-articulated practice standards further fuels variation within and across states. For example, some states dismiss charges if a youth is found incompetent, other states divert a youth before a finding of incompetency, and still others attempt to remediate almost all youths impaired in their legal decisional capacity. Kruh et al. (2006) reported that youths referred for a competency evaluation in Washington State were more likely to have a mental illness than youths in South Carolina or Chicago, which may result in more youths in Washington State being deemed incompetent. However, Warren, Rosenfeld, Fitch, and Hawk (1997) found that even when state standards were identical, states differed in their rates of referral and interpretation of the legal standards, resulting in different rates of (adult) incompetence. Likewise, Burrell et al. (2008) surveyed counties in California and, among other findings, found large variation in the proportion of juvenile defendants deemed incompetent across counties.

Evaluation Report

The juvenile competency report provides the platform through which the evaluator can convey to all parties the relevant information concerning each youth and its integration into a final opinion concerning competency, treatment, and the potential for attainment of competency in the foreseeable future. When the report is being sent to all parties including the defense attorney, the district attorney, and the judge, regardless of who ordered the assessment it is imperative that no information concerning the offense and the youth's possible involvement in it be included in the report. As with all forensic reports, all the relevant sources of information consulted or used in reaching these opinions should be clearly laid out at the beginning of the report, with each fact being attributed to its appropriate source.

Larson and Grisso (2011) recommended a five-part evaluation report: assessment of mental disorder and intellectual disability, assessment of developmental status, assessment of functional abilities for competency to stand trial, causes of deficits in competency abilities, and potential for remediation or restoration (if in the opinion of the evaluator the defendant is incompetent to stand trial). Sufficient background information is also included to provide context for the clinical information being presented and a summary of relevant mental health treatment and prior educational testing to better inform the description of the current clinical condition. A segment devoted to the evaluator's efforts to obtain informed (and possibly research) assent from the juvenile, and in many instances permission from the parent or guardian, is also commonly included at the beginning of the report.

Over the past decade, some common problems in report writing have been observed among trainees at the University of Virginia's juvenile forensic training program. This observation prompted the development of a report writing checklist that is now required as part of the final submission of the case report for successful completion of the training (Warren, 2013). The most common problem observed was the evaluator's inclusion of information relevant to the defendant's guilt. This error occurred despite lengthy discussions during the training of the importance of excluding this type of information, as well as other types of aggravating information, because the report is not privileged or protected. When this information is found in the practice reports that are submitted to us, we have observed that this information has often crept in while quoting the youth's ability to describe and convey a memory at the time of the offense, in understanding the seriousness of his or her crime and possible sentences, or in the youth's description of the evidence that might be relevant to his or her defense. Unrelated aggravating information is also often inadvertently included in the education and testing sections of the report in which aggressive and threatening behavior at school or in other locations has been reported.

Whatever the evaluator's motivation for including such information, it provides material for arguing risk for violence in another context. Irrelevant information, gratuitous and imprecise diagnoses (e.g., conduct disorder), and nonspecific psychological testing are also not uncommon, at times creating the impression of precision and comprehensiveness to more inexperienced readers, but ultimately confusing and at times distorting the competency opinion.

Research concerning the content of competency reports has found that more than one third of evaluators fail to provide information on the causal explanation for a youth's deficits, compromising the quality of the reports (Christy et al., 2004; Nicholson & Norwood, 2000; Ryba, Cooper, & Zapf, 2003). This lack of integration and explanation may reflect the additional time and independent deliberation needed to consider and explain such deficits. Many forms of psychological assessment require a consistent and structured method not only for collecting data but also for summarizing it into a conclusion. In contrast, competency assessments ultimately involve the presentation of a psycholegal opinion that requires some ingenuity to integrate the different legal dimensions of competency with the clinical and functional assessment that is unique to each youth. Mental health, developmental, and crime-related factors have to be assessed not in terms of current ability but in terms of perceived capacity in the context of a decisional bar that is defined by context. This assessment is compounded by the necessity of offering opinions on whether the youth is likely to be restored to competency in the foreseeable future and the nature of the needed relevant interventions.

Research has demonstrated that some forensic psychologists use clinical rather than legal information to determine competence (G. H. Morris, Haroun, & Naimark, 2004). Larson and Grisso (2011) suggested that greater specificity in the statutory language regarding areas to be considered by evaluators could contribute to greater uniformity in how evaluators assess juvenile competency and write reports. This type of detail, however, is uncommon in most statutes addressing various aspects of mental health law, suggesting that more extensive training and sustained supervision is a more viable option for obtaining a higher standard of practice and reasonable degree of consistency across evaluators and states.

COMPETENCY HEARING AND JUDICIAL ORDERS FOR RESTORATION SERVICES

On receipt of the juvenile competency evaluation report, a competency hearing is held in which the judge makes a determination of competency. Research has found that a judge's opinion of a juvenile's adjudicative competence is influenced by characteristics of the youth him- or herself. Older youths and more mature youths are more likely to be deemed competent by judges, suggesting that judges may be heavily influenced by chronological age rather than the detailed descriptions in evaluation reports outlining competence-related capacities (Cox et al., 2012). Furthermore, although judges and attorneys recognize immaturity as a cause for incompetence, they rate it as less important than mental illness or mental retardation (Viljoen & Wingrove, 2007), with only 26% of judges rating immaturity as essential in juvenile competence evaluations (Viljoen, Wingrove, & Ryba, 2008).

Most judges appear to agree with or possibly abdicate to clinicians' opinions in determining competence (Melton et al., 2007; G. H. Morris et al., 2004). In one study directly comparing a judge's competency decision with that of the evaluator's recommendation, Kruh et al. (2006) found 91% agreement for incompetence and 99% agreement for competence, with an overall agreement of 95%. This finding underscores the importance of the accuracy of the forensic clinician's opinion in the evaluation report. If the judge deems the youth incompetent but amenable to treatment, the judge will very likely order remediation services for the youth.

REMEDIATION PROGRAMS

As of yet, few integrated remediation programs have been developed specifically for youths. To some extent, this may reflect the complex intermingling of mental health, intellectual, and developmental issues that need to be addressed using multidimensional programming that is relevant to different-aged youths (Schwalbe & Medalia, 2007; C. L. Scott, 2003; Viljoen & Grisso, 2007; Viljoen, Odgers, Grisso, & Tillbrook, 2007). It may also reflect the rather nascent stage of juvenile competency legislation and the current focus on defining the law rather than providing the services that are responsive to it. Experience has demonstrated, however, that youths require a different array of services to be assisted in attaining competency than do adults and that the experience gained in providing services to the latter is not particularly useful in designing responsive programming for the former.

Remediation programs typically tend to emphasize one of four approaches: psychotropic medication, educational treatment, treatment programs geared toward those with intellectual deficits, and interventions for youths with developmental immaturity (Viljoen & Grisso, 2007; Zapf & Roesch, 2011). Ultimately, programming that is truly responsive to youths of varying ages requires that all of these components be integrated into a single program, with trained service providers administering a tailored intervention to each youth individually as they progress through remediation services.

Medication Issues

In some instances, medication management can be relevant or even central to the remediation process. In *Sell v. United States* (2003), the U.S. Supreme Court held that antipsychotic drugs could be administered against the adult defendant's wishes for the purpose of restoring competency, but only in rare, limited circumstances (Slobogin, 2012). In most instances, the issue with youths does not reach the level of forcing medication, but rather providing assistance to the youth and the family in obtaining and dispensing the proper medication. This goal may require arranging for a psychiatric assessment, obtaining support for the family in paying for the medication, and assisting the family in transporting forgotten or lost medication to the location where the youth is residing. It might also entail encouraging or educating the youth and family about the importance of full compliance with prescribed medication and checking to ensure that the youth has taken prescribed medication before attending any hearing. Growing sophistication in identifying the prodromal symptoms of schizophrenia and other psychotic disorders also requires the ongoing training and education of remediation service providers so they can be aware of and sensitive to the more subtle indices of serious mental illness in youths.

Educational Issues

Educational treatment programs are designed to increase a defendant's understanding of the legal process or remedy situations that in some way prohibit the defendant from participating in the defense (Zapf & Roesch, 2011). In their review of the literature, Zapf and Roesch (2011) concluded that the research could not determine at this point whether education programs that teach adult defendants about their legal rights are any more effective than individualized treatment programs that target specific underlying deficits. Viljoen et al. (2007) compared pre–post scores on training items from the MacArthur Competence Assessment Tool—Criminal Adjudication for a sample of 11- to 24-year-olds. Participants younger in age and those with lower IQs showed less improvement in scores after participating in the program, although minority participants showed greater improvement. Viljoen et al.'s findings further suggest that some concepts are easier to learn than others. They found considerable variability in the improvement of participant scores across six concepts. For example, 73.5% of participants who were taught about the consequences of conviction improved after teaching, whereas only 26.8% who were taught about the consequences of a guilty plea showed improvement. This is consistent with a satisfaction survey of youths receiving remediation services in Virginia. Jackson et al. (2014) found that some concepts were self-reported by youths as more difficult to learn (e.g., plea bargain) than others. More important, rote memorization of responses is inadequate to demonstrate competence (*United States v. Duhon*, 2000).

The complexity underlying these processes of learning involves ensuring that the learning is not only factual but also rational in nature as required by the *Dusky v. United States* (1960) standard. This element of rational understanding has been interpreted widely as the ability to apply the information to one's own situation and to use it to inform the decisions that are being made by the youth. This interplay among teaching, extrapolating, and reviewing the impact of this new knowledge on the behavior and decision making of youth is best observed in a one-to-one relationship that allows an iterative process specific to each child and that is sustained and internalized over time.

Special Needs Issues

Many youths who are found incompetent to stand trial have varying levels of intellectual disability and different elements of the communication and relational impairments associated with autism spectrum disorders (Warren et al., 2009). Some of these youths can respond to interventions that are interactive and repetitive and in which information is presented in narrative form. However, the available research has indicated that this group of juveniles is the least likely to attain competency despite the type and length of services offered to them (McGaha, Otto, McClaren, & Petrila, 2001; Warren et al., 2009).

When working with this group of youths, service providers must skillfully balance attempts to provide services and gauge progress while constantly remaining aware of the ruling in *Jackson v. Indiana* (1972) that states that a defendant cannot be held for longer than the reasonable time necessary to determine whether there is substantial probability that he or she will attain competency in the foreseeable future. Practice standards in Virginia require that eight sessions be provided to all youths even when all evaluators have opined that a youth is likely unrestorably incompetent, so as to demonstrate conclusively that progress cannot and will not occur. With less-impaired youths, progress is assessed every 3 months to ensure that there remains a possibility that progress and attainment is possible. If this is not the case, an independent evaluation is ordered to determine whether the youth should be returned to the court as unrestorably incompetent.

Developmental Immaturity Issues

It was initially believed that incompetence predicated on developmental immaturity would require the passage of time to remediate (O'Donnell & Gross, 2012). However, Kivisto, Moore, Fite, and Seidner (2011) found that the relationship between age and competence was partially explained by the development of a future orientation (i.e., the extent to which long-range consequences influence decision-making processes), suggesting that although age is untreatable, methods for facilitating future orientation are potentially possible.

Similarly, the construction of interactive programming at the University of Virginia has demonstrated that when developmental issues such as future orientation, peer influence, and risk perception are included in the narratives and exercises used to teach youths legal constructs, progress can be made in helping younger youths separate their initial age-appropriate thinking from the approach that might be more advantageous to them in court (Warren, 2013). This process seems to be significantly mediated by intelligence, with youths of higher intellectual capacity better able to grasp a new or different perspective and apply it to their unique situation in court and those with more limited cognitive abilities not able to attain this level of abstraction and learning (Warren, Aaron, Ryan, Chauhan, & DuVal, 2003; Warren et al., 2009).

Remediation Service Providers

The remediation service providers who deliver the direct services to youths undergoing remediation services generally hold a bachelor's degree in psychology, social work, criminal justice, or education and have had some prior experience working with children or adolescents. In Virginia, remediation service providers are referred to as *restoration counselors*. Restoration counselors undergo a 3-day training before being contracted to provide services and are supervised by a restoration supervisor in the field at least once every 30 days. Larson and Grisso (2011) emphasized that remediation service providers must possess specialized knowledge of the developmental capabilities of youths as well as methods for teaching youths information related to their state's definition of competence.

Location of Remediation Services

Remediation services for youths are increasingly offered in the least restrictive setting allowed by the court. Such settings include the youth's home, a relative's home, a foster home, or possibly a group home. When mandated by the court, youths will be placed in detention because of security concerns, with services optimally being provided to them in this setting until their security risk diminishes, and they return home.

This emphasis on the least restrictive setting is particularly appropriate for youths because it allows them to stay in their homes with access to school and other community supports while their remediation is implemented (Burrell et al., 2008; Ferguson et al., 2010). In contrast to incompetent adults, who often have treatment-resistant psychosis or refuse medication, most youths do not have mental health conditions that warrant inpatient hospitalization, and the majority can be assisted with medication management in the community. When outpatient programs are compared with programs using residential treatment, the cost of the services is reduced substantially.

Length of Remediation Services

Some states specify a period of time during which services must be provided and completed, and others use a formula based on the offense (for example, one third of the time the defendant would have served if convicted of the same crime; Finkle et al., 2009). The inclusion of a periodic review is also embedded in most state statutes. There has been little research comparing juveniles with adults to determine the length of time juveniles take to attain competency. Warren et al. (2009) found that the majority of youths were restored within 90 days, and McGaha et al. (2001) found that most youths who were restored in a secure setting were restored within 217 days. Among adults, the majority (75%) of incompetent defendants are returned to court as competent within 6 months (Bennett & Kish, 1990; D. R. Morris & Parker, 2008).

FOUR JUVENILE COMPETENCY REMEDIATION SERVICES PROGRAMS

Four long-standing juvenile competency remediation services programs are situated in Virginia, Florida, Maryland, and Louisiana. We briefly describe each program in the following sections.

Restoring Youths in the Community

The Restoring Youth program was developed in Virginia through a 4-year grant awarded to the University of Virginia by the Virginia Department of Criminal Justice Services in collaboration with the Virginia Department of Behavioral Health and Disability Services (see http://www.juvenilecompetency.com). Building on the original community-based program established in 2000, it was formalized into a theory-based program (Lipsey, Howell, Kelly, Chapman, & Carver, 2010) built on the system of care framework (Finkle et al., 2009; Keith Matthews, Krivelyova, Stephens, & Bilchik, 2013; Pires, 2002) that is increasingly used in the context of the juvenile justice system (Burrell et al., 2008; MacKinnon-Lewis, Kaufman, & Frabutt, 2002). It is based on differentiated (Santamaria, 2009; G. E. Smith & Throne, 2007; J. C. Smith, 2011; Tomlinson, 2000) and personalized (Corno & Snow, 1986; Jenkins, 2000; Keefe & Jenkins, 2008) instruction research. The program is currently being replicated in other locations with the goal of establishing it as an evidence-based practice by 2020.

The Restoring Youth program is based on eight service-related principles that dictate that services be time sensitive, community based, individualized and integrative, developmental and culturally appropriate, dyadic in nature, training based, dose sensitive, and data driven. The program is manualized with ongoing training and supervision, and it includes a toolkit of activities to teach juveniles of varying ages the skills necessary for adjudicative competence (Warren, 2013). Each activity can be adapted to appeal to a variety of interests and learning styles (e.g., tactile–kinesthetic, visual, auditory) and unique developmental, cognitive, and cultural requirements. These educational tools include digital (animated) storytelling with a multicultural cast of characters that serves to amalgamate storytelling and learning (Figg, McCartney, & Gonsoulin, 2009). A variety of media (flashcards, workbooks, coloring books) are included that appeal to individual interests and are designed to reinforce concepts learned in the digital stories. A courtroom board game teaches courtroom personnel roles, and a range of other engaging and developmentally appropriate materials have been created for use with youths of different ages.

Barriers to competency, such as a mental health disorder, are addressed through intensive case management in which restoration counselors make referrals for services to mitigate identified barriers. The dosage of education required depends on the youth. On average, however, each juvenile participates individually in two to three 1-hour face-to-face restoration sessions per week with his or her restoration counselor for an average of 116 days (range = 2 weeks–6 months). Services are provided in the least restrictive setting allowed by the court (typically in the home), thus eliminating unnecessary hospitalizations or residential placements while facilitating parental involvement (Tomlinson, 2000). More important, the successful transfer of knowledge depends on highly skilled restoration counselors who are able to identify different learning styles and adapt to the needs of each youth (Tricarico & Yendol-Hoppey, 2012), requiring strict adherence to training requirements for restoration counselors.

The Restoring Youth program is also supported by the Restoring Youth case management software, which contains all the information relevant to the care of each youth and the operation of the overall program (see http://www.juvenilecompetency.com). Developed by custom application designers at the University of Virginia, this software allows for web-based storage of all records and documents concerning each individual youth; the detailing of individual sessions and progress notes for each contact with the youth; the documentation and saving of all reviews, reports, documents, and decisions submitted to and reviewed by the court; and the barriers to competency that are being addressed with each youth by the restoration counselor. The software allows for different levels of access: Restoration counselors have access to all case notes and information relevant to their individual caseloads, restoration supervisors have access to all the cases under their direct supervision, and the program administrator has access to all cases that are currently active (or closed) within the system. The 24-chapter interactive DVD, titled *DJ and Alicia*, has been programmed to allow users to download the performance of each youth during each session for research purposes—for example, how youths of different ages with different types of impairment learn the different legal constructs and demonstrate the ability to apply that information to their own legal situation.

Florida's Restoration Services Program

Florida's Juvenile Incompetence to Proceed program was developed in 1997 in response to the juvenile competence legislation that was passed that same year. The Juvenile Incompetence to Proceed program provides competency restoration services to youths who have been found incompetent as a result of a predicate condition including mental illness (Chapter 394 and Chapter 916, Florida Statutes) or intellectual disability or autism (Chapter 393, Florida Statutes). The principles of the program require that the restoration services be provided with dignity and fairness and in the least restrictive setting allowed by the courts; some juveniles receive services in a community outpatient setting and some in a secure residential placement. The goal of Juvenile Incompetence to Proceed is identified as helping each youth to become knowledgeable about the delinquency process and his or her legal situation so as to best ensure appropriate due process in the legal system.

Youths receiving services in the community receive services in their home, detention facility, or at their school by Twin Oaks Forensic Outpatient Services, a private corporation that provides case management and competency training as needed by youths of varying ages. Mental health services are not provided directly, but rather are coordinated through a case manager who arranges for referral to the statewide Agency for Persons With Disabilities. Youths receiving services in a secure residential setting are served at Apalachicola Forest Youth Camp, located in Liberty County, Florida. The youth camp is a 39-bed facility operated by Twin Oaks Juvenile Development, Inc., under contract with the Department of Children and Families. It is located on a 78-acre site in a wilderness area. Security measures include cameras and a 14-foot-high fence. The buildings are constructed as log homes. The facility consists of six 7- to 8-person cabins with individual bedrooms, an education building with six classrooms, a professional building with 24-hour nursing coverage, and an administrative building.

Maryland's Remediation Program

Maryland's juvenile competency attainment program was established in October 2006.[1] Since that time, approximately 350 youths have been served, with all but 75 youths having attained competency and returned to court, most within 3 months of referral. Maryland's competency attainment program was modeled on Virginia's program, described above. The program is administered by the Office of Forensic Services in the state's Mental Hygiene Administration (the state's mental health authority). The director of the program is a social worker who is assisted by a part-time consulting psychiatrist with board certification in child and adolescent psychiatry and forensic psychiatry. The program contracts with a cadre of community-based psychiatrists and psychologists who conduct evaluations of youths referred by the courts. In addition, the program contracts with a dozen professionals who provide competency attainment services for youths found incompetent to proceed. These professionals include social workers, licensed professional counselors, and special educators, all of whom receive specialized training in the provision of attainment services.

Nearly all attainment services are provided on an outpatient basis in the community. A child found incompetent may not be placed in a psychiatric hospital except pursuant to civil admission procedures. Except for a small number who were hospital patients at the time they were found incompetent (and remained afterward), no youths have been hospitalized for attainment services.

Furthermore, no child found incompetent may remain in or be placed in a juvenile justice detention facility. If a child is in detention when found incompetent and continues to meet criteria for detention, the court may order the child to a facility for children. The Mental Hygiene Administration uses beds at a state-operated residential treatment center for this purpose. Only about 45 youths have been admitted in the 7 years that the program has been in place.

Youths referred for competency attainment services are assigned a competency attainment provider. The provider meets with the youth two to three times per week. If the youth is in the community (85% are), these meetings occur most often in the youth's home. Sometimes providers will meet with youths at their school. If a youth is in the facility for children, the provider meets with the youth there.

Providers take a psychoeducational approach to competency attainment. Relying in part on materials

[1]Our sincerest appreciation to W. Lawrence Fitch, former director of forensic services for Maryland's Mental Hygiene Administration, with responsibility for the state's program for competency attainment services for youths found incompetent to proceed in juvenile court, for authoring this section.

developed by the Maryland Administrative Office of the Courts for general use by youths in the juvenile justice system (and their families), providers educate the youth about juvenile justice charges, procedures, and dispositions. A provider may arrange for a youth to watch a television show or movie with courtroom scenes and discuss what he or she has seen. Sometimes a provider will use flash cards to test a youth's understanding of terminology. If a youth has special needs (e.g., medication), the provider will work with the family to ensure that the needs are met. In nearly all such cases, the youth will already have been referred for services, and the encouraging of family cooperation becomes an important part of the attainment provider's role.

Maryland law requires dismissal of the charges if a youth has not attained competency within 6 months (most misdemeanors) or 18 months (felonies and some serious misdemeanors). Of the approximately 20% of youths who do not attain competency within this period (or who are found not to be attainable sooner), 35% were diagnosed with mental retardation or borderline intellectual functioning, 26% had cognitive disorder not otherwise specified, 9% had attention-deficit/hyperactivity disorder (as a primary diagnosis), 7% had a psychotic disorder, 6% had a communication or language disorder, 4% had a mood disorder, 4% had a learning disability (as a primary diagnosis), and the remaining youths had a variety of other diagnoses or disabilities. The average Global Assessment of Functioning score was 54.4. Of the 72% for whom an IQ score was reported, the average was a full-scale IQ of 64. Case reviews indicated that 87% of the sample had an individualized education program in place when the charges were lodged. Twenty-five percent were living with a nonparental guardian.

Louisiana's Remediation Program

The Louisiana Juvenile Competency Restoration Program was developed in 2006 in response to the Louisiana Laws Children's Code 837.1-2 (2005). The code provides the qualifications necessary for providing services to incompetent youths with these services differing on the basis of the underlying impairment that is contributing to the limitations in the youth's legal decisional capacity. For those incompetent because of an ignorance of court procedures and legal rights, psychiatrists, psychologists, medical psychologists, certified educational teachers, social workers, and counselors are identified as qualified to provide services and submit review reports to the court. For those youths with some form of mental illness or intellectual deficit, the list of qualified providers includes psychiatrists, licensed psychologists, medical psychologists, licensed clinical social workers, qualified mental retardation professionals, and licensed professional counselors, all of whom have been involved in the provision of clinical services to youths in the immediate 3 years and who have specific expertise in child development specific to severe disabilities in children.

The code identifies the process by which a restoration provider will submit a report to the court, district attorney, and defense counsel every 90 days, describing the services provided to the youth including medication, education, and counseling; the likelihood that the mental capacity to proceed will be restored in the foreseeable future; and the progress the youth has made in the intervening period on 12 specific abilities. This section of the Louisiana Children's Code also requires that if the youth has been placed in an out-of-home placement, the report will include an assessment of the danger the child poses to him- or herself and others and the appropriateness of the placement. A section pertaining to Fifth Amendment protections against self-incrimination affirms that testimony from a restoration service provider cannot include any statements from the youth concerning the alleged delinquent behavior and that no such statements can be used in subsequent court proceedings.

The educational content of the restoration program is based on the Bennett criteria, which are specific abilities and capacities identified in the landmark case *Louisiana v. Bennett* (1977). These 12 criteria include a number of factual criteria such as understanding the nature of certain legal rights, the delinquency allegations, the range of possible dispositions, the different legal defenses that are available to the youth, the underlying adversarial nature of the court process, and the roles of the judge and defense counsel. It also underscores the importance of the youth's disclosing all the relevant facts to the defense attorney, being able to testify at trial, maintaining appropriate courtroom behavior, listening effectively to witness testimony for errors, and being able to comprehend his or her situation in relation to the proceedings. The program was designed to educate youths ages 9 to 17 years. It provides repetition and simplicity so children and adolescents with developmental or mental health diagnoses will be able to engage with the material, and it proceeds through consecutive steps that progress from the more simple concepts (e.g., appropriate attire for court) to the more complex (e.g., plea bargain).

To promote this progression of learning, the Louisiana Department of Health and Hospitals created and approved a training manual that includes 10 lesson plans including a pretest and posttest for each youth. If the juvenile is unable to read, the restoration service provider reads each lesson and uses visual aids for additional assistance. The lessons consist of matching, filling in the blanks, and short answers. The competency restoration providers are encouraged to be creative by gearing the program to each individual's specific need.

The Louisiana Juvenile Competency Restoration Program provides competency restoration services to approximately 40 youths each year in 10 different regions of the state, with sessions being provided both individually and in a group format. The meetings occur once a week for 1 hour and include both the review of information covered previously and progressively more complex information. The average length of competency restoration services is 10 weeks, with the majority of youths being restored to competency. Each month statistical data are reported to the program director, including the number of juveniles served for the month; race, age, charge, and parish or county; the number of youths who have completed the program; and the final decision by the court.

JUVENILE COMPETENCY RESTORATION SERVICES RESEARCH

According to Heilbrun and Brooks (2010), the field of forensic psychology has focused on legal decision making to the exclusion of other pertinent inquiries. This may help explain why so little is empirically known about restoration services for adults (Pinals, 2005) as well as for youths (Grisso, 2004; C. L. Scott, 2003). Only two studies have examined restoration services programs as they pertain to youths being adjudicated in juvenile court. McGaha et al. (2001) examined more than 400 youths ordered into restoration services in Florida. The most common diagnosis was conduct disorder (57%), followed by attention-deficit/hyperactivity disorder (37%). Only 17% of the juveniles carried a psychotic diagnosis. Each of these juveniles was subject to residential treatment in a secure setting, averaging 217.5 days (per youth) of restoration treatment. After this type of restoration effort, the majority (71%) of youths were recommended by the evaluating clinician and determined by the court to be competent. Ultimately, 44% of the juveniles with mental retardation (without a co-occurring diagnosed mental illness), 34% with a co-occurring mental illness and mental retardation, and 8% with a mental illness only were found to be unrestorably incompetent after treatment.

Most recently, Warren et al. (2009) examined the restoration outcomes of 563 youths referred to the program in the Commonwealth of Virginia. Among this group, 73% were determined to have been restored to competence after services had been provided for between 61 and 90 days. No juveniles were admitted for inpatient hospitalization for the purpose of restoration; only 5% were hospitalized on the basis of civil commitment criteria for further psychiatric evaluation or stabilization. Warren et al. found the highest rate of achieved competence among youths without a mental illness or mental retardation (91%) and the lowest rate of achieved competence among youths with mental retardation (47%).

POSTJUVENILE COMPETENCY RESTORATION SERVICES

Among adults, 80% to 90% are restored to competence, with approximately 7% remaining unrestorable (Pinals, 2005). Among juveniles, on average 71% are returned to the court as competent after receiving restoration services (McGaha et al., 2001; Warren et al., 2009). McGaha et al. (2001) speculated that the rates of restoration are lower among juveniles because of the higher rates of mental retardation, a condition that is generally resistant to intervention, with developmental immaturity further increasing the rate of incompetency among juveniles. Viljoen et al. (2012) also suggested that restoration rates may in fact be lower but that pressure is at times exerted on the evaluator to deem a youth competent so that the trial may proceed, even when the youth's competence remains in question.

After a specified period of time, or periodically, the youth is returned to court for a competency hearing so the court can either opine on the juvenile's competence or check the status of the youth's progress. Because of the fluidity of competency, Finkle et al. (2009) recommended that a competency hearing be held as soon as possible on completion of the postrestoration services evaluation. For example, Seattle has adopted a competency court model in which competency hearings can be scheduled in as little as 2 hours.

RELEVANT POLICY AND RESEARCH DIRECTIONS

Several policy issues emerge from this chapter. First, there is a need for greater clarity in raising the issue of competence. When defense attorneys were asked what would help them better defend a youth who might be incompetent to stand trial, half identified better access to mental health evaluations and more than one third sought better guidance about when to request a competency evaluation (Viljoen et al., 2010). Second, because of differences among juvenile competency evaluators, some youths are being tried who may not have the capacity to be considered competent by many judges. Greater statutory clarity and practice guidelines would facilitate improved consistency among and between evaluators and jurisdictions. Finally, this approach should be augmented with an abundance of formal training and certification.

Cultural competency is another significant but seldom articulated barrier to optimal service delivery with incompetent youths and their families. With few exceptions (i.e., Heilbrun & Brooks, 2010; Viljoen & Roesch, 2005), academics or practitioners seldom mention or address culture, whether in the context of evaluation practice, assessment of competency via clinician judgment or assessment tools, or remediation services. Yet, the majority of juveniles who are arrested are of minority status and increasingly are nonnative English speakers. Although practice standards are beginning to appear that concern the exclusive use of court-certified interpreters, and some of the restoration tools are being translated into Spanish, the more subtle aspects of culture and how youths from different countries proceed through the adjudicative process in the United States remains a largely unexplored area of practice.

In this chapter, we clearly identified a number of areas requiring further research. The vast majority of youths whose competence is questioned are recommended as competent to stand trial after a competency evaluation. Future research should test the degree of concordance between attorneys' perceptions of juveniles' incompetence to stand trial and clinicians' competency evaluation opinion to identify the level of consistency between these two sources of information (Viljoen et al., 2010). An important component of a competency evaluation involves making a prediction of restorability, yet limited research is available—all pertaining to adults—that identifies factors relevant to the prediction of restorability by mental health clinicians (Parker, 2012; Warren et al., 2013). Scholars are also advocating for the development of new juvenile competence instruments that assess for developmental immaturity, are normed on youths of varying ages, and include an assessment of malingering (Heilbrun & DeMatteo, 2012). Standardized instruments in conjunction with more rigorous training of evaluators would undoubtedly facilitate greater consistency among juvenile competence evaluators within and across the various states that recognize juvenile competency.

Finally, although more courts are recognizing juvenile incompetence, most states lack a uniform or empirically sound programmatic response to it (Viljoen et al., 2012). Current remediation models are based primarily on incapacity predicated on mental illness or intellectual deficits, and even in these domains little is empirically known about the process and outcome that are relevant to these particular populations. There is also little research into remediation for immaturity. A further standardization and the establishment of best practices could ensure the development of more effective, efficient, and cost-effective programming for youths.

CONCLUSIONS

The study of adjudicative competency in juvenile court is one of more interesting and evolving areas of forensic practice and research today. It is replete with legal ambiguities, unanswered questions concerning forensic assessment and opinion formation, insufficiently articulated standards for training, and an emerging legal mandate with few youth-specific tools and programs designed to respond to it. Despite its nascent stage of development, it has been enriched by sophisticated research that has provided important insight into the impact of development on the competency of some youths. As observed by E. S. Scott and Steinberg (2008), however, these advances must now be integrated into juvenile justice policy and the programming that is embedded in it.

The current challenge clearly lies in the development of well-trained juvenile forensic evaluators and remediation service providers coupled with creative, flexible, and compelling interventions that respond to youths of all ages and cultural backgrounds. Only through these practice enhancements can we ensure that competency is not an empty right but rather an extension of established law into a new context capable of protecting the integrity and fairness of the juvenile justice system. Embedded in all of these challenges is the need to integrate the best of what has been learned in diverse fields such as education, mental health, neurobiology, human development, legal decision making, forensic assessment, program development, and the development of evidence-based practices to create an exciting new frontier in the field of forensic research and practice that is responsive to youths of all ages.

References

Advokat, C. D., Guidry, D., Burnett, D. M. R., Manguno-Mire, G., & Thompson, J. W., Jr. (2012). Competency restoration treatment: Differences between defendants declared competent or incompetent to stand trial. *Journal of the American Academy of Psychiatry and the Law*, *40*, 89–97.

American Bar Association. (1982). Criminal justice mental health standards. *Mental Disability Law Reporter*, *6*, 269–295.

American Psychological Association. (2013). Specialty guidelines for forensic psychology. *American Psychologist*, *68*, 7–19. http://dx.doi.org/10.1037/a0029889

Baerger, D. R., Griffin, E. F., Lyons, J. S., & Simmons, R. (2003). Competency to stand trial in preadjudicated and petitioned juvenile defendants. *Journal of the American Academy of Psychiatry and the Law*, *31*, 314–320.

Bennett, G., & Kish, G. (1990). Incompetency to stand trial: Treatment unaffected by demographic variables. *Journal of Forensic Sciences*, *35*, 403–412.

Birckhead, T. R. (2010). Culture clash: The challenge of lawyering across difference in juvenile court. *Rutgers Law Review*, *62*, 959–991.

Bonnie, R. J. (1992). The competence of criminal defendants: A theoretical reformulation. *Behavioral Sciences and the Law*, *10*, 291–316. http://dx.doi.org/10.1002/bsl.2370100303

Bonnie, R. J., & Grisso, T. (2000). Adjudicative competence and youthful offenders. In T. Grisso & R. G. Schwartz (Eds.), *Youth on trial: A developmental perspective on juvenile justice* (pp. 73–103). Chicago, IL: University of Chicago Press.

Bonnie, R. J., & Scott, E. S. (2013). The teenage brain: Adolescent brain research and the law. *Current Directions in Psychological Science*, *22*, 158–161. http://dx.doi.org/10.1177/0963721412471678

Burrell, S., Kendrick, C., & Blalock, B. (2008). Incompetent youth in California justice. *Stanford Law and Policy Review*, *19*, 198–250.

Cauffman, E., & Steinberg, L. (2000). (Im)maturity of judgment in adolescence: Why adolescents may be less culpable than adults. *Behavioral Sciences and the Law*, *18*, 741–760. http://dx.doi.org/10.1002/bsl.416

Cauffman, E., & Steinberg, L. (2012). Emerging findings from research on adolescent development and juvenile justice. *Victims and Offenders*, *7*, 428–449. http://dx.doi.org/10.1080/15564886.2012.713901

Christy, A., Douglas, K. S., Otto, R. K., & Petrila, J. (2004). Juveniles evaluated incompetent to proceed: Characteristics and quality of mental health professionals' evaluations. *Professional Psychology: Research and Practice*, *35*, 380–388. http://dx.doi.org/10.1037/0735-7028.35.4.380

Colwell, K., Colwell, L. H., Perry, A. T., Wasieleski, D., & Billings, T. (2008). The Test of Malingered Incompetence (TOMI): A forced-choice instrument for assessing cognitive malingering in competence to stand trial evaluations. *American Journal of Forensic Psychology*, *26*, 17–42.

Corno, L., & Snow, R. E. (1986). Adapting teaching to individual differences among learners. In M. Wittrock (Ed.), *Handbook of research on teaching* (pp. 605–699). New York, NY: Macmillan.

Cowden, V. L., & McKee, G. R. (1995). Competency to stand trial in juvenile delinquency proceedings: Cognitive maturity and the attorney-client relationship. *Journal of Family Law, 33*, 629–660.

Cox, J. M., Goldstein, N. E. S., Dolores, J., Zelechoski, A. D., & Messenheimer, S. (2012). The impact of juveniles' ages and levels of psychosocial maturity on judges' opinions about adjudicative competence. *Law and Human Behavior, 36*, 21–27. http://dx.doi.org/10.1037/h0093953

Drope v. Missouri, 420 U.S. 162 (1975).

Dusky v. United States, 362 U.S. 402 (1960).

Everington, C., & Luckasson, R. (1992). *Competence assessment for standing trial for defendants with mental retardation: CAST–MR test manual*. Worthington, OH: International Diagnostic Services.

Felthous, A. R. (2011). Commentary: Competence to stand trial in juveniles and the judgment model. *Journal of the American Academy of Psychiatry and the Law, 39*, 327–331.

Ferguson, A. C., Jimenez, M. M., & Jackson, R. L. (2010). Juvenile false confessions and competency to stand trial: Implications for policy reformation and research. *New School Psychology Bulletin, 7*, 62–77.

Figg, C., McCartney, R. W., & Gonsoulin, W. (2009). Differentiating instruction with digital storytelling while making connections to critical literacy. *Teaching and Learning, 5*, 31–44.

Finkle, M. J., Kurth, R., Cadle, C., & Mullan, J. (2009). Competency courts: A creative solution for restoring competency to the competency process. *Behavioral Sciences and the Law, 27*, 767–786. http://dx.doi.org/10.1002/bsl.890

Fogel, M. H., Schiffman, W., Mumley, D., Tillbrook, C., & Grisso, T. (2013). Ten year research update (2001–2010): Evaluations for competence to stand trial (adjudicative competence). *Behavioral Sciences and the Law, 31*, 165–191. http://dx.doi.org/10.1002/bsl.2051

Frost, L. E., & Volenik, A. E. (2004). The ethical perils of representing the juvenile defendant who may be incompetent. *Washington University Journal of Law and Policy, 14*, 327–358.

Furby, L., & Beyth-Marom, R. (1992). Risk taking in adolescence: A decision-making perspective. *Developmental Review, 12*, 1–44. http://dx.doi.org/10.1016/0273-2297(92)90002-J

Godinez v. Moran, 509 U.S. 389 (1993).

Grisso, T. (2000). What we know about youths' capacities as trial defendants. In T. Grisso & R. G. Schwartz (Eds.), *Youth on trial: A developmental perspective on juvenile justice* (pp. 139–171). Chicago, IL: University of Chicago Press.

Grisso, T. (2004). *Double jeopardy: Adolescent offenders with mental disorders*. Chicago, IL: University of Chicago Press.

Grisso, T. (2005). *Evaluating juveniles' adjudicative competence: A guide for clinical practice*. Sarasota, FL: Professional Resource Press.

Grisso, T., Steinberg, L., Woolard, J., Cauffman, E., Scott, E., Graham, S., . . . Schwartz, R. (2003). Juveniles' competence to stand trial: A comparison of adolescents' and adults' capacities as trial defendants. *Law and Human Behavior, 27*, 333–363. http://dx.doi.org/10.1023/A:1024065015717

Group for the Advancement of Psychiatry. (1974). *Misuse of psychiatry in the criminal courts: Competency to stand trial*. New York, NY: Brunner/Mazel.

Heilbronner, R. L. (2011). Structured Interview of Reported Symptoms (SIRS). In J. S. Kreutzer, J. DeLuca, & B. Caplan (Eds.), *Encyclopedia of clinical neuropsychology* (Vol. 99, pp. 2417–2418). New York, NY: Springer. http://dx.doi.org/10.1007/978-0-387-79948-3_848

Heilbrun, K., & Brooks, S. (2010). Forensic psychology and forensic science: A proposed agenda for the next decade. *Psychology, Public Policy, and Law, 16*, 219–253. http://dx.doi.org/10.1037/a0019138

Heilbrun, K., & DeMatteo, D. (2012). Toward establishing standards of practice in juvenile forensic mental health assessment. In E. L. Grigorenko (Ed.), *Handbook of juvenile forensic psychology and psychiatry* (pp. 145–156). http://dx.doi.org/10.1007/978-1-4614-0905-2_10

Hoge, R. D. (2012). Forensic assessments of juveniles: Practice and legal considerations. *Criminal Justice and Behavior, 39*, 1255–1270. http://dx.doi.org/10.1177/0093854812444024

Hoge, S. K., Bonnie, R. J., Poythress, N., Monahan, J., Eisenberg, M., & Feucht-Haviar, T. (1997). The MacArthur Adjudicative Competence Study: Development and validation of a research instrument. *Law and Human Behavior, 21*, 141–179. http://dx.doi.org/10.1023/A:1024826312495

In re Gault, 387 U.S. 1 (1967).

In re Winship, 397 U.S. 358 (1970).

Jackson, S. L., Warren, J. I., & Jones Coburn, J. (2014). A community-based model for remediating juveniles adjudicated incompetent to stand trial: Feedback from youth, attorneys, and judges. *Juvenile and Family Court Judges Journal, 65*, 23–38.

Jackson v. Indiana, 406 U.S. 715 (1972).

Jenkins, J. M. (2000). Looking backward: Educational reform in the twentieth century. *International Journal of Educational Reform, 9*, 74–78.

Keefe, J. W., & Jenkins, J. M. (2008). *Personalized instruction: The key to student achievement* (2nd ed.). Lanham, MD: Rowman & Littlefield Education.

Keith Matthews, S., Krivelyova, A., Stephens, R. L., & Bilchik, S. (2013). Juvenile justice contact of youth in systems of care. *Criminal Justice Policy Review, 24,* 143–165. http://dx.doi.org/10.1177/0887403411422409

Kent v. United States, 383 U.S. 541 (1966).

Kivisto, A. J., Moore, T. M., Fite, P. A., & Seidner, B. G. (2011). Future orientation and competence to stand trial: The fragility of competence. *Journal of the American Academy of Psychiatry and the Law, 39,* 316–326.

Kruh, I., & Grisso, T. (2009). *Evaluation of juveniles' competence to stand trial.* New York, NY: Oxford University Press.

Kruh, I. P., Sullivan, L., Ellis, M., Lexcen, F., & McClellan, J. (2006). Juvenile competence to stand trial: A historical and empirical analysis of a juvenile forensic evaluation service. *International Journal of Forensic Mental Health, 5,* 109–123. http://dx.doi.org/10.1080/14999013.2006.10471236

Larson, K., & Grisso, T.; National Youth Screening & Assessment Project. (2011). *Developing statutes for competence to stand trial in juvenile delinquency proceedings: A guide for law makers.* Worcester, MA: Center for Mental Health Services Research. Retrieved from http://escholarship.umassmed.edu/psych_cmhsr/502

Lipsey, M., Howell, J. C., Kelly, M., Chapman, G., & Carver, D. (2010). *Improving the effectiveness of juvenile justice programs: A new perspective on evidence-based practice.* Washington, DC: Center for Juvenile Justice Reform.

Lipsitt, P. D., Lelos, D., & McGarry, A. L. (1971). Competency for trial: A screening instrument. *American Journal of Psychiatry, 128,* 105–109.

Louisiana Laws, Children's Code 837.1-2 (2005).

Louisiana v. Bennett, 345 So.2d 1129 (1977).

MacKinnon-Lewis, C., Kaufman, M., & Frabutt, J. M. (2002). Juvenile justice and mental health: Youth and families in the middle. *Aggression and Violent Behavior, 7,* 353–363. http://dx.doi.org/10.1016/S1359-1789(01)00062-3

Mayzer, R., Bradley, A. R., Rusinko, H., & Ertelt, T. W. (2009). Juvenile competency to stand trial in criminal court and brain function. *Journal of Forensic Psychiatry and Psychology, 20,* 785–800. http://dx.doi.org/10.1080/14789940903174089

McGaha, A., Otto, R. K., McClaren, M. D., & Petrila, J. (2001). Juveniles adjudicated incompetent to proceed: A descriptive study of Florida's Competence Restoration program. *Journal of the American Academy of Psychiatry and the Law, 29,* 427–437.

McKee, G. R. (1998). Competency to stand trial in preadjudicatory juveniles and adults. *Journal of the American Academy of Psychiatry and the Law, 26,* 89–99.

McKee, G. R., & Shea, S. J. (1999). Competency to stand trial in family court: Characteristics of competent and incompetent juveniles. *Journal of the American Academy of Psychiatry and the Law, 27,* 65–73.

Melton, G. B., Petrila, J., Poythress, N. G., & Slobogin, C. (2007). *Psychological evaluations for the courts: A handbook for mental health professionals and lawyers* (3rd ed.). New York, NY: Guilford Press.

Morris, D. R., & DeYoung, N. J. (2012). Psycholegal abilities and restoration of competence to stand trial. *Behavioral Sciences and the Law, 30,* 710–728. http://dx.doi.org/10.1002/bsl.2040

Morris, D. R., & Parker, G. F. (2008). Jackson's Indiana: State hospital competence restoration in Indiana. *Journal of the American Academy of Psychiatry and the Law, 36,* 522–534.

Morris, G. H., Haroun, A. M., & Naimark, D. (2004). Assessing competency competently: Toward a rational standard for competency-to-stand-trial assessments. *Journal of the American Academy of Psychiatry and the Law, 32,* 231–245.

Mossman, D. (2007). Predicting restorability of incompetent criminal defendants. *Journal of the American Academy of Psychiatry and the Law, 35,* 34–43.

Mossman, D., Noffsinger, S. G., Ash, P., Frierson, R. L., Gerbasi, J., Hackett, M., . . . Zonana, H. V. (2007). AAPL practice guideline for the forensic psychiatric evaluation of competence to stand trial. *Journal of the American Academy of Psychiatry and the Law, 35*(Suppl.), S3–S72.

Murrie, D. C., Boccaccini, M. T., Zapf, P. A., Warren, J. I., & Henderson, C. E. (2008). Clinician variation in findings of competence to stand trial. *Psychology, Public Policy, and Law, 14,* 177–193. http://dx.doi.org/10.1037/a0013578

Nicholson, R. A., Briggs, S. R., & Robertson, H. (1988). Instruments for assessing competency to stand trial: How do they work? *Professional Psychology: Research and Practice, 19,* 383–394. http://dx.doi.org/10.1037/0735-7028.19.4.383

Nicholson, R. A., & Norwood, S. (2000). The quality of forensic psychological assessments, reports, and testimony: Acknowledging the gap between promise and practice. *Law and Human Behavior, 24,* 9–44. http://dx.doi.org/10.1023/A:1005422702678

O'Donnell, P. C., & Gross, B. (2012). Developmental incompetence to stand trial in juvenile courts. *Journal of Forensic Sciences, 57,* 989–996. http://dx.doi.org/10.1111/j.1556-4029.2012.02093.x

Parker, G. F. (2012). The quandary of unrestorability. *Journal of the American Academy of Psychiatry and the Law, 40*, 171–176.

Pate v. Robinson, 383 U.S. 375 (1966).

Pinals, D. A. (2005). Where two roads meet: Restoration of competence to stand trial from a clinical perspective. *New England Journal on Criminal and Civil Confinement, 31*, 81–108.

Pires, S. A. (2002). *Building systems of care: A primer*. Washington, DC: National Technical Assistance Center for Children's Mental Health, Georgetown University Center for Child and Human Development.

Poythress, N., Lexcen, F. J., Grisso, T., & Steinberg, L. (2006). The competence-related abilities of adolescent defendants in criminal court. *Law and Human Behavior, 30*, 75–92. http://dx.doi.org/10.1007/s10979-006-9005-4

Redding, R. E. (2002). Adjudicative competence in the modern juvenile court. *Virginia Journal of Social Policy and the Law, 9*, 353–410.

Redding, R. E., Floyd, M. Y., & Hawk, G. L. (2001). What judges and lawyers think about the testimony of mental health experts: A survey of the courts and bar. *Behavioral Sciences and the Law, 19*, 583–594. http://dx.doi.org/10.1002/bsl.455

Redding, R., & Frost, L. (2001). Adjudicative competence in the modern juvenile court. *Virginia Journal of Social Policy and the Law, 9*, 353–410.

Redlich, A. D. (2007). Double jeopardy in the interrogation room for youths with mental illness. *American Psychologist, 62*, 609–611. http://dx.doi.org/10.1037/0003-066X62.6.609

Rogers, R., & Cruise, K. R. (1998). Assessment of malingering with simulation designs: Threats to external validity. *Law and Human Behavior, 22*, 273–285. http://dx.doi.org/10.1023/A:1025702405865

Rogers, R., & Ewing, C. (2003). The prohibition of ultimate opinions: A misguided enterprise. *Journal of Forensic Psychology Practice, 3*, 65–75. http://dx.doi.org/10.1300/J158v03n03_04

Rogers, R., Grandjean, N., Tillbrook, C. E., Vitacco, M. J., & Sewell, K. W. (2001). Recent interview-based measures of competency to stand trial: A critical review augmented with research data. *Behavioral Sciences and the Law, 19*, 503–518. http://dx.doi.org/10.1002/bsl.458

Rotter, M., & Greenspan, M. (2011). Commentary: Competency restoration research—Complicating an already complex process. *Journal of the American Academy of Psychiatry and the Law, 39*, 307–310.

Ryba, N. L., Cooper, V. G., & Zapf, P. A. (2003). Juvenile competence to stand trial evaluations: A survey of current practices and test usage among psychologists. *Professional Psychology: Research and Practice, 34*, 499–507. http://dx.doi.org/10.1037/0735-7028.34.5.499

Sanborn, J. B. (2009). Juveniles' competency to stand trial: Wading through the rhetoric and the evidence. *Journal of Criminal Law and Criminology, 99*, 135–213.

Santamaria, L. J. (2009). Culturally responsive differentiated instruction: Narrowing gaps between best pedagogical practices benefiting all learners. *Teachers College Record, 111*, 214–247.

Sarkar, S. P. (2011). In the twilight zone: Adolescent capacity in the criminal justice arena. *Advances in Psychiatric Treatment, 17*, 5–11. http://dx.doi.org/10.1192/apt.bp.108.006254

Schwalbe, E., & Medalia, A. (2007). Cognitive dysfunction and competency restoration: Using cognitive remediation to help restore the unrestorable. *Journal of the American Academy of Psychiatry and the Law, 35*, 518–525.

Scott, C. L. (2003). Commentary: A road map for research in restoration of competency to stand trial. *Journal of the American Academy of Psychiatry and the Law, 31*, 36–43.

Scott, E. S., Reppucci, D., & Woolard, J. L. (1995). Evaluating adolescent decision making in legal contexts. *Law and Human Behavior, 19*, 221–244. http://dx.doi.org/10.1007/BF01501658

Scott, E. S., & Steinberg, L. (2008). Adolescent development and the regulation of youth crime. *Future of Children, 18*, 15–33. http://dx.doi.org/10.1353/foc.0.0011

Sell v. United States, 539 U.S. 166 (2003).

Siegel, D. M. (2008). The growing admissibility of expert testimony by clinical social workers on competence to stand trial. *Social Work, 53*, 153–163. http://dx.doi.org/10.1093/sw/53.2.153

Slobogin, C. (2012). Sell's conundrums: The right of incompetent defendants to refuse anti-psychotic medication. *Washington University Law Review, 90*, 1523–1543.

Smith, G. E., & Throne, S. (2007). *Differentiating instruction with technology in K–5 classrooms*. Retrieved from http://www.iste.org/images/excerpts/DIFFK5-excerpt.pdf

Smith, J. C. (2011). *Differentiated instruction: Exploring implementation at the middle level* (Doctoral dissertation). Available from ProQuest Dissertations and Theses database. (UMI No. 3449941)

Soulier, M. (2012). Juvenile offenders: Competence to stand trial. *Psychiatric Clinics of North America, 35*, 837–854. http://dx.doi.org/10.1016/j.psc.2012.08.005

Soulier, M. F., & Scott, C. L. (2010). Juveniles in court. *Harvard Review of Psychiatry, 18*, 317–325. http://dx.doi.org/10.3109/10673229.2010.527518

Steinberg, L. (2007). Risk-taking in adolescence: New perspectives from brain and behavioral science. *Current Directions in Psychological Science*, *16*, 55–59. http://dx.doi.org/10.1111/j.1467-8721.2007.00475.x

Steinberg, L., Graham, S., O'Brien, L., Woolard, J., Cauffman, E., & Banich, M. (2009). Age differences in future orientation and delay discounting. *Child Development*, *80*, 28–44. http://dx.doi.org/10.1111/j.1467-8624.2008.01244.x

Teichner, G., & Wagner, M. T. (2004). The Test of Memory Malingering (TOMM): Normative data from cognitively intact, cognitively impaired, and elderly patients with dementia. *Archives of Clinical Neuropsychiatry*, *19*, 455–464. http://dx.doi.org/10.1016/S0887-6177(03)00078-7

Tillbrook, C., Mumley, D., & Grisso, T. (2003). Avoiding expert opinions on the ultimate legal question: The case for integrity. *Journal of Forensic Psychology Practice*, *3*, 77–87. http://dx.doi.org/10.1300/J158v03n03_05

Tomlinson, C. A. (2000). *Differentiation of instruction in the elementary grades*. Retrieved from http://www.ericdigests.org/2001-2/elementary.html

Tricarico, K., & Yendol-Hoppey, D. (2012). Teacher learning through self-regulation: An exploratory study of alternatively prepared teachers' ability to plan differentiated instruction in an urban elementary school. *Teacher Education Quarterly*, *39*, 139–158.

United States v. Duhon, W.D. La. (2000).

Varela, J. G., Boccaccini, M. T., Gonzalez, E., Jr., Gharagozloo, L., & Johnson, S. M. (2011). Do defense attorney referrals for competence to stand trial evaluations depend on whether the client speaks English or Spanish? *Law and Human Behavior*, *35*, 501–511. http://dx.doi.org/10.1007/s10979-010-9253-1

Viljoen, J. L., & Grisso, T. (2007). Prospects for remediating juveniles' adjudicative incompetence. *Psychology, Public Policy, and Law*, *13*, 87–114. http://dx.doi.org/10.1037/1076-8971.13.2.87

Viljoen, J. L., McLachlan, K., Wingrove, T., & Penner, E. (2010). Defense attorneys' concerns about the competence of adolescent defendants. *Behavioral Sciences and the Law*, *28*, 630–646. http://dx.doi.org/10.1002/bsl.954

Viljoen, J. L., Odgers, C., Grisso, T., & Tillbrook, C. (2007). Teaching adolescents and adults about adjudicative proceedings: A comparison of pre- and post-teaching scores on the MacCAT-CA. *Law and Human Behavior*, *31*, 419–432. http://dx.doi.org/10.1007/s10979-006-9069-1

Viljoen, J. L., Penner, E., & Roesch, R. (2012). Competence and criminal responsibility in adolescent defendants: The role of mental illness and adolescent development. In B. C. Feld & D. Bishop (Eds.), *The Oxford handbook on juvenile crime and juvenile justice* (pp. 526–548). New York, NY: Oxford University Press.

Viljoen, J. L., & Roesch, R. (2005). Competence to waive interrogation rights and adjudicative competence in adolescent defendants: Cognitive development, attorney contact, and psychological symptoms. *Law and Human Behavior*, *29*, 723–742. http://dx.doi.org/10.1007/s10979-005-7978-y

Viljoen, J. L., Vincent, G. M., & Roesch, R. (2006). Assessing adolescent defendants' adjudicative competence: Interrater reliability and factor structure of the Fitness Interview Test–Revised. *Criminal Justice and Behavior*, *33*, 467–487. http://dx.doi.org/10.1177/0093854806287317

Viljoen, J. L., & Wingrove, T. (2007). Adjudicative competence in adolescent defendants: Judges' and defense attorneys' views of legal standards for adolescents in juvenile and criminal court. *Psychology, Public Policy, and Law*, *13*, 204–229. http://dx.doi.org/10.1037/1076-8971.13.3.204

Viljoen, J. L., Wingrove, T., & Ryba, N. L. (2008). Adjudicative competence evaluations of juvenile and adult defendants: Judges' views regarding essential components of competence reports. *International Journal of Forensic Mental Health*, *7*, 107–119. http://dx.doi.org/10.1080/14999013.2008.9914408

Virginia Code § 16.1–356.

Warren, J. I. (2013). *Manual for RestoringYouth Program*. Unpublished manual, University of Virginia.

Warren, J. I., Aaron, J., Ryan, E., Chauhan, P., & DuVal, J. (2003). Correlates of adjudicative competence among psychiatrically impaired juveniles. *Journal of the American Academy of Psychiatry and the Law*, *31*, 299–309.

Warren, J. I., Chauhan, P., Kois, L., Dibble, A., & Knighton, J. (2013). Factors influencing 2,260 opinions of defendants' restorability to adjudicative competency. *Psychology, Public Policy, and Law*, *19*, 498–508. http://dx.doi.org/10.1037/a0034740

Warren, J. I., Duval, J., Komarovskaya, I., Chauhan, P., Buffington-Vollum, J., & Ryan, E. (2009). Developing a forensic service delivery system for juveniles adjudicated incompetent to stand trial. *International Journal of Forensic Mental Health*, *8*, 245–262. http://dx.doi.org/10.1080/14999011003635670

Warren, J. I., Rosenfeld, B., Fitch, W. L., & Hawk, G. (1997). Forensic mental health clinical evaluation: An analysis of interstate and intersystemic differences. *Law and Human Behavior*, *21*, 377–390. http://dx.doi.org/10.1023/A:1024855118855

Zapf, P. A., & Roesch, R. (2006). Competency to stand trial: A guide for evaluators. In A. K. Hess & I. B. Weiner (Eds.), *Handbook of forensic psychology* (3rd ed., pp. 305–331). New York, NY: Wiley.

Zapf, P. A., & Roesch, R. (2011). Future directions in the restoration of competency to stand trial. *Current Directions in Psychological Science*, *20*, 43–47. http://dx.doi.org/10.1177/0963721410396798

Part VII

INTERVENTIONS AND COSTS

CHAPTER 24

RISK REDUCTION INTERVENTIONS FOR ADOLESCENT OFFENDERS

Jodi L. Viljoen, Etta Brodersen, Catherine Shaffer, and Robert J. McMahon

When an adolescent commits a crime, youth justice professionals must make important decisions about which interventions to provide. Judges must decide whether to incarcerate an adolescent or use community-based treatments. Youth probation officers and case managers face decisions regarding whether to refer the adolescent to therapy and, if so, what kind. Also, mental health professionals must make ongoing decisions about specific issues to address in therapy (e.g., anger management skills, problem-solving skills) and specific techniques to use (e.g., cognitive–behavioral therapy [CBT], specific skills training).

The treatment-related decisions that professionals make have a tremendous impact; if effective and empirically supported approaches are used, many adolescents can successfully desist from offending and achieve important developmental milestones (e.g., complete high school, obtain a stable job, develop healthy relationships; Henggeler & Sheidow, 2012). Furthermore, preventing a single youth from engaging in a life of crime saves society $2.6 million to $5 million, including savings in the costs of operating the justice system (e.g., running youth detention facilities) and addressing harms that victims experience (e.g., providing medical and mental health treatment to victims; Cohen & Piquero, 2009).

Conversely, if ineffective strategies are used, adolescents' criminal behavior can escalate, become entrenched, and spiral into other difficulties, such as substance abuse, unemployment, early parenthood, and perpetration of family violence, such as violence toward their children or intimate partners (Moffitt, Caspi, Harrington, & Milne, 2002). In fact, although theory from the 1990s asserted that most adolescent offenders are adolescent-limited offenders who desist from offending as they mature and enter adulthood, more recent research has shown that individuals who start offending during adolescence do not necessarily spontaneously desist (Moffitt et al., 2002; Piquero, Diamond, Jennings, & Reingle, 2013). Furthermore, individuals who begin offending at an earlier age, in childhood, show high persistence in reoffending. In other words, it is not feasible to simply wait until youths mature out of their offending behavior. Instead, implementation of effective interventions is essential.

To guide intervention planning and delivery, two independent bodies of research have developed. The first focuses on risk assessment and risk management (Heilbrun, 2003). It is led primarily by forensic researchers, who have developed risk assessment tools and intervention-matching principles. The second body of research is often referred to as "what-works" research. It is led by intervention researchers and child clinical or developmental psychologists who have identified empirically supported intervention programs. In general, risk assessment and risk management research tends to focus heavily on front-line assessments by professionals from various disciplines (e.g., youth probation officers, psychologists) and overarching principles of risk reduction (e.g., matching services to youths' needs). In comparison, research on what works focuses on specific interventions provided by trained therapists. However, these models are

http://dx.doi.org/10.1037/14643-024
APA Handbook of Psychology and Juvenile Justice, K. Heilbrun (Editor-in-Chief)

not mutually exclusive. In fact, as we argue, there is a strong need for better integration, because both assessment and intervention are important to facilitate risk reduction efforts. As a starting point, we briefly describe the history of relevant laws and policies pertaining to interventions for adolescent offenders. We highlight ways in which policy developments have driven research on risk reduction, as well as how research has influenced policies.

REHABILITATIVE FOCUS OF THE JUVENILE JUSTICE SYSTEM: HISTORY OF LAWS AND POLICIES

Early juvenile justice systems in the United States, Canada, and elsewhere developed with a focus on interventions and a strong belief in adolescents' potential for change (Illinois Juvenile Court Act, 1899; Mack, 1909). In writing about the early juvenile court, Judge Julian Mack (1909) wrote "The work of the juvenile court, is at best, palliative, curative. The most important, indeed the vital thing, is to prevent the children from reaching that condition in which they have to be dealt with in any court" (p. 122).

In the ensuing decades, however, sociologists came to view rehabilitation efforts (for juveniles and adults) with increasing skepticism (Cullen, 2012). Their primary concern centered on the enormous discretion afforded to social welfare agencies and the possibility that this discretion could lead to abuses of power. During the 1970s, serious criticisms were also raised regarding the effectiveness of rehabilitative approaches. This attack is often traced to an article titled "What Works?—Questions and Answers About Prison Reform" (Martinson, 1974). In this review, Martinson concluded that "with few and isolated exceptions, the rehabilitative efforts that have been reported so far have had no appreciable effect on recidivism" (p. 25). Martinson noted that although juvenile offenders might presumably be more amenable to treatment than adults, he did not find clear evidence of this. He offered two possible explanations for his bleak conclusions. First, "it may be simply that our programs aren't good enough" (p. 223). Second, it could be that current rehabilitative strategies, more generally, simply "cannot overcome, or even appreciably reduce, the powerful tendency of offenders to continue in criminal behavior" (p. 49). Lawmakers and policymakers quickly latched onto Martinson's article, interpreting his results to mean that nothing works and rallying for a punitive approach to crime control.

At around this same time, courts started to raise concerns that juvenile offenders were sometimes given lengthy periods of detention under the guise of treatment and with little consideration to their rights. For instance, in the case of *In re Gault* (1967), a 15-year-old boy made a lewd and indecent prank telephone call to his neighbor. He was sentenced to a state industrial school until age 21 (i.e., the equivalent of a 6-year sentence) in an effort to rehabilitate him. In comparison, had Gault been an adult, he would have received a fine of $5 to $50 or been sentenced to up to 2 months in jail.

Thus, this case and the cases that followed extended various adult rights to adolescents, such as the right to an attorney and the right against self-incrimination (*Breed v. Jones*, 1975; *Fare v. Michael C.*, 1979; *In re Winship*, 1970). With these reforms, the distinction between the juvenile and adult criminal justice system began to blur. Against this backdrop, courts continued to grapple with the issue of "should we punish?" or "should we treat?" (Reader, 1996, p. 477). Noting this ambivalence between treatment and punishment, Roscoe Pound, dean of the Harvard Law School, described the juvenile court as being like the child of "an illicit relationship between the legal profession and the social work profession," noting that "now no one wants to claim the little bastard" (Reader, 1996, p. 477).

In the 1990s, the balance again tipped to emphasize punitive approaches to youth crime. At this time, crime statistics showed some increases in rates of adolescent offending (Snyder, Sickmund, & Poe-Yamagata, 1996). As public concerns about youth violence and juvenile superpredators soared, many states implemented punitive laws (Grisso, 2001). Lawmakers lowered the age at which a child could be transferred to adult court to as young as 12 (or younger in some jurisdictions) and implemented rules whereby adolescents could be automatically transferred if they committed certain types of crime, violent or nonviolent. Schools also started to funnel youths toward the juvenile justice system at high rates. Under zero-tolerance policies, youths were automatically expelled from schools if they engaged in any form of deviant or disallowed behaviors (American Psychological Association, 2008). For instance, in one case, a child was reportedly expelled for pointing a chicken wing as a weapon (Steinberg, 2003).

The so-called epidemic of youth violence turned out to be relatively short lived. Juvenile crime rates had stabilized or even declined by the early 2000s (Snyder, 2004). However, the reactive laws and policies that were set in motion during this era remain. In some contexts, there are signs of a return to a less punitive and more rehabilitative ethos. In 2005, for example, the U.S. Supreme Court overturned the death penalty for juvenile offenders, arguing that adolescents lack the maturity of judgment and culpability of adults (*Roper v. Simmons*, 2005). More recently, the U.S. Supreme Court placed greater restrictions on the use of life sentences for adolescents (*Graham v. Florida*, 2010; *Miller v. Alabama*, 2012).

In other contexts, however, there is a general disregard for treatment and developmental issues. For example, in the United States, sex offender registry laws have been extended to youths; under these new laws, adolescents who commit certain sexual offenses are automatically placed on registries (including publicly accessible registries), potentially for the rest of their life (Adam Walsh Child Protection and Safety Act, 2006). This practice is inconsistent with research that has shown that many adolescents who have committed sexual offenses do not sexually reoffend and that treatment for this population can be very effective (Letourneau et al., 2013). In Canada, recent government reforms require courts to consider the possibility of adult sentences for youths in a broader set of cases (Cook & Roesch, 2012). However, adultlike penalties have not been found to reduce reoffending (e.g., Bishop, Frazier, Lanza-Kaduce, & Winner, 1996; Lanza-Kaduce, Lane, Bishop, & Frazier, 2005).

In the remainder of this chapter, we describe risk assessment and risk management research and what-works research. These two different streams of research were both born out of a general concern about an indiscriminate reliance on punitive approaches and a desire to identify more effective strategies to reduce crime.

RISK ASSESSMENT AND RISK MANAGEMENT RESEARCH

Risk assessment research first arose in forensic (i.e., legal) settings involving adults (Skeem & Monahan, 2011). In these contexts, legal decisions, such as whether to incarcerate an offender, are based on a consideration of the individual's "dangerousness" or risk to others, among other factors (e.g., severity of offense). To inform these decisions, courts often seek guidance from mental health professionals, assigning them the challenging task of identifying whether an individual is at high risk for future violence. To provide professionals with an evidence-based approach for these assessments, researchers compiled empirically supported risk (and protective) factors to form risk assessment tools.

Early risk assessment tools quickly took off and rapidly spread throughout justice and forensic systems (Archer, Buffington-Vollum, Stredny, & Handel, 2006). Given their popularity, researchers soon made efforts to develop risk assessment tools designed specifically for adolescents (Viljoen, Cruise, Nicholls, Desmarais, & Webster, 2012; Vincent, Terry, & Maney, 2009). Rather than solely predicting whether an adolescent will offend, many of these tools also aim to guide intervention planning. Indeed, juvenile risk assessment reports tend to place a greater focus on intervention planning than do adult risk assessment reports (Viljoen, McLachlan, & Vincent, 2010).

At its core, research on risk assessment is based on an assumption that one size does not fit all and that justice-involved adolescents are a very heterogeneous group. Although some adolescent offenders pose a high risk for reoffending, many are relatively low risk and can be safely managed in community settings. In addition, adolescents offend for many different reasons. For instance, one adolescent might commit violence because of callous and unemotional personality features, whereas another might do so as a result of emotional reactivity or affiliations with delinquent peers (Frick, 2012). As a result, youths might require tailored interventions.

Thus, the goal of risk assessment is to identify youths' needs in order to assist in planning individualized risk management or risk reduction efforts. Risk management is typically defined broadly to include not only formal therapy programs, but also other approaches (e.g., supervision, monitoring, and victim safety planning) that are used by justice and mental health professionals (Doyle & Logan, 2012; Hart et al., 2003). The risk–need–responsivity (RNR) model provides a framework that bridges risk assessment to risk management efforts.

Risk–Need–Responsivity Model of Offender Rehabilitation

The RNR model is based on an integrated theory of crime that Andrews and Bonta (1994, 2010a) referred to as the personal, interpersonal, and community reinforcement perspective. This perspective draws from general personality and cognitive social learning approaches. Although originally developed for adult offenders, the RNR model has been extended to adolescents. The RNR model offers three main principles for risk management: the risk principle, the needs principle, and the responsivity principle. A meta-analysis found that interventions that adhered to these principles showed a moderate effect size in reducing recidivism ($r = .26$), whereas those that did not showed no effect ($r = -.02$; Andrews & Bonta, 2010).

Risk principle: More intense intervention for higher risk youths. The risk principle asserts that interventions should match the youth's level of risk, with more intensive interventions for higher risk youths than for lower risk youths (Andrews & Bonta, 2010a, 2010b). As the RNR model notes, more crime can be prevented by targeting high-risk youths because they are responsible for more crime than low-risk youths. Furthermore, overprogramming youths who are low risk may not only waste limited resources but even increase risk. For instance, referring low-risk youths to group therapy with high-risk youths could expose youths to antisocial peers and serve as a gateway to more serious crime (Dodge, Dishion, & Lansford, 2007).

Consistent with the risk principle, a meta-analysis showed that intensive interventions were associated with greater reductions in offending among high-risk adolescents than among low-risk adolescents (Andrews & Dowden, 2006; see also Conduct Problems Prevention Research Group, 2010; Lipsey, 2009). In comparison, intensive interventions for low-risk youths appear to simply produce a small and negligible impact (Andrews & Dowden, 2006). However, more services for high-risk youths do not necessarily result in reduced reoffending (Singh et al., 2014). Instead, reoffense risk is likely contingent on the quality of services, their intensity, and the extent to which they address youths' individual needs.

Needs principle: Target criminogenic needs. The needs principle states that adolescents should be matched to interventions that target their criminogenic needs (Andrews & Bonta, 2010a, 2010b). Criminogenic needs are defined as dynamic or changeable risk factors that, when decreased, can reduce risk of offending; they include antisocial personality patterns, antisocial attitudes and beliefs, antisocial peers and associates, family circumstances, school and work, leisure and recreation, and substance abuse (Andrews & Bonta, 2010b; Simourd & Andrews, 1994). In contrast, factors such as low self-esteem or vague personal or emotional problems are not considered criminogenic needs, because these variables are generally not strong predictors of offending (Andrews & Bonta, 2010b).

Consistent with the needs principle, meta-analyses have indicated that interventions are most effective when they target well-established criminogenic needs (Andrews & Bonta, 2010b; Dowden & Andrews, 2000). In contrast, interventions that target noncriminogenic needs (e.g., vague emotional problems, fear of punishment) yield poor effects. The RNR model asserts not only that should interventions address criminogenic needs, but also that individual youths should be provided with interventions that address their particular criminogenic needs. For instance, if substance use is a primary risk factor for a youth's offending, then he or she should receive substance use treatment, whereas if antisocial peers drive the adolescent's offending, then interventions should focus on reducing these negative peer affiliations. Several recent studies have found that the individualized matching of interventions to juveniles' criminogenic needs results in decreased reoffending (Luong & Wormith, 2011; Singh et al., 2014). In a 3-year follow-up study, youths who had many unaddressed criminogenic needs (i.e., youths for whom only 0%–25% of needs were addressed through interventions) were 18 times more likely to reoffend than youths whose criminogenic needs were generally addressed (i.e., youths for whom 75%–100% of needs were addressed; Vieira, Skilling, & Peterson-Badali, 2009). That said, one study reported that matching services to criminogenic needs is associated with decreased offending in boys but not in girls (Vitopoulos, Peterson-Badali, & Skilling, 2012). One possible explanation is that girls may have some additional needs, beyond those included in the RNR model, that are important to address in interventions (e.g., history of victimization, relationship difficulties; Cauffman, 2008), but further research is needed.

Responsivity principle: Tailor interventions to youths' characteristics. Whereas the need principle focuses on what to address in interventions, the responsivity principle focuses on how to deliver interventions (Polaschek, 2011). The responsivity principle has two components (Andrews & Bonta, 2010a, 2010b). First, it emphasizes that service providers should maximize the effectiveness of interventions by providing cognitive–behavioral treatment. This is referred to as *general responsivity*, in that the RNR model considers cognitive social learning approaches (e.g., positive reinforcement, prosocial modeling, problem solving) to be relevant to all offenders. Second, the responsivity principle asserts that interventions should be fine-tuned and tailored to a particular youth's strengths, abilities, motivation, and learning style; this is referred to as *specific responsivity* because it is specific to a youth. For instance, if a youth has a learning disability, he or she should receive interventions that are appropriate for this population, such as interventions that use simplified materials and visual aids.

Consistent with the general responsivity principle, research has supported the effectiveness of cognitive–behavioral interventions for adolescent offenders (Landenberger & Lipsey, 2005; Lipsey, 2009). Limited research, however, has examined the specific responsivity principle. In one study, Vieira et al. (2009) reported that match to five potential responsivity factors (e.g., mental health functioning, cognitive functioning, culture and language) did not significantly affect reoffense rates. However, the authors noted that this null finding may be the result of challenges in measuring responsivity factors. In comparison, Singh et al. (2014) found that matching interventions to key strengths resulted in reduced reoffending among youths in custody, providing some support for strengths as a responsivity consideration in this context.

Risk Assessment Tools as a Method to Facilitate Adherence to RNR Principles

Within the RNR model, risk assessment tools are viewed as a vehicle to transport the RNR principles to practice (Andrews & Bonta, 2010b). In other words, professionals are supposed to use risk assessment tools to match a youth to interventions that are the appropriate level of intensity (i.e., risk principle) and that target that youth's particular needs (i.e., needs principle). The uptake of adolescent risk assessment tools has been remarkable. In a clinician survey, 97% of forensic psychologists reported using violence risk assessment tools in their adolescent risk assessment (Viljoen et al., 2010).

Numerous studies have indicated that adolescent risk tools can significantly predict reoffending and violence; the predictive validity of leading tools, such as the Structured Assessment of Violence Risk in Youth (SAVRY; Borum, Bartel, & Forth, 2006) and the Youth Level of Service/Case Management Inventory (YLS/CMI; Hoge & Andrews, 2011), generally falls in the moderate range (Olver, Stockdale, & Wormith, 2009; Viljoen, Mordell, & Beneteau, 2012). However, virtually nothing is known about whether risk assessment tools help to match adolescent offenders to appropriate interventions. Research has started to examine this area.

In one of the earliest studies on this topic, Flores, Travis, and Latessa (2003) observed that youth probation officers generally did not use their risk assessments (with the YLS/CMI) to plan their risk reduction strategies. Specifically, only 43% of practitioners reported that they used YLS/CMI assessments to guide treatment goals. In addition, this study did not find significant associations between youths' identified needs and the interventions they received, with the exception being that youths at one study site were more likely to receive substance abuse treatment if they had identified needs in this area.

Other researchers have found similar results. Vieira et al. (2009) reported that the average match between youths' needs (as identified with the YLS/CMI) and the interventions they received was 35%, meaning that only 35% of youths' identified needs were addressed. Risk–need matching was lowest in the following domains: family problems, antisocial attitudes, and peer relationships. Singh et al. (2014) found that, after the implementation of the Short-Term Assessment of Risk and Treatability: Adolescent Version (Nicholls, Viljoen, Cruise, Desmarais, & Webster, 2010; Viljoen, Nicholls, Cruise, Desmarais, & Webster, 2014), critical vulnerabilities were comprehensively addressed by case managers in only about half of youths' intervention plans. Key strengths were addressed less often (i.e., a quarter of cases).

Luong and Wormith (2011) reported somewhat more promising results, which they attributed to the careful policies and intensive training that the study site implemented. They reported a significant correlation between risk level, as identified by the Level of Service Inventory—Saskatchewan Youth Edition and the level of supervision that youth probation officers provided ($r = .66$), meaning that higher risk youths received more intensive supervision. Furthermore, for most of the inventory's subscales, the interventions that youths received corresponded with their needs in the area (i.e., needs and intervention matched for 60% or more youths). However, Luong and Wormith reported that many youths received more interventions than needed in the area of education and employment (i.e., 79% of youths with low or very low needs in this area received education or employment interventions). Conversely, a substantial proportion of youths with moderate or high antisocial patterns (31%) did not receive interventions in this domain.

The above-described studies examine risk reduction after the implementation of risk assessment tools. Given that they examined only a single time period (i.e., postimplementation), this research cannot say whether the implementation of a risk assessment tool improves or changes risk reduction efforts. For instance, it is possible that adherence to the RNR principles was poor at these study sites before the implementation of a tool and that implementation improved adherence somewhat, although it remained inadequate.

To date, only one set of studies has tested the impact of adolescent risk assessment on risk reduction using a pre- and postimplementation design (Vincent, Guy, Gershenson, & McCabe, 2012; Vincent, Paiva-Salisbury, Cook, Guy, & Perrault, 2012). In this seminal research, Vincent, Guy, et al. (2012) and Vincent, Paiva-Salisbury, et al. (2012) implemented the SAVRY and the YLS/CMI in several U.S. states. Ten months after the implementation of these tools, 80% of juvenile probation officers reported that they used the tools to guide youths' referrals to services, and 90% reported using the tools to inform their decisions about youths' supervision level (e.g., frequency of contacts with youths; Vincent, Paiva-Salisbury, et al., 2012). Moreover, at one study site, the implementation of the SAVRY resulted in significant reductions in incarceration rates, increased rates of youths being supervised in the community, and increased service referrals for high-risk youths (Vincent, Guy, et al., 2012). However, the implementation of a risk assessment tool did not directly result in reduced youth reoffending rates. Given that many steps must occur between risk assessment and reductions in reoffending, this finding is not surprising. In particular, even if risk assessment tools help front-line staff identify needs, staff must then be able to determine which particular risk reduction strategies can effectively target those needs. Furthermore, these strategies and services (e.g., evidence-based treatment programs such as CBT and functional family therapy, or FFT) must be locally available, and adolescents (and their families) must be willing to participate in them.

Overall, these studies have demonstrated that the adoption of a risk assessment tool does not automatically increase adherence to the RNR principles, although it has the potential to help. Instead, additional efforts (e.g., policies, training, access to evidence-based treatments) must be put in place to translate risk assessments into effective interventions.

Summary and Challenges

The RNR model has provided a much-needed framework for linking research on risk and protective factors to interventions and risk reduction strategies. In general, research has provided support for the risk, need, and responsivity principles (Andrews & Bonta, 2010b). Currently, one of the biggest hurdles that professionals face is how to translate the RNR model to practice, especially because the implementation of a risk assessment tool does not, in and of itself, ensure adherence to the RNR principles. As we discuss later, however, some efforts are being made to increase the uptake of RNR principles.

Several additional concerns have been raised about the RNR model. Some authors have asserted that it leads to an overfocus on prevention of reoffending rather than bringing about positive outcomes, such as contributing to an adolescent's overall healthy development (e.g., school success, healthy relationships; Ward, Yates, & Willis, 2012). In other words, it tends to focus on what benefits society rather than on what benefits the adolescent, although it can be argued that reduced offending benefits not only society but the adolescent as well (Polaschek, 2011).

Because the RNR model was developed primarily for adult offenders, it emphasizes individually oriented CBT rather than family approaches. Given that family approaches have strong support for adolescents (Henggeler & Schoenwald, 2011), this is a potential limitation. However, RNR principles appear relevant to family therapy in that family therapy is more effective when it targets criminogenic needs (Dowden & Andrews, 2003). Finally, as Polaschek (2011) described, the RNR model is a broad framework that provides some overarching principles to guide interventions. However, it does not provide a specific treatment guide or program, nor does it offer much guidance on intervention design, treatment plans, or measuring treatment-related change (Polaschek, 2011). However, research on what works has helped to fill this gap through the development and evaluation of specific intervention programs. Key findings from this body of research are described next.

WHAT-WORKS RESEARCH

Research on what works for adolescent offenders exploded in the 1990s. The Blueprints for Violence Prevention Project took on a pivotal role in reviewing existing programs and cataloguing effective and ineffective approaches (Elliot & Mihalic, 2004; Mihalic, Irwin, Elliott, Fagan, & Hansen, 2001; Muller & Mihalic, 1999). From more than 100 programs that were reviewed, the Blueprints Project identified three programs for adolescent offenders that had adequate support: multisystemic therapy (MST; Henggeler, Schoenwald, Borduin, Rowland, & Cunningham, 2009), FFT (Alexander & Parsons, 1973, 1982), and multidimensional treatment foster care (MTFC; Muller & Mihalic, 1999). Adequate support was defined as experimental evidence that the intervention significantly reduced offending and that this effect was sustained for at least 1 year, replication of positive findings in at least one additional site, and use of a randomized or quasi-experimental design with random assignment or a matched control group (Muller & Mihalic, 1999).

Research on these model programs (i.e., MST, FFT, MTFC) attracted the attention of youth justice agencies, policymakers, and practitioners alike. This was particularly true of MST (Henggeler, Melton, & Smith, 1992), which emerged at a crucial point in history. At a time when adolescents were being incarcerated at higher rates than before, MST provided evidence that community-based interventions could provide a safer, more effective, and cheaper alternative to incarceration (Borduin et al., 1995; Henggeler et al., 1992). MST has also turned attention to the importance of proper implementation, fidelity, and adherence to interventions (Henggeler, Melton, Brondino, Scherer, & Hanley, 1997). Even the best interventions do not work if agencies and practitioners do not adhere to them.

Since the 1990s, research on evidence-based interventions has continued to grow at a rapid pace. Hundreds of studies have now been conducted on interventions for adolescent offenders, including more than 20 meta-analyses of various interventions such as Scared Straight, boot camps, and family and parenting interventions (e.g., Petrosino, Turpin-Petrosino, & Buehler, 2003; D. B. Wilson, MacKenzie, & Mitchell, 2008; Woolfenden, Williams, & Peat, 2001). Researchers have increasingly focused on the specific mechanisms that underlie effective interventions (S. J. Huey, Henggeler, Brondino, & Pickrel, 2000), as well as on strategies by which to successfully implement interventions in real-world settings

(Schoenwald, McHugh, & Barlow, 2012). Below, we review major findings from what-works research, starting with those interventions that have been disproven or lack research support.

What Does Not Work?

Most interventions and approaches to reduce adolescent offending were developed with good intentions. Nevertheless, some of these well-intentioned approaches simply do not work; worse yet, some have harmful effects on youths. As Cullen (2012) noted, the justice field is "littered with interventions—from the penitentiary to boot camps—that were 'creative' but proved to be examples of quackery" (pp. 12–13).

Severe penalties. Although the public and policymakers often call for more serious penalties for youth crime (e.g., transfer to adult court, long periods of incarceration), research has shown that severe penalties generally do not reduce adolescent offending (Lambie & Randell, 2013). For instance, youths who are transferred to adult courts have been found to reoffend at equally high rates (or higher rates, in some cases) than matched youths who are retained in juvenile court (e.g., Bishop et al., 1996; Lanza-Kaduce et al., 2005). One reason that punitive sanctions are ineffective is that, to be effective, punishments must be immediate and consistently delivered (Andrews & Bonta, 2010b). In practice, however, significant delays exist between the time at which an adolescent commits an offense and his or her punishment. Another reason that punishment has little deterrent value is that, compared with adults, adolescents have more limited capacities to consider the long-term consequences of their actions because the brain regions responsible for planning (i.e., frontal lobes) have not yet fully developed (Steinberg, 2010). Finally, many crimes go undetected, so there is no punishment at all.

Although harsh sanctions generally do not appear effective, it is likely that courts will continue to use these penalties in at least some cases. As such, rather than simply asking "whether transfer is good or bad, research must offer guidance on where to redraw the line for determining transfer to do the most good and the least harm" (Loughran et al., 2010, p. 486). For instance, the Pathways to Desistance Study (Loughran et al., 2010) reported that although transfer to adult court had an overall null effect on reoffending, it was associated with somewhat reduced rates of reoffending among adolescents who had committed violent offenses. Additional research is needed. Even at this time, however, it is clear that courts should opt for less restrictive options, such as diversion or juvenile court, as a first course of action (Johnson, Lanza-Kaduce, & Woolard, 2011), and administer sanctions with graduated severity and matched to a youth's particular risk level (Lambie & Randell, 2013).

Scare tactics. Scared Straight programs, also known as juvenile awareness programs, typically involve arranging for at-risk youths to meet incarcerated adult offenders who describe the dangers and downsides of a criminal lifestyle. The most famous of these programs was implemented in New Jersey in the 1970s and involved adult male inmates describing exaggerated experiences of prison violence and rape to at-risk and delinquent adolescents (Finckenauer, 1982). An award-winning documentary followed the New Jersey program and reported that 94% of youths who participated did not commit offenses within the first 3 months after program completion (Petrosino et al., 2003). Fueled by this positive media attention, these programs rapidly spread throughout the United States.

However, research has since shown Scared Straight programs to be ineffective. A follow-up study on the New Jersey program revealed that, contrary to initial reports, it had no effect on youths' attitudes toward crime, and it appeared to increase reoffending (Finckenauer, 1982). Specifically, 41% of youths who participated in this program committed new offenses within 6 months of program completion compared with 11% of youths in the control group. More recently, a meta-analysis concluded that Scared Straight programs "result in an increase in criminality" and "doing nothing would have been better than exposing juveniles to the program" (Petrosino et al., 2003, p. 58). The iatrogenic effects could be because these programs glamorize criminal lifestyles, lack a rehabilitative component, and are too short in duration to have a meaningful long-term impact (Klenowski, Bell, & Dodson, 2010). Furthermore, whereas these programs focus on scaring adolescents about the costs of crime, adolescents are hard-wired to place an emphasis on the rewards and benefits of their behaviors rather than their costs.

As a result of the negative findings regarding these programs, the Office of Juvenile Justice and Delinquency Program has refused to fund Scared Straight programs and cautioned agencies against these programs (Office of Juvenile Justice and Delinquency Prevention, 2011). Nevertheless, these programs continue to be used in the United States, Canada, Australia, Germany, Norway, and the United Kingdom (Petrosino, Turpin-Petrosino, Hollis-Peel, & Lavenberg, 2013). Furthermore, media sources, such as the popular television series "Beyond Scared Straight," continue to portray these programs as more effective than they actually are.

Group therapy. Given that group therapy is more cost-effective than individual approaches, youth justice agencies often rely on group therapy (Dodge et al., 2007; Handwerk, Field, & Friman, 2000). However, concerns have been raised that group interventions with antisocial youths may result in a peer-contagion or iatrogenic effect (Dodge et al., 2007). Specifically, when antisocial youths are included in groups, they can exert a powerful antisocial influence on their peers through modeling and reinforcement of antisocial behavior; this is referred to as *deviancy training* (Dishion, Spracklen, Andrews, & Patterson, 1996).

Indeed, several studies have found increases in delinquent behavior, such as offending and substance use, as a result of youth participation in group intervention programs (e.g., Dishion et al., 1996; Poulin, Dishion, & Burraston, 2001). Other studies, however, have failed to find iatrogenic effects (Lipsey, 2006; Weiss et al., 2005). As such, some authors have asserted that the iatrogenic effect may be overstated, especially given that group therapy constitutes only a very limited proportion of the total time that adolescents spend with peers (Handwerk et al., 2000; Weiss et al., 2005).

The effectiveness of group therapy, and its potential iatrogenic effects, may vary depending on the type of group. In particular, structured groups may be less vulnerable to iatrogenic effects than groups that are relatively unstructured and peer directed. In addition, groups might have a more negative impact on some youths than on others; low-risk youths who are placed in a group consisting primarily of higher risk youths may be more likely to be negatively influenced than youths who are already well entrenched in delinquent peer groups (Arnold & Hughes, 1999). At this time, however, limited research has examined which populations are most vulnerable to iatrogenic effects or what factors may mediate or moderate the relationship.

Wilderness challenge programs. Wilderness challenge programs were first introduced in the 1960s for adolescents engaging in problem behaviors (e.g., offending, substance abuse). These group-based programs typically teach adolescents survival skills in a wilderness setting (e.g., building shelter, preparing food) and engage adolescents in physically challenging activities (e.g., long hikes, canoeing, rafting). Some wilderness challenge programs offer group, individual, and family therapy as part of the program; however, this is not commonplace (Becker, 2010).

In general, wilderness challenge programs have limited research support (Cason & Gillis, 1994; Hattie, Marsh, Neill, & Richards, 1997). Unfortunately, the vast majority of wilderness challenge programs are not evaluated (Gillis, Gass, & Russell, 2008), resulting in uncertainty regarding their effectiveness (Tarolla, Wagner, Rabinowitz, & Tubman, 2002). In addition, improvements from wilderness challenge programs quickly disappear after program completion (Lipsey & Wilson, 1998; Russell, 2000), possibly because it is difficult to generalize skills that youths learn in wilderness environments back in their natural setting. That said, wilderness challenge programs tend to be more successful if they include therapy, are physically intense, involve a residential format, and are multidimensional (i.e., target multiple domains of youth functioning; Hattie et al., 1997; S. J. Wilson & Lipsey, 2000). Programs such as Wilderness Adventure Therapy (Crisp & Hinch, 2004) and Behavior Management Through Adventure (Gillis et al., 2008) are examples of programs that are standardized and have shown positive effects such as decreasing offending and improving mental health, coping skills, and family functioning (Crisp & Hinch, 2004; Gillis et al., 2008).

Boot camps. Boot camps are short term (e.g., 2- to 14-month) incarceration programs that are modeled after basic training in the military with military-style structures, rules, and discipline (Gover, MacKenzie, & Armstrong, 2000; MacKenzie & Herbert, 1996). Adolescents participate in drills, ceremonies, and physical training and receive punishment for misbehavior (e.g., push-ups, running laps). Boot camps are primarily intended for nonviolent, first-time offenders and implemented with the goal of improving an offender's attitudes and behaviors to reduce the likelihood of recidivism, as well as to reduce prison populations and costs (MacKenzie, 1990; MacKenzie, Wilson, & Kider, 2001).

Although advocates in favor of boot camps have argued that they are conducive to positive growth and change (Clark & Aziz, 1996; MacKenzie & Herbert, 1996), there is little evidence to suggest that boot camps have any positive effects in treating delinquency (Lipsey, 1992). For example, a review conducted by MacKenzie et al. (2001) found equal odds of recidivism between boot camps and comparison groups (i.e., 49% and 50%, respectively), suggesting that boot camps do not offer any advantages over incarceration or community supervision.

What Works? Empirically Supported Approaches

Although some risk reduction strategies, such as harsh penalties, scare tactics, and unstructured group therapy, have limited research support, research has dispelled the myth that nothing works. Indeed, effective reoffense reduction strategies can reduce reoffending by as much as 50% (Andrews & Bonta, 2006). Below, we discuss supported approaches, including the impact of the intervention on reoffending, as well as whether it reduces risk factors for offending (e.g., anger management difficulties, coping problems) or builds protective factors (e.g., connections to others). We highlight effectiveness across gender and ethnicity when such information is available.

Approaches that target family and social environment. Family and multicomponent social-ecological interventions are among the most widely supported intervention strategies for adolescent offenders. For instance, each of the three model programs that the Blueprints for Violence Prevention identified (i.e., MST, FFT, MTFC) focuses on the youth's environment and family context (Henggeler & Schoenwald, 2011).

Multisystemic therapy. MST is a highly individualized, ecologically-based treatment for adolescent offenders (Henggeler, Schoenwald, et al., 2009). MST is provided over a 4- to 6-month period by a therapist who is available to the family 24 hours a day, 7 days a week. Therapists draw from a variety of approaches, including strategic family therapy, behavioral parent training, and CBT (Borduin & Schaeffer, 2002). Rather than focusing solely on the individual adolescent, MST addresses the systems surrounding the youth, including family, peer, school, and community settings, and it is highly individualized to each youth. Examples of goals at the family level are to treat barriers affecting caregivers' ability to be a strong support for their children (e.g., substance abuse, mental illness, community supports), increase family communication, and teach parenting skills and techniques (Borduin & Schaeffer, 2002). Goals at the individual level are addressed with the assistance of youths' parents and focus on improving adolescents' social skills, connection to prosocial peers, academic or occupational performance, and problem-solving capacities (Borduin & Schaeffer, 2002).

MST is used in numerous states in the United States (currently 34), as well as in 15 countries (Henggeler & Schaeffer, 2010; see also http://mstservices.com). As of 2012, MST had been evaluated in 20 outcome studies (Henggeler & Sheidow, 2012). MST has been shown to decrease general and violent offending in adolescent offenders, as measured by both official records and adolescents' self-reports (Butler, Baruch, Hickey, & Fonagy, 2011; Curtis, Ronan, & Borduin, 2004). Youths completing MST have lower rates of incarceration (Henggeler et al., 1997) and out-of-home placements (Henggeler & Schaeffer, 2010) than youths who obtain only the usual treatment services (e.g., individual therapy). Positive treatment effects have been sustained for as long as 22 years posttreatment (Sawyer & Borduin, 2011). Also, economic research has shown that MST yields cost savings of $75,110 to $199,374 per participant when considering value to taxpayers (e.g., cost of police, jails, probation) and both tangible (e.g., property damage) and intangible (e.g., suffering to crime victims) costs (Klietz, Borduin, & Schaeffer, 2010). Drake et al. (2009) reported lower cost savings of $17,694 per participant.

In addition to decreasing offending, MST appears effective in targeting a number of risk factors for offending. In comparison with usual services, MST produces larger decreases in association with antisocial peers (Henggeler et al., 1986), more substantial improvements in family relations (i.e., increased support, decreased conflict, improved cohesion; Borduin et al., 1995), and lower rates of substance use (Curtis, Ronan, Heiblum, & Crellin, 2009). MST is also associated with reductions in caregiver stress (Brunk, Henggeler, & Whelan, 1987), improved academic performance (Borduin, Schaeffer, & Heiblum, 2009), and decreased callous and unemotional traits (Butler et al., 2011). In addition, MST has higher rates of treatment completion than treatment as usual (Hunsley & Lee, 2007), with an average completion rate of 86% (Curtis et al., 2004).

Studies have found that, consistent with other types of interventions, the effect sizes for MST are larger in efficacy trials (i.e., delivered by graduate students supervised by MST developers, $d = 0.81$) than in effectiveness trials (i.e., delivered in real-world settings, $d = 0.26$; Curtis et al., 2004). Although much of the research on the effectiveness of MST has been conducted by MST developers, several independent replications have yielded positive results, including a four-way randomized trial in Norway (Ogden & Hagen, 2006) and several independent studies in the United States (Stambaugh et al., 2007; Timmons-Mitchell, Bender, Kishna, & Mitchell, 2006). That said, several independent studies did not find a significant effect, including evaluations in Sweden (Sundell et al., 2008) and Canada (Leschied & Cunningham, 2002). These null findings could be the result of limited therapist adherence. Also, some authors have asserted that MST could have a more limited impact in countries that offer higher quality treatment as usual (Butler et al., 2011; Leschied & Cunningham, 2002; Sundell et al., 2008).

Several studies have formally tested gender as a moderator and found that MST has similar effectiveness for boys and girls (Henggeler, Melton, & Smith, 1992; Sawyer & Borduin, 2011). Also, MST has demonstrated efficacy with youths from a variety of ethnic backgrounds, including African American and Hawaiian youths (S. R. Huey & Polo, 2010). Research on mechanisms of change has shown that improved family functioning and decreased affiliation with delinquent peers are key to MST's ability to decrease antisocial behavior (Henggeler, Letourneau, et al., 2009; S. J. Huey et al., 2000). Furthermore, therapist adherence is a critical predictor of success (S. J. Huey et al., 2000).

Functional family therapy. FFT (Alexander & Parsons, 1973, 1982) is a short-term intervention for youths (ages 10–18 years) with conduct disorder, early and persistent antisocial behavior or violence, and alcohol or substance abuse issues. It provides families with eight to 30 weekly sessions of family therapy over a 3- to 6-month period. FFT has a relational focus; it aims to improve family relationships and the manner in which the adult caregiver and the youth interact and communicate with one another and to increase the caregiver's parenting abilities (e.g., rule setting, family routines, problem-solving skills). In the first stage of FFT, practitioners attempt to increase motivation to change and therapy engagement by addressing factors in the family environment that may interfere with therapy (e.g., negative attitudes). Once these factors are successfully addressed, practitioners work with families to build skills; promote protective factors in the individual, environmental, and family systems (e.g., parental monitoring, coping skills, communication skills); and enhance family relationship quality. In the final stage of FFT, practitioners help families and youths generalize and apply their new skills to promote long-lasting change (Alexander, Pugh, & Parsons, 1998).

FFT has been implemented at more than 270 sites and is delivered to more than 12,000 youths annually (Functional Family Therapy, n.d.). As of 2010, approximately seven efficacy studies and five effectiveness studies had studied the impact of FFT (Functional Family Therapy, 2015). According to this research, completion of FFT is associated with reduced reoffending among adolescent offenders (Sexton & Alexander, 2003), with positive effects being sustained over periods of as much as 5 or 6 years and into adulthood (Gordon, Graves, &

Arbuthnot, 1995). As with MST, findings have emphasized the importance of adherence; a large randomized trial found that rates of reoffending at 1-year posttreatment did not differ significantly between FFT and traditional probation services (Sexton & Turner, 2010). However, therapist adherence had an impact on results. When therapist adherence was high, youths showed significant reductions in offending compared with youths who received usual services (i.e., probation; Sexton & Turner, 2010).

In addition to directly reducing reoffending, FFT has been found to decrease risk factors for offending. For instance, FFT is associated with improved family interactions (Alexander & Parsons, 1982) and reduced adolescent substance use (Barrett, Slesnick, Brody, Turner, & Peterson, 2001). Also, it has been shown to weaken the association between callous and unemotional traits and violent behavior (White, Frick, Lawing, & Bauer, 2013). FFT treatment completion rates are high, with only 10% of youths dropping out of treatment compared with the 50% to 70% of youths who drop out of routine community treatments (Sexton & Alexander, 2003). Several independent evaluations of FFT in Sweden have found favorable results (Hansson, Cederblad, & Höök, 2000; Hansson, Johansson, Drott-Englen, & Benderix, 2004). Research has also indicated that FFT carries economic benefits of $49,776 per participant when benefits to both victims and taxpayers are included (Drake et al., 2009).

FFT has been implemented throughout the United States, Europe, and New Zealand (Functional Family Therapy, n.d.). Studies have reported that FFT is helpful to diverse ethnic groups (Alexander et al., 1998). To date, however, ethnicity research has focused on Hispanic and Caucasian youths. Although research on FFT has made explicit efforts to include high proportions of female participants, research has in general not examined effects separately for male and female adolescents (Alexander, Waldron, Robbins, & Neeb, 2013).

Multidimensional treatment foster care. MTFC (Chamberlain, 2003) is designed for serious juvenile offenders who cannot live with their biological parents because of severe behavioral problems. As an alternative to incarceration or group homes, this program places youths with carefully trained foster parents who provide close supervision and fair, consistent, and appropriate rules and consequences (Fisher & Chamberlain, 2000). MTFC provides foster parents with ongoing support and assistance. Also, it provides family therapy to the youth's biological family and individual therapy to the youth, including customized aftercare services. An emphasis is on teaching the youth relationship skills and reducing contact with delinquent peers. In addition, to facilitate the youth's academic and work success, MTFC works with schools to develop strategies to assist and support the youth.

MTFC has strong research support, and has been examined in eight randomized control studies (TFC Consultants, 2013). Youths completing MTFC have significantly lower rates of reoffending and subsequent incarceration (according to official records and adolescents' self-reports) than youths who are incarcerated, in group homes, or in residential treatment programs (Barth, Greeson, Zlotnik, & Chintapalli, 2009; Chamberlain & Reid, 1998). Furthermore, these positive effects appear to be sustained over time for periods of at least 18 months (Chamberlain, Leve, & DeGarmo, 2007; Eddy, Bridges Whaley, & Chamberlain, 2004; Harold et al., 2013). According to economic research, MTFC is cost effective and yields a cost savings of $88,953 per participant when cost savings for both taxpayers and crime victims are combined (Drake et al., 2009).

In addition to directly reducing reoffending, MTFC has also been shown to help reduce or treat well-established risk factors for offending and violence. For instance, studies have reported that youths who complete MTFC show reduced contact with delinquent peers, reduced substance use, and improved school performance and attendance (Leve & Chamberlain, 2007; Smith, Chamberlain, & Eddy, 2010). Also, youths completing MTFC have higher levels of successful reintegration with their biological family and higher rates of treatment completion than youths placed in community group homes (Chamberlain & Reid, 1998).

To address female adolescents' unique risks and needs, MTFC's developers adapted the intervention for girls by adding a focus on social–relational aggression, emotional regulation, skills in building age-appropriate peer relationships, strategies to reduce sexual risk taking and avoid sexual coercion, and motivational interviewing and education pertaining to drug use (Leve, Chamberlain, Smith, & Harold, 2012). Studies have indicated that this adaptation is associated with reduced offending, incarceration, and delinquent peer contact in female adolescents (Chamberlain et al., 2007; Leve, Chamberlain, & Reid, 2005; Leve & Chamberlain, 2007). Studies have also reported improved school attendance (Leve & Chamberlain, 2007), decreased rates of unplanned pregnancy (Kerr, Leve, & Chamberlain, 2009), and reduced depression (Harold et al., 2013). Thus far, little research has examined cultural differences in the impact of MTFC.

Approaches that target the individual youth. Although family approaches have gained considerable momentum, some individual approaches also have support, particularly in addressing individual risk factors such as difficulties in anger management and impulse control.

Cognitive–behavioral therapy. CBT is based on the principle that cognitive processes influence emotion, motivation, and behavior and that problematic behaviors (such as offending) develop as a result of dysfunctional thinking patterns (Lipsey, Chapman, & Landenberger, 2001). CBT programs for adolescent offenders vary in their focus (e.g., anger management, relapse prevention) and modality (e.g., individual or group). However, CBT typically includes a focus on (a) identifying high-risk situations, thoughts, and feelings that precede offending; (b) helping adolescents replace antisocial thoughts with prosocial ones; and (c) improving youths' problem-solving, coping, and social skills (MacKenzie, 2006; Vaske, Galyean, & Cullen, 2011). Often, CBT teaches these skills through various behavioral learning techniques, such as role playing, reward and punishment contingencies, and modeling (Hubbard & Latessa, 2004). The duration of CBT programs varies from weeks to years, and intensity varies from many meetings per week to less than once per week (Landenberger & Lipsey, 2005).

Several meta-analyses have demonstrated the effectiveness of CBT for reducing recidivism in youths and adults with antisocial behavior (Landenberger & Lipsey, 2005; Lipsey, 1995; Pearson, Lipton, Cleland, & Lee, 2002; D. B. Wilson, Bouffard, & MacKenzie, 2005). For example, meta-analyses have found recidivism rates are 10% to 32% lower in offenders who completed CBT compared with offenders who did not receive this type of treatment, including mixed samples of youths and adults. Effect sizes are even greater when CBT programs target high-risk offenders, have a high-quality implementation of treatment, and include anger control and interpersonal problem-solving components (Landenberger & Lipsey, 2005). Furthermore, in studies with youths and combined samples of youths and adults, CBT has been found to outperform other treatment approaches, such as behavioral approaches (e.g., contingency contracting; token economy), nonbehavioral therapy, deterrence, and vocational programs (Andrews et al., 1990; Dowden & Andrews, 2000; Lipsey & Wilson, 1998; Pearson et al., 2002).

CBT interventions have also been shown to reduce specific risk factors for reoffending, including antisocial attitudes (Sukhodolsky, Kassinove, & Gorman, 2004), anger management difficulties (Beck & Fernandez, 1998), social problem-solving skills and impulse control (Dowden & Andrews, 2003; Sukhodolsky et al., 2004), and school attendance and academic performance (Lipsey, 1995). Because CBT is short term, time-limited, and focuses on current problems, it is well suited for application in the criminal justice system (Desai et al., 2006). Many CBT interventions are manualized, which makes them relatively easy to implement. Also, an analysis of the economic benefits of CBT programs for youth offenders found that CBT programs are cost effective, yielding a cost savings of $5,007 to victims and $2,356 to taxpayers per participant (Drake et al., 2009).

Several different brand-name CBT programs exist, such as Aggression Replacement Training (Goldstein & Glick, 1994) and Moral Reconation Therapy (Little & Robinson, 1988). Lipsey and Cullen (2007) argued that the general CBT approach, rather than any specific brand-name version, is responsible for overall positive effects on offending, but within this framework the inclusion of certain components (e.g., anger control) may enhance CBT effects, and other components may diminish their effects (e.g., victim impact and behavior modification; see Landenberger & Lipsey, 2005). In contrast, MacKenzie (2006) found that certain brand-name programs performed better than others (i.e., Moral Reconation Theory was more effective than Reasoning and Rehabilitation). However, these differences could be due to a different emphasis between programs on components found to be more or less effective.

CBT interventions have often been found to be effective for both male and female offenders (Lipsey, 2009). In addition, some evidence has suggested that CBT may be effective for adolescents with various ethnic backgrounds (Krishnan, Yeo, & Cheng, 2013; Lipsey, 2009), but research has been limited. In general, most studies have been conducted in North America and Europe and have consisted mainly of Caucasian and African American participants.

Dialetical behavioral therapy. Dialectical behavioral therapy (DBT) is a cognitive–behavioral treatment that was developed by Linehan (1993) to address the needs of adult women with a history of chronic self-injurious behaviors or borderline personality disorder. DBT is similar to CBT in that it includes components such as problem-solving and skills training. However, it departs from standard CBT by emphasizing a dialectical approach to behavior change, meaning that it encourages the client or patient to accept him- or herself and at the same time teaches skills for behavioral change. DBT aims to build skills in four areas: mindfulness (i.e., the ability to experience one's environment without trying to change it), distress tolerance (i.e., the use of strategies to tolerate distress), emotion regulation (i.e., the ability to reduce negative emotions and increase positive ones), and interpersonal effectiveness (i.e., the ability to achieve objectives in interpersonal interactions while maintaining positive relationships and self-respect). DBT is highly structured and typically consists of individual and group therapy sessions as well as phone support. When used with youths, additional components may be included, such as family therapy sessions (MacPherson, Cheavens, & Fristad, 2013). Usually, DBT is conducted over a time period of 16 weeks to more than 1 year.

Most studies of DBT have been conducted with adults. However, DBT has also been found to reduce suicide, nonsuicidal self-injury, depression, and anger in adolescents with mental health difficulties and improve overall psychiatric and psychosocial functioning (Fleischhaker et al., 2011; Woodberry & Popenoe, 2008). Few studies have tested DBT specifically with adolescent offenders. However, one study found that adolescent offenders (male and female) with mental illness who completed DBT showed significantly lower recidivism than those who received treatment as usual (Barnoski, 2002). Several studies have found that DBT is associated with reduced institutional misconduct among incarcerated youths (Shelton, Kesten, Zhang, & Trestman, 2011; Trupin, Stewart, Beach, & Boesky, 2002).

In addition, DBT may help to address risk factors for adolescent offending. For instance, it has been found to reduce aggression, antisocial attitudes, and risk taking and improve affect, self-control, and coping abilities (Shelton et al., 2011; Trupin et al., 2002). It has also been found to reduce suicidal and nonsuicidal self-injurious behaviors in adolescent offenders (Trupin et al., 2002). Despite some promising findings, more research is required regarding DBT's effectiveness with adolescent offenders (Shelton et al., 2011).

Motivational interviewing. Motivation to change is often thought to be particularly low in justice settings, because individuals are typically mandated to receive treatment (McMurran, 2009). Interest in motivational interviewing (MI) has thus grown as a potential means to increase treatment engagement (Miller & Rollnick, 2012). MI approaches are typically delivered in brief, individualized sessions (15–45 minutes) that focus on increasing problem acceptance and recognition, addressing ambivalence to change, and highlighting the benefits of behavioral change (Anstiss, Polaschek, & Wilson, 2011). MI emphasizes empathy, optimism, respect for client choice, and conversation about change. It is not a replacement for other treatment programs (e.g., CBT); rather, it is an additional tool to use, particularly with individuals who have limited motivation.

MI has been found to be effective in reducing a variety of risk behaviors such as drug and alcohol abuse, sexual risk taking, and medication noncompliance among adolescents and adults (Jensen et al., 2011; Rubak, Sandbaek, Lauritzen, & Christensen, 2005). However, research on its application to adolescent offenders has been limited (McMurran, 2009). One study found that male youth offenders who participated in MI showed greater treatment gains (e.g., more confident in ability to resist drugs, improved parent–youth communication) than those in a control group (Slavet et al., 2005). Another study found that MI resulted in reduced offending (i.e., impaired driving) among adolescents who were low on depression but not among those who were high in depression (Stein et al., 2006). To our knowledge, no studies have examined the impact of MI on reoffending in juveniles. However, Anstiss et al. (2011) found that adult male prisoners who completed MI had 21% lower reconviction and a 17% lower reimprisonment rate 4 years after release compared with the control group.

Gender-specific interventions. Concern has been expressed that programs designed for male young offenders may not adequately address the needs of their female counterparts (Bloom, Owen, Rosenbaum, & Deschenes, 2003). According to theory and research, factors such as victimization, mental health, family discord, and relationships with antisocial boyfriends may provide a particularly important role in female offending (Kerig & Schindler, 2013). As a result, efforts have been made to develop gender-specific interventions.

In a review conducted by the Office of Juvenile Justice and Delinquency Prevention's Girls Study Group, Zahn, Day, Mihalic, and Tichavsky (2009) reported that only 18 of the 62 gender-specific programs they identified had been evaluated. Thus, given the lack of research, most gender-specific programs cannot currently be considered evidence based (Kerig & Schindler, 2013). Furthermore, outcomes of gender-specific programs have been somewhat mixed. Although gender-specific programs showed positive effects in academic, interpersonal, and psychological domains, they did not show long-term reductions in recidivism (Zahn et al., 2009). Even some of the most promising gender-specific programs (e.g., Working to Insure and Nurture Girls' Success [Burke, Keaton, & Pennell, 2003], Reaffirming Young Sisters' Excellence [National Council on Crime and Delinquency, 2001]) have not produced significant long-term reductions in reoffending (i.e., at periods of 1 year or longer).

Rather than developing separate gender-specific programs, research has also started to investigate whether well-established programs are effective with girls or can be successfully adapted for girls. Some well-established, evidence-based interventions, such as MST, already have some support across gender (Henggeler et al., 1992; Sawyer & Borduin, 2011). Other model programs, such as MTFC, have successfully accommodated female populations (Leve et al., 2012). Thus, rather than developing entirely different programs, it may be possible to adapt or tailor existing evidence-based programs for girls (Kerig & Schindler, 2013).

Summary and Challenges

Over the past several decades, research has made significant progress in developing, evaluating, and disseminating evidence-based interventions. This research has convincingly demonstrated that community-based interventions not only can serve as an effective alternative to incarceration but also carry impressive cost benefits (Klietz et al., 2010). Findings have demonstrated the importance of targeting youths' family, peer, and school environments rather than relying solely on efforts to change individual adolescents (Henggeler & Sheidow, 2012). In addition, given that considerable drift can occur when programs are transferred from controlled research environments to real-world contexts (S. J. Huey et al., 2000; Sexton & Turner, 2010), leading programs such as MST, FFT, and MTFC place an emphasis on therapist adherence, proper implementation, and ongoing support.

One of the challenges that evidence-based programs face is in their dissemination to youth justice professionals. Although evidence-based programs have been implemented widely (Henggeler & Sheidow, 2012), many agencies and professionals perceive evidence-based programs such as MST to be a significant commitment that requires extensive time and resources. Another potential challenge is that such evidence-based programs place relatively limited emphasis on the front-end process of program referral, triage, or standardized assessments (e.g., risk assessment). That said, they often do include some assessment. In MST, therapists conduct a strength and needs assessment (Henggeler, Schoenwald, et al., 2009). This assessment is not a formal questionnaire but instead a form on which a therapist records strengths (e.g., protective factors) and weaknesses (e.g., risk factors) in family, individual, peer, and school domains. In addition, MST therapists identify how adolescents' behaviors fit into and are maintained through their social context. Thus, in many ways, this process parallels the task in risk assessment.

EFFORTS TO BRIDGE RISK ASSESSMENT TO EVIDENCE-BASED INTERVENTIONS

The fields of risk assessment–risk management and evidence-based interventions (i.e., what-works research) have operated as separate and distinct fields. However, recently, several efforts have been made to bridge these domains (see Dvoskin, Skeem, Novaco, & Douglas, 2012). Below, we review examples of these efforts. Given the dearth of strategies that focus on adolescents, we include descriptions of efforts in child, adult, and adolescent contexts.

Stop Now and Plan Program

The Stop Now and Plan Program (SNAP) is a cognitive–behavioral intervention for children (ages 12 years and younger) with anger management difficulties and impulsivity. It is designed specifically for children at increased risk for later contact with the youth justice system. It includes a 12-week parent group and 12-week child skills group to teach children to stop, think, and plan their behavior. Research has found that children who complete SNAP showed decreased parent-rated delinquency and aggression and lower rates of subsequent convictions than children in a control group (Augimeri, Farrington, Koegl, & Day, 2007; Koegl, Farrington, Augimeri, & Day, 2008). SNAP has been adapted for girls and has support as a gender-appropriate intervention (Kerig & Schindler, 2013). In addition, although originally designed for children, an adolescent version of SNAP was recently developed (e.g., SNAP: Youth Outreach; Child Development Institute, n.d.), including an approach for justice-involved youth (Leena Augimeri, personal communication, June 19, 2013).

As part of SNAP, professionals are encouraged to use risk assessment tools, namely the Early Assessment of Risk List for Boys Version 2 (Augimeri, Koegl, Webster, & Levene, 1998) and the Early Assessment Risk List for Girls, Consultation Version 1 (Levene et al., 2001). These tools are designed to help predict antisocial behavior in boys and girls who are 12 years old and younger and to guide intervention planning. Thus, the SNAP program nicely combines risk assessment and interventions.

Formulation and Scenario Planning

In the adult risk assessment field, a major area of initiative is formulation (e.g., Hart & Logan, 2011). The goal of formulation is to prioritize treatment targets by developing a case conceptualization of the factors that cause (i.e., motivate) or contribute to an individual's violence. Hart and Logan (2011) also introduced scenario planning, used in the military, health care, and business, to the field of risk assessment (Schoemaker, 1995). Scenario planning is the process of identifying plausible scenarios or events that might happen in the future (i.e., different situations in which an individual might engage in particular types of violence). The goal of scenario planning is to trouble shoot and problem solve around possible situations. For instance, rather than simply stating that an individual is at high risk for future violence, scenario planning encourages professionals to identify more specific situations of concern (e.g., that a youth will stab or seriously assault the peer whom he perceives as having stolen his girlfriend). By identifying these scenarios, the professional can then take steps to prevent that particular situation (e.g., warn the peer, help the school develop strategies to avoid or reduce contact between the youth and his peer, problem solve nonaggressive strategies to resolve the conflict).

Several adult risk assessment tools, including the Revised Sexual Violence Protocol (Hart et al., 2003) and Historical Clinical Risk Management–20, Version 3 (Douglas, Hart, Webster, & Belfrage, 2013), include an emphasis on formulation and scenario planning, as does a recent adolescent measure, the Short-Term Assessment of Risk and Treatability: Adolescent Version (Viljoen, Nicholls, et al., 2014). Thus far, one study has found that professionals show consistency in the violence-related scenarios they identify (C. M. Wilson, 2013). However, further research is needed.

Strategic Training in Community Supervision

The Strategic Training in Community Supervision (STICS) is a training program for probation officers that is designed to increase the uptake of RNR principles (Bonta, Rugge, Scott, Bourgon, & Yessine, 2008). It provides probation officers (POs) with a 3-day course that teaches the RNR principles and specific social learning techniques such as prosocial modeling and reinforcement. After this training, POs meet in small groups once a month over a 1-year period to practice learned skills. Also, POs submit audiotaped sessions for which they are then provided individualized feedback to identify areas that need improvement.

Pilot implementations of the STICS program have occurred in several Canadian provinces (British Columbia, Prince Edward Island, and Saskatchewan; Bonta et al., 2011). At these sites, POs (who supervise adult offenders) were randomly assigned to STICS training or a control group. POs submitted a pretraining audiotape, which recorded a session that they had with a client before the training. They then collected posttraining audiotapes from POs. Bonta et al. (2011) found that POs who participated in the STICS program spent more time focusing on criminogenic needs and procriminal attitudes during their sessions with clients than POs without this training. STICS POs also showed better adherence to the RNR principles and greater use of skills (e.g., cognitive techniques, relationship-building skills). The STICS program was developed primarily for adult offenders. Thus, its main focus is on individually oriented techniques (e.g., problem-solving skills) rather than family approaches. However, many of the principles could be applied to youths.

Adolescent Risk Reduction and Resilience Work-Plan

In our own work, we have recently developed the Adolescent Risk Reduction and Resilient Outcomes Work-Plan (ARROW; Viljoen, Brodersen, Shaffer, & Muir, 2014) to provide youth justice professionals with additional support and guidance on risk reduction interventions. The ARROW draws from the RNR model and what-works research. It lays out a general model by which to bridge a risk assessment tool to interventions; this model starts with formulation and scenario planning, followed by intervention planning, implementation of interventions, and the refinement of interventions based on ongoing monitoring and risk reassessments.

In the ARROW guide (Viljoen, Brodersen, et al., 2014), we compiled evidence-based risk reduction strategies for each specific factor on the SAVRY (e.g., peer delinquency, impulsivity and risk taking, anger management difficulties, substance use). The guide includes a discussion of specialized evidence-based interventions that are relevant to particular factors (e.g., MST, DBT) but also of broader types of risk reduction strategies, including strategies to

- plan for safety (e.g., warn potential victims, monitor no-contact orders),
- supervise the adolescent (e.g., arrange positive activities, help caregivers monitor the youth),
- engage the youth and build his or her motivation (e.g., understand the youth's perspectives and his or her own reasons to change),
- engage families and social supports (e.g., offer caregivers information and support),
- build the youth's skills (e.g., help the youth to problem solve and identify triggers), and
- build and leverage protective factors (e.g., support and facilitate existing strengths, such as by encouraging continued involvement in prosocial activities or ties with prosocial peers).

To help implement the ARROW, we have developed accompanying forms (e.g., a checklist of strategies for each factor), worksheets and discussion aids for sessions with youths (e.g., triggers worksheet, a rules chart), and training and implementation materials (e.g., training cases). The ARROW also includes an adherence checklist that professionals, supervisors, and researchers can use to check compliance with the ARROW strategies. Work on the ARROW is at a very early stage; we are currently conducting pilot research that we will use to refine it.

Summary and Next Steps

Risk assessment and risk management research and what-works research share common goals: to help prevent adolescent offending and to offer alternatives to an overreliance on incarceration. Over the past few decades, both fields of research have advanced knowledge and improved practice. However, these fields have operated fairly independently, with little dialogue between them. The field of risk assessment undoubtedly has much it could learn and gain from the field of intervention. Improved ties could move the field of risk assessment from principles (e.g., "match interventions to target youth's needs") to practice (e.g., developing specific training programs and guides to help professionals implement this principle). It is also possible that risk assessment and risk management research might have some value to intervention researchers. The justice system, for better or worse, adopts a language that centers on risk and public protection. Thus, evidence-based interventions may gain wider acceptance in justice contexts if interventions include risk assessment tools or if intervention researchers show how their program yields reductions in risk, as measured by well-established risk assessment tools. Below, we offer additional recommendations for research and practice.

Systematically test the relevance of risk tools to treatment. Although risk assessments may be a first step to effective interventions, it is unlikely that simply implementing a risk assessment tool will reduce reoffending. This is because numerous steps must occur between risk assessment and reoffense reduction. For instance, using a risk assessment tool to identify that a youth lacks adequate parental supervision is of limited value if effective interventions to address this need (e.g., evidence-based family therapy) are not locally available.

Although risk assessment tools may not directly reduce reoffending, they could play at least two roles in risk reduction. First, they might aid in treatment selection. Second, they might help measure the degree to which youth improve over the course of treatment by measuring treatment-related change. At this point, we do not know the extent to which adolescent risk assessment tools successfully fulfill either of these roles. To evaluate their utility in this regard, the field must shift focus and expand beyond the present fixation on the ability of tools to predict reoffending. Of particular value will be studies that compare treatment selection and matching (e.g., the degree to which youths receive services that address their needs and are commensurate with their risk level) before and after the implementation of risk assessment tools (e.g., Vincent, Guy, et al., 2012). Also, studies are needed that examine the ability of risk assessment tools to detect treatment-related change, such as comparisons between risk assessment tools and other measures of change (e.g., self-report questionnaires, goal attainment scales).

Develop enhanced strategies by which to link risk assessments to risk reduction. Most manuals for risk assessment tools offer little explicit guidance as to how to use the tools in treatment planning efforts. Thus, professionals require further support. One strategy might be to offer enhanced training. For instance, the STICS program includes didactic training in risk reduction strategies, careful review of and feedback on POs' audiotaped sessions with clients, and ongoing support over a 1-year period (Bonta et al., 2008). Another approach may be to develop enhanced guidelines to accompany risk assessment tools. For instance, the ARROW Guide compiles evidence-based risk reduction strategies for each risk and protective factor on the SAVRY. Similarly, the Risk Management Historical Clinical–20 Guide describes interventions relevant dynamic factors on the Historical Clinical Risk Management–20, a widely used adult tool (Douglas et al., 2001).

In developing these types of strategies to link risk assessment to evidence-based interventions, we can draw from the field of implementation science. Implementation science studies methods to increase the uptake and dissemination of evidence-based approaches into routine practice (Eccles et al., 2009). As implementation science emphasizes, whether approaches (such as STICS or the ARROW) work depends not only on the soundness of the approach but also on how it is implemented (e.g., if the approach is implemented in an appropriate and effective manner; Proctor et al., 2011). Rather than simply focusing on standard psychometric properties (e.g., validity), implementation science examines outcomes such as whether an approach (e.g., ARROW, STICS) is acceptable (e.g., whether professionals are satisfied with the approach) and feasible (e.g., whether professionals find it useful and adhere to it and deliver it as intended; Proctor et al., 2011). Thus, these outcomes will be important to examine in research on approaches such as the ARROW.

Increase the feasibility and uptake of evidence-based interventions. Many evidence-based interventions have gained wide uptake. MST is used with 17,000 families each year (Henggeler & Sheidow, 2012) and FFT with 12,000 families annually (http://www.fftllc.com). However, this falls short of what is needed; it has been estimated that "fewer than 5% of eligible high risk juvenile offenders in the U.S. are treated with an evidence-based intervention" (Henggeler & Schoenwald, 2011, p. 8). What are the barriers to effective implementation of evidence-based programs? One is cost; despite strong evidence of cost-effectiveness, administrators and service providers may perceive interventions to be expensive and time consuming to implement. Also, practitioners often view some manualized interventions, such as CBT programs, as being overly rigid and lacking attention to clinical judgment (Addis & Krasnow, 2000).

As a means to increase the adoption of evidence-based approaches, some professionals have developed modular interventions (Chorpita & Weisz, 2009). In this approach, a series of stand-alone modules is developed (e.g., psychoeducation, self-calming techniques for anger management). These models can then be rearranged to meet a particular youth's needs; specifically, professionals can decide which modules to implement and in what order. Also, whereas traditional interventions often treat only one problem at a time (e.g., conduct problems), a modular approach enables professionals to address multiple problems simultaneously; e.g., conduct problems and depression. Recent findings have provided support for modular approaches (Chorpita et al., 2013; Weisz et al., 2012). Furthermore, one study found that professionals have a more positive view of modular approaches than standard interventions, possibly because of their increased flexibility (Borntrager, Chorpita, Higa-McMillan, & Weisz, 2009). Thus, it is possible that modular approaches could facilitate a wider adoption of evidence-based practice.

CONCLUSION

During the past several decades, research has made some important contributions to risk reduction strategies for adolescent offenders. Research has tested (and convincingly disproven) the assumption that offender treatment does not work (e.g., Andrews & Bonta, 2010b). It has revealed that harsh punitive laws and policies often do not have the desired effect of improving public safety (e.g., Petrosino et al., 2003, 2013). It has developed evidence-based principles to reduce risk for reoffending (i.e., match interventions to youths' risk levels and needs) and identified and evaluated evidence-based interventions that provide an effective alternative to incarceration (such as MTFC, MST, and FFT). Indeed, we have come a long way since Martinson's (1974) erroneous conclusion that nothing works. However, a long road lies ahead. Most urgent, we must work to effectively implement the approaches we now know work. To achieve this, it will be critical to build bridges between risk assessment and risk reduction and to draw from the field of implementation science.

References

Adam Walsh Child Protection and Safety Act, 42 U.S.C. §16911 et seq. (2006).

Addis, M. E., & Krasnow, A. D. (2000). A national survey of practicing psychologists' attitudes toward psychotherapy treatment manuals. *Journal of Consulting and Clinical Psychology*, *68*, 331–339. http://dx.doi.org/10.1037/0022-006X.68.2.331

Alexander, J. F., & Parsons, B. V. (1973). Short-term behavioral intervention with delinquent families: Impact on family process and recidivism. *Journal of Abnormal Psychology*, *81*, 219–225. http://dx.doi.org/10.1037/h0034537

Alexander, J. F., & Parsons, B. V. (1982). *Functional family therapy*. http://dx.doi.org/10.1037/11621-000

Alexander, J. F., Pugh, C., & Parsons, B. V. (1998). Functional family therapy. In D. S. Elliott (Ed.), *Blueprints for violence prevention* (Vol. 2, Book 3, pp. 13–47). Boulder: University of Colorado, Institute of Behavioral Science.

Alexander, J. F., Waldron, H., Robbins, M. S., & Neeb, A. A. (2013). *Functional family therapy for adolescent behavior problems*. http://dx.doi.org/10.1037/14139-000

Andrews, D. A., & Bonta, J. (1994). *The psychology of criminal conduct*. Cincinnati, OH: Anderson.

Andrews, D. A., & Bonta, J. (2006). *The psychology of criminal conduct* (4th ed.). Newark, NJ: LexisNexis.

Andrews, D. A., & Bonta, J. (2010a). *The psychology of criminal conduct* (5th ed.). Cincinnati, OH: Anderson.

Andrews, D. A., & Bonta, J. (2010b). Rehabilitating criminal justice policy and practice. *Psychology, Public Policy, and Law*, *16*, 39–55. http://dx.doi.org/10.1037/a0018362

Andrews, D. A., & Dowden, C. (2006). Risk principle of case classification in correctional treatment: A meta-analytic investigation. *International Journal of Offender Therapy and Comparative Criminology*, *50*, 88–100. http://dx.doi.org/10.1177/0306624X05282556

Andrews, D. A., Zinger, I., Hoge, R. D., Bonta, J., Gendreau, P., & Cullen, F. T. (1990). Does correctional treatment work? A clinically relevant and psychologically informed meta-analysis. *Criminology*, *28*, 369–404. http://dx.doi.org/10.1111/j.1745-9125.1990.tb01330.x

Anstiss, B., Polaschek, D. L., & Wilson, M. (2011). A brief motivational interviewing intervention with prisoners: When you lead a horse to water, can it drink for itself? *Psychology, Crime, and Law*, *17*, 689–710. http://dx.doi.org/10.1080/10683160903524325

Archer, R. P., Buffington-Vollum, J. K., Stredny, R. V., & Handel, R. W. (2006). A survey of psychological test use patterns among forensic psychologists. *Journal of Personality Assessment*, *87*, 84–94. http://dx.doi.org/10.1207/s15327752jpa8701_07

Arnold, M. E., & Hughes, J. N. (1999). First do no harm: Adverse effects of grouping deviant youth for skills training. *Journal of School Psychology*, *37*, 99–115. http://dx.doi.org/10.1016/S0022-4405(98)00027-2

Augimeri, L. K., Farrington, D. P., Koegl, C. J., & Day, D. M. (2007). The SNAP Under 12 Outreach Project: Effects of a community based program for children with conduct problems. *Journal of Child and Family Studies*, *16*, 799–807. http://dx.doi.org/10.1007/s10826-006-9126-x

Augimeri, L. K., Koegl, C. J., Webster, C. D., & Levene, K. S. (1998). *The Early Assessment of Risk List for Boys (EARL–20B), Version 2*. Toronto, Ontario, Canada: Earlscourt Child and Family Centre.

Barnoski, R. (2002). *Preliminary findings for the Juvenile Rehabilitation Administration's mentoring program* (Research Rep. No. 02–07-1202). Olympia: Evergreen State College, Washington State Institute for Public Policy.

Barrett, H., Slesnick, N., Brody, J. L., Turner, C. W., & Peterson, T. R. (2001). Treatment outcomes for adolescent substance abuse at 4- and 7-month assessments. *Journal of Consulting and Clinical Psychology*, *69*, 802–813. http://dx.doi.org/10.1037/0022-006X.69.5.802

Barth, R. P., Greeson, J. K. P., Zlotnik, S. R., & Chintapalli, L. K. (2009). Evidence-based practice for youth in supervised out-of-home care: A framework for development, definition, and evaluation. *Journal of Evidence-Based Social Work*, *6*, 147–175. http://dx.doi.org/10.1080/15433710802683796

Beck, R., & Fernandez, E. (1998). Cognitive-behavioral therapy in the treatment of anger: A meta-analysis. *Cognitive Therapy and Research*, *22*, 63–74. http://dx.doi.org/10.1023/A:1018763902991

Becker, S. P. (2010). Wilderness therapy: Ethical considerations for mental health professionals. *Child and Youth Care Forum*, *39*, 47–61. http://dx.doi.org/10.1007/s10566-009-9085-7

Bishop, D. M., Frazier, C. E., Lanza-Kaduce, L., & Winner, L. (1996). The transfer of juveniles to criminal court: Does it make a difference? *Crime and Delinquency*, *42*, 171–191. http://dx.doi.org/10.1177/0011128796042002001

Bloom, B., Owen, B., Rosenbaum, J., & Deschenes, E. P. (2003). Focusing on girls and young women: A gendered perspective on female delinquency. *Women and Criminal Justice*, *14*, 117–136. http://dx.doi.org/10.1300/J012v14n02-136

Bonta, J., Bourgon, G., Rugge, T., Scott, T., Yessine, A. K., Gutierrez, L., & Li, J. (2011). An experimental demonstration of training probation officers in evidence-based community supervision. *Criminal Justice and Behavior*, *38*, 1127–1148. http://dx.doi.org/10.1177/0093854811420678

Bonta, J., Rugge, T., Scott, T., Bourgon, G., & Yessine, A. K. (2008). Exploring the black box of community supervision. *Journal of Offender Rehabilitation*, *47*, 248–270. http://dx.doi.org/10.1080/10509670802134085

Borduin, C. M., Mann, B. J., Cone, L. T., Henggeler, S. W., Fucci, B. R., Blaske, D. M., & Williams, R. A. (1995). Multisystemic treatment of serious juvenile offenders: Long-term prevention of criminality and violence. *Journal of Consulting and Clinical Psychology*, *63*, 569–578. http://dx.doi.org/10.1037/0022-006X.63.4.569

Borduin, C. M., & Schaeffer, C. M. (2002). Multisystemic treatment of juvenile sex offenders: A progress report. *Journal of Psychology and Human Sexuality*, *13*, 25–42. http://dx.doi.org/10.1300/J056v13n03_03

Borduin, C. M., Schaeffer, C. M., & Heiblum, N. (2009). A randomized clinical trial of multisystemic therapy with juvenile sexual offenders: Effects on youth social ecology and criminal activity. *Journal of Consulting and Clinical Psychology*, *77*, 26–37. http://dx.doi.org/10.1037/a0013035

Borntrager, C. F., Chorpita, B. F., Higa-McMillan, C., & Weisz, J. R. (2009). Provider attitudes toward evidence-based practices: Are the concerns with the evidence or with the manuals? *Psychiatric Services*, *60*, 677–681. http://dx.doi.org/10.1176/appi.ps.60.5.677

Borum, R., Bartel, P., & Forth, A. (2006). *SAVRY: Structured Assessment of Violence Risk in Youth: Professional manual*. Toronto, Ontario, Canada: Psychological Assessment Resources.

Breed v. Jones, 421 U.S. 519 (1975).

Brunk, M., Henggeler, S. W., & Whelan, J. P. (1987). Comparison of multisystemic therapy and parent training in the brief treatment of child abuse and neglect. *Journal of Consulting and Clinical Psychology*, *55*, 171–178. http://dx.doi.org/10.1037/0022-006X.55.2.171

Burke, C., Keaton, S., & Pennell, S. (2003). *Addressing the gender-specific needs of girls: An evaluation of San Diego's WINGS program* (Board of Corrections final report). San Diego, CA: San Diego County Probation Department & San Diego Association of Governments.

Butler, S., Baruch, G., Hickey, N., & Fonagy, P. (2011). A randomized controlled trial of multisystemic therapy and a statutory therapeutic intervention for young offenders. *Journal of the American Academy of Child and Adolescent Psychiatry*, *50*, 1220–35.e2. http://dx.doi.org/10.1016/j.jaac.2011.09.017

Cason, D., & Gillis, H. L. (1994). A meta-analysis of outdoor adventure programming with adolescents. *Journal of Experiential Education*, *17*, 40–47. http://dx.doi.org/10.1177/105382599401700109

Cauffman, E. (2008). Understanding the female offender. *Future of Children*, *18*, 119–142. http://dx.doi.org/10.1353/foc.0.0015

Chamberlain, P. (2003). *Treating chronic juvenile offenders: Advances made through the Oregon multidimensional treatment foster care model*. http://dx.doi.org/10.1037/10596-000

Chamberlain, P., Leve, L. D., & DeGarmo, D. S. (2007). Multidimensional treatment foster care for girls in the juvenile justice system: 2-year follow-up of a randomized clinical trial. *Journal of Consulting and Clinical Psychology*, *75*, 187–193. http://dx.doi.org/10.1037/0022-006X.75.1.187

Chamberlain, P., & Reid, J. B. (1998). Comparison of two community alternatives to incarceration for chronic juvenile offenders. *Journal of Consulting and Clinical Psychology*, 66, 624–633. http://dx.doi.org/10.1037/0022-006X.66.4.624

Child Development Institute. (n.d.). *SNAP*. Retrieved from http://www.childdevelop.ca/programs/snap

Chorpita, B. F., & Weisz, J. R. (2009). *Modular approach to therapy for children with anxiety, depression, trauma, or conduct problems (MATCH–ADTC)*. Satellite Beach, FL: PracticeWise.

Chorpita, B. F., Weisz, J. R., Daleiden, E. L., Schoenwald, S. K., Palinkas, L. A., Miranda, J., . . . Gibbons, R. D.; Research Network on Youth Mental Health. (2013). Long-term outcomes for the Child STEPs randomized effectiveness trial: A comparison of modular and standard treatment designs with usual care. *Journal of Consulting and Clinical Psychology*, *81*, 999–1009. http://dx.doi.org/10.1037/a0034200

Clark, C. L., & Aziz, D. W. (1996). Shock incarceration in New York State: Philosophy, results, and limitations. In D. L. MacKenzie & E. E. Hebert (Eds.), *Correctional boot camps: A tough intermediate sanction* (pp. 39–68). Washington, DC: U.S. Department of Justice.

Cohen, M., & Piquero, A. (2009). New evidence on the monetary value of saving a high risk youth. *Journal of Quantitative Criminology*, *25*, 25–49. http://dx.doi.org/10.1007/s10940-008-9057-3

Conduct Problems Prevention Research Group. (2010). Fast Track intervention effects on youth arrests and delinquency. *Journal of Experimental Criminology*, *6*, 131–157. http://dx.doi.org/10.1007/s11292-010-9091-7

Cook, A. N., & Roesch, R. (2012). "Tough on crime" reforms: What psychology has to say about the recent and proposed justice policy in Canada. *Canadian Psychology/Psychologie Canadienne*, *53*, 217–225. http://dx.doi.org/10.1037/a0025045

Crisp, S. R., & Hinch, C. M. (2004). *Treatment effectiveness of wilderness adventure therapy: Summary findings*. Clifton Hill, Victoria, Australia: Neo Psychology.

Cullen, F. T. (2012). Taking rehabilitation seriously: Creativity, science, and the challenge of offender change. *Punishment and Society*, *14*, 94–114. http://dx.doi.org/10.1177/1462474510385973

Curtis, N. M., Ronan, K. R., & Borduin, C. M. (2004). Multisystemic treatment: A meta-analysis of outcome studies. *Journal of Family Psychology*, *18*, 411–419. http://dx.doi.org/10.1037/0893-3200.18.3.411

Curtis, N. M., Ronan, K. R., Heiblum, N., & Crellin, K. (2009). Dissemination and effectiveness of multisystemic treatment in New Zealand: A benchmarking study. *Journal of Family Psychology*, *23*, 119–129. http://dx.doi.org/10.1037/a0014974

Desai, R. A., Goulet, J. L., Robbins, J., Chapman, J. F., Migdole, S. J., & Hoge, M. A. (2006). Mental health care in juvenile detention facilities: A review. *Journal of the American Academy of Psychiatry and the Law*, *34*, 204–214.

Dishion, T. J., Spracklen, K. M., Andrews, D. W., & Patterson, G. R. (1996). Deviancy training in male adolescent friendships. *Behavior Therapy*, *27*, 373–390. http://dx.doi.org/10.1016/S0005-7894(96)80023-2

Dodge, K. A., Dishion, T. J., & Lansford, J. E. (Eds.). (2007). *Deviant peer influences in programs for youth: Problems and solutions*. New York, NY: Guilford Press.

Douglas, K. S., Hart, S. D., Webster, C. D., & Belfrage, H. (2013). *HCR–20V3: Assessing risk for violence—User guide*. Burnaby, British Columbia, Canada: Mental Health, Law, and Policy Institute, Simon Fraser University.

Douglas, K. S., Webster, C. D., Hart, S. D., Eaves, D., & Ogloff, J. R. P. (Eds.). (2001). *HCR-20: Violence risk management companion guide*. Burnaby, British Columbia, Canada: Simon Fraser University, Mental Health,

Law, and Policy Institute, and University of South Florida, Department of Mental Health Law & Policy.

Dowden, C., & Andrews, D. A. (2000). Effective correctional treatment and violent recidivism: A meta-analysis. *Canadian Journal of Criminology*, *42*, 449–467.

Dowden, C., & Andrews, D. A. (2003). Does family intervention work for delinquents? Results of a meta-analysis. *Canadian Journal of Criminology and Criminal Justice*, *45*, 327–342. http://dx.doi.org/10.3138/cjccj.45.3.327

Doyle, M., & Logan, C. (2012). Operationalizing the assessment and management of violence risk in the short-term. *Behavioral Sciences and the Law*, *30*, 406–419. http://dx.doi.org/10.1002/bsl.2017

Drake, E. K., Aos, S., & Miller, M. G. (2009). Evidence-based public policy options to reduce crime and criminal justice costs: Implications in Washington State. *Victims and Offenders*, *4*, 170–196. http://dx.doi.org/10.1080/15564880802612615

Dvoskin, J. A., Skeem, J. L., Novaco, R. W., & Douglas, K. S. (2012). *Using social science to reduce violent offending*. New York, NY: Oxford University Press.

Eccles, M. P., Armstrong, D., Baker, R., Cleary, K., Davies, H., Davies, S., . . . Sibbald, B. (2009). An implementation research agenda. *Implementation Science*, *4*, 18–25. http://dx.doi.org/10.1186/1748-5908-4-18

Eddy, J., Bridges Whaley, R., & Chamberlain, P. (2004). The prevention of violent behavior by chronic and serious male juvenile offenders: A 2-year follow-up of a randomized clinical trial. *Journal of Emotional and Behavioral Disorders*, *12*, 2–8. http://dx.doi.org/10.1177/10634266040120010101

Elliott, D. S., & Mihalic, S. (2004). Issues in disseminating and replicating effective prevention programs. *Prevention Science*, *5*, 47–53. http://dx.doi.org/10.1023/B:PREV.0000013981.28071.52

Fare v. Michael C., 442 U.S. 707 (1979).

Finckenauer, J. (1982). *Scared straight and the panacea phenomenon*. Englewood Cliffs, NJ: Prentice Hall.

Fisher, P. A., & Chamberlain, P. (2000). Multidimensional treatment foster care: A program for intensive parenting, family support, and skill building. *Journal of Emotional and Behavioral Disorders*, *8*, 155–164. http://dx.doi.org/10.1177/106342660000800303

Fleischhaker, C., Böhme, R., Sixt, B., Brück, C., Schneider, C., & Schulz, E. (2011). Dialectical behavioral therapy for adolescents (DBT-A): A clinical trial for patients with suicidal and self-injurious behavior and borderline symptoms with a one-year follow-up. *Child and Adolescent Psychiatry and Mental Health*, *5*, 3. http://dx.doi.org/10.1186/1753-2000-5-3

Flores, A. W., Travis, L. F., & Latessa, E. J. (2003). *Case classification for juvenile corrections: An assessment of the Youth Level of Service/Case Management Inventory (YLS/CMI): Final report*. Washington, DC: National Institute of Justice.

Frick, P. J. (2012). Developmental pathways to conduct disorder: Implications for future directions in research, assessment, and treatment. *Journal of Clinical Child and Adolescent Psychology*, *41*, 378–389. http://dx.doi.org/10.1080/15374416.2012.664815

Functional Family Therapy. (2015). *FFT: Functional family therapy*. Retrieved from http://functionalfamilytherapy.com

Functional Family Therapy (n.d.). *Functional family therapy*. Retrieved from http://fftinc.com

Gillis, H. L., Gass, M. A., & Russell, K. C. (2008). The effectiveness of Project Adventure's behavior management programs for male offenders in residential treatment. *Residential Treatment for Children and Youth*, *25*, 227–247. http://dx.doi.org/10.1080/08865710802429689

Goldstein, A. P., & Glick, B. (1994). Aggression replacement training: Curriculum and evaluation. *Simulation and Gaming*, *25*, 9–26. http://dx.doi.org/10.1177/1046878194251003

Gordon, D. A., Graves, K., & Arbuthnot, J. (1995). The effect of functional family therapy for delinquents on adult criminal behavior. *Criminal Justice and Behavior*, *22*, 60–73. http://dx.doi.org/10.1177/0093854895022001005

Gover, A. R., MacKenzie, D. L., & Armstrong, G. S. (2000). Importation and deprivation explanations of juveniles' adjustment to correctional facilities. *International Journal of Offender Therapy and Comparative Criminology*, *44*, 450–467. http://dx.doi.org/10.1016/S0047-2352(99)00032-X

Graham v. Florida, 130 S. Ct. 2011 (2010).

Grisso, T. (2001). Why juvenile justice will survive its centennial. In L. E. Frost & R. J. Bonnie (Eds.), *The evolution of mental health law* (pp. 167–180). http://dx.doi.org/10.1037/10414-008

Handwerk, M. L., Field, C. E., & Friman, P. C. (2000). The iatrogenic effects of group intervention for antisocial youth: Premature extrapolations? *Journal of Behavioral Education*, *10*, 223–238. http://dx.doi.org/10.1023/A:1012299716053

Hansson, K., Cederblad, M., & Höök, B. (2000). Funktionell familjeterapi [Functional family therapy]. *Socialvetenskaplig Tidskrift*, *3*, 231–243. Retrieved from http://www.fft-sverige.se

Hansson, K., Johansson, P., Drott-Englen, G. U. N., & Benderix, Y. (2004). Funktionell familjeterapi i barnpsykiatrisk praxis: Om behandling av ungdomskriminalitet utanför universitetsforskningen [Functional family therapy in child psychiatric practice]. *Nordisk Psykologi*, *56*, 304–320. http://dx.doi.org/10.1080/00291463.2004.10637451

Harold, G. T., Kerr, D. C., Van Ryzin, M., DeGarmo, D. S., Rhoades, K. A., & Leve, L. D. (2013). Depressive symptom trajectories among girls in the juvenile justice system: 24-month outcomes of an RCT of multidimensional treatment foster care. *Prevention Science*, *14*, 437–446. http://dx.doi.org/10.1007/s11121-012-0317-y

Hart, S. D., Kropp, P. R., Laws, D. R., Klaver, J., Logan, C., & Watt, K. A. (2003). *The Risk for Sexual Violence Protocol (RSVP): Structured professional guidelines for assessing risk of sexual violence*. Burnaby, British Columbia, Canada: Mental Health, Law, and Policy Institute, Simon Fraser University; Pacific Psychological Assessment Corporation; & the British Columbia Institute Against Family Violence.

Hart, S. D., & Logan, C. (2011). Formulation of violence risk using evidence-based assessments: The structured professional judgment approach. In P. Sturmey & M. McMurran (Eds.), *Forensic case formulation* (pp. 83–106). Chichester, England: Wiley.

Hattie, J., Marsh, H. W., Neill, J. T., & Richards, G. E. (1997). Adventure education and outward bound: Out-of-class experiences that make a lasting difference. *Review of Educational Research*, *67*, 43–87. http://dx.doi.org/10.3102/00346543067001043

Heilbrun, K. (2003). Violence risk: From prediction to management. In D. Carson & R. Bull (Eds.), *Handbook of psychology in legal contexts* (2nd ed., pp. 127–142). New York, NY: Wiley.

Henggeler, S. W., Letourneau, E. J., Chapman, J. E., Borduin, C. M., Schewe, P. A., & McCart, M. R. (2009). Mediators of change for multisystemic therapy with juvenile sexual offenders. *Journal of Consulting and Clinical Psychology*, *77*, 451–462. http://dx.doi.org/10.1037/a0013971

Henggeler, S. W., Melton, G. B., Brondino, M. J., Scherer, D. G., & Hanley, J. H. (1997). Multisystemic therapy with violent and chronic juvenile offenders and their families: The role of treatment fidelity in successful dissemination. *Journal of Consulting and Clinical Psychology*, *65*, 821–833. http://dx.doi.org/10.1037/0022-006X.65.5.821

Henggeler, S. W., Melton, G. B., & Smith, L. A. (1992). Family preservation using multisystemic therapy: An effective alternative to incarcerating serious juvenile offenders. *Journal of Consulting and Clinical Psychology*, *60*, 953–961. http://dx.doi.org/10.1037/0022-006X.60.6.953

Henggeler, S. W., Rodick, J. D., Borduin, C. M., Hanson, C. L., Watson, S. M., & Urey, J. R. (1986). Multisystemic treatment of juvenile offenders: Effects on adolescent behavior and family interaction. *Developmental Psychology*, *22*, 132–141. http://dx.doi.org/10.1037/0012-1649.22.1.132

Henggeler, S. W., & Schaeffer, C. (2010). Treating serious antisocial behavior using multisystemic therapy. In J. R. Weisz & A. E. Kazdin (Eds.), *Evidence-based psychotherapies for children and adolescents* (2nd ed., pp. 259–276). New York, NY: Guilford Press.

Henggeler, S. W., & Schoenwald, S. K. (2011). Evidence-based interventions for juvenile offenders and juvenile justice policies that support them. *Social Policy Report*, *25*(1), 1–28.

Henggeler, S. W., Schoenwald, S. K., Borduin, C. M., Rowland, M. D., & Cunningham, P. B. (2009). *Multisystemic therapy for antisocial behavior in children and adolescents* (2nd ed.). New York, NY: Guilford Press.

Henggeler, S. W., & Sheidow, A. J. (2012). Empirically supported family-based treatments for conduct disorder and delinquency in adolescents. *Journal of Marital and Family Therapy*, *38*, 30–58. http://dx.doi.org/10.1111/j.1752-0606.2011.00244.x

Hoge, R. D., & Andrews, D. A. (2011). *Youth Level of Service/Case Management Inventory 2.0 (YLS/CMI 2.0): User's Manual*. North Tonawanda, NY: Multi-Health Systems.

Hubbard, D. J., & Latessa, E. J. (2004). *Evaluation of cognitive-behavioral programs for offenders: A look at outcome and responsivity in five treatment programs*. Cincinnati, OH: University of Cincinnati, Center for Criminal Justice Research, Division of Criminal Justice. Retrieved from http://www.uc.edu/content/dam/uc/ccjr/docs/reports/project_reports/CogEvaluationFINAL_REPORT.pdf

Huey, S. J., Jr., Henggeler, S. W., Brondino, M. J., & Pickrel, S. G. (2000). Mechanisms of change in multisystemic therapy: Reducing delinquent behavior through therapist adherence and improved family and peer functioning. *Journal of Consulting and Clinical Psychology*, *68*, 451–467. http://dx.doi.org/10.1037/0022-006X.68.3.451

Huey, S. R., & Polo, A. J. (2010). Assessing the effects of evidence-based psychotherapies with ethnic minority youths. In J. R. Weisz & A. E. Kazdin (Eds.), *Evidence-based psychotherapies for children and adolescents* (2nd ed., pp. 451–465). New York, NY: Guilford Press.

Hunsley, J., & Lee, C. M. (2007). Research-informed benchmarks for psychological treatments: Efficacy studies, effectiveness studies, and beyond. *Professional Psychology: Research and Practice*, *38*, 21–33. http://dx.doi.org/10.1037/0735-7028.38.1.21

Illinois Juvenile Court Act, Ill. Laws 132 et seq. (1899).

In re Gault, 387 U.S. 1 (1967).

In re Winship, 397 U.S. 358 (1970).

Jensen, C. D., Cushing, C. C., Aylward, B. S., Craig, J. T., Sorell, D. M., & Steele, R. G. (2011). Effectiveness of motivational interviewing interventions for adolescent substance use behavior change: A meta-analytic review. *Journal of Consulting and Clinical Psychology, 79*, 433–440. http://dx.doi.org/10.1037/a0023992

Johnson, K., Lanza-Kaduce, L., & Woolard, J. (2011). Disregarding graduated treatment: Why transfer aggravates recidivism. *Crime and Delinquency, 57*, 756–777. http://dx.doi.org/10.1177/0011128708328867

Kerig, P. K., & Schindler, S. R. (2013). Engendering the evidence base: A critical review of the conceptual and empirical foundations of gender-responsive interventions for girls' delinquency. *Laws, 2*, 244–282. http://dx.doi.org/10.3390/laws2030244

Kerr, D. R., Leve, L. D., & Chamberlain, P. (2009). Pregnancy rates among juvenile justice girls in two randomized controlled trials of multidimensional treatment foster care. *Journal of Consulting and Clinical Psychology, 77*, 588–593. http://dx.doi.org/10.1037/a0015289

Klenowski, P. M., Bell, K. J., & Dodson, K. D. (2010). An empirical evaluation of juvenile awareness programs in the United States: Can juveniles be "scared straight"? *Journal of Offender Rehabilitation, 49*, 254–272. http://dx.doi.org/10.1080/10509671003716068

Klietz, S. J., Borduin, C. M., & Schaeffer, C. M. (2010). Cost–benefit analysis of multisystemic therapy with serious and violent juvenile offenders. *Journal of Family Psychology, 24*, 657–666. http://dx.doi.org/10.1037/a0020838

Koegl, C. J., Farrington, D. P., Augimeri, L. K., & Day, D. M. (2008). Evaluation of a targeted cognitive-behavioral program for children with conduct problems—The SNAP Under 12 Outreach Project: Service intensity, age and gender effects on short- and long-term outcomes. *Clinical Child Psychology and Psychiatry, 13*, 419–434. http://dx.doi.org/10.1177/1359104508090606

Krishnan, P., Yeo, L., & Cheng, Y. (2013). School-based cognitive-behavioral therapy for academically underachieving Singaporean adolescents with aggressive and rule-breaking behavior. *Asia Pacific Journal of Counselling and Psychotherapy, 4*, 3–17. http://dx.doi.org/10.1080/21507686.2012.722553

Lambie, I., & Randell, I. (2013). The impact of incarceration on juvenile offenders. *Clinical Psychology Review, 33*, 448–459. http://dx.doi.org/10.1016/j.cpr.2013.01.007

Landenberger, N. A., & Lipsey, M. W. (2005). The positive effects of cognitive-behavioral programs for offenders: A meta-analysis of factors associated with effective treatment. *Journal of Experimental Criminology, 1*, 451–476. http://dx.doi.org/10.1007/s11292-005-3541-7

Lanza-Kaduce, L., Lane, J., Bishop, D. M., & Frazier, C. E. (2005). Juvenile offenders and adult felony recidivism: The impact of transfer. *Journal of Criminal Justice, 28*, 59–77.

Leschied, A. W., & Cunningham, A. (2002). *Seeking effective interventions for serious young offenders: Interim results of a four-year randomized study of multisystemic therapy in Ontario, Canada*. London, Ontario, Canada: Centre for Children and Families in the Justice System of the London Family Court Clinic. Retrieved from http://www.lfcc.on.ca

Letourneau, E. J., Henggeler, S. W., McCart, M. R., Borduin, C. M., Schewe, P. A., & Armstrong, K. S. (2013). Two-year follow-up of a randomized effectiveness trial evaluating MST for juveniles who sexually offend. *Journal of Family Psychology, 27*, 978–985. http://dx.doi.org/10.1037/a0034710

Leve, L. D., & Chamberlain, P. (2007). A randomized evaluation of multidimensional treatment foster care: Effects on school attendance and homework completion in juvenile justice girls. *Research on Social Work Practice, 17*, 657–663. http://dx.doi.org/10.1177/1049731506293971

Leve, L. D., Chamberlain, P., & Reid, J. B. (2005). Intervention outcomes for girls referred from juvenile justice: Effects on delinquency. *Journal of Consulting and Clinical Psychology, 73*, 1181–1184. http://dx.doi.org/10.1037/0022-006X.73.6.1181

Leve, L. D., Chamberlain, P., Smith, D. K., & Harold, G. T. (2012). Multidimensional treatment foster care as an intervention for juvenile justice girls in out-of-home care. In S. Miller, L. D. Leve, & P. K. Kerig (Eds.), *Delinquent girls: Contexts, relationships, and adaptation* (pp. 147–160). http://dx.doi.org/10.1007/978-1-4614-0415-6_9

Levene, K. S., Augimeri, L. K., Pepler, D. J., Walsh, M. M., Koegl, C. J., & Webster, C. D. (2001). *The Early Assessment Risk List for Girls (EARL–21G), Version 1* [Consultation edition]. Toronto, Ontario, Canada: Child Development Institute.

Linehan, M. (1993). *Cognitive behavioral treatment of borderline personality disorder*. New York, NY: Guilford Press.

Lipsey, M. W. (1992). Juvenile delinquency treatment: A meta-analytic inquiry into the variability of effects. In T. D. Cook, H. Cooper, D. S. Cordray, H. Hartmann, L. V. Hedges, R. J. Light, . . . Mosteller, F. (Eds.), *Meta-analysis for explanation: A casebook* (pp. 83–127). New York, NY: Russell Sage Foundation.

Lipsey, M. W. (1995). What do we learn from 400 research studies on the effectiveness of treatment with juvenile delinquents? In J. McGuire (Ed.), *What works: Reducing reoffending? Guidelines from research and practice* (pp. 63–78). London, England: Wiley/Blackwell.

Lipsey, M. W. (2006). The effects of community-based group treatment for delinquency: A meta-analytic search for cross-study generalizations. In K. A. Dodge, T. J. Dishion, & J. E. Lansford (Eds.), *Deviant peer influences in programs for youth* (pp. 162–184). New York, NY: Guilford Press.

Lipsey, M. W. (2009). The primary factors that characterize effective interventions with juvenile offenders: A meta-analytic overview. *Victims and Offenders*, *4*, 124–147. http://dx.doi.org/10.1080/15564880802612573

Lipsey, M. W., Chapman, G. L., & Landenberger, N. A. (2001). Cognitive-behavioral programs for offenders. *Annals of the American Academy of Political and Social Science*, *578*, 144–157. http://dx.doi.org/10.1177/0002716201578001009

Lipsey, M. W., & Cullen, F. T. (2007). The effectiveness of correctional rehabilitation: A review of systematic reviews. *Annual Review of Law and Social Science*, *3*, 297–320. http://dx.doi.org/10.1146/annurev.lawsocsci.3.081806.112833

Lipsey, M. W., & Wilson, D. B. (1998). Effective intervention for serious juvenile offenders: A synthesis of research. In R. Loeber & D. P. Farrington (Eds.), *Serious and violent juvenile offenders: Risk factors and successful interventions* (pp. 313–345). Thousand Oaks, CA: Sage.

Little, G. L., & Robinson, K. D. (1988). Moral reconation therapy: A systematic step-by-step treatment system for treatment resistant clients. *Psychological Reports*, *62*, 135–151. http://dx.doi.org/10.2466/pr0.1988.62.1.135

Loughran, T. A., Mulvey, E. P., Schubert, C. A., Chassin, L. A., Steinberg, L., Piquero, A. R., . . . Losoya, S. (2010). Differential effects of adult court transfer on juvenile offender recidivism. *Law and Human Behavior*, *34*, 476–488. http://dx.doi.org/10.1007/s10979-009-9210-z

Luong, D., & Wormith, J. (2011). Applying risk/need assessment to probation practice and its impact on the recidivism of young offenders. *Criminal Justice and Behavior*, *38*, 1177–1199. http://dx.doi.org/10.1177/0093854811421596

Mack, J. W. (1909). The juvenile court. *Harvard Law Review*, *23*, 104–122. http://dx.doi.org/10.2307/1325042

MacKenzie, D. L. (1990). Boot camp prisons: Components, evaluations, and empirical issues. *Federal Probation*, *54*, 44–52.

MacKenzie, D. L. (2006). *What works in corrections: Reducing the criminal activities of offenders and delinquents*. http://dx.doi.org/10.1017/CBO9780511499470

MacKenzie, D. L., & Herbert, E. E. (Eds.). (1996). *Correctional boot camps: A tough intermediate sanction*. Rockville, MD: National Institute of Justice.

MacKenzie, D. L., Wilson, D. B., & Kider, S. B. (2001). Effects of correctional boot camps on offending. *Annals of the American Academy of Political and Social Science*, *578*, 126–143. http://dx.doi.org/10.1177/0002716201578001008

MacPherson, H. A., Cheavens, J. S., & Fristad, M. A. (2013). Dialectical behavior therapy for adolescents: Theory, treatment adaptations, and empirical outcomes. *Clinical Child and Family Psychology Review*, *16*, 59–80. http://dx.doi.org/10.1007/s10567-012-0126-7

Martinson, R. (1974). What works? Questions and answers about prison reform. In P. Bean (Ed.), *Critical concepts in sociology* (pp. 200–232). London, England: Routledge.

McMurran, M. (2009). Motivational interviewing with offenders: A systematic review. *Legal and Criminological Psychology*, *14*, 83–100. http://dx.doi.org/10.1348/135532508X278326

Mihalic, S., Irwin, K., Elliott, D., Fagan, A., & Hansen, D. (2001, July). Blueprints for Violence Prevention. *Juvenile Justice Bulletin*, pp. 1–16.

Miller, W. R., & Rollnick, S. (2012). *Motivational interviewing: Preparing people for change* (3rd ed.). New York, NY: Guilford Press.

Miller v. Alabama, 132 S. Ct. 2455 (2012).

Moffitt, T. E., Caspi, A., Harrington, H., & Milne, B. J. (2002). Males on the life-course-persistent and adolescence-limited antisocial pathways: Follow-up at age 26 years. *Development and Psychopathology*, *14*, 179–207. http://dx.doi.org/10.1017/S0954579402001104

Muller, J., & Mihalic, S. (1999). *Blueprints: A violence prevention initiative* (Fact Sheet). Washington, DC: US Department of Justice, Office of Justice Programs, Office of Juvenile Justice and Delinquency Prevention.

National Council on Crime and Delinquency. (2001). *Evaluation of the RYSE program, Alameda County Probation Department: A report prepared for Alameda County Probation Department*. Oakland, CA: Author.

Nicholls, T. L., Viljoen, J. L., Cruise, K. R., Desmarais, S. L., & Webster, C. D. (2010). *Short-Term Assessment of Risk and Treatability: Adolescent Version (START:AV) (abbreviated manual)*. Coquitlam, British Columbia, Canada: BC Mental Health and Addiction Services.

Office of Juvenile Justice and Delinquency Program. (2011, March/April). Justice Department discourages the use of "Scared Straight" programs. *OJJDP News at a Glance*. Retrieved from https://www.ncjrs.gov/html/ojjdp/news_at_glance/234084/topstory.html

Ogden, T., & Hagen, K. (2006). Multisystemic treatment of serious behavior problems in youth: Sustainability of effectiveness two years after intake. *Child and Adolescent Mental Health*, *11*, 142–149. http://dx.doi.org/10.1111/j.1475-3588.2006.00396.x

Olver, M. E., Stockdale, K. C., & Wormith, J. (2009). Risk assessment with young offenders: A meta-analysis of three assessment measures. *Criminal Justice and Behavior*, *36*, 329–353. http://dx.doi.org/10.1177/0093854809331457

Pearson, F. S., Lipton, D. S., Cleland, C. M., & Yee, D. S. (2002). The effects of behavioral/cognitive-behavioral programs on recidivism. *Crime and Delinquency*, *48*, 476–496. http://dx.doi.org/10.1177/0011128702048003006

Petrosino, A., Turpin-Petrosino, C., & Buehler, J. (2003). Scared Straight and other juvenile awareness programs for preventing juvenile delinquency: A systematic review of the randomized experimental evidence. *Annals of the American Academy of Political and Social Science*, *589*, 41–62. http://dx.doi.org/10.1177/0002716203254693

Petrosino, A., Turpin-Petrosino, C., Hollis-Peel, M. E., & Lavenberg, J. G. (2013). Scared Straight and other juvenile awareness programs for preventing juvenile delinquency: A systematic review. *Campbell Systematic Reviews*, *9*, 1–55. Retrieved from http://www.campbellcollaboration.org/lib/project/3

Piquero, A. R., Diamond, B., Jennings, W. G., & Reingle, J. M. (2013). Adolescence-limited offending. In C. L. Gibson & M. D. Krohn (Eds.), *Handbook of life-course criminology: Emerging trends and directions for future research* (pp. 129–142). http://dx.doi.org/10.1007/978-1-4614-5113-6_8

Polaschek, D. L. (2011). Many sizes fit all: A preliminary framework for conceptualizing the development and provision of cognitive–behavioral rehabilitation programs for offenders. *Aggression and Violent Behavior*, *16*, 20–35. http://dx.doi.org/10.1016/j.avb.2010.10.002

Poulin, F., Dishion, T. J., & Burraston, B. (2001). 3-year iatrogenic effects associated with aggregating high-risk adolescents in cognitive-behavioral preventive interventions. *Applied Developmental Science*, *5*, 214–224. http://dx.doi.org/10.1207/S1532480XADS0504_03

Proctor, E., Silmere, H., Raghavan, R., Hovmand, P., Aarons, G., Bunger, A., . . . Hensley, M. (2011). Outcomes for implementation research: Conceptual distinctions, measurement challenges, and research agenda. *Administration and Policy in Mental Health and Mental Health Services Research*, *38*, 65–76. http://dx.doi.org/10.1007/s10488-010-0319-7

Reader, W. D. (1996). The laws of unintended results. *Akron Law Review*, *29*, 477–489.

Roper v. Simmons, 543 U.S. 551 (2005).

Rubak, S., Sandbaek, A., Lauritzen, T., & Christensen, B. (2005). Motivational interviewing: A systematic review and meta-analysis. *British Journal of General Practice*, *55*, 305–312.

Russell, K. C. (2000). Exploring how the wilderness therapy process relates to outcomes. *Journal of Experiential Education*, 23, 170–176. http://dx.doi.org/10.1177/105382590002300309

Sawyer, A. M., & Borduin, C. M. (2011). Effects of multisystemic therapy through midlife: A 21.9-year follow-up to a randomized clinical trial with serious and violent juvenile offenders. *Journal of Consulting and Clinical Psychology*, *79*, 643–652. http://dx.doi.org/10.1037/a0024862

Schoemaker, P. (1995). Scenario planning: A tool for strategic thinking. *Sloan Management Review*, *4*, 25–40.

Schoenwald, S. K., McHugh, R., & Barlow, D. H. (2012). The science of dissemination and implementation. In R. McHugh & D. H. Barlow (Eds.), *Dissemination and implementation of evidence-based psychological interventions* (pp. 16–42). New York, NY: Oxford University Press.

Sexton, T., & Turner, C. W. (2010). The effectiveness of functional family therapy for youth with behavioral problems in a community practice setting. *Journal of Family Psychology*, *24*, 339–348. http://dx.doi.org/10.1037/a0019406

Sexton, T. L., & Alexander, J. F. (2003). Functional family therapy: A mature clinical model for working with at-risk adolescents and their families. In T. L. Sexton, G. R. Weeks, & M. S. Robbins (Eds.), *Handbook of family therapy* (pp. 323–348). New York, NY: Brunner-Routledge.

Shelton, D., Kesten, K., Zhang, W., & Trestman, R. (2011). Impact of a dialectic behavior therapy–corrections modified (DBT-CM) upon behaviorally challenged incarcerated male adolescents. *Journal of Child and Adolescent Psychiatric Nursing*, *24*, 105–113. http://dx.doi.org/10.1111/j.1744-6171.2011.00275.x

Simourd, L., & Andrews, D. A. (1994). Correlates of delinquency: A look at gender differences. *Forum on Corrections Research*, *6*, 26–31.

Singh, J. P., Desmarais, S. L., Sellers, B. G., Hylton, T., Tirotti, M., & Van Dorn, R. A. (2014). From risk assessment to risk management: Matching interventions to adolescent offenders' strengths and vulnerabilities. *Children and Youth Services Review*, *47*, 1–9.

Skeem, J. L., & Monahan, J. (2011). Current directions in violence risk assessment. *Current Directions in Psychological Science*, *20*, 38–42. http://dx.doi.org/10.1177/0963721410397271

Slavet, J. D., Stein, L. A., Klein, J. L., Colby, S. M., Barnett, N. P., & Monti, P. M. (2005). Piloting the family check-up with incarcerated adolescents and their parents. *Psychological Services*, 2, 123–132. http://dx.doi.org/10.1037/1541-1559.2.2.123

Smith, D. K., Chamberlain, P., & Eddy, J. M. (2010). Preliminary support for multidimensional treatment foster care in reducing substance use in delinquent boys. *Journal of Child and Adolescent Substance*

Abuse, 19, 343–358. http://dx.doi.org/10.1080/1067828X.2010.511986

Snyder, H. N. (2004). *Juvenile arrests 2002*. Washington, DC: Office of Juvenile Justice and Delinquency Prevention.

Snyder, H. N., Sickmund, M., & Poe-Yamagata, E. (1996). *Juvenile offenders and victims: 1996 update on violence*. Washington, DC: U.S. Department of Justice, Office of Justice Programs, Office of Juvenile Justice and Delinquency Prevention.

Stambaugh, L. F., Mustillo, S. A., Burns, B. J., Stephens, R. L., Baxter, B., Edwards, D., & DeKraai, M. (2007). Outcomes from wraparound and multisystemic therapy in a center for mental health services system-of-care demonstration site. *Journal of Emotional and Behavioral Disorders, 15*, 143–155. http://dx.doi.org/10.1177/10634266070150030201

Stein, L. A. R., Colby, S. M., Barnett, N. P., Monti, P. M., Golembeske, C., & Lebeau-Craven, R. (2006). Effects of motivational interviewing for incarcerated adolescents on driving under the influence after release. *American Journal on Addictions, 15*(Suppl. 1), 50–57. http://dx.doi.org/10.1080/10550490601003680

Steinberg, L. (2003, April). *Less guilty by reason of adolescence: A developmental perspective on adolescence and the law*. Invited Master Lecture, Biennial Meeting of the Society for Research in Child Development, Tampa, FL.

Steinberg, L. (2010). A dual systems model of adolescent risk-taking. *Developmental Psychobiology, 52*, 216–224.

Sukhodolsky, D. G., Kassinove, H., & Gorman, B. S. (2004). Cognitive-behavioral therapy for anger in children and adolescents: A meta-analysis. *Aggression and Violent Behavior, 9*, 247–269. http://dx.doi.org/10.1016/j.avb.2003.08.005

Sundell, K., Hansson, K., Löfholm, C. A., Olsson, T., Gustle, L. H., & Kadesjö, C. (2008). The transportability of multisystemic therapy to Sweden: Short-term results from a randomized trial of conduct-disordered youths. *Journal of Family Psychology, 22*, 550–560. http://dx.doi.org/10.1037/a0012790

Tarolla, S. M., Wagner, E. F., Rabinowitz, J., & Tubman, J. G. (2002). Understanding and treating juvenile offenders: A review of current knowledge and future directions. *Aggression and Violent Behavior, 7*, 125–143. http://dx.doi.org/10.1016/S1359-1789(00)00041-0

TFC Consultants. (2013). *Multidimensional treatment foster care*. Retrieved from http://www.mtfc.com

Timmons-Mitchell, J., Bender, M. B., Kishna, M. A., & Mitchell, C. C. (2006). An independent effectiveness trial of multisystemic therapy with juvenile justice youth. *Journal of Clinical Child and Adolescent Psychology, 35*, 227–236. http://dx.doi.org/10.1207/s15374424jccp3502_6

Trupin, E. W., Stewart, D. G., Beach, B., & Boesky, L. (2002). Effectiveness of dialectical behavior therapy program for incarcerated female juvenile offenders. *Child and Adolescent Mental Health, 7*, 121–127. http://dx.doi.org/10.1111/1475-3588.00022

Vaske, J., Galyean, K., & Cullen, F. T. (2011). Toward a biosocial theory of offender rehabilitation: Why does cognitive-behavioral therapy work? *Journal of Criminal Justice, 39*, 90–102. http://dx.doi.org/10.1016/j.jcrimjus.2010.12.006

Vieira, T. A., Skilling, T. A., & Peterson-Badali, M. (2009). Matching court-ordered services with treatment needs: Predicting treatment success with young offenders. *Criminal Justice and Behavior, 36*, 385–401. http://dx.doi.org/10.1177/0093854808331249

Viljoen, J. L., Brodersen, E., Shaffer, C., & Muir, N.; ARROW Advisory Board (2014). *Adolescent Risk Reduction and Resilient Outcomes Work-Plan*. Burnaby, British Columbia, Canada: Simon Fraser University.

Viljoen, J. L., Cruise, K. R., Nicholls, T. L., Desmarais, S. L., & Webster, C. (2012). Taking stock and taking steps: The case for an adolescent version of the Short-Term Assessment of Risk and Treatability. *International Journal of Forensic Mental Health, 11*, 135–149. http://dx.doi.org/10.1080/14999013.2012.737406

Viljoen, J. L., McLachlan, K., & Vincent, G. M. (2010). Assessing violence risk and psychopathy in juvenile and adult offenders: A survey of clinical practices. *Assessment, 17*, 377–395. http://dx.doi.org/10.1177/1073191109359587

Viljoen, J. L., Mordell, S., & Beneteau, J. L. (2012). Prediction of adolescent sexual reoffending: A meta-analysis of the J-SOAP-II, ERASOR, J-SORRAT-II, and Static-99. *Law and Human Behavior, 36*, 423–438. http://dx.doi.org/10.1037/h0093938

Viljoen, J. L., Nicholls, T. L., Cruise, K. R., Desmarais, S. L., & Webster, C. D.; with contributions by Douglas-Beneteau, J. (2014). *Short-Term Assessment of Risk and Treatability: Adolescent Version (START:AV)–User Guide*. Burnaby, British Columbia, Canada: Mental Health, Law, and Policy Institute.

Vincent, G. M., Guy, L. S., Gershenson, B. G., & McCabe, P. (2012). Does risk assessment make a difference? Results of implementing the SAVRY in juvenile probation. *Behavioral Sciences and the Law, 30*, 384–405. http://dx.doi.org/10.1002/bsl.2014

Vincent, G. M., Paiva-Salisbury, M. L., Cook, N. E., Guy, L. S., & Perrault, R. T. (2012). Impact of risk/needs assessment on juvenile probation officers' decision making: Importance of implementation. *Psychology, Public Policy, and Law, 18*, 549–576. http://dx.doi.org/10.1037/a0027186

Vincent, G. M., Terry, A. M., & Maney, S. M. (2009). Risk/needs tools for antisocial behavior and violence among youthful populations. In J. T. Andrade (Ed.), *Handbook of violence risk assessment and treatment: New approaches for mental health professionals* (pp. 377–423). New York, NY: Springer.

Vitopoulos, N. A., Peterson-Badali, M., & Skilling, T. A. (2012). The relationship between matching service to criminogenic need and recidivism in male and female youth: Examining the RNR principles in practice. *Criminal Justice and Behavior, 39,* 1025–1041. http://dx.doi.org/10.1177/0093854812442895

Ward, T., Yates, P., & Willis, G. (2012). The good lives model and the risk need responsivity model: A critical response to Andrews, Bonta, and Wormith (2011). *Criminal Justice and Behavior, 39,* 94–110. http://dx.doi.org/10.1177/0093854811426085

Weiss, B., Caron, A., Ball, S., Tapp, J., Johnson, M., & Weisz, J. R. (2005). Iatrogenic effects of group treatment for antisocial youths. *Journal of Consulting and Clinical Psychology, 73,* 1036–1044. http://dx.doi.org/10.1037/0022-006X.73.6.1036

Weisz, J. R., Chorpita, B. F., Palinkas, L. A., Schoenwald, S. K., Miranda, J., Bearman, S. K., . . . Gibbons, R. D.; Research Network on Youth Mental Health. (2012). Testing standard and modular designs for psychotherapy treating depression, anxiety, and conduct problems in youth: A randomized effectiveness trial. *Archives of General Psychiatry, 69,* 274–282. http://dx.doi.org/10.1001/archgenpsychiatry.2011.147

White, S. F., Frick, P. J., Lawing, K., & Bauer, D. (2013). Callous-unemotional traits and response to functional family therapy in adolescent offenders. *Behavioral Sciences and the Law, 31,* 271–285. http://dx.doi.org/10.1002/bsl.2041

Wilson, C. M. (2013). *Reliability and consistency of risk formulations in assessments of sexual violence risk* (Doctoral dissertation). Retrieved from http://summit.sfu.ca/item/13599

Wilson, D. B., Bouffard, L. A., & MacKenzie, D. L. (2005). A quantitative review of structured, group-oriented, cognitive–behavioral programs for offenders. *Criminal Justice and Behavior, 32,* 172–204. http://dx.doi.org/10.1177/0093854804272889

Wilson, D. B., MacKenzie, D. L., & Mitchell, F. N. (2008). Effects of correctional boot camps on offending. *Annals of the American Academy of Political and Social Science, 578,* 126–143.

Wilson, S. J., & Lipsey, M. W. (2000). Wilderness challenge programs for delinquent youth: A meta-analysis of outcome evaluations. *Evaluation and Program Planning, 23,* 1–12. http://dx.doi.org/10.1016/S0149-7189(99)00040-3

Woodberry, K. A., & Popenoe, E. J. (2008). Implementing dialectical behavior therapy with adolescents and their families in a community outpatient clinic. *Cognitive and Behavioral Practice, 15,* 277–286. http://dx.doi.org/10.1016/j.cbpra.2007.08.004

Woolfenden, S. R., Williams, K., & Peat, J. (2001). Family and parenting interventions in children and adolescents with conduct disorder and delinquency aged 10–17. *Cochrane Database of Systematic Reviews, 2,* CD003015.

Zahn, M. A., Day, J. C., Mihalic, S. F., & Tichavsky, L. (2009). Determining what works for girls in the juvenile justice system: A summary of evaluation evidence. *Crime and Delinquency, 55,* 266–293. http://dx.doi.org/10.1177/0011128708330649

CHAPTER 25

TRAUMA-INFORMED JUVENILE JUSTICE SYSTEMS AND APPROACHES

Jessica Feierman and Julian D. Ford

Emerging research about psychological trauma holds potential to shape legal advocacy as well as treatment and services for youths in the juvenile justice system. In this chapter, we examine these issues from the perspective of an attorney (Feierman) and a psychologist (Ford), discussing opportunities, pitfalls, and complexities. The opportunities to improve outcomes for youths by applying the research on traumatic stress are significant: An understanding of trauma can improve diagnoses, better match youths with needed trauma-informed services, improve conditions of confinement, and prevent harmful system involvement. Moreover, to the extent that traumatic stress is identified as a risk factor for juvenile justice involvement, a focus on resilience is vital. The potential pitfalls of bringing traumatic stress research into the juvenile justice arena are also substantial: Raising evidence of trauma in court creates a risk of harsher treatment for youths, gathering information about trauma can lead to youth self-incrimination, and urging policy change regarding trauma without simultaneously examining the social context of the juvenile justice system could inadvertently stigmatize or pathologize individual youths or communities. In this chapter, we urge a careful consideration of both risks and opportunities. We also highlight areas of complexity. Although prior traumatic experiences are common for youths in the juvenile justice system, they are not universal. Moreover, psychological trauma and its sequelae (including but not limited to posttraumatic stress disorder [PTSD]) occur in many complex ways that require correspondingly thoughtful and careful responses from both the legal and the mental health fields. Applying a thoughtful approach to trauma and the juvenile justice system will better position both psychologists and attorneys to support positive outcomes for youths.

More than three quarters of youths involved in the juvenile justice system have been exposed to traumatic stressors, including abuse or family or community violence, life-threatening accidents or disasters, and interpersonal losses (Ford, Grasso, Hawke, & Chapman, 2013). For most of these youths, exposure to trauma is a repetitive or continuous condition involving multiple incidents and multiple types of victimization (polyvictimization; Finkelhor, Ormrod, & Turner, 2007). Although exposure to adversity on its own does not automatically traumatize youths, this type of repetitive victimization or harm generally does have a lasting, and troubling, impact. Polyvictimized children must adapt to survive, thus relying on ways of thinking and behaving that may involve aggression, impulsivity, risk taking, self-medication (e.g., with alcohol or drugs), hypervigilance, and isolation or affiliation with peers engaging in similar delinquent behavior (Ford, Chapman, Mack, & Pearson, 2006). These survival adaptations arise in an attempt to protect themselves and others from the danger and harm caused by trauma. Yet they regularly cause problems for youths in relationships, at home, at school, and in the broader community. As a result,

http://dx.doi.org/10.1037/14643-025
APA Handbook of Psychology and Juvenile Justice, K. Heilbrun (Editor-in-Chief)

traumatized youths may face academic failure, disciplinary sanctions, stigma, delinquency, and ultimately contact with law enforcement and the juvenile justice system.

Trauma-related survival adaptations map precisely onto the symptoms of PTSD, particularly as it has been reformulated in the most recent edition of the guidebook to mental health diagnoses, the American Psychiatric Association's (2013) *Diagnostic and Statistical Manual of Mental Disorders, Fifth Edition* (*DSM–5*). Not surprisingly, therefore, PTSD among juvenile justice–involved youths is 3 to 10 times more prevalent than in community samples (Ford, 2012). Not only do the trauma-related survival adaptations of PTSD put youths at risk of entering the juvenile justice system, they may also lead youths to become trapped in the juvenile justice and, subsequently, the adult criminal justice systems. The majority of adolescent offenders do not reoffend after delinquency. However, for some youths, the harsh and restrictive sanctions in the juvenile justice system may exacerbate their own vulnerabilities, including mental health challenges stemming from trauma exposure. A small percentage of such youths fall into persistent life-course delinquency that may lead to social and vocational challenges and failures persisting into adulthood (Moffitt & Caspi, 2001).

Trauma-related emotional, behavioral, and interpersonal problems may also compromise youths' ability to safely engage in programs and services while in legal custody or supervision (Ford & Blaustein, 2013). Moreover, even for youths who enter the juvenile justice system without a history of trauma, justice involvement itself can be traumatic: In many secure placements, youths face not only separation from their families, but also the exacerbation of trauma-related problems or even direct traumatization or retraumatization by strip searches, isolation, and physical or sexual abuse (Burrell, 2013). When the justice system itself traumatizes or retraumatizes youths, this increases the likelihood of persistent recidivism.

Thus, it is incumbent on juvenile justice leaders and advocates to develop policies, programs, and practices that reduce the burden that psychological trauma places on youths, their families and communities, and the justice system itself. Failing to address psychological trauma leads the justice system to incur direct economic costs, the potential for legal sanctions for failure to protect and rehabilitate, and a political and public opinion backlash that can compromise continued future funding and programs.

In this chapter, we describe the history of efforts to make juvenile justice systems and services trauma informed, as well as the scientific research and legal analysis that can guide the design and implementation of trauma-informed practices and policies within the juvenile justice system. We highlight how trauma-informed practices and policies are of particular relevance to vulnerable subpopulations, including girls, youths of color, and juveniles charged with sexual offenses. We conclude with a discussion and recommendations for trauma-informed policies and practices in the justice system, including community-based programs, family-based supports, and residential programming for juvenile justice facilities.

RELEVANT HISTORY

In the final decades of the 19th century, children and adolescents were formally accorded separate status from adults in psychological theory and science[1] and legal theory and practice.[2] The concept of a separate juvenile court, first put into practice with the 1899 founding of the juvenile court in Chicago, established that children should be treated differently than adults under the law. "The child offender ought to be kept separate from the adult criminal, and should receive at the hands of the law a treatment differentiated to suit his special needs; that the courts should be agencies for the rescue as well as

[1]Evidenced, for example, in the 1893 founding by G. Stanley Hall of the *Pedagogical Seminary*, the first psychology journal devoted to the study of child development.

[2]Separate trials for children were first held on a statewide basis in Massachusetts in 1872; in 1899, the first juvenile court was established in Chicago.

the punishment of children" (Mack, 1909, p. 104). Children's cases would be heard in different courtrooms from adult cases, with the public excluded from admission. To rehabilitate youths, an understanding of the origins of delinquent behavior and attitudes was viewed as necessary: "Instead of asking merely whether a boy or a girl has committed a specific offense," the court would

> find out what he is, physically, mentally, morally, and then if it learns that he is treading the path that leads to criminality, to take him in charge, not so much to punish as to reform, not to degrade but to uplift, not to crush but to develop, not to make him a criminal but a worthy citizen. (Mack, 1909, p. 107)

To this end, reformers suggested that a child study team be available to conduct physical and psychological exams and then to advise the court. They also argued that the courtroom layout itself should reflect the juvenile court's more therapeutic goals; rather than sitting up on a bench looking down, the judge should be seated "with the child at his side, where he can on occasion put his arm around his shoulder and draw the lad to him" (Mack, 1909, p. 120).

For youths adjudicated delinquent, the system would continue its focus on rehabilitation. Probation officers would demonstrate "guidance and friendly interest" in their charges.[3] Reformers asserted that children should not be imprisoned (Mack, 1909). Parents were viewed as the best source of rehabilitation—and children were to remain with their parents when possible. However, if a child must be removed from the home, a rehabilitative placement would be sought.

> If a child must be taken away from its home, if for the natural parental care that of the state is to be substituted, a real school, not a prison in disguise, must be provided. . . . This cannot be done in one great building, with a single dormitory for all of the two or three or four hundred or more children, in which there will be no possibility of classification along the lines of age or degrees of delinquency, in which there will be no individualized attention. (Mack, 1909, p. 114)

Instead, reformers advocated for children to be placed in cottages in the country:

> Locks and bars and other indicia of prisons must be avoided; human love, supplemented by human interest and vigilance, must replace them. In such schools there must be opportunity for agricultural and industrial training, so that when the boys and girls come out, they will be fitted to do a man's or woman's work in the world, and not be merely a helpless lot. (Mack, 1909, p. 114)[4]

The core elements of the juvenile justice system spread from Judge Mack's court across the country. Within 20 years, each state had a designated juvenile court in which children were treated differently than adults, with a more informal approach focused on rehabilitation and education rather than incarceration with adults.

Proponents saw the juvenile justice system as a step toward a more humane treatment of youths. Critics, however, have sine raised concerns about the juvenile system's role in punishing youths for failing to comply with race-, ethnicity-, and class-based norms. Early reformers described the youths who would come into the juvenile justice system as coming from the "dangerous classes," "little Arabs,"

[3]Mack (1909) further explained that the probation officer's

> duties are oftentimes of the most delicate nature. Tact, forbearance, and sympathy with the child, as well as a full appreciation of the difficulties that the poorer classes, and especially the immigrants . . . are indispensable. . . . The probation officers obtaining the best results enter into intimate friendly relations with their probationers, and bring into play as many factors as possible, such as, for instance, securing employment for their probationers, readjusting family difficulties, securing medical treatment or charity if necessary, interesting helpful friends and relatives, getting the cooperation of churches, social settlements and various other organizations, encouraging probationers to start bank accounts, to keep better hours, to associate with better companions, and so forth. (p. 117)

[4]This approach was consistent with the moral treatment paradigm (Bockoven, 1956; Rowley, 1845) that was in ascendance in the mental health field in the 19th and early 20th centuries. Moral treatment fell into disfavor (Peloquin, 1994) because of the warehousing of disturbed people in institutions that were the prisons in disguise that Judge Mack had decried.

and "foreign childhood that floats along the streets and docks of the city—vagabondish, thievish, familiar with the vicious ways and places of the town" (Platt, 1974, p. 373). Reformers also noted that such youths are "mainly American-born, but the children of Irish and German immigrants. They are as ignorant as London fishmen or costermongers. They are far more brutal than the peasantry from whom they descend, and much banded together" (Platt, 1974, p. 374). If the "civilizing influences of American life" failed to reach them, "we should see an explosion from this class which might leave this city in ashes and blood" (Platt, 1974, p. 374).

In the more than 100 years since its inception, the juvenile justice system has gone through several paradigmatic changes. In the 1960s, the U.S. Supreme Court launched an era of constitutionalization, which established increased procedural protections for youths (Levick, Feierman, Kelley, Goldstein, & Mordecai, 2012, p. 288). As the Court explained, a judicial system that had begun with the goals of reform and rehabilitation had given way to one marked by procedural irregularities; children faced harsh punitive consequences without minimal procedural protections. Referring to an earlier case noting that the "powers of the Star Chamber were a trifle in comparison with those of our juvenile courts" (*In re Gault*, 1967, p. 18), the Supreme Court underscored the risks of procedural arbitrariness in the existing juvenile system. Because "the condition of being a boy does not justify a kangaroo court" (*In re Gault*, 1967, p. 28), juveniles were entitled to key due process protections, including the right to counsel, the right to notice of charges, and the right to confront witnesses, and the right against self-incrimination. Significant distinctions remained between juvenile and adult court: Not all constitutional protections guaranteed in criminal court attached in juvenile proceedings. For example, juveniles did not have a right to trial by jury (*McKeiver v. Pennsylvania*, 1971). Moreover, states still were free to (and did) create unique and rehabilitative juvenile dispositions. The informality of the courtroom, however, gave way to a more formal, and generally more adversarial, structure.

In the 1980s, during a period of economic recession and escalating crime, public attitudes and justice policies took a sharp turn toward a conservative "get tough" approach (Scott & Steinberg, 2008). Rather than seeing young offenders as wayward children, advocates for legislative reform "seemed to view juveniles involved in crime as *more* culpable and dangerous than adult criminals . . . 'super-predators[,]' . . . remorseless teenage criminals" (Scott & Steinberg, 2008, p. 17). This research, later discredited even by some of its own authors predicted that youth crime rates would continue to rise (Becker, 2001). Relying on the research, state legislatures passed increasingly punitive laws, directing many more cases to the adult system, through transfer statutes in which youths of a certain age, or charged with certain crimes, would automatically be charged as adults. This led to an estimated 250,000 youths per year being transferred to the adult criminal justice system (Scott & Steinberg, 2008). At the same time, legislation reshaped the juvenile justice system to focus increasingly on punishment and accountability. Youths were subjected to longer juvenile dispositions in secure placement not only for violent offenses, but also for property crimes, other nonviolent offenses, and school-based behavior that were once the purview of the school disciplinary system (Scott & Steinberg, 2008, p. 48). Although the dire predictions about youth criminality that spurred these changes turned out to be misguided, the policies remained for decades, and continue to hold sway in many juvenile justice systems.

The next significant shift in juvenile policy began in the early 2000s, with a heightened focus on adolescent development and a responsiveness to both psychological and neuroscience research. In 2005, the U.S. Supreme Court struck down the death penalty as applied to minors, noting key distinctions between youths and adults (*Roper v. Simmons*, 2005). According to the Court, juveniles were less culpable than adults because they lacked maturity and responsibility—as evidenced by their "impetuous and ill-considered actions and decisions," they are more "vulnerable or susceptible to negative influences and outside pressures, including peer pressure" (*Roper v. Simmons*, 2005, p. 569) than adults, and their character is less well-formed, more transitory, than that of an adult. In establishing these distinctions, the Court relied not only on common sense, but also referred to psychological research submitted in *amicus* briefs. In subsequent cases, the emphasis on psychology and, increasingly, neuroscience, was even more solidly established. The Court subsequently used the research to strike down as unconstitutional life without parole for juveniles convicted of nonhomicide offenses (*Graham v. Florida*, 2010) or through mandatory sentencing schemes (*Miller v. Alabama*, 2012) and to establish that police must give *Miranda* warnings if a "reasonable child" would have perceived that he or she was not free to leave (*J.D.B. v. North Carolina*, 2011). The Supreme Court's recognition that psychological research and neuroscience play a role in defining how the law should be applied to teenagers has led to a shift from the punitive laws of the 1990s to a new, evidence-based response to juvenile offending, in both the juvenile and the criminal justice systems.

Contemporary juvenile courts reflect their history. Each state retains elements of the original juvenile court separate from the adult criminal justice system, with an ongoing attention to rehabilitation (although often balanced with other penological goals). All states also include procedural protections, such as the right to counsel, for juveniles. Although many states still have adult sentencing and other harsh dispositions for juveniles, the past 10 years have turned the focus to the need for evidence-based and developmentally appropriate interventions for youths. Moreover, as the neuroscience on adolescent development has developed, emerging research has also provided more clarity to researchers' understanding of psychological trauma and PTSD (Ford, 2009).

Despite significant changes in the juvenile justice system over the past century, contemporary research demonstrates that we have not left behind the problems of racial and ethnic bias that were part and parcel of the formation of the juvenile court. A youth of color is much more likely than a White youth to enter the juvenile justice system, even though White youths are more likely to engage in unlawful behavior (Desai, Falzer, Chapman, & Borum, 2012; Piquero, 2008; Vazsonyi & Chen, 2010). White children and families are more likely to receive private mental health care, whereas children and families of color, particularly those with lower incomes, are more likely to be brought under the supervision of public systems (Davis & Ford, 2004; Stagman & Cooper, 2010). Moreover, many youths of color are brought into the juvenile justice system for normative adolescent behavior that is not a sign of a troubled past but instead of heightened policing in their schools and communities (Kim, Losen, & Hewitt, 2010). Youths of color therefore disproportionately face a risk of psychological trauma, as a direct result of their placement in a juvenile justice facility.

It is within the context of this history that we explore how juvenile justice systems respond to psychological trauma. The focus on psychology and neuroscience over the past 10 years provided courts and agencies with a precedent for forging important links between science and law (Ford, 2012). The scientific lens, in turn, has provided a new approach to the juvenile justice system's focus on rehabilitation. History suggests that research can and should influence policies and practices in the juvenile justice system. History also warns that good intentions, unchecked by procedural protections, are not the answer.

CURRENT EVIDENCE AND STANDARDS

A growing body of scientific and clinical evidence about the impact of trauma on children and families provides a foundation for reforms in juvenile justice systems. While there is increasing clarity about clinical interventions, case law and legal standards are still in flux. In various legal contexts and different jurisdictions, courts and legislatures respond differently to the research on trauma. In some instances, the research is used as mitigation evidence, or to connect youth with needed services. In other instances, however, the research is used to justify longer or more secure placement for youth. These inconsistencies suggest the need for ongoing attention to the interplay between clinical research and legal and policy development.

Scientific and Clinical Evidence

Since the diagnosis of PTSD was first formally recognized in the American Psychiatric Association's *Diagnostic and Statistical Manual of Mental Disorders* 35 years ago, scientific and clinical studies have refined our understanding of the nature and impact of psychological trauma. The field has shifted from viewing PTSD primarily as a disorder of anxiety to a broader view that psychological trauma can alter youths' fundamental capacities for self-regulation.

Exposure to psychological trauma and posttraumatic stress sequelae. The definition of psychological trauma has undergone many revisions and was most recently reformulated in the *DSM–5*. The *DSM–5* criteria of PTSD and acute stress disorder include underlying traumatic experience such as directly experiencing, witnessing (immediately or in the aftermath), or indirectly learning about a close family member or friend being subjected to events involving "exposure to actual or threatened death, serious injury, or sexual violence" (American Psychiatric Association, 2013, p. 271). Whether the experience then leads to PTSD will depend on the individual's response, which, in turn, is shaped by his or her internal and external resources (DiGangi et al., 2013). Any close encounter of this kind with death or imminent threat of death, physical devastation, or betrayal and violation can lead to a lasting sense of profound fear, shock, or horror. In PTSD, this is seen in spontaneous memories of traumatic events, including recurrent dreams, flashbacks, or other intense physical or psychological distress; hypervigilance; heightened arousal; avoidance of reminders; persistent negative thoughts (including blame of self or others) and emotions (including anger, guilt, shame, horror, terror, and grief) or absent or numbed emotions; and problems with aggressive, isolative, impulsive, and intentionally or accidentally self-injuring behavior.

Most children are remarkably resilient, even in the face of harmful or traumatic events. However, when trauma is complex, even the most resilient child or youth, without needed supports, tends to develop serious and persistent emotional and behavioral problems (D'Andrea, Ford, Stolbach, Spinazzola, & van der Kolk, 2012; Ford, 2005). Complex psychological trauma often involves multiple types—not just incidents, but types (e.g., physical abuse, sexual abuse, domestic violence, community violence, life-threatening neglect)—of adversity or victimization. Complex trauma thus usually involves polyvictimization (Finkelhor et al., 2007; Finkelhor, Ormrod, Turner, & Hamby, 2005). Tragically, complex trauma does not take any single universal form but can occur in many ways when trauma exposure involves prolonged or unrelentingly repeated intentional acts that violate the social compact and the integrity of the individual (e.g., torture, captivity, battering, molestation).

Posttraumatic stress and self-regulation. Pervasive traumatic exposure can be profoundly harmful for children and youths (Shonkoff & Garner, 2012) because the brain's and body's stress response systems become chronically activated as if constantly struggling to survive in the face of extreme threats (Ford, 2009). In essence, traumatization severely undermines a youth's capacity for self-regulation. Self-regulation is a fundamental psychological capacity acquired in childhood that involves the ability to deploy several basic psychobiological competences to achieve allostatic (homeostasis-promoting; McEwen, 2006) balance in body state, psychological state, and relationship to the physical and interpersonal environment. Buckner, Mezzacappa, and Beardslee (2009) defined self-regulation as "an integrated set of abilities or skills that draw from both executive function and emotion regulation capacities, which are . . . interrelated and act in a collaborative manner when an individual engages in goal-directed behavior" (p. 19). Their research has pointed to the pivotal role of self-regulation in increased adaptive functioning across a wide range of outcomes (e.g., social competence, academic achievement, maintaining or regaining emotional equilibrium). Markers of successful self-regulation in youths are not just superficially or transiently compliant behavior but an enhanced ability to cope with stressors without self-defeating attitudes and behavior (Compas, 2006).

Self-regulation requires the intentional gathering and processing of information to selectively and successfully pursue goals (Thayer, Hansen, Saus-Rose, & Johnsen, 2009) that, when achieved, increase the overall well-being of both the individual and her or his social and physical environment. Active pursuit of goals requires a complex harnessing of self-organizational and emotion regulation capacities. To organize behavior effectively for this purpose, one must shift from being either passive (unresponsive) or reflexively reactive (automatic response tendency) to finding and selectively activating an intentional action strategy (contextually appropriate response) that is not interrupted or distorted by habitual reactions (automatic response tendencies) but draws on the person's past successful responses (general response bias; J. W. Sherman et al., 2008). Put more basically, to be self-regulated is to be able to (a) stop and think, (b) learn from past experiences, and (c) be ready and aim before firing (Ford, 2009).

Self-regulation thus involves the ability to (a) consciously focus attention, (b) be aware of the environment and one's own physical and emotional body states, (c) draw on memory to learn from the past and adapt effectively in the present, and (d) maintain or regain emotion states that provide a genuine sense of well-being and lead to further self-regulation. Although these competencies may seem obvious, they are deceptively difficult for traumatized youths to achieve on a reliable basis. Structuring programs serving youths in the juvenile justice system to elicit, support, and foster self-regulation is therefore a direct way both to help youths recover from complex trauma and to make courts, services, and facilities—and their communities—safer and healthier. Self-regulation is a normative developmental challenge for all children and adolescents; thus, approaches to juvenile justice policies, operations, and services that are designed to enhance self-regulation may have broader benefits for all youths, not just those who have experienced psychological trauma (Ford & Blaustein, 2013).

Self-regulation begins with the selective and sustained deployment of attention (Ayduk et al., 2000). Children (Turner, Finkelhor, & Ormrod, 2006) and adolescents (Ford, Elhai, Connor, & Frueh, 2010) who have experienced complex traumatic stressors often have pervasive problems with concentration. This is a hallmark of PTSD that can be difficult to distinguish from, and may be misdiagnosed as, attention-deficit disorder symptoms (Ford & Connor, 2009). Attention-deficit/hyperactivity disorder is a common comorbidity of PTSD in children and adolescents that may be better diagnosed as PTSD alone in some cases (Ford & Connor, 2009). The attentional focusing problems in both of these disorders are similar but distinct, and each can put adolescents at risk for more severe disruptive behavior disorders (e.g., oppositional defiant disorder; Ford et al., 2000). Therefore, whether the source is attention deficit disorder, PTSD, or a combination of both, enhancing attention-focusing skills is a key first step in addressing the complicated self-regulation deficits of many youths in the justice system.

A second critical component of self-regulation is awareness of sensory–perceptual input from the environment and sensorimotor (e.g., kinesthetic and vagal tone or heart rate rhythm feedback; Porges, 2007) information from within the body. Sensory–perceptual awareness enables the person to consciously select and accurately perceive relevant information from the environment (Ford, 2005). Instead of approaching the external environment and their own internal environment including emotions and body states, with confidence and interest, children who have experienced complex traumatic stressors such as maltreatment and are experiencing PTSD or related posttraumatic reactions tend instead to experience hypervigilance (constantly scanning for danger and becoming flooded with too much sensory–perceptual information) or dissociation (a blunted awareness of important information) from their bodies and the environment (Cicchetti & Curtis, 2005).

Several related forms of memory are a third component of self-regulation. These include working (short-term processing), declarative (verbal), and narrative (autobiographical) memory. PTSD involves impairment in all three types of memory (Jelinek, Randjbar, Seifert, Kellner, & Moritz, 2009). Verbal memory is susceptible to interruption or inaccuracy when psychological trauma occurs (Elzinga, Bakker, & Bremner, 2005). Moreover, PTSD may have a particularly marked influence on autobiographical memory (Jelinek et al., 2009). Memory that draws on past experience as a guide for goals and plans is most useful if it includes not just the scattered details but meaningful stories or narratives that represent a logical and chronological depiction of how things have happened and, therefore, how events may occur or can be influenced in the future. Autobiographical memory enables a person to make sense of, learn from, and use what has been most important in her or his life. People with PTSD tend to report traumatic memories in response to cues that would generally elicit positive memories in nontraumatized individuals (Sutherland & Bryant, 2008). Posttraumatic impairment in autobiographical memory may undermine the child's or adolescent's core sense of self, potentially contributing to a sense of being "fragile in a dangerous world" and having experienced "permanent and disturbing change" (Meiser-Stedman, Dalgleish, Glucksman, Yule, & Smith, 2009, p. 232).

Finally, emotion regulation (Goldsmith, Pollak, & Davidson, 2008) and interpersonal connectedness (attachment; Lyons-Ruth, Dutra, Schuder, & Bianchi, 2006) are essential higher order capacities that enable youths to translate sensory–perceptual/sensorimotor and cognitive/memory information into emotion states and relational connections that reinforce and sustain the continued use and development of all other self-regulatory competences. Emotion regulation involves being able to sustain euthymic emotion states (e.g., a balance of feeling calm and energized, satisfied and motivated) and to recover from dysthymic emotion states (Ford, 2005). Relational connectedness involves a parallel combination of being able to sustain secure attachment working models (i.e., trust, closeness, affection) while recovering from insecure and disorganized attachment working models (e.g., viewing relationships as abandoning, betrayals, exploitive, rejecting, unloving, or worthless). Developmentally, emotion regulation competences are learned through interactions from the first days of life with primary caregivers who are responsive, attuned, and reliable (Lyons-Ruth et al., 2006)—that is, through modeling of emotion regulation in caring and trustworthy relationships (Ford, 2005). Although internalization of the sense of security established in the first years of life with primary caregivers is essential for children to become able to autonomously regulate their emotions, interpersonal connectedness continues to be an essential element in emotion regulation throughout the life span.

The central (brain) and peripheral (autonomic) nervous system alterations associated with childhood exposure to maltreatment and violence (Teicher & Samson, 2013) are likely to increase stress reactivity, anger, and impulsivity while reducing the youth's ability to self-regulate (Weder et al., 2009; P. Yang, Wu, Hsu, & Ker, 2004; S. J. Yang, Shin, Noh, & Stein, 2007). Complex trauma exposure is also associated with altered cognitive information processing, schemas, and expectations that may lead the youth to be prone to endorse aggression (Bradshaw & Garbarino, 2004; Dodge, Pettit, Bates, & Valente, 1995), submit to victimization (Ponce, Williams, & Allen, 2004), or experience high levels of self-criticism and shame (Alessandri & Lewis, 1996; Glassman, Weierich, Hooley, Deliberto, & Nock, 2007; Sachs-Ericsson, Verona, Joiner, & Preacher, 2006)—all of which are associated with increased risk of reactive aggression (Crick & Dodge, 1996; Hudley & Friday, 1996; Shields & Cicchetti, 1998). Moreover, complex trauma may lead to involvement with peers who engage in, model, and encourage delinquent behavior (Ford, Elhai, et al., 2010). Such problems can occur from childhood exposure to domestic violence or abuse (Choi, Jeong, Rohan, Polcari, & Teicher, 2009; De Bellis & Kuchibhatla, 2006), childhood sexual abuse (Kitayama et al., 2007; Lanius et al., 2005; Schmahl, Vermetten, Elzinga, & Douglas Bremner, 2003), combinations of these traumatic adversities (i.e., polyvictimization; Ford et al., 2013), and multiple out-of-home placements (Ford, Connor, & Hawke, 2009).

As a result of these impairments in self-regulation, youths with complex trauma histories often develop externalizing problems (e.g., hostility, oppositionality, impulsivity) in childhood (Ford,

Fraleigh, & Connor, 2010; Ford et al., 1999; Mongillo, Briggs-Gowan, Ford, & Carter, 2009) and adolescence (Farrington, 1993; Ford et al., 2009; Ford, Hartman, Hawke, & Chapman, 2008; Ruchkin, Henrich, Jones, Vermeiren, & Schwab-Stone, 2007; Turner et al., 2006). These youths tend to be diagnosed with externalizing disorders such as attention-deficit/hyperactivity disorder, oppositional defiant disorder, and conduct disorder; personality disorders; or behavioral dyscontrol syndromes (e.g., psychopathy, substance use, intermittent explosive disorders). Although those diagnoses may sometimes be warranted, this diagnostic profile fits many youths in secure justice settings who are primarily reactively aggressive and not intractable to treatment or rehabilitation. Assessing and treating the sequelae of undetected complex trauma provide an alternative approach to remediating complicated and severe behavior problems in justice-involved youths and can thus promote more effective management and treatment options.

Risk and Protective Factors

Psychologically traumatic experiences affect children and youths differently at different ages and in different familial and community contexts; youths vary greatly in their degree of resilience to traumatic events. The traumatic stress research field has dealt with this heterogeneity by identifying measurable factors that either increase the risk of a child having chronic adverse posttraumatic reactions or have a protective effect in the aftermath of trauma exposure. Age (whether in childhood or later in life), race, and ethnic or cultural background have not been found to consistently be either a risk or protective factor for traumatized children (Copeland, Keeler, Angold, & Costello, 2007; McLaughlin et al., 2013). The prevalence of exposure to traumatic stressors and posttraumatic stress problems is comparable for White youth and youth of color in the community (Copeland et al., 2007; McLaughlin et al., 2013) and in the juvenile justice system (Abram et al., 2004; Ford et al., 2008, 2013).

In contrast, gender has repeatedly been identified as a risk factor. Although exposure to trauma puts youths and adults of both genders at risk not just for PTSD but for a wide range of serious and persistent emotional and behavioral problems, traumatized girls and women are twice as likely as boys and men to develop PTSD or other inward-directed (internalizing) disorders involving anxiety, depression, dissociation, or eating problems (Tolin & Foa, 2006). Traumatized boys are more likely than girls to have severe problems in adolescence with aggression, delinquency, and substance abuse—although traumatized girls can also develop severe problems of these types (Leve & Chamberlain, 2004).

A careful look at gender and trauma reveals a somewhat more nuanced picture. Boys' externalizing problems are often preceded by internalized anxiety or depression that is typically less well recognized (Ford et al., 2006) and more adversely affected by family breakdown than girls' (Nilsson, Gustafsson, & Svedin, 2012). Moreover, a traumatized girl is also at risk for externalizing behavior problems, which unfortunately also often go undetected until the girl's behavior has become sufficiently severe to result in juvenile justice involvement, serious health risks, or intensive psychiatric treatment (Smith, Leve, & Chamberlain, 2006).

Most traumatized youths, male and female, are remarkably resilient, but this does not mean that they are unaffected by traumatic experiences. Resilience is the capacity to retain and continue to develop self-regulation (Dishion & Connell, 2006) despite experiencing the aftereffects of psychological trauma. Most youths who have experienced traumatic stressors, particularly when they take the form of interpersonal victimization, betrayal, exploitation, or loss, have traumatic stress reactions during and for some time afterward (Copeland et al., 2007; McLaughlin et al., 2013). These posttraumatic reactions are expected biological adaptations to the survival threat posed by trauma (Ford, 2005), not signs of physical or psychological weakness or pathology. Resilient youths go on to either cope with or resolve these reactions before they develop into a persistent impairment in their ability to function and mature, or they are able to recover physiologically (Vaisvaser et al., 2013) and psychologically with effective help if they develop PTSD or a related behavioral or emotional disorder (Brom & Kleber, 2008).

Key protective factors that increase the likelihood of resilience among youths in the wake of psychological trauma include parental support and role modeling, involvement and achievement in school and other prosocial activities, social support from other trusted adults and peers, the development of strong emotion regulation capacities, and a sense of optimism and self-efficacy (either before or after the trauma; DiGangi et al., 2013; Hoge, Austin, & Pollack, 2007). The dynamic nature of many of the protective factors underscores the extent to which systems and policies, as well as families and communities, can support resilience.

Psychological Trauma and Youths in the Juvenile Justice System[5]

Between 25% (Costello, Fairbank, Erklani, & Angold, 2002) and 43% (Silverman, Reinherz, & Giaconia, 1996) of children in the United States are estimated to experience at least one traumatic stressor (Seedat, Nyamai, Njenga, Vythilingum, & Stein, 2004), with an estimated 60% to 75% of adolescents (McLaughlin et al., 2013; Seedat et al., 2004) reporting having experienced at least one traumatic stressor in their lifetime. Focusing specifically on complex trauma, the lowest epidemiological prevalence estimate for children and youths in the United States is 5% (Costello et al., 2002). Other studies have indicated that as many as one in five 3-year-olds in community samples has experienced potentially traumatic family violence (Mongillo et al., 2009), and almost one in three adolescents (Kilpatrick et al., 2000) has experienced potentially traumatic physical or sexual assault. Between 50% (Kilpatrick et al., 2000) and 80% (Finkelhor, Ormrod, & Turner, 2009) of children and adolescents in the United States have reported some form of victimization, including sexual assault (5%–8%), physical assault (22%–61%), abuse (16%), witnessing family violence or abuse (10%), or murder of a family member or friend (8%).

Youths can become involved in the delinquency system for a host of reasons unrelated to their mental health or even their actions. In certain schools or neighborhoods, normative adolescent behavior regularly leads to juvenile court involvement. This is particularly true for youth of color, including African American and Latino youths (Davis & Ford, 2004). Moreover, many youths who experience trauma and engage in delinquent acts never become involved in the juvenile justice system. Often, these disparities also reflect social realities, with wealthier youths and white youths less likely to face system involvement for their behavior (Annie E. Casey Foundation, 2006).

Nonetheless, the prevalence of trauma histories is much higher for youths in the juvenile justice system than in the larger community. Approximately 90% of youths in juvenile detention facilities reported a history of exposure to at least one potentially traumatic event in two independent surveys of representative samples (Abram et al., 2004; Ford et al., 2008). Prevalence estimates of being threatened with a weapon (58%; Abram et al., 2004), traumatic loss (48%; Ford et al., 2008), and physical assault (35%; Abram et al., 2004; Ford, Hawke, & Chapman, 2010) were particularly high in the juvenile detention samples compared with community samples. A hierarchical cluster analysis of a large representative sample of youths in juvenile detention revealed two complex trauma subgroups: 20% of those in detention reported some combination of sexual or physical abuse or family violence, and 15% of the sample had experienced emotional abuse and family violence but not physical or sexual abuse (Ford, Hawke, & Chapman, 2010). The resultant combined prevalence estimate of 35% for complex trauma history is about 3 times higher than the 10% to 13% estimates of polyvictimization from an epidemiological study of children and adolescents (Finkelhor et al., 2009) and adolescents (Ford, Elhai, et al., 2010). High prevalence estimates of PTSD have been reported for youths in justice settings—as many as 10% to 19% of detained youths in the United States meet criteria for PTSD (Abram et al., 2004; Cauffman, Feldman, Waterman, & Steiner, 1998; Ford et al., 2008; Steiner, Garcia, & Matthews, 1997).

[5]Portions of this section are from *Trauma and Resilience: A New Look at Advocacy for Youth in the Juvenile Justice and Child Welfare Systems*, by J. Feierman and L. Fine, 2014, Philadelphia, PA: Juvenile Law Center. Adapted with permission.

Gender, Sexual Identity, and Posttraumatic Stress in the Juvenile Justice System

In the past 2 decades, the incidence of juvenile justice involvement among girls has risen substantially, compared with relatively stable levels for boys (Leve & Chamberlain, 2004). Girls enter the juvenile justice system with higher rates of exposure to childhood maltreatment than their male counterparts (King et al., 2011). Between 70% and 90% of girls who are placed in secure juvenile justice settings report trauma histories, usually with multiple ongoing incidents consistent with complex trauma (Abram et al., 2004; Cauffman et al., 1998; Steiner et al., 1997). Many of these girls are involved in the child welfare system and are at high risk for problems with substance abuse, risky sexual behavior, teen pregnancy, intergenerational family and domestic violence, community violence, physical illness, unemployment, school failure, and adult incarceration (Kerr, Leve, & Chamberlain, 2009; Smith et al., 2006). Overall, although girls make up 20% to 35% of the overall juvenile delinquency population, they account for 33% to 50% of the "crossover" population, or group of youths who have had contact with both the juvenile justice and the child welfare systems.

Girls' experiences of family violence frequently influence their pathways into the juvenile justice system. Girls tend to be detained or incarcerated for less serious offenses than boys, including technical probation violations and status offenses, often as a result of self-protective behavior such as running away from violence in the home. Similarly, to the extent that girls are arrested for violent crimes, their offenses disproportionately involve family members or others with whom they have relationships, often when they are witnesses to or victims of domestic violence. Thus, reactive aggression in defense of self or others may be a substantial problem legally and interpersonally for traumatized girls. Self-directed aggression (i.e., self-harm) is also more common among traumatized girls than boys (Bilén et al., 2010; Muehlenkamp, Williams, Gutierrez, & Claes, 2009; Olfson, Gameroff, Marcus, Greenberg, & Shaffer, 2005).

Studies with girls have found them to be less likely to be overtly aggressive than boys (Card, Stucky, Sawalani, & Little, 2008) but equally or more likely to be persistently physically aggressive (Lynne-Landsman, Graber, Nichols, & Botvin, 2011), especially if they have been victimized (Cullerton-Sen et al., 2008; O'Leary, Smith Slep, Avery-Leaf, & Cascardi, 2008). Girls have also been found to use covert forms of relational aggression such as intentionally humiliating or rejecting other people more frequently than boys (Bowie, 2007; Ostrov & Godleski, 2010), particularly if they have been sexually abused (Cullerton-Sen et al., 2008). Emotion regulation problems are associated with the use of relational aggression only for girls, and youths who engage in relational aggression are likely to behave in socially deviant ways (Bowie, 2010).

Although girls are more likely than boys to have histories of sexual abuse, boys in the juvenile justice system (King et al., 2011) are more likely than other boys (McLaughlin et al., 2013) to have been sexually abused. For boys or girls in the juvenile justice system who have histories of sexual abuse, gender influences the sequelae: Girls have been found to be more likely than their male peers to respond to violent sexual abuse with anxiety and affective disorders, and boys have been found more likely to have attention-deficit/hyperactivity disorder or disruptive behavior disorders and substance use disorders (King et al., 2011). Girls entering the juvenile justice system are in general more likely than boys to have affective or anxiety disorders and conditions frequently comorbid with them, such as eating disorders.

Girls may also face distinct issues once they enter juvenile justice facilities. They are at higher risk for sexual abuse at the hands of staff than are their male peers. Programs operating in juvenile justice facilities have often not been tested on or validated for use with girls, or they may not be available to girls because of the smaller population size. Even medical providers in juvenile facilities are often ill equipped to address girls' health issues. A lack of program options may also mean that girls are likely to be sent farther away because no appropriate options exist in their communities (F. Sherman & Levick, 2003).

As with gender, sexual orientation and gender identity often inform a youth's pathway into the juvenile justice system, his or her treatment needs, and the risk of victimization within the system. Indeed, youths who are gender nonconforming may be at a greater risk for exposure to psychological trauma both before entering and within the juvenile justice system. Lesbian, gay, bisexual, transgender, and questioning (LGBTQ) youths are more likely than their straight peers to experience rejection or abuse by their families (both biological and foster), victimization at school, homelessness, and certain types of criminal charges, such as prostitution (Majd, Marksamer, & Reyes, 2009). Although LGBTQ youths, like all youths, enter the justice system for a variety of reasons, many become involved for reasons relating to their gender identities or sexual orientation, such as chronic truancy because of fear of harassment at school, running away because of harassment or abuse at home, and survival crimes once they have run away, including prostitution (Majd et al., 2009; Wilber, Ryan, & Marksamer, 2006).

Despite the increased presence of LGBTQ youths in the juvenile justice system, most programs that provide services to youths fail to consider sexual orientation or gender identity in the development of their policies and professional standards (Estrada & Marksamer, 2006). LGBTQ youths are thus more likely to continue experiencing rejection, harassment, and other victimization once in placement, at the hands of both other youths and staff. Few placements or jurisdictions have developed policies to house gender-nonconforming youths according to gender identity rather than physical characteristics. This can lead to further harassment and, in the juvenile justice system, to gender-nonconforming youths being placed in solitary confinement for extended periods of time (Wilber et al., 2006).

Youths of Color and Posttraumatic Stress in the Juvenile Justice System

As we have noted, youths of color are overrepresented in the juvenile justice system and in secure settings specifically (Iguchi, Bell, Ramchand, & Fain, 2005), with research demonstrating racial biases in case processing at each stage of the system, including arrest, pretrial detention, adjudication, disposition, and transfer to adult court (Annie E. Casey Foundation, 2006; Teplin, McClelland, Abram, & Mileusnic, 2005). This holds true even when controlling for factors such as category of offense, and it is particularly true in cases of drug and weapons possession offenses, for which youths of color are more likely to be sentenced despite higher rates of drug use and possession among White youths than among youths of color. Researchers have compellingly identified systemic biases contributing to these imbalances (Alexander, 2010). As a result, in major cities, "as many as 80 percent of young African American men now have criminal records" (Alexander, 2010, p. 7).

Once in the juvenile or criminal justice system, youths of color continue to receive harsher treatment than White youths. For example, White youths involved with law enforcement are more likely to receive community-based mental health services, whereas youths of color are more likely to receive detention, even when their circumstances are comparable. African American adolescents are also more likely than White adolescents to be diagnosed with disorders considered to be less treatable, leading to a psychiatric hospitalization rate 2 or 3 times higher than that of White adolescents (Williams & Mohammed, 2009). Incarceration of youths of color not only potentially perpetuates societal stigma and cultural trauma, it places them at risk for illness (Iguchi et al., 2005) and violent death (Teplin et al., 2005).

Because cultural norms and practices influence how people define traumatic events and posttraumatic symptoms (Pole, Gone, & Kulkarni, 2008), it is difficult to draw solid conclusions about the link among race, ethnicity, and psychological trauma. Two independent studies reported few differences between youths of different ethnic and racial backgrounds in likelihood of trauma exposure or trauma-related psychological and behavioral problems (Abram et al., 2004; Ford et al., 2008). However, Ford et al. (2008) found that detained Hispanic–Latino youths were twice as likely as White or Black youths to report a history of traumatic loss, neglect, or community violence, yet White youths reported more severe suicidality and alcohol abuse risk than Black or Hispanic/Latino youths. It is not clear whether research about traumatic exposure reflects different exposures, differences in reporting, or differences in resilience factors (e.g., cultural norms or supports mitigating depression or substance use; Ford et al., 2008).

Youths of color have not been found to be more prone to either adolescent-limited or life-course-persistent aggression than White youths (Lynne-Landsman et al., 2011). However, youths who experience racial discrimination are more likely to engage in physical aggression than their peers (Tobler et al., 2013), which may help to account for the finding that, when youths of color are in ethnically heterogeneous settings (as is the case in most juvenile justice services), they are more prone to engage in physical aggression as a defensive behavior (Vervoort, Scholte, & Overbeek, 2010).

Cultural norms and practices also influence youths' and caregivers' responsiveness to treatment (Pole et al., 2008; Vazsonyi & Keiley, 2007). Culturally sensitive practices to prevent exposure to complex trauma, and to assist youths in secure juvenile justice programs to recover from the aftereffects of complex trauma, are being developed nationally (Ko et al., 2008) and in several statewide juvenile justice systems (Chapman, 2010; Ford, Chapman, Hawke, & Albert, 2007). Culturally adapted interventions for traumatized children (Jaycox et al., 2009; Morsette et al., 2009; Ngo et al., 2008), particularly those with an evidence base for youths of color in, or at risk of involvement in, the juvenile justice system (Ford & Hawke, 2012; Ford, Steinberg, Hawke, Levine, & Zhang, 2012; Marrow, Knudsen, Olafson, & Bucher, 2012), are essential to establish best practices that reduce disparities that are associated with disproportionate minority contact in juvenile justice.

CASE LAW AND LEGAL STANDARDS[6]

Information about psychological trauma is regularly introduced in court through psychological evaluations, through presentencing reports, and by prosecution or defense attorneys. In one study of cases in which judges were deciding whether youths charged in adult court should have their cases transferred to juvenile court, researchers found information about possible traumatic experiences in 71% of the psychological evaluations (Riggs Romaine, Goldstein, Hunt, & DeMatteo, 2011). As the U.S. Court of Appeals for the Fifth Circuit has explained, evidence about childhood harms can be double edged in court:

> Although the evidence of [a defendant's] inadequate supervision as a child might permit an inference that he or she is not as morally culpable for his [or her] behavior, it also might suggest [that the defendant], as a product of his environment, is likely to continue to be dangerous in the future. (*Ladd v. Cockrell*, 2002, p. 360)

In this section, we highlight relevant law on the impact of psychological trauma and identify some of the legal proceedings in which traumatic stress research may be most effectively raised to link youths to needed services.

Diversion

Although case law is not settled on this point, some court decisions have suggested that evidence of psychological trauma or traumatic stress problems may support diverting youths from the juvenile justice system based on a youth's diminished culpability resulting from past trauma or his or her increased risk of exposure to psychological trauma from the juvenile justice system itself. In *In re Kemmo N.* (1988), a Maryland appellate court upheld an intake officer's decision to avoid formal prosecution for a juvenile's drug and robbery charges. The Court recognized that "the informal adjustment . . . enables the juvenile to avoid the trauma of full involvement in the court system" (*In re Kemmo N.*, 1988, p. 1206). Similarly, in *In the Matter of Tristan C.* (1993), for example, the Family Court in New York considered the case of a

[6]The legal analysis in this section is from *Trauma and Resilience: A New Look at Advocacy for Youth in the Juvenile Justice and Child Welfare Systems*, by J. Feierman and L. Fine, 2014, Philadelphia, PA: Juvenile Law Center. Adapted with permission.

10-year-old who accidentally shot his best friend. The court noted that the respondent suffered from extreme guilt, suicidal thoughts, flashbacks, and nightmares and had been diagnosed with PTSD and major depressive disorder. The court granted a motion to dismiss the case in the interest of justice, noting that "the present juvenile delinquency proceeding by itself has aggravated [Respondent's] psychological trauma and could well impede his recovery" (*In the Matter of Tristan C.*, 1993, p. 637). Another court established that dismissal would be appropriate when youths demonstrate symptoms of "any mental illness, incapacity, or other sensitivity which might render him particularly susceptible to undue trauma" (*In re Angel R.*, 2008, p. 4).

These cases are consistent with numerous others in which judges recognize the harm or trauma of the juvenile justice court proceedings. The D.C. Court of Appeals, for example, noted that "[a] delinquency hearing, while hopefully characterized by a degree of informality and flexibility, still may be a traumatic experience for a juvenile" (applying the double jeopardy rule in juvenile court); *District of Columbia v. I.P.*, 1975, p. 229.

Transfers to and From Adult Court

There is no settled case law on the role of trauma in the decision to transfer youths to or from adult court. Reported cases have suggested, however, that this may be an area in which some judges consider psychological trauma or traumatic stress problems as a risk factor and basis for harsher and more stringent sanctions rather than an opportunity to connect youths with needed services. In *United States v. Sealed Appellant* (2009), the U.S. Court of Appeals for the Fifth Circuit upheld a trial court's decision to transfer a juvenile with PTSD to adult criminal court. In concluding that the 15-year-old posed a serious risk of future violence, the court emphasized his lack of stability and support, his exposure to violence, and his anger management problems (*United States v. Sealed Appellant*, 2009). Similarly, in *State in the Interest of C.A.H.* (1982), the Supreme Court of New Jersey held that two children should be transferred to adult court, in part because of the challenges of rehabilitation for youths with PTSD. Rejecting expert testimony about the boys' increased impulsivity, the high court also characterized the juvenile's conduct as "purposeful," "calculated," "premeditated," and deserving of more stringent punishment reserved for "volitional, deliberate and nonimpulsive behavior" (*State in the Interest of C.A.H.* 1982, p. 335).

Defenses

Some jurisdictions have recognized, through case law or statute, that battered child syndrome is a defense in manslaughter or murder against an abuser. In *State v. Hines* (1997), for example, the Superior Court of New Jersey held that testimony regarding the defendant's PTSD was admissible as "directly relevant to the issues of the honesty and reasonableness of defendant's purported belief that she had to resort to deadly force in order to repel the victim's [her abusive father's] assault" (p. 787). The court observed that certain PTSD symptoms, such as

> hyper-vigilance and re-experiencing of prior trauma, are particularly relevant to claims of self-defense by a person afflicted with PTSD because these symptoms can affect a person's state of mind when confronted with a situation similar to the initial traumatic event. (*State v. Hines*, 1997, p. 786)

Similarly, in *In the Matter of the Appeal in Maricopa County* (1994), an Arizona court held that expert testimony regarding "examples of the terrible and degrading physical and emotional abuse suffered by the juvenile [defendant] and her younger sister" were admissible to show how "such a mental state would cause someone to do an act otherwise violative of her own moral standards" (p. 63). In *State v. Janes* (1993), the Washington Supreme Court opined that chronic abuse resulting in PTSD is "an extreme stressor that exceeds a child's capacity to cope with it or integrate it into their personality, their awareness, their consciousness" (p. 501). The court added that "although PTSD is classified as a mental disorder, it is one of the few kinds of psychiatric disorders that is considered a *normal response* to an *abnormal situation*" (*State v. Janes*, 1993, p. 501).

Although the case law provides strong language about the effect of PTSD on a child's mental state, the cases occur in a narrow legal context: children harming or killing abusive adults. For obvious reasons, the battered child syndrome defense is generally applied when a child lashes out at an abuser rather than at an innocent party, despite research suggesting that hypervigilance is not limited to responses to abusers (Daniels, Lamke, Gaebler, Walter, & Scheel, 2013).

Sentencing and Disposition

As the U.S. Supreme Court noted in *Miller v. Alabama* (2012), judges must make an individualized determination of the defendant's circumstances, including the child's exposure to psychological trauma, before imposing a life-without-parole sentence. According to the Court, proceeding without such an assessment unconstitutionally precludes the sentencing judge from considering the "family and home environment that surrounds [the youth]—and from which he cannot usually extricate himself—no matter how brutal or dysfunctional" (*Miller v. Alabama*, 2012, p. 2468). This language not only recognizes the importance of a defendant's trauma history, but also that such experiences are particularly relevant to assessing culpability for youthful offenders, who may have little or no control over their environments. Even before the *Miller* decision, other courts recognized the importance of childhood trauma to juvenile life-without-parole sentences (*United States v. Juvenile*, 2003). In the context of life without parole, courts must (and do) consider the impact of psychological trauma and resultant survival adaptations as a mitigating factor. The open question is whether this reasoning can be extended to other sentencing contexts. For some courts, at least, public safety concerns will outweigh the potential for mitigation raised by trauma evidence.

A few appellate courts have recognized the relevance of psychological trauma to the application of federal sentencing guidelines. Both the Ninth Circuit and the D.C. Circuit have recognized that "youthful lack of guidance" may justify a court imposing a sentence lower than the recommended range when "a past condition . . . may have led a convicted defendant to criminality" (*United States v. Floyd*, 1991, p. 1101; see also *United States v. Clark*, 1993). The Ninth Circuit explained that a "lack of guidance and education, abandonment by parents and imprisonment at age 17 constitute the elements of this mitigating circumstance" (*United States v. Floyd*, 1991, p. 1099). Although cases have articulated this standard, however, few, if any, have applied it to reduce an offender's sentence. Thus, even in this context, there is a chance that evidence of a history of psychological trauma or problems with traumatic stress reactions will be used as a risk factor rather than as a mitigator.

How providing information about psychological trauma and PTSD plays out in juvenile dispositions will obviously depend on the jurisdiction, the judge, and the available services. However, case law suggests that, as in the adult context, judges may at times be more swayed by concerns around public safety than by the need to connect youths with effective services. For example, in *In the Matter of Johnny S.* (2010), a New York Family Court judge recognized that, as a result of his serious history of victimization, the defendant "perceives his environment as threatening, . . . has difficulty regulating his anger and emotions[, and] acts out through intimidation and violence" (p. 843). The court acknowledged evidence that the state's detention "facilities provide inadequate treatment planning and services for children with diagnosed mental illnesses, including PTSD" (*In the Matter of Johnny S.*, 2010, p. 845). Ultimately, however, the court placed Johnny in a secure setting (*In the Matter of Johnny S.*, 2010). Unlike adult sentencing cases, which generally impose serious prison time regardless of downward departures, juvenile disposition determinations require judges to make difficult decisions about whether a youth will be safe in a less secure setting. For that reason, in the absence of strong policies protecting youths, there is a risk that the information will be interpreted to support a more secure placement rather than a community-based treatment approach.

Procedural Determinations

Case law is not clear about the extent to which entering facts or expert opinions about the impact of psychological trauma into evidence will be taken into account in procedural decisions such as an individual's competency to stand trial or his or her rights during an interrogation. Regarding competency, the Michigan Court of Appeals considered evidence of a defendant's PTSD, attention-deficit/hyperactivity disorder, impulse control disorder, and developmental delay as relevant to the competency determination (*In re Landfair*, 2010). Ultimately, however, the Court concluded that the

> respondent's circumstances, standing alone, did not indicate that his mental condition was such that he was unable to understand the nature and object of the proceedings against him and his statements to the court showed a sufficient level of comprehension. (*In re Landfair*, 2010, p. 1)

Thus, the defendant was found competent to stand trial.

In determining the admissibility of a confession, courts must look at whether the confession was voluntary in light of the totality of the circumstances. Courts have long recognized that adolescents are more susceptible to coercion than adults and that this difference is legally relevant in determining whether a confession was voluntary (*Haley v. Ohio*, 1948). Few published cases have addressed the role of traumatic stress problems such as PTSD in the voluntariness determination. In one case, however, a California appellate court did factor in a youth's PTSD as part of the totality-of-the-circumstances analysis (*People v. Pratcher*, 2009). The expert had opined that "an adolescent who had suffered trauma would operate at a lower level than an adolescent with a normal developing brain" (*People v. Pratcher*, 2009, p. 10). The court agreed that the youth's psychological trauma history and traumatic stress symptoms were relevant but ultimately concluded that the confession was voluntary (*People v. Pratcher*, 2009).

Juvenile Conditions

Too often, the juvenile justice system itself causes harm to the youth it is intended to serve. Simply being separated from family and placed in a secure facility, locked in a unit or cell, can be highly stressful and can become traumatic. Youths are often traumatized or retraumatized by harsh conditions such as shackling, strip searches, and solitary confinement. Many also face physical or sexual abuse by other youths or by staff members and harassment along the lines of gender and sexuality (Burrell, 2013). It is clear that evidence about institutional exposure to psychological trauma can be helpful in constitutional litigation regarding conditions. In assessing the constitutionality of strip searches, for example, courts have recognized that being forced to strip in front of a stranger can be "demeaning, dehumanizing, undignified, humiliating, terrifying, unpleasant, embarrassing, repulsive, signifying degradation and submission" (*Mary Beth G. v. City of Chicago*, 1983, p. 1272) and that "children are especially susceptible to possible traumas from strip searches" (*Flores v. Meese*, 1988, p. 667).[7]

Similarly, courts have recognized the severe harm that can be caused by placing youths in solitary confinement. In one case, for example, a federal court in New York placed great weight on the testimony of experts that solitary confinement would cause serious psychological damage. As one expert noted,

> What is true in this case for adults is of even greater concern with children and adolescents. Youngsters are in general more vulnerable to emotional pressures than mature adults; isolation is a condition of extraordinarily severe psychic stress; the resultant impact on the mental health of the individual exposed to such stress will always be serious, and can occasionally be disastrous. (*Lollis v. New York State Department of Social Services*, 1970, p. 481)

Courts have applied similar reasoning to the use of restraints (*In re Jonathon C.B.*, 2011) and the problem of sexual and physical abuse and harassment

[7]See also *Thomas ex. rel. Thomas v. Roberts* (2001; strip searches represented a serious intrusion on the rights of the children); *Jenkins v. Talladega City Board of Education* (1996, "the perceived invasiveness and physical intimidation intrinsic to strip searches may be exacerbated for children"; p. 1044); *Cornfield v. Consolidated High School District No. 230* (1993, a strip search was particularly intrusive for a 16-year-old because that is the "age at which children are extremely self-conscious about their bodies"; p. 1323); and *Doe v. Renfrow* (1980, a strip search of a 13-year-old was a "violation of any known principle of human decency."; p. 93).

(*R.G. v. Koller*, 2006) recognizing that institutional hazards are fundamentally psychologically traumatic.

Although courts have recognized that harsh conditions can traumatize youths, this does not mean that they always prohibit such conditions or hold them unconstitutional. Indeed, in a number of strip search cases, courts justified imposing the strip search despite the trauma it would impose, in the name of protecting incarcerated youths (*N.G. v. Connecticut*, 2004; *Smook v. Minnehaha County*, 2006). Nonetheless, evidence on the trauma imposed by harsh conditions (including expert testimony) has played a significant role in conditions litigation.

Case law can also support the argument that youths should receive thoughtful, trauma-informed services, even when in a secure placement. In *In the Matter of Johnny S.* (2010), for example, a New York Family Court judge explained that "there is a substantive due process right to treatment" (p. 846) for those detained by the juvenile court and that the type and extent of treatment provided must be related to the reason the person is detained. The court further explained that "the conditions of placement may not be punitive nor exclusively designed to incapacitate, but must include treatment and rehabilitation consistent with the needs and best interests of the juvenile" (*In the Matter of Johnny S.*, 2010, p. 846). This framework can support the argument that a child who has experienced trauma and is demonstrating related symptoms must be given access to appropriate, targeted treatment.

IMPLICATIONS

The high rates of trauma for youth in juvenile justice settings suggest a need for significant changes in juvenile justice policies, practices, and programs. Services provided to youth must, at a minimum, be designed to help youth heal from past trauma. When possible, these services should be provided in the homes and communities to which youth will ultimately return. At the same time, the system must avoid retraumatizing youth through harmful interventions such as strip searches, solitary confinement, and separation from home and family.

Practice Implications: Interventions for Traumatized Youths in the Juvenile Justice System

If the dilemmas faced by trauma-affected youths are viewed as the result of a dysregulation of core self-regulatory competences (Ford, 2005), then enhancement of self-regulation provides a focus for trauma-informed juvenile justice services at all levels. To some degree, specific educational or mental health services such as groups, classes, counseling, or therapy can provide youths with preparation and guidance for self-regulation.[8] However, self-regulation is primarily acquired through social learning: by modeling (observational learning) and reinforcement (consequences that enhance the motivational value of behaviors in youths' support systems). As a result, interventions that address the behavior and culture for adult staff or that support families, schools, and other key adults, and provide targeted therapeutic interventions for youths, may be particularly effective.

Support a positive culture and environment in which traumatized children live, including home, community programs, schools, and residential facilities, plays a crucial role in helping youths learn to regulate their emotions more effectively. Indeed, serving youths in their own homes and communities will generally be the most effective way to help traumatized youth. Thus, youth should be kept out of institutional placement whenever possible.

When a youth must be placed in a residential setting, a focus on social learning will often necessitate culture change. The primary source of social learning for youths is the example set by adult staff and the milieu, which in turn substantially sets the tone for a second critical influence—peer role modeling. The actions of supervisors and administrators, the formal and informal performance expectations and evaluation processes, and the policies and procedures in place in juvenile justice residential facilities provide

[8]For example, teaching basic concepts or skills; coaching to facilitate practice and application of skills; enhancing motivation and trust; and medications that reduce affective, cognitive, or biological instability.

powerful sources of modeling and reinforcement for staff as they respond to work stressors and challenges. When these sources consistently set an example that encourages self-regulation (e.g., modeling mindful responses to stressful events), they increase staff capacity to manage the challenging nature of the juvenile justice environment. Specific educational practices to meet these goals include psychoeducation, supervision, and skills development, with a focus on youth support, coaching, and deescalation strategies. In many juvenile facilities that currently apply a punitive correctional model of interaction with the youths in their care, shifting to a trauma-informed model will require a significant shift in approach. Highlighting the potential positive impact on recidivism rates, the cost-effectiveness of this approach, and the rehabilitative history of the juvenile court may all be helpful in supporting such a shift.

It is worth noting that home-, clinic-, and school-based interventions for delinquency and substance abuse have been found to have broad based benefits, including improvements in parent and family functioning as well as child behavior and functioning (see Chapter 26, this handbook). Therefore, they may have an impact on the self-regulation problems associated with complex trauma, although no study has yet explicitly tested this hypothesis.

Following are some promising approaches to interventions that address the need for both social learning and therapeutic care for traumatized youths in the juvenile justice system.

Attachment, self-regulation, and competency. The attachment, self-regulation, and competency treatment framework (Kinniburgh, Blaustein, Spinazzola, & van der Kolk, 2005) is a flexible, components-based model of intervention designed to translate across service settings. The model identifies 10 core intervention targets, nine of which fall within the three domains of attachment (building and supporting a safe and responsive caregiving system by primary caregivers, providers, and milieus), self-regulation (supporting youth capacity to identify, modulate, and express emotional and physiological experiences), and competency (building core self-reflective capacities, including problem-solving skills and a coherent and positive understanding of self); the 10th core target involves processing and integration of life experiences, including but not limited to traumatic events. A core concepts framework guides the provider in using each target clinically as well as in integrating them into systemic or milieu functioning, staff training, and other modalities. The framework emphasizes the importance of whole systems change in supporting youth development and caregiver safety and has been applied in juvenile justice facilities, residential treatment programs, inpatient hospitals, group homes and therapeutic foster care, and outpatient treatment. Although not yet empirically validated by systematic research, the attachment, self-regulation, and competency framework has shown promise in evaluations with youth in, or at risk for involvement in, juvenile justice, when done either as a therapy or as a milieu intervention (Ford, Blaustein, Habib, & Kagan, 2013).

Sanctuary. This organizational change model (Bloom, 2013) emphasizes the development of a trauma-informed culture that supports recovery from the impacts of traumatic stress while simultaneously providing safety for clients, families, staff, and administrators. Seven features of the environment are addressed, with an emphasis on building a culture of nonviolence, emotional intelligence, inquiry and social learning, shared governance, open communication, social responsibility, and growth and change. Across intervention components, treatment is approached within an understanding of the core areas, or phases, of safety, emotion management, loss, and future. Intervention components highlight the role of training, organizational development, development of collaborative teams that include clients, and trauma-informed and trauma-specific treatment. This model has been implemented extensively in inpatient and residential programs. Although not yet empirically validated by systematic research, Sanctuary has been successfully disseminated in several juvenile justice systems.

Structured Psychotherapy for Adolescents Responding to Chronic Stress. Structured Psychotherapy for Adolescents Responding to Chronic Stress (SPARCS; DeRosa & Pelcovitz,

2008) is a group intervention designed to address the needs of adolescents who have experienced chronic trauma and whose stress may be ongoing. The model integrates key concepts from three evidence-based treatment programs: dialectical behavior therapy (DeRosa & Rathus, 2013), Trauma Affect Regulation: Guide for Education and Therapy (TARGET; Ford et al., 2013), and the UCLA Trauma/Grief Program (Layne et al., 2008). SPARCS targets core areas known to be disrupted by chronic exposure to trauma, including challenges with self-regulation, relationships, self-perception, and future goals, and emphasizes the building of adolescent capacity to cope with current stressors, build effective relationships, and develop a sense of meaning and purpose. Although not yet empirically validated by systematic research, SPARCS has been successfully implemented in a wide range of child- and adolescent-serving programs and with ethnically diverse groups (Ford et al., 2013).

Trauma Affect Regulation: Guide for Education and Therapy. TARGET (Ford et al., 2013) is an educational and therapeutic intervention for trauma-affected adolescents and adults that may be implemented as an individual or group therapy or as a milieu intervention (Ford & Blaustein, 2013; Ford & Hawke, 2012). The model emphasizes an understanding of trauma-related self-dysregulation through the lens of the brain's emotion regulation and executive function systems, and it reframes symptoms as adaptive responses. TARGET is an empirically supported intervention for delinquent or justice-involved youths with dual-diagnosis substance use and trauma-related disorders (Ford, Steinberg, et al., 2012). Evidence of TARGETS effectiveness as a milieu social learning intervention with detained or incarcerated youths is provided by two quasi-experimental studies (Ford & Hawke, 2012; Marrow et al., 2012). TARGET teaches a seven-step sequence of self-regulation skills summarized by the acronym FREEDOM. The first two skills, focusing and recognizing triggers, provide a foundation for shifting from hypervigilance to mentalizing (Allen, Fonagy, & Bateman, 2008). The next four skills represent a dual-processing approach to differentiating stress-related and core value–grounded emotions, thoughts, goals, and behavioral options. The final skill teaches ways to enhance self-esteem and self-efficacy, recognizing how being self-regulated makes a contribution to the world. TARGET has been disseminated in several juvenile justice, child welfare, and mental health systems (Ford et al., 2013).

Trauma systems therapy. Trauma systems therapy (TST; Navalta, Brown, Nisewaner, Ellis, & Saxe, 2013) is a therapeutic intervention that emphasizes the importance of (a) building the trauma-affected child's capacity to regulate emotional state and (b) building a self-regulating system and of being able to support the child in managing emotions. TST actively targets the social environment, including the treatment system, and tailors treatment using a matrix system that identifies levels of the child's emotion regulation and the social environment's capacities to support this. Treatment is designed to encompass five phases: surviving, stabilizing, enduring, understanding, and transcending. Within each phase, psychotherapy (e.g., cognitive processing, emotional regulation skills training, or both; psychopharmacology) and home- and community-based services and advocacy are provided. TST has been successfully used with ethnically and culturally diverse populations of troubled youths and families. Although not yet empirically validated by systematic research, TST has been successfully implemented in a wide range of child- and adolescent-serving programs and with ethnically diverse groups (Navalta et al., 2013).

Policy Recommendations

Too often, the best intentions lead to harmful outcomes for youth in the juvenile justice system. Trauma-informed policies must recognize the potential harm youth face when they are placed in institutional settings, exposed to harsh conditions, and separated from family and community. Careful policies can help jurisdictions benefit from the latest research on trauma while still protecting youth from such troubling and potentially harmful conditions.

Provide early identification of trauma issues in the juvenile justice system, but only with procedural protections for youth and for targeted purposes. A common recommendation regarding trauma-informed systems, services, and advocacy, and one embraced by the Attorney General's National Task Force on Children Exposed to Violence, is to screen youths for exposure to violence. As the task force's report indicates,

> all children who enter the juvenile justice system should be screened for exposure to violence . . . upon the child's first contact with the juvenile justice system and should include youth who meet the criteria for diversion from the system. (Listenbee et al., 2012, p. 21)

Although this general goal is important, such screening can create problems for youths if not accompanied by procedural protections. As described in the Case Law and Legal Standards section, there are numerous instances in which a child's trauma history is used to establish risk but not to provide services. For this reason, states should establish policies to ensure that information gathered in screens and subsequent evaluations—including the factual history and any resulting diagnoses—is used only to provide services, and cannot be used in court without the consent of the youth and his or her counsel (see, e.g., Rosado & Shah, 2007).

Moreover, the juvenile justice system is not designed to provide mental health services, and it may indeed lead to long-term harmful collateral consequences for youths who enter it, including difficulties remaining in school, obtaining higher education, or finding employment (Henning, 2004). Thus, procedural protections should also ensure that screening does not lead to net widening, that is, to an increase in the number of youths in juvenile justice supervision or facilities or reliance on the juvenile justice system as a means for traumatized youths to get needed treatment. Evidence of psychological trauma or PTSD should not itself provide cause for justice system involvement. Instead, it should help ensure that youths who would otherwise be in the juvenile justice system receive appropriately matched care and services.

Increase access to trauma-informed services in the least restrictive environment. There is an urgent need for effective interventions for youths and families in the least restrictive environment. Such programs should be available from the first identification of need, and they should be available at various levels of security. Although this is vital for all youths who are experiencing behavioral or psychological problems, it is particularly urgent for traumatized youths (Ford, 2012; Ford, Chapman, Connor, & Cruise, 2012).

It is crucial that preventive and voluntary programs be available to traumatized youths and families at risk. Too often, families seek assistance for troubled youths through the juvenile justice system, having been denied community-based supports (Listenbee et al., 2012). Ensuring that positive, nonpunitive, trauma-informed interventions are available in schools, homes, and the child welfare system can help to address the serious problems created by trauma before youths become justice involved (Listenbee et al., 2012).

Programs must also be available in and by referral from the juvenile justice system. Without an accurate understanding that trauma exposure and PTSD are associated with mental health problems that are actually highly responsive to evidence-based treatment (Ford, Chapman, et al., 2012) and trauma-informed juvenile justice services (Ford & Hawke, 2012; Marrow et al., 2012), youths may be denied effective treatment and ordered to receive inappropriate treatment, including psychotropic medication (Ipser & Stein, 2012). To avoid this result, courts need information about programs that prevent recidivism and increase the safety of youths and the community by reducing traumatic stress reactions and enhancing self-regulation.

Once a youth enters the juvenile justice system, effective trauma-informed services should be available in community settings and in secure and nonsecure juvenile justice settings. The availability of programming at various levels of security allows judges to place youths in the least restrictive alternative possible (e.g., in the community instead of in a residential setting or in a juvenile facility rather than an adult prison). Such programs are crucial to address the needs of youths of color, girls, and LGBTQ youths (Listenbee et al., 2012). Creating these programs and ensuring that they work effectively will require collaboration among various stakeholders within the juvenile justice system and also across systems, including child welfare, education, and mental health agencies (Listenbee et al., 2012).

Eliminate or reform procedures that harm or traumatize youths. Exposing youths to harm, psychological trauma, or retraumatization undermines the juvenile justice system's goals of rehabilitation and promoting responsible youth conduct and public safety. Practices that require careful scrutiny to assess potentially traumatizing impacts, in individual cases and at the system level, include removal from the community, placement in a secure facility, and transfer to adult correctional settings. Particular attention should be paid to the potential for harm and trauma from boot camps, prolonged isolation, physical and mechanical restraints, and strip searches (Burrell, 2013; Listenbee et al., 2012). Youths in secure facilities may be especially vulnerable to physical and sexual abuse as well as to traumatizing correctional practices. Internal and external monitoring systems must be in place and fully functioning to prevent such practices.

Gather data and respond to findings with particular attention to racial disparities. Too often, juvenile justice system interventions actually cause harm and even increase recidivism rates (Soler, Shoenberg, & Schindler, 2009). Tracking data on the effectiveness of interventions will help to ensure that trauma-informed responses help—and do not hurt—those they are designed to serve. Moreover, given the persistent race-based disparities in the juvenile justice system, data systems should be designed to track youths by race and ethnicity, to identify any disparate treatment, and to immediately correct for problems identified. To the extent possible, data systems should also be set up to assess whether juvenile justice services are being used for youths and families who could benefit from voluntary or preventive services or who may not need system involvement at all. Tracking the outcomes for traumatized youths over time, throughout and after their juvenile justice involvement, is vital to identifying approaches that can yield the best developmental and public safety outcomes.

Ensure that evidence about a child's trauma history is used in court to connect the youth with services and to protect him or her from harmful consequences rather than to punish. Both attorneys and psychologists should be attentive to the possibility that courts, if focused on the risk factors associated with traumatic stress problems, will fail to connect youths with needed services and will instead order harsher sanctions, transfer to adult systems, and secure placement in conditions likely to exacerbate trauma. Thoughtful decisions regarding the evidence introduced in court can help to address this problem. More effective, however, are policies that clarify that psychological trauma and PTSD evidence should be used to mitigate, divert, and assist, and guidance for legal professionals in accessing trauma-informed and evidence-based services and interventions, such as the Bench Card for the Trauma-Informed Judge produced by the National Childhood Traumatic Stress Network's Justice Consortium (n.d.).

State policies could require that youths be diverted from the juvenile justice system and provided with needed treatment when (a) their offense stems from a traumatic stress response or (b) the youth might be uniquely vulnerable to exposure to trauma in the system (Listenbee et al., 2012). This approach will be particularly effective if diversion programs are also trauma informed. In many jurisdictions, youths may have their case dismissed if they comply with certain requirements, such as attending school and going to counseling. If the school is not aware of the youth's traumatic stress triggers and self-regulation strengths and difficulties, or if the counseling program offered is not appropriate for a traumatized child, the youth may fail to comply with the program and end up in the juvenile justice system (Listenbee et al., 2012).

States can also develop legislation to ensure that information about youths' history of psychological trauma and traumatic stress problems is not misused in the transfer decision. For example, statutes could require judges to consider a child's trauma history, PTSD symptoms, or risk for exposure to psychological trauma as indications that the child should remain in juvenile court rather than be transferred to adult court. Similarly, the availability of a battered child defense could be written into state law, establishing a defense to criminal responsibility, the requirement of a transfer from adult court to juvenile court, or diversion to an alternative mental health treatment program when a child's actions were an understandable response to traumatic stress. More generally, sentencing laws can explicitly require that trauma be considered as a mitigating, and not an aggravating, factor. State legislation can also require consideration of trauma as relevant to various procedural decisions in the juvenile justice system. For example, states could require trauma to be considered in a totality-of-the-circumstances test regarding the admissibility of a juvenile confession. They could also require that a child's trauma be considered in decisions about the child's capacity to stand trial determinations. In fact, a court rule to this effect has been adopted in Vermont (Rule 1: Procedure for Juvenile Delinquency Proceedings—Reporter's Notes, 2006 Amendment).

Further Research

The legal research in this chapter is limited to an analysis of published opinions, most frequently appellate court decisions. Although these decisions provide an overview of possible issues in court responses to trauma, they are not necessarily representative. More research is needed in the legal community to identify trends regarding the use of psychological trauma and PTSD as evidence or as a factor in judicial decision making in trial courts, particularly in juvenile courts. Additional research could also identify the extent to which judges and attorneys have the knowledge base they need to interact with traumatized clients and to advocate for appropriate trauma-informed services.

From the standpoint of psychology and mental health, research is needed to determine how to identify traumatized youths without involving them or pushing them deeper into the juvenile and criminal justice systems. More specifically, in light of the frequent reliance on psychological testimony on matters related to juvenile confessions, competency, and culpability, research is critically needed to determine whether, when, and how a history of psychological trauma and PTSD and other posttraumatic survival adaptations (e.g., reactive aggression; Ford, Chapman, et al., 2012) can validly be relied on to inform those judgments.

In addition, it is vital to continue building on the emerging research on interventions for traumatized youths in the juvenile justice system, with a particular eye to the impact on youth recidivism. Case law research has demonstrated that judges have real concerns about public safety for youths who have experienced trauma. Demonstrating successful programs, such as the evidence-based intervention TARGET and several promising interventions for traumatized youths (attachment, self-regulation, and competency framework; Sanctuary; SPARCS; TST), would set the stage for juvenile courts to connect youths with services rather than confine them for their risk. Studies accruing evidence of effectiveness in a variety of juvenile justice settings (e.g., probation and diversion as well as detention and incarceration) would provide courts, advocates, administrators, and policymakers with information needed to respond more effectively to traumatized youths. Ultimately, research is needed to determine how to prevent exposure to psychological trauma and how to build universal resilience to adversity in children and in the system that serves them.

References

Abram, K. M., Teplin, L. A., Charles, D. R., Longworth, S. L., McClelland, G. M., & Dulcan, M. K. (2004). Posttraumatic stress disorder and trauma in youth in juvenile detention. *Archives of General Psychiatry*, *61*, 403–410. http://dx.doi.org/10.1001/archpsyc.61.4.403

Alessandri, S. M., & Lewis, M. (1996). Differences in pride and shame in maltreated and nonmaltreated preschoolers. *Child Development*, *67*, 1857–1869. http://dx.doi.org/10.2307/1131736

Alexander, M. (2010). *The new Jim Crow: Mass incarceration in the age of colorblindness*. New York, NY: New Press.

Allen, J. G., Fonagy, P., & Bateman, A. (2008). *Mentalizing in clinical practice*. Arlington, VA: American Psychiatric Publishing.

American Psychiatric Association. (2013). *Diagnostic and statistical manual of mental disorders* (5th ed.). Arlington, VA: Author.

Annie E. Casey Foundation. (2006). *Race matters: Unequal opportunities for juvenile justice*. Baltimore, MD: Author.

Becker, E. (2001, February 9). As ex-theorist on young "superpredators," Bush aide has regrets. *New York Times*. Retrieved from http://www.nytimes.com/2001/02/09/us/as-ex-theorist-on-young-superpredators-bush-aide-has-regrets.html

Bilén, K., Ottosson, C., Castrén, M., Ponzer, S., Ursing, C., Ranta, P., . . . Pettersson, H. (2010). Deliberate self-harm patients in the emergency department: Factors associated with repeated self-harm among 1524 patients. *Emergency Medical Journal, 28*, 1019–1025. http://dx.doi.org/emj.2010.102616

Bloom, S. (2013). The sanctuary model. In J. D. Ford & C. A. Courtois (Eds.), *Treating complex traumatic stress disorders in children and adolescents: Scientific foundations and therapeutic models* (pp. 277–294). New York, NY: Guilford Press.

Bockoven, J. S. (1956). Moral treatment in American psychiatry. *Journal of Nervous and Mental Disease, 124*, 167–194, 292–321. http://dx.doi.org/10.1097/00005053-195608000-00008

Bowie, B. H. (2007). Relational aggression, gender, and the developmental process. *Journal of Child and Adolescent Psychiatric Nursing, 20*, 107–115. http://dx.doi.org/10.1111/j.1744-6171.2007.00092.x

Bowie, B. H. (2010). Understanding the gender differences in pathways to social deviancy: Relational aggression and emotion regulation. *Archives of Psychiatric Nursing, 24*, 27–37. http://dx.doi.org/10.1016/j.apnu.2009.04.007

Bradshaw, C. P., & Garbarino, J. (2004). Social cognition as a mediator of the influence of family and community violence on adolescent development: Implications for intervention. *Annals of the New York Academy of Sciences, 1036*, 85–105. http://dx.doi.org/10.1196/annals.1330.005

Brom, D., & Kleber, R. (2008). Resilience as the capacity for processing traumatic experiences. In D. Brom, R. Pat-Horenczyk, & J. Ford (Eds.), *Treating traumatized children* (pp. 133–149). London, England: Routledge.

Buckner, J. C., Mezzacappa, E., & Beardslee, W. R. (2009). Self-regulation and its relations to adaptive functioning in low income youths. *American Journal of Orthopsychiatry, 79*, 19–30. http://dx.doi.org/10.1037/a0014796

Burrell, S. (2013). *Trauma and the environment of care in juvenile institutions*. Los Angeles, CA: National Center for Child Traumatic Stress.

Card, N. A., Stucky, B. D., Sawalani, G. M., & Little, T. D. (2008). Direct and indirect aggression during childhood and adolescence: A meta-analytic review of gender differences, intercorrelations, and relations to maladjustment. *Child Development, 79*, 1185–1229. http://dx.doi.org/10.1111/j.1467-8624.2008.01184.x

Cauffman, E., Feldman, S. S., Waterman, J., & Steiner, H. (1998). Posttraumatic stress disorder among female juvenile offenders. *Journal of the American Academy of Child and Adolescent Psychiatry, 37*, 1209–1216. http://dx.doi.org/10.1097/00004583-199811000-00022

Chapman, E. J. (2010). *Healing invisible wounds: Why investing in trauma-informed care for children makes sense*. Retrieved from http://www.justicepolicy.org/images/upload/10-07_REP_HealingInvisibleWounds_JJ-PS.pdf

Choi, J., Jeong, B., Rohan, M. L., Polcari, A. M., & Teicher, M. H. (2009). Preliminary evidence for white matter tract abnormalities in young adults exposed to parental verbal abuse. *Biological Psychiatry, 65*, 227–234. http://dx.doi.org/10.1016/j.biopsych.2008.06.022

Cicchetti, D., & Curtis, W. J. (2005). An event-related potential study of the processing of affective facial expressions in young children who experienced maltreatment during the first year of life. *Development and Psychopathology, 17*, 641–677. http://dx.doi.org/10.1017/S0954579405050315

Compas, B. E. (2006). Psychobiological processes of stress and coping: Implications for resilience in children and adolescents—Comments on the papers of Romeo & McEwen and Fisher et al. *Annals of the New York Academy of Sciences, 1094*, 226–234. http://dx.doi.org/10.1196/annals.1376.024

Copeland, W. E., Keeler, G., Angold, A., & Costello, E. J. (2007). Traumatic events and posttraumatic stress in childhood. *Archives of General Psychiatry, 64*, 577–584. http://dx.doi.org/10.1001/archpsyc.64.5.577

Cornfield v. Consolidated High School District No. 230, 991 F.2d 1316, 1323 (7th Cir. 1993)

Costello, E. J., Erkanli, A., Fairbank, J. A., & Angold, A. (2002). The prevalence of potentially traumatic events in childhood and adolescence. *Journal of Traumatic Stress, 15*, 99–112. http://dx.doi.org/10.1023/A:1014851823163

Crick, N. R., & Dodge, K. A. (1996). Social information-processing mechanisms in reactive and proactive aggression. *Child Development, 67*, 993–1002. http://dx.doi.org/10.2307/1131875

Cullerton-Sen, C., Cassidy, A. R., Murray-Close, D., Cicchetti, D., Crick, N. R., & Rogosch, F. A. (2008). Childhood maltreatment and the development of relational and physical aggression: The importance of a gender-informed approach. *Child Development, 79*, 1736–1751. http://dx.doi.org/10.1111/j.1467-8624.2008.01222.x

D'Andrea, W., Ford, J., Stolbach, B., Spinazzola, J., & van der Kolk, B. A. (2012). Understanding interpersonal trauma in children: Why we need a developmentally appropriate trauma diagnosis. *American Journal of Orthopsychiatry*, *82*, 187–200. http://dx.doi.org/10.1111/j.1939-0025.2012.01154.x

Daniels, J. K., Lamke, J. P., Gaebler, M., Walter, H., & Scheel, M. (2013). White matter integrity and its relationship to PTSD and childhood trauma—A systematic review and meta-analysis. *Depression and Anxiety*, *30*, 207–216. http://dx.doi.org/10.1002/da.22044

Davis, S. D., & Ford, M. E. (2004). A conceptual model of barriers to mental health services among African Americans. *African American Research Perspectives*, *10*, 44–54.

De Bellis, M. D., & Kuchibhatla, M. (2006). Cerebellar volumes in pediatric maltreatment-related posttraumatic stress disorder. *Biological Psychiatry*, *60*, 697–703. http://dx.doi.org/10.1016/j.biopsych.2006.04.035

DeRosa, R., & Pelcovitz, D. (2008). Group treatment of chronically traumatized adolescents: Igniting SPARCS of change. In D. Brom, R. Pat-Horenczyk, & J. D. Ford (Eds.), *Treating traumatized children: Risk, resilience, and recovery* (pp. 225–239). London, England: Routledge.

DeRosa, R. R., & Rathus, J. H. (2013). Dialectical behavior therapy with adolescents. In J. D. Ford & C. A. Courtois (Eds.), *Treating complex traumatic stress disorders in children and adolescents: Scientific foundations and therapeutic models* (pp. 225–246). New York, NY: Guilford Press.

Desai, R. A., Falzer, P. R., Chapman, J., & Borum, R. (2012). Mental illness, violence risk, and race in juvenile detention: Implications for disproportionate minority contact. *American Journal of Orthopsychiatry*, *82*, 32–40. http://dx.doi.org/10.1111/j.1939-0025.2011.01138.x

DiGangi, J. A., Gomez, D., Mendoza, L., Jason, L. A., Keys, C. B., & Koenen, K. C. (2013). Pretrauma risk factors for posttraumatic stress disorder: A systematic review of the literature. *Clinical Psychology Review*, *33*, 728–744. http://dx.doi.org/10.1016/j.cpr.2013.05.002

Dishion, T. J., & Connell, A. (2006). Adolescents' resilience as a self-regulatory process: Promising themes for linking intervention with developmental science. *Annals of the New York Academy of Sciences*, *1094*, 125–138. http://dx.doi.org/10.1196/annals.1376.012

District of Columbia v. I.P., 335 A.2d 224 (D.C. 1975).

Dodge, K. A., Pettit, G. S., Bates, J. E., & Valente, E. (1995). Social information-processing patterns partially mediate the effect of early physical abuse on later conduct problems. *Journal of Abnormal Psychology*, *104*, 632–643. http://dx.doi.org/10.1037/0021-843X.104.4.632

Doe v. Renfrow, 631 F.2d 91, 93 (7th Cir. 1980).

Elzinga, B. M., Bakker, A., & Bremner, J. D. (2005). Stress-induced cortisol elevations are associated with impaired delayed, but not immediate recall. *Psychiatry Research*, *134*, 211–223. http://dx.doi.org/10.1016/j.psychres.2004.11.007

Estrada, R., & Marksamer, J. (2006). The legal rights of LGBT youth in state custody: What child welfare and juvenile justice professionals need to know. *Child Welfare*, *85*, 171–194.

Farrington, D. P. (1993). Childhood origins of teenage antisocial behaviour and adult social dysfunction. *Journal of the Royal Society of Medicine*, *86*, 13–17.

Feierman, J., & Fine L. (2014). *Trauma and resilience: A new look at advocacy for youth in the juvenile justice and child welfare systems*. Philadelphia, PA: Juvenile Law Center.

Finkelhor, D., Ormrod, R. K., & Turner, H. A. (2007). Poly-victimization: A neglected component in child victimization. *Child Abuse and Neglect*, *31*, 7–26. http://dx.doi.org/10.1016/j.chiabu.2006.06.008

Finkelhor, D., Ormrod, R. K., & Turner, H. A. (2009). Lifetime assessment of poly-victimization in a national sample of children and youth. *Child Abuse and Neglect*, *33*, 403–411. http://dx.doi.org/10.1016/j.chiabu.2008.09.012

Finkelhor, D., Ormrod, R. K., Turner, H. A., & Hamby, S. L. (2005). Measuring poly-victimization using the Juvenile Victimization Questionnaire. *Child Abuse and Neglect*, *29*, 1297–1312. http://dx.doi.org/10.1016/j.chiabu.2005.06.005

Flores v. Meese, 681 F. Supp. 665 (C.D. Cal. 1988).

Ford, J. D. (2005). Treatment implications of altered neurobiology, affect regulation and information processing following child maltreatment. *Psychiatric Annals*, *35*, 410–419.

Ford, J. D. (2009). Neurobiological and developmental research: Clinical implications. In C. A. Courtois & J. D. Ford (Eds.), *Treating complex traumatic stress disorders: An evidence-based guide* (pp. 31–58). New York, NY: Guilford Press.

Ford, J. D. (2012). Posttraumatic stress disorder (PTSD) among youth involved in juvenile justice. In E. Grigorenko (Ed.), *Handbook of juvenile forensic psychology and psychiatry* (pp. 485–503). http://dx.doi.org/10.1007/978-1-4614-0905-2_31

Ford, J. D., & Blaustein, M. (2013). Systemic self-regulation: A framework for trauma-informed services in residential juvenile justice programs. *Journal of Family Violence*, *28*, 655–677.

Ford, J. D., Blaustein, M., Habib, M., & Kagan, R. (2013). Developmental trauma-focused treatment models. In J. D. Ford & C. A. Courtois (Eds.), *Treating complex traumatic stress disorders in children and adolescents: Scientific foundations and therapeutic models* (pp. 261–276). New York, NY: Guilford Press.

Ford, J. D., Chapman, J., Mack, M., & Pearson, G. (2006). Pathway from traumatic child victimization to delinquency: Implications for juvenile and permanency court proceedings and decisions. *Juvenile and Family Court Journal*, *57*, 13–26. http://dx.doi.org/10.1111/j.1755-6988.2006.tb00111.x

Ford, J. D., Chapman, J. C., Connor, D. F., & Cruise, K. C. (2012). Complex trauma and aggression in secure juvenile justice settings. *Criminal Justice and Behavior*, *39*, 695–724.

Ford, J. D., Chapman, J. F., Hawke, J., & Albert, D. B. (2007). *Trauma among youth in the juvenile justice system critical issues and new directions*. Retrieved from http://www.ncmhjj.com/pdfs/Trauma%5Fand%5FYouth.pdf

Ford, J. D., & Connor, D. (2009). ADHD and posttraumatic stress disorder (PTSD). *Current Attention Disorders Reports*, *1*, 61–66. http://dx.doi.org/10.1007/s12618-009-0009-0

Ford, J. D., Connor, D. F., & Hawke, J. (2009). Complex trauma among psychiatrically impaired children: A cross-sectional, chart-review study. *Journal of Clinical Psychiatry*, *70*, 1155–1163. http://dx.doi.org/10.4088/JCP.08m04783

Ford, J. D., Elhai, J. D., Connor, D. F., & Frueh, B. C. (2010). Poly-victimization and risk of posttraumatic, depressive, and substance use disorders and involvement in delinquency in a national sample of adolescents. *Journal of Adolescent Health*, *46*, 545–552. http://dx.doi.org/10.1016/j.jadohealth.2009.11.212

Ford, J. D., Fraleigh, L. A., & Connor, D. F. (2010). Child abuse and aggression among psychiatrically impaired children. *Journal of Clinical Child and Adolescent Psychology*, *39*, 25–34.

Ford, J. D., Grasso, D. J., Hawke, J., & Chapman, J. F. (2013). Poly-victimization among juvenile justice-involved youths. *Child Abuse and Neglect*, *37*, 788–800. http://dx.doi.org/10.1016/j.chiabu.2013.01.005

Ford, J. D., Hartman, J. K., Hawke, J., & Chapman, J. C. (2008). Traumatic victimization, posttraumatic stress disorder, suicidal ideation, and substance abuse risk among juvenile justice-involved youths. *Journal of Child and Adolescent Trauma*, *1*, 75–92. http://dx.doi.org/10.1080/19361520801934456

Ford, J. D., & Hawke, J. (2012). Trauma affect regulation psychoeducation group and milieu intervention outcomes in juvenile detention facilities. *Journal of Aggression, Maltreatment, and Trauma*, *21*, 365–384. http://dx.doi.org/10.1080/10926771.2012.673538

Ford, J. D., Hawke, J., & Chapman, J. C. (2010). *Complex psychological trauma among juvenile justice-involved youth*. Farmington: University of Connecticut.

Ford, J. D., Racusin, R., Daviss, W. B., Ellis, C. G., Thomas, J., Rogers, K., . . . Sengupta, A. (1999). Trauma exposure among children with oppositional defiant disorder and attention deficit-hyperactivity disorder. *Journal of Consulting and Clinical Psychology*, *67*, 786–789. http://dx.doi.org/10.1037/0022-006X.67.5.786

Ford, J. D., Racusin, R., Ellis, C. G., Daviss, W. B., Reiser, J., Fleischer, A., & Thomas, J. (2000). Child maltreatment, other trauma exposure, and posttraumatic symptomatology among children with oppositional defiant and attention deficit hyperactivity disorders. *Child Maltreatment*, *5*, 205–217. http://dx.doi.org/10.1177/1077559500005003001

Ford, J. D., Steinberg, K. L., Hawke, J., Levine, J., & Zhang, W. (2012). Randomized trial comparison of emotion regulation and relational psychotherapies for PTSD with girls involved in delinquency. *Journal of Clinical Child and Adolescent Psychology*, *41*, 27–37. http://dx.doi.org/10.1080/15374416.2012.632343

Glassman, L. H., Weierich, M. R., Hooley, J. M., Deliberto, T. L., & Nock, M. K. (2007). Child maltreatment, non-suicidal self-injury, and the mediating role of self-criticism. *Behaviour Research and Therapy*, *45*, 2483–2490. http://dx.doi.org/10.1016/j.brat.2007.04.002

Goldsmith, H. H., Pollak, S. D., & Davidson, R. J. (2008). Developmental neuroscience perspectives on emotion regulation. *Child Development Perspectives*, *2*, 132–140. http://dx.doi.org/10.1111/j.1750-8606.2008.00055.x

Graham v. Florida, 130 S. Ct. 2011 (2010).

Haley v. Ohio, 332 U.S. 596 (1948).

Henning, K. N. (2004). Eroding confidentiality in delinquency proceedings: Should schools and public housing authorities be notified? *New York University Law Review*, *79*, 520–611.

Hoge, E. A., Austin, E. D., & Pollack, M. H. (2007). Resilience: Research evidence and conceptual considerations for posttraumatic stress disorder. *Depression and Anxiety*, *24*, 139–152. http://dx.doi.org/10.1002/da.20175

Hudley, C., & Friday, J. (1996). Attributional bias and reactive aggression. *American Journal of Preventive Medicine*, *12*(5, Suppl.), 75–81.

Iguchi, M. Y., Bell, J., Ramchand, R. N., & Fain, T. (2005). How criminal system racial disparities may translate into health disparities. *Journal of Health Care for the Poor and Underserved*, *16*(4, Suppl. B), 48–56. http://dx.doi.org/10.1353/hpu.2005.0114

In re Angel R., No. D-21296-08, slip op. (N.Y. Fam. Ct. Oct. 24, 2008).

In re Gault, 387 U.S. 1 (1967).

In re Jonathon C.B., 2011 IL 107750 (Ill. 2011).

In re Kemmo N., 540 A.2d 1202 (Md. Ct. Spec. App. 1988).

In re Landfair, No. 289942, 2010 WL 1629072 (Mich. Ct. App. Apr. 22, 2010).

In the Matter of Johnny S., 896 N.Y.S.2d 842 (N.Y. Fam. Ct. 2010).

In the Matter of the Appeal in Maricopa County, 893 P.2d 60 (Ariz. Ct. Ap., 1994).

In the Matter of Tristan C., 595 N.Y.S.2d 635 (N.Y. Fam. Ct. 1993).

Ipser, J. C., & Stein, D. J. (2012). Evidence-based pharmacotherapy of post-traumatic stress disorder (PTSD). *International Journal of Neuropsychopharmacology, 15*, 825–840. http://dx.doi.org/10.1017/S1461145711001209

Jaycox, L. H., Langley, A. K., Stein, B. D., Wong, M., Sharma, P., Scott, M., & Schonlau, M. (2009). Support for students exposed to trauma: A pilot study. *School Mental Health, 1*, 49–60. http://dx.doi.org/10.1007/s12310-009-9007-8

J.D.B. v. North Carolina, 131 S. Ct. 2394 (2011).

Jelinek, L., Randjbar, S., Seifert, D., Kellner, M., & Moritz, S. (2009). The organization of autobiographical and nonautobiographical memory in posttraumatic stress disorder (PTSD). *Journal of Abnormal Psychology, 118*, 288–298. http://dx.doi.org/10.1037/a0015633

Jenkins v. Talladega City Board of Education, 95 F.3d 1036, 1044 (11th Cir. 1996).

Kerr, D. C., Leve, L. D., & Chamberlain, P. (2009). Pregnancy rates among juvenile justice girls in two randomized controlled trials of multidimensional treatment foster care. *Journal of Consulting and Clinical Psychology, 77*, 588–593. http://dx.doi.org/10.1037/a0015289

Kilpatrick, D. G., Acierno, R., Saunders, B., Resnick, H. S., Best, C. L., & Schnurr, P. P. (2000). Risk factors for adolescent substance abuse and dependence: Data from a national sample. *Journal of Consulting and Clinical Psychology, 68*, 19–30. http://dx.doi.org/10.1037/0022-006X.68.1.19

Kim, C. Y., Losen, D. J., & Hewitt, D. T. (2010). *The school-to-prison pipeline: Structuring legal reform.* New York, NY: NYU Press.

King, D. C., Abram, K. M., Romero, E. G., Washburn, J. J., Welty, L. J., & Teplin, L. A. (2011). Childhood maltreatment and psychiatric disorders among detained youths. *Psychiatric Services, 62*, 1430–1438. http://dx.doi.org/10.1176/appi.ps.004412010

Kinniburgh, K. J., Blaustein, M., Spinazzola, J., & van der Kolk, B. A. (2005). Attachment, self-regulation, and competency. *Psychiatric Annals, 35*, 424–430.

Kitayama, N., Brummer, M., Hertz, L., Quinn, S., Kim, Y., & Bremner, J. D. (2007). Morphologic alterations in the corpus callosum in abuse-related posttraumatic stress disorder: A preliminary study. *Journal of Nervous and Mental Disease, 195*, 1027–1029. http://dx.doi.org/10.1097/NMD.0b013e31815c044f

Ko, S. J., Ford, J. D., Kassam-Adams, N., Berkowitz, S. J., Wilson, C., Wong, M., . . . Layne, C. M. (2008). Creating trauma-informed systems: Child welfare, education, first responders, health care, juvenile justice. *Professional Psychology: Research and Practice, 39*, 396–404. http://dx.doi.org/10.1037/0735-7028.39.4.396

Lanius, R. A., Williamson, P. C., Bluhm, R. L., Densmore, M., Boksman, K., Neufeld, R. W., . . . Menon, R. S. (2005). Functional connectivity of dissociative responses in posttraumatic stress disorder: A functional magnetic resonance imaging investigation. *Biological Psychiatry, 57*, 873–884. http://dx.doi.org/10.1016/j.biopsych.2005.01.011

Layne, C. M., Saltzman, W. R., Poppleton, L., Burlingame, G. M., Pasalic, A., Durakovic, E., . . . Pynoos, R. S. (2008). Effectiveness of a school-based group psychotherapy program for war-exposed adolescents: A randomized controlled trial. *Journal of the American Academy of Child and Adolescent Psychiatry, 47*, 1048–1062. http://dx.doi.org/10.1097/CHI.0b013e31817eecae

Leve, L. D., & Chamberlain, P. (2004). Female juvenile offenders: Defining an early-onset pathway for delinquency. *Journal of Child and Family Studies, 13*, 439–452. http://dx.doi.org/10.1023/B:JCFS.0000044726.07272.b5

Levick, M., Feierman, J., Kelley, S. M., Goldstein, N. E. S., & Mordecai, K. (2012). The Eighth Amendment evolves: Defining cruel and unusual punishment through the lens of childhood and adolescence. *University of Pennsylvania Journal of Law and Social Change, 15*, 285–321.

Listenbee, R. L., Jr., Torre, J., Boyle, G., Cooper, S. W., Deer, S., Durfee, D. T., . . . Taguba, A. (2012). *Report of the Attorney General's National Task Force on Children Exposed to Violence.* Retrieved from http://www.justice.gov/defendingchildhood/cev-rpt-full.pdf

Lollis v. New York State Department of Social Services, 322 F. Supp. 473 (S.D.N.Y. 1970).

Lynne-Landsman, S. D., Graber, J. A., Nichols, T. R., & Botvin, G. J. (2011). Trajectories of aggression, delinquency, and substance use across middle school among urban, minority adolescents. Advance online publication. *Aggressive Behavior, 37*, 161–176.

Lyons-Ruth, K., Dutra, L., Schuder, M. R., & Bianchi, I. (2006). From infant attachment disorganization to adult dissociation: Relational adaptations or traumatic experiences? *Psychiatric Clinics of North America, 29*, 63–86.

Mack, J. (1909). The juvenile court. *Harvard Law Review*, *23*, 104–122.

Majd, K., Marksamer, J., & Reyes, C. (2009). *Hidden injustice: Lesbian, gay, bisexual, and transgender youth in juvenile courts*. Berkeley, CA: Autumn Press.

Marrow, M., Knudsen, K., Olafson, E., & Bucher, S. (2012). The value of implementing TARGET within a trauma-informed juvenile justice setting. *Journal of Child and Adolescent Trauma*, *5*, 257–270. http://dx.doi.org/10.1080/19361521.2012.697105

Mary Beth G. v. City of Chicago, 723 F.2d 1263 (7th Cir. 1983).

McEwen, B. (2006). Stress, adaptation, and disease. *Annals of the New York Academy of Sciences*, *840*, 33–44.

McKeiver v. Pennsylvania, 403 U.S. 528 (1971).

McLaughlin, K. A., Koenen, K. C., Hill, E. D., Petukhova, M., Sampson, N. A., Zaslavsky, A. M., & Kessler, R. C. (2013). Trauma exposure and posttraumatic stress disorder in a national sample of adolescents. *Journal of the American Academy of Child and Adolescent Psychiatry*, *52*, 815–830 e814. http://dx.doi.org/10.1016/j.jaac.2013.05.011

Meiser-Stedman, R., Dalgleish, T., Glucksman, E., Yule, W., & Smith, P. (2009). Maladaptive cognitive appraisals mediate the evolution of posttraumatic stress reactions: A 6-month follow-up of child and adolescent assault and motor vehicle accident survivors. *Journal of Abnormal Psychology*, *118*, 778–787. http://dx.doi.org/10.1037/a0016945

Miller v. Alabama, 132 S. Ct. 2455 (2012).

Moffitt, T. E., & Caspi, A. (2001). Childhood predictors differentiate life-course persistent and adolescence-limited antisocial pathways among males and females. *Development and Psychopathology*, *13*, 355–375. http://dx.doi.org/10.1017/S0954579401002097

Mongillo, E. A., Briggs-Gowan, M., Ford, J. D., & Carter, A. S. (2009). Impact of traumatic life events in a community sample of toddlers. *Journal of Abnormal Child Psychology*, *37*, 455–468. http://dx.doi.org/10.1007/s10802-008-9283-z

Morsette, A., Swaney, G., Stolle, D., Schuldberg, D., van den Pol, R., & Young, M. (2009). Cognitive behavioral intervention for trauma in schools (CBITS): school-based treatment on a rural American Indian reservation. *Journal of Behavior Therapy and Experimental Psychiatry*, *40*, 169–178. http://dx.doi.org/10.1016/j.jbtep.2008.07.006

Muehlenkamp, J. J., Williams, K. L., Gutierrez, P. M., & Claes, L. (2009). Rates of non-suicidal self-injury in high school students across five years. *Archives of Suicide Research*, *13*, 317–329. http://dx.doi.org/10.1080/13811110903266368

National Childhood Traumatic Stress Network's Justice Consortium. (n.d.). *Bench card for the trauma-informed judge*. Retrieved from http://www.nctsn.org/sites/default/files/assets/pdfs/judge_bench_cards_final.pdf

Navalta, C. P., Brown, A. D., Nisewaner, A., Ellis, B. H., & Saxe, G. N. (2013). Trauma systems therapy. In J. D. Ford & C. A. Courtois (Eds.), *Treating complex traumatic stress disorders in children and adolescents: Scientific foundations and therapeutic models* (pp. 329–348). New York, NY: Guilford Press.

Ngo, V., Langley, A., Kataoka, S. H., Nadeem, E., Escudero, P., & Stein, B. D. (2008). Providing evidence-based practice to ethnically diverse youths: Examples from the Cognitive Behavioral Intervention for Trauma in Schools (CBITS) program. *Journal of the American Academy of Child and Adolescent Psychiatry*, *47*, 858–862. http://dx.doi.org/10.1097/CHI.0b013e3181799f19

N.G. v. Connecticut, 382 F.3d 225 (2d Cir. 2004).

Nilsson, D. K., Gustafsson, P. E., & Svedin, C. G. (2012). Polytraumatization and trauma symptoms in adolescent boys and girls: Interpersonal and noninterpersonal events and moderating effects of adverse family circumstances. *Journal of Interpersonal Violence*, *27*, 2645–2664. http://dx.doi.org/10.1177/0886260512436386

O'Leary, K. D., Smith Slep, A. M., Avery-Leaf, S., & Cascardi, M. (2008). Gender differences in dating aggression among multiethnic high school students. *Journal of Adolescent Health*, *42*, 473–479. http://dx.doi.org/10.1016/j.jadohealth.2007.09.012

Olfson, M., Gameroff, M. J., Marcus, S. C., Greenberg, T., & Shaffer, D. (2005). National trends in hospitalization of youth with intentional self-inflicted injuries. *American Journal of Psychiatry*, *162*, 1328–1335. http://dx.doi.org/10.1176/appi.ajp.162.7.1328

Ostrov, J. M., & Godleski, S. A. (2010). Toward an integrated gender-linked model of aggression subtypes in early and middle childhood. *Psychological Review*, *117*, 233–242. http://dx.doi.org/10.1037/a0018070

Peloquin, S. M. (1994). Moral treatment: How a caring practice lost its rationale. *American Journal of Occupational Therapy*, *48*, 167–173. http://dx.doi.org/10.5014/ajot.48.2.167

People v. Pratcher, No. A117122, 2009 WL 2332183 (Cal. Ct. App. 2009).

Piquero, A. R. (2008). Disproportionate minority contact. *Future of Children*, *18*, 59–79. http://dx.doi.org/10.1353/foc.0.0013

Platt, A. (1974). The triumph of benevolence: The origins of the juvenile justice system in the United States.

In R. Quinney (Ed.), *Criminal justice in America: A critical understanding* (pp. 366–389). Boston, MA: Little, Brown.

Pole, N., Gone, J. P., & Kulkarni, M. (2008). Posttraumatic stress disorder among ethnoracial minorities in the United States. *Clinical Psychology: Science and Practice, 15*, 35–61. http://dx.doi.org/10.1111/j.1468-2850.2008.00109.x

Ponce, A. N., Williams, M. K., & Allen, G. J. (2004). Experience of maltreatment as a child and acceptance of violence in adult intimate relationships: Mediating effects of distortions in cognitive schemas. *Violence and Victims, 19*, 97–108. http://dx.doi.org/10.1891/vivi.19.1.97.33235

Porges, S. W. (2007). The polyvagal perspective. *Biological Psychiatry, 74*, 116–143. http://dx.doi.org/10.1016/j.biopsycho.2006.06.009

R.G. v. Koller, 415 F. Supp. 2d 1129 (D. Haw. 2006).

Riggs Romaine, C. L., Goldstein, N. E. S., Hunt, E., & DeMatteo, D. (2011). Traumatic experiences and juvenile amenability: The role of trauma in forensic evaluations and judicial decision making. *Child and Youth Care Forum, 40*, 363–380. http://dx.doi.org/10.1007/s10566-010-9132-4

Roper v. Simmons, 543 U.S. 551 (2005).

Rosado, L., & Shah, R. (2007). *Protecting youth from self-incrimination when undergoing screening, assessment, and treatment within the juvenile justice system.* Philadelphia, PA: Juvenile Law Center.

Rowley, E. B. (1845). Observations on the advantages to be derived from increased accommodation for the insane; on the beneficial effects that would attend a more extended application of moral treatment; and on the probable cause of the high rate of mortality in almost all county asylums. *Provincial Medical and Surgical Journal, 9*, 301–306.

Ruchkin, V., Henrich, C. C., Jones, S. M., Vermeiren, R., & Schwab-Stone, M. (2007). Violence exposure and psychopathology in urban youth: The mediating role of posttraumatic stress. *Journal of Abnormal Child Psychology, 35*, 578–593. http://dx.doi.org/10.1007/s10802-007-9114-7

Sachs-Ericsson, N., Verona, E., Joiner, T., & Preacher, K. J. (2006). Parental verbal abuse and the mediating role of self-criticism in adult internalizing disorders. *Journal of Affective Disorders, 93*, 71–78. http://dx.doi.org/10.1016/j.jad.2006.02.014

Schmahl, C. G., Vermetten, E., Elzinga, B. M., & Douglas Bremner, J. (2003). Magnetic resonance imaging of hippocampal and amygdala volume in women with childhood abuse and borderline personality disorder. *Psychiatry Research: Neuroimaging, 122*, 193–198. http://dx.doi.org/10.1016/S0925-4927(03)00023-4

Scott, E. S., & Steinberg, L. (2008). Adolescent development and the regulation of youth crime. *Future of Children, 18*, 15–33. http://dx.doi.org/10.1353/foc.0.0011

Seedat, S., Nyamai, C., Njenga, F., Vythilingum, B., & Stein, D. J. (2004). Trauma exposure and post-traumatic stress symptoms in urban African schools. Survey in Cape Town and Nairobi. *British Journal of Psychiatry, 184*, 169–175. http://dx.doi.org/10.1192/bjp.184.2.169

Sherman, F., & Levick, M. L. (2003). When individual differences demand equal treatment: An equal rights approach to the special needs of girls in the juvenile justice system. *Wisconsin Women's Law Journal, 18*, 9–50.

Sherman, J. W., Gawronski, B., Gonsalkorale, K., Hugenberg, K., Allen, T. J., & Groom, C. J. (2008). The self-regulation of automatic associations and behavioral impulses. *Psychological Review, 115*, 314–335. http://dx.doi.org/10.1037/0033-295X.115.2.314

Shields, A., & Cicchetti, D. (1998). Reactive aggression among maltreated children: The contributions of attention and emotion dysregulation. *Journal of Clinical Child Psychology, 27*, 381–395. http://dx.doi.org/10.1207/s15374424jccp2704_2

Shonkoff, J. P., Garner, A. S.; Committee on Psychosocial Aspects of Child and Family Health; Committee on Early Childhood, Adoption, and Dependent Care; & Section on Developmental and Behavioral Pediatrics. (2012). The lifelong effects of early childhood adversity and toxic stress. *Pediatrics, 129*, e232–e246. http://dx.doi.org/10.1542/peds.2011-2663

Silverman, A. B., Reinherz, H. Z., & Giaconia, R. M. (1996). The long-term sequelae of child and adolescent abuse: A longitudinal community study. *Child Abuse and Neglect, 20*, 709–723. http://dx.doi.org/10.1016/0145-2134(96)00059-2

Smith, D. K., Leve, L. D., & Chamberlain, P. (2006). Adolescent girls' offending and health-risking sexual behavior: The predictive role of trauma. *Child Maltreatment, 11*, 346–353. http://dx.doi.org/10.1177/1077559506291950

Smook v. Minnehaha County, 457 F.3d 806 (8th Cir. 2006).

Soler, M., Shoenberg, D., & Schindler, M. (2009). Juvenile justice: Lessons for a new era. *Georgetown Journal on Poverty Law and Policy, 16*, 483–541.

Stagman, S., & Cooper, J. L. (2010). *Children's mental health: What every policymaker should know.* New York, NY: National Center for Children in Poverty.

State in the Interest of C.A.H., 446 A.2d 93 (N.J. 1982).

State v. Hines, 696 A.2d 780 (N.J. Super. Ct. App. Div. 1997).

State v. Janes, 850 P.2d 495 (Wash. 1993).

Steiner, H., Garcia, I. G., & Matthews, Z. (1997). Posttraumatic stress disorder in incarcerated juvenile delinquents. *Journal of the American Academy of Child and Adolescent Psychiatry*, *36*, 357–365. http://dx.doi.org/10.1097/00004583-199703000-00014

Sutherland, K., & Bryant, R. A. (2008). Autobiographical memory and the self-memory system in posttraumatic stress disorder. *Journal of Anxiety Disorders*, *22*, 555–560. http://dx.doi.org/10.1016/j.janxdis.2007.03.008

Teicher, M. H., & Samson, J. A. (2013). Childhood maltreatment and psychopathology: A case for ecophenotypic variants as clinically and neurobiologically distinct subtypes. *American Journal of Psychiatry*, *170*, 1114–1133. http://dx.doi.org/10.1176/appi.ajp.2013.12070957

Teplin, L. A., McClelland, G. M., Abram, K. M., & Mileusnic, D. (2005). Early violent death among delinquent youth: A prospective longitudinal study. *Pediatrics*, *115*, 1586–1593. http://dx.doi.org/10.1542/peds.2004-1459

Thayer, J. F., Hansen, A. L., Saus-Rose, E., & Johnsen, B. H. (2009). Heart rate variability, prefrontal neural function, and cognitive performance: The neurovisceral integration perspective on self-regulation, adaptation, and health. *Annals of Behavioral Medicine*, *37*, 141–153. http://dx.doi.org/10.1007/s12160-009-9101-z

Thomas ex. rel. Thomas v. Roberts, 261 F.3d 1160, 1167 (11th Cir. 2001).

Tobler, A. L., Maldonado-Molina, M. M., Staras, S. A., O'Mara, R. J., Livingston, M. D., & Komro, K. A. (2013). Perceived racial/ethnic discrimination, problem behaviors, and mental health among minority urban youth. *Ethnicity and Health*, *18*, 337–349. http://dx.doi.org/10.1080/13557858.2012.730609

Tolin, D. F., & Foa, E. B. (2006). Sex differences in trauma and posttraumatic stress disorder: A quantitative review of 25 years of research. *Psychological Bulletin*, *132*, 959–992. http://dx.doi.org/10.1037/0033-2909.132.6.959

Turner, H. A., Finkelhor, D., & Ormrod, R. (2006). The effect of lifetime victimization on the mental health of children and adolescents. *Social Science and Medicine*, *62*, 13–27. http://dx.doi.org/10.1016/j.socscimed.2005.05.030

United States v. Clark, 8 F.3d 839 (D.C. 1993).

United States v. Floyd, 945 F.2d 1096 (9th Cir. 1991).

United States v. Juvenile, 347 F.3d 778 (9th Cir. 2003).

United States v. Sealed Appellant, 591 F.3d 812 (5th Cir. 2009).

Vaisvaser, S., Lin, T., Admon, R., Podlipsky, I., Greenman, Y., Stern, N., . . . Hendler, T. (2013). Neural traces of stress: Cortisol related sustained enhancement of amygdala-hippocampal functional connectivity. *Frontiers in Human Neuroscience*, *7*, 313. http://dx.doi.org/10.3389/fnhum.2013.00313

Vazsonyi, A. T., & Chen, P. (2010). Entry risk into the juvenile justice system: African American, American Indian, Asian American, European American, and Hispanic children and adolescents. *Journal of Child Psychology and Psychiatry*, *51*, 668–678. http://dx.doi.org/10.1111/j.1469-7610.2010.02231.x

Vazsonyi, A. T., & Keiley, M. K. (2007). Normative developmental trajectories of aggressive behaviors in African American, American Indian, Asian American, Caucasian, and Hispanic children and early adolescents. *Journal of Abnormal Child Psychology*, *35*, 1047–1062. http://dx.doi.org/10.1007/s10802-007-9154-z

Vervoort, M. H., Scholte, R. H., & Overbeek, G. (2010). Bullying and victimization among adolescents: The role of ethnicity and ethnic composition of school class. *Journal of Youth and Adolescence*, *39*, 1–11. http://dx.doi.org/10.1007/s10964-008-9355-y

Weder, N., Yang, B. Z., Douglas-Palumberi, H., Massey, J., Krystal, J. H., Gelernter, J., & Kaufman, J. (2009). MAOA genotype, maltreatment, and aggressive behavior: The changing impact of genotype at varying levels of trauma. *Biological Psychiatry*, *65*, 417–424. http://dx.doi.org/10.1016/j.biopsych.2008.09.013

Wilbur, S., Ryan, C., & Marksamer, J. (2006). *Best practice guidelines: Serving LGBT youth in out-of-home care*. Washington, DC: Child Welfare League of America.

Williams, D. R., & Mohammed, S. A. (2009). Discrimination and racial disparities in health: Evidence and needed research. *Journal of Behavioral Medicine*, *32*, 20–47. http://dx.doi.org/10.1007/s10865-008-9185-0

Yang, P., Wu, M. T., Hsu, C. C., & Ker, J. H. (2004). Evidence of early neurobiological alternations in adolescents with posttraumatic stress disorder: A functional MRI study. *Neuroscience Letters*, *370*, 13–18. http://dx.doi.org/10.1016/j.neulet.2004.07.033

Yang, S. J., Shin, D. W., Noh, K. S., & Stein, M. A. (2007). Cortisol is inversely correlated with aggression for those boys with attention deficit hyperactivity disorder who retain their reactivity to stress. *Psychiatry Research*, *153*, 55–60. http://dx.doi.org/10.1016/j.psychres.2006.04.001

CHAPTER 26

COMMUNITY-BASED INTERVENTIONS FOR JUVENILE OFFENDERS

Scott W. Henggeler

In this chapter, I present extensive evidence for the effectiveness of several well-validated community-based treatments for juvenile offenders presenting with serious clinical problems. When implemented with fidelity, these interventions have reduced rates of criminal behavior and residential placements, which, in turn, have produced considerable cost savings. Concomitantly, the interventions have improved family relations and the functioning of youths within the community (e.g., decreased association with deviant peers, increased school attendance). In addition to reviewing the outcome literature, I synthesize the commonalities in content and process of effective interventions—commonalities that derive from the work of many researchers in the fields of developmental psychopathology, psychotherapy, and criminology.

Before I examine the literature on community-based interventions for juvenile offenders, it is important to provide a context from which to view the implementation of community-based services and evidence-based practices, because these services compete with residential placements for public support. Although the number of juveniles in residential placement facilities has decreased substantially from 1997 to 2010 (i.e., 1-day census from 116,701 to 79,165), their profile has changed little (Hockenberry, 2013). Thirty-seven percent of youths in residential placement had perpetrated crimes against people (e.g., robbery, assault), 24% had committed property crimes, and 20% had committed status offenses (e.g., running away) or technical violations of probation or parole (e.g., breaking curfew, testing positive for drugs). Youths committed to state custody made up about two thirds of confined juveniles, and their average length of stay was 4 months, primarily in long-term secure facilities or group home settings. Detained juveniles made up about one third of confined juveniles, and they were housed primarily in detention centers with an average length of stay of 19 days. In light of the large differences in lengths of stay between committed and detained youths, one might hypothesize that youths perpetrating more serious offenses were more likely to be committed, whereas youths with less serious violations were more likely to be detained. The offense profiles of committed and detained offenders, however, are virtually identical. The personal, family, social, and fiscal costs of these placements are substantive.

COSTS OF JUVENILE CONFINEMENT

The United States leads the world in the incarceration of adults and juveniles (Trzcinski & Allen, 2012). Although, as noted previously, considerable decline in youth confinement has been achieved during the past 15 years (Hockenberry, 2013), the United States still locks up a higher percentage of youths than any other developed country (Annie E. Casey Foundation, 2013). More important,

Scott W. Henggeler is a board member and stockholder of MST Services LLC, the Medical University of South Carolina–licensed organization that provides training in multisystemic therapy.

http://dx.doi.org/10.1037/14643-026
APA Handbook of Psychology and Juvenile Justice, K. Heilbrun (Editor-in-Chief)

the reduction in confinement has not led to an increase in juvenile crime—juvenile crime has actually decreased during this time (Annie E. Casey Foundation, 2013). The costs of confinement have been described in several recent reviews (Lambie & Randell, 2013; Mendel, 2011; Petteruti, Walsh, & Velazquez, 2009), and these costs are summarized next.

Iatrogenic Effects on Youth Mental Health

Juvenile facilities can be dangerous places to live, with considerable exposure to violence as well as physical, emotional, and sexual abuse from residents and staff. Such exposure and victimization can lead to or exacerbate anxiety and depressive disorders as well as suicidal ideation and suicide attempts, especially in a context in which youths are isolated from family support. Moreover, many facilities have been cited for overreliance on isolation and restraint to control youth behavior. In spite of considerable need, mental health and substance abuse treatment resources are scarce.

Decreased Education and Employment Outcomes

Removing youths from their local school for several months does not enhance academic achievement. Correctional programs often fail to meet the challenging academic needs of confined youths. Moreover, many juveniles do not reenroll in school after returning to their community, and schools often set up barriers to enrollment for such youths. Unfortunately, decreased education and the stigma of incarceration often lead to fewer employment opportunities and concomitant socioeconomic disadvantage.

Disrupted Family and Relationships

Removal from the family can present emotional and instrumental hardships for youths and family members. Confined youths lose the emotional support of parents, siblings, and extended family while they are away. Likewise, many adolescents play important roles in caring for younger siblings and contributing to the economic well-being of the family, and these valuable contributions are disrupted by out-of-home placement as well.

High Recidivism Rates

Confining an adolescent with problem behavior with a broad array of other antisocial youths cannot reasonably be expected to decrease his or her antisocial tendencies. Indeed, extensive evidence has demonstrated the detrimental effects of programs that place deviant youths together for prolonged periods of time in facilities that separate them from prosocial peer influences (see, e.g., Robst, Armstrong, & Dollard, 2011). These difficulties are compounded by the negative effects of placement noted previously.

Financially Wasteful

The confinement of juveniles is not cost-effective, especially compared with evidence-based alternatives delivered in the community. For example, the average cost of 4 months of confinement in 2005 was approximately $30,000 (Justice Policy Institute, 2009), whereas effective community-based alternatives are delivered at a fraction of the cost. Indeed, confinement produces multiple types of poor outcomes at very high cost, whereas evidence-based interventions can result in considerable cost savings as well as crime reduction and improved youth and family functioning.

Conclusion

Making a case for the continued high rates of incarceration is difficult. In addition to negative mental health and social outcomes, the confinement of juvenile offenders leads to high rates of recidivism at very high cost. Fortunately, in recent years advocates and stakeholders across the nation have recognized the deleterious outcomes associated with residential placements and have promoted and enacted several substantive reforms aimed at improving outcomes for juvenile offenders (Bryer & Levin, 2013). These reforms (e.g., disallowing incarceration for minor offenses, closing down youth confinement facilities, restructuring juvenile justice responsibilities and finances) are largely responsible for the decrease in juvenile confinement noted previously. Indeed, Bryer and Levin (2013) highlighted nine states that have led the movement to reduce juvenile confinement. On average, confinement was reduced by 38% across these states between 2001 and 2010 and, concomitantly, arrests were reduced by 24%. Although these reductions were associated with several important juvenile justice reforms, Bryer and Levin (2013) emphasized that the adoption of evidence-based community practices has played a central role as one of the reforms.

COMMUNITY-BASED SERVICES WITHIN THE JUVENILE JUSTICE SYSTEM

In 2010, 1,642,600 juvenile arrests were made (Puzzanchera, 2013). After arrest, juvenile justice stakeholders (e.g., juvenile court intake worker, solicitor, judge) decide whether the youth should be officially processed through the court system, diverted from the system to a variety of community-based services, or released without referral to services. Of the juvenile arrests in 2010, 76% were referred to juvenile court or criminal court (Puzzanchera, 2013). Subsequently, as emphasized by Mears, Cochran, Greenman, Bhati, and Greenwald (2011), juveniles can receive a wide array of sanctions that vary in focus (e.g., restorative justice programs, probation, diversion to a variety of programs), intensity, and duration. The heterogeneity of these services makes it challenging to conduct well-specified outcome studies (e.g., examining specific theories of change) and to synthesize the literature.

Processing in the Juvenile Justice System

Two recent reviews have examined the results of studies that compared outcomes of arrested juveniles diverted from the system with those of juveniles receiving traditional juvenile court processing. Petrosino, Turpin-Petrosino, and Guckenburg (2010) included 29 studies and Schwalbe, Gearing, MacKenzie, Brewer, and Ibrahim (2012) included 28, with less overlap in the reviewed studies than might be expected. Although their results were heterogeneous, Petrosino et al. (2010) concluded that rather than providing a public safety benefit, processing juvenile offenders through the system resulted in increased criminal behavior. The negative effects of processing were greater when diverted youths received services than when they were simply released. Thus, overall, juveniles diverted with services had the most favorable outcomes, followed by juveniles diverted with no services, followed by juveniles processed in the juvenile justice system.

Schwalbe et al. (2012) classified diversion programs into five mutually exclusive program categories: case management, individually oriented treatment with or without case management, family treatment with or without case management, youth court, and restorative justice (also see Restorative Justice section below). These authors drew several pertinent conclusions from their results. First, as with Petrosino et al. (2010), the results were heterogeneous, and moderation analyses were therefore appropriate. Second, diversion programs were associated with lower rates of recidivism than court processing, but not significantly so. Third, only family-based programs had significantly better outcomes than traditional court processing. Fourth, similar to the findings in the area of child mental health (e.g., Bickman, Lambert, Andrade, & Penaloza, 2000), outcomes from widely used case management approaches were not encouraging. Fifth, the use of treatment manuals, researcher involvement, and fidelity monitoring tended to increase the effectiveness of diversion approaches.

Together, the findings from these two reviews suggest two inferences that are pertinent to this chapter. First, as with confinement, penetration into the juvenile justice system does not, in general, seem to be associated with positive juvenile outcomes. Second, more favorable outcomes are associated with family-based interventions and with those that are well specified and well implemented.

Restorative Justice

Restorative justice (Zehr & Mika, 1997) is a movement within criminal justice that represents a philosophical shift from punishment and rehabilitation of the offender to promoting accountability and repairing the harm caused by the offender to the victim and community. As such, restorative justice includes a range of interventions such as victim–offender mediation, family group counseling, and community service. These interventions are not uniformly specified or implemented. In general, restorative justice programs take a nonadversarial approach and seem to focus on first-time offenders and youths committing property offenses. Results from outcome reviews have been mixed (e.g., Bonta, Jesseman, Rugge, & Cormier, 2006; Schwalbe et al., 2012), and the research literature includes many poorly designed studies that bias findings (Bergseth & Bouffard, 2007). Nevertheless, it seems reasonable to conclude that restorative justice programs hold promise as alternatives to traditional juvenile court processing.

Juvenile Drug Court

Juvenile drug courts (JDC) combine close judicial oversight (e.g., weekly meetings, frequent drug testing, rewards and sanctions based on specified youth behaviors) with substance use treatment provided by therapists who are typically from community-based provider organizations. The interventions provided by these therapists are usually not family based and rarely include evidence-based treatment (Stein, Deberard, & Homan, 2013). JDCs have proliferated to more than 500 sites nationwide in spite of mixed results. Most recently, Drake (2012) and Stein, Deberard, and Homan (2015) both calculated average effect sizes slightly above .10 for JDC outcomes studies, the majority of which have been unpublished. In light of very heterogeneous outcomes in the JDC literature, reviewers (e.g., Belenko & Logan, 2003; Hills, Shufelt, & Cocozza, 2009) have suggested that the effectiveness of JDCs has been attenuated by their difficulty engaging parents in treatment as well as by a failure to integrate evidence-based substance abuse treatments. Most evidence-based treatments of adolescent substance abuse are family based (Waldron & Turner, 2008).

Henggeler and colleagues evaluated whether the integration of family- and evidence-based interventions improved JDC outcomes in two randomized controlled trials (RCTs). In the first study (Henggeler et al., 2006), substance-abusing juvenile offenders in JDC evidenced greater decreases in criminal behavior and substance use than counterparts in family court, and the integration of family- and evidence-based treatment within JDC improved youth substance-related outcomes. Supporting the importance of family functioning in achieving favorable JDC outcomes, improved caregiver supervision was a key determinant of favorable outcomes for juveniles in JDC (Schaeffer et al., 2010), and caregiver substance use predicted youth nonresponse to JDC interventions (Halliday-Boykins et al., 2010). The second study included six JDCs randomized to conditions that included a family- and evidence-based treatment versus treatment as usual. Substance-abusing juvenile offenders in the family- and evidence-based condition showed greater decreases in substance use and criminal behavior than did counterparts in the JDCs that included substance abuse treatment as usual (Henggeler, McCart, Cunningham, & Chapman, 2012). Consistent with the suggestion of reviewers (e.g., Belenko & Logan, 2003; Hills et al., 2009), the findings of this research program suggest that JDC outcomes can be enhanced through the integration of family- and evidence-based interventions.

Scared Straight and Juvenile Awareness Programs

In Scared Straight and similar programs, juveniles are brought into adult prison and, through interaction with prisoners and observation of prison life, "scared" out of their delinquent behavior. Reviews (e.g., Drake, Aos, & Miller, 2009; Petrosino, Turpin-Petrosino, Hollis-Peel, & Lavenberg, 2013) of experimental and quasi-experimental evaluations of the shock approach have consistently concluded that they increase the risk of subsequent criminal behavior.

Conclusion

In a long-term longitudinal study of high-risk boys, Gatti, Tremblay, and Vitaro (2009) concluded that intervention by the juvenile justice system during adolescence has an overall iatrogenic effect and that its negative impact increases as the type of intervention becomes more intensive and restrictive. Labeling and deviant peer contagion were hypothesized as the most likely mediating mechanisms for these results. Findings from the preceding review of juvenile justice interventions tend to support the conclusions of Gatti et al. Processing in the juvenile justice system was not associated with positive juvenile outcomes, and confinement of juveniles had myriad deleterious effects. However, the interventions that showed the most promise (see, e.g., diversion to family-based programs and JDC outcomes when evidence-based treatments are integrated) tended to be family based, well specified, and implemented with fidelity. As discussed next, the best validated interventions with serious juvenile offenders have these same characteristics—as well as other key commonalities that likely account for their effectiveness.

EVIDENCE-BASED TREATMENTS IMPLEMENTED WITH SUPPORT OF THE JUVENILE JUSTICE SYSTEM

The development and validation of effective interventions based on behavioral science during the past 4 decades occurred against a background in which many criminal justice stakeholders believed that nothing works (Martinson, 1974). Assuming that the failure of past efforts to achieve favorable outcomes with juvenile offenders was a product of poorly conceived interventions rather than an inherent intransigence of adolescent antisocial behavior, several independent treatment development research teams capitalized on emerging findings on the determinants of delinquent behavior (e.g., Elliott, Huizinga, & Ageton, 1985) as well as advances in psychotherapy research—especially pertaining to behavior therapy, cognitive–behavioral therapy, and structural and strategic family therapy approaches. Their work has been expanded to many collaborative research teams worldwide as well as to investigators fully independent of the original treatment developers, as presented subsequently.

During the past decade, foundations and state, federal, and international organizations have compiled lists of effective treatments of antisocial behavior in adolescents. Arguably, the most prominent of these lists is the Blueprints for Violence Prevention originally developed by the Office of Juvenile Justice and Delinquency Prevention (Elliott, 1998) and updated continuously (Blueprints, 2013). More than 1,000 programs that aim to reduce antisocial behavior in youths have been reviewed, and only eight have been identified as model prevention–intervention programs. Model programs are well specified, have strong evidence of effectiveness, achieved favorable outcomes with sustained treatment effects for at least a year, and have the capacity to be disseminated to community settings with fidelity. Only three treatment programs met these criteria, and each is family based: multisystemic therapy (MST), functional family therapy (FFT), and multidimensional treatment foster care (MTFC). Although other treatments, also family based, have shown promise in the treatment of delinquency (i.e., brief strategic family therapy, multidimensional family therapy), I focus on the Blueprints models programs to (a) clearly document their success in reducing serious antisocial behavior in adolescents and (b) highlight clinical commonalities that likely account for their success.

Multisystemic Therapy

The MST clinical approach is specified in Henggeler, Schoenwald, Borduin, Rowland, and Cunningham (2009), and the journey from small efficacy studies conducted in a university context in the 1980s to international transport and multisite RCTs has been described by Henggeler (2011).

Clinical approach. MST is based on a social-ecological theoretical model (Bronfenbrenner, 1979) that views all behavior as multidetermined (i.e., by interrelated individual, family, peer, school, and neighborhood factors). More important, the social-ecological model is highly compatible with findings from extensive longitudinal research on the determinants of antisocial behavior in adolescents (Liberman, 2008). For example, research has demonstrated the significance of family functioning (e.g., parental supervision and monitoring, affective relations), peer relations (e.g., association with deviant peers as a powerful predictor of antisocial behavior), and community (e.g., school performance, availability of prosocial activities) in the development and maintenance of antisocial behavior. Viewing the family as central to child and adolescent functioning, the MST theory of change proposes that improved family functioning (especially instrumental aspects, such as monitoring, discipline, and supervision) can lead to reduced risk factors (e.g., decreased association with deviant peers) and improved protective factors (e.g., improved school performance and community engagement).

To accomplish these aims, the therapist's primary clinical task is to determine the key proximal variables (e.g., poor parental monitoring, association with deviant peers) contributing to the youth's antisocial behavior. These variables are then prioritized on the basis of salience and amenability to change, and well-operationalized interventions are designed to address any barriers to change. For example, perhaps parental depression is a key barrier to effective monitoring of the youth's whereabouts and implementation of productive discipline strategies. In such a case, the therapist might deliver an evidence-based mental health treatment (e.g., cognitive–behavioral therapy) to the parent while concurrently developing more effective parenting skills. Youth and family outcomes are tracked continuously, and interventions are modified in an ongoing process until the desired outcomes are achieved. Importantly, a primary aim of treatment is to empower the parents to be more effective with their children. Thus, for example, therapists might coach parents in how to promote their child's problem-solving skills, disengage the adolescent from deviant peers, or negotiate desired support from teachers and school administrators.

MST uses a model of service delivery designed to overcome barriers to service access for this challenging clinical population. MST is a home-based intervention delivered by master's-level therapists who work within teams of two to four therapists and a half-time supervisor. Caseloads are low to facilitate family engagement and the delivery of intensive services, which are on average of 4 months duration. MST programs are self-contained, and therapists and supervisors receive intensive training and ongoing quality assurance to promote treatment fidelity and youth outcomes. Importantly, key aspects of effectiveness of the MST quality assurance system have been supported in large-scale longitudinal research (Schoenwald, Chapman, Sheidow, & Carter, 2009).

Outcomes research. Twenty controlled evaluations (17 RCTs and three quasi-experimental) of MST with juvenile offenders or with adolescents presenting with serious behavior problems have been published. Table 26.1 provides a list and brief summaries of these studies including authors, design, independence, sample size, population, comparison condition, length of follow-up, and significant MST outcomes. The studies include 12 trials with juvenile offenders and eight with youths presenting with serious conduct problems. Four RCTs were conducted in Europe, and the remainder were conducted in the United States. Comparison groups have ranged from youths receiving usual community services to youths receiving very intensive services and other evidence-based approaches. The vast majority of studies had follow-ups of at least a year, and one RCT had a 21.9-year follow-up. As one might expect, most of the early MST trials were conducted by MST developers, whereas most of the eight independent evaluations have been published in recent years.

Rather than listing study findings in the text, several summary conclusions are presented, and the reader is referred to Table 26.1 for more details. First, MST research has intentionally focused on very challenging clinical populations, such as violent and chronic juvenile offenders, juvenile sex offenders, substance-abusing juvenile offenders, and youths in the mental health system presenting with significant externalizing problems. Second, across studies with juvenile offenders, the median reduction in rearrest was 39%, and the median reduction in out-of-home placement was 53% (Henggeler, 2015). Third, in general, favorable outcomes have been achieved for key targets of MST interventions, including improved parenting and family relations, increased school attendance, improved parental mental health, decreased youth symptoms and substance use, and improved peer relations, and consumer satisfaction with MST services has been high. Fourth, and also important, several RCTs as well as the large-scale MST transportability study (Schoenwald et al., 2009) have demonstrated significant associations between treatment fidelity and youth recidivism.

Mediation research. As noted previously, the MST theory of change posits that reductions in adolescent antisocial behavior are mediated by improved family functioning, especially more effective parenting. This perspective has been supported by mediational and qualitative studies with substance-abusing juvenile offenders and chronic and violent juvenile offenders (Huey, Henggeler, Brondino, &

TABLE 26.1

Published MST Outcome Studies Addressing Serious Antisocial Behavior in Adolescents

Study, sample size, and design	Population	Comparison	Follow-up	MST outcomes
Henggeler et al. (1986) *N* = 80 Quasi-experimental	Delinquents	Diversion services	Posttreatment	Improved family relations; decreased behavioral and emotional problems and association with deviant peers
Borduin, Henggeler, Blaske, & Stein (1990) *N* = 16 RCT	Adolescent sexual offenders	Individual counseling	3 yr	Reduced sexual offending (93%) and other criminal offending (72%)
Henggeler, Melton, & Smith (1992) *N* = 84 RCT	Violent and chronic juvenile offenders	Usual community services; high rates of incarceration	59 wk	Improved family relations and peer relations; decreased recidivism (43%) and out-of-home placement (64%)
Henggeler, Melton, Smith, Schoenwald, & Hanley (1993)	Same sample as Henggeler et al. (1992)		2.4 yr	Decreased recidivism (24%, doubled survival rate)
Borduin et al. (1995) *N* = 176 RCT	Violent and chronic juvenile offenders	Individual counseling	4 yr	Improved family relations; decreased psychiatric symptomatology for parents, youth behavior problems, and recidivism (63%)
Schaeffer & Borduin (2005)	Same sample as Borduin et al. (1995)		13.7 yr	Decreased rearrests (54%) and days incarcerated (57%)
Sawyer & Borduin (2011)	Same sample as Borduin et al. (1995)		21.9 yr	Decreased felony arrests (36%), violent felony arrests (75%), and days in adult confinement (33%)
Henggeler, Melton, Brondino, Scherer, & Hanley (1997) *N* = 155 RCT	Violent and chronic juvenile offenders	Juvenile probation services; high rates of incarceration	1.7 yr	Decreased youth psychiatric symptomatology, incarceration (53%), and recidivism (26%, nonsignificant); treatment adherence linked with recidivism outcomes
Henggeler, Rowland, et al. (1999) *N* = 116 (final sample, *N* = 156) RCT	Youths presenting with psychiatric emergencies	Psychiatric hospitalization	4 mo postrecruitment	Decreased externalizing problems (Child Behavior Checklist); improved family relations; increased school attendance; higher consumer satisfaction
Schoenwald, Ward, Henggeler, & Rowland (2000)	Same sample as Henggeler, Rowland, et al. (1999)		4 mo postrecruitment	73% reduction in days hospitalized and 49% reduction in days in other out-of-home placements
Henggeler et al. (2003)	Same sample as Henggeler, Rowland, et al. (1999)		16 mo postrecruitment	Favorable outcomes at 4 mo dissipated

(*continues*)

TABLE 26.1 (*Continued*)

Published MST Outcome Studies Addressing Serious Antisocial Behavior in Adolescents

Study, sample size, and design	Population	Comparison	Follow-up	MST outcomes
Henggeler, Pickrel, & Brondino (1999) $N = 118$ RCT	Substance-abusing and dependent delinquents	Usual community services	11 mo postrecruitment	Decreased drug use at posttreatment; decreased days in out-of-home placement (50%) and criminal arrests (25%, nonsignificant); treatment adherence linked with decreased drug use and other outcomes
Henggeler, Clingempeel, Brondino, & Pickrel (2002)	Same sample as Henggeler et al. (1999)		4 yr	Decreased violent crime (74%) and increased marijuana abstinence
Ogden & Halliday-Boykins (2004) $N = 100$ RCT; independent	Norwegian youths with serious antisocial behavior	Usual child welfare services	6 mo postrecruitment	Decreased externalizing and internalizing symptoms and out-of-home placements (78%); increased social competence and consumer satisfaction; differential site effects
Ogden & Hagen (2006)	Sample from three sites with fidelity		24 mo postrecruitment	Decreased internalizing symptoms and out-of-home placements (56%)
Rowland et al. (2005) $N = 31$ RCT	Youths with serious emotional and behavioral disturbances at risk for out-of-home placement	Hawaii's intensive Continuum of Care	6 mo postrecruitment	Decreased symptoms and arrests (34%; nonsignificant); increased days in regular school (42%; marginally significant) and social support (marginally significant); and decreased days in out-of-home placement (68%)
Timmons-Mitchell, Bender, Kishna, & Mitchell (2006) $N = 93$ RCT; independent	Juvenile offenders (felons) at imminent risk of placement	Usual community services	18-mo posttreatment follow-up	Improved youth functioning and school functioning; decreased substance use problems, rearrests (37%), and out-of-home placements (68%)
Henggeler et al. (2006) $N = 161$ RCT	Substance-abusing and substance-dependent juvenile offenders in drug court	Four treatment conditions, including family court with usual services and drug court with usual services	12 mo postrecruitment	MST enhanced substance use outcomes for alcohol and marijuana; drug court was more effective than family court at decreasing self-reported substance use and criminal activity
Stambaugh et al. (2007) $N = 267$ Quasi-experimental; independent	Youths with serious emotional disturbance and antisocial behavior at risk for out-of-home placement	Wraparound	18-mo follow-up	Improved functioning; decreased symptoms and out-of-home placements (54%)

Sundell et al. (2008) $N = 156$ RCT; independent	Swedish youths who met diagnostic criteria for conduct disorder	Usual child welfare services in Sweden	7 mo postrecruitment	No outcomes favoring either treatment condition; low treatment fidelity associated with recidivism
Löfholm, Olsson, Sundell, & Hansson (2009)	Same sample as Sundell et al. (2008)		2 yr postreferral	No outcomes favoring either treatment condition
Borduin, Schaeffer, & Heiblum (2009) $N = 48$ RCT	Juvenile sexual offenders	Usual community services	9 yr	Decreased behavior problems and symptoms; improved family relations, peer relations, and academic performance; decreased caregiver distress, sex crime recidivism (83%), recidivism for other crimes (50%), and days incarcerated (80%)
Painter (2009) $N = 174$ Quasi-experimental; independent	Youths with externalizing disorders	Case management and family skills training	Pre–post	Improved youth functioning across multiple domains; decreased juvenile justice involvement
Letourneau et al. (2009) $N = 127$ RCT	Juvenile sexual offenders	Usual sex offender–specific treatment	12 mo postrecruitment	Decreased sexual behavior problems, delinquency, substance use, externalizing symptoms, and out-of-home placements (59%)
Letourneau et al. (2013)	Same sample as Letourneau et al. (2009)		2 yr postrecruitment	12-mo outcomes sustained for problem sexual behavior, self-reported delinquency, and out-of-home placements (50% decrease), but no difference for criminal arrests
Glisson et al. (2010) $N = 615$ RCT; independent	Juvenile offenders	Usual community services	18 mo postrecruitment	Reduced out-of-home placements (53%); reduced symptoms in sites with organizational intervention, but dissipated at 18-month follow-up
Butler, Baruch, Hickley, & Fonagy (2011) $N = 108$ RCT; independent	British juvenile offenders	Multicomponent evidence-based interventions	18 mo postrecruitment	Reduced offenses (41%) and placements (41% during past 6 months); reduced self-reported and parent-reported delinquency and psychopathic symptoms, improved parenting
Asscher, Deković, van der Laan, & Prins (2013) $N = 256$ RCT; independent	Dutch youths with severe and violent antisocial behavior	Usual community services	6 mo postrecruitment	Decreased youth antisocial behavior; increased parental sense of competence, positive discipline, and relationship quality; increased youth association with prosocial peers

(*continues*)

TABLE 26.1 (*Continued*)

Published MST Outcome Studies Addressing Serious Antisocial Behavior in Adolescents

Study, sample size, and design	Population	Comparison	Follow-up	MST outcomes
Weiss et al. (2013) N = 164 RCT; independent	Adolescents with serious conduct problems in self-contained classrooms	Usual services	18 mo postrecruitment for self-report measures and 2.5 yr for arrests	Reduced externalizing problems but not arrests; decreased school absences, improved parenting and parental mental health symptoms

Note. Citations with the same superscript represent multiple publications based, at least in part, on the same dataset. MST = multisystemic therapy; RCT = randomized clinical trial. From "Empirically Supported Family-Based Treatments for Conduct Disorder and Delinquency," by S. W. Henggeler and A. J. Sheidow, 2012, *Journal of Marital and Family Therapy, 38*, pp. 36–40. Copyright 2012 by Wiley. Adapted with permission.

Pickrel, 2000), juvenile sex offenders (Henggeler, Letourneau, et al., 2009), juvenile offenders in England (Tighe, Pistrang, Casdagli, Baruch, & Butler, 2012), and Dutch youths with severe and violent antisocial behavior (Deković, Asscher, Manders, Prins, & van der Laan, 2012).

Functional Family Therapy

In one of the first RCTs published in the emerging field of family therapy more than 40 years ago, Alexander and Parsons (1973) demonstrated favorable treatment effects for juvenile offenders. Currently, FFT is one of the most widely transported family therapies, and FFT clinical procedures are specified most extensively in Alexander, Waldron, Robbins, and Neeb (2013).

Clinical approach. Conceptually, FFT is based largely on an integration of family systems theory and behavioral approaches. Adolescent antisocial behavior is viewed as a symptom of dysfunctional family relationships. As such, rather than focusing on problem behaviors per se, interventions aim to change patterns of family behavior in ways that lead to symptom change.

The implementation of FFT includes five phases that aim to attenuate behavioral problems presented by the adolescent and the family difficulties associated with these problems.

1. During the engagement phase, the therapist aligns with the family through active listening, respect, and empathetic behaviors. A strengths-based approach is taken with the entire family, and the therapist is highly available for communication and interactions (e.g., telephone outreach, home visits, arranging for transportation).
2. The motivation phase engenders hope and positive expectations among family members. Confrontation is avoided, negative interaction patterns are interrupted, and the therapist takes a nonblaming stance. Reframing is often used to shift the family's focus from the problem behavior to a more positive relationship emphasis.
3. A primary therapeutic task is to understand the association between the presenting problems and the family's relations with themselves and others outside the family (i.e., relational assessment). Through discussions with family members (e.g., to understand their values) and observations of their interactions (e.g., to understand the affective and instrumental nature of family relationships), the therapist analyzes information and develops plans for behavior change.
4. On the basis of the relational assessment, the primary aim of the behavior change phase is to affect the problem behavior by establishing new patterns of family interaction that replace the old patterns. Therapists use behavioral techniques, such as communication training, modeling, teaching, assigning homework, and training in conflict resolution, to change family interactions in ways that decrease the identified problem behaviors.

5. Finally, the generalization phase aims to extend the favorable family changes to their social network (e.g., school, juvenile justice authorities) and to create plans for relapse prevention.

As with MST, FFT programs are self-contained. These programs typically include a team of three to eight master's-level therapists who carry caseloads of 12 to 15 families, and treatment duration averages about 12 sessions over 3 to 4 months. Services are delivered in home, clinic, and other community settings. The implementation of FFT includes strong training and quality assurance protocols, and FFT has been a focus in research on the transport of evidence-based treatments to community settings (Zazzali et al., 2008).

Outcomes research. As presented in Table 26.2, seven controlled evaluations of FFT have been published. Five of these were RCTs, and four were conducted by researchers independent of the treatment developers. Four studies included juvenile offenders ranging in seriousness from status offenders to serious offenders released from incarceration, and three samples focused on youths with substance use problems. Likewise, comparison groups varied considerably, including, for example, youths receiving psychodynamic family treatment, youths in Homebuilders Family Preservation, and youths confined in residential facilities. Studies typically included at least a 12-month follow-up, and one follow-up was extended to 5 years postrecruitment.

Most of the studies demonstrated significant reductions in either criminal offending or substance use, with independent quasi-experimental studies showing the strongest effects. Importantly, and consistent with MST findings, in a large multisite study that did not demonstrate treatment effects (Sexton & Turner, 2010), FFT treatment adherence was associated with recidivism outcomes.

Mediation research. Although formal mediational analyses have not been conducted with FFT, results from several studies are suggestive. For example, Alexander, Barton, Schiaro, and Parsons (1976) observed that improved family communication was associated with decreased youth recidivism. More recently, Robbins, Turner, Alexander, and Perez (2003) showed that therapeutic alliances in which the therapist was not equally aligned with the youth and parents were associated with higher dropout rates.

Multidimensional Treatment Foster Care

MTFC is designed for the most challenging youths in the juvenile justice system—those who have been committed to out-of-home placements. In addition to the evaluations with serious juvenile offenders noted subsequently, MTFC has also proven effective in treating youths in the child welfare system. The model has been most extensively specified by Chamberlain (2003).

Clinical approach. Social learning theory provides the primary conceptual framework for MTFC. Though more explicitly behavioral and less systemic than most family-based approaches, MTFC attends closely to the broader social ecology in which juvenile offenders are embedded (e.g., minimizing youth association with deviant peers is a central goal of treatment). The overriding purpose of MTFC interventions is to surround youths with competent adults who are positive and encouraging, model responsible behavior, and provide a highly structured context. Youths are placed in a foster home for 6 to 9 months, one youth per placement, with specially trained foster parents who have continuous access to an MTFC program supervisor. The foster parents implement a highly structured behavioral plan that specifies contingencies for desired and inappropriate behaviors occurring at home, school, or elsewhere. Youth behavior is closely tracked, and rewards and sanctions are applied as specified in the plan. Concomitantly, a therapist works with the youth to address individual-level deficits (e.g., social skills, emotion management), and a skills trainer provides real-world opportunities to practice newly developed skills. Finally, a family therapist works with the youth's biological family to facilitate a smooth and effective transition back home. As with MST and FFT, MTFC includes extensive training of all members of the treatment team and provides continuous support for the foster parents and treatment professionals to promote program fidelity.

TABLE 26.2

Published FFT Outcome Studies Addressing Antisocial Behavior in Adolescents

Study, sample size, and design	Population	Comparison	Follow-up	FFT outcomes
Alexander & Parsons (1973) *N* = 86 RCT	Juvenile status offenders	Three control conditions: client-centered family groups, psychodynamic family treatment, and no treatment	6–18 mo posttreatment	Improved family communication; decreased status offending (53%) and criminal offending (29%; nonsignificant)
Barton, Alexander, Waldron, Turner, & Warburton (1985) *N* = 74 Quasi-experimental	Serious juvenile offenders released from incarceration	Primarily youths in group homes and other placements	15 mo posttreatment	Decreased criminal offending (57%)
Gordon, Arbuthnot, Gustafson, & McGreen (1988) *N* = 54 Quasi-experimental; independent	Status offenders and juvenile offenders	Lower risk delinquents receiving probation	2.5 yr postrecruitment	Decreased recidivism (84%)
Gordon, Graves, & Arbuthnot (1995)	Same sample as Gordon et al. (1988)		5 yr postrecruitment	Decreased adult criminal offenses (78%)
Friedman (1989) *N* = 121 RCT; independent	Substance-abusing adolescents	Parent group treatment	15 mo postrecruitment	No treatment effects
Slesnick & Prestopnik (2009) *N* = 119 RCT; independent	Runaway adolescents with alcohol problems	Homebuilders Family Preservation and services as usual	15 mo postrecruitment	Decreased alcohol use in comparison with services as usual
Barrett, Slesnick, Brody, Turner, & Peterson (2001) *N* = 114 RCT	Substance-abusing adolescents	Four treatment conditions: FFT, CBT, FFT and CBT combined, and group therapy	3 mo posttreatment	Favorable outcomes for marijuana use at posttreatment dissipated at 3-month follow-up
Sexton & Turner (2010) *N* = 917 RCT; independent	Juvenile offenders	Probation services as usual	12 mo posttreatment	No treatment effects; treatment adherence linked with recidivism outcomes

Note. CBT = cognitive–behavioral therapy; FFT = functional family therapy; RCT = randomized clinical trial. From "Empirically Supported Family-Based Treatments for Conduct Disorder and Delinquency," by S. W. Henggeler and A. J. Sheidow, 2012, *Journal of Marital and Family Therapy, 38*, p. 45. Copyright 2012 by Wiley. Adapted with permission.

Outcomes research. As noted previously, MTFC targets serious juvenile offenders who have been committed to residential care. As such, control conditions for the three trials conducted in the United States by Chamberlain and her colleagues have been group care placements (see Table 26.3 for a summary of outcome studies). The control condition in the Swedish independent evaluations included youths in residential foster care or home-based treatment. Follow-ups have been for at least 2 years postbaseline, and one study included a 7- to 9-year follow-up. Also, MTFC is one of the few evidence-based treatments that, in one study, focused specifically on female chronic offenders committed to out-of-home care.

MTFC has achieved the types of outcomes for which all interventions for juvenile offenders should strive. Substantive reductions in criminal offending, including violent offending, and rates of confinement have been achieved. MTFC has also achieved

TABLE 26.3

Published MTFC Outcome Studies Addressing Serious Antisocial Behavior in Adolescents

Study, sample size, and design	Population	Comparison	Follow-up	MTFC outcomes
Chamberlain (1990) $N = 32$ Quasi-experimental	Delinquents committed to confinement	Group care placements	2 yr posttreatment	Decreased incarceration (47%)
Chamberlain & Reid (1998) $N = 79$ RCT	Male chronic and serious juvenile offenders committed to confinement	Group care placements	1 yr postbaseline; 1 yr postdischarge	60% fewer days incarcerated; decreased self-reported delinquency (56%); decreased criminal charges (52%)
Eddy, Whaley, & Chamberlain (2004)	Same sample as Chamberlain & Reid (1998)		2 yr postdischarge	Decreased violent recidivism (45%), repeat violent recidivism (79%), and delinquency
Smith, Chamberlain, & Eddy (2010)	Same sample as Chamberlain & Reid (1998)		18 mo postbaseline	Decreased substance use
Leve, Chamberlain, & Reid (2005) $N = 81$ RCT	Female chronic juvenile offenders committed to out-of-home care	Group care placements	1 yr postbaseline	62% fewer days incarcerated; decreased criminal charges (42%; nonsignificant)
Chamberlain, Leve, & DeGarmo (2007)	Same sample as Leve et al. (2005)		2 yr postbaseline	Decreased incarceration (67%) and criminal charges (41%; marginally significant)
Leve & Chamberlain (2007)	Same sample as Leve et al. (2005)		1 yr postbaseline	Increased school attendance and homework completion
Leve & Chamberlain (2005)	Same sample as Leve et al. (2005) plus sample from Chamberlain & Reid (1998)		1 yr postbaseline	Decreased association with delinquent peers
Kerr, Leve, & Chamberlain (2009)	Same sample as Leve et al. (2005) plus 85 additional female offenders randomized to same intervention conditions		2 yr postbaseline	Decreased pregnancies (43%)
Harold et al. (2013)	Same sample as Kerr et al. (2009)		2 yr postbaseline	Decreased depressive symptoms
Rhoades, Leve, Harold, Kim, & Chamberlain (2014)	Same sample as Kerr et al. (2009)		7–9 yr postbaseline	Decreased drug use
Westermark, Hansson, & Olsson (2011) $N = 35$ RCT; independent	Youths with antisocial behavior	Residential, foster care, or home-based treatment	2 yr postbaseline	Decreased externalizing symptoms, depression, and psychiatric distress
Westermark, Hansson, & Vinnerljung (2008) $N = 306$ Quasi-experimental; independent	Same MTFC sample, large community sample		1 yr	Decreased placement disruptions (62%)

Note. Citations with the same superscript letter represent multiple publications based, at least in part, on the same dataset. MTFC = multidimensional treatment foster care; RCT = randomized clinical trial. From "Empirically Supported Family-Based Treatments for Conduct Disorder and Delinquency," by S. W. Henggeler and A. J. Sheidow, 2012, *Journal of Marital and Family Therapy*, *38*, pp. 49–50. Copyright 2012 by Wiley. Adapted with permission.

favorable reductions in externalizing symptoms, depression and psychiatric distress, substance use, and pregnancies. As noted next, such outcomes have been mediated by key risk factors for serious antisocial behavior in adolescents.

Mediational studies. Mediators of MTFC effectiveness have been evaluated in three articles pertaining to two outcome studies, and these articles have supported the model's clinical emphases. Eddy and Chamberlain (2000) found that favorable MTFC outcomes were mediated by improved foster parent supervision, discipline, and relations with the youth as well as by decreased association with deviant peers. Leve and Chamberlain (2005, 2007) showed that MTFC outcomes were mediated by decreased association with deviant peers and increased completion of schoolwork, respectively. Such findings are consistent with the known determinants of serious antisocial behavior by adolescents as well as the mediational findings of MST.

Summary and Conclusions

The effectiveness of MST, FFT, and MTFC with juvenile offenders and adolescents presenting with serious externalizing problems has been evaluated in more than 30 controlled studies. The vast majority of these studies were RTCs, and many were conducted in community settings independent of the treatment developers. Although significant treatment effects were not observed in all studies, the vast majority demonstrated meaningful decreases in recidivism and confinement, which were sometimes sustained for many years posttreatment. Moreover, the outcome studies often showed significant improvements in youth and family functioning, including decreased internalizing and externalizing symptoms, improved parenting, less association with delinquent peers, and improved school performance and attendance.

BASES OF SUCCESS

In a context in which juvenile justice interventions are often iatrogenic and few interventions have proven effective in treating serious antisocial behavior (Blueprints, 2013), why has this small subset of family-based interventions demonstrated favorable outcomes across multiple challenging adolescent populations (e.g., violent offenders, sex offenders, substance-abusing offenders, youth with serious externalizing problems) and nations? Although this question cannot be answered definitively, general agreement exists among most reviewers of this issue (e.g., Boxer & Goldstein, 2012; Caldwell & Van Rybroek, 2013; Henggeler & Schoenwald, 2011) as well as among the leaders in the larger field of offender rehabilitation (e.g., Andrews & Bonta, 1998; Gendreau & Goggin, 1996). The best validated treatments of juvenile offenders share several key commonalities.

Family Is the Primary Change Agent

Although extensive evidence has supported the role of the family in the etiology and maintenance of youth antisocial behavior (e.g., Petrosino, Derzon, & Lavenberg, 2009), evidence-based treatments also view the parents or caregivers as central to attenuating such problems. These treatments identify and build on family strengths rather than being deficit focused. Each intervention devotes considerable resources to engaging the entire family in treatment, determining barriers to more effective parenting, and implementing specific interventions that build competencies for families to better manage their problems. Critically, the aforementioned mediational studies have validated the important roles that improved family functioning (especially supervision, monitoring, and discipline strategies) plays in decreasing antisocial behavior in adolescents.

A Social-Ecological Theoretical and Clinical Perspective Is Taken

In addition to the family, other systems in which the family and youths are embedded play important roles in the development and maintenance of antisocial behavior in adolescents (Liberman, 2008). Each of the evidence-based treatments carefully considers the impact of peer (e.g., association with deviant peers) and school (e.g., low attendance, poor performance) risk factors. Therapists implement specific interventions to help caregivers minimize youths' association with problem peers, build more prosocial peer relations, and enhance school or vocational performance. Such interventions contrast dramatically with many approaches in the mental health, substance abuse, and juvenile justice systems that congregate problem adolescents together, often for prolonged periods of time.

Interventions Are Delivered in Community Settings

The evidence-based approaches deliver their interventions where youth problems occur—in homes, schools, and other community settings. These intervention models are committed to overcoming barriers to service access, and very high rates of treatment completion demonstrate their success at such. Although youth behavior can certainly be modified (e.g., less aggressive behavior, completion of chores, desired participation in therapeutic activities) in residential facilities that are well managed and staffed with competent professionals, such behavior change is unlikely to generalize to the real world when youths return home. Behavioral contingencies in home neighborhoods are vastly different from those in confinement. Evidence-based treatments overcome this generalization problem by making changes directly in the settings in which problems occur.

Interventions Are Behavioral, Individualized, and Comprehensive

Although the conceptual frameworks of MST, FFT, and MTFC are largely social-ecological, each model uses behavioral and cognitive–behavioral intervention techniques—but within a systemic framework (i.e., always considering the broader social network in treatment implementation). Interventions are generally structured, pragmatic, and present oriented. Importantly, treatment is not provided in a cookbook fashion. Across the evidence-based models, interventions are individualized to the specific strengths and needs of the youth and family and are comprehensive in their consideration of familial and extrafamilial factors that are contributing to problems or that might facilitate solutions.

Quality Assurance Is Used to Promote Treatment Fidelity and Youth Outcomes

The adoption and transport of MST, FFT, and MTFC programs to community settings involves extensive commitment to site development (e.g., assurance of appropriate referrals, hiring of appropriate staff, organizational realignment to support evidence-based treatments), training and support of therapists and supervisors (e.g., initial training, ongoing clinical and administrative support), community collaboration (e.g., with juvenile justice and child welfare authorities), and outcome monitoring. The overriding purpose of this work is to optimize treatment fidelity and, hence, youth and family outcomes.

CONCLUSION

In this chapter, I provided summaries of generally poor findings for juvenile justice interventions and discussed the bases of success of a select set of effective family- and community-based treatments. As a final and concluding point, however, Löfholm, Eichas, and Sundell (2014) provided important lessons regarding the need for fidelity monitoring in both RCTs and the transport of effective treatments to community settings. As noted in Table 26.1, favorable MST treatment effects were not observed in a large multisite RCT of MST with conduct-disordered youths (Sundell et al., 2008) that was conducted during the initial transport of MST to Sweden. Sundell et al. (2008) reported that treatment fidelity was low in that trial and, in light of the established relationship between treatment fidelity and youth outcomes, low fidelity was hypothesized as one possible explanation for the lack of treatment effects. In a subsequent study that included 68 therapists and almost a thousand families, Löfholm et al. examined MST implementation during the 6 years after the initiation of the RCT. Steady increases in treatment fidelity and concomitant youth outcomes were observed during those years. These findings have at least two critical implications for the conduct and interpretation of RCTs, as well as for the transport of effective community-based approaches.

First, as noted by the authors, an outcome evaluation initiated during early stages of implementation may fail to find treatment effects as a result of low treatment fidelity. Treatment fidelity should be established before an RCT begins. Second, program experience and continuous quality assurance can improve both fidelity and outcomes of evidence-based treatments over years of implementation. The implications of these findings underscore the importance of procedures for promoting therapist fidelity (e.g., supervision, ongoing training) and the continuous monitoring of program implementation and youth outcomes—a continuous improvement system.

References

Alexander, J. F., Barton, C., Schiaro, R. S., & Parsons, B. V. (1976). Systems-behavioral intervention with families of delinquents: Therapist characteristics, family behavior, and outcome. *Journal of Consulting and Clinical Psychology*, *44*, 656–664. http://dx.doi.org/10.1037/0022-006X.44.4.656

Alexander, J. F., & Parsons, B. V. (1973). Short-term behavioral intervention with delinquent families: Impact on family process and recidivism. *Journal of Abnormal Psychology*, *81*, 219–225. http://dx.doi.org/10.1037/h0034537

Alexander, J. F., Waldron, H. B., Robbins, M. S., & Neeb, A. A. (2013). *Functional family therapy for adolescent behavior problems*. http://dx.doi.org/10.1037/14139-000

Andrews, D., & Bonta, J. (1998). *The psychology of criminal conduct* (2nd ed.). Cincinnati, OH: Anderson.

Annie E. Casey Foundation. (2013). *Reducing youth incarceration in the United States*. Baltimore, MD: Author.

Asscher, J. J., Deković, M., Manders, W. A., van der Laan, P. H., & Prins, P. J. M. (2013). A randomized controlled trial of the effectiveness of multisystemic therapy in the Netherlands: Post-treatment changes and moderator effects. *Journal of Experimental Criminology*, *9*, 169–187. http://dx.doi.org/10.1007/s11292-012-9165-9

Barrett, H., Slesnick, N., Brody, J. L., Turner, C. W., & Peterson, T. R. (2001). Treatment outcomes for adolescent substance abuse at 4- and 7-month assessments. *Journal of Consulting and Clinical Psychology*, *69*, 802–813. http://dx.doi.org/10.1037/0022-006X.69.5.802

Barton, C., Alexander, J. F., Waldron, H., Turner, C. W., & Warburton, J. (1985). Generalizing treatment effects of functional family therapy: Three replications. *American Journal of Family Therapy*, *13*, 16–26. http://dx.doi.org/10.1080/01926188508251260

Belenko, S., & Logan, T. K. (2003). Delivering more effective treatment to adolescents: Improving the juvenile drug court model. *Journal of Substance Abuse Treatment*, *25*, 189–211. http://dx.doi.org/10.1016/S0740-5472(03)00123-5

Bergseth, K. J., & Bouffard, J. A. (2007). The long-term impact of restorative justice programming for juvenile offenders. *Journal of Criminal Justice*, *35*, 433–451. http://dx.doi.org/10.1016/j.jcrimjus.2007.05.006

Bickman, L., Lambert, E. W., Andrade, A. R., & Penaloza, R. V. (2000). The Fort Bragg continuum of care for children and adolescents: Mental health outcomes over 5 years. *Journal of Consulting and Clinical Psychology*, *68*, 710–716. http://dx.doi.org/10.1037/0022-006X.68.4.710

Blueprints. (2013). *Blueprints database standards*. Boulder, CO: Author.

Bonta, J., Jesseman, R., Rugge, T., & Cormier, R. (2006). Restorative justice and recidivism: Promises made, promises kept? In D. Sullivan & L. Tifft (Eds.), *Handbook of restorative justice: A global perspective* (pp. 108–120). New York, NY: Routledge.

Borduin, C. M., Henggeler, S. W., Blaske, D. M., & Stein, R. (1990). Multisystemic treatment of adolescent sexual offenders. *International Journal of Offender Therapy and Comparative Criminology*, *34*, 105–113. http://dx.doi.org/10.1177/0306624X9003400204

Borduin, C. M., Mann, B. J., Cone, L. T., Henggeler, S. W., Fucci, B. R., Blaske, D. M., & Williams, R. A. (1995). Multisystemic treatment of serious juvenile offenders: Long-term prevention of criminality and violence. *Journal of Consulting and Clinical Psychology*, *63*, 569–578. http://dx.doi.org/10.1037/0022-006X.63.4.569

Borduin, C. M., Schaeffer, C. M., & Heiblum, N. (2009). A randomized clinical trial of multisystemic therapy with juvenile sexual offenders: Effects on youth social ecology and criminal activity. *Journal of Consulting and Clinical Psychology*, *77*, 26–37. http://dx.doi.org/10.1037/a0013035

Boxer, P., & Goldstein, S. E. (2012). Treating juvenile offenders: Best practices and emerging critical issues. In E. L. Grigorenko (Ed.), *Handbook of juvenile forensic psychology and psychiatry* (pp. 323–340). http://dx.doi.org/10.1007/978-1-4614-0905-2_21

Bronfenbrenner, U. (1979). *The ecology of human development: Experiments by design and nature*. Cambridge, MA: Harvard University Press.

Bryer, S., & Levin, M. (2013). *The comeback states: Reducing youth incarceration in the United States*. Washington, DC: National Juvenile Justice Network and the Center for Effective Justice, Texas Public Policy Foundation.

Butler, S., Baruch, G., Hickley, N., & Fonagy, P. (2011). A randomized controlled trial of multisystemic therapy and a statutory therapeutic intervention for young offenders. *Journal of the American Academy of Child and Adolescent Psychiatry*, *12*, 1220–1235. http://dx.doi.org/10.1016/j.jaac.2011.09.017

Caldwell, M. F., & Van Rybroek, G. (2013). Effective treatment programs for violent adolescents: Programmatic challenges and promising features. *Aggression and Violent Behavior*, *18*, 571–578. http://dx.doi.org/10.1016/j.avb.2013.06.004

Chamberlain, P. (1990). Comparative evaluation of specialized foster care for seriously delinquent youths: A first step. *Community Alternatives: International Journal of Family Care*, *2*, 21–36.

Chamberlain, P. (2003). *Treating chronic juvenile offenders: Advances made through the Oregon multidimensional treatment foster care model*. http://dx.doi.org/10.1037/10596-000

Chamberlain, P., Leve, L. D., & DeGarmo, D. S. (2007). Multidimensional treatment foster care for girls in the juvenile justice system: 2-year follow-up of a randomized clinical trial. *Journal of Consulting and Clinical Psychology*, *75*, 187–193. http://dx.doi.org/10.1037/0022-006X.75.1.187

Chamberlain, P., & Reid, J. B. (1998). Comparison of two community alternatives to incarceration for chronic juvenile offenders. *Journal of Consulting and Clinical Psychology*, *66*, 624–633. http://dx.doi.org/10.1037/0022-006X.66.4.624

Deković, M., Asscher, J. J., Manders, W. A., Prins, P. J. M., & van der Laan, P. (2012). Within-intervention change: Mediators of intervention effects during multisystemic therapy. *Journal of Consulting and Clinical Psychology*, *80*, 574–587. http://dx.doi.org/10.1037/a0028482

Drake, E. (2012). *Chemical dependency treatment for offenders: A review of the evidence and benefit-cost findings* (Document No. 12-12-1201). Olympia: Washington State Institute for Public Policy.

Drake, E. K., Aos, S., & Miller, M. G. (2009). Evidence-based public policy options to reduce crime and criminal justice costs: Implications in Washington State. *Victims and Offenders*, *4*, 170–196. http://dx.doi.org/10.1080/15564880802612615

Eddy, J. M., & Chamberlain, P. (2000). Family management and deviant peer association as mediators of the impact of treatment condition on youth antisocial behavior. *Journal of Consulting and Clinical Psychology*, *68*, 857–863. http://dx.doi.org/10.1037/0022-006X.68.5.857

Eddy, J. M., Whaley, R., & Chamberlain, P. (2004). The prevention of violent behavior by chronic and serious male juvenile offenders: A 2-year follow-up of a randomized clinical trial. *Journal of Emotional and Behavioral Disorders*, *12*, 2–8.

Elliott, D. S. (Series Ed.). (1998). *Blueprints for violence prevention*. Boulder, CO: Blueprints.

Elliott, D. S., Huizinga, D., & Ageton, S. S. (1985). *Explaining delinquency and drug use*. Beverly Hills, CA: Sage.

Friedman, A. S. (1989). Family therapy vs. parent groups: Effects on adolescent drug abusers. *American Journal of Family Therapy*, *17*, 335–347. http://dx.doi.org/10.1080/01926188908250780

Gatti, U., Tremblay, R. E., & Vitaro, F. (2009). Iatrogenic effect of juvenile justice. *Journal of Child Psychology and Psychiatry*, *50*, 991–998. http://dx.doi.org/10.1111/j.1469-7610.2008.02057.x

Gendreau, P., & Goggin, C. (1996). Principles of effective correctional programming. *Forum on Corrections Research*, *8*, 38–41.

Glisson, C., Schoenwald, S. K., Hemmelgarn, A., Green, P., Dukes, D., Armstrong, K. S., & Chapman, J. E. (2010). Randomized trial of MST and ARC in a two-level evidence-based treatment implementation strategy. *Journal of Consulting and Clinical Psychology*, *78*, 537–550. http://dx.doi.org/10.1037/a0019160

Gordon, D. A., Arbuthnot, J., Gustafson, K. E., & McGreen, P. (1988). Home-based behavioral-systems family therapy with disadvantaged juvenile delinquents. *American Journal of Family Therapy*, *16*, 243–255. http://dx.doi.org/10.1080/01926188808250729

Gordon, D. A., Graves, K., & Arbuthnot, J. (1995). The effect of functional family therapy for delinquents on adult criminal behavior. *Criminal Justice and Behavior*, *22*, 60–73. http://dx.doi.org/10.1177/0093854895022001005

Halliday-Boykins, C. A., Schaeffer, C. M., Henggeler, S. W., Chapman, J. E., Cunningham, P. B., Randall, J., & Shapiro, S. B. (2010). Predicting nonresponse to juvenile drug court interventions. *Journal of Substance Abuse Treatment*, *39*, 318–328. http://dx.doi.org/10.1016/j.jsat.2010.07.011

Harold, G. T., Kerr, D. C. R., Van Ryzin, M., DeGarmo, D. S., Rhoades, K. A., & Leve, L. D. (2013). Depressive symptom trajectories among girls in the juvenile justice system: 24-month outcomes of an RCT of multidimensional treatment foster care. *Prevention Science*, *14*, 437–446. http://dx.doi.org/10.1007/s11121-012-0317-y

Henggeler, S. W. (2011). Efficacy studies to large-scale transport: The development and validation of multisystemic therapy programs. *Annual Review of Clinical Psychology*, *7*, 351–381. http://dx.doi.org/10.1146/annurev-clinpsy-032210-104615

Henggeler, S. W. (2015). Preventing youth violence through therapeutic interventions for high-risk youth. In P. D. Donnelly & C. L. Ward (Eds.), *Oxford textbook of violence prevention: Epidemiology, evidence, and policy* (pp. 161–167). http://dx.doi.org/10.1093/med/9780199678723.003.0022

Henggeler, S. W., Clingempeel, W. G., Brondino, M. J., & Pickrel, S. G. (2002). Four-year follow-up of multisystemic therapy with substance-abusing and substance-dependent juvenile offenders. *Journal of the American Academy of Child and Adolescent Psychiatry*, *41*, 868–874. http://dx.doi.org/10.1097/00004583-200207000-00021

Henggeler, S. W., Halliday-Boykins, C. A., Cunningham, P. B., Randall, J., Shapiro, S. B., & Chapman, J. E. (2006). Juvenile drug court: Enhancing outcomes by integrating evidence-based treatments. *Journal of Consulting and Clinical Psychology*, *74*, 42–54. http://dx.doi.org/10.1037/0022-006X.74.1.42

Henggeler, S. W., Letourneau, E. J., Chapman, J. E., Borduin, C. M., Schewe, P. A., & McCart, M. R. (2009). Mediators of change for multisystemic therapy with juvenile sexual offenders. *Journal of Consulting and Clinical Psychology*, *77*, 451–462. http://dx.doi.org/10.1037/a0013971

Henggeler, S. W., McCart, M. R., Cunningham, P. B., & Chapman, J. E. (2012). Enhancing the effectiveness of juvenile drug courts by integrating evidence-based practices. *Journal of Consulting and Clinical Psychology*, *80*, 264–275. http://dx.doi.org/10.1037/a0027147

Henggeler, S. W., Melton, G. B., Brondino, M. J., Scherer, D. G., & Hanley, J. H. (1997). Multisystemic therapy with violent and chronic juvenile offenders and their families: The role of treatment fidelity in successful dissemination. *Journal of Consulting and Clinical Psychology*, *65*, 821–833. http://dx.doi.org/10.1037/0022-006X.65.5.821

Henggeler, S. W., Melton, G. B., & Smith, L. A. (1992). Family preservation using multisystemic therapy: An effective alternative to incarcerating serious juvenile offenders. *Journal of Consulting and Clinical Psychology*, *60*, 953–961. http://dx.doi.org/10.1037/0022-006X.60.6.953

Henggeler, S. W., Melton, G. B., Smith, L. A., Schoenwald, S. K., & Hanley, J. H. (1993). Family preservation using multisystemic treatment: Long-term follow-up to a clinical trial with serious juvenile offenders. *Journal of Child and Family Studies*, *2*, 283–293. http://dx.doi.org/10.1007/BF01321226

Henggeler, S. W., Pickrel, S. G., & Brondino, M. J. (1999). Multisystemic treatment of substance-abusing and dependent delinquents: Outcomes, treatment fidelity, and transportability. *Mental Health Services Research*, *1*, 171–184. http://dx.doi.org/10.1023/A:1022373813261

Henggeler, S. W., Rodick, J. D., Borduin, C. M., Hanson, C. L., Watson, S. M., & Urey, J. R. (1986). Multisystemic treatment of juvenile offenders: Effects on adolescent behavior and family interactions. *Developmental Psychology*, *22*, 132–141. http://dx.doi.org/10.1037/0012-1649.22.1.132

Henggeler, S. W., Rowland, M. D., Halliday-Boykins, C., Sheidow, A. J., Ward, D. M., Randall, J., . . . Edwards, J. (2003). One-year follow-up of multisystemic therapy as an alternative to the hospitalization of youths in psychiatric crisis. *Journal of the American Academy of Child and Adolescent Psychiatry*, *42*, 543–551. http://dx.doi.org/10.1097/01.CHI.0000046834.09750.5F

Henggeler, S. W., Rowland, M. D., Randall, J., Ward, D. M., Pickrel, S. G., Cunningham, P. B., . . . Santos, A. B. (1999). Home-based multisystemic therapy as an alternative to the hospitalization of youths in psychiatric crisis: Clinical outcomes. *Journal of the American Academy of Child and Adolescent Psychiatry*, *38*, 1331–1339. http://dx.doi.org/10.1097/00004583-199911000-00006

Henggeler, S. W., & Schoenwald, S. K. (2011). Evidence-based interventions for juvenile offenders and juvenile justice policies that support them. *Society for Research in Child Development: Social Policy Report*, *25*, 1–20.

Henggeler, S. W., Schoenwald, S. K., Borduin, C. M., Rowland, M. D., & Cunningham, P. B. (2009). *Multisystemic therapy for antisocial behavior in children and adolescents* (2nd ed.). New York, NY: Guilford Press.

Hills, H., Shufelt, J. L., & Cocozza, J. J. (2009). *Evidence-based practice recommendations for juvenile drug courts*. Delmar, NY: National Center for Mental Health and Juvenile Justice.

Hockenberry, S. (2013). *Juveniles in residential placement, 2010*. Washington, DC: U.S. Department of Justice, Office of Justice Programs, Office of Juvenile Justice and Delinquency Prevention.

Huey, S. J., Jr., Henggeler, S. W., Brondino, M. J., & Pickrel, S. G. (2000). Mechanisms of change in multisystemic therapy: Reducing delinquent behavior through therapist adherence and improved family and peer functioning. *Journal of Consulting and Clinical Psychology*, *68*, 451–467. http://dx.doi.org/10.1037/0022-006X.68.3.451

Justice Policy Institute. (2009). *The costs of confinement: Why good juvenile justice policies make good fiscal sense*. Washington, DC: Author.

Kerr, D. C. R., Leve, L. D., & Chamberlain, P. (2009). Pregnancy rates among juvenile justice girls in two randomized controlled trials of multidimensional treatment foster care. *Journal of Consulting and Clinical Psychology*, *77*, 588–593. http://dx.doi.org/10.1037/a0015289

Lambie, I., & Randell, I. (2013). The impact of incarceration on juvenile offenders. *Clinical Psychology*

Review, *33*, 448–459. http://dx.doi.org/10.1016/j.cpr.2013.01.007

Letourneau, E. J., Henggeler, S. W., Borduin, C. M., Schewe, P. A., McCart, M. R., Chapman, J. E., & Saldana, L. (2009). Multisystemic therapy for juvenile sexual offenders: 1-year results from a randomized effectiveness trial. *Journal of Family Psychology*, *23*, 89–102. http://dx.doi.org/10.1037/a0014352

Letourneau, E. J., Henggeler, S. W., McCart, M. R., Borduin, C. M., Schewe, P. A., & Armstrong, K. S. (2013). Two-year follow-up of a randomized effectiveness trial evaluating MST for juveniles who sexually offend. *Journal of Family Psychology*, *27*, 978–985. http://dx.doi.org/10.1037/a0034710

Leve, L. D., & Chamberlain, P. (2005). Association with delinquent peers: Intervention effects for youth in the juvenile justice system. *Journal of Abnormal Child Psychology*, *33*, 339–347. http://dx.doi.org/10.1007/s10802-005-3571-7

Leve, L. D., & Chamberlain, P. (2007). A randomized evaluation of multidimensional treatment foster care: Effects on school attendance and homework completion in juvenile justice girls. *Research on Social Work Practice*, *17*, 657–663. http://dx.doi.org/10.1177/1049731506293971

Leve, L. D., Chamberlain, P., & Reid, J. B. (2005). Intervention outcomes for girls referred from juvenile justice: Effects on delinquency. *Journal of Consulting and Clinical Psychology*, *73*, 1181–1184. http://dx.doi.org/10.1037/0022-006X.73.6.1181

Liberman, A. M. (Ed.). (2008). *The long view of crime: A synthesis of longitudinal research*. http://dx.doi.org/10.1007/978-0-387-71165-2

Löfholm, C. A., Eichas, K., & Sundell, K. (2014). The Swedish implementation of multisystemic therapy for adolescents: Does treatment experience predict treatment adherence? *Journal of Clinical Child and Adolescent Psychology*, *43*, 643–655. http://dx.doi.org/10.1080/15374416.2014.883926

Löfholm, C. A., Olsson, T., Sundell, K., & Hansson, K. (2009). Multisystemic therapy with conduct-disordered young people: Stability of treatment outcomes two years after intake. *Evidence and Policy*, *5*, 373–397.

Martinson, R. (1974). What works? Questions and answers about prison reform. *Public Interest*, *35*, 22–54.

Mears, D. P., Cochran, J. C., Greenman, S. J., Bhati, A. S., & Greenwald, M. A. (2011). Evidence of the effectiveness of juvenile court sanctions. *Journal of Criminal Justice*, *39*, 509–520. http://dx.doi.org/10.1016/j.jcrimjus.2011.09.006

Mendel, R. A. (2011). *No place for kids: The case for reducing juvenile incarceration*. Baltimore, MD: Annie E. Casey Foundation.

Ogden, T., & Hagen, K. A. (2006). Multisystemic therapy of serious behaviour problems in youth: Sustainability of therapy effectiveness two years after intake. *Journal of Child and Adolescent Mental Health*, *11*, 142–149. http://dx.doi.org/10.1111/j.1475-3588.2006.00396.x

Ogden, T., & Halliday-Boykins, C. A. (2004). Multisystemic treatment of antisocial adolescents in Norway: Replication of clinical outcomes outside of the US. *Child and Adolescent Mental Health*, *9*, 77–83. http://dx.doi.org/10.1111/j.1475-3588.2004.00085.x

Painter, K. (2009). Multisystemic therapy as community-based treatment for youth with severe emotional disturbance. *Research on Social Work Practice*, *19*, 314–324. http://dx.doi.org/10.1177/1049731508318772

Petrosino, A., Derzon, J., & Lavenberg, J. (2009). The role of the family in crime and delinquency: Evidence from prior quantitative reviews. *Southwest Journal of Criminal Justice*, *6*, 108–132.

Petrosino, A., Turpin-Petrosino, C., & Guckenburg, S. (2010). Formal system processing of juveniles: Effects on delinquency. *Campbell Systematic Reviews*. Advance online publication.

Petrosino, A., Turpin-Petrosino, C., Hollis-Peel, M. E., & Lavenberg, J. G. (2013). "Scared Straight" and other juvenile awareness programs for preventing juvenile delinquency. *Cochrane Database of Systematic Reviews, 2013*, CD002796.

Petteruti, A., Walsh, N., & Velazquez, T. (2009). *The costs of confinement: Why good juvenile justice policies make good fiscal sense*. Washington, DC: Justice Policy Institute.

Puzzanchera, C. (2013). *Juvenile arrests 2010* (Juvenile Justice Bulletin). Washington, DC: U.S. Department of Justice, Office of Justice Programs, Office of Juvenile Justice and Delinquency Prevention.

Rhoades, K. A., Leve, L. D., Harold, G. T., Kim, H., & Chamberlain, P. (2014). Drug use trajectories after a randomized controlled trial of MTFC: Associations with partner drug use. *Journal of Research on Adolescence*, *24*, 40–54.

Robbins, M. S., Turner, C. W., Alexander, J. F., & Perez, G. A. (2003). Alliance and dropout in family therapy for adolescents with behavior problems: Individual and systemic effects. *Journal of Family Psychology*, *17*, 534–544. http://dx.doi.org/10.1037/0893-3200.17.4.534

Robst, J., Armstrong, M., & Dollard, N. (2011). Peer contagion among youth in Medicaid-funded residential mental health treatment programs. *Children and Youth Services Review*, *33*, 651–655. http://dx.doi.org/10.1016/j.childyouth.2010.11.007

Rowland, M. R., Halliday-Boykins, C. A., Henggeler, S. W., Cunningham, P. B., Lee, T. G., Kruesi, M. J. P., & Shapiro, S. B. (2005). A randomized trial of multisystemic therapy with Hawaii's Felix Class youths. *Journal of Emotional and Behavioral Disorders*, *13*, 13–23. http://dx.doi.org/10.1177/10634266050130010201

Sawyer, A. M., & Borduin, C. M. (2011). Effects of multisystemic therapy through midlife: A 21.9-year follow up to a randomized clinical trial with serious and violent juvenile offenders. *Journal of Consulting and Clinical Psychology*, *79*, 643–652. http://dx.doi.org/10.1037/a0024862

Schaeffer, C. M., & Borduin, C. M. (2005). Long-term follow-up to a randomized clinical trial of multisystemic therapy with serious and violent juvenile offenders. *Journal of Consulting and Clinical Psychology*, *73*, 445–453. http://dx.doi.org/10.1037/0022-006X.73.3.445

Schaeffer, C. M., Henggeler, S. W., Chapman, J. E., Halliday-Boykins, C. A., Cunningham, P. B., Randall, J., & Shapiro, S. B. (2010). Mechanisms of effectiveness in juvenile drug court: Altering risk processes associated with delinquency and substance abuse. *Drug Court Review*, *7*, 57–94.

Schoenwald, S. K., Chapman, J. E., Sheidow, A. J., & Carter, R. E. (2009). Long-term youth criminal outcomes in MST transport: The impact of therapist adherence and organizational climate and structure. *Journal of Clinical Child and Adolescent Psychology*, *38*, 91–105. http://dx.doi.org/10.1080/15374410802575388

Schoenwald, S. K., Ward, D. M., Henggeler, S. W., & Rowland, M. D. (2000). Multisystemic therapy vs. hospitalization for crisis stabilization of youth: Placement outcomes 4 months post-referral. *Mental Health Services Research*, *2*, 3–12. http://dx.doi.org/10.1023/A:1010187706952

Schwalbe, C. S., Gearing, R. E., MacKenzie, M. J., Brewer, K. B., & Ibrahim, R. (2012). A meta-analysis of experimental studies of diversion programs for juvenile offenders. *Clinical Psychology Review*, *32*, 26–33. http://dx.doi.org/10.1016/j.cpr.2011.10.002

Sexton, T., & Turner, C. W. (2010). The effectiveness of functional family therapy for youth with behavioral problems in a community practice setting. *Journal of Family Psychology*, *24*, 339–348. http://dx.doi.org/10.1037/a0019406

Slesnick, N., & Prestopnik, J. L. (2009). Comparison of family therapy outcome with alcohol-abusing, runaway adolescents. *Journal of Marital and Family Therapy*, *35*, 255–277. http://dx.doi.org/10.1111/j.1752-0606.2009.00121.x

Smith, D. K., Chamberlain, P., & Eddy, J. M. (2010). Preliminary support for multidimensional treatment foster care in reducing substance use in delinquent boys. *Journal of Child and Adolescent Substance Abuse*, *19*, 343–358. http://dx.doi.org/10.1080/1067828X.2010.511986

Stambaugh, L. F., Mustillo, S. A., Burns, B. J., Stephens, R. L., Baxter, B., Edwards, D., & DeKraai, M. (2007). Outcomes from wraparound and multisystemic therapy in a center for mental health services system-of-care demonstration site. *Journal of Emotional and Behavioral Disorders*, *15*, 143–155. http://dx.doi.org/10.1177/10634266070150030201

Stein, D. M., Deberard, S., & Homan, K. (2013). Predicting success and failure in juvenile drug treatment court: A meta-analytic review. *Journal of Substance Abuse Treatment*, *44*, 159–168. http://dx.doi.org/10.1016/j.jsat.2012.07.002

Stein, D. M., Deberard, S., & Homan, K. (2015). The effectiveness of juvenile drug treatment courts: A meta-analytic review of literature. *Journal of Child and Adolescent Substance Abuse*, *24*, 80–93.

Sundell, K., Hansson, K., Lofholm, C. A., Olsson, T., Gustle, L. H., & Kadesjo, C. (2008). The transportability of multisystemic therapy to Sweden: Short-term results from a randomized trial of conduct-disordered youth. *Journal of Family Psychology*, *22*, 550–560. http://dx.doi.org/10.1037/a0012790

Tighe, A., Pistrang, N., Casdagli, L., Baruch, G., & Butler, S. (2012). Multisystemic therapy for young offenders: Families' experiences of therapeutic processes and outcomes. *Journal of Family Psychology*, *26*, 187–197. http://dx.doi.org/10.1037/a0027120

Timmons-Mitchell, J., Bender, M. B., Kishna, M. A., & Mitchell, C. C. (2006). An independent effectiveness trial of multisystemic therapy with juvenile justice youth. *Journal of Clinical Child and Adolescent Psychology*, *35*, 227–236. http://dx.doi.org/10.1207/s15374424jccp3502_6

Trzcinski, E., & Allen, T. (2012). Justice toward youth: Investigating the mismatch between current policy and public opinion. *Children and Youth Services Review*, *34*, 27–34. http://dx.doi.org/10.1016/j.childyouth.2011.07.014

Waldron, H. B., & Turner, C. W. (2008). Evidence-based psychosocial treatments for adolescent substance abuse. *Journal of Clinical Child and Adolescent Psychology*, *37*, 238–261. http://dx.doi.org/10.1080/15374410701820133

Weiss, B., Han, S., Harris, V., Catron, T., Ngo, V. K., Caron, A., . . . Guth, C. (2013). An independent randomized clinical trial of multisystemic therapy with non-court-referred adolescents with serious conduct problems. *Journal of Consulting and Clinical Psychology*, *81*, 1027–1039. http://dx.doi.org/10.1037/a0033928

Westermark, P. K., Hansson, K., & Olsson, M. (2011). Multidimensional treatment foster care (MTFC): Results from an independent replication. *Journal of Family Therapy*, *33*, 20–41. http://dx.doi.org/10.1111/j.1467-6427.2010.00515.x

Westermark, P. K., Hansson, K., & Vinnerljung, B. (2008). Does multidimensional treatment foster care (MTFC) reduce placement breakdown in foster care? *International Journal of Child and Family Welfare*, *4*, 155–171.

Zazzali, J. L., Sherbourne, C., Hoagwood, K. E., Greene, D., Bigley, M. F., & Sexton, T. L. (2008). The adoption and implementation of an evidence based practice in child and family mental health services organizations: A pilot study of functional family therapy in New York State. *Administration and Policy in Mental Health and Mental Health Services Research*, *35*, 38–49. http://dx.doi.org/10.1007/s10488-007-0145-8

Zehr, H., & Mika, H. (1997). *Fundamental concepts of restorative justice*. Akron, PA: Mennonite Central Committee.

CHAPTER 27

INTERVENING IN THE COMMUNITY TO TREAT TRAUMA IN YOUNG MEN OF COLOR

John Rich, Erica J. Harris, Sandra L. Bloom, Linda Rich, and Theodore Corbin

In this chapter, we apply a trauma-informed public health approach to men of color, a population that is disproportionately affected by crime, violence, and involvement with the criminal justice system. Men of color are also disproportionately victims of violence, which results in higher rates of death by homicide than any other group of males, as well as higher rates of nonfatal injury. Nonfatal injury itself carries with it the risk of reinjury and death. Less often recognized are the psychological wounds of violence, trauma, and adversity, which may lead to intrusive symptoms of posttraumatic stress and depression and may predispose men of color to substance use and further violence. All of these factors together contribute to the overall poorer health of men of color, including higher rates of chronic disease, higher mortality, and a lower position on the social ladder.

We examine the complex interplay of race, gender, social context, and poverty in creating traumatizing circumstances for poor boys and men, particularly brown and Black. We describe a growing movement toward understanding and addressing the consequences of trauma in the health care and criminal justice systems, especially involving both working in cross-system partnership.

RELEVANT BACKGROUND AND HISTORY

Youth violence is a major public health problem in the United States. Although youth homicide rates have declined in the United States since the mid-1990s, in 2010 the total homicide rate among people ages 10 to 24 was 7.5 per 100,000 (Annest, 2013)—the lowest homicide rate for youths since 1981. Throughout this period, males—particularly those between the ages of 15 and 24—had a significantly higher homicide rate than females. Similarly, despite a decline in homicide rates, Black non-Hispanic people had a significantly higher youth homicide rate than White people. Hispanic people also had a higher homicide rate than did White people (David-Ferdon, Dahlberg, & Kegler, 2013).

Nonfatal violence harms even more youths. In 2012, more than 599,000 young people ages 10 to 24 were treated in emergency departments for injuries sustained from violence. Of these victims, 37,000 were admitted to U.S. hospitals for intentional injuries and more than 531,000 were treated and released from emergency departments (Centers for Disease Control and Prevention [CDC], 2008). In a 2007 study of violence in schools, 4.2% of high school students reported that in the previous 12 months, they were in one or more physical fights that resulted in injuries that had to be treated by a doctor or nurse (CDC, 2009). Although those who have sustained intentional injuries requiring hospital admission may receive a number of supports and services, their treatment and release involve little beyond the physical care required to treat their acute injuries. Intentional injuries are among the most costly health problems in the United States, accounting for $75 to $100 billion yearly in disability and lost productivity (Reiner, Pastena, Swan, Lindenthal, & Tischler, 1990).

http://dx.doi.org/10.1037/14643-027
APA Handbook of Psychology and Juvenile Justice, K. Heilbrun (Editor-in-Chief)

Youths of color, particularly males, also suffer disproportionately from violent assault and criminal victimization. In 2012, 377,302 males ages 10 to 24 were treated in emergency departments for nonfatal violent injuries (CDC, 2008). Of these, 23% were Black—although individuals who are Black make up only 17% of the overall population of 10- to 24-year-olds. A 2007 report from the Bureau of Justice Statistics found that Blacks were victims of 15% of nonfatal assaults and 50% of all homicides despite making up just 13% of the U.S. population in 2005 (Harrell, 2007). The report also noted that younger Black people, particularly males, were more likely to be victims of violent crime than were other groups. According to the report, 85% of Black victims of homicide were male, and 51% were between the ages of 17 and 29.

Young Black males are also disproportionately represented among prisoners in local, state, and federal jails and prisons. Overall, Black males are 6 times more likely than White males to be incarcerated and 2.5 times more likely than Hispanic males (Carson & Sabol, 2012). According to a 2013 Bureau of Justice Statistics report, nearly 60% of the state prison population of the United States is made up of racial and ethnic minorities (Carson & Golinelli, 2013). Of particular concern is the fact that one of every 10 Black males in their 30s is in prison or jail on any given day (Bonczar, 2003). For all men, the lifetime likelihood of imprisonment is one in nine. For Black men, this likelihood is one in three—as opposed to one in six for Latino men and one in 17 for White men.

At the same time, Black and Latino males are disproportionately affected by other preventable health problems and by indicators of social inequality. Young African American males have an all-cause mortality rate that is 1.5 times higher than that for young White males (Kaiser Family Foundation, 2006). The homicide rate for young African American males between the ages of 15 and 24 is 19 times higher than that for similarly aged White males (CDC, 2008). According to the CDC (2008), new HIV infections for African American men (103.6 per 100,000 population) occur at a rate 7 times that of White men and twice that of Latino men (CDC, 2012). Of new infections among African American men, 72% occurred in gay or bisexual men, with 45% of these occurring in African American gay or bisexual men between the ages of 13 and 24. HIV death rates for African American men ages 25 to 44 are more than 7 times as high as those for White men. Despite these health disparities, more than a third of African American men between the ages of 18 and 29 lack health insurance (Kaiser Family Foundation, 2006).

The homicide rate for Latino males ages 15 to 24 is 6 times higher than the rate for similarly aged White males. The AIDS rate for Latino males is almost 3 times that for White males, and they are 2.5 times as likely to die from HIV/AIDS as White males (Heron, 2010). Still, despite these health problems, in 2006, 56% of Latino males between the ages of 18 and 29 lacked health insurance, more than any racial or ethnic group in this age range (Kaiser Family Foundation, 2006). Educational disparities are also apparent for Latino males, because only 61% have a high school diploma—the lowest high school graduation percentage of any racial or ethnic group of men. Young Latino men ages 18 to 29 are also disproportionately incarcerated; the percentage of those in prison in 2005 (3.6%) was more than twice that of White men (1.5%) in the same age group (Kaiser Family Foundation, 2006).

In addition, access to employment limits the opportunities for Black and Latino men. According to a 2013 report by the Urban Institute examining the impact of the 2008 recession, 30% of young Black males and 25% of young Hispanic males were unemployed in January 2010, compared with 15.6% of young White males (Kuehn, 2013).

As these statistics demonstrate, young men of color are at a higher risk of violence and trauma. This increased risk, however, must be understood in light of contextual factors and the important confluence of masculinity, racism, and social class.

ROLE OF MASCULINITY

There is a paucity of literature examining the role of masculinity in the emotional navigation of trauma. There has been no empirical examination of masculinity and trauma, and the available analyses have probed existing psychosocial theories on gender (Eagan Chamberlin, 2012; Fox & Pease, 2012; Mejía, 2005; Ridge, Emslie, & White, 2011). Trauma and masculinity are commonly explored through the experience of military engagement and posttraumatic stress disorder experienced by veterans (Eagan Chamberlin, 2012; Fox & Pease, 2012).

Gender and masculinity are regarded as social constructs, and the process of socialization into masculinity can itself be forceful and traumatizing (Fox & Pease, 2012; Mejía, 2005). Masculinity confers toughness and a denial of vulnerability, which leads to both internal and external conflict when victimization occurs, and these can further emotional distress (Fox & Pease, 2012). The construct of masculinity also disconnects individuals from the necessary processing of emotions and blunts their natural responses to trauma (Eagan Chamberlin, 2012; Fox & Pease, 2012; Mejía, 2005; Ridge et al., 2011), which can lead to internalization and violent defense mechanisms, perpetuating the cycle of violence (Mejía, 2005; Ridge et al., 2011). Masculinity also limits help-seeking behaviors, thus further hindering the ability to address trauma within the context of socialized masculinity (Fox & Pease, 2012; Mejía, 2005; Ridge et al., 2011). Gender-specific trauma interventions sensitive to the constraints of masculinity are lacking (Fox & Pease, 2012).

ROLE OF RACE AND RACISM

When examining the health of young men of color, it is appropriate to consider the meaning of race. It has been widely agreed that race has no biological or genetic correlate, but rather is a social construction (Krieger, 2000, 2005; A. Smedley & Smedley, 2005; B. Smedley, Stith, & Nelson, 2002; Williams, Mohammed, Leavell, & Collins, 2010).
In the context of young men of color, this means that differences observed by race, or ethnicity for that matter, are serving as proxies for other important factors such as poverty, low social class, or racism. Substantial evidence has supported the conclusion that young men of color are poorer, are lower on the social ladder, and experience greater levels of racism and discrimination than their White counterparts.

With regard to racism, Dr. Camara Jones (2000) has developed a framework for understanding levels of racism, suggesting that racism exists at institutional, personally mediated, and internalized levels. Within this framework, she has defined institutional racism as "differential access to the goods and services of a society based on race" (p. 1212). Personally mediated racism includes both prejudice—"judging another individual's abilities on the basis of race"—and discrimination—"acting and behaving differently toward individuals on the basis of race" (pp. 1212–1213). Finally, internalized racism is defined as the way in which members of a stigmatized group incorporate negative stereotypes and reflect those negative stereotypes through behavior.

These concepts can facilitate an understanding of the risks facing young men of color. To the extent that deeply embedded discriminatory policies differentially harm males of color—for example, longer sentences imposed for possession of crack cocaine than powder cocaine—these young men will suffer disproportionately. To the extent that the range of systems that serve young men of color have embedded biases and racism, these young men will receive inferior care within the health care system, will have lesser access to quality education and employment, and will face greater risks in contact with law enforcement, criminal justice personnel, and the courts.

Personally mediated racism also has a powerful effect on the overall status of young males of color. Although these young men are likely to face direct and overt prejudice and discrimination—such as being denied employment or housing—such treatment may be decreasing over time. However, recent studies about implicit bias, or those biases that are deeply held but of which the holder is unaware, may reflect their devastating impact (Kang, 2005). For example, researchers in Massachusetts and Illinois studied whether the names of applicants on fictional resumes submitted to advertised jobs could offer insight into implicit bias. They assigned to the resumes either "Black-sounding" or "White sounding" names to see whether the names of these fictional applicants affected the likelihood of being interviewed. They discovered that applicants with "Black sounding" names were less likely to be called in for an interview than applicants with "White-sounding" names (Bertrand & Mullainathan, 2004). Law enforcement data also support the impression that men of color are more likely to be stopped and searched by the police during a routine stop (Lundman & Kaufman, 2003).

Internalized racism may also affect how these young men see themselves. African American and Latino men are often negatively depicted in the media as criminal, aggressive, or hypersexual. Research has shown that negative self-perception can take hold early in a child's life and that it can have a powerful effect on that child's view of the future (Jones, 2000; Krieger, Smith, Naishadham, Hartman, & Barbeau, 2005; Paradies, 2006; Pyke, 2010).

POVERTY

To the extent that men of color are disproportionately poor, owing mainly to historical discrimination and the lack of opportunity for high-quality education and employment, they also disproportionately suffer the adverse health consequences related to poverty, particularly when one considers violence and trauma. Many of these young people are trapped in communities with a high level of crime, an abundance of firearms, and a shared perception that the police are not effective in protecting them. When these young people suffer trauma or victimization, symptoms of hyperarousal often lead them to take self-protective actions such as securing a weapon (Rich & Grey, 2005). Although health care and mental health providers might believe that possession of a weapon is a sign of involvement in criminal activity, for many young people a consequence of trauma is that they never feel safe. This has important implications for how clinicians address trauma in this population, especially given that a number of treatment modalities presume that the trauma survivor is reacting in a phobic way to a threat that no longer exists. For many of these young people, the threat of violence is very real and constant in their lives, and therefore traditional approaches may be less salient for this population. Moreover, to the extent that these young men believe that they do not have a future of promise, given the extreme concentrated poverty in which they live and the discrimination they face on a daily basis, trauma and violence may intensify their sense of a foreshortened future, a common symptom of posttraumatic stress (Rich, 2009; Rich & Stone, 1996).

A PUBLIC HEALTH AND TRAUMA-INFORMED LENS

Although there might be many explanations for the disparities facing Black and Latino men from a criminal justice or law enforcement perspective, justice systems are increasingly looking to public health approaches and trauma-informed strategies to decrease the impact of crime victimization and disproportionate incarceration of men of color. The National Institute of Justice (Schweig, 2014) has advocated a public health approach to preventing community violence that calls for the four pillars of public health practice: defining and monitoring the problem, identifying risk and protective factors, developing and testing prevention strategies, and ensuring widespread adoption. Implicit in this viewpoint is the idea that public health, health care and criminal justice agencies, and professionals must work together to identify risk factors and protective factors for violence and develop effective interventions (Schweig, 2014).

Over the past 20 years, there has been an outpouring of biological, psychological, and public health knowledge about the damaging impact of stress, adversity, and trauma on the human brain and body (Adler & Stewart, 2010; Barbeau, Krieger, & Soobader, 2004; McEwen & Gianaros, 2010; Seeman, Epel, Gruenewald, Karlamangla, & McEwen, 2010). Although a full delineation of this evidence is beyond the scope of this chapter, the fundamentals of this approach formed the foundation of the Attorney General's Defending Childhood Task Force Report. The authors of this landmark report, a committee of experts in law enforcement and trauma, conducted hearings across the United States, gathering testimony from a broad spectrum of communities affected by violence. Their key findings support the idea that early childhood exposure to violence and adversity is not only a significant cause of behavioral problems, but also results in significant physical and emotional disease. Furthermore, the report suggested that, rather than address only the delinquency and criminal justice consequences of this adversity, systems actively work to prevent childhood adversity and help victims heal (Holder, Leary, & Hanes, 2012).

The literature on trauma is clear that not only do violence and trauma affect those who are directly victimized by violence but they have a dramatic indirect effect on those who witness violence (Bain & Brown, 1996; Farrell & Bruce, 1997; Osofsky, 1995; Rich & Sullivan, 2001; Rosenthal, 2000; Scarpa, 2003). For every violent episode, there are an untold number of witnesses to the event. Most young people who experience intentional injuries are likely to have witnessed violence before their injuries and, if they survive, are likely to be witnesses to more violence after discharge. Witnessing community violence is related to substance abuse, aggression, anxiety, depression and antisocial behavior in adolescence. Adolescent delinquency and substance abuse can further prime a pattern of chronic violent offending in adulthood (Zinzow et al., 2009). In one large study of more than 8,000 sixth-, seventh-, and eighth-grade urban students, children exposed to high levels of community violence were more than 7 times as likely to carry a handgun, 6 times as likely to use marijuana, 5 times as likely to binge drink or to be involved in a gang, and almost 3 times as likely to be injured in a fight (Barroso et al., 2008). A 2013 study by Abram et al. found that among juvenile detainees in Chicago, 92.5% had experienced at least one major trauma and that witnessing violence was common among both males (74.9%) and females (63.5%). In addition, they found that 11.2% of the youths had posttraumatic stress disorder (PTSD), with more than half of the participants citing witnessing trauma as the precipitating event for their PTSD (Abram et al., 2013).

Involvement in violent behavior is a recurrent problem. Sims and colleagues (Goins, Thompson, & Simpkins, 1992; Sims et al., 1989) showed that as many as 45% of victims who suffered a penetrating injury were reinjured over the 5 years after the first injury and 20% were dead within those 5 years. Other studies in urban trauma centers have found similar violence recidivism rates. Youths who are victims of violence are likely to respond with retaliation. According to the American Academy of Pediatrics (1999), when children are exposed to violence, they are more likely to engage in later acts of violence. The underlying cause of this relationship between exposure to violence and later offending was suggested by a study of African American men, ages 18 to 25, who had been shot or stabbed (Rich & Stone, 1996). Qualitative interviews and narrative analysis revealed that young male victims of violence perceive that if they fail to respond violently to an assault, they will be at further risk of victimization. In this way, violence breeds violence. In researching repeated injury, Cooper, Eslinger, Nash, al-Zawahri, and Stolley (2000) found that prominent risk factors associated with further involvement in violence were being an African American man age 31 or younger, being unemployed, having an annual income of less than $10,000, lacking medical insurance, using drugs currently, and having a history of drug dealing. Moreover, 86% of these men felt that disrespect was involved in their injury.

Research has suggested a link between past trauma and future violence (Cooper et al., 2000; Goins et al., 1992; Sims et al., 1989). Many young people who grow up in urban environments are traumatized in their youth. Many subsequently become victims or perpetrators. In-depth interviews with African American men who are victims of violence have shown that symptoms of trauma combine with the so-called "code of the street" to compel them to self-medicate with drugs, carry a weapon, and sometimes seek retaliation, all to reestablish a sense of safety (Rich, 2009; Rich & Grey, 2005). This dynamic is not limited to African American men; it also resonates with other men of color who face limited life possibilities in communities perceived as hostile.

The problem has reached dramatic proportions. In a recently released national survey sponsored by the Office of Juvenile Justice and Delinquency Prevention and supported by the Centers for Disease Control and Prevention (Finkelhor, Turner, Ormrod, Hamby, & Kracke, 2009), more than 60% of the children surveyed (age 17 and younger) had been exposed to violence within the past year, either directly or indirectly. Nearly half of the children and adolescents surveyed (46.3%) had been assaulted at least once in the past year, and more than 10% had been injured in an assault. Almost one quarter had been victims of robbery, vandalism, or theft or had witnessed a violent act, often within their own family. Multiple victimizations were common. A majority of those children who reported being exposed to violence during their lifetime also reported being exposed to violence within the past year, strongly suggesting that these children were at ongoing risk of violent victimization.

Apart from physical pain and injury, violence causes significant psychological outcomes for the victim (Corbin et al., 2011). In the United States, more than 20% of injured trauma survivors have symptoms consistent with a diagnosis of PTSD 12 months after acute care inpatient hospitalization (Zatzick et al., 2007). As Corbin et al. (2013) showed in their study of a population of young men and boys of color, the rate of exposure to violence, trauma, and adversity is high, as is the rate of PTSD. For example, in a Chicago study of young men in the juvenile justice system, more than 90% of detained youths had experienced at least one type of psychological trauma at some point in their lives and more than 50% of those had been exposed to six or more potentially traumatic adversities by the time of detention. Of these, 90% were male, and most were ethnic or racial minorities (Abram et al., 2004).

SYSTEM-LEVEL BARRIERS

For young men of color, particularly those who have been exposed to violence, access to treatment is limited as a result of many barriers: transportation, cost, availability of trauma-specific treatment, and perhaps most important, their perceived stigmatization by peers if they become part of the mental health system. In Philadelphia, Dr. Arthur Evans, commissioner of Philadelphia's Department of Behavioral Health and Intellectual disAbility Services, recognized these barriers and has been making significant efforts to get mental health services into the community (see, e.g., http://healthymindsphilly.org/blog).

At the same time, the mental health system is not the only system in which these young people will seek or be sent to services. Child welfare; juvenile and adult justice systems; homeless and housing systems; primary, secondary, and higher educational systems; and health care systems all are likely to have multiple interfaces with young boys and men of color and their families.

The diversity of services often provides its own unintentional barrier, because managers and staff within each system have their own language, beliefs, procedures, policies, practices, and cognitive models. Any of these can create barriers to communication between systems. In addition, the work of helping traumatized people to heal within each system is complicated, complex, and interactive, demanding complex skills and awareness on the part of helpers who need a level of emotional stability and maturity that surpasses that of their clients.

Research has increasingly identified the systems that serve young victims as playing a key role in their retraumatization through what Bloom (2010, 2011, 2014; Bloom & Farragher, 2010) has called "trauma-organized systems." In many helping organizations, acute crisis often leads to chronic states of organizational crisis and organizational hyperarousal. A lack of safety may present as a lack of physical safety, workplace violence, abusive behavior on the part of managers or staff, and a pervasive mistrust of the organization. Bloom and Farragher (2010) noted,

> a perceived lack of safety erodes trust, which is the basis for positive social relationships. As a result these organizations are very tightly wrapped and tensions run high. Under such unrelenting stress, helping professionals and the agencies themselves become more highly reactive and are more ready to see threat rather than opportunity, pathology rather than strength, and risk rather than reward. (p. 155)

A core challenge for providers delivering human services is to develop the ability to simultaneously manage distressing emotions and extend empathy to their clients. Emotional intelligence is recognized as an important component of any workplace environment that is productive and healthy. However, emotional intelligence is slow to develop or is eroded when fear, recurrent crisis, unrelenting stress, and unmanaged conflict come to dominate a work environment. Emotions are contagious, and under any circumstances, human service delivery environments demand high levels of emotional labor from workers. Stress and trauma exacerbate those demands. Atmospheres of recurrent or constant crisis severely constrain the ability of staff to manage their own emotions, making it difficult to provide healing environments for their clients and thus contributing to poor services. Negative emotions become collective emotions. Under these circumstances, conflict escalates, and both relationships and problem-solving suffer (Bloom & Farragher, 2010).

KNOWLEDGE GAPS ABOUT TRAUMA AND YOUNG MEN OF COLOR

There is a lack of research and knowledge about the prevalence of PTSD and other symptoms of trauma among urban young men of color. Early studies by Breslau found that about 13% of youths in Detroit had PTSD (Breslau & Davis, 1992). Liebschutz et al. (2007), working in an urban primary care clinic, found that 23% of patients had PTSD, but in only 11% of these cases was the diagnosis noted in the chart. More specific research about the impact of trauma on young men of color has been sparse. Rich and Grey (2005) conducted qualitative research on young male victims of violence in Boston and found that 67% of those who were available to be evaluated at 3 months had PTSD. Corbin et al. (2013) studied a subsample of participants in Healing Hurt People, a hospital-based violence intervention program, and found that 74% of these victims had PTSD. Larger community-based assessments of problems have been lacking.

Both case-based and qualitative research have supported the idea that PTSD contributes to the cycle of violence. Rich and Grey (2005) found that victims of violence were frequently unaware of the cause of their intrusive symptoms. Having received little or no education about the consequences of trauma at the time of their injuries, many young people turned to alcohol or marijuana to self-treat their symptoms. This in turn put them at increased risk for involvement with the juvenile justice system or exclusion from legitimate work due to drug testing. In addition, intense feelings of danger were related to hyperarousal and flashbacks, often leading these patients to either obtain weapons or consider doing so. This defensive action set the stage for future juvenile justice involvement, reinjury, or death.

PROVIDING EFFECTIVE TRAUMA TREATMENT TO YOUNG MEN OF COLOR

Given the challenges to effectively serving young urban men, a key starting point is to address the pervasive trauma-organized culture that leads to retraumatization of victims. Bloom (1997) proposed the sanctuary model and its conceptual framework of four key interdependent aspects of recovery from traumatic and other adverse experience—safety, emotions, loss, and future (SELF)—as a remedy to the previously described trauma-organized systems. The sanctuary model is an organizational intervention that is grounded in constructivist self-development theory (Pearlman & Saakvitne, 1995a, 1995b), burnout theory (Maslach & Leiter, 1997), and systems theory (Von Bertalanffy, 1974), using the valuation theory of organizational change (Hermans, 1991; Weatherbee, Dye, Bissonnette, & Mills, 2009) to improve organizational culture. The goal of the sanctuary model is to improve organizational culture by educating staff on the effects of trauma and stress on behavior, changing the mindset of staff about client behaviors from a pejorative view ("sick") to an alternative view ("injured"), and providing tools to change both individual and group behavior. By addressing these critical dynamics at both the individual and group levels, the sanctuary model can be used to improve the quality of service delivery as well as client outcomes (Esaki et al., 2013).

SELF provides a shared language and organizing framework and a nonlinear, cognitive–behavioral, psychoeducational approach for facilitating movement for the individual client, family, staff, or entire organization. It is a framework that helps to organize what are often chaotic amounts of information and as a result imposes a sense of coherence on that information, making it more comprehensible, manageable, and meaningful (Antonovsky, 1987).

SELF is a compass that allows exploration of all four key domains of healing. Safety is about attaining physical, psychological, social, and moral safety with oneself, in relationships, and in a variety of different environments. Emotional management focuses on identifying levels of various emotions and developing skills to modulate emotion in response to memories, people, or events in a way that fosters safety for self and others. Loss addresses feelings of grief in dealing with personal losses and recognizing that all change involves loss, that working through loss is a process, and that letting go can be facilitated by the support of others. Future is about vision and encourages people to try new roles, ways of relating, and behaving as survivors to ensure personal safety, envisioning a different and better future. The belief is that the energy for change actually resides in the future and is always there to be drawn on as a motivating force. By using SELF for assessment, problem solving, psychoeducational groups, and service delivery planning, the recipients of services (clients, families, and staff) are able to embrace a shared, nontechnical, and nonpejorative language that allows everyone to see the larger recovery process in perspective.

At the individual level, little is known about the effectiveness of different treatment approaches for trauma among urban men of color. Certainly a number of treatments such as cognitive–behavioral therapy, exposure therapy, eye movement desensitization and reprocessing therapy, and medications have been shown to be effective with combat veterans, some of whom are men of color from urban areas (Institute of Medicine, 2012). For certain treatments, such as prolonged exposure, extrapolations from returning combat veterans and inner-city youths may only go so far. Exposure therapies assume that phobic responses persist despite the resolution of the preexisting threat. As noted earlier, urban youths many find themselves constantly surrounded by an unsafe environment.

Recently, a number of hospital-based violence intervention programs have been established across the country in an attempt to intervene with injured youths in the window of vulnerability that opens after a violent injury. These programs, which currently exist under the umbrella of the National Network of Hospital based Violence Intervention Programs (http://www.nnhvip.org; Purtle et al., 2013), provide important supports such as case management and referral at a critical moment in the lives of these young people. A substantial body of research has demonstrated that such programs decrease violent reinjury, substance use, and involvement with the criminal justice system (Cooper, Eslinger, & Stolley, 2006; Cooper et al., 2000; Cunningham et al., 2009; Dicker et al., 2009; Purtle et al., 2013; Smith, Dobbins, Evans, Balhotra, & Dicker, 2013; Zun, Downey, & Rosen, 2006). Although such programs may differ in the extent to which they focus on trauma, one program in particular—Healing Hurt People (HHP) at the Drexel College of Medicine, affiliated with Hahnemann Hospital and St. Christopher's Hospital for Children—has built its intervention on trauma theory and the sanctuary model to specifically address the psychological consequences of trauma, particularly in children and young adults.

HHP is a trauma-informed, hospital-based violence intervention program, designed to address the mental health consequences of violent injury, prevent reinjury, and improve the life-course trajectories of violently injured youths in Philadelphia. Established at Hahnemann University Hospital in 2008 within Drexel's Center for Nonviolence and Social Justice and expanded to St. Christopher's Hospital for Children in 2009, HHP serves approximately 125 victims of violence annually—50 of whom are children. HHP practice is guided by the sanctuary model (Bloom, 1997). Within the practice, HHP is guided by the SELF concepts. The HHP model uses the SELF concepts throughout the program to guide clients to recovery from traumatic events.

HHP serves young victims of intentional injury (assaults, gunshot wounds, and stabbings) between the ages of 8 and 30 who are seen in the emergency department for their injuries and referred to the program by treating clinicians. Specifically, HHP staff—a social worker and community outreach worker—meet the client soon after his or her injury and assess key issues of safety, past trauma, and pressing physical and mental health needs while also educating the client about what symptoms he or she should expect as a result of the trauma. Staff members then perform a home visit and conduct a more thorough assessment in the week after the injury. The results of the assessment are used to design a customized service plan to meet the client's self-identified needs and goals. After the assessment phase, staff members provide intensive case management, navigation to needed services, and mentoring. In addition, clients are enrolled in psychoeducational SELF groups. These groups provide a trauma-informed safe environment for youths to process their trauma with the grounded support of their peers.

A cross-sectional analysis of HHP clients showed that 75% met full diagnostic criteria for PTSD, highlighting the tremendous need for trauma-informed mental health interventions in this population (Corbin et al., 2013). Trauma-specific interventions, such as cognitive–behavioral therapy, trauma art narrative therapy, and other modalities are available to those who need trauma-specific treatments, and staff are able to navigate clients to providers who are skilled in these methods. Many of the foregoing activities are critical to prepare clients for more intensive engagement with a therapist because many clients arrive with deep and justified suspicion of the mental health system and its stigma. Because HHP clients are predominantly boys and men of color, and many lack previous positive experience with mental health and primary care providers, the support of trusted and culturally competent staff is a critical ingredient in connecting these young patients to care. To this end, HHP appeals to the client or patient by offering support services that will benefit them while delivering behavioral health counseling. This allows behavioral health service delivery to a population that has historically associated stigma with such services.

HHP has been supported by the Philadelphia Department of Behavioral Health and Intellectual disAbility Services. With this support, HHP is currently expanding to additional Level 1 trauma centers in the Philadelphia area. This expansion is aligned with Philadelphia's strategic plan (http://www.phila.gov/Newsletters/Youth_Violence_Strategic_Plan_%20FINAL%20September%202013.pdf) to decrease youth violence in one of the most crime-ridden police districts in the city. Simultaneously, HHP is currently engaged in rigorous quantitative and qualitative evaluation to determine its effectiveness in decreasing recurrent violence and involvement with the criminal justice system and in decreasing PTSD and depression. With support from the Annie E. Casey Foundation and the Stoneleigh Foundation, the HHP replication is being evaluated using a stepped-wedge research design (Brown & Lilford, 2006), in which the control group is recruited at the new replication site while the research team prepares the intervention team by means of training and implementation of fidelity measures. Once the intervention is ready to launch, participants are offered the opportunity to receive the intervention. This staged approach allows for rigorous evaluation of the program while maintaining the ethically responsible obligation to provide the needed intervention to participants once available.

Consistent with HHP's focus on trauma and the behavioral health consequences of violence, the evaluation will focus on mental health outcomes including PTSD, sleep quality health status, social support, health care utilization, depression, substance use, and personal mastery, as well as involvement with the criminal justice system and recurrent injury. A qualitative component of the research will seek to identify those aspects of engagement with the program that are most critical to addressing the key outcomes.

If the program is shown to be effective, then broad replication of such interventions in health care settings and communities may be the indicated next step in decreasing the effects of trauma on young men of color. In addition, work is currently underway with the Department of Behavioral Health and Intellectual disAbility Services to design a clinical model under which the behavioral health services delivered under HHP will be reimbursable under Medicaid. Although many HHP participants qualify for Medicaid coverage, either because they are juveniles whose families live in poverty or, for older adolescents, as a result of their injuries, the potential for expanded Medicaid coverage under the Patient Protection and Affordable Care Act (2010) could result in more consistent health insurance coverage for this population. Reimbursement to hospitals and health centers that provide a full range of healing services to young victims of violence would provide incentives for the adoption of proven models and allow for sustainability over time.

CONCLUSION

Although the examples presented here are largely based in public health and health care institutions, awareness of the impact of trauma is growing among a range of systems that touch the lives of young men of color. The previously mentioned Attorney General's Defending Childhood Task Force (Holder et al., 2012) included among its many recommendations the following:

- Recognize and support the critical role of law enforcement's participation in collaborative responses to violence. (p. xv)
- Involve men and boys as critical partners in preventing violence. (p. xv)
- Develop and provide trauma-informed care in all hospital-based trauma centers and emergency departments for all children exposed to violence. (p. x)

The implementation of such recommendations would promote a multisystem and multidisciplinary approach to trauma and violence. This would bring us one step closer to achieving a coordinated response to violence and healing from trauma in boys and young men of color.

References

Abram, K. M., Teplin, L. A., Charles, D. R., Longworth, S. L., McClelland, G. M., & Dulcan, M. K. (2004). Posttraumatic stress disorder and trauma in youth in juvenile detention. *Archives of General Psychiatry, 61,* 403–410. http://dx.doi.org/10.1001/archpsyc.61.4.403

Abram, K. M., Teplin, L. A., King, D. C., Longworth, S. L., Emanuel, K. M., Romero, E. G., . . . Welty, L. J. (2013). PTSD, *trauma, and comorbid psychiatric disorders in detained youth* (Juvenile Justice Bulletin). Retrieved from http://www.ojjdp.gov/pubs/239603.pdf

Adler, N. E., & Stewart, J. (2010). Preface to *The biology of disadvantage: Socioeconomic status and health. Annals of the New York Academy of Sciences, 1186,* 1–4. http://dx.doi.org/10.1111/j.1749-6632.2009.05385.x

American Academy of Pediatrics Task Force on Violence. (1999). The role of the pediatrician in youth violence prevention in clinical practice and at the community level. *Pediatrics, 103,* 173–181. http://dx.doi.org/10.1542/peds.103.1.173

Annest, J. (2013). Homicide rates among persons aged 10–24 years—United States, 1981–2010. *Morbidity and Mortality Weekly Report, 62,* 545–548.

Antonovsky, A. (1987). *Unraveling the mystery of health: How people manage stress and stay well.* San Francisco, CA: Jossey-Bass.

Bain, J. E., & Brown, R. T. (1996). Adolescents as witnesses to violence. *Journal of Adolescent Health, 19,* 83–85. http://dx.doi.org/10.1016/1054-139X(96)00129-2

Barbeau, E. M., Krieger, N., & Soobader, M. J. (2004). Working class matters: Socioeconomic disadvantage, race/ethnicity, gender, and smoking in NHIS 2000. *American Journal of Public Health, 94,* 269–278. http://dx.doi.org/10.2105/AJPH.94.2.269

Barroso, C. S., Peters, R. J., Jr., Kelder, S. J., Conroy, J., Murray, N., & Orpinas, P. (2008). Youth exposure to community violence: Association with aggression, victimization, and risk behaviors. *Journal of Aggression, Maltreatment, and Trauma, 17,* 141–155. http://dx.doi.org/10.1080/10926770802374916

Bertrand, M., & Mullainathan, S. (2004). Are Emily and Greg more employable than Lakisha and Jamal? A field experiment on labor market discrimination. *American Economic Review, 94,* 991–1013. http://dx.doi.org/10.1257/0002828042002561

Bloom, S. L. (1997). *Creating sanctuary: Toward the evolution of sane societies.* New York, NY: Routledge.

Bloom, S. L. (2010). Organizational stress as a barrier to trauma-informed service delivery. In M. Becker & B. Levin (Eds.), *A public health perspective of women's mental health* (pp. 295–311). http://dx.doi.org/10.1007/978-1-4419-1526-9_15

Bloom, S. L. (2011). Trauma-organized systems and parallel process. In N. Tehrani (Ed.), *Managing trauma in the workplace: Supporting workers and organizations* (pp. 139–153). London, England: Routledge.

Bloom, S. L. (2014). Creating, destroying and restoring sanctuary within caregiving organisations. In A. Odgers (Ed.), *From broken attachment to earned security: The role of empathy in therapeutic change* (pp. 55–89). London, England: Karnac.

Bloom, S. L., & Farragher, B. (2010). *Destroying sanctuary: The crisis in human service delivery systems.* http://dx.doi.org/10.1093/acprof:oso/9780195374803.001.0001

Bonczar, T. (2003). *Prevalence of imprisonment in the U.S. population, 1974–2001*. Washington, DC: U.S. Department of Justice.

Breslau, N., & Davis, G. C. (1992). Posttraumatic stress disorder in an urban population of young adults: Risk factors for chronicity. *American Journal of Psychiatry*, *149*, 671–675.

Brown, C. A., & Lilford, R. J. (2006). The stepped wedge trial design: A systematic review. *BMC Medical Research Methodology*, *6*, 54. http://dx.doi.org/10.1186/1471-2288-6-54

Carson, E., & Golinelli, D. (2013). *Prisoners in 2012: Advance counts*. Washington, DC: Bureau of Justice Statistics. Retrieved from http://www.bjs.gov/content/pub/pdf/p12ac.pdf

Carson, E., & Sabol, W. (2012). *Prisoners in 2011*. Washington, DC: Bureau of Justice Statistics.

Centers for Disease Control and Prevention. (2008). *Web-based Injury Statistics Query and Reporting System (WISQARS)*. Retrieved from http://www.cdc.gov/injury/wisqars/index.html

Centers for Disease Control and Prevention. (2009). *Youth violence: Facts at a glance*. Retrieved from http://www.cdc.gov/violenceprevention/pdf/YV_DataSheet_Summer2009-a.pdf

Centers for Disease Control and Prevention. (2012). *Estimated HIV incidence among adults and adolescents in the United States, 2007–2010* (HIV Surveillance Supplemental Report, Vol. 17). Atlanta, GA: Author.

Cooper, C., Eslinger, D., Nash, D., al-Zawahri, J., & Stolley, P. (2000). Repeat victims of violence: Report of a large concurrent case-control study. *Archives of Surgery*, *135*, 837–843. http://dx.doi.org/10.1001/archsurg.135.7.837

Cooper, C., Eslinger, D. M., & Stolley, P. D. (2006). Hospital-based violence intervention programs work. *Journal of Trauma*, *61*, 534–537. http://dx.doi.org/10.1097/01.ta.0000236576.81860.8c

Corbin, T. J., Purtle, J., Rich, L. J., Rich, J. A., Adams, E. J., Yee, G., & Bloom, S. L. (2013). The prevalence of trauma and childhood adversity in an urban, hospital-based violence intervention program. *Journal of Health Care for the Poor and Underserved*, *24*, 1021–1030. http://dx.doi.org/10.1353/hpu.2013.0120

Corbin, T. J., Rich, J. A., Bloom, S. L., Delgado, D., Rich, L. J., & Wilson, A. S. (2011). Developing a trauma-informed, emergency department-based intervention for victims of urban violence. *Journal of Trauma and Dissociation*, *12*, 510–525. http://dx.doi.org/10.1080/15299732.2011.593260

Cunningham, R., Knox, L., Fein, J., Harrison, S., Frisch, K., Walton, M., . . . Hargarten, S. W. (2009). Before and after the trauma bay: The prevention of violent injury among youth. *Annals of Emergency Medicine*, *53*, 490–500. http://dx.doi.org/10.1016/j.annemergmed.2008.11.014

David-Ferdon, C., Dahlberg, L., & Kegler, S. (2013). Homicide rates among persons aged 10–24 years: United States, 1981–2010. *Morbidity and Mortality Weekly Report*, *62*, 545–548.

Dicker, R. A., Jaeger, S., Knudson, M. M., Mackersie, R. C., Morabito, D. J., Antezana, J., & Texada, M. (2009). Where do we go from here? Interim analysis to forge ahead in violence prevention. *Journal of Trauma and Acute Care Surgery*, *67*, 1169–1175. http://dx.doi.org/10.1097/TA.0b013e3181bdb78a

Eagan Chamberlin, S. (2012). Emasculated by trauma: A social history of posttraumatic stress disorder, stigma, and masculinity. *Journal of American Culture*, *35*, 358–365. http://dx.doi.org/10.1111/jacc.12005

Esaki, N., Benamati, J., Yanosy, S., Middleton, J., Hopson, L., Hummer, V., & Bloom, S. L. (2013). The sanctuary model: Theoretical framework. *Families in Society*, *94*, 87–95. http://dx.doi.org/10.1606/1044-3894.4287

Farrell, A. D., & Bruce, S. E. (1997). Impact of exposure to community violence on violent behavior and emotional distress among urban adolescents. *Journal of Clinical Child Psychology*, *26*, 2–14. http://dx.doi.org/10.1207/s15374424jccp2601_1

Finkelhor, D., Turner, H., Ormrod, R., Hamby, S., & Kracke, K. (2009). *Children's exposure to violence: A comprehensive national survey* (Juvenile Justice Bulletin). Retrieved from http://www.ncjrs.gov/pdffiles1/ojjdp/227744.pdf

Fox, J., & Pease, B. (2012). Military deployment, masculinity and trauma: Reviewing the connections. *Journal of Men's Studies*, *20*, 16–31. http://dx.doi.org/10.3149/jms.2001.16

Goins, W. A., Thompson, J., & Simpkins, C. (1992). Recurrent intentional injury. *Journal of the National Medical Association*, *84*, 431–435.

Harrell, E. (2007). *Black victims of violent crime*. Washington, DC: Department of Justice.

Hermans, H. (1991). The person as co-investigator in self-research: Valuation theory. *European Journal of Personality*, *5*, 217–234. http://dx.doi.org/10.1002/per.2410050304

Heron, M. (2010). Deaths: Leading causes for 2006. *National Vital Statistics Report*, *58*(14).

Holder, E. H., Leary, M., & Hanes, M. (2012). *Report of the Attorney General's National Task Force on Children Exposed to Violence*. Washington, DC: Defending Childhood Taskforce, U.S. Department of Justice.

Institute of Medicine. (2012). *Treatment for posttraumatic stress disorder in military and veteran populations: Initial assessment*. Washington, DC: National Academies Press.

Jones, C. P. (2000). Levels of racism: A theoretic framework and a gardener's tale. *American Journal of Public Health, 90*, 1212–1215. http://dx.doi.org/10.2105/AJPH.90.8.1212

Kaiser Family Foundation (2006). *Young African American men in the United States* (fact sheet). Menlo Park, CA: Author.

Kang, J. (2005). Trojan horses of race. *Harvard Law Review, 118*, 1489–1593.

Krieger, N. (2000). Refiguring "race": Epidemiology, racialized biology, and biological expressions of race relations. *International Journal of Health Services, 30*, 211–216. http://dx.doi.org/10.2190/672J-1PPF-K6QT-9N7U

Krieger, N. (2005). Stormy weather: Race, gene expression, and the science of health disparities. *American Journal of Public Health, 95*, 2155–2160. http://dx.doi.org/10.2105/AJPH.2005.067108

Krieger, N., Smith, K., Naishadham, D., Hartman, C., & Barbeau, E. M. (2005). Experiences of discrimination: Validity and reliability of a self-report measure for population health research on racism and health. *Social Science and Medicine, 61*, 1576–1596. http://dx.doi.org/10.1016/j.socscimed.2005.03.006

Kuehn, D. (2013). *The labor market performance of young Black men in the Great Recession*. Washington, DC: Urban Institute.

Liebschutz, J., Saitz, R., Brower, V., Keane, T. M., Lloyd-Travaglini, C., Averbuch, T., & Samet, J. H. (2007). PTSD in urban primary care: High prevalence and low physician recognition. *Journal of General Internal Medicine*, 22, 719–726. http://dx.doi.org/10.1007/s11606-007-0161-0

Lundman, R., & Kaufman, R. (2003). Driving while Black: Effects of race, ethnicity, and gender on citizen self-reports of traffic stops and police actions. *Criminology, 41*, 195–220. http://dx.doi.org/10.1111/j.1745-9125.2003.tb00986.x

Maslach, C., & Leiter, M. P. (1997). *The truth about burnout: How organizations cause personal stress and what to do about it*. San Francisco, CA: Jossey-Bass.

McEwen, B. S., & Gianaros, P. J. (2010). Central role of the brain in stress and adaptation: Links to socioeconomic status, health, and disease. *Annals of the New York Academy of Sciences, 1186*, 190–222. http://dx.doi.org/10.1111/j.1749-6632.2009.05331.x

Mejía, X. E. (2005). Gender matters: Working with adult male survivors of trauma. *Journal of Counseling and Development*, 83, 29–40. http://dx.doi.org/10.1002/j.1556-6678.2005.tb00577.x

Osofsky, J. D. (1995). The effects of exposure to violence on young children. *American Psychologist, 50*, 782–788. http://dx.doi.org/10.1037/0003-066X.50.9.782

Paradies, Y. (2006). A systematic review of empirical research on self-reported racism and health. *International Journal of Epidemiology, 35*, 888–901. http://dx.doi.org/10.1093/ije/dyl056

Patient Protection and Affordable Care Act, Pub. L. 111-148, 42 U.S.C. §§ 18001–18121 (2010).

Pearlman, L., & Saakvitne, K. (1995a). *Trauma and the therapist: Countertransference and vicarious traumatization in psychotherapy with incest survivors*. New York, NY: Norton.

Pearlman, L., & Saakvitne, K. (1995b). Vicarious traumatization: How trauma therapy affects the therapist. In L. A. Pearlman & K. W. Saakvitne (Eds.), *Trauma and the therapist: Countertransference and vicarious traumatization in psychotherapy with incest survivors* (pp. 279–294). New York, NY: Norton.

Purtle, J., Dicker, R., Cooper, C., Corbin, T., Greene, M. B., Marks, A., . . . Moreland, D. (2013). Hospital-based violence intervention programs save lives and money. *Journal of Trauma and Acute Care Surgery, 75*, 331–333. http://dx.doi.org/10.1097/TA.0b013e318294f518

Pyke, K. D. (2010). What is internalized racial oppression and why don't we study it? Acknowledging racism's hidden injuries. *Sociological Perspectives, 53*, 551–572. http://dx.doi.org/10.1525/sop.2010.53.4.551

Reiner, D. S., Pastena, J. A., Swan, K. G., Lindenthal, J. J., & Tischler, C. D. (1990). Trauma recidivism. *American Surgeon, 56*, 556–560.

Rich, J. (2009). *Wrong place, wrong time: Trauma and violence in the lives of young Black men*. Baltimore, MD: Johns Hopkins University Press.

Rich, J. A., & Grey, C. M. (2005). Pathways to recurrent trauma among young Black men: Traumatic stress, substance use, and the "code of the street." *American Journal of Public Health, 95*, 816–824. http://dx.doi.org/10.2105/AJPH.2004.044560

Rich, J. A., & Stone, D. A. (1996). The experience of violent injury for young African-American men. *Journal of General Internal Medicine, 11*, 77–82. http://dx.doi.org/10.1007/BF02599582

Rich, J. A., & Sullivan, L. M. (2001). Correlates of violent assault among young male primary care patients. *Journal of Health Care for the Poor and Underserved, 12*, 103–112. http://dx.doi.org/10.1353/hpu.2010.0538

Ridge, D., Emslie, C., & White, A. (2011). Understanding how men experience, express and cope with mental distress: Where next? *Sociology of Health and Illness, 33*, 145–159. http://dx.doi.org/10.1111/j.1467-9566.2010.01266.x

Rosenthal, B. S. (2000). Exposure to community violence in adolescence: Trauma symptoms. *Adolescence, 35*, 271–284.

Scarpa, A. (2003). Community violence exposure in young adults. *Trauma, Violence, and Abuse, 4*, 210–227. http://dx.doi.org/10.1177/1524838003004003002

Schweig, S. (2014). *Healthy communities may make safe communities: Public health approaches to violence prevention*. Retrieved from http://nij.gov/journals/273/Pages/violence-prevention.aspx

Seeman, T., Epel, E., Gruenewald, T., Karlamangla, A., & McEwen, B. S. (2010). Socio-economic differentials in peripheral biology: Cumulative allostatic load. *Annals of the New York Academy of Sciences, 1186*, 223–239. http://dx.doi.org/10.1111/j.1749-6632.2009.05341.x

Sims, D. W., Bivins, B. A., Obeid, F. N., Horst, H. M., Sorensen, V. J., & Fath, J. J. (1989). Urban trauma: A chronic recurrent disease. *Journal of Trauma, 29*, 940–946. http://dx.doi.org/10.1097/00005373-198907000-00006

Smedley, A., & Smedley, B. D. (2005). Race as biology is fiction, racism as a social problem is real: Anthropological and historical perspectives on the social construction of race. *American Psychologist, 60*, 16–26. http://dx.doi.org/10.1037/0003-066X.60.1.16

Smedley, B., Stith, A., & Nelson, A. (Eds.). (2002). *Unequal treatment: Confronting racial and ethnic disparities in health care*. Washington, DC: National Academies Press.

Smith, R., Dobbins, S., Evans, A., Balhotra, K., & Dicker, R. A. (2013). Hospital-based violence intervention: Risk reduction resources that are essential for success. *Journal of Trauma and Acute Care Surgery, 74*, 976–980. http://dx.doi.org/10.1097/TA.0b013e31828586c9

Von Bertalanffy, L. (1974). General systems theory and psychiatry. In S. Arieti (Ed.), *American handbook of psychiatry: Vol. 1. The foundations of psychiatry* (pp. 1095–1117). New York, NY: Basic Books.

Weatherbee, T., Dye, K., Bissonnette, A., & Mills, A. (2009). Valuation theory and organizational change: Towards a sociopsychological method of intervention. *Journal of Change Management, 9*, 195–213. http://dx.doi.org/10.1080/14697010902879152

Williams, D. R., Mohammed, S. A., Leavell, J., & Collins, C. (2010). Race, socioeconomic status, and health: Complexities, ongoing challenges, and research opportunities. *Annals of the New York Academy of Sciences, 1186*, 69–101. http://dx.doi.org/10.1111/j.1749-6632.2009.05339.x

Zatzick, D. F., Rivara, F. P., Nathens, A. B., Jurkovich, G. J., Wang, J., Fan, M. Y., . . . Mackenzie, E. J. (2007). A nationwide US study of posttraumatic stress after hospitalization for physical injury. *Psychological Medicine, 37*, 1469–1480. http://dx.doi.org/10.1017/S0033291707000943

Zinzow, H. M., Ruggiero, K. J., Hanson, R. F., Smith, D. W., Saunders, B. E., & Kilpatrick, D. G. (2009). Witnessed community and parental violence in relation to substance use and delinquency in a national sample of adolescents. *Journal of Traumatic Stress, 22*, 525–533.

Zun, L. S., Downey, L., & Rosen, J. (2006). The effectiveness of an ED-based violence prevention program. *American Journal of Emergency Medicine, 24*, 8–13. http://dx.doi.org/10.1016/j.ajem.2005.05.009

CHAPTER 28

RESIDENTIAL INTERVENTIONS WITH JUSTICE-INVOLVED YOUTHS

Keith R. Cruise, Samantha L. Morin, and Katelyn Affleck

Residential care is an umbrella term used to describe a higher level of intervention outside of a community setting. Such care is delivered across a range of residentially based living arrangements that vary from shelters or group homes to large secure institutions, often serving youths across multiple systems including child welfare, mental health, and juvenile justice (James, Alemi, & Zepeda, 2013). Reflecting a shift away from punitive sanctions to reembracing a rehabilitation response to juvenile crime, there is a nationwide trend away from overreliance on out-of-home placements for juveniles toward community-based alternatives (42% reduction in residential placements from 1997 to 2011; see Hockenberry, 2014).

Multiple factors have been implicated in this reduction. First, basic cost–benefit analyses have often cited the high costs associated with corrections and residential placement (see Hussey, Drinkard, Falletta, & Flannery, 2008; Sunseri, 2005) relative to the benefits in recidivism reduction (see Cameron, Frensch, Preyde, & Quosai, 2011; Robst, Armstrong, Dollard, & Rohrer, 2013).

Second, federal legislation such as the 2002 reauthorization of the Juvenile Justice and Delinquency Prevention Act has mandated states to implement strategies targeting reductions in racial and ethnic disparities and created financial incentives for states to increase use of research-based delinquency reduction interventions and community-based alternatives to out-of-home placements (see Soler, Schoenberg, & Schindler, 2009). The U.S. Department of Justice, empowered through the Civil Rights of Institutionalized Persons Act (1997), continues to investigate conditions and practices in juvenile facilities that may reflect systematic patterns of practice resulting in harm. These investigations often involve the care and confinement conditions of youths with medical and mental health problems, as well as protection from victimization in secure settings. According to information on the Department of Justice's website (http://www.justice.gov/crt/about/spl/findsettle.php#juv), the Civil Rights Division has open investigations in nine states, with most current investigations focusing on conditions of confinement in juvenile detention and correctional centers.

Third, state legislatures have directed financial resources away from large corrections-based models of care to smaller, treatment-oriented models (Lipsey, Howell, Kelly, Chapman, & Carver, 2010). For example, the New York State Close to Home Initiative decreased the size of the state-operated juvenile secure custody system by 320 beds over a 2-year period and shifted resources toward development of smaller community-based residential programs, at an estimated cost saving of $31.5 million over a 2-year period (New York State Office of the Governor, 2012).

Fourth, the Blueprints for Violence Prevention report (Mihalic, Irwin, Elliott, Fagan, & Hansen, 2011) identified 11 model programs on the basis of research-based criteria of program effectiveness. Only three programs specific to justice-involved youths were identified as model programs (Functional Family Therapy, Multisystemic Therapy, and

http://dx.doi.org/10.1037/14643-028
APA Handbook of Psychology and Juvenile Justice, K. Heilbrun (Editor-in-Chief)

Multidimensional Treatment Foster Care). All three of these programs are community based. Research evidence supporting reductions in recidivism and improvements in functional outcomes with these three models (see Butler, Baruch, Hickey, & Fonagy, 2011; Chamberlain, Leve, & DeGarmo, 2007; Curtis, Ronan, & Borduin, 2004; Glisson et al., 2010; Leve & Chamberlain, 2007; Sexton & Turner, 2011) has supported the idea that successful rehabilitation of justice-involved youths can be achieved in the community without risking the potential negative effects of peer contagion and deviancy training (see Dodge, Dishion, & Lansford, 2006) and developmental disruption (see Dmitrieva, Monahan, Cauffman, & Steinberg, 2012; E. S. Scott & Steinberg, 2008; Steinberg, 2009) from out-of-home placements.

Considering this context, in this chapter we review the current state of knowledge regarding the effectiveness of residential interventions for juveniles. We begin by reviewing national juvenile justice trends regarding placement of juveniles in residential settings. Next, we provide a historical perspective, tracking results of large-scale meta-analyses addressing juvenile justice interventions in general, and residential treatments in particular, to review evidence of the general effectiveness of residential interventions. Third, we examine both individual- and system-level barriers found in residential treatment settings that can attenuate treatment effectiveness and reduce recidivism. Fourth, we highlight promising programs for juveniles drawn from research on residential settings. Finally, we offer suggestions for policy, practice, and future research to promote a better understanding of the effectiveness of residential interventions for justice-involved youths.

JUVENILES IN RESIDENTIAL PLACEMENT

Three surveys conducted by the Office of Juvenile Justice and Delinquency Prevention have provided complementary information describing juveniles in some form of residential placement in the United States (Sedlack, 2010). The Census of Juveniles in Residential Placement (CJRP) is a biennial, point-prevalence (e.g., 1-day population counts) survey of secure and nonsecure, public and private residential placement facilities housing juveniles (i.e., people younger than age 21) in the United States. Facility types included in the CJRP reflect multiple points along a continuum of care available to the juvenile justice system (i.e., group homes, ranch and wilderness camps, detention centers, long-term secure facilities). The most recent CJRP data indicated that 116,701 juveniles were held in residential placements in October 2011; the majority were individuals with delinquency offenses (86%) or status offenses (3%; Hockenberry, 2014). These data reflect that 196 juveniles were in residential placement for every 100,000 youths in the United States. The 2011 census showed a 42% reduction in total number of juveniles placed since the CJRP was initiated in 1997, with the largest reduction in public facilities (76% reduction from 1997 to 2011). Despite the decrease in total number of juveniles in placement, CJRP data reflect stability in the percentage of juveniles placed for person and violent offenses from 1997 to 2011 (30%–33% for person offenses; 23% for violent offenses). During this time period, the percentage of juveniles in placement for status offenses dropped (from 5% in 1997 to 3% in 2011).

Basic demographic information collected as part of the 2011 CJRP indicated a gender breakdown in residential placement that roughly approximates the gender breakdown of juvenile arrests. For example, while accounting for 70% of juvenile delinquency arrests in 2011, boys represented 86% of the juveniles in residential placement (Puzzanchera, 2013). Girls in placement tended to be younger than their male counterparts (38% of girls were younger than 16, compared with 28% of boys; Hockenberry, 2014). Despite nationwide efforts to reduce racial and ethnic disparities (Kempf-Leonard, 2007; Piquero, 2008), minority youths accounted for 68% of juveniles in residential placement in 2011 (including 40% Black, 32% White, and 23% Hispanic). CJRP data indicated that the overall decline in the residential placement population from 1997 to 2011 has not affected Black youths (41% reduction) and Hispanic youths (28% reduction) at the same rate as White youths (49% reduction). To further illustrate, 521 Black juveniles were in placement for every 100,000 Black youths, whereas 112 White juveniles were in placement per 100,000 White youths.

The Juvenile Residential Facility Census (JRFC) is a biennial, point-prevalence survey that collects information about type, characteristics, capacity, and level of security in residential facilities across the United States (Sedlack, 2010). In October 2010, the JRFC collected data from 2,111 juvenile facilities (1,074 public, 1,037 private), with public facilities housing 70% of the juvenile residential placement population (Hockenberry, Sickmund, & Sladky, 2013). Of this total, 760 facilities were identified as residential treatment centers (36%), 530 facilities as group homes or halfway houses (25%), 705 as detention centers (33%), and 188 as training schools (9%). More than 50% of facilities reported using one or more confinement procedures (e.g., locking youths in single rooms during sleeping hours), with this percentage logically increasing for detention centers (95%) and training schools (96%) versus residential treatment centers (48%). Fifty-five percent of facilities reported a census of fewer than 20 youths. Large facilities (census ≥ 50 residents) made up only 19% of the total facilities but housed 61% (40,262 youths) of the residential facility population.

Over the past decade, significant attention has been paid to establishing practice standards for screening and assessment for youths in the areas of mental health (Grisso, Vincent, & Seagrave, 2005; Wasserman et al., 2003) and education (Cruise, Evans, & Pickens, 2011) within the juvenile justice system. Data collected from the 2010 JRFC indicated that 86% of facilities reported screening all youths for educational needs at admission (i.e., within 24 hours to 7 days). Seventy-four percent of facilities reported screening all youths for substance abuse problems, with 55% completing this evaluation within 24 hours of admission. In addition, more than 50% of facilities reported providing substance abuse counseling or therapy, with individual (>90%) and group (>85%) services as the most common modalities. Fifty-seven percent of facilities reported completion of a mental health evaluation (most commonly reported as a mental health screen) of all youths by an in-house mental health professional, with mental health evaluations more common in private (79%) than in public (49%) facilities. Fifty-eight percent of facilities reported completing screenings within 7 days of admission. Eighty-nine percent of facilities reported screening all youths for suicide risk, with 86% indicating that this screen was conducted within 24 hours of admission.

The final survey conducted by the Office of Juvenile Justice and Delinquency Prevention is the Survey of Youth in Residential Placement (SYRP; Sedlack, 2010). The SYRP sampled youths between ages 10 and 20 in all facilities surveyed through the CJRP and the JRFC by randomly selecting facilities and then using a proportional-to-size sample design to ensure representation of pre- and postadjudication facilities as well as adequate representation of female and Hispanic youths (see Sedlack, 2010). Comprehensive in nature, the survey provides unique information regarding the self-reported experiences of youths in residential placement, with the 2003 SYRP findings reflecting a nationally representative sample of 7,073 youths in custody. Conditions of confinement data from the 2003 SYRP were summarized by Sedlack and McPherson (2010a). Ninety-three percent of youth reported placement at a facility designed as a single-program type (i.e., residential treatment center vs. detention), with 35% of youths reporting a coed facility placement (housing both male and female youths in separate units). Placement with older youths appeared common (20% living on units with youths more than 3 years older; 43% reporting being placed with young adults). Only 36% of juveniles reported sleeping in a private room, with sleeping arrangements varying by facility along security level.

General attitudes regarding facility amenities, facility safety, access to support, and family contact reflected divergent views regarding the conditions of confinement reported by youths. To illustrate, 25% of youths surveyed reported no positive features (e.g., good food, good school program, good recreational program) in describing the facility, 38% reported that they feared a physical attack by either other youths or staff, and 43% reported living in a unit described as having poor youth or staff relations. Sixty percent of youths cited the presence of gangs in the placement facilities.

In contrast, 84% identified knowing how to locate a staff member when support was needed, and 92% reported having some level of contact with families during placement. Discipline measures used in residential facilities varied from removal of privileges (43% of youths reporting) to room confinement and solitary confinement (26% and 24% of youths reporting, respectively). Although restrictive discipline measures were described across all facility types, secure facilities (e.g., detention, corrections) were more likely to be identified as using these strategies.

Sedlack, McPherson, and Basena (2013) summarized data regarding the self-reported victimization experiences of youths surveyed in the 2003 SYRP. They reported that victimization is quite common for youths in residential placement. Of youths, 46% reported theft of personal property (average report of six episodes), 10% reported being a victim of robbery (28% involving use of a weapon; 20% reporting multiple incidents of being robbed of property), and 29% reported being physically assaulted or threatened with physical assault. Between 60% and 70% of the reported incidents involved peer-to-peer victimizations. Four percent of youths in custody reported being the victim of a sexual assault. Fifty percent of youths reporting sexual assaults identified a facility staff person as the assailant; 41% of all sexual assaults included some form of penetration. Fifty-six percent of youths in custody reported experiencing more than one type of victimization, and 61% reported being injured during these experiences.

Predictors of any violent victimization included a combination of youth and facility characteristics. For example, youths reporting an abuse history or having a learning disability were 1.5 times more likely to report being a victim of violence. Age had an inverse association with victimization risk, with youths identified as serious offenders 1.3 times as likely to report victimization. An ineffective grievance process ($OR = 2.1$) and greater use of physical control methods ($OR = 1.5$) were consistent facility-level predictors of all types of violent victimization (e.g., robbery, physical assault, sexual assault).

The 2003 SYRP also provided a snapshot of youths' self-reported needs and services received (Sedlack & McPherson, 2010b). Mental health needs were surveyed using items drawn from the Massachusetts Youth Screening Instrument (Grisso & Barnum, 2006). Although not diagnostic, the results provide a snapshot of the self-reported mental health concerns of youths in residential placements. Problems with anger were common, with more than 60% reporting difficulties with temper control or becoming easily upset; attention problems were also reported by 40% of youths. A majority of youths endorsed indicators of depression (loneliness) and anxiety (nervous or worried feelings; 52% and 51%, respectively). Indicators of suicide risk varied from 15% (felt like killing yourself) to 26% (felt like life was not worth living). Youths endorsed possible psychotic symptoms: heard voices (12%) and seeing things others do not see (14%). Finally, 70% of youths endorsed an item reflecting exposure to a potentially traumatic event.

Reflecting mental health disorder prevalence (reviewed later), more female than male youths reported each type of mental health problem. In addition to the high rate of mental health needs, 69% of youths reported some type of basic health care need, ranging from basic dental care to injury or illness. Almost all youths (97%) reported that some form of mental health services were available at the placement facility, with 53% of youths reporting meeting with a counselor frequently. Eighty percent of respondents reported counseling services as being "somewhat helpful" to "very helpful." Qualifications of mental health staff were reported as limited, with 88% of youths residing in facilities in which some or all counselors were not mental health professionals.

A few general conclusions can be made on the basis of these three complementary surveys. First, use of out-of-home, residential placements for juveniles has dropped substantially (42%) over the past decade; however, more than 100,000 male and female adolescents reside in placements ranging from group homes to long-term secure custody facilities. Second, despite this overall reduction, minority youths remain overrepresented in residential placements relative to their percentage of the U.S. population. Third, although there is a trend toward residential treatment facilities with a smaller average census, data on conditions of confinement reflect ongoing concerns about safety and self-reported victimization rates. Fourth, systematic screening and assessment for education, mental health, and substance use problems has increased but is still not universal across residential facilities. Fifth, despite a smaller overall number, between 20% and 30% of youths charged with a violent offense were currently in placements, with the majority acknowledging mental health difficulties and access to mental health services of unknown effectiveness or quality.

IS THERE EVIDENCE SUPPORTING THE EFFECTIVENESS OF RESIDENTIAL TREATMENT FOR JUVENILES? LESSONS LEARNED FROM META-ANALYTIC RESULTS

There has been a long-standing debate regarding the effectiveness of treatment for adult and juvenile offenders. The nothing-works conclusion is often attributed to Martinson (1974), who wrote, "With few isolated exceptions the rehabilitative efforts that have been reported so far have no appreciable effects on recidivism" (p. 25). The rebuttal by Gendreau and Ross (1979) focused on methodological issues and is often cited as a catalyst for subsequent meta-analytic reviews of offender rehabilitation programs. The debate regarding effectiveness of offender rehabilitation programs continues today (see Cullen, Smith, Lowenkamp, & Latessa, 2009; Farabee, 2005). However, numerous meta-analyses have provided a basis for greater optimism about offender treatment programs in general (see Andrews & Dowden, 2006; Dowden & Andrews, 2000) and juvenile rehabilitation programs specifically (Baldwin, Christian, Berkeljon, & Shadish, 2012; Dowden & Andrews, 2003; Latimer, 2001; van der Stouwe, Asscher, Stams, Deković, & van der Laan, 2014), with more recent meta-analyses typically reporting small to medium effect sizes in reducing recidivism.

Specifically focusing on juveniles, meta-analytic results and systematic reviews have concluded that juvenile awareness programs (e.g., Scared Straight) are more harmful than doing nothing (see Petrosino, Turpin-Petrosino, & Buehler, 2003); boot camps and wilderness camps have demonstrated variable to modest overall effects (MacKenzie, Brame, MacDowall, & Souryal, 1995; Wilson & Lipsey, 2000), and cognitive–behavioral interventions have demonstrated significant effects on multiple outcomes (e.g., recidivism, mental health disorders, violence; see Cameron & Telfer, 2004; Özabacı, 2011; Townsend et al., 2010), particularly when implemented consistent with the risk–need–responsivity model (see Andrews & Bonta, 2010). Currently, the debate regarding juvenile rehabilitation programs has focused on the relative effectiveness of community-based programs versus programs delivered in residential or secure settings (see Greenwood, 1996, 2008; Henggeler & Schoenwald, 2011; Lipsey, 2009), including whether setting has an impact on effectiveness and under what conditions residential treatments achieve maximum recidivism reduction.

Grietens and Hellinckx (2004) provided a systematic review of five meta-analyses that focused exclusively on residential treatment programs (see Dowden & Andrews, 1999; Garrett, 1985; Lösel & Körferl, 1989; Lipsey & Wilson, 1998; Redondo, Sanchez-Meca, & Garrido, 1999). Collectively, these meta-analyses were published from 1985 to 1999, incorporated effects from 304 studies conducted between 1950 and 1995, and represented both North American and European countries. The overall mean effect size was 0.19 (SD = 0.09, 95% CI [0.08, 0.30]), reflecting average recidivism rates of 45.5% in the treatment group and 54.5% in the control group—an overall recidivism difference of 9%. Comparable recidivism rates drawn from studies of juveniles in nonresidential settings ranged from 0.12 to 0.70. Grietens and Hellinckx concluded that delinquent behavior appeared difficult to treat in residential settings. However, it is important to note that these authors did not conduct any formal analysis of moderators or provide any direct statistical comparisons of effect sizes between residential and nonresidential treatments.

De Swart et al. (2012) conducted a meta-analysis (k = 27) involving 17,038 youths to examine effectiveness of residential care. A unique focus of this meta-analysis was examining quasi-experimental studies or randomized controlled trials published from 1980 to 2011 that addressed the effectiveness of residential treatments by comparing effect sizes obtained for (a) institutional evidence-based treatment (EBT) compared with institutional care as usual (CAU; $k = 17$), (b) institutional EBT with noninstitutional EBT ($k = 1$), (c) institutional CAU with noninstitutional CAU ($k = 3$), and (d) institutional CAU with noninstitutional EBT ($k = 6$). Studies were coded as EBT using the definition supported by Weisz, Jenson-Doss, and Hawley (2006): an intervention that is structured and manual based with demonstrated empirical evidence.

Of the 27 studies, 15 involved a criminal justice intervention, with 12 studies classified as being conducted in a secure setting. A small overall effect size was obtained ($d = 0.129$, 95% CI [−0.69, 1.81]) with significant heterogeneity across effect sizes. Age, gender, study design, and type of outcome measure (i.e., delinquency, skills, problem behavior) did not affect effect sizes for institutional care. Two moderators uniquely contributed to the overall variation in effect size: (a) comparison between EBTs versus CAU in institutional settings ($d = 0.337$, 95% CI [0.138, 0.537]) and (b) cognitive–behavioral therapy (CBT) interventions ($d = 0.520$, 95% CI [0.281, 0.759]). In comparing the different types of interventions, only the comparison between institutional EBTs and institutional CAU yielded a small to medium effect size. All other comparisons were nonsignificant, indicating that care in institutional settings can be as effective as noninstitutional care, but that better results were obtained for EBTs in institutional settings relative to institutional CAU. De Swart et al. (2012) noted that variables generally viewed as responsivity factors (e.g., youth IQ, length of stay, size of living groups, and characteristics of youth care workers) could not be tested as moderators of treatment effectiveness.

With previous meta-analyses supporting the overall effectiveness of cognitive–behavioral programs in reducing recidivism risk, Landenberger and Lipsey (2005) conducted a meta-analysis of experimental and quasi-experimental CBT treatment studies ($k = 58$) to investigate potential moderators of treatment effects on 12-month posttreatment recidivism rates. The CBT studies included in this meta-analysis involved both adult ($n = 41$; 71%) and juvenile ($n = 17$; 29%) samples drawn from correctional ($n = 27$; 47%) and community ($n = 31$; 53%) settings. A major component of this meta-analysis was determining whether brand-name CBT treatments (e.g., Aggression Replacement Training; Goldstein & Glick, 1987) achieved greater recidivism reduction than programs that contained generic CBT elements (e.g., cognitive restricting, interpersonal problem solving). The average odds of success for offenders in the treatment group was 1.5 times the odds for those in the control group, reflecting a recidivism reduction of 25% to 30%. Consistent with previous meta-analyses, significant heterogeneity in effect size was detected. After controlling for method characteristics (e.g., intention to treat, randomized designs, type of recidivism), Landenberger and Lipsey determined that neither participant type (juvenile or adult) nor treatment setting (community or correctional) predicted treatment effect sizes. This result suggested that subsequent analyses of moderators were applicable to juveniles in secure settings.

Landenberger and Lipsey (2005) drew three major conclusions. First, after controlling for method effects, specific CBT therapies (e.g., brands such as Moral Reconation Therapy) did not account for differences in recidivism effect sizes. Second, CBT elements were positively associated with effect sizes; programs including interpersonal problem solving ($\beta = 0.32$, $p < .03$) and anger control ($\beta = 0.36$, $p < .03$) were associated with greater recidivism reduction. Conversely, victim impact ($\beta = -0.31$, $p < .02$) and behavior modification ($\beta = -0.31$, $p < .09$) were associated with lower recidivism reduction. Third, participant characteristics (recidivism risk rating), CBT quantity (e.g., sessions per week, hours per week), and quality of CBT implementation (e.g., training, fidelity monitoring) were stronger predictors than either CBT brand or CBT generic elements. On the basis of these results, Landenberger and Lipsey estimated that a best-practice CBT program would treat moderately high-risk offenders, use any brand-name CBT intervention, and stress anger control and interpersonal problem-solving skills over at least 16 weeks in a well-designed and well-implemented program (i.e., no design flaws, zero attrition, intention-to-treat analysis). This optimized best-practice program was estimated to yield a recidivism reduction of 52%, favoring treatment.

Lipsey (2009) conducted a meta-analysis that attempted to determine the primary factors affecting successful juvenile interventions by disentangling two key delinquency intervention characteristics: general level of juvenile justice supervision (e.g., no supervision, diversion, probation or parole, incarceration) and type of intervention philosophy (surveillance, deterrence, discipline, restorative, counseling, skill building, multiple coordinated services). Lipsey was interested in determining whether different programs were differentially effective on the basis of level of juvenile justice supervision. This analysis was conducted on the basis of an updated meta-analytic database of juvenile delinquency interventions (548 independent study samples; see Lipsey, 1992; Lipsey & Wilson, 1998), with the primary outcome being 12-month recidivism rate postintervention. After accounting for methodological differences, characteristics of the juvenile sample (i.e., gender mix, delinquency risk, aggression history) and intervention philosophy were associated with recidivism outcomes; however, level of supervision (probation vs. corrections) was not. Notably, after controlling for methodological differences and juvenile risk level, intervention effects were comparable across programs delivered in community and incarcerated settings. In contrast, quality of implementation (βs ranging from 0.13 to 0.25) and level of delinquency risk (βs ranging from 0.21 to 0.46) consistently predicted positive recidivism effects across the four major categories of intervention philosophies.

Although Lipsey's (2009) analysis suggested an optimistic overall appraisal of the effectiveness of juvenile justice interventions, isolating effect sizes for intervention philosophy within supervision settings indicated that counseling skills (i.e., individual counseling, group counseling, peer programs) were less effective in incarcerated settings ($\beta = -0.29$, $p < .05$). Consistent with earlier meta-analytic results, cognitive–behavioral interventions ($n = 14$) demonstrated a mean recidivism reduction of 26% ($\phi = .13$) after covarying methodological differences, type of juvenile sample, and juvenile justice supervision. The overarching conclusion reached by Lipsey (2009) was that after controlling for level of risk and other juvenile sample characteristics, interventions were equally effective regardless of supervision level, underscoring that institutionally based programs can achieve recidivism reductions similar to those of programs delivered in community settings.

What conclusions can be reached about the effectiveness of residential treatments for juveniles based on meta-analyses conducted over the past 2 decades? First, although significant, the average recidivism reduction achieved in residential programs varies from 10% to 30%, with significant variation in effect sizes attributed primarily to the methodologies used and the quality of treatment implementation. Second, regardless of treatment setting, cognitive–behavioral interventions result in larger recidivism reduction effects; however, specific CBT brands do not produce superior results when differences in methodology (i.e., intention to treat, experimental vs. quasi-experimental designs) and treatment implementation factors (i.e., level of training of treatment providers, fidelity monitoring, low dropout rate) are controlled. Third, quality of treatment implementation has consistently been associated with greater recidivism reduction. Although supporting cautious optimism about the effectiveness of residential treatments for juveniles, these results reinforce the need to carefully and critically examine potential barriers to implementing programs in residential treatment settings.

BARRIERS AFFECTING TREATMENT IMPLEMENTATION IN RESIDENTIAL SETTINGS

Implementing effective treatment programs in residential settings is challenging. Some of these challenges are common across community-based and residential treatment programs (e.g., staff training, treatment fidelity, and quality assurance monitoring; Penn, Esposito, Stein, Lacher-Katz, & Spirito, 2005; Schoenwald & Henggeler, 2003; Schoenwald, Henggeler, Brondino, & Rowland, 2000). However, residential treatment settings are often described as having a specific culture (see James et al., 2013; Lane, Goldstein, Heilbrun, Cruise, & Pennacchia, 2012) that can require organizational change to yield positive outcomes (Bloom, 2005; Rivard et al., 2004). For example, staff retention and turnover (Connor et al., 2003), burnout (Seti, 2008), compassion fatigue (Eastwood & Ecklund, 2008), staff attitudes toward treatment (Ahonen & Degner, 2013), and safety concerns (Orlando, Chan, & Morral, 2003) have all been related to implementing effective programs in residential settings. In addition, the effectiveness of behavior management programs (Holmqvist, Hill, & Lang, 2009; Taylor & Mudford, 2012), size of the youth census (Sternberg et al., 2013; Walker & McCormick, 2004), proportion of highly delinquent peers relative to total census (Dodge & Sherrill, 2006), length of stay (Jones, Chancey, Lowe, & Risler, 2010; Sternberg et al., 2013), and physical plant issues (e.g., layout, surveillance; M. Scott, 2009; Underwood, Warren, Talbott, Jackson, & Daily, 2014) have been related to program implementation and outcomes. More recently, empirical attention has been devoted to three specific factors as potential barriers to successful residential treatment of juveniles: (a) high prevalence of mental health disorders, (b) peer contagion and deviance training, and (c) youth and staff attitudes and facility safety.

Mental Health Disorders

Prevalence studies conducted with male and female justice-involved youths across a range of juvenile justice settings (e.g., probation, residential treatment centers, detention and secure custody) have concluded that approximately 65% of male and female juveniles meet diagnostic criteria for a mental health disorder (Schufelt & Coccoza, 2006; Teplin, Abram, McClelland, Dulcan, & Mericle, 2002; Wasserman et al., 2003). This rate surpasses mental health disorder prevalence estimates for males and female juveniles in community settings (42.6% in the National Comorbidity Survey Replication—Adolescent Supplement study; Kessler et al., 2012). Using a structured diagnostic interview, Teplin et al. (2002) reported that 73.8% of female offenders in this detained sample were identified with any disorder, compared with 66.3% of male offenders. Among female offenders, 30.8% were identified with anxiety disorders, 27.6% with any affective disorder, 21.4% with attention-deficit/hyperactivity disorder, and 46.8% with any substance use disorder, with rates varying little by age group (66.7%, age 13 or younger; 72.2%, ages 14–15; 77.6%, age 16 or older). A similar trend was found for male offenders, with overall prevalence rates lower for each diagnostic category except substance use disorders. Among male offenders, 18.7% were identified with anxiety disorders, 21.3% with any affective disorder, 16.6% with attention-deficit/hyperactivity disorder, and 50.7% with substance use disorders. Mental health disorders also varied little by age group for male offenders (52.7%, age 13 or younger; 68.0%, ages 14–15; 67.3%, age 16 or older).

Comorbidity is also quite common, with 46% of detained boys and 57% of detained girls diagnosed with two or more disorders (Teplin et al., 2013). Multiple substance use disorders are equally common among juvenile detainees (Teplin, Welty, Abram, Dulcan, & Washburn, 2012), as are co-occurring disorders (Hussey, Drinkard, & Flannery, 2007; Vaughn, Freedenthal, Jenson, & Howard, 2007). Substance use, conduct, and anxiety problems are common comorbid diagnoses that have also been documented as correlates of recidivism risk (Cottle, Lee, & Heilbrun, 2001). Among adolescent offenders, comorbid disorders also predict an escalating pattern of more frequent and severe future offenses relative to no disorders (Hoeve, McReynolds, Wasserman, & McMillan, 2013), and they differentially affect female adolescents, with mental health disorders being a stronger predictor of multiple delinquency outcomes (number of offenses, days in detention) among female than male offenders (Welch-Brewer, Stoddard-Dare, & Mallett, 2011). In fact, Hussey et al. (2008) determined that the complexity of overlapping problems for adolescent female offenders was associated with much higher use of residential treatment, individual counseling, and case management, increasing the overall treatment costs within facilities. Level of substance use problems was specifically associated with more risk factors and fewer protective factors, indicating that the presence of substance use disorders can attenuate general delinquency reduction interventions unless substance use problems are also addressed

(Hussey et al., 2008; Mulder, Vermunt, Brand, Bullens, & van Marle, 2012; van der Put, Creemers, & Hoeve, 2014).

Exposure to potential traumatic events is very common among juveniles, with 90% of male and female youths in detention settings reporting exposure to at least one lifetime potentially traumatic event (Abram et al., 2004; Ford, Hartman, Hawke, & Chapman, 2008) and 56.8% reporting six or more exposures (Abram et al., 2004). Previous maltreatment and violence exposure account for the vast majority of traumatic event exposures (Kerig, Ward, Vanderzee, & Arnzen Moeddel, 2009; Stimmel, Cruise, Ford, & Weiss, 2014) reported by youths in secure settings. However, female adolescent offenders endorse much higher rates of exposure to interpersonal traumas including sexual abuse (Kerig et al., 2009; Wasserman & McReynolds, 2011) than do male adolescent offenders. Yet for both male and female detainees, history of interpersonal trauma was a significant predictor of posttraumatic stress disorder (PTSD) symptoms, which subsequently predicted increased rates of other mental health difficulties in both male and female adolescent offenders (Kerig et al., 2009). As such, the number and type of trauma exposures have important implications for the behavioral and mental health functioning of juveniles in secure settings (Abram et al., 2004; Abram, Teplin, McClelland, & Dulcan, 2003; Becker & Kerig, 2011; Ford, Chapman, Connor, & Cruise, 2012; Kerig et al., 2009).

Rates of mental health disorders increase as male and female offenders penetrate further into the juvenile justice system (Espinosa, Sorensen, & Lopez, 2013; Wasserman, McReynolds, Schwalbe, Keating, & Jones, 2010). To illustrate, Wasserman et al. (2010) compared reports of mental health disorders across three different juvenile justice entry points (intake via probation or juvenile court, detention, or postadjudication or secure custody). Rates of any mental health disorder increased dramatically across these entry points (35.1% at system intake, 58.9% detention, and 63.7% postadjudication or secure custody), with the same trend being detected across affective, anxiety, disruptive, and substance use disorders. More specifically, with youths at system intake serving as the reference group, youths in detained and postadjudication or secure custody were 2.22 and 2.5 times as likely, respectively, to meet criteria for an externalizing disorder and 1.77 and 1.22 times as likely to meet criteria for an anxiety disorder.

Wasserman et al. (2010) found similar trends regarding lifetime and recent (e.g., past-month) suicide attempt history, with reported rates increasing across entry points for lifetime attempts (10.8% system intake, 17.7% detention, and 16.3% postadjudication or secure) and past-month attempt (1.9% system intake, 3.7% detention, and 2.5% postadjudication or secure). Even though female offenders represent a lower percentage of the overall population in secure settings, they are much more likely to be identified with mental health disorders than their male counterparts (Cruise, Marsee, Dandreaux, & DePrato, 2007; Teplin et al., 2002). Concerns have been raised that female adolescents are placed either in intervention programs designed for male adolescents or in programs that focus on putative gender-specific factors (self-esteem, empowerment) that are neither empirically tested nor adequately matched to criminogenic needs (Antonishak, Reppucci, & Mulford, 2004; Miller, Leve, & Kerig, 2012).

Recent data have reflected that mental health disorders persist during periods of incarceration. Karnik et al. (2009) measured mental health disorders in 790 youths (18% female) 9 months after incarceration. They specifically hypothesized that disorder rates would be lower than rates found by other researchers who have estimated prevalence at intake. After controlling for conduct disorder (CD) and oppositional defiant disorder (ODD), 88% of male and 92% of female youths were diagnosed with a mental health disorder after 9-month custody stays. Anxiety disorders (26% male youths, 55% female youths) and substance use disorders (86% male youths, 84% female youths) were quite common, indicating that time in custody could affect disorder rates. However, availability and impact of treatment were not addressed, and Karnik et al. acknowledged that the referral process within the jurisdiction could also have accounted for the consolidation of youths with serious psychopathology in the facility.

The prevalence and severity of mental health disorders reviewed here are consistent with the snapshot of mental health problems documented via surveys of youths in custody (Sedlack & McPherson, 2010b). Recent data have suggested that rates of disorders increase as youths penetrate further into the juvenile justice system, with severity of disorders being associated with higher risk and lower protective factors as well as increased risk for continued offending behavior (Chitsabesan et al., 2012). As such, the presence and persistence of mental health disorders require careful assessment and management when youths are placed in residential treatment programs, because the data suggest that the presence of mental health problems is one factor that could moderate the overall effectiveness of general rehabilitation programs (Chitsabesan et al., 2012; Starnes, 2013).

It is unfortunate that mental health factors have not yet been systematically studied to gauge their impact on recidivism reduction interventions. However, studies have indicated that patterns of psychopathology vary within subtypes of delinquent youths, which has important implications for assessing needs and matching to individualized treatment. Linking assessment and treatment in this manner will most likely reduce the likelihood of attenuated treatment effects when placing high-risk and high-mental-health-need youths into general delinquency reduction programs (Mulder et al., 2012).

Deviance Training

Deviance training refers to the process by which deviant peers positively reinforce deviant communication and behavior (see Dishion, Dodge, & Lansford, 2006), with evidence supporting the effects of deviance training as a form of negative peer contagion on subsequent delinquent behavior among adolescents in community settings (Dishion, Véronneau, & Myers, 2010; Freeman, Hadwin, & Halligan, 2011; Van Ryzin & Dishion, 2013). The consolidation of delinquent youths prone to reinforce deviant communication and behavior within group settings, including residential treatment settings, has raised concerns about residential treatments leading to iatrogenic harm (Bayer, Pintoff, & Pozen, 2003). However, results of meta-analyses specifically investigating iatrogenic harm in adolescent group treatment in general, and as a result of deviancy training specifically, have not been consistent.

For example, in their meta-analysis Weiss et al. (2005) defined an iatrogenic effect as "an effect wherein treatments involving peer groups were associated with significantly smaller or a significantly greater likelihood of a negative effect size" (p. 1041). Their results did not support the proposition that treatments with a peer group component were associated with greater likelihood of having a negative effect size. Other variables, including age, gender, degree of treatment structure, and length of treatment, also did not affect the likelihood of a negative effect size, suggesting little support for the deviancy training hypothesis (Weiss et al., 2005). These results were based on group treatments drawn from the general psychotherapy research and were not specific to either residential treatment or juvenile justice. Therefore, we review studies that have specifically addressed iatrogenic harm and the deviancy training hypothesis in these settings.

Shapiro, Smith, Malone, and Collaro (2010) conducted a study investigating iatrogenic harm effects among juveniles with first-time offenses placed in either a residential center (n = 1,255) or a community setting (n = 752). After they controlled for five predictors of recidivism (gender, age, race, severity of initial offense, family history of criminal behavior), they found that youths placed in a residential setting for a 4-week evaluation period had a significantly higher recidivism rate relative to similar youths who completed the same type of evaluation but in a community setting. Results from an unmatched sample were confirmed by matching youths across the two settings via propensity scores to control for the potential impact of placement. Through use of propensity matching, and controlling for other delinquent risk factors, Shapiro et al. concluded that the increased recidivism rate among youths in the residential setting could be attributed to the forced interactions with peers in this setting. This conclusion seemed reasonable, given that all youths were first-time offenders, other delinquency risk factors were controlled, and length of time for deviant peer exposure in the residential group was constant. However, a limitation of this study was the inability to specifically test the density of deviant peer contact in either setting.

Robst, Armstrong, and Dollard (2011) examined juvenile justice contacts among youths with mental health needs receiving care in residential treatment settings, specifically investigating whether the severity of delinquent behavior among peers in three types of residential settings (psychiatric inpatient, therapeutic group home, specialized therapeutic foster care) was associated with increased risk of juvenile justice contact during and after treatment. Robst et al. documented an association between peer delinquency at the end of treatment and juvenile justice contacts during and after treatment, with the rate of juvenile justice contacts increasing for youths treated in larger facilities.

In contrast, a series of studies conducted by Huefner and colleagues did not support a peer contagion effect in residential care settings. Huefner, Handwerk, Ringle, and Field (2009) studied youths with CD at admission and measured whether CD or ODD symptom severity at the end of treatment was predicted by conduct problems within units as measured by daily incident reports. They documented decreases in daily conduct problems during treatment and a significant reduction in ODD and CD symptoms among youths 1 year after admission, with the greatest reduction seen in youths in the CD diagnosis group. Huefner et al. concluded that these results did not support the deviance training hypothesis.

In a subsequent study, Huefner and Ringle (2012) examined negative peer contagion on the level of problem behavior (measured by daily incident reports) within residential care programs, addressing whether level of caregiver experience and length of stay in the program mediated this effect. Using hierarchical linear modeling, they determined that greater exposure to conduct-disordered peers was not related to higher CD or ODD behavior; neither staff level of experience nor youth time in the program affected the rate of CD or ODD behavior. More specifically, as the percentage of youths with CD in a residential group home increased, there was no association with change in CD or ODD behavior and no interaction between negative peer density (e.g., percentage of youths with CD diagnoses) and youth length of stay or staff level of experience.

Lee and Thompson (2009) conducted a sophisticated study of peer contagion in residential care settings using latent class analysis and growth curve modeling to determine whether youths placed in residential treatment environments with peers exhibiting high or increasing levels of externalizing behavior would display more externalizing behaviors over time. A particular strength of this study was the overall size of the study sample ($N = 744$ youths) in residential placement for more than 90 days, with all youths receiving the same model of residential care (the teaching family model) that included monitoring for fidelity and quality assurance. Individual-level trajectory class, representing change in problem behavior, was merged with data reflecting trajectory class membership of proximal peers to examine the degree of fit between change in problem behavior during residential care.

Lee and Thompson (2009) determined that individual youths had the highest probability of having the same trajectory as their proximal peers. Youths identified as having an individual trajectory group membership of gradual increasers had a 28% probability of proximal peers being in the same trajectory group. However, Lee and Thompson also found a similar pattern for gradual decreasers, with a 30% probability of individual or group trajectory match. Individual or group trajectory match for low problem (44%) and high flyers (55%) reflected a pattern of relative satiability at the lower and upper range of behavior problems. The results of this study demonstrated that there is some evidence to support a peer contagion effect in residential treatment settings (e.g., increases in problem behaviors matching trajectory of problem behavior of peers), but this effect appeared specific to about 10% of the overall sample, with 90% showing no increase in problem behaviors—or even a decrease in problem behaviors.

Results of recent studies investigating iatrogenic harm as a result of peer deviance training have produced mixed results regarding the extent to which the density of negative peers in residential settings has a significant impact on increasing problem behaviors. Commentators have specifically documented the challenges of delivering mental health services in juvenile justice facilities (Desai et al., 2006; Myers & Farrell, 2008), with negative peer effects seen as significantly contributing to diminished or ineffective services (Osgood & Briddell, 2006). A limited number of studies have empirically tested the magnitude of the negative peer-group effect in juvenile justice settings (Shapiro et al., 2010) or on new juvenile justice contacts during and after residential treatment (Robst et al., 2011). The peer contagion literature has broadly suggested that within residential treatment settings, exposure to youths with more conduct problems may negatively affect only a small number of youths (Huefner & Ringle, 2012; Lee & Thompson, 2009). It is not entirely clear from these studies how treatment programming, staff training, and monitoring youth–staff interactions influence the likelihood of iatrogenic harm from deviance training.

Youth–Staff Attitudes Toward Rehabilitation and Facility Safety

Another barrier to effective residential treatment can include (a) perceptions of rehabilitation effectiveness of the youths mandated to residential settings and the staff responsible for delivering care and (b) the availability of those services. A series of recent quantitative and qualitative studies has addressed these potential barriers.

Using qualitative methods, researchers have documented themes in adolescent attitudes toward rehabilitation during and after placement in residential treatment settings. Abrams (2006) conducted an ethnographic study of 19 male adolescents after institutional confinement to document their experiences with residential care and how they thought this care affected their motivation to desist from crime. A unique focus of this study involved comparing adolescent experiences across residential programs using varied treatment approaches (family systems versus cognitive–behavioral). Regardless of treatment type, adolescents consistently identified confusion regarding the purpose and goals of programming. Also, the level of structure did not affect the adolescents' perspectives on deterrence from future offending, and adolescents remained uncertain about their ability to change until they were discharged—reinforcing a concern regarding skill generalization from residential to community contexts (see also Abrams & Aguilar, 2005).

Holmqvist, Hill, and Lang (2007) investigated adolescent and treatment staff ratings of alliance and its impact on treatment outcome for treatments delivered in residential care settings. By measuring adolescent and treatment staff alliance, they examined the association between youths and staff and its relation to outcome. Data from this study indicated a positive association between adolescent and staff ratings of the collaborative alliance ($r = .45, p < .05$) and a general trend demonstrating that this reciprocal alliance was associated with a decrease in subsequent criminal justice contact. Collaborative alliance had a stronger impact than perceived emotional bond between adolescents and staff, indicating that when youths rated staff as active participants focused on treatment, this collaborative, task-focused approach was associated with better outcomes.

By measuring attributions of responsibility (internal or external) and attributions about reason for placement (internal or external), Englebrecht, Peterson, Scherer, and Naccarato (2008) determined that adolescents who accepted responsibility for their behavior that resulted in placement, and perceived that the treatment programming could help them, had higher overall rates of treatment engagement. Youths who did not accept responsibility, but perceived the treatment program as offering some benefit, also demonstrated higher rates of treatment engagement. However, this study revealed a significant attribution–engagement effect by gender; female offenders were more likely to endorse external attributions in both domains (responsibility and reason for placement) and reported the lowest levels of treatment engagement.

Marsh and Evans (2010) also found significant support for a combination of individual, relational, and program factors affecting adolescents' perceived likelihood of success postincarceration. In a large sample of male and female adolescent offenders ($N = 543$; 29% female), they predicted perceived likelihood of success on the basis of self-reported relationship quality, social support, and sense of program belonging. After controlling for ethnicity, age, time at facility, and social desirability, Marsh and Evans found that relationship quality, social support, and sense of program belonging predicted perceived likelihood of success for males, whereas only program belonging predicted the same outcome for females. For both genders, self-reported ability to regulate or cope with anger was also associated with greater perceived success.

Reflecting the theme of task orientation by treatment staff, Ahonen and Degner (2013) examined both quantitative and qualitative data to categorize staff into levels of staff group unanimity on how well they agreed to deliver treatment and achieve behavior change. They noted that residential units high in staff group unanimity had greater contact between staff and youths and higher levels of staff-supervised activities with youths in the residential programs. They concluded that fostering staff group unanimity among staff within units was important to achieving treatment change for adolescents in residential care settings.

Youth perceptions of safety within residential and correctional settings are implicated in effective treatment response. To illustrate, van der Laan and Eichelsheim (2013) investigated adolescents' perceptions of safety during institutional confinement and determined that higher ratings of safety were associated with the number of previous detentions ($\beta = 0.16, p < .05$) and more positive interactions with peer inmates ($\beta = 0.44, p < .001$). Positive interactions with staff promoted higher perceptions of autonomy ($\beta = 0.69, p < .001$) and well-being ($\beta = 0.30, p < .001$).

Rates of institutional misconduct are also relevant to effective treatment (see Levitt, 2010, for a review of juvenile victimization in institutional settings). Drawing on both the importation model (e.g., individual-level risk factors) and the deprivation model (e.g., negative or abusive conditions experienced within facilities), Kupchik and Snyder (2009) predicted victimization experiences based on Council of Juvenile Corrections Administrators Performance-based Standards data collected from juvenile detention and correctional programs across the United States. They found that a combination of facility- and individual-level variables (focusing on youth perceptions of the facility) best predicted victimization experiences within facilities. More specifically, facility type (correctional) and index of violent incidents at the facility predicted overall victimization rates. However, individual-level variables (understands facility rules, staff helpfulness index, positive school environment, and previous experiences with being locked up) were all significant predictors of victimization. Youths who understood facility rules, rated staff as helpful, and rated the school environment as positive were less likely to experience victimization. These same variables explained victimization experiences specific to fear, theft, physical abuse, sexual abuse, and fights with peers.

In summary, we have reviewed three potential barriers to effective intervention and recidivism reduction programming for youths in juvenile justice facilities: prevalence of mental illness, deviance training, and youth and staff attitudes toward treatment and safety. We selected these three factors because of the attention devoted to each in the empirical literature—and their possible contribution to the heterogeneity in recidivism effect sizes found in meta-analyses of juvenile justice interventions. The factor that has often been cited as negatively affecting treatment outcome (iatrogenic harm stemming from the large number of negative peers in residential treatment units) appears to have the least empirical support. The prevalence of mental health disorders among justice-involved youths has been well documented, with recent data suggesting that the deeper youths penetrate the juvenile justice system, the higher the rates of disorder (including comorbid disorders) and the greater the service utilization. Although studies have recently established links among mental illness, patterns of broader risk and needs, and future delinquent behavior, researchers have not yet addressed specific types of mental illness as moderators of response to general delinquency intervention programs. Similarly, the culture of residential treatment (youth attitudes, staff attitudes, and experiences within facilities) has not been investigated as a moderator of treatment effects, despite data linking each domain to perceptions of alliance, treatment engagement, and physical safety.

CURRENT RESEARCH EVIDENCE FOR RESIDENTIAL INTERVENTIONS

We now address results from recent studies of residential interventions tested with justice-involved youths. We focus on studies published in the past 10 years that have documented specific programs implemented within residential settings with juveniles. We exclude studies testing interventions only in community settings and meta-analyses that included only a small number of juvenile studies (see Ferguson & Wormith, 2013). The recent nature of this review allows us to address newly developing programs that were often not included in recent meta-analyses. We also focus on treatment programs that target general delinquency risk factors, specific mental health problems, or both when there is published evidence of intervention effectiveness consisting of (a) pilot studies demonstrating outcomes, (b) randomized controlled trials, or (c) quasi-experimental designs.

Trauma Response or Posttraumatic Stress Disorder

With the high documented histories of trauma exposure and PTSD among justice-involved youths, researchers have recently studied trauma-informed or trauma-focused interventions with juveniles in residential settings. Thoder and Cautilli (2011) examined the effectiveness of Mode Deactivation Therapy in a sample of 39 adjudicated boys (ages 14–17) in a residential treatment center. Mode deactivation therapy is a form of CBT that includes cognitive, affective, motivational, and behavioral components delivered using an individual and family manualized approach (Apsche, Bass, & Houston, 2007). Researchers reported a reduction in overall symptomatology, as measured by the Devereux Scales of Mental Disorders (a reduction of 1 standard deviation in the total score from 58.6 to 48.5) and Child Behavior Checklist (Internalizing Problems mean score reduced from a 63 to 53 at 12 months and Externalizing Problems mean score reduced from 63 to 42 at 12 months). Over a 4-year period, the sample had no felony arrests. Two (5%) had criminal charges during the first 6 months after discharge; the overall recidivism rate was 7%.

One program designed to promote psychoeducation about trauma response and to enhance current coping is Trauma Affect Regulation: Guide for Education and Therapy (TARGET; Ford & Russo, 2006). TARGET provides an educational and life skills curriculum and has been adapted for juvenile justice settings to address barriers to treatment in these facilities (e.g., mental health staffing is limited, addressing trauma may cause behavioral management problems or interfere with maintaining discipline). TARGET provides staff with tools to teach youths to better manage their emotions, thoughts, and behaviors using skills that enable them to better adhere to the rules and expectations of the placement. As such, TARGET is a manualized, gender-specific treatment and prevention intervention for traumatized adolescents or adults.

Ford and Hawke (2012) examined the effectiveness of TARGET in three juvenile detention facilities, controlling for site, length of stay, ethnicity, number of arrests, mental health and traumatic stress problems, and cohort effects. Data were collected from a sample of 394 admissions to three juvenile detention centers from 2006 to 2008. Of these youths, 197 received at least one group session of TARGET. A matched sample of 197 youths admitted to detention centers at which TARGET was not used made up the comparison group. At admission, two thirds of the youths reported at least one traumatic stressor in their lifetime, and 21% had full or partial PTSD. Ford and Hawke reported that every session of TARGET received in the first 7 days of detention was associated with a 54% reduction in disciplinary incidents and 72 fewer minutes of disciplinary seclusion for each youth during a modal stay (14 days). TARGET group participation was unrelated to recidivism; however, recidivism did decline significantly after implementation of TARGET (Ford & Hawke, 2012).

Although it was not specific to residential settings, Ford, Steinberg, Hawke, Levine, and Zhang (2012) conducted a randomized controlled trial comparing TARGET and a relational supportive therapy (enhanced treatment as usual) with 59 delinquent girls ages 13 to 17 ($M = 14.7$ years, $SD = 1.2$) who met full or partial criteria for PTSD. They reported that both therapies demonstrated large effect sizes for pre–post change in PTSD symptoms ($ds = 0.75–1.35$). Both had small to medium effect-size changes in anxiety ($ds = 0.27–0.61$), anger ($d = 0.46$), depression ($d = 0.65$), and posttraumatic cognitions ($d = 0.53$). A Treatment ×

Time interaction reflected small to medium effects favoring TARGET for change in PTSD ($d = 1.26$) and anxiety ($d = 0.61$) symptoms, posttraumatic cognitions ($d = 0.53$), and emotion regulation ($d = -0.35$) and favoring enhanced treatment as usual for change in hope ($d = -0.85$) and anger ($d = 0.46$). Although not specific to only residential treatment, these two studies (Ford & Hawke, 2012; Ford et al., 2012) demonstrated promising results among justice-involved youths and possible generalizability to residential settings.

Raider, Steele, Delillo-Storey, Jacobs, and Kuban (2008) suggested that CBT approaches to treating traumatized adolescent offenders may need to be supplemented with sensory-based therapeutic activities to assist with the processing of the implicit memories of trauma and to restore more effective emotional functioning. Raider et al. developed a structured trauma treatment (the Structured Sensory Intervention for Traumatized Children, Adolescents, and Parents—Adjudicated and At Risk Youth) that targets the major sensations experienced in a traumatic event (e.g., terror, worry, powerlessness) and conducted a randomized controlled trial to assess its efficacy with traumatized, adjudicated adolescents in a residential treatment setting. The sample consisted of 23 youths with a documented history of multiple trauma exposure. The participants were randomly assigned to the treatment group ($n = 13$) or the waitlist-control group ($n = 10$). Three participants dropped out during the treatment process. Two thirds of participants were between 16 and 17 years old; 11 were male and 9 were female. Study participants demonstrated statistically significant reductions in trauma symptoms, depression, rule-breaking behaviors, aggressive behaviors, and other mental health problems.

Substance Use

Several substance abuse treatment models have been evaluated in residential settings. They include gender-specific, integrated, aftercare, and promising unique treatment approaches.

Gender specific. Many of the studies evaluating the effectiveness of treatments with juveniles have been conducted with primarily male samples, limiting their generalizability to female offenders. Because girls often present with high levels of substance use problems, there is a need for effective treatments to address their substance-related problems and criminogenic behaviors. One such treatment developed for use with female adolescents is the Holistic Enrichment for At-Risk Teens (HEART; Roberts-Lewis, Parker, Welch, Wall, & Wiggins, 2009) program. HEART is a multicomponent, female gender–sensitive residential substance abuse treatment program that targets girls between ages 12 and 18 with substance abuse or dependence. HEART uses a therapeutic community model of service delivery that involves intensive and comprehensive residential treatment in which the participants take part in the management of the program. It uses a hierarchical treatment model that consists of five stages (orientation, adjustment, transition, honors, and community) that reflect increased levels of personal and social responsibility. Each stage has clearly defined written goals, activities, and expectations (Roberts & Welch, 2008). Treatment staff and participants are also trained in the use of CBT approaches such as problem solving, cognitive restructuring, self-control, social perception, and coping skills.

Roberts-Lewis et al. (2009) conducted a pilot study that evaluated HEART's effectiveness in changing the behavioral and cognitive skills of 34 incarcerated girls with substance abuse or dependence. They reported that the participants' behaviors and cognitive skills improved significantly as a result of treatment. More specifically, social involvement ($F = 3.61$, $p < .05$), social competence ($F = 6.12$, $p < .01$), self-control ($F = 10.59$, $p < .01$), self-monitoring ($F = 7.04$, $p < .01$), and prosocial behaviors ($F = 10.29$, $p < .01$) all significantly improved over the course of treatment. In addition, cognitive concentration skills ($F = 4.82$, $p < .05$), consequential thinking skills ($F = 5.28$, $p < .01$), and critical thinking ($F = 4.20$, $p < .05$) significantly improved as well (Roberts-Lewis et al., 2009).

Roberts-Lewis, Welch-Brewer, Jackson, Pharr, and Parker (2010) examined the effectiveness of the HEART program on the psychosocial functioning of 30 females in the pilot sample who completed both pretest and posttest measures. They reported that participants demonstrated significant improvement in eight of 10 areas of psychosocial functioning measured via the Problem Oriented Screening Instrument for Teenagers: mental health ($F = 11.107$, $p < .01$), family relations ($F = 11.187, p < .01$), peer relations ($F = 31.611, p < .01$), educational status ($F = 6.456, p < .05$), vocational status ($F = 4.258$, $p < .05$), leisure and recreational skills ($F = 30.621$, $p < .01$), and decreases in aggressive behaviors ($F = 10.208, p < .05$). The researchers concluded that the HEART program may be effective in decreasing some of the difficult psychosocial problems that females in juvenile correctional facilities experience before incarceration (Roberts-Lewis, Welch-Brewer, Jackson, Pharr, & Parker, 2010).

The HEART program was also evaluated to determine its effectiveness in improving problems related to personal and social functioning (Roberts-Lewis, Welch-Brewer, Jackson, Kirk, & Pharr, 2010). A quasi-experimental, two-group pretest–posttest repeated-measures design compared incarcerated female adolescents participating in HEART with 70 girls who received the standard substance abuse treatment intervention: group and individual counseling, substance abuse treatment based on the 12-step approach, and educational services based on a traditional education model. The researchers reported group differences favoring the HEART participants on posttest measures of three of the four social functioning scales: problems with friends ($F = 7.66, p < .05$), problems with family ($F = 5.28$, $p < .05$), and problems with school ($F = 7.66, p < .05$).

Integrated model. One evidence-based program for substance use and HIV prevention (SUHIP) was adapted for use with high-risk juveniles detained in secure correctional facilities. The SUHIP program combines two evidence-based interventions, Reconnecting Youth (Eggert, Herting, McCauley, & Randell, 2003) and Street Smart (Rotheram-Borus et al., 2003), adapting both for use with adolescent detainees. Reconnecting Youth is a school-based prevention program originally designed for high school students with the primary goal of eliminating substance use by developing various life skills (e.g., decision making, interpersonal communication). Street Smart is a program for high-risk youths that was designed to reduce HIV risk behaviors by influencing outcome expectancies, social skills, and self-efficacy. The SUHIP curriculum is a condensed version of both interventions that retains core elements of each.

Mouttapa, Watson, McCuller, Reiber, and Tsai (2009) conducted a pilot study comparing juveniles who received SUHIP intervention with a control group on several factors: knowledge of HIV prevention behaviors, attitudes and beliefs about HIV, attitudes toward condom use, rates of stimulant use, and self-efficacy for being drug free. The sample consisted of 48 participants (21 in the SUHIP group, 27 in the control group) from two all-male and two all-female 24-hour probation camps. Assessments were completed at baseline and 2 months after release to the community. Researchers reported that relative to the control group, SUHIP treatment participants demonstrated greater increases in knowledge of HIV prevention behaviors, $F = 7.46$, $p < .01$; decreases in erroneous beliefs regarding HIV vulnerability and testing, $t(20) = -2.32, p < .03$; increased ease in carrying and using condoms, $F = 5.20, p < .03$; lower stimulant use by females, $F = 7.30, p < .01$; and increased self-efficacy in avoiding drug and alcohol use, $t(20) = -4.48$, $p < .001$. In addition, SUHIP participants reported greater improvements in attitudes about school atmosphere, $t(20) = -3.31, p < .001$, and greater reductions in problem behaviors including fights, $t(20) = 4.42, p < .001$, and trouble with the law, $t(20) = 2.89, p < .01$. Mouttapa et al. concluded that incorporation of evidence-based HIV and substance use prevention programs into one integrated model was feasible in effectively targeting multiple risk behaviors for high-risk youths in juvenile correctional facilities.

Aftercare programs. Adolescents in juvenile justice facilities are among the least adequately served high-risk populations, experiencing service delivery gaps that may contribute to increased problems in mental health, substance use, and delinquency (Liddle, Dakof, Henderson, & Rowe, 2011). Aftercare services may help to ameliorate some of these issues when a juvenile is released from custody or a residential setting. One such program was adapted from an existing empirically validated intervention for drug-using adolescents (Multidimensional Family Therapy [MDFT]), adding a detention-to-community (DTC) component. The DTC component required development of a variation of MDFT. First, an in-detention module was added so individual and family interventions could begin rapidly after arrest. This module was delivered in the 3 to 14 days that youths were held in detention facilities. The second variation was the addition of a family-oriented HIV and sexually transmitted disease prevention module. Youths and their parents participated in three 2-hour multifamily groups designed to enhance their awareness of the nature of sexually transmitted diseases and HIV, personalize their sexual and drug-associated risk behaviors, and improve communication and prevention skills. The major components of MDFT–DTC are context and time specific, with in-detention and postdetention/community-based interventions among the key components.

Liddle et al. (2011) conducted a two-site randomized controlled trial to assess implementation outcomes and the effectiveness of MDFT–DTC for use in detention and aftercare. The MDFT–DTC group consisted of 76 participants (83% male) with a mean age of 15.5 (SD = 1.19), and the services-as-usual (SAU) group consisted of 78 participants (83% male) with a mean age of 15.4 (SD = 1.06). Liddle et al. reported that MDFT–DTC demonstrated better treatment enrollment and retention than SAU, with only 3% of MDFT youths failing to enroll compared with 45% of SAU youths. About 87% of MDFT–DTC youths and families were retained in treatment for 3 months or more compared with 23% of SAU youths. Youths and parents receiving MDFT–DTC were reportedly more satisfied with their treatment services than those receiving SAU: youth, $t(149) = 2.63$, $p = .010$; parents, $t(146) = 3.23$, $p = .002$. MDFT clinicians reported high levels of collaboration with juvenile justice professionals, achieving average values of 4 or higher (on a 5-point scale) on each of the Interdisciplinary Index of Collaboration items. In addition, when youths were discharged from detention, higher levels of collaboration with the MDFT–DTC group were associated with improvement in adolescent outcome, including decreases in substance use ($F = 3.54$, $p = .017$), marginal decreases in delinquency ($F = 2.40$, $p = .070$), and marginal decreases in the frequency of unprotected sex ($F = 2.63$, $p = .062$). Researchers concluded that results supported the effectiveness of the MDFT–DTC intervention and the need to develop an expanded model.

Promising programs using unique approaches. Orlando Edelen, Cerully, Verni, Tucker, and Fox (2013) explored whether mindfulness training could be successfully implemented with youths undergoing residential substance abuse treatment. Nine adolescent males in residential substance use treatment were enrolled in voluntary mindfulness training consisting of eight 90-minute sessions. Researchers reported that the mindfulness training program was perceived as helpful, acceptable, and feasible in the residential setting (Orlando Edelen et al., 2013).

Psychopathy

Little research has been conducted to assess the effectiveness of residential treatment with juveniles demonstrating psychopathic traits. Those researchers who have examined such treatment have used samples drawn from the Mendota Juvenile Treatment Center (MJTC), a program established in 1995 to treat aggressive, severely behaviorally disordered delinquent boys who were found to be unmanageable in other secure corrections settings. The MJTC program is operated as a secure juvenile corrections institution but housed on the grounds of a state forensic hospital. Thus, this program has a relatively high staff-to-adolescent ratio and access to a wide range of ancillary services from the hospital. Youths are typically transferred to MJTC when they have repeatedly failed to respond to rehabilitative services offered in the usual juvenile corrections institutions. The MJTC has 14- to 15-bed units and greater treatment resources than standard juvenile corrections institutions (JCIs). The treatment philosophy of the MJTC draws on the theory of defiance (Sherman, 1993) that describes a minority of offenders who react to deterrent sanctions with an increase in the frequency, persistence, and seriousness of violent or other antisocial behavior. The MJTC attempts to erode this defiance cycle with intensive treatment, replacing antagonistic bonds with conventional ones.

Caldwell, Skeem, Salekin, and Van Rybroek (2006) examined the treatment response of 141 male juveniles with high scores (*M* [mt] 27) on the Psychopathy Checklist: Youth Version. Youths were divided into two groups: a group that participated in the intensive treatment program at MJTC ($n = 56$) and a comparison group that participated in a less intensive treatment-as-usual program in a standard JCI ($n = 85$). Clinical assessment variables were measured for each youth; these variables included cognitive functioning, CD, psychopathy features, and treatment needs. Recidivism variables were also collected, including the number and type of charges filed over the 730 days after release from secure custody. Researchers reported that youths treated in the MJTC were significantly less likely to recidivate generally in the institution or community than youths treated in the JCI (57% vs. 78%). Only 21% of MJTC youths were involved in institutional or community violence within 2 years after release compared with 49% of JCI youths. After controlling for a number of covariates, researchers concluded that MJTC did not have an impact on general and nonviolent misdemeanor offending; however, MJTC-treated youths were 2.7 times less likely to become violent in the community than those in JCI.

Caldwell (2011) examined the associations among psychopathy, institutional behavior, and posttreatment offending in 248 male juveniles treated in the MJTC. The average age of the juveniles when released from treatment was 17 years, 1 month ($SD = 13$ months). The measures used in the study were the Psychopathy Checklist: Youth Version (Forth, Kosson, & Hare, 2003), institutional adjustment data, and recidivism data over a mean follow-up period of 54 months. Caldwell reported that the Psychopathy Checklist: Youth Version Interpersonal facet was significantly related to admission behavior problems, whereas other facets were not ($F = 3.80$, $p < .05$). Juveniles with higher Interpersonal facet scores demonstrated the greatest improvement in institutional behavior during treatment.

Overall, treatment group youths were charged with fewer crimes after release than were comparison group youths (3.27 vs. 4.88; $F = 6.36$, $p < .05$). Treatment was also associated with a significant decrease in general and violent offending for each facet. The Interpersonal facet was related to institutional and community violence for the sample ($F = 7.02$, $p < .01$) in a particularly important way, because those who score high on this facet may have skills that can be more readily used in pursuit of goals that are more conventional. Caldwell (2011) concluded that the treatment appeared to disrupt the link between violence and psychopathy in adolescents high on psychopathic traits.

Aggression Reduction

In recent years, a number of interventions targeting aggression reduction have been implemented and tested with juveniles in residential settings.

Aggression Replacement Training (Goldstein, Glick, & Gibbs, 1998; Hollin, 2004). Currie, Wood, Williams, and Bates (2012) illustrated some of the challenges in carrying out treatment research with an incarcerated population. With a sample of Australian male adolescents, they conducted a 2-year longitudinal study investigating aggression replacement training. Aggression Replacement Training encompasses three CBT components delivered in three separate 1-hour group sessions per week over a 10-week period. Specifically, skill streaming teaches effective social skills aimed at addressing aggressive behavior, anger control training aims to reduce frequency of anger arousal and teach techniques of self-control, and moral reasoning training facilitates moral–cognitive development (Currie et al., 2012). Currie et al. attempted to include a wait-list control group, but institutional factors did not allow them to recruit a group sizable enough for statistical comparison. Factors included variations in length of custody before parole and scheduling conflicts with vocational or education programs in which the potential participants were involved.

Twenty male adolescent participants completed self-report measures assessing aggressive behaviors, problem solving, and impulsivity at intake, posttreatment, 6-month follow-up, and

24-month follow-up (Currie et al., 2012). A significant main effect for time of total aggression score, $F(1, 19) = 12.65$, $p = .002$, partial $\eta^2 = .40$, was observed from pre- to postintervention, reflecting a significant reduction in self-reported aggression. In addition, participant self-reports on specific subscales—including physical aggression, $F(1, 19) = 16.43$, $p = .001$, partial $\eta^2 = .46$; hostility, $F(1, 19) = 8.70$, $p = .008$, partial $\eta^2 = .31$; and indirect aggression, $F(1, 19) = 11.04$, $p = .004$, partial $\eta^2 = .37$—reflect reductions in scores from pre- to postintervention.

EQUIP (Gibbs, Potter, & Goldstein, 1995). In a quasi-experimental study, Helmond, Overbeek, and Brugman (2012) evaluated a cognitive–behavioral program, EQUIP, for integrity and effectiveness in a sample of incarcerated adolescents. The EQUIP program was designed to teach peer helping and skill-building approaches to justice-involved adolescents by addressing cognitive distortions, social skills deficiencies, and moral developmental delays. EQUIP emphasizes both group culture and cognitive restructuring through curriculum (e.g., anger management, social skills training, social decision making) and mutual help (i.e., identify and replace problem-naming and thinking errors) meetings. The sample included 115 incarcerated adolescents (89 in the experimental group, 26 in the control group; 69% male; mean age at pretest = 15.54 years). Measures completed at pre- and postintervention included an adaptation of the How I Think Questionnaire (Barriga, Gibbs, Potter, & Liau, 2001) to capture cognitive distortions, an adaptation of the Inventory of Adolescent Problems—Short Form (Gibbs et al., 1995) to measure social skills, and the Sociomoral Reflection Measure—Short Form Objective (Brugman, Basinger, & Gibbs, 2007) to measure moral value evaluation and moral judgment.

Helmond et al. (2012) observed significant differences for social skills, $F(1, 97) = 4.799$, $p = .16$, partial $\eta^2 = .47$, and development of moral values, $F(1, 97) = 5.002$, $p = .014$, partial $\eta^2 = .49$, with the experimental group remaining stable and the control group showing a decrease in both areas. However, they observed no significant differences for cognitive distortions or moral judgment. These findings suggest that the EQUIP program can stabilize social skills and moral evaluation development for incarcerated adolescents (Helmond et al., 2012). More important, program integrity played a moderating role in EQUIP intervention effectiveness. Helmond et al. defined low program integrity as less than half of the EQUIP program being implemented as intended and moderate program integrity as more than half of the program being implemented as intended. Although they observed no differences between low versus moderate program integrity groups for cognitive distortions and moral judgment, low and moderate program integrity groups significantly differed from the control group on participant reports of social skills and moral value evaluation. Helmond et al. posited that the EQUIP intervention delivered at higher levels of program integrity could achieve stronger results but was adversely affected by a high program participant turnover rate (Helmond et al., 2012).

Responsive Aggression Regulation Therapy. Hoogsteder et al. (2014) conducted a quasi-experimental study assessing Responsive Aggression Regulation Therapy (Re-ART) in a sample of Dutch incarcerated juveniles. Re-ART (Hoogsteder, 2007) is a largely individualized intervention for aggressive youths based on principles of the risk–need–responsivity model, especially the responsivity principle (Andrews & Bonta, 2010). To increase responsivity to treatment, the therapy addresses obstructions such as demotivation, distrust, attention deficits, and low impulse control. The intervention is informed by the transactional model (Sameroff & Fiese, 2000), the theory of social information processing (Crick & Dodge, 1994; Dodge, 2006), CBT, drama-therapeutic techniques (e.g., role-playing games), and mindfulness. In Re-ART, a juvenile receives individual and group training over 12 to 14 sessions.

The Hoogsteder et al. (2014) sample consisted of an experimental group receiving Re-ART and a comparison group receiving treatment as usual. The participants completed multiple measures to assess treatment outcomes at pre- and postintervention, including assessment of risk of recidivism

(Structured Assessment of Violent Risk in Youth; Borum, Bartel, & Forth, 2002; Lodewijks, de Ruiter, & Doreleijers, 2003), aggressive incidents and aggression-related skills from the Re-ART list (e.g., self-control, assertiveness, and dealing with anger; Hoogsteder, 2012a), coping (Utrecht Coping List; Evers, Vliet-Mulder, & Groot, 2000), and cognitive distortions (Brief Irrational Thoughts Inventory [Hoogsteder, 2012b]; How I Think Questionnaire [Barriga et al., 2001]). At postintervention assessment, Hoogsteder et al. observed that the participants in the Re-ART group had significantly lower violent recidivism risk scores on the Structured Assessment of Violent Risk in Youth, $F(1, 84) = 19.78$, $p < .001$, reflecting a large effect size ($ES = 1.01$). In addition, for aggression reduction skills, Re-ART participants showed greater change in self-reported self-control than adolescents in the treatment-as-usual group, $F(1, 84) = 240.14$, $p < .001$; this pattern was also observed by adult mentors, $F(1, 84) = 51.41$, $p < .001$, reflecting large effect sizes (2.36 and 1.38, respectively). Moreover, a significant posttest difference was observed regarding aggression incidents in the sample. During the treatment period, fewer aggressive incidents were registered by staff for the Re-ART participants than for the treatment-as-usual participants, $F(1, 84) = 7.08$, $p = .009$, $d = 0.70$ (Hoogsteder et al., 2014). As such, Re-START was found to be more effective than treatment as usual in reducing recidivism risk and aggressive behavior in incarcerated juveniles.

CONCLUSIONS AND FUTURE DIRECTIONS

Despite significant reductions in the use of out-of-home placements, more than 100,000 juveniles continue to be placed in residential facilities as a result of contact with the juvenile justice system, and data reflect that minority youths continue to be disproportionately placed in such placements (Hockenberry, 2014). Regardless of race and gender, juvenile offenders in residential placements have extremely high rates of mental health disorders, are frequently exposed to victimization, and exhibit a pattern of general delinquency risk factors that collectively contribute to high recidivism rates after being discharged from residential placements (Chitsabesan et al., 2012; Espinosa et al., 2013; Sedlack & McPherson, 2010b; Teplin et al., 2002).

Even when placed outside of the community, juveniles should receive interventions that have demonstrated empirical support for reducing delinquency risk factors, enhancing positive development, and addressing frequently occurring mental health impairment. Meta-analyses reviewed in this chapter have indicated that the average recidivism reduction achieved in residential programs varies from 10% to 30%, with significant variation in effect sizes attributed primarily to the research methodologies used (intention to treat, experimental vs. quasi-experimental designs) and the quality of treatment implementation (level of treatment provider training, fidelity monitoring, dropout rate; see De Swart et al., 2012; Landenberger & Lipsey, 2005; Lipsey, 2009).

Our review indicates that the number of studies incorporating more rigorous research designs to test effectiveness of interventions delivered to youths in residential settings is small but growing (Caldwell et al., 2006; Ford & Hawke, 2012; Hoogsteder et al., 2014; Liddle et al., 2011; Roberts-Lewis, Welch-Brewer, Jackson, Kick, & Pharr, 2010). Although we are cautiously optimistic about the current level of effectiveness of residential treatment for juvenile offenders, if the current research trajectory continues, we will soon have an evidence base supporting effective treatment models that draw on promising or developing evidence-based practices to treat aggression, substance abuse, and trauma—critical, high-prevalence problems found among justice-involved youths in residential settings. Despite this cautious optimism, however, relatively small sample sizes, absence of replication, and inability to address moderators of treatment effectiveness remain as barriers to determining the overall effectiveness of residential treatments.

It is critical that researchers partner with local and state juvenile justice systems to select and implement programs with evidence of effectiveness and rigorously test such models in residential facilities against the accepted definition of evidence-based programming used for community interventions. This definition has two parts: (a) The program is manualized and (b) there is independent scientific evidence of its effectiveness in two separate juvenile offender samples (see Lipsey et al., 2010). Until widespread use of evidence-based intervention is achieved, residential programs should use interventions that are theory based or have some empirical support.

In evaluating residential interventions, researchers must investigate potential mediators and moderators of treatment effectiveness. This will help refine our knowledge of key treatment mechanisms and under what conditions or with whom treatments are most effective. The moderators that we have reviewed here include presence and severity of mental health problems (Chitsabesan et al., 2012; Espinosa et al., 2013), negative peer density and peer contagion (Huefner & Ringle, 2012; Lee & Thompson, 2009), and staff and youth perceptions of program integrity and safety (Holmqvist et al., 2007; van der Laan & Eichelsheim, 2013). The trend toward downsizing residential programs means that generating evidence of treatment effectiveness will often require using multiple facilities to obtain a sufficiently large sample. This in turn will require the use of nested research designs to examine the impact of facility-level differences.

With the increasing use of structured risk and needs assessments across the juvenile justice system (Viljoen, McLachlan, & Vincent, 2010), it is critical that juvenile justice researchers continue to study the implementation of such tools and their impact on placement decisions. A structured review of risk and needs can yield valuable observations of how needs are matched to services and when a youth is recommended for placement outside the community. Risk–needs–responsivity guided and empirically supported assessments should help inform residential placement decisions, just as they now often do in the community (Vincent, Guy, Gershenson, & McCabe, 2012; Vincent, Paiva-Salisbury, Cook, Guy, & Perrault, 2012; Vitopoulos, Peterson-Badali, & Skilling, 2012). Juvenile courts should adopt policies supporting communication of assessment results, with disposition decisions informed by the results of these assessments, and quality assurance monitoring of relevant outcomes. Unless research clearly establishes that general delinquency intervention programs are equally effective for youths with mental health difficulties, juvenile justice systems should consider expanding their use of diversion programs for youths with low recidivism risk and high mental health needs (see Colwell, Villarreal, & Espinosa, 2012; Sullivan, Veysey, Hamilton, & Grillo, 2007). Formal processing in the juvenile system increases the likelihood of out-of-home placement and may also limit the availability of mental health treatment.

In conclusion, recognizing that the juvenile justice system will continue to rely on and need a full continuum of care, it is imperative that resources be dedicated to examining the effectiveness of residential interventions. Such efforts will require continued investment by researchers, practitioners, and policymakers. But the return on this investment—ensuring that juveniles in residential placements can successfully reintegrate into the community at lower risk—means that it is critically important that it be made.

References

Abram, K. M., Teplin, L. A., Charles, D. R., Longworth, S. L., McClelland, G. M., & Dulcan, M. K. (2004). Posttraumatic stress disorder and trauma in youth in juvenile detention. *Archives of General Psychiatry*, *61*, 403–410. http://dx.doi.org/10.1001/archpsyc.61.4.403

Abram, K. M., Teplin, L. A., McClelland, G. M., & Dulcan, M. K. (2003). Comorbid psychiatric disorders in youth in juvenile detention. *Archives of General Psychiatry*, *60*, 1097–1108. http://dx.doi.org/10.1001/archpsyc.60.11.1097

Abrams, L. S. (2006). Listening to juvenile offenders: Can residential treatment prevent recidivism? *Child and Adolescent Social Work Journal*, *23*, 61–85. http://dx.doi.org/10.1007/s10560-005-0029-2

Abrams, L. S., & Aguilar, J. P. (2005). Negative trends, possible selves, and behavior change. *Qualitative Social Work: Research and Practice*, *4*, 175–196. http://dx.doi.org/10.1177/1473325005052392

Ahonen, L., & Degner, J. (2013). Staff group unanimity in the care of juveniles in institutional treatment: Routines, rituals, and relationships. *Journal of Offender Rehabilitation*, *52*, 119–137. http://dx.doi.org/10.1080/10509674.2012.751953

Andrews, D. A., & Bonta, J. (2010). Rehabilitating criminal justice policy and practice. *Psychology, Public Policy, and Law*, *16*, 39–55. http://dx.doi.org/10.1037/a0018362

Andrews, D. A., & Dowden, C. (2006). Risk principle of case classification in correctional treatment: A meta-analytic investigation. *International Journal of Offender Therapy and Comparative Criminology*, *50*, 88–100. http://dx.doi.org/10.1177/0306624X05 282556

Antonishak, J., Reppucci, N. D., & Mulford, C. F. (2004). Girls in the justice system: Treatment and intervention. In M. M. Moretti, C. L. Odgers, & M. A. Jackson (Eds.), *Girls and aggression: Contributing factors and intervention principles* (pp. 165–180). http://dx.doi.org/10.1007/978-1-4419-8985-7_12

Apsche, J. A., Bass, C. K., & Houston, M. A. (2007). Family mode deactivation therapy as a manualized cognitive behavioral therapy treatment. *Behavior Analyst Today*, *8*, 363–378.

Baldwin, S. A., Christian, S., Berkeljon, A., & Shadish, W. R. (2012). The effects of family therapies for adolescent delinquency and substance abuse: A meta-analysis. *Journal of Marital and Family Therapy*, *38*, 281–304. http://dx.doi.org/10.1111/j.1752-0606. 2011.00248.x

Barriga, A. Q., Gibbs, J. C., Potter, G. B., & Liau, A. K. (2001). *How I Think (HIT) questionnaire manual*. Champaign, IL: Research Press.

Bayer, P., Pintoff, R., & Pozen, D. E. (2003). *Building criminal capital behind bars: Social learning in juvenile corrections* (Center Discussion Paper No. 864). New Haven, CT: Economic Growth Center, Yale University.

Becker, S. P., & Kerig, P. K. (2011). Posttraumatic stress symptoms are associated with the frequency and severity of delinquency among detained boys. *Journal of Clinical Child and Adolescent Psychology*, *40*, 765–771. http://dx.doi.org/10.1080/15374416.2011. 597091

Bloom, S. L. (2005). The sanctuary model of organizational change for children's residential treatment. *Therapeutic Communities*, *26*, 61–78.

Borum, R., Bartel, P., & Forth, A. (2002). *Manual for the Structured Assessment of Violence Risk in Youth (SAVRY)*. Tampa, FL: University of South Florida.

Brugman, D., Basinger, K. S., & Gibbs, J. C. (2007). *Measuring adolescents' moral judgment: An evaluation of the Sociomoral Reflection Measure—Short Form Objective (SRM–SFO)*. Unpublished manuscript, University of Utrecht, Utrecht, the Netherlands.

Butler, S., Baruch, G., Hickey, N., & Fonagy, P. (2011). A randomized controlled trial of multisystemic therapy and a statutory therapeutic intervention for young offenders. *Journal of the American Academy of Child and Adolescent Psychiatry*, *50*, 1220–35.e2. http://dx.doi.org/10.1016/j.jaac.2011.09.017

Caldwell, M. F. (2011). Treatment-related changes in behavioral outcomes of psychopathy facets in adolescent offenders. *Law and Human Behavior*, *35*, 275–287. http://dx.doi.org/10.1007/s10979-010-9239-z

Caldwell, M., Skeem, J., Salekin, R., & Van Rybroek, G. (2006). Treatment response of adolescent offenders with psychopathy features: A 2-year follow-up. *Criminal Justice and Behavior*, *33*, 571–596. http://dx.doi.org/10. 1177/0093854806288176

Cameron, G., Frensch, K., Preyde, M., & Quosai, T. S. (2011). Community adaptation of youth accessing residential programs or a home-based alternative: Contact with the law and delinquent activities. *Residential Treatment for Children and Youth*, *28*, 150–175. http://dx.doi.org/10.1080/0886571X.2011. 577344

Cameron, H., & Telfer, J. (2004). Cognitive-behavioural group work: Its application to specific offender groups. *Howard Journal of Criminal Justice*, *43*, 47–64. http://dx.doi.org/10.1111/j.1468-2311.2004.00310.x

Chamberlain, P., Leve, L. D., & DeGarmo, D. S. (2007). Multidimensional treatment foster care for girls in the juvenile justice system: 2-year follow-up of a randomized clinical trial. *Journal of Consulting and Clinical Psychology*, *75*, 187–193. http://dx.doi.org/ 10.1037/0022-006X.75.1.187

Chitsabesan, P., Rothwell, J., Kenning, C., Law, H., Carter, L., Bailey, S., & Clark, A. (2012). Six years on: A prospective cohort study of male juvenile offenders in secure care. *European Child and Adolescent Psychiatry*, *21*, 339–347. http://dx.doi.org/ 10.1007/s00787-012-0266-9

Civil Rights of Institutionalized Persons Act, Pub. L. 96–247, 42 U.S.C. 1997 *et seq*.

Colwell, B., Villarreal, S. F., & Espinosa, E. M. (2012). Preliminary outcomes of a pre-adjudication diversion initiative for juvenile justice involved youth with mental health needs in Texas. *Criminal Justice and Behavior*, *39*, 447–460. http://dx.doi.org/10.1177/ 0093854811433571

Connor, D. F., McIntyre, E. K., Miller, K., Brown, C., Bluestone, H., Daunais, D., & LeBeau, S. (2003). Staff retention and turnover in a residential treatment center. *Residential Treatment for Children and Youth*, *20*, 43–53. http://dx.doi.org/10.1300/J007v20n03_04

Cottle, C. C., Lee, R. J., & Heilbrun, K. (2001). The prediction of criminal recidivism in juveniles: A meta-analysis. *Criminal Justice and Behavior*, *28*, 367–394. http://dx.doi.org/10.1177/0093854801028003005

Crick, N. R., & Dodge, K. A. (1994). A review and reformulation of social information-processing mechanisms in children's social adjustment. *Psychological Bulletin*, *115*, 74–101. http://dx.doi.org/ 10.1037/0033-2909.115.1.74

Cruise, K. R., Evans, L. J., & Pickens, I. B. (2011). Integrating mental health and special education needs into comprehensive service planning for juvenile offenders in long-term custody settings. *Learning and Individual Differences*, *21*, 30–40. http://dx.doi.org/10.1016/j.lindif.2010.11.004

Cruise, K. R., Marsee, M. A., Dandreaux, D. M., & DePrato, D. K. (2007). Mental health screening of female juvenile offenders: Replication of a subtyping strategy. *Journal of Child and Family Studies*, *16*, 615–625. http://dx.doi.org/10.1007/s10826-006-9111-4

Cullen, F. T., Smith, P., Lowenkamp, C. T., & Latessa, E. J. (2009). Nothing works revisited: Deconstructing Farabee's *Rethinking rehabilitation*. *Victims and Offenders*, *4*, 101–123. http://dx.doi.org/10.1080/15564880802612565

Currie, M. R., Wood, C. E., Williams, B., & Bates, G. W. (2012). Aggression replacement training (ART) in Australia: A longitudinal justice evaluation. *Psychiatry, Psychology and Law*, *19*, 577–604. http://dx.doi.org/10.1080/13218719.2011.615807

Curtis, N. M., Ronan, K. R., & Borduin, C. M. (2004). Multisystemic treatment: A meta-analysis of outcome studies. *Journal of Family Psychology*, *18*, 411–419. http://dx.doi.org/10.1037/0893-3200.18.3.411

Desai, R. A., Goulet, J. L., Robbins, J., Chapman, J. F., Migdole, S. J., & Hoge, M. A. (2006). Mental health care in juvenile detention facilities: A review. *Journal of the American Academy of Psychiatry and the Law*, *34*, 204–214.

De Swart, J. W., Van den Broek, H. H., Stams, G. M., Asscher, J. J., Van der Laan, P. H., Holsbrink-Engels, G. A., & Van der Helm, G. P. (2012). The effectiveness of institutional youth care over the past three decades: A meta-analysis. *Children and Youth Services Review*, *34*, 1818–1824. http://dx.doi.org/10.1016/j.childyouth.2012.05.015

Dishion, T. J., Dodge, K. A., & Lansford, J. E. (2006). Findings and recommendations: A blueprint to minimize deviant peer influence in youth interventions and programs. In K. A. Dodge, T. J. Dishion, & J. E. Lansford (Eds.), *Deviant peer influences in programs for youth: Problems and solutions* (pp. 366–394). New York, NY: Guilford Press.

Dishion, T. J., Véronneau, M. H., & Myers, M. W. (2010). Cascading peer dynamics underlying the progression from problem behavior to violence in early to late adolescence. *Development and Psychopathology*, 22, 603–619. http://dx.doi.org/10.1017/S0954579410000313

Dmitrieva, J., Monahan, K. C., Cauffman, E., & Steinberg, L. (2012). Arrested development: The effects of incarceration on the development of psychosocial maturity. *Development and Psychopathology*, *24*, 1073–1090. http://dx.doi.org/10.1017/S0954579412000545

Dodge, K. A. (2006). Translational science in action: Hostile attributional style and the development of aggressive behavior problems. *Development and Psychopathology*, *18*, 791–814. http://dx.doi.org/10.1017/S0954579406060391

Dodge, K. A., Dishion, T. J., & Lansford, J. E. (Eds.). (2006). *Deviant peer influences in programs for youth: Problems and solutions*. New York, NY: Guilford Press.

Dodge, K. A., & Sherrill, M. R. (2006). Deviant peer group effects in youth mental health interventions. In K. A. Dodge, T. J. Dishion, & J. E. Landsford (Eds.), *Deviant peer influences in programs for youth: Problems and solutions* (pp. 97–121). New York, NY: Guilford Press.

Dowden, C., & Andrews, D. A. (1999). What works in young offender treatment: A meta-analysis. *Forum on Corrections Research*, *11*, 21–24.

Dowden, C., & Andrews, D. A. (2000). Effective correctional treatment and violent reoffending: A meta-analysis. *Canadian Journal of Criminology*, *42*, 449–467.

Dowden, C., & Andrews, D. A. (2003). Does family intervention work for delinquents? Results of a meta-analysis. *Canadian Journal of Criminology and Criminal Justice*, *45*, 327–342. http://dx.doi.org/10.3138/cjccj.45.3.327

Eastwood, C. D., & Ecklund, K. (2008). Compassion fatigue risk and self-care practices among residential treatment center childcare workers. *Residential Treatment for Children and Youth*, *25*, 103–122. http://dx.doi.org/10.1080/08865710802309972

Eggert, L. L., Herting, J. R., McCauley, E., & Randell, B. (2003). *Reconnecting youth: Replication of an indicated prevention program in multicultural settings*. Washington, DC: U.S. Department of Education.

Englebrecht, C., Peterson, D., Scherer, A., & Naccarato, T. (2008). "It's not my fault": Acceptance of responsibility as a component of engagement in juvenile residential treatment. *Children and Youth Services Review*, *30*, 466–484. http://dx.doi.org/10.1016/j.childyouth.2007.11.005

Espinosa, E. M., Sorensen, J. R., & Lopez, M. A. (2013). Youth pathways to placement: The influence of gender, mental health need and trauma on confinement in the juvenile justice system. *Journal of Youth and Adolescence*, 42, 1824–1836. http://dx.doi.org/10.1007/s10964-013-9981-x

Evers, A., Vliet-Mulder, J. C., & Groot, C. J. (2000). *Documentatie van tests en testresearch in Nederland, deel 1 en 2* [Documentation of tests and test research in the Netherlands, Parts 1 and 2]. Amsterdam, the Netherlands: NIP/Van Gorcum.

Farabee, D. (2005). *Rethinking rehabilitation: Why can't we reform our criminals?* Washington, DC: AEI Press.

Ferguson, L. M., & Wormith, J. S. (2013). A meta-analysis of moral reconation therapy. *International Journal of Offender Therapy and Comparative Criminology*, *57*, 1076–1106. http://dx.doi.org/10.1177/0306624X12447771

Ford, J. D., Chapman, J. F., Connor, D. F., & Cruise, K. R. (2012). Complex trauma and aggression in secure juvenile justice settings. *Criminal Justice and Behavior*, *39*, 694–724. http://dx.doi.org/10.1177/0093854812436957

Ford, J. D., Hartman, J. K., Hawke, J., & Chapman, J. F. (2008). Trauamatic victimization, posttraumatic stress disorder, suicidal ideation, and substance abuse risk among juvenile justice-involved youth. *Journal of Child and Adolescent Trauma*, *1*, 75–92. http://dx.doi.org/10.1080/19361520801934456

Ford, J. D., & Hawke, J. (2012). Trauma affect regulation psychoeducation group and milieu intervention outcomes in juvenile detention facilities. *Journal of Aggression, Maltreatment, and Trauma*, *21*, 365–384. http://dx.doi.org/10.1080/10926771.2012.673538

Ford, J. D., & Russo, E. (2006). Trauma-focused, present-centered, emotional self-regulation approach to integrated treatment for posttraumatic stress and addiction: Trauma adaptive recovery group education and therapy (TARGET). *American Journal of Psychotherapy*, *60*, 335–355.

Ford, J. D., Steinberg, K. L., Hawke, J., Levine, J., & Zhang, W. (2012). Randomized trial comparison of emotion regulation and relational psychotherapies for PTSD with girls involved in delinquency. *Journal of Clinical Child and Adolescent Psychology*, *41*, 27–37. http://dx.doi.org/10.1080/15374416.2012.632343

Forth, A. E., Kosson, D., & Hare, R. D. (2003). *Psychopathy Checklist: Youth Version.* Toronto, Ontario, Canada: Multi Health Systems.

Freeman, K., Hadwin, J. A., & Halligan, S. L. (2011). An experimental investigation of peer influences on adolescent hostile attributions. *Journal of Clinical Child and Adolescent Psychology*, *40*, 897–903. http://dx.doi.org/10.1080/15374416.2011.614582

Garrett, C. J. (1985). Effects of residential treatment on adjudicated delinquents: A meta-analysis. *Journal of Research in Crime and Delinquency*, *22*, 287–308. http://dx.doi.org/10.1177/0022427885022004002

Gendreau, P., & Ross, R. R. (1979). Effective correctional treatment: Bibliotherapy for cynics. *Crime and Delinquency*, *25*, 463–489. http://dx.doi.org/10.1177/001112877902500405

Gibbs, J. C., Potter, G. B., & Goldstein, A. P. (1995). *The EQUIP program: Teaching youth to think and act responsibly through a peer-helping approach.* Champaign, IL: Research Press.

Glisson, C., Schoenwald, S. K., Hemmelgarn, A., Green, P., Dukes, D., Armstrong, K. S., & Chapman, J. E. (2010). Randomized trial of MST and ARC in a two-level evidence-based treatment implementation strategy. *Journal of Consulting and Clinical Psychology*, *78*, 537–550. http://dx.doi.org/10.1037/a0019160

Goldstein, A. P., & Glick, B. (1987). *Aggression replacement training: A comprehensive intervention for aggressive youth.* Champaign, IL: Research Press.

Goldstein, A. P., Glick, B., & Gibbs, J. C. (1998). *Aggression replacement training: A comprehensive intervention for aggressive youth* (Rev. ed.). Champaign, IL: Research Press.

Greenwood, P. W. (1996). Responding to juvenile crime: Lessons learned. *Future of Children*, *6*, 75–85. http://dx.doi.org/10.2307/1602595

Greenwood, P. W. (2008). Prevention and intervention programs for juvenile offenders. *Future of Children*, *18*, 185–210. http://dx.doi.org/10.1353/foc.0.0018

Grietens, H., & Hellinckx, W. (2004). Evaluating effects of residential treatment for juvenile offenders by statistical meta-analysis: A review. *Aggression and Violent Behavior*, *9*, 401–415. http://dx.doi.org/10.1016/S1359-1789(03)00043-0

Grisso, T., & Barnum, R. (2006). *Massachusetts Youth Screening Instrument, Version 2: User's manual and technical report.* Sarasota, FL: Professional Resources Press.

Grisso, T., Vincent, G., & Seagrave, D. (2005). *Mental health screening and assessment in juvenile justice.* New York, NY: Guilford Press.

Helmond, P., Overbeek, G., & Brugman, D. (2012). Program integrity and effectiveness of a cognitive behavioral intervention for incarcerated youth on cognitive distortions, social skills, and moral development. *Children and Youth Services Review*, *34*, 1720–1728. http://dx.doi.org/10.1016/j.childyouth.2012.05.001

Henggeler, S., & Schoenwald, S. K. (2011). Evidence-based interventions for juvenile offenders and juvenile justice policies that support them. *Social Policy Report*, *25*, 1–28.

Hockenberry, S. (2014). *Juveniles in residential placement, 2011.* Washington, DC: Office of Juvenile Justice and Delinquency Prevention.

Hockenberry, S., Sickmund, M., & Sladky, A. (2013). *Juvenile residential facility census, 2010: Selected findings.* Washington, DC: Office of Juvenile Justice and Delinquency Prevention.

Hoeve, M., McReynolds, L. S., Wasserman, G. A., & McMillan, C. (2013). The influence of mental health disorders on severity of reoffending in juveniles. *Criminal Justice and Behavior*, *40*, 289–301. http://dx.doi.org/10.1177/0093854812459639

Hollin, C. R. (2004). Aggression replacement training: The cognitive-behavioural context. In A. P. Goldstein, R. Nensén, B. Daleflod, & M. Kalt (Eds.), *New perspectives on aggression replacement training: Practice, research and application* (pp. 51–72). New York, NY: Wiley.

Holmqvist, R., Hill, T., & Lang, A. (2007). Treatment alliance in residential treatment of criminal adolescents. *Child and Youth Care Forum*, *36*, 163–178. http://dx.doi.org/10.1007/s10566-007-9037-z

Holmqvist, R., Hill, T., & Lang, A. (2009). Effects of aggression replacement training in young offender institutions. *International Journal of Offender Therapy and Comparative Criminology*, *53*, 74–92. http://dx.doi.org/10.1177/0306624X07310452

Hoogsteder, L. M. (2007). *Theoretical manual of the responsive aggressive regulation therapy*. Den Helder, the Netherlands: R. I. J. De Doggershoek.

Hoogsteder, L. M. (2012a). *Manual aggression related cognitive and social skills list*. Castricum, the Netherlands: Tingkah.

Hoogsteder, L. M. (2012b). *Manual list irrational thoughts*. Castricum, the Netherlands: Tingkah.

Hoogsteder, L. M., Kuijpers, N., Stams, G. J. J. M., van Horn, J. E., Hendriks, J., & Wissink, I. B. (2014). Study on the effectiveness of responsive aggression regulation therapy (Re-ART). *International Journal of Forensic Mental Health*, *13*, 25–35. http://dx.doi.org/10.1080/14999013.2014.893711

Huefner, J. C., Handwerk, M. L., Ringle, J. L., & Field, C. E. (2009). Conduct disordered youth in group care: An examination of negative peer influence. *Journal of Child and Family Studies*, *18*, 719–730. http://dx.doi.org/10.1007/s10826-009-9278-6

Huefner, J. C., & Ringle, J. L. (2012). Examination of negative peer contagion in a residential care setting. *Journal of Child and Family Studies*, *21*, 807–815. http://dx.doi.org/10.1007/s10826-011-9540-6

Hussey, D. L., Drinkard, A. M., Falletta, L., & Flannery, D. J. (2008). Understanding clinical complexity in delinquent youth: Comorbidities, service utilization, cost, and outcomes. *Journal of Psychoactive Drugs*, *40*, 85–95. http://dx.doi.org/10.1080/02791072.2008.10399764

Hussey, D. L., Drinkard, A. M., & Flannery, D. J. (2007). Comorbid substance use and mental disorders among offending youth. *Journal of Social Work Practice in the Addictions*, *7*, 117–138. http://dx.doi.org/10.1300/J160v07n01_07

James, S., Alemi, Q., & Zepeda, V. (2013). Effectiveness and implementation of evidence-based practices in residential care settings. *Children and Youth Services Review*, *35*, 642–656. http://dx.doi.org/10.1016/j.childyouth.2013.01.007

Jones, C. D., Chancey, R., Lowe, L. A., & Risler, E. A. (2010). Residential treatment for sexually abusive youth: An assessment of treatment outcomes. *Research on Social Work Practice*, *20*, 172–182. http://dx.doi.org/10.1177/1049731509333349

Juvenile Justice and Delinquency Prevention Act of 2002, Pub. L. 107–273, No. 42 U.S.C. 5602.

Karnik, N. S., Soller, M., Redlich, A., Silverman, M., Kraemer, H. C., Haapanen, R., & Steiner, H. (2009). Prevalence of and gender differences in psychiatric disorders among juvenile delinquents incarcerated for nine months. *Psychiatric Services*, *60*, 838–841. http://dx.doi.org/10.1176/appi.ps.60.6.838

Kempf-Leonard, K. (2007). Minority youths and juvenile justice: Disproportionate minority contact after nearly 20 years of reform efforts. *Youth Violence and Juvenile Justice*, *5*, 71–87. http://dx.doi.org/10.1177/1541204006295159

Kerig, P. K., Ward, R. M., Vanderzee, K. L., & Arnzen Moeddel, M. (2009). Posttraumatic stress as a mediator of the relationship between trauma and mental health problems among juvenile delinquents. *Journal of Youth and Adolescence*, *38*, 1214–1225. http://dx.doi.org/10.1007/s10964-008-9332-5

Kessler, R. C., Avenevoli, S., Costello, J., Green, J. G., Gruber, M. J., McLaughlin, K. A., . . . Merikangas, K. R. (2012). Severity of 12-month *DSM–IV* disorders in the National Comorbidity Survey Replication Adolescent Supplement. *Archives of General Psychiatry*, *69*, 381–389. http://dx.doi.org/10.1001/archgenpsychiatry.2011.1603

Kupchik, A., & Snyder, R. (2009). The impact of juvenile inmates' perceptions and facility characteristics on victimization in juvenile correctional facilities. *Prison Journal*, *89*, 265–285. http://dx.doi.org/10.1177/0032885509339505

Landenberger, N. A., & Lipsey, M. W. (2005). The positive effects of cognitive-behavioral programs for offenders: A meta-analysis of factors associated with effective treatment. *Journal of Experimental Criminology*, *1*, 451–476. http://dx.doi.org/10.1007/s11292-005-3541-7

Lane, C., Goldstein, N. E., Heilbrun, K., Cruise, K. R., & Pennacchia, D. (2012). Obstacles to research in residential juvenile justice facilities: Recommendations for researchers. *Behavioral Sciences and the Law*, *30*, 49–68. http://dx.doi.org/10.1002/bsl.1991

Latimer, J. (2001). A meta-analytic examination of youth delinquency, family treatment, and recidivism. *Canadian Journal of Criminology*, *43*, 237–253.

Lee, B. R., & Thompson, R. (2009). Examining externalizing behavior trajectories of youth in group homes:

Is there evidence for peer contagion? *Journal of Abnormal Child Psychology*, *37*, 31–44. http://dx.doi.org/10.1007/s10802-008-9254-4

Leve, L. D., & Chamberlain, P. (2007). A randomized evaluation of multidimensional treatment foster care: Effects on school attendance and homework completion in juvenile justice girls. *Research on Social Work Practice*, *17*, 657–663. http://dx.doi.org/10.1177/1049731506293971

Levitt, L. (2010). The comparative risk of mistreatment for juveniles in detention facilities and state prisons. *International Journal of Forensic Mental Health*, *9*, 44–54. http://dx.doi.org/10.1080/14999013.2010.483344

Liddle, H. A., Dakof, G. A., Henderson, C., & Rowe, C. (2011). Implementation outcomes of multidimensional family therapy-detention to community: A reintegration program for drug-using juvenile detainees. *International Journal of Offender Therapy and Comparative Criminology*, *55*, 587–604. http://dx.doi.org/10.1177/0306624X10366960

Lipsey, M. W. (1992). Juvenile delinquency treatment. A meta-analytic inquiry into the variability of effects. In T. D. Cook, H. Cooper, D. S. Cordray, H. Hartmann, L. V. Hedges, R. J. Light, . . . Mosteller, F. (Eds.), *Meta-analysis for explanation: A casebook* (pp. 83–127). New York, NY: Russell Sage Foundation.

Lipsey, M. W. (2009). The primary factors that characterize effective interventions with juvenile offenders: A meta-analytic overview. *Victims and Offenders*, *4*, 124–147. http://dx.doi.org/10.1080/15564880802612573

Lipsey, M. W., Howell, J. C., Kelly, M. R., Chapman, G., & Carver, D. (2010). *Improving the effectiveness of juvenile justice programs: A new perspective on evidence-based practices*. Retrieved from http://cjjr.georgetown.edu/pdfs/ebp/ebppaper.pdf

Lipsey, M. W., & Wilson, D. B. (1998). Effective intervention for serious juvenile offenders: A synthesis of research. In R. Loeber & D. Farrington (Eds.), *Serious and violent juvenile offenders: Risk factors and successful interventions* (pp. 313–345). Thousand Oaks, CA: Sage.

Lodewijks, H. P., de Ruiter, C., & Doreleijers, T. A. (2003). Risk assessment and risk management of violent behaviour of adolescents. *Directive Therapy*, *23*, 25–42. http://dx.doi.org/10.1007/BF03060301

Lösel, F., & Köferl, P. (1989). Evaluation research on correctional treatment in West Germany: A meta-analysis. In H. Wegener, F. Lösel, & J. Haisch (Eds.), *Criminal behavior and the justice system: Psychological perspectives* (pp. 334–355). http://dx.doi.org/10.1007/978-3-642-86017-1_21

MacKenzie, D. L., Brame, R., MacDowell, D., & Souryal, G. (1995). Boot camp prisons and recidivism in eight states. *Criminology*, *33*, 327–358. http://dx.doi.org/10.1111/j.1745-9125.1995.tb01181.x

Marsh, S. C., & Evans, W. P. (2010). Personal and social characteristics associated with perceived likelihood of success in incarcerated youth. *Residential Treatment for Children and Youth*, *27*, 304–313. http://dx.doi.org/10.1080/0886571X.2010.522895

Martinson, R. (1974). What works? Questions and answers about prison reform. *Public Interest*, *35*, 22–54.

Mihalic, S., Irwin, K., Elliott, D., Fagan, A., & Hansen, D. (2011). *Blueprints for violence prevention*. Washington, DC: Office of Juvenile Justice and Delinquency Prevention.

Miller, S., Leve, L. D., & Kerig, P. K. (Eds.). (2012). *Delinquent girls: Contexts, relationships, and adaptation*. http://dx.doi.org/10.1007/978-1-4614-0415-6

Mouttapa, M., Watson, D. W., McCuller, W. J., Reiber, C., & Tsai, W. (2009). Substance use and HIV prevention for youth in correctional facilities. *Journal of Correctional Education*, *60*, 289–315.

Mulder, E., Vermunt, J., Brand, E., Bullens, R., & van Marle, H. (2012). Recidivism in subgroups of serious juvenile offenders: Different profiles, different risks? *Criminal Behaviour and Mental Health*, *22*, 122–135. http://dx.doi.org/10.1002/cbm.1819

Myers, D. M., & Farrell, A. F. (2008). Reclaiming lost opportunities: Applying public health models in juvenile justice. *Children and Youth Services Review*, *30*, 1159–1177. http://dx.doi.org/10.1016/j.childyouth.2008.03.002

New York State Office of the Governor. (2012). *Governor Cuomo, Majority Leader Skelos, and Speaker Silver announce agreement on 2012–2013 budget*. Retrieved from http://www.governor.ny.gov/news/governor-cuomo-majority-leader-skelos-and-speaker-silver-announce-agreement-2012-2013-budget

Orlando, M., Chan, K. S., & Morral, A. R. (2003). Retention of court-referred youths in residential treatment programs: Client characteristics and treatment process effects. *American Journal of Drug and Alcohol Abuse*, *29*, 337–357. http://dx.doi.org/10.1081/ADA-120020518

Orlando Edelen, M., Cerully, J. L., Verni, K. A., Tucker, J. S., & Fox, E. (2013). Implementation of mindfulness training for adolescent residential clients. *Therapeutic Communities*, *34*, 96–103. http://dx.doi.org/10.1108/TC-03-2013-0003

Osgood, D. W., & Briddell, L. O. (2006). Peer effects in juvenile justice. In K. A. Dodge, T. J. Dishion, & J. E. Landsford (Eds.), *Deviant peer influences in programs for youth: Problems and solutions* (pp. 141–161). New York, NY: Guilford Press.

Özabacı, N. (2011). Cognitive behavioural therapy for violent behaviour in children and adolescents:

A meta-analysis. *Children and Youth Services Review*, *33*, 1989–1993. http://dx.doi.org/10.1016/j.childyouth.2011.05.027

Penn, J. V., Esposito, C., Stein, L. A., Lacher-Katz, M., & Spirito, A. (2005). Juvenile correctional workers' perceptions of suicide risk factors and mental health issues of incarcerated juveniles. *Journal of Correctional Health Care*, *11*, 333–346. http://dx.doi.org/10.1177/107834580401100403

Petrosino, A., Turpin-Petrosino, C., & Buehler, J. (2003). Scared Straight and other juvenile awareness programs for preventing juvenile delinquency: A systematic review of the randomized experimental evidence. *Annals of the American Academy of Political and Social Science*, *589*, 41–62. http://dx.doi.org/10.1177/0002716203254693

Piquero, A. R. (2008). Disproportionate minority contact. *Future of Children*, *18*, 59–79. http://dx.doi.org/10.1353/foc.0.0013

Puzzanchera, C. (2013). *Juvenile arrests 2011*. Washington, DC: Office of Juvenile Justice and Delinquency Prevention.

Raider, M. C., Steele, W., Delillo-Storey, M., Jacobs, J., & Kuban, C. (2008). Structured sensory therapy (SITCAP-ART) for traumatized adjudicated adolescents in residential treatment. *Residential Treatment for Children and Youth*, *25*, 167–185. http://dx.doi.org/10.1080/08865710802310178

Redondo, S., Sanchez-Meca, J., & Garrido, V. (1999). The influence of treatment programs on the recidivism of juvenile and adult offenders: A European meta-analytic review. *Psychology, Crime, and Law*, *5*, 251–278. http://dx.doi.org/10.1080/10683169908401769

Rivard, J. C., McCorkle, D., Duncan, M. E., Pasquale, L. E., Bloom, S. L., & Abramovitz, R. (2004). Implementing a trauma recovery framework for youths in residential treatment. *Child and Adolescent Social Work Journal*, *21*, 529–550. http://dx.doi.org/10.1023/B:CASW.0000043363.14978.e6

Roberts, A., & Welch, C. (2008). Incarcerated teens and substance abuse: The HEART Program. In C. LeCroy & J. Mann (Eds.), *Handbook of prevention and intervention programs for adolescent girls* (pp. 269–304). Hoboken, NJ: Wiley.

Roberts-Lewis, A. C., Parker, S., Welch, C., Wall, A., & Wiggins, P. (2009). Evaluating the cognitive and behavioral outcomes of incarcerated adolescent females receiving substance abuse treatment: A pilot study. *Journal of Child and Adolescent Substance Abuse*, *18*, 157–171. http://dx.doi.org/10.1080/10678280902724093

Roberts-Lewis, A. C., Welch-Brewer, C. L., Jackson, M. S., Kirk, R., & Pharr, O. (2010). Assessing change in psychosocial functioning of incarcerated girls with a substance use disorder: Gender sensitive substance abuse intervention. *Journal of Offender Rehabilitation*, *49*, 479–494. http://dx.doi.org/10.1080/10509674.2010.510771

Roberts-Lewis, A. C., Welch-Brewer, C. L., Jackson, M. S., Pharr, O., & Parker, S. (2010). Female juvenile offenders with HEART: Preliminary findings of an intervention model for female juvenile offenders with substance use problems. *Journal of Drug Issues*, *40*, 611–625. http://dx.doi.org/10.1177/002204261004000304

Robst, J., Armstrong, M., & Dollard, N. (2011). Peer contagion among youth in Medicaid-funded residential mental health treatment programs. *Children and Youth Services Review*, *33*, 651–655. http://dx.doi.org/10.1016/j.childyouth.2010.11.007

Robst, J., Armstrong, M., Dollard, N., & Rohrer, L. (2013). Arrests among youth after out-of-home mental health treatment: Comparisons across community and residential treatment settings. *Criminal Behaviour and Mental Health*, *23*, 162–176. http://dx.doi.org/10.1002/cbm.1871

Rotheram-Borus, M. J., Song, J., Gwadz, M., Lee, M., Van Rossem, R., & Koopman, C. (2003). Reductions in HIV risk among runaway youth. *Prevention Science*, *4*, 173–187. http://dx.doi.org/10.1023/A:1024697706033

Sameroff, A. J., & Fiese, B. H. (2000). Transactional regulation: The developmental ecology of early intervention. In J. P. Shonkoff & S. J. Meisels (Eds.), *Handbook of early childhood intervention* (pp. 135–159). http://dx.doi.org/10.1017/CBO9780511529320.009

Schoenwald, S. K., & Henggeler, S. W. (2003). Introductory comments. *Cognitive and Behavioral Practice*, *10*, 275–277. http://dx.doi.org/10.1016/S1077-7229(03)80045-7

Schoenwald, S. K., Henggeler, S. W., Brondino, M. J., & Rowland, M. D. (2000). Multisystemic therapy: Monitoring treatment fidelity. *Family Process*, *39*, 83–103. http://dx.doi.org/10.1111/j.1545-5300.2000.39109.x

Schufelt, J., & Coccoza, J. J. (2006). *Youth with mental health disorders in the juvenile justice system: Results from a multi-state prevalence study*. Delmar, NY: National Center for Mental Health and Juvenile Justice.

Scott, E. S., & Steinberg, L. (2008). *Rethinking juvenile justice*. Cambridge, MA: Harvard University Press.

Scott, M. (2009). Treating youths in correctional facilities. *Psychiatric Services*, *60*, 1142. http://dx.doi.org/10.1176/appi.ps.60.8.1142

Sedlack, A. J. (2010). *Introduction to the Survey of Youth in Residential Placement*. Washington, DC: Office of Juvenile Justice and Delinquency Prevention.

Sedlack, A. J., & McPherson, K. S. (2010a). *Conditions of confinement: Findings from the Survey of Youth in*

Residential Placement. Washington, DC: Office of Juvenile Justice and Delinquency Prevention.

Sedlack, A. J., & McPherson, K. S. (2010b). *Youth's needs and services: Findings from the Survey of Youth in Residential Placement*. Washington, DC: Office of Juvenile Justice and Delinquency Prevention.

Sedlack, A. J., McPherson, K. S., & Basena, M. (2013). *Nature and risk of victimization: Findings from the Survey of Youth in Residential Placement*. Washington, DC: Office of Juvenile Justice and Delinquency Prevention.

Seti, C. L. (2008). Causes and treatment of burnout in residential child care workers: A review of the research. *Residential Treatment for Children and Youth*, *24*, 197–229. http://dx.doi.org/10.1080/08865710802111972

Sexton, T., & Turner, C. W. (2011). The effectiveness of functional family therapy for youth with behavioral problems in a community practice setting. *Journal of Family Psychology*, *24*, 339–348. http://dx.doi.org/10.1037/a0019406

Shapiro, C. J., Smith, B. H., Malone, P. S., & Collaro, A. L. (2010). Natural experiment in deviant peer exposure and youth recidivism. *Journal of Clinical Child and Adolescent Psychology*, *39*, 242–251. http://dx.doi.org/10.1080/15374410903532635

Sherman, L. (1993). Defiance, deterrence, and irrelevance: A theory of the criminal sanction. *Journal of Research in Crime and Delinquency*, *30*, 445–474. http://dx.doi.org/10.1177/0022427893030004006

Soler, M., Schoenberg, D., & Schindler, M. (2009). Juvenile justice: Lessons for a new era. *Georgetown Journal on Poverty Law and Policy*, *16*, 483–541.

Starnes, T. (2013). Altering outcomes in juvenile offending: The evidence base. *Adolescent Psychiatry*, *3*, 316–323. http://dx.doi.org/10.2174/22106766030414012117370l

Steinberg, L. (2009). Adolescent development and juvenile justice. *Annual Review of Clinical Psychology*, *5*, 459–485. http://dx.doi.org/10.1146/annurev.clinpsy.032408.153603

Sternberg, N., Thompson, R. W., Smith, G., Klee, S., Cubellis, L., Davidowitz, J., . . . Schnur, E. (2013). Outcomes in children's residential treatment centers: A national survey 2010. *Residential Treatment for Children and Youth*, *30*, 93–118. http://dx.doi.org/10.1080/0886571X.2013.785221

Stimmel, M. A., Cruise, K. R., Ford, J. D., & Weiss, R. A. (2014). Trauma exposure, posttraumatic stress disorder symptomatology, and aggression in male juvenile offenders. *Psychological Trauma*, *6*, 184–191. http://dx.doi.org/10.1037/a0032509

Sullivan, C. J., Veysey, B. M., Hamilton, Z. K., & Grillo, M. (2007). Reducing out-of-community placement and recidivism: Diversion of delinquent youth with mental health and substance use problems from the justice system. *International Journal of Offender Therapy and Comparative Criminology*, *51*, 555–577. http://dx.doi.org/10.1177/0306624X06296237

Sunseri, P. A. (2005). Children referred to residential care: Reducing multiple placements, managing costs and improving treatment outcomes. *Residential Treatment for Children and Youth*, *22*, 55–66. http://dx.doi.org/10.1300/J007v22n03_04

Taylor, S., & Mudford, O. C. (2012). Improving behavior in a residential service for youth in drug and alcohol rehabilitation. *Behavioral Interventions*, *27*, 109–128. http://dx.doi.org/10.1002/bin.1342

Teplin, L. A., Abram, K. M., McClelland, G. M., Dulcan, M. K., & Mericle, A. A. (2002). Psychiatric disorders in youth in juvenile detention. *Archives of General Psychiatry*, *59*, 1133–1143. http://dx.doi.org/10.1001/archpsyc.59.12.1133

Teplin, L. A., Abram, K. M., Washburn, J. J., Welty, L. J., Hershfield, J. A., & Dulcan, M. K. (2013). *The Northwestern Juvenile Project Overview* (Juvenile Justice Bulletin). Washington, DC: Office of Juvenile Justice and Delinquency Prevention.

Teplin, L. A., Welty, L. J., Abram, K. M., Dulcan, M. K., & Washburn, J. J. (2012). Prevalence and persistence of psychiatric disorders in youth after detention: A prospective longitudinal study. *JAMA Psychiatry*, *69*, 1031–1043.

Thoder, V. J., & Cautilli, J. D. (2011). An independent evaluation of mode deactivation therapy for juvenile offenders. *International Journal of Behavioral and Consultation Therapy*, *7*, 41–46.

Townsend, E., Walker, D. M., Sargeant, S., Vostanis, P., Hawton, K., Stocker, O., & Sithole, J. (2010). Systematic review and meta-analysis of interventions relevant for young offenders with mood disorders, anxiety disorders, or self-harm. *Journal of Adolescence*, *33*, 9–20. http://dx.doi.org/10.1016/j.adolescence.2009.05.015

Underwood, L. A., Warren, K. M., Talbott, L., Jackson, L., & Dailey, F. L. (2014). Mental health treatment in juvenile justice secure care facilities: Practice and policy recommendations. *Journal of Forensic Psychology Practice*, *14*, 55–85. http://dx.doi.org/10.1080/15228932.2014.865398

van der Laan, A., & Eichelsheim, V. (2013). Juvenile adaptation to imprisonment: Feelings of safety, autonomy and well-being, and behaviour in prison. *European Journal of Criminology*, *10*, 424–443. http://dx.doi.org/10.1177/1477370812473530

van der Put, C. E., Creemers, H. E., & Hoeve, M. (2014). Differences between juvenile offenders with and without substance use problems in the prevalence and impact of risk and protective factors for criminal recidivism. *Drug and Alcohol Dependence*,

134, 267–274. http://dx.doi.org/10.1016/j.drugalcdep.2013.10.012

van der Stouwe, T., Asscher, J. J., Stams, G. J., Deković, M., & van der Laan, P. H. (2014). The effectiveness of multisystemic therapy (MST): A meta-analysis. *Clinical Psychology Review*, *34*, 468–481. http://dx.doi.org/10.1016/j.cpr.2014.06.006

Van Ryzin, M. J., & Dishion, T. J. (2013). From antisocial behavior to violence: A model for the amplifying role of coercive joining in adolescent friendships. *Journal of Child Psychology and Psychiatry*, *54*, 661–669. http://dx.doi.org/10.1111/jcpp.12017

Vaughn, M. G., Freedenthal, S., Jenson, J. M., & Howard, M. O. (2007). Psychiatric symptoms and substance use among juvenile offenders: A latent profile investigation. *Criminal Justice and Behavior*, *34*, 1296–1312. http://dx.doi.org/10.1177/0093854807304624

Viljoen, J. L., McLachlan, K., & Vincent, G. M. (2010). Assessing violence risk and psychopathy in juvenile and adult offenders: A survey of clinical practices. *Assessment*, *17*, 377–395. http://dx.doi.org/10.1177/1073191109359587

Vincent, G. M., Guy, L. S., Gershenson, B. G., & McCabe, P. (2012). Does risk assessment make a difference? Results of implementing the SAVRY in juvenile probation. *Behavioral Sciences and the Law*, *30*, 384–405. http://dx.doi.org/10.1002/bsl.2014

Vincent, G. M., Paiva-Salisbury, M. L., Cook, N. E., Guy, L. S., & Perrault, R. T. (2012). Impact of risk/needs assessment on juvenile probation officers' decision making: Importance of implementation. *Psychology, Public Policy, and Law*, *18*, 549–576. http://dx.doi.org/10.1037/a0027186

Vitopoulos, N. A., Peterson-Badali, M., & Skilling, T. A. (2012). The relationship between matching service to criminogenic need and recidivism in male and female youth: Examining the RNR principles in practice. *Criminal Justice and Behavior*, *39*, 1025–1041. http://dx.doi.org/10.1177/0093854812442895

Walker, C., & McCormick, D. (2004). Current practices in residential treatment for adolescent sex offenders: A survey. *Journal of Child Sexual Abuse*, *13*, 245–255.

Wasserman, G. A., Jensen, P. S., Ko, S. J., Cocozza, J., Trupin, E., Angold, A., . . . Grisso, T. (2003). Mental health assessments in juvenile justice: Report on the consensus conference. *Journal of the American Academy of Child and Adolescent Psychiatry*, *42*, 752–761. http://dx.doi.org/10.1097/01.CHI.0000046873.56865.4B

Wasserman, G. A., & McReynolds, L. S. (2011). Contributors to traumatic exposure and posttraumatic stress disorder in juvenile justice youths. *Journal of Traumatic Stress*, *24*, 422–429. http://dx.doi.org/10.1002/jts.20664

Wasserman, G. A., McReynolds, L. S., Schwalbe, C. S., Keating, J. M., & Jones, S. A. (2010). Psychiatric disorder, comorbidity, and suicidal behavior in juvenile justice youth. *Criminal Justice and Behavior*, *37*, 1361–1376. http://dx.doi.org/10.1177/0093854810382751

Weiss, B., Caron, A., Ball, S., Tapp, J., Johnson, M., & Weisz, J. R. (2005). Iatrogenic effects of group treatment for antisocial youths. *Journal of Consulting and Clinical Psychology*, *73*, 1036–1044. http://dx.doi.org/10.1037/0022-006X.73.6.1036

Weisz, J. R., Jensen-Doss, A., & Hawley, K. M. (2006). Evidence-based youth psychotherapies versus usual clinical care: A meta-analysis of direct comparisons. *American Psychologist*, *61*, 671–689. http://dx.doi.org/10.1037/0003-066X.61.7.671

Welch-Brewer, C. L., Stoddard-Dare, P., & Mallett, C. A. (2011). Race, substance abuse, and mental health disorders as predictors of juvenile court outcomes: Do they vary by gender? *Child and Adolescent Social Work Journal*, *28*, 229–241. http://dx.doi.org/10.1007/s10560-011-0229-x

Wilson, S., & Lipsey, M. W. (2000). Wilderness challenge programs for delinquent youth: A metaanalysis of outcome evaluations. *Evaluation and Program Planning*, *23*, 1–12. http://dx.doi.org/10.1016/S0149-7189(99)00040-3

Chapter 29

SEXUAL OFFENDING: ASSESSMENT AND INTERVENTION

Robert A. Prentky, Sue Righthand, and Raina Lamade

Charles Dickens walked the streets of London in the early 19th century. When his father was arrested and put into a debtors' prison, Charles was 12 years old. As was the custom, Charles's mother and her children moved into the prison. Charles boarded with a family friend and lived on the street earning money for his family by pasting labels on bottles in a blacking warehouse. From his own daunting childhood experiences, Charles wrote one of his masterpieces, *Oliver Twist*, published in 1838. Through the character of Oliver, Dickens described the worst of life in the orphanages and the worst of child labor. Social reformers, libertarians, and academics decried the abuses and demanded laws to protect children from exploitation. In the judicial system, however, the age at which children were distinguished from adults for the purpose of determining criminal responsibility was quite young compared with modern standards. Questions were not raised as to whether the youth's behavior deserved punishment, whether adverse life experiences should mitigate punishment, or whether the state should play a role in treating the youth.

Today, some 175 years after *Oliver Twist* was published and almost 50 years after the landmark case of *In re Gault* (1967), management strategies are routinely implemented for juvenile sex offenders (e.g., mandatory registration on public registries, in some cases lifetime registration; residency restrictions, in some cases for a lifetime; civil commitment in at least 20 states) that are far more deleterious in their potential influence on the outcomes of the youth they affect than anything in the pre-*Gault* era. Title 1 of the Adam Walsh Child Protection and Safety Act of 2006 established the Sex Offender Registration and Notification Act, a national sex offender registration system. The act requires that all juveniles age 14 and older who have committed a sex offense be included on both state and national public sex offender registries (Council of State Governments, 2010; Pittman, 2013). The juvenile's addresses (home, school, work), photograph and physical description, and license plate number can be made public (Council of State Governments, 2010). One is reminded of Chaffin and Bonner's (1998) sardonic warning: "Don't shoot, we're your children."

Moreover, courts today are often provided evaluations that are not based on objective scientific evidence, with conclusions based on results that misinterpret—and occasionally flagrantly distort—the research, fail to address the limitations of the evaluation, and generally ignore practice guidelines (Zimring, 2004). Assessment of juveniles has, overwhelmingly, become a nomothetic focus on the presumptive risk of dangerousness, not a comprehensive, idiographic assessment of the youth's needs. Risk assessment, moreover, has become a tool for justifying denial of liberty and removal from caregivers and the community (Vitacco, Caldwell, Ryba, Malesky, & Kurus, 2009). We would argue that this is especially the case with adolescents who have committed sex offenses.

We wish to acknowledge our esteem and admiration for a young attorney, Nicole Pittman, who has invested her heart and soul in promoting the rational care and management of youth with sexual behavior problems.

http://dx.doi.org/10.1037/14643-029
APA Handbook of Psychology and Juvenile Justice, K. Heilbrun (Editor-in-Chief)

The mission of this chapter is to provide an overview and update on assessment and interventions with juvenile sex offenders. As noted, assessment has, overwhelmingly, focused on the question of risk, hence most of our review is dominated by that central theme. Even Fanniff and Becker (2006), one of very few articles that has focused on the broader question of assessment, addressed only cognitive distortions, sexual interest, and polygraphy, not other critical areas, such as personality, cognitive, or trauma assessment. Advances in treatment certainly eclipse what was available in the 1960s and offer promise—contingent on the conditions and circumstances of the treatment. We have done our best to offer a fair appraisal of the state of the art, although it does not appear that we have moved as far beyond *In re Gault* (1967) as the time elapsed might suggest.

RELEVANT HISTORY

Over the past few decades, a quantum change has occurred in attitudes about youths with sex-offending behaviors, moving from one extreme in which frank instances of sexual battery were attributed to adolescent sexual experimentation to the opposite extreme in which juveniles are labeled as sexually violent predators, subject, in some jurisdictions in the United States, to indeterminate civil commitment (Trivits & Reppucci, 2002). Barbaree, Marshall, and Hudson (1993) observed that

> prior to the 1980s, the predominant view of the sexual offences committed by juveniles was that they constituted a nuisance value only reflecting a "boys-will-be-boys" attitude . . . these acts were seen as examples of experimentation and therefore as innocent. (p. 10)

Barbaree et al. (1993) went on to note, however, that by the early 1990s this view had changed, principally in response to a wave of juvenile crime. This attitudinal shift in the direction of harsh sanctions was eloquently captured by Chaffin and Bonner (1998) in their article titled "Don't Shoot, We're Your Children: Have We Gone Too Far in Our Response to Adolescent Sexual Abusers and Children With Sexual Behavior Problems?" During the past decade, however, the pendulum has once again begun to move slowly back in the opposite direction, principally in response to (a) declining juvenile crime rates, (b) recognition that incarcerating juveniles may be yielding suboptimal results, and (most important) (c) the impact of developmental neuroscience and research on the juvenile brain (Bonnie & Scott, 2013). In *Roper v. Simmons* (2005), the Court rejected the death penalty sentence as disproportionate and a violation of the Eighth Amendment banning cruel and unusual punishment. *Graham v. Florida* (2010) and *Miller v. Alabama* (2012) both rejected sentences of life without parole for juveniles. In all three cases, the Court relied on cognitive neuroscience research, pointing to developmental immaturity and diminished decision making capacity in adolescents.

At one time, polarized reactions to sexual offending by juveniles could be explained, in part, by two separate realities. One reality, according to the extant empirical literature, is that rates of sexual reoffending by juveniles are indeed quite low—according to meta-analytic studies, generally in the range of 5% to 15% (e.g., Caldwell, 2010; Heilbrun, Lee, & Cottle, 2005; McCann & Lussier, 2008; Reitzel & Carbonell, 2006; Viljoen, Mordell, & Beneteau, 2012). A second reality is that data from multiple sources, in addition to these meta-analyses, have suggested that a small group of juveniles persist in offending beyond their adolescence (e.g., Rubinstein, Yeager, Goodstein, & Lewis, 1993) and pose a genuine ongoing risk. Juveniles with a first sexual offense may be subject to highly punitive practices and laws fueled by profound misconceptions about the magnitude of risk posed by these youths (cf. Caldwell & Dickinson, 2009; Trivits & Reppucci, 2002), such as indeterminate confinement, mandated registration, notification, and residency restrictions. Not only may such policies and practices not have the intended positive effect of reducing sexual violence, but they may have serious unintended negative effects (Dierkhising, Lane, & Natsuaki, 2014), such as (a) diminishing positive social and interpersonal skills and prosocial beliefs and promoting criminogenic attitudes when youths are isolated from normative developmental experience or placed with delinquent peers; (b) experiencing rejection and isolation by peers, family, former friends, potential employers, and others, further eroding self-esteem, undermining attempts at achieving normal, developmentally appropriate relationships and successfully reintegrating into society; and (c) thereby marginalizing youngsters who ultimately place demands on society rather than contribute positively.

This rush to policies advocating costly management strategies has occurred in the absence of research supporting their effectiveness (Vitacco et al., 2009). Relevant studies (e.g., Caldwell & Dickinson, 2009) have found no evidence of reduced sexual or violent reoffending for juveniles subjected to registration and notification. Furthermore, juvenile registration and notification have been associated with increases in plea bargaining as well as prosecutorial dismissals of sex offense cases, perhaps as attorneys seek to divert youths from what appear to be unduly harsh outcomes. Well intended as such actions may be, some youths who might benefit from treatment are excluded when they are diverted from the juvenile justice system.

Unstable Course of Adolescent Development

The single most obvious risk-relevant difference between adults and juveniles is age. Even under normal conditions, adolescence is a time of extraordinary maturational change in virtually all domains of development, from physical and biological to emotional, cognitive, neurocognitive, social, sexual, and behavioral (e.g., Bonnie & Scott, 2013; Casey, Getz, & Galvan, 2008; Dahl, 2001; Iselin, DeCoster, & Salekin, 2009; Modecki, 2008; Reyna & Farley, 2006; Steinberg, 2007; Steinberg & Scott, 2003; van den Bos, van Dijk, Westenberg, Rombouts, & Crone, 2011). The prestigious New York Academy of Sciences devoted a 2003 conference entirely to the topic of adolescent brain development (Dahl & Spear, 2004). Recently, a special issue of *Current Directions in Psychological Science* (Engle, 2013), featuring 14 articles, was devoted to the teenage brain. Assessing risk in the presence of such developmental change introduces extraordinary uncertainty.

Risk taking, sensation seeking, impulsivity, poor decision making, illegal behaviors, and intense, unstable emotions are all normative in adolescence, not something idiosyncratic to delinquent youths. Although scientific support for this observation has been fairly recent, it is not a startling revelation. Aristotle quipped, more than 2,300 years ago, that "young people are in a condition like permanent intoxication, because youth is sweet and they are growing" (Höffe, 2010). And Shakespeare added, almost 400 years ago in *The Winter's Tale* (Act III), "I would that there were no age between 10 and 23, for there's nothing in between but getting wenches with child, wrongdoing the ancientry, stealing, fighting" (Shakespeare, 1974, p. 1585).

Because what is truly normative may appear problematic in a youngster who has been flagged because of problematic behavior, it is critically important to distinguish between expected adolescent behavior and a pattern of behavior that is nonnormative and unacceptable. Change, by definition of adolescent development, is also normative and not something idiosyncratic to delinquent youths. Change must be controlled for with (a) repeated, short-term assessments and (b) change-sensitive markers that are built into the assessment. Assessing risk in adolescents is akin to hitting a moving target. Unlike adults, who typically present with decades of stable behavior patterns, adolescents have very limited life experience and may offer little reliable evidence of a stable pattern that is useful for gauging risk. Adolescents reliably exhibit unreliability.

What happens to all adolescents in the normal course of development is further complicated by varying degrees of maltreatment to which many, if not most, juvenile sex offenders are subjected (e.g., Burton, 2003; Ford & Linney, 1995; Knight & Prentky, 1993). Abuse and neglect is often real time (i.e., occurring within roughly the same time frame as the risk assessment). Family circumstances, home environment, placements, caregivers, school, peers, and other life situations of adolescents may change rapidly or within a short time frame. Hence, the social ecology of youth may increase risk or be protective (Henggeler et al., 2009). In sum, the risk temperature of adolescents is arguably much more variable and unstable than that of adults.

Although capturing this variability is a significant methodological challenge, it is essential for improving the accuracy of clinicians' assessments, as well as improving their management decisions.

Not only is child maltreatment potentially destabilizing from the standpoint of assessing risk—precipitating reactive but otherwise short-lived behavioral responses to situational or environmental catalysts—it may also lead to invisible, hard-wired brain damage that contributes to longer term maladaptation (e.g., De Bellis, Baum, et al., 1999; De Bellis, Keshavan, et al., 1999; Ferris, 1996; Ito, Teicher, Glod, & Ackerman, 1998; Ito et al., 1993; Perry, 1994; Perry, Pollard, Blakley, Baker, & Vigilante, 1995; Stein, Koverola, Hanna, Torchia, & McClarty, 1997; Stien & Kendall, 2004; Teicher, 2000, 2002; Teicher, Glod, Surrey, & Swett, 1993; Teicher et al., 1997; Thomas & Johnson, 2008). As De Bellis et al. (1991) concluded, "the overwhelming stress of maltreatment experiences in childhood is associated with alterations of biological stress systems and with adverse influences on brain development" (p.1281).

An important study in this regard examined age-related differences and dynamic risk factors in a large sample (N = 674) of adjudicated youthful offenders (Vincent, Perrault, Guy, & Gershenson, 2012). Vincent et al. (2012) examined Structured Assessment of Violence Risk in Youth (SAVRY) scores in three age groups: 12 and younger, 13–15, and 16–18. At follow-up (14.5 months, on average), group assignment by age did not moderate the association between SAVRY scores and reoffense, regardless of how reoffense was assessed (petitions for [a] violent offenses [including sex offenses], [b] nonviolent offenses, [c] probation violations [including status offenses and minor traffic violations], and [d] any petition). Vincent et al. found, simply summarized, that the SAVRY identified risk levels accurately across all three periods of development.

A similar finding was reported for a large child welfare sample of children and juveniles who engaged in problematic and assaultive sexual behavior (Prentky et al., 2010). In that study, the Juvenile Sex Offender Assessment Protocol—II (J-SOAP–II) performed with comparable accuracy for the preadolescents (age 11 and younger; n = 336) and the adolescents (age 12 and older; n = 223). Notably, Viljoen et al. (2008) found the opposite for both the SAVRY and the J-SOAP–II, namely that both risk scales were more accurate with older adolescents. Viljoen et al. (2008) raised the important question of inconsistency of results across studies, finding that none of the nine moderators they tested reached statistical significance. Two of the nine are critical: base rate (examined as less than or more than 10%) and exposure time (less than or more than 5 years). From their meta-analysis, Viljoen et al. (2012) reported an average 10.9% sexual reoffense rate and a 49.4% general reoffense rate over a median exposure period of 6 years. A criterion that is limited to sexual reoffense and a base rate that hovers around 10% impose a daunting challenge to predictive accuracy. Extending the exposure time, as we point out subsequently, does not improve (increase) the base rate significantly and renders sensitive analysis of dynamic risk predictors moot.

We maintain in this chapter that risk assessment with children and adolescents cannot simply mimic risk assessment with adults; a prospective developmental model that accounts for discontinuity of risk (frequent fluctuations with highly variable time lags) is essential. Unlike the assumed temporal stability of risk in adults, the opposite must be assumed with juveniles. Viljoen et al. (2012) seemed to offer a tentative conclusion that "it is possible that certain risk factors, such as dynamic factors, may be particularly important during adolescence" (p. 433). We would argue that the sensitivity of risk scales will only be advanced by adopting procedures that permit close to real-time analysis of changes in risk.

Vincent et al. (2012) reported, for example, that dynamic risk factors contributed to the explanatory variance, as did age. To return momentarily to the discussion about age, presumably some dynamic risk factors are indeed highly age sensitive (e.g., placement and caregiver instability, substance abuse, social skills, social isolation vs. social and peer involvement). One might hypothesize that certain discrete subgroups of juvenile sex offenders (i.e., the ones characterized by marked psychosocial immaturity who target much younger victims) would be more likely to evidence a moderating effect of age.

An interesting corollary to Vincent et al. (2012) was Modecki's (2008) five-sample study that included 56 male and 80 female adolescents, along with college students (ages 18–21), young adults (ages 22–27), adults, and 91 male delinquents. Modecki found no differences in maturity of judgment, assessed using Cauffman and Steinberg's (2000) three factors (Responsibility, Perspective, and Temperance), between delinquent and nondelinquent adolescents. They did find, however, significant differences in maturity of judgment between high- and low-delinquency youths. Moreover, maturity of judgment predicted self-reported delinquency beyond the contributions of age, gender, race, education level, socioeconomic status, and antisocial decision making. Although Modecki was comparing comparably aged adolescents, immaturity of judgment and decision making is a well-known feature of adolescence, and it typically improves with age and can be targeted with effective interventions.

Daunting Base-Rate Challenge

Crime rarely conforms to Gauss's normal distribution. Rather, Pareto's power law distribution (e.g., Schroeder, 1991) or the closely related J-curve (e.g., Clarke, 1996), both characterized by a marked positive skew, seem to do a much better job. In both distributions, there are a few atypical (or extreme) events on the left side and a very long tail of more common (or much less extreme) events on the right side. In popular terms, this has also been referred to as the "80/20" rule (Kock, 1999), wherein 20% of something is responsible for 80% of some outcome. Although the ratio is rarely 80/20, the principle holds—a small proportion of something accounts for a large proportion of something else. The power law distribution has been applied to everything from earthquakes (a very few earthquakes cause most of the damage) to wealth (a very small proportion of the population holds most of it) to crime (a small number of offenders are responsible for a disproportionate amount of crime; Eck, Clarke, & Guerette, 2007). Not surprisingly, delinquency follows a power law distribution as well.

Perhaps the single most often cited longitudinal study of delinquent youths illustrating the J-curve or power law distribution was conducted by Marvin Wolfgang (Wolfgang, Figlio, & Sellin, 1972). This birth-cohort study involved close to 10,000 boys in Philadelphia. About one third of the boys ($n = 3{,}475$) had had at least one documented contact with the police. Out of the entire cohort, 627 (6%) were chronic offenders charged with five or more offenses; this 6% was responsible for 71% of the homicides, 77% of the rapes, 70% of the robberies, and 69% of the aggravated assaults.

The prospective longitudinal Cambridge Study in Delinquent Development study, conducted by West and subsequently by Farrington, followed 411 boys, most 8 to 9 years old at the beginning of the study, from 1961 through 1981 (e.g., Blumstein, Farrington, & Moitra, 1985; Farrington, 1986; Farrington & West, 1981). Extensive data were gathered on most of the boys ($N = 395$). The boys were interviewed and tested at ages 8, 10, and 14 and again at ages 16, 18, 21, and 24. As in the Philadelphia Cohort Study, about one third of the youths in the sample were convicted at least once—and a small proportion (7%) of those youths accounted for about half of all the offenses in the study and were labeled as chronic offenders.

The Pittsburgh Youth Survey began in 1987 with 1,500 youths in the first, fourth, and seventh grades (Loeber, Farrington, Stouthamer-Loeber, Moffitt, & Caspi, 1998). The study, directed by Loeber, followed about 500 boys from ages 7 to 17 and another 500 boys from ages 13 to 23. Almost the entire sample (87%) reported at least one delinquent act, with a maximum of 20 delinquent acts. Although this study relied on self-report, the results were similar to those of the Cambridge Study in Delinquent Development: About two thirds of the youths reported no delinquent acts; of those that did, the range was from one to 20. Once again, a power law frequency distribution applied both to the entire sample and to the subsample when the two thirds of youth reporting no delinquency were removed.

A longitudinal study of 1,037 New Zealand children compared the base rates of persistent and temporary antisocial behavior problems (Moffitt, Caspi, Rutter, & Silva, 2001). The boys were rated as very antisocial by three sources (parents, teachers, youths), and 5% of the boys met these selection criteria. Moffitt found clear evidence that the temporal stability of delinquency was attributable to these 5% of youths whose behavior was most extreme and most persistent.

Many other studies have reported essentially the same findings: A small percentage of the delinquent or criminal population is responsible for most of the crime. These studies of youths have consistently found that roughly 5% or 6% of the offenders commit roughly 50% of all known crimes (cf. Farrington, Ohlin, & Wilson, 1986). As counterintuitive as it may be, given the rather draconian nature of the laws enacted to manage juvenile sex offenders, the proportion of youths that poses a significant risk to reoffend is quite small. There is no theoretical, empirical, or clinical reason to believe that youths who commit sex offenses are any different from those who apparently do not. In our own dataset on 667 boys in the child welfare system who had been flagged for sexually inappropriate and coercive behaviors (Prentky, Pimental, Cavanaugh, & Righthand, 2009; Prentky et al., 2010), we found evidence of the same power law distribution of reoffenses after a 7-year follow-up (Exhibit 29.1).

In attempting to assess the sexual reoffense risk posed by juvenile sex offenders, we are trying to capture the most persistent of these youths. If the base rate hovers around 10% or less, the true positive target is extraordinarily small, and a very high false positive rate is virtually inevitable. As noted earlier, reported rates of sexual reoffending by juveniles are generally around 10% over 5 years (e.g., Caldwell, 2007, 2010; Heilbrun et al., 2005; McCann & Lussier, 2008; Reitzel & Carbonell, 2006; Viljoen et al., 2012). Caldwell (2010) examined 63 datasets consisting of 11,219 youths who committed sexual offenses. Over a 5-year follow-up period, the average sexual reoffense rate was 7%, with most rates falling between 5% and 15%. Caldwell (2010) further found that when these juveniles did reoffend, the offense was more likely to be nonsexual than sexual. A long-term (20-year) prospective follow-up study by Worling, Litteljohn, and Bookalam (2010) yielded similarly low rates even over the long term. A long-term (10-year) follow-up study of preadolescent children with sexual behavior problems also found very low repetition, ranging from 2% to 10%, depending on type of treatment received (Carpentier, Silovsky, & Chaffin, 2006).

Exhibit 29.1
Reoffense Distribution of 667 Boys After a 7-Year Follow-Up

Total number of sexual, victim-involved offenses at follow-up (skew = +3.64, *SE* = 0.472):

0	1	2	3	4	13
96.4%	1.9%	0.7%	0.3%	0.4%	0.1%

Total number of victims at follow-up (skew = +4.04, *SE* = .098):

0	1	2	> 2
75.6%	9.0%	4.9%	4.3%

Total number of separate incidents at follow-up (skew = +3.52, *SE* = .098):

0	1	2	3	4	5	6–25
59.5%	10.5%	5.2%	5.5%	2.4%	4.3%	6.3%

Heterogeneity and Attempts at Differentiation

Fifteen years after Knight and Prentky (1993) pointed out the marked heterogeneity of juvenile sex offenders, Chaffin (2008) identified it as "one of the likely culprits for some of the poor juvenile justice policies" (p. 117). Chaffin went on to comment,

> The term *juvenile sex offender*, as a taxonomic category has virtually no value other than as an administrative classification for crimes. Taxonomically, the term misleads more often than it informs. . . . It has little value as a risk marker, as a prognostic indicator, or prescriptively for intervention purposes. The problem is that youth captured under the sex offender label, although presumed to share common features, are actually incredibly diverse and may have little in common with each other aside from their administrative classification under law and policy. . . . Youth labeled as juvenile sex offenders include:

- traumatized young girls reacting to their own sexual victimization;
- persistently delinquent teens who commit both sexual and nonsexual crimes;
- otherwise normal early-adolescent boys who are curious about sex and act experimentally but irresponsibly;
- generally aggressive and violent youth;
- immature and impulsive youth acting without thinking;
- so-called Romeo and Juliet cases;
- those who are indifferent to others and selfishly take what they want;
- youth misinterpreting what they believed was consent or mutual interest;
- children imitating actions they have seen in the media;
- youth ignorant of the law or the potential consequences of their actions;
- youth attracted to the thrill of rule violation;
- youth imitating what is normal in their own family or social ecology;
- depressed or socially isolated teens who turn to younger juveniles as substitutes for agemates;
- seriously mentally ill youth;
- youth responding primarily to peer pressure;
- youth preoccupied with sex;
- youth under the influence of drugs and alcohol;
- youth swept away by the sexual arousal of the moment; and
- youth with incipient sexual deviancy problems. (p. 117)

As mentioned earlier, distinguishing between what is normative and what is maladaptive and problematic is critical. Several of Chaffin's (2008) aforementioned features or motives are illustrative: "otherwise normal early-adolescent boys who are curious about sex and act experimentally but irresponsibly" or "Romeo and Juliet cases" compared with "traumatized young girls reacting to their own sexual victimization" or "persistently delinquent teens who commit both sexual and nonsexual crimes" (p. 117).

The diversity of motives highlighted by Chaffin (2008) illustrates a critical point: Uninformed or misinformed policies leading to rigid, one-size-fits-all legal strategies are doomed to fail. A second important point is that diversity of motives is not equivalent to a classification system. An empirically informed taxonomy must be designed and tested with a particular purpose in mind. If the purpose is improving the predictive efficacy of decisions about likelihood of reoffense, then the taxonomy must incorporate dimensions demonstrated to discriminate with respect to reoffense. Perhaps the single most important theoretical and practical contribution to taxonomic differentiation among delinquent children and adolescents was Moffitt's (1993) pioneering research on developmental trajectories of antisocial behavior that revealed a childhood-onset life-course-persistent pattern with strong links to severe adverse childhood events and antisocial behavior that persists into adulthood and a juvenile-onset adolescence-limited pattern that desists with transition into adulthood. The principal task, which has been achieved with only moderate success in the extant juvenile sexual offending risk assessment scales, is identifying the life-course-persistent sexually offending youths.

With the exception of Ryan, Hunter, and Murrie (2012), Moffitt's (1993) taxonomy has rarely been applied to juveniles who have offended sexually. Although the Moffitt taxonomy supports the connection between early-onset conduct disorder–antisociality and persistence, no clear empirical support has been found for a similar connection between atypical sexual interests and persistence. Nevertheless, the importance of Moffitt's two trajectories from the standpoint of risk, needs, and effective interventions clearly underscores the critical need to infuse assessment and intervention models with sensitive markers for developmental epochs beginning early in childhood. It makes little sense theoretically or clinically to combine 11- to 13-year-olds with 16- to 18-year-olds when examining risk or needs (Viljoen et al., 2008). That is, however, often seen in current practice. As Cicchetti (1990) and Moffitt (1993) pointed out, the pathway to chronicity is marked by milder expressions of delinquency leading to increasingly serious forms of delinquency over time. It is this pattern that must be captured to reflect the full spectrum of troubled, antisocial behaviors. It is this pattern, when adequately captured, that will shed light on life-course-persistent sex offending. This need was pointed out by Thomas and Johnson (2008).

At present, the only programmatic research on heterogeneity among juveniles with sexual offenses has been conducted by Hunter (e.g., Hunter, 2006, 2008; Hunter, Figueredo, Malamuth, & Becker, 2003; Ryan et al., 2012), who described three subtypes, two of which derive from Moffitt's (1993) work: (a) life-course-persistent (early-onset, temporally stable patterns of delinquent and antisocial behavior) and (b) adolescent nonparaphilic (transient sexual offending as an expression of adolescent experimentation or psychosocial deficits). Hunter's third subtype was an early-adolescence-onset paraphilic type, hypothesized to involve early-onset pedophilia. In all three cases, age of onset is important.

In a subsequent study of 256 male juvenile sex offenders, Hunter (2006) derived five subgroups using cluster analysis, the first two again being essentially replications of Moffitt's taxonomy (a life-course-persistent antisocial type and an adolescent-onset "experimenter" type). The other three subgroups were (a) a socially impaired, anxious, depressed group; (b) an antisocial group with pedophilic interest; and (c) a nonantisocial group with pedophilic interest. The first group had the highest arrest rate for nonsexual crimes and the highest reported rate of childhood maltreatment and exposure to violence. The second group was the least psychosocially and psychosexually disturbed of all the groups. Hunter and his colleagues have thus far provided evidence of increasingly clear developmentally distinctive paths, two of which follow Moffitt's taxonomy and two of which (the last two groups) identify a pedophilic preferential interest, one more antisocial than the other.

Risk–Need–Responsivity Model

The risk–need–responsivity (RNR) model has been reported on and discussed in the criminal justice literature for decades (cf. Andrews & Bonta, 2010). It is an integrative, unifying model that underscores the criticality of all phases: a comprehensive assessment of needs as well as risk, evaluation-driven treatment plans and all other client-specific interventions, and the responsivity interface between needs and interventions. RNR had its beginning at a time when the nothing-works attitude in correctional rehabilitation prevailed. Researchers (e.g., Andrews & Bonta, 2010) found that the programs that were most successful at reducing recidivism rates had certain characteristics, which they described as the principles of risk, need, and responsivity.

According to the risk principle, the greatest reductions in recidivism will result when individuals who present with most risk factors associated with reoffending receive the most intensive, relevant interventions. Providing intensive interventions to those with relatively few risks may not only deplete scarce resources but may do more harm than good, particularly when individuals with few risk factors are mixed with those who have substantial risk factors and intervention needs and may model antisocial behaviors or exploit or abuse others.

The need principle asserts that effective interventions are those that target dynamic (changeable) risk-relevant factors (criminogenic needs). Some risk factors are historical and static; the need principle directs practitioners' focus to factors that can change and that, if changed, can decrease risk. Risk reduction requires practitioners to adhere to this principle while strengthening protective factors that increase prosocial behavior.

The responsivity principle emphasizes that interventions are most likely to be effective when they are designed in ways that are generally and specifically the best fit for a particular individual. Among the general considerations are whether the proposed intervention is a well-validated and empirically supported approach to targeting the outcome of interest. Specific responsivity considerations encompass individual learning styles, cognitive or developmental challenges, psychological characteristics, and motivation to change as well as relevant cultural, gender, and other factors (e.g., individual and family characteristics that affect an adolescent and his or her family's ability to positively engage in and respond to interventions).

Subsequent research has shown that programs that apply these principles of effective intervention have greater reductions in criminal recidivism among both adults (Andrews & Bonta, 2010) and juveniles (e.g., Pealer & Latessa, 2004), including adults and juveniles who have committed sexual offenses (Hanson, Bourgon, Helmus, & Hodgson, 2009). One-size-fits-all approaches are not likely to be very effective.

To be most useful, and consistent with the RNR model, assessments of adolescents who have sexually offended should consider factors associated with sexual and nonsexual reoffending that either increase the likelihood of reoffending (risk factors) or mitigate the risk (protective factors). This consideration does not focus only on individual (ontogenic) factors but extends to family (microsystemic), community (exosystemic), and cultural (macrosystemic) factors as well (Belsky, 1980; Bronfrenbrenner, 1979). In addition, although historical factors that are associated with recidivism or desistance may be useful for assessing risk and understanding needs, identifying dynamic risk and protective factors (i.e., criminongenic needs) is essential because they are primary targets for intervention. In addition, as the RNR model purports, assessments that identify traits or characteristics that, if effectively addressed, can enhance treatment responsiveness (i.e., treatment responsivity) are needed as well.

In addition, depending on the youth, special issues may require assessment because they are related to the offending, selection of intervention priorities, or facilitation of treatment responsiveness. Such factors may include substance abuse, trauma symptoms, cognitive functioning, and serious mental health issues. Similarly, socioecological factors that can affect service delivery and treatment responsiveness must be considered. These factors include, for example, caregivers' willingness to actively supervise the youth or be involved in the youth's treatment, school and community sentiment and response, and cultural practices and beliefs. By considering these varied factors, assessments that use the RNR model can provide a road map for effective interventions.

ASSESSMENT

Good assessments respond to clinical referral questions (e.g., what risk and protective factors associated with sexual and nonsexual offending are present). Examiners gather detailed information about the youth, his or her family, their situation, and circumstances that can facilitate good case plans that guide effective interventions and help decision makers facilitate desistance from offending and promote positive outcomes. By responding to appropriate and answerable referral questions, practitioners can conduct assessments that are likely to be more relevant and useful.

Good assessments guide effective interventions. The focus, approach, and comprehensiveness of the assessment will depend on the referral questions and purpose of the evaluation—for example, to guide treatment planning or legal decisions (e.g., Melton, Petrila, Poythress, & Slobogin, 2007; Ryan, 2012).

Although psychosocial and psychosexual assessments are still routinely sought at the time of commitment, assessments executed to aid or assist with legal decisions typically focus on the presumptive risk posed by the adolescent. Development and testing of risk scales for juvenile sex offenders began in some earnest in the mid-1990s, with the first scale reaching publication in 2000 (Prentky, Harris, Frizzell, & Righthand, 2000). A recent survey reported that two structured professional judgment risk assessment scales, the J-SOAP–II (Prentky et al., 2000; Prentky & Righthand, 2001, 2003) and the Estimate of Risk of Adolescent Sexual Offense Recidivism (ERASOR; Worling & Curwen, 2000), are currently used by more than half of all outpatient and residential treatment providers in the United States (McGrath, Cumming, Burchard, Zeoli, & Ellerby, 2010). Moreover, these same risk scales are used in numerous countries around the world. From the widespread use of these scales, not to mention the many other scales used for assessing risk with juvenile sex offenders (e.g., Juvenile Sexual Offense Recidivism Risk Assessment Tool—II [Epperson & Ralston, 2014; Epperson, Ralston, Fowers, DeWitt, & Gore, 2006], Juvenile Risk Assessment Scale [Hiscox, Witt, & Haran, 2007], Juvenile Risk Assessment Tool [Rich, 2009]), one may reasonably infer widespread demand. This is not surprising given the numerous decision points at which a juvenile's risk may be assessed: (a) in the Dispositional Planning Unit of Family Court, (b) by probation officers before adjudication, (c) in court during the adjudicatory process, (d) by child welfare workers responding to reports of a child who is sexually abusive or sexually acting out, (e) by therapists considering discharging a youth from residential placement, (f) by therapists receiving postadjudication referrals for treatment, (g) by the Sex Offender Assessment Board or judges considering registration level, and (h) by examiners evaluating a youngster for civil commitment.

All of these decisions hinge on reliable, valid assessments of risk and (we would argue) needs. An evidence-driven risk and needs assessment can provide the juvenile justice system, the child protection and welfare system, and practitioners in the community with an empirically based roadmap for (a) informing discretionary decisions about safe management of juveniles with sexual offending behavior, ensuring that the most intensive and restrictive interventions are reserved strictly for those who pose the greatest risk; (b) informing placement decisions by assisting decision makers in determining the least restrictive placement possible for promoting community safety and positive youth development; (c) informing community-based aftercare planning when youths are placed in juvenile correctional facilities or treatment programs; and (d) informing treatment planning with respect to risk-relevant needs that, once addressed, can support youths in developing prosocial, healthy relationships and lifestyles. Any progress that lays the groundwork for more effective (and more humane) management strategies, improved treatment interventions, and more accurate and informative screening tools that reduce contact with the juvenile justice or child welfare system is clearly beneficial.

When the purpose of the assessment is to guide treatment planning, it does not need to be as detailed because the therapists gather information about the youth and his or her family over time. They can revise their assessments and treatment plans accordingly. By contrast, when evaluations are used to inform legal decisions, the evaluations are likely to be a single snapshot of the youngster, often relying on nomothetic measures. These evaluations may result in conclusions and recommendations that can have significant and sometimes very severe life-altering consequences that may curtail the youth's liberty for long periods of time. Thus, given the high stakes associated with forensic evaluations, they should (a) be comprehensive (both individualized and incorporating validated measures), (b) be detailed in explaining and justifying recommendations, (c) describe all information relied on, and (d) note any limitations of the data or assessment procedures. Last, it is imperative that evaluators recognize that any assessment of a youth with problematic or illegal sexual behavior could be used for unintended reasons, such as when an assessment is released or subpoenaed to assist with legally mandated decisions regarding registration and notification.

Standards and Guidelines

Recently, the Association for the Treatment of Sexual Abusers (ATSA; 2012) adopted *Adolescents Who Have Engaged in Sexually Abusive Behavior: Effective Policies and Practices*. This document briefly reviews developments in the field regarding these adolescents; an increased research base, albeit one with significant limitations; and current practices and recommendations for future research.

As discussed earlier, adolescence is a time of rapid social, emotional, and cognitive development that extends not only through the teenage years but well into the early to the mid-20s. Thus, standards and guidelines increasingly call on practitioners who provide assessments to be knowledgeable about adolescent development and its implications for risk and needs assessment and recognize that maturational processes vary between, as well as within, individual youths (ATSA, 2012).

Developmental knowledge includes understanding the range of normative sexual behavior in youths and recognizing that sexual behaviors that may reflect significant problems in adults, such as sex with children, may not have the same serious prognostic implications when exhibited by teenagers. Inappropriate or even illegal sexual behaviors by youths may occur with other children who do not differ substantially in age. As the aforementioned base rate of 5% to 15% suggests, the problematic or illegal sexual behavior is often experimental, situational, and opportunistic and does not persist, especially after appropriate interventions.

Furthermore, adolescents typically do not have the cognitive capacity required for the detailed planning that may be a significant risk factor in adults. More often, they are impulsive and opportunistic. The capacity for impulse control, emotional regulation, perspective taking, and empathy, as well as thinking of the future consequences of one's behaviors, is still developing. Clearly, the fundamental differences between adolescence and adulthood must be well understood and heeded when assisting youths, their families, and other involved parties.

A number of useful books provide assessment and practice guidelines as well as specific assessment strategies and methods. A thorough review of these suggestions and guidelines is beyond the scope of this chapter but is recommended for practitioners who are new to the field, and more seasoned clinicians and other professionals may want to review them as well. For example, in the third edition of *Psychological Evaluations for the Courts*, Melton et al. (2007) have discussed very relevant information on risk and needs assessment, forensic evaluation and working with the courts, consultation, report writing, and court testimony. Ryan et al. (2012) has presented a guide to evaluating and treating youths with sex-offending behavior. Hoge and Andrews (2010) have provided guidance on preparing to conduct an assessment, collecting relevant information, and interpreting findings and report writing. Others (e.g., Rich, 2009) have outlined relevant assessment domains and provided practical information on structuring and conducting interviews with youths, caregivers, and additional collateral sources.

Briefly, these guidelines stress the importance of using multiple sources of information and varied assessment methods that cover pertinent domains, using relevant and adequately validated tests and measures when indicated, and presenting the strengths and limitations of procedures and results. Especially in view of adolescent development and treatment responsiveness, it is important that assessment reports emphasize findings that describe current functioning and circumstances and are relevant to the foreseeable future, absent significant life changes. Furthermore, the necessity of timely, periodic reassessments—in view of developmental and situational fluctuations, maturation and treatment responsiveness, and current needs—is stressed. The short shelf life of the report, often 6 months or less depending on the youth's age and circumstances, is emphasized.

Adolescents referred for problematic sexual behaviors are typically referred because of sex-offending (i.e., illegal) behaviors. Consequently, the client or parent is typically not the referent. Usually the youth has been referred by a third party, such as a child welfare worker, juvenile justice staff member, school personnel, attorney, or judge. As such, these evaluations are not confidential (the adolescent and guardian must sign consent forms allowing assessment results to be shared), and the findings may have significant and even severe consequences for the youth and his or her family.

Assessment approaches that adhere to the RNR model are likely to be most useful for triaging youths, as well as allocating resources. As an introduction to our following discussion of how the RNR model can be integrated into assessments, we emphasize that our discussion of risk and protective factors and criminogenic needs is hampered by significant limitations in the quantity and quality of research regarding risk factors and protective factors, assessment protocols, and interventions associated with juvenile sex reoffending and desistance.

Assessment and the RNR Model

When referring adolescents for evaluation, the bottom-line question referents want answered is whether the youth will engage in illegal sexual behavior again. Because of the dynamic nature of human behavior, developmental flux, and situational factors, predictions of future offending are often inaccurate. We know, however, that given the low base rates of sexual reoffending, repeat sexual offending is unlikely, especially when the youth is provided with appropriate treatment. Yet, some youths do reoffend, and evaluators can be most helpful to referral sources, the youth, his or her family, and ultimately the community by providing structured, focused, and holistic assessments that are consistent with the RNR framework. Such assessments

- identify individual, family, and social and circumstantial risk and protective factors associated with repeated, illegal sexual behaviors and other conduct problems;
- identify other factors relevant for facilitating effective interventions (e.g., developmental disabilities, learning challenges, co-occurring disorders, culture, degree of motivation for change);
- provide clear, practical, and case-relevant recommendations that are based on the best evidence; and
- match interventions with individual risk and protective factors, dynamic risk-relevant needs and circumstances, and factors that may increase treatment responsiveness.

An important caveat at the outset is the frequent disconnect between assessment and interventions in RNR programs (DeMatteo, Hunt, Batastini, & LaDuke, 2010). As DeMatteo Hunt, et al. (2010) noted, "There is often a weak link between the assessment of risk and the selection of needs-appropriate intervention strategies for specific offender populations. This disconnect can reduce the likelihood of achieving optimal or even minimal reductions in reoffense rates" (p. 62). DeMatteo, Hunt, et al. identified three specific conditions in which this disconnect occurs: (a) at the beginning of the assessment phase and trickling down to the implementation phase; (b) when recommendations, based on well-conducted assessments, are inadequately communicated or improperly applied or administered; and (c) in the absence of any equivalent of a risk and needs assessment. The second circumstance, the "one-size-fits-all trap in which individual treatment needs are ignored" (p. 63), may be most prevalent. A one-size-fits-all program is likely to be most cost efficient.

There is, moreover, a tendency for clinicians conducting assessments to identify needs that are unrelated to risk and fail to identify needs that are (Borum, 2003; DeMatteo, Hunt, et al., 2010). The principal reason for targeting noncriminogenic needs is that, from a clinical standpoint, they appear very compelling. Enhancing self-esteem, as DeMatteo, Hunt, et al. (2010) pointed out, may be laudable, but it is unlikely to mitigate risk of reoffense. Mulvey and Iselin (2008) offered a further reason for why assessments may lack empirical rigor, noting that the ethos of juvenile courts encourages reliance on unstructured judgments and opinions (p. 39).

Risk and Protective Factors

Risk factors are rarely demonstrated to be causal. To establish causality, it must be empirically demonstrated that changing the risk factor produces changes in the onset or rate of offending. Rather, most risk factors are correlated with offending behavior. Similarly, protective factors have not, thus far, been demonstrated to prevent reoffending; they may mitigate risk, thereby reducing the likelihood of recidivism. Broadly speaking, the greater the number of risk factors and the fewer the number of protective factors that are present, the greater the risk of repeat offending is.

One of the earliest, often-cited comprehensive reviews of the then-extant research on risk factors for adolescent sex offenders was that of Worling and Långström (2003). Those risk factors with the best support were (a) deviant sexual interests (Kenny, Keogh, & Seidler, 2001; Worling & Curwen, 2000), (b) prior criminal sanctions for sexual assault (Långström, 2002; Schram, Milloy, & Rowe, 1992), (c) past sexual offenses against two or more victims (Långström, 2002; Worling, 2002), (d) selection of a stranger victim (Långström, 2002; Smith & Monastersky, 1986), (e) lack of intimate peer relationships or social isolation (Kenny et al., 2001; Långström & Grann, 2000), and (f) incomplete offense-specific treatment (Borduin, Henggeler, Blaske, & Stein, 1990; Worling & Curwen, 2000).

A subsequent review by Gerhold, Browne, and Beckett (2007) reported that "the single most documented and significantly correlated factor related to general and sexual recidivism in adolescents appears to be a prior offense history, either general offending, sexual offending, or both" (p. 434). What was inconclusive from Gerhold et al.'s review was whether juveniles who have committed a sex offense are more—or less—likely to reoffend sexually or nonsexually and the extent to which these juveniles differ from other youths who commit only nonsexual offenses. This question has begun to be sorted out with recent empirical research on taxonomic differentiation.

Seto and Lalumière's (2010) meta-analysis collapsed 59 studies ($N = 3{,}855$ adolescent sexual offenders and 13,393 adolescent nonsexual offenders). The results revealed marked similarities between the two groups of juveniles: traits of antisocial personality, antisocial attitudes and beliefs, early conduct problems, social problems, intelligence, and general psychopathology. The adolescent sex offenders differed from their non–sex-offending counterparts by having less extensive criminal histories, fewer delinquent peers, less substance abuse, and more serious and varied histories of maltreatment (more likely to have been sexually, physically, and emotionally abused; more likely to have had early exposure to sex or pornography; more likely to have been exposed to sexual violence in the family; and more likely to have atypical sexual interests, such as sexual fantasies involving younger children or sexual fantasies involving force or coercion).

Kjellgren, Priebe, Svedin, and Långström (2010) administered a school-based survey to 1,933 male youths in Sweden. Of that sample, 101 (5.2%) reported sexually coercive behavior and an additional 6.8% reported nonsexual conduct problems. The key findings reported by Kjellgren et al. were as follows:

- Risk factors common to general antisocial behavior are noted in youths with sexual offenses.
- Gender-specific distorted attitudes and rape myths, not surprisingly, were much more common among youths with sexual offenses.
- Similarly, pro-rape attitudes and sexual preoccupation were most commonly observed among the youths with sexual offenses.
- "Penetrative sexual victimization, almost continuous experiencing of sexual lust, frequent use of porn and having watched violent porn, younger age at first sexual intercourse, 6 or more sexual partners, and having sold sex were all more common among *both*" (pp. 1167–1168) the youths with sexual offenses and youths with nonsexual conduct problems, compared with the normal controls.

Kjellgren et al. concluded that their findings were entirely in line with those of Seto and Lalumière (2010) and "strongly support the idea that sexuality-related variables are necessary to consider for improved etiological understanding, assessment, and treatment of sexually coercive youth" (p. 1168). A more recent review by Pullman and Seto (2012) supported the conclusion that a majority of adolescent sexual offenders are generalists (i.e., similar to other adolescent nonsexual offenders), whereas a minority of adolescent sexual offenders are specialists (possess unique risk and etiological factors, such as a history of maltreatment and atypical sexual interests).

Uncertain Role (and Conceptualization) of Protective Factors

In the domain of forensic adult risk assessment, existing models have consistently focused on risk factors and ignored or disregarded protective factors (Rogers, 2000). The same holds true for juvenile risk assessment. It remains an empirical question whether inclusion of protective factors that may reduce the likelihood of reoffending and promote prosocial behavior and lifestyles in youths may increase the efficacy of risk and needs assessment scales. Risk assessment measures such as the ERASOR and J-SOAP–II do not directly assess the presence of protective factors. The role of protective factors in delinquency, however, has been discussed for decades. Stattin and Magnusson (1996) noted that

> empirical studies have started to consider (a) the home-upbringing conditions and the individual characteristics that appear to help some individuals remain well, despite being brought up in adverse environments, (b) the conditions that may protect subjects with seemingly risky behaviors from developing more serious problems, and (c) the individual characteristics and environmental conditions that may change the course of life into a more positive direction. (p. 636)

In some cases, the apparent absence of risk (a score indicating the risk factor is not present) mighty be considered a strength or possibly protective. For example, the apparent absence of high sexual drive, high sexual preoccupation, or poorly managed anger could be considered a strength. By contrast, although social isolation may be a risk factor for repeated sexual offending, a lack of social isolation may not necessarily be a strength or protective factor if the adolescent's social life involves delinquency-minded peers. Pardini, Loeber, Farrington, and Stouthamer-Loeber (2012) reported from their Pittsburgh Youth Study that low peer delinquency was a direct protective factor for 13- to 14-year-olds ($OR = 0.44$) and 15- to 18-year-olds ($OR = 0.41$). A negative attitude toward delinquency was also protective for the 13- to 14-year-olds ($OR = 0.50$).

Few attempts have been made to develop and test protective factor assessment scales with adolescents who have sex-offending behaviors. Bremer (2006) developed the Protective Factors Scale to assess personal, family, and community assets that support positive behavior and prosocial development in general and including sexual behavior. Bremer noted that when used with the ERASOR (Worling & Curwen, 2000), which focuses on risk factors associated with sexual offending behaviors, the tools can facilitate appropriate interventions that can promote treatment progress as well as community safety. The Protective Factors Scale's utility for facilitating treatment and reducing sex offense recidivism has not been evaluated empirically.

Spice, Viljoen, Latzman, Scalora, and Ullman (2013) examined both risk and protective factors related to sexual and nonsexual recidivism in a sample of 193 youths. All protective factors were taken from the SAVRY (prosocial involvement, strong social support, strong attachments and bonds, positive attitude toward intervention and authority, strong commitment to school, resilient personality traits). Spice et al. found no protective factors to be associated with sexual recidivism and only strong attachments and bonds, as measured by the SAVRY, to be negatively related to nonsexual recidivism.

Although little is known about protective factors that are unique to juveniles who have committed sex offenses, ATSA (2012) proposed several from the delinquency literature, including positive family functioning (e.g., adequate supervision, consistent and fair discipline), positive peer social group, supportive adults, commitment to school, prosocial and noncriminogenic attitudes, and emotional maturity. Many of these, as Stattin and Magnusson (1996) suggested, are simply the inverse of risk factors (e.g., positive peer social group, prosocial and noncriminogenic attitudes).

More recently, Worling (2013) developed the Desistence for Adolescents Who Sexually Harm. Worling noted the dearth of research regarding strengths and protective factors and their relation to desistence from sexual offending. In his monograph on the measure, Worling reported that research pertaining to its psychometric properties and validity are in progress. As we noted earlier, capturing what is truly protective for a given youth may need to rely on self-report (i.e., a structured interview).

Risk and Needs Assessment Protocols

An exhaustive review of risk and needs assessment tools for adolescents with sexual behavior problems is well beyond the scope of this chapter. We have tried, however, to provide a reasonable snapshot. The literature on adolescent risk factors and assessment scales is not nearly as extensive as it is for adults who have offended sexually, but research (e.g., Viljoen et al., 2012) has suggested that the use of one or more validated risk measures can help prioritize cases for treatment and supervision, titrate intervention intensity to risks and needs, and maximize the efficient and effective use of limited resources. Furthermore, as Viljoen et al. (2012) noted, these assessment protocols yield incremental validity in risk assessment compared with unstructured clinical judgment or individual risk factors alone.

In spite of the seeming urgency for advances in developmentally appropriate risk and needs assessment, progress has been limited. As Viljoen et al. (2012) and others (e.g., Hempel, Buck, Cima, & van Marle, 2013) have noted, findings from individual studies of juvenile sex-offending risk assessment tools have yielded mixed results. Some of the weak or inconsistent findings are due to obvious methodological problems. Such problems include (a) limited sample sizes and low base rates of sexual reoffending; (b) differences in sample characteristics, such as outpatient versus residential placement; (c) samples with a greater proportion of youths with a delinquency history; and (d) studies that included youths for whom the risk scale was not intended (e.g., 20% sexual harassers in Aebi, Plattner, Steinhausen, & Bessler, 2011). Moreover, the length of follow-up and quality of outcome data undoubtedly contribute to disparate findings. Challenges with archival research, on which such studies often rely, probably also contribute to variable outcomes. These challenges include vague, ambiguous, or incomplete records and lax attention to detail or coding criteria when rating scale items, resulting in compromised accuracy and interrater reliability (although, according to Rajlic and Gretton, 2010, most studies of the J-SOAP–II and the ERASOR have found interrater reliability to be adequate or better). The single most daunting methodological problem, however, has been the low base rates for sexual reoffending, which have generally averaged around 10%. Such low (known) base rates for sexual reoffense (and commensurately high false positive rates) have posed a formidable obstacle to improving accuracy.

Empirical Findings on Validity of Risk Assessment Scales

Clearly, uninformed and inaccurate risk assessment decisions increase the number of mistakes, often resulting in unintended negative consequences that translate into significant and unnecessary human and monetary costs to society (Caldwell, Ziemke, & Vitacco, 2008; Chaffin, 2008). The goal of avoiding these false-positive and false-negative errors requires a sophisticated, empirically informed understanding of how to assess risk and needs in adolescents with sexual offending behaviors. Understanding the often subtle, complexly interactive effects of dynamic risk and protective factors is a more difficult task than static risk assessment but is essential for arriving at recommendations and conclusions that are remedial, reliable, efficacious, and humane.

Although programmatic research began in the mid-1990s with the development of the first version of the J-SOAP, and considerable research has taken place since, we are a long way from achieving our goal of creating and field testing an efficacious risk and needs protocol that can serve as a platform for implementing a more humane management strategy for juvenile sex offenders. When Bert Harris, Kate Frizzell, Sue Righthand, and Robert Prentky began work on a risk assessment scale intended for a new outpatient treatment program for juvenile sex offenders at the Joseph J. Peters Institute in Philadelphia, Pennsylvania, it was 1994 and fully in the throes of a wave of actuarial excitement, primarily for adult sex offenders. Naively, we jumped on board the actuarial wagon and set off to create an equivalent scale for adolescents. We have all learned a great deal over the past 2 decades, not the least of which is that an actuarial scale (i.e., a risk scale with life tables of probabilistic estimates) makes little sense for adolescents, unless the predictive window is exceptionally small (e.g., 6 months) and reassessments are frequent (e.g., at least one every 6 months). We further discuss this issue of developing life tables for adolescents in the Recommendations section of this chapter.

A notable study by Griffin, Beech, Print, Bradshaw, and Quayle (2008) regarding adolescent illegal sexual behaviors provided support for Bremer's (2006) assessment model of integrating risk and protective factors to identify relevant treatment targets and guide effective interventions. In this study, Griffin et al. described the development of the draft Assessment, Intervention, and Moving On—2 (AIM–2), a holistic research-based structured assessment guide designed for boys, ages 12 through 18 years, who have sexually abused others. The AIM–2 included 75 static and dynamic individual, family or caregiver, and environmental factors that are scored as concerns (risk factors) or strengths (protective factors) and categorized as low, medium, or high on each domain.

The AIM–2's predictive validity was tested with a randomly selected subsample of 70 adolescents who were followed for a minimum of 2 years (average follow-up of 6 years). Findings indicated that seven adolescents (10%) committed a new sexual offense. All of the sexual recidivists had high concern ratings (i.e., risk factors) and low strengths (i.e., protective factors). Moreover, participants with high concern ratings but also high protective ratings were less likely to reoffend than those with similar concern ratings but few strengths, suggesting that a cumulative effect of multiple protective factors may reduce the likelihood of repeat offending.

Although protective factors and nonsexual reoffending by youths who have committed a range of nonviolent or violent offenses have received greater research attention than studies of adolescent illegal sexual behaviors, this literature also is limited. The SAVRY (Borum, Bartel, & Forth, 2003) is particularly noteworthy in this regard.

The SAVRY was developed to assess risk factors associated with any kind of violent offending, including sexual reoffending (Borum et al., 2003). It is similar to the AIM–2 in that it has integrated six prosocial protective factors with risk factors to facilitate structured clinical judgments about repeat violent offending of any kind and to facilitate effective interventions. The protective factors are individual and related environmental factors that are generally considered inconsistent with antisocial orientations: prosocial involvement, social support, strong attachment bonds, a positive attitude toward authority and intervention and commitment to school or work, and a resilient personality.

The SAVRY has been the focus of various predictive validity studies and has demonstrated a positive association with repeated, nonspecified, general, or violent behavior (e.g., McGowan, Horn, & Mellott, 2011; Meyers & Schmidt, 2008; Vincent, Chapman, & Cook, 2011). Furthermore, in a study of adolescent illegal sexual behaviors, Viljoen et al., 2008) found the SAVRY predicted serious nonsexual violent recidivism, although its accuracy was better with older adolescents. It did not predict sexual reoffending. The SAVRY protective items were not associated with reoffending of any kind after discharge from the treatment program, but they had small to moderate associations with nonsexual aggression during treatment, which would suggest they are relevant targets of intervention.

In sum, research regarding adolescent illegal sexual behaviors, protective factors, and sexual reoffending has been minimal. Yet research regarding offending in general has suggested that the presence of protective factors, especially multiple ones, may have a moderating or buffering effect on risk factors associated with sexual and nonsexual recidivism. Thus, identifying treatment targets and treatment needs empirically associated with reoffending, developing individualized interventions that reduce recidivism of any kind, and promoting multiple protective factors are likely to facilitate desistance from repeat offending while promoting prosocial lifestyles.

Viljoen et al. (2012) aggregated 33 studies (published and unpublished) yielding a total of 6,196 male adolescents who had committed a sexual offense. Total scores on the ERASOR (Worling & Curwen, 2000), J-SOAP–II (Prentky & Righthand, 2003), Juvenile Sexual Offense Recidivism Risk Assessment Tool—II (Epperson & Ralston, 2014; Epperson et al., 2006), and the Static-99 (Hanson & Thornton, 1999) all predicted sexual recidivism with relatively equal efficacy (aggregated area under the curve values ranged from .64 to .67). Although the aggregated correlations were quite low (.12–.20), Viljoen et al. pointed out, citing Rice and Harris (2005), that correlations underestimate predictive validity when base rates are low. The primary reason why receiver operating characteristic area under the curve is the standard metric for reporting predictive accuracy of risk assessment scales is precisely because it is independent of base rates (Mossman, 1994).

Knight, Ronis, and Zakireh (2009) offered specific recommendations for future research on risk assessment:

- A "major deficiency of the three risk instruments [JSOAP–II, ERASOR, & JSORRAT–II] may . . . be the restrictive truncation of the range of information available on the domains . . . evaluated" (p. 899); the typical 0, 1, 2 ratings, Knight et al. pointed out, may optimize interrater reliability but at the price of sacrificing a range of severity needed for more accurate prediction.
- "If one's task were risk management instead of prediction . . . more differentiated scales standardized against both offender populations and community controls, are required to provide a richer and more empirically informed basis for treatment planning and needs targeting" (p. 899).
- The accomplishment of the aforementioned objectives necessitates multiple sources of input for ratings.

We absolutely agree with Knight et al. (2009) and have recommended that proceeding forward the next generation of risk scales for juveniles must include a structured clinical interview to augment structured professional judgment.

We also note that the reportedly low base rate of sexual reoffense must be addressed if offense prediction—as opposed to risk management—continues to be the objective. Aebi et al. (2011) found, for example, a total of seven detected cases of sexual recidivism in their sample of 223 youths (3.1%) after an average 4.3 year follow-up. The multivariate model they reported was thus based on seven cases. Similarly, the construction and validation sample for the first version of J-SOAP included 96 youths in community-based treatment. Twelve-month follow-up data on criminal reoffense were obtained on 75 of the youths, revealing a sexual recidivism rate of 4% ($n = 3$; Prentky et al., 2000). We made no attempt to analyze predictive validity based on three cases. If predictive accuracy continues to be the primary goal and sexual recidivism continues to be the criterion, either the criterion will have to broadened or higher risk samples will have to be targeted—or both.

Worling and Langton (2012) also offered a variety of risk assessment–related recommendations for communication of risk: (a) an explicit time frame over which the assessment may be considered valid; Worling and Langton recommended 1 year or less (we recommend, depending on the case, an even more conservative estimate of 6 months or less); (b) caveats about the reliability of individual risk factors over time, implying the need for developmentally sensitive risk factors; (c) addressing both risk of sexual reoffending and risk of nonsexual, violent reoffending as well, making the SAVRY (Borum et al., 2003) or the Youth Level of Service/Case Management Inventory (Hoge & Andrews, 2002) possibly important additions to the assessment; and (d) examining the personal strengths of the youth and incorporating those strengths into the case formulation and intervention plan.

Worling and Langton (2012) further pointed out, in this regard, that a similar analysis of protective factors is also important, including the potential mitigatory impact of such factors on risk. This should also be incorporated into a comprehensive intervention plan. We would add a fifth recommendation: to document the limitations of the evaluation and their potential impact on the conclusions and recommendations, including the adequacy and reliability of the archival data and the conditions of the evaluation (including ambient noise and privacy).

Risk Communication: A Caveat

Research support for the use of cutoff scores with risk labels (*low, moderate, high*) with juveniles is lacking. When drawing conclusions about the assessment, practitioners should be cautious about applying risk-level labels and refrain from using any labels that cannot be supported by the data. This means not affixing a label based solely on the cutoff score of a risk scale. The preponderance of the evidence gathered in an evaluation should support the label, if one is used. The most problematic concern with individual-specific risk-level labels is the temporal stability of the label. The label may define the youth long after it is no longer valid. Because risk assessments should be revisited as frequently as every 2 to 3 months, and certainly within 6 months, the label may well change; the original label, however, remains in the record permanently. Stated otherwise, normative data do not account for the fluidity of adolescent development and environmental flux. Furthermore, labels increase error. Because one is placing all youths into one of three bins (low, medium, or high risk), the inevitable result is a large number of youths classified as high risk when they are not, resulting in false-positive judgment errors and associated unintended but serious negative consequences of such a classification. False-negative errors may also occur when the label, derived from the results of completing a risk scale, reflects a low-risk classification but a careful, idiographic analysis of risk reveals a higher risk to reoffend.

Similarly, a score derived from a risk scale, or the labeled bin that the score falls into, should never be used in isolation to support or to justify subjecting a youth to long-term statutory requirements, such as registration or community notification (ATSA, 2012). When assistance with such determinations is sought, the recommendations should be firmly anchored in a comprehensive assessment.

A potentially very troubling concern is raised with the introduction of life tables with probabilistic estimates of reoffense. These life tables, derived from reference groups or development samples of actuarial risk scales, place the client into a bin on the basis of scale score. As we noted earlier, these scores are particularly subject to change in adolescents. Unlike adult actuarial risk assessment tables, which reflect estimates going out many years, juveniles must be reassessed frequently and any meaningful prediction should not be for more than 6 months. Of greater concern, however, is the potential for misuse or abuse of any estimate derived from a life table. As with a cutoff score with an associated label (low, moderate, high), life table estimates pose a similar, if not greater, danger of becoming an inexpungible, defining feature of the youth, regardless of their accuracy.

There is no defensible substitute for an idiographic evaluation that addresses individual, contextual, and situational dynamic needs and protective factors that may exacerbate or mitigate risk, as well as the extent to which these factors are currently present or are likely to be present in the near future, in combination with nomothetic data. DeMatteo, Batastini, Foster, and Hunt (2010) provided helpful guidelines for integrating idiographic and nomothetic data, including (a) use of structured professional judgment measures, (b) critical evaluation of the risk factors determined to be present, (c) an anamnestic approach to gathering client-specific information relevant to the assessment of risk (Heilbrun, Yasuhara, & Shah, 2010; Melton et al., 2007), (d) use of a model to guide data collection and interpretation (Heilbrun, 2001), and (e) awareness of heuristics that contribute to bias, including over- or underemphasis of specific risk or protective factors.

INTERVENTIONS

In the sections that follow, we turn our attention to the role of treatment as an intervention strategy for juvenile sex offenders, attempts at estimating the efficacy of treatment, and the critical role of public policy in formulating and promoting interventions.

Treatment and the RNR Model

As noted earlier, the RNR model (Andrews & Bonta, 2010) describes three major principles of correctional rehabilitation and human service delivery that, if met, are associated with reductions in criminal recidivism among both adults (Andrews & Bonta, 2010) and juveniles (e.g., Pealer & Latessa, 2004), including adults and juveniles who have committed sexual offenses (Hanson et al., 2009). RNR, more than anything else, is integrative. As a model, it begins with comprehensive assessment and targeted recommendations that issue from the assessment, proceeds to treatment, and embraces a wide range of rehabilitative options. In 2012, ATSA, in its policy statement on juveniles who commit sexually abusive offenses, recommended that risk, need, and responsivity principles be adhered to when working with adolescents who have engaged in sexually abusive behavior.

Marlatt developed a cognitive–behavioral model (relapse prevention) for treatment of alcoholics (Marlatt & Gordon, 1985). This relapse prevention model was adapted for use with sex offenders (Pithers, Marques, Gibat, & Marlatt, 1983) and has long been the most widely applied model in treatment programs for sex offenders (Laws, 1989; Laws, Hudson, & Ward, 2000). Relapse prevention is also the most commonly used model for treating juvenile sex offenders (McGrath et al., 2010). In addition to teaching the principles of relapse prevention, the most commonly addressed needs of juvenile sex offenders include positive self-esteem, clarifications of values, sex education, social skills training, impulse control and coping skills, assertiveness training and conflict resolution, and empathy training (Hunter, 2000). Importantly, relapse prevention has not been supported by the empirical research on juvenile sex offenders, and thus is not recommended.

From a strictly clinical standpoint, buy in is essential. Treatment that is imposed is likely to elicit grudging (or worse) participation. Rather than feeling like a helpless pawn being ordered into treatment by the system, youths who are both fully informed and engaged in the decision-making process, perceiving some degree of ownership of their fate and their behavior, are more likely to work toward interventions that are put in place—including their treatment goals. Similarly, transparency goes hand in hand with buy-in and is essential. This can be accomplished by means of a case review conference that brings all parties together with the youth to (a) discuss options, (b) solicit feedback from the youth, and (c) convey a sense of concern and flexibility rather than indifference, rigidity, or insensitivity. This can be accomplished with a modicum of sensitivity while simultaneously setting limits and realistic expectations. The overarching goal must involve moving youths, as expeditiously as possible, along a path toward psychological health; this goal demands a risk management plan that does no further harm to youths and at the same time protects against any further victimization. The process of moving treatment-resistant youths down this rehabilitative path will be immensely improved by making youngsters allies of their own health.

Treatment Efficacy

Assessments of youths with sex-offending behavior are not complete without consideration of factors that may increase treatment responses and positive outcomes. These factors may include learning styles, co-occurring disorders or substance abuse problems, limited motivation to change, cultural beliefs, attitudes about sexuality and relationships, self-esteem, and so forth. Some responsivity factors (e.g., chronic substance abuse, an acute episode of mental illness, symptoms of posttraumatic stress disorder associated with childhood sexual abuse) may not be empirically associated with reoffense risk, but may impede treatment progress. Other factors, such as atypical sexual interests, including much younger children (e.g., 4 years or more younger than the youth) are risk relevant. Atypical sexual interests, which appear to be rather infrequent, may require appropriate interventions. Such assessment and interventions must be based on the best available research and provided by appropriately trained clinicians. Worling (2012) reviewed the research literature on the assessment and treatment of atypical sexual arousal and found it to be sparse and fraught with methodological limitations. He noted that visual reaction-time methods of assessing sexual interest have received some research support with adolescents, but noted that for some youth sexual interests are not firmly established and may become age appropriate over time, with maturation.

Appropriate psychological tests can provide objective nomothetic information in addition to information derived from client interviews, collateral interviews, and historical records. Testing may help confirm or disconfirm hypotheses and may be especially useful when evaluating questions concerning responsivity factors, such as learning disorders, attachment disorders, trauma, and other psychiatric disorders. Testing also can serve to establish a pretreatment baseline, against which treatment progress and outcomes can be objectively evaluated. Although the literature on general assessment with juveniles who have sexually offended is sparse, several sources are noteworthy (Fanniff & Becker, 2006; O'Reilly & Carr, 2006; Ryan, 2012; Worling & Langton, 2012).

A comprehensive review of treatment outcome studies is well beyond the scope of this chapter. We provide, however, an overview of findings from selected individual studies and meta-analyses. More detailed discussions of the treatment literature may be found elsewhere (Becker & Hunter, 1997; Bourke & Donohue, 1996; Efta-Breitbach & Freeman, 2005; Fanniff & Becker, 2006; Hunter & Figueredo, 1999; Reitzel & Carbonell, 2006; Righthand & Welch, 2001, 2005; Walker, McGovern, Poey, & Otis, 2004; Worling & Langton, 2012).

Meta-analyses of treatment with adolescents who have offended sexually have suggested that treatment may reduce the likelihood of sexual recidivism. Reitzel and Carbonell (2006) conducted a meta-analysis of nine published and unpublished studies, finding an 11.5% difference in sexual recidivism rates between adolescents who completed a sex offense–specific treatment program (7.4%) and those receiving no treatment (18.9%). Comparisons regarding treatment modality (e.g., cognitive–behavioral treatment vs. other treatment methods) were not significant. Reitzel and Carbonell noted, however, that multisystemic therapy (MST) was not included as a cognitive–behavioral intervention, although it is described as emphasizing such techniques (http://mstservices.com). In the Reitzel and Carbonell analysis, MST was categorized as a socioecological intervention and was found to be the most robust treatment method. Thus, this categorization of MST as noncognitive behavior may explain this study's finding regarding cognitive–behavioral therapy and suggests that socioecological interventions using cognitive–behavioral therapy may be most effective. Appropriately, Reitzel and Carbonell urged caution when interpreting these meta-analytic findings, citing an array of methodological limitations such as the small number of studies, small sample sizes, varying follow-up periods, and divergent strategies for controlling for treatment dropouts.

Heilbrun et al. (2005) identified nine published studies to include in their meta-analysis focusing on risk factors and needs of adolescents who had offended sexually. They found that too few of the studies provided sufficient information about the specific types of treatment that were offered. Therefore, they created a composite intervention item that included studies that provided information about outcomes from any type of treatment that had reducing sexual recidivism as a goal. Their findings indicated that this intervention variable was significantly related to sexual recidivism, suggesting that treatment efforts with adolescent illegal sexual behaviors were effective at reducing sexual recidivism.

Walker et al. (2004) appear to have been the first researchers to conduct a meta-analysis of treatment studies of juveniles who offended sexually. Their study included 10 published and unpublished studies. Findings indicated that all of the treatments used in their aggregated pool of studies positively reduced sexual recidivism. Cognitive–behavioral therapy had the strongest effects, and MST appeared promising.

Results from individual studies of MST for problematic sexual behavior (MST–PSB) are also noteworthy and encouraging. MST–PSB is an adaptation of the MST model that is designed specifically for youths who engage in sex-offending behaviors. MST is the only treatment approach for adolescents who have offended sexually that has been empirically validated by several randomized controlled studies, albeit with very small samples (Borduin, Schaeffer, & Heiblum, 2009, $N = 48$). A randomized MST–PSB study with a larger sample ($N = 127$) reported preliminary findings consistent with earlier research (Letourneau et al., 2009). When compared with community-based services currently provided to adolescents who offend sexually, MST demonstrated improvements in family and peer relations and academic performance and evidenced reductions in problematic sexual behavior, substance use, and criminal behavior (Henggeler et al., 2009). At present, it appears "that the only treatment approach that has been empirically demonstrated to reduce recidivism and other negative outcomes for adolescent sexual offenders, using the gold standard evaluation design of randomized clinical trials, is multisystemic therapy" (Pullman & Seto, 2012, p. 206).

Additional support for community-based sex offense–specific treatment that involves caregivers was provided by Worling et al.'s (2010) 10-year follow-up of an outpatient sex offense–specific treatment program. Overall, 67% of the comparison group in Worling et al.'s study received some treatment, although the details and duration were unknown. The adolescents were followed for 12 to 20 years. Rates of sexual recidivism were 9% for youths in the specialized treatment group and 21% for the comparison group; 22% for violent nonsexual recidivism for the specialized treatment group and 39% for the comparison group; and 28% for nonviolent, nonsexual recidivism and 52% for the comparison group. Because the Worling et al. study was not a randomized trial, it is not possible to rule out inadvertent bias in assignment to the treatment group or the comparison group.

Although it appears that relatively few youths have persistent patterns of deviant sexual interests, such as recurring atypical sexual fantasies involving prepubescent children or coercive sexual acts, the presence of such atypical sexual interests may be an important risk factor for sexual recidivism. If identified, such an interest requires monitoring and, if indicated, appropriate intervention. Yet, as Worling found in his 2012 review, specific treatment interventions that target atypical arousal have limited research support. Although Worling provided some suggestions that may be helpful, overfocusing on sexual interests, fantasies, and urges may do more harm than good for some youths (Fanniff & Becker, 2006). As Worling noted, atypical arousal may be a risk factor for a minority of adolescents, whereas factors such as attitudes and beliefs that justify sex offending, impulsivity, insufficient monitoring, and, for some, an antisocial orientation are more likely to be risk relevant for most youths who have offended sexually.

It is apparent that many of the risk and protective factors related to juvenile sex offending are those that are relevant for juvenile offending in general. Definitive evidence of the need for special sex offense–specific treatment is lacking. In the one study that specifically investigated this question, Lab, Shields, and Schondel (1993) compared sex offense–specific treatment with treatment typically provided for adolescents who committed non–sex offenses. They found low recidivism rates for both groups. The low base rate of sexual reoffending may have obscured real differences, although it may be that the criminogenic needs of these groups were, in fact, similar, as seems to be the case among some adolescents who have offended sexually and others who have been delinquent but have not offended sexually.

In sum, effective interventions are those that provide the most intensive interventions to those with the greatest needs and fewest protective factors, are assessment driven and match interventions to relevant criminogenic and responsivity needs, are based on the best available evidence, and are applied with fidelity to the treatment model. For example, in his meta-analysis of interventions with juveniles who offended with a range of offenses (i.e., not sex offense specific), Lipsey (2009) found that generic therapeutic interventions that were provided by well-trained and supervised staff who monitored client progress and treatment fidelity were effective and were as effective as model interventions such as MST. The crux of the message from Lipsey's meta-analysis was that "the largest and most consistent relationship with recidivism effects is the quality of program implementation with, of course, higher quality associated with bigger effects on recidivism" (p. 141). What Lipsey found that was most striking was the lack of differential efficacy of interventions ("most of the interventions were about equally effective irrespective of whether the youth was under no official supervision, had been diverted, was under probation supervision, or was in a juvenile custodial facility") and "the robustness of intervention effects" (p. 143), leading to his conclusion that effective treatment is not highly context dependent. The important caveat is that although Lipsey's dataset was large, based on 548 independent studies of juveniles ranging in age from 12 to 21, it did not target youths who committed sexual offenses. Thus, these findings may more properly apply to subtypes of juvenile sex offenders, such as Hunter's (2006) Type 1 (life-course-persistent antisocial type).

PUBLIC POLICY AND INTERVENTION

In 2012, ATSA adopted policies and practices for adolescents who engaged in sexually abusive behavior, in which it noted,

> as of 2011, laws in 35 states require adolescents who have been adjudicated for sexual crimes to register with law enforcement, sometimes for life; 18 of these states disclose juveniles' private information to the public. Some registered youths are also required to comply with residency restrictions prohibiting them from living near schools, parks or other places where children may congregate. Sometimes registered youths are expelled from schools or not allowed to participate in activities that can promote healthy development, such as school clubs, sports, and dances.
>
> Like registered adults, registered youth who do not comply with mandated public registration requirements may be subject to prosecution for a felony and attendant severe consequences, including lengthy incarceration. Such policies not only have detrimental life altering consequences for the youth, but his or her family members as well.
>
> Increasingly, research findings show that registration and public notification policies, especially when applied to youth, are not effective; and may do more harm than good. Such laws may

> have deleterious effects on prosocial development by disrupting positive peer relationships and activities and interfering with school and work opportunities, resulting in housing instability or homelessness, harassment and ostracization, social alienation and lifelong stigmatization and instability. Such practices are inconsistent with community safety and promotion of prosocial development and, in fact, may actually elevate a youth's risk by increasing known risk factors for sexual and nonsexual offending such as social isolation. (pp. 5–6).

Fueled by profound misconceptions about the magnitude of risk posed by youths who have offended sexually, even juveniles with a first sexual offense may be subject to highly punitive practices and laws (Caldwell & Dickinson, 2009; Trivits & Reppucci, 2002), such as indeterminate confinement, mandated registration, notification, and residency restrictions. Not only may such policies and practices not have the intended positive effect of reducing sexual violence, but they may have serious unintended negative effects. These effects may include (a) deteriorating positive social and interpersonal skills and prosocial beliefs and promotion of criminogenic attitudes when youths are isolated from normative developmental experiences or placed with delinquent peers; (b) experiencing rejection and isolation by peers, family, former friends, potential employers, and others, further eroding self-esteem and undermining attempts at achieving normal, developmentally appropriate relationships and successfully reintegrating into society; and thereby (c) marginalizing youngsters who ultimately place demands on society rather than contributing positively.

Severe overreactions to sexual offending by juveniles can be explained, in part, by two separate realities. According to the extant empirical literature, rates of sexual reoffending by juveniles are indeed quite low—according to meta-analytic studies, generally in the range of 5% to 15% (e.g., Caldwell, 2010; Heilbrun et al., 2005; McCann & Lussier, 2008; Reitzel & Carbonell, 2006; Viljoen et al., 2012). However, sexual abuse is a very serious offense that may have severe and long-term consequences. Moreover, in spite of the relatively low base rate of sexual recidivism, data from multiple sources have suggested that a small group of juveniles persist (e.g., Rubinstein et al., 1993). High-quality assessments and effective interventions are necessary for increasing community safety while simultaneously facilitating desistence from sexual and nonsexual offending among adolescents who have offended sexually and promoting prosocial development.

This rush to policies advocating costly management strategies has occurred absent research supporting their effectiveness (Vitacco et al., 2009). Relevant studies (e.g., Caldwell & Dickinson, 2009) have found no evidence of reduced sexual or violent reoffending for juveniles subjected to registration and notification. Moreover, juvenile registration and notification has been associated with an increase in plea bargaining as well as prosecutorial dismissal of sex offense cases, perhaps as attorneys seek to divert youths from what appear to be unduly harsh outcomes. As well intended as such actions may be, some youths who might benefit from treatment are excluded when they are diverted from the juvenile justice system.

As Garfinkle (2003) concluded in her law review article, "Children who commit sexual offenses generally have the same vulnerabilities and are in the same need of protection as the child victims whom the proponents of Megan's Laws claim to protect" (p. 205).

Illustration of Continuum of Services and Placements

In Figure 29.1, we use the subtype descriptors discussed earlier in this chapter, based on the work of Hunter (2006, 2008; Hunter et al., 2003). In the case of the situational offender, depending on the youth and his or her treatment needs, required interventions may be minimal (e.g., some isolated instances of sexual offending and family members who believe sex offending occurred and increased monitoring is needed). In such cases, being caught and sanctioned by parents, recognizing harm done to a sibling, or talking with law enforcement or child welfare professionals about the abusive behavior

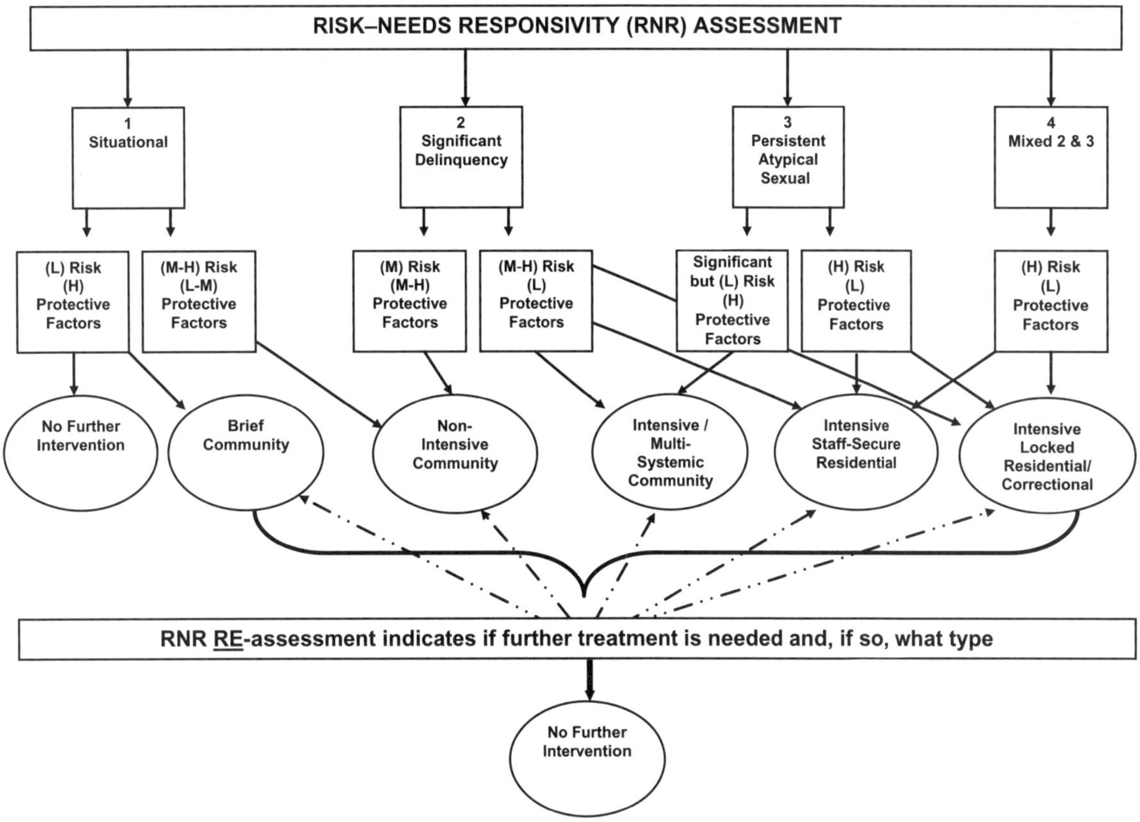

FIGURE 29.1. RNR model as applied to youth with varying degrees of risk and protective factors. Bracket indicates reassessments. Dashed lines indicate that more treatment is needed; type depends on RNR findings. L= lower or fewer; M = moderate; H = higher or more.

may be sufficient for the youth to recognize the wrongfulness of the sexually abusive behavior and stop. With other youths, brief interventions focusing on erroneous or distorted attitudes or beliefs that fostered the sexually abusive behavior or interventions that may facilitate reunification, when appropriate, and repairing family relationships may be all that is needed. In both types of cases, the offending may be situational and transitory.

In other instances, when there is a history of early onset or serious delinquency, depicted in Figure 29.1 as significant delinquency, interventions may primarily focus on delinquency factors, such as criminogenic attitudes that support illegal behavior, negative or delinquent peer relationships, substance abuse issues, and nonsexual antisocial behavior. The focus on sexual behavior may be limited, addressing beliefs and attitudes that support coercive sexual behavior and promoting consensual, healthy sexual relationships. In cases involving persistent atypical or non-normative sexual arousal (labeled *persistent atypical sexual* in Figure 29.1), treatment related to the atypical arousal is indicated and is part of a holistic treatment package that addresses those and other relevant treatment needs.

When multiple criminogenic needs are present, interventions are prioritized to address those that are most urgent for facilitating safety and promoting progress. Furthermore, as indicated by the RNR model (Andrews & Bonta, 2010), those youths with the most risk factors and criminogenic needs and limited or few protective factors (labeled *Mixed 2 and 3* in Figure 29.1) require the greatest intensity of treatment in terms of frequency and duration (dosage) and the most supervision. Youths with many risk factors and few protective factors who have histories of multiple victims, violent behavior, noncompliance with treatment, and eloping from home or treatment settings may require placement in a locked setting. Triaging limited treatment resources to those with the greatest risk factors and treatment needs is likely to reduce reoffense risk, promote prosocial behavior, and be more cost effective.

As shown in Figure 29.1, a continuum of treatment intensity is necessary to appropriately match interventions to current individual risks and needs. Timely reassessments are required to monitor the youth's current treatment needs. The guiding principle should always be continuity along a continuum of care that moves in the direction of decreasing intensity and decreasing restrictiveness. As youths develop, mature, and respond more positively to treatment, they should be moved along the continuum, benefiting from less intensive interventions and more opportunities to participate in normative adolescent activities. If a good-faith effort is made to address problematic sexual behavior assertively and competently with best-practice modalities, most youths will reach a point at which no further intervention is required.

Sometimes, however, a youth's behavior, response to treatment, and reassessment may indicate the need for more intensive interventions. The youth may not be positively engaged in treatment, he or she may have more risks and fewer protective factors than previously thought, and more intensive treatment interventions may be needed. For these reasons, the continuum of treatment intensity must be fluid and bidirectional, because risk, protective, and treatment response factors change. To be most effective, as Bengis (1986) noted decades ago, the continuum of treatment should be consistent in approach, relying on relevant and effective interventions.

In Figure 29.2, a Venn diagram illustrates the continuum of treatment intensity as well as the range of placement possibilities. Decision makers, such as judges, probation officers, and child welfare workers, ultimately determine placement in treatment settings. These decisions, however, should be informed by competent clinical input regarding the current status of risk and protective factors and needed treatment intensity. Consistent with ATSA's (2012) policies and practices, these decisions should always favor, whenever possible, the least restrictive placement.

As the arrows in the Venn diagram reflect, a variety of treatment options are available for youths in the community. With increasingly effective community interventions that involve caregivers and increased parental monitoring and support, relatively few youths may require the intensity and

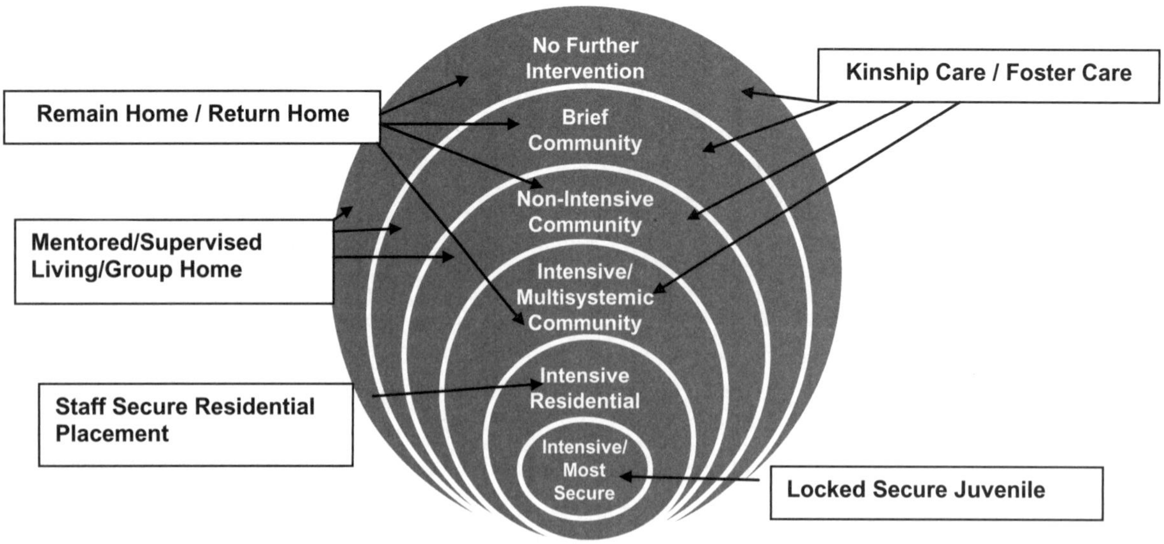

FIGURE 29.2. Placements along the treatment continuum.

supervision provided by treatment in a residential or correctional facility. When such placements are deemed necessary, a flexible continuum of services, including a consistent approach to treatment, is critical for fostering growth and transitioning youths back to the community or home as soon as possible.

Providing interventions along a flexible, responsive, and effective continuum of care enables treatment providers to match client needs to the most appropriate interventions at a particular time. As RNR research has shown (e.g., Hanson et al., 2009), the approach of tailoring interventions to current treatment needs is most likely to increase positive outcomes such as reducing recidivism and promoting prosocial development. Such an approach is not only more humane—avoiding unnecessary, severe, punitive, and ineffective interventions—but it is also more likely to reduce the incidence of further sexual victimization and be more cost effective in the process.

Intervention recommendations that provide the referring party (court, attorney, probation officer) with a clear and practical road map for reducing risk factors and promoting protective factors should be standard operating procedure. Consistent with the RNR model, interventions that have the strongest research support for matching individual criminogenic needs with caregiver and community resources should be emphasized. Depending on the youth and his or her treatment needs, the indicated interventions may be minimal (e.g., some isolated instances of sexual offending). Interventions may also primarily focus on delinquency factors, such as attitudes that support illegal behavior and negative peer relationships, while the focus on sexual behavior may be limited. In cases involving atypical or non-normative sexual arousal, treatment related to such arousal is indicated as part of a treatment package that addresses those needs. When multiple criminogenic needs are present, recommendations for interventions are prioritized to address those that are most urgent for facilitating safety and promoting progress. Recommendations also include intensity (dosage) of treatment, duration of treatment, and location of services. The risks and benefits associated with various treatment or placement options should also be discussed.

Concluding Thoughts on Promoting Health

A 1999 New York Academy of Sciences Conference was devoted to the question of uncertainty in the risk assessment of environmental and occupational hazards (Bailer et al., 1999). Of particular note was the session devoted to risk assessment for children (Landrigan, 1999). Landrigan (1999) noted in his preliminary remarks that "if high-risk groups, such as children, do not receive appropriate consideration, then risk assessment and the regulatory decisions that follow from it will . . . fail to adequately protect the most vulnerable members of society" (pp. 1–2).

Landrigan (1999) further remarked that "adoption of a new child-centered agenda for research and risk assessment is necessary" (p. 1). Although Landrigan's remarks were in reference to a different threat and admittedly the analogy is not direct (i.e., in the present context, children and adolescents are held responsible for the threat, not victimized by it), the central point remains—a child-centered, developmentally sensitive agenda that applies equally to the child welfare system and the juvenile justice system must replace the current punitive, offender-centered agenda.

The good news is that children and adolescents do not present the stark threat that they have been assumed to. The bad news is that good news is not always welcome news:

> Vested political or financial interests and highly emotional advocacy agendas will complicate healthy skepticism about the facts or their dispassionate consideration. Moral panic, righteous indignation, and truthiness have their own allure and satisfaction. The sound bite that we should put our kids' safety before the rights of sexual offenders, adult or juvenile, sounds so intuitively correct that it is a guaranteed political winner, even if the policy it promotes is ultimately destructive and fails to deliver the child protection goods. (Chaffin, 2008, p. 120)

The task at hand is vastly more encompassing than testing the latest version of a new risk assessment scale. No risk assessment scale, no matter what its presumptive accuracy, will solve the systemic problem of how youths who have committed sexual offenses should be managed. The quintessential issue may be seen as part of the interminable debate over retributive versus restorative justice for juveniles. We would argue, however, that the most prudent answer transcends this philosophical conundrum and could be resolved less contentiously with data-informed, cost-effective (viable) responses to the problem.

There is no debate that sexual abuse by juveniles is a serious problem. Even one more victim is one too many. Fortunately, as the empirical literature has suggested, the base rate of known sexual recidivism is relatively low (5% to 15% in most samples). Every realistic option to further reduce the likelihood of reoffending, sexually or otherwise, should be considered. Our most earnest efforts, however, must not be at the expense of those children and juveniles responsible for the abuse—most of whom were themselves subject to varying degrees of abuse. In the collective interests of society, as well as of all children, both the victimized and the victimizers, the most constructive response is also the most salutary and humane response—providing the best possible therapeutic care for victims and victimizers, because all of these children are the next generation of adults. At present, the most useful framework for achieving this goal is the RNR model of assessment and treatment. Embedded within the assessment phase of RNR should be a conceptual, theoretical, and clinical appreciation that juveniles with sexual offending behaviors are, as Stattin and Magnusson (1996) reminded us, whole persons. The totality of a youngster is not his or her offending behavior. Our assessments should be as holistic a snapshot of the youth as the data permit. As we have attempted to illustrate, the passageway through the system should flow in one direction—toward increasingly greater reintegration into a normal life. This goal becomes increasingly remote when normality has been supplanted by many years of incarceration, replacing normal adolescent development with tedium (at best) and further indoctrination in criminal behavior and maltreatment (at worst). To be sure, some youths' problematic behavior is so intractable that management in a secure facility is the only viable option. Even with those youth, however, the ultimate goal should remain the same; the only difference is that these youth require the most intensive treatment.

Juveniles who have harmed other children are themselves often victims of harm, sometimes grievous harm. If we fail, for whatever myriad reasons (or excuses), in caring for all of the children that we as a society have harmed, we will pay a far greater price in their outcomes as damaged young adults.

References

Aebi, M., Plattner, B., Steinhausen, H. C., & Bessler, C. (2011). Predicting sexual and nonsexual recidivism in a consecutive sample of juveniles convicted of sexual offences. *Sexual Abuse: A Journal of Research and Treatment*, *23*, 456–473.

Andrews, D. A., & Bonta, J. (2010). *The psychology of criminal conduct* (5th ed.). New Providence, NJ: LexisNexis/Anderson.

Association for the Treatment of Sexual Abusers. (2012). *Adolescents who have engaged in sexually abusive behavior: Effective policies and practices*. Beaverton, OR: Author. Retrieved from http://www.atsa.com/adolescents-engaged-in-sexually-abusive-behavior

Bailer, A. J., Maltoni, C., Bailar, J. C., Belpoggi, F., Brazier, J. V., & Soffritti, M. (Eds.). (1999). Uncertainty in the risk assessment of environmental and occupational hazards. *Annals of the New York Academy of Sciences*, *895*, ix–xii, 1–376.

Barbaree, H. E., Marshall, W. L., & Hudson, S. M. (Eds.). (1993). *The juvenile sex offender*. New York, NY: Guilford Press.

Becker, J. V., & Hunter, J. A. (1997). Understanding and treating child and adolescent sexual offenders. In T. H. Ollendick & R. J. Prinz (Eds.), *Advances in clinical child psychology* (Vol. 19, pp. 177–197). http://dx.doi.org/10.1007/978-1-4757-9035-1_5

Belsky, J. (1980). Child maltreatment: An ecological integration. *American Psychologist*, *35*, 320–335. http://dx.doi.org/10.1037/0003-066X.35.4.320

Bengis, S. (1986). *A comprehensive continuum of care for adolescent sexual offenders*. Orwell, VT: Safer Society Program.

Blumstein, A., Farrington, D. P., & Moitra, S. (1985). Delinquency careers: Innocents, desisters, and persisters. In M. Tonry & N. Morris (Eds.), *Crime and justice: An annual review of research* (Vol. 6, pp. 187–219). Chicago, IL: University of Chicago Press.

Bonnie, R. J., & Scott, E. S. (2013). The teenage brain: Adolescent brain research and the law. *Current Directions in Psychological Science*, *22*, 158–161. http://dx.doi.org/10.1177/0963721412471678

Borduin, C. M., Henggeler, S. W., Blaske, D. M., & Stein, R. J. (1990). Multisystemic treatment of adolescent sexual offenders. *International Journal of Offender Therapy and Comparative Criminology*, *34*, 105–113. http://dx.doi.org/10.1177/0306624X9003400204

Borduin, C. M., Schaeffer, C. M., & Heiblum, N. (2009). A randomized clinical trial of multisystemic therapy with juvenile sexual offenders: Effects on youth social ecology and criminal activity. *Journal of Consulting and Clinical Psychology*, *77*, 26–37. http://dx.doi.org/10.1037/a0013035

Borum, R. (2003). Managing at-risk juvenile offenders in the community: Putting evidence-based principles into practice. *Journal of Contemporary Criminal Justice*, *19*, 114–137. http://dx.doi.org/10.1177/1043986202239745

Borum, R., Bartel, P., & Forth, A. (2003). *Manual for the Structured Assessment of Violence Risk in Youth*. Odessa, FL: Psychological Assessment Resources.

Bourke, M. L., & Donohue, B. (1996). Assessment and treatment of juvenile sex offenders: An empirical review. *Journal of Child Sexual Abuse*, *5*, 47–70. http://dx.doi.org/10.1300/J070v05n01_03

Bremer, J. (2006). Protective Factors Scale: Determining the level of intervention for youth with harmful sexual behavior. In D. S. Prescott (Ed.), *Risk assessment of youth who have sexually abused* (pp. 195–221). Oklahoma City, OK: Wood & Barnes.

Bronfrenbrenner, U. (1979). *The ecology of human development: Experiments by nature and design*. Cambridge, MA: Harvard University Press.

Burton, D. (2003). Male adolescents: Sexual victimization and subsequent sexual abuse. *Child and Adolescent Social Work Journal*, *20*, 277–296. http://dx.doi.org/10.1023/A:1024556909087

Caldwell, M. F. (2007). Sexual offense adjudication and sexual recidivism among juvenile offenders. *Sexual Abuse: A Journal of Research and Treatment*, *19*, 107–113.

Caldwell, M. F. (2010). Study characteristics and recidivism base rates in juvenile sex offender recidivism. *International Journal of Offender Therapy and Comparative Criminology*, *54*, 197–212. http://dx.doi.org/10.1177/0306624X08330016

Caldwell, M. F., & Dickinson, C. (2009). Sex offender registration and recidivism risk in juvenile sexual offenders. *Behavioral Sciences and the Law*, *27*, 941–956. http://dx.doi.org/10.1002/bsl.907

Caldwell, M. F., Ziemke, M. H., & Vitacco, M. J. (2008). An examination of the Sex Offender Registration and Notification Act as applied to juveniles: Evaluating the ability to predict sexual recidivism. *Psychology, Public Policy, and Law*, *14*, 89–114. http://dx.doi.org/10.1037/a0013241

Carpentier, M. Y., Silovsky, J. F., & Chaffin, M. (2006). Randomized trial of treatment for children with sexual behavior problems: Ten-year follow-up. *Journal of Consulting and Clinical Psychology*, *74*, 482–488. http://dx.doi.org/10.1037/0022-006X.74.3.482

Casey, B. J., Getz, S., & Galvan, A. (2008). The adolescent brain. *Developmental Review*, *28*, 62–77. http://dx.doi.org/10.1016/j.dr.2007.08.003

Cauffman, E., & Steinberg, L. (2000). (Im)maturity of judgment in adolescence: Why adolescents may be less culpable than adults. *Behavioral Sciences and the Law*, *18*, 741–760. http://dx.doi.org/10.1002/bsl.416

Chaffin, M. (2008). Our minds are made up—Don't confuse us with the facts: Commentary on policies concerning children with sexual behavior problems and juvenile sex offenders. *Child Maltreatment*, *13*, 110–121. http://dx.doi.org/10.1177/1077559508314510

Chaffin, M., & Bonner, B. (1998). Don't shoot, we're your children: Have we gone too far in our treatment of adolescent sexual abusers and children with sexual behavior problems? *Child Maltreatment*, *3*, 314–316. http://dx.doi.org/10.1177/1077559598003004003

Cicchetti, D. (1990). A historical perspective on the discipline of developmental psychopathology. In J. Rolf, A. Masten, D. Cicchetti., K. Nucchtelein, & S. Weintraub (Eds.), *Risk and protective factors in the development of psychopathology* (pp. 2–28). http://dx.doi.org/10.1017/CBO9780511752872.003

Clarke, R. V. (1996). The distribution of deviance and exceeding the speed limit. *British Journal of Criminology*, *36*, 169–181. http://dx.doi.org/10.1093/oxfordjournals.bjc.a014080

Council of State Governments. (2010). *Legislating sex offender management: Trends in state legislation 2007 and 2008* (Report from Grant No. 2006-WP-BX-K003). Lexington, KY: Author.

Dahl, R. E. (2001). Affect regulation, brain development, and behavioral/emotional health in adolescence. *CNS Spectrums*, *6*, 60–72.

Dahl, R. E. , & Spear, L. P. (2004). Adolescent brain development: A period of vulnerabilities and opportunities. Keynote address. *Annals of the New York Academy of Sciences*, *1021*, 1–22. http://dx.doi.org/10.1196/annals.1308.001

De Bellis, M. D., Baum, A. S., Birmaher, B., Keshavan, M. S., Eccard, C. H., Boring, A. M., . . . Ryan, N. D. (1999). Developmental traumatology part I: Biological stress systems. *Biological Psychiatry*, *45*, 1259–1270. http://dx.doi.org/10.1016/S0006-3223(99)00044-X

De Bellis, M. D., Keshavan, M. S., Clark, D. B., Casey, B. J., Giedd, J. N., Boring, A. M., . . . Ryan, N. D.

(1999). Developmental traumatology part II: Brain development. *Biological Psychiatry*, *45*, 1271–1284. http://dx.doi.org/10.1016/S0006-3223(99)00045-1

DeMatteo, D., Batastini, A., Foster, E., & Hunt, E. (2010). Individualizing risk assessment: Balancing idiographic and nomothetic data. *Journal of Forensic Psychology Practice*, *10*, 360–371. http://dx.doi.org/10.1080/15228932.2010.481244

DeMatteo, D., Hunt, E., Batastini, A., & LaDuke, C. (2010). The disconnect between assessment and intervention in the risk management of criminal offenders. *Open Access Journal of Forensic Psychology*, *2*, 59–74. Retrieved from http://www.forensicpsychologyunbound.ws/OAJFP/Risk_Management.html

Dierkhising, C. B., Lane, A., & Natsuaki, M. N. (2014). Victims behind bars: A preliminary study of abuse during juvenile incarceration and post-release social and emotional functioning. *Psychology, Public Policy, and Law*, *20*, 181–190. http://dx.doi.org/10.1037/law0000002

Eck, J. E., Clarke, R. V., & Guerette, R. T. (2007). Risky facilities: Crime concentration in homogeneous sets of establishments and facilities. *Crime Prevention Studies*, *21*, 225–264.

Efta-Breitbach, J., & Freeman, K. A. (2005). Treatment of juveniles who sexually offend: An overview. *Journal of Child Sexual Abuse*, *13*, 125–138. http://dx.doi.org/10.1300/J070v13n03_07

Engle, R. W. (Ed.). (2013). Special issue on the teenage brain. *Current Directions in Psychological Science*, *22*(2).

Epperson, D. L., & Ralston, C. A. (2014). Development and validation of the Juvenile Sexual Offense Recidivism Risk Assessment Tool–II. *Sexual Abuse: A Journal of Research and Treatment*. Advance online publication. http://dx.doi.org/10.1177/1079063213514452

Epperson, D. L., Ralston, C. A., Fowers, D., DeWitt, J., & Gore, K. S. (2006). Actuarial risk assessment with juveniles who offend sexually: Development of the Juvenile Sexual Offense Recidivism Risk Assessment Tool–II (JSORRAT–II). In D. Prescott (Ed.), *Risk assessment of youth who have sexually abused: Theory, controversy, and emerging strategies* (pp. 118–169). Oklahoma City, OK: Wood & Barnes.

Fanniff, A. M., & Becker, J. V. (2006). Specialized assessment and treatment of adolescent sex offenders. *Aggression and Violent Behavior*, *11*, 265–282. http://dx.doi.org/10.1016/j.avb.2005.08.003

Farrington, D. P. (1986). Stepping stones to adult criminal careers. In D. Olweus, J. Block, & M. R. Yarrow (Eds.), *Development of antisocial and prosocial behavior: Research, theories, and issues* (pp. 359–384). New York, NY: Academic Press.

Farrington, D. P., Ohlin, L. E., & Wilson, J. Q. (1986). *Understanding and controlling crime: Toward a new research strategy*. http://dx.doi.org/10.1007/978-1-4612-4940-5

Farrington, D. P., & West, D. J. (1981). The Cambridge Study in Delinquent Development. In S. A. Mednick & A. E. Baert (Eds.), *Prospective longitudinal research* (pp. 137–145). New York, NY: Oxford University Press.

Ferris, C. (1996). The rage of innocents: Childhood trauma may string the biochemical trip wires that can set off later explosions of violence. *Sciences*, *36*, 22–26. http://dx.doi.org/10.1002/j.2326-1951.1996.tb03241.x

Ford, M., & Linney, J. A. (1995). Comparative analysis of juvenile sexual offenders, violent nonsexual offenders and status offenders. *Journal of Interpersonal Violence*, *10*, 56–70. http://dx.doi.org/10.1177/088626095010001004

Garfinkle, E. (2003). Coming of age in America: The misapplication of sex-offender registration and community notification laws to juveniles. *California Law Review*, *91*, 163–208. http://dx.doi.org/10.2307/3481385

Gerhold, C. K., Browne, K. D., & Beckett, R. (2007). Predicting recidivism in adolescent sexual offenders. *Aggression and Violent Behavior*, *12*, 427–438. http://dx.doi.org/10.1016/j.avb.2006.10.004

Graham v. Florida, 130 S. Ct. 2011 (2010).

Griffin, H. L., Beech, A., Print, B., Bradshaw, H., & Quayle, J. (2008). The development and initial testing of the AIM2 framework to assess risk and strengths in young people who sexually offend. *Journal of Sexual Aggression*, *14*, 211–225. http://dx.doi.org/10.1080/13552600802366593

Hanson, R. K., Bourgon, G., Helmus, L., & Hodgson, S. (2009). The principles of effective correctional treatment also apply to sexual offenders: A meta-analysis. *Criminal Justice and Behavior*, *36*, 865–891. http://dx.doi.org/10.1177/0093854809338545

Hanson, R. K., & Thornton, D. (1999). *Static-99: Improving actuarial risk assessment for sex offenders* (User Report No. 1999–02). Ottawa, Ontario, Canada: Department of the Solicitor General of Canada.

Heilbrun, K. (2001). *Principles of forensic mental health assessment*. New York, NY: Kluwer Academic/Plenum.

Heilbrun, K., Lee, R. J., & Cottle, C. C. (2005). Risk factors and intervention outcomes: Meta-analyses of juvenile offending. In K. Heilbrun, N. E. S. Goldstein, & R. E. Redding (Eds.), *Juvenile delinquency: Prevention, assessment, and intervention* (pp. 111–133). New York, NY: Oxford University Press.

Heilbrun, K., Yasuhara, K., & Shah, S. (2010). Approaches to violence risk assessment: Overview and critical analysis. In R. Otto & K. Douglas (Eds.), *Handbook of violence risk assessment* (pp. 1–17). New York, NY: Routledge.

Hempel, I., Buck, N., Cima, M., & van Marle, H. (2013). Review of risk assessment instruments for juvenile sex offenders: What is next?

International Journal of Offender Therapy and Comparative Criminology, 57, 208–228. http://dx.doi.org/10.1177/0306624X11428315

Henggeler, S. W., Letourneau, E. J., Chapman, J. E., Borduin, C. M., Schewe, P. A., & McCart, M. R. (2009). Mediators of change for multisystemic therapy with juvenile sexual offenders. *Journal of Consulting and Clinical Psychology, 77*, 451–462. http://dx.doi.org/10.1037/a0013971

Hiscox, S. P., Witt, P. H., & Haran, S. J. (2007). Juvenile Risk Assessment Scale (JRAS): A predictive validity scale. *Journal of Psychiatry and Law, 35*, 503–539.

Höffe, O. (Ed.). (2010). *Aristotle's "Nicomachean Ethics."* Leiden, the Netherlands: Brill Academic.

Hoge, R. D., & Andrews, D. A. (2002). *Youth Level of Service/Case Management Inventory: User's manual.* Toronto, Ontario, Canada: Multi-Health Systems.

Hoge, R. D., & Andrews, D. A. (2010). *Evaluation for risk of violence in juveniles.* http://dx.doi.org/10.1093/med/9780195370416.001.0001

Hunter, J. A. (2000). *Understanding juvenile sex offenders: Research findings and guidelines for effective management and treatment* (Juvenile Justice Fact Sheet; NCJ No. 183507). Retrieved from https://www.ncjrs.gov/pdffiles1/Digitization/183507NCJRS.pdf

Hunter, J. A. (2006). Understanding diversity in juvenile sexual offenders: Implications for assessment, treatment, and legal management. In R. E. Longo & D. S. Prescott (Eds.), *Current perspectives: Working with sexually aggressive youth and youth with sexual behavior problems* (pp. 63–77). Holyoke, MA: NEARI Press.

Hunter, J. A. (2008). The sexual crimes of juveniles. In R. R. Hazelwood & A. W. Burgess (Eds.), *Practical aspects of rape investigation* (4th ed., pp. 409–427). http://dx.doi.org/10.1201/9781420065053.ch21

Hunter, J. A., & Figueredo, A. J. (1999). Factors associated with treatment compliance in a population of juvenile sexual offenders. *Sexual Abuse: A Journal of Research and Treatment, 11*, 49–67. http://dx.doi.org/10.1177/107906329901100105

Hunter, J. A., Figueredo, A. J., Malamuth, N. M., & Becker, J. V. (2003). Juvenile sex offenders: Toward the development of a typology. *Sexual Abuse: A Journal of Research and Treatment, 15*, 27–48. http://dx.doi.org/10.1177/107906320301500103

In re Gault, 387 U.S. 1 (1967).

Iselin, A.-M. R., DeCoster, J., & Salekin, R. T. (2009). Maturity in adolescent and young adult offenders: The role of cognitive control. *Law and Human Behavior, 33*, 455–469. http://dx.doi.org/10.1007/s10979-008-9160-x

Ito, Y., Teicher, M. H., Glod, C. A., & Ackerman, E. (1998). Preliminary evidence for aberrant cortical development in abused children: A quantitative EEG study. *Journal of Neuropsychiatry and Clinical Neurosciences, 10*, 298–307.

Ito, Y., Teicher, M. H., Glod, C. A., Harper, D., Magnus, E., & Gelbard, H. A. (1993). Increased prevalence of electrophysiological abnormalities in children with psychological, physical, and sexual abuse. *Journal of Neuropsychiatry and Clinical Neurosciences, 5*, 401–408.

Kenny, D. T., Keogh, T., & Seidler, K. (2001). Predictors of recidivism in Australian juvenile sex offenders: Implications for treatment. *Sexual Abuse: A Journal of Research and Treatment, 13*, 131–148.

Kjellgren, C., Priebe, G., Svedin, C. G., & Långström, N. (2010). Sexually coercive behavior in male youth: Population survey of general and specific risk factors. *Archives of Sexual Behavior, 39*, 1161–1169. http://dx.doi.org/10.1007/s10508-009-9572-9

Knight, R. A., & Prentky, R. A. (1993). Exploring characteristics classifying juvenile sexual offenders. In H. E. Barbaree, W. L. Marshall, & S. M. Hudson (Eds.), *The juvenile sexual offender* (pp. 45–83). New York, NY: Guilford Press.

Knight, R. A., Ronis, S. T., & Zakireh, B. (2009). Bootstrapping persistence risk indicators for juveniles who sexually offend. *Behavioral Sciences and the Law, 27*, 878–909. http://dx.doi.org/10.1002/bsl.908

Kock, R. (1999). *80–20 principle: The secret to success by achieving more with less.* New York, NY: Doubleday.

Lab, S., Shields, G., & Schondel, C. (1993). Research note: An evaluation of juvenile sexual offender treatment. *Crime and Delinquency, 39*, 543–553. http://dx.doi.org/10.1177/0011128793039004008

Landrigan, P. J. (1999). Risk assessment for children and other sensitive populations. *Annals of the New York Academy of Sciences, 895*, 1–9. http://dx.doi.org/10.1111/j.1749-6632.1999.tb08073.x

Långström, N. (2002). Long-term follow-up of criminal recidivism in young sex offenders: Temporal patterns and risk factors. *Psychology, Crime, and Law, 8*, 41–58. http://dx.doi.org/10.1080/10683160208401808

Långström, N., & Grann, M. (2000). Risk for criminal recidivism among young sex offenders. *Journal of Interpersonal Violence, 15*, 855–871. http://dx.doi.org/10.1177/088626000015008005

Laws, D. R. (Ed.). (1989). *Relapse prevention with sex offenders.* New York, NY: Guilford Press.

Laws, D. R., Hudson, S. M., & Ward, T. (2000). *Remaking relapse prevention with sex offenders: A source book.* http://dx.doi.org/10.4135/9781452224954

Letourneau, E. J., Henggeler, S. W., Borduin, C. M., Schewe, P. A., McCart, M. R., Chapman, J. E., & Saldana, L. (2009). Multisystemic therapy for juvenile sexual offenders: 1-year results from a randomized effectiveness trial. *Journal of Family Psychology, 23*, 89–102. http://dx.doi.org/10.1037/a0014352

Lipsey, M. W. (2009). The primary factors that characterize effective interventions with juvenile offenders: A meta-analytic overview. *Victims and Offenders, 4*, 124–147. http://dx.doi.org/10.1080/15564880802612573

Loeber, R., Farrington, D. P., Stouthamer-Loeber, M., Moffitt, T., & Caspi, A. (1998). The development of male offending: Key findings from the first decade of the Pittsburgh Youth Study. *Studies in Crime and Crime Prevention, 7*, 141–172.

Marlatt, G. A., & Gordon, J. R. (Eds.). (1985). *Relapse prevention: Maintenance strategies in the treatment of addictive behaviors*. New York, NY: Guilford Press.

McCann, K., & Lussier, P. (2008). Antisociality, sexual deviance, and sexual reoffending in juvenile sex offenders: A meta-analytical investigation. *Youth Violence and Juvenile Justice, 6*, 363–385. http://dx.doi.org/10.1177/1541204008320260

McGowan, M. R., Horn, R. A., & Mellott, R. N. (2011). The predictive validity of the Structured Assessment of Violence Risk in Youth in secondary educational settings. *Psychological Assessment, 23*, 478–486. http://dx.doi.org/10.1037/a0022304

McGrath, R. J., Cumming, G. F., Burchard, B. L., Zeoli, S., & Ellerby, L. (2010). *Current practices and trends in sexual abuser management: The Safer Society 2009 North American Survey*. Brandon, VT: Safer Society.

Melton, G. B., Petrila, J., Poythress, N. G., & Slobogin, C. (2007). *Psychological evaluations for the courts: A handbook for mental health professionals and lawyers* (3rd ed.). New York, NY: Guilford Press.

Meyers, J. R., & Schmidt, F. (2008). Predictive validity of the Structured Assessment for Violence Risk in Youth (SAVRY) with juvenile offenders. *Criminal Justice and Behavior, 35*, 344–355. http://dx.doi.org/10.1177/0093854807311972

Miller v. Alabama, 132 S. Ct. 2455 (2012).

Modecki, K. L. (2008). Addressing gaps in the maturity of judgment literature: Age differences and delinquency. *Law and Human Behavior, 32*, 78–91. http://dx.doi.org/10.1007/s10979-007-9087-7

Moffitt, T. E. (1993). Adolescence-limited and life-course-persistent antisocial behavior: A developmental taxonomy. *Psychological Review, 100*, 674–701. http://dx.doi.org/10.1037/0033-295X.100.4.674

Moffitt, T. E., Caspi, A., Rutter, M., & Silva, P. A. (2001). *Sex differences in antisocial behavior*. Cambridge, England: Cambridge University Press.

Mossman, D. (1994). Assessing predictions of violence: Being accurate about accuracy. *Journal of Clinical and Consulting Psychology, 62*, 783–792. http://dx.doi.org/10.1037/0022-006X.62.4.783

Mulvey, E. P., & Iselin, A. M. (2008). Improving professional judgments of risk and amenability in juvenile justice. *Future of Children, 18*, 35–57. http://dx.doi.org/10.1353/foc.0.0012

O'Reilly, G., & Carr, A. (2006). Assessment and treatment of criminogenic needs. In H. E. Barbaree & W. L. Marshall (Eds.), *The juvenile sex offender* (2nd ed., pp. 189–218). New York, NY: Guilford Press.

Pardini, D. A., Loeber, R., Farrington, D. P., & Stouthamer-Loeber, M. (2012). Identifying direct protective factors for nonviolence. *American Journal of Preventive Medicine, 43*(Suppl. 1), S28–S40. http://dx.doi.org/10.1016/j.amepre.2012.04.024

Pealer, J. A., & Latessa, E. J. (2004, December). Applying the principles of effective interventions to juvenile corrections. *Corrections Today*, pp. 26–29.

Perry, B. D. (1994). Neurobiological sequelae of childhood trauma: PTSD in children. In M. Murburg (Ed.), *Catecholamine function in posttraumatic stress disorder: Emerging concepts* (pp. 233–255). Washington, DC: American Psychiatric Publishing.

Perry, B. D., Pollard, R. A., Blakley, T. L., Baker, W. L., & Vigilante, D. (1995). Childhood trauma, the neurobiology of adaptation, and "use-dependent" development of the brain: How states become "traits." *Infant Mental Health Journal, 16*, 271–291. http://dx.doi.org/10.1002/1097-0355(199524)16:4<271::AID-IMHJ2280160404>3.0.CO;2-B

Pithers, W. D., Marques, J. K., Gibat, C. C., & Marlatt, G. A. (1983). Relapse prevention: A self-control model of treatment and maintenance of change for sexual aggressives. In J. G. Greer & I. R. Stuart (Eds.), *The sexual aggressor: Current perspectives on treatment* (pp. 214–239). New York, NY: Van Nostrand Reinhold.

Pittman, N. (2013). *Raised on the registry: The irreparable harm of placing children on sex offender registries in the U.S.* New York, NY: Human Rights Watch.

Prentky, R. A., Harris, B., Frizzell, K., & Righthand, S. (2000). Development and validation of an actuarial instrument for assessing risk among juvenile sex offenders. *Sexual Abuse: A Journal of Research and Treatment, 12*, 71–93.

Prentky, R. A., Li, N. C., Righthand, S., Schuler, A., Cavanaugh, D., & Lee, A. F. (2010). Assessing risk of sexually abusive behavior among youth in a child welfare sample. *Behavioral Sciences and the Law, 28*, 24–45. http://dx.doi.org/10.1002/bsl.920

Prentky, R. A., Pimental, A., Cavanaugh, D., & Righthand, S. (2009). Predicting risk of sexual recidivism in juveniles: Predictive validity of the J-SOAP-II. In A. R. Beech, L. A. Craig, & K. D. Browne (Eds.), *Assessment and treatment of sexual offenders: A handbook* (pp. 265–292). http://dx.doi.org/10.1002/9780470714362.ch15

Prentky, R. A., & Righthand, S. (2001). *Juvenile Sex Offender Assessment Protocol manual*. Bridgewater, MA: Author.

Prentky, R. A., & Righthand, S. (2003). *Juvenile Sex Offender Assessment Protocol-II: J-SOAP-II manual*. Bridgewater, MA: Author.

Pullman, L., & Seto, M. C. (2012). Assessment and treatment of adolescent sexual offenders: Implications of recent research on generalist versus specialist explanations. *Child Abuse and Neglect, 36*, 203–209. http://dx.doi.org/10.1016/j.chiabu.2011.11.003

Rajlic, G., & Gretton, H. M. (2010). An examination of two sexual recidivism risk measures in adolescent offenders: The moderating effect of offender type. *Criminal Justice and Behavior, 37*, 1066–1085. http://dx.doi.org/10.1177/0093854810376354

Reitzel, L. R., & Carbonell, J. L. (2006). The effectiveness of sexual offender treatment for juveniles as measured by recidivism: A meta-analysis. *Sexual Abuse: A Journal of Research and Treatment, 18*, 401–421.

Reyna, V. F., & Farley, F. (2006). Risk and rationality in adolescent decision-making: Implications for theory, practice, and public policy. *Psychological Science in the Public Interest, 7*, 1–44.

Rice, M. E., & Harris, G. T. (2005). Comparing effect sizes in follow-up studies: ROC Area, Cohen's d, and r. *Law and Human Behavior, 29*, 615–620.

Rich, P. (2009). *Understanding, assessing, and rehabilitating juvenile sexual offenders*. Hoboken, NJ: Wiley.

Righthand, S., & Welch, C. (2001). *Youths who have sexually offended: A review of the professional literature*. Washington, DC: Office of Juvenile Justice and Delinquency Prevention.

Righthand, S., & Welch, C. (2005). Characteristics of youth who sexually offend. *Journal of Child Sexual Abuse, 13*, 15–32. http://dx.doi.org/10.1300/J070v13n03_02

Rogers, R. (2000). The uncritical acceptance of risk assessment in forensic practice. *Law and Human Behavior, 24*, 595–605. http://dx.doi.org/10.1023/A:1005575113507

Roper v. Simmons, 543 U.S. 551 (2005).

Rubinstein, M., Yeager, C. A., Goodstein, C., & Lewis, D. O. (1993). Sexually assaultive male juveniles: A follow-up. *American Journal of Psychiatry, 150*, 262–265.

Ryan, E. (2012). Interviewing, evaluation, & risk assessment. In E. Ryan, J. A. Hunter, & D. Murrie (Eds.), *Evaluation of juveniles who sexually offend: A guide for mental health clinicians* (pp. 119–160). Oxford, England: Oxford University Press.

Ryan, E., Hunter, J. A., & Murrie, D. (2012). *Evaluation of juveniles who sexually offend: A guide for mental health clinicians*. Oxford, England: Oxford University Press.

Schram, D. D., Milloy, C. D., & Rowe, W. E. (July, 1992). Juvenile sex offenders: A follow-up study of re-offense behavior. *Interchange*, 1–3.

Schroeder, M. (1991). *Fractals, chaos, power laws: Minutes from an infinite universe*. New York, NY: W. H. Freeman.

Seto, M. C., & Lalumière, M. L. (2010). What is so special about male adolescent sexual offending? A review and test of explanations through meta-analysis. *Psychological Bulletin, 136*, 526–575. http://dx.doi.org/10.1037/a0019700

Shakespeare, W. (1974). The winter's tale. In G. B. Evans (Textual Ed.), *The Riverside Shakespeare*. Boston, MA: Houghton Mifflin.

Smith, W. R., & Monastersky, C. (1986). Assessing juvenile sexual offenders' risk for reoffending. *Criminal Justice and Behavior, 13*, 115–140. http://dx.doi.org/10.1177/0093854886013002001

Spice, A., Viljoen, J. L., Latzman, N. E., Scalora, M. J., & Ullman, D. (2013). Risk and protective factors for recidivism among juveniles who have offended sexually. *Sexual Abuse: A Journal of Research and Treatment, 25*, 347–369. http://dx.doi.org/10.1177/1079063212459086

Stattin, H., & Magnusson, D. (1996). Antisocial development: A holistic approach. *Development and Psychopathology, 8*, 617–645. http://dx.doi.org/10.1017/S0954579400007331

Stein, M. B., Koverola, C., Hanna, C., Torchia, M. G., & McClarty, B. (1997). Hippocampal volume in women victimized by childhood sexual abuse. *Psychological Medicine, 27*, 951–959. http://dx.doi.org/10.1017/S0033291797005242

Steinberg, L. (2007). Risk-taking in adolescence: New perspectives from brain and behavioral science. *Current Directions in Psychological Science, 16*, 55–59. http://dx.doi.org/10.1111/j.1467-8721.2007.00475.x

Steinberg, L., & Scott, E. S. (2003). Less guilty by reason of adolescence: Developmental immaturity, diminished responsibility, and the juvenile death penalty. *American Psychologist, 58*, 1009–1018. http://dx.doi.org/10.1037/0003-066X.58.12.1009

Stien, P. T., & Kendall, J. (2004). *Psychological trauma and the developing brain: Neurologically based interventions for troubled children*. New York, NY: Haworth Press.

Teicher, M. H. (2000). Wounds that time won't heal: The neurobiology of child abuse. *Cerebrum, 2*, 50–67.

Teicher, M. H. (2002). Scars that won't heal: The neurobiology of child abuse. *Scientific American, 286*, 68–75. http://dx.doi.org/10.1038/scientificamerican0302-68

Teicher, M. H., Glod, C. A., Surrey, J., & Swett, C., Jr. (1993). Early childhood abuse and limbic system ratings in adult psychiatric outpatients. *Journal of Neuropsychiatry and Clinical Neurosciences, 5*, 301–306.

Teicher, M. H., Ito, Y., Glod, C. A., Andersen, S. L., Dumont, N., & Ackerman, E. (1997). Preliminary evidence for abnormal cortical development in physically and sexually abused children using EEG coherence and MRI. *Annals of the New York Academy of Sciences, 821*, 160–175. http://dx.doi.org/10.1111/j.1749-6632.1997.tb48277.x

Thomas, M. S. C., & Johnson, M. H. (2008). New advances in understanding sensitive periods in brain development. *Current Directions in Psychological Science, 17*, 1–5. http://dx.doi.org/10.1111/j.1467-8721.2008.00537.x

Trivits, L. C., & Reppucci, N. D. (2002). Application of Megan's law to juveniles. *American Psychologist, 57*, 690–704. http://dx.doi.org/10.1037/0003-066X.57.9.690

van den Bos, W., van Dijk, E., Westenberg, M., Rombouts, S. A. R. B., & Crone, E. A. (2011). Changing brains, changing perspectives: The neurocognitive development of reciprocity. *Psychological Science, 22*, 60–70. http://dx.doi.org/10.1177/0956797610391102

Viljoen, J. L., Mordell, S., & Beneteau, J. L. (2012). Prediction of adolescent sexual reoffending: A meta-analysis of the J-SOAP-II, ERASOR, J-SORRAT-II, and Static-99. *Law and Human Behavior, 36*, 423–438. http://dx.doi.org/10.1037/h0093938

Viljoen, J. L., Scalora, M., Cuadra, L., Bader, S., Chavez, V., Ullman, D., & Lawrence, L. (2008). Assessing risk of violence in adolescents who have sexually offended: A comparison of the J-SOAP-II, J-SORRAT-II, and SAVRY. *Criminal Justice and Behavior, 35*, 5–23. http://dx.doi.org/10.1177/0093854807307521

Vincent, G. M., Chapman, J., & Cook, N. E. (2011). Risk-needs assessment in juvenile justice: Predictive validity of the SAVRY, racial differences, and the contribution of needs factors. *Criminal Justice and Behavior, 38*, 42–62. http://dx.doi.org/10.1177/0093854810386000

Vincent, G. M., Perrault, R. T., Guy, L. S., & Gershenson, B. G. (2012). Developmental issues in risk assessment: Implications for juvenile justice. *Victims and Offenders, 7*, 364–384. http://dx.doi.org/10.1080/15564886.2012.713900

Vitacco, M. J., Caldwell, M., Ryba, N. L., Malesky, A., & Kurus, S. J. (2009). Assessing risk in adolescent sexual offenders: Recommendations for clinical practice. *Behavioral Sciences and the Law, 27*, 929–940. http://dx.doi.org/10.1002/bsl.909

Walker, D. F., McGovern, S. K., Poey, E. L., & Otis, K. E. (2004). Treatment effectiveness for male adolescent sexual offenders: A meta-analysis and review. *Journal of Child Sexual Abuse, 13*, 281–293.

Wolfgang, M. E., Figlio, R. M., & Sellin, T. (1972). *Delinquency in a birth cohort*. Chicago, IL: University of Chicago Press.

Worling, J. R. (2002). Assessing risk of sexual assault recidivism with adolescent sexual offenders. In M. C. Calder (Ed.), *Young people who sexually abuse: Building the evidence base for your practice* (pp. 365–375). Lyme Regis, England: Russell House.

Worling, J. R. (2012). The assessment and treatment of deviant sexual arousal with adolescents who have offended sexually. *Journal of Sexual Aggression, 18*, 36–63. http://dx.doi.org/10.1080/13552600.2011.630152

Worling, J. R. (2013). *Desistence for adolescents who sexually harm*. Retrieved from http://www.erasor.org/new-protective-factors.html

Worling, J. R., & Curwen, T. (2000). Adolescent sexual offender recidivism: Success of specialized treatment and implications for risk prediction. *Child Abuse and Neglect, 24*, 965–982. http://dx.doi.org/10.1016/S0145-2134(00)00147-2

Worling, J. R., & Långström, N. (2003). Assessment of criminal recidivism risk with adolescents who have offended sexually: A review. *Trauma, Violence, and Abuse, 4*, 341–362. http://dx.doi.org/10.1177/1524838003256562

Worling, J. R., & Langton, C. M. (2012). Assessment and treatment of adolescents who sexually offend: Clinical issues and implications for secure settings. *Criminal Justice and Behavior, 39*, 814–841. http://dx.doi.org/10.1177/0093854812439378

Worling, J. R., Litteljohn, A., & Bookalam, D. (2010). 20-year prospective follow-up study of specialized treatment for adolescents who offended sexually. *Behavioral Sciences and the Law, 28*, 46–57. http://dx.doi.org/10.1002/bsl.912

Zimring, F. E. (2004). *An American travesty: Legal responses to adolescent sexual offending*. http://dx.doi.org/10.7208/chicago/9780226983592.001.0001

Part VIII

TRAINING AND ETHICS

CHAPTER 30

TRAINING MENTAL HEALTH AND JUVENILE JUSTICE PROFESSIONALS IN JUVENILE SCREENING, ASSESSMENT, AND EVALUATION

Lourdes M. Rosado and Mary Ann Scali

That minors are different is a principle that permeates U.S. law. Indeed, U.S. Supreme Court jurisprudence in the past 70 years has consistently taken account of the developmental differences between minors and adults in determining the breadth and scope of minors' constitutional and legal rights. Thus, juvenile and criminal court professionals can and do consider the unique developmental attributes of youths—such as differences in their cognitive reasoning, perception of risk, present versus future orientation, susceptibility to peer influence, and capacity for change—at different junctures in the court process, starting with initial intake and charging; through detention, adjudication, and disposition; and ultimately to discharge.

Consequently, these professionals—who include judges, prosecutors, defense attorneys, and probation officers—use forensic assessments to aid them in critical decision making with regard to youths who become involved in the justice system. On one level, these professionals often call on the expertise of psychologists and psychiatrists to help them answer key legal questions regarding individual youths who come before the court. Such questions include issues of competence, culpability, amenability to rehabilitation and treatment, and appropriate treatment planning. On a second level, forensic psychologists and psychiatrists help to guide court professionals in the latter's distinct roles as policymakers and resource allocators for the justice system.

Often, however, these collaborations do not work as effectively as they could because court professionals and forensic evaluators lack sufficient shared knowledge and common language from which to operate. For example, most judges and lawyers still do not receive formal education or training in adolescent development and psychology. Conversely, many mental health professionals receive no formal education on the law pertaining to the specific legal questions on which they are asked to opine. Although more forensic training is available today for psychiatrists and psychologists than there was a decade or two ago, such training is not universal—and the availability of juvenile forensic training is even more limited.

The challenge is to expand the shared base of substantive knowledge for use by legal, mental health, and juvenile justice professionals, in and out of court. In this chapter, we explore professional education and training of judges, lawyers, and probation officers as an important strategy for expanding that base. Clinicians with expertise in assessing juvenile offenders can play a critical role in training legal professionals to more effectively use that expertise to address the overarching goals of better outcomes for court-involved youths, including reducing their risk of recidivism. In the first part of this chapter, we review recent U.S. Supreme Court case law, particularly the Court's reliance on the expanding knowledge of adolescent development to inform important rulings affecting youths in the justice system. The key findings in this series of Supreme Court cases underscore the importance of the evaluator's role in assisting juvenile justice professionals who make decisions about a particular

http://dx.doi.org/10.1037/14643-030
APA Handbook of Psychology and Juvenile Justice, K. Heilbrun (Editor-in-Chief)

youth, as well as informing these professionals in their roles as policymakers. We also describe the expanded use of screening, assessment, and evaluations for different purposes in the justice system.

In the second part of the chapter, we then discuss the development and implementation of a national training curriculum specifically designed to enhance that shared knowledge and language to facilitate collaboration between juvenile court professionals and forensic clinicians.

LEGAL DECISION MAKING AND FORENSIC EVALUATION: WHY JUDGES, LAWYERS, AND PROBATION OFFICERS NEED TO WORK WITH EVALUATORS

Since 2005, the U.S. Supreme Court has issued four watershed decisions that reinforce the primacy of a key principle: Adolescents are different under the law. The Court has observed in these landmark decisions that professionals must adequately consider the particular attributes of adolescents in all aspects of juvenile court decision making. That same time period has witnessed increased use of various screening and assessment instruments—for example, to identify mental health disorders or substance abuse problems or assess the level of risk—with justice-involved youths around the country.

Simultaneously, the issue of adjudicative competence is now being raised more frequently in juvenile cases, and some states have adopted juvenile-specific competency standards to determine whether a youth should stand trial. Also, even more studies and scholarship on adolescent development have been released (and are ongoing) that further inform the field and necessitate juvenile professionals' outreach and collaboration with forensic evaluators when making legal decisions about court-involved youths.

Consequently, juvenile justice professionals and evaluators are working together more closely than ever. As an individual youth's case proceeds through the different stages of the court process, legal professionals must make a number of critical decisions. An understanding of adolescent development generally, as well as of the specific information about the individual youth that an evaluator can provide (e.g., level of development in different domains, learning disabilities or special education needs, mental health disorders), can and should inform such decisions. In addition, juvenile justice professionals who play policymaking roles in their jurisdictions greatly rely on the forensic clinical community to guide implementation of developmentally appropriate and evidence-based policies and programming.

Constitutional Jurisprudence and Its Implications for Juvenile Forensic Evaluation

Shortly after publication of the first edition of *Understanding Adolescents: A Juvenile Court Training Curriculum* (Youth Law Center, Juvenile Law Center, & American Bar Association, 2000; see the Development of *Toward Developmentally Appropriate Practice* section), the U.S. Supreme Court issued the first of a series of landmark decisions affecting youths in the justice system. In *Roper v. Simmons* (2005), the Court held that imposing the death penalty on individuals who committed murders as juveniles violated the Eighth Amendment's prohibition against cruel and unusual punishment. In the years after publication of the curriculum's second edition (National Juvenile Defender Center & Juvenile Law Center, 2009), the Court handed down three more decisions: In *Graham v. Florida* (2010), the Court held that it is unconstitutional to impose life-without-parole sentences on juveniles convicted of nonhomicide offenses; in *J.D.B. v. North Carolina* (2010), the Court held that a child's age must be taken into account when determining whether a youth is in custody, because custody triggers *Miranda* warnings before questioning, thus enunciating a "reasonable child" test for custody; and in *Miller v. Alabama* (2012), the Court prohibited the imposition of mandatory life-without-parole sentences on youths. The Court's findings in these cases—on the lesser level of maturity, decision-making capacity, and culpability of minors compared with adults, as well as their greater capacity for change—are buttressed by a body of developmental and neuroscience research demonstrating significant psychological and physiological differences between youths and adults (see Chapters 4, 5, and 6, this handbook). The Court's holdings also confirm that juvenile courts must take into account a youth's unique developmental status at all decision-making stages of his or her case. Thus, these cases presage an even closer partnership between justice professionals and forensic evaluators, because the latter can provide critical information regarding a particular youth's developmental status as it relates to legal decisions.

Many juvenile justice professionals also have policymaking duties and make decisions that greatly affect the overall functioning of the system and thus the outcomes for many youths. Courts and legislatures must decide, for example, what safeguards must be in place when police take statements from youths (e.g., Should statements be videotaped? Should youths only be questioned with a parent present?); what words the court should use in a guilty plea colloquy so that a youth truly understands the consequences of waiving his or her rights embodied in trial; and what factors the court should consider in deciding whether a youth is amenable to further treatment in the juvenile versus the adult criminal court. Probation officers and court personnel also make decisions about which programs and facilities should provide services to court-involved youths, from community supervision to placement in a residential facility for intensive treatment. How can they determine which programs are best suited for which youth? These decisions should be guided by knowledge of adolescent development, and forensic clinicians can play an important role in applying developmental concepts to legal issues.

Indeed, three key findings in this series of Supreme Court cases (*Graham v. Florida*, 2010; *J.D.B. v. North Carolina*, 2010; *Roper v. Simmons*, 2005) signal the importance of the evaluator's role in assisting juvenile justice professionals who make decisions about a particular youth, as well as informing these professionals in their roles as policymakers.

Lesser maturity and decision-making capacity. "First, children have a 'lack of maturity and an underdeveloped sense of responsibility,' leading to recklessness, impulsivity, and heedless risk-taking" (*Miller v. Alabama*, 2012, p. 2464; see also *Graham v. Florida*, 2010; *Roper v. Simmons*, 2005). Research has demonstrated that adolescents, compared with adults, generally have less decision-making capacity and judgment, particularly in stressful situations, and "considerable evidence supports the conclusion that children and adolescents are less capable decision makers than adults in ways that are relevant to their criminal choices" (Scott & Steinberg, 2008b, p. 20). Psychosocial factors that influence adolescents' perceptions, judgments, and abilities to make decisions limit their capacity for autonomous choice (Cauffman & Steinberg, 2000; Modecki, 2008). Research on adolescent decision making has suggested that youths are heavily influenced by these social and emotional factors (Albert & Steinberg, 2011, as cited in Levick, Feierman, Kelley, & Goldstein, 2012). "Adolescents lack mature capacity for self-regulation in emotionally charged contexts, relative to adults and children" (Somerville, Fani, & McClure-Tone, 2011, as cited in Bonnie, Johnson, Chemers, & Schuck, 2013, p. 91). Thus, for example, adolescent decision making is characterized by sensation- and reward-seeking behavior (Steinberg, 2010). Greater impulsivity during adolescence may stem from adolescents' weak future orientation and more limited capacity to anticipate the consequences of decisions (Steinberg et al., 2009; see also Bonnie et al., 2013).

Advances in neuroscience have confirmed the lesser decision-making capacities of youths compared with adults. The parts of the brain controlling higher order functions—such as reasoning, judgment, and inhibitory control—develop after other parts of the brain controlling more basic functions (e.g., vision, movement) and do not fully develop until an individual is in his or her early 20s. Specifically, the prefrontal cortex—the brain's "CEO" that controls important decision-making processes—is the last to develop (Baird et al., 1999; Gogtay et al., 2004; Rubia et al., 2000). Because the prefrontal cortex governs so many aspects of complex reasoning and decision making, it is possible that adolescents' undesirable behavior—risk taking, impulsivity, and poor judgment—may be significantly influenced by their incomplete brain development (Steinberg, 2010). Indeed,

> the latest studies suggest that much of what distinguishes adolescents from children and adults is an *imbalance among*

> *developing brain systems* [italics added]. . . . This imbalance model implies dual systems: one that is involved in cognitive and behavioral control and one that is involved in socioemotional processes. Accordingly, adolescents lack mature capacity for self-regulation because the brain system that influences pleasure-seeking and emotional reactivity develops more rapidly than the brain system that supports self-control. (Bonnie et al. 2013, p. 97)

These key attributes of adolescent thinking have important implications for many aspects of juvenile court practice. For example, these attributes must inform a court's decision regarding whether to admit into evidence a youth's confession to police. Specifically, courts must routinely answer several important questions. Was a youth's confession voluntary? Would a reasonable youth have thought he or she was in custody when he or she was questioned by police, thus warranting *Miranda* warnings (*J.D.B. v. North Carolina*, 2011)? Did the juvenile make a knowing, voluntary, and informed waiver of his or her *Miranda* rights (*Miranda v. Arizona*, 1966) before making a statement to police? The particular characteristics of adolescent thinking discussed above—such as less mature decision making in stressful situations and short-term orientation—are directly relevant to these questions, and clinicians can provide assessments of the influence of such factors on the interrogation or confession at issue. Moreover, the troubling phenomenon of false confessions by youths reinforces the need for courts to adequately account for these cognitive and psychosocial factors in ruling on the admissibility of confessions (Kassin et al., 2010).[1] Kassin (2007) pointed out that psychologists are increasingly serving as consultants and expert witnesses in cases involving possible false confessions. These characteristics of adolescent thinking also have important implications regarding the safeguards states adopt for police interrogations of youths. For example, some psychologists have strongly recommended electronic recording of youth interrogations given youths' heightened susceptibility (Kassin et al., 2010).

Susceptibility to peer and outside pressures. The U.S. Supreme Court recognizes that "children are more vulnerable to negative influences and outside pressures, including from their family and peers; they have limited control over their own environment and lack the ability to extricate themselves from horrific, crime-producing settings" (*Miller v. Alabama*, 2012, p. 2464; *Roper v. Simmons*, 2005). That teenagers are more susceptible to peer pressure has wide support in the social science literature (Figner et al., 2009, as cited in Bonnie et al., 2013; Gardner & Steinberg, 2005, as cited in Bonnie et al., 2013; Steinberg & Scott, 2003).

> Peer influence affects adolescent judgment both directly and indirectly. In some contexts, adolescents make choices in response to direct peer pressure to act in certain ways. More indirectly, adolescents' desire for peer approval—and fear of rejection—affect their choices, even without direct coercion. (Steinberg & Scott, 2003, p. 1012)

Recent brain imaging findings have further supported the observation that adolescent behavior is greatly affected by peer influence:

> Chein and colleagues examined the neural basis of riskier driving decisions by adolescents relative to adults in the presence of peers during a simulated driving task. Adolescents, but not adults, showed heightened activity in reward-related circuitry, including the ventral striatum, in the presence of peers. This activity was inversely correlated with subjective ratings on resistance to peer influences. Individuals rating themselves low on this scale showed more reward-related brain activity in the presence of peers. Not only are peers influential but also positive

[1]See, for example, Goldstein, Condie, Kalbeitzer, Osman, and Geier's (2003) study examining whether age, IQ, and history of special education predicted *Miranda* rights comprehension and the self-reported tendency to falsely confess to a crime among 55 delinquent boys; when *Miranda* comprehension, age, and IQ were simultaneously tested as predictor variables of the self-reported likelihood of false confessions, only age served as an independent predictor.

> exchanges with others may be powerful motivators. Asynchronous development of brain systems appears to correspond with a shift from thinking about self to thinking about others from early adolescence to young adulthood. Together these studies suggest that in the heat of the moment, as in the presence of peers or rewards, functionally mature reward centers of the brain may hijack less mature control systems in adolescents. (Bonnie et al., 2013, p. 98)

The influence of peers on adolescents must be considered, for example, at the adjudicatory phase, when the court must determine the youth's culpability or level of blameworthiness when a crime is committed by a group (Bonnie et al. 2013). Research has shown that juveniles who engage in offending behavior typically do so in the company of their peers (U.S. Department of Justice, 2005). Evaluators can assist the court by opining on whether and how peer pressure played a role in the offense in question. As well, at the final disposition or sentencing stage the court must assess the youth's amenability to treatment and rehabilitation, special needs, and capacity to develop competencies (as in the mastery of skills) in fashioning an appropriate disposition plan or sentence (Woolard, Gross, Mulvey, & Reppucci, 1992). A clinician's assessment of a youth's susceptibility to peer influences also has important implications for a youth's disposition. It is particularly problematic when a youth who is greatly influenced by peers is placed in a facility where he or she will be exposed to negative peers. But this youth may greatly benefit from community programming with prosocial peers that also guides the youth's family on techniques for supporting him or her. Indeed, the role of peers in adolescent decision making also has key implications for the type of programs and facilities with which the juvenile court contracts.

Lesser culpability, greater capacity for change. "And third, a child's character is not as 'well formed' as an adult's; his traits are 'less fixed' and his actions less likely to be 'evidence of irretrievabl[e] deprav[ity]'" (*Miller v. Alabama*, 2012, p. 2464; *Roper v. Simmons*, 2005). Indeed, "the character of a juvenile is not as well formed as that of an adult. The personality traits of juveniles are more transitory, less fixed" (*Roper v. Simmons*, 2005, p. 570). They "are more capable of change than are adults, and their actions are less likely to be evidence of 'irretrievably depraved character' than are the actions of adults," such that "a greater possibility exists that a minor's character deficiencies will be reformed" (*Graham v. Florida*, 2010, pp. 2026–2027). Developmental research has reached the same conclusions. It is well known that "[adolescence] is transitional because it is marked by rapid and dramatic change within the individual in the realms of biology, cognition, emotion, and interpersonal relationships" (Scott & Steinberg, 2008a, p. 32). The research has confirmed that "many of the factors associated with antisocial, risky, or criminal behavior lose their intensity as individuals become more developmentally mature" (Levick et al., 2012, p. 297) and "the period of risky experimentation does not extend beyond adolescence, ceasing as identity becomes settled with maturity. Only a small percentage of youth who engage in risky experimentation persist in their problem behavior into adulthood" (Bonnie et al., 2013, p. 90).[2]

An evaluator's assessment of a youth's capacity for change is particularly important in the decision about whether a youth will be prosecuted in juvenile versus adult criminal court. Most states have one or more mechanisms by which juveniles charged with offenses may be tried in adult criminal court. For example, in 46 states, a juvenile court judge may waive juvenile court jurisdiction in certain juvenile cases, thus authorizing a transfer to criminal court. In addition, prosecutors in about 15 states have the authority to file certain juvenile cases directly in criminal court. Finally, in certain states, statutes provide that cases meeting certain age and offense criteria are to be excluded from juvenile court jurisdiction and must be filed directly in criminal court (Adams & Addie, 2012; Griffin, Addis, Adams, & Firestine, 2011; Puzzanchera,

[2]See also Scott and Steinberg (2008a), explaining that "most teenagers desist from criminal behavior . . . [as they] develop a stable sense of identity, a stake in their future, and mature judgment" (p. 31).

Adams, & Hockenberry, 2012; see also Ziedenberg, 2011).

However, many states also have reverse waiver laws that allow youths whose cases are in adult criminal court to petition to have the case transferred or decertified to the juvenile court (Griffin et al., 2011). In making these decisions, prosecutors, judges, or both must consider a number of factors, usually including the youth's age and previous delinquency record, the alleged offense, and the youth's amenability to treatment and rehabilitation within the juvenile justice system (Griffin et al., 2011), and the forensic evaluator plays a key role in informing these decisions. Clinicians can also work with justice professionals and legislatures to ensure that the criteria used to make these determinations are developmentally appropriate.

Increased Use of Screening, Assessment, and Evaluation Tools in Juvenile Court

Since publication of the curriculum's first edition (Youth Law Center et al., 2000), the use of validated screening and assessment instruments has increased in the juvenile court context, as have forensic evaluations. Many of these instruments and evaluations are administered by clinicians, but nonclinicians are increasingly using certain instruments, particularly screening tools, directly with the juvenile justice population. Forensic clinicians have long used validated instruments to assist in assessing youths on various dimensions, such as their amenability to treatment. Clinicians also play a critical role in supporting juvenile justice stakeholders in their use of instruments. For example, clinicians train these stakeholders on instrument administration, how to score and interpret results, and what are and are not valid uses of test results. Instruments administered by nonclinician juvenile justice professionals, such as probation officers, court intake personnel, and detention center staff, can contribute to better informed and less biased decision making.

Currently, screening and assessment instruments and diagnostic evaluations are being used to assess a variety of questions for court-involved youths. We discuss these briefly in the following sections.

Existence of mental health and substance abuse disorders. Empirical studies have suggested that 65% to 70% of youths involved in the justice system have one or more diagnosable psychiatric disorders, including major depression, mood, anxiety, and substance use disorders (Shufelt & Cocozza, 2006; Teplin, Abram, McClelland, Dulcan, & Mericle, 2002; Wasserman, McReynolds, Ko, Katz, & Carpenter, 2005; Wasserman, McReynolds, Lucas, Fisher, & Santos, 2002). In addition, the majority of youths in the juvenile justice system have experienced trauma, either through exposure to community and family violence or being the direct victim of such violence (Buffington, Dierkhising, & Marsh, 2010). "The ways that mental illness presents itself in juveniles can be far more complex both diagnostically and with regard to treatment" (Larson & Grisso, 2012, p. 10) because "symptoms of mental illness are just emerging in adolescence and are complicated by ongoing developmental processes in several ways" (Larson & Grisso, 2012, p. 11).

For example, a behavior may be seen as normative development at one age but be regarded as a symptom of mental illness at another age. It is also difficult to distinguish between symptoms and behavior (e.g., of depression) that will change as a child grows up and those that will persist and develop into a lifelong mental disorder (Larson & Grisso, 2012). Nonclinicians can administer screens at the early stages of court cases, specifically at intake and pretrial detention, to flag youths who may be exhibiting symptoms of mental health disorders. Clinicians may then conduct full evaluations that include the use of validated assessment tools to diagnose these youths.

Existence of learning or developmental disability. Screening, assessment, and evaluation are also used to identify learning or developmental disabilities among youths in the juvenile justice system. Learning disabilities, emotional disturbance, intellectual disability, and speech or language impairments are more prevalent among the delinquency population (Leone, Wilson, Mulcahy, & Krezmien, 2009). Different theories are posited for why youths with disabilities are overrepresented in the juvenile court. The differential treatment theory hypothesizes that because juvenile justice stakeholders do not understand that certain youth characteristics and behaviors may be linked to a disability, they may treat disabled youths more harshly than their nondisabled peers for comparable behavior (Leone et al., 2009). The metacognitive deficit theory posits that because youths with disabilities have poorer problem-solving strategies, they are more likely to engage in delinquent behavior (Leone et al., 2009).

Students with disabilities are suspended and expelled at disproportionate rates (St. George, 2012) and are more likely to be referred into the juvenile justice system through the school-to-prison pipeline (Burdick, Feierman, & McInerney, 2011). Federal special education law imposes additional substantive limitations on school discipline. Under the Individuals With Disabilities Education Improvement Act of 2004 (IDEIA) and Section 504 of the Rehabilitation Act of 1973, students may not be removed for more than 10 days if their behavior is related to their disability. In addition, under IDEIA, students have a right to alternative education when suspended or expelled. Even students who are not yet identified as special education students may be entitled to some protection against school disciplinary practices. A student who the school district knew, or should have known, needed a special education evaluation is entitled to an expedited evaluation and alternative education during the time of the disciplinary exclusion (IDEIA, 2004).

Justice system personnel can play an important role in helping youths and families access educational assessments. When an evaluator identifies a youth as having a learning disability, or the evaluator determines that the offending behavior is a manifestation of a disability, the justice system can use the above-described legal tools to keep the youth in school and divert him or her from an unnecessary adjudication of delinquency. The identification of a youth's intellectual disability can have an impact on various decisions, including whether the youth made a knowing, intelligent, and voluntary waiver of his or her *Miranda* rights before being interrogated or whether the youth is competent to stand trial (see the Juvenile Adjudicative Competence section).

Risk of reoffending. Juvenile justice professionals—particularly court intake personnel and probation officers—are increasingly using risk assessment instruments at different points in the juvenile court process (Vincent, Guy, & Grisso, 2012). The use of risk assessment tools has been on the rise since the mid-1990s as result of recommendations in the Juvenile Justice and Delinquency Prevention Act of 1974 and the increased availability of validated tools to use with youths (Models for Change Research Initiative, 2011).

Risk assessment is

> the practice of using a structured tool that combines information about youth to classify them as being low, moderate or high risk for reoffending or continued delinquent activity, as well as identifying factors that might reduce that risk on an individual basis. (Vincent et al., 2012, p. 5)

Risk assessments can help inform decisions about the level of supervision that a youth needs and what type of intervention will reduce the youth's level of risk by targeting dynamic (changeable) risk factors (Vincent et al., 2012). A risk assessment will estimate the likelihood that a youth will continue in delinquent behaviors if nothing is done to intervene, and thus such an assessment may also be particularly helpful in identifying which youths can be diverted from formal court processing while protecting community safety. "Many adolescents who come into contact with the law will not reoffend even if they receive only minimal intervention, because most of those adolescents are at low risk for reoffending" (Vincent et al., 2012, p. 5). Probation offices can also collect data on prevalent dynamic risk factors in the population of youths and families they serve, which can help inform the type of programming the agency should provide (Vincent et al., 2012).

Juvenile Adjudicative Competence

The issue of juvenile competence to stand trial was rarely raised in juvenile court before the mid-1990s, but in the past 10 years it has been raised with increasing frequency in most jurisdictions (Larson & Grisso, 2012). As a consequence, forensic clinicians are increasingly being called on to evaluate youths on this issue. Although states may enact their own competency standards, those standards must at a minimum meet the criteria set forth in *Dusky v. United States* (1960)—whether the defendant "has sufficient present ability to consult with his lawyer with a reasonable degree of rational understanding and . . . a rational as well as factual understanding of the proceedings against him" (Larson & Grisso, 2012, p. 8). If the defendant is adjudicated competent, the legal proceedings continue. For defendants who are not competent, most statutes provide for a period of treatment or programming to remediate competence-relevant deficits.

A juvenile may be incompetent to stand trial because of mental illness, intellectual disability, or simply developmental immaturity (Larson & Grisso, 2012). Indeed, the most comprehensive examination of juveniles' trial-related abilities to date, the MacArthur Juvenile Adjudicative Competence Studies, found juveniles younger than age 15 performed more poorly, on average, than young adults with regard to their understanding and reasoning about trial-related matters. For juveniles in detention centers, about 35% of 11- to 13-year-olds and 22% of 14- to 15-year-olds were significantly impaired in relevant areas of competence.

In an effort to seed the field with the developmental research and learning that has taken place in the past decade, Larson and Grisso (2012) produced a manual to assist jurisdictions in crafting juvenile competence to stand trial statutes.[3] The manual offers input on how jurisdictions can apply developmental concepts to their laws regulating determinations of juvenile competence. Most states have not yet developed statutes regarding juvenile-specific competence to stand trial (Larson & Grisso, 2012). Juvenile justice professionals and forensic clinicians will need to work together in the coming years to fill this gap.

DEVELOPMENT OF *TOWARD DEVELOPMENTALLY APPROPRIATE PRACTICE: A JUVENILE COURT TRAINING CURRICULUM*

In the first part of this chapter, we described why justice professionals need ongoing training and a common language to work together in service of youths who come into contact, or are at risk of contact, with the courts. In the second part, we focus on the *Juvenile Court Training Curriculum*[4] created and subsequently revised to facilitate and expand the collaboration of juvenile justice professionals and forensic evaluators.

The curriculum originally grew out of a national assessment of the access to defense counsel and quality of representation in juvenile court that identified several critical areas in which defender training was inadequate or nonexistent, including child and adolescent development (American Bar Association Juvenile Justice Center, Juvenile Law Center, & Youth Law Center, 2002). The U.S. Supreme Court's jurisprudence of the past 10 years, and other trends during this period, reaffirm the need to provide training to all juvenile justice professionals on normative adolescent development and a wide variety of issues, including mental health and substance abuse disorders, learning and intellectual disabilities, risk assessment, and juvenile competence to stand trial. The *Juvenile Court Training Curriculum* covers all of these issues.

With funding from the John D. and Catherine T. MacArthur Foundation, in 1996 the project team—which consisted of the American Bar Association Juvenile Justice Center (now the National Juvenile Defender Center), Juvenile Law Center, and Youth Law Center—embarked on a multiyear project to fill the void in professional legal education. The project team was assisted by a multidisciplinary advisory group that included psychologists, psychiatrists, social workers, special education experts, adult education consultants and professional trainers, and social scientists representing a wide range of disciplines, as well as juvenile court judges, prosecutors, defense attorneys, and probation officers from around the country.

In its initial investigation of existing training, the team found that court professionals lacked a foundation in what is normative adolescent development. How do teenagers develop their cognitive

[3]Larson and Grisso's (2011) publication provides excellent guidance to lawmakers on this subject.

[4]The first edition of the curriculum was titled *Understanding Adolescents: A Juvenile Court Training Curriculum* (Youth Law Center, Juvenile Law Center, & American Bar Association, 2000). The second, current edition of the curriculum is titled *Toward Developmentally Appropriate Practice: A Juvenile Court Training Curriculum* (National Juvenile Defender Center & Juvenile Law Center, 2009). Hereinafter, we refer to it as the *Juvenile Court Training Curriculum*.

skills, moral framework, social relations, and sense of identity? What aspects of youthful offending can be viewed as symptomatic of normal adolescent development as opposed to a pathology or abnormality? If some offending behavior can indeed be characterized as normal adolescent development, what are the implications for juvenile court practice, both in individual cases and in overall policymaking? The answers to these questions are relevant to the legal decisions that must be made at different stages of the court process. For example, in assessing a youth's culpability in an offense, the court should consider the youth's level of cognitive thinking. In fashioning a rehabilitation plan for an adjudicated youth, it would be helpful for the court to know his or her educational needs and functioning. The Supreme Court's jurisprudence of the past decade has confirmed that the U.S. Constitution requires courts to consider a youth's developmental status in making these critical decisions.

The subject areas described above were not typically covered in a comprehensive way in traditional continuing education for juvenile court judges, prosecutors, defense attorneys, and probation officers. Thus, the project team set as its goal the creation of an interdisciplinary curriculum that would not only educate juvenile court professionals on all of these issues, but also inform clinicians as to what juvenile court professionals need to know from them about these subjects. The team wanted to put the clinician in the role of educator so that the clinician would be able to more effectively interact with juvenile court professionals when assuming his or her role as evaluator. The main purpose of such a curriculum would be to teach juvenile court practitioners how they can apply the findings of adolescent development and related research to improve decision making at every stage of the court process. The curriculum would also give juvenile court professionals the background information they need for global planning in their jurisdictions (e.g., to develop prevention and diversion programming, develop or contract with appropriate programming for adjudicated youths) and for legislative and regulatory advocacy (e.g., enacting or amending statutes that set forth the criteria for juvenile vs. adult criminal court jurisdiction or that govern residential programs for adjudicated youth).

The project team identified two pilot sites—the juvenile courts in West Palm Beach, Florida, and Oakland, California—and worked with the sites as well as with clinicians and social scientists to develop a list of prospective training topics. The project team then recruited experts from around the country to develop and present initial trainings to the juvenile court professionals in the pilot sites from 1997 to 1999. The team applied the feedback from these pilot sites to write the curriculum for national publication and distribution. One of the key pieces of feedback from the sites was that the curriculum needed to clarify the connection between the information presented and actual juvenile court practice so that juvenile court professionals saw the relevance and potential applications of what they were learning. Consequently, the team structured the modules so they could be delivered by teams of attorneys and clinicians rather than simply by clinicians alone. Some pilot site trainees commented that they found initial sessions informative but not useful. Attorneys as cotrainers could particularly speak to the relevance of the training material to daily practice in a way that clinicians alone could not.

On the heels of the 2005 Supreme Court decision in *Roper v. Simmons* that relied heavily on the emerging adolescent development research, the Models for Change partners at the John D. and Catherine T. MacArthur Foundation agreed it was time to update the first edition of the curriculum. The National Juvenile Defender Center and Juvenile Law Center worked together on the update and revision process. The project team hosted two meetings of experts with significant experience in writing about the substantive issues and in delivering training based on the Juvenile Court Training Curriculum to discuss how it was being used, gaps in information, and recommendations for revisions. The National Juvenile Defender Center and Juvenile Law Center created a topical bibliography with the latest developmental research and law reforms to guide the discussions.

From these meetings, a review of training evaluations, and consultation with additional experts, the project team drafted outlines with proposed content for the modules to be included in the second edition of the *Juvenile Court Training Curriculum*: (a) understanding adolescent development; (b) evaluation, screening, and assessment in juvenile justice; (c) special education and disability rights; (d) forensic questions about youth capacities; and (e) communicating with youths, including interviews and client counseling. The National Juvenile Defender Center and Juvenile Law Center secured the leading experts in the country to work on drafting each of the new modules. Lead authors worked with teams of reviewers and editors to develop each lesson. The revised *Juvenile Court Training Curriculum* is an excellent example of a cross-disciplinary product.

REVISED CURRICULUM: *TOWARD DEVELOPMENTALLY APPROPRIATE PRACTICE* AND IMPLICATIONS FOR SCREENING, ASSESSMENT, AND EVALUATION OF YOUTHS

The second edition of the curriculum, *Toward Developmentally Appropriate Practice: A Juvenile Court Training Curriculum* (National Juvenile Defender Center & Juvenile Law Center, 2009), consists of five separate modules:

Module 1: Adolescent Development

Module 2: Screening, Assessing, and Evaluating Youth

Module 3: Special Education and Disability Rights

Module 4: Legal Questions About Youth's Capacities

Module 5: Communicating With Youth: Interviews and Colloquies

The curriculum is a boxed set available on request at no cost through the Models for Change website (http://modelsforchange.wufoo.com/forms/z7x4a9/). Intended for juvenile court judges, defense attorneys, prosecutors, and probation staff, the curriculum provides in-depth training materials on the most up-to-date adolescent development research and its application to juvenile court practice. As a part of the MacArthur Foundation's project (*Models for Change: Systems Reform in Juvenile Justice*), this curriculum is available to jurisdictions across the country to enhance the capacity of professionals to make high-quality, developmentally appropriate decisions about the court-involved youths with whom they work.

Each module contains an estimate of presentation duration, a list of learning objectives, a summary of key concepts, and comprehensive substantive material on the particular topic. To promote interaction within trainings, the modules include several exercises, including hypothetical case scenarios, discussion guides for video clips, and other training tools. All of the topics in the revised modules implicate screening, assessment, and evaluation of youths in the juvenile court, and Module 2 (Screening, Assessing, and Evaluating Youth) provides a targeted discussion about juvenile court professionals' access and understanding of these tools.

Curriculum Modules

Module 1: Adolescent development. This first module describes key aspects of adolescent development and their application to decision making at critical junctures in the juvenile court process. Participants in training programs learn how teenagers develop their cognitive skills, moral framework, social relations, and identity, as well as how various factors, including brain development, disabilities, and the environment in which they live affect their behavior and decision making. Specifically, this module is designed to provide juvenile justice professionals with a better understanding of those factors that led to a particular youth's involvement in the court system and thereby inform decision making at important stages in the juvenile court process, such as intake, detention, waiver to adult court, adjudication, and disposition.

In Module 1, juvenile court professionals learn how adolescent thinking differs from that of children and adults and how it increases the likelihood of taking risks and engaging in undesirable behavior. They also gain an appreciation of how adolescents develop an identity—more specifically, the roles that family, peers, and the larger community play in identity development. With respect to moral development, the module covers how adolescents develop and express concepts of right and wrong and the influence of peers and family on the development of moral reasoning. The second edition of the curriculum includes a special section on brain development, because advances in brain imaging have demonstrated how changes in the adolescent brain can affect teenage behavior. Juvenile court practitioners increasingly call on forensic evaluators and others to weigh in on a number of legal decisions in which these developmental concepts are relevant, including competence, amenability to rehabilitation, and appropriate treatment planning.

Module 2: Screening, assessing, and evaluating youth. This second module provides juvenile court professionals with information about forensic evaluations, as well as screening and assessment instruments used in juvenile justice systems. Participants learn how forensic evaluations and other screening and assessment tools can inform legal decisions and the type of information that must go into evaluations. The module covers key components of the mental health evaluation process, the importance of finding qualified examiners and focusing referral questions appropriately, tips for reviewing and understanding reports, and the importance of confidentiality protections for information obtained through evaluations and screening and assessment.

Module 2 helps juvenile court professionals understand that mental health evaluations conducted for the purpose of addressing a legal issue (i.e., forensic evaluations) differ from those conducted for the purpose of informing treatment decisions (i.e., therapeutic evaluations). The module discusses how evaluations used in juvenile court are guided by the legal question before the court, and the youth's developmental issues should be described as they relate to this legal question and its associated functional–legal capacities.

Juvenile court professionals are encouraged to request written evaluations in language and a format that they can understand. Juvenile court professionals are also reminded that psychiatric diagnoses and the results of psychological testing on their own typically do not answer legal questions before the court (e.g., whether the youth is competent to stand trial or whether the youth should be transferred to adult court). Participants in training based on Module 2 learn that diagnoses and psychological tests, in and of themselves, do not provide enough relevant information about adolescents and their functioning to make legal determinations. However, diagnoses and psychological constructs (e.g., intelligence, academic achievement, depression, and memory functioning) are described in the module as parts of complete evaluations that help inform the court's decisions about youths.

Module 2 also provides information about selecting a qualified mental health professional. It describes a competent evaluator as one who is knowledgeable about (a) child development; (b) emotional, behavioral, and cognitive impairments in childhood and adolescence; (c) the legal process and commonly encountered legal issues for which there is a psychological component; (d) the juvenile justice system and services available in the community; and (e) cultural competence across race, ethnicity, socioeconomic class, sexual orientation, and gender.

The module also provides juvenile justice professionals with guidance on how they can improve the quality of mental health evaluations. Several relevant steps include identifying psychological and legal issues that are to be addressed by the examiner, providing relevant collateral information about the youth to the mental health professional, and ensuring that the mental health professional conducting the evaluation has the required knowledge, training, and experience.

After the details on forensic evaluation, Module 2 then offers participants an overview of distinctions between forensic evaluations and other screening and assessment activities that may be conducted with youths who are involved with the juvenile justice system. The module describes screening instruments as brief tools used that can be used with all youths to identify immediate concerns or those that potentially require more comprehensive assessment. The module also discusses how screens should not be used to provide diagnoses or unequivocal conclusions about youths. It further outlines some screening tools that can be administered by juvenile justice staff (rather than mental health professionals), such as recidivism risk instruments and several mental health instruments.

The module then contrasts assessment instruments as more in-depth tools that are used when screening indicates a need for further evaluation. For example, screening instruments may reveal the need for a mental health assessment to identify in greater detail potential mental health problems or treatment planning. Training based on Module 2 emphasizes outreach to mental health professionals for administration and interpretation of mental health assessment instruments and psychological tests.

The final section of this module discusses the need to establish adequate legal protections for youths who are administered screens, assessments, and evaluations. Youths may reveal personal and highly sensitive information about themselves when they are screened, assessed, and evaluated. The module offers some examples of policies to ensure that screening, assessing, and evaluating youths in delinquency proceedings does not lead to further prosecution. Juvenile justice professionals must be aware of the information-sharing implications and possibilities for self-incrimination that arise in these contexts.

Module 3: Special education and disability rights. The third module provides an overview of education-related disabilities, the laws pertaining to special education and disability rights, and the relevance of special education and disability rights for juvenile courts. In particular, the module covers the major provisions of the IDEIA, the Americans With Disabilities Act of 1990, and Section 504 of the Rehabilitation Act of 1973. The applicability of each of these statutes to juvenile court processing and advocacy is explained. In addition, the module includes discussion of school discipline practices and policies that affect the court involvement of youths with disabilities, with a particular focus on the IDEIA school discipline protections. The module also covers the challenges faced by youths, their parents, and advocates in securing special education rights and describes the importance of identifying youths who are eligible for special education services.

Legal professionals receiving training based on this module learn how they can better recognize and treat youths in the justice system who have, or may have, disabilities that compromise their ability to comprehend, learn, or behave in socially acceptable ways. The module reviews the types of disabilities commonly found among justice-involved youths as well as different theories about the possible relationship between disabling conditions and delinquency (e.g., are there different attributes of these disabling conditions that may predispose youths to offending behaviors?). More important, the module also covers the federal legal entitlements to special education (when children are both in and outside of the juvenile justice system), including their rights to continue their education when they get into trouble at school. Because juvenile court professionals grapple with a high number of school-related cases, this module underscores the need for educational and other evaluators' expertise and input when making legal decisions about youths with education-related learning or other disabilities.

Module 4: Legal questions about youths' capacities. The fourth module reviews legal issues in delinquency cases that require an understanding of an individual youth's capacities, including the validity of a waiver of *Miranda* rights, the voluntariness of a confession, the competence of the youth to participate in the legal process, and the transfer of the youth to criminal court. For each of these legal concepts, the module provides information about relevant developmental, behavioral, and social science research that can be applied when these questions are raised. The updated version of this module contemplates a differential juvenile jurisprudence that has since been established through the decisions issued by the Supreme Court. This evolving juvenile jurisprudence calls on juvenile justice professionals and forensic evaluators to carefully analyze individual youth's capacities to engage in particular legal tasks such as waiving rights and voluntarily confessing.

This module also includes information about the distinct aspects of obtaining and reviewing a forensic evaluation. With the abundance of screens, assessments, and evaluations being used in juvenile court, it is essential that juvenile court professionals know how to ask the right questions. Forensic evaluators must know the legal criteria that their evaluation is to address so they can select the appropriate evaluation methods and tools. Participants in training on this module learn about the elements of each legal issue discussed (*Miranda* waivers, confessions, competence, and transfer) and the central components of an effective forensic evaluation on each issue. The module contains specific descriptions of the characteristics and capacities of youths that need to be explored by the forensic evaluator and gives participants information about how to obtain and review such evaluations.

Module 5: Communicating with youth—Interviews and colloquies. This final module describes techniques for effective communication with youths involved in the juvenile court system, including respondents, witnesses, and complaining witnesses. In particular, the module covers how professionals can incorporate developmental considerations into their communications with youths in both providing and seeking information. By teaching participants self-awareness as interviewers, this module helps participants to interview youths in developmentally sound and culturally competent ways, including understanding girls; youths of color; and lesbian, gay, bisexual, and transgender youths. In addition, the module highlights the importance of sensitive interviewing of youths with disabilities, traumatized youths, and youths with mental health needs.

Although not discussed in the module itself, there is a growing body of research about the prevalence of speech and language disorders among youths in the delinquency system (Bryan, Freer, & Furlong, 2007; Sanger, Hux, & Belau, 1997; Sanger, Moore-Brown, Magnuson, & Svoboda, 2001; Snow & Powell, 2008). Effective communication is the foundation of all of interactions with youths. Speech and language disorders therefore have an impact on youths' abilities to understand and communicate with all juvenile justice professionals about their experiences relevant to juvenile court. As this research on speech and language disorders progresses, it will be important for juvenile justice professionals to learn about accessing and working with speech-language pathologists.

This module includes several interactive exercises to assist juvenile court professionals with strategies for successful interviewing and communication with youths in the delinquency system. The module offers recommendations for audiovisual aids and even movie scenes that provide a basis for discussion and learning about communication skills.

HOW THE JUVENILE COURT TRAINING CURRICULUM IS CURRENTLY USED

As discussed, the revised curriculum grew out of the John D. and Catherine T. MacArthur Foundation's Models for Change: Systems Reform in Juvenile Justice project. Having supported the development and release of a rich empirical research agenda through the Network on Adolescent Development and Juvenile Justice, and having seen tremendous advances in juvenile justice practice, policy, and legal reforms, the foundation sought a revised curriculum that would include the latest developmental research and the latest law reforms. The revision process began in 2006 after the 2005 U.S. Supreme Court decision in *Roper v. Simmons* and was ongoing until December 2009, when the updated curriculum was released at the Models for Change conference. Since December 2009, more than 3,000 copies of *Toward Developmentally Appropriate Practice: A Juvenile Court Training Curriculum* have been distributed to juvenile court practitioners in every state and the District of Columbia and to more than a dozen foreign countries.

The *Juvenile Court Training Curriculum* is used by training groups for all juvenile court actors, including judges, probation officers, public defenders, private defense counsel, and prosecutors. Training based on the updated *Juvenile Court Training Curriculum* has been provided to thousands of juvenile court professionals and has reached juvenile professionals in every state, the District of Columbia, and Puerto Rico. As with the previous version, portions of the revised curriculum have been taught at national training venues for legal and mental health professionals, including the National Council of Juvenile and Family Court Judges, the National Juvenile Defender Leadership Summit, the Leadership Institute for the National Juvenile Justice Network, and the American Psychology–Law Society Conference. In addition, the project team receives requests from criminal and juvenile justice colleges, law schools, and clinical programs. Much of the training, however, has taken place at the state and local level as juvenile courts and probation offices have sought to expand the training opportunities available to their professionals.

The project team has learned quite a bit about training and assessing the utility of training since the release of the first edition of the curriculum. In the revision process, they learned that participants were most interested in the application of the developmental science to their work with youths in the delinquency system. Consequently, the revised modules include more examples and exercises to engage training participants in thoughtful discussions about how developmental science can and should affect their decision making about youths in the delinquency process.

The project team continues to conduct immediate training evaluations and has also conducted follow-up evaluations to determine whether the *Juvenile Court Training Curriculum* is meeting the needs of its recipients. Some examples of feedback from participants include an appreciation for "group activities and the way that it incorporates both national and local knowledge." Participants and trainers have praised the functionality and versatility of the *Juvenile Court Training Curriculum*, using it to provide context in discussions of new competency statutes and preparing lawyers to represent juvenile clients, and of the curriculum's provision of quality information to inform day-to-day practice. Some curriculum training recipients have said that they were able to use what they have learned to better empower young people.

The ultimate goal of the curriculum design and training was to foster more developmentally appropriate decision making in juvenile delinquency courts. The project team has been very pleased to receive feedback stating that the curriculum has improved the decision making of many juvenile court actors. Curriculum recipients report gaining "a fuller understanding of the issues involved with at-risk youths." It has reinforced the idea "that a youth's age, maturity level, and overall cognitive functioning must be taken into account in all cases." This has helped courtroom actors engage with youths and become more willing to "look beyond the surface . . . in fashioning remedies and ordering services" for youths. The *Juvenile Court Training Curriculum* has spread beyond its initial recipients. Survey respondents say the curriculum "has helped to convince others that the developmental approach is helpful."

Recipients appreciate the curriculum and have noted its strongest components. Several have highlighted its usefulness in sentencing practices and its overview on adolescent brain development. Others like the curriculum's comprehensive yet straightforward organization. The easy-to-access format makes it simple to share with interagency training partners.

Most heartening are comments from judges trained with the curriculum. One judge reported using the curriculum training to gain a "fuller understanding of the issues involved with at-risk youth and more often look beyond the surface now in fashioning remedies and ordering services." One expert offering training based on the curriculum reported that it has broadened the perspective of court personnel. In Utah, recipients "used it as part of a literature review to help the State of Utah draft a training protocol and standard of practice to evaluate the adjudicative competencies of juveniles." The curriculum has been invaluable in informing courtroom actors on competency and capacity issues and has helped public defenders better communicate with their clients. Probation officers are trained in the curriculum in several jurisdictions. Many localities use it as both a training and a reference tool.

The project team continues to work to facilitate the curriculum's use around the country. The team helps training organizations and individual juvenile courts to identify and cultivate experts to deliver the trainings. The team also works with the expert trainer and training organizers to tailor the material to the local audience. For example, the team can advise trainers on how to incorporate information about local law and practice into the training and what interactive exercises would be most relevant to that particular audience. Individuals and organizations who are interested in conducting trainings using the *Juvenile Court Training Curriculum* are encouraged to contact the National Juvenile Defender Center (http://www.njdc.info).

CONCLUSION

Despite aggressive distribution and training, the need for training based on the *Juvenile Court Training Curriculum* persists. The application of developmental concepts to law is a complex endeavor. Juvenile court professionals and forensic evaluators alike have a long way to go before juvenile courts across the country are fully implementing developmentally appropriate practice. Training based on the revised curriculum is an important step in promoting the reform of juvenile court practices since the quartet of Supreme Court cases discussed in this chapter opened the door for the application of developmental science into other areas of juvenile jurisprudence. We can expect to see legal advocates urge courts, legislators, and other policymakers to apply the developmental scholarship that the Supreme Court has cited to a wide range of issues, from how intake officers evaluate risk to determine which youths to divert to how courts evaluate searches and seizures of youths and from what protections legislators must put into place for a youth to enter a valid guilty plea to what programming probation offices provide to youths to decrease their chances of recidivating. As this trend unfolds, juvenile court professionals and forensic evaluators will be working together as never before. Training is an important tool to facilitate this ongoing collaboration.

References

Adams, B., & Addie, S. (2012). *Delinquency cases waived to criminal court 2009*. Washington, DC: National Center for Juvenile Justice & Office of Juvenile Justice and Delinquency Prevention.

American Bar Association Juvenile Justice Center, Juvenile Law Center, & Youth Law Center. (2002). *A call to justice: An assessment of access to counsel and quality of representation in delinquency proceedings*. Retrieved from http://www.njdc.info/pdf/cfjfull.pdf

Americans With Disabilities Act of 1990, Pub. L. No. 101-336, 42 U.S.C. §§ 12101–12213 (2000).

Ayduk, O., Mendoza-Denton, R., Mischel, W., Downey, G., Peake, P. K., & Rodriguez, M. (2000). Regulating the interpersonal self: Strategic self-regulation for coping with rejection sensitivity. *Journal of Personality and Social Psychology*, *79*, 776–792. http://dx.doi.org/10.1037//0022-3514.79.5.776

Baird, A. A., Gruber, S. A., Fein, D. A., Maas, L. C., Steingard, R. J., Renshaw, P. F., . . . Yurgelun-Todd, D. A. (1999). Functional magnetic resonance imaging of facial affect recognition in children and adolescents. *Journal of the American Academy of Child and Adolescent Psychiatry*, *38*, 195–199. http://dx.doi.org/10.1097/00004583-199902000-00019

Bonnie, R., Johnson, R., Chemers, B., & Schuck, J. (Eds.). (2013). *Reforming juvenile justice: A developmental approach*. Washington, DC: National Research Council.

Bryan, K., Freer, J., & Furlong, C. (2007). Language and communication difficulties in juvenile offenders. *International Journal of Language and Communication Disorders*, *42*, 505–520. http://dx.doi.org/10.1080/13682820601053977

Buffington, K., Dierkhising, C. B., & Marsh, S. C. (2010). *Ten things every juvenile court judge should know about trauma and delinquency*. Washington, DC: National Council of Juvenile and Family Court Judges, National Child Traumatic Stress Network, and Office of Juvenile Justice and Delinquency Prevention. http://dx.doi.org/10.1111/j.1755-6988.2010.01044.x

Burdick, K., Feierman, J., & McInerney, M. (2011). Creating positive consequences: Improving education outcomes for youth adjudicated delinquent. *Duke Forum for Law and Social Change*, *3*, 5–28.

Cauffman, E., & Steinberg, L. (2000). Researching adolescents' judgment and culpability. In T. Grisso & R. Schwartz (Eds.), *Youth on trial: A developmental perspective on juvenile justice* (pp. 325–343). Chicago, IL: University of Chicago Press.

Dusky v. United States, 362 U.S. 402 (1960).

Gogtay, N., Giedd, J. N., Lusk, L., Hayashi, K. M., Greenstein, D., Vaituzis, A. C., . . . Thompson, P. M. (2004). Dynamic mapping of human cortical development during childhood through early adulthood. *Proceedings of the National Academy of Sciences, USA*, *101*, 8174–8179. http://dx.doi.org/10.1073/pnas.0402680101

Goldstein, N. E. S., Condie, L. O., Kalbeitzer, R., Osman, D., & Geier, J. L. (2003). Juvenile offenders' *Miranda* rights comprehension and self-reported likelihood of offering false confessions. *Assessment*, *10*, 359–369. http://dx.doi.org/10.1177/1073191103259535

Graham v. Florida, 560 U.S. 2011 (2010).

Griffin, P., Addis, S., Adams, B., & Firestine, K. (2011). *Trying juveniles as adults: An analysis of state transfer laws and reporting*. Washington, DC: Office of Juvenile Justice and Delinquency Prevention. Retrieved from https://www.ncjrs.gov/pdffiles1/ojjdp/232434.pdf

Individuals With Disabilities Education Improvement Act of 2004, Pub. L. No. 108-446, 20 U.S.C. §§ 1400–1482.

J.D.B. v. North Carolina, 131 S. Ct. 2394 (2011).

Juvenile Justice and Delinquency Prevention Act of 1974, Pub. L. No. 93-415, 42 U.S.C. § 5601 *et seq.*

Kassin, S. (2007). Expert testimony on the psychology of confessions: A pyramidal framework of the relevant science. In E. Borgida & S. Fisk (Eds.), *Beyond common sense: Psychological science in the courtroom* (pp. 195–218). http://dx.doi.org/10.1002/9780470696422.ch10

Kassin, S. M., Drizin, S. A., Grisso, T., Gudjonsson, G. H., Leo, R. A., & Redlich, A. D. (2010). Police-induced confessions: Risk factors and recommendations. *Law and Human Behavior*, *34*, 3–38. http://dx.doi.org/10.1007/s10979-009-9188-6

Ladd v. Cockrell, 311 F.3d 349 (5th Cir. 2002).

Larson, K., & Grisso, T. (2011). *Developing statues to stand trial in juvenile delinquency proceedings: A guide for lawmakers*. Retrieved from http://www.modelsforchange.net/publications/330

Larson, K., & Grisso, T. (2012). *Developing statutes for competence to stand trial in juvenile delinquency proceedings: A guide for lawmakers*. Retrieved from http://www.modelsforchange.net/publications/330

Leone, P., Wilson, M., Mulcahy, C., & Krezmien, M. (2009). *Special education and disability rights: Module 3*. Retrieved from http://udcdcslclinicmanuals.pbworks.com/f/Special+Education+and+Disability+Rights+Module.pdf

Levick, M., Feierman, J., Kelley, S., & Goldstein, N. E. S. (2012). The Eighth Amendment evolves: Defining cruel and unusual punishment through the lens of childhood and adolescence. *University of Pennsylvania Journal of Law and Social Change*, *15*, 285–321.

Miller v. Alabama, 132 S. Ct. 2455 (2012).

Miranda v. Arizona, 384 U.S. 436 (1966).

Modecki, K. L. (2008). Addressing gaps in the maturity of judgment literature: Age differences and delinquency. *Law and Human Behavior*, *32*, 78–91. http://dx.doi.org/10.1007/s10979-007-9087-7

Models for Change Research Initiative. (2011). *Knowledge brief: Can risk assessment improve juvenile justice practice?* Retrieved from http://www.modelsforchange.net/publications/313

National Juvenile Defender Center & Juvenile Law Center. (2009). *Toward developmentally appropriate practice: Juvenile court training curriculum* (2nd ed.). Retrieved from http://www.modelsforchange.net/publications/255

Puzzanchera, C., Adams, B., & Hockenberry, S. (2012). *Juvenile court statistics 2009*. Washington, DC: Office of Juvenile Justice and Delinquency Prevention. Retrieved from http://www.ojjdp.gov/pubs/239114.pdf

Rehabilitation Act of 1973, Pub. L. No. 93-112, 29 U.S.C. §§ 701–796.

Roper v. Simmons, 543 U.S. 551 (2005).

Rubia, K., Overmeyer, S., Taylor, E., Brammer, M., Williams, S. C., Simmons, A., . . . Bullmore, E. T. (2000). Functional frontalisation with age: Mapping neurodevelopmental trajectories with fMRI. *Neuroscience and Biobehavioral Reviews*, *24*, 13–19. http://dx.doi.org/10.1016/S0149-7634(99)00055-X

Sanger, D. D., Hux, K., & Belau, D. (1997). Oral language skills of female juvenile delinquents. *American Journal of Speech-Language Pathology*, 6, 70–76. http://dx.doi.org/10.1044/1058-0360.0601.70

Sanger, D. D., Moore-Brown, B., Magnuson, G., & Svoboda, N. (2001). Prevalence of language problems among adolescent delinquents. *Communication Disorders Quarterly*, *23*, 17–26. http://dx.doi.org/10.1177/152574010102300104

Scott, E., & Steinberg, L. (2008a). *Rethinking juvenile justice*. Cambridge, MA: Harvard University Press.

Scott, E. S., & Steinberg, L. (2008b). Adolescent development and the regulation of youth crime. *Future of Children*, *18*, 15–33. http://dx.doi.org/10.1353/foc.0.0011

Shufelt, J., & Cocozza, J. (2006). *Youth with mental health disorders in the juvenile justice system: Results from a multi-state prevalence study*. Retrieved from http://www.unicef.org/tdad/usmentalhealthprevalence06(3).pdf

Snow, P. C., & Powell, M. B. (2008). Oral language competence, social skills and high-risk boys: What are juvenile offenders trying to tell us? *Children and Society*, 22, 16–28. http://dx.doi.org/10.1111/j.1099-0860.2006.00076.x

St. George, D. (2012, February 28). Maryland school board moves to limit student suspension. *Washington Post*, p. B1.

Steinberg, L. (2010). A dual systems model of adolescent risk-taking. *Developmental Psychobiology*, *52*, 216–224.

Steinberg, L., Graham, S., O'Brien, L., Woolard, J., Cauffman, E., & Banich, M. (2009). Age differences in future orientation and delay discounting. *Child Development*, *80*, 28–44. http://dx.doi.org/10.1111/j.1467-8624.2008.01244.x

Steinberg, L., & Scott, E. S. (2003). Less guilty by reason of adolescence: Developmental immaturity, diminished responsibility, and the juvenile death penalty. *American Psychologist*, *58*, 1009–1018. http://dx.doi.org/10.1037/0003-066X.58.12.1009

Teplin, L. A., Abram, K. M., McClelland, G. M., Dulcan, M. K., & Mericle, A. A. (2002). Psychiatric disorders in youth in juvenile detention. *Archives of General*

Psychiatry, *59*, 1133–1143. http://dx.doi.org/10.1001/archpsyc.59.12.1133

U.S. Department of Justice, Office of Justice Programs. (2005). *Co-offending and patterns of juvenile crime*. Retrieved from https://www.ncjrs.gov/pdffiles1/nij/210360.pdf

Vincent, G., Guy, L., & Grisso, T. (2012). *Risk assessment in juvenile justice: A guidebook for implementation*. Retrieved from http://njjn.org/uploads/digital-library/Risk_Assessment_in_Juvenile_Justice_A_Guidebook_for_Implementation.pdf

Wasserman, G. A., McReynolds, L. S., Ko, S. J., Katz, L. M., & Carpenter, J. R. (2005). Gender differences in psychiatric disorders at juvenile probation intake. *American Journal of Public Health*, *95*, 131–137. http://dx.doi.org/10.2105/AJPH.2003.024737

Wasserman, G. A., McReynolds, L. S., Lucas, C. P., Fisher, P., & Santos, L. (2002). The voice DISC-IV with incarcerated male youths: Prevalence of disorder. *Journal of the American Academy of Child and Adolescent Psychiatry*, *41*, 314–321. http://dx.doi.org/10.1097/00004583-200203000-00011

Woolard, J. L., Gross, S. L., Mulvey, E. P., & Reppucci, N. D. (1992). Legal issues affecting mentally disordered youth in the juvenile justice system. In J. Cocozza (Ed.), *Responding to the mental health needs of youth in the juvenile justice system* (pp. 89–106). Seattle, WA: National Coalition for the Mentally Ill in the Criminal Justice System.

Youth Law Center, Juvenile Law Center, & American Bar Association. (2000). *Understanding adolescents: A juvenile court training curriculum*. Retrieved from http://www.modelsforchange.net/publications/178

Ziedenberg, J. (2011). *You're an adult now: Youth in adult criminal justice systems*. Washington, DC: U.S. Department of Justice.

CHAPTER 31

ETHICAL ISSUES IN PSYCHOLOGY AND JUVENILE JUSTICE

Gerald P. Koocher and Robert T. Kinscherff

We address the ethical issues arising in the juvenile justice system by first reflecting on the principles and rationale for treating juvenile offenders differently from adult offenders. A more complete account of juvenile court history appears elsewhere in this handbook (see Chapter 1). However, the gradual development of a separate legal framework for juveniles probably had its origins in the 1820s when the New York House of Refuge became the first juvenile reform school in the United States. Previously, youthful offenders were tried and incarcerated in the same system used for adults. In 1899, the first juvenile court was established in Chicago (Cook County), and by the 1920s virtually every state had established similar courts with jurisdiction over juvenile delinquency and child protection cases.

Juvenile courts became an important part of the Progressive Era's (1890–1920) broad social movement, which included the legal doctrine of *parens patriae*. This doctrine casts the state as a benevolent parentalistic authority and the juvenile court as making decisions for the benefit of the child much as a parent would. Other Progressive Era initiatives involving children included compulsory education and the development of public education systems, restrictions on child labor, and efforts to improve access to medical care and social services.

Guided by *parens patriae*, juvenile court decisions were to focus on the protection and rehabilitation of juvenile offenders, in contrast to the social control and punishment arising from the state's exercise of police powers through the adult criminal justice system. Youths were redefined as adolescents by Hall (1904), who described them as having less-developed maturity, reasoning, and capacities to manage impulsivity or anticipate consequences—and as thus being more vulnerable to unsavory environmental influences but still less morally culpable than adults for their misconduct. This approach to the role of the juvenile court and to adolescents was reflected in the incorporation of court clinics in the original juvenile court in Chicago and subsequent early incarnations of the approach such as the Boston Juvenile Court.

As the juvenile courts and the juvenile justice system evolved at the beginning of the 20th century, different theoretical models existed for understanding and treating delinquent behavior. These models included a developmental perspective that focused on the maturational differences between adolescents and adults, an ecological view that focused on the role of destructive outside influences (family, peers, societal), and a medical model that focused on the individual characteristics of youths (genetic, temperament, intelligence, internal conflicts, attitudes; Abrams, 2013). The tensions among proponents of these models have again become apparent more than a century later in contemporary practices and policy debates.

In practice, juvenile courts and the juvenile justice system frequently fell short of their benign, protective, and rehabilitative aspirations. In addition, inherent tensions arising from deep ambivalence over whether or how juveniles should be punished for misconduct have never been truly

http://dx.doi.org/10.1037/14643-031
APA Handbook of Psychology and Juvenile Justice, K. Heilbrun (Editor-in-Chief)

resolved. Paralleling the criminal justice system, both therapeutic and punitive interventions were largely shaped by the medical model and focused on the individual level rather than the social ecology of youths (Abrams & Snyder, 2010). Through the early 20th-century, juveniles were not afforded basic legal rights and protections because juvenile court proceedings were presumed to be benign and rehabilitative rather than punitive. In reality, juveniles were commonly sent to poorly funded and inadequately staffed reform schools for periods of time far longer than any adult would have served if incarcerated for the same offense. Juveniles with very minor offenses were placed in the same facilities as youths who had committed major violent and sexual offenses. Youths were often released with poor educational or vocational preparation, attenuated ties with their families and communities, and their strongest peer relationships with other delinquent youths.

The juvenile justice system received renewed attention by policymakers, advocates, and the courts during the 1960s and early 1970s because of rising rates of delinquency, high recidivism rates of youths who penetrated the juvenile justice system, and increased attention to civil rights and deinstitutionalization of youthful offenders as well as people with mental illness. Three landmark U.S. Supreme Court cases would radically reshape the practices of juvenile court. In *Kent v. United States* (1966), the Court held that juveniles are entitled to proceedings sufficient to meet basic constitutional protections of due process and fundamental fairness. The issue in that case was whether the juvenile court had afforded the juvenile defendant minimal fairness and due process in making the determination that he should be transferred for trial as an adult on very serious charges.

In essence, the *Kent v. United States* (1966) decision articulated the view that a constitutional tradeoff between due process and benignly well-intended efforts at rehabilitation of a juvenile "is not an invitation to procedural arbitrariness" (pp. 554–556). This thinking particularly applied when there "may be grounds for concern that the child receives the worst of both worlds: that he gets neither the protections accorded to adults nor the solicitous care and regenerative treatment postulated for children" (p. 556).

In re Gault (1967) then established that juveniles are entitled to many of the constitutional rights afforded adult defendants. The Court found that the juvenile court proceedings involving Gerald Gault and other juvenile defendants across the country in similar proceedings amounted to acting as kind of a kangaroo court because they occurred without rights to counsel, notice of charges, and privilege against self-incrimination. *In re Winship* (1970) established that in prosecutions of juveniles, just as with adult defendants, every element of a charge must be proven beyond a reasonable doubt. However, in *McKeiver v. Pennsylvania* (1971), the Supreme Court held that youths in juvenile court proceedings are not entitled to trial by jury under the U.S. Constitution. Some states do afford juveniles a trial by jury under state law. Taken together, these cases provided most constitutional protections for youths in delinquency proceedings and sharply limited the previously almost unlimited discretion of juvenile courts to order conditions or confinement simply if doing so was deemed consistent with rehabilitation.

Additional Supreme Court cases elaborated the federal constitutional contours of juvenile proceedings. In *Fare v. Michael C.* (1979), the Court ruled that a juvenile's asking to speak with his probation officer is not the same as asking to speak with an attorney and so is insufficient to halt interrogation after *Miranda* warnings. *Schall v. Martin* (1984) held that a New York statute allowing preventive detention of a juvenile charged as a delinquent but before adjudication on the charge is permissible because of the community's interest in avoiding criminal misconduct but also the state's interest in preventing potential harm to the juvenile during the commission of crimes and from spiraling downward into further criminality as a result of peer pressure.

As the Supreme Court was beginning to review federal constitutional issues in juvenile justice, the President's Commission on Law Enforcement and the Administration of Justice (1967) concluded that the juvenile justice system was largely failing to rehabilitate youths. This prompted a trend to divert lower level offenders into community-based services that was further accelerated by passage of the Juvenile Justice and Delinquency Prevention Act of

1974, federal legislation that shaped juvenile justice for decades by founding the Office of Juvenile Justice and Delinquency Prevention.

The act also distinguished status offenders from delinquents and mandated that status offenders cannot be held in a detention facility or committed to a juvenile or adult criminal justice authority. Status offenders are youths who have become court involved because of their status as being minors rather than legal adults and for conduct that would not bring an adult before a court, such as truancy, running away, being stubborn with their parents or legal guardians, being disruptive (but not delinquent) in school, violating curfew, and the like. Which behaviors can trigger a status offender proceeding vary by state; these proceedings are variously called Child in Need of Services, Person in Need of Services, Family in Need of Services, Child Requiring Assistance, or other similar term.

In addition, the act also redeployed federal resources to establish or expand community-based services and conditioned federal juvenile justice block grants to the states on showing that the states were effectively engaged in several initiatives. These initiatives included addressing disproportionate minority contact or confinement in the juvenile justice system; requiring sight and sound separation of juvenile and adult defendants or offenders in courthouses, detention facilities, or incarceration facilities; and limits on the time a juvenile can be held in an adult facility while awaiting arraignment or a hearing before a court.

The mid-1980s saw a significant upswing in juvenile violent crime associated with trafficking in crack cocaine and the readily availability of firearms. In particular, the alarming increases in juvenile homicides contributed to the public perception that violent juvenile crime was out of control and the portent of the emergence of a youthful generation of "superpredators." Although rates of violent juvenile and adult crime had begun sharply and consistently dropping by the mid-1990s, legislative steps to make it easier to treat juveniles as adults in the criminal justice system won support as a result of continuing public fears of youth crime and events such as the mass shooting at Columbine High School in 1999. By the early 2000s, 47 states and the District of Columbia had passed legislation making it easier to prosecute and punish youths as adults by requiring that some youths be tried as adults, shifting decision making from judges to prosecutors, and other such measures. Juvenile detention and correctional facilities also came to increasingly resemble adult correctional facilities (Krisberg, 2006).

Concern about violent crime by juveniles led to an emphasis on accountability that was often the justification for more readily prosecuting youths and sentencing youths through the adult criminal justice system. However, there was also renewed emphasis on the accountability of juvenile courts. Juvenile justice system policymakers became aware of the unintended consequences of treating youthful offenders as adult criminals (such as even higher recidivism rates) and the unrealized potential of the juvenile justice system to successfully rehabilitate youths by incorporating research-informed and largely community-based interventions into juvenile justice practices. The federal Omnibus Crime Control and Safe Streets Act (2002) reflected this shift of emphasis by its attention to accountability for both individual offenders and juvenile justice systems. Individual offenders were to face systems of graduated sanctions, and juvenile justice systems were to develop capacities to support positive developmental competencies of youths, keep track of youths in contact with juvenile justice, and develop a broader range of alternatives such restorative justice alternatives. This shift in emphasis to mutual accountability for juveniles and juvenile justice systems was also shaped by major evidence-driven reform initiatives by the MacArthur Foundation (Models for Change); Annie E. Casey Foundation (Juvenile Alternatives to Detention); the Justice Project of the Council of State Governments; and other professional, philanthropic, and governmental organizations.

The new century has also seen extraordinary Supreme Court rulings dramatically shifting the constitutional landscape for youths charged with homicide and other serious misconduct. These landmark rulings have occurred in the context of renewed and intense policy debate regarding juvenile justice based in emerging research in developmental neuroscience, developmental trajectories of antisocial behavior and orientation, the characteristics of youths who penetrate the juvenile justice system, the limits of clinical prognostication, and empirically based interventions for youths who engage in delinquent misconduct. The shifting landscape of law, policy, and research will continue to have significant implications for professional practice for psychologists and others involved in juvenile justice, including ethical and legal implications.

The Supreme Court issued some rulings on juvenile justice after the landmark cases of the late 1960s and early 1970s, but these rulings did not qualify as landmark decisions shifting the constitutional landscape. However, the Supreme Court did issue a landmark ruling in *Roper v. Simmons* (2005) that held that execution is unconstitutional when applied to persons committing capital crimes before age 18. In doing so, the Court rejected case-by-case sentencing determinations in favor of a bright-line constitutional bar on execution for such crimes on grounds including diminished moral culpability reflecting the developmental immaturity of youths, the greater amenability of youths to change and rehabilitation, and the lack of a scientific basis to reliably predict at the time of sentencing that a youthful defendant is forever beyond rehabilitation and therefore warrants execution. Relying on the same lines of analysis, the Supreme Court extended its reach in *Graham v. Florida* (2010). In *Graham*, the Court held as unconstitutional the imposition of a sentence of life without the possibility of parole for a nonhomicide crime committed by a youth younger than age 18.

The lines of analysis relied upon in the *Roper v. Simmons* (2005) and *Graham v. Florida* (2010) majority opinions framed the issues squarely: Is it constitutional for statutes to mandate life without the possibility of parole for homicides committee by juveniles? If not, is it constitutional to impose life without the possibility of parole that was not mandated by statute but was imposed after an individualized sentencing hearing? If so, what factors should a court rely on in imposing a sentence of life with or without the possibility of parole? Also, would a constitutional bar on mandatory life without the possibility of parole for homicides committed by juveniles apply retroactively to people already serving these sentences?

The Supreme Court answered some, but not all, of these questions in *Miller v. Alabama* (2012). *Miller* held as unconstitutional sentencing schemes imposing mandatory life without the possibility of parole for juveniles for capital crimes committed when they were younger than age 18. The Court held open the possibility that there may be the "rare juvenile offender whose crime reflects irreparable corruption" (*Miller v. Alabama*, 2012, p. 2469, quoting *Roper v. Simmons*, 2005) for whom life without parole is warranted but opined that such cases would be "uncommon" (*Miller v. Alabama*, 2012, p. 2469). By citing *Graham* with approval in its analysis, the *Miller* majority also suggested that most youths incarcerated for some time after conviction for murder would warrant at least "some meaningful opportunity to obtain release based on demonstrated maturity and rehabilitation" (*Miller v. Alabama*, 2012, p. 2469).

The Court did not comment on whether the *Miller v. Alabama* (2012) ruling should apply retroactively to the approximately 2,000 people serving mandatory life without the possibility of parole after juvenile convictions for capital crimes. It also left to the states the precise definition of a meaningful opportunity to demonstrate capacity for rehabilitation at the time of sentencing or subsequent achievement of rehabilitation after some term of incarceration. There is currently intense legislative controversy and continuing litigation among the states about how to implement the *Miller* decision.

State and federal appellate decisions interpreting and implementing *Miller v. Alabama* (2012) have come to different results. In November 2012, the Michigan Court of Appeals in *People v. Carp* found that *Miller* does not apply retroactively and does not preclude a sentencing court from imposing life without parole provided there is a constitutionally adequate sentencing hearing. However, in a one-page order issued in August 2013 in the case of *Hill v. Snyder* the U.S. District Court for the Eastern District of Michigan (Southern Division) found unconstitutional—when applied to persons convicted of first-degree murder committed as a juvenile—a Michigan law barring parole consideration for persons sentenced to life imprisonment after conviction on first-degree murder. As a result, there is "an obligation to desist from enforcing that statute" and so the federal court ordered that "every person convicted of first degree murder in the State of Michigan as a juvenile and who was sentenced to life in prison shall be eligible for parole" (*Hill v. Snyder*, 2013, p. 2). An Illinois appellate court held in the November 2012 decision in *People v. Williams* that *Miller* applies retroactively, and the Massachusetts Supreme Judicial Court held in December 2013 in *Diatchenko v. District Attorney* that *Miller* applied retroactively and that no juvenile may be sentenced to life without possibility of parole. Legislatures continue to debate what minimum mandatory sentences might be imposed on juveniles that do not amount to unconstitutionally long terms of incarceration. Forensic psychologists involved in these kinds of cases are advised to remain abreast of developments of relevant law in their jurisdictions.

Roper v. Simmons (2005), *Graham v. Florida* (2010), and *Miller v. Alabama* (2012) understandably generated a focus on the constitutional limits to punishment of juveniles. However, in the interim, the Supreme Court decided the case of *J.D.B. v. North Carolina* in 2011. At its simplest, this case merely determined that a youth's age "has an objectively discernible relationship" (*J.D.B. v. North Carolina*, 2011, p. 2404) to considering how a youth might reasonably respond when police initiate an interrogation with a juvenile. However, *J.D.B.* may ultimately have far-reaching constitutional implications for legal practice if it is understood as shifting the legal standard from the reasonable person standard that does not distinguish between adults and juveniles to a more developmentally nuanced reasonable juvenile standard. This is because "there are numerous instances when the characteristics of youth might dictate a different view of the reasonableness of the defendant's conduct or mental state, or otherwise require different treatment of youth" (Levick & Tierney, 2012, p. 517). In other words, "the adoption of a reasonable juvenile standard has the potential to alter longstanding views about a juvenile's criminal responsibility and guilt" (Levick & Tierney, 2012, p. 517).

Currently, debate rages about how to best develop and implement the line of cases from *In re Gault* (1967) through *Roper v. Simmons* (2005), *Graham v. Florida* (2010), and *Miller v. Alabama* (2012) that reflect constitutional "children are different" jurisprudence even for youths who have committed homicides and other very serious crimes. At the same time, the less prominent but potentially expansive majority holding in *J.D.B. v. North Carolina* (2011) articulating a distinct reasonable juvenile standard arguably,

> precludes uniform treatment of juvenile and adult defendants on issues where youths' understanding, judgment, or mental state reflects their developmental status and distinguishes them from adults in legally and constitutionally relevant ways. In the juvenile justice system, courts must likewise acknowledge relevant characteristics of youth in deciding such fundamental questions as the scope of a child's blameworthiness, the voluntariness of a child's confession, the reasonableness of the child's belief that she was threatened with or subject to force, or the reasonableness of her belief that she could not extricate herself from peers or circumstances resulting in criminal conduct. (Levick & Tierney, 2012, p. 33)

IMPLICATIONS FOR PSYCHOLOGISTS OF DEVELOPMENTS IN LAW, POLICY, AND RESEARCH

For psychologists and others practicing in a juvenile justice context, these jurisprudential trends pose important ethical challenges in (a) keeping abreast of constitutional and other legal developments, including the articulation of factors to be relied on by courts in cases involving juveniles; (b) maintaining sufficient professional familiarity with relevant research (e.g., child and adolescent development, patterns of delinquency); and (c) maintaining sufficient competency in professional practice in applying research and practice to specific juvenile forensic contexts (e.g., *Miranda* waivers, competence-to-stand-trial evaluations, transfer evaluations, aid in disposition evaluations).

In addition, to ethically maintain competent practice, psychologists providing forensic mental health services in juvenile justice cases will need to maintain sufficient familiarity with less visible but equally important shifts in policy and practice that are underway. Psychologists will also need to keep abreast of existing and emerging bodies of research

- indicating that more punitive approaches toward youths generally result in higher recidivism rates with little deterrent effect on other adolescents (Redding, 2008);
- finding that even youths who have been chronic, violent offenders tend to desist as they mature (Mulvey et al., 2004) and describing social mechanisms, characterized as a cradle-to-prison pipeline, that tend to disproportionately drive some youths—especially youths who are impoverished, of color, or both—into penetrating the juvenile and then the criminal justice system (Children's Defense Fund, 2007);
- describing the disproportionate impact of community violence—especially gun violence—on a variety of disparate populations (e.g., characterized by age, gender, ethnicity, region, level of poverty, and other factors);
- articulating the promise and limitations of developmental psychology and developmental neuroscience (the adolescent brain) for legal and social policy (Steinberg, 2009; Steinberg & Scott, 2003);
- documenting the highly disproportionate prevalence of youths in the juvenile justice system with behavioral health disorders, cognitive impairments and learning disabilities, acquired (e.g., fetal alcohol spectrum disorders) and congenital (e.g., autism spectrum disorders) developmental and intellectual disabilities, and exposures to adverse childhood experiences yielding toxic stress and trauma;
- supporting the use of strategies to divert youths from unwarranted penetration into the juvenile justice system, including use of evidence-based models for specialty courts to identify, divert, and treat juveniles with behavioral health disorders (especially co-occurring mental health and substance use disorders); supporting and critiquing the use of models such as the risk–need–responsivity approach to identify risk and protective factors, criminogenic needs, and individual factors in assessing and intervening with delinquent misconduct to manage and reduce risk of recidivism (Andrews, Bonta, & Wormith, 2006); and
- demonstrating the effectiveness of empirically based screening, assessment, and treatment approaches in reducing delinquent recidivism.

The confluence of these lines of research and growing dissatisfaction with the results of approaches toward juvenile offenders that were more punitive and expensive but less effective in reducing recidivism led to governmental and philanthropic initiatives to change juvenile justice policy and practice. Many other foundations also fund local and regional initiatives aimed at juveniles.

Increasing emphasis was placed by federal and state government agencies, philanthropic organizations seeking to spur juvenile justice reform, and juvenile courts and juvenile justice agencies themselves on developing multiple strategies as alternatives to traditional juvenile case processing and disposition, such as diversion to community-based services, limiting the use of detention facilities, devising specialized courts such as juvenile drug courts or juvenile mental health courts, incorporating empirically supported screening and assessment into case decision making, devising and disseminating empirically based interventions, and more effective reentry planning for incarcerated youths. These lines of research reflect familiar perspectives in tension at the inception of the juvenile court, including developmental (e.g., desistance of misconduct with maturation, risk-resiliency models), biological–medical (e.g., the adolescent brain, childhood psychopathy, diagnoses such as conduct disorder), and ecological (e.g., cradle-to-prison pipeline, positive youth development assets, systems interventions) approaches to youths and delinquency.

A major challenge for the 21st century will involve developing a coherent view of juveniles that incorporates these perspectives as complementary rather than competing perspectives, and to do so in a way that can inform law and public policy as well as the role of psychologists who play a part in juvenile justice legal proceedings and assessment or treatment of juvenile offenders. Juvenile cases at the extreme as reflected in the *Roper v. Simmons* (2005), *Graham v. Florida* (2010), and *Miller v. Alabama* (2012) cases pose significant challenges for ethical practice at the limits of existing behavioral science and capacities to prognosticate about a youth's potential for long-term rehabilitation. However, seemingly mundane cases may pose deceptively complex ethical issues that should not be overlooked by psychologists involved in them as professionals. Even seemingly minor decisions involving first offenders or lower level offenders may ultimately result in significant consequences for the youth, the community, or both.

ETHICAL CHALLENGES BY PRINCIPLE AND STANDARDS

Simply reading the existing professional guidelines and standards may fail to provide sufficient guidance in identifying and resolving the often-complex ethical challenges that may arise when psychologists work with court-involved youths or youths who have further penetrated the juvenile justice system. Nonetheless, it is essential that psychologists working in a juvenile justice context be closely familiar with relevant sources of ethical guidance. The existing ethical rules of the road address the issues discussed in the first section of this chapter across several different sections and content areas. The starting point is the *Ethical Principles of Psychologists and Code of Conduct* (American Psychological Association [APA], 2010), beginning with the aspirational *Ethical Principles*. The *Ethical Principles* provide essential context to guide application of the enforceable sections of the *Code of Conduct*. In addition, although specific context and facts will greatly shape the ethical analysis of each situation (e.g., the specific role of the psychologist as forensic examiner, treating or supervising clinician, consultant, administrator, or researcher), professional activities by psychologists in the juvenile justice context are informed by the aspirational *Ethical Principles*. Specific behaviors that might come to the attention of ethics committees or statutory licensing boards as actionable or warranting enforcement would fall under the *Code of Conduct*.

Competence

Consider what a psychologist must know to practice ethically in this arena. The *Ethical Principles* requires psychologists to do good (beneficence), to do no harm (nonmaleficence), and to demonstrate both responsibility and integrity. All of these principles require competence, but the nature of the competence required also involves specific ethical standards (referred to by their respective numbering) that concern negotiating between ethical and legal demands (1.02), staying within one's established areas of competence in terms of clinical populations and in different professional practice contexts (2.01), maintaining competence as practices and laws change (2.03), maintaining and appropriately disposing of records (6.01–6.02), and using appropriate assessments procedures (9.01, 9.02, 9.06, and 9.08).

Competent clinical skills in working with child and adolescent clients is necessary, but not sufficient. APA's (2013) *Specialty Guidelines for Forensic Psychology* clearly advise "obtaining a fundamental and reasonable level of knowledge and understanding of the legal and professional standards, laws, rules, and precedents that govern their participation in legal proceedings and that guide the impact of their services on service recipients" (p. 9). In this context, the psychologist should have sufficient knowledge of the local court system, relevant law and procedure, the practices and services of the local juvenile justice system, and community-based alternatives to the juvenile justice system for essential or recommended services and interventions.

Clinical competence related to child and adolescent assessment and treatment alone will generally prove insufficient to function competently in the juvenile justice context. Competent psychologists should also have additional familiarity with several domains of professional practice and research. Although not all of these domains will apply to every case, psychologists have an obligation not to take on cases for which they lack essential knowledge and skills (Hoge, 2013). Arguably, the higher the stakes of the case, the greater the burden on the psychologist to ensure requisite competence in relevant professional practice skills and familiarity with relevant research and professional practice literature.

Specialized knowledge domains relevant to competent practice in the juvenile justice context include

- understanding developmental research and research on psychopathology relevant to adolescent normative and non-normative misconduct, including developmental trajectories and patterns of chronic and violent delinquency and normative self-desistence of misconduct with maturity;
- remaining current on research underpinnings and implications for policy and professional practice of the cradle-to-prison pipeline trajectory (Children's Defense Fund, 2007);
- having knowledge of the significantly higher prevalence of mental disorders, substance use disorders, co-occurring mental and substance use disorders, cognitive disabilities, and learning disabilities in juvenile justice populations (Redlich, 2007; Shufelt & Cocozza, 2006);
- having familiarity with research regarding disproportionate prevalence of youths involved in the justice system with exposures to adverse childhood experiences, manifestations of psychological trauma, and methods of trauma-informed assessment, clinical management, and intervention (Kinscherff, 2012);
- understanding the elevated prevalence of a variety of risk behaviors among delinquent youths, including higher rates of sexual risk behaviors for HIV/AIDS, particularly among youths with substance use disorders and mental disorders (Teplin et al., 2005);
- distinguishing between treatment and rehabilitation (Kinscherff, 2012; Tate, Reppucci, & Mulvey, 1995; see also Chapter 18, this handbook);
- evidencing informed practices in screening, assessment, treatment, and other interventions in juvenile justice populations in the community, in residential treatment facilities, and in juvenile justice secure facilities (Wu & Thompson, 2010);
- having an awareness of practice areas in which empirically derived tools and interventions may exist, even when not broadly disseminated;
- having familiarity in professional practice with special populations as necessary in individual cases, such as gang-involved youths, including their social anthropology and organization (Wu & Thompson, 2010); juvenile sexual offenders; juvenile fire setters; lesbian, gay, bisexual, transgender, and questioning youths; youths dually involved with child protection and juvenile justice systems; cultural and linguistic minorities; youths with emerging psychotic disorders; youths with developmental disabilities, intellectual disabilities, or significant learning disabilities; exploited youths in sexual and labor trafficking; immigrant (first- and second-generation) and refugee youths and families; and, because most research and practice has involved male adolescents, female offenders and younger offenders;
- understanding family factors, including evidence-informed practices for effective and sustained family engagement;
- recognizing contextual contributions from overlapping systems—family, extended family, peers, neighborhood, school, and community—and their impact on risk, protective, and mediating factors;
- having familiarity with the possible iatrogenic effects of unwarranted penetration into the juvenile justice system, detention, confinement with more seriously delinquent peers or criminal adults, or referral for generic mental health services unlikely to yield results in reducing recidivism;
- having familiarity with research regarding programs without demonstrated efficacy for delinquent youths (e.g., boot camps, wilderness programs) or, worse, programs that increase the risk of juvenile offending (e.g., Scared Straight; Petrosino, Turpin-Petrosino, Hollis-Peel, & Lavenberg, 2013); and
- having an awareness of research regarding positive youth development assessment, assets, and intervention strategies (Butts, Mayer, & Ruth, 2005); disproportionate representation of minorities in contact with the juvenile justice system or confined as juvenile offenders; and the scientific limits of clinical prognostication (Kahneman & Tversky, 1973), as well as the scientific limits on offering longer term prognostication regarding

the likelihood of amenability to rehabilitation of individual youths and the serious ethical pitfalls arising when prognosticating at or beyond the limits of science, especially in high-stakes cases (Kinscherff & Grisso, 2013).

Psychologists must exercise considerable self-awareness and discipline to rigorously reflect about their professional competence before agreeing to take on a case in a juvenile justice context. We strongly recommended consultation with expert colleagues when self-assessment of professional competence is poorly informed because of lack of familiarity with the specific juvenile justice proceedings or population or otherwise potentially compromised. Declining the case or referring it elsewhere is one option, but a psychologist may ethically proceed if adequate arrangements are made for relevant skill and information acquisition and effective consultation and supervision.

Integrity

Once professional competence has been reasonably established, our ethical analysis turns to questions of integrity. The specialty guidelines (APA, 2013) advise that "forensic psychologists strive for accuracy, honesty, and truthfulness in the science, teaching, and practice of forensic psychology and they strive to resist partisan pressures to provide services in any ways that might tend to be misleading or inaccurate" (p. 8).

The most persistent themes relevant to maintaining ethical integrity in forensic work involve clear and appropriate disclosures and professional boundaries with a recognition that third parties often have an interest in the proceedings. In the juvenile justice system, the focus of the psychologist may not rest with a sole or primary client. For example, when the psychologist is conducting a court-ordered evaluation, the court will be the primary identified client but the psychologist clearly has ethical duties (including competence and integrity) to the juvenile being evaluated, to defense counsel and prosecutor (including management of professional role and issues of confidentiality or privilege), and perhaps to others such as probation officers, juvenile justice facility staff, or treating clinicians. In such settings, the psychologist may owe differing levels or kinds (e.g., legal, ethical, forensic, clinical) of professional duty in rippling fashion to many entities including the juvenile offender, the family, the defense attorney or prosecutor, the court, the juvenile justice authority, or other retaining entity. Accurate identification of the client and the radiating or hierarchical professional obligations of the psychologist is essential to determine much of what follows with respect to boundaries and all other issues involving ethical professional practice.

Practitioners must first consider their role in the case at hand in the context of their obligations of fairness, impartiality, and conflicts of interest. This begins with a clarification of the psychologists' role in the case. The role may involve formal evaluation, treatment, consultation, or some specialized activity such as triage for diversion or rapid suicide risk assessment. Once the psychologist determines client status or hierarchy and roles requested, the next ethical obligation involves obtaining appropriate consent.

Although many people think of informed consent as having someone sign a document, obtaining consent involves a process marked by offering all of the information that a person would need to make an informed voluntary decision (Berg, Appelbaum, Parker, & Lidz, 2001; Koocher & Keith-Spiegel, 2008) and updating that process as events in service delivery (or the legal system) progress. Making a fully informed decision requires access to information presented in a manner that one can understand and the ability to make a reasoned decision on the basis of that information. Individuals who have trouble with the language, for whatever reason, require special consideration. Non-native English speakers have the right to appropriate translations, and those with poor reading skills or with a limited vocabulary should also receive special assistance. The process requires a degree of interactivity that allows the decision maker to ask questions and get clarification. The process also involves an expectation that the person giving the information and eliciting the decision will ensure that the recipient decision maker understands and that no relevant facts that might influence the decision are withheld.

In research paradigms outside the realm of juvenile justice, when participants are not legally capable of giving consent, permission (i.e., proxy consent) must be obtained from authorized others. Legally incompetent people are generally offered the opportunity to assent. When engaged in the juvenile justice system, many niceties that apply in general research contexts do not exist, unless one solicits the juvenile for research participation. Juveniles in the justice system are entitled to all of the research protections afforded their peers, with special attention to avoiding coercion associated with limitations on their freedom imposed on them by the system.

Juvenile offenders facing psychological treatment or evaluation services are entitled to explanations in terms they can understand, but they often have little choice other than participating (at least to some extent), declining any participation, or remaining mute in the presence of the psychologist—particularly when services are court ordered. Juveniles cannot offer informed consent in most circumstances because they are legal minors and are therefore legally incapable of offering informed consent, although psychologists are required to attempt to secure an adequate assent from them. Because juveniles cannot offer informed consent, those making decisions on their behalf, such as parents or attorneys, need full access to sufficient information that will permit them to make genuinely informed decisions. In addition, some juvenile offenders may lack the capacity to grasp the meaning of information provided to them (e.g., their *Miranda* rights; Grisso, 1980) or to understand the current implications or the future consequences of decisions they have a voice in making. Thus, crafting an adequate informed consent–assent requires a thorough and accurate identification of the client, the anticipated goals or outcomes of the psychologist's involvement, clarity about the psychologist's role, and transparency about any limits of confidentiality and testimonial privilege, the course and nature of the psychologist's work product, and the context in which the work will apply.

A key element of the integrity principle comes into play when services are requested or ordered by third parties (e.g., courts, attorneys, juvenile justice authorities). During the consent process, juveniles and their legal representatives must have full information about the psychologist's responsibilities to the various parties, the work to be done, and the uses to be made of the work. Psychologists must also remain prepared to uphold the scientific and professional integrity of their work regardless of who has requested their services or who has responsibility for paying their bill.

Another application of the integrity principle involves distinguishing among the roles of fact witness, expert witness, and advocate. Fact witnesses, or percipient witnesses, may testify about events they have directly perceived. Such witnesses typically cannot offer opinions, but rather simply testify with factual reports of their own experiences and perceptions. Expert witnesses have credentials that may qualify them to offer opinions of a professional and scientific nature to help the trier of fact (i.e., judge or jury) weigh evidence. Sometimes such psychologists also have clinical treatment roles with the person about whom testimony is required. In these instances, they may be termed *treating experts*. Psychologists who are treating experts must be cautious to remain within the scope of their expertise. For example, a psychologist who has been treating a juvenile defendant for depression is properly able to offer opinions regarding the clinical assessment of depression, diagnosis and impact on functioning, treatment methods, prognosis with and without treatment, and other clinical matters. However, unless the treating psychologist has also conducted additional examination sufficient to serve as an adequate foundation, the psychologist should be very wary about offering forensic opinions such as whether the depression specifically caused or led to the delinquent misconduct, the youth's risks of delinquent recidivism, or whether the youth should be committed to a juvenile justice authority.

Potential expert witnesses will typically undergo a *voir dire* examination, with direct and cross-examination about their credentials, before the judge qualifies them as experts on particular content areas and allows their opinion testimony. Although experts are typically recruited and paid by one side or the other in a legal dispute, they should retain their integrity by accurately representing the science (and its limitations) underlying their testimony.

This is also the case when experts are court ordered and the court is the primary identified client. One way of considering the role of expert witnesses is that they aspire to bring the best of psychology as a science into the courtroom in an effort to provide essential information to the legal finders of fact (judge or jury). In doing so, they avoid skewing or withholding information or informed opinions, disclose any reasonable plausible alternative explanations or hypotheses, and avoid cloaking what is actually advocacy under the guise of neutral, objective professionalism.

In some instances, psychologists may serve as advocates for their clients, and this role may involve applying their expertise. However, a psychologist serving as an advocate must be transparent in adopting an advocacy role and be prepared to discuss how that role may have shaped their clinical methods, inferences, or opinions. Similarly, a treating expert who also seeks to advocate on behalf of a patient or client must exercise care to retain scientific and professional integrity. This can raise role conflicts at times, particularly when a client expects the therapist to offer unmitigated support, despite data with some limitations.

Psychologists should also consider whether presenting as an advocate may actually undermine the interests of their therapy client. For example, judges may discount the professional opinions of psychologists whom they consider to be less credible simply as a result of adopting an advocacy stance, especially if the psychologist in an advocacy stance either seems to be withholding information intentionally or is inadequately informed about the therapy client. For example, this can occur when a treating psychologist who has (in an effort to be helpful) characterized a juvenile therapy client as engaged and making very good progress in treatment when other information disclosed in court (but not by the juvenile or family to the therapist) indicates that the juvenile has continued to persistently engage in delinquent misconduct or other very concerning behavior.

One illustration of how psychologists have taken embarrassing stances as advocates in juvenile cases became evident in Justice Scalia's dissent to the majority decision in *Roper v. Simmons* (2005). In this case, the APA had adopted a stance contradicting a line of reasoning used in a prior brief. As Justice Scalia wrote,

> We need not look far to find studies contradicting the Court's conclusions. As petitioner points out, the American Psychological Association (APA), which claims in this case that scientific evidence shows persons under 18 lack the ability to take moral responsibility for their decisions, has previously taken precisely the opposite position before this very Court. In its brief in *Hodgson v. Minnesota*, 497 U.S. 417 (1990), the APA found a "rich body of research" showing that juveniles are mature enough to decide whether to obtain an abortion without parental involvement. Brief for APA as Amicus Curiae, O. T. 1989, No. 88–805 etc., p. 18. The APA brief, citing psychology treatises and studies too numerous to list here, asserted: "[B]y middle adolescence (age 14–15) young people develop abilities similar to adults in reasoning about moral dilemmas, understanding social rules and laws, [and] reasoning about interpersonal relationships and interpersonal problems." Id., at 19–20. Given the nuances of scientific methodology and conflicting views, courts—which can only consider the limited evidence on the record before them—are ill equipped to determine which view of science is the right one. Legislatures "are better qualified to weigh and 'evaluate the results of statistical studies in terms of their own local conditions and with a flexibility of approach that is not available to the courts.'" *McCleskey v. Kemp*, 481 U.S. 279, 319 (1987) (quoting *Gregg, supra*, at 186). (*Roper v. Simmons*, 2005; see http://www.law.cornell.edu/supct/html/03-633.ZD1.html)

In essence, Justice Scalia called out the APA for using selected psychological research to make conceptually conflicting arguments about adolescent maturity and responsibility. On the one hand, APA has staked out advocacy positions for freedom of choice in the context of abortion and against a juvenile death penalty. On the other hand, each amicus brief chose to deliberately cite only supporting data while overlooking contrary scientific data arguments opposing the position. Although different committees 2 decades apart wrote the two briefs, the contrasts illustrate the APA's fairly liberal political position and the willingness of the experts involved to ignore science that did not support their arguments. Authors of amicus briefs are rarely subject to cross-examination. Such advocacy would qualify as unethical if it came as expert testimony at trial from a psychologist who declined to acknowledge its limits.

Professional and Scientific Responsibility

The dissent by Justice Scalia in *Roper v. Simmons* (2005), cited above, provides a good transition to the realm of professional and scientific responsibility in juvenile justice contexts. Stepping away from the organizational issues illustrated in the amicus briefs to individual practices issues, a key ethical problem involves scientific foundations in clinical practice with juvenile justice populations. Because youthful offenders often evoke emotional reactions by virtue of the situations in which they often find themselves and the nature of the crimes involved (i.e., ranging from minor property offenses to brutal homicides), psychologists must take extra care to ensure a solid scientific foundation for their opinions and avoid relying on personal intuitions, values, or political positions.

Kahneman and Tversky (1973) have clearly demonstrated how people often make predictions by naming the most representative outcome—a form of judgmental heuristic representativeness. In this mode, people typically predict outcomes that appear most representative of the evidence available to them. Such intuitive predictions fail to address the reliability of the evidence or the prior probability of the outcome, ignoring the logic of statistical prediction. Debates over the relative merits of unstructured clinical assessments, structured clinical judgment approaches, and actuarial prediction tools are not new in psychology, but the heavy consequences of poor decisions make it all the more necessary that psychologists working in all forensic arenas rely on evidence-based methods of screening, assessment, intervention, and treatment. Psychologists are reminded that standard clinical training and reliance on standard clinical methods of assessment are ordinarily insufficient in a juvenile forensic mental health context. Professional competence for psychologists working in this context calls for familiarity with forensic applications of standard clinical methods as well as with specialized forensic assessment tools and approaches. At the end of the process, the psychological assessment or recommendation is only as good as the least valid bit of data relied on in reaching the conclusion (Faust, 2013).

In this context, psychologists should make use of specialized tools designed for the assessment of court-involved youths or juvenile offenders when making recommendations. Such clinicians should draw on appropriate research regarding the effects of community-based or institution-based interventions on recidivism rates. Research should also govern recommendations regarding the effects on public safety of community-versus institution-based programs. When data to inform a decision do not exist, clinicians should not imply that there is a scientific foundation for their recommendation.

Respect for People's Rights and Dignity

This section of the aspirational principles has special relevance for juvenile justice contexts in which potential conflicts exist between domestic policies and with international human rights law. The issue of sentencing juvenile offenders for life without parole is such an example. Research regarding disproportionate adjudication or confinement of minorities would also inform ethical practice in this category. It also applies in contexts in which practices that might advantage an adult offender are not extended to juveniles, as was the situation in *In re Gault* (1967), described earlier.

Concern for the Welfare of Others

Avoiding harm becomes an ethical challenge for psychologists working in any arena of the juvenile justice system, particularly when the offender poses a significant danger to others or faces dispositions ranging from prolonged juvenile incarceration or even a potential life sentence. The psychologist must first consider what constitutes harm in this complex context. For example, juvenile incarceration might ordinarily be considered a harm to be avoided, but a facility-based intervention may constitute the only rehabilitative option that also controls risks to the community. Tracking with a GPS bracelet, a restrictive curfew, and psychological treatment imposed as a condition of intensive probation may be considered a harm by some because it is quasi-coercive, but it may be the best option to prevent a youth from even more onerous consequences should he or she reoffend. One must also consider to whom any protection from harm is owed: the youthful offender, one or more victims, all potential future victims, the identified client (if not the offending youth), or someone else. The clinician must also consider whether the duty differs depending on whether the psychologist's client is the court, the defense, the prosecution, or another entity.

THEMES INVOLVING ENFORCEABLE STANDARDS OF THE APA CODE OF CONDUCT

This section addresses the section of the *Ethical Principles of Psychologists and Code of Conduct* (APA, 2010) that is enforceable: the Code of Conduct. Our discussion is divided according to major themes associated with the code.

Clarity of Role and Decision Making

Multiple relationships may occur in many juvenile justice contexts, particularly in settings in which psychologists may be called on to provide assessments or treatment that may also form the basis of decisions by courts or juvenile justice authorities. Anticipating, identifying, clarifying, and resolving expectations regarding professional roles, issues of confidentiality and testimonial privilege, potential third-party uses of records, and other issues become especially important because of the potential consequences of court involvement, commitment to a juvenile justice authority, or transfer for adult criminal justice trial and sentencing.

An adequate process of analyzing and establishing informed consent is essential. A psychologist always retains responsibility for identifying the key variables and obtaining appropriate consent for professional services in legal contexts. Other authorities may seek to prescribe procedures and forms, but the ultimate professional responsibility rests with the individual clinician. Important legal and ethical duties arise primarily out of the professional relationship between the psychologist and the identified client. The scope of the psychologist's role in providing professional services to the legal client will ordinarily define the psychologist's role, goals, and the appropriate methods to be used. As a result, the legal client must be identified (e.g., court, attorney, juvenile justice authority, other) in explaining the psychologist's role, scope of professional activities, goals, and methods. The nature of confidentiality and testimonial privilege—and any limits on them—must be clearly conveyed. Relevant risks and benefits to proceeding with professional services or declining them must be discussed as well as other elements of informed consent.

Informed consent is provided by a person legally competent to consent to specified professional services. With some exceptions (i.e., emancipated minors or, in some states, the ability to seek reproductive health care, treatment for sexually transmitted diseases, substance abuse treatment, or mental health care), people younger than age 18 are legal minors and not generally able to authorize professional services by psychologists, so parents or legal guardians ordinarily provide informed consent for professional services on their behalf. The Code of Conduct requires that a psychologist attempt to obtain assent when a person is a legal incompetent (such as being a minor) or the purpose of assessment is to investigate possible legal incompetence (see APA, 2010, Standards 3.07 and 3.10).

When the professional service is ordered by the court (such as a court-ordered evaluation), the court is ordinarily the identified client although the juvenile is the direct recipient of the professional services. In such instances, the parent or legal guardian must be informed that because the court is the client, there is no psychotherapist–client or doctor–patient privilege. All must understand that the court will receive reports of the results of the professional services, but that the youth can assent to personally participate (or not) in the court-ordered evaluation or treatment. The legal representative of the youth and the youth must understand that an evaluation will proceed (even if with some limits) even if the juvenile declines to personally participate.

For example, if the evaluation is for competence to stand trial and the juvenile will not directly participate, the psychologist may rely on collateral informants, documents, and observations of the juvenile (such as observing on a detention unit without interviewing the client) to gather information regarding likely level of functioning, capacity to communicate with defense counsel, and other relevant factors. Of course, treatment of a youth who declines personal participation raises additional challenges that may or may not be subject to resolution. For example, a court may commit a juvenile to a juvenile justice treatment facility whether or not the youth assents to participate.

One way of thinking about this is that the court order authorizes the psychologist to proceed on behalf of the court and that the usual rules of confidentiality or doctor–patient testimonial privilege do not apply because the court is the identified client rather than the juvenile. The court order authorizes professional activity by the psychologist, but it does not compel direct participation by the juvenile (who may receive legal advice to not participate).

Similar issues arise when the psychologist is retained by an attorney. The psychologist will need to clarify with the attorney, the juvenile, and the juvenile's parents or guardian that the attorney is the identified client, that there is no doctor–patient privilege so the attorney will be provided information, and that the work product of professional services belongs to the attorney. Because the professional work product belongs to the attorney, the parents or guardian of the juvenile cannot authorize its release to third parties (e.g., school, pediatrician, treating clinician) unless doing so is authorized by the attorney. Psychologists should also determine whether there is clear guidance in the jurisdiction about whether a condition ordinarily triggering a mandated report (e.g., child abuse) continues to trigger that duty or if being retained by an attorney places all communications within the attorney–client privilege. Unless there is abundantly clear guidance in the jurisdiction about how to proceed when a mandated reporting duty comes into direct conflict with attorney–client privilege, psychologists are urged to clarify this issue as part of negotiating involvement when an attorney seeks to retain them.

In reality, potential negative consequences may accrue to a youthful defendant or offender who chooses not to directly participate in a court-ordered evaluation or treatment. This can contribute to a coercive context for obtaining informed consent or assent. The greater the degree of coercion, the greater the vulnerability of deciding to directly participate, and the more onerous the consequences for declining to participate, the more attentive the psychologist must be to ensuring that the youth and legal guardian fully understand the elements of informed consent–assent and appreciate the risks and benefits of both participating in and declining to participate in the court-ordered activity.

As mentioned above, when the professional service is retained by an attorney, the youth and parent or legal guardian are informed that the psychologist's activities are governed by attorney–client privilege (if defense) or the government's duties to disclose information, especially if exonerating or exculpating (if prosecution). In these situations, psychologists recognize that the attorney retaining their services is the identified client. Psychologists should remain mindful that because the attorney is the client (and so owns and controls the work product), juveniles or their parents or legal guardians do not ordinarily have the authority to subsequently sign releases for reports or communications about work conducted by the psychologist for the attorney. Releasing reports or communicating about psychological services provided under attorney–client privilege without clear authorization from the attorney risks sabotaging the protection available to the juvenile by the attorney–client privilege and could form the basis of an ethics or license complaint for unauthorized release or disclosure of information. Psychologists are advised to clarify potentially ambiguous circumstances such as the situation described above when a psychologist's mandated reporting obligation may conflict with attorney–client privilege.

When the professional service is retained, contracted, or employed for a juvenile justice authority, the presumptive client becomes the juvenile justice authority. Psychologists should clarify for the jurisdiction in which they are practicing whether committing a youth to a juvenile justice authority supersedes the authority of the parent or legal guardian to authorize professional services. For example, in some jurisdictions commitment of a youth gives the juvenile justice authority the ability to physically place a youth—including confinement in a locked setting—but does alter or disrupt the authority of parents or legal guardians to authorize or decline professional clinical services. In those jurisdictions, a youth placed in a locked or group setting would still require a parent's or legal guardian's authorization for clinical assessments or treatments. Other jurisdictions may have a range of assessments or interventions that can occur without authorization by a parent or legal guardian on commitment of a youth.

In addition, there may be special organizational rules or contractual agreements regarding the provision of assessments, treatments, or other psychological services. In some cases, mental health professionals may be contracted to provide services with the understanding that—despite being contracted by the juvenile justice authority—the usual rules regarding confidentiality and testimonial privilege apply. In other cases, the contract will specify that there is no confidentiality of records or information provided by the juvenile and no testimonial privilege protecting communications by the juvenile from being introduced into legal proceedings. In either case, the psychologist must seek and obtain a clear understanding of any limits on confidentiality and privilege to complete an adequate informed consent–assent process. Once again, others may seek to dictate terms, but clinicians retain responsibility for their own actions.

An adequate process of informed consent or assent will take into account (a) the age and developmental status of the juvenile client; (b) the legal status of the juvenile or parent or legal guardian in being able to offer informed consent or, alternatively, assent; (c) the expressed preference of the juvenile; and (d) the ability of the juvenile to appreciate the role of the psychologist and the purposes, methods, risks and benefits, considerations of confidentiality and privilege, and other aspects relevant to informed consent–assent.

In situations in which the juvenile does not clearly understand his or her relationship with the psychologist, the nature and anticipated purpose of professional activities by the psychologist, or potential future consequences of the information the juvenile provides, the psychologist should notify the identified client (e.g., court, defense attorney or prosecutor, juvenile justice authority). Sometimes, a process must be engaged in that results in clarifying who can authorize the psychologist's professional activities through court order, informed consent, or adequately obtained consent. Legally incompetent persons have the right to veto a decision about enrolling them as participants in research projects not likely to provide therapeutic benefits, but such veto rights do not apply in nonresearch juvenile court processes or procedures. For example, although a juvenile as legal incompetent cannot veto a court-ordered evaluation to preclude assessment of competence to stand trial or aid in disposition (although the court cannot force a juvenile defendant to participate in an interview), an adjudicated juvenile offender recruited as a potential participant in a research project that offered no benefit to him or her as an individual would ordinarily have the right to decline participation even if the juvenile's parent or guardian had granted permission.

Interprofessional Relationships

The psychologist must also maintain clear professional boundaries with respect to the other parties in the juvenile justice arena, including prosecutors, defense attorneys, probation officers, and others (see APA, 2010, Standards 3.07 and 3.09). Such clarity becomes essential in understanding one's role as a neutral expert, providing litigation support to one side, or advocating for a juvenile offender or victim. At times, the psychologist's role will flow from a third party's request for services, and the obligation to resolve conflicting expectations for services belongs to the psychologist at the outset of the professional relationship. The ethical standards of the legal profession differ from psychology's standards in several important ways. For example, attorneys can often consult with multiple experts and choose to use or disclose only those who seem likely to help provide the best case for their client. Psychologists are expected to uphold their integrity on the basis of the knowledge base of the field rather than shopping only for data that support a particular position staked out in advance.

Privacy and confidentiality. Apart from the usual expectations of psychologists with respect to privacy and confidentiality, some special obligations are incurred with court involvement, institutional controls, and Fifth Amendment considerations. Most of these parallel similar requirements for psychologists who work with adult offenders in legal and correctional settings (see APA, 2010, Standards 4.01–4.02 and 4.05–4.06). A key difference sometimes occurs in juvenile settings in which, in an effort to exercise less formality or a less parentalistic ambience, a more casual attitude may prevail among some professionals in the system. In this context, the psychologist must focus on the identified client with privacy–confidentiality issues and give notification of these parameters at the outset of the professional relationship.

When there are doubts about the examinee's ability to fully grasp these parameters, the psychologist should consider engaging the examinee's legal representative for the purpose of exercising any waivers or releases. Although parents are often able to act as their child's surrogate in such situations (e.g., health and educational contexts), some parents may not have the ability to adequately represent their child's best interests in a legal context. Court-appointed counsel may stand in a better position to serve that function in many cases.

Record keeping and fees. Psychologists working the juvenile justice system should keep records in a manner consistent with the professional standards for the services offered and in compliance with applicable laws regarding retention (see APA, 2010, Standards 6.01–6.04). For example, those conducting assessments should preserve both raw data and completed reports. Those conducting psychotherapy should create adequate records to reflect the nature and course of treatment including date, time, and duration of sessions; observations about mental status; key issues addressed; and progress toward treatment goals. Storing and maintain such records depends on the site and context. For example, psychologists conducting an assessment as an independent practitioner will typically maintain records at their private office, whereas those who work as institutional employees will follow the procedures of the institution.

Access to records would also follow from the nature of the services provided and the releases or waivers authorized. All of this information should be explained to the identified client at the outset of service delivery. For example, when participating in a court-ordered evaluation, the juvenile should understand that the results of the assessment will be made available in court. Clinical records that originate in other ways can be shared only with a release signed by the juvenile and the juvenile's legal guardian or under court order. This would include private treatment records or assessments.

Fee arrangements should also be agreed to and explained at the outset of the professional relationship, and they will vary as a function of the context and setting. The most common problem encountered in forensic contexts involves the use of retainers and interruption of services based on nonpayment. This happens most commonly when a substantial amount of time is invested (e.g., data collection for a forensic assessment) and payment for services is delayed. In such situations, it is not inappropriate to suspend service delivery until payment is made. However, it is ethically inappropriate to withhold records on the basis of unpaid fees (APA, 2010, Standard 6.03). The most ethical strategy for avoiding this problem is to reach agreement on a timely payment schedule in advance and suspend future services if payment ceases. This might include ceasing work on an assessment report if partial payment does not follow data collection. Many ethical clinicians will consider adjusting their fees if clients experience an unanticipated financial hardship, but in no case should one hold records needed for patient care or legal defenses hostage to payment.

Research in Juvenile Justice Populations

Research focused on juvenile offenders can add significant value to improve psychologists' assessment, intervention, and prevention strategies. However, the same ethical problems that apply to research with adult correctional populations (Gostin, Vanchieri, & Pope, 2007) not only apply but assume even greater importance when the potential participants are juveniles (Mulvey & Phelps, 1988; see also APA, 2010, Standards 8.01–8.02). Apart from the challenges of consent and confidentiality described earlier, problem definition, overidentification, and adverse self-fulfilling prophecies linked to labeling pose additional problems (Mulvey & Phelps, 1988), as does potential coercion to participate that can radiate down to siblings (Koocher, 2005). In some instances the potential participants, or those granting permission on their behalf, may have a misconception that participation will provide some potential therapeutic or administrative benefits even when none are mentioned. Special institutional review board protections, including the use of data safety monitoring boards, may be warranted to ensure appropriate protections.

Assessment

Assessments of juveniles' competency to stand trial, suggestibility and judgment, criminal responsibility, amenability to rehabilitation, and qualification for waiver or transfer to adult courts raise many complex assessment issues, as psychologists try to translate their findings into ethically sound recommendations in the context of legal standards (see APA, 2010, Standards 9.01–9.04). Clinical and scientific rigor become prime assessment considerations.

At the outset, it is important to distinguish routine screenings from assessment. Psychological assessment involves formal data collection followed by analysis and reporting intended to answer particular diagnostic or treatment questions (Rey-Casserly & Koocher, 2012). Such detailed and integrative work does not apply to screening instruments, normally intended to be brief, easily administered tools to quickly assess some particular risk that may warrant further assessment or intervention. In a juvenile justice setting, screening might focus on issues such as suicide risk or depression and involve symptom or observational checklists that can alert those charged with monitoring the welfare of a particular individual or population to probe more deeply in response to elevated scores.

The clinical competence and integrity concerns discussed earlier have special relevance when selecting assessment tools for use in juvenile justice, similar to the issues of concern when evaluating adults in forensic context. Unfortunately, most forensic adaptations of psychological assessment tools (e.g., forensic scoring for the Minnesota Multiphasic Personality Inventory—2) have not been adapted for use with child or adolescent populations. The same situation applies when clinicians seek to apply culturally adapted tools but ignore the fact that no adjustment has been made for developmental differences. As a result, psychologists must use special caution when trying to adapt existing instruments to juvenile justice contexts. Any modified test use or other validity considerations should be discussed in resulting reports or testimony.

Police interrogations and *Miranda* warnings provide a good example. Scott and Grisso (1997) reviewed the decision making of juveniles in terms of cognitive capacity and judgment factors, including attitudes toward risk and temporal perspective. They reviewed research findings demonstrating that by about age 14, adolescents' cognitive decision-making abilities are similar to those of adults. However, they noted that the studies they found tended to have small sample sizes, were conducted in laboratory settings, used homogeneous middle-class participants, and rarely compared the decision making of minors with that of adults. They concluded, "This format yields little useful data about how decisions are made in informal unstructured settings in which decision-makers must rely on their own experience and knowledge in making choices" (p. 160). Regarding judgment factors, Scott and Grisso described how factors such as attitude toward and perception of risk and temporal perspective lead adolescents to make choices different from those of adults. "Whereas cognitive competence affects the process of decision-making, immature judgment is reflected in outcomes, in that developmental factors influence values and preferences, which in turn shape the cost–benefit calculus" (p. 161).

The prevalence of mental illness among justice-involved youths is alarmingly high, and mental illness by itself represents a risk factor for false confession. These two facts place suspected youths in double jeopardy in an interrogation room (Owen-Kostelnik, Reppucci, & Meyer, 2006; Redlich, 2007). Research by Shufelt and Cocozza (2006) across multiple sites and levels of care found that among youths involved in the juvenile justice system, approximately 70% warranted diagnosis of a mental disorder, with most youths warranting two or more diagnoses; some 60% with a mental disorder also had a co-occurring substance use disorder; and 27% presented with mental disorders sufficiently impairing to warrant an urgent and significant clinical response.

Taking 2011 as a sample index year, the U.S. Department of Justice reported 4,467 arrests per 100,000 youths between ages 10 and 17 (Office of Juvenile Justice and Delinquency Prevention, 2014). Thus, assuming continued similar statistics, one can predict that as many as an estimated 3,126 per 100,000 (70%) of youths warranting diagnosis of one or more mental disorders come into contact with police en route to the juvenile justice system.

Research in one urban juvenile facility holding youths detained after arrest (a detention center rather than a juvenile correctional or treatment center) found approximately 60% of male and 70% of female youths warranted one or more mental disorder diagnosis when conduct disorder diagnosis was excluded (Teplin, Abram, McClelland, Dulcan, & Mericle, 2002), suggesting that police are commonly interacting with and interrogating youths who have some degree of clinical impairment. The Shufelt and Cocozza (2006) finding that 27% of youths involved in the juvenile justice system present with serious mental health needs warranting urgent care strongly suggests that police are engaging with a significant number of youths in significant mental health crisis and vulnerable to processes of interrogation that contribute to false confession. Prevalence rates for serious mental illness among juvenile justice–involved youths of approximately 20% (Cocozza & Skowyra, 2000) suggest that some 893 per 100,000 youths are seriously mentally ill at the time they are arrested and presumably questioned by police. This would translate to approximately 220,000 arrests of seriously mentally ill youths per year, a number that is much higher if all youths with less seriously impairing mental disorders are considered. Thus, mental health screening and more comprehensive assessments sensitive to the complex clinical and forensic issues involved raise a range of critically important ethical issues in juvenile justice contexts.

Psychotherapy

As discussed earlier, situations in which psychotherapeutic treatment is court ordered can raise complex issues regarding coercive role played by involvement in court proceedings. Dewey and Gottlieb (2011) described issues that can arise when providing court-ordered treatment, many of which also apply when a youth is committed to a juvenile justice authority and participation in treatment is expected as part of a program of rehabilitation. Each of these issues has implications for obtaining adequate informed consent or assent (see APA, 2010, Standards 10.01 and 3.04–3.07).

First, the psychologist must have sufficient information about the court's expectations about the nature and course of treatment, goals of treatment, the nature and quality of the youth's engagement in the treatment process, confidentiality, duration of treatment or conditions to be met to terminate treatment, and any consequences to the juvenile of failing to progress in treatment toward the court's identified goals. The psychologist will need this information in detail to complete an adequate informed consent or assent.

Second, the psychologist must be able to confidently identify the juvenile's legal guardian capable of offering an informed consent. Dewey and Gottlieb (2011) observed that in one research study, "43% of juvenile detainees did not have a legal guardian that could be successfully contacted" (p. 7) and that many youths live with extended family members or other adults who are not their legal guardians. Indeed, some youths may still be living with one or both parents but be in the temporary or permanent legal custody of the state child protection agency, although still living at home. This difficulty may also extend to obtaining permission to exchange information about the youth with schools, previous evaluating or treating professionals, and others who may have invaluable information about the youth.

Third, a psychologist must consider whether or how to elicit an informed consent or assent when the court has ordered a treatment that, in the psychologist's professional judgment, is poorly matched to actual needs, clinically unnecessary, carries significant risks of iatrogenic effects, or is otherwise counterindicated. In these circumstances, psychologists need to consider whether, and under what circumstances, they will decline to provide the court-ordered treatment and how they would communicate the decision to the juvenile, the juvenile's family or legal guardian, and the court.

DISTINGUISHING TREATMENT FROM REHABILITATION

The terms *treatment* and *rehabilitation* are sometimes used interchangeably by legal and clinical professionals. The two terms are often found in statutes or court opinions as though they are identical terms and concepts. Whatever their use in the law in the jurisdiction in which a psychologist practices, it is useful and ethically important to distinguish the terms conceptually. *Treatment* consists of interventions typically provided by, or under the supervision of, licensed clinical professionals to remedy a diagnosed mental health problem. *Rehabilitation* is a broader concept that refers to specifically addressing factors that, if neglected, are likely to increase the risk of delinquent recidivism. These may be nonclinical factors such as a youth's academic achievement, vocational readiness, or housing needs. Treatment may be part of a broader program of rehabilitation, but not all rehabilitation interventions or supports are treatment.

Treatment may or may not have an impact on reducing recidivism risk. In some cases, treatment may reduce recidivism risk by addressing a clinical target that is also a recidivism risk factor (e.g., reducing substance abuse) or a psychological factor closely linked to a target behavior (e.g., treating a teen with depression who had no history of aggression until the onset of a depression characterized by marked irritability and disregard for consequences to him- or herself). In other cases, treatment may have little or no impact on recidivism risk (e.g., tobacco smoking cessation or enhancing self-esteem). In still other situations, treatment may actually increase recidivism risk (e.g., treating a low-risk offender in groups or facilities with high-risk offenders, or treating the debilitating depression of a gang-involved youth and thereby restoring energy, motivation, and the decision to leave the house to rejoin the gang). Psychologists providing treatment to juveniles with problem behaviors that can be or have been charged as offenses must carefully consider what, if any, links there are between the treatment offered and empirically derived risk, contextual, and protective factors for delinquent misconduct (see Chapter 18, this handbook).

Most mental health treatments were not designed to address key factors associated with juvenile offender recidivism or to robustly engage protective factors that contribute to desistance from delinquent misconduct as a youth ages and matures. Psychologists providing treatment to youths engaged in delinquent misconduct have an ethical duty ensure their competence in the provision of psychological services. In this context, the psychologist must be familiar with empirically supported treatments for delinquent misconduct that may be described in a diagnosis such as conduct disorder and to clarify with all concerned what, if any, contribution an effective treatment may offer to reduction of recidivism (rehabilitation). For example, treatment of depression or attention-deficit/hyperactivity disorder manifesting in a youth whose behavior warrants a diagnosis of conduct disorder will ordinarily not prove sufficient to eliminate the conduct disorder. Successful treatment of depression or attention-deficit/hyperactivity disorder alone may lead the youth diagnosed with conduct disorder to be more euthymic, energetic, or less impulsive when engaging in delinquent misconduct but will not likely prove sufficient to reduce recidivism. However, successful treatment of depression or attention-deficit/hyperactivity disorder can contribute significantly but indirectly if it allows the youth to be more motivated to avoid negative consequences for misconduct, engage more effectively in the normative social learning processes that contribute to self-desistance of misconduct, or to learn relevant social, cognitive, or other skills (e.g., developing social skills that allow the youth to affiliate successfully with non-delinquent youths or to hold a job, identifying and replacing criminal thinking patterns, developing a talent or interest that is incompatible with continued misconduct).

SUMMARY

The ethical challenges involved in providing psychological services within the juvenile justice system revolve around a cluster of important standards above and beyond the APA's aspirational ethical principles. The cluster includes special competence requirements, managing complex interprofessional relationships, grasping and managing systemic boundary and role problems, helping clients understand and protect their confidentiality rights, and ensuring that assessment and treatment take place in an evidence-based context. Psychologists who choose to tread clinically into this arena should have competence in child and adolescent clinical psychology as well as forensic practice. They will need an understanding of the history, case law, and general principles that distinguish the juvenile courts from adult courts. They will also need to recognize the special vulnerabilities inherent in serving juveniles who must often rely on others to represent their best interests. They will do all this in a complex system of adjudication, incarceration, assessment, treatment, rehabilitation, and probation that demands a firm evidentiary basis and resistance to cutting corners or taking shortcuts that can seriously compromise the lives of juveniles. All of this can and should be done by our best-trained and most dedicated colleagues.

References

Abrams, L. S. (2013). Juvenile justice at a crossroads: Science, evidence, and twenty-first century reform. *Social Service Review*, *87*, 725–752. http://dx.doi.org/10.1086/674074

Abrams, L. S., & Snyder, S. M. (2010). Youthful offender re-entry: Models for intervention and directions for future inquiry. *Children and Youth Services Review*, *32*, 1787–1795. http://dx.doi.org/10.1016/j.childyouth.2010.07.023

American Psychological Association. (2010). *Ethical principles of psychologists and code of conduct (2002, Amended June 1, 2010)*. Retrieved from http://www.apa.org/ethics/code/index.aspx

American Psychological Association. (2013). Specialty guidelines for forensic psychology. *American Psychologist*, *68*, 7–19. http://dx.doi.org/10.1037/a0029889

Andrews, D. A., Bonta, J., & Wormith, J. S. (2006). The recent past and near future of risk and/or need assessment. *Crime and Delinquency*, *52*, 7–27. http://dx.doi.org/10.1177/0011128705281756

Berg, J. W., Appelbaum, P. S., Parker, L. S., & Lidz, C. W. (2001). *Informed consent: Legal theory and clinical practice*. New York, NY: Oxford University Press.

Butts, J., Mayer, S., & Ruth, G. (2005). *Focusing juvenile justice on positive youth development* (Issue Brief). Chicago, IL: University of Chicago, Chapin Hall Center for Children. Retrieved from http://www.chapinhall.org/sites/default/files/publications/249.pdf

Children's Defense Fund. (2007). *America's cradle to prison pipeline report*. Retrieved from http://www.childrensdefense.org/library/data/cradle-prison-pipeline-report-2007-full-highres.html

Cocozza, J. J., & Skowyra, K. R. (2000). Youth with mental health disorders: Issues and emerging responses. *Office of Juvenile Justice and Delinquency Prevention Journal*, *7*, 3–13.

Dewey, L. M., & Gottlieb, M. C. (2011). Ethical guidelines for providing court-ordered outpatient psychotherapy to juvenile offenders. *Journal of Forensic Psychology Practice*, *11*, 1–20. http://dx.doi.org/10.1080/15228932.2011.521694

Diatchenko v. District Attorney for the Suffolk District, 466 Mass. 655, 1 N.E.3d 270 (2013).

Fare v. Michael, C., 442 U.S. 707 (1979).

Faust, D. (2013). Increasing the accuracy of clinical judgment (and thereby improving patient care). In G. P. Koocher, J. C. Norcross, & B. A. Greene (Eds.), *The psychologists' desk reference* (pp. 26–30). New York, NY: Oxford University Press.

Gostin, L. O., Vanchieri, C., & Pope, A. (Eds.). (2007). *Ethical considerations for research involving prisoners*. Washington, DC: National Academies Press.

Graham v. Florida, 560 U.S. 48 (2010).

Grisso, T. (1980). Juveniles' capacities to waive *Miranda* rights: An empirical analysis. *California Law Review*, *68*, 1134–1166. http://dx.doi.org/10.2307/3480263

Hall, G. S. (1904). *Adolescence: Psychology and its relations to physiology, anthropology, sociology, sex, crime, religion and education*. New York, NY: Appleton.

Hill v. Snyder, United States District Court, E. D. Michigan, Southern Division (Order Granting

Plaintiff's Motion for Ruling on Scope of Summary Judgment Order and Denying Plaintiff's Motion for Class Action Certification as Moot, Case No. 10-14568, August 12, 2013).

Hoge, R. D. (2013). Best practices in forensic mental health assessment. In R. Roesch & P. Zapf (Eds.), *Forensic assessments in criminal and civil law: A handbook for lawyers* (pp. 237–248). New York, NY: Oxford University Press.

In re Gault, 387 U.S. 1 (1967).

In re Winship, 397 U.S. 358 (1970).

J.D.B. v. North Carolina, 131 S. Ct. 2394 (2011).

Juvenile Justice and Delinquency Prevention Act of 1974, Pub. Law 93–415, 42 U.S.C. § 5601 *et seq.*

Kahneman, D., & Tversky, A. (1973). On the psychology of prediction. *Psychological Review*, *80*, 237–251. http://dx.doi.org/10.1037/h0034747

Kent v. United States, 383 U.S. 541 (1966).

Kinscherff, R. (2012). *A primer for mental health practitioners working with youth involved in the juvenile justice system.* Washington, DC: Technical Assistance Partnership for Child and Family Mental Health, American Research Institutes.

Kinscherff, R., & Grisso, T. (2013). Human rights violations and Standard 1.02: Intersections with human rights law and applications in juvenile capital cases. *Ethics and Behavior*, *23*, 71–76. http://dx.doi.org/10.1080/10508422.2013.757963

Koocher, G. P. (2005). Behavioral research with children: The fenfluramine challenge. In E. Kodesh (Ed.), *Learning from cases: Ethics and research with children* (pp. 179–193). New York, NY: Oxford University Press.

Koocher, G. P., & Keith-Spiegel, P. C. (2008). *Ethics in psychology and the mental health professions: Standards and cases.* New York, NY: Oxford University Press.

Krisberg, B. (2006). Rediscovering the juvenile justice ideal in the United States. In J. Muncie & B. Goldson (Eds.), *Comparative youth justice* (pp. 6–18). http://dx.doi.org/10.4135/9781446212608.n2

Levick, M. L., & Tierney, E. A. (2012). The United States Supreme Court adopts a reasonable juvenile standard in *JDB v. North Carolina* for purposes of the *Miranda* custody analysis: Can a more reasoned justice system for juveniles be far behind? *Harvard Civil Rights-Civil Liberties Law Review*, *47*, 3–33.

McKeiver v. Pennsylvania, 403 U.S. 528 (1971).

Miller v. Alabama, 132 S. Ct. 2455 (2012).

Mulvey, E. P., & Phelps, P. (1988). Ethical balances in juvenile justice research and practice. *American Psychologist*, *43*, 65–69. http://dx.doi.org/10.1037/0003-066X.43.1.65

Mulvey, E. P., Steinberg, L., Fagan, J., Cauffman, E., Piquero, A. R., Chassin, L., . . . Losoya, S. H. (2004). Theory and research on desistance from antisocial activity among serious adolescent offenders. *Youth Violence and Juvenile Justice*, 2, 213–236. http://dx.doi.org/10.1177/1541204004265864

Office of Juvenile Justice and Delinquency Prevention. (2014). *Statistical briefing book.* Retrieved from http://www.ojjdp.gov/ojstatbb/crime/JAR_Display.asp

Omnibus Crime Control and Safe Streets Act of 2002, 42 U.S.C. 3796 *et seq.*

Owen-Kostelnik, J., Reppucci, N. D., & Meyer, J. R. (2006). Testimony and interrogation of minors: Assumptions about maturity and morality. *American Psychologist*, *61*, 286–304. http://dx.doi.org/10.1037/0003-066X.61.4.286

People v. Carp, 298 Mich. App. 472 (2012).

People v. Williams, 982 N.E.2d 181 (Ill. App. Ct. 2012).

Petrosino, A., Turpin-Petrosino, C., Hollis-Peel, M. E., & Lavenberg, J. G. (2013). "Scared Straight" and other juvenile awareness programs for preventing juvenile delinquency. *Cochrane Database of Systematic Reviews, 2013*, CD002796. http://dx.doi.org/10.1002/14651858.CD002796.pub2

President's Commission on Law Enforcement and the Administration of Justice. (1967). *Task force report: Juvenile delinquency and youth crime—Report on juvenile justice and consultants' papers.* Washington, DC: U.S. Government Printing Office.

Redding, R. E. (2008). *Juvenile transfer laws: An effective deterrent to delinquency?* Washington, DC: U.S. Department of Justice, Office of Juvenile Justice and Delinquency Prevention.

Redlich, A. D. (2007). Double jeopardy in the interrogation room for youths with mental illness. *American Psychologist*, *62*, 609–611. http://dx.doi.org/10.1037/0003-066X62.6.609

Rey-Casserly, C., & Koocher, G. P. (2012). Ethical issues in psychological assessment. In J. R. Graham & J. A. Naglieri (Eds.), *Handbook of psychology: Vol. 10. Assessment psychology* (2nd ed., pp. 295–330). Hoboken, NJ: Wiley.

Roper v. Simmons, 543 U.S. 551 (2005).

Schall v. Martin, 467 U.S. 253 (1984).

Scott, E. S., & Grisso, T. (1997). The evolution of adolescence: A developmental perspective on juvenile justice reform. *Journal of Criminal Law and Criminology*, *88*, 137–189. http://dx.doi.org/10.2307/1144076

Shufelt, J. L., & Cocozza, J. J. (2006). *Youth with mental health disorders in the juvenile justice system: Results from a multi-state prevalence study*. Delmar, NY: National Center for Mental Health and Juvenile Justice.

Steinberg, L. (2009). Should the science of adolescent brain development inform public policy? *American Psychologist*, *64*, 739–750. http://dx.doi.org/10.1037/0003-066X.64.8.739

Steinberg, L., & Scott, E. S. (2003). Less guilty by reason of adolescence: Developmental immaturity, diminished responsibility, and the juvenile death penalty. *American Psychologist*, *58*, 1009–1018. http://dx.doi.org/10.1037/0003-066X.58.12.1009

Tate, D. C., Reppucci, N. D., & Mulvey, E. P. (1995). Violent juvenile delinquents. Treatment effectiveness and implications for future action. *American Psychologist*, *50*, 777–781. http://dx.doi.org/10.1037/0003-066X.50.9.777

Teplin, L. A., Abram, K. M., McClelland, G. M., Dulcan, M. K., & Mericle, A. A. (2002). Psychiatric disorders in youth in juvenile detention. *Archives of General Psychiatry*, *59*, 1133–1143. http://dx.doi.org/10.1001/archpsyc.59.12.1133

Teplin, L. A., Elkington, K. S., McClelland, G. M., Abram, K. M., Mericle, A. A., & Washburn, J. J. (2005). Major mental disorders, substance use disorders, comorbidity, and HIV-AIDS risk behaviors in juvenile detainees. *Psychiatric Services*, *56*, 823–828. http://dx.doi.org/10.1176/appi.ps.56.7.823

Wu, S., & Thompson, C. (2010). Juvenile offenders. In C. Scott (Ed.), *Handbook of correctional mental health* (2nd ed., pp. 543–572). Arlington, VA: American Psychiatric Publishing.

Index